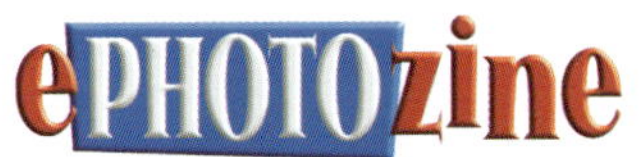

GUIDE TO GREAT PHOTOGRAPHY

ESSENTIAL REFERENCE MANUAL FOR FILM AND DIGITAL CAMERA OWNERS

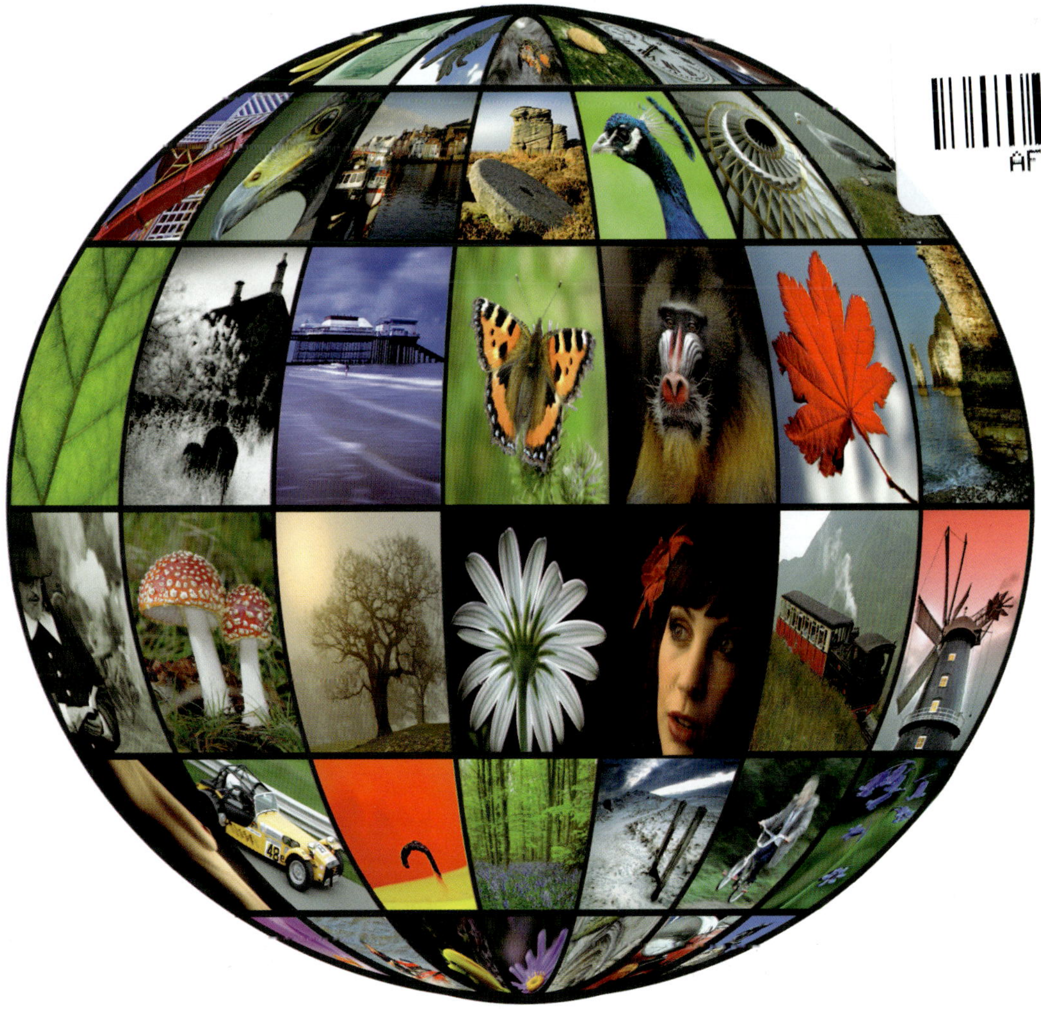

EDITED BY PETER BARGH

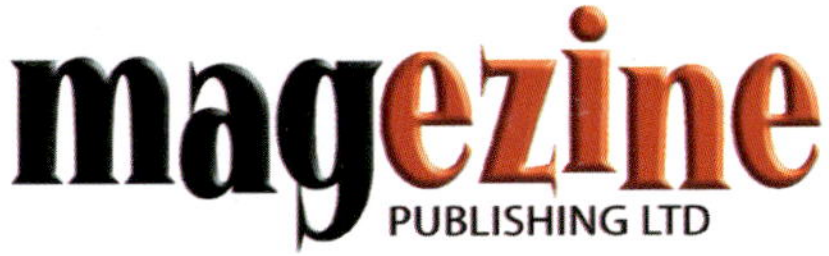

An ePHOTOzine book
Published by Magezine Publishing Ltd
The Turbine
Shireoaks Triangle Business Park
Coach Close
Shireoaks
S81 8AP
England

Tel: +44 (0)1909 512111
Fax: +44 (0)1909 512147

Email: info@magezinepublishing.com
www.magezinepublishing.com

FIRST EDITION
Copyright © Magezine Publishing Ltd 2006

A Catalogue record for this book is available from the
British Library.

ISBN 0-9551760-0-X   Paperback
978-0-9551760-0-5

ISBN 0-9551760-1-8   Hardback
978-0-9551760-1-2

Who created the book

Editor: Peter Bargh

Writers: Ian Andrews, Karen Bacon, Peter Bargh,
                  Jeanette Lazenby, Will Smith,
                  Heather Turner, Rob Webb, Gary Wolstenholme

Sub Editor: Rob Webb
Proof reading: Tracey Johnson, Rose Teal, Rob Webb

Picture research: Kate Barclay, Peter Bargh, Jamie
                  Emerson, Keith Henson, Lauren Malley,
                  Steve Neil, Anthony Smith, Luke
                  Smith, Paul Stefan, Emma Tumman,
                  Matt Wagster

Design concept: Steve Handley

Design: Peter Bargh

Production: Rose Teal

Photographs: © ePHOTOzine members 2001-2006

Print management: Imago Publishing Ltd
Printed in Singapore

Magezine Publishing books are available from all good bookshops.
Alternatively contact our order line on +44(0)1909) 512111, write
to us at the address at the top of this page or visit our online shop
at: www.ephotozine.com/shop

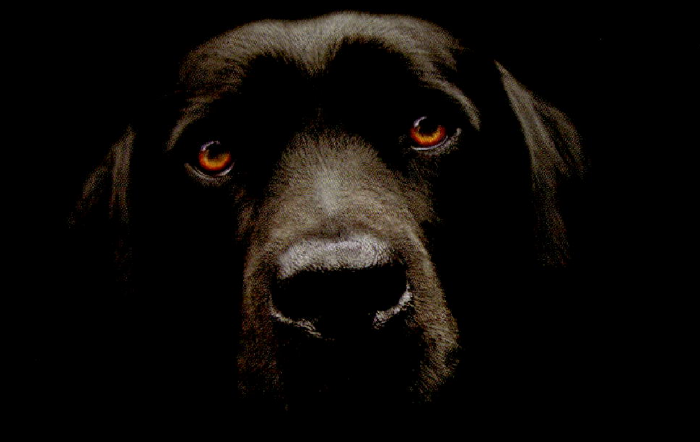

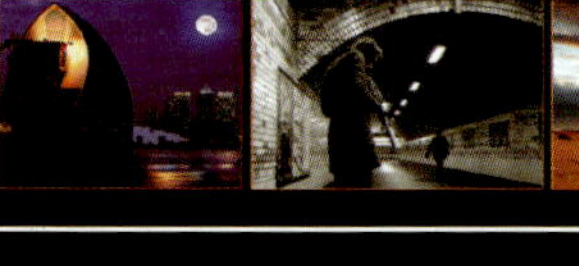
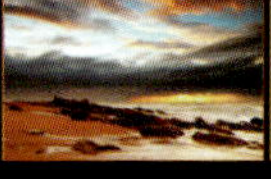
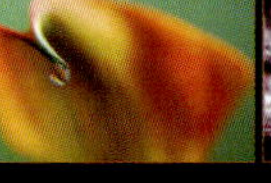
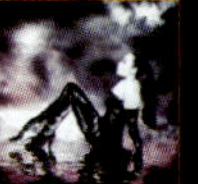

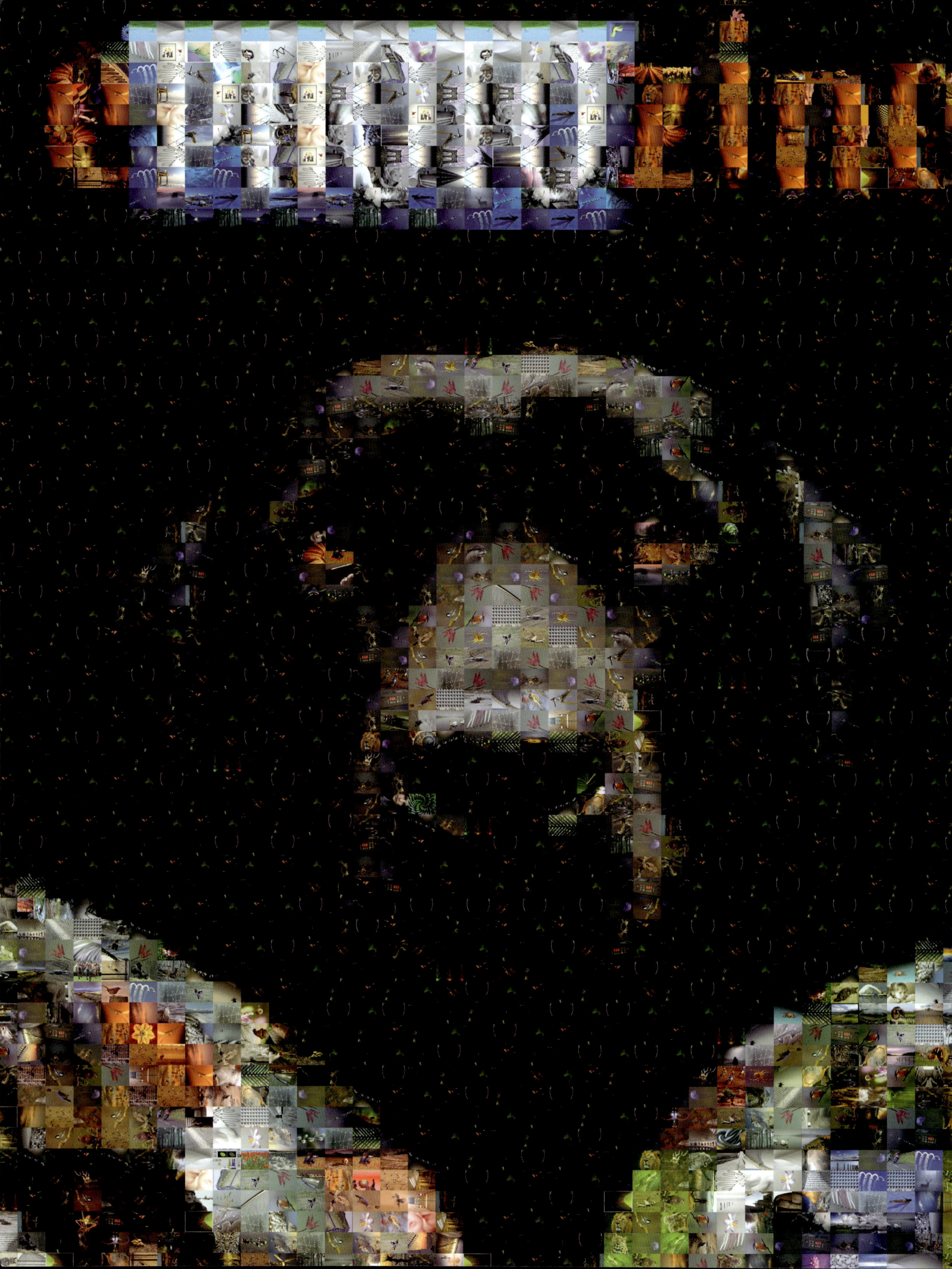

About The Book

The Guide to Great Photography brings together some of the finest images uploaded to ePHOTOzine over the course of its five year history. The pictures were selected from over a quarter of a million that have been uploaded into one of the 13 gallery subsections. These, along with hundreds of facts, tips and techniques, bring together a superb resource for anyone interested in photography who wants to gain inspiration, learn new tricks or just enjoy great images.

When an ePHOTOzine member, Seb Wheeler, suggested in our forums two years ago that we create a book of images, I had no idea what a mammoth task I was about to embark on!

At that time we had a gallery of around 153,000 images, split into 13 categories. A book, full of the best images and accompanied by tips and techniques, seemed like a simple plan to pull together. After sounding it out with members to see whether it would be something they'd like, the answer was a resounding 'Yes'. The nightmare began!

What I hadn't envisaged, those many moons ago, was that the gathering of the images would be such an arduous task. For starters, I had to look through our gallery of 250,000 photos and choose ones to go in. After around four hours of looking through one of the smallest sections, Sports, I'd delved through just 70 pages. I was only a quarter of the way through one section which equated to just 3% of the gallery! A quick calculation made me realise that I had another 243 hours to go just to choose the photos. Time to ask for help. I soon had several volunteer picture editors, and two months later I had a set of pictures. Following a template format created by my designer friend, Steven Handley, I began to lay out the pages.

Challenge two: over 200 pages of photos, all of different shapes and sizes needed to be placed. This reminded me of a complex jigsaw. Fortunately, I enjoyed jigsaws as a kid – sadly, I couldn't start with the edges! This took ages to get right, but once completed gave me a great sense of satisfaction. This satisfaction was soon to be shattered.

Our policy on ePHOTOzine is that copyright of uploaded photographs remains with the photographer. If we want to use photos, we will contact each photographer. The email correspondence began. We sent out about 1,800 emails requesting the use of a photo. This generated many responses asking questions, many bounce backs and lots of clarification. Total estimate of email correspondence over the two years has been over 5,500! In one week last year we had four members of staff working almost full-time sending, receiving and administrating emails.

In the end, through reasons including lost photos, non-answered emails, members not wanting to be in the book, non-signed model releases, and size-too-small problems, we ended up with 70% of the photographs submitted, many incorrectly. This meant a total redesign of the pages and lots more organisational headaches. More jigsaw puzzles! If anyone ever says to me "It's just pictures and words – how come it's taken so long?" I'll scream!

The fruit of all this hard work is the kind of book that I believe you will have never seen before and will never see again. The Guide to Great Photography features outstanding photos, useful captions and panels of advice throughout to help you improve your photography. Flick through the pages for inspiration, pore over the techniques for advice and guides and dip into sections to improve your skills. There's something in this book for everyone, from beginner to professional. Enjoy the book, and, now the hard work's over, I'm off to relax until the next great idea! ∎

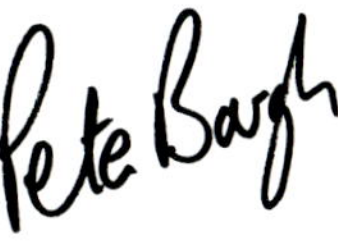

Peter Bargh, May 2006

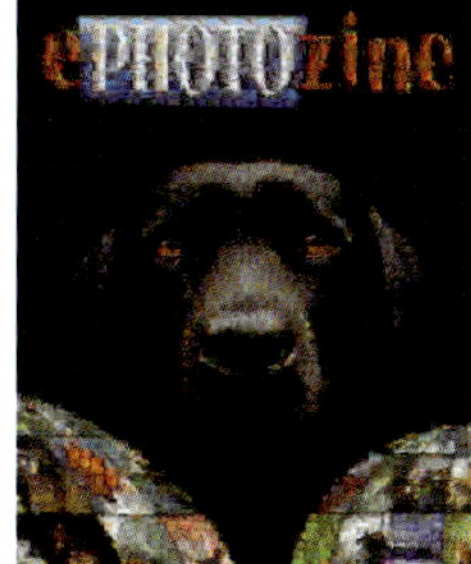

● This photograph of Max, by Martin Wait, is the most popular image on ePHOTOzine. I ran it through AndreaMosaic, using a folder full of photos selected for the book to create the mosaic. You may need to squint your eyes to see the original clearly. The tutorial showing how this fascinating effect is done can be viewed on ePHOTOzine, along with over 300 other film and digital techniques.

FORUMS – OUR COMMUNITY

■ Here's the place to ask questions and share ideas with like-minded photographers about current issues, techniques, equipment and more. If you're having difficulty, help is at hand from ePHOTOzine's broad base of members, no matter how specialised the problem. You can also make new friends, and meet up on group trips organised by members.

PHOTO-LOCATIONS

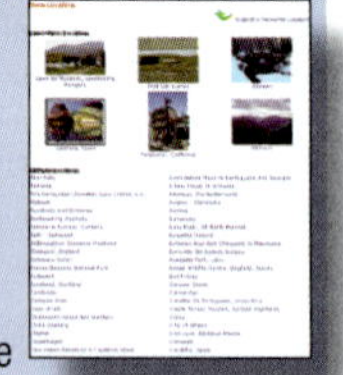

■ Are you struggling for ideas of where to go? Then take a look at the photo locations section of ePHOTOzine. This is where members list their absolute favourite and most impressive locations. By browsing through these pages, you are bound to find somewhere inspirational.

SHOPS

■ ePHOTOzine has a number of shops, run either by us or in partnership with photographic industry leaders. ePHOTOzine Direct can be found at www.ephotozine.com/shop. Other shops include a camera phone shop, and an online printing service.

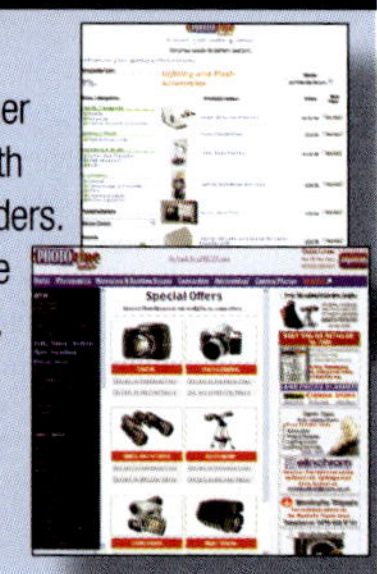

GLOSSARY

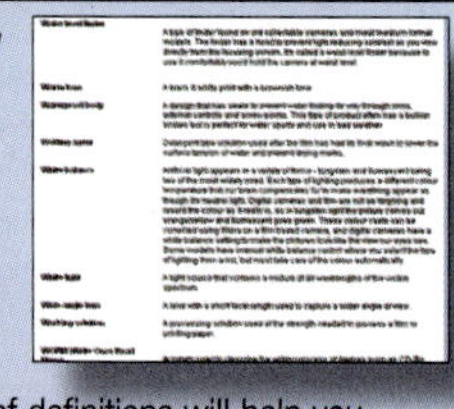

■ If you don't know your aspherical elements from your chromatic aberrations, this is the place to find answers. Our comprehensive list of definitions will help you improve your understanding.

PRO PORTFOLIOS

■ A place for those who earn a living from their photography to showcase a selection of their finest work. Check out some classic interviews in this section too.

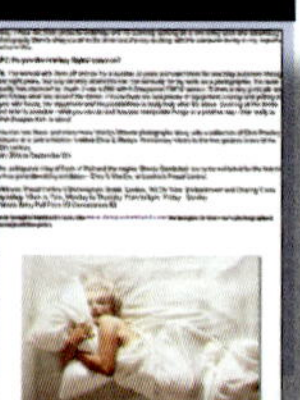

THE GALLERY

■ The gallery displays over 275,000 pictures, with over 4000 new images added every week. Each of ePHOTOzine's 41,000 members have their own portfolio to display their photos so that other photographers can critique, comment on, or simply admire images. Pictures uploaded can also win awards such as the 'Readers' Choice' award, which is decided by members' votes, along with 'Highly Commended' and the coveted 'Editor's Choice' award, selected by Peter Bargh, editor of ePHOTOzine.

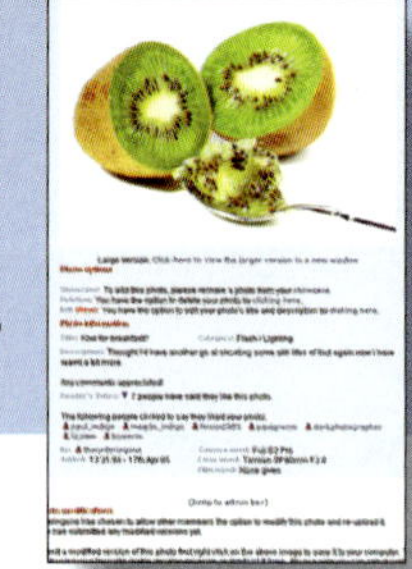

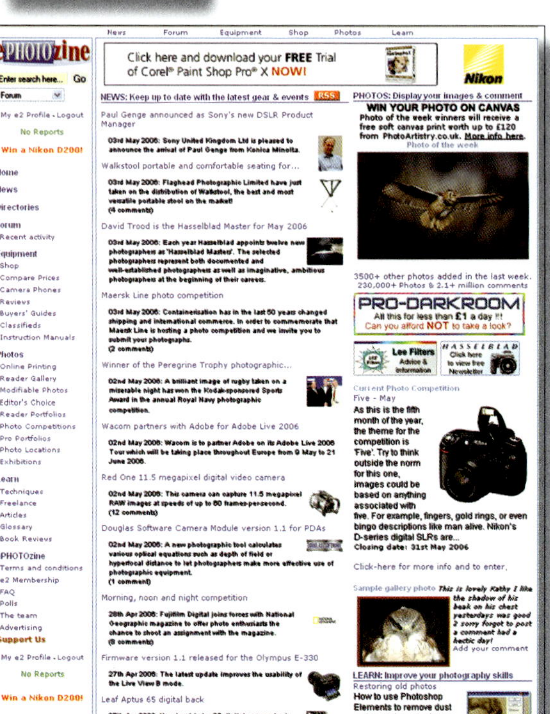

TECHNIQUES

■ Over 300 techniques covering all aspects of photography are provided to help you improve your images. Whatever level of expertise you have there is always something new to learn, whether it is a subject-based technique, a particular image editing technique, or something more specialist such as stereo-photography, this is the place to find the answers.

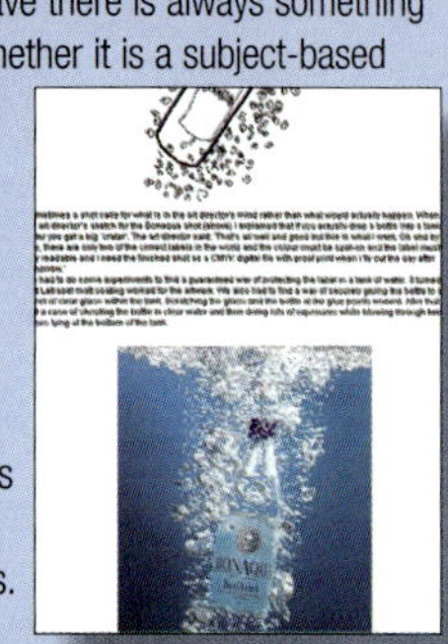

DIRECTORIES

■ A comprehensive resource of manufacturers, repair agencies, processing labs, photo courses, insurance companies and hire centres. Find contact details and website addresses for photography related companies, large or small. Other listings include model agencies, book publishers, stock libraries, and other useful websites.

NEWS

■ Keep abreast of the latest happenings in the world of photography. Our coverage is among the most comprehensive on the internet, covering news on the latest gear, events, competitions and industry gossip as it breaks.

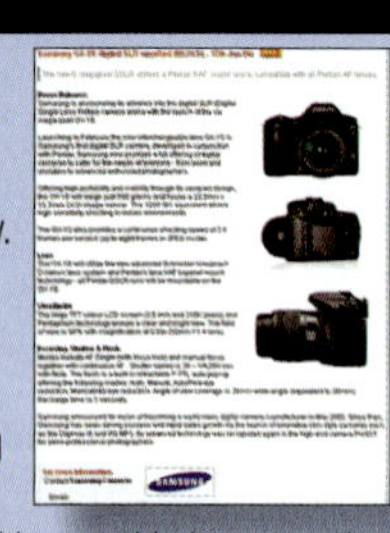

COMPETITIONS

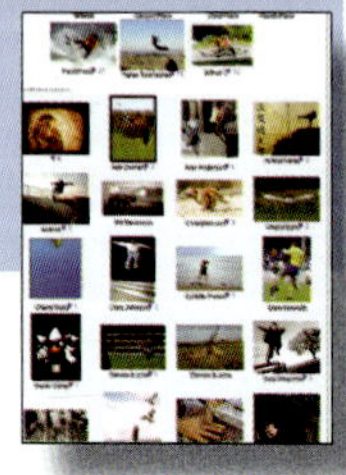

■ Every month a themed photo competition is open to members, giving you the opportunity to win fantastic prizes worth thousands of pounds. Fun one-hour challenges and caption competitions are held weekly by members too. See page 18-21 for details of previous winners.

EQUIPMENT REVIEWS

■ Sporting one of the most comprehensive ranges of lens tests on the web, the reviews section contains information on every different type of photographic equipment, helping you to make the right decision for your next purchase.

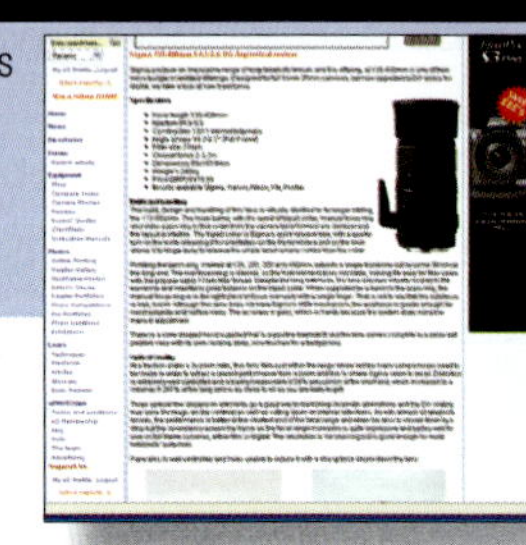

In the beginning...

Having just celebrated its fifth year, we take a look at ePHOTOzine's rise to become the UK's leading online photography magazine. What made Peter Bargh leave a secure job and go it alone in, at that time, the very precarious and unstable world of the internet? Premonition, stupidity or just adventure? Enjoy our insight into the making of ePHOTOzine.

The idea for ePHOTOzine came while I was working for one of the UK's largest publishers, EMAP. I was launch editor of *Digital PhotoFX* magazine – a well paid role, with some great benefits, including a lovely car. While the benefits were great, I seemed to have a new boss every five minutes. With each one bringing new ideas about how things should be run, the environment was quite volatile. I saw great people pushed sideways and poor people rise to the top. But these were not sound reasons to leave. It was more about motivation.

My reward for coming up with the concept for the digital magazine, and its subsequent development, was to be taken out for a curry! That £20 curry was a great investment – the magazine has now dropped FX from the title, but it's still the leading digital newsstand magazine. I'd also suggested that we introduce a website to bring extra features to *Digital PhotoFX*. The publisher seemed interested, but I could see it was way down in her priorities, so I started thinking that I could do this myself.

Over lunch with an old friend I started discussing this concept. He was excited and arranged a meeting with his financial partner and web development colleague Between us we came up with a very sketchy business plan for a new photography resource – OneWorld Photography.

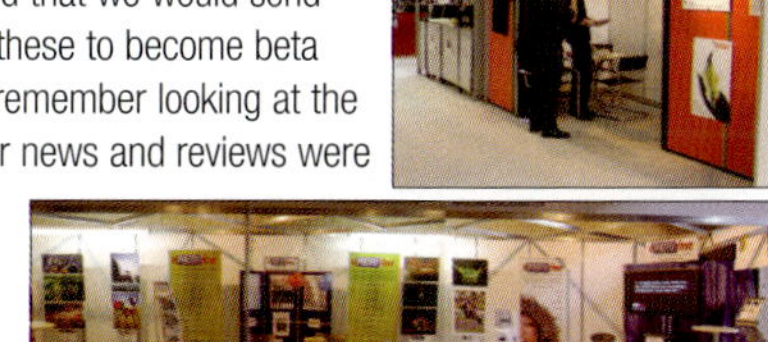

I handed in my notice in September 2000. It was one of the scariest moments of my life. I knew most things about magazines, editing, writing, design, but web? Apart from a few bits of HTML code to change text from plain to bold or create a new paragraph, I was completely in the dark.

I came up with a concept for the site – how I wanted it to look and what I wanted included. Some of the first drafts are to the right. I also came up with the name. The company was publishing and our plan was to create several web sites in a magazine format so Magezine Publishing Limited was registered. The first project, ePHOTOzine, was born. I had ambitious plans to come up with eHIFIzine eCARAVANzine and many more as soon as I got the photography one off the ground. How naive!

What followed was the most exciting, but also most frustrating year of my life. I wanted lush designs with complex search features to make the site the most original thing going, yet I had no idea how to brief the web development team or how it would all work. We muddled through and a concept was taken to Focus on Imaging at the Birmingham NEC in February 2001. I invited members of the trade to view and presented the concept on a Plasma TV in a small booth in Hall 9.

The interest from the trade and visitors was fantastic and many of those visitors are still members today. We asked people to register and explained that we would send them an email when it went live. We also asked 100 or so of these to become beta testers. In May 2001 the site went live. Months passed and I remember looking at the gallery and forums and thinking how quiet they were. Also, our news and reviews were not being indexed. I'd had the first UK hands-on experience with Minolta's Dimage 7 and wrote enthusiastically about this in a review. Weeks later nothing! Had I made the right move?

On several occasions I felt like throwing in the towel, but I was encouraged to stick at it. Fortunately, I did! It wasn't long before the numbers started to grow. 15,000 unique visitors per month gave us a story to tell the advertisers and, thanks to the likes of Nikon, Samsung and Jessops, we started to become viable.

Katie Teesdale joined as advertising manager and, shortly after, Will Smith as technical assistant. By the end of the first year we were starting to make great progress – 60,000 unique visitors, many more advertisers and, most importantly lots of regular members giving valuable feedback to the way the site should be developed. Tracey Johnson replaced Katie and the three of us made huge progress taking the site to new heights.

In the last year our membership has reached 297,000, we've moved offices into a business innovation centre and have been joined by Rose Teal (admin), Gary Wolstenholme (editorial), Rob Webb (development), Tom Cupr (web developer) and Tricia Aylward (advertising).

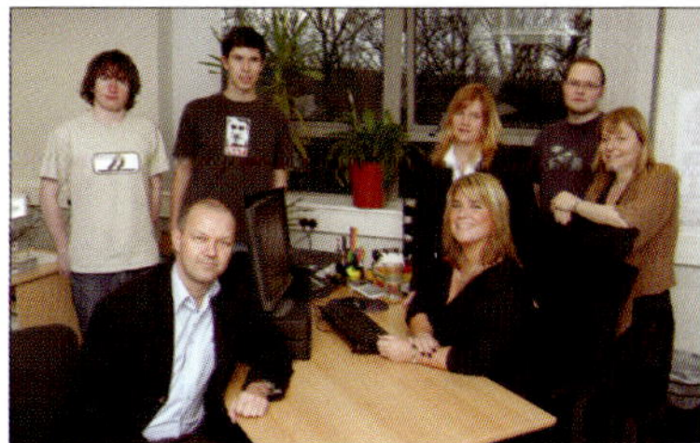

● Our small stand at the NEC 2003 and huge in 2006! Keith Henson pulls the crowds with his landscape talk.

● The team at the Turbine offices in Shireoaks. Back row: Rob, Will, Tricia, Gary and Rose; front Peter and Tracey.

ePHOTOzine has grown from under ten thousand unique visitors a month to ten thousand unique visitors a day and over three million a year! This increase in popularity has been caused by a steady improvement in the usability of the website and the features it offers.

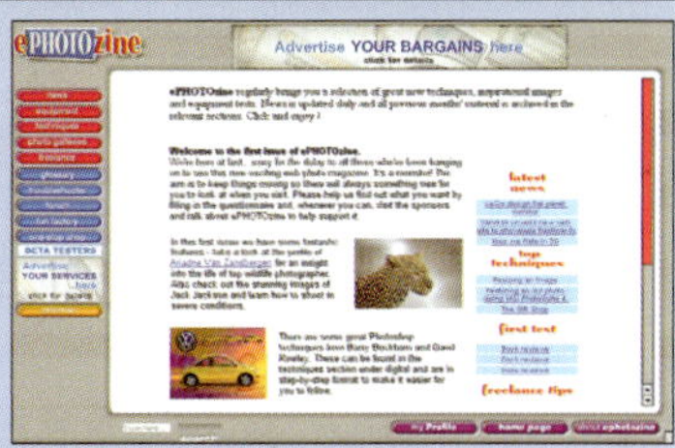

● The original build/layout of ePHOTOzine was a frame based model, run with ColdFusion. When Will Smith came onboard we changed over to PHP and a design with a more modern feel. This format has been adhered to with just slight tweaks.

Taking the reader gallery section of the website as an example, it has gone from simply offering the browsing of images to being able to browse, comment on, rate and modify them as well.

The overall experience for readers is now a lot more interactive and there is a much stronger community feel thanks to the way the main sections of the gallery, forum and reader portfolios all link together.

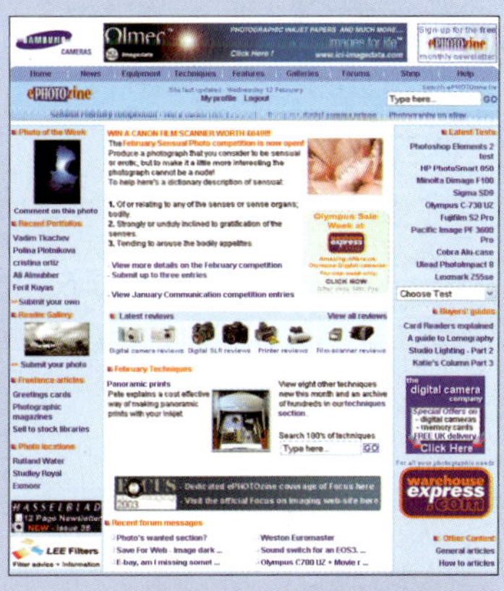

The improvements have, in part, been driven by the readers themselves, with the ePHOTOzine team always ready to listen to suggestions on how to improve the website.

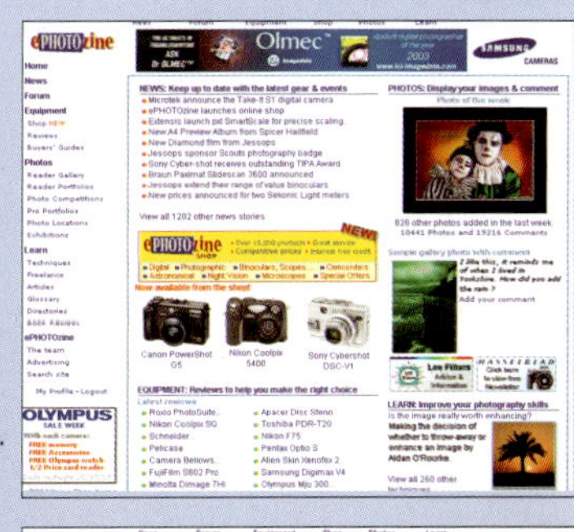

As well as the reader-suggested improvements there are all sorts of new features in the pipeline that will make ePHOTOzine an even more enjoyable experience in the future.

Will Smith
ePHOTOzine
Web developer

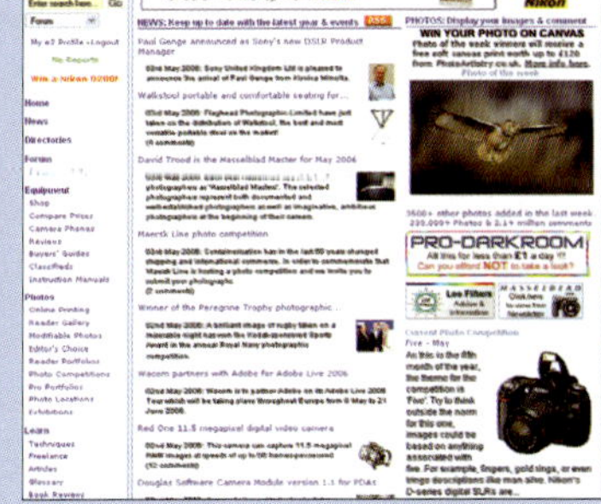

MEMBERS MEETING TIPS

The art of planning
■ When planning the initial meet online, it's important that you state a positive date and venue or the thread will become full of 'Yes, just let me know where and when' posts and will disappear without trace.
■ Plan everything in plenty of time. Late planning for a meet usually means only one or two people turn up.
■ The organiser really needs to take a bit of a 'lead' to avoid chaos.
■ Do your homework first. Visit the area if you don't know it well, check out important details like car parking.
■ Get the date included in the header of the forum message – it makes it easier to search and find older threads.

Location, location, location
■ Make sure the meeting point is very obvious. Provide good details of how to get there. Send out maps and directions if needed.
■ Use famous landmarks or beauty spots as meeting points to avoid confusion (e.g. under Blackpool Tower or the big clock at Waterloo).
■ Have a plan so people know what to do if they turn up late.
■ Post repeatedly in the forum (at least every couple of days) with a list of those attending to let as many people as possible know about the meet.
■ Be prepared with a backup location should something prevent you from getting to the original place or if the weather is poor.
■ If there are only going to be two or three of you, when you meet up decide if you all want to do things together or if you also want time to do your own thing. This saves misunderstandings.
■ Try to have a 'please most people most of the time' approach when planning – a gentle undulating walk in the Lakes will suit more people than a viciously difficult climb (although some will want to do the latter).
■ Carry a list of expected attendees.
■ Make a list of mobile numbers to contact people or swap mobile numbers with at least one other person who will be at the meet if you get separated from the main group. Make sure there will be mobile phone reception.
■ Check out where you're going using **www.multimap.com** and use Route Master to see how long it takes to get there.
■ Remember where you parked.
■ Take ear plugs on overnight stays – you never know who's going to be snoring fit to lift the roof!
■ Take your sense of humour.

Safety in numbers
■ Don't go on a meeting with one other person unless you know them.
■ Don't accept a lift from someone you don't know – it's tempting to accept a lift from the station, but be safe. Make other arrangements tactfully or see if other people can be in the car too.
■ Always tell someone where you are going and when you expect to return.
■ It's the individuals' responsibility to look after themselves. People who organise meets aren't there to look after the welfare of others.
■ Try to make sure you have enough petrol in the car. There's nothing worse than hunting for a petrol station in the middle of nowhere and holding up others in the group.
■ The days are long, especially if people stay from sunrise to sunset so make sure you have plenty of food and water.
■ Consider when and where people might like food or refreshments.
■ Make sure you have plenty of batteries and memory cards/film with you.

Fun and interaction
■ Have fun and take lots of photographs – that's what you're there for!
■ Take lots of incriminating photos of all other attendees!
■ Study the forum for a week before to keep up to date on the ePHOTOzine gossip.
■ Most importantly – never, ever, accidentally go to sleep where other ePHOTOzine members can see you – the embarrassing shots will be posted before you know what's happening!

MEETINGS AT ZOOS

■ Trips have been arranged to most zoos in the UK now. One of the highest turnouts was to **Chester Zoo in September 2004,** organised by Andy Wilmore (zippie). With over 30 members, including ePHOTOzine editor Pete and technical writer Gary Wolstenholme, they ventured around the grounds shooting everything that moved!

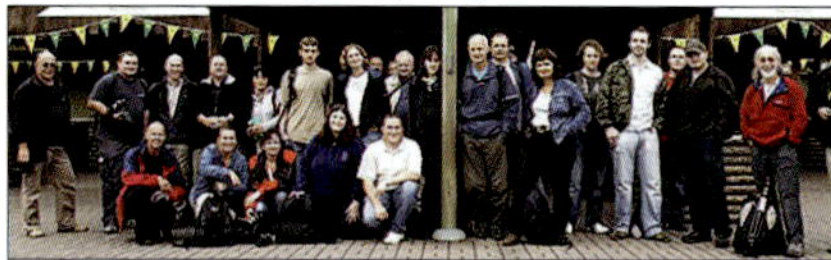

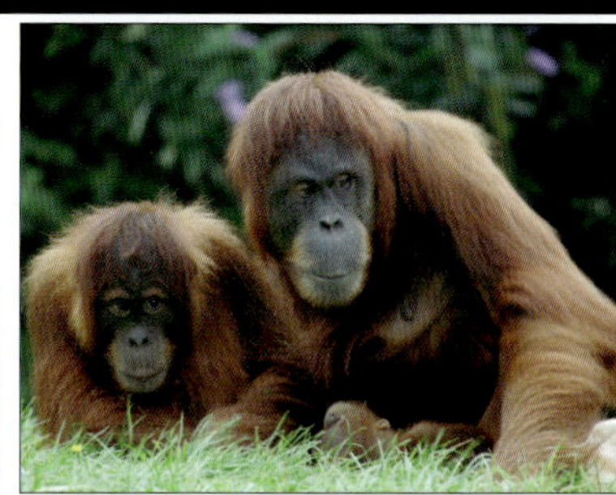

MEETINGS AT THE YORKSHIRE SCULPTURE PARK

Yorkshire Sculpture Park October 2005
Caleb Daniels suggested a meeting at the home of Henry Moore and Elizabeth Fink Sculptures. He was joined by several members including Alex Brookes, Colin Walden, Chris Ceaser, Ian Jackson and ePHOTOzine editor, Peter Bargh. Despite a rainy start, and losing one member, the day was a good one and included opportunities to photograph a wide variety of fungi, cows and horses at nose distance, and an unusual building, as well as the usual array of interesting sculptures. Caleb enjoyed the day so much he's since organised two more trips there. The photograph to the right is one of his from the third visit.

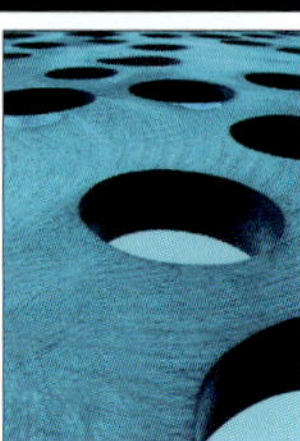

MEETINGS IN THE FORESTS

It's not surprising with user names like Carabosse, FrancisR, Greyheron53, JimboT, Kit-Monster, Lobsterboy, Randomrubble, RoyBoy and VFR400 that a fungi foray in **Epping Forest** might take their fancy. And that's exactly what happened in October 2004 when these nine members spent between 6 and 10 hours shooting the earthy 'shrooms. Many other forest meets have been held including ones at the New Forest, Forest of Dean, Sherwood and Burnham Beeches.

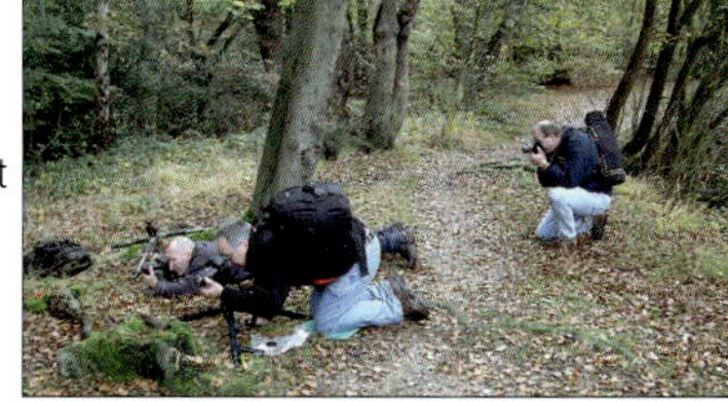

MEETINGS AT THE COAST

Matt Wagster has become known as the meetings king - he's attended more than any other member and, along with Stevie B, Edward Norton, Brian Price and Andy Dippie, camped over at **Flamborough**. They were joined the following day by Magda & Paul Indigo and Keith Henson, and it was that meeting that was to spark the partnership of Keith and Andy and the formation of Northscape (see page 38). We've had meetings all around the country's coastline, from the smooth white cliffs of Dorset to the rugged Scottish coastline.

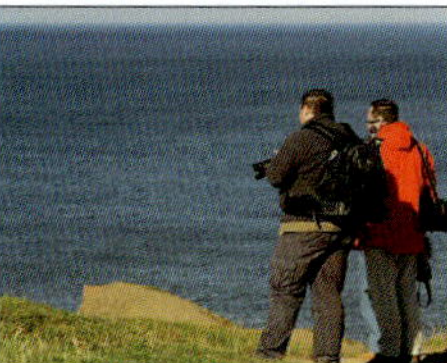

MEETINGS IN WALES

Alethea Hollis, Malcolm Johns, Mari Sterling, Gerwyn Gibbs, Dave Farmer and Robert Taylor formed a South Wales group whose meetings have included a trip to photograph the waterfalls of the **Ystradfellte valley**. Since that very wet day the group has grown in size and met on several occasions. Mari went on to organise the **Southerndown** meet as she lives nearby. They also met up at **Raglan Castle** and more recently at **Elan Valley**.

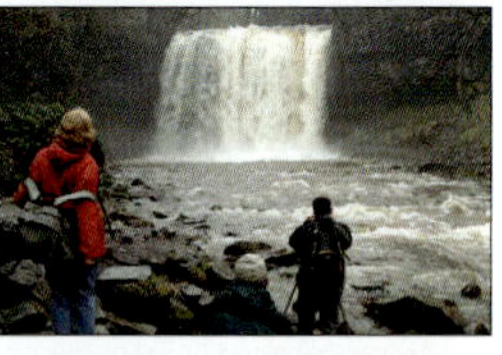

INTERNATIONAL MEETINGS

Amsterdam May 2005
It was thanks to Conrad Heijdemann that the first ePHOTOzine international meet took place in Holland. UK participants Ian (digicammad), Roger (ziggy), Suzi (suziblue) and Emma (ejtumman), met Dutch members John (johnvanbeers) & Tanja, and Conrad (conrad) and were treated to a fantastically well-organised event. The tour took them to Keukenhof, the well-known bulb flower show gardens, then to the Zaanse Schans, a preservation area north of Amsterdam where there used to be over 1000 windmills. Then to the city, where they walked along the typical canals and, finally, to the picture postcard area of Kinderdijk featuring no less than 19 windmills. Suzi and Ian, pictured right, went on to organise the next meeting in **Paris, April 2006,** although due to others' commitments only Suzi, SheilaC and Ziggy could attend.

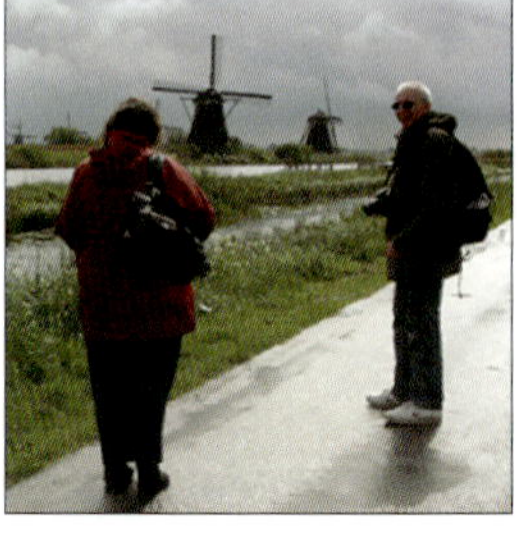

Meeting members

Over the last five years ePHOTOzine has grown to be one of the biggest photography communities on the internet, but this virtual club has also moved into the real world with at least one members' meeting now taking place every week. The meeting phenomena was never planned, it all started way back in 2002 when Big Bri asked, "Anyone fancy a day trip?"

When one of ePHOTOzine's founder members, Brian Price (Big Bri), posted a thread up in November 2002 asking "Is there anyone on here thinks it would be good fun to meet up for a day of happy snapping somewhere? Or am I just bonkers?" we never expected the direction the site was about to go in.

Our forums were starting to get busier and friendships were beginning to form, but this suggestion started a ball rolling that has turned ePHOTOzine into probably the largest camera club going.

From that first meeting, which became a visit to Westonbirt Arboretum, we have had members meet up all over the country and had several overseas events too. It's a great way to meet like-minded photographers. Here are just a few of the recorded highlights.

ONE THAT STARTED THE BALL ROLLING – WESTONBIRT ARBORETUM

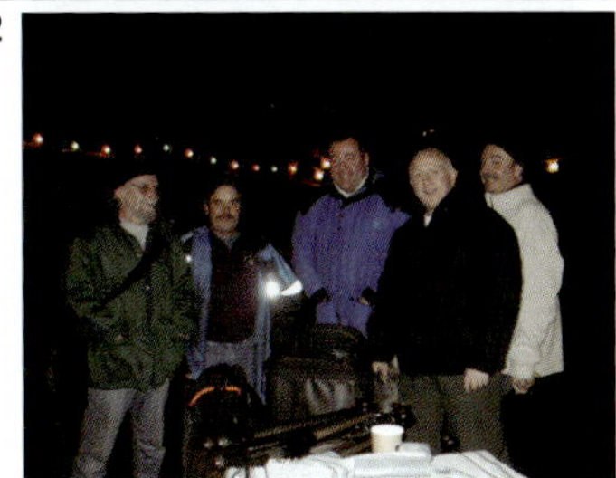

Westonbirt Arboretum in Gloucestershire – December 2002
This was the first ever recorded ePHOTOzine meeting of five members – Chris Taylor, Roy Heath, Brian Price, Alan Benson and Barry Thomas. With the exception of Roy and Alan, who are neighbours, this was a first meeting for our group, although everyone knew each other through ePHOTOzine.

At this time of the year Westonbirt Arboretum has a tour called "The Enchanted Wood" – a one mile walk through the woods where a series of coloured lights are used to illuminate some of their very fine specimen trees and bushes.

THE BIG ONE! – MEETINGS IN SCOTLAND

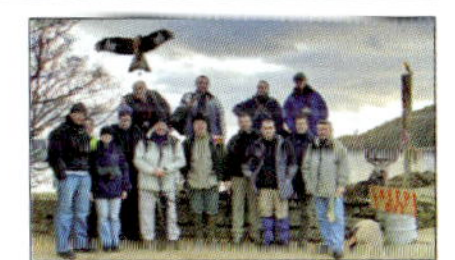

David Watson, Noel Cummins, Adam Pratt, Roy Mathieson, Rich Jobling, Mike Fisher, Laura Stevenson, Adam McCormack, Andy Currie, Ian Oliver, Alan Humphris, Paul Barr, Paul Gaughan, Adrian Carr, Suzanne Lebrun and Colin McGregor met at Balmaha on Loch Lomondside. This meeting led on to the gargantuan organisation of **Rowardennan November 2005** by David Watson, who runs a Scottish youth hostel with his wife. Rowardennan has been the biggest ePHOTOzine event yet, with over 45 members staying for the weekend.

MEETINGS AT WILDLIFE CENTRES

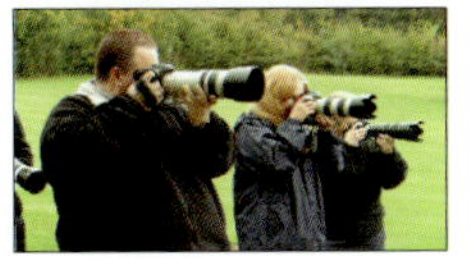

We have a diverse range of photographers, ranging from beginners to pros, who shoot everything from abstracts to flowers. One of the main groups are wildlife photographers and they've met up all over the place. Wildlife centres provide one of the better meeting points and are a great way to spend a day learning from the experts.

THE NOW LEGENDARY NORTH WEST MEET

Blubberhouses near West End village, North Yorkshire
Following on from the first meeting in Westonbirt, Bill Tavenar (sinargee), invited members to join him for a weekend meeting staying at the West End Outdoor Centre near Blubberhouses. The location

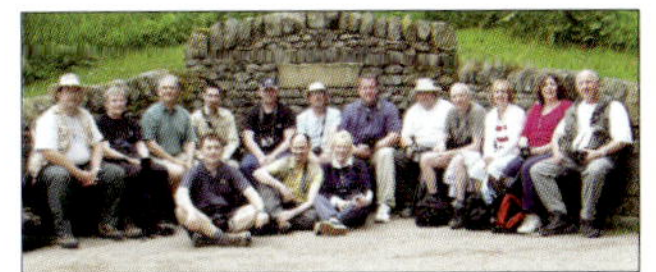

offered members a chance to meet, but also take fabulous scenic shots of the surrounding areas including Fountains Abbey.

MEETINGS AT BIRD RESERVES

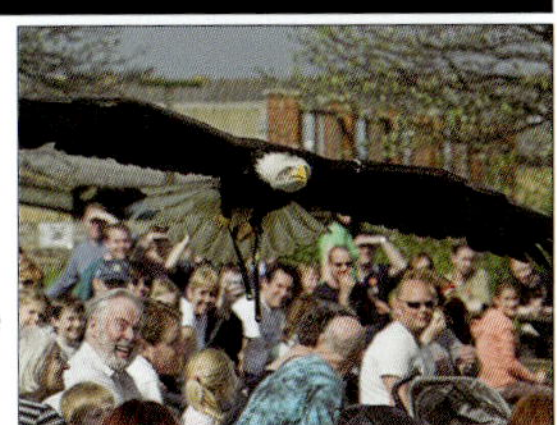

Eagle Heights was the location for this bird of prey flying display. It's just one of the centres where meetings have been held. We even have members, such as Vince Jones, who run centres and arrange special meetings. Vince runs the Barn Owl Centre in Gloucester.

ORGANISING MEETS

■ We have a forum section just for meetings. Simply post a new topic with the subject heading relevant to the meeting you want to organise and then give a few details of your suggested location/itinerary.

■ Meetings can be anywhere you like. If you're planning to visit a stately home, gardens, countryside, wildlife reserve, rural location, town centre, sporting event or even just stay locally, you will usually find several other members who'd be more than happy to join you.

■ Check out the tips opposite to help you plan one.

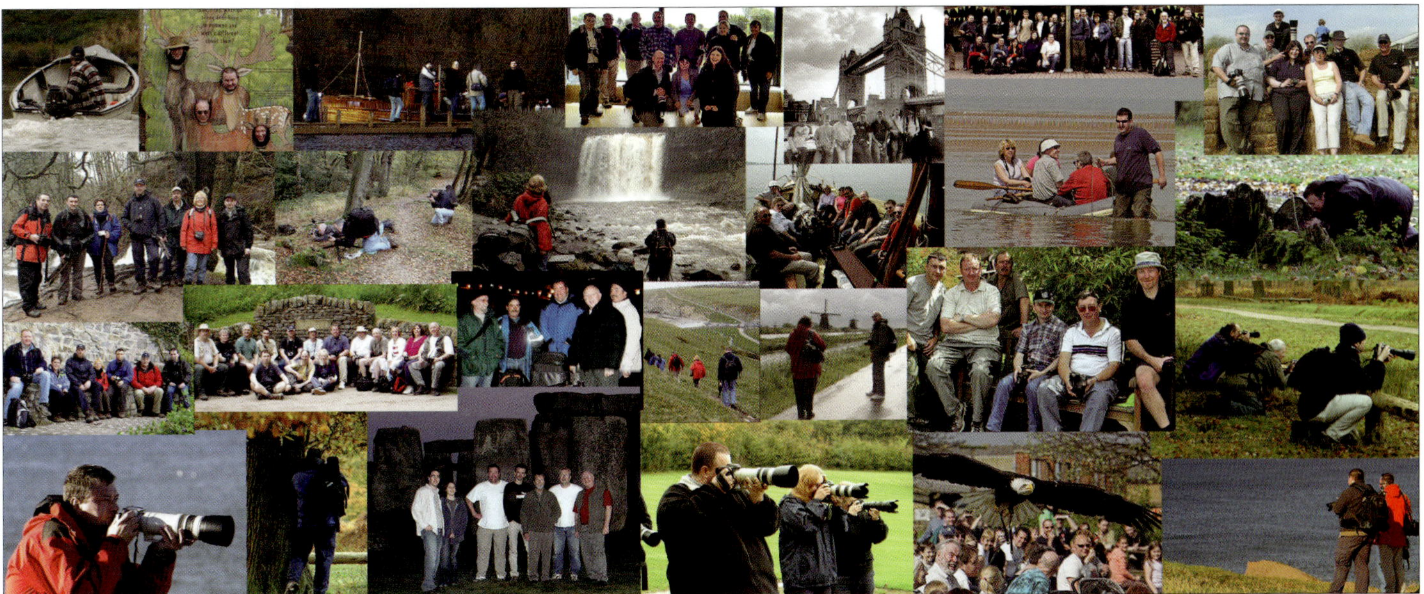

CAMERA TYPES

Throughout the history of photography we've seen many formats come and go. The pioneers shot on glass plates, which were replaced by sheet film and then large sized roll film, such as 120 and 620.

What followed, driven by Kodak, was a range of easier-to-use formats, from smaller 127 roll film to cartridge loading 110 and 126. Then came the short-lived Disc system and, most recently, the biggest film flop to date, the APS system. 35mm introduced in 1913 outlived them all, that was until digital.

Digital photography has now surpassed most other forms of image recording – it's killed the Polaroid instant camera and has torn the foundations away from the seemingly infallible 35mm camera.

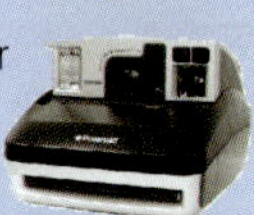

Digital camera

A digital camera records the image onto a light sensitive CCD (charge-coupled device). This converts light into a huge array of coloured squares known as pixels (picture elements). These make up the digital photograph and the more pixels in a photo the bigger you can produce it without seeing the squares. This is known as resolution. Most cameras today are at least two million pixel resolution, creating photos with a pixel grid of 1800x1660.

35mm camera

The most popular film camera uses a roll of film available in lengths up to 36 exposures. The film is exposed in the camera and then processed to produce prints or transparencies. Single-lens reflex (SLR) versions are still popular amongst camera enthusiasts, but the mass market that shot on 35mm compacts has largely moved to digital compacts.

Compact vs SLR

A compact camera has a built in lens, usually a zoom, and the image is viewed through a viewfinder or LCD. It's small and easy to carry around, but not as versatile as an SLR.

An SLR is a bigger camera, but usually has a lens that can be removed and replaced with more specialist optics. Huge magnification options are available and also extreme wide-angles and specialist macro gear. You see through the lens that takes the photo so they are more accurate when composing your shot. The cameras generally have a wider range of features, allowing more complex photos to be taken. The SLR is the choice of the enthusiast.

Medium-format

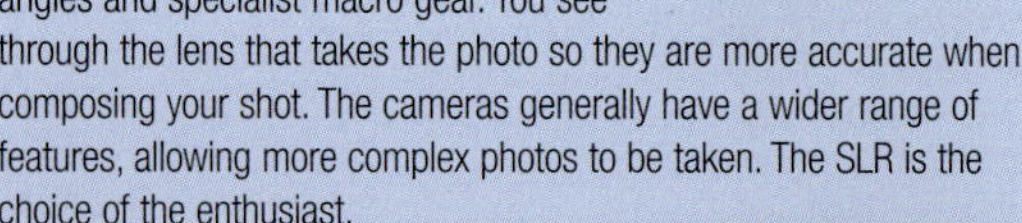

Cameras that use 120 and 220 roll film to deliver negatives with sizes from 6x4.5cm up to 6x17cm. Although this area of photography has also suffered with the rise of digital, there are still many photographers who prefer the larger format and enjoy the benefits it brings. It tends to be the professional advertising and fashion photographers, supplying to agencies, who still demand a film-based result and medium-format gives the desired results, but with the rate digital is going the days of medium-format are numbered.

Large format

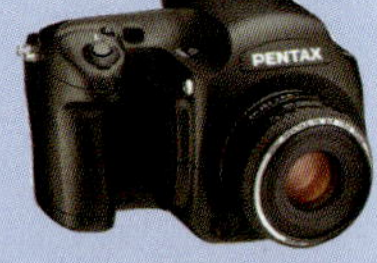

Going right back to the roots these cameras, with anything upwards from 5x4in, are now used by high end advertising, architecture and fine art photographers. The sheet film allows image by image processing so users can expose and develop each exposure to specific needs. The results leap off a light box too, but the size of camera and fiddly nature of the equipment make them too slow and hindering for most photographers.

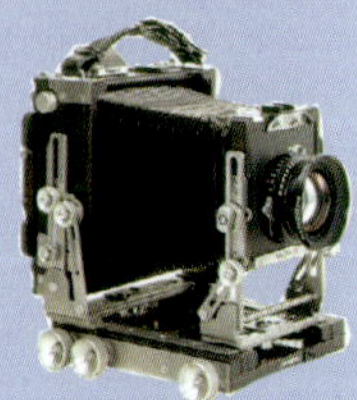

SLR CAMERA FEATURES

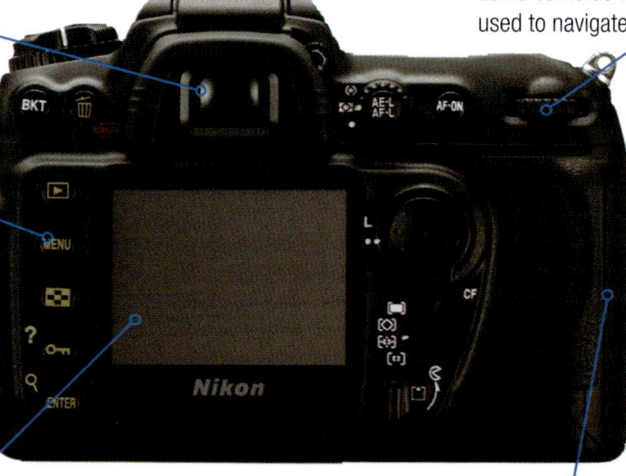

Shutter Release

This is the button you press to take a photo. Pressing this lightly will also focus the camera. Some cameras have a separate button on the back for focusing continuously.

Built-in flash

Most cameras have a low-powered built in flash which will help you to take pictures in low light. A more powerful flash can be added to the hotshoe on top of the camera.

Mode dial

Selecting the required exposure mode is done with the mode dial. Some cameras have many preset automatic scene modes covering all sorts of different shooting scenarios.

Depth-of-field preview

Pressing this button closes down the aperture so that you can see its effect on the area you have in focus. When using this control the viewfinder will darken depending on what aperture setting is being previewed.

Interchangeable lens

A wide range of lenses for every purpose are available for most SLR camera systems. Special purpose lenses such as fish-eyes and ultra-telephotos provide unique perspectives.

Viewfinder

On an SLR the image in the viewfinder is directed through the picture taking lens, allowing you to see exactly what you are taking. Other features such as exposure and focusing information are also displayed here.

Flash hot-shoe

Primarily, the hotshoe is intended for the connection of a more powerful external flashgun. Other useful accessories such as a spirit-level, can be attached here as well.

Command dial

Most cameras have one or two dials to control the shutter speed, aperture and exposure compensation. On some cameras the dials are used to navigate the menus.

Menu controls

Controls for the digital side of the camera are revealed in the menu. Settings normally found here include colour preferences, quality settings and custom functions.

LCD screen

The screen will display pictures that have been taken along with exposure information and the time and date that your images were taken.

Memory card slot

This is where your digital 'film' goes. Memory cards are available in many different formats and capacities, the most common being CompactFlash and Secure Digital.

ACCESSORIES

An SLR offers an expanding range of equipment versatility. Through the lens mount you have access to a wide range of lenses from ultra wide-angle to super powerful telephoto. You can also buy converters and adaptors to get you ultra close to the subject. There are attachments to look round 90° and even ones to turn your camera into a pinhole camera. Then there's the hotshoe giving you access to a much more powerful flash and the viewfinder can be modified to be viewed at right angles so you can see more comfortably when shooting at low level. Many cameras have a cable release socket to fire the camera from a distance and all have a tripod mount to allow the camera to be mounted on a solid platform. The latest digital cameras can be connected to a computer and operated from software, known as tethered shooting, which is handy for on-the-move photography with a laptop or for accurate studio use.

Back to basics

If you are new to photography or require a refresher course in the basics of camera features check this section out first. Here we explain about focusing, exposure metering and composition as well as giving you a rundown on camera types, lens options, flash and other vital information you need to know.

We've kept the information short and simple, but it should be enough to whet your appetite. If you want more advanced advice you can either view our wide range of free tutorials on ePHOTOzine or join the forums and ask as many questions as you like. With over 270,000 visitors each month there's always someone around to help.

CAMERA HANDLING

How you use your camera is a matter of personal preference, but good handling can lead to sharper pictures.

Holding a compact camera

When using a camera with an LCD screen, it is important to ensure that the camera is held steady. By keeping your elbows into your body you can hold the camera much steadier than you can at arms length. The LCD screen also frees you up to use other, less conventional objects to support your camera. Squeeze the shutter release rather than stabbing it in a jerky fashion.

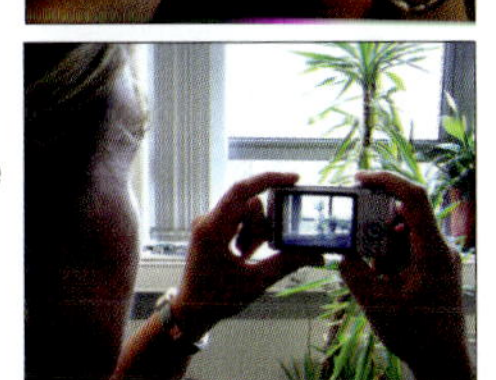

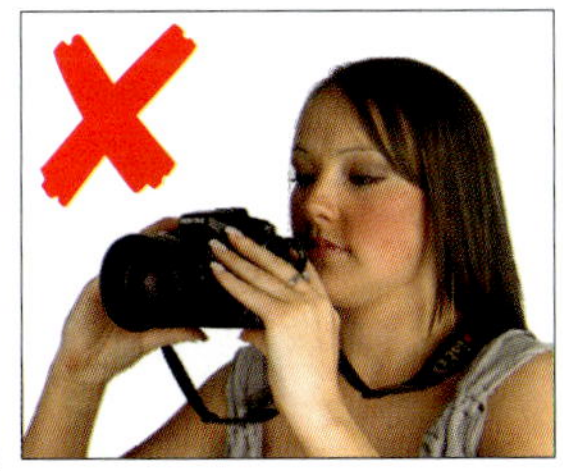

■ Holding your camera against a wall or any other solid object will allow you to take longer exposures when light levels drop.

Holding an SLR

We gave a compact camera user an SLR and she held it like this (see pic right). Wrong!
Hold the camera with two hands, supporting most of the weight of the camera under the lens with your left hand, and one around the finger grip to release the shutter. A good way to improve the steadiness of the camera is to keep your left elbow pressed against your body and to widen your stance.

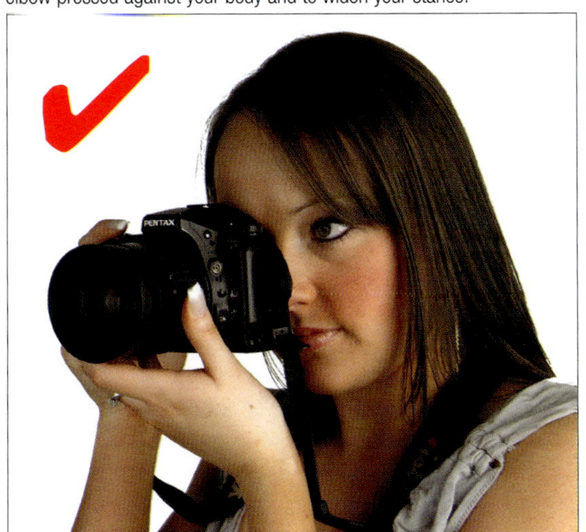

DIGITAL OR FILM – FROM CAPTURE TO REVIEW

■ Both the latest digital cameras and older film cameras work in a similar way. You point the camera at your chosen subject, look through a viewfinder to compose the shot and press a button to take the photograph. As you press the button a shutter opens and allows light in through the lens which is focused on a light sensitive receptor. In film cameras the film is the receptor and in digital cameras it's a CCD. The image is then either in latent form when shooting with film or converted to pixels when using digital.

■ You then send the film to a lab who use chemicals to develop the image into a strip of negatives and print onto paper to make your photos.

■ The digital files can either be emailed to a lab for prints to be made, burned onto a CD and taken to a shop, or mailed, or output on a home inkjet printer. Models specifically designed for photo printing will give the best results.

■ Digital photos can be improved before they are printed using image editing software, such as Photoshop, Elements or Paint Shop Pro. You can use this for basic enhancements such as tighter cropping, retouching spots or increasing contrast or saturation. It can also be used for more complex things such as removing articles from shots, adding things, combining elements or complex layer jobs with lots of extra manipulation. The other good thing about digital is that you can preview the shot on the camera's LCD as soon as you've taken it, delete a bad one and reshoot.

■ Film users don't have to miss out. A scanner can be used to convert the film or prints into digital files and then edit them, so they can be just as good as those from a digital camera.

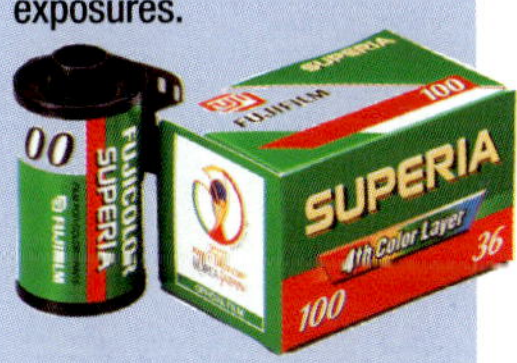

● Above: the CCD that you'd find in a digital camera is the modern film. Below: 35mm film comes in sizes from 12 to 36 exposures.

COMPACT CAMERA FEATURES

Shutter Release
This button has two stages of control. Lightly press the button to focus and press it all the way to take a photo.

Mode dial
Used to access exposure modes, scene assist programs and movie mode and voice memo recording.

Zoom control
Most cameras use a switch to change the focal length as you move it back and forth. Some more advanced cameras have a manual zoom ring.

Viewfinder
Many digital compacts no longer have an optical viewfinder. Instead you see the image on an LCD screen on the back of the camera. Models that do have a separate optical viewfinder can suffer from parallax error. This means you don't get exactly what you composed for, but you do save on battery power and see easier in bright light.

Built-in flash
Provides illumination when light levels drop or for fill-in in harsh light. Only a few compacts have a hotshoe to connect an external flash, so the way to add extra power is using an external slave.

LCD screen
Located on the back to serve as a viewfinder as well as allowing you to playback images. The main problem with LCD screens is the delay between displaying the scene and taking the picture. This 'shutter lag' can be frustrating, especially when trying to capture fast moving subjects.

Built in zoom lens
Compact digital cameras do not have an interchangeable lens like on an SLR. To make up for this many cameras sport a large zoom range of 10x to maximise the flexibility of the camera.

FOCAL LENGTH

What is it?

Most cameras have either a built-in zoom lens or a choice of interchangeable lenses. The numbers on the lens in millimetres refer to the focal length. 35mm format has been the standard for so long that all focal lengths for digital cameras are given with the equivalent in 35mm format. In 35mm format the standard lens is 50mm. It's called standard because it gives roughly the same magnification as the human eye, which is actually around 43mm.

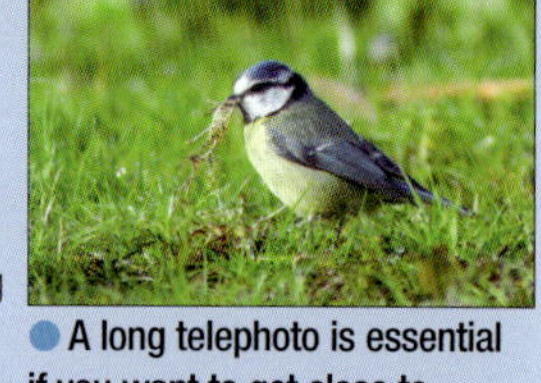

Anything longer than a standard lens is classed as a telephoto lens and magnifies the subject. Anything shorter than 50mm is classed as wide-angle and decreases magnification but gains a wider angle of view to capture more of the scene in the frame.

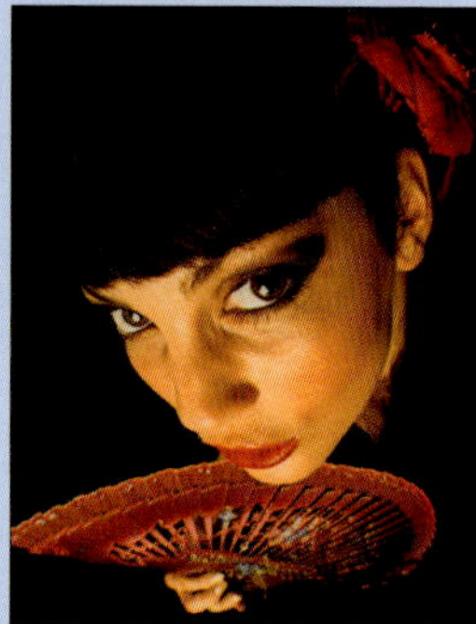

● A long telephoto is essential if you want to get close to nature. This nest gathering Blue Tit was taken with a 600mm.

Ultra wide-angles are lenses wider than 21mm and super telephotos are lenses longer than 300mm. There are also special lenses, such as macros, that allow superb close up facilities and fish-eye lenses that have a 180 degree angle-of-view and produce circular images.

In most cases the physical size of a lens is relative to the focal length, a 400mm lens will be bigger than a 28mm lens for example. One exception to this is a mirror or reflex lens, so called because it has a set of mirrors inside the lens to fold the light, making the lens about half as long as a conventional telephoto.

● This unusual portrait was taken using a fish-eye adaptor – a low-cost accessory that converts a standard or wide lens to give a distorted, super wide-angle view.

There are times when your budget may not allow the purchase of a super long telephoto or an ultra-wide lens. Or you may have a camera with a non-interchangeable lens. If so there are attachments made to go wider or longer. Designed for camcorders these tele and wide adaptors can be used on still cameras, although the quality isn't fantastic. There are also 1.4x, 2x and 3x converters for interchangeable lens users that turn a 80-200mm zoom into a 112-280mm, 160-400mm and 240-600mm respectively.

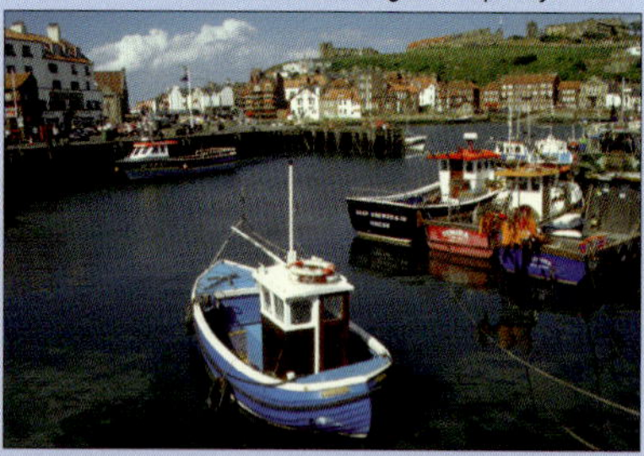

● A 28mm wide angle is perfect for most landscapes and scenic shots like this.

ANGLE-OF-VIEW

What is it?

The angle-of-view is basically how wide an area is covered by a given lens.

How does it affect me?

Angle-of-view is influenced by two variables – the focal length of the lens, and the size of the area of light sensitive material used to capture your image. Typically, if you double the focal length of your lens you will get half as much in the frame.

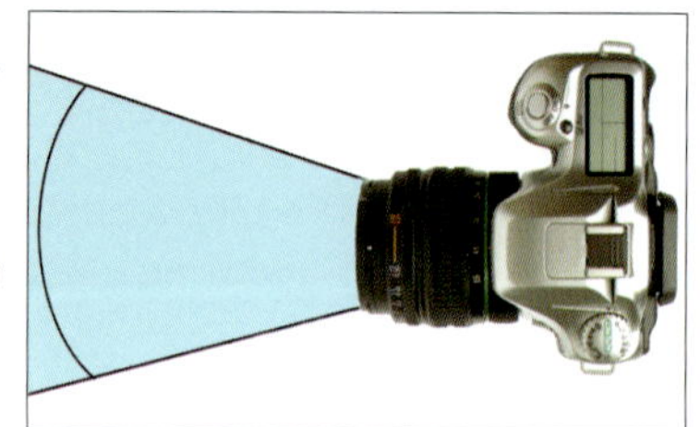

Different image formats also affect the angle-of-view. For example, a 50mm lens is considered to be a standard lens on a 35mm camera. On larger formats, a 50mm lens would be considered to be a wide-angle lens, and on smaller formats 50mm is a telephoto. This difference in the angle of view will also affect the depth of field. Smaller format cameras will have more in sharp focus for a particular angle-of-view than larger format cameras because the focal length of the lens used will be shorter.

The focal length table below gives a rough idea of the equivalent focal lengths of lenses on a compact digital camera with a 2/3inch digital sensor, through to a 5x4in large format camera. Below that is an illustration to show the approximate crop of digital sensors with 1.3x, 1.5x and 2x crop factors.

FOCAL LENGTH EQUIVALENTS

2/3inch sensor	4/3rds sensor	APS-C sensor	35mm film	6x4.5cm film	6x6cm film	6x7cm film	5x4in film
6mm	14mm	18mm	28mm	35mm	40mm	65mm	90mm
8mm	17mm	24mm	35mm	40mm	50mm	80mm	105mm
10mm	25mm	30mm	50mm	75mm	80mm	105mm	150mm
18mm	45mm	55mm	90mm	125mm	150mm	180mm	270mm
30mm	70mm	90mm	135mm	200mm	250mm	270mm	400mm
45mm	100mm	135mm	200mm	300mm	350mm	400mm	600mm
66mm	150mm	200mm	300mm	450mm	500mm	600mm	900mm

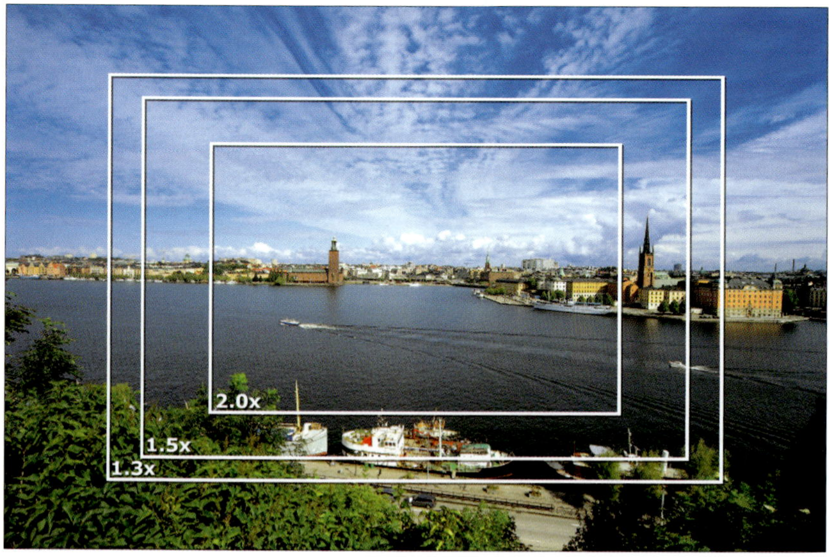

FOCAL LENGTH COMPARISON

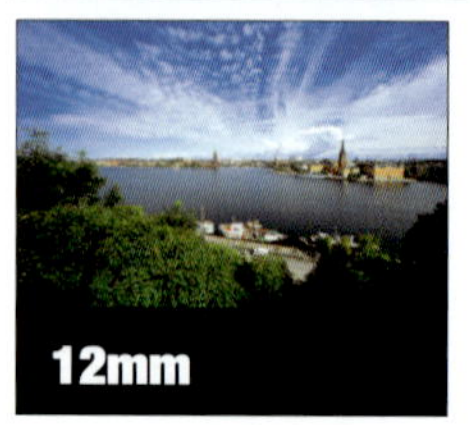

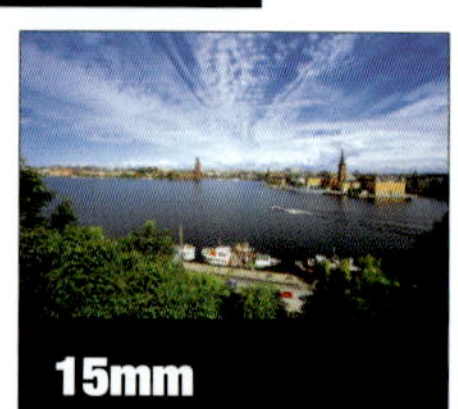

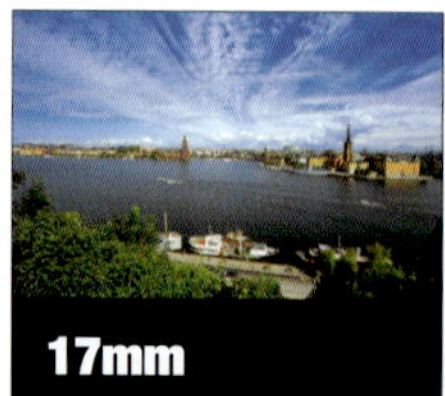

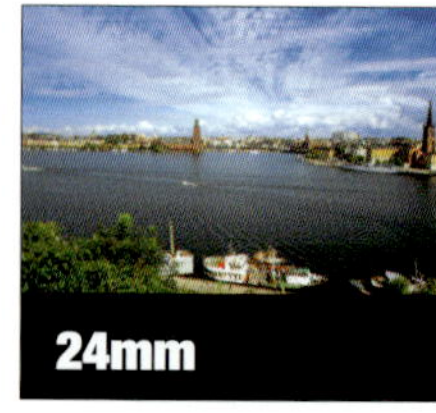

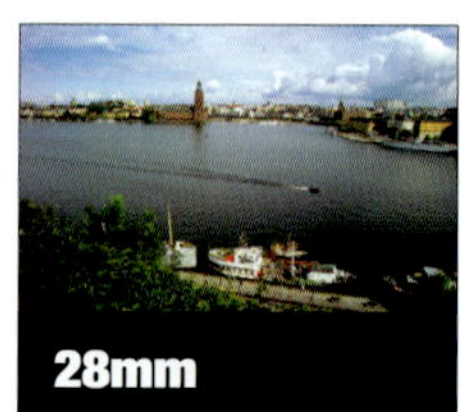

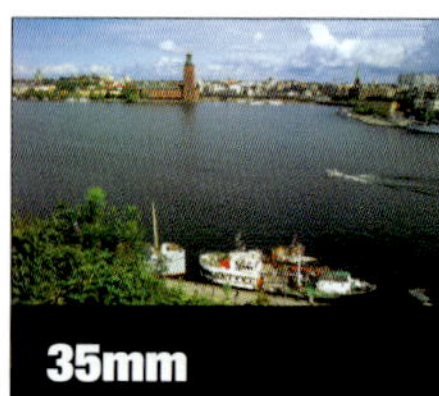

● Thanks to Sigma Imaging UK for use of this picture sequence.

WHICH LENS?

How do I choose?
Choosing which lens is best for you can be a mind boggling task. The list of different manufacturers and specifications can seem never ending.

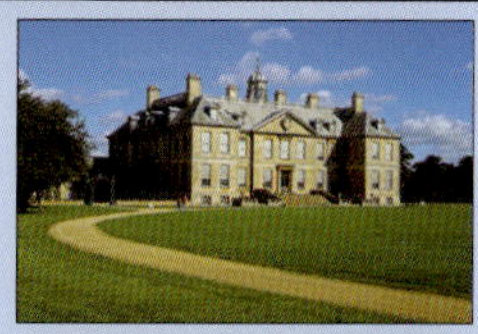

Independents or camera manufacturer's own?
There are lenses available by third party manufacturers, such as Sigma or Tamron, who offer similarly specified lenses at a fraction of the price of those made by camera companies. Often third party lenses aren't quite as good at some things as the professional camera manufacturers' lenses, such as resolution or build quality, but will offer a viable alternative for those without an endless budget. ePHOTOzine has reviews of many of these lenses so you can compare how well each lens performs, and whether one lens may be worth paying more for than another.

Prime or zoom?
Choosing a fixed or a zoom lens depends entirely on your requirements. Zoom lenses are popular because they allow you to recompose your shot in seconds, and will generally do the job of three or more fixed lenses without the bulk. On the other hand prime lenses tend to have higher optical quality and brighter maximum apertures than zooms so are the preferred choice for low light and action photography.

Wide-angle or telephoto?
Wide angles allow you to emphasize perspective by getting in close to your subject. This makes them great for sweeping landscapes where objects in the foreground appear much larger and the horizon appears much further away. Telephoto lenses not only bring a distant subject closer, they also have the effect of compressing perspective because you will generally be further from your subject. Lenses from this range are useful for landscapes or sports and wildlife, where access is restricted.
Visit **www.photodo.com** for a huge range of lens tests and buying advice.

COMPOSITION

What is it?
Composition is the art of placing the various elements of the subject in a suitable place in the viewfinder so they appear aesthetically pleasing or challenging in the photograph.

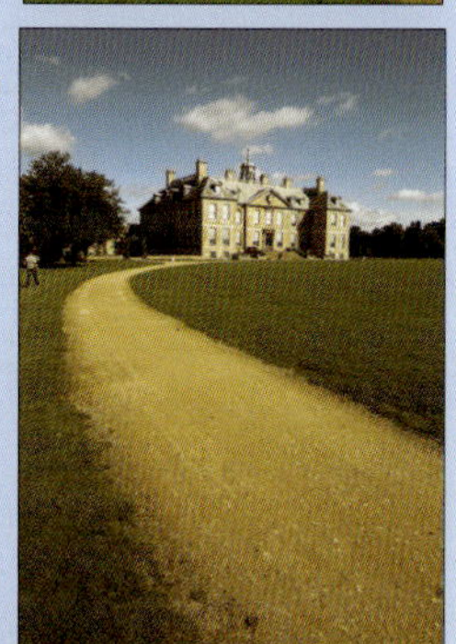

How will it improve my photography?
Beginners tend to always fix the subject bang in the centre of the frame with loads of wasted space around. They also shoot with the camera in horizontal position, called landscape format.

Try to move closer and fill the frame with the subject. Consider turning the camera through 90deg into portrait format when the subject suits the upright format. Also, consider shooting with the subject off-centre – use focus lock to ensure it comes out sharp.

In this architectural shot on the right the photographer has moved closer and used a wide-angle to allow the path to lead our eyes to the building.

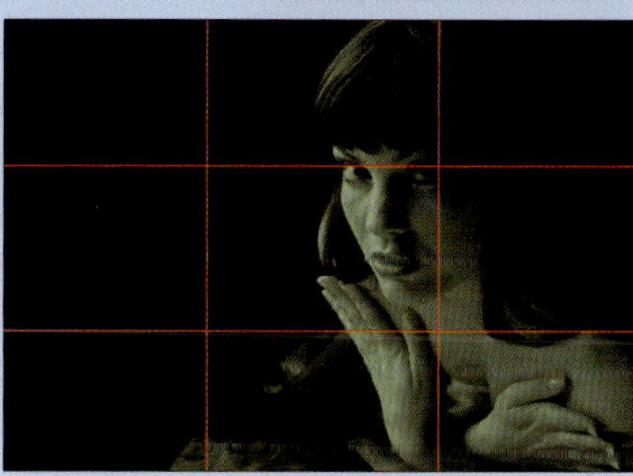

The Rule of Thirds suggests you place the subject on one of the red intersections in your photo. By doing so you will create a far more pleasing result. In this portrait the girl's face was positioned on the right third and her eye on the upper horizontal third. It creates a far more striking portrait than one in the centre of the frame.

FOCUSING

What are the options?
Generally, cameras have two or three auto-focus modes to choose from, such as: Single Servo, Continuous Servo and Auto or AI Servo.

How do they work?
In **Single Servo** mode the camera locks-on to your subject when it is in focus. Unfortunately, if your subject moves it will not keep up with it. This makes Single Servo ideal for static or slow moving subjects.

Continuous Servo mode is designed to keep track of moving subjects as efficiently as possible and, because the camera is always expecting your subject to move, it never locks-on.

Auto or AI Servo modes are designed to give the best of both the other two modes. The camera will lock on to static subjects and detect if your subject is in motion.

Modern 35mm SLRs often have five or more focusing points spread across the area of the viewfinder. These allow you to quickly compose shots with your subject off-centre.

What about manual focusing?
Manual focusing is performed by either turning the lens barrel or by moving the whole lens back and forth as with large format cameras. Manual focusing is necessary in situations where the exact point of focus is critical, for example macro photography.

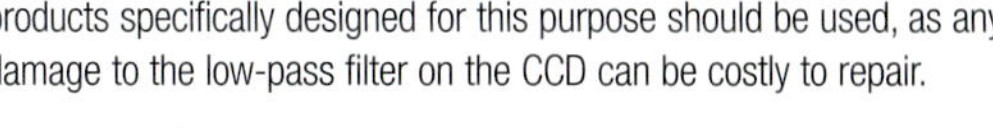

● Continuous servo was used to keep up with this fast moving bike.

KEEP YOUR CAMERA CLEAN

Why bother?
Any specs of dust on the lens or CCD will make the results inferior than if it was spotless. Dust or grime on a lens can cause flare and uneven exposure. Dust on a CCD means you waste time spotting, using the Clone or Heal tool.

What do I use for lenses?
For a lens the best thing to do is attach a skylight or UV glass filter as soon as you buy it. This not only protects the lens from dust but also looks after the front if you accidentally knock the lens. Get a dent on the filter and it's far cheaper to replace than a lens.
To clean a lens or filter use either a lint free cloth, or a special device like this lens pen, sold through the ePHOTOzine shop. It has a brush on one side to sweep away dust and a soft pad on the other to wipe away grime.

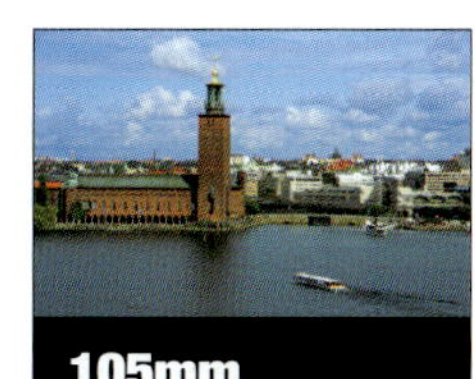

What do I use for CCDs?
Swabs, brushes, pads and even miniature vacuums are available to remove dust particles that collect on your camera's CCD. Only products specifically designed for this purpose should be used, as any damage to the low-pass filter on the CCD can be costly to repair.

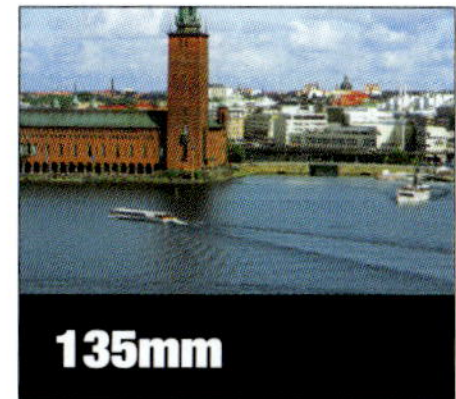

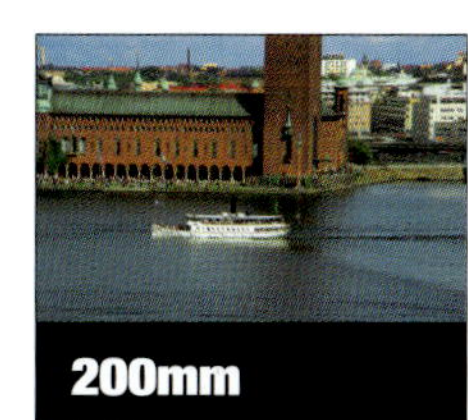

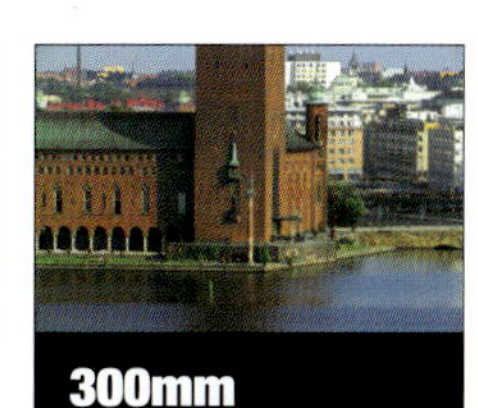

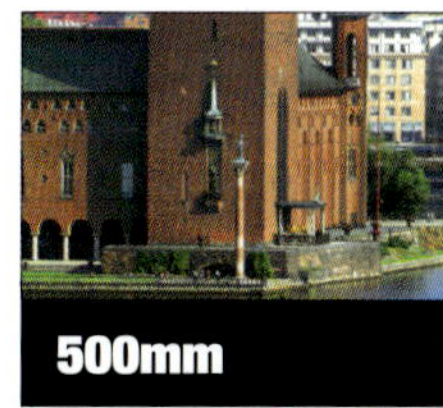

APERTURES EXPLAINED

What is it?
The aperture is an opening in the lens, made by a group of thin metal blades, which controls the amount of light that enters your camera to form an image. The aperture has two main effects on exposure – it alters the amount 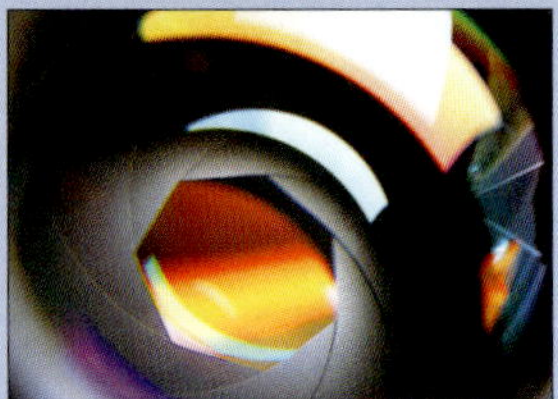 of your image that appears in focus, and it also affects how long you will need to open the shutter for the correct exposure.

What's an 'f' stop?
The word 'stop' comes from the very first cameras. Instead of a diaphragm of blades as used in modern lenses, early photographers had to insert a piece of metal into the lens with a hole drilled through it. This piece of metal was called a stop because it stopped some of the light getting through the lens.

Numbers marked on a lens are sometimes referred to as relative brightness and are expressed as a ratio to one. e.g. 1:2.8 would be f/2.8. The closer to zero the number is, the brighter the aperture.

Why have more blades?
The curvature of the aperture and the number of blades it's made of has a direct effect on how smooth out-of-focus backgrounds appear. The more blades used the rounder the aperture, 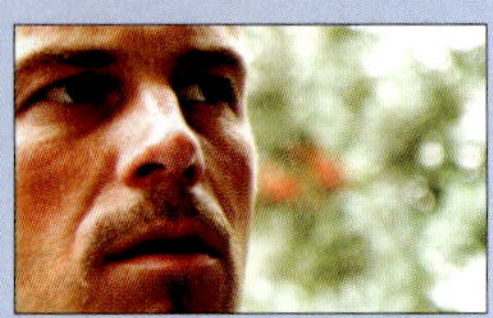 leading to smoother background blur, known as bokeh.

Another phenomenon affected by the aperture are diffraction stars. These occur when a strong point source of light is partially obscured in the image. The result is a bright, multi-pointed star radiating from the light source. The number of points on the star is influenced directly by the number of aperture blades. Lenses with an even number of blades create stars with an equal number of points, so a lens with a six-blade diaphragm creates a six pointed star. Apertures made from an odd number of blades create stars with double the number of points. A nine bladed diaphragm creates a beautiful 18 point star.

What is depth-of-field
Simply put, depth-of-field, or front to back sharpness, is the amount of your image that is in focus. The brighter the aperture used, the less of your image will be in focus. This can be useful for isolating your subject by blurring the background. The focal length of the lens you use will also determine the depth-of-field. Longer focal length lenses reduce the amount of your image that is in focus, whereas shorter focal length lenses (wide-angles) increase the amount in focus. 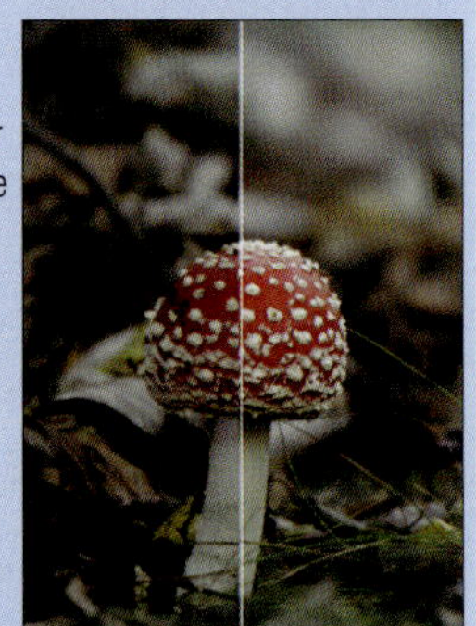

Technique – Hyper-focal focusing
When you focus on your subject there is an area in front and behind the point of focus that is still sharp. Hyperfocal focusing allows you to maximise the area that appears in focus whilst keeping the horizon sharp. Older manual focus lenses have a depth-of-field scale marked on the barrel which allows you to use this technique quickly 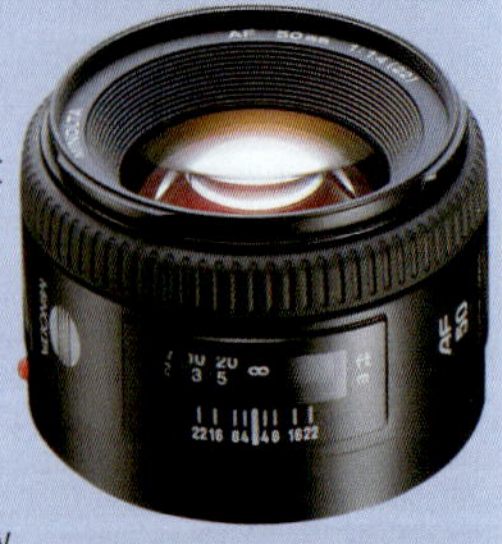 and precisely. To do this, simply align the infinity symbol with the mark that corresponds to the aperture you have selected. Newer autofocus lenses rarely display this scale. Instead, focus about a third of the way into your picture to maximise the area in focus.

EXPOSURE

What is it?
Exposure is basically the combination of shutter speed and aperture you use to take your picture. When both are correctly selected the photo will be accurately exposed. Getting this balance right is critical for producing stunning images. Get it wrong and you'll have a dark (under-exposed) or light (over-exposed) result.

Which metering mode is most suitable?
Most modern cameras include two or three different metering options, such as matrix or evaluative, centre weighted and spot.

Matrix or Evaluative metering (green grid on photo) splits the
image up into separate segments and uses a complex algorithm to calculate the correct exposure by taking readings from each segment. This mode is accurate under most conditions, and is great for general photography and snapshots.

Centre weighted metering (yellow oval on photo) takes the whole
frame into consideration but with an emphasis on a defined area in the centre of the image. This mode is great for portraits or for scenes of low contrast. In backlit situations, centre weighted metering will under-expose your image.

Spot metering (blue circle on photo) uses a small
point either located at the centre of the frame or selectable by the user for exposure calculation. Spot metering is great for shooting in high contrast situations, or when your subject is brightly backlit, as you can choose exactly where you obtain your meter reading from.

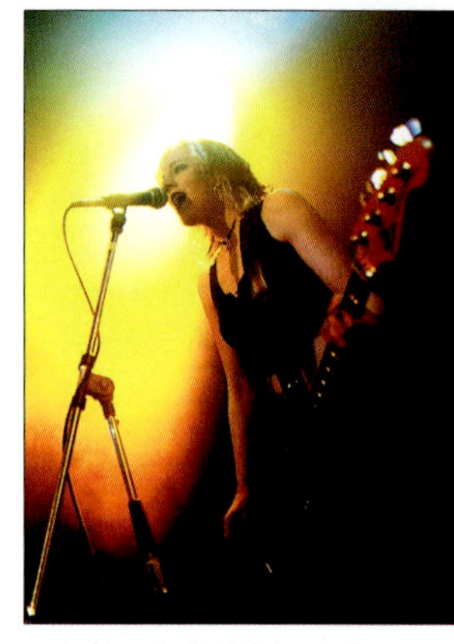

● GARY WOLSTENHOLME Spot metering was essential for this backlit stage shot.

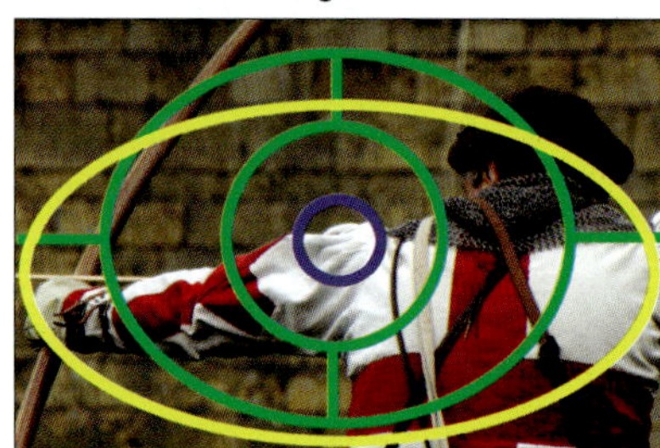

SHUTTER SPEEDS EXPLAINED

What is it?
The shutter controls the duration that the light sensitive area inside your camera is exposed to light. The speed you choose will depend on the light available. Longer exposures are needed in dim light and shorter in bright conditions.

If you are hand-holding your camera there is a general rule of thumb that you should select a shutter speed that is at least equal to the focal length of your lens. This will reduce the chances of your image being ruined by camera-shake. For example, a shutter speed of at least 1/300th of a second should be selected when using a 300mm lens. For digital cameras with sensors smaller than 35mm film, the rule still stands, except it will apply to the equivalent angle-of-view rather than the actual focal length of the lens. For example, a digital compact camera may only have a 6mm lens, but because the 35mm angle-of-view is 28mm, then the longest shutter speed for hand-held sharp shots should be around 1/30th of a second.

How does it affect my images?
Different shutter speeds can also be used for creative effect. By choosing a slow shutter speed you can choose to blur moving objects, or, as in this example of the canoeist, you can freeze them by choosing a fast one.

Technique – Panning
Panning is a useful technique which helps produce an impression of speed when taking pictures of moving subjects. A correctly panned shot will keep your subject sharp while blurring the background. To create this 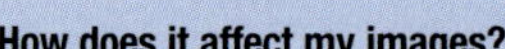 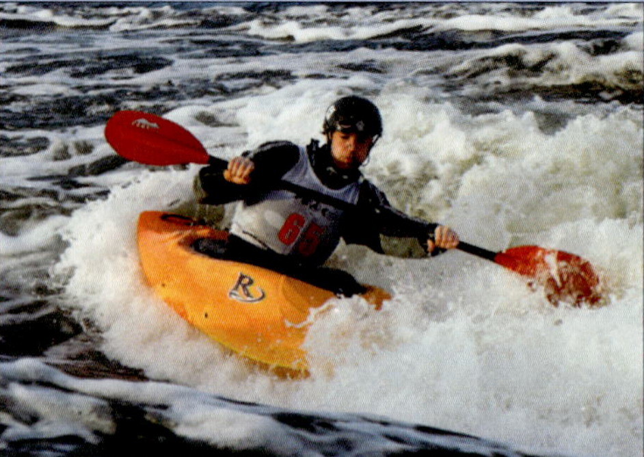 effect you first need to select an appropriate shutter speed. Normally between 1/8th and 1/30th of a second is ideal, although this will vary depending on how quickly your subject moves. As your subject moves past, start to follow it in the viewfinder, keeping it in the same part of the frame. As you are moving, take your picture. If you have matched the speed of your subject it should be acceptably sharp, whilst the background is blurred.

Turn to the Sports section on page 66 for more details on panning and other shutter techniques.

WHITE BALANCE & COLOUR TEMPERATURE

What is it?

White light consists of light of every different colour in the visible spectrum. Sometimes there can be a greater proportion of one colour than the others, for example, tungsten light-bulbs will produce white light with a strong orange cast, whereas daylight contains equal proportions of all colours.

This cast is the colour temperature and the strength of hue of this cast is measured in degrees Kelvin – shown on the scale to the right.

Blue sky	10,000
Shade from blue sky	7500
Shade from partly cloudy sky	7000
Shade in daylight	6500
Overcast sky	6000
Average noon daylight (Summer)	5500
Early afternoon sunlight	5000
Mid afternoon sunlight	4500
Early morning/evening sunlight	3500
Sunrise/sunset	2500

How can I correct it?

The household tungsten lamp I mentioned before would have a colour temperature of around 2500K, whereas typical daylight has a temperature of around 5500K. These colour casts can either be corrected or enhanced by using a complimentary colour filter on film cameras or by adjusting the white balance settings on your digital camera.

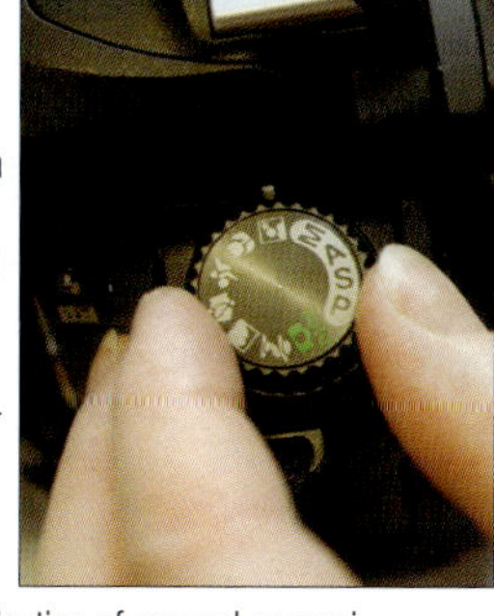

Digital cameras often have pre-set white balance settings for tungsten, fluorescent and daylight as well as an automatic mode which will attempt to correct the colour for you.

Turn to the colour wheel on page 211.

EXPOSURE MODES

What are they?

Many 35mm and digital auto cameras have a selection of different modes that allow you to affect the exposure in a number of ways.

Automatic point & shoot cameras tend to have scene assist modes. These are a selection of pre-set exposure settings that are tailored to a particular scene. Common scene modes include ones for portraits, landscapes, close ups and sports.

More advanced cameras have a selection of manual or semi-manual modes for controlling each aspect of exposure individually.

Program mode takes over full control of both the aperture and shutter speed selection, only allowing you control over exposure compensation. It's useful for fast, no-thinking photography.

Aperture-priority gives you control over the aperture value used and the camera matches this with the correct shutter speed. This is used for those who care about the depth of field and critical focus point.

Shutter-priority works in the same way, but you have control over the shutter speed used and the camera sets the aperture. This is used by sports and action photographers who need to freeze the subject.

Manual exposure puts you in full control of everything, so you can decide for yourself exactly what effect you wish to produce. This is used by creative photographers wanting to totally override the camera in tricky lighting set-ups.

ELECTRONIC FLASH

What is it?

Most cameras now have a built-in flash. This will help when you want to take pictures in low light, as the camera detects the lack of light and fires the flash automatically to illuminate the subject with a natural colour light.

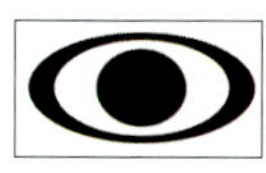 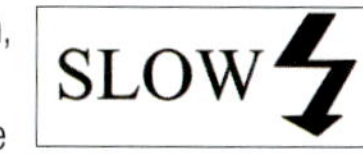

A built-in flash is fine for basic photography, but for better lighting you would use a separate detachable flash, either attached to the camera or triggered using a slave system. These allow you to produce less harsh results and are available from manufacturers such as Metz, Cullmann and Sunpak as well as the major camera brands. One with a bounce head is more versatile.

Camera flash modes

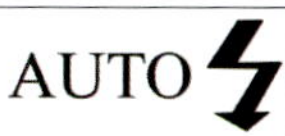

Auto: Most cameras have an auto low light detector that activates the flash to fire.

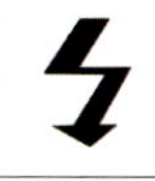

On: Sometimes the light is bright enough to prevent flash being needed, but you may still want it. This mode forces the flash to fire and is used for fill-in or to illuminate close subjects when shooting a scene at sunrise or sunset

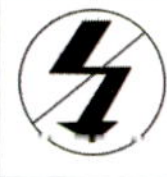

Off: Prevents flash firing when you want a shot taken in natural light, such as at dawn and dusk, or to record candle light or neons

Red-eye reduction: Fires a pre-flash to reduce the size of the subject's pupils and, in doing so, prevents harsh looking red pupils that occur when the flash bounces back off the eye's capillaries.

Slow-sync: Fires the flash, but uses a slow shutter speed so you get a balance

of flash and ambient light. This is often used for special effects photos and sports & action (below).

Rear curtain sync: Used on more advanced camera/flash systems to give more natural looking slow sync shots of moving subjects.

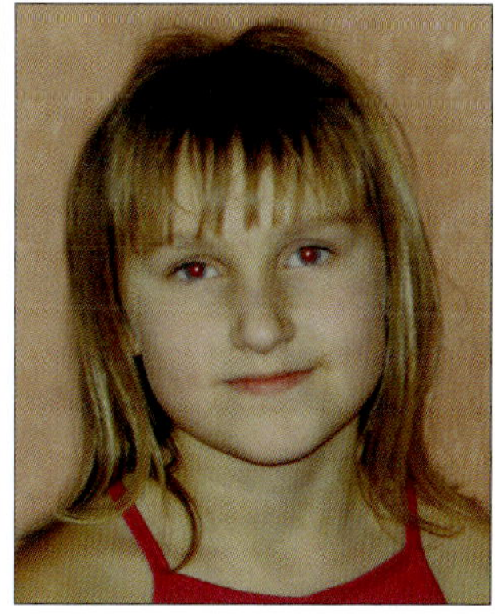 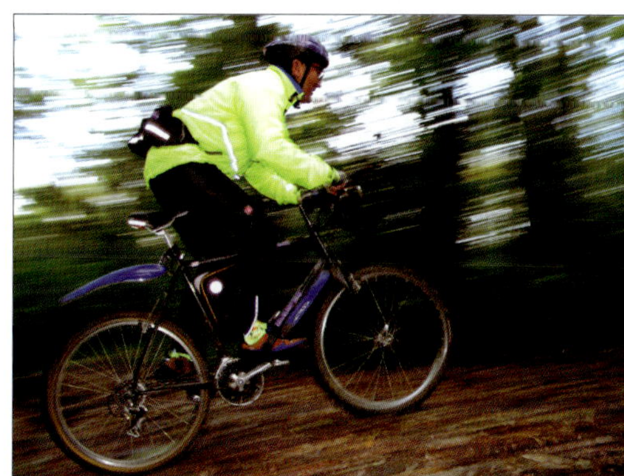

Studio flash

Enthusiast photographers often invest in studio systems with many more power and accessory options, such as softboxes and light tents to produce more natural light. The photograph below of model Nichole was taken using a Bowens Esprit 250DX studio head. This sort of photography is easy with studio lighting. All you need is a willing model, a suitable clean background, a flash head and some space.

The flash can be pointed directly at the subject, but the light is quite harsh so most photographers invest in a brolly or softbox to diffuse the light. A brolly is the lowest cost option, but a softbox gives more natural light. Studio lighting manufacturers such as Bowens, Elinchrom and Paterson make a wide range of attachments to suit all types of studio work from portraiture and glamour through pack shots to car photography.

A flash meter is also worth having to ensure the exposure is measured correctly.

Turn to the lighting section on page 152 for more details of flash and flash techniques.

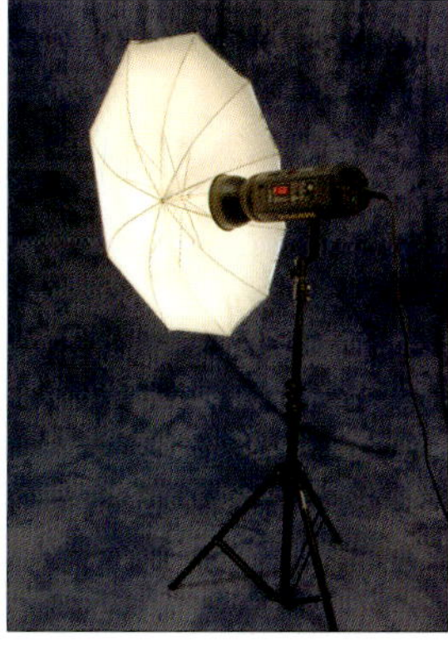 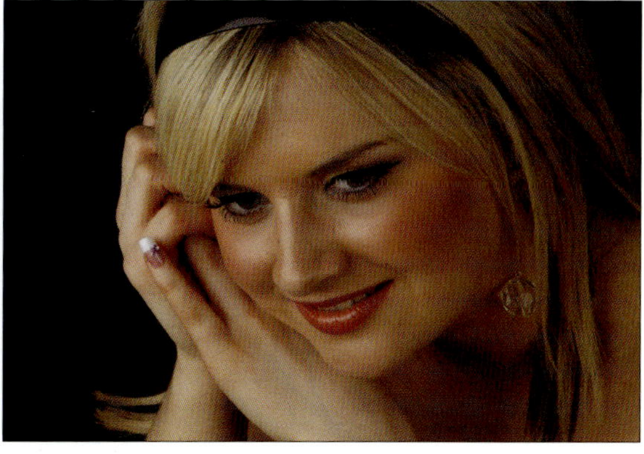

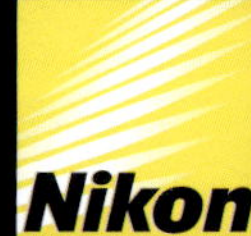

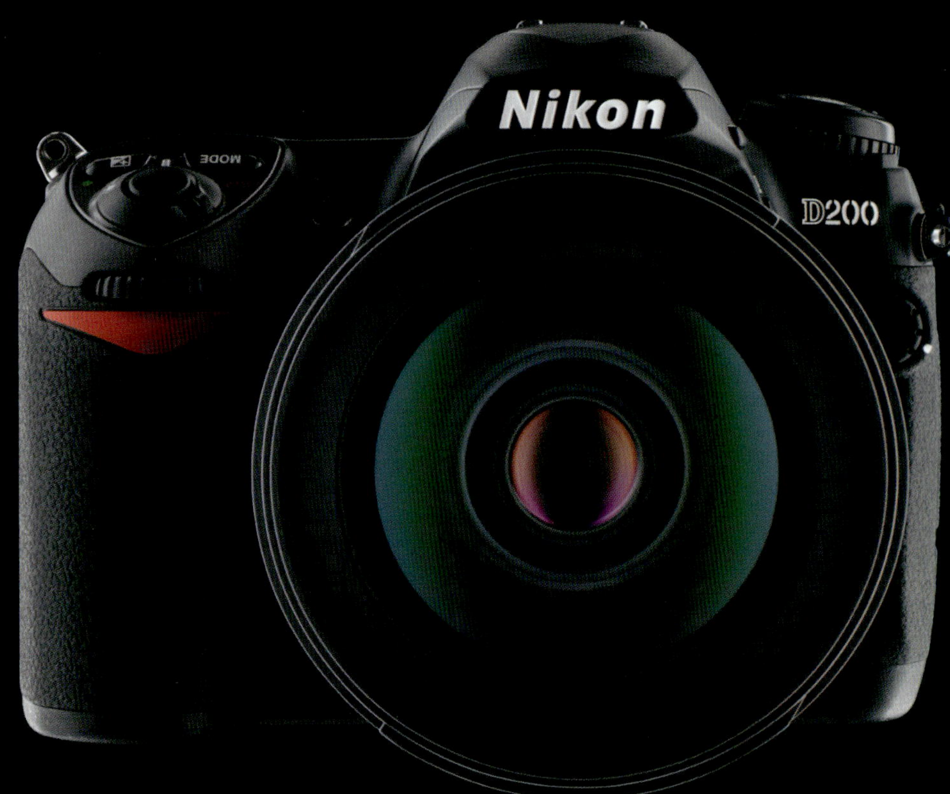

The Nikon D200. Our rivals want to see the back of it.

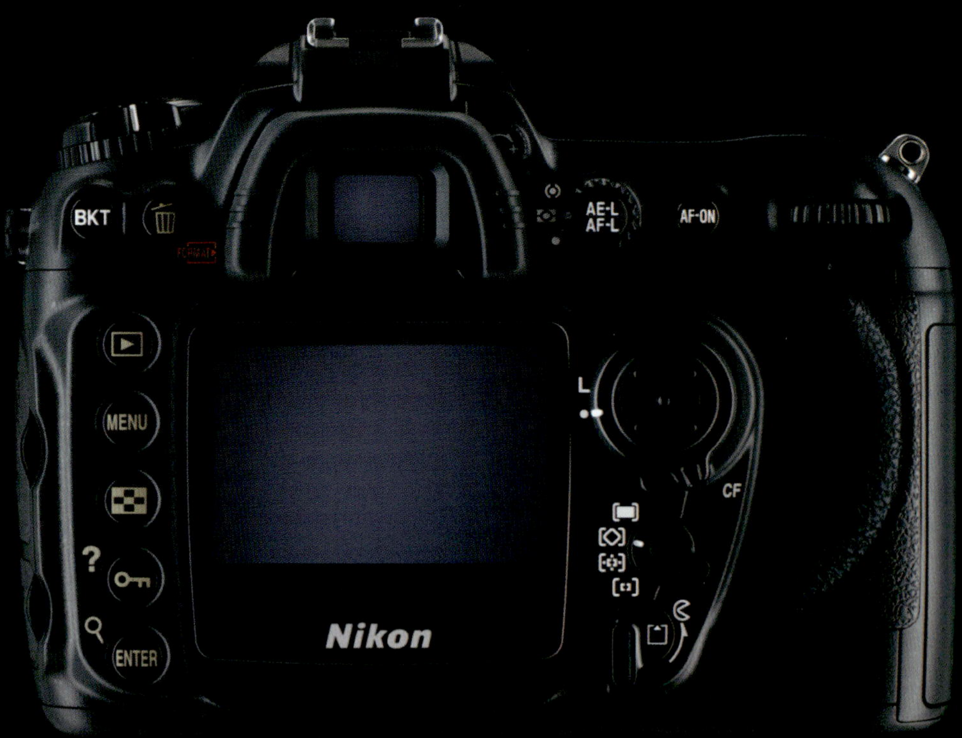

Ok.

10.2 MegaPixel DX sensor to deliver sharp images even under high enlargement. Super fast start-up, 0.15 sec. 5 fps continuous shooting. New, flexible auto focus system. 11-area or 7 wide-area. 0.94 x magnification viewfinder. 3D colour matrix II metering. Magnesium-alloy body with specially developed sealing system. **Welcome to Nikon.**

Most Improved

When Annaliese Bending discovered ePHOTOzine she was searching the internet looking for information on how to take better photos and use Adobe Photoshop Elements. It wasn't long before she was hooked and in the year and a half she's been with the site her photography has shown dramatic improvements, earning her the title *Most Improved Photographer*.

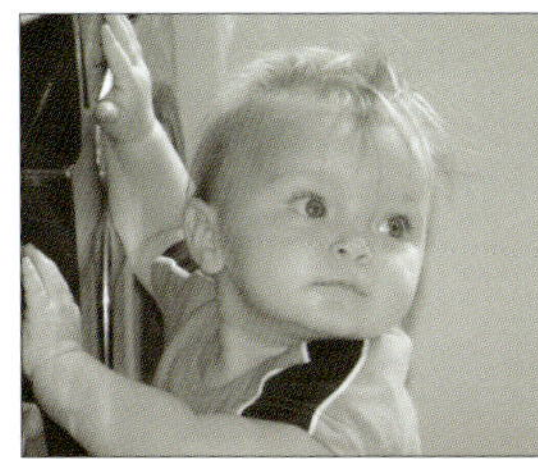

Cornish family photographer, Annaliese Bending's main drive for joining ePHOTOzine was to receive advice and help from more experienced members that she'd found on the site.

Over the short time Annaliese's been a member her photography has improved dramatically. One of the main things that's attributed to this is the encouragement she gets from all on ePHOTOzine. Her family are very proud of what she's achieved.

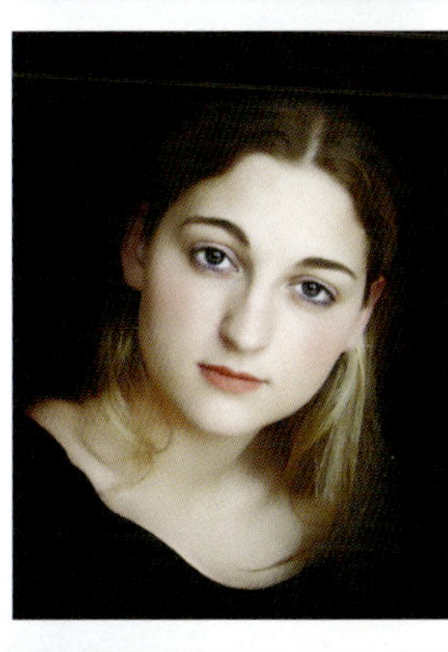

Annaliese believes ePHOTOzine is a rapid learning resource and without it she feels she would still be snapping away cluelessly. "Its helped me accept where I was going wrong, put me in touch with people that have helped greatly, and most of all given me confidence that I was lacking," she explains

But it's not just help in taking photos that's part of the improvement. The change from the basic program Photoshop Elements to Photoshop CS and Corel Painter IX using various plug ins has given her the tools to develop into new areas of image manipulation.

She found out about these and how to use them from other photographers in the ePHOTOzine forums and in magazines. Photoshop CS is her preferred program and has opened up endless possibilities. "I've been using it for just over a year and I'm still finding so much new stuff."

Another common aspect of Annaliese's images is her good range of very attractive models. These started out as family members who, after much begging, decided to help out. As time progressed and people saw her

pictures, they offered to model in exchange for prints. "A local salon owner saw my work on the internet and decided to try me out, and people in the salon, hairdressers and clients let me practice on them".

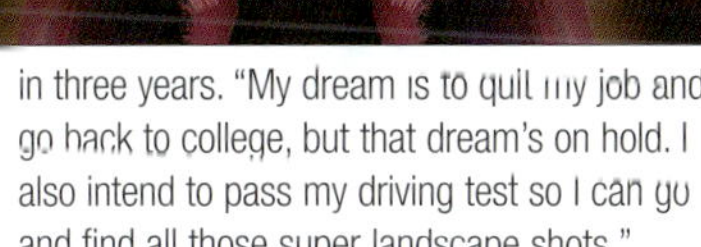

One of the key aspects of model photography is putting the sitter at ease, unless they are natural in front of the camera. Annaliese is fortunate that one or two of her models are complete naturals, but others do need a bit of encouragement. "I'm quite a bubbly person and I find they relax quite easily after a few test shots. I find posing the models one of the hardest aspects."

Getting published in the *Western Morning News* has been Annaliese's biggest accomplishment, along with a £250 repro fee for four shots.

"I'm very interested in landscape photography and still life – both areas I have yet to explore. I am limited as I have a very young daughter, work nights and don't drive, so I plan to put more effort in as soon as my daughter starts school

in three years. "My dream is to quit my job and go back to college, but that dream's on hold. I also intend to pass my driving test so I can go and find all those super landscape shots."

Annaliese's long term plan is to offer a portrait service with a difference – we don't think it will be too difficult!

Take a look at more beautiful portraits on Annaliese's web site. **www.annaliese.co.uk** ■

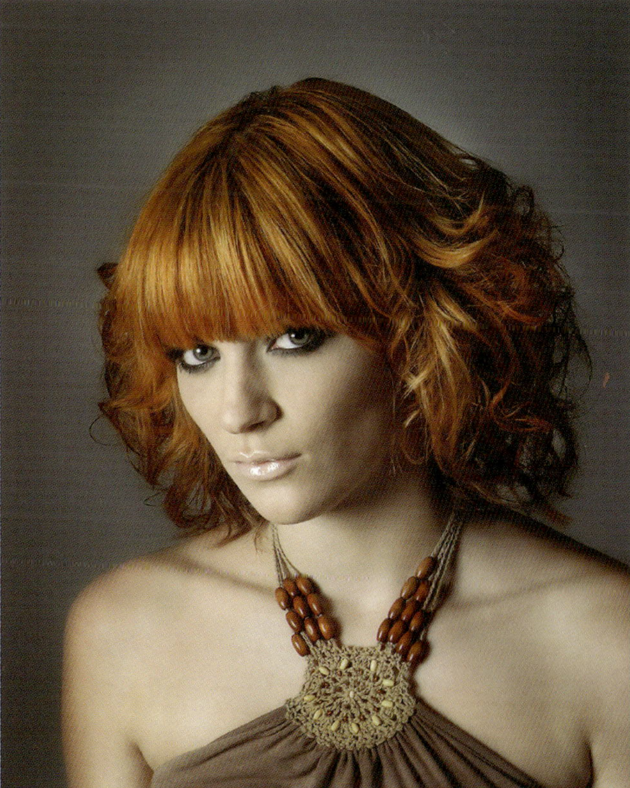

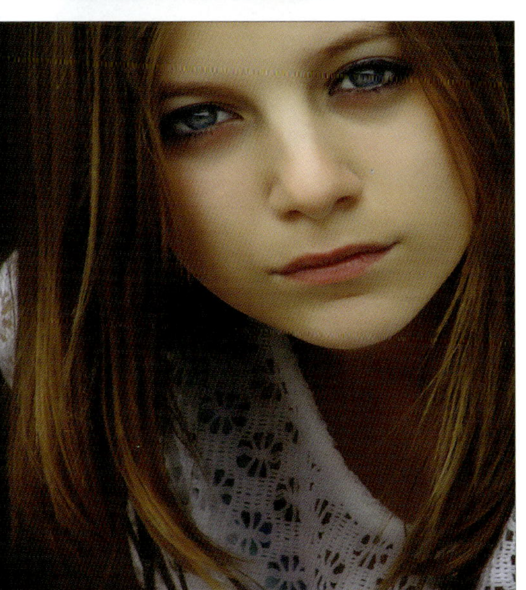

● Top left: Annaliese's first upload – a shot of her daughter taken on a Fuji Finepix 4900. Sept 2004.
● Middle: Sarah next to a window and tinfoil reflector. Nov 2004.
● Bottom: Sarah enhanced using Photoshop diffuser. April 2005.
● Left: Taken with Canon EOS 300D, starting to use less Photoshop treatments and more work with light. June 2005.
● Top right: Taken on a Canon EOS 20D, window lit and reflector used to bounce light. The right side was copied and flipped to create symmetry. Oct 2005.
● Right: One of a selection of images from Annaliese's first paid shoot. This was lit using studio flash with one softbox and a reflector. Taken on a Canon EOS 20D with 50mm f/2.8 in Feb 2006.

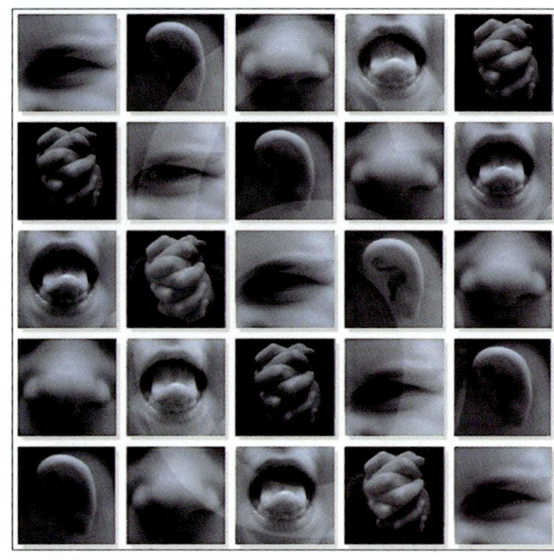

THEME: Senses **PRIZE:** Gaskin Canvas print
MONTH: Oct 2004 **NUMBER OF ENTRIES:** 394
WINNER: Jason Long
Jason has shown a novel way of displaying the senses and, at the same time, given a suggestion of a sixth sense!

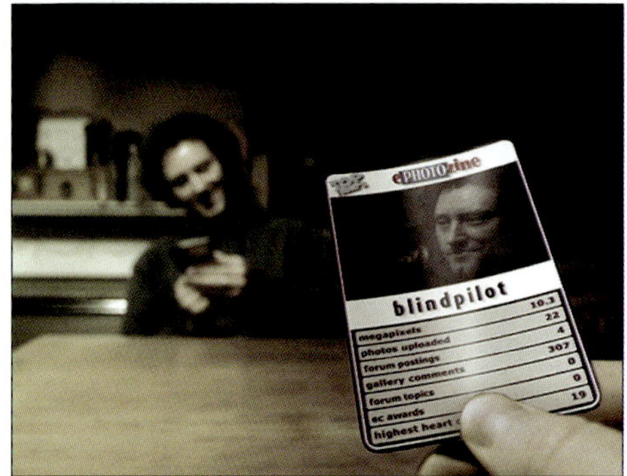

THEME: Self portrait **PRIZE:** Metz flash and Gitzo tripod
MONTH: March 2004 **NUMBER OF ENTRIES:** 302
WINNER: Fergus Davidson
The photographer playing himself at ePHOTOzine Top Trumps. He used Fireworks and 3DMax to combine the three photos. It stood out from the rest – pure genius!

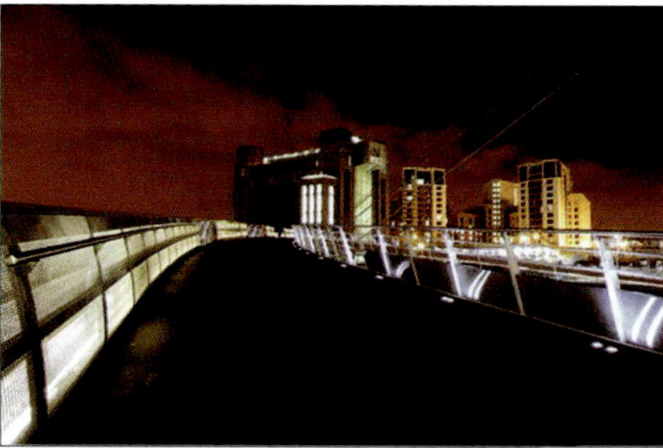

THEME: Low light **PRIZE:** Extensis Portfolio 6
MONTH: Oct 2003 **NUMBER OF ENTRIES:** 320
WINNER: Dave Fletcher
Guest judge, William Cheung, picked this low light shot of the Millennium bridge in Newcastle because he felt it oozed with atmosphere and the sky's colour amazed him.

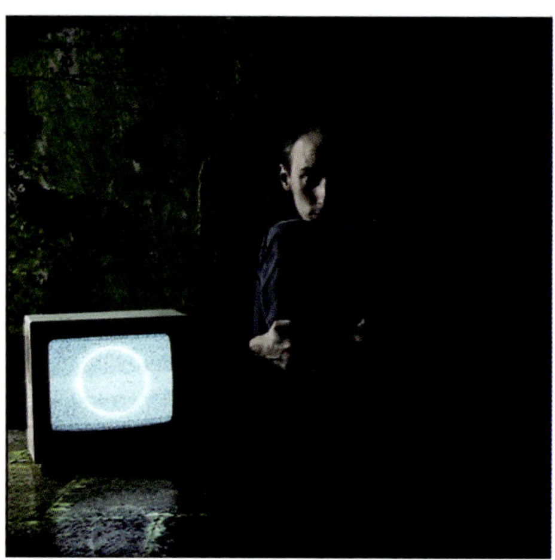

THEME: Film titles **PRIZE:** Archos Media Player
MONTH: March 2005 **NUMBER OF ENTRIES:** 357
WINNER: Aleksey Lapkovsky
Aleksey's representation of the film The Ring. This was quite topical as The Ring 2 had only just been released at the cinema. Very dark and moody shot – just like the film.

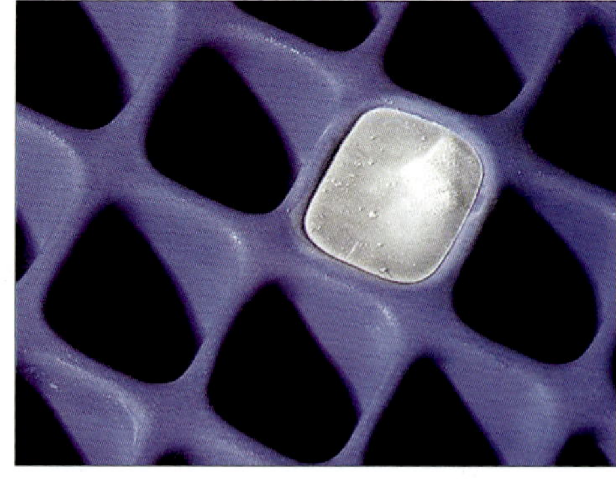

THEME: Cube **PRIZE:** AVITechnologies Cube
MONTH: August 2004 **NUMBER OF ENTRIES:** 345
WINNER: Martin Stewart
Here's a strong and bold shot that's also clean and sharp so the ice stands out well against the contrasting blue tray.

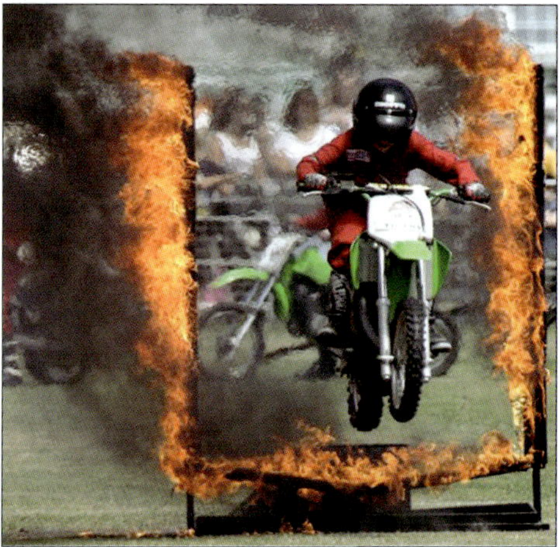

THEME: Action **PRIZE:** Roxio Creator 7
MONTH: April 2004 **NUMBER OF ENTRIES:** 751
WINNER: Matt Adams
This previous Editor's Choice winner sums up the theme perfectly and offers a real sense of action.

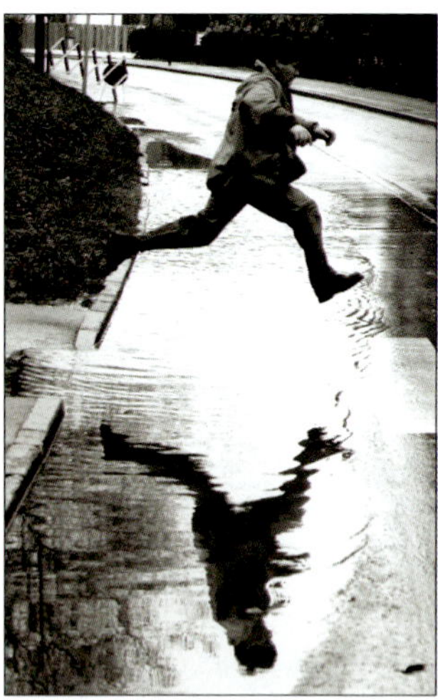

THEME: Water
MONTH: May 2004
WINNER: Jaka Adamic
NUMBER OF ENTRIES: 552
PRIZE: Amazing Internet website
A very well captured moment that reminds us of a shot by Henri Cartier-Bresson.

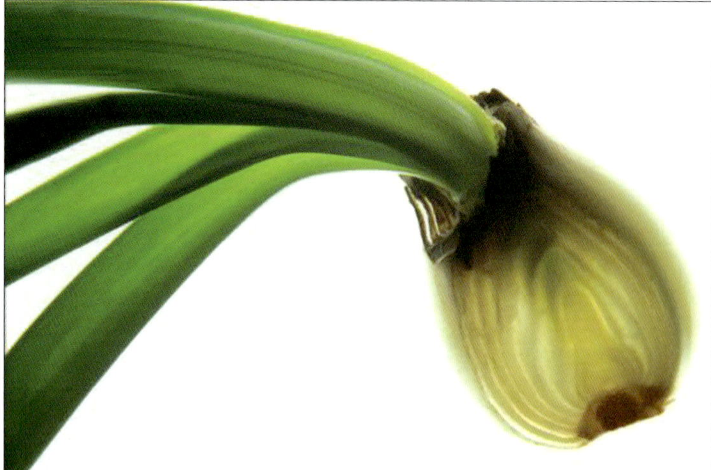

THEME: Spring **PRIZE:** Samsung Digimax 4mp camera
MONTH: March 2003 **NUMBER OF ENTRIES:** 261
WINNER: Stuart Porter
Stu wanted this picture to illustrate the daffodil bulb which is the secret to how it is able to be one of the first spring plants to produce flowers. Daffodils draw on stored energy to produce their flowers, whilst other plants build up energy as the sun's rays get stronger.

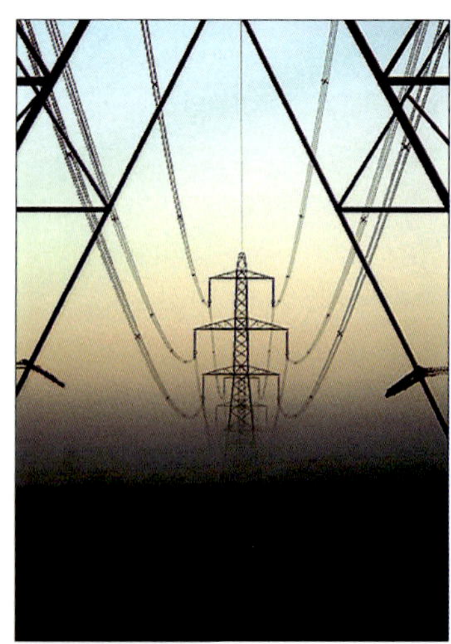

THEME: Power
MONTH: November 2003
WINNER: Andrew Frost
NUMBER OF ENTRIES: 329
PRIZE: Canon EOS 30
Most imaginative of the pylon images, with very striking lighting and excellent framing.

Competitions

Since its launch ePHOTOzine has introduced over 36 photo competitions and given away over £19,000 worth of prizes to successful members. With a total of 16,905 entries submitted so far, these are some of the winning pictures.

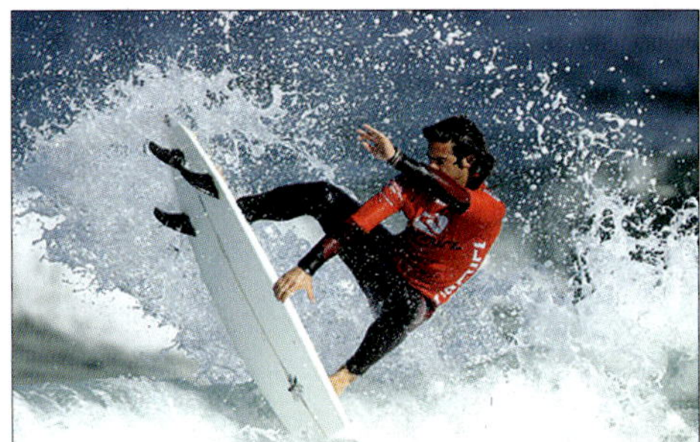

THEME: Action   **PRIZE:** Adobe Photoshop CS
MONTH: Nov 2004   **NUMBER OF ENTRIES:** 671
WINNER: Paul Frost

A 360° grab air taken at Rip Curl Masters, Newquay and he landed it as well! You don't get much more action packed than this from our loading surf photographer.

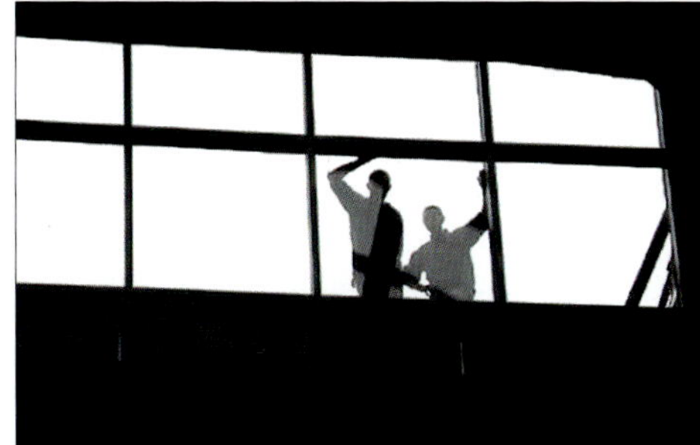

THEME: Squares   **PRIZE:** Epson Inkjet printer
MONTH: August 2003   **NUMBER OF ENTRIES:** 201
WINNER: Bernard Caulfield

A very simple, but effectively framed subject that was a little different than most of the others, making it stand out.

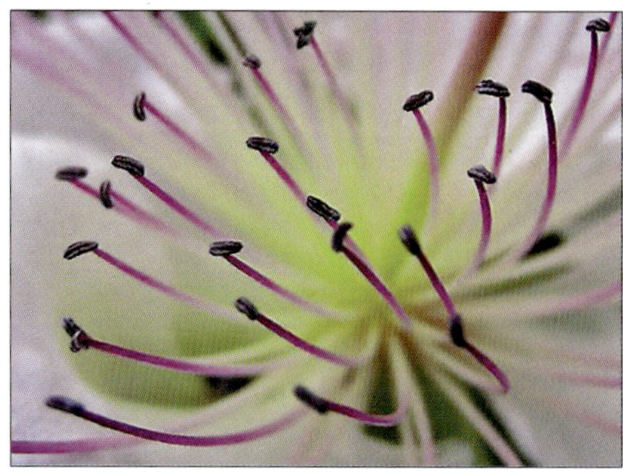

THEME: Flowers   **PRIZE:** Epson Inkjet printer
MONTH: June 2004   **NUMBER OF ENTRIES:** 1079
WINNER: Hermin Abramovitch

Although obviously an image of a flower, our judge loved this shot because it had an air of 'other world' mystery.

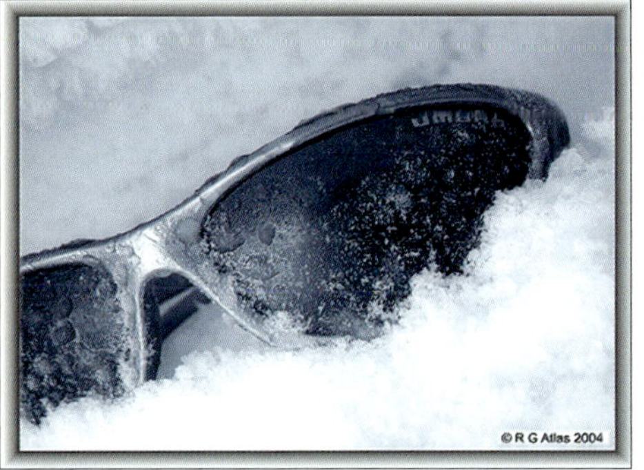

THEME: Cool   **PRIZE:** Nikon Coolpix 8700
MONTH: Sept 2004   **NUMBER OF ENTRIES:** 724
WINNER: Rob Atlas

We picked this one because Rob's interpretation was spot on, combining the coolness of ice with the cool image of a pair of shades. It stood out as soon as we saw it uploaded mid way through the competition.

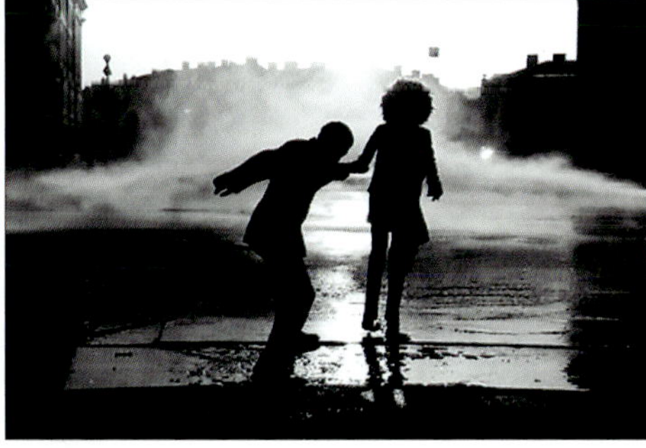

THEME: Silhouettes   **PRIZE:** Sony Cybershot camera
MONTH: July 2003   **NUMBER OF ENTRIES:** 528
WINNER: Aleksey Lapkovsky

This photo breathes life. It met the theme perfectly, but rather than a typical black silhouette against a colour backwash it has fantastic depth and emotion that perfectly freezes a moment in time.

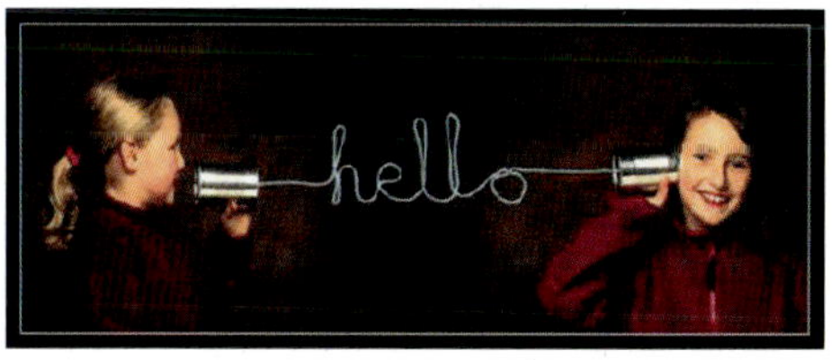

THEME: Communication **PRIZE:** Olympus Camedia
MONTH: Jan 2003   **NUMBER OF ENTRIES:** 210
WINNER: Dave Ellison

Dave worked on two images with this lettered wire theme. We thought it was an excellent interpretation of the competition.

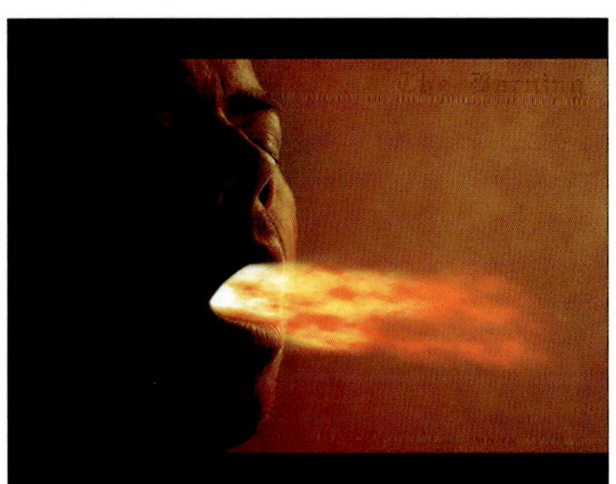

THEME: Fire   **PRIZE:** Adobe Photoshop CS
MONTH: Nov 2005   **NUMBER OF ENTRIES:** 477
WINNER: Martin Wait

A fantastic dark portrait of a fire breather, created in Photoshop using a subtle texture layer. The tones are superb, the fire very realistic and the overall balance excellent.

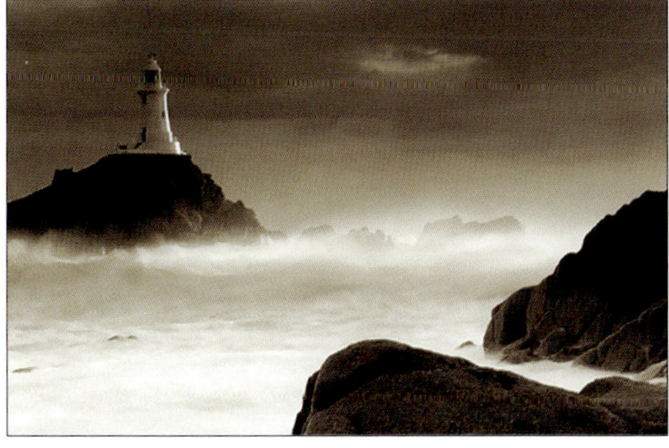

THEME: Long exposure **PRIZE:** Manfrotto tripod & Northscape course
MONTH: August 2005   **NUMBER OF ENTRIES:** 662
WINNER: David Bosomworth

Taken at Dusk - this is a picture of Corbierre Lighthouse on Jersey. It was pretty rough, so hard to get the long exposure and keep the lighthouse sharp. He used a Canon EOS 10D and Sigma 28-300mm zoom.

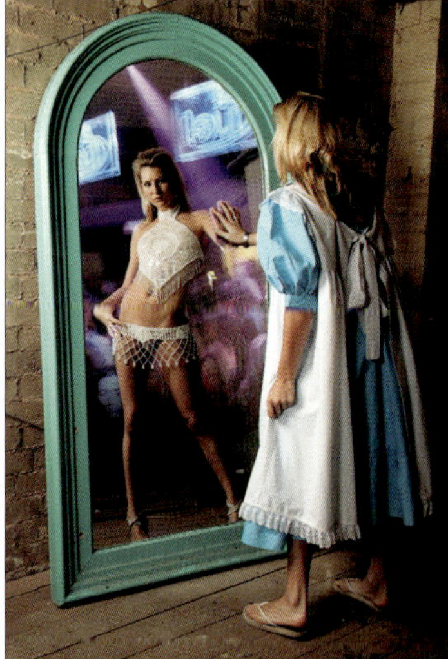

THEME: Reflections   **PRIZE:** Amazing Internet website
MONTH: April 2005   **NUMBER OF ENTRIES:** 57
WINNER: Paul Ward

Alice through the looking glass. This encapsulates the theme in such a clever way.

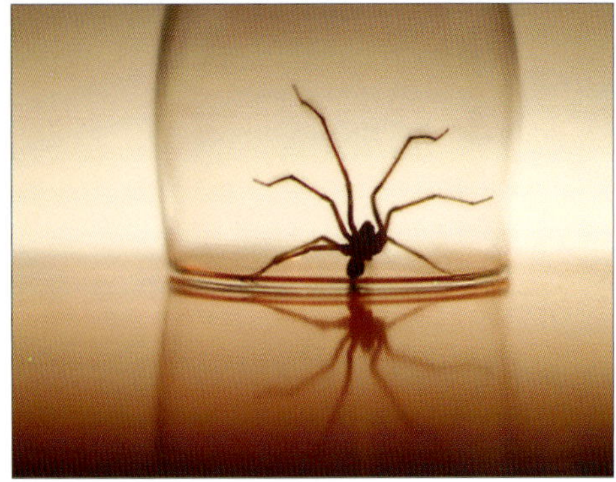

THEME: Solitude **PRIZE:** Minolta Film Scanner
MONTH: Sept 2003 **NUMBER OF ENTRIES:** 444
WINNER: Steve Sharp
An excellent shot, providing you are not Arachnophobic! Highly original and well executed. We love the softness and unusual depth.

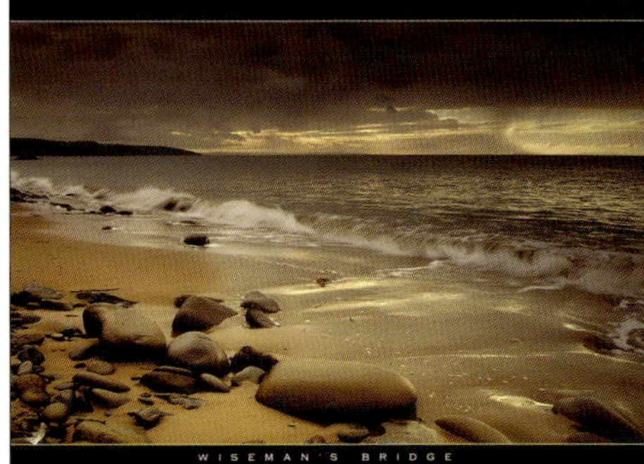

THEME: Filter effects **PRIZE:** Lee Filters kit
MONTH: Sept 2005 **NUMBER OF ENTRIES:** 264
WINNER: Angela Joel
This beach scene is at Wiseman's Bridge, between Saundersfoot & Tenby, is a strong landscape with subtle colours and shows great use of a graduated ND filter.

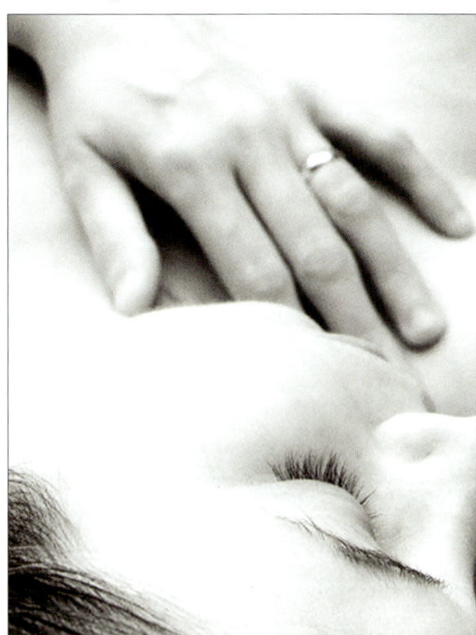

THEME: Sensual **PRIZE:** Canon Film Scanner
MONTH: Feb 2003 **NUMBER OF ENTRIES:** 112
WINNER: John Morley
Titled "asleep", this high key shot was taken using an Olympus Camedia E-10 and it was the first competition that John had ever entered.

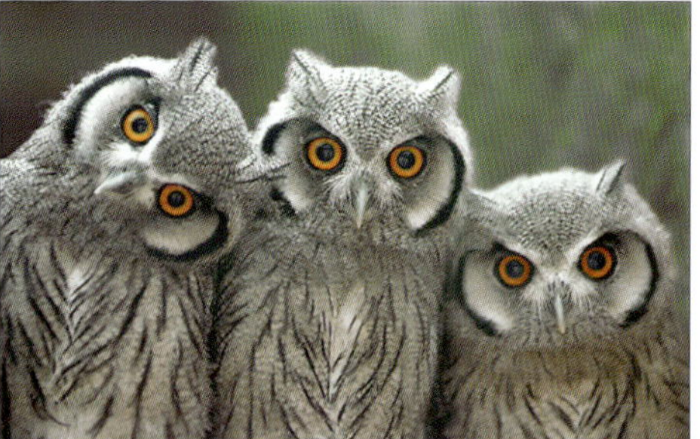

THEME: Birds **PRIZE:** Waterproof jacket
MONTH: July 2004 **NUMBER OF ENTRIES:** 712
WINNER: Linda Wright
It's easy to see why this cute picture of three baby owls gained Linda a resounding victory.

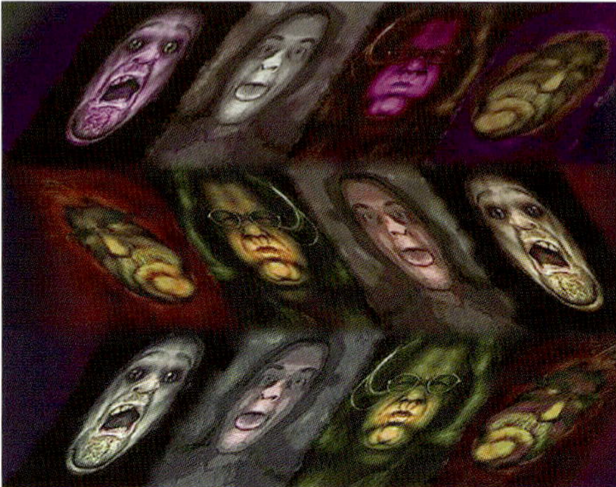

THEME: Panels **PRIZE:** Lowepro waterproof bag
MONTH: April 2003 **NUMBER OF ENTRIES:** 164
WINNER: Steve Bentley
A series of scans of a face, then individually treated in the image-editing program and distorted to fit the panels.

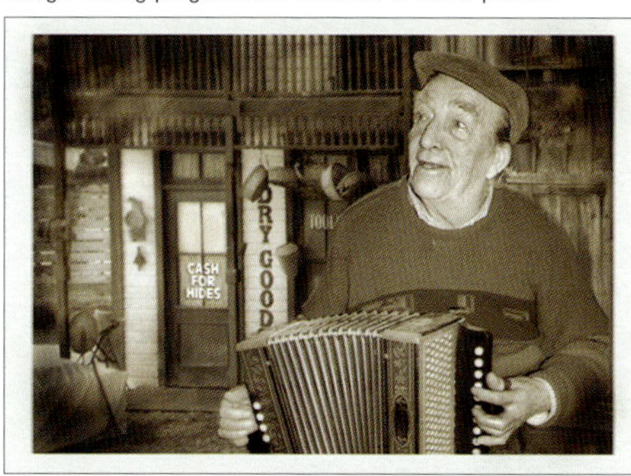

THEME: Sound **PRIZE:** Ticket to see Robbie Williams
MONTH: June 2003 **NUMBER OF ENTRIES:** 92
WINNER: Steve Le Prevost
We liked this for the wonderful balance, carefully focused shot with superb detail and excellent tonal range.

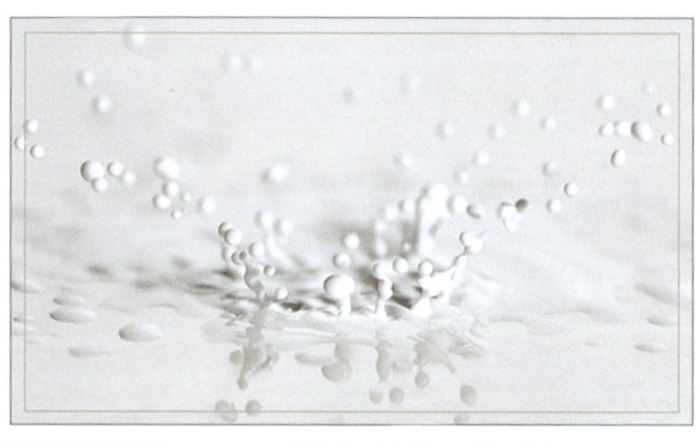

THEME: White **PRIZE:** Olympus Camedia camera
MONTH: Dec 2005 **NUMBER OF ENTRIES:** 499
WINNER: Marc Whitburn
Another splash made with a mixture of glycerin, water, white paint and rubbing alcohol, landing on white Formica. Captured using a Canon EOS 300D and Tamron 90mm macro lens.

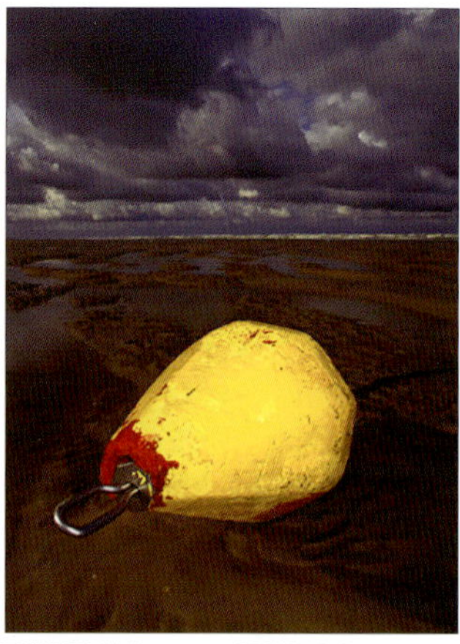

THEME: Yellow **MONTH:** Dec 2004
WINNER: St.John Pope
NUMBER OF ENTRIES: 726
Slightly underexposed with fill-in flash on Calais Beach. Enhanced in Photoshop.

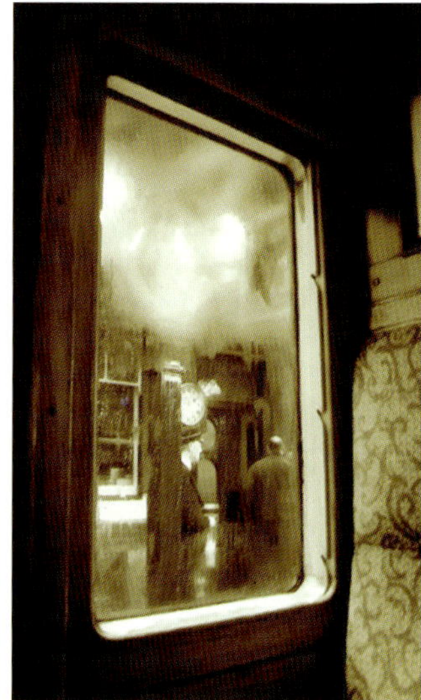

THEME: Through the Window
MONTH: Dec 2003 **WINNER:** John Short
NUMBER OF ENTRIES: 365
This one gave us a nostalgic through-the-window insight into the past.

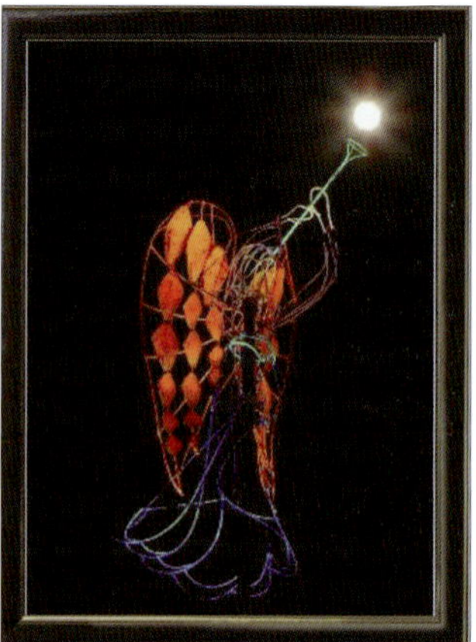

THEME: Christmas **MONTH:** Dec 2002
WINNER: Alan Benson
NUMBER OF ENTRIES: 72
Alan saw this sculpture above the Roman Baths in Bath and it reminded him of the Carol announcing the arrival of Jesus.

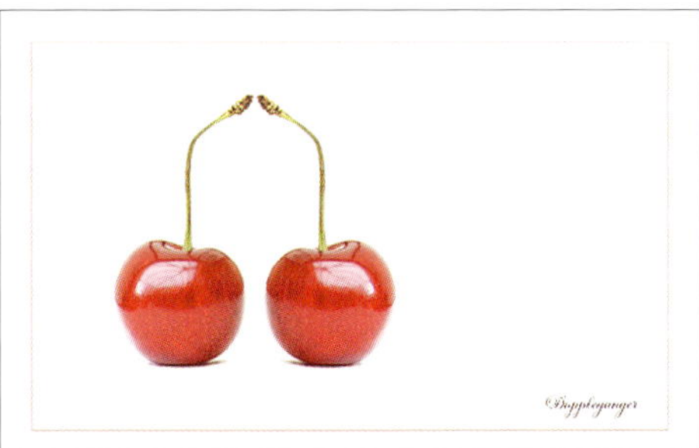

THEME: Double **PRIZE:** Minolta Dimage SLR
MONTH: July 2005 **NUMBER OF ENTRIES:** 392
WINNER: Chris Miles
A simpl but beautifully placed and lit pair of cherries, taken using a Nikon D70

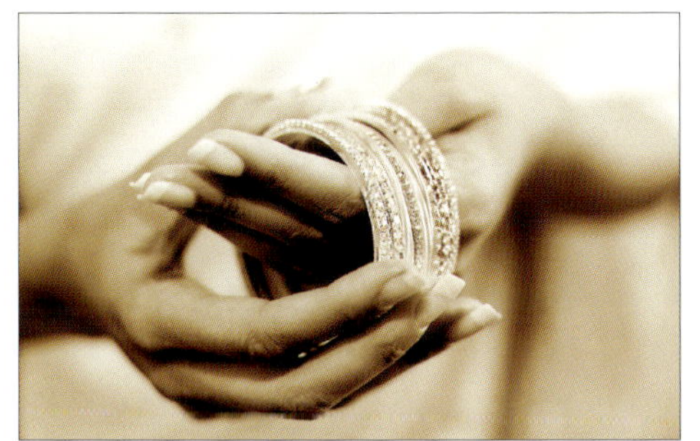

THEME: Events **PRIZE:** Hi-Ti dye sub printer
MONTH: March 2006 **NUMBER OF ENTRIES:** 370
WINNER: Darrin James
A Mauritian bride puts on her grandmother's bracelets as she prepares for her wedding day. This demonstrates careful use of toning and a sensitive crop.

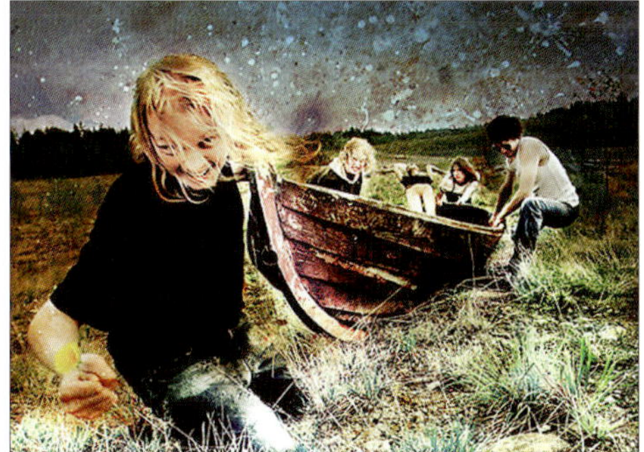

THEME: New Year Resolution **PRIZE:** Fo2PiX software
MONTH: Jan 2006 **NUMBER OF ENTRIES:** 174
WINNER: Aleksi Koskinen
It's just bursting with energy, life, movement and excitement.

THEME: Lines **PRIZE:** Nikon D50 SLR
MONTH: May 2005 **NUMBER OF ENTRIES:** 671
WINNER: Penny Piddock
The Zebra was taken in Kenya using a Canon EOS 10D and 100-400mm lens. The barcode was composed to complement the animal's stripes.

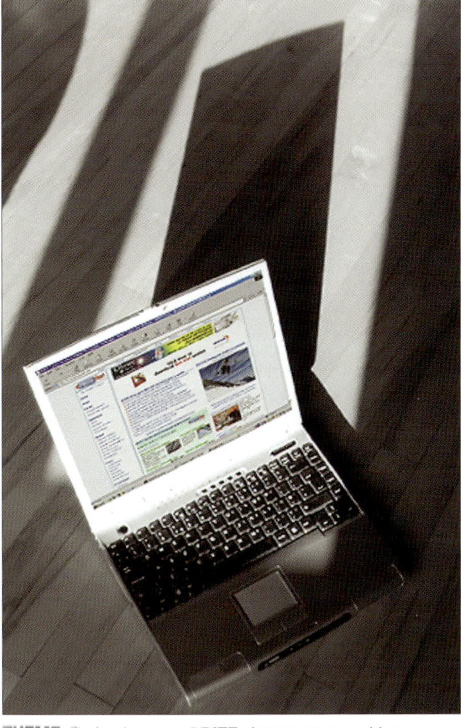

THEME: Technology **PRIZE:** Apacer storage drive
MONTH: Feb 2004 **NUMBER OF ENTRIES:** 237
WINNER: Chris Clowe
A very strong, simple image that embodies the theme very well and turns it into a strong and very pleasing image. Great, clean, modern ambience.

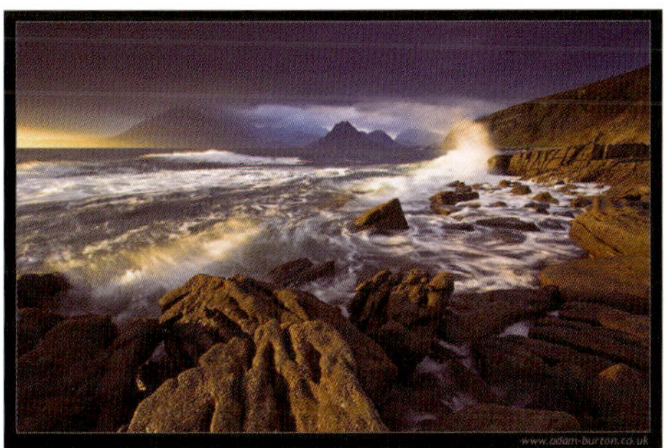

THEME: The Bigger Picture **PRIZE:** Photo Artistry Canvas
MONTH: Feb 2006 **NUMBER OF ENTRIES:** 345
WINNER: Adam Burton
"TOAST" judge, Claire Winter, felt the vastness reflected the enormity that people often feel when suffering from obesity.

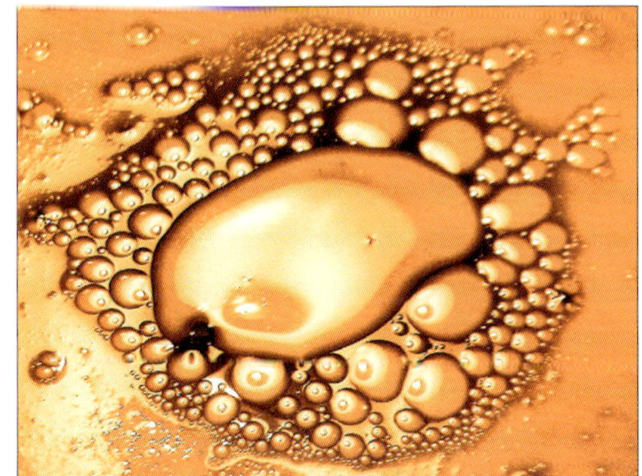

THEME: Patterns & Textures **PRIZE:** Paint Shop Pro 8
MONTH: May 2003 **NUMBER OF ENTRIES:** 317
WINNER: Brian Mossemenear
Brian spotted this mixture of Olive Oil and Balsamic Vinegar left on a plate and interrupted his meal to grab the camera and capture the image. 1/10sec at f/3.4.

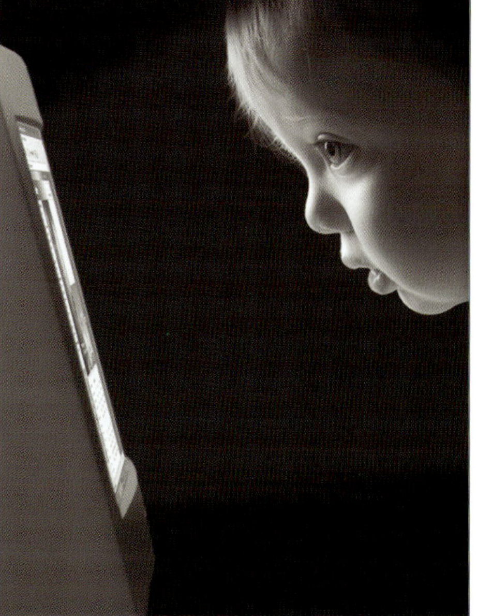

THEME: Connection **PRIZE:** Canon EOS outfit
MONTH: Feb 2005 **NUMBER OF ENTRIES:** 429
WINNER: Chris Clowe
An obvious option to attempt, but this version is extremely well executed and, as such, took first place

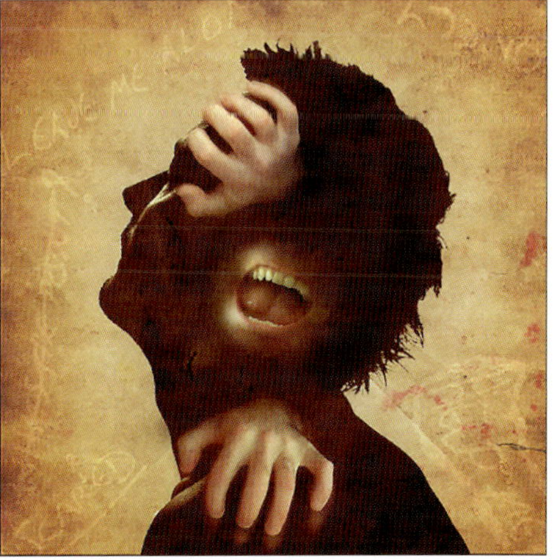

THEME: Inside **PRIZE:** Amazing Internet website
MONTH: Oct 2005 **NUMBER OF ENTRIES:** 375
WINNER: Chris Conway
A clever digital manipulation draws on the fact that we all have a voice inside trying to get out. Great treatment.

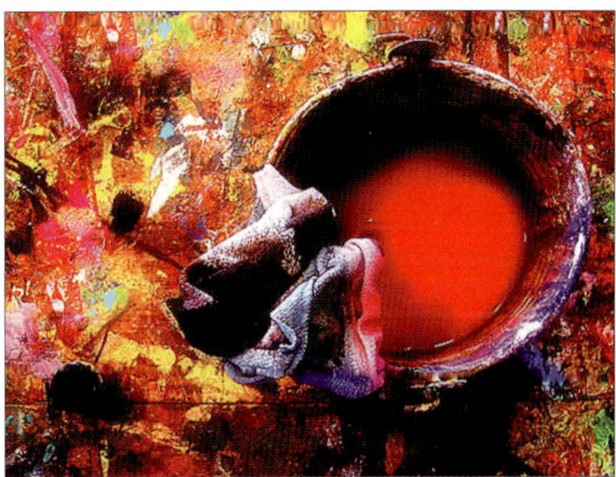

THEME: Paint **PRIZE:** Corel Paint Shop Pro 9
MONTH: June 2005 **NUMBER OF ENTRIES:** 224
WINNER: Hermin Abramovitch
Here's an amazingly colourful paint study. It leaps off the page. With such a simple theme it was inevitable that the shot may have paint in, but we didn't expect anything this good.

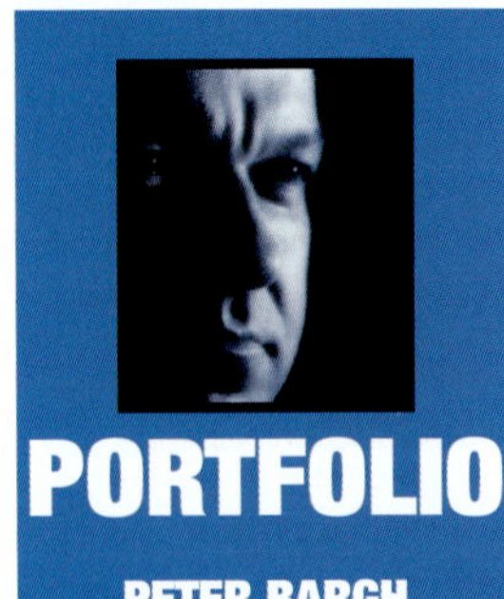

PORTFOLIO

PETER BARGH
Pete's the publisher of ePHOTOzine and an enthusiast photographer with an interest in shooting everything and anything.

It seems appropriate that the editor/publisher has a portfolio too so please excuse my self indulgence...

An awareness of photography goes way back in my life. In my early years I used to look at pictures taken by my mum on her Kodak 126-cartridge Instamatic.

She was an artist who photographed local village scenes and then painted them for friends, but her technical skills were limited to a bright or cloudy setting.

So I was aware of photography as a recording medium, but not artistically. It wasn't until I was about 13 and heavily into music that I discovered a proper camera would help me record pictures of my favourite pop stars – at that time David Bowie – off TV!

I bought my first magazine, *Practical Photography*, in 1977 and started to become more and more serious. My first job was a Saturday position at Dixons (when they were a camera retailer and sold darkroom kit and everything for the hobby photographer). I moved to the Sheffield Co-op and helped developed the photo department into an enthusiast's place. We bought in all sorts of weird and wonderful stuff!

I then moved to Jessops and spent about eight years in their Sheffield branch. I often used to have queues waiting for me because of my knowledge!

Throughout this period I built up a huge collection of kit that I used. I have, at some stage, owned most medium-format brands – my favourite was the Mamiya RB67. I had a Sinar Wolf and an MPP 5x4 for a number of years too. I've owned Pentax, Olympus, Contax and Nikon 35mm systems.

At home I had a room converted to a permanent darkroom with MPP 54 and LPL 67 enlargers

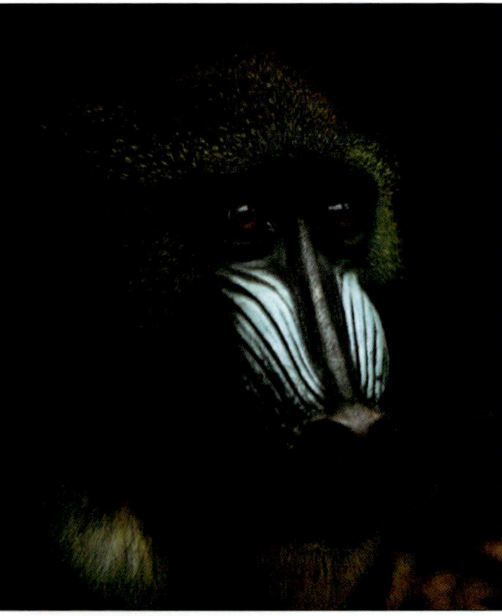

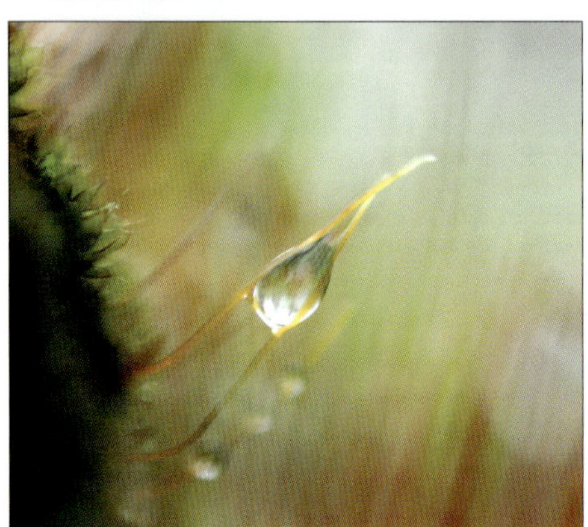

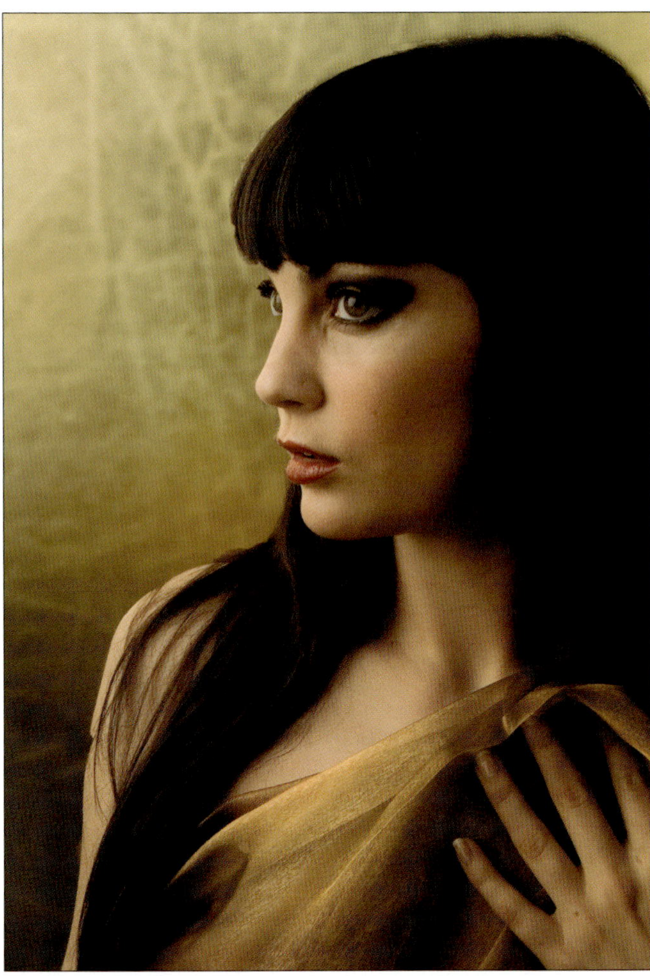

● **Top left:** A mandrill at Chester Zoo in the Monkey house taken on a Pentax *ist D at a member's meet. ● **Left:** I went to Critch Tramway museum and ended up shooting moss! I liked the fact this naturally looks like a watercolour painting, due to the out of focus tones created by the very shallow depth of field. It was taken on the Pentax *ist D with Tamron 90mm. ● **Right:** Angelina taken using a gold reflector as a background and a Lastolite Tri-flector to light the foreground. Lit with Bowens Esprit 250DX.

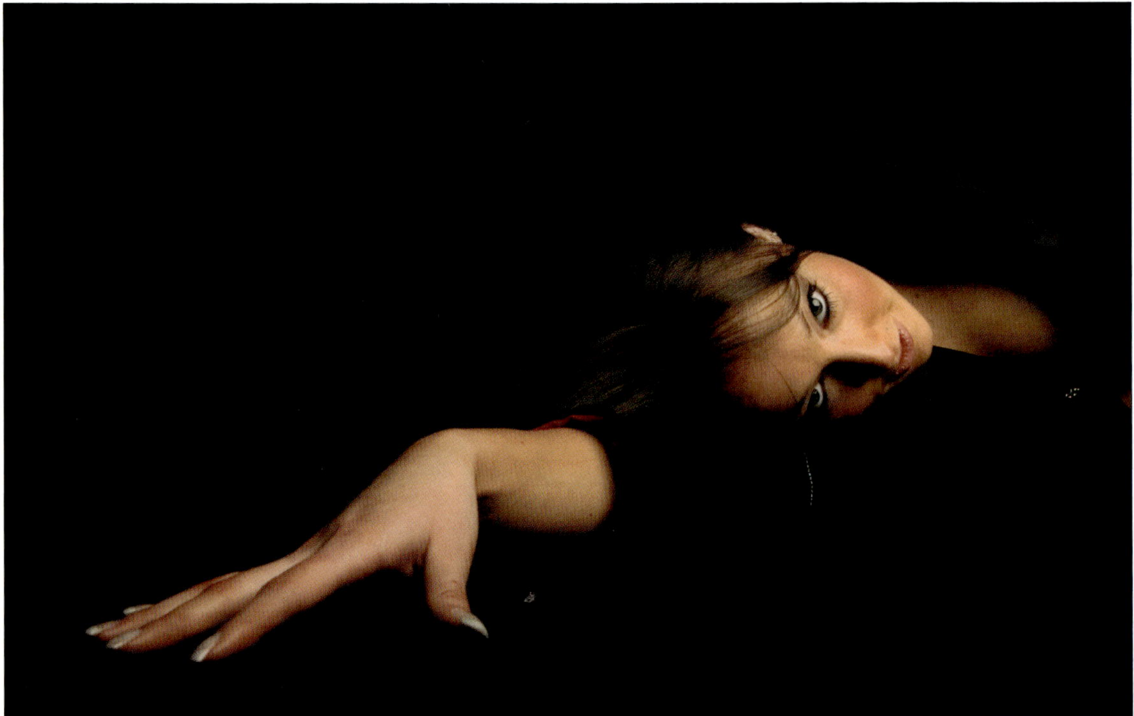

● I wanted to get something a little more unusual, so I asked Rachel to spread her arm out and raise her palm. I used the Pentax 16-45mm wide angle lens and shot from near the hand to change the perspective. Lit from front right with a Bowens Esprit 500 and Octo 150 softbox.

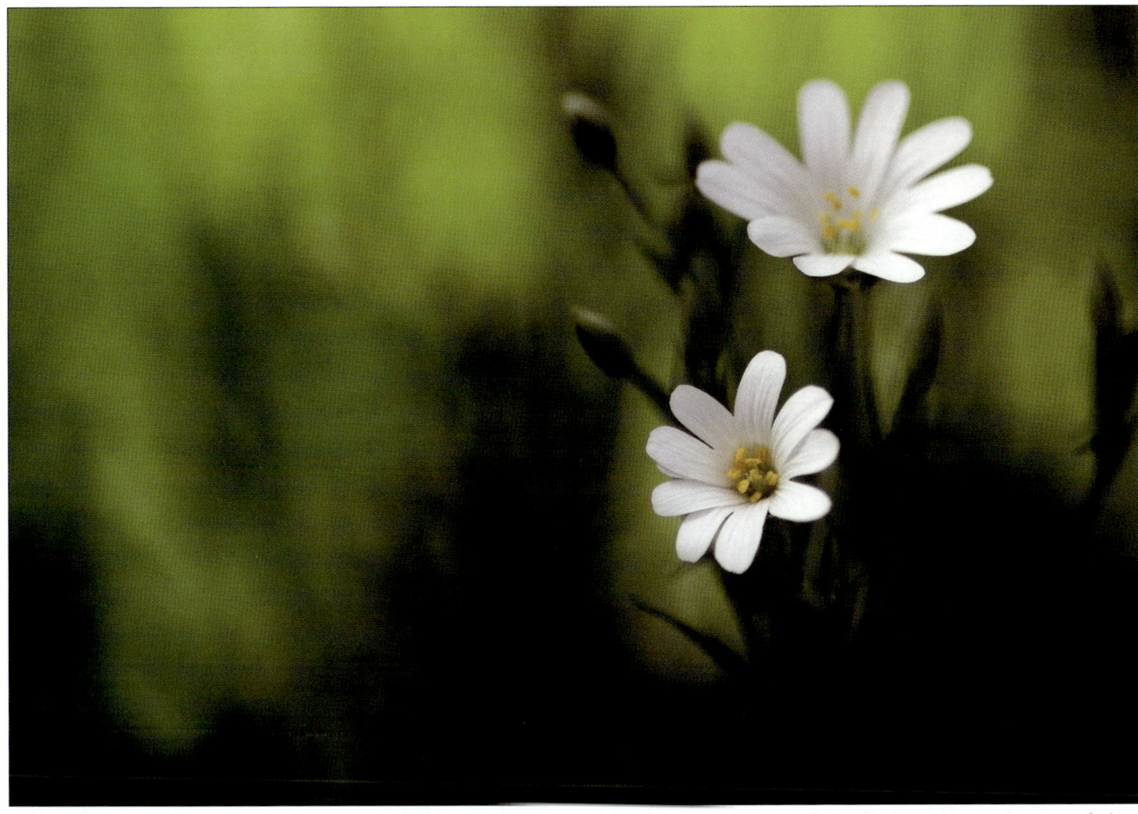

● I've taken thousands of flower photographs over the years, but this stitchwort is by far my favourite. It's pin sharp in the right spots and has a wonderfully soft natural background created using the Tamron 90mm macro lens wide open.

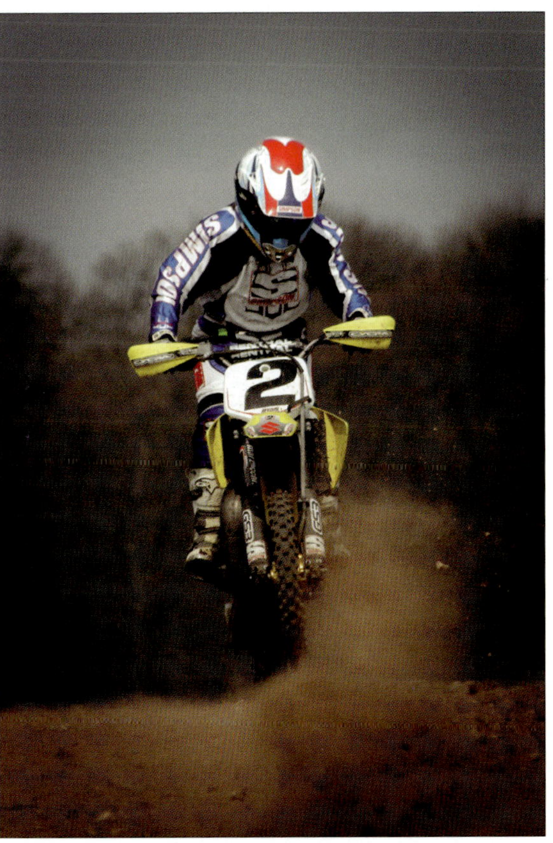

● While visiting a car boot sale in Sherwood forest I saw a motocross event taking place in an adjacent field. It was my first attempt at this kind of photography. I had a quick word with the organisers and they gave me access to the best positions on the track.

and huge things like an Ademco Dry Mounting Press and Kodak Fibre Based glazer. I was a fanatic, trying everything from darkroom to filter tricks.

Because of my thirst for experimentation I found working in retail couldn't pay enough to feed me and my expensive hobby, so I started submitting photos to magazines and initially got very little response.

My first success was a photo in the *Sheffield Star's Calendar* and then I had a photo printed on the cover of the *British Amateur Photographers Association* magazine – a club run by David Kilpatrick. The payment was a selection of books worth £25!

I then realised I could write how-to articles to go with my photos and that's when my life changed.

From being an amateur snapper with no qualifications, apart from an O-level in woodwork, I soon secured a job on *Practical Photography* as technical writer. A year later I became technical editor, and then I took over *Buying Cameras* magazine as editor. I also launched the UK's first Digital Photography magazine *Digital PhotoFX*. I've written articles for many papers and magazines, have produced a video and several books…and I still only have a CSE in English!

I launched ePHOTOzine over five years ago and it's gone from strength to strength.

Today I spend too much time working and little time taking photographs, but I love ePHOTOzine and the members. We have a great crowd and I enjoy the activity. Although occasionally one or two have spoilt this, overall it's a huge buzz!

When I do get to take photos it's at the weekend and I tend to spend that time either trawling around my old haunts in Derbyshire, doing landscape and floral photography or visiting stately homes and National Trust style properties photographing their homes and gardens.

I've recently started to diversify my portfolio by including a selection of glamour and fine art nude photographs and have started to do more studio work. I've been using one of the larger offices at the Turbine in Shireoaks with a Bowens studio lighting set up. I've also acquired a 600mm and intend to do some bird photography. ■

SOME OF THE PROJECTS PETE'S WORKED ON

■ **DIRECTOR** Magazine
Publishing Ltd

■ **PUBLISHER**
Guide to Great Photography
ePHOTOzine
Pentax User Club
Freelance Photography Made Easy

■ **DESIGNER**
Guide to Great Photography
Pentax User Club
Photoshop 5.5 A to Z
Photoshop 6.0 A to Z
Photoshop 7.0 A to Z
Photoshop CS A to Z

■ **EDITOR**
Guide to Great Photography
ePHOTOzine
Pentax User Magazine
Digital PhotoFX
Buying Cameras
Getting Started in Digital Photography

■ **TECHNICAL EDITOR**
Practical Photography

■ **BOOK AUTHOR**
Guide to Great Photography
Photoshop CS A to Z
Photoshop 7.0 A to Z
Photoshop 6.0 A to Z
Photoshop 5.5 A to Z
Teach Yourself Digital Photo

■ **VIDEO PRESENTER**
The Definitive Guide to Digital Photography

■ **PHOTOGRAPHER**
Cambridge Press
Corel PhotoCD Europe
Euro PhotoWeb
John Hinde
Marshall Editions
Sheffield Newspapers
Sheffield Education
World of Discovery

■ **COMMISSIONS**
Amateur Photographer
Black & White Photographer
BPI News
Computer Arts
Dixons Complete Guide to APS
EMAP Advantage
Golf World
HP PhotoWorld
Ilex Press
International Traveller
Jessops Catalogue
Jessops Website
Mailroom
Nikon Owners' Club
Nikon Fotoshare
Nikon In Touch
Photo Answers
The Photographer
Photography Monthly
Readers Digest
WHSmith Guide to Photography
Yours Specials

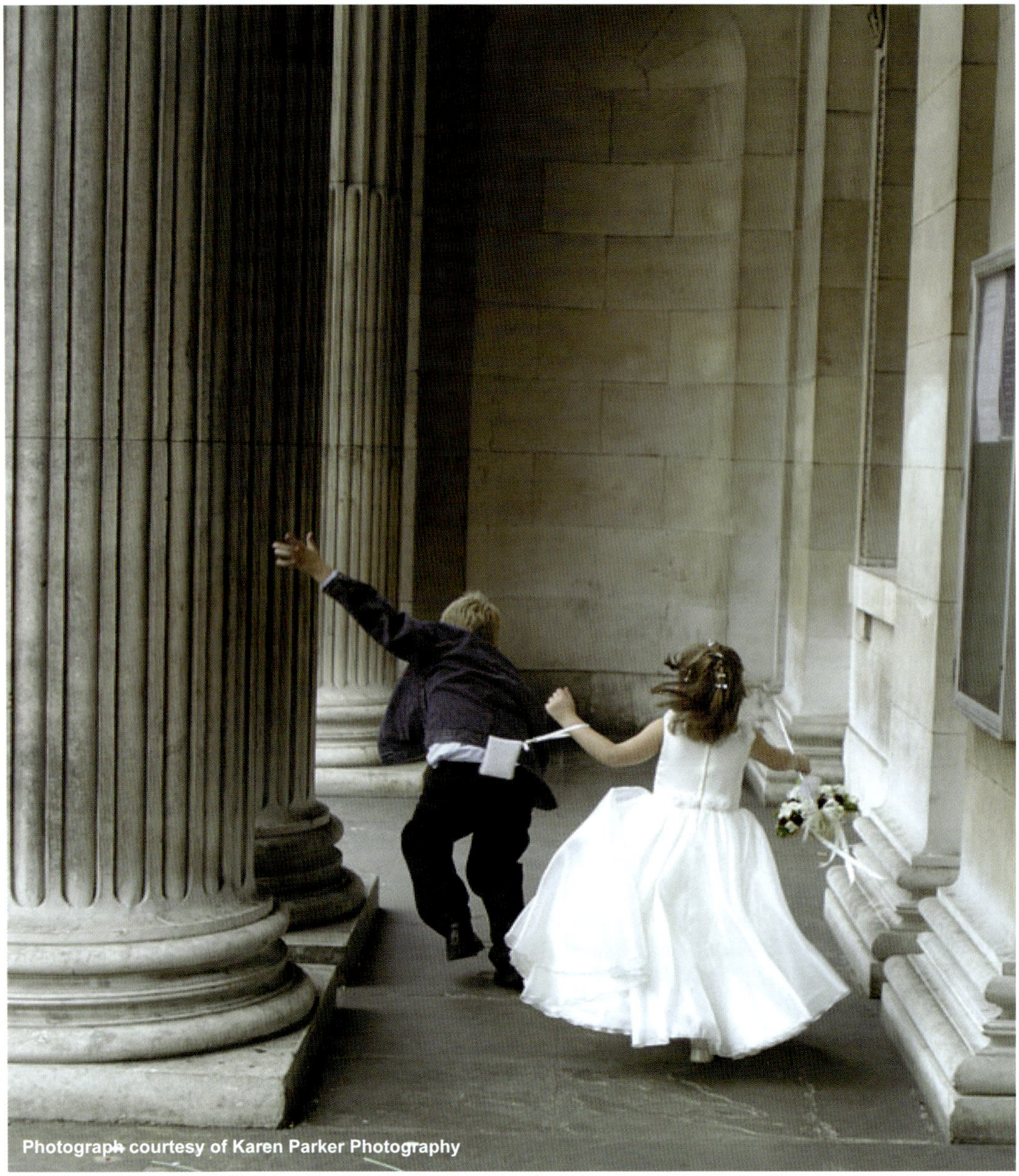

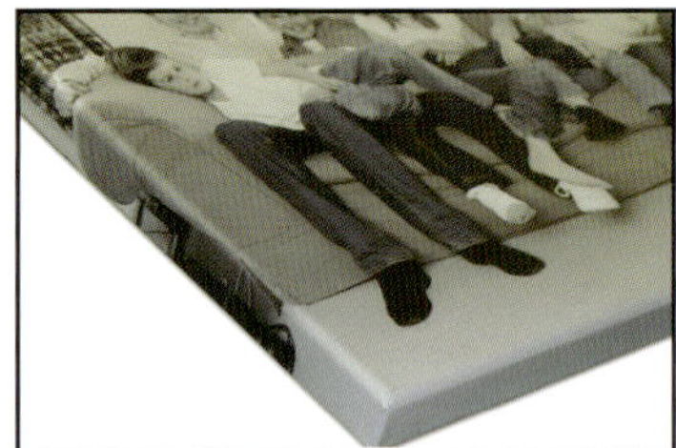

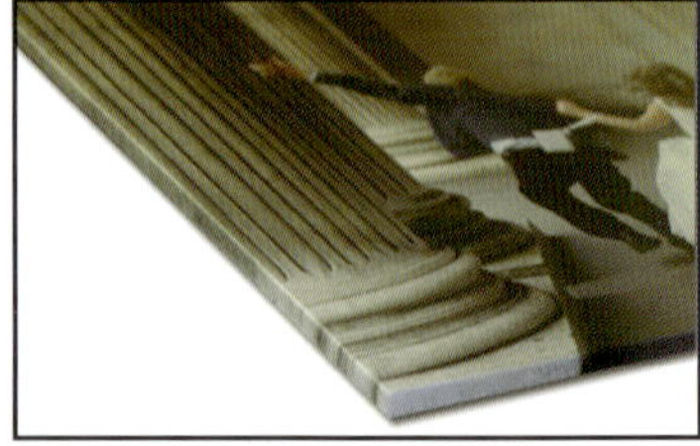

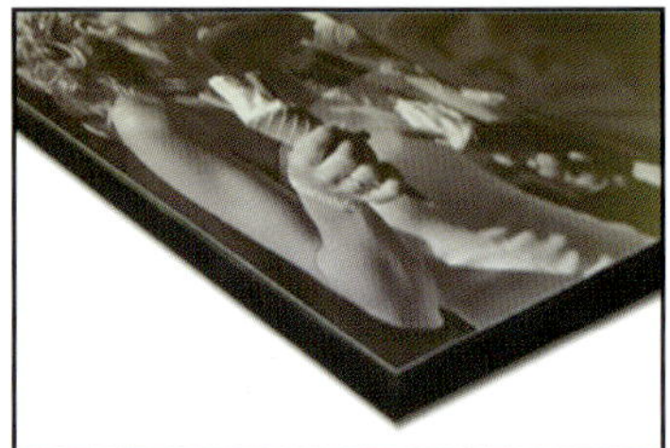

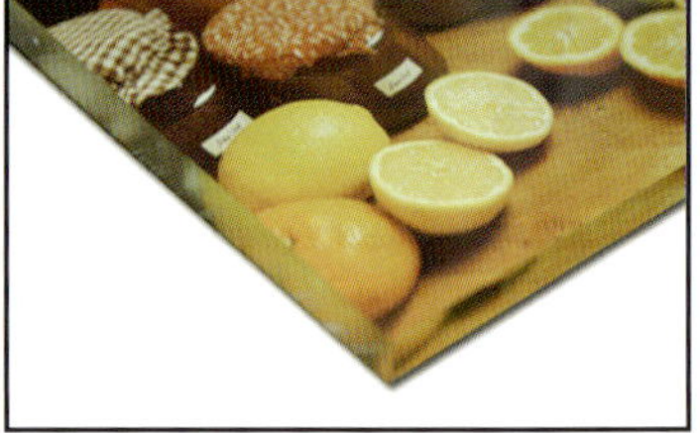

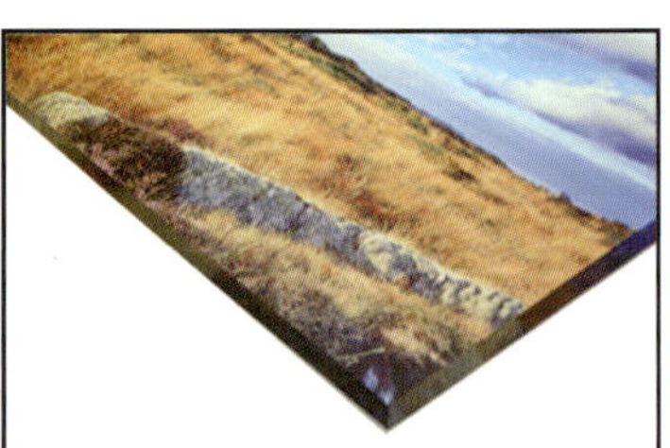

Photograph courtesy of Karen Parker Photography

In Pursuit Of The Perfect Printer?

You've just taken the perfect photograph. Your feeling is one of intense satisfaction. Now you need a professional printer; not any printer, but one who will work with you to achieve the best results in print quality.

PhotoArtistry specialises in innovative printing techniques using the latest in digital print technology. Working from your digital files or from scanned images, we will print your photos onto canvas, inkjet paper, or a range of digital fine art papers and offer the following mounted options:-

- **Stretched Canvas Prints**
- **Acrylic Perspex Block Mounts**
- **Aluminium Block Mounts**
- **Traditional Block Mounts**

www.photoartistry.co.uk
Creative Print Solutions For Creative People

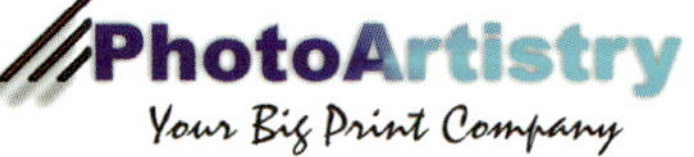

PhotoArtistry

Your Big Print Company

Photo of the week

Every photo uploaded to the ePHOTOzine gallery is viewed by editor, Peter Bargh. He selects his favourites each day and gives them an Editor's Choice Award (EC). These photographs are then considered for the coveted title of Photo of the Week (POTW) and every winner receives a free canvas mounted photo from our sponsor, PhotoArtistry. Here are some of the latest.

The idea of the EC is to provide a selection of superb images that could inspire and encourage development, but most of all it's a showcase for brilliant photography. The editor selects pictures that he thinks stand out for one or more of the following reasons:

Technical excellence Includes photographs that are razor sharp, perfectly exposed, superbly composed, fantastically edited.

Innovative Includes photographs that are original, not run of the mill, different than the norm. Ones that make him think, "Wow, I've never seen that before!"

Treatment of the subject matter The way a particular subject is approached, e.g. shallow depth-of-field for a wild flower may do better than a front to back sharp meadow. A side profile of a fox may do better than a head on shot, a racing car panned is likely to work better than one that looks as though it's stood still etc.

Creativity Includes photographs that break the rules, stand out for odd colours, interesting compositions, selective focus etc.

Personal appeal "Yes I do have a liking of certain styles. I think paintings by Salvador Dali and surrealists like him are fascinating. I find Bob Carlos Clarke's pictures highly erotic. I love the infrared work of Simon Marsden. I enjoy the still lifes of Irvin Penn. I admire the landscapes of Ansel Adams. As a youth I was often engrossed in books of birds of prey by Eric Hoskins."

Presentation A badly framed or titled photo may lose mental points and a perfectly presented photo may gain points, but essentially it's the centre that counts.

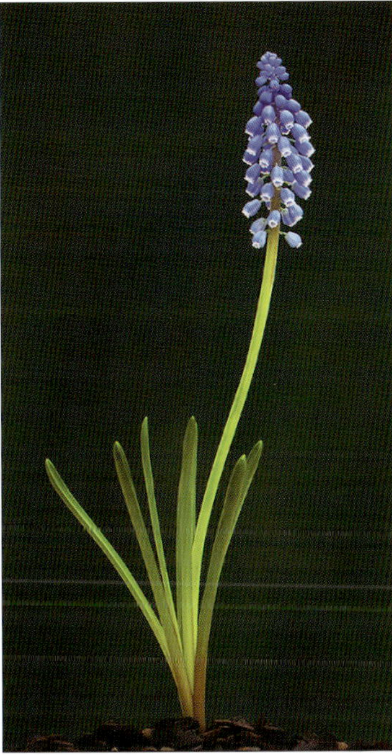

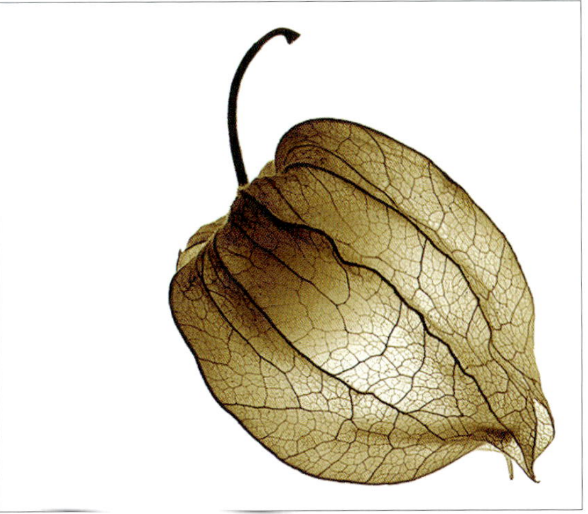

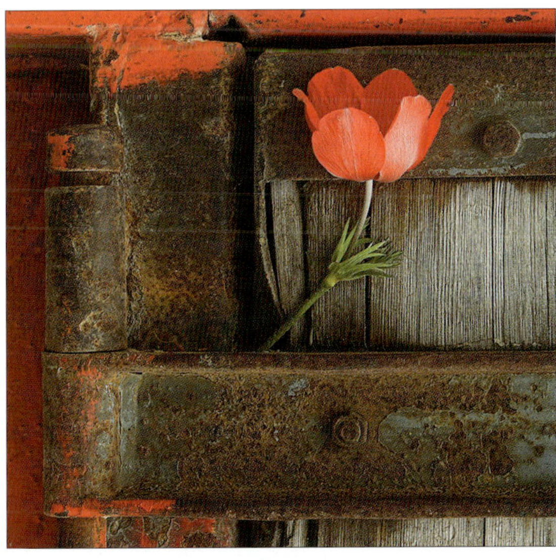

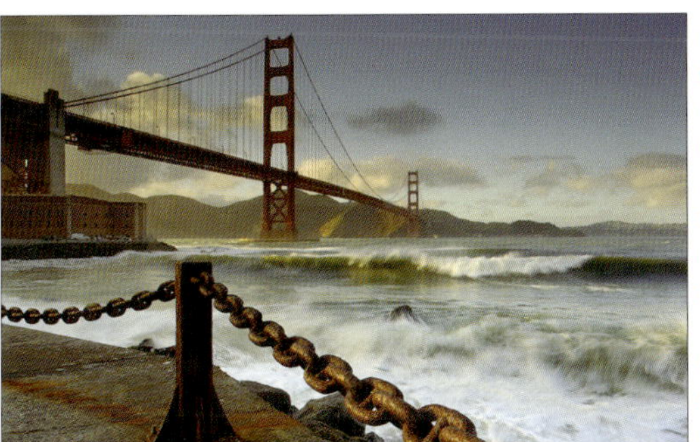

From the top, clockwise:
- Muscari against dark background by Chris Miles.
- Physalis on white background by Angela Joel.
- Anenome placed on Rusty lorry by Lydia Moore.
- Glen Etive Mountain Scene by Jeanette Lazenby.
- Stile on Welsh beach by Mari Sterling.
- San Francisco's Golden Gate Bridge by Patrick Smith.

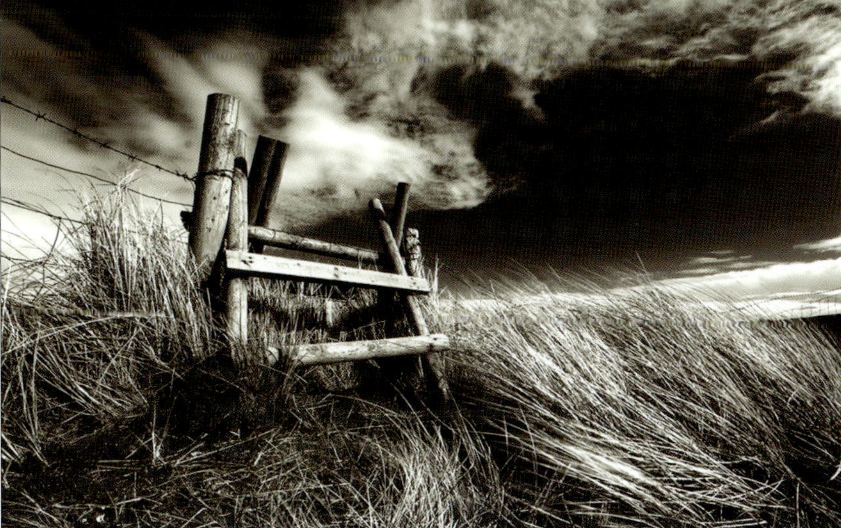

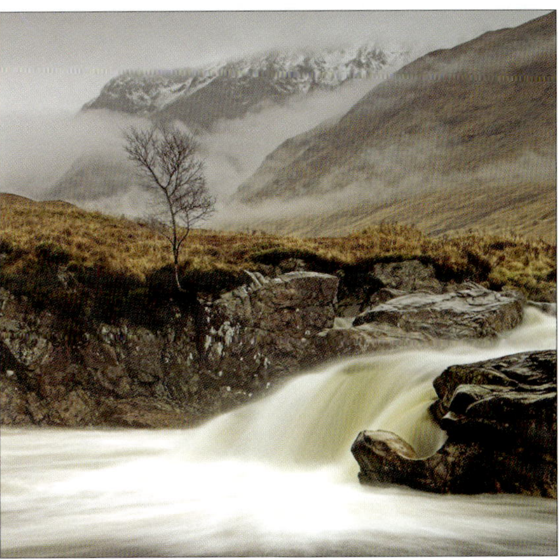

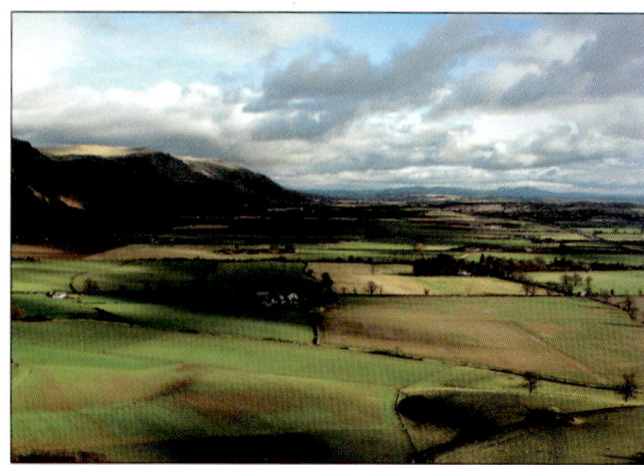

● GILL BRETT Climbing a hill to a landmark, such as Wallace Monument, Stirling, can give a better viewpoint.

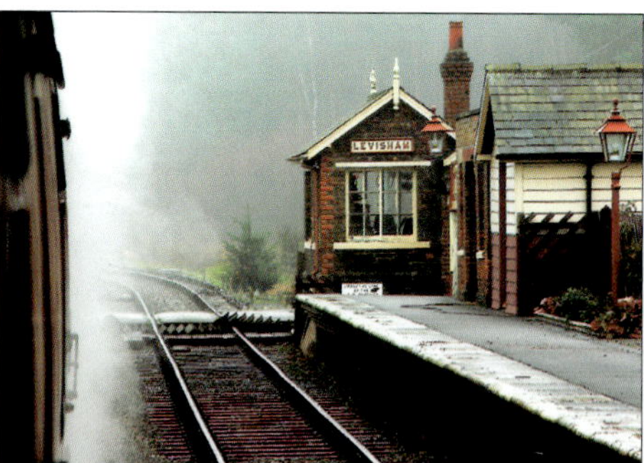

● IAIN JOHNSTONE A rather dull December day on the North Yorkshire Moors Railway at Levisham.

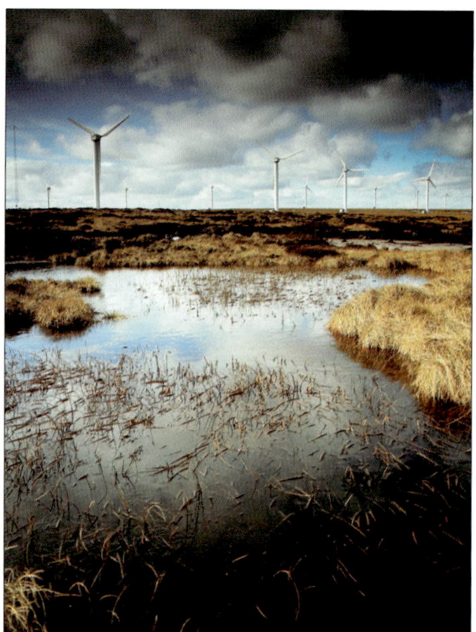

● AL MULROONEY A fast shutter speed was used to freeze these turbines at Ovenden Moor.

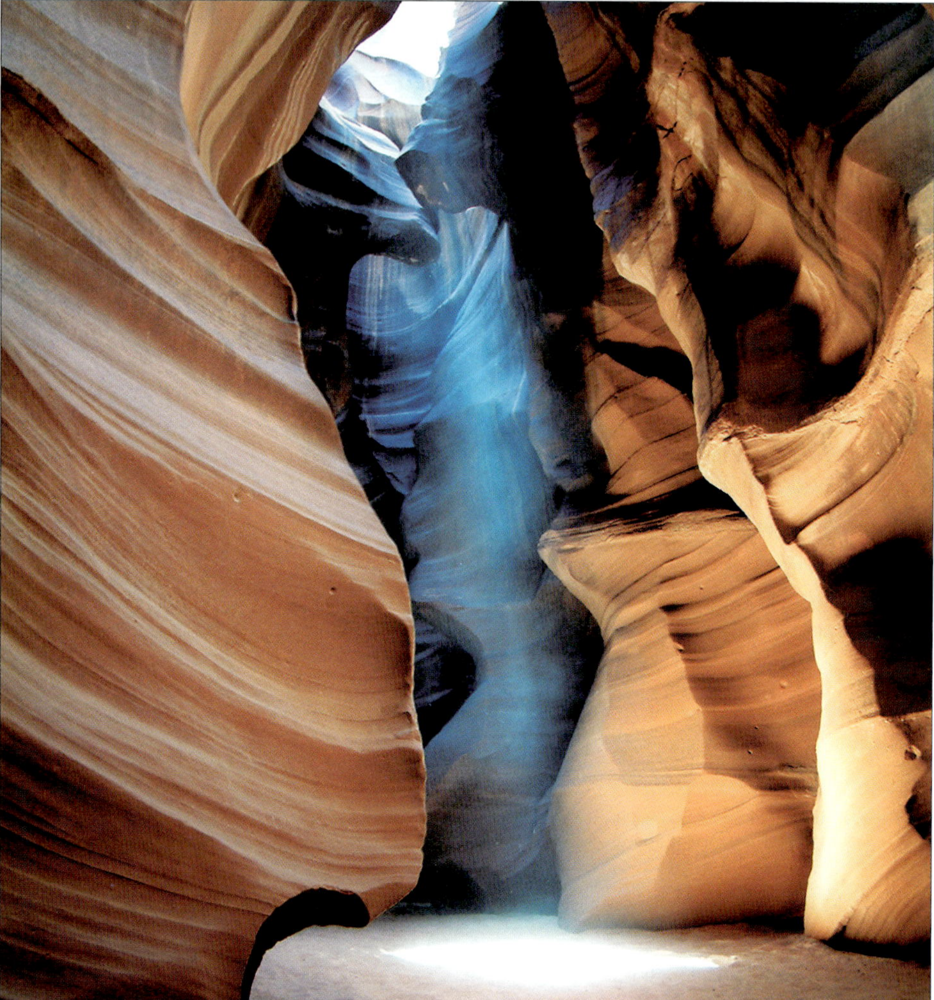

● ALETHEA HOLLIS We hired a guide to take us over a dry river bed by Land Rover to Antelope Canyon, Arizona, USA. It was taken at midday when shafts of light burst through the slits in the canyon ceiling.

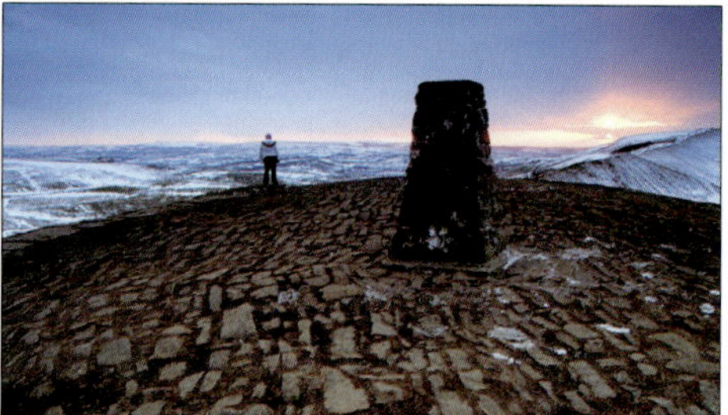

● CHRIS HERRING This sunset, following a snow fall on the top of Mam Tor in the Peak District, was taken on a Canon EOS 20D with a Sigma 18-50mm f/2.8 lens.

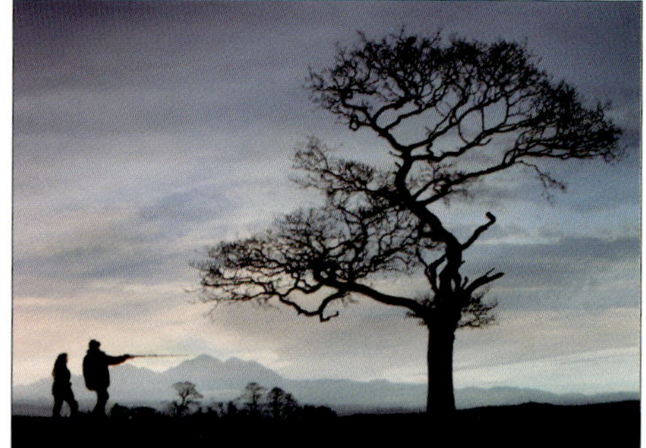

● JOHN POWELL Including people in a scene adds a sense of scale. This dramatic silhouette was taken in Hagley, West Midlands, using an Olympus E10.

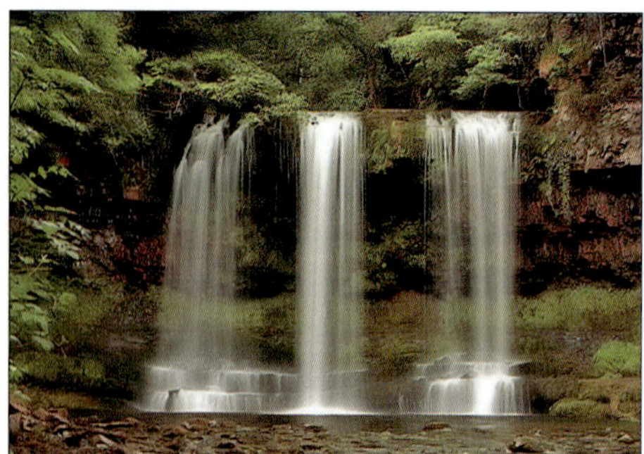

● ANDREW ROBERTS Sgwd-yr-Eira (waterfall of snow) taken at Ystradfellte, South Wales.

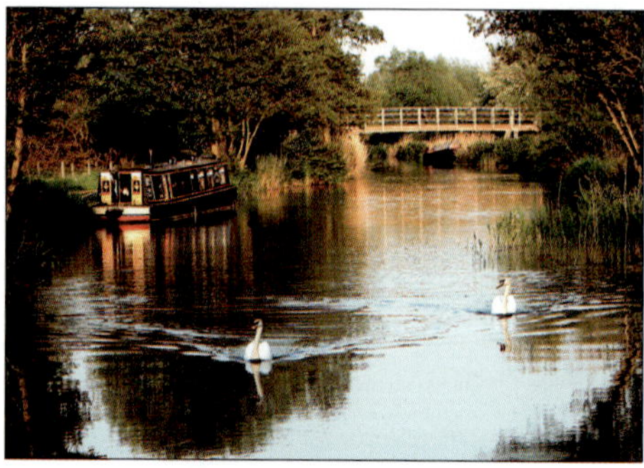

● GRAHAM MULROONEY Kennett and Avon Canal in Berkshire. The swans draw your eye into the scene.

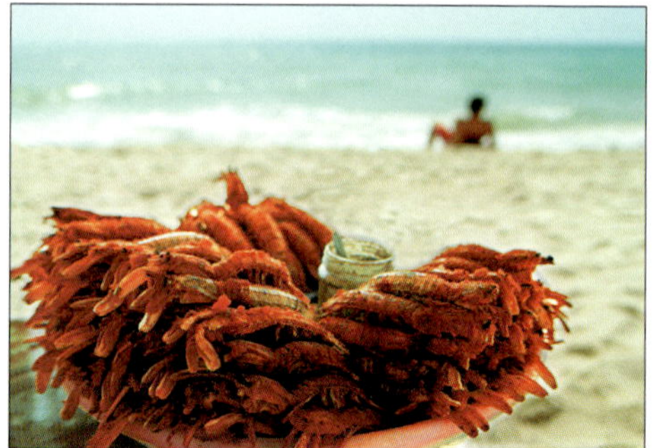

● NIAMH BALDOCK Baby lobsters on Sihanoukville beach, Cambodia, taken with a wide aperture.

Landscapes

Our world is full of natural beauty and to capture this well it's all about light and being in the right place at the right time. ePHOTOzine photographers will think nothing about arriving at a scene at the crack of dawn to photograph the sunrise and cut through the early morning mist, or trudge miles with a heavy rucksack to search out the unphotographed.

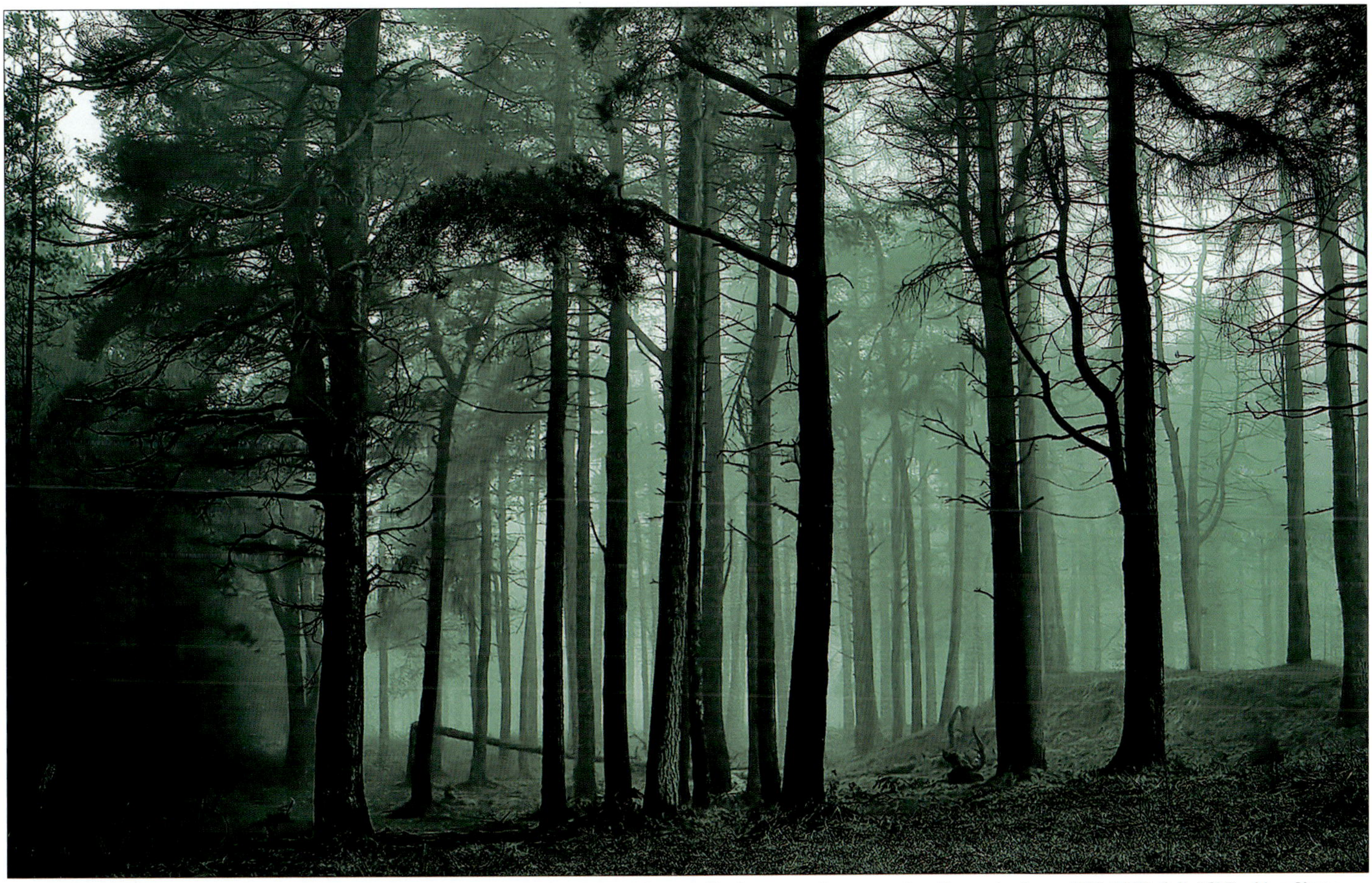

● ANDREW ROBERTS This haunting woodland scene was taken at Andrew's local forest in Tredegar on a foggy morning. He used a Canon EOS 300D digital SLR with a Sigma 18-55mm zoom and an exposure of 1/160sec at f/4. The result was then toned in Photoshop CS. There are many more like this in Andrew's ePHOTOzine portfolio.

Landscapes are, undoubtedly, the most photographed subjects around. You may be fortunate enough to step out of your door to a stunning vista, take a holiday in some beautiful location or spend time hiking around our more remote settings, but either way there's something for everyone in landscape photography.

Over the following 38 pages you will see some of the most impressive scenes, exposed in some of the most creative ways, from some of the most talented ePHOTOzine members.

We've split this section up into popular sub-sections and have included tips throughout to help you make the most of our countryside. You'll see that a landscape doesn't have to be just a pasture or woodland scene. You can move in close to crop out most of the surrounds or include buildings, objects or people as points of interest.

Hopefully, from the images that follow, you'll gain a huge amount of inspiration to shoot better landscapes. Each picture has a short caption that either explains how the photo was taken or where it is, so you can follow in the footsteps of previous photographers.

There are certain pieces of photographic equipment that will help you improve your photographs – you will see many of our photographers use filters, so we've included a guide to the 10 essential landscape filters. Most serious landscape photographers use a tripod to prevent camera shake and a wide-angle lens is usually found in the outfit bag.

Whether you shoot film or digital you should be prepared for certain problems that might occur. Cold weather affects batteries so keep your camera in warmth when not in use. Also ensure you carry a spare battery – you won't find a friendly dealer at the top of a mountain!

When shooting digital avoid using the LCD too much as this drains batteries quickly. Make sure you have enough storage space (memory cards) to shoot the pictures you hope to take. Cards are no longer expensive, so it's worth having more than you need to ensure you don't miss a shot.

It's not just the equipment that makes a good landscape. The time of day is vital. It's widely believed that midday sun is a no go when shooting landscapes, but you can get some interesting graphical effects at this time, with deep shadows. However, early morning and late evening tend to be more suitable for most scenes.

Many ePHOTOzine photographers think nothing of setting their alarms for the early hours so they can arrive at a chosen scene at the crack of dawn. It's hit and miss whether they'll see a spectacular sunrise or ethereal blanket of mist, but when the timing's right the results speak for themselves.

You'll see from the following photos that depth-of-field (front to back sharpness) is an important consideration when using film or digital cameras and this is explained on page 28

It's also important to consider the position of the horizon and how straight it is. There are several rules of composition that we cover on page 29 and these can, and often are, broken, but there's no excuse for a wonky horizon – apart from maybe one too many beers! Some tripods have a spirit level built in to give you the benefit of the doubt, or you can buy one to slip onto the hot-shoe of your camera.

So, without further ado, turn the page to begin your journey into the wonderful world of landscapes. ■

● JOHN SIMMONS This photographer likes to get into the middle of the field for frame-filling poppy detail.

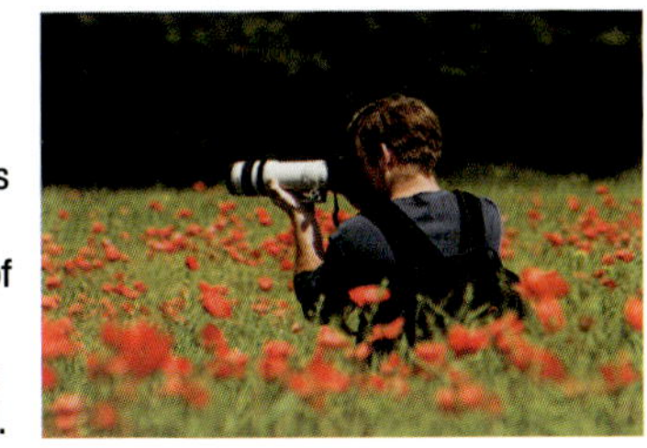

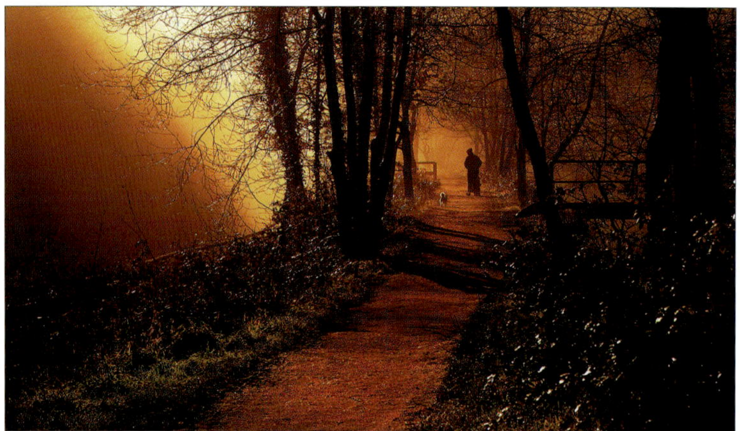

● IAN HUTCHINSON This elderly lady waiting for her dog was taken at Etherow Country Park, Stockport, on a cold December morning.

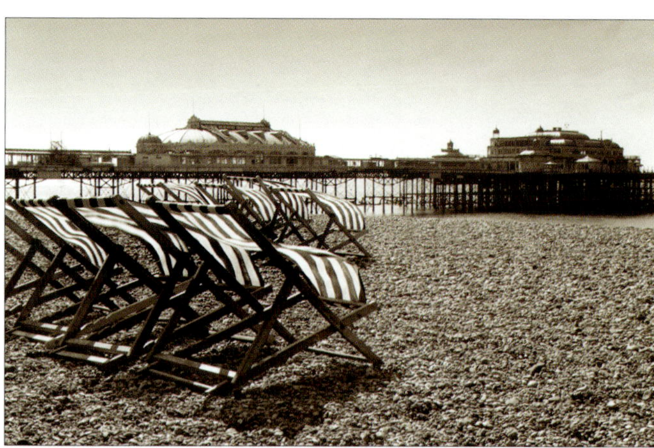

● DAVE CLARKE Palace Pier, Brighton, Sussex, taken in 1987 on a Canon T70 using Ilford FP4 film with an exposure of 1/4sec at f/22.

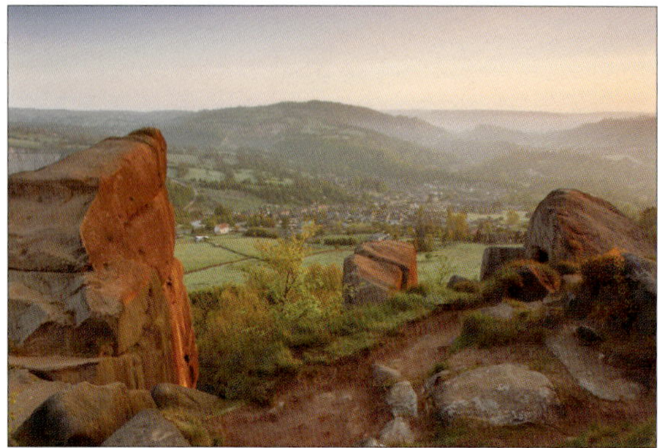

● IAN DAISLEY Black Rock, Derbyshire, with the village of Cromford nestled in the valley, looking towards Matlock in the distance.

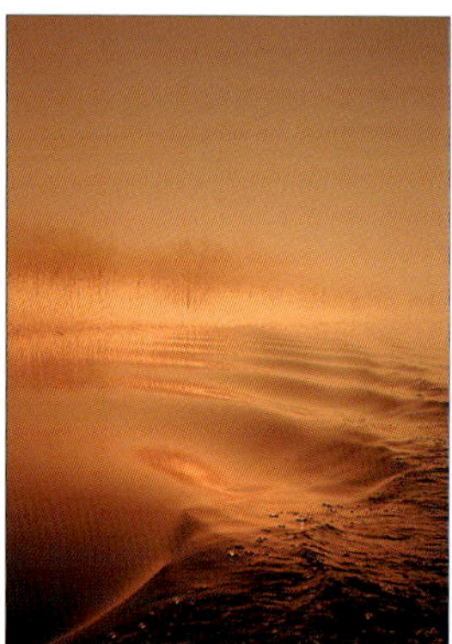

● ANGELA JOEL Ripples on Llangors Lake, Brecon Beacons.

DEPTH-OF-FIELD

■ Depth-of-field is one of the more important aspects of photography and is something that confuses newcomers learning about photography and bypasses those who just take snapshots. In simple terms depth-of-field is the amount of sharp focus in front and behind the main point of focus.

■ The amount of depth-of-field is controlled by one of three things: camera to subject distance, the aperture or the focal length of the lens. The further the camera is away from the subject the greater the depth-of-field. A smaller aperture increases depth-of-field. A wider angle lens increases depth-of-field.

■ Once the basics are grasped this technique can be used to make a photograph appear incredibly sharp from the nearest to far point, or throw everything totally out of focus apart from a very shallow plane.

■ While portrait photographers may want shallow depth-of-field so all the attention is placed on the model and not the background, landscape photographers generally want everything sharp from the nearby grass or rocks to the distant hills or woodland.

■ Some photographers go to great lengths to confuse you about how to work out the depth-of-field, mentioning things such as circles of confusion and depth of focus. There are even calculators available to work out the exact focus to the millimetres. Look at the diagram here and you'll see how it works:

■ The basic principle is that the amount of extra sharpness behind the main point of focus, represented by the dark line, will be twice as much as that in front. Learn to focus at a specific point in the scene so that all the elements you want sharp are within the necessary depth-of-field – the diagram's dark shaded area.

■ Many SLR cameras have a depth-of-field preview button that stops the lens down to the aperture selected so you can see how sharp different planes will be when the photograph is taken. The viewfinder appears dark but once your eyes become accustomed you'll see a difference as you press down and release the preview button. If you have a digital camera use the zoom LCD preview to confirm focus by scrolling around the magnified image looking at various elements.

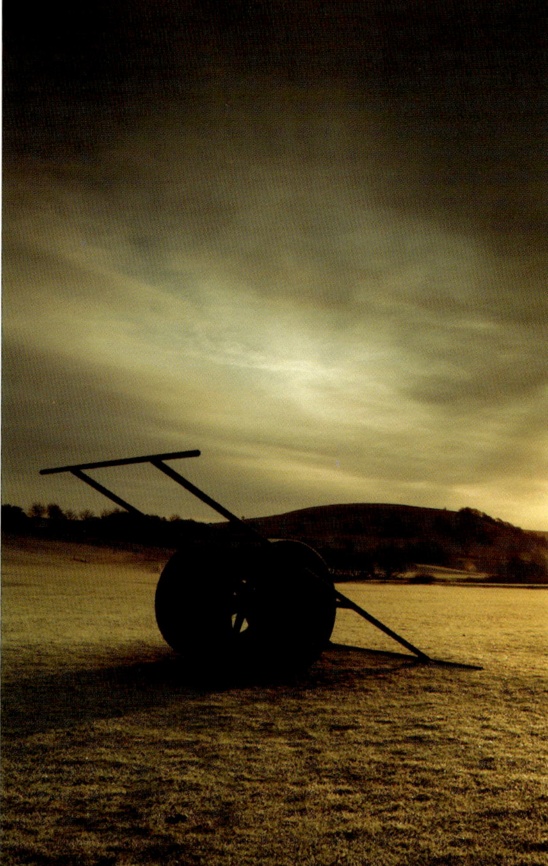

● MATT WAGSTER A cricket roller taken on a cold winter morning at Burnsall Village, Yorkshire. The exposure was 1/2sec at f/22.

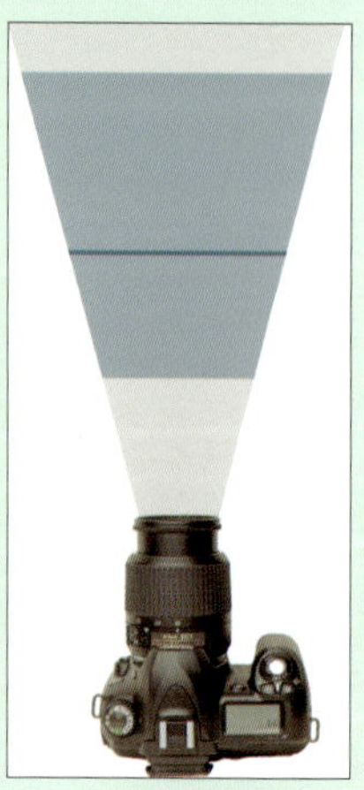

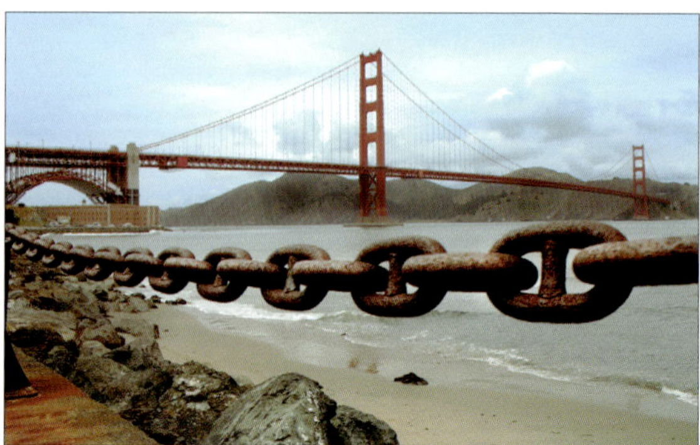

● GIUSEPPE LIPARI Including the foreground chain gives a different view of Golden Gate Bridge taken from Crissy Fields, San Francisco.

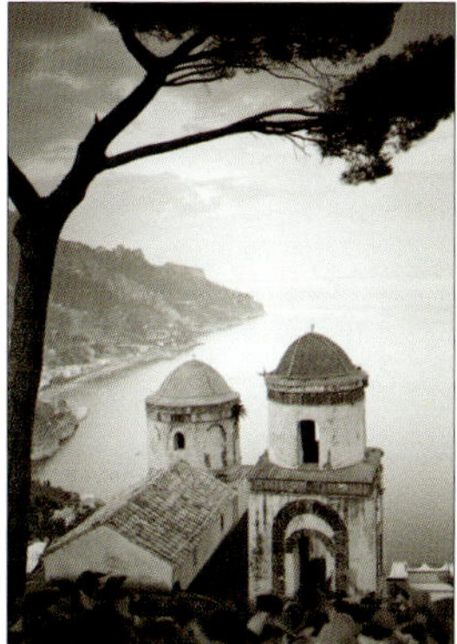

● JOANNE DUNN View from Villa Ruffolo, Ravello in Italy.

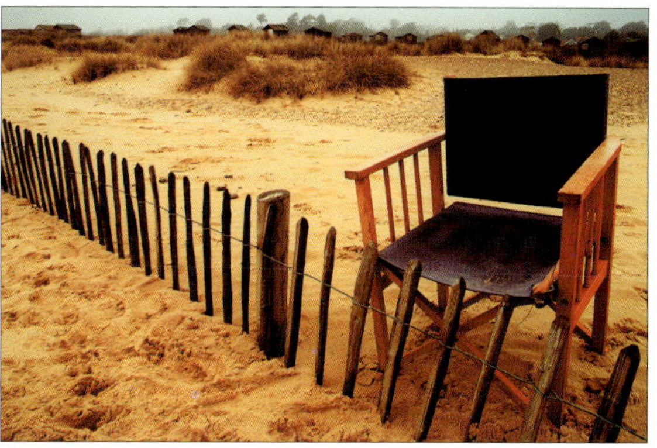

● JOHN DUCKETT This deckchair, abandoned on a North Suffolk beach, seemed to sum up a typical wet Bank Holiday Monday.

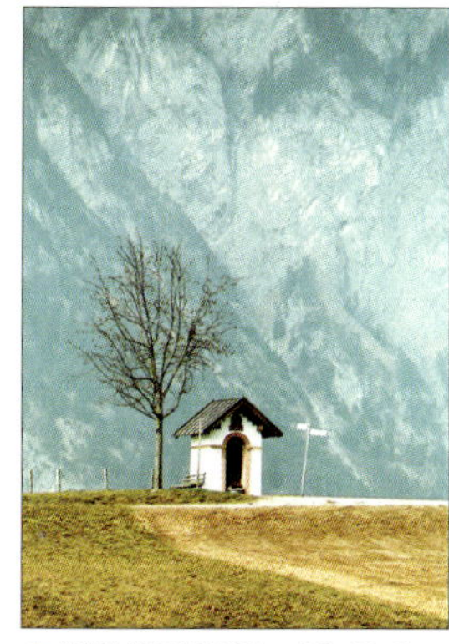

● IVAN HARRIS Wayside Shrine near Goetzens in Austria.

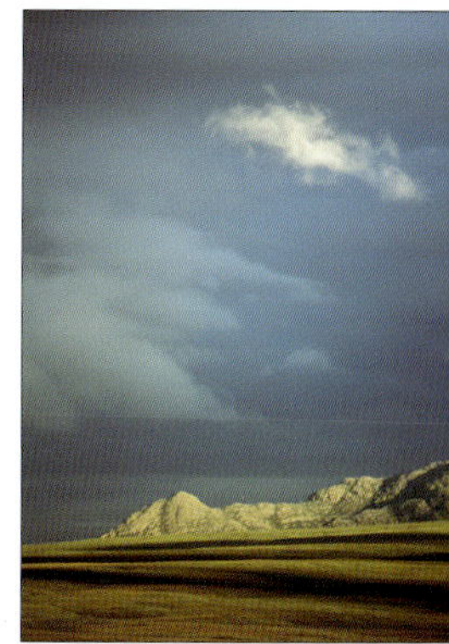

● REAGAN PANNELL Shot after a storm for atmosphere.

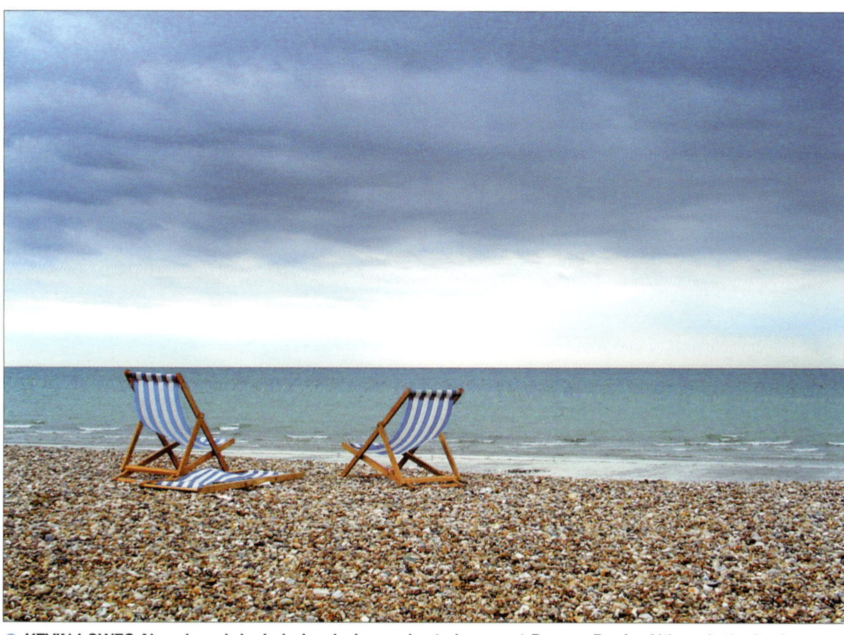

● KEVIN LOWES Abandoned deckchairs during a short shower at Bognor Regis. Although the horizon splits the photo across the middle, the main subject has been placed on the lower third.

COMPOSITION – RULE OF THIRDS

■ Composition, or the way elements in a photograph are arranged, is one of those things that can make all the difference between a snapshot and a great photograph. Look around your camera's viewfinder just before you take a photograph and you'll start to see better compositions. Look at the subject and its surrounds. Take care to avoid things that could spoil the balance of elements, such as a tree near the edge or a litter bin or road sign bang in the middle.

■ You may wish to include an extra element, or a focal point, to a scene to enhance or balance the elements. A rock in the foreground, positioned left or right, may add depth. An arch or doorway will naturally frame the subject, also a tree branch can be positioned across the top to provide a frame over the skyline.

■ Try using a different lens to change the composition, a wide-angle lens will allow more to be included in the frame for creating sweeping vistas and a telephoto narrows down the angle to help you hone in on a subject and remove all the nearby clutter. Move closer, step back, shoot from a higher viewpoint or crouch down.

■ There are several classic composition theories where you place elements of a photograph into naturally pleasing zones that balance the overall image. Most of these techniques are easy to follow and subliminally improve the visual appearance of a photograph. The most popular is the rule of thirds.

■ The rule of thirds is where you visualise lines that split the photograph into thirds, horizontally and vertically, creating a nine section grid. You position the main point of focus on one or more of the four intersecting lines. A landscape would have the horizon either one or two thirds of the way up the photograph, while a tree would be placed on the left or right third, creating an L shape composition.

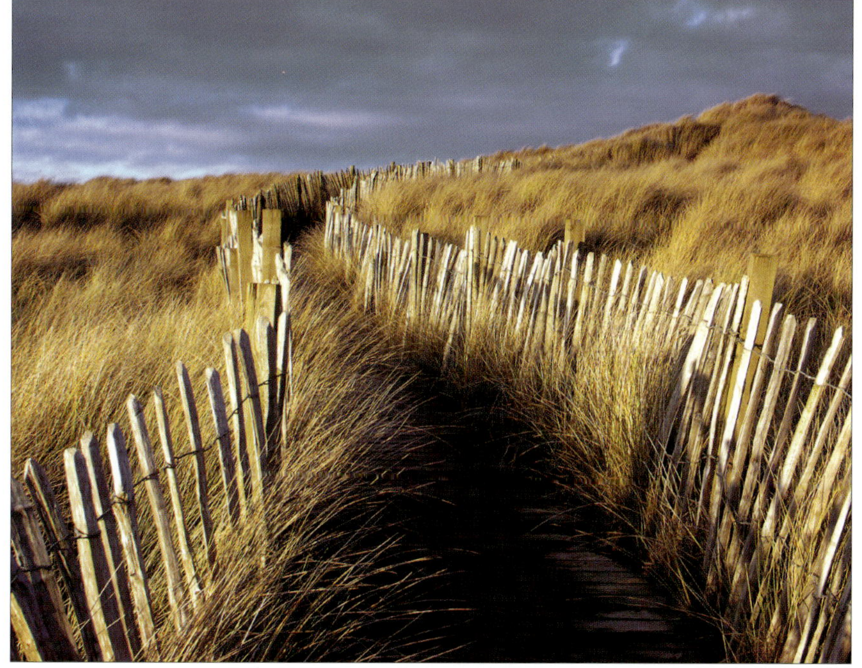

● BRIAN SLESSOR A path leading to the beach at the Waters of Philorth, Fraserburgh, taken at f/5.6 on a Konica Minolta A2. The horizon has been placed on the top third and the path leads your eye there.

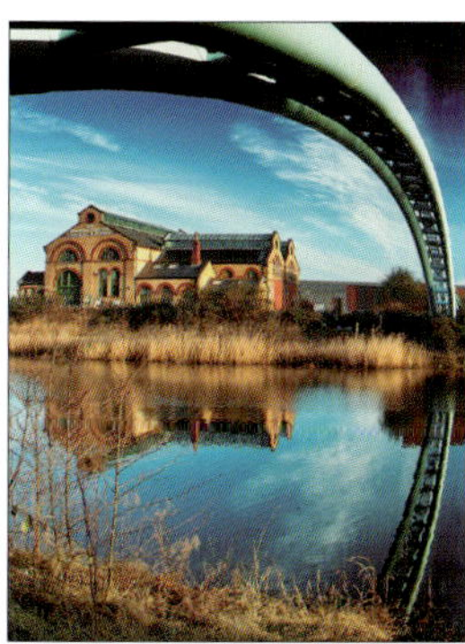

● MARK CAVENDISH An old Pumping Station in Cardiff, carefully framed by a modern curved bridge.

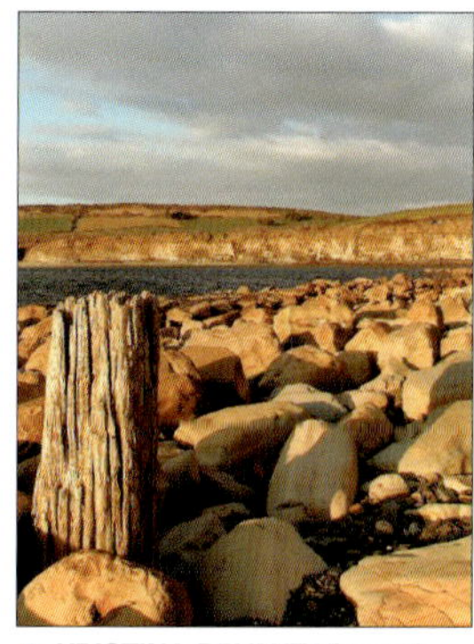

● KRISTINA BRYANT View of Kimmeridge, Dorset on Fuji S5000. The foreground post seeks our attention.

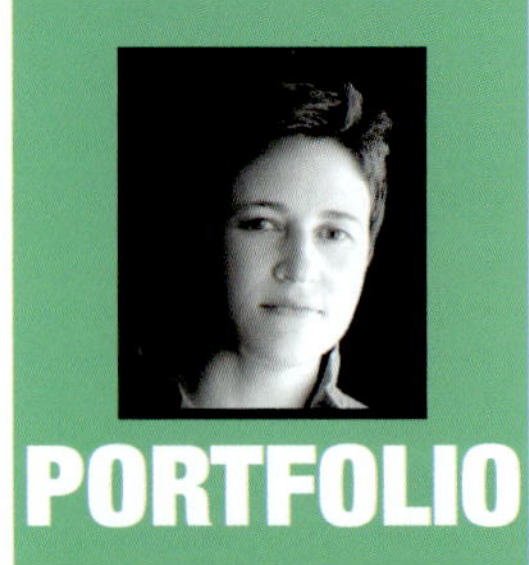

PORTFOLIO

HELEN DIXON
Helen specialises in
landscape photography
and hopes to break into the
stock library market soon.

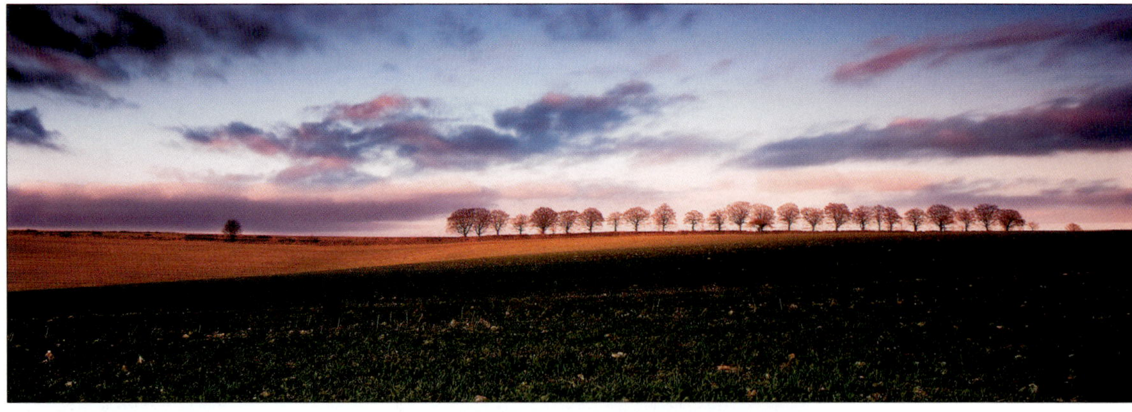

**My passion for photography
began after buying my first
computer in June 2003, closely
followed by the purchase of my
first camera – a Canon G5.**

In October 2003 I entered a
competition with the theme 'Autumn'.
Taking pictures for this inspired me
to get out and discover the beauty
landscapes have to offer. To my
amazement, I won first prize – a copy
of Photoshop CS.

That's when I began to get
serious. I realised my heart lay
with photographing landscapes
and anything to do with nature.
Landscapes offer so many different
options to the photographer. I
especially like the way the same
scene looks so different from day to
day. Many factors affect this, but light
is one of the most important.

I love the way light can totally
change an image and have such
an effect on the beautiful world we
live in. It gives me so much pleasure
to try and capture some of these
magical moments.

I didn't want to be limited in
my photography, so I upgraded to
a Canon EOS 10D which helped
me develop immensely. I now use
a Canon 1D Mark II. I always use
a sturdy tripod, if conditions and
circumstances allow, and find an
angle-finder useful for low shots.

I try to capture the best picture
possible in-camera, that way it
doesn't require too much post-
processing. To give myself the best
chance of this I use various filters,
including a circular polariser and a
set of hard and soft edged ND grads
to help control exposure.

Occasionally I also use an 81c
warm up. I shoot in RAW format, and
convert the images using Capture
One or Photoshop to give me the
best possible quality.

In future I'd like to have work
accepted by a stock library. ■
www.helendixonphotography.co.uk

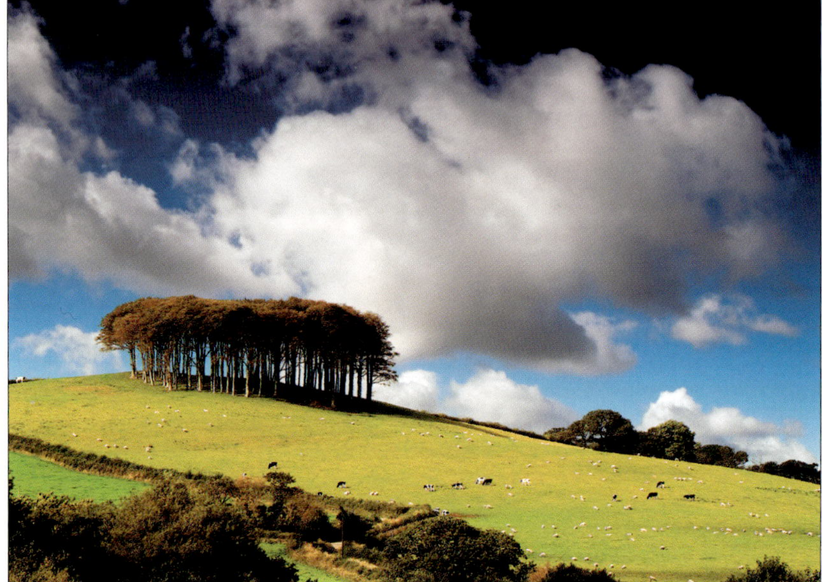

● All photos taken with Canon
EOS 10D. Above: The setting sun,
taken using a Canon 17-40mm
and cropped to panoramic format.
Left: taken on the Cornwall/Devon
border alongside the busy A303.
I parked in a lay-by and used the
Sigma 70-300mm set to 300mm.
Below left: Frosty mornings may be
cold, but the atmosphere can be the
best condition to capture nature's
wonders. I was trying to keep as
much of the sky and retain the
foreground too, so I broke the rule
about splitting a landscape in half
with the horizon. Below right:
The sunset was disappointing but
the clouds behind and to the side
really caught the last of the sun. I
changed viewpoints and snapped
away at the little clump of trees. I
like the simplicity of this shot.

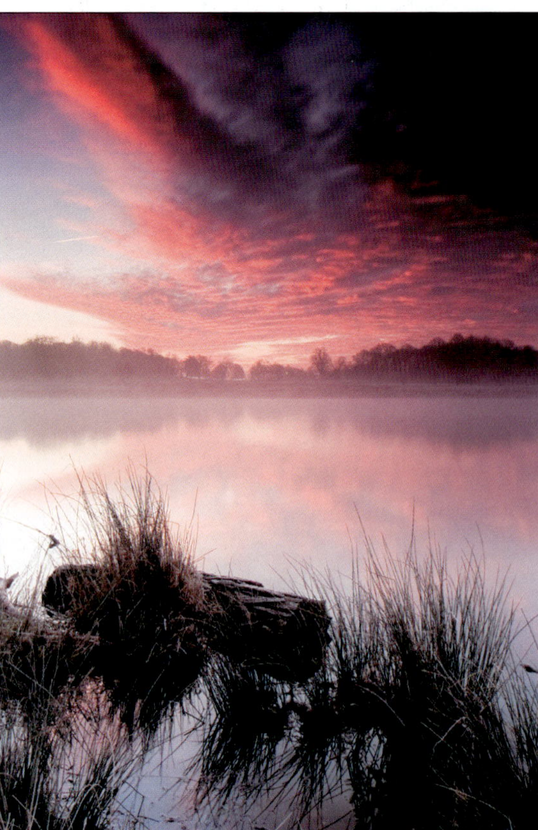

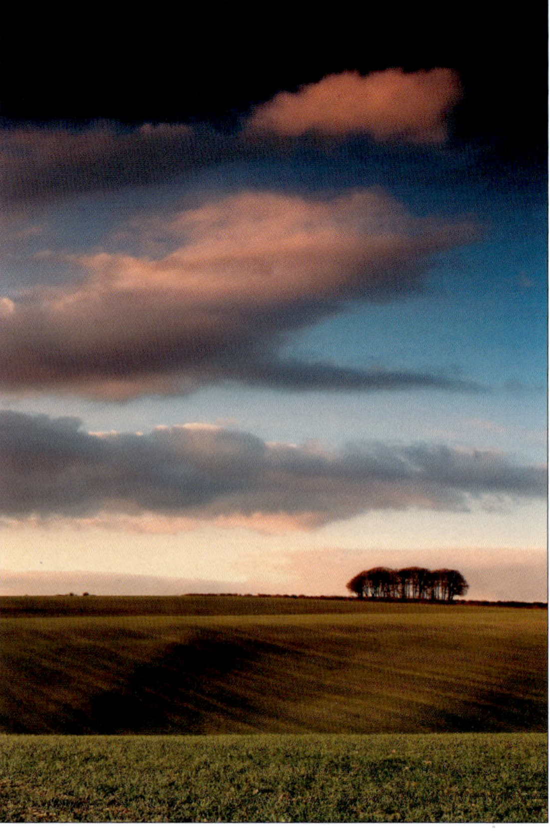

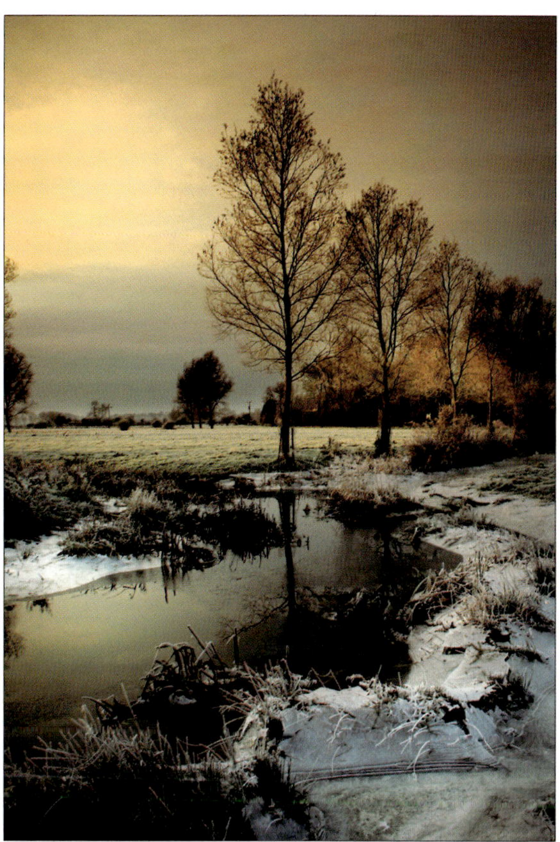

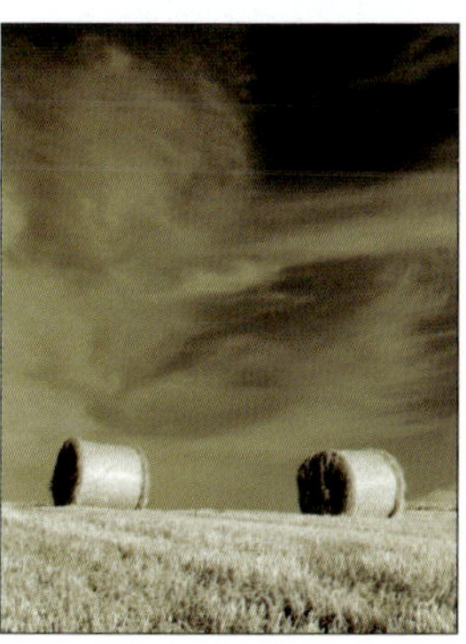

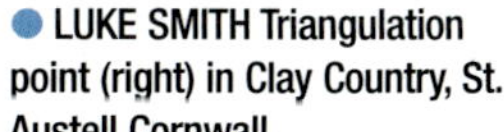

KATHY WRIGHT Bat Willows, Waveney Valley, Norfolk.

STEVE HANNAH Circular polariser and digitally toned.

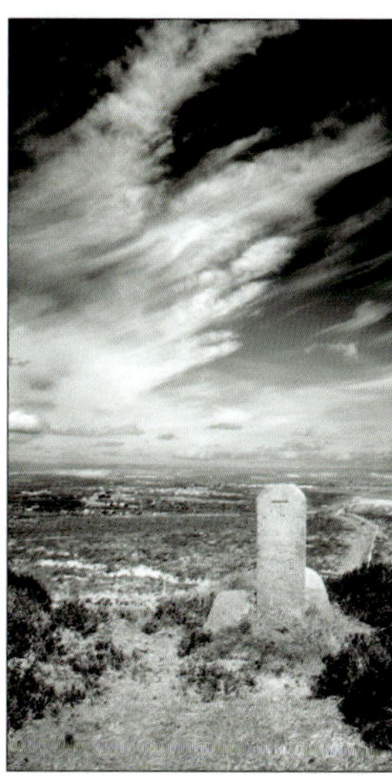

LUKE SMITH Triangulation point (right) in Clay Country, St. Austell Cornwall.

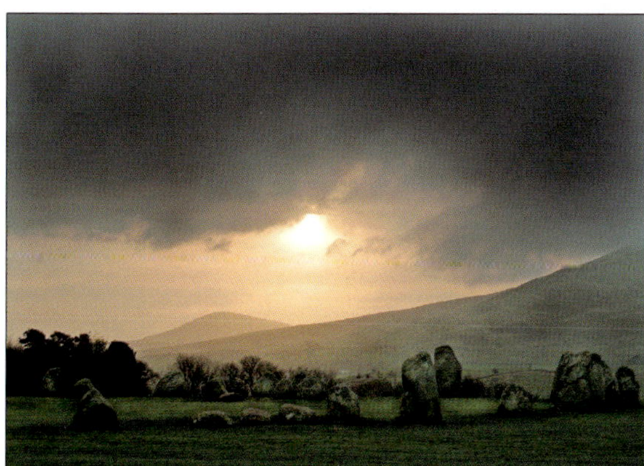

MARTIN WESTON Castlerigg stone circle near Keswick in Cumbria. Taken using a 121F filter on a Leica Digilux camera.

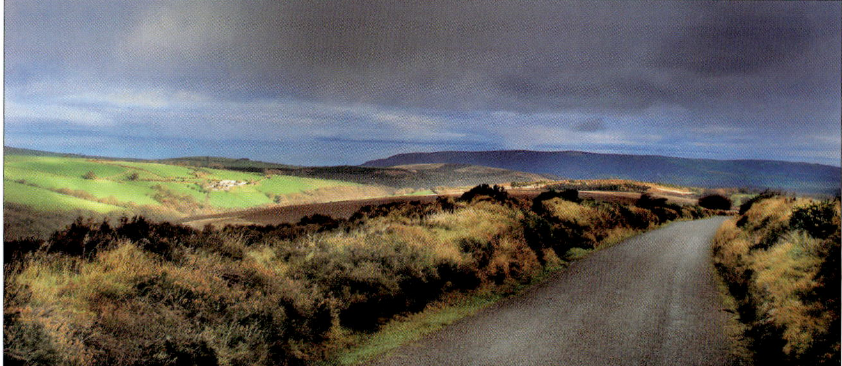

PETER MURRELL This sort of scene, taken in Exmoor, screams out to be cropped in the panoramic format, as the detail above and below the crop really won't add value to the photograph.

DIGITAL TECHNIQUE – ADDING A GRADUATED COLOUR TO THE SKY

■ Many of the photographs in this section were taken with a graduated filter positioned over the lens to either help balance the exposure of the bright sky and the darker ground, or to add colour to an otherwise dreary looking sky. A similar effect can be created digitally using Photoshop.

1 This shot of a typically dull Derbyshire day was taken at one of my favourite walking locations, Monsal Dale, between rain showers. The rainbow appeared but the light was awful. A graduated filter would have helped enhance the sky, but so will a digital gradient. Open your photograph and select the gradient tool from the toolbar.

2 Click on the gradient strip icon in the top horizontal bar that appears and select Foreground to Transparent. Then click inside this to open the gradient editor.

3 Select the bottom 'Colour Stop' left hand slider and click on it to open the colour picker. Choose a suitable colour – it doesn't have to be the final colour at this stage because we can edit later. I selected an orange to emulate a sunset filter. Click OK to close the window.

4 Create a new layer (Shift+Ctrl+N) and with the gradient tool selected click at the top of the photo, hold down the mouse button and draw a line so it goes about half way into the landscape. Let go of the mouse. You should now have an orange sky on the new layer.

5 The good thing about creating the colour gradient on a new layer is that you can experiment with blend modes, opacity and colour. I find Multiply blend mode suits this technique which is selected from the drop down list in the layers palette.

6 To change the colour select the Hue/Saturation option (Ctrl+U), making sure you still have the gradient layer selected. Drag the hue slider to the left to change the colour from orange through red, pink, purple and blue, or to the right to go through brown, yellow, green and blue.

7 While you're in the Hue/Saturation palette you have the option to tweak the colour further. Adjusting the Saturation slider changes the richness of the colour and the lightness slider controls the strength of the colour.

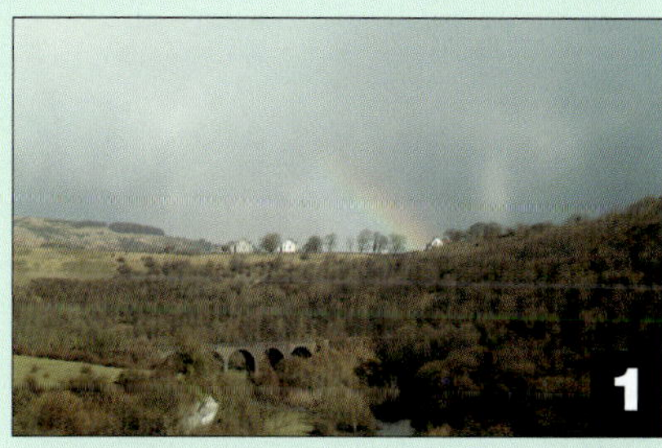

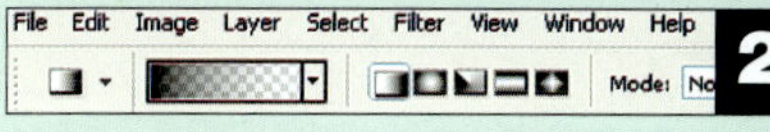

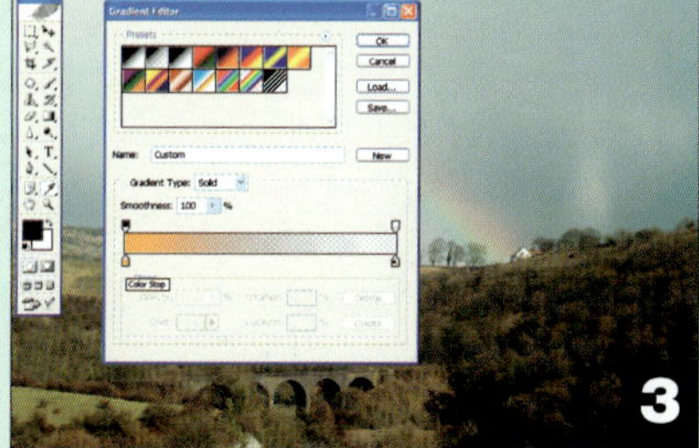

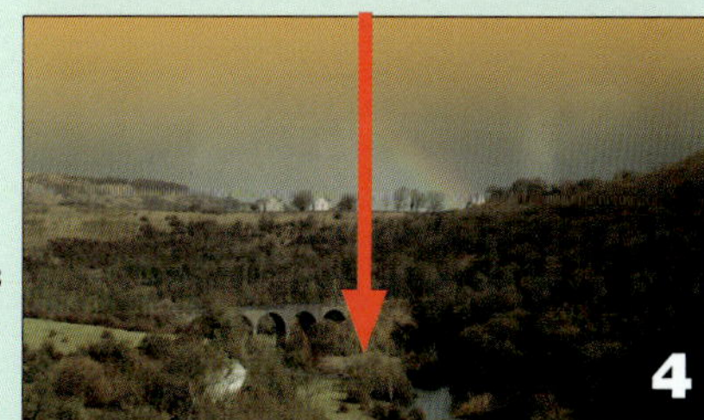

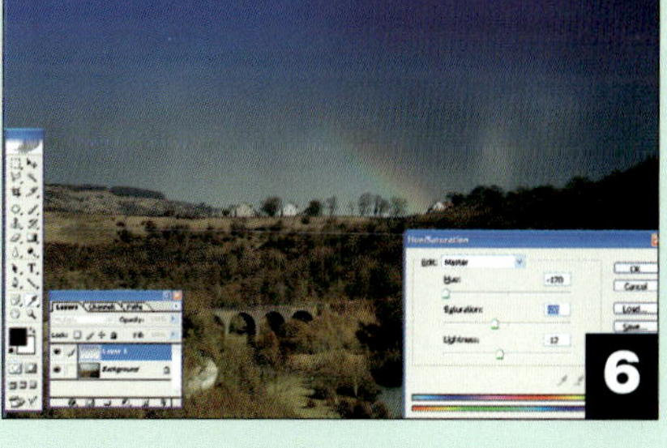

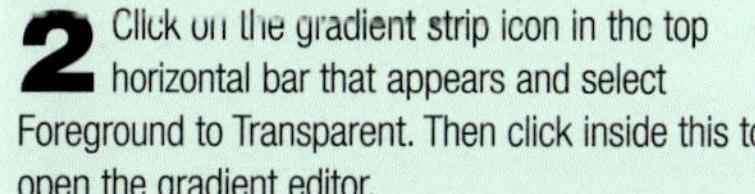

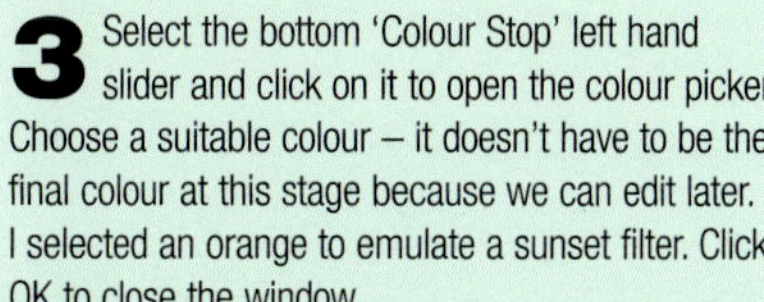

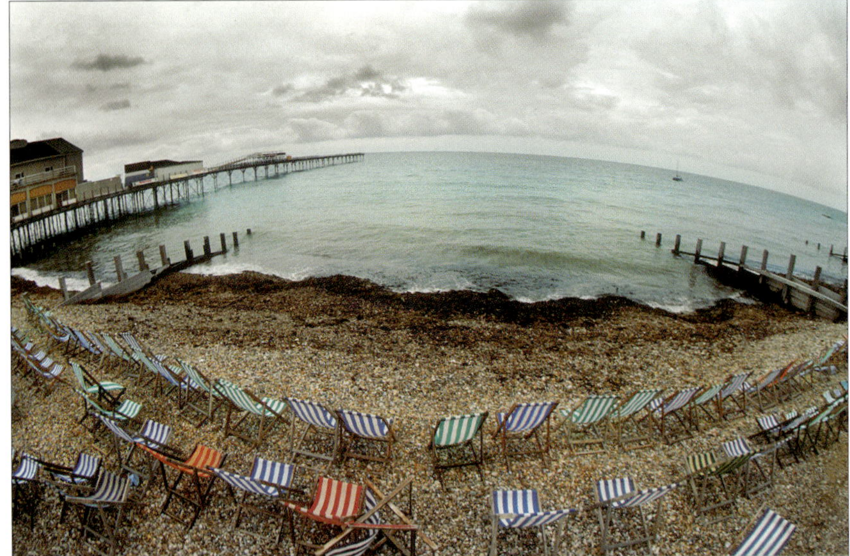

● PAUL BAILEY August in Bognor, shot using Canon 15mm full frame fish-eye lens on the Canon EOS 1N. Taken early on the day of the International Bird Man Rally, before the crowds arrived!

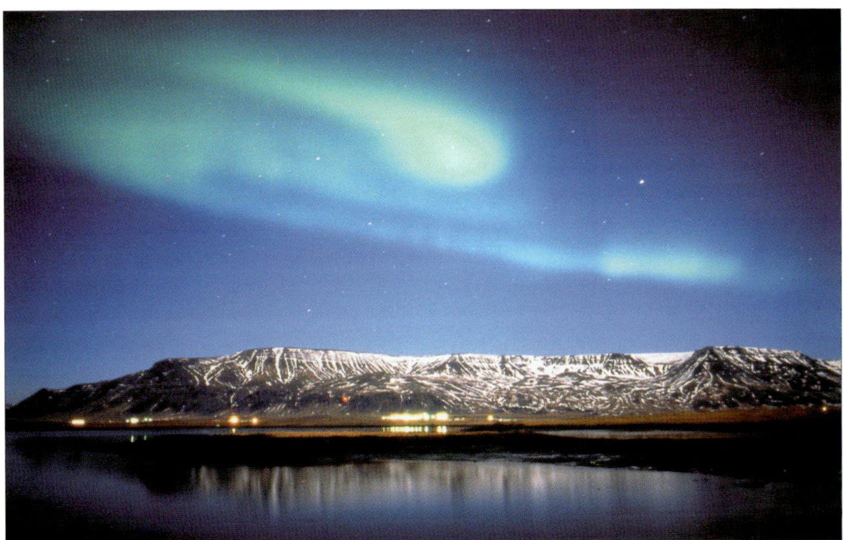

● TONY PROWER A 30 second exposure of The Northern Lights over a Reykjavik mountain in Iceland. Olympus OM1 and Fuji Provia 400F.

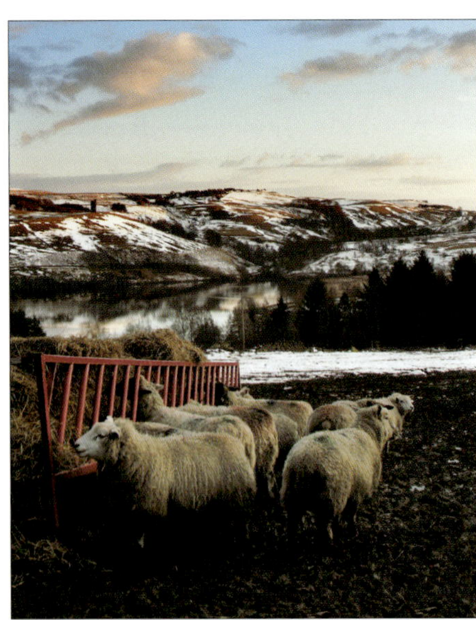

● TOM SANDERSON This scene would be dull without the sheep.

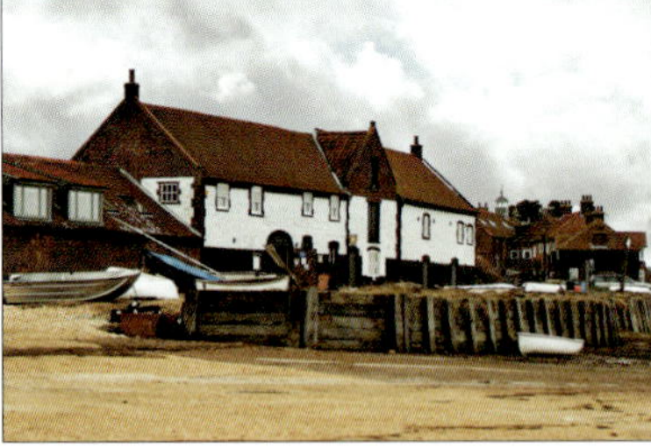

● SANDY BUNT Burnham Overy Staithe is one of my favourite places – it's as if time stood still. Taken using Canon EOS 20D.

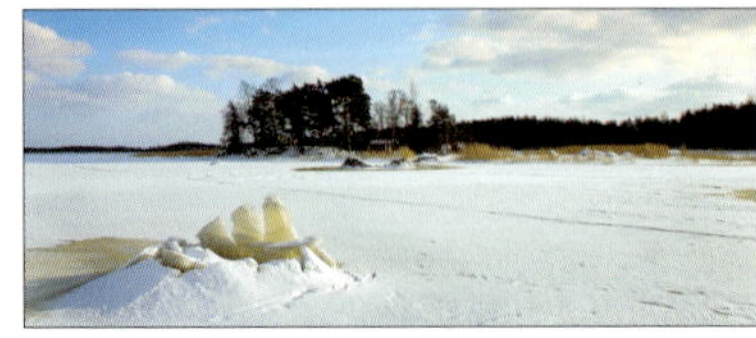

● DENNIS BAVENAMARK This one second exposure was taken in Porvoo, Finland, on the icy lake in -17C weather conditions.

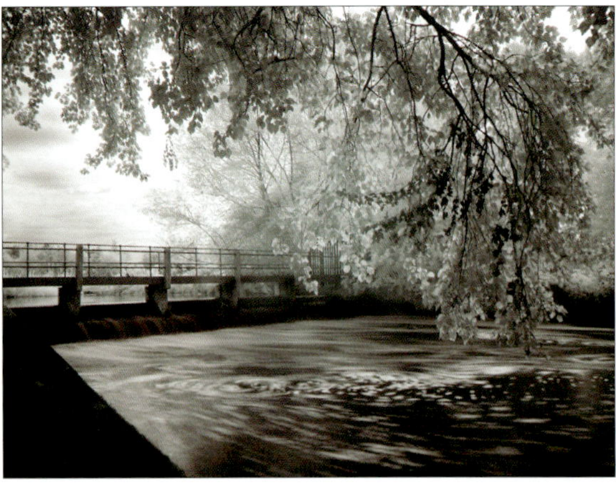

● ROY ROBERTS Weir pool on the River Colne. Taken using a Nikon Coolpix 5000 with a Hoya R72 Infrared filter and 2sec exposure.

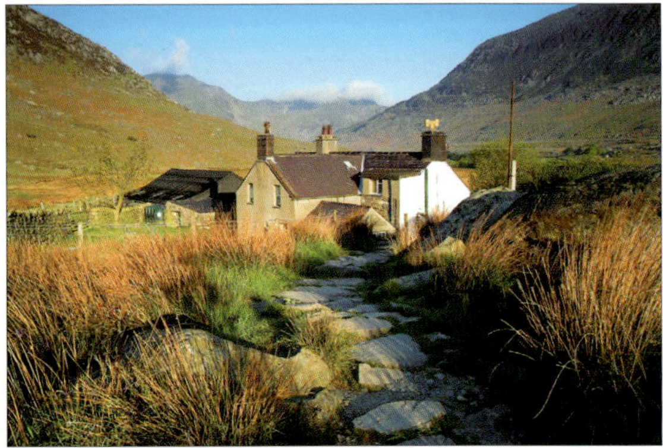

● RICHARD NICOLLS Shot in Ogwen Valley, North Wales, with the camera on a Manfrotto tripod to prevent camera shake at 1/15sec.

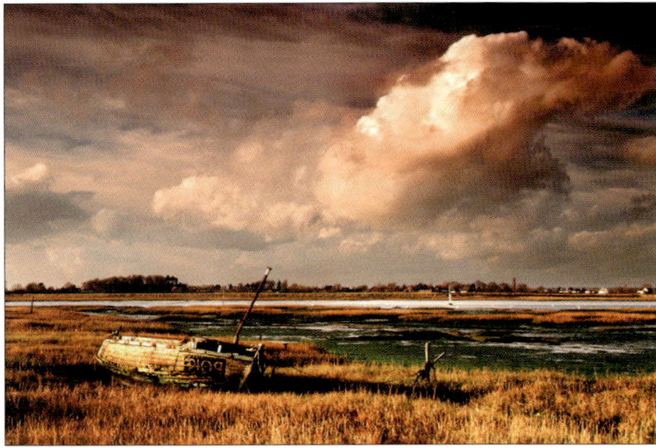

● STEPHEN WEBSDALE I was lucky enough to have good light and a great sky at Bosham estuary, West Sussex. This was enhanced using a full grad, 81C warm up and polarising filters.

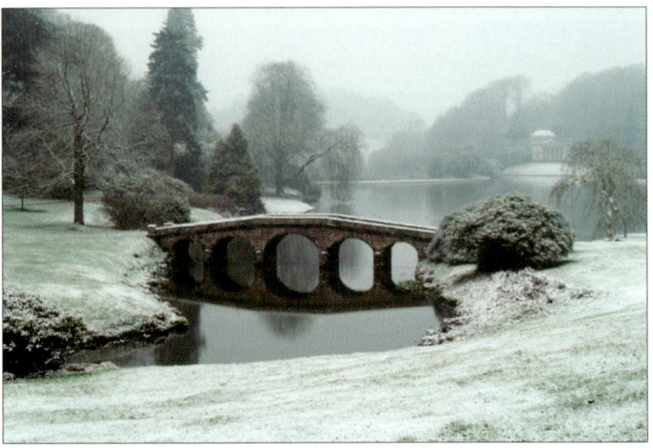

● ALAN BENSON The season can have a real influence on the scene. Stourhead has a vast variation of colour throughout the year.

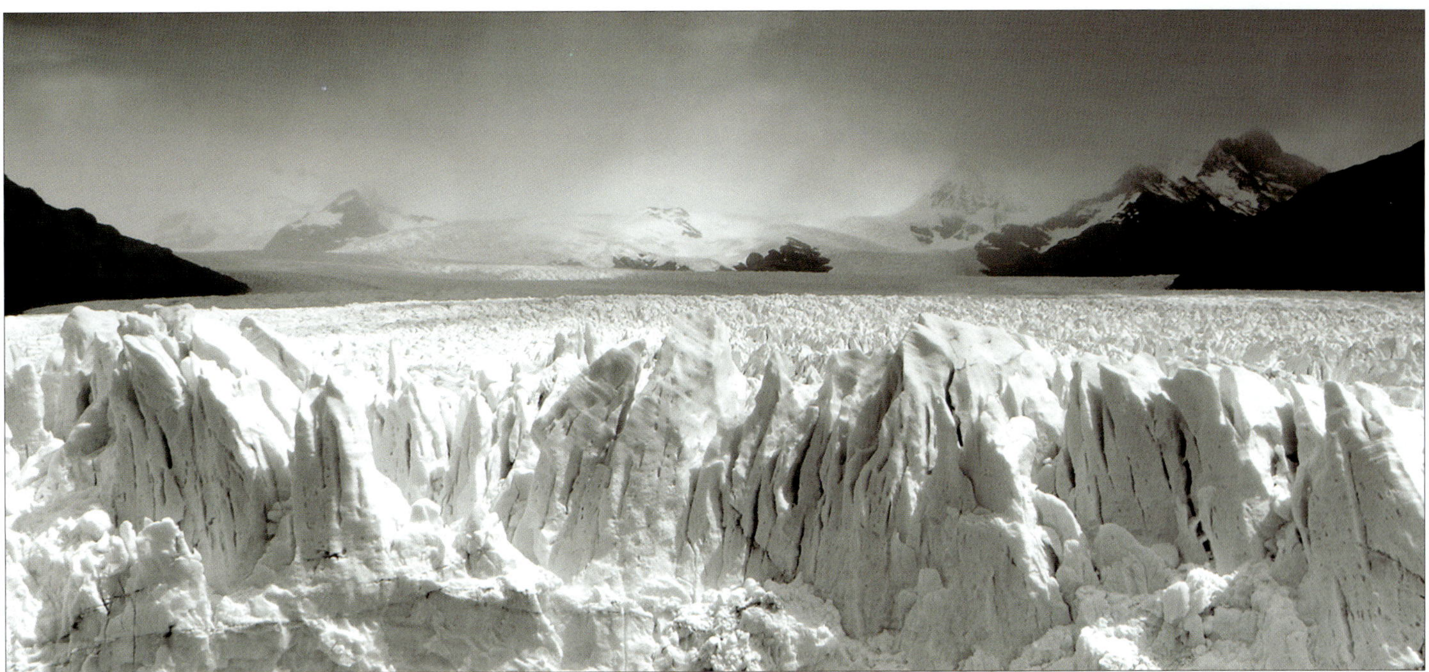

● NICHOLAS FROST Moreno Glacier, Argentina, using a Fuji S7000 with ND grad filter and cropped to panoramic format afterwards.

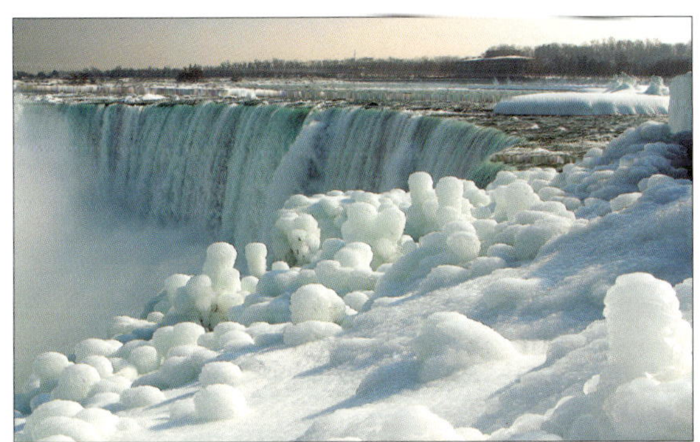

● ANDY GRANT Shot from the Canadian side of Niagara Falls during the cold spell in Jan 2005. Canon 300D with Sigma 28-300mm lens.

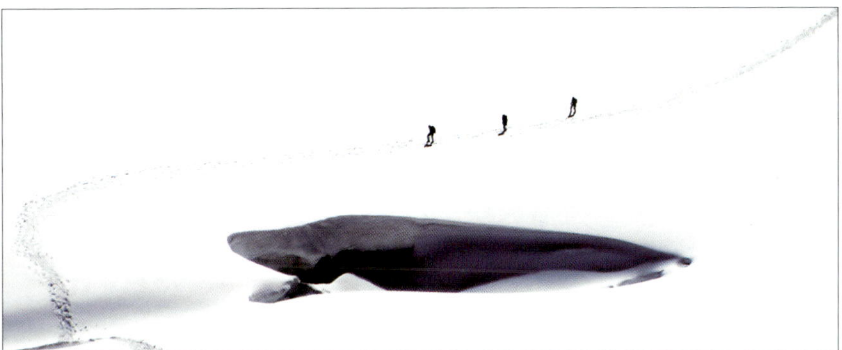

● CHRIS FROUD Three mountaineers give a sense of scale to this enormous crevasse on the Trient Glacier in the French Alps.

DIGITAL TECHNIQUE – CREATING DIGITAL SNOW

■ Many natural weather effects can be created using an image editing program and a little knowledge. Here we'll show you how to add a touch of snow to your winter scene. Choose a photo that doesn't have too much contrast – one like this taken on a misty day out at Crich Tramway Museum, Derbyshire, will be perfect.

1 To add some falling snow create a new layer Layer⇨New⇨Layer (Shift+Ctrl+N) and, using the Rectangular Marquee tool, draw a box about 1/4 the size of the main image over the image.

2 Fill the box with black – Edit⇨Fill (Shift + F5), select black from the Use drop down.

3 Then go to Filter⇨Noise⇨Add Noise and set Distribution to Gaussian and tick Monochromatic. This will give a random spread of white pixels. Drag the amount slider to around 60% to make them quite thick.

4 Go to Image⇨Adjustments⇨Threshold to control the density of snow. Dragging the slider to the left increases the snow particles

and to the right reduces them. I dragged a touch to the right to create a thinner snow fall.

5 Next give a sense of movement using Filter⇨Blur⇨Motion Blur. Set the angle in the direction you want the snow to fall and adjust the Distance slider so it creates the motion blur. Don't set this too high or it will no longer look like snow drops and just streaks.

6 Choose Edit⇨Transform⇨Scale and drag the corners of the box so that it fills the whole image area. You should now have a black canvas with white blurred dots of noise all over. This "digital snow" is now appearing as larger flakes and spread more over the picture so it looks less like noise.

7 Set the snow layer's blend mode to Screen so that the black disappears and the image below can be seen again.

8 If you prefer the snow to look less prominent you can adjust the opacity of the snow layer. Or try duplicating the snow layer and applying the threshold adjustment from step 4 again to give two levels of snow depth.

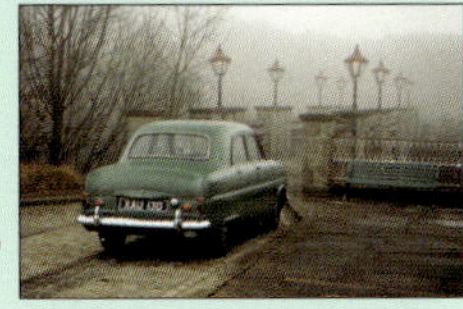

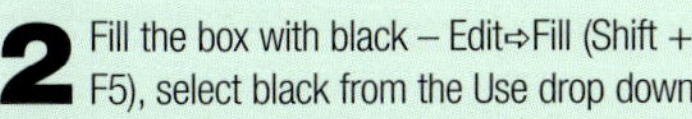

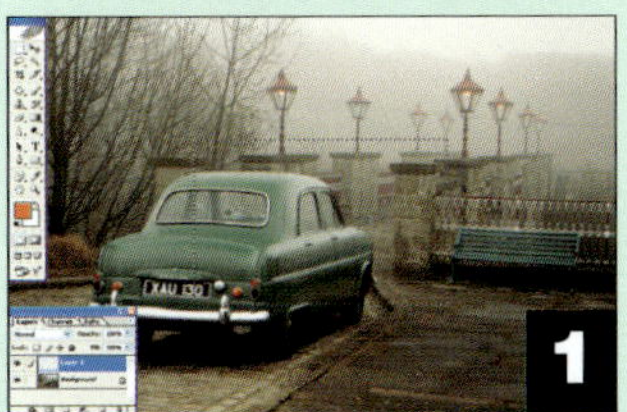

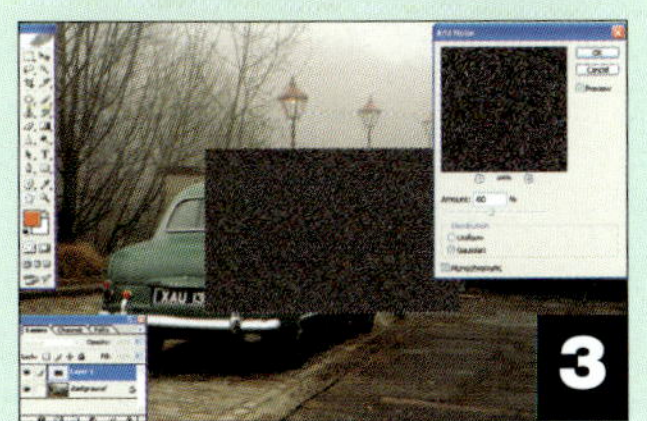

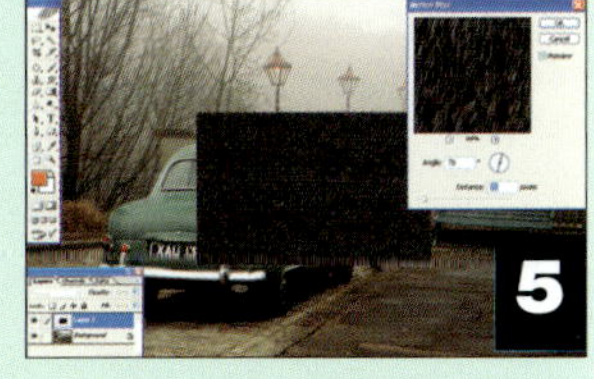

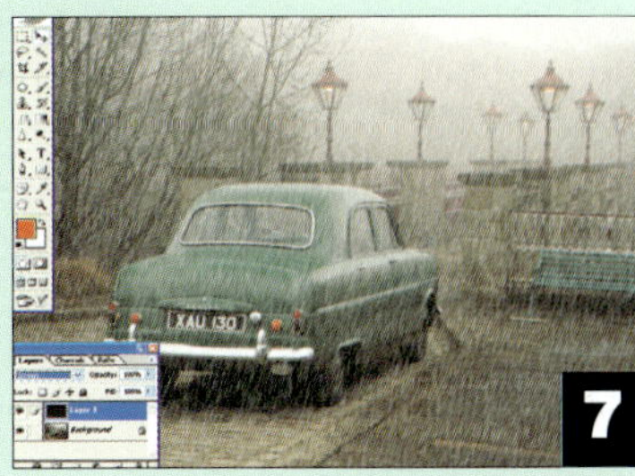

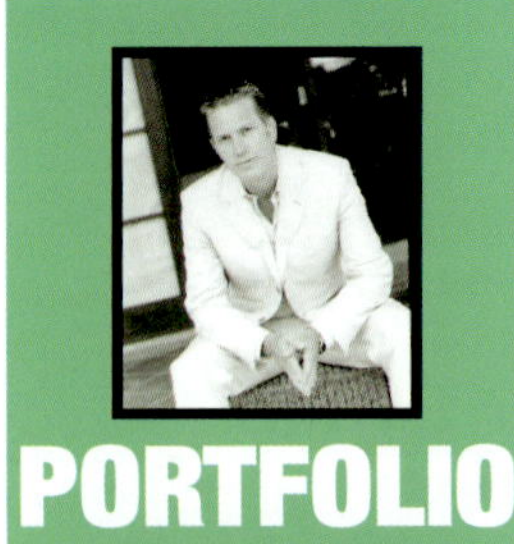

PORTFOLIO

DARRIN JAMES
Photography has been in Darrin's blood since he took his first photograph at the age of six.

After leaving school I continued to flirt with photography on a semi-professional basis, but it wasn't until I was in my thirties that I decided to leave the corporate world and dedicate myself to this incredibly rewarding art form.

The passion really kicked in after some extended travel in South America, Europe and Asia. I found that photography is an amazing medium through which to be involved in some of the most incredible cultures on our planet.

I've gained an incredible experience and richness sharing time with some truly remarkable people. Quite a lot of the photos I take are for sale through various outlets and a percentage of the proceeds goes directly to charities such as UNICEF who are involved in the education of children in developing countries.

My concentration now is on a hugely important part of all cultures – the celebration of marriage. To date I've been incredibly lucky to have covered hundreds of weddings, involving over 20 distinct cultures across many different countries in The Americas, Europe, Asia Pacific and The Middle East.

With all types of cultural based photography, whether living with villagers in remote parts of Northern Laos or being trusted to cover a society wedding in London, I have always found the key to getting the best results is to know and respect those who you are privileged to be sharing those moments with.

Immerse yourself in the celebration of life rather than stand on the edge looking at it through a camera lens – this will bring more reward than just great photos. ■
www.djphotography.net
+44 7800 626 789.

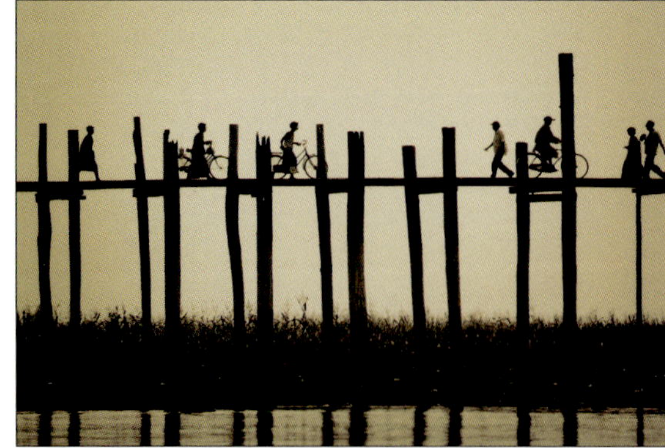

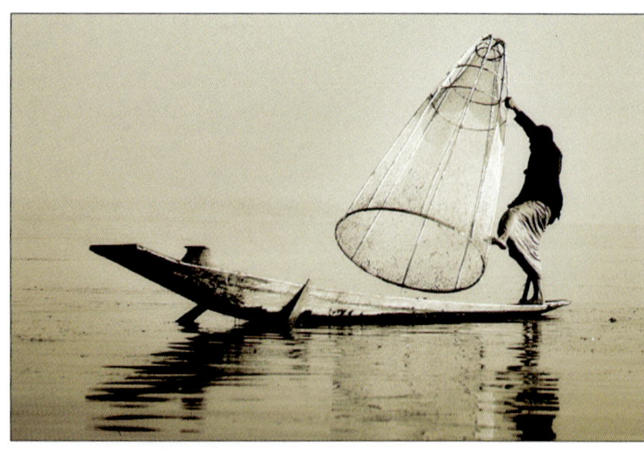

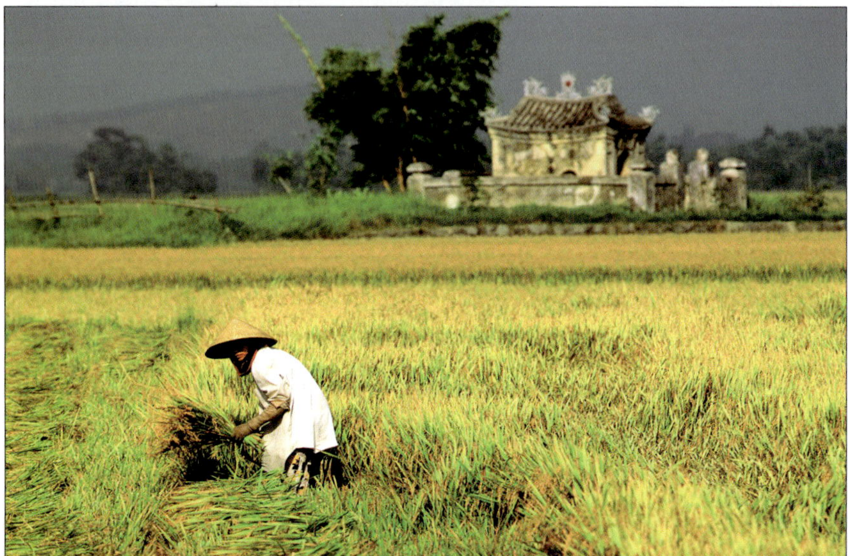

● Above left: Rush hour on U Bien Bridge, Mandalay, Myanmar, taken with Canon EOS-1V and then sepia toned

● Above right: The time tested method of fishing on Lake Inle, Myanmar. It was captured on Fuji Velvia with the Canon EOS-1V and 28-70mm f/2.8 lens. The image was then scanned and toned in Photoshop.

● Left: This shot of a rice farmer, near Hue, Vietnam, was taken at dawn on Fuji Velvia in a Canon EOS-1V fitted with the Canon EF 100-400 lens. The composition ensures he balances with the distant building.

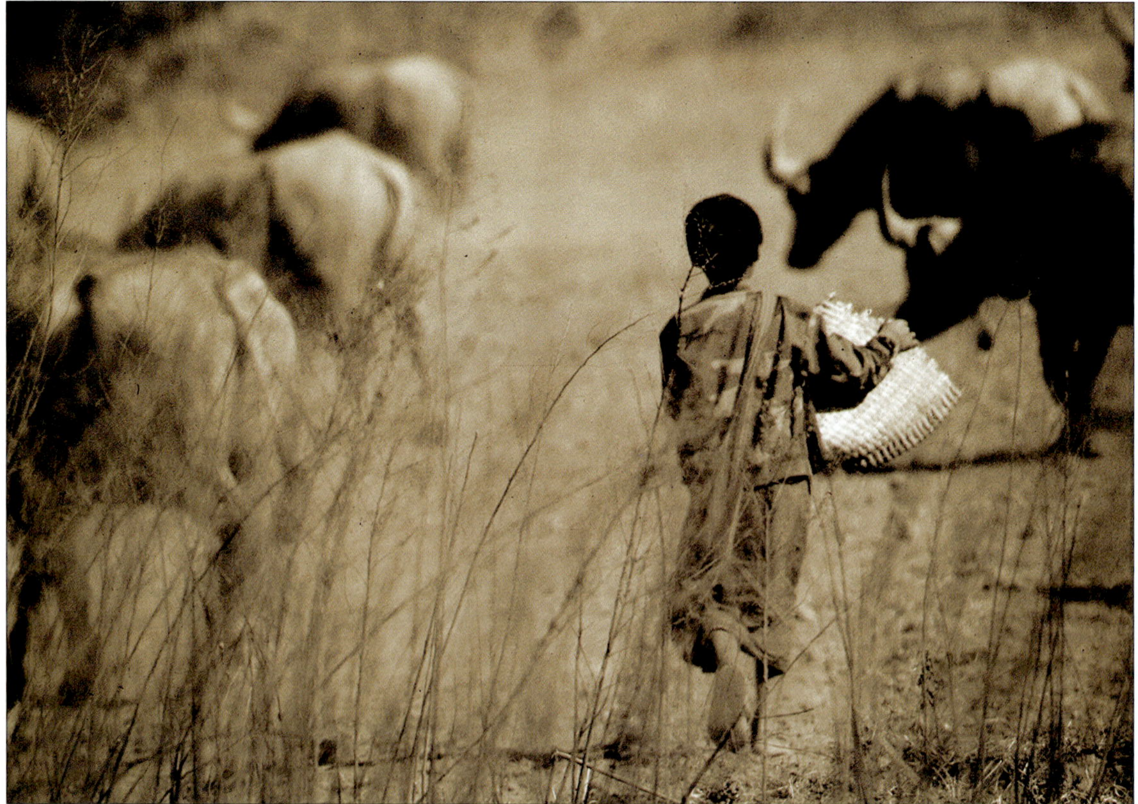

● A young boy tends to the family herd of buffalos as they make their way across the dusty plain in central Myanmar. Darrin used the Canon EOS1-VHS SLR loaded with Fuji Provia and a Canon 100-400mm IS lens was attached. Using a longer focal length lens allows you to compress perspective, which has worked really well here.

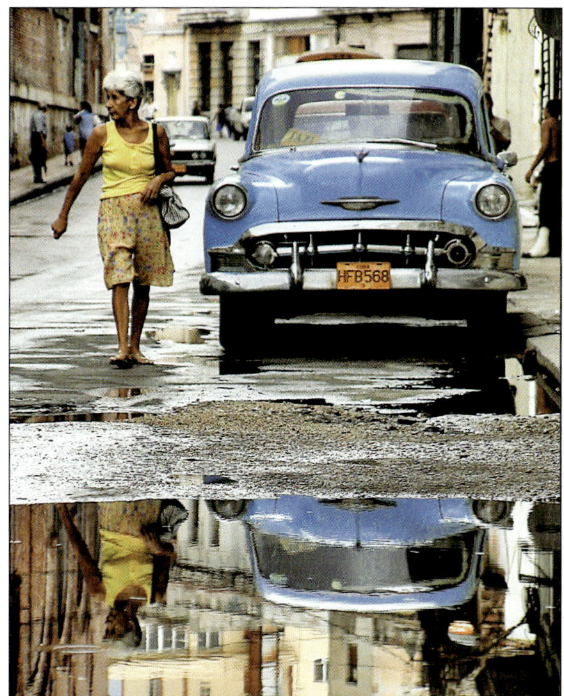

● TIM PERCIVAL Taken shortly after a tropical rain storm in the heart of Havana, Cuba.

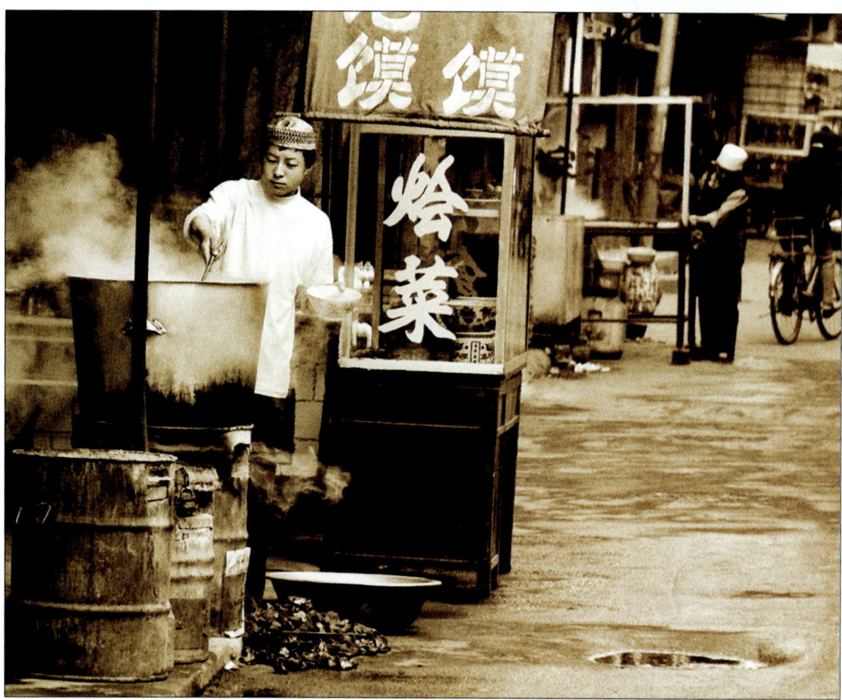

● MARK KEELAN This was taken in the Muslim Quarter, Xian, China, on Ilford 400 black & white film and converted to sepia in Photoshop.

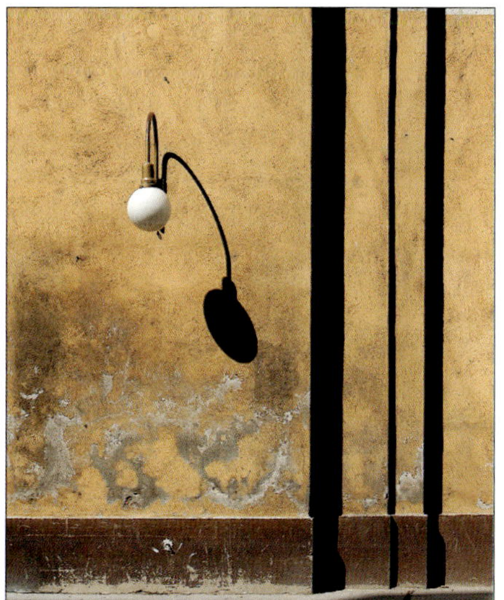

● JIM MACBRAYNE Street lamp on derelict cinema in Vienna. Harsh sunlight creates strong shadows.

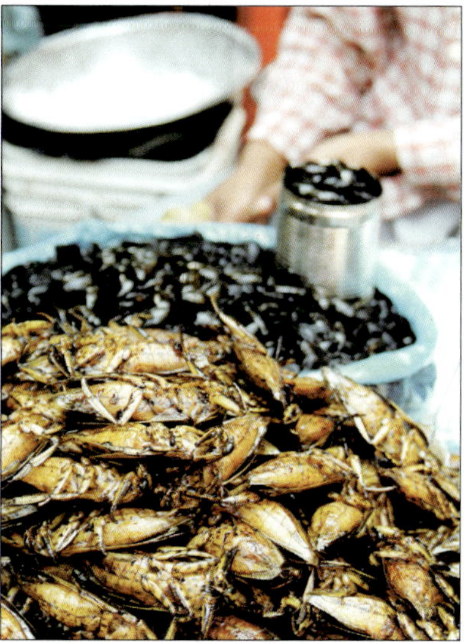

● NIAMH BALDOCK Anyone for fried cockroach or beetles?

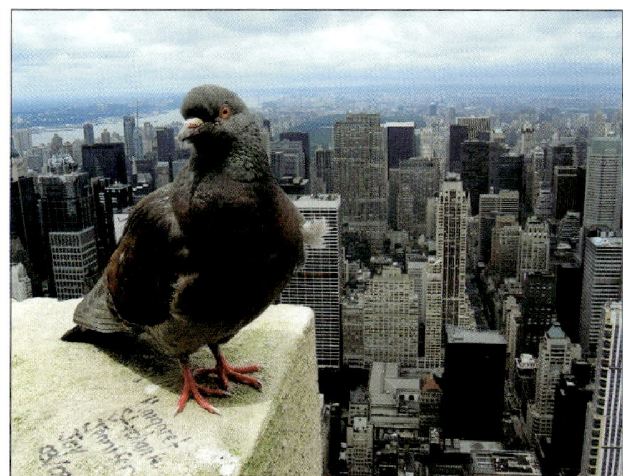

● MIZ POLATAJKO Empire State pigeon taken with a Canon Ixus 400. This combination of two photos gives a representation of what I saw.

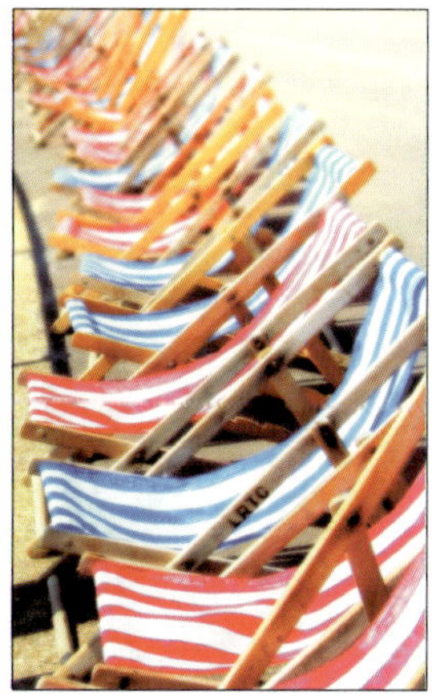

● PAUL TURNER Bright colours of unoccupied deck chairs.

TRAVEL TIPS

■ Consider what equipment you need to take with you on a trip. You don't want to take bits you won't use, but equally it's no use getting to your destination and wishing you'd brought the lens you left behind.

■ Do some research before you set off. The internet has some excellent sites that will help you know what clothing to take, what the power plug size is, how safe the area is and also which are the most scenic places in your chosen area.

■ If you intend going off the beaten track, be warned that maps in many countries aren't always as good as those in the UK. It may be worth investing in a compass as it's easy to become disorientated.

■ If you're a film user make sure you have plenty of film, take it in your hand luggage to avoid harmful baggage X-rays and don't go trigger happy as soon as you reach your destination. Spend some time looking around and familiarising yourself with the area before you start to take photographs.

■ If you're visiting a city for a few days it's worth taking a tour bus on day one to have a fast track tour of the city and then on the following days you can revisit the places you found interesting at your leisure.

■ When photographing people of other cultures respect their privacy and ask for permission if you want to take their photograph. Be aware that it's taboo to photograph people in some countries – ask your guide or hotel reception if you're unsure.

■ Avoid taking photographs of military areas, and of anyone in uniform – In some countries you will be arrested.

■ Visit the local markets or craft fairs. The stalls will be heaving with colour and activity. Fish and fruit markets are especially interesting places to take a camera.

■ When in unfamiliar territory keep your camera equipment secure. Thieves can easily slip a camera bag from your feet without you noticing. Keep everything in sight at all times.

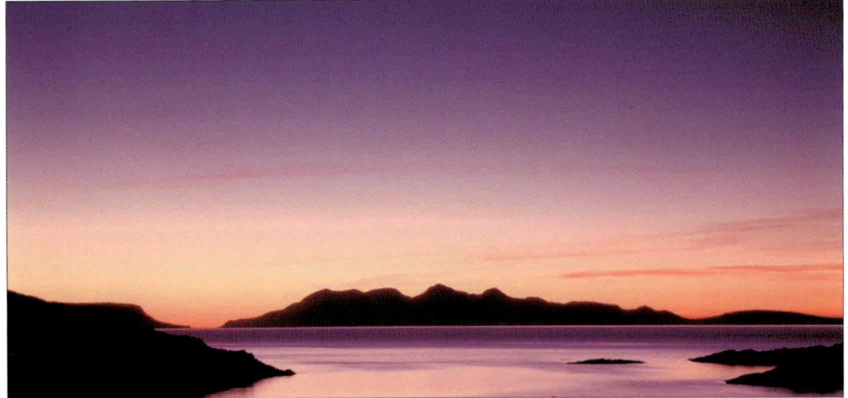

● ARTHUR CAMPBELL The Isle of Rum, west coast of Scotland, shot from Morar. A Cokin graduated filter was held over the Fujifilm 4900's lens to further enhance this wonderful sunset.

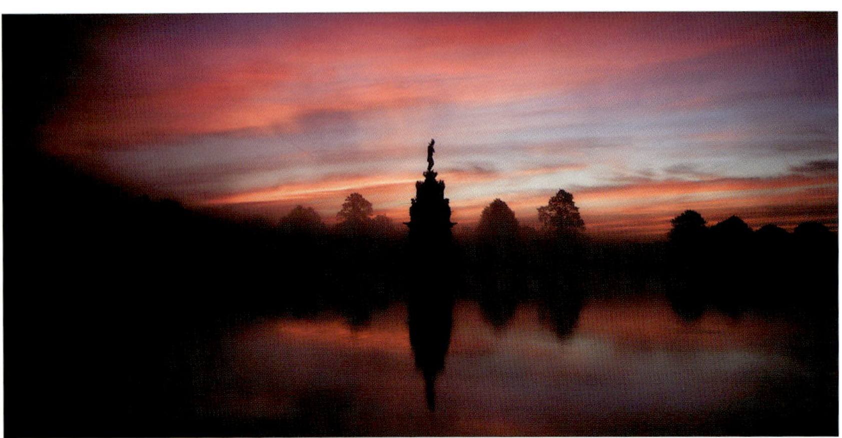

● NIK HOLGATE The Arethusa "Diana" statue in Bushy Park, 6.30am late September, taken using a Canon EOS 300D. The exposure was 2.5 secs at f/22 exposure with a 22mm lens and Cokin 121S grad.

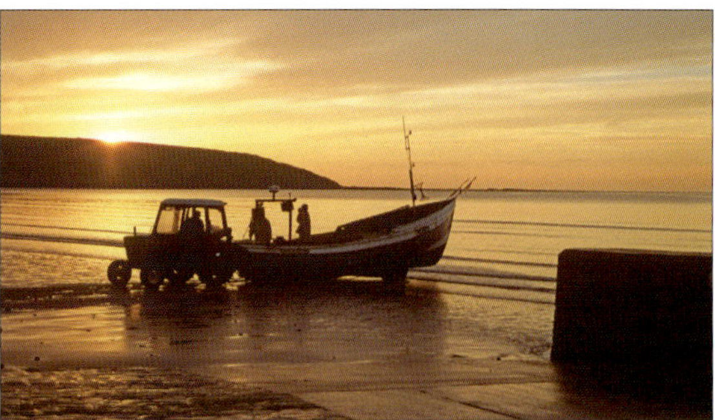

● KENNETH PECK A morning departure for the Filey Coble, going fishing, taken using a Nikon F50 and 28-80mm on Fuji Provia 400.

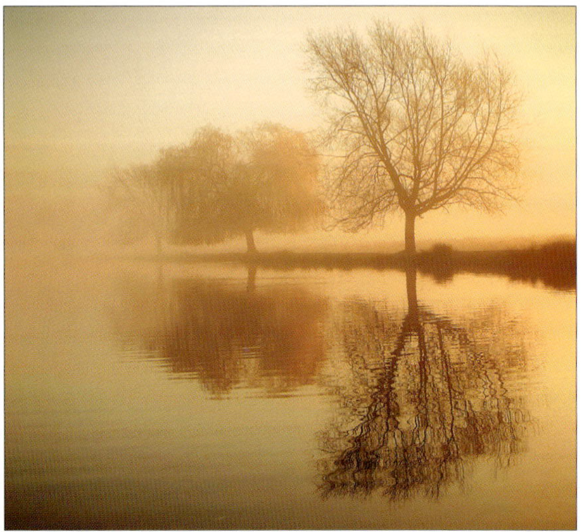

● GARETH BODRELL A local lake at dawn on a misty winter's morning. The calmness of the lake is perfect for mirror reflections.

SHOOTING SUNSETS

Things you can do to give your sunsets WOW factor.

■ To avoid underexposure make sure the sun is to one side of the frame when you take a meter reading and lock the exposure before placing the sun back in the centre.

■ Use a grey graduated filter to tone down the brighter sun if you don't want foreground detail to be silhouetted.

■ Use a longer lens to give the sun more impact, but don't look through the viewfinder when taking the shot as it could damage your eyes.

■ Switch the focusing system to manual or landscape mode to ensure the camera's autofocus isn't fooled.

■ Don't use a digital camera's auto white balance mode as the sun's intense colour can fool the system.

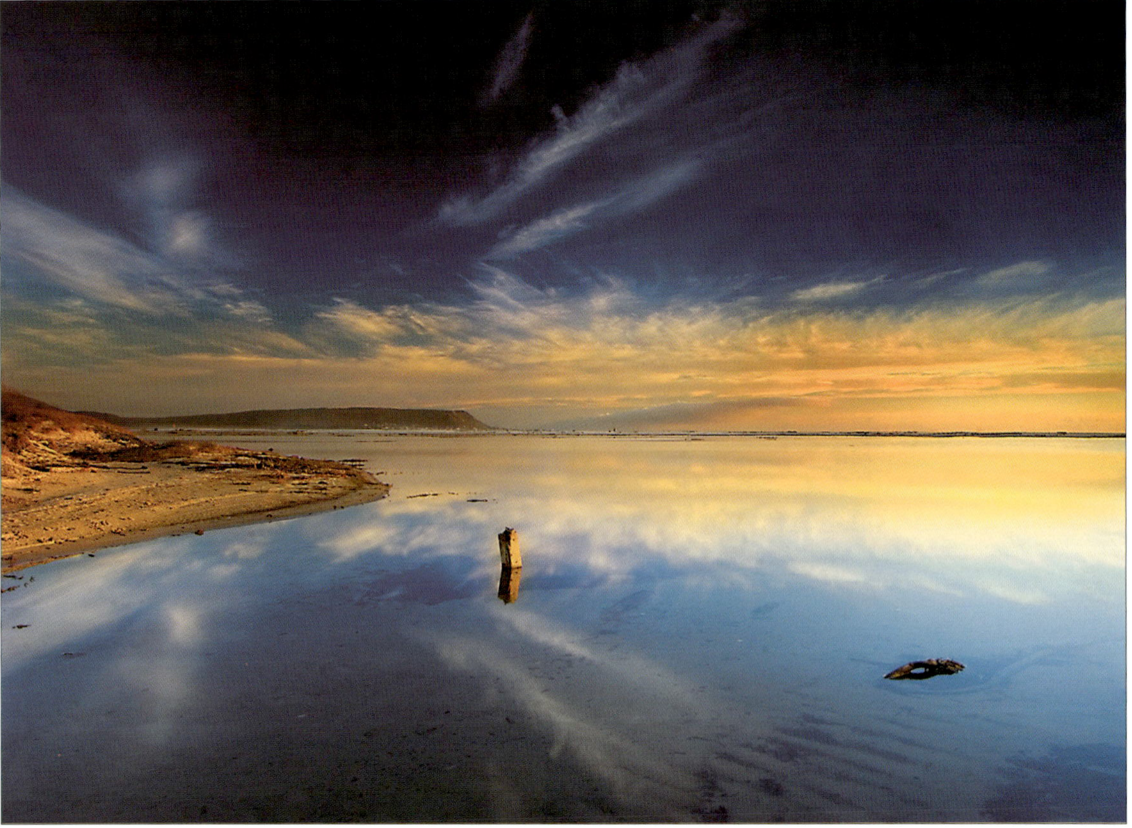

● STEPHAN SMITH The setting sun brings the last of its warmth on a blustery cold evening in Noordhoek, Cape Town, South Africa. The shot was taken on a Canon 20D and 10-22mm lens.

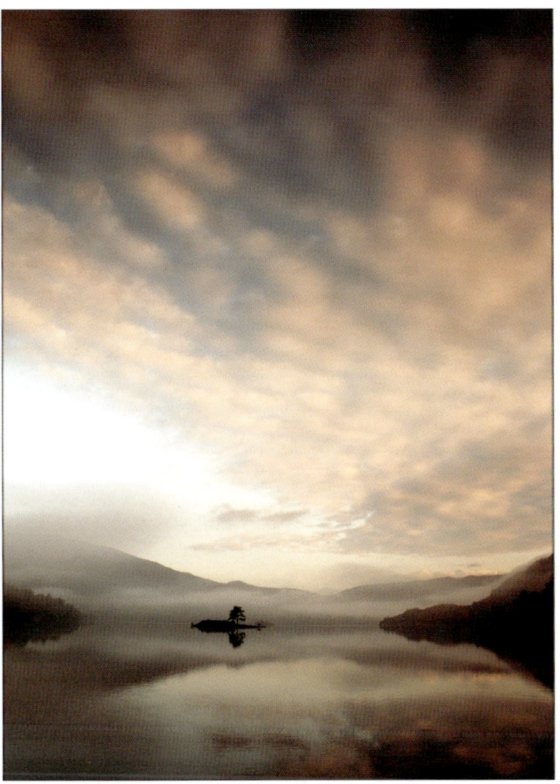

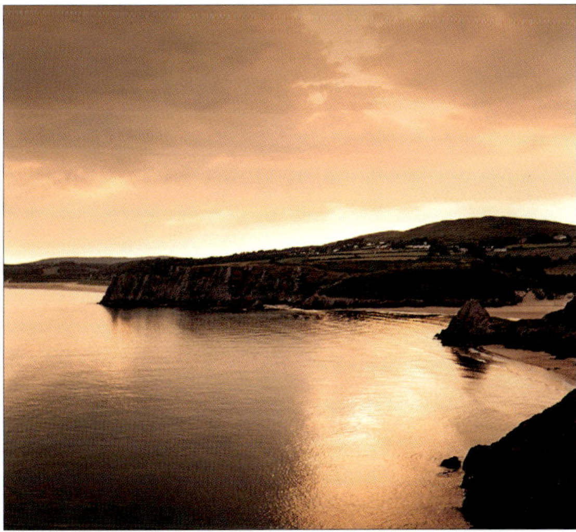

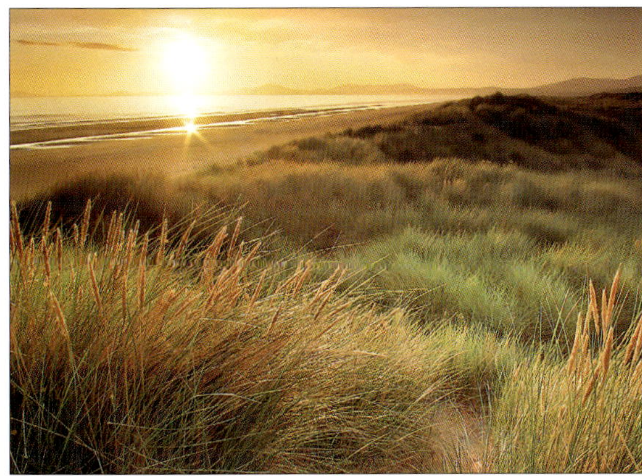

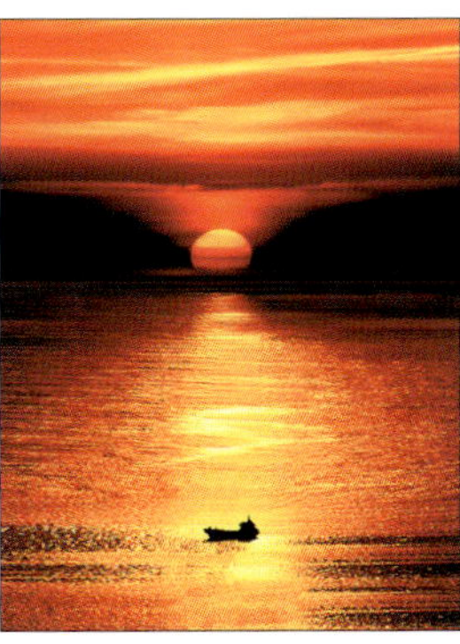

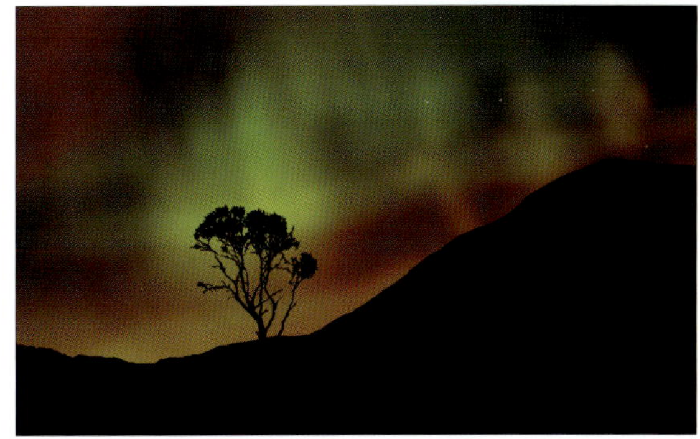

● HERMIN ABRAMOVITCH The boat looks tiny as the sun sets.

● DAVID BRENNAN The Aurora Borealis, shot north of Haggerston Castle using a 40sec exposure at f/6.3 with white balance on cloudy.

● DAVE HUDSPETH Dawn mist at Glenridding, Lake District.

● AFRON JOHN Three Cliffs Bay, Gower, late evening light, taken on a vintage Zeiss Nettar. The result was toned In Photoshop.

● ANDREW KIME A summer evening at Harlech Dunes, using a Canon G3 with Cokin 3 and 1 stop ND grads, plus an 81B warm-up.

DIGITAL TECHNIQUE – SUBTLE COLOUR ADJUSTMENTS

■ As well as graduated filters, covered on the previous page, landscape photographers are often armed with an 81 series warm filter or two. These pale orange filters are used to subtly enhance the scene, and are really important for film photographers who don't have complete control of the colour balance of a scene due to characteristics of the film they use and the conditions they shoot in. Some photographers choose certain films for specific subjects, and the range of light balancing filters, which also includes the 82 blue series, helps them fine tune the results.

Digital photographers have a white balance setting to help with extreme lighting changes, but subtle changes are often not recorded and it's here where image editing can be used to fine tune results.

1 Many image editing programs have a fairly simple automated colour correction option. In Photoshop it's called Variations. Here you have the current image surrounded by versions showing how it would look if you clicked on that photo and applied the indicated colour. Each click of an outer colour changes the centre original and before and after photos appear above. In this shot I've added a small amount of blue and cyan to remove an overtly warm hue on the building caused by the setting sun.

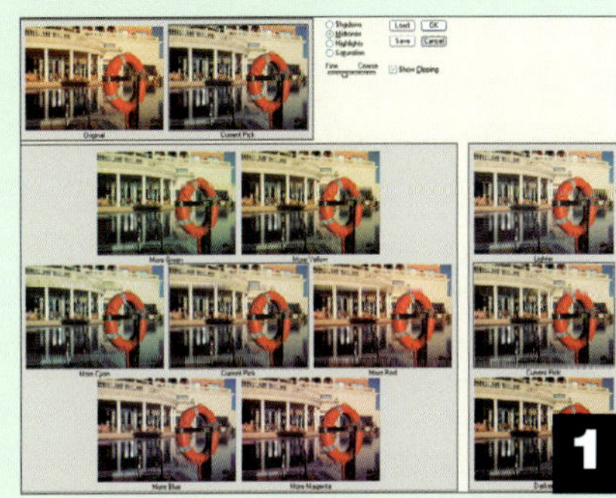

2 Photoshop has made it easy for those who want to simply apply the 81 warm filter or 82 cool, along with many other correction filters. Since CS users can go to Image⇔Adjustments⇔Photo Filter and select the correction filter of their choice and then adjust the strength of correction, I've split the photo so you can see the before (right) and after (left) effects.

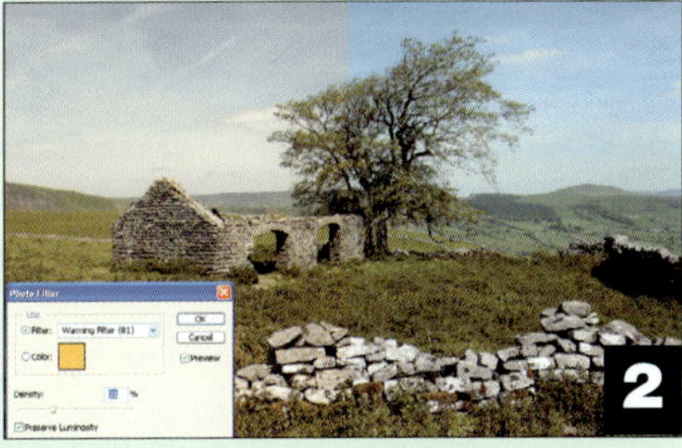

3 Those who like to go a stage further can select Photoshop's colour balance option. You'll find this option in just about every good image editing program but it does need a level of skill to use, including a well calibrated monitor and a good eye for colour. You have to adjust the highlights, midtones and shadows separately. The left half of photo 3 shows what happens when you increase the amount of yellow and red slightly in all three areas.

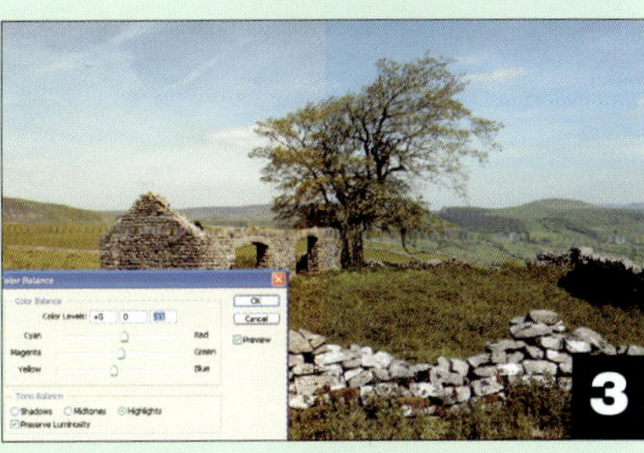

4 Advanced programs, such as Photoshop, go much further to help you adjust the colour. The most advanced being the curves option Image⇔Adjustments⇔Curves (Ctrl+M). Here you can select each channel and adjust the colour using a graph that represents all the tonal range from highlight to shadow. Dragging from a specific point will affect the colour more in that area. Here I selected the blue channel and dragged it down to increase warmth.

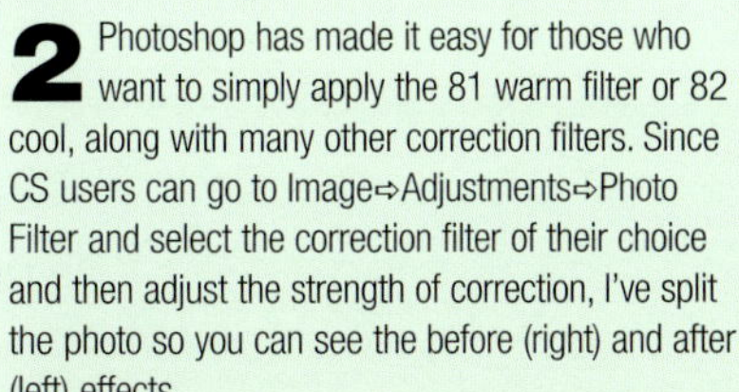

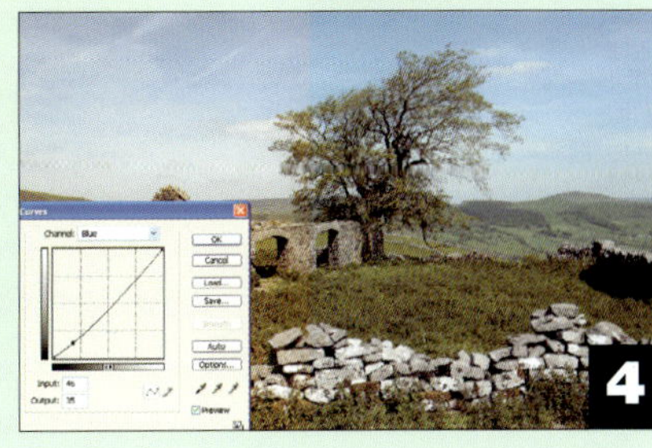

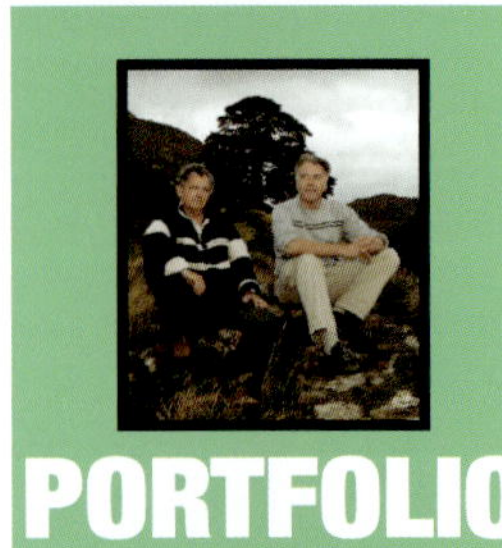

PORTFOLIO

NORTHSCAPE
Two of ePHOTOzine's best known landscape photographers join forces.

Northscape was formed in the spring of 2005, by Keith Henson and Andy Dippie. The idea was to take two photographers whose work differed yet complimented one another, and this premise was met in the merging of Andy's brooding landscapes and Keith's own often-surreal images.

The original intention was to build a website as a publicity vehicle, but that quickly expanded into photographic workshops, publishing interest, sponsorship from Manfrotto and our work being taken on by new and exciting galleries.

Andy took up photography seriously just four years ago, when the purchase of a Fuji 602 for a family holiday sparked a talent for capturing landscapes in a unique way that he was previously unaware of. Applying knowledge gained during his many years working as a BBC cameraman to still capture, Andy soon developed a style that was instantly recognisable. For Andy, photographing landscapes is an attitude of mind; to have the eye to see and the patience to wait for that one instant when the light is right to bring out the full drama of the scenery.

Andy's main influence is Joe Cornish and if he had to choose a favourite location it would be anywhere on Britain's beautiful coastline – Whitby especially has always been an unavoidable magnet to him. If I had to choose a signature of Andy's it would be boats in all their guises, the grace of the tall ships in particular.

My own work reflects my love of the abstract and the yearning to capture moments of fantasy in a real world. Influenced originally by artists such as Turner and

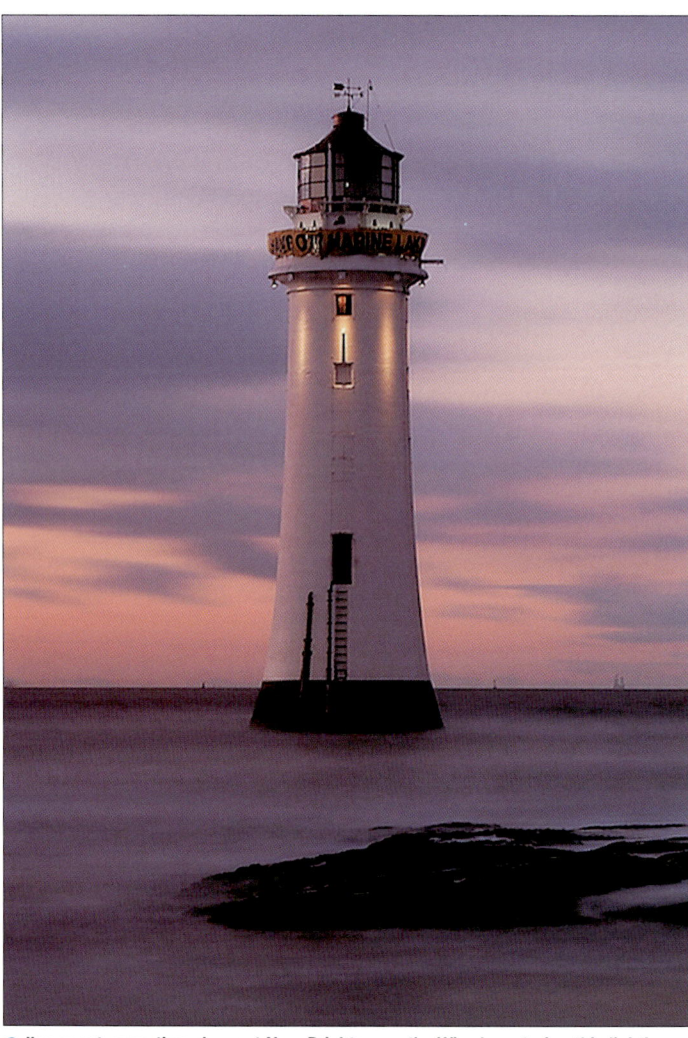

● I've spent some time down at New Brighton, on the Wirral, capturing this lighthouse in all kinds of weather. On this occasion I was looking for a postcard effect. ISO 100 18secs at f/22, with Lee 0.6 ND Grad and 81B warm-up filters attached.

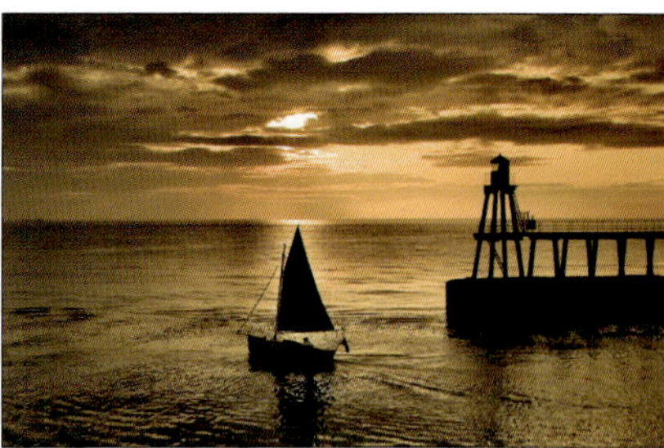

● As the boat leaves the harbour, the position of the setting sun ensures perfect backlight and a partial silhouette effect. Taken on the Fuji S2 Pro.

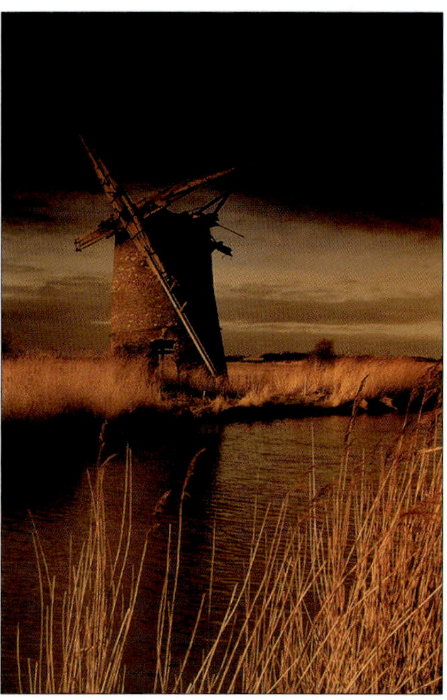

● Brograve mill, Norfolk, is one of the oldest mills in the country, built around 1771. It was taken in early January on ISO100, 1/125sec at f/18.

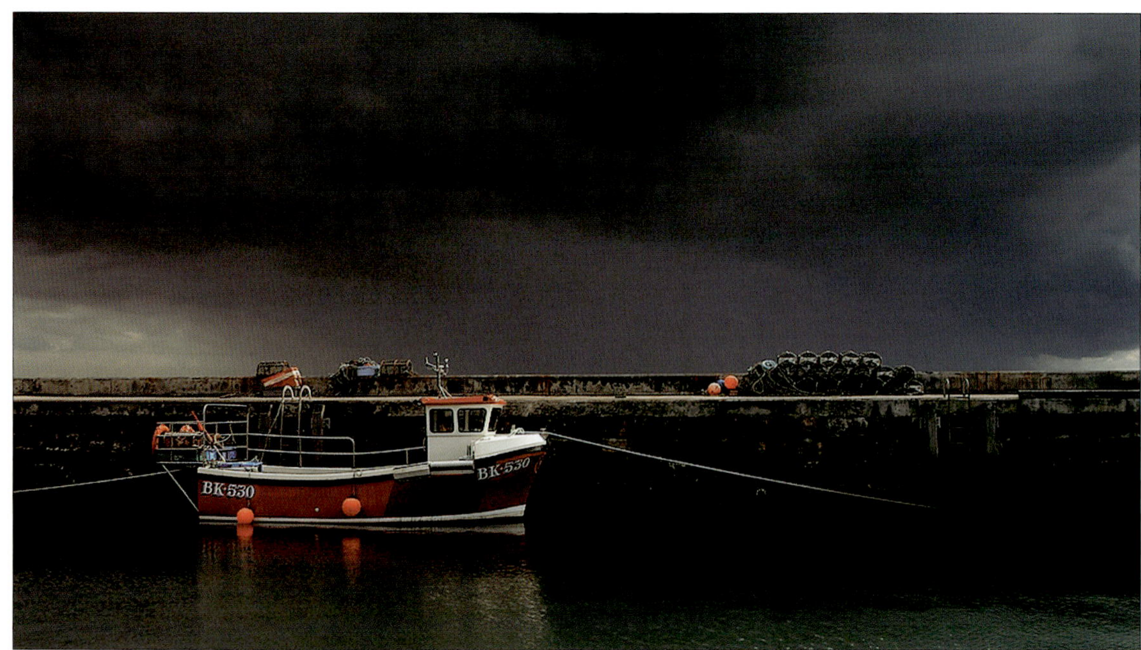

● On my first visit to Beadnell Harbour on the Northumbrian coast, I spotted this fishing boat and the lobster pots. The light wasn't right, but I awoke the following morning to find a good storm blowing. I returned to the harbour and it was just a matter of waiting for the light to punch through and catch the tops of the lobster pots and the superstructure of the boat. The exposure was 1/25sec at f/22 using a Lee 0.8 ND Grad and warm-up filter with the camera set at ISO 100.

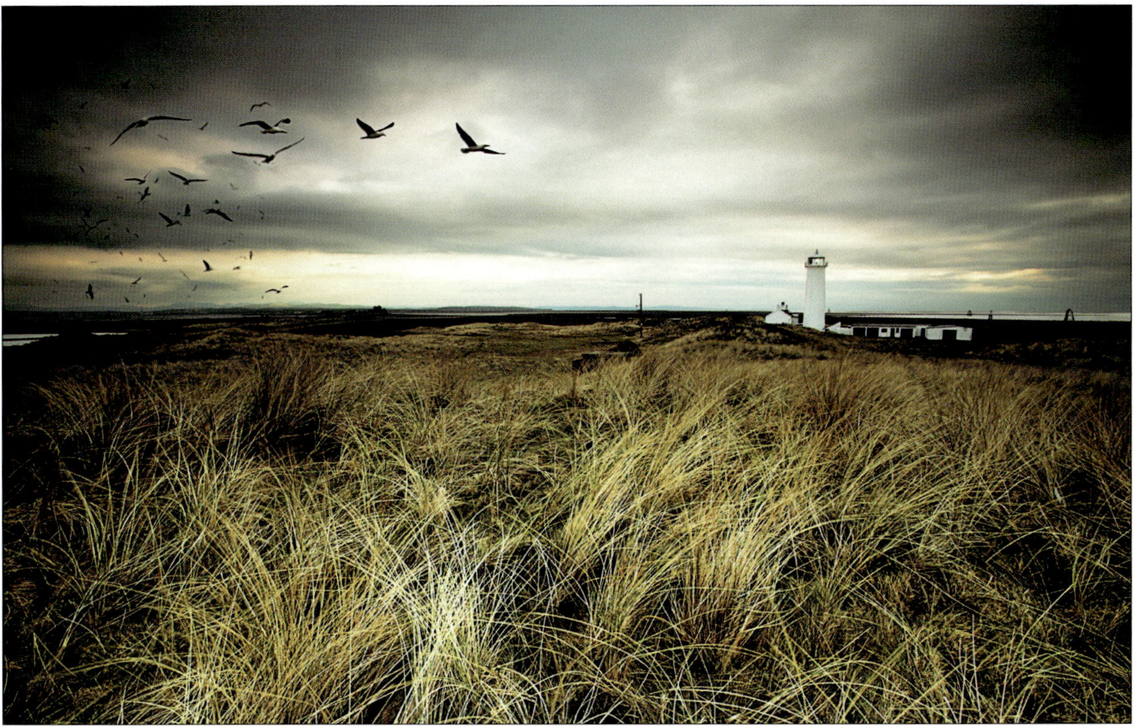

● Walney Island, Cumbrian Coast, Barrow in Furness, is reached by bridge. I wanted to capture the important elements of the island – the lighthouse, the dunes, the gulls and in the distance, Piel Castle. I used a relatively fast shutter speed, but even so several fast moving gulls had to be cloned out of the final image and the lighthouse required some careful dodging to bring it out of the final print.

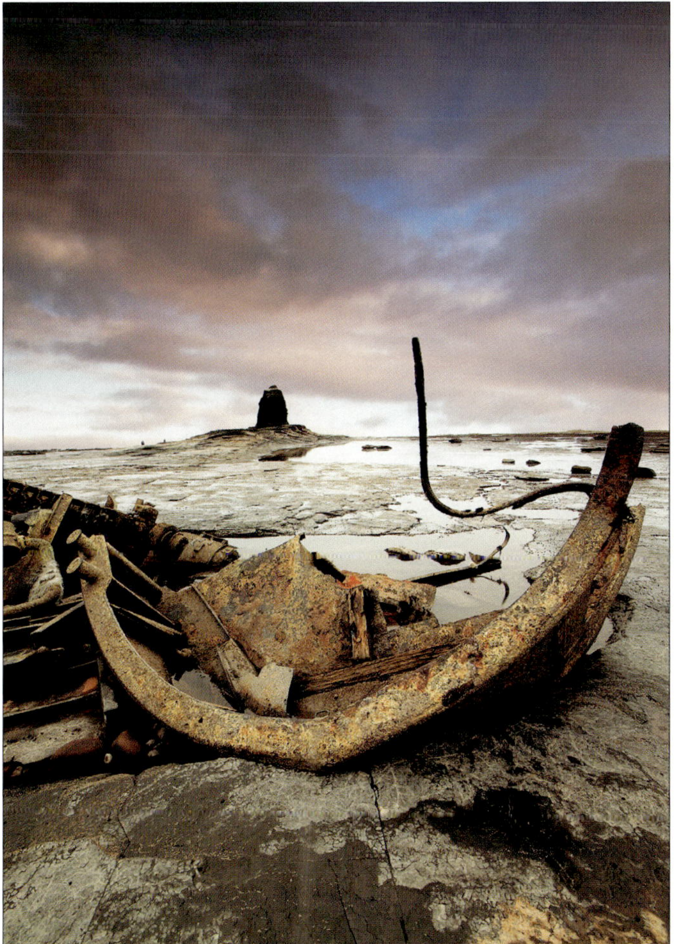

● Here I wanted to use the wreck at Saltwick Bay on the Yorkshire Coast as a very strong part of the composition, while framing Black Nab in the background.

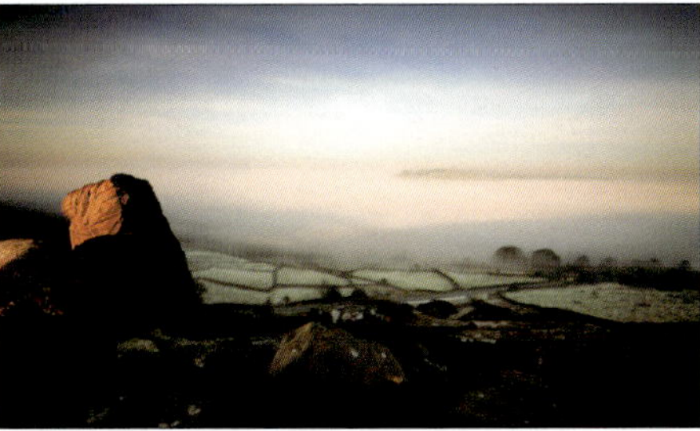

● Curbar, one of Derbyshire's gritstone edges taken as the sun rose over a frosty landscape.

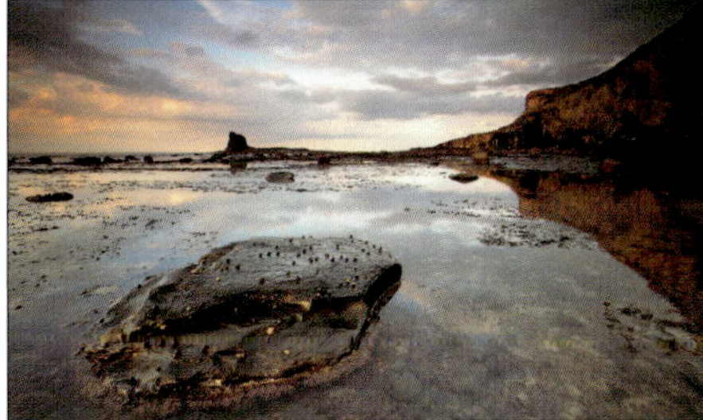

● Using the shell-covered rock as a foreground, the long exposure strengthened the reflections in the sea.

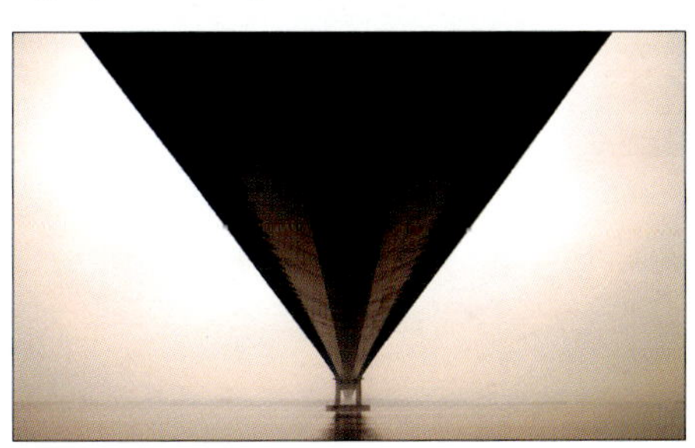

● Taken just before dawn with a strong mist, lit with the red light spill from Hull and the Humber bridge.

Ruskin, landscape photography was a chance to escape the sterile world of the studio. There is no greater pleasure than to be alone in the world with a camera as the morning sun comes up over the horizon – much of my work is done in the first hour of the day. If I had just one place to be with a camera it would be Saltwick Bay on the Yorkshire Coast. There's something ethereal about the bay, with it's shale nab jutting above the tide and, despite being close to Whitby, it has a remote and unnerving feel in the cold of a winter's dawn. Each visit throws up new images as you wander its fossil strewn rock shelves, although for anybody intending to visit, the tide rises quickly.

Though Andy and I both use digital cameras we believe that, even in this software age, the camera should still be the photographer's main tool and we work at producing images that require as little post-shooting work on the screen as possible.

We'll both spend hours in search of locations and, if necessary, return again and again until we get that moment we first envisaged when finding it. You always have an impression in your mind of where you need the light to be and the one thing to remember as a landscape photographer is that sometimes you have to walk away. Planning is so important. If you don't know a location already then arrive early - nothing ruins the shot more than having to rush your work. Think of composition, where the light will strike the land, then wait - patience will get you the image you always dreamed of. Most of all enjoy being with your camera and the beauty that's out there waiting to be captured.

As for our future plans for Northscape, if the first few months are anything to go by the years will pass very quickly indeed - hopefully, successfully. The photographic workshops will be core to the business and we have already explored the potential of opening a photographic gallery in the north of England, something sadly missing at the moment. ■

www.northscape.co.uk
Tel: 01302 371961

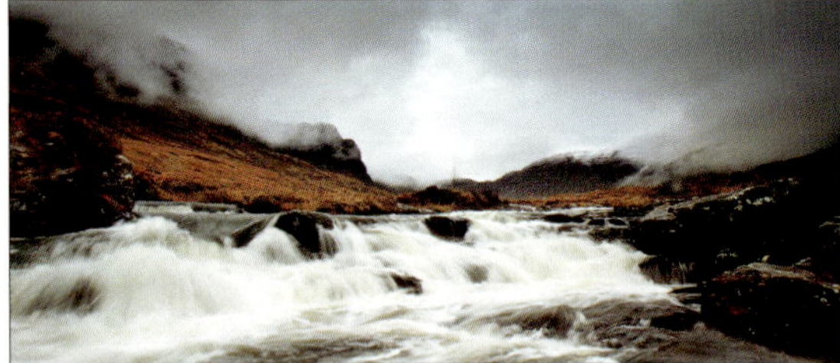

● TONY PERRYMAN Taken on a very rainy Autumn day on the Isle of Skye using a Minolta 700si with 18-35mm lens on Velvia 50.

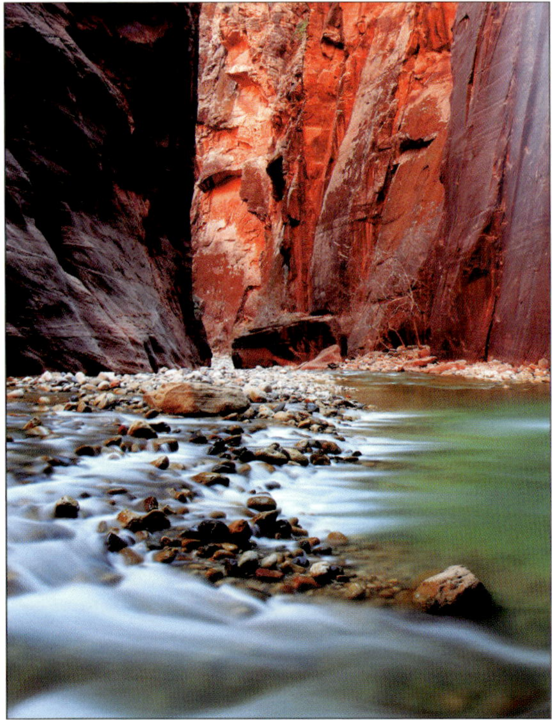

● LEE BEEL The Narrows, Virgin River, Zion National Park, Utah.

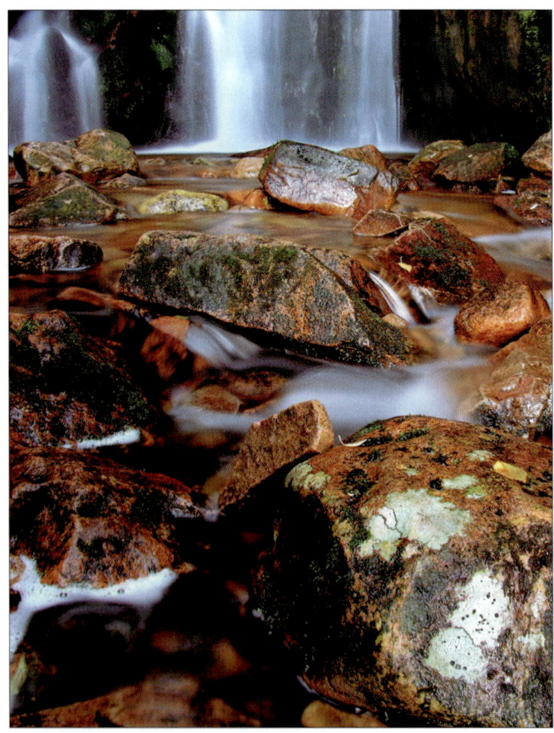

● KRISTINA SMITH A tripod mounted Nikon Coolpix 8700 was used to take this 4 sec exposure of Scale Force n the Lake District.

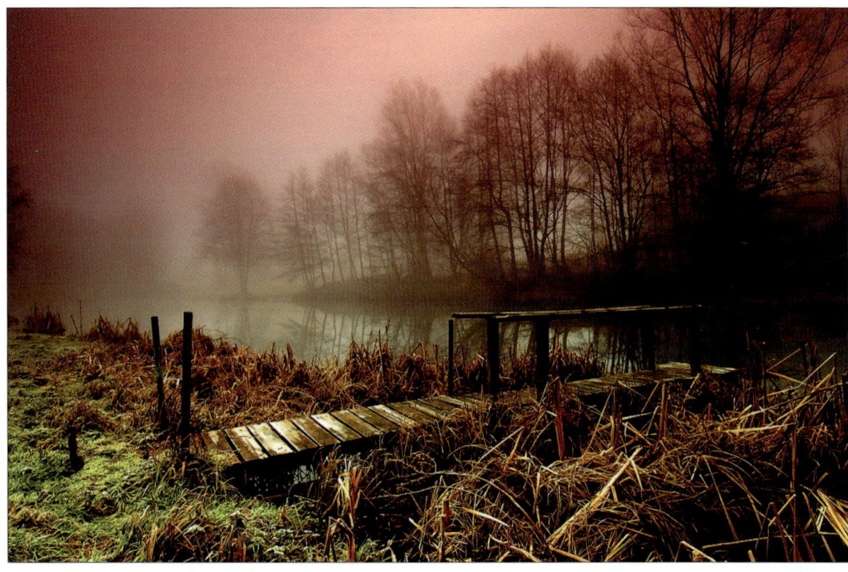

● CHRIS RUDLAND A very frosty morning in Suffolk, taken using a Nikon D70. A Cokin Polariser, 121M and 121L ND grad filters were combined to create the moody atmosphere to the otherwise plain sky.

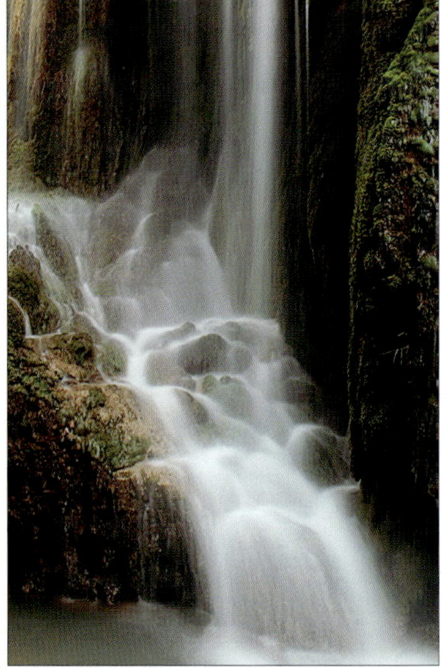

● ANTONIO ALOMAR A 3 sec exposure of a waterfall at the Monasterio de Piedra Aragón.

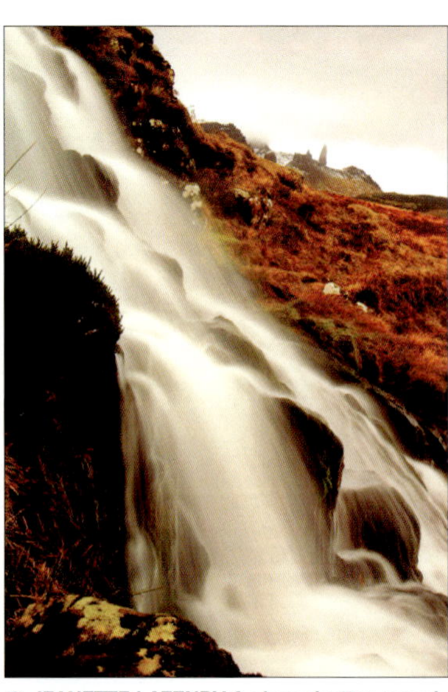

● JEANETTE LAZENBY A slow shutter speed has captured the force of the waterfall.

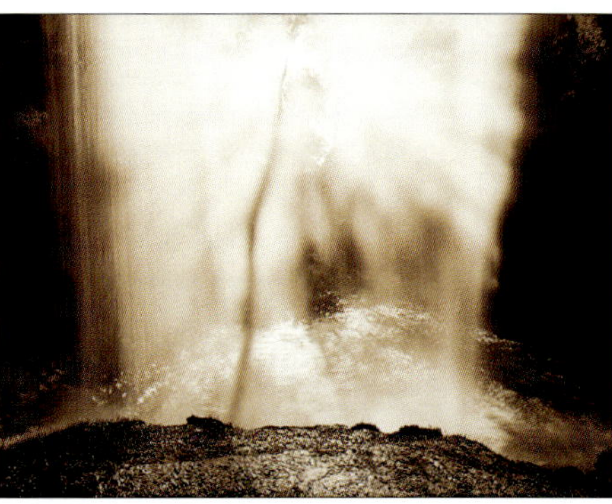

● STEVE GARRETT Taken from behind the Henrhyd Falls at Brecon Beacons, Wales.

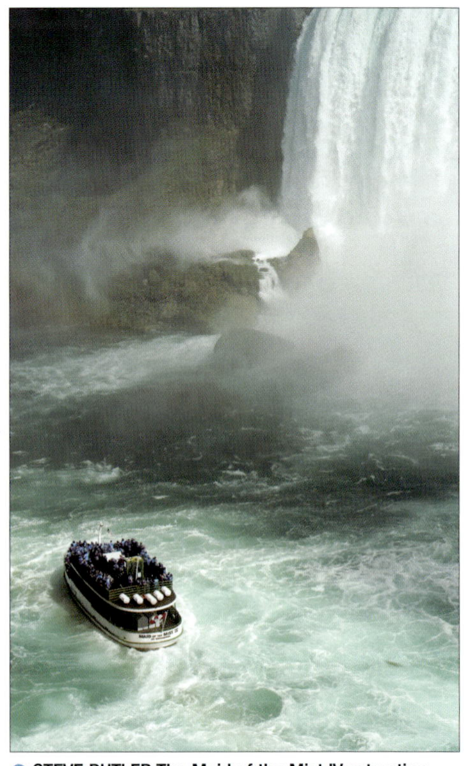

● STEVE BUTLER The Maid of the Mist IV, retreating from the Niagara Falls, Canada.

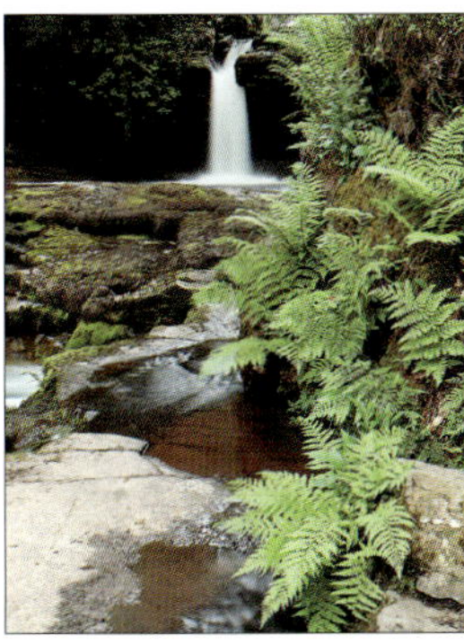

● ROBERT TAYLOR A selective view of falls near Ystradfellte.

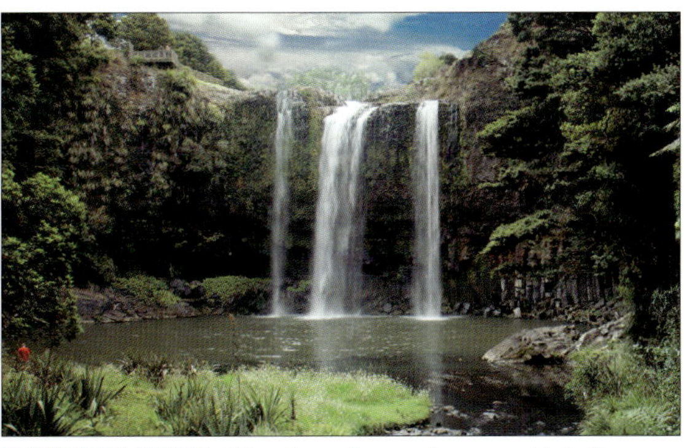

● RAYMOND KING The blue sky and green foreground help the Whangarei Falls in New Zealand look like an image from a fairytale.

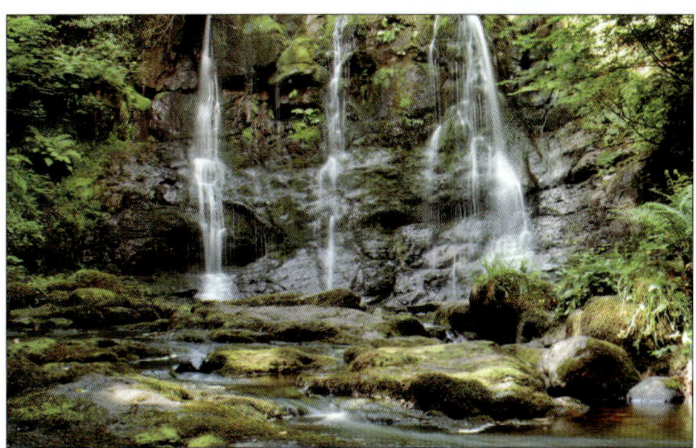

● DEREK CLEGG Glenariff Forest Park in Northern Ireland, taken using a Fuiji S1 Pro on a slow shutter to introduce water blur.

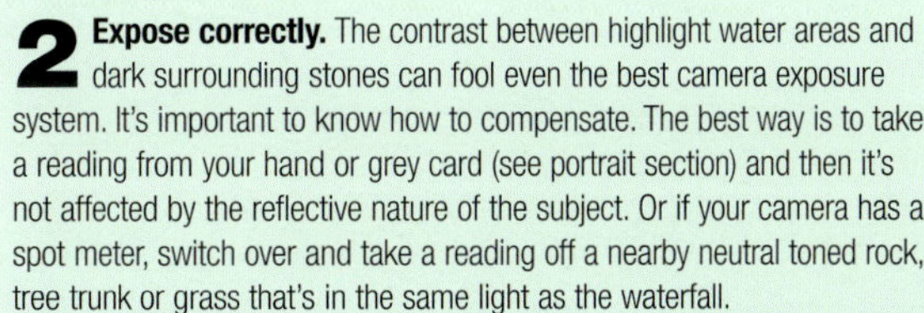

● BERNARD CAULFIELD West Burton Falls are also known locally as Cauldron Falls and are easy to access from West Burton village.

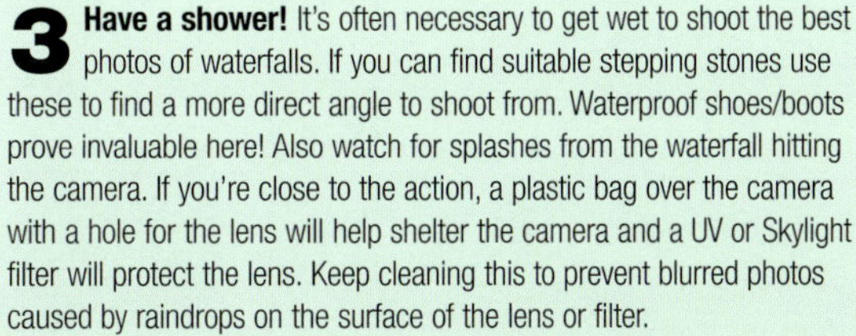

● MARTIN WEST Early October sun illuminating the water at Padley Gorge, Derbyshire. Canon 20D, Canon 17-85 lens and warm-up filter.

SHOOTING TIPS — WATERFALLS

■ Waterfalls may look easy to photograph but there's a lot of skill involved in making them look as good as those on these pages. A good waterfall needs very careful control of exposure, lighting and camera position. The time of day the shot is taken is also crucial in obtaining a great photo.

1 Which shutter speed? If you want to show the power of a waterfall and catch the spray you need to use a fast shutter speed of around 1/250sec or faster, but most photographers prefer a slower approach. Choose a shutter speed slower than 1/15sec and the water will blur, creating really beautiful results. The speed you set depends on the power and fall of the water. If the exposure is too long you can sometimes lose some of the finer detail. If you use a film camera, bracket exposures and shoot at several speeds from 1/15sec to one second. Digital camera users can confirm the result on the LCD and re-shoot if necessary.

2 Expose correctly. The contrast between highlight water areas and dark surrounding stones can fool even the best camera exposure system. It's important to know how to compensate. The best way is to take a reading from your hand or grey card (see portrait section) and then it's not affected by the reflective nature of the subject. Or if your camera has a spot meter, switch over and take a reading off a nearby neutral toned rock, tree trunk or grass that's in the same light as the waterfall.

3 Have a shower! It's often necessary to get wet to shoot the best photos of waterfalls. If you can find suitable stepping stones use these to find a more direct angle to shoot from. Waterproof shoes/boots prove invaluable here! Also watch for splashes from the waterfall hitting the camera. If you're close to the action, a plastic bag over the camera with a hole for the lens will help shelter the camera and a UV or Skylight filter will protect the lens. Keep cleaning this to prevent blurred photos caused by raindrops on the surface of the lens or filter.

4 Use a tripod. With shutter speeds longer than 1/30sec it's safer to support the camera on a tripod or nearby rock/tree. A tripod gives you most scope to get the shot you want. Choose one with waterproof feet and preferably with legs that can splay individually so you can arrange the tripod over uneven rocky foreground.

5 Tidy up the scene. I often remove fallen leaves or distracting twigs from the water or surrounding rocks. While you can easily clone these out digitally, it makes sense to remove them before you take the shot. Take care if you have to balance on uneven or slippy rocks.

6 Sensitivity. Use a slow speed film with ISO25 to ISO100 setting or force the CCD of your digital camera to shoot at the slowest setting, which is usually ISO100. This ensures highest quality with least noise.

7 Use a filter. A neutral density filter will ensure you can shoot at lower shutter speeds in bright light. Better still, use a polarizing filter which also reduces the light but removes glare and reflections to make the water see-through and the colouring of surrounding foliage vibrant. Use an 81 series filter to warm up water, which can often look a touch blue.

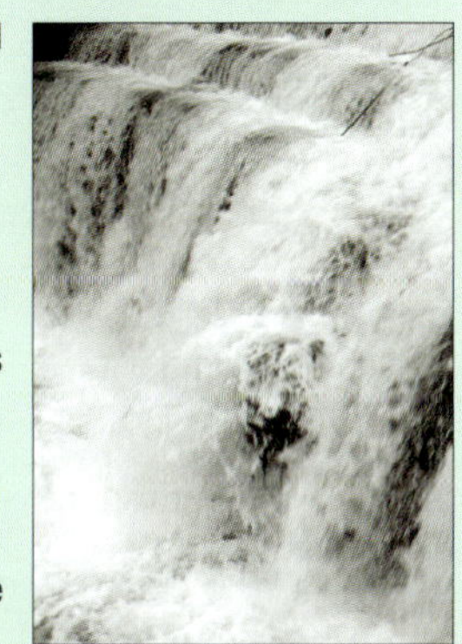

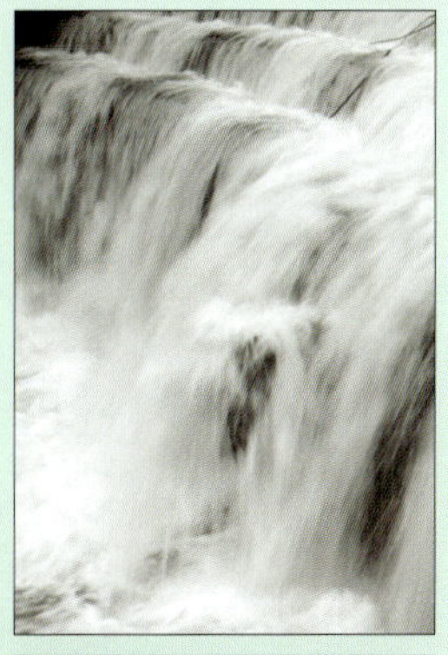

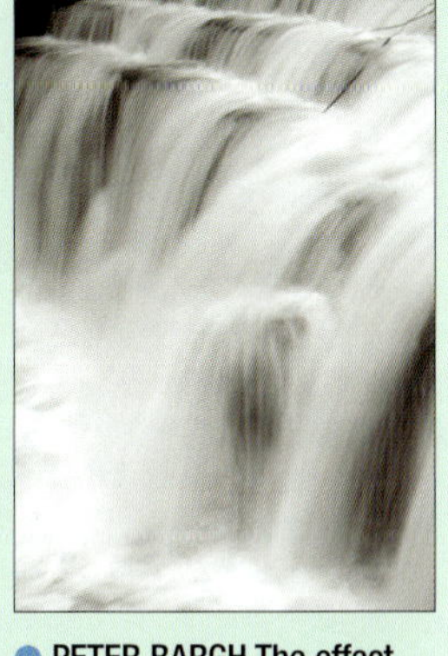

● PETER BARGH The effect of changing shutter speed from 1/90sec (top), to 1/25sec (middle) and 1/6sec (bottom).

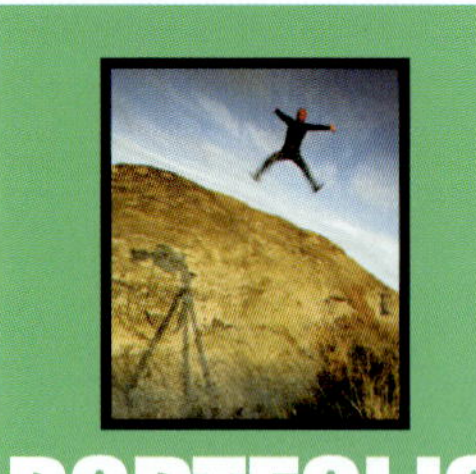

PORTFOLIO

STEVE SHARP
Steve likes nothing more than to be out walking at dawn or dusk in an inspiring landscape.

I became interested in photography in 2001, after becoming hooked on the internet. Looking at all the photography sites was a real eye opener and I finally realised what a camera could actually do.

Almost overnight I went from a point and clicker into someone who wanted to create more than just snapshots. I bought my first digital compact camera, a Casio QV-3EX with 3.3 megapixels. This was a great camera for me at the time and certainly gave me the bug to do more.

About a year later I decided I needed something with more flexibility so I upgraded to a Canon digital SLR with interchangeable lenses and have never looked back!

I also continued to use the internet which was a great learning tool and after a bit of trial and error, I had soon got to grips with the basics of photography and was totally hooked.

My essential equipment is a wide-angle lens, a good solid tripod, a set of neutral density graduated filters, IR filter and a shutter release cable, which cannot be underestimated for crucial timing on certain shots.

These days I like nothing more than to be out walking at dawn or dusk in an inspiring landscape, hoping for that perfect moment when all the elements come together, allowing me to capture the moment forever.

I also enjoy experimenting with more fun images, taking pictures of people and animals using wide-angle and fisheye lenses for that extraordinary perspective.

In the future I plan to build up my images with a view to selling some prints and perhaps even write a book of my own. ■
www.sbsharp.co.uk

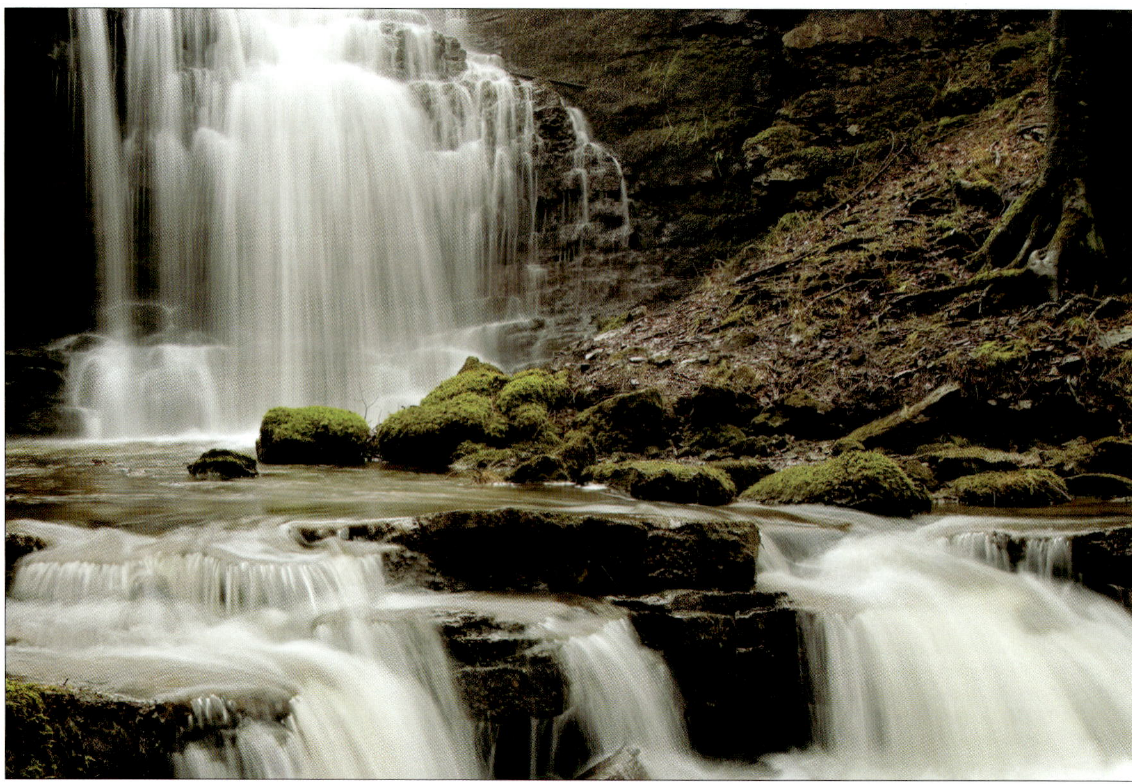

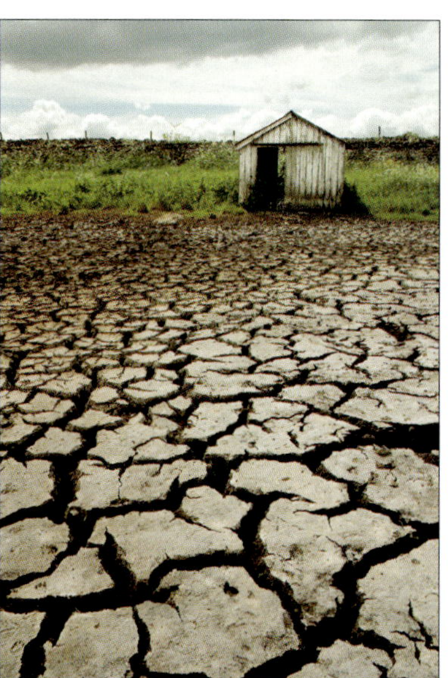

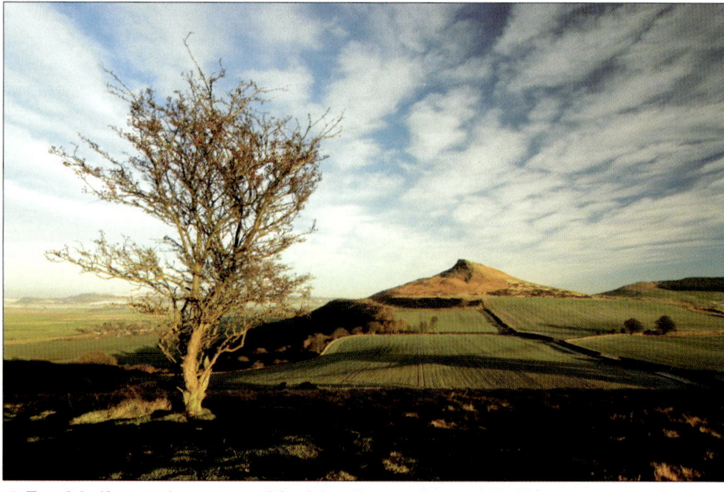

● Top: A half second exposure of Scaleber Force using an 81b filter to warm-up the colours. Left: The mud cracks lead us to the derelict shack. Above: Roseberry Topping is the cone shaped hill, near Great Ayton village, Cleveland.

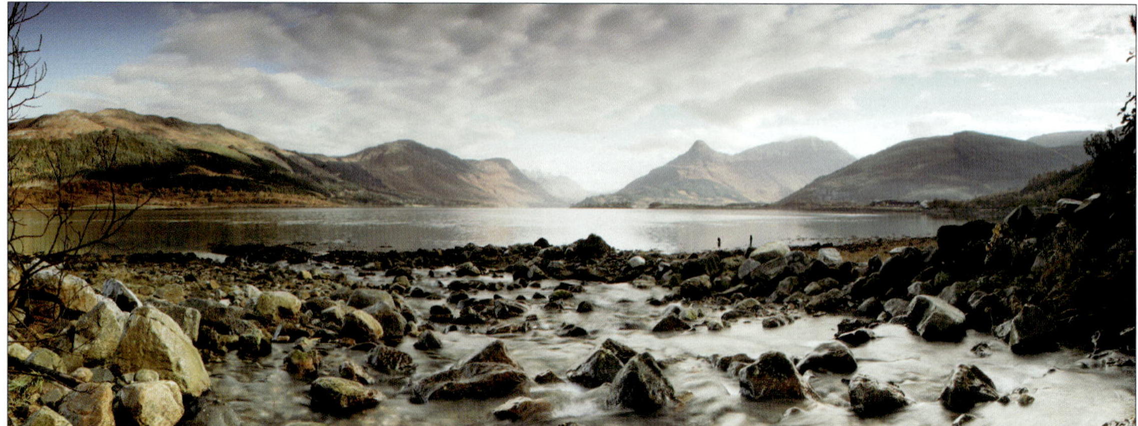

● Loch Leven is the largest loch in lowland Scotland. This photograph was made by combining five upright shots stitched together in Photoshop. Quite a bit of mask work was needed to reduce the levels of the over exposed foreground.

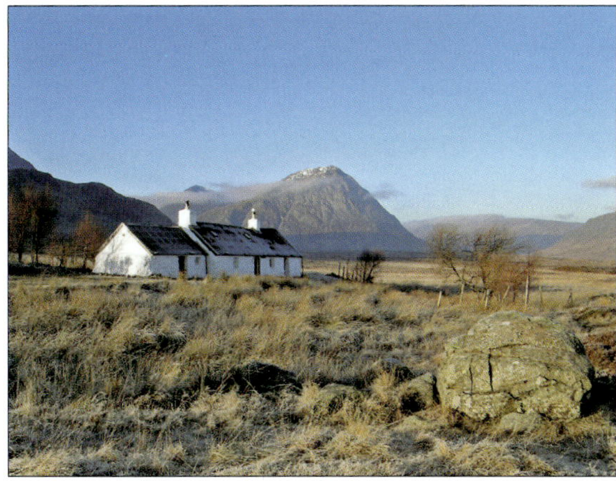

● LOUISE MCGILVIRAY Blackrock Cottage, Rannoch Moor, with its impressive mountain backdrop, is an ideal landscape location.

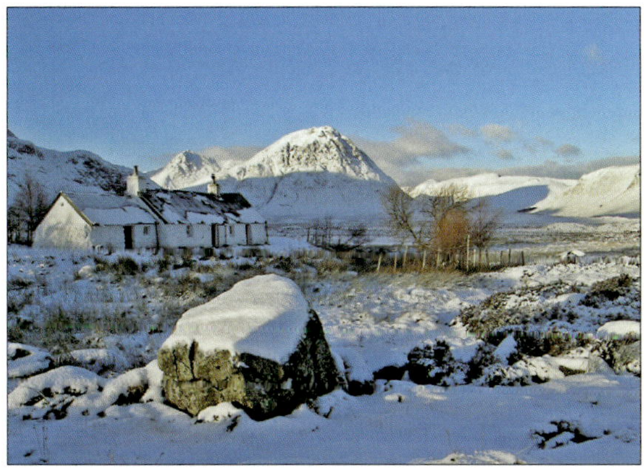

● LOUISE MCGILVIRAY A winter view of the cottage with the distinctive shape of Buachaille Etive Mor in the background.

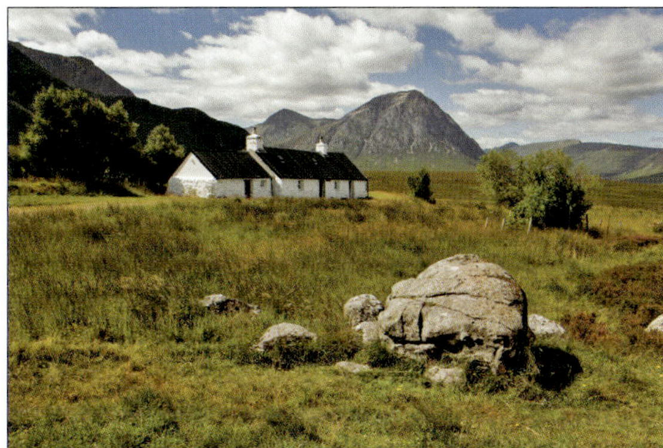

● DOUGLAS MCGILVIRAY A sunny version with fluffy clouds and a blue sky is the type that a postcard company would more likely use.

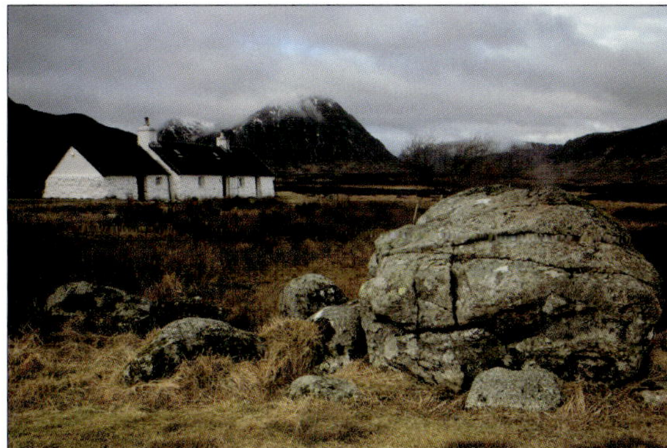

● HELEN TRUST Taken in February using a Canon 300D with an f/22 aperture and a 1/2sec shutter speed to ensure everything is sharp.

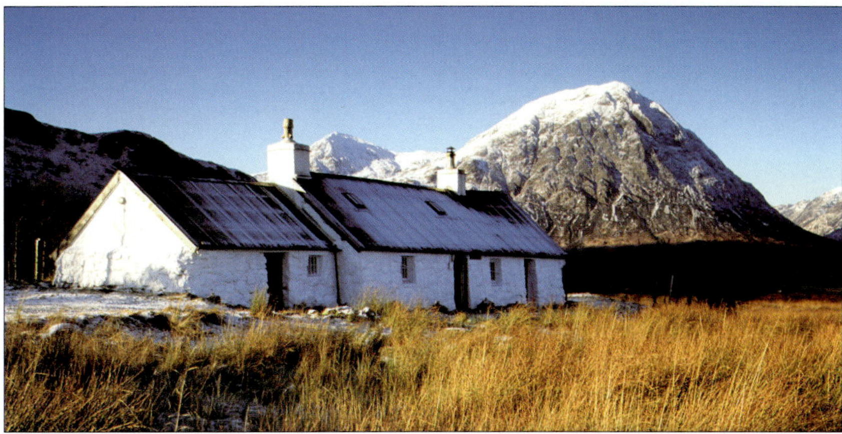

● JOHN CARROLL A closer shot of the Cottage, taken using a Canon EOS 20D with EF 17-40mm L.

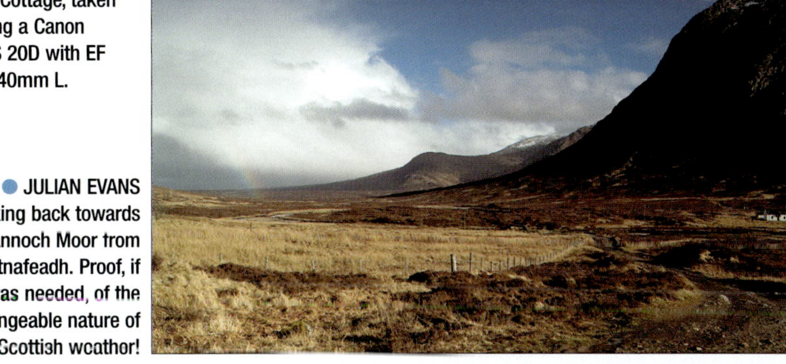

● JULIAN EVANS Looking back towards Rannoch Moor from Altnafeadh. Proof, if it was needed, of the changeable nature of Scottish weather!

SHOOTING TIPS – A CHANGE OF VIEWPOINT

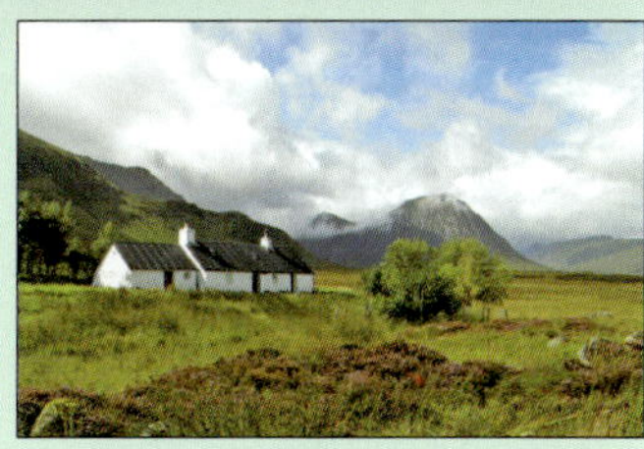

There are many locations around the world that crop up regularly in the gallery on ePHOTOzine. The good thing about seeing the same shot recorded by different photographers is that it gives you ideas how to take photos from different viewpoints and, as the examples shown here of Black Rock cottage also illustrate, how the time of year can totally affect the look and feel of the subject.

■ When you're about to take a scenic photograph look for interesting foreground detail. In the case of Black Rock Cottage notice how many of the photographers have stepped back to include the boulder – some positioned to the right, another to the left. This can make the overall balance much more pleasing.

■ Try changing the camera to subject distance and use a different focal length lens. Moving further away and using a longer telephoto lens setting will make the elements appear closer together as it compresses perspective. Using a wider angle lens will make distant subjects appear further away and smaller in the photo.

■ Moving closer to the ground will make the closer, foreground subject tower above in the scene and have higher proportions to the background.

■ Look around for options to shoot from a higher vantage point to get a different angle on the scene. There's often a nearby hill, a building with access to high levels or road that will gain you height. Some professionals will use step ladders to raise them above obstructions, such as hedgerows or fencing.

■ Prepare to go back and visit the same location again if the conditions aren't right. Each day can bring a wide variety of conditions. Some photographers wait all day for the elusive moment when the sun breaks through the dark clouds and illuminates a vital part of the scene.

■ Shooting the same scene throughout the seasons will give a varied range of images, from the fresh look of spring through the lush green of summer, to the rustic autumn and the barren winter. Each season brings a range of skies, from travel agent blue to dreary grey.

■ A useful item to have in your camera bag is a Sun Position Compass. This little gadget indicates all sunrise and sunset positions throughout the year. It comes with a table showing the hours of daylight all through the year. This enables you to plot the sun's course during the day and determine where shadows will form.

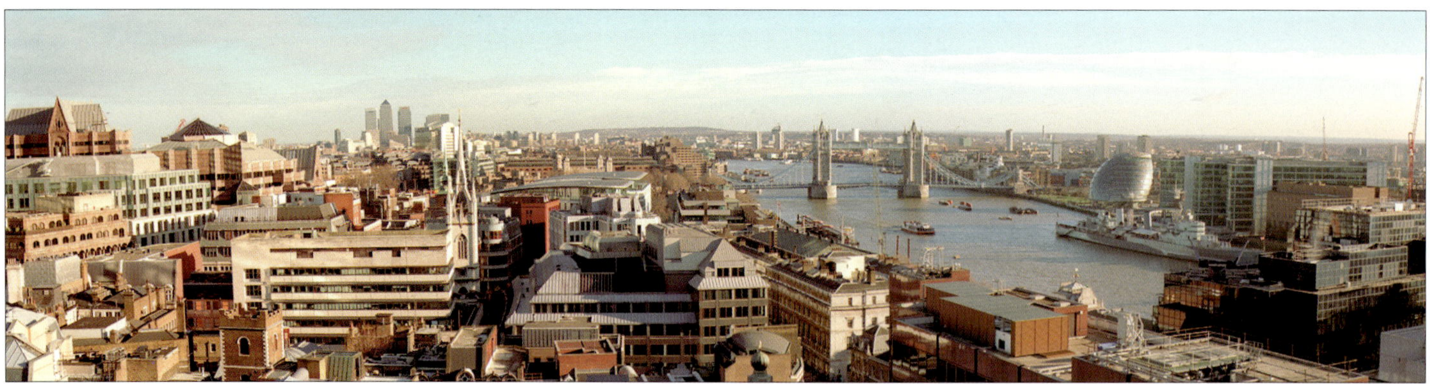

● YAT TANG View of the City of London, including the river Thames and London Bridge. It was taken as four separate photographs on Fuji Reala, using a Canon EOS 50E with a 50mm f/1.7 lens. The four photographs were then merged digitally to create this panorama. If you want to try this method, use a tripod to ensure consistency across the photos.

DIGITAL PANORAMAS

■ If you're ever faced with a scene that you can't squeeze in when looking through the camera's viewfinder, consider using a technique that's almost as old as photography. By taking a series of photos side by side photographers have been able to join them together and create a much wider panoramic view. The technique, known as a joiner, is made easier with digital technology and many image editing programs have a feature to join, or stitch, photos together. In Photoshop Elements and Photoshop CS it's called PhotoMerge.

1 Take a series of photos from the same position each with a different camera angle. To make it easier for the software to join them, set the camera to manual exposure or use the AE lock so all the shots have the same exposure value and shoot, allowing around 15-20% overlap. Ideally use a tripod to keep everything straight. Place the photos in a folder and name it panoramics.

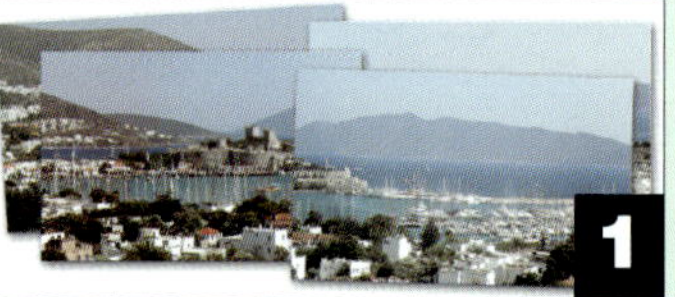

2 Open File⇨Automate⇨Photomerge and select the panoramics folder for the source files. The program will then pull all the photos into a large preview window or come up with a message asking you to do it manually from a thumbnail it collects. Drag the pictures into place in the preview pane.

3 Settings gives you the choice of a normal stitch or one that adjusts the perspective. Select whichever gives you the preferred result, previewed in the pane. Choose advanced blending to minimise colour changes where images with different exposures overlap. Click OK and the image will be merged.

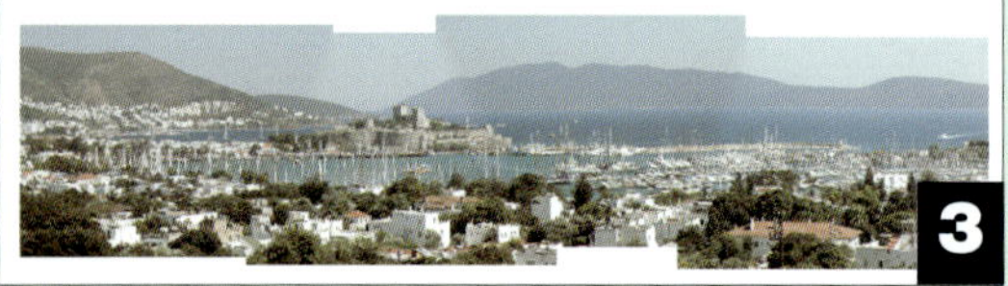

4 Use the Patch and Clone tools to edit areas where the merged sections are a different tone.

5 Crop and save composite as a .pmg file which can be opened and reworked in the future.

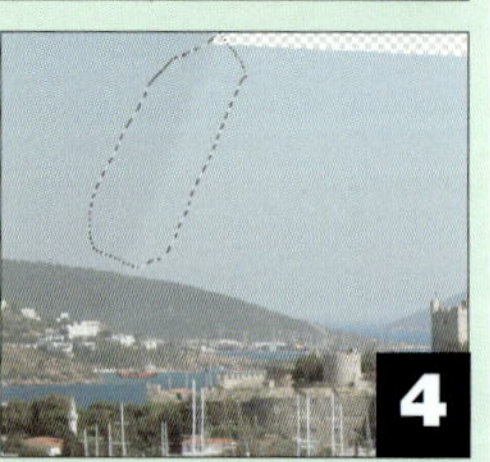

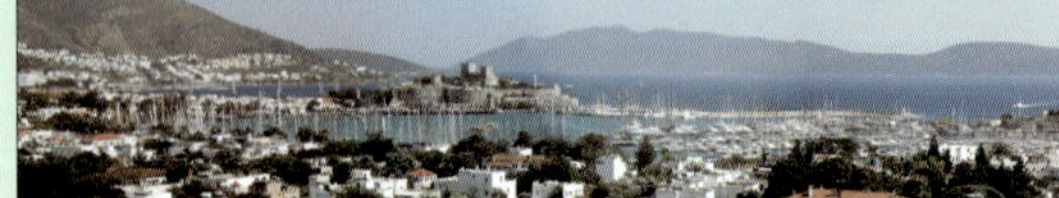

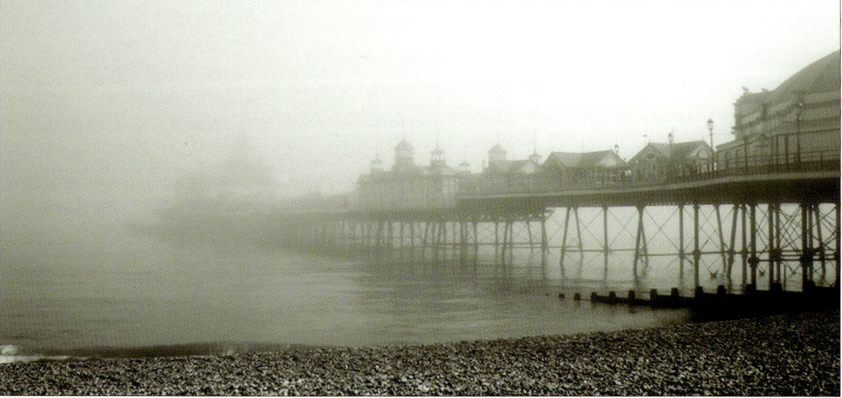

● DENNIS GREY Eastbourne Pier captured using a Canon EOS 300D. The pier was shrouded in an incredible sea mist, despite the beach being bathed in late afternoon sunshine.

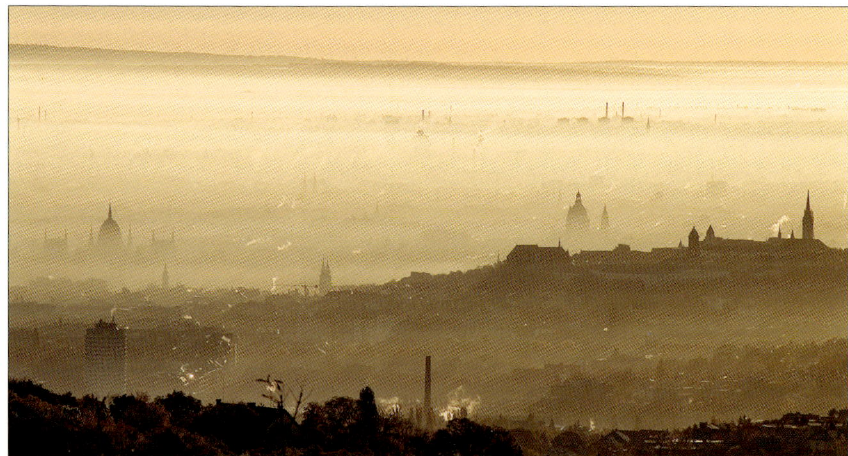

● TERENCE AMOS Sunrise and mist appeared soon after heavy rain in this view that overlooks Budapest, taken with a Canon EOS10D and Sigma 18-125mm. The exposure was 1/180 at f/13.

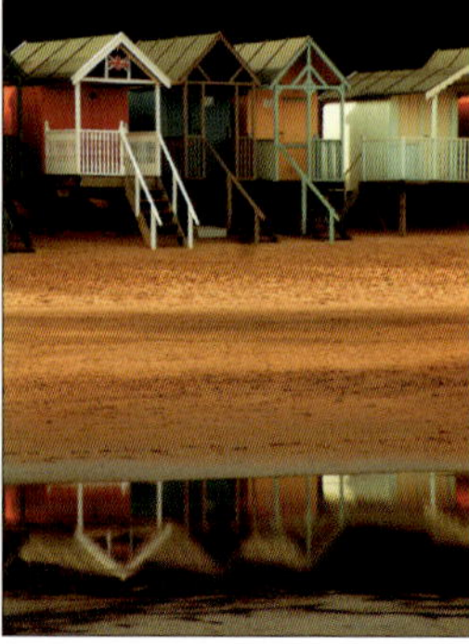

● JOAN DUCKETT Beach huts and reflections in Wells, Norfolk.

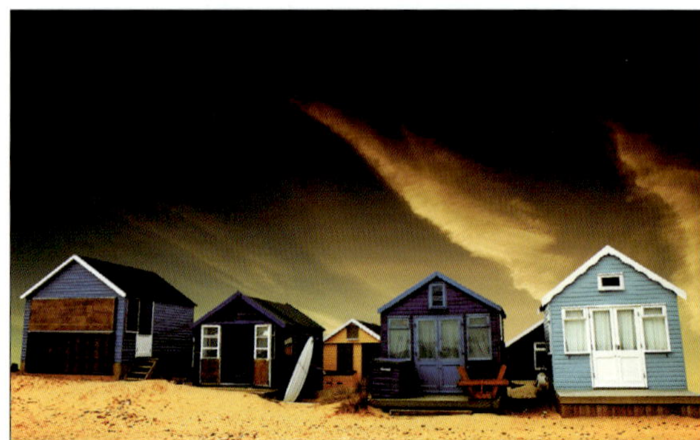

● MARTIN WAIT After replacing the original sky I introduced a colour boost that gave it a quirky "place at the edge of the world" feel.

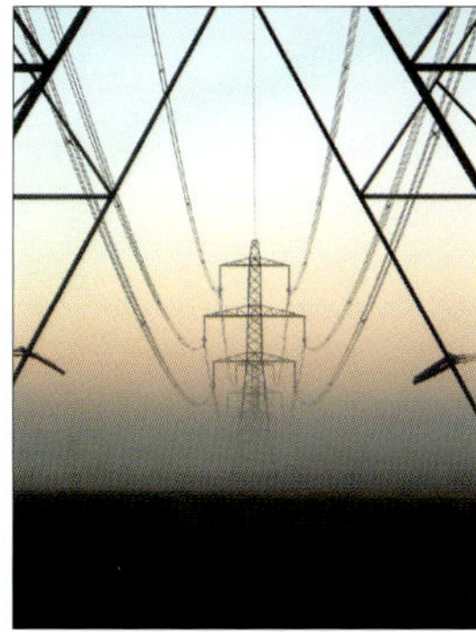

● ANDREW FROST Subjects that you drive past every day!

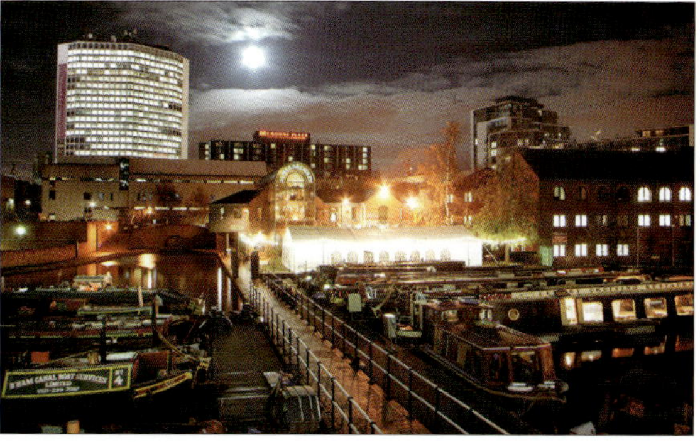

● PAUL WARD A chance shot spotted while on a job, taken at Gas St Basin, Birmingham, on a Canon EOS 1Ds and 17-40mm L lens.

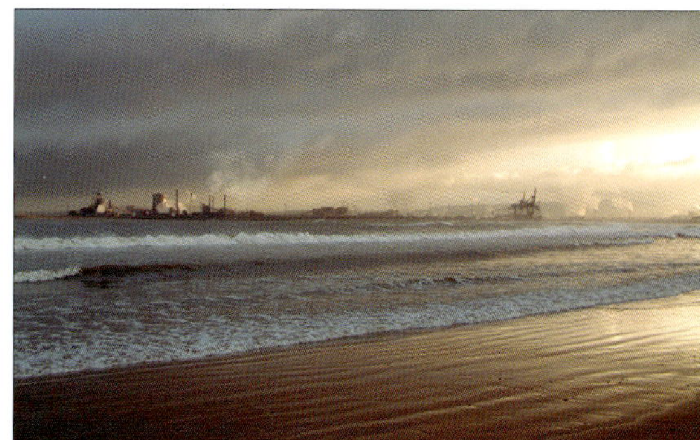

● EDWARD MCKILLOP NICHOLL The North Gare beach at the mouth of the River Tees, photographed late on a January afternoon.

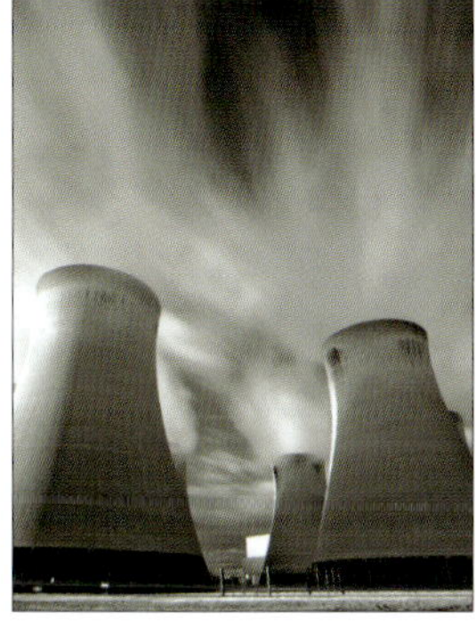

● JAMES QUINN Drax Power Station in North Yorkshire taken with an infrared filter and a 10sec exposure.

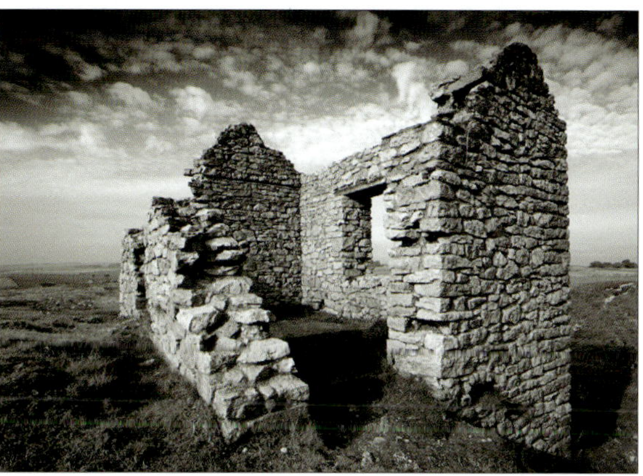

● ANDY BOTT Magpie Mine, Derbyshire, using a Canon EOS3 and Fuji Sensia film, converted to black and white in Photoshop.

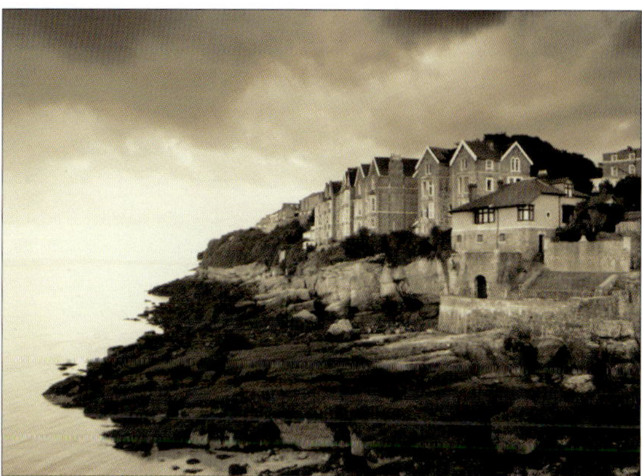

● ADE OSMANT An ND grad filter was used to enhance the sky of this view from Clevedon Pier. It was then converted to sepia tone.

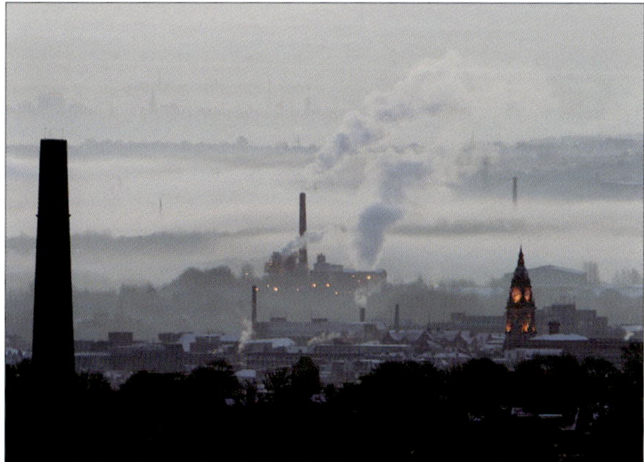

● STEVE LANGTON December dawn over Bolton, Lancashire, taken with a two second exposure on a Canon EOS 10D and 300mm lens.

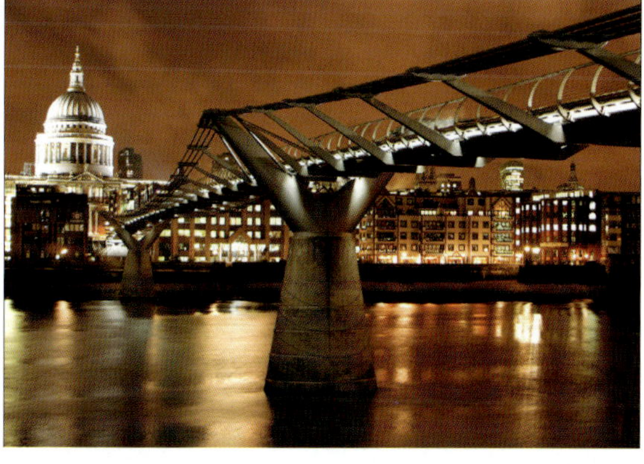

● ALAN HUGHES I waited for the clouds to clear to get rid of the orange sky/light pollution in this scene of St Paul's Cathedral, London.

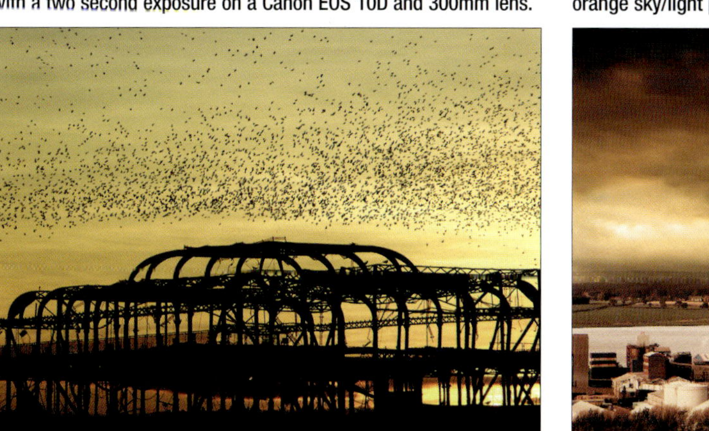

● CHRIS MOLE This silhouette shows a flight of Starlings flocking around Brighton's West Pier at sunset. A Minolta A1 was used.

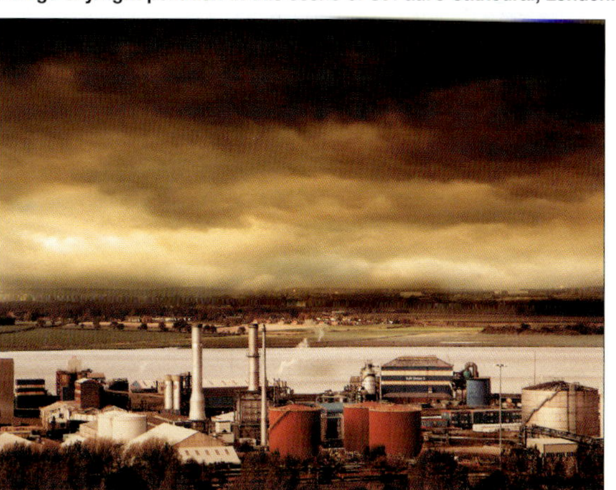

● FRANK MARSH The colours of this ICI chemical plant at Runcorn, looking over the Mersey towards Speke, enhanced in Photoshop.

TIME OF DAY

■ We previously mentioned the importance of shooting scenes at different times of the year and from different viewpoints. Another thing to consider is the time of day.

■ Shooting at dawn or dusk creates photos with incredible colour, as the sun rises or sets, because the colour temperature is at its warmest.

■ Avoid shooting at midday when shadows are harsh and the light is blue.

■ Shooting in misty/foggy conditions enhances the colour of a sunrise/sunset.

■ A tripod is essential at these times to prevent camera shake and allow shutter speeds that are longer than one second.

■ Beware if your shot includes illumination from buildings and street lights – the camera will see the main part of the scene as black and overexpose. Make sure you compensate to avoid this.

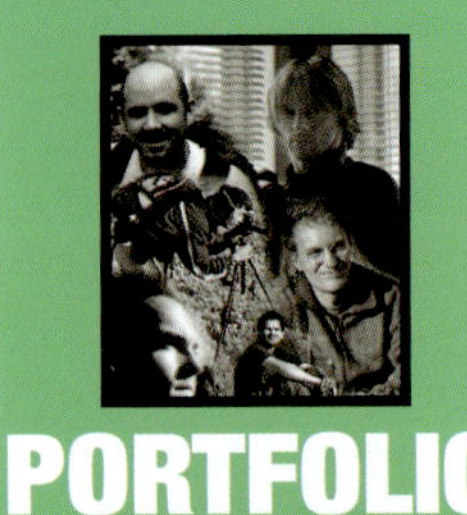

PORTFOLIO

TIMECATCHER
A group of photographers brought together with one aim – to promote the natural beauty of the landscape.

The TimeCatcher.com project was initially created by Canadian landscape photographer Patrick Di Fruscia. Patrick's vision was to create a unique website to promote the natural beauty and variety within our world's environments.

To achieve this aim, Patrick invited a small, international group of respected landscape and nature photographers to form the TimeCatcher team.

The first team members were Adam Burton, Ian Cameron and Richard Nicholls. Patrick met all these UK-based landscape photographers through the ePHOTOzine website after admiring their individual styles.

They were soon joined by the other team members from the USA; Francis Cailles, Kenneth Kwan and Jay Patel, whose work has been featured on various photographic websites.

Having made a significant contribution, Richard Nicholls decided to leave the team to pursue his personal website www.magicallandscape.com.

All of the TimeCatcher photographers possess a distinct individual style, which each has developed through dedication and practice over the years, learning through experience what works best for them. Although individual, these styles have many consistencies, which help to make the TimeCatcher photographs instantly recognisable.

The team all place great emphasis on capturing images in the most special light the day has to offer, namely that of dawn and dusk. Neutral density graduated and polarizing filters are used to help each photographer faithfully record on film or digital what the eye can see naturally. No unnatural

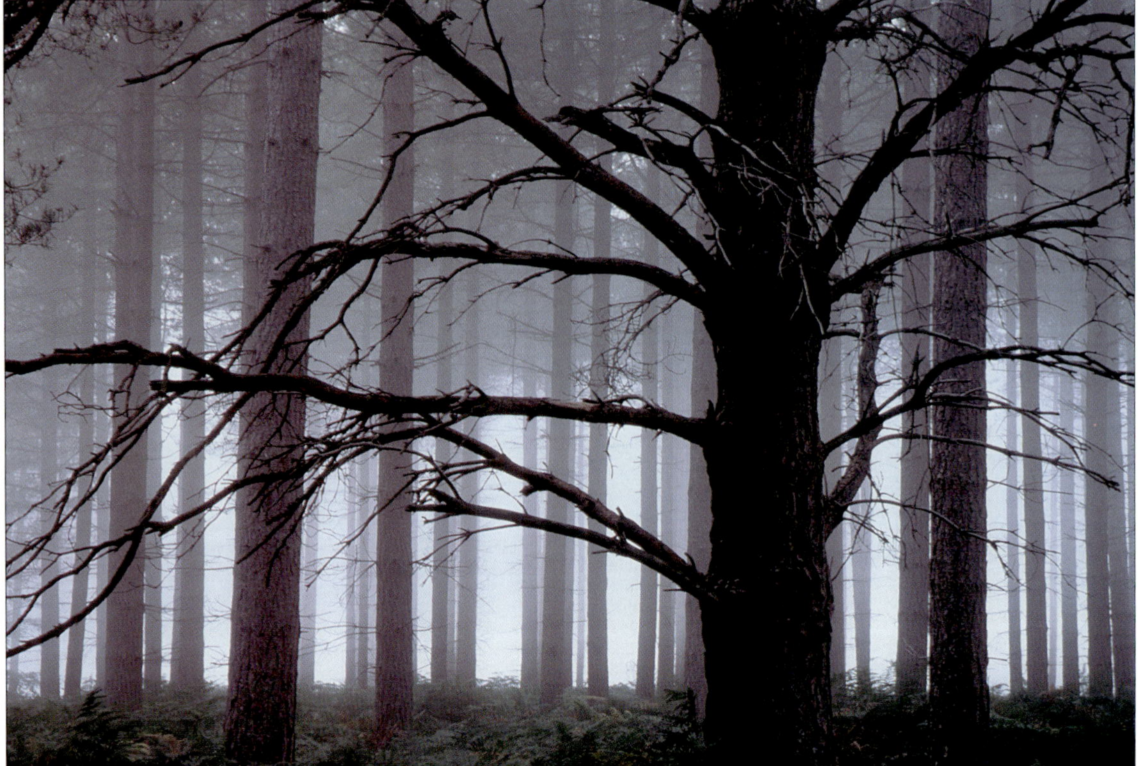

● This shot was taken early one October morning in the New Forest. Adam Burton was trying to make the most of the mist by taking one of those 'trees in mist' shots when he came across this amazing tree. It really contrasted well with the vertical trees behind so he positioned it on the right third and captured it on his Nikon F80 loaded with Fuji Velvia.

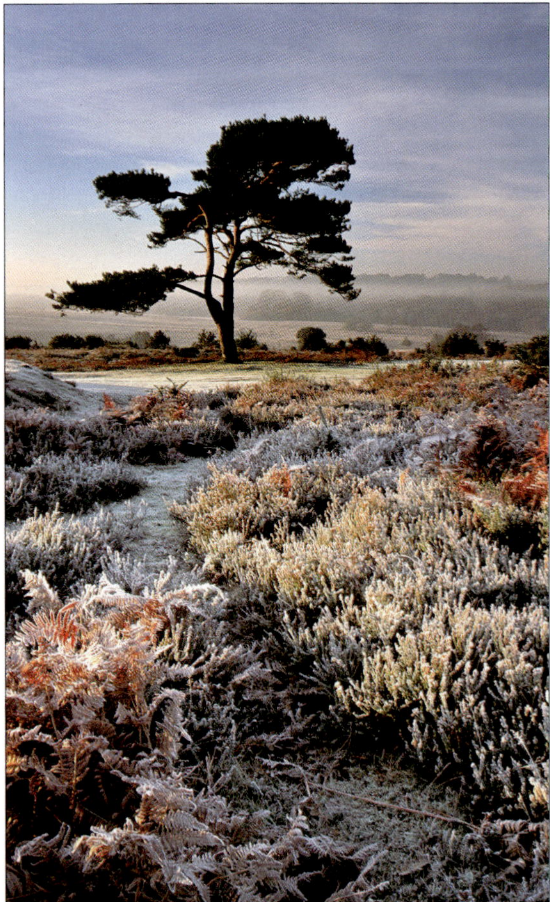

● The path leads your eye to the tree in this frosty morning shot in the New Forest. Adam has several variations of this on ePHOTOzine but it's a version with tree on the right that's been his best seller.

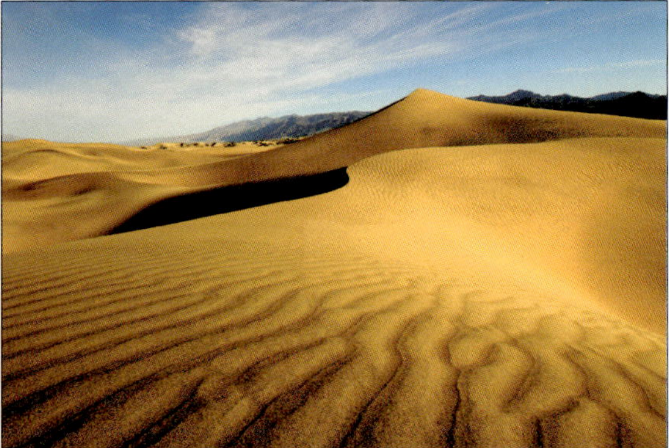

● This scene by American photographer Francis Cailles shows the rich colour of the sand and harsh sunlight that casts strong shadows, adding a great outline to the dunes.

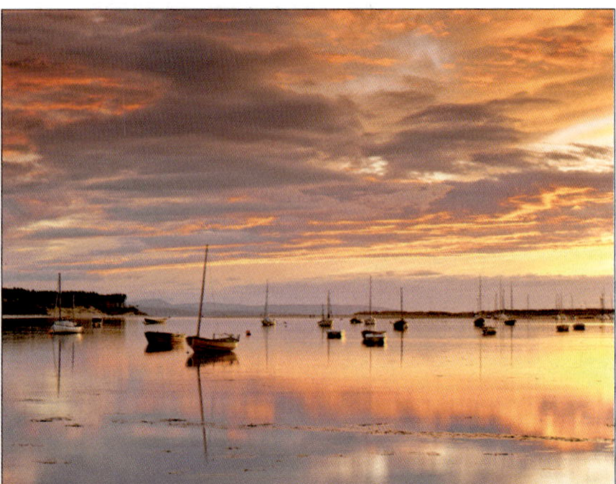

● Findhorn Bay, Scotland, has always been a great source of dramatic sunsets for Ian Cameron. The setting sun has reflected off the base of low clouds staining them a vivid red.

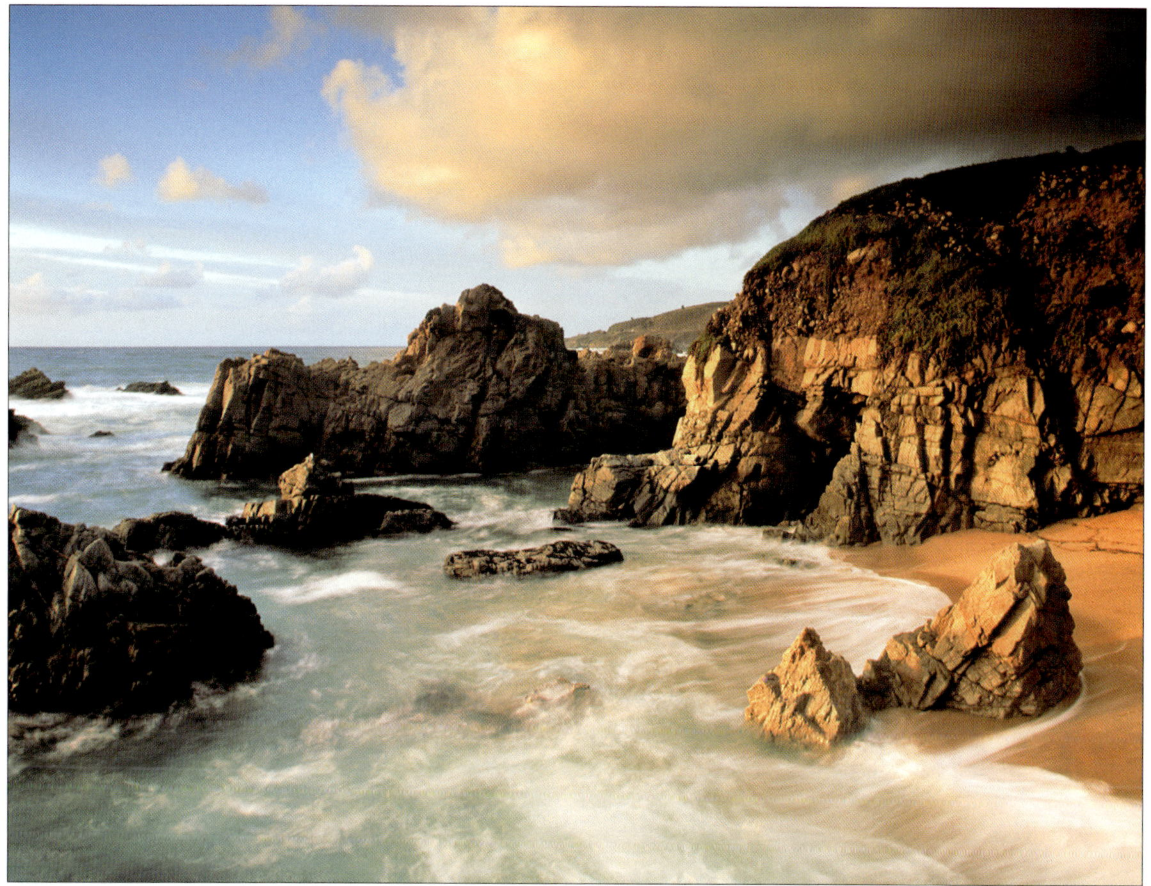

● Kenneth Kwan used a Canon Elan 7E with a 24mm fixed focal length lens to take the sun setting at Garrapata State Beach, California. A polariser and ND grad filter have helped cut down reflections and balance the sky with the ground. Fuji Velvia 50 film was used.

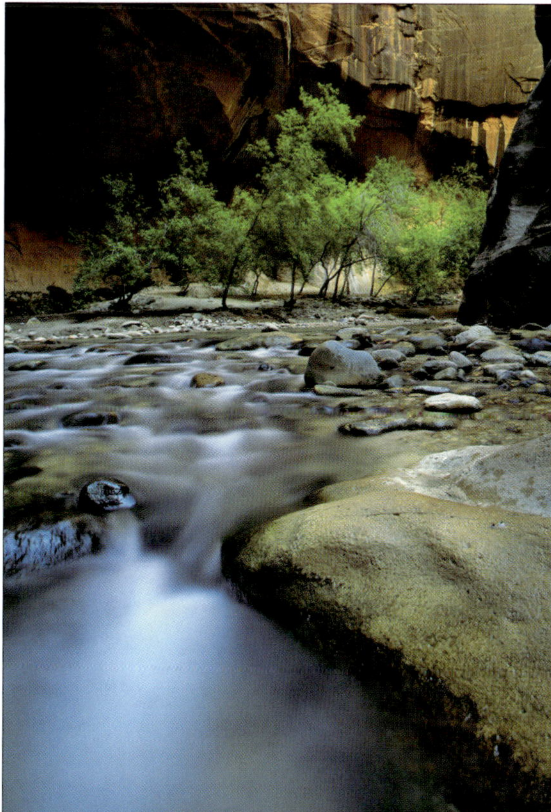

● Patrick Di Fruscia's shot, titled "A river runs through it", was taken in Zion National Park. It offers spectacular scenery all year round and the red cliffs contrast against the lush green leaves.

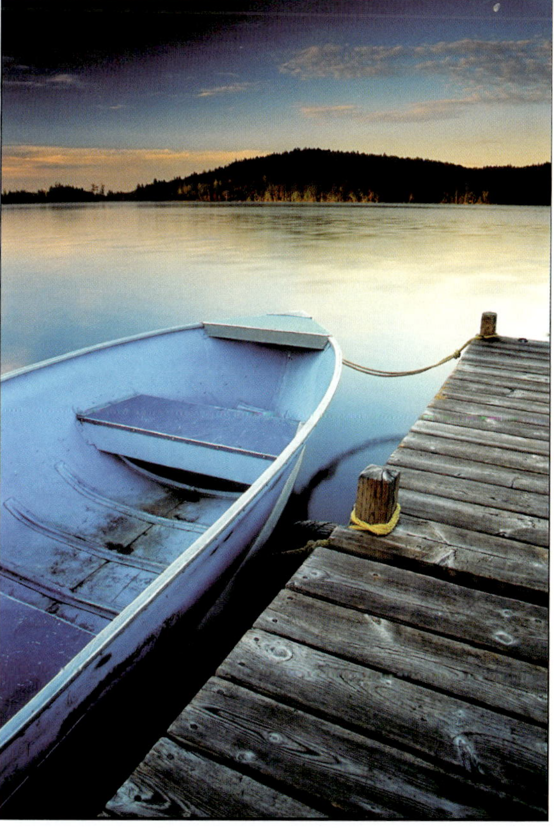

● Patrick Di Fruscia took this shot at the Manoir du Lac Delage in Quebec, Canada at around 4.30am using a two-stop ND Grad and a warming filter on his Minolta Dynax 7 and 24-105mm f/3.5-4.5.

sunset style filters are used, as the team believes there can be no alternative to the natural capture of light.

Some of the team continues to use film cameras, such as the Pentax 67 and Minolta Dynax 7, while others have moved across to the digital format and use either Nikon or Canon digital SLRs. It matters little which format is used – for the TimeCatcher team the camera is but a tool used to capture the moment. All that matters is that the camera can accurately capture an image in high quality.

Each team member contributes to the site by displaying photographs which they believe capture the essence of the natural world.

Since they use photography as a means to promote conservation, each photographer makes it their priority to only display images of the highest quality.

This will often involve many repeated long trips to remote locations in many different weather conditions, until the magical light can be witnessed and recorded in that special image.

Additionally, the TimeCatcher team is committed to sharing the approach they take to capture the images shown on the site to encourage and inspire other photographers.

One of the ways in which they achieve this is by providing the technical specifications behind every photo displayed. More recently, images have begun to feature a short story describing the motivation, inspiration and actions of the photographer.

When contacted by the readers via email, TimeCatcher team members are more than willing to share technical information and/or their experiences in capturing the photographs displayed on the site.

In the future, the TimeCatcher team members will continue to write more articles, as time permits, describing recent photographic trips on the 'Through the Lens' website feature.

TimeCatcher will also continue to display images representing our natural world and aims to inspire fellow photographers and captivate people all over the world with their photographic creations. ∎

www.timecatcher.com

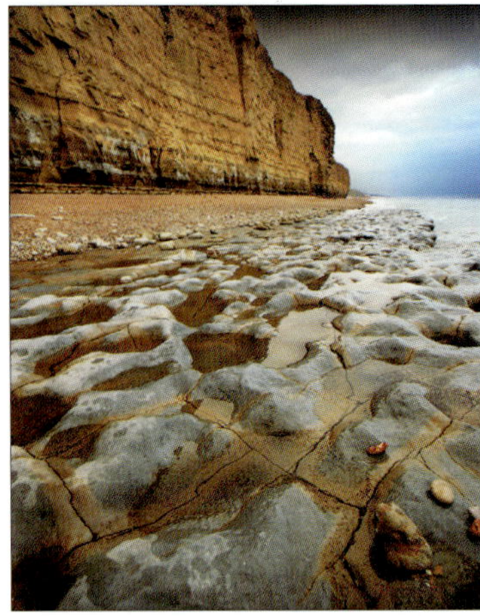

● NIGEL SHARMAN Burton Beach at the western end of the Chesil Beach in Dorset.

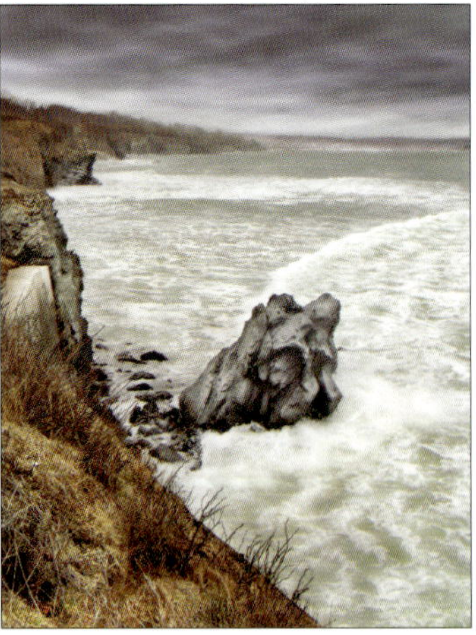

● DAVID PRITCHARD Newport, Rhode Island. Converted to mono and re-coloured.

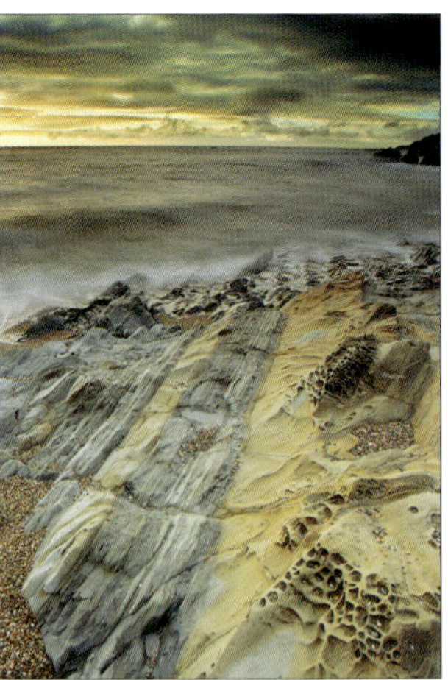

● PATRICK SMITH A one second exposure with polariser and ND grad.

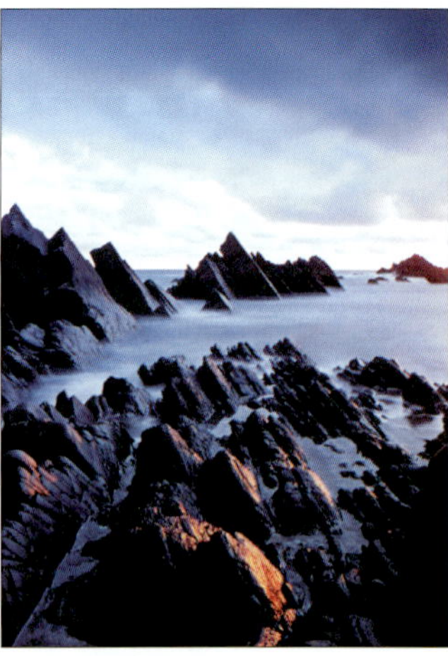

● STEPHEN SMITH Jagged rocks along the North Cornish coast.

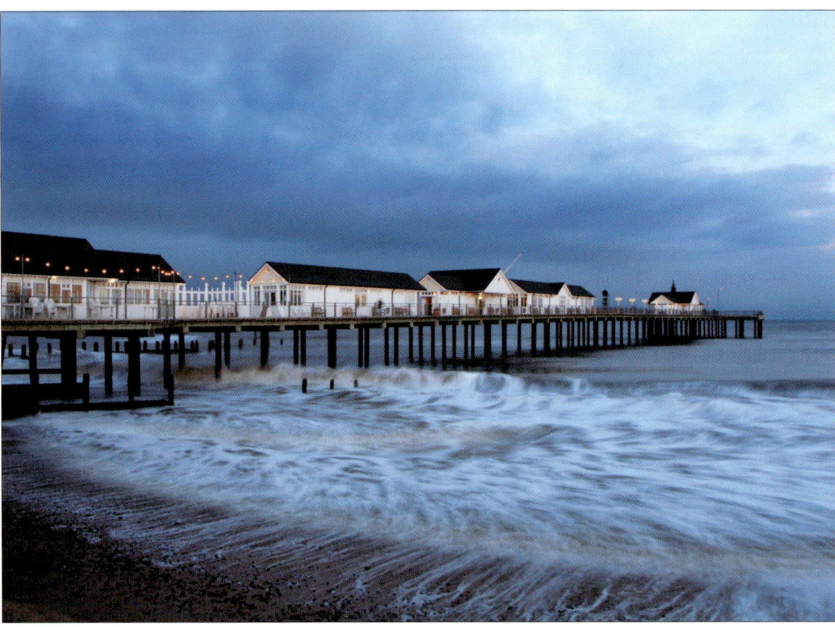

● JULIAN MITCHELL A long exposure at Southwold pier in Suffolk, with the saturation increased a little and sharpened.

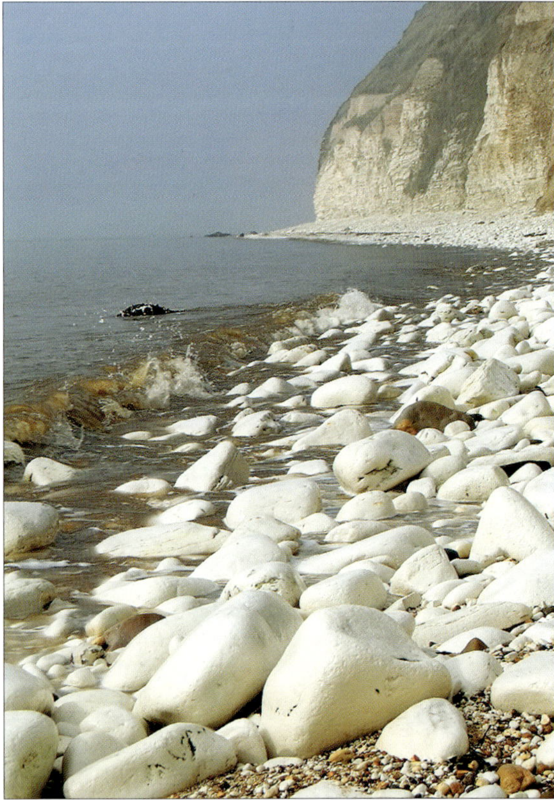

● MARK CURRY Dane's Dyke, near Flamborough, has this quiet beach of large stones and shingle. Photoshop helped darken the sky.

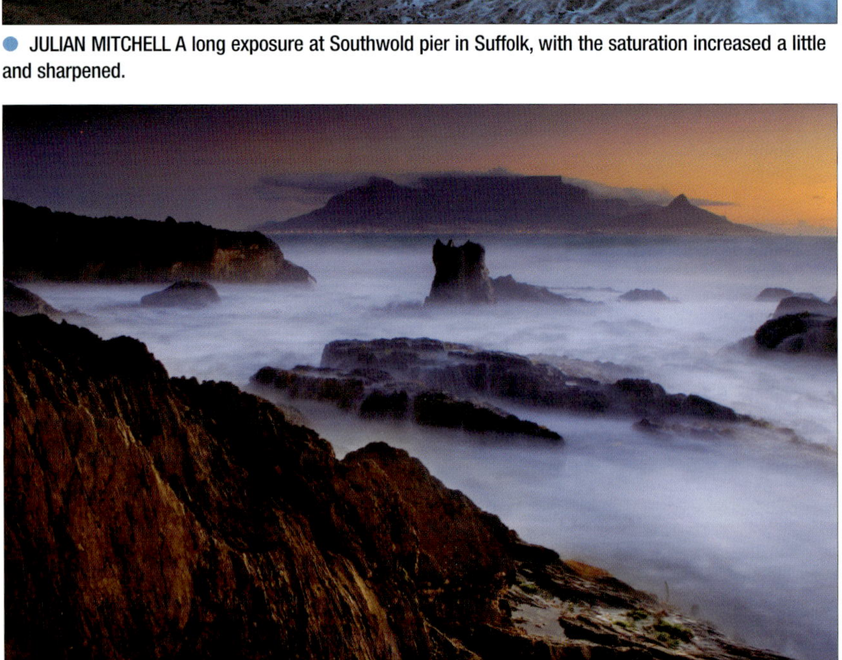

● STEPHEN SMITH The setting sun brings the last of its warmth on a blustery cold evening in Noordhoek, Cape town, South Africa.

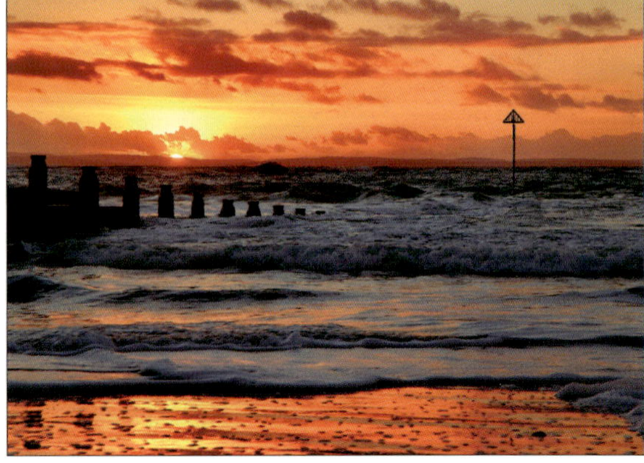

● DUNCAN ROBINS View over Chichester Harbour, West Wittering, taken at sunset with an 18-70mm lens and a 1/40sec exposure.

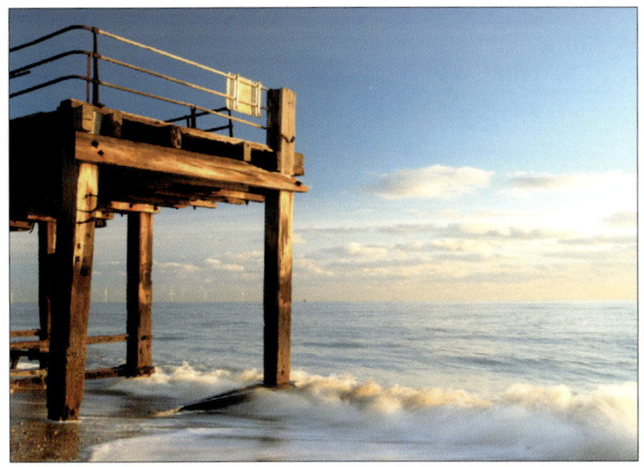

● JON GIBBS Britannia Pier at Great Yarmouth, taken on a November morning with a 1/3 second exposure at f/22.

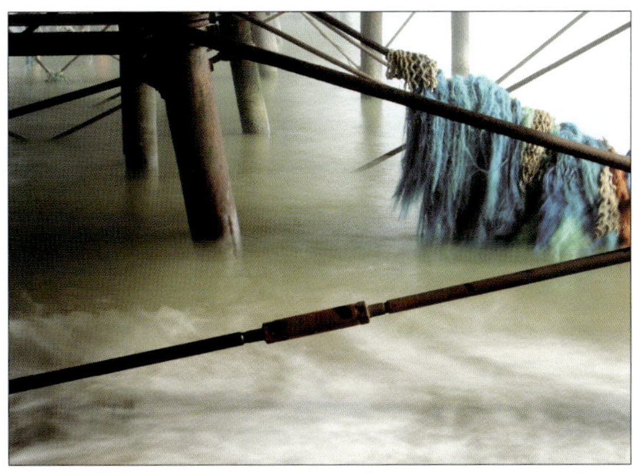

● DENNIS GRAY was quite taken with this colourful fishing net caught under the pier and the movement of the water.

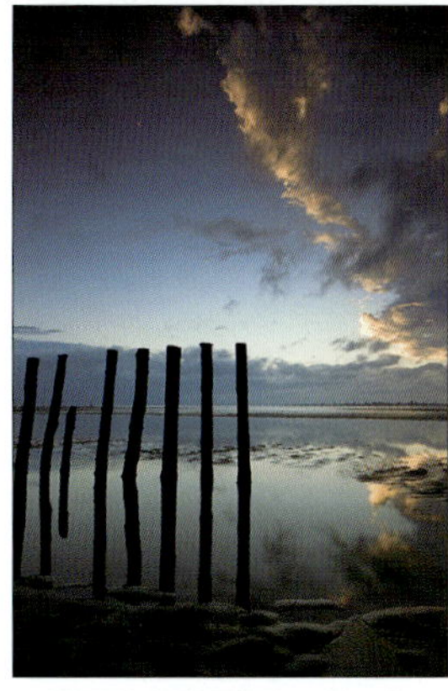

● PETER GRAVES East Head, Sussex, from Chichester Harbour.

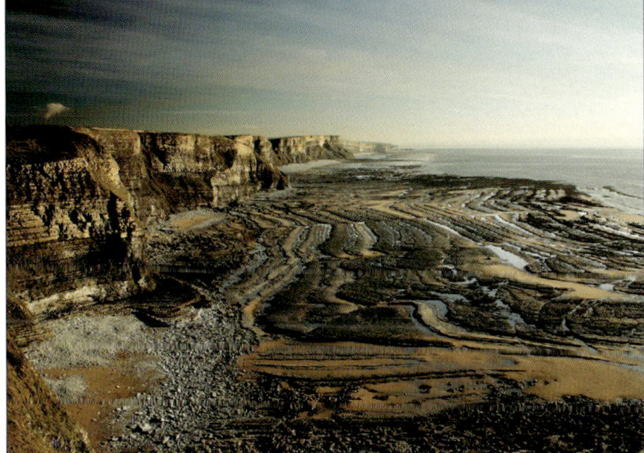

● MARI STERLING A beautiful view of the cliffs at Southerndown, Dunraven Bay, taken in afternoon winter light.

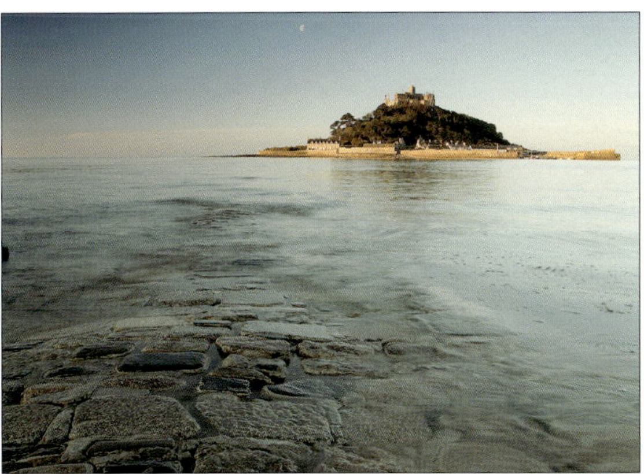

● MATT WHORLOW St Michael's Mount at sunrise. "Unfortunately, the tide was higher than I'd hoped so the causeway is under water."

● ANGELA JOEL Red flag taken in Egypt at sunset. The island in the background is Tiran Island. The red flag indicates strong currents.

DIGITAL TECHNIQUE – A DIFFERENT USE FOR MOTION BLUR

■ Sometimes you'll visit a location that has no atmosphere or you don't have the correct filters to lift the sky. You take the photograph anyway and have a shot like the one below, at Cromer. Cromer pier has been photographed many times by ePHOTOzine members and the best shots are usually taken at dawn or dusk. This was a dull spring day, but I had an idea how to rescue it.

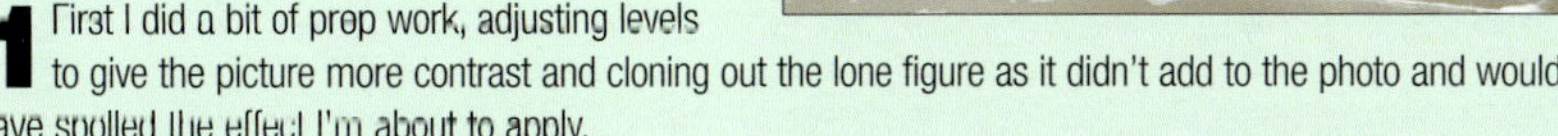

1 First I did a bit of prep work, adjusting levels to give the picture more contrast and cloning out the lone figure as it didn't add to the photo and would have spoiled the effect I'm about to apply.

2 I'm going to give the scene a feeling of motion, which you'd normally see applied to an action photo. I'll use Photoshop's motion Blur filter. Filter⇨Blur⇨Motion Blur. A pop-up window appears allowing you to set the direction and distance of the blur. In this example I set the direction to a slight angle to follow the surf in the sea. I adjusted the distance so there was obvious blur but not too much to destroy the detail in the sea or clouds. I applied it to the whole photo and will remove the filter from the pier in the next stage.

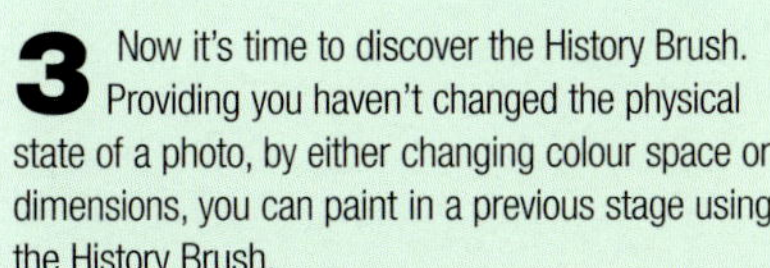
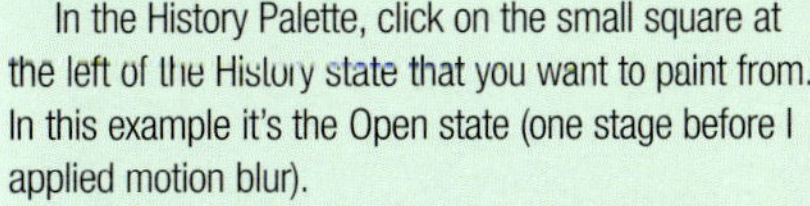

3 Now it's time to discover the History Brush. Providing you haven't changed the physical state of a photo, by either changing colour space or dimensions, you can paint in a previous stage using the History Brush.

In the History Palette, click on the small square at the left of the History state that you want to paint from. In this example it's the Open state (one stage before I applied motion blur).

Now select the History Brush from the toolbar and paint in the areas you want to be reverted to the unblurred state. Use a brush with a feathered edge to avoid a sharp change from the before and after filter effect. Also change the size of the brush depending on the size of the area you're working on.

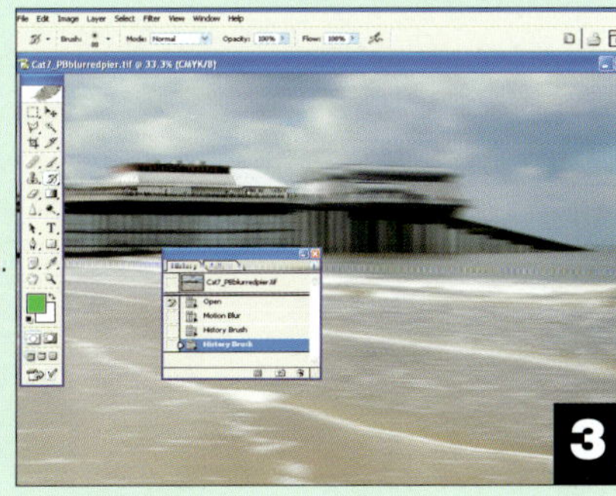

4 Once I'd worked around all of the pier I still didn't think the photo had quite the right amount of interest to make it worth displaying so I adjusted the contrast and hue/saturation and then used the History brush to paint back the brilliant white of the pier.

5 As a final stage, I applied a blue gradient to the sky and a green one to the sea, using the technique on page 31. This may be too unnatural for many, but I quite like it.

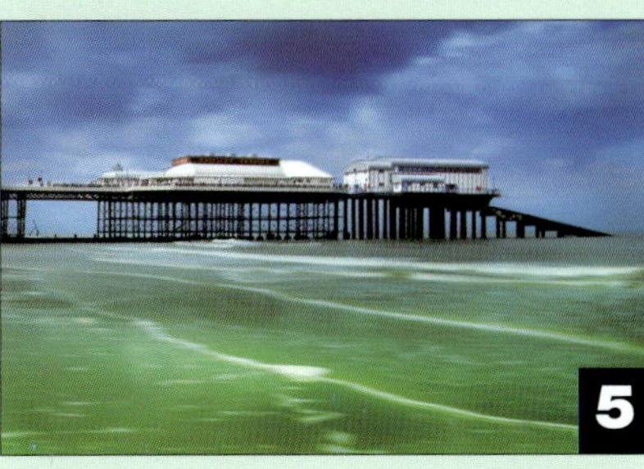
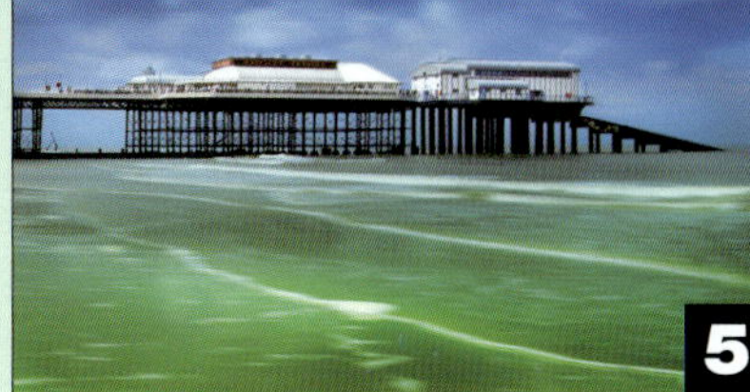

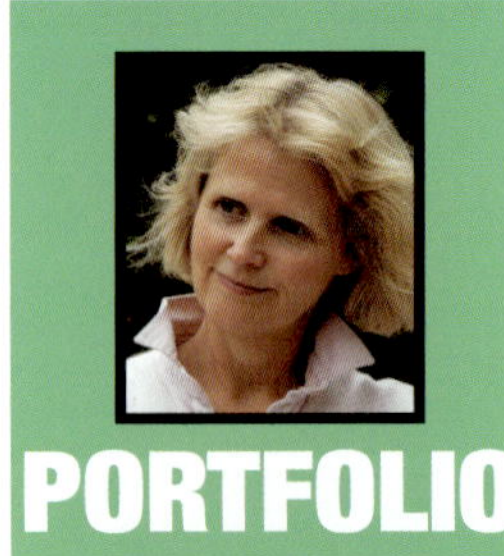

PORTFOLIO

KATE BARCLAY
finds her passion for landscape photography challenging but very rewarding.

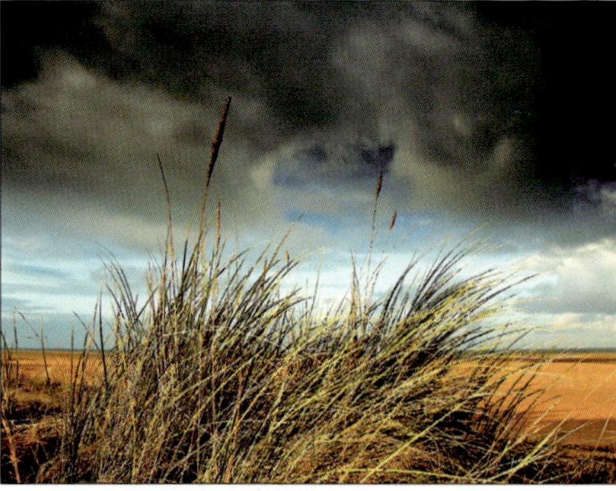

My love of photography began just over a year ago when a friend lent me his compact digital camera. I borrowed books from friends and the local library and began teaching myself the basics.

My creative background, working as a theatre costume designer in New Zealand before moving to the UK, provided me with a good foundation to develop.

My first camera was a Nikon Coolpix 4300 digital, which was great for learning the fundamentals of photography. At first I shot everything, experimenting with the minimal settings the camera had and the various lighting conditions nature throws at us.

My current passion is landscape photography, particularly low light and night time photography. These are challenging but very rewarding if you get it right. I'm fortunate enough to live near the sea on the North Norfolk coast, where we get stunning skies and wonderful natural light. Mix this with sand, sea and reflections and I'm in seventh (photography) heaven!

I now use a Nikon D70 with 18-70mm lens and various filters. My essential is a tripod – a must for low light. Using this helps focus my mind; it stops me getting snap happy and makes me think about composition and camera settings.

The beauty of photography is that the possibilities are endless and there's so much more I want to do. In future I want to experiment with black and white, macro work and have a play around with more abstract images.

To do all this I would like a macro lens and 70-300mm zoom. I also want to have a go at using film instead of digital for some of the black and white photography I'm planning to do. ■
www.katebarclay.co.uk

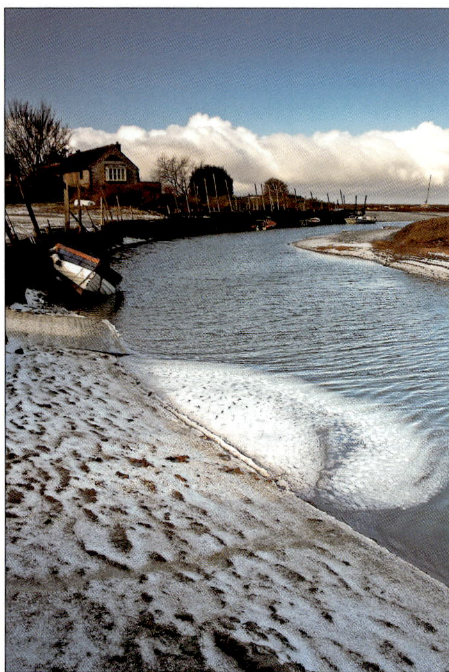

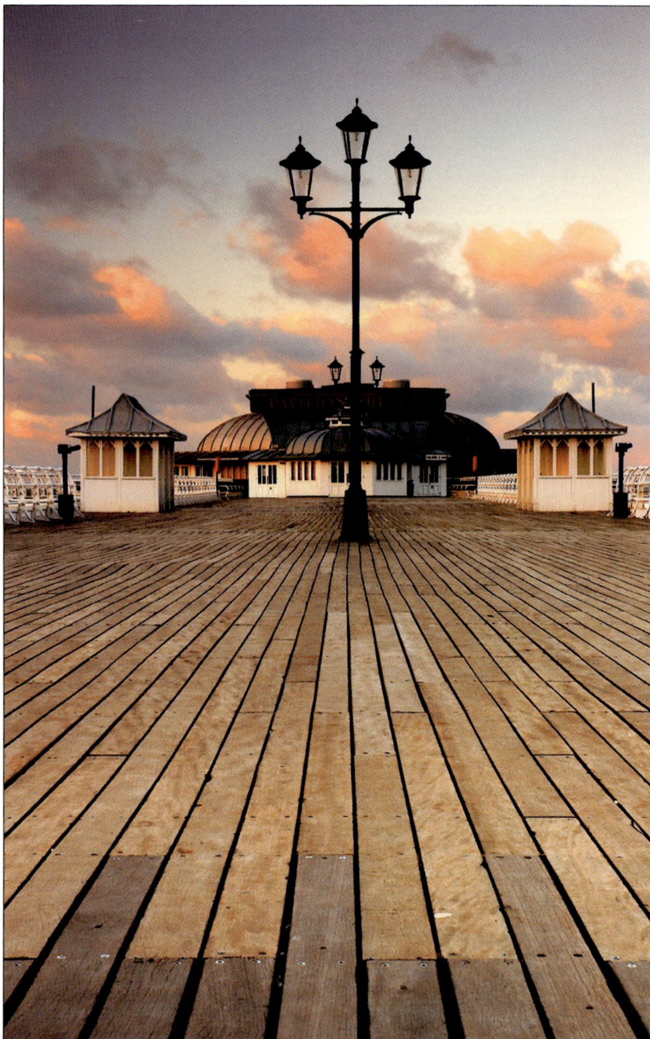

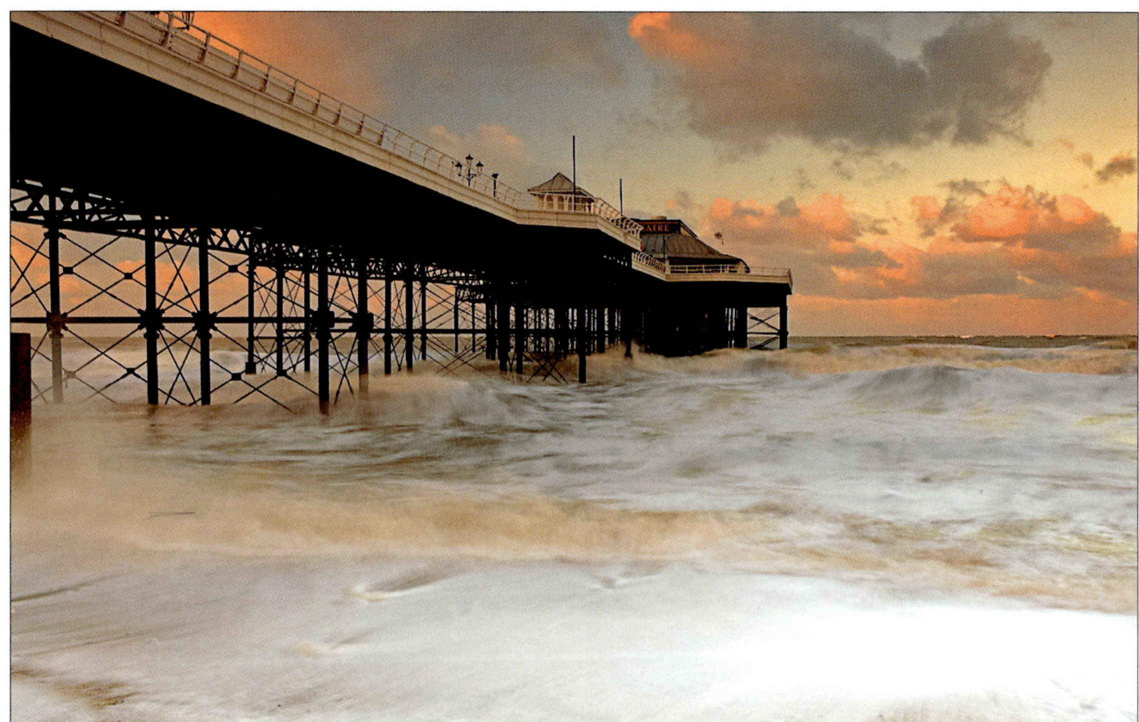

● All four shots taken using the Nikon D70 and RAW mode, at ISO200. Top: Holkham beach, Norfolk, with a 1/160sec at f/6 and a polariser + ND grad 0.6 filter. Middle: A 1/10sec exposure at f/22 of snow on the river at Blakeney, North Norfolk coast. Top right: The setting sun illuminates Cromer Pier, Norfolk. An ND Grad soft 0.9 has darkened the sky. Bottom: The same pier from the beach with a 1sec exposure.

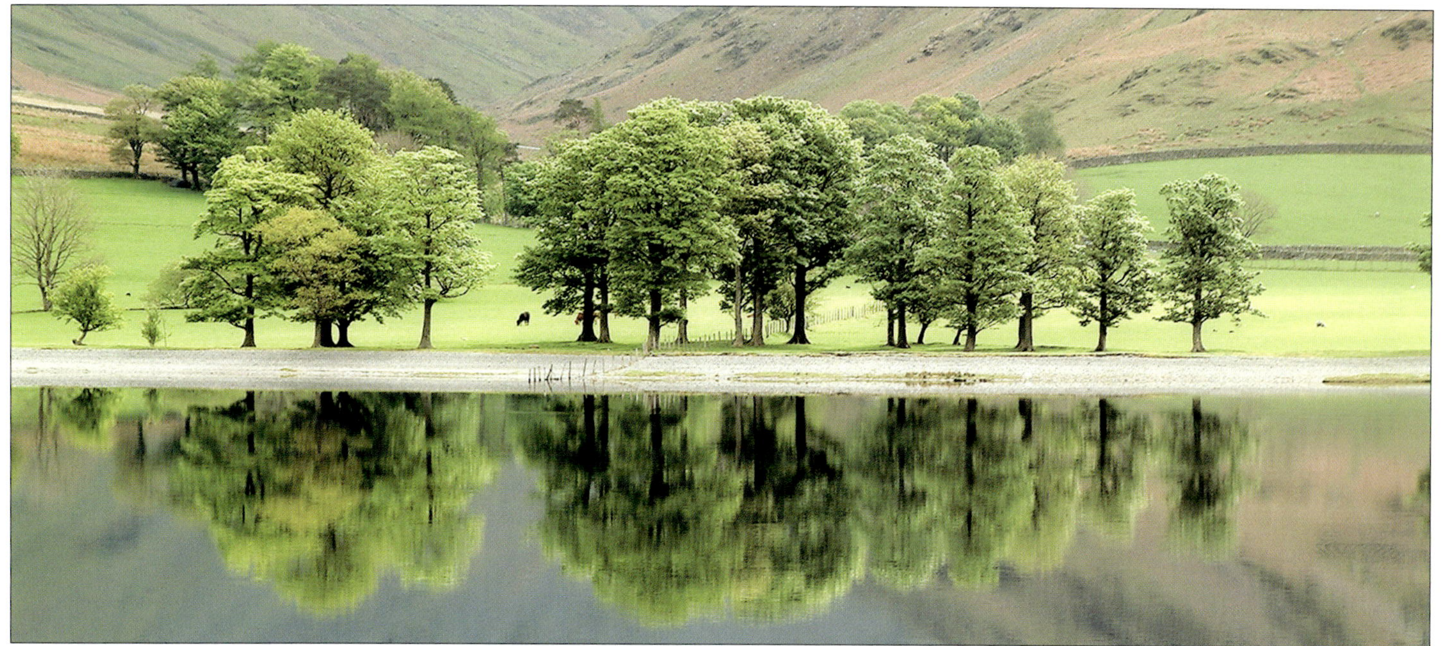

TERESA HILL When a lake is calm you can get some superb colourful reflections, like this example – taken using a Fuji Finepix S602 of Lake Buttermere in the Lake District.

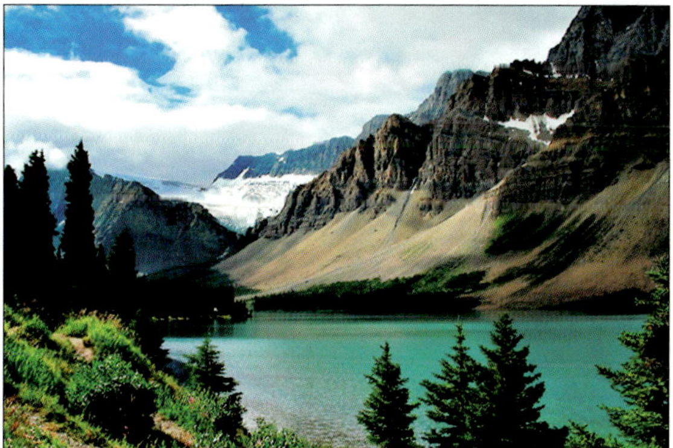

XIANG GUI Bow Lake in the Canadian Rockies. This scene sets off the spectacular mountains and the vivid green glacial waters.

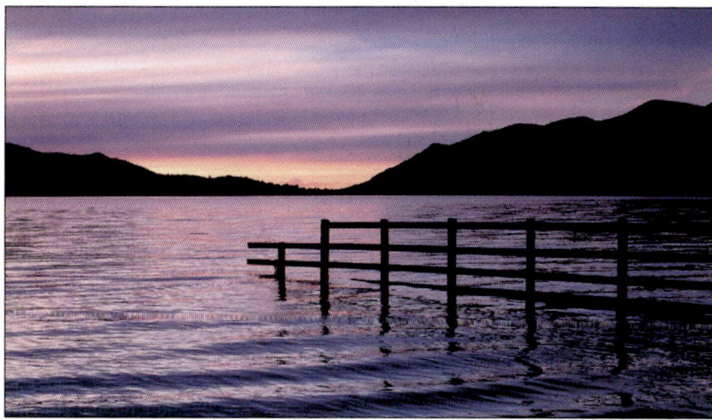

CHRIS GIRLING The end of a beautiful evening at Derwent Water, taken using a tripod mounted Fuji S602, fitted with a 0.6 grad filter.

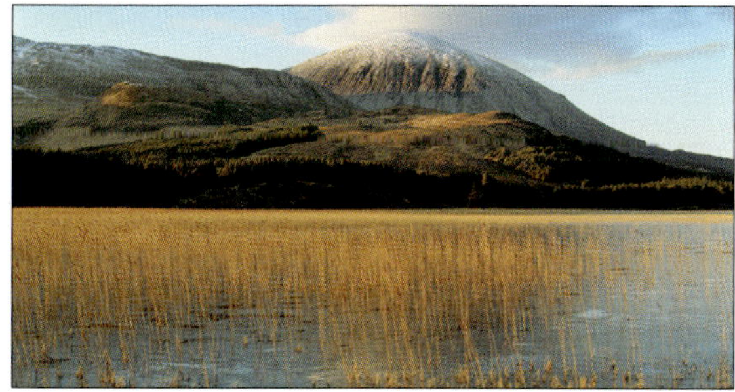

DOUGLAS SALTERI Beinn na Caillich looks down on Loch Cill Chriosd on the Isle of Skye as the reeds sway in the wind.

DIGITAL TECHNIQUE – CREATING MIRROR STYLE REFLECTIONS

Nothing beats the serene stillness of a lake to deliver a mirror reflection of your surrounding scenery – unless, of course, you have access to a computer!

1 Copy the photography. Select⇨ALL (Ctrl+A) and then extend the canvas size – Image⇨Canvas size. From the pop up window double the height measurement and select the top centre square. Click OK. Go to Edit⇨Paste and you should have an image with an equal amount of blank space at the bottom and a second layer with the pasted image in the centre.

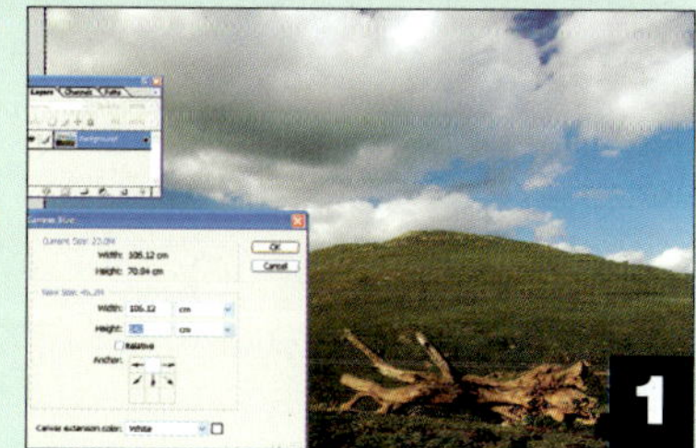

2 To position the image go to Edit⇨Transform⇨Flip Vertical and use the Move tool to drag the new pasted image so the two line up. You can use the keyboard's arrow keys to align precisely.

3 Go to Filter⇨Distort⇨Ocean Ripple and set a large Ripple size and a small ripple magnitude. Use the preview window to adjust to your preference. Once applied, you'll notice this filter has made the edge that lines up ragged. Use the rectangle marquee to trim off the ragged edge and then move the picture again so it lines up to the layer below.

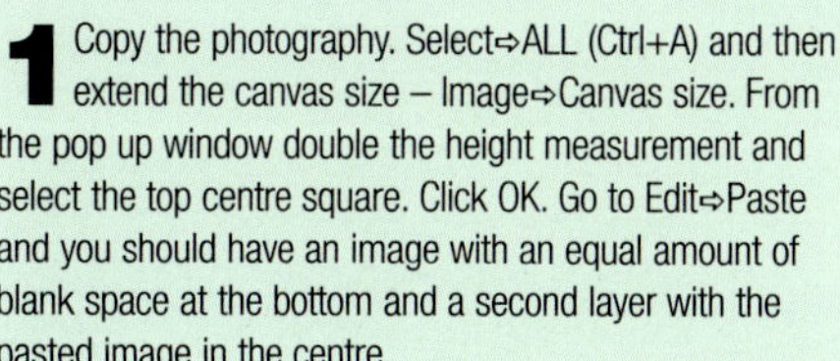

4 At the moment the lower layer looks too bright and unrealistic. You could use the lightness slider in the Hue/Saturation Adjustment, but I find it better to add a black fill layer and reduce the opacity of this for a more varied and natural looking effect. Create a new layer Layer⇨New⇨Layer (Shift+Ctrl+N). Make a selection the same size as the bottom layer, using the rectangle Marquee tool. Feather this by around 5 pixels to avoid a sharp edge – Select⇨Feather and fill with black Edit⇨Fill (Shift+F5). Set the opacity to around 50%.

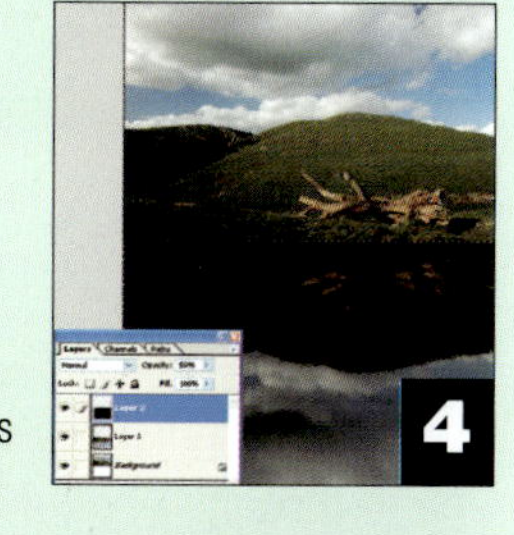

5 Now adjust the perspective of the reflection so it looks more natural. Make sure the reflection layer is active. Reduce the size of the canvas on screen (Ctrl -). Go to Edit⇨Transform⇨Distort. Click on the centre bottom square and drag down to stretch the image vertically. Then click on the left and right squares in turn and pull left and right to stretch the image a little.

6 Finally, select the black fill layer and, using the Eraser, set at a large, feathered brush size and paint over the edge to remove the sharp line, making the reflection below appear as though it's blending with the upper layer.

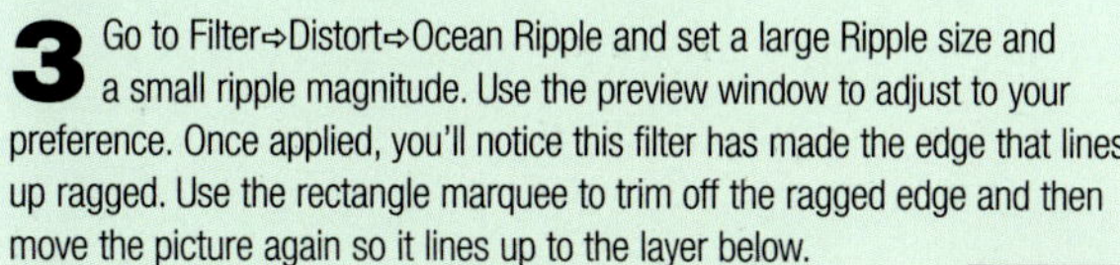

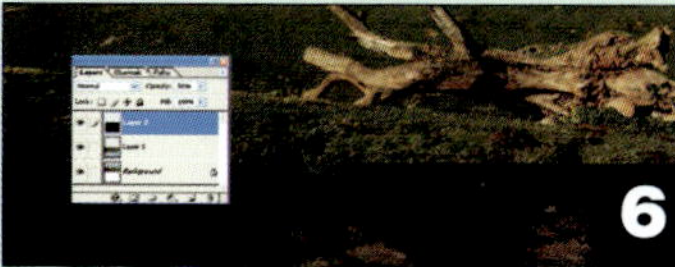

GRADUATING WITH HONOUR

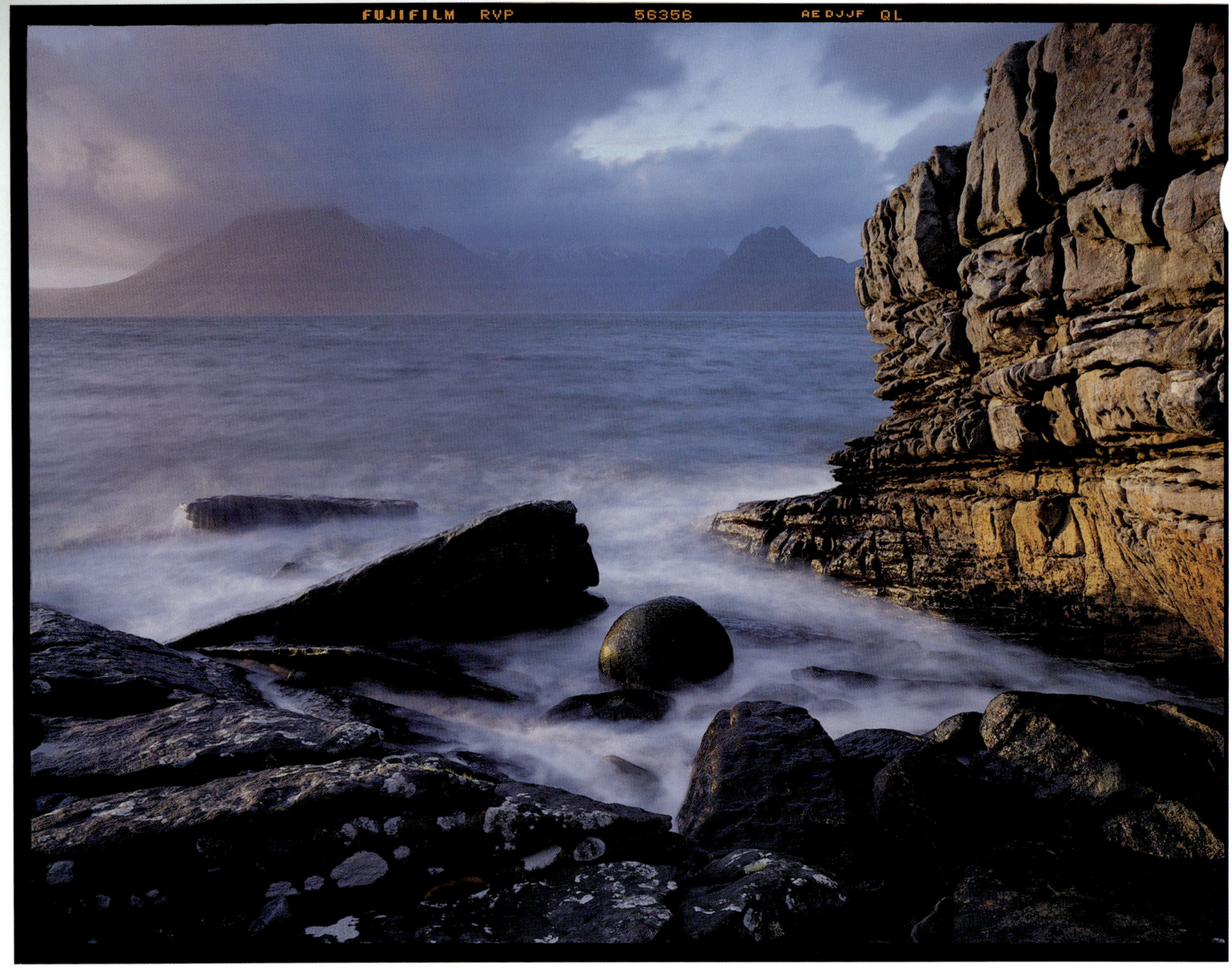

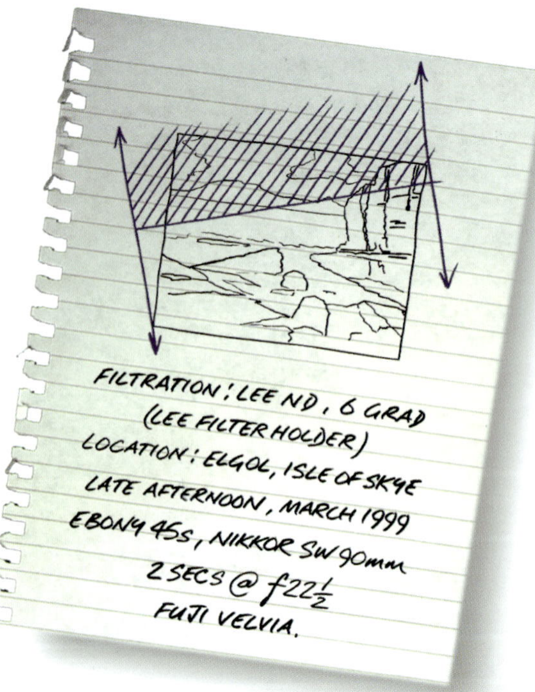

In the final analysis, all technique is there to serve a purpose. When photographing wild landscape, my aim is to reflect its raw beauty and emotional power and, hopefully, honour the earth through photography. Shooting on transparency film, I need to achieve perfection in camera rather than at a printing stage. Top quality N.D. graduated filters go a long way to helping me realise my goal. In this example, the filter darkened down the otherwise too bright sky and mountains without corrupting their colour, so containing the energy of the composition and opening up the foreground. Lens performance was unaffected.

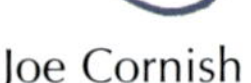

Joe Cornish

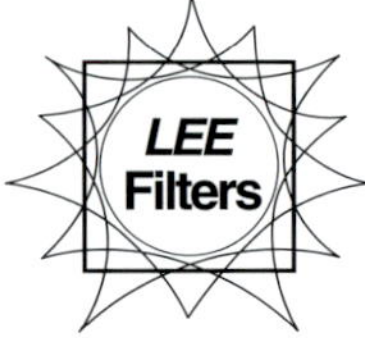

INSPIRING PROFESSIONALS

Tel: (01264) 335919   Fax: 355058   www.leefilters.com

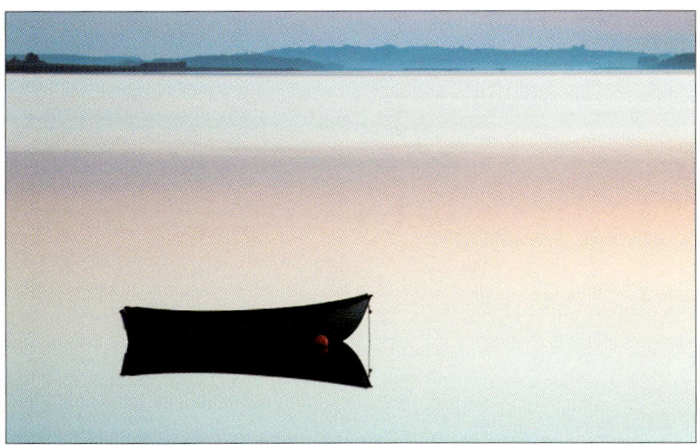

● PETER STEWART A 15sec exposure at f/8 gave the smooth tones Peter was looking for and saturation was increased in Photoshop.

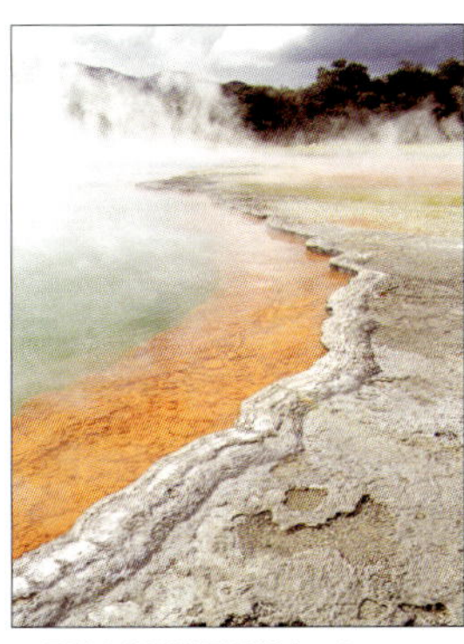

● TOM COWLEY Wai-o-tapu Thermal Park, New Zealand.

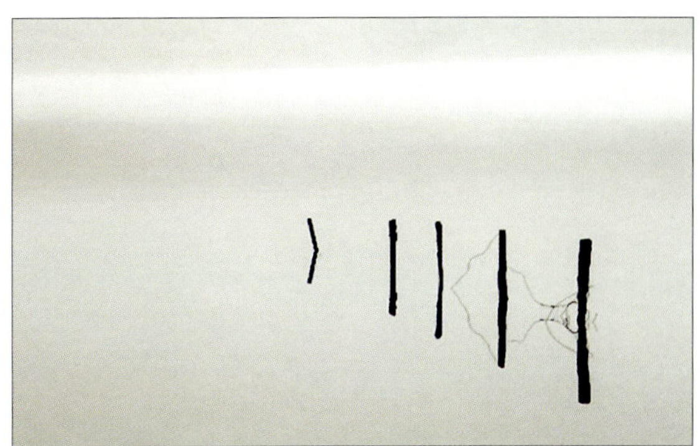

● DAVID WATSON Fence posts appear to be floating on Loch Lomond in Scotland, shot with an Olympus C920z digital camera.

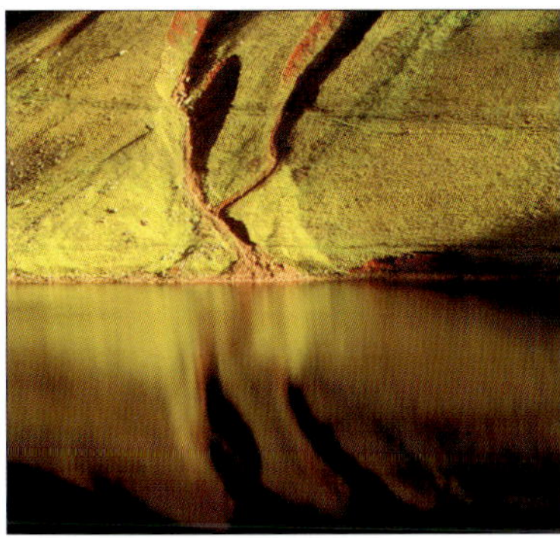

● JON DIXON Evening sunlight on Bannau Sir Gaer, South Wales.

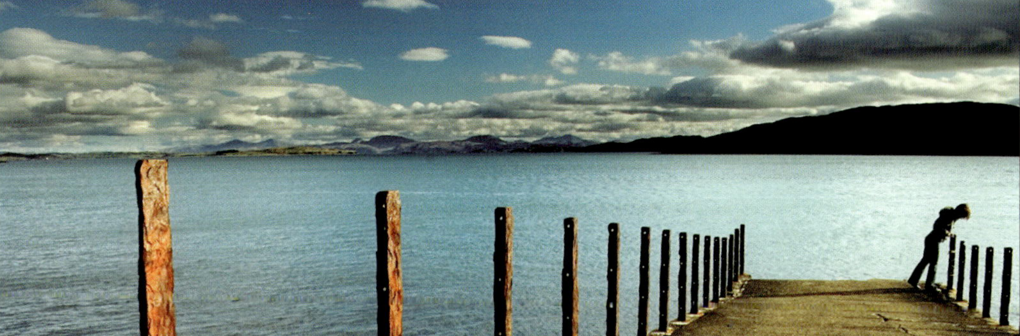

● PAUL GAUGHAN The standard 18-55mm was set at f/22 on the Canon EOS 300D to take this scene looking across to the Isle of Jura. A polarising filter was attached and the shutter speed was 1/30sec.

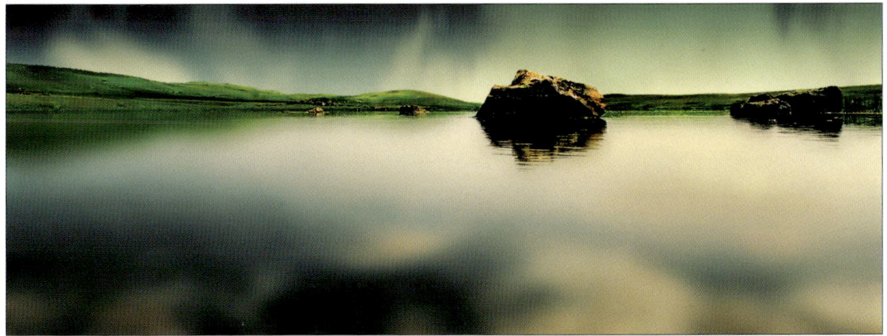

● EWAN RAYMENT Lying on the ground with his elbows in the water allowed Ewan to take this panoramic image of a small lake in Shetland, Scotland.

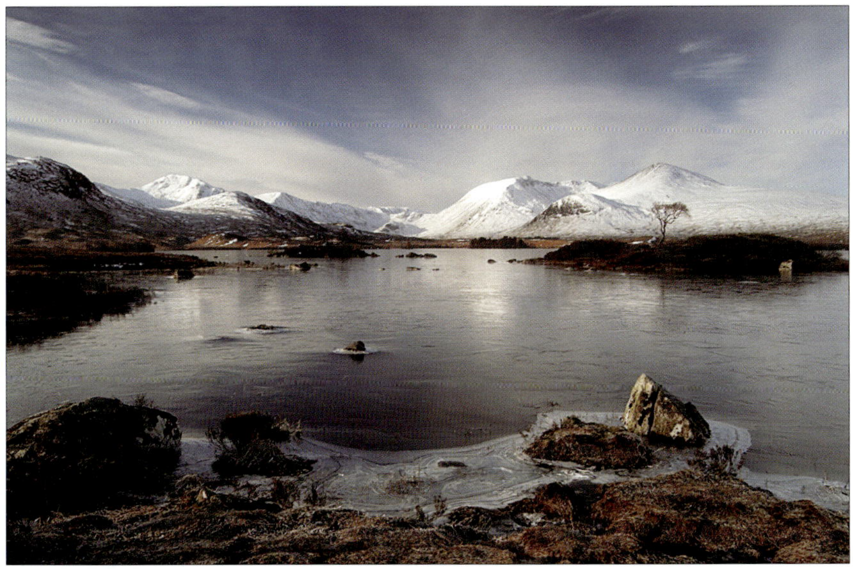

● JULIAN EVANS The Blackmount looking across a frozen Lochan na h-Achlaise, Scotland, using the Fuji S2 Pro and Nikkor 18-35mm.

EQUIPMENT – ESSENTIAL LANDSCAPE FILTERS

Digital photography has made most of the special effects filters that we've encountered over the years redundant. Most of the effects can be created using an image editing program. There are a few optical filters, however, that any landscape photographer shouldn't be without.

■ **Polariser** The most useful filter in any landscape photographer's bag. Rotates in its mount to reduce reflections on any non-metallic surface. Use this to reduce reflections on foliage, water and wet rocks while at the same time deepening blue skies, making scenes look vivid in colour. Buy a linear variety for older mechanical cameras and a circular for all modern digitals.

■ **Neutral density** Essential for those who shoot waterfalls and want a slow blurring effect. The ND filter is a neutral grey colour and reduces the exposure by one stop (NDx2), two stops (NDx4) or 3 stops (NDx8). Some manufacturers make stronger ones up to 6 stops (NDx64). B+W go right up to the 20 stop Sun filter, but that would have little use for landscape photographers.

■ **Neutral density grad** Similar to a normal ND filter but half of the filter is clear and a gradient of tone between the two ensures you don't see a line across the photo. These are used to balance the exposure of the lighter tone of a sky with the darker tone of the ground. Like ND filters they are available in different strengths.

■ **81 Series Warm** This is a light brown/straw coloured filter that gives the scene a warm glow and is perfect for shooting at midday where the scene may have a slight blue tone. It can also be useful in the morning or evening to enhance the golden tones of the sun.

■ **UV or Skylight 1B** The UV is a clear filter and the skylight has a slight pink tone, both are used to reduce haze. Most people buy this kind of filter to protect the front element of their lens from dust, scratches or knocks. It's obviously cheaper to replace a £10 filter than a £300 lens!

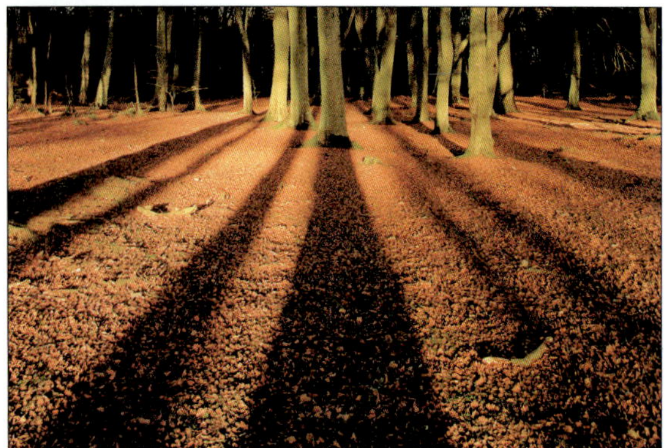

● MAGGIE BRODIE These shadows of beech trees were taken in a local wood on a December afternoon, using a Nikon D70.

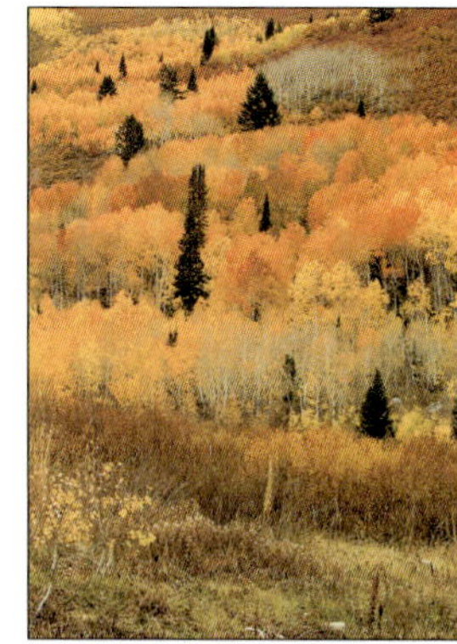

● BILL MATSON Autumn in the mountains of Utah, Alpine Loop.

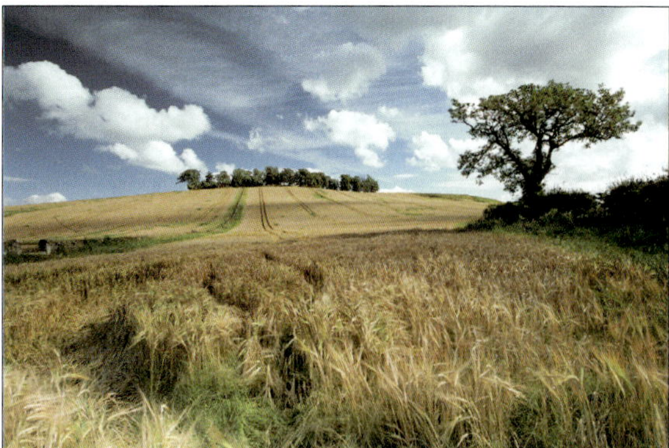

● BRIAN D CLARKE A barley field in Fife, Scotland, taken using a Nikon F5 with 17-35mm Nikkor lens set at 17mm.

DIGITAL TECHNIQUE – CREATE AN AUTUMN EFFECT

■ Use Photoshop's Replace Colour option to replace a season. Here we show you how to turn Summer into Autumn in a few simple steps.

1 I've chosen a photo that only has a few leaves because it's easier to illustrate the effect and less complicated but will give you an idea of what's possible using Photoshop's Replace Colour mode.

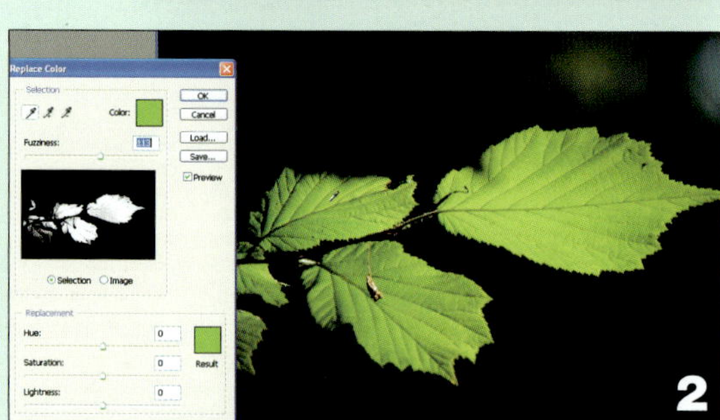

2 Go to Image⇒Adjustments⇒ Replace colour. From the pop-up palette make sure Selection is chosen so you see a small black and white preview image. Click anywhere on the image in this window or on the actual photo you are editing and a selection will be made. The black and white preview will show areas of colour that will change as white and unaffected areas as black. In this example I clicked on the centre of one of the green leaves.

3 Adjust the fuzziness slider until all the area you want to change is white. The small colour square at the top of the palette represents the average colour value of the area you have selected.

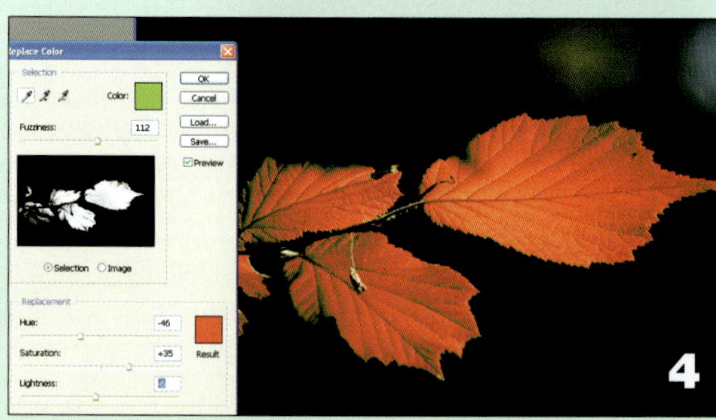

4 The other colour square, bottom right of the palette, indicates the colour that you are now going to change your selection to using the three Hue, Saturation and Lightness sliders. Adjust these until you achieve the desired colour in the image on screen. Notice in this screengrab that there's still some green that hasn't been picked up in our first selection.

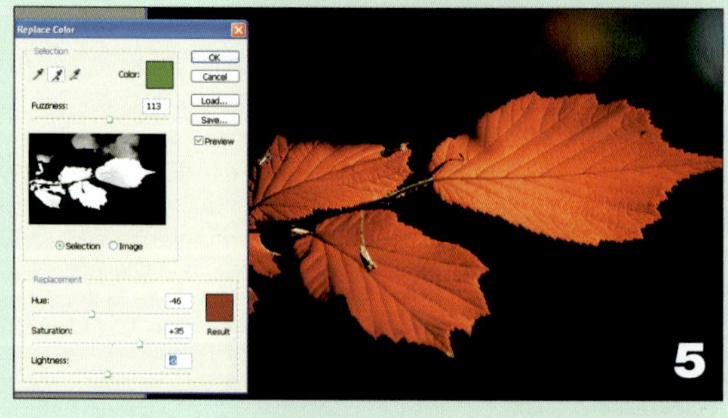

5 To rectify this, either move the threshold slider further to the right or, as I did here, click on the + Eyedropper tool and on one of the remaining green colour values within the photo that needs to be included. This colour replacement technique is very useful for many areas of photography.

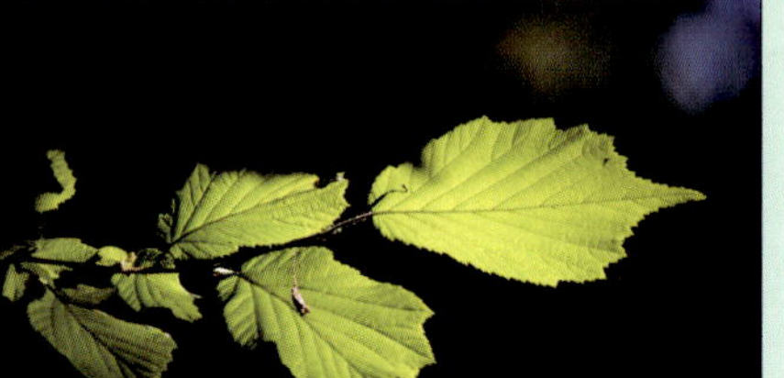

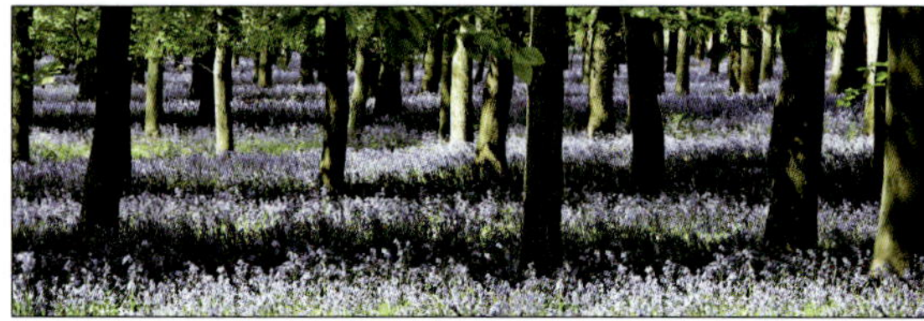

● CHRIS SHEPHERD In early May, Ashridge Forest on the outskirts of Berkhamsted is covered in a carpet of bluebells.

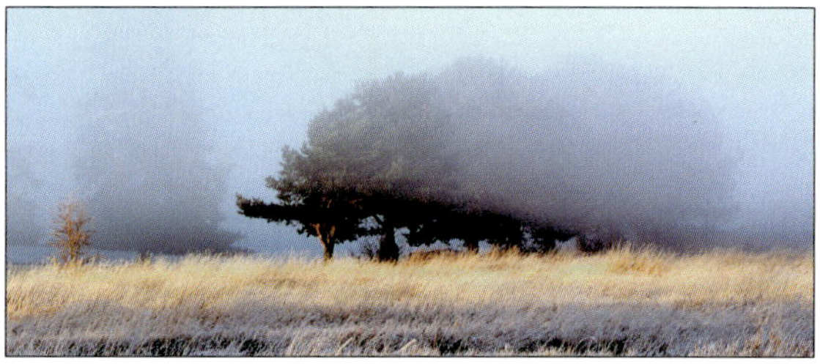

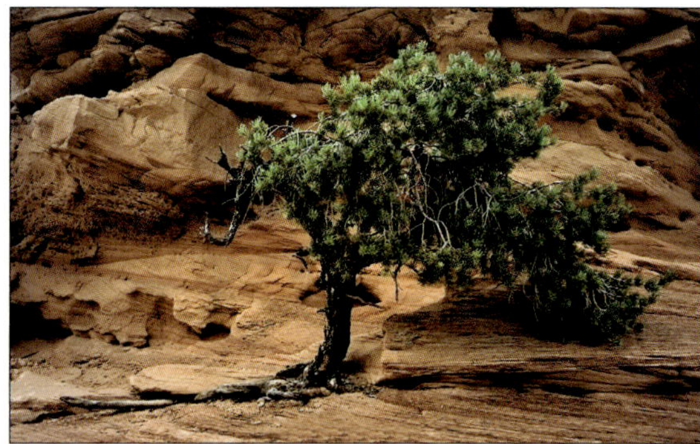

● CHRISTOPHER YUCHYM The fog was created by the sunlight hitting the frozen grass, melting and creating this beautiful scene.

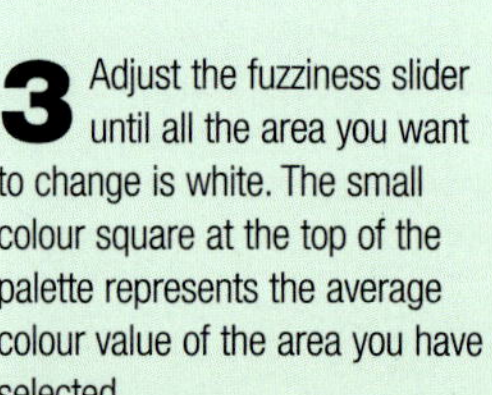

● ALAN WILLIAMS Dwarf juniper tree at Canyonlands National Park, Utah, taken using a Leica Minilux Zoom loaded with Fuji Provia 100F.

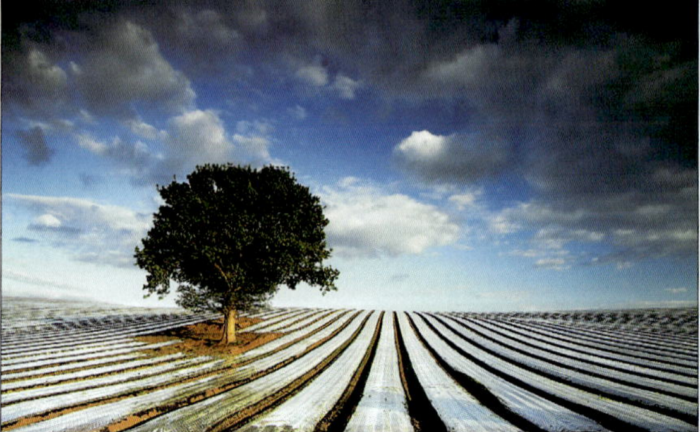

● IAN WESTLAKE The lines and contrast between the polythene and trees attracted me to this scene, shot using a Cokin 121S ND grad.

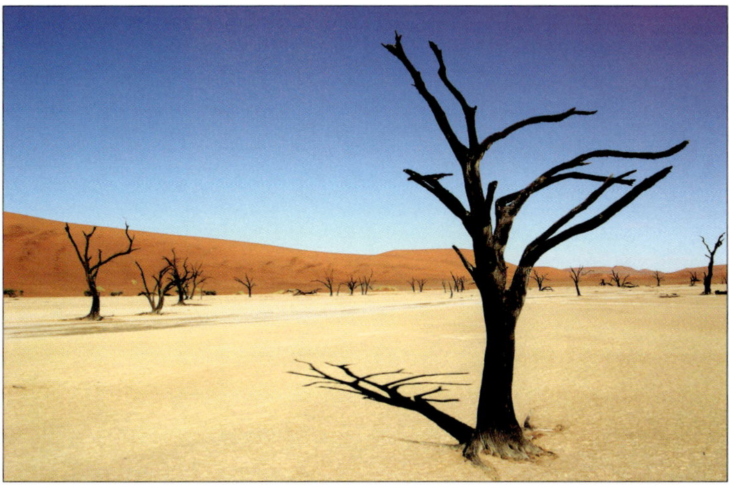

● CAROLINE BEEVIS Ancient Friends, 600-year-old dead trees in Dead Vlei, Sossusvlei, Namibia, taken using a Nikon Coolpix 4300.

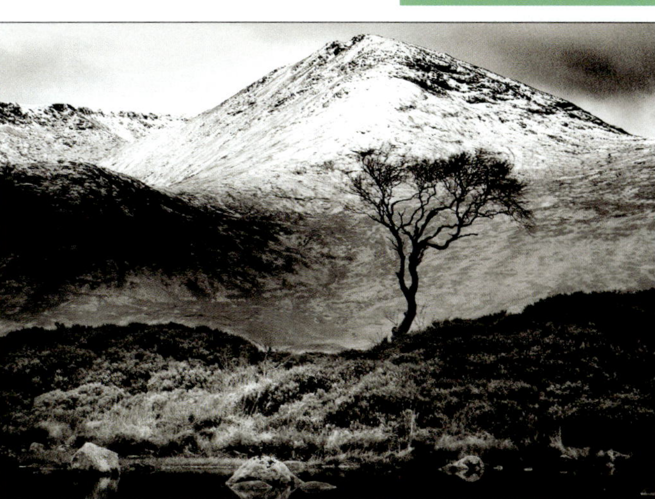

● DAVID DUNN Rannoch, shot on a very bad weather day to show that not all good landscapes have to be taken on sunny days.

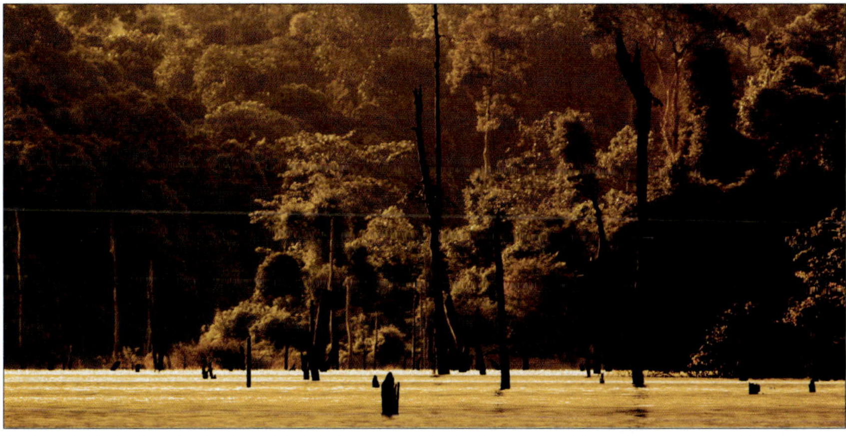

● KEN SU Lake Kenyir, Southeast Asia's largest artificial lake, taken with a 300mm lens and an exposure of 1/500sec at f/5.6. A warming filter was attached to give the golden hue.

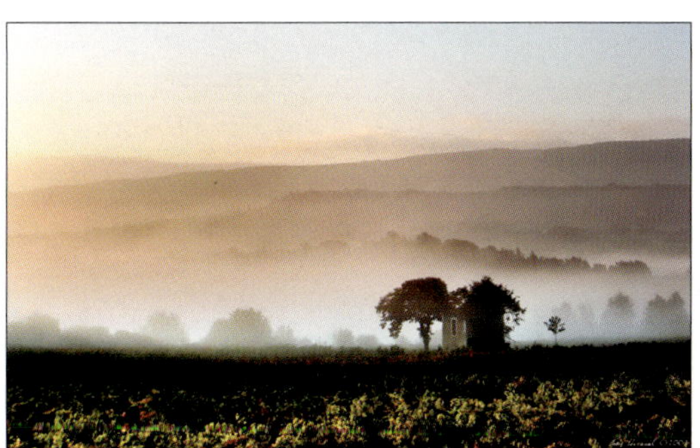

● TIM PERCIVAL Early morning at the village of Goult, Provence. It's classic wine country and I like the wine in the mist!

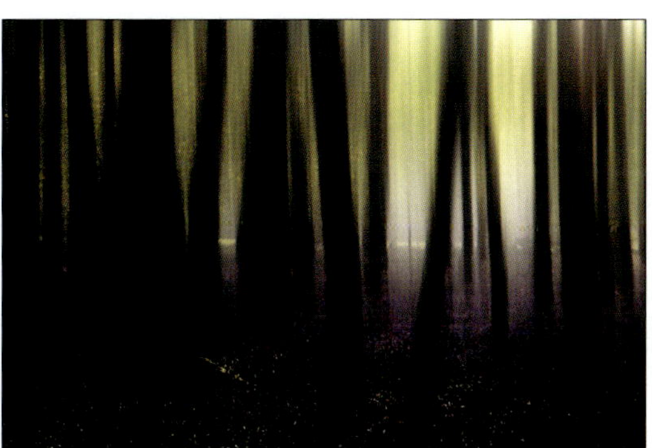

● COLIN MILL Bluebell woods at Ashridge. A vaseline smeared filter was placed over the lens to get this streaky effect.

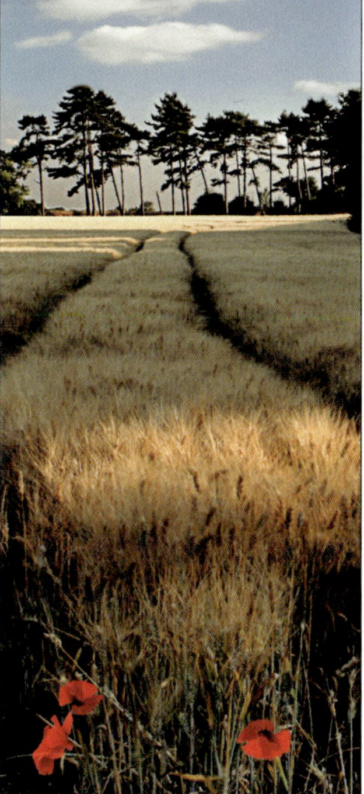

● TONY HEPWORTH Poppies on the edge of a field in Hertfordshire.

LOCATION GUIDE – FORESTS TO VISIT

■ **Sherwood Forest**, Nottinghamshire. One of the most visited woods in England, partly because of tourists attracted by the legend of Robin Hood. It has some of the oldest trees in Europe, including the 800 year old major oak. As well as oak, you'll find silver birch, Scots pine, small-leafed lime, birch, holly, hawthorn and wild cherry. **www.sherwoodforest.org.uk**

■ **The Forest of Dean** in Gloucestershire is one of England's last remaining ancient forests and occupies an area of 27,000 acres. Around 20 million trees can be found including oak, beech, ash, birch and holly. **www.forestofdean.gov.uk**

■ **The National Forest**, set up in 1990, covers 200 square miles, spanning Derbyshire, Leicestershire and Staffordshire in the Midlands. It blends ancient woodlands and new planting to frame a variety of farms, open country, towns and villages. **www.nationalforest.org**

■ **The New Forest,** Hampshire, is a photographer's paradise with an area of around 93,500 acres, including around 30,000 acres of woodland, 20,000 acres of heathland, 10,000 acres of grassland and 133 ponds. Attractions include the New Forest Ponies and around 46 species of rare plants. Trees include Beech, Oak and Pine. Over 1000 species of fungi have been recorded! **www.thenewforest.co.uk**

■ **Burnham Beeches**, Buckinghamshire is regarded as one of the best examples of ancient woodland in Britain and includes 500 year old beech trees. Covering 540 acres it attracts around 500,000 visitors a year who will see a population of woodpeckers, woodcock, tawny owls, foxes, dragonflies and some of Britain's rarest invertebrates. **www.cityoflondon.gov.uk**

■ **Epping Forest** is the largest open space available to the public in the London area, measuring 6000 acres. Two-thirds of the forest is wooded, with 50 different types of trees and large shrubs. Residents include all three species of woodpecker, plus nightingales, hawfinch, tree creepers and nuthatches. There are also over 80 artificial ponds and lakes, 650 plant species and more than 1500 species of fungi. **www.cityoflondon.gov.uk**

■ **Glen Finglas**, Loch Lomond and the Trossachs is a 4085 hectare woodland at the heart of Scotland's first National Park. The woodlands include willow, oak, birch, hazel, rowan and alder with scattered areas of juniper, ash, bird cherry and aspen. **www.glen-finglas.info**

■ **Westonbirt,** Gloucester is open 365 days a year with a collection containing around 18,000 trees and shrubs, covering 600 acres. It's well worth a visit in autumn for the colourful maples. **www.forestry.gov.uk**

■ **Afan Forest Park,** West Glamorgan, is part of the 30,000 hectare Valleys Forest – the largest urban forest in Europe. It includes a colourful mixture of maturing larch crops, ancient oak woodlands, varied evergreen conifers, open areas of green fields, bracken and heather. **www.forestry.gov.uk**

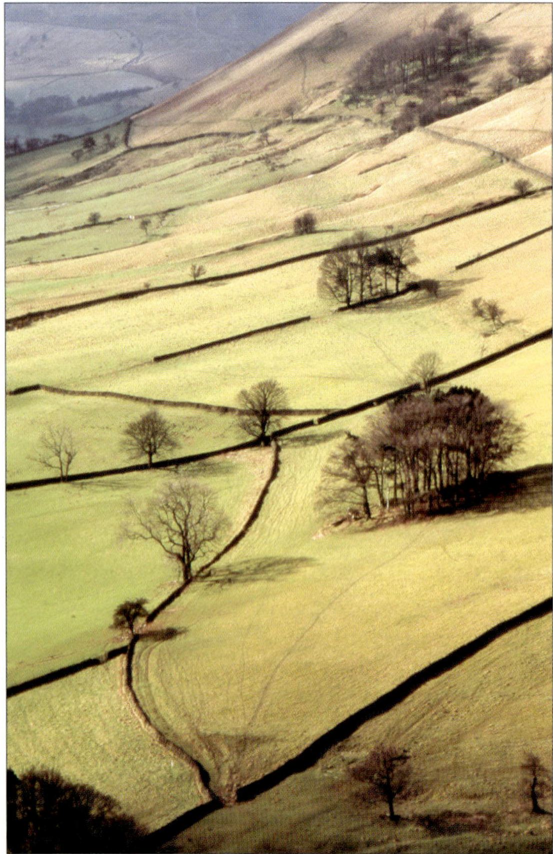

● SIMON FALCONER View Near Edale, Derbyshire, using Fuji Sensia 100 film in a Nikon F-801 with Nikon 70-210mm zoom at 210mm.

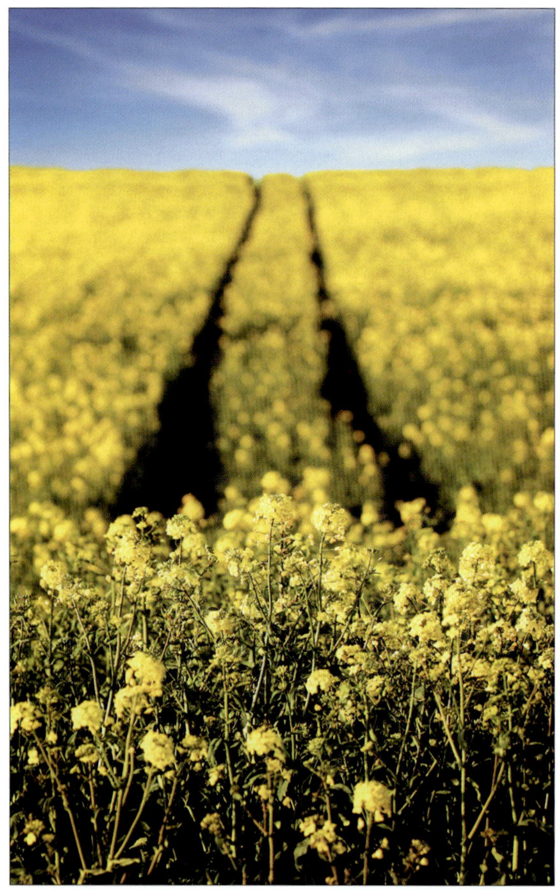

● NIGEL SHARMAN Great use of rule of thirds, sharp foreground, shallow focus and plough lines going off towards a vanishing point.

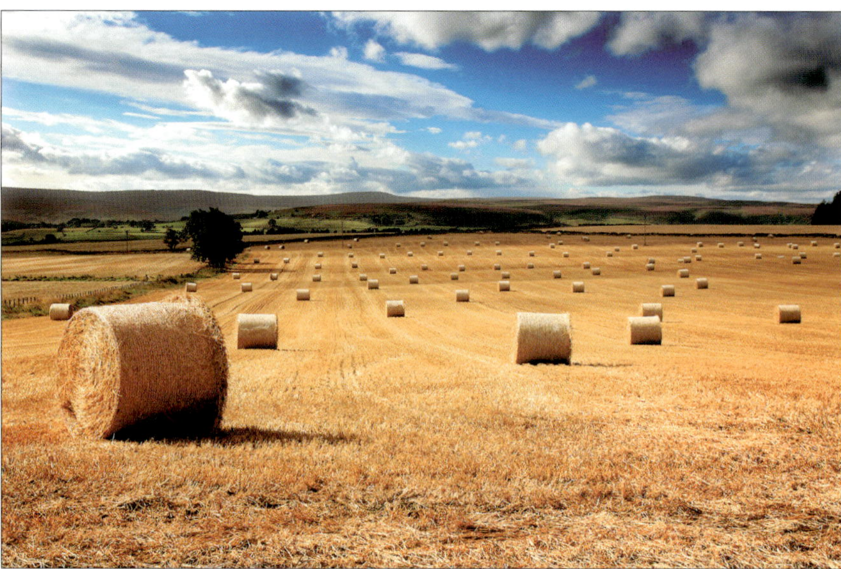

● CHRIS CEASER Sunkissed hay bales on the edge of the Derwent Valley, Co Durham, taken using a 1/250sec exposure at f/13. Move around while looking through the viewfinder to avoid overlapping bales.

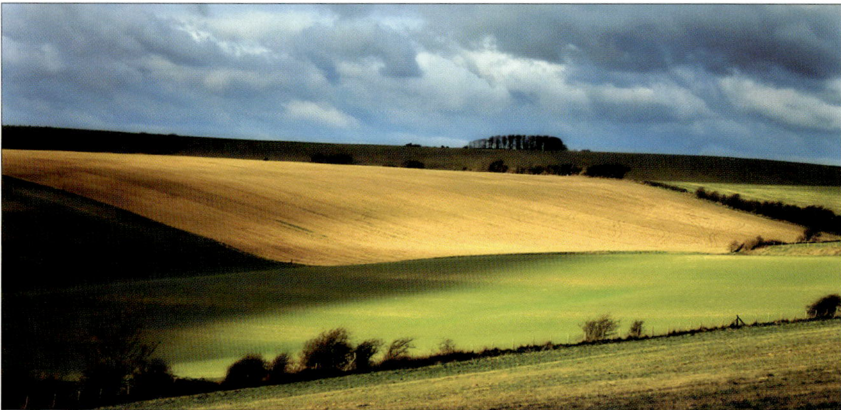

● DENNIS REDDICK To get the balance, I combined two different exposures – one of the fields, the other of the broody sky, both from a Canon 300D, into one image using Photoshop 7.

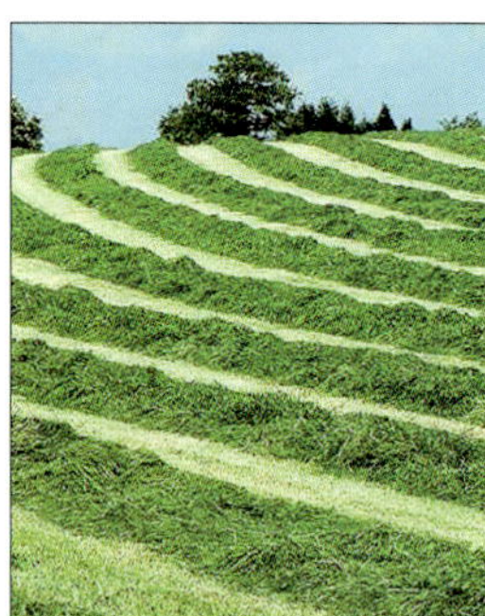

● BRIAN GRIFFITHS Look out for interesting patterns in fields!

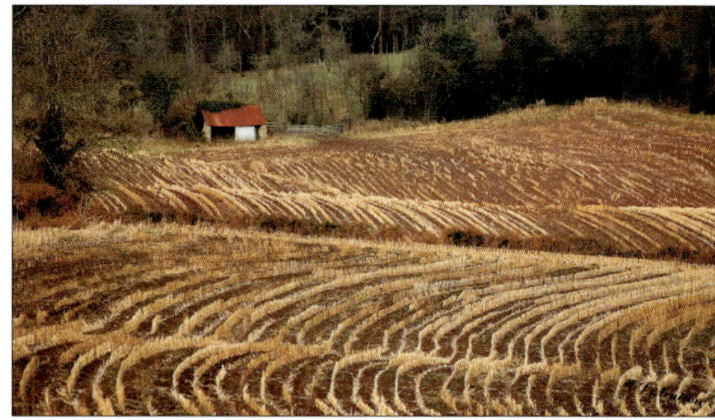

● MICHAEL ARNISON Straw stubble, taken in January when the sun was quite low, using a zoom lens set at 200mm and f/4.5.

LANDSCAPE TIPS

■ Use plough lines to split the photographs or guide your eye to a specific part of the scene.
■ Ask for the farmer's permission if you intend going into farm fields that aren't marked as public pathways.
■ On cloudy days wait for a break and the sun to spill across the fields.

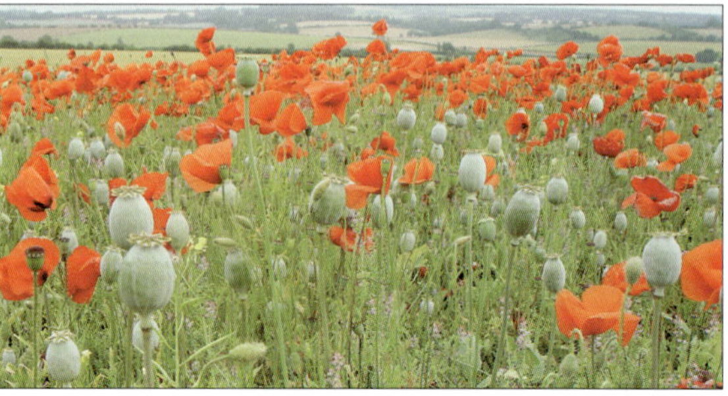

● PADDY HINTON A low level shot of a flowering poppy field near King Somborne in Hampshire.

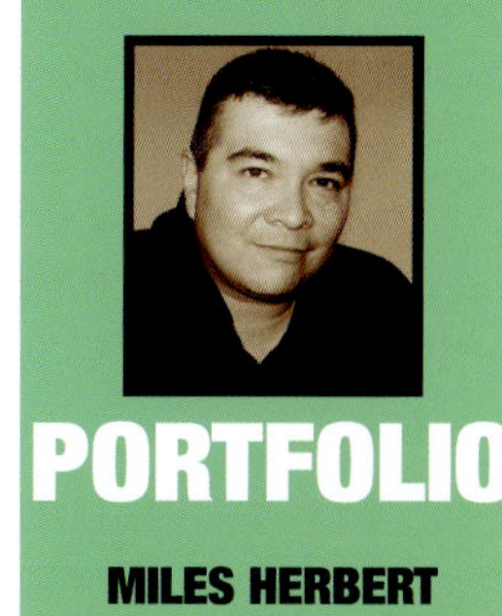

PORTFOLIO

MILES HERBERT
Miles is a landscape
enthusiast who is starting to
turn passion into profit

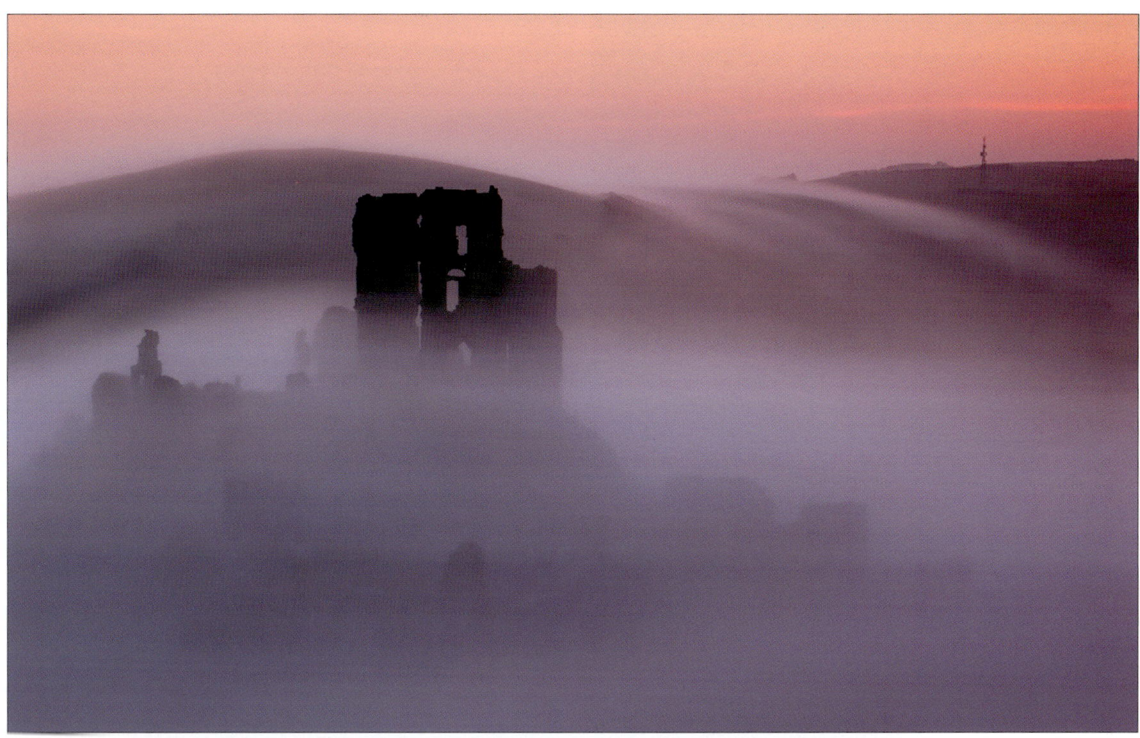

● Corfe Castle in Dorset
emerges from the mist in
the cold pre-dawn light,
taken with a Lee 0.6ND
Grad and 81B warm-up
filter. Having climbed the
hill in the dark, I sat down
to wait for the light and
as it got lighter I could
see the mist flowing
through the gaps in the
hills and rolling down into
the valley. That was when
I started to get that tingle
of excitement and I knew
it was going to be one of
those special days!

**It was in summer 2002, after
watching an amazing sunset
on Chesil Beach in Dorset,
that photography became a
serious hobby. I realised my
digital point and shoot camera
just wasn't up to the job and
since then have used several
different cameras, before finally
settling on my current Nikons.**

I particularly enjoy landscape
photography; there is something
magical in being sat up on a
hill, shivering and alone in the
pre-dawn darkness and trying to
capture that special moment.

I must confess to being
somewhat of a perfectionist though
– if the scene isn't right, I'm quite
happy to walk away empty handed
and return another day when
conditions look right again.

For landscape photography
you need patience and dedication
– these will be rewarded in the
long run. It also pays to know your
camera and equipment inside out.
When you know the strengths and
limitations of your equipment it will
be easier to get the most out of it.

I always make sure I have a
good look around the frame before
pressing the shutter button. It's
surprising how many times there's
something in the frame that goes
unnoticed in the background
because you're concentrating so
hard on the main subject. But that
one little thing can ruin the image.

As well as landscape
photography I also enjoy
photographing nature, especially
shots of animals and birds.

My future in photography is
looking bright. What started off
as just a hobby is slowly heading
off in a different direction and
has reached a point where it may
become my main source of income.
With a little more time invested in
the business, who knows what the
future may bring! ■
www.captive-light.com

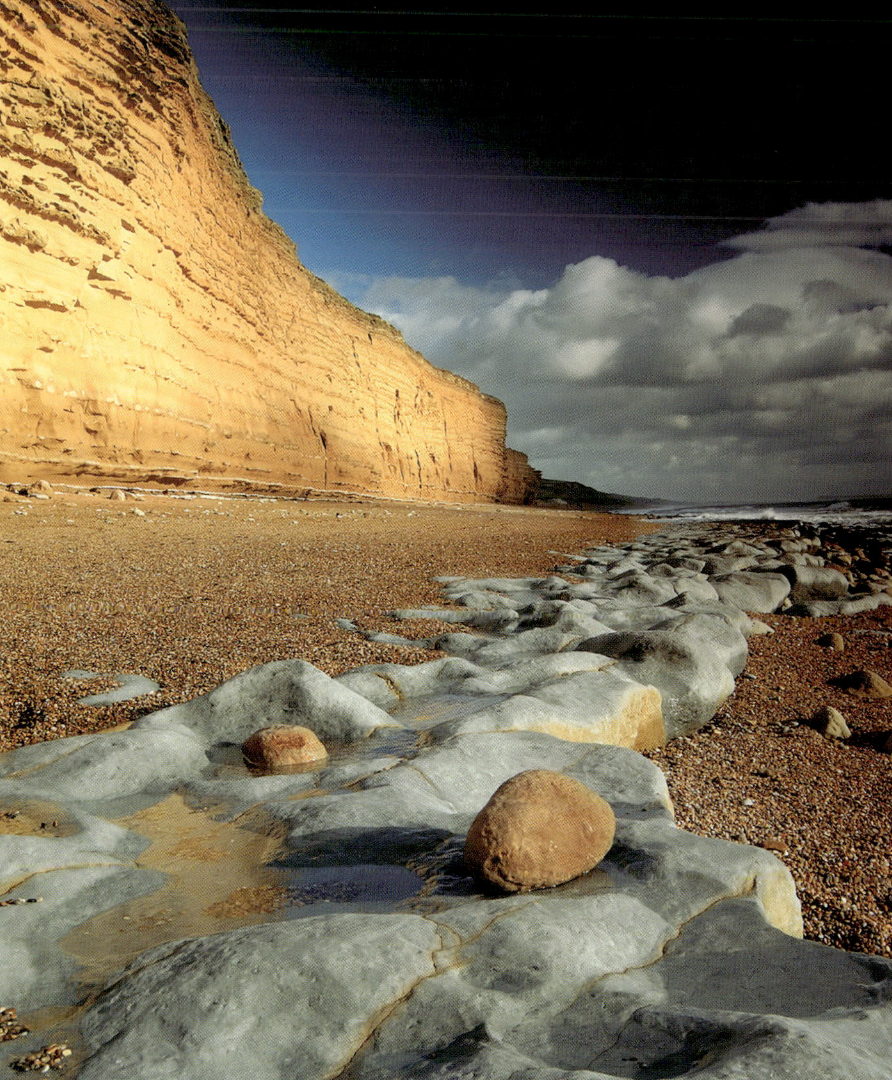

● The cliffs and rock
ledges at Burton
Bradstock at low tide in
Dorset. I was hoping for
better weather and had
to wait about an hour for
a whole five minutes of
patchy sunlight to take
this shot.

PLACES TO GO

■ **Want to photograph lighthouses?** Check out these around the UK: Arbroath Signal Tower, Scotland ● Ardnamurchan, Argyll ● Beachy Head, Sussex ● Blacknore Point, Bristol ● Dungeness Old, Kent ● Eddystone, Plymouth ● Flamborough, North Yorkshire ● Flatholm, Bristol ● Godrevy, Cornwall ● Happisburgh, Norfolk ● Killantringan, Galloway ● Kinnaird Head, Fraserburgh ● Leasowe, Wirral ● Lizard, Cornwall ● Longships, Cornwall ● Maughold Head, Isle of Man ● New Brighton, Wirral ● Orfordness, Suffolk ● Pendeen, Cornwall ● Portland Bill, Dorset ● Skerries, Anglesey ● Smeaton's Tower, Plymouth Hoe ● Souter, Sunderland ● South Foreland, Kent ● South Stack, Anglesey ● St. Anthony's, Cornwall ● St Catherine's Oratory, Isle of Wight ● St Mary's, Tyne and Wear ● Start Point, Dartmouth ● Trevose Head, Cornwall ● Trwyn Du, Anglesey ● Withernsea, East Yorkshire.

■ **Prefer windmills?** Check out these around the UK:
Kent: Herne Hill ● Drapers, Margate ● Chillenden Mill ● West Kingsdown ● Meopham ● Union Mill ● Cranbrook ● Stelling Minnis ● Stocks Mill ● Wittersham.
Lincolnshire: Sibsey Trader Mill ● Ellis Mill ● Dobson's Mill ● Maud Foster Mill ● Alford Mill ● Heckington Windmill.
Cambridgeshire: Bourn Post Mill ● Barnack ● Burwell tower ● Fulbourn Windmill; Foster's Mill ● Swaffham Prior, Wicken.
Norfolk: Berney Arms ● Brograve Mill ● Denver Mill ● Horsey Mill ● Dereham Mill ● Lingford Cornmill ● Stow Mill, Paston ● Stracey Arms Drainage Mill ● Old Buckenham Cornmill ● Thurne Dyke Drainage Mill ● Wicklewood Cornmill.
Others: Wilton Mill, Wiltshire ● Arnesby, Leicestershire ● Lowe's Mill Thaxted, Essex ● Lytham Mill, Lancashire ● Chesterton Windmill, Warwickshire ● Wilton Windmill, Wiltshire ● Pakenham Windmill, Suffolk ● Saxtead Green Post Mill, Suffolk ● Polegate Windmill, Sussex ● Stott Park Bobbin Mill, Cumbria ● Shipley WindmilL, Sussex
Visit **www.windmillworld.com**

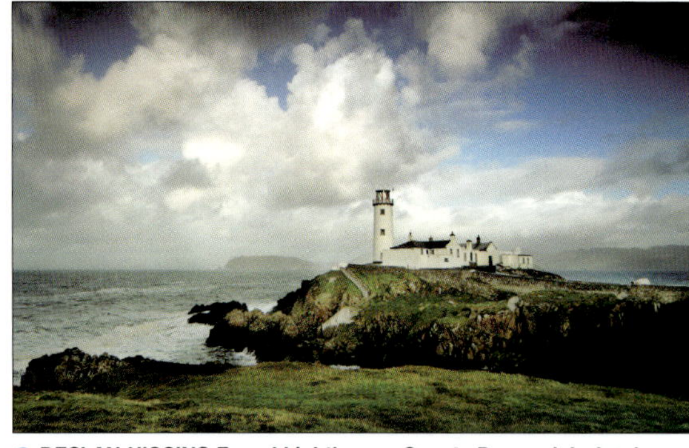

● **DECLAN HIGGINS** Fanad Lighthouse, County Donegal, Ireland, taken just before a storm. A polariser and ND grad were used.

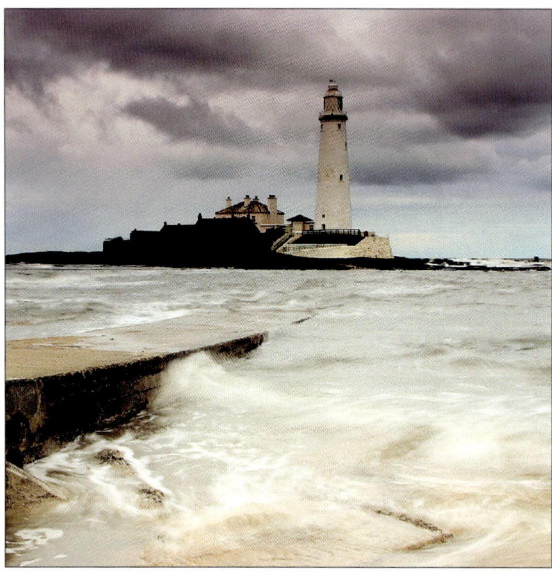

● **MARK MULCAHY** St Mary's, Whitley Bay on a blustery day, taken using a Canon EOS 10D with a 24mm lens, polariser and ND Grad.

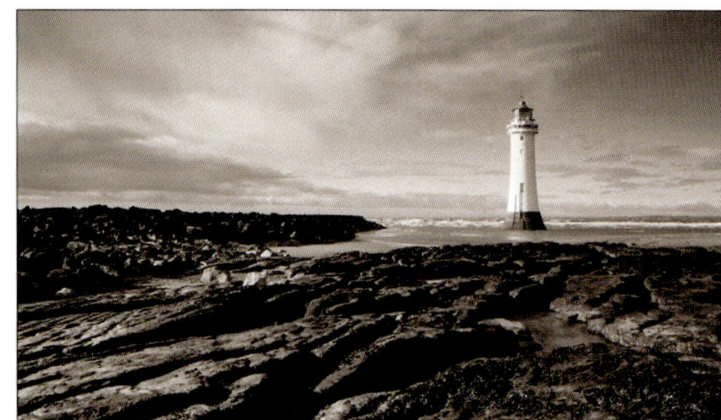

● **STUART WHITTINGHAM** New Brighton Lighthouse, taken using a Canon EOS 300D and Tamron 17-35mm set at f/22.

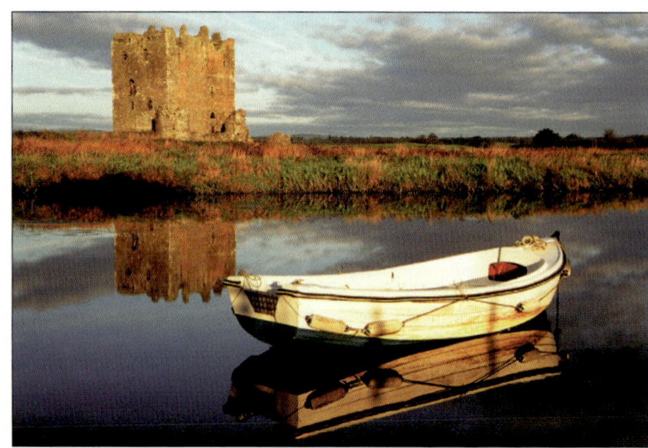

● **DAVID DALZIEL** Threave Castle, Dumfries and Galloway, taken shortly after sunrise on a perfectly calm, late summer morning.

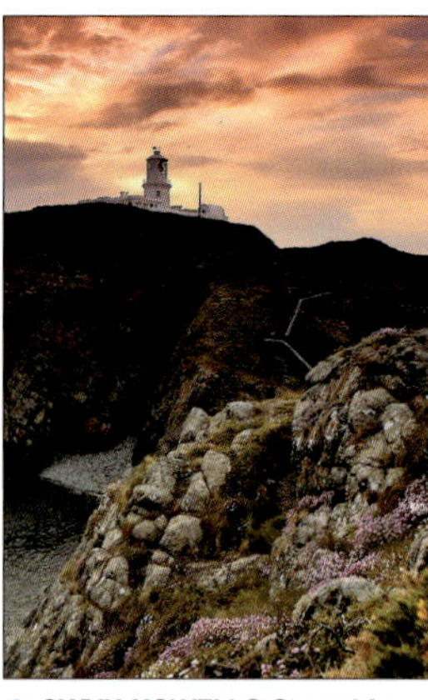

● **GWYN HOWELLS** Strumble Head lighthouse, Pembrokeshire.

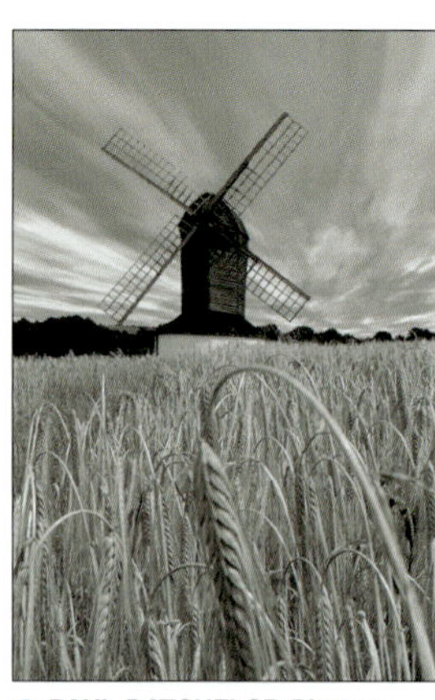

● **PAUL BATCHELOR** Pitstone Windmill, Ivinghoe, Bucks

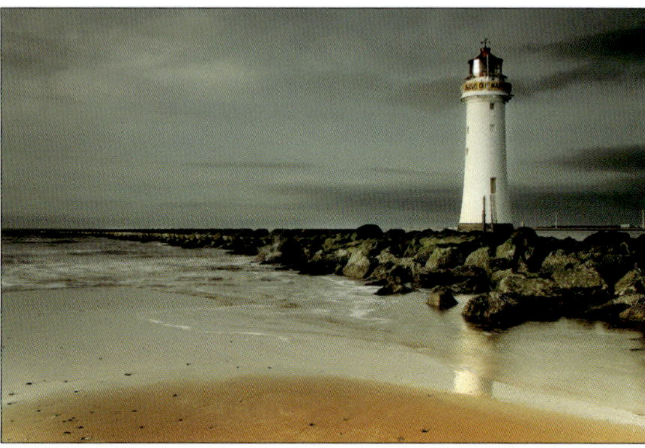

● **PAUL STEFAN** New Brighton Lighthouse on a cold winter afternoon, taken with a Canon EOS 20D.

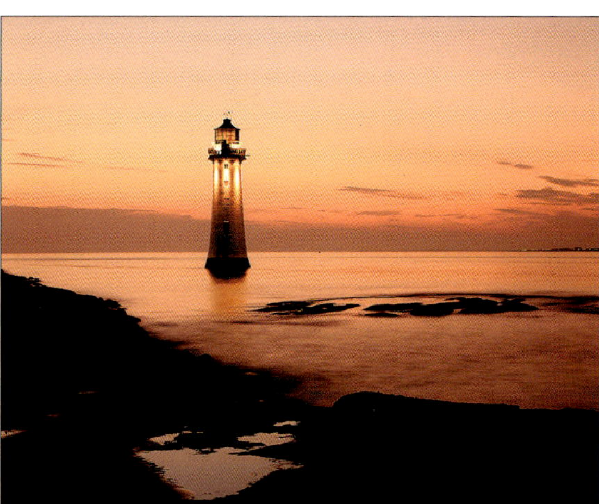

● **ANTHONY SMITH** New Brighton Lighthouse, Wirral, at sunset, taken using a Cokin sunset filter along with a medium ND grad.

PLACES TO GO

■ Here are just a few of the many castles, and their websites, that are well worth a trip to visit and photograph.
● Chillingham Castle: **www.chillingham-castle.com**
● Warwick Castle: **www.warwick-castle.co.uk**
● Bamburgh Castle: **www.bamburghcastle.com**
● St. Michael's Mount: **www.stmichaelsmount.co.uk**
● Bolsover Castle: **www.english-heritage.org.uk**
● Dartmouth Castle: **www.english-heritage.org.uk**
● Old Wardour Castle: **www.english-heritage.org.uk**

■ Both the English Heritage and the National Trust represent a number of castles. More information can be found by visiting: **www.english-heritage.org.uk** and **www.nationaltrust.org.uk**

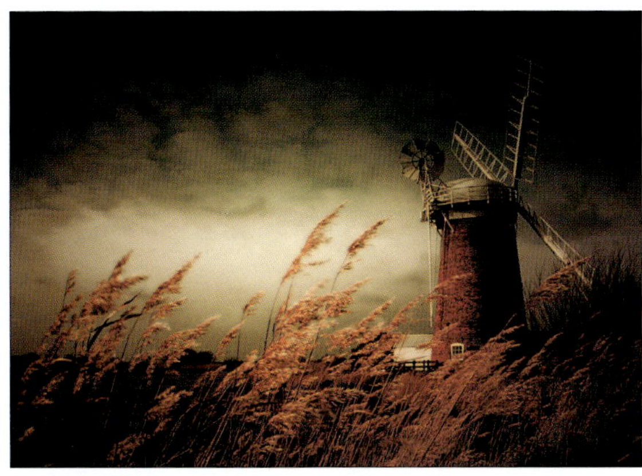

● IAN FLINDT This dramatic image of Horsey Windpump was created using the Lighting and Diffuse Glow filters in Photoshop.

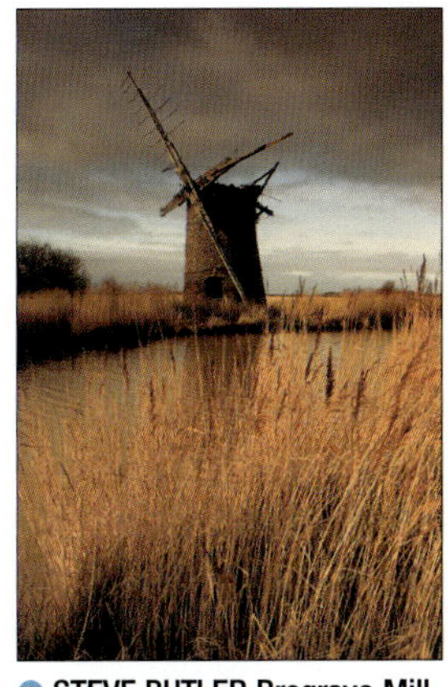

● STEVE BUTLER Brograve Mill on the Norfolk Broads.

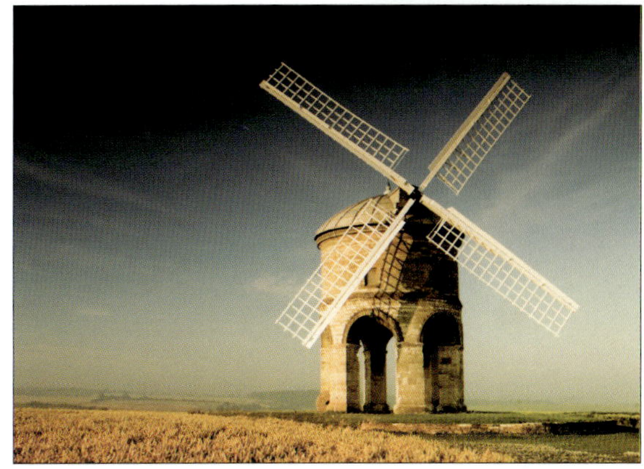

● IAN WALKER Chesterton Windmill in Warwickshire, taken on a Canon EOS 20D with a 24mm lens, polariser and warm-up filters.

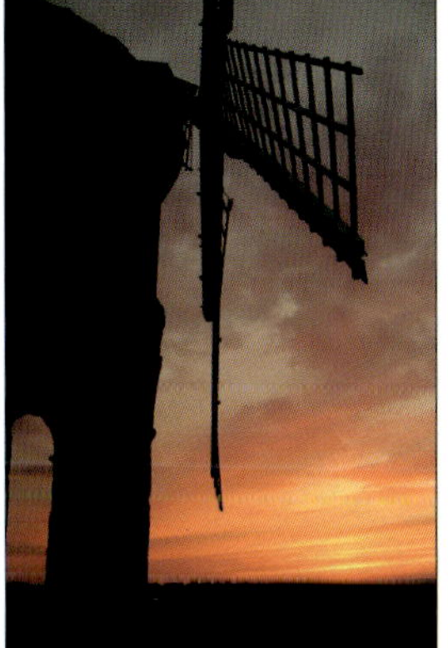

● PHIL DRINKWATER Chesterton Windmill as sun sets.

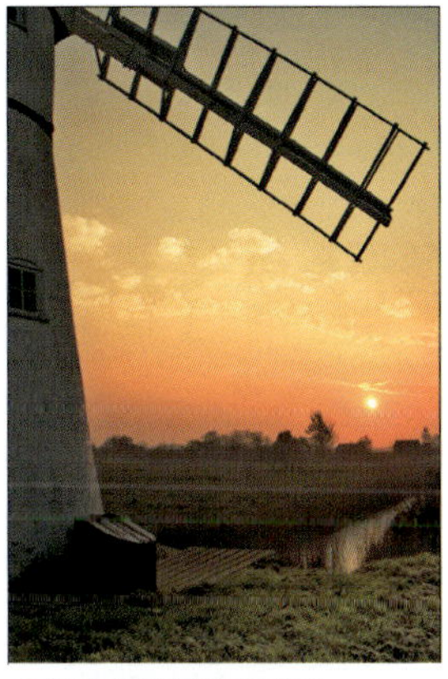

● PHIL NIGHTINGALE Thurne, Norfolk Broads: a different view.

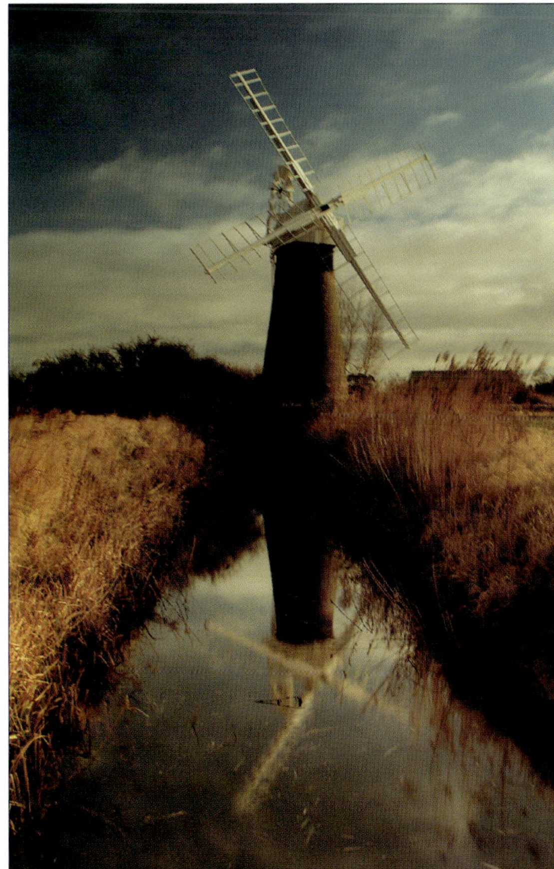

● JOHN DUCKETT Thurne Windpump taken early in the morning with a long shutter speed to convey some movement in the image.

DIGITAL TECHNIQUE – ADDING CLOUDS TO A BLAND SKY

■ It's surprising how a collection of sky photographs can come in handy when you have a dull looking image that needs salvaging. In this technique we'll photograph the sky and then use one of the photos as an element within another photograph.

1 When you're out on a good day, shoot a few sky shots. Blue skies with fluffy clouds are always worth recording and they are relatively easy to expose. Just select a suitable area, looking for the best range of clouds and also the bluest area of sky. You'll find this is about 90 degrees to the sun. Also consider using a polarising filter which will make the blue more saturated so the white clouds stand out more. It's fairly easy to expose for clouds and normally you can rely on the camera's built-in meter, especially when it's a multi-pattern variety.

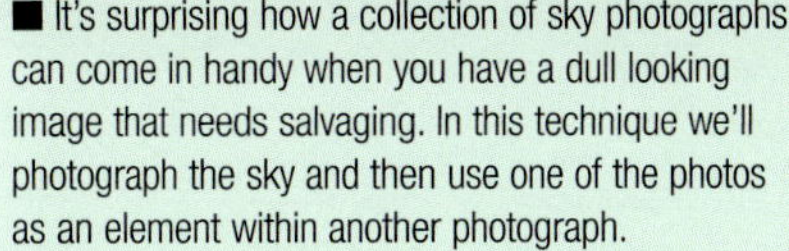

2 Here's a typical east coast beach scene with an uneventful sky. We'll first make a selection around the sky using your image editing software's Lasso or, as the sky's so uniformly dull, it's easier to select using the Magic Wand tool. Set the tolerance to around 30 to pick up large areas of the sky and have the Magic Wand on the "Add to selection" mode so you can click around to build up the whole sky area. When it's all selected feather the selection by one pixel Select⇨Feather (Alt+Ctrl+D) and expand Select⇨Modify⇨Expand by 2 or 3 pixels to ensure the edge around the cliffs doesn't have a white outline.

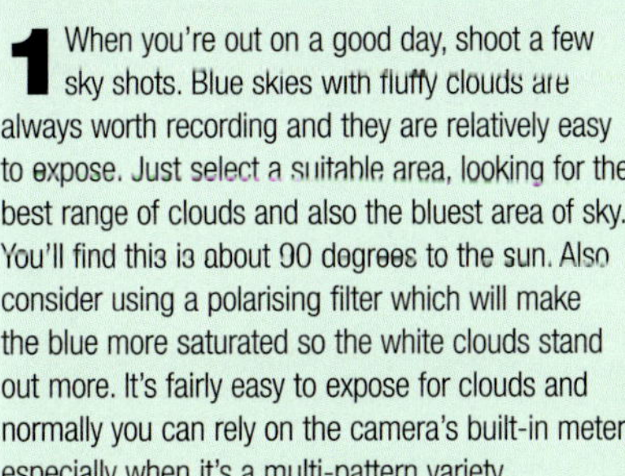

3 Find a suitable cloud photo, making sure it matches the scene you're going to drop it into. Open in Photoshop, Select⇨All (Ctrl+A), Edit⇨Copy (Ctrl+C) to copy the cloud photo and then click back on your original scene and Paste into the selection Edit⇨Paste Into (Shift+Ctrl+V).

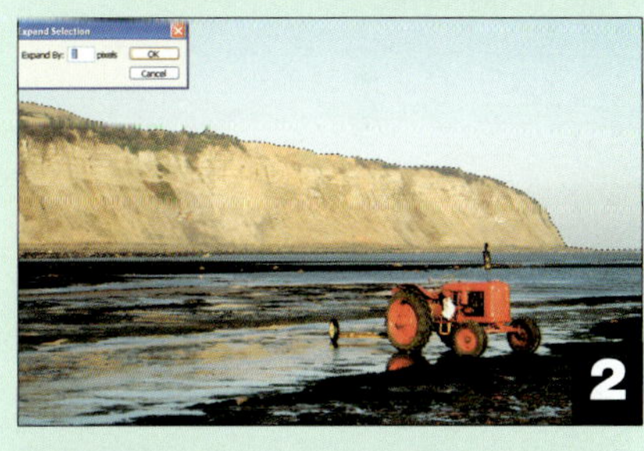

4 The sky photo will now appear in the area selected and can be adjusted using the Edit⇨Transform⇨Scale option and the Move Tool. Notice that the layers palette now shows a second layer and has a Layer mask (the black and white box to the right). If you click on this you can reveal more of the background or the sky using the eraser and brush tools.

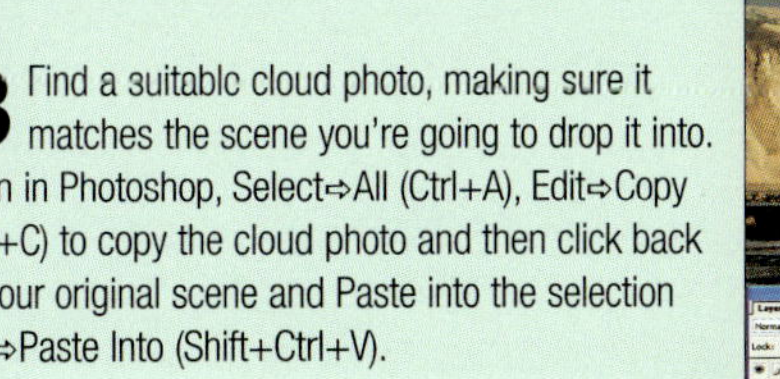

5 Adjust the hue/saturation or curves to balance the tones of the sky with the background.

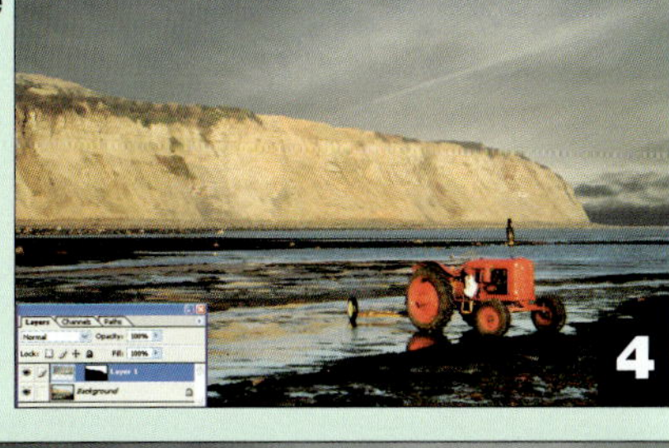

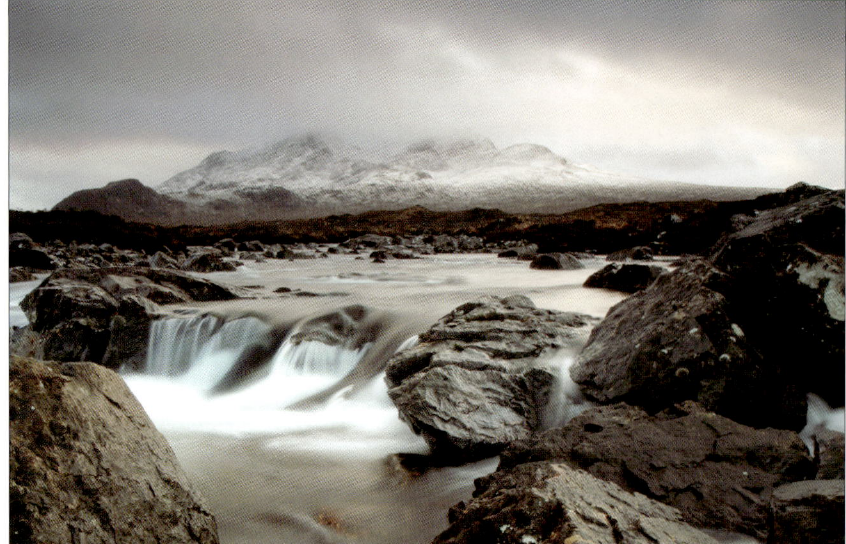

● STEWART CAIE A January view from the river Sligachan looking towards the Cuillins, Isle of Skye, captured on the Canon EOS 10D with a lengthy 3.2sec exposure.

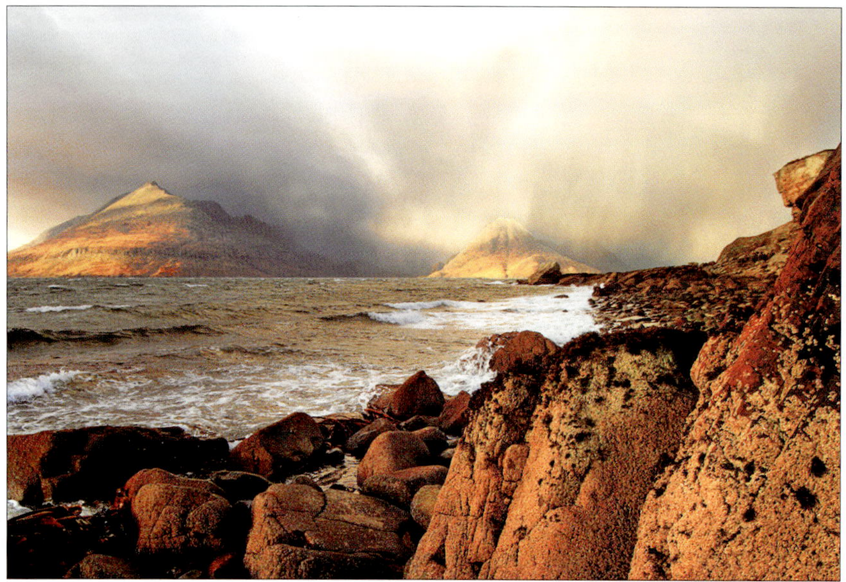

● BILL STEVENSON Winter at Elgol, on the Isle of Skye, taken using a tripod mounted Canon EOS 10D with a 28-135mm IS zoom lens. The foreground rocks form a lower frame for the mountains.

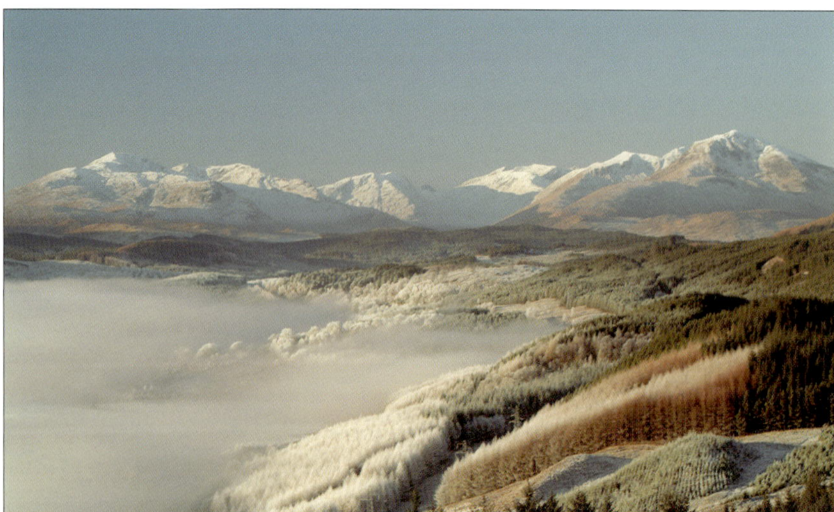

● DAVE FARMER Mist over Loch Garry, taken with a Fuji S2 Pro and Nikon 24-70mm from the A87 Invergarry to Kyle of Lochalsh road.

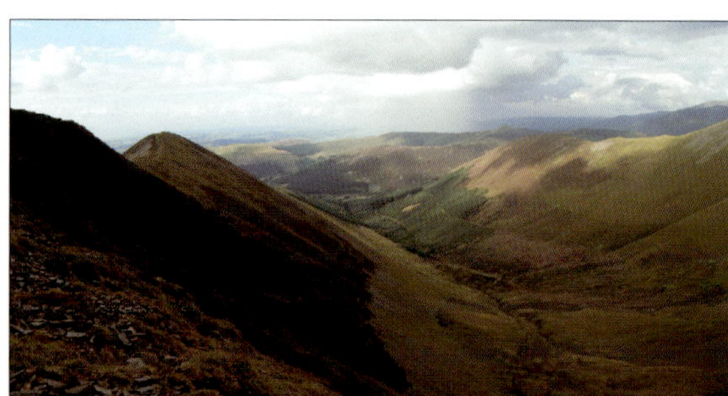

● PETER HAYES The Lake District provides some spectacular scenes, like this at Coledale Horseshoe. The image, taken on a thundery August day, is a panoramic stitch of two seperate shots from the Fuji S2 Pro.

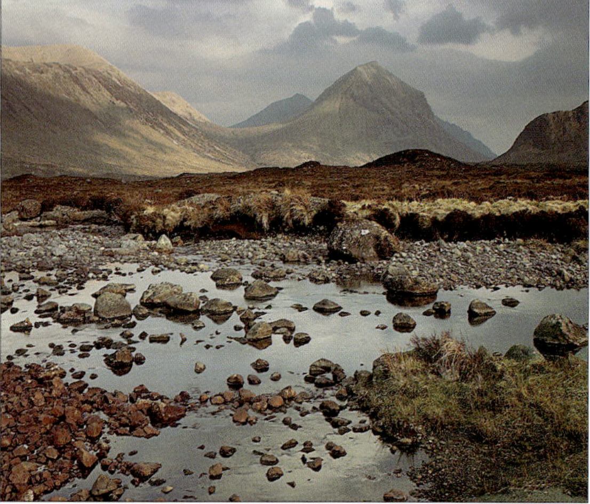

● THOMAS GORMAN A glimmer of hope – even on a dull day it can appear in the form of light breaking through the clouds. A view toward Marsco and the Red Cuillin from Sligachan, the Cuillin range, Isle of Skye.

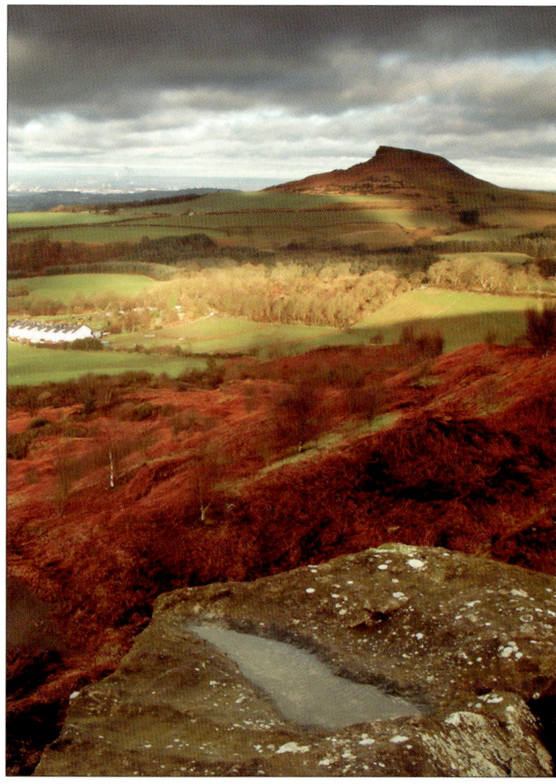

● TONY MARSH Roseberry Topping, viewed from Gribdale on a January morning, with Middlesbrough in the distance.

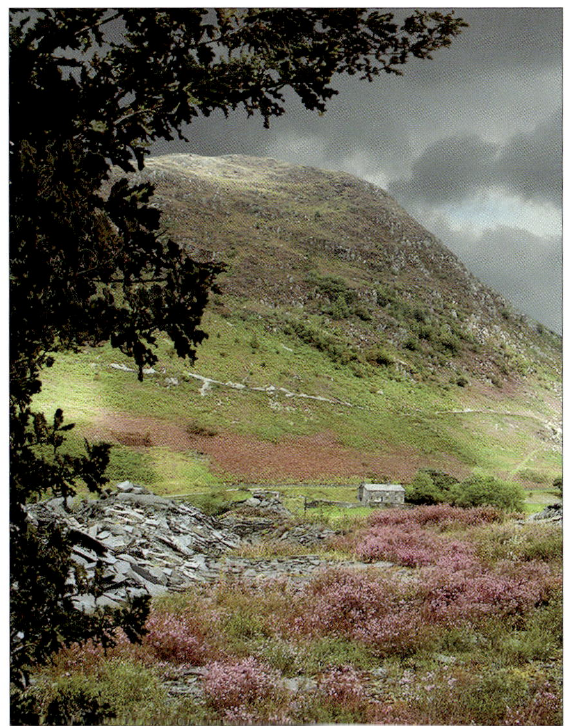

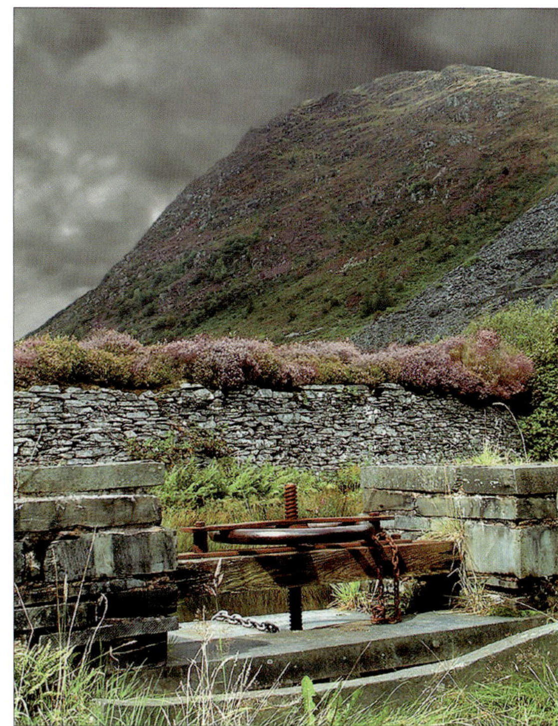

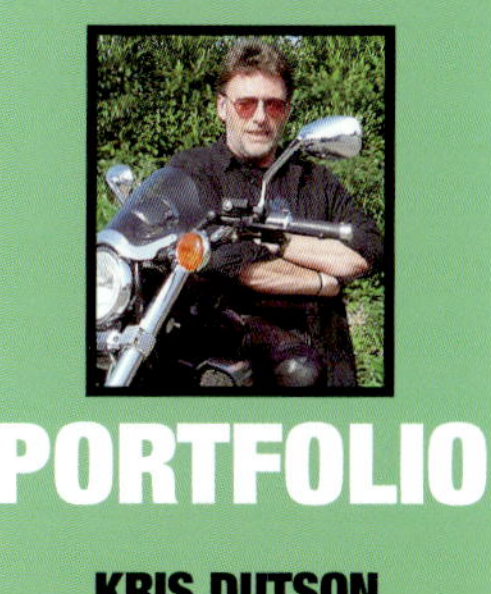

PORTFOLIO

KRIS DUTSON
used a basic exposure
system to take these photos
and combined two exposures
to get the desired results.

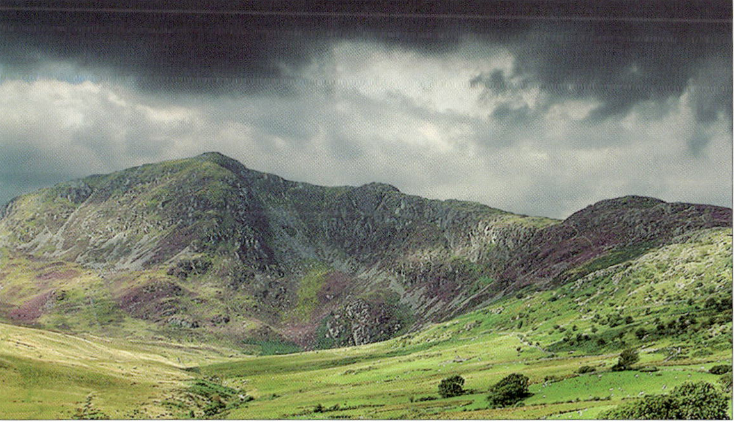

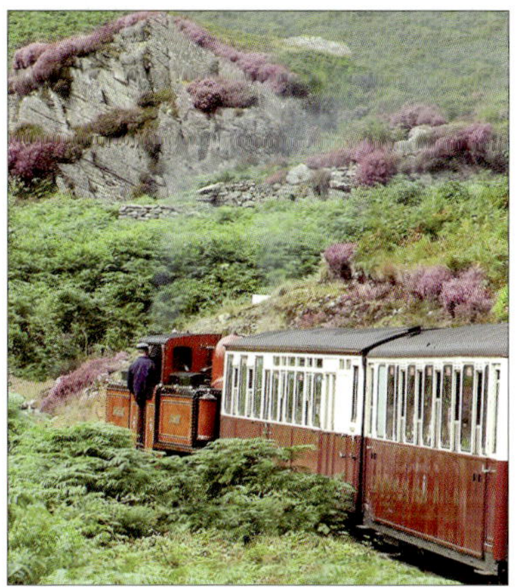

● Shots in Snowdonia National Park. Top left: A stone cottage sits alone in a field of heather, beneath an unnamed Welsh mountain near Corris. Top right: Heather and Rust, taken near to the slate cottage. Above left: Mynydd Moel is part of the Cader Idris range. Above right: A little bit different from my normal landscape shot. This one incorporates another of my loves – steam. It was taken from the carriage window of a train on the Ffestiniog railway. Bottom left: Slate Hut in a disused slate quarry near Aberllefenni. This image consists of two exposures, one for the sky and one for the foreground, merged together in Photoshop. Bottom right: Eventually the sun came out long enough to light the mine entrance on the mountain side.

I became interested in photography in the late '80s, capturing memories of the many motorcycle races and airshows I attended, as well as the English landscapes that I've always loved in photographs.

I bought a Canon AE1P, 35-70mm and 100–300mm zoom lenses and set about teaching myself the dark art of photography. I achieved reasonable results, but the bug didn't really take hold.

That changed in 2000 after I bought my first PC that came with a Kodak DC215 digital camera. Before I knew it, I was hooked! I loved the way digital offered me total control over my images – I could shoot, edit and print images in a way that film couldn't offer.

I soon realised I'd need a camera with more resolution to capture landscapes with good detail, so I upgraded to a Fuji S602z. I didn't possess any filters so the images here, from a holiday in Wales, are of the two exposure variety. I set the camera up on a tripod, set the required aperture and took two photos – one exposed for the foreground and the other for the sky.

After opening both images in Photoshop, I dragged the correctly exposed foreground shot on top of the other and used the eraser tool to erase the sky on the top image and reveal the correctly exposed one underneath.

Some tidying up of the image, along with judicious use of the Sponge tool on the heather and foliage to increase saturation, produced the desired result.

I now use a digital SLR with filters, but will still use the two exposure method if I believe it will achieve the best result.

In my book it's the final image that counts – it doesn't matter how you get there. ■
www.southernscenicphotography.co.uk

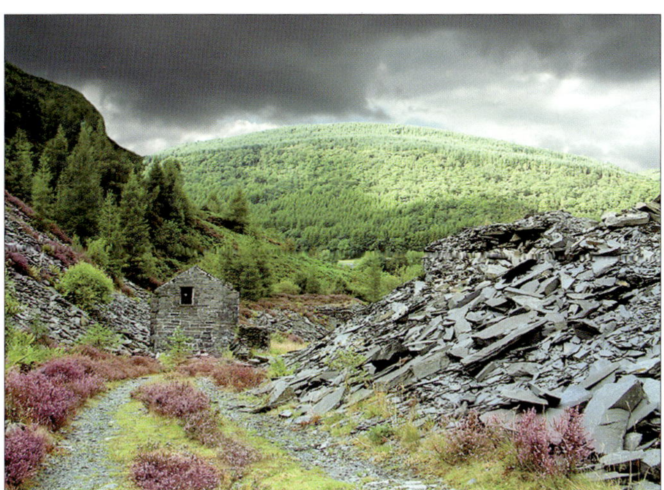

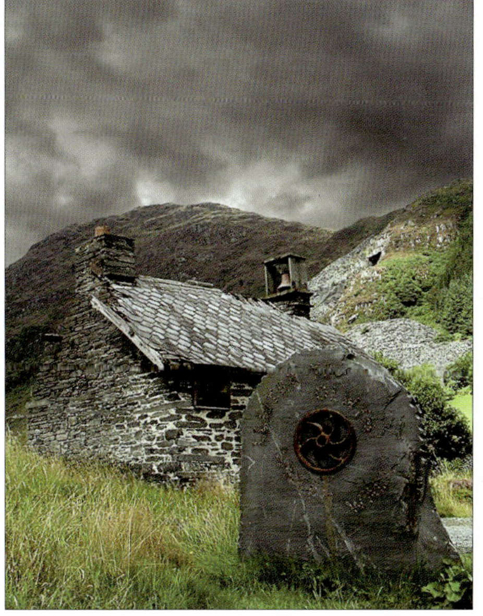

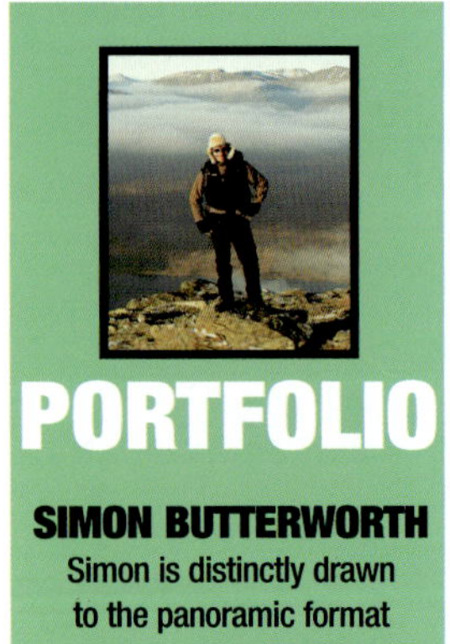

PORTFOLIO

SIMON BUTTERWORTH
Simon is distinctly drawn to the panoramic format and uses a Hasselblad X-pan camera.

My interest in serious photography began about two and a half years ago, shortly after moving to Scotland. I rapidly realised that my compact camera was not up to the job of capturing the grandeur of the highlands and islands.

At first, I took pictures of things I saw on my walks but, more recently, the photography has become paramount with my expeditions planned around areas and features I would like to photograph. I plan walks to coincide with the best light falling on the most important features of the picture. Waiting for the light to happen is not often an option in Scotland; it's either too cold, or the midges are after blood.

As an admirer of Colin Prior's photographs, I'm instinctively drawn to the panoramic format. I tried digital stitching, but found the situations I wanted to capture were so fleeting and ephemeral that I missed many opportunities.

I decided to buy an X-pan. I now use this together with a digital SLR, in whichever situation seems most appropriate. The digital is fantastic for those difficult light situations and for experimental shots.

ePHOTOzine has been very important to me as an apprentice snapper. Seeing hundreds of pictures a day, as well as getting expert feedback on my own submissions, is an invaluable help. I feel I've had 10 years' experience in the last year, thanks to members.

I very quickly learned that it's not the subject, but how it's handled that matters. A well composed pile of dustbins with good light is worth 100 Grand Canyons taken in average light with poor composition. It's all about encapsulating mood and emotion. This is hard to grasp at first, but the realisation soon dawns that people tire of postcard views with cloudless blue skies. ■

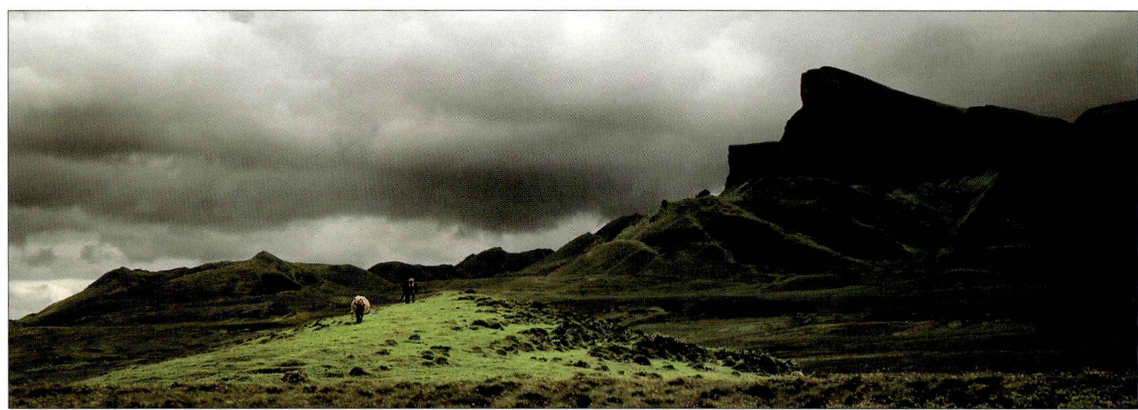

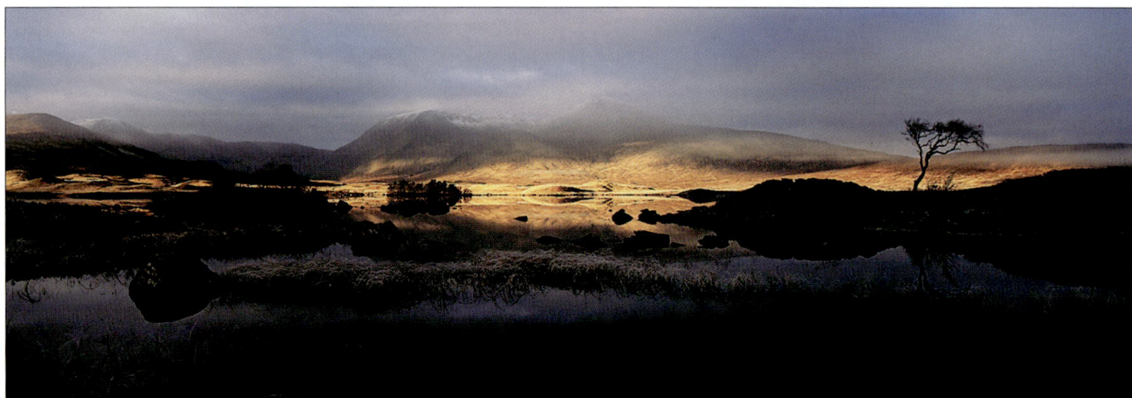

● From top to bottom: first two panoramics using the Hasselblad X-Pan with a 45mm lens on Fuji Velvia 50 film. Cows standing under the dramatic cliffs of the Quirang on north Skye, and early morning mist lifting on Lochan na h-Achlaise, Rannoch Moor, Scotland.
The bottom two shots are taken using a Canon EOS 20D digital SLR. Dawn light over Loch Ba, Rannoch Moor Scotland, was taken using a Sigma 28-300mm at an ungodly 4.30am. Very tough for a nocturnal musician!
A stripe of late evening sun falling on The Pap of Glencoe was seen from the north shore of Loch Leven. This was taken using the Sigma 12-24mm lens.

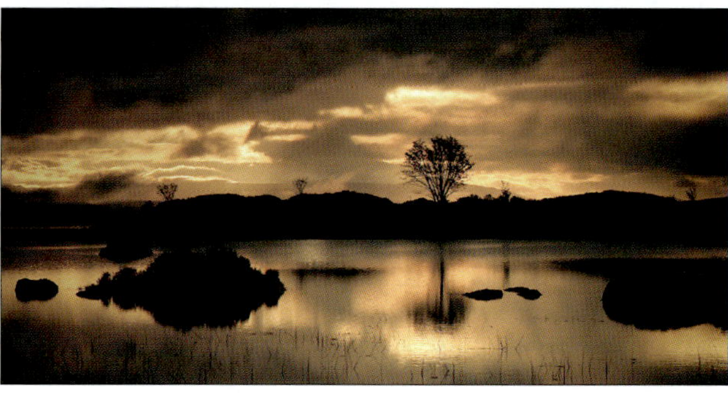

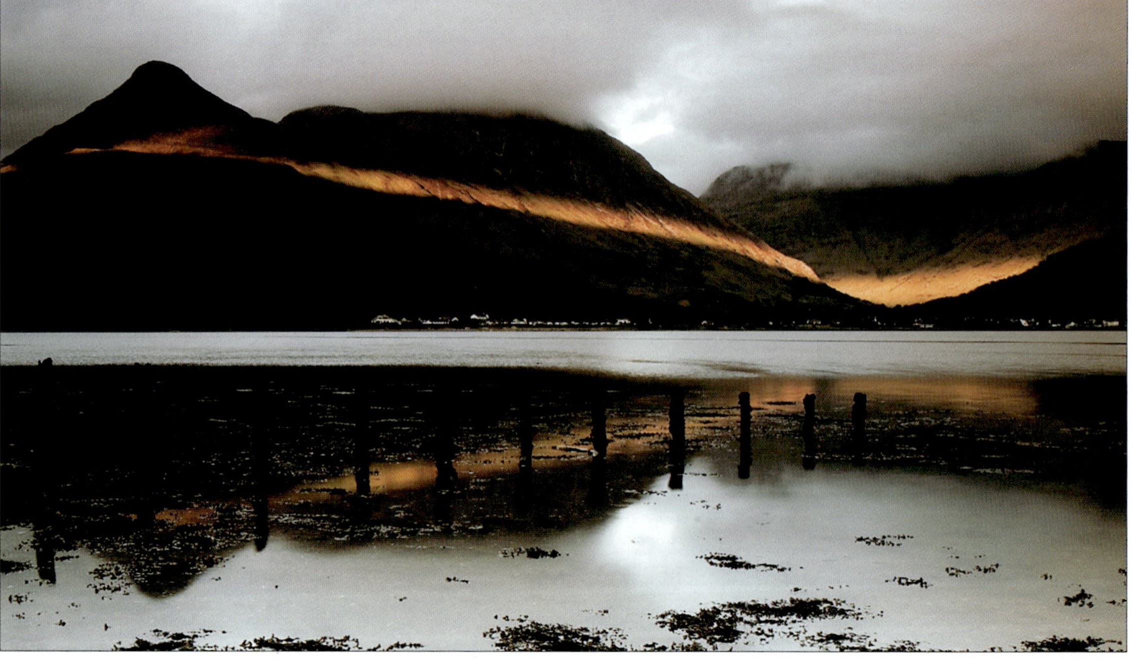

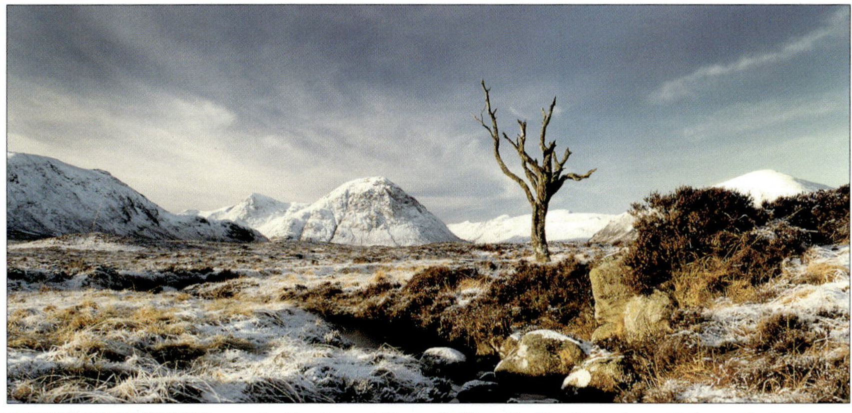

● PETER PATTERSON This spectacular tree on Rannoch Moor, Scotland, has been photographed many times by ePHOTOzine members and this mid winter, panoramic crop shows it at its best.

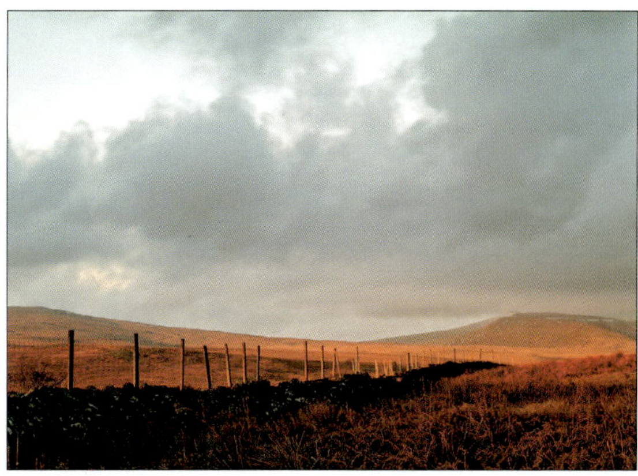

● GERWYN GIBBS Taken late on a winter afternoon, just off the side of the road crossing the high moor of the Brecon Beacons.

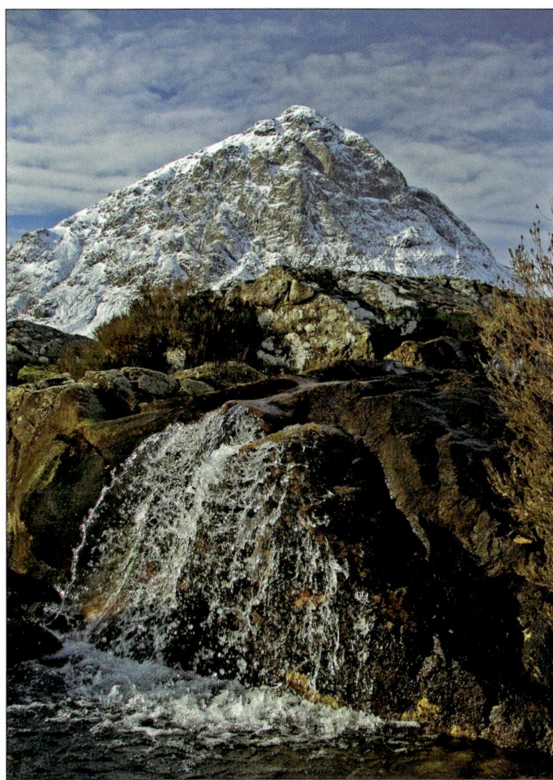

● PAUL BARR February shot of Buachaille Etive Mor, Glencoe.

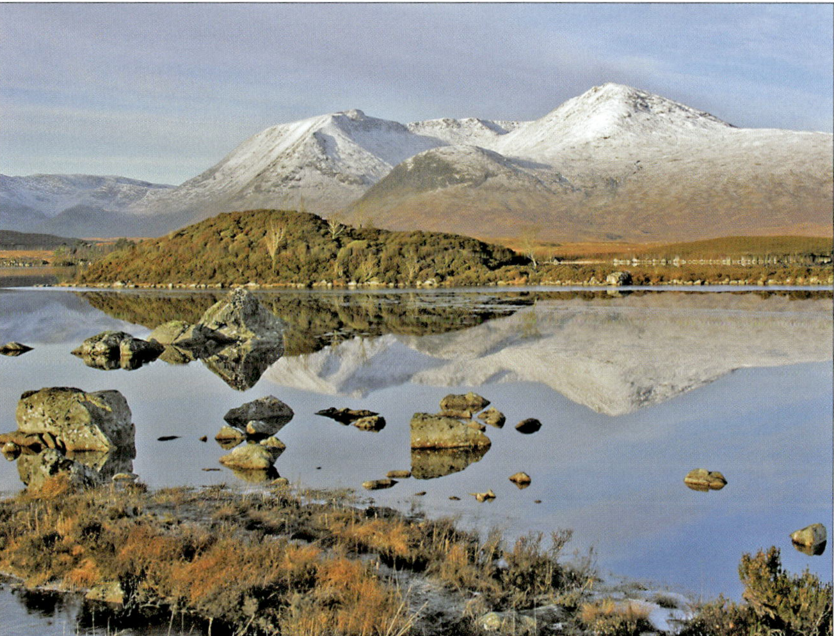

● DOUGLAS MCGILVIRAY An early morning December shot, taken on Rannoch Moor with Blackmount in the background. The winter light briefly rewarded our patience – five minutes later it was gone!

SHOOTING TIPS – USING GRADUATED FILTERS

Graduated filters are one of the most popular filters used by landscape photographers. To make the most of them, follow these simple pointers:

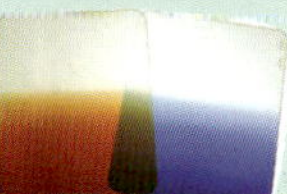

■ The reason a graduated filter is used is to help you balance the exposure from the sky to the ground. To ensure you expose correctly there are a few guidelines you can follow. First, take a meter reading from the ground without the filter in place. Lock this exposure using your camera's AE lock option or switch to manual and set the exposure suggested when you were in auto mode. Then slide the filter into place and take a photo. You can use exposure compensation if you prefer a darker or light foreground than suggested by the meter.

■ Avoid buying circular graduated filters – these give you limited control as the gradient is always placed in the centre. With the slip in system variety, from the likes of Cokin and Lee, you have the option of adjusting the filter up or down in the holder so the gradient appears above or below centre.

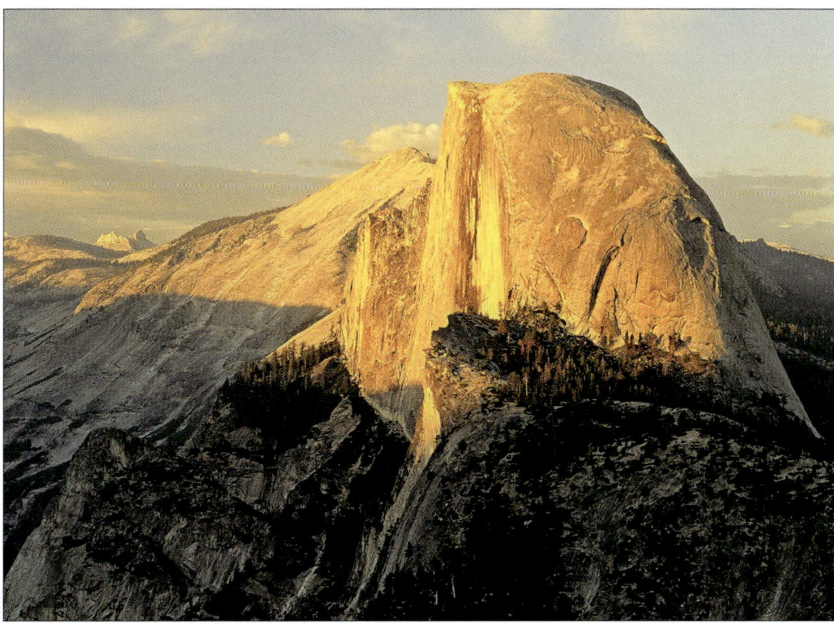

● IAN JONES Sunset on Half Dome, Yosemite, USA, using a Pentax MZ30 with a Sigma 28-300mm lens and a 0.6 ND grad & 81D filter. The exposure of 1/60sec at f/22 was recorded on Fuji Velvia 50 film.

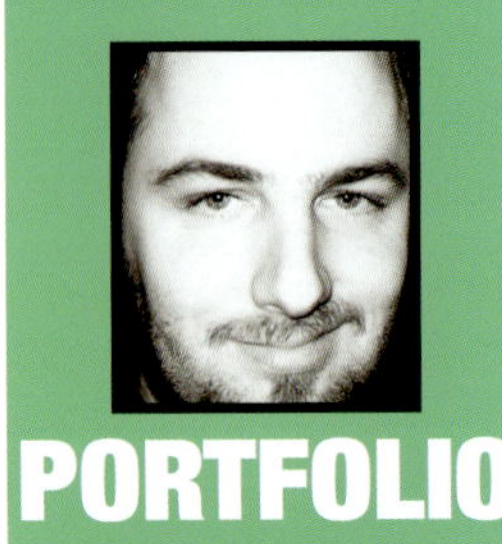

PORTFOLIO

BRUCE MORGAN has a fantastic portfolio of photographs of the coastline of South Africa, all taken in the space of just one year.

I bought my first digital camera, a Canon A80, in 2004. At first, I took pictures of anything that stood still for long enough, but after being invited to an early morning shoot on the beach I became serious about photography.

From these first attempts on the beach I was hooked, but I wasn't getting the compositions I desired. I bought a Canon EOS 300D digital SLR, which I still use. This helped my photography develop, allowing me to experiment with my images.

I have a Canon 18-55mm and Sigma 70-300mm telephoto lens. Other essentials include a range of ND Grad filters – which are handy for tricky light conditions – and a sturdy tripod, used with the timer or remote switch for the best results. Selecting the right aperture and shutter combination is also critical.

My main interest is landscapes and I love how the weather affects these type of photographs – sunrises can be bland or full of colour and clouds can light up the sky or not even feature at all.

Composition is essential; if there's not much happening in the sky I won't include it, preferring to use the foreground as my main focus. Light is the most essential element in photography and I'm still learning how to get the best results out of first light – this can transform a dreary scene into a delightful painting.

I love to witness nature in all its glory; waking up early to watch the sun paint the landscape, wondering if the display is just for me. Moments like these are why I love photography.

In future I'd like to travel more – there are many beautiful places in South Africa that I'd love to photograph. Buying more lenses is definitely on the cards and I also hope to sell some of my images. ■
www.pasteldreams.za

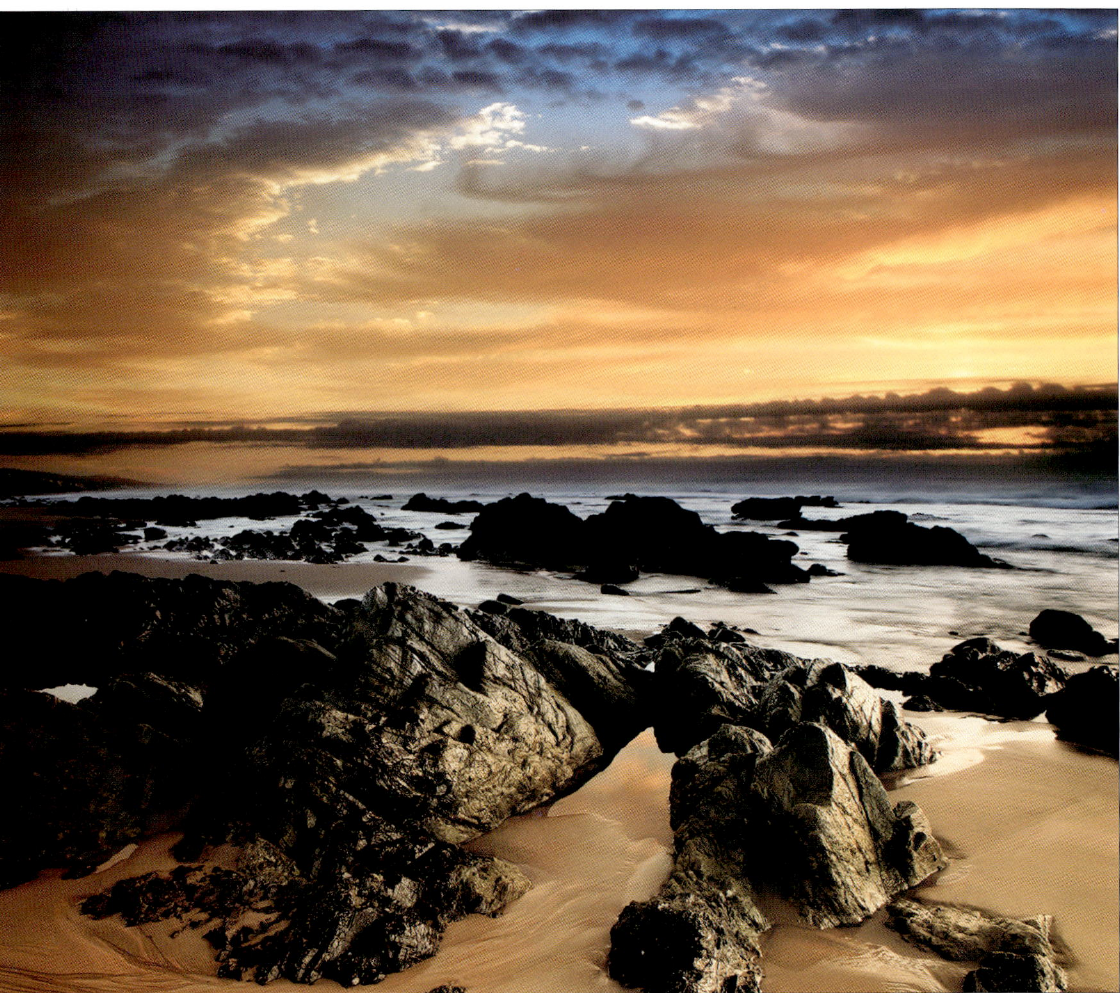

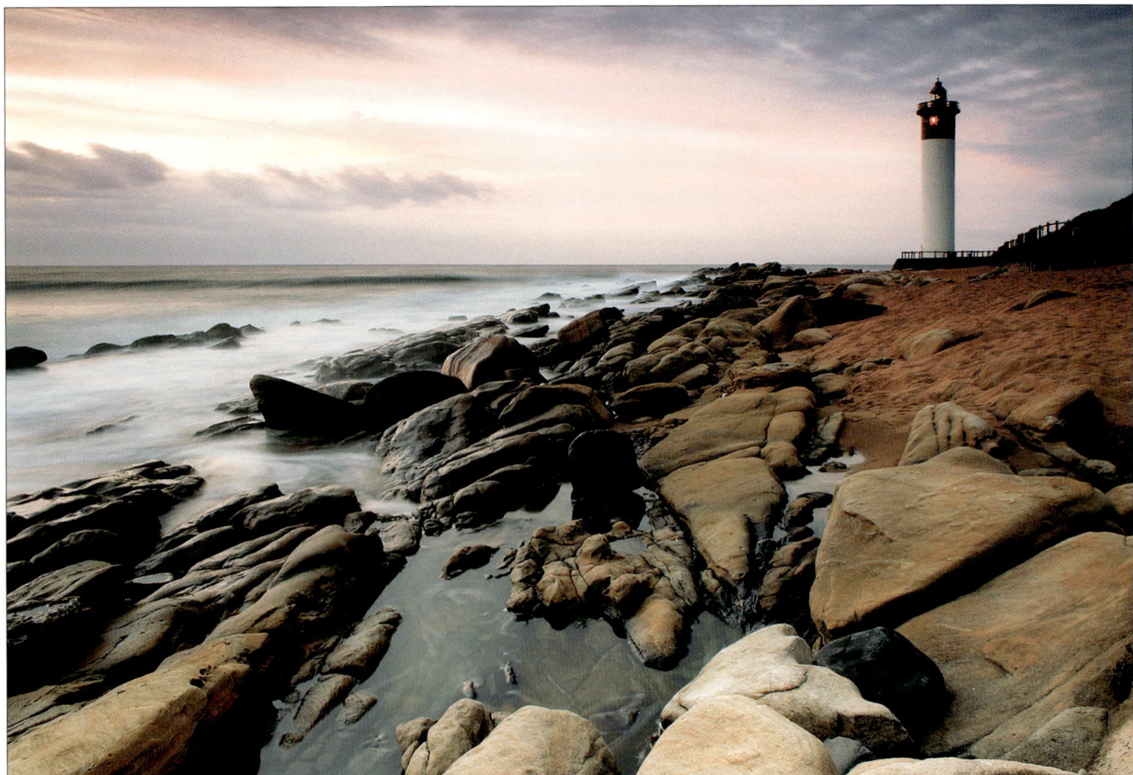

● Bruce is lucky enough to live near the magnificent Sugar Coast which offers golden sunsets and rich, saturated colour. Photographs like the rocky Umdloti Beach, top, and Umhlanga Rocks Lighthouse, Durban, South Africa, above, were taken using a Cokin P121S graduated filter and a circular polarizing filter with an f/11 aperture. The exposure in Umdloti beach was 20 seconds and Umhlanga Rocks was 8 seconds.

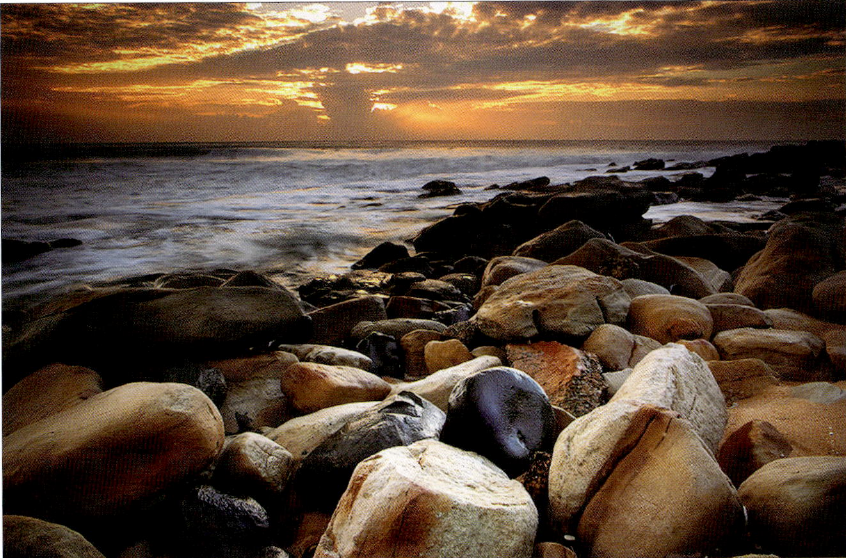

● A 1sec exposure at f/11 with Cokin P121S, P121M and P164 filters on the Canon EOS 300D with an 18-55mm lens. Bruce increased the saturation in Photoshop to make the colours even more dramatic.

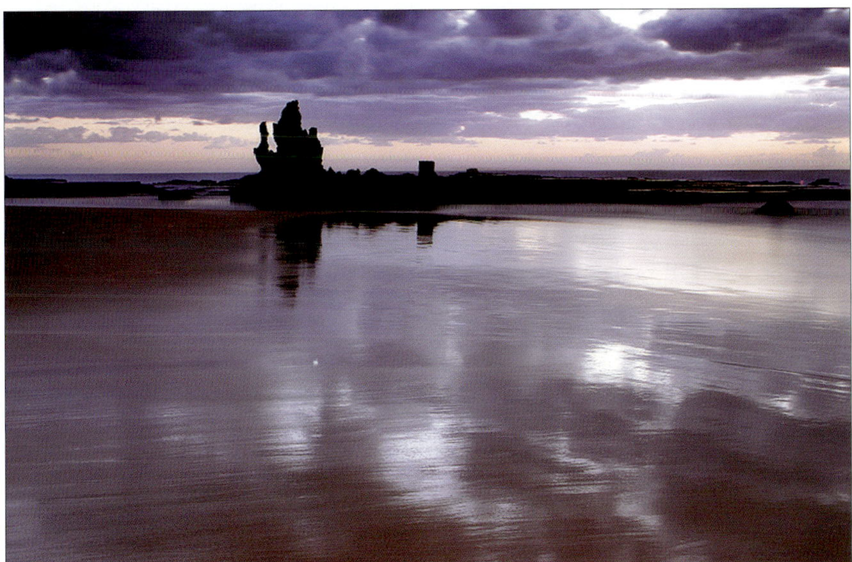

● There's nothing like waking up at 3am to drive to a location like this and take some photos. It's up the coast at a place called Umdloti. 20sec at f/11 Cokin 121S and polariser filter.

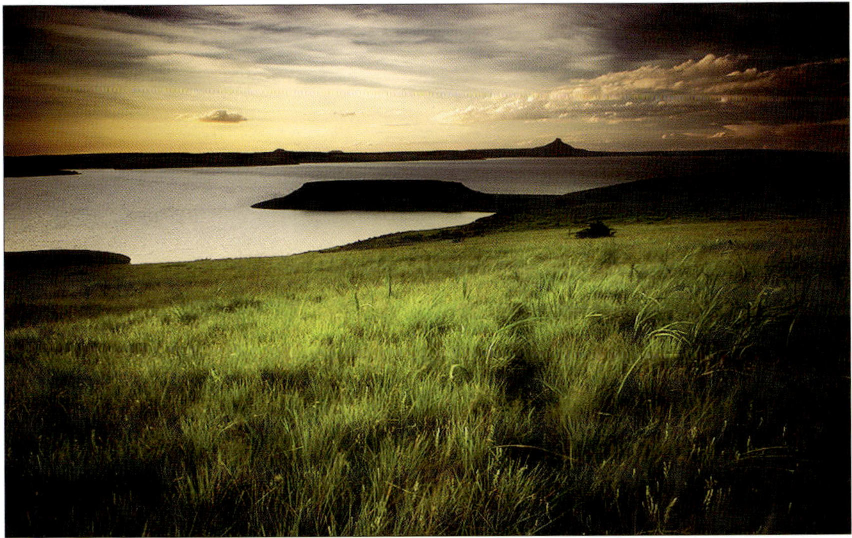

● Valley of Hills in Johannesburg, taken using the Canon EOS 300D and 18-55mm lens with the ISO100. A graduated filter was used to tone down the sky.

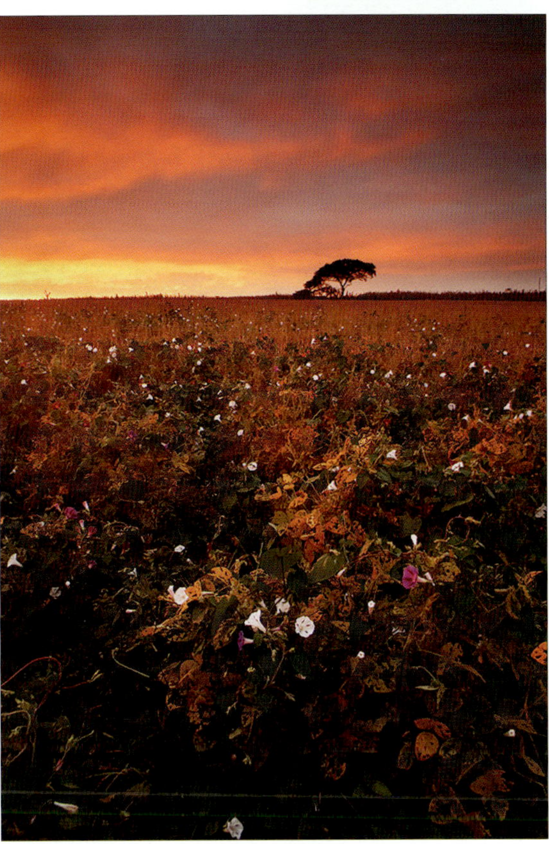

● An early morning rise again to capture this stunning dawn in a field of flowers. The tree was positioned on the right third intersection to give it a small but important place in the scene.

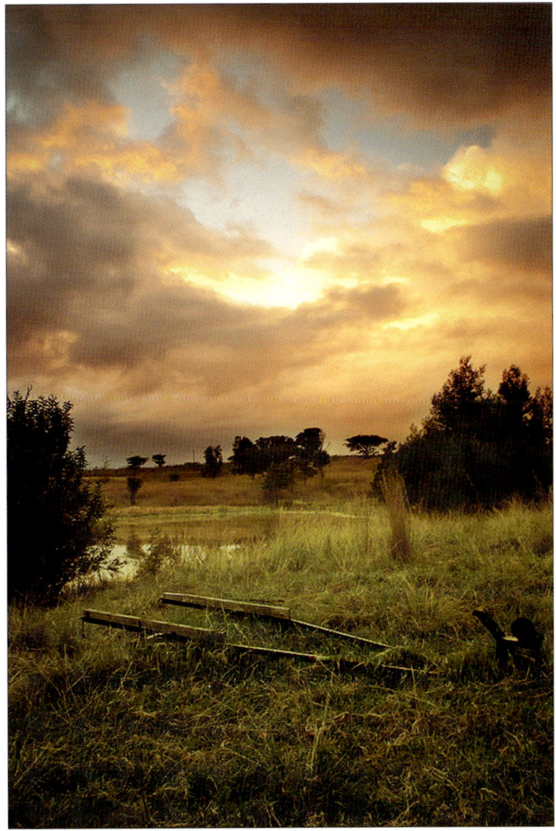

● Remains of an old boat trailer, taken early morning with a 10sec exposure at f/11 and a Cokin Circular Polariser and 121F filter.

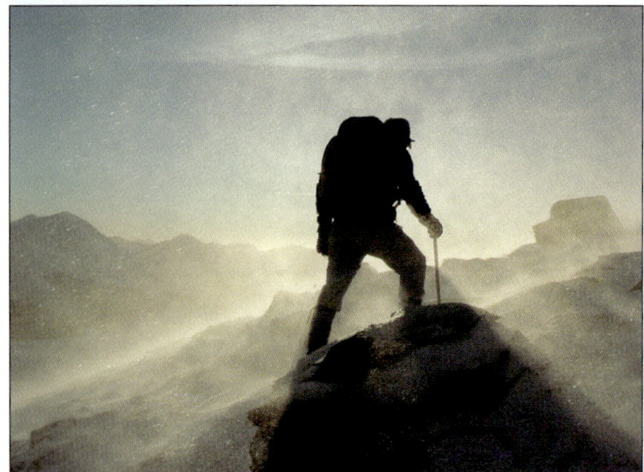

● BRYAN FISH A backlit climber on the west face of Meall Glas (957m), north east of Crianlarich, Scotland.

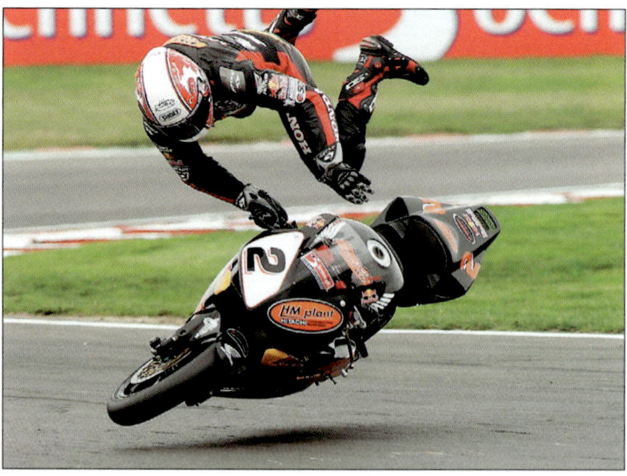

● RUSSELL LEE Michael Rutter flies through the air after a highside at Russell's chicane at the Snetterton Race Track.

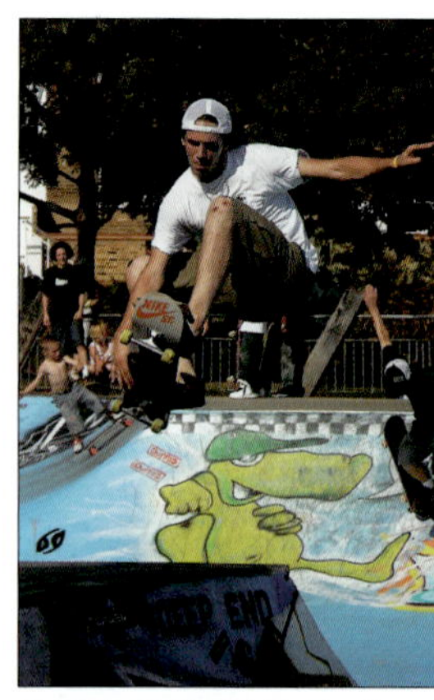

● SCOTT MARTIN Shutter lag on digital needs to be planned.

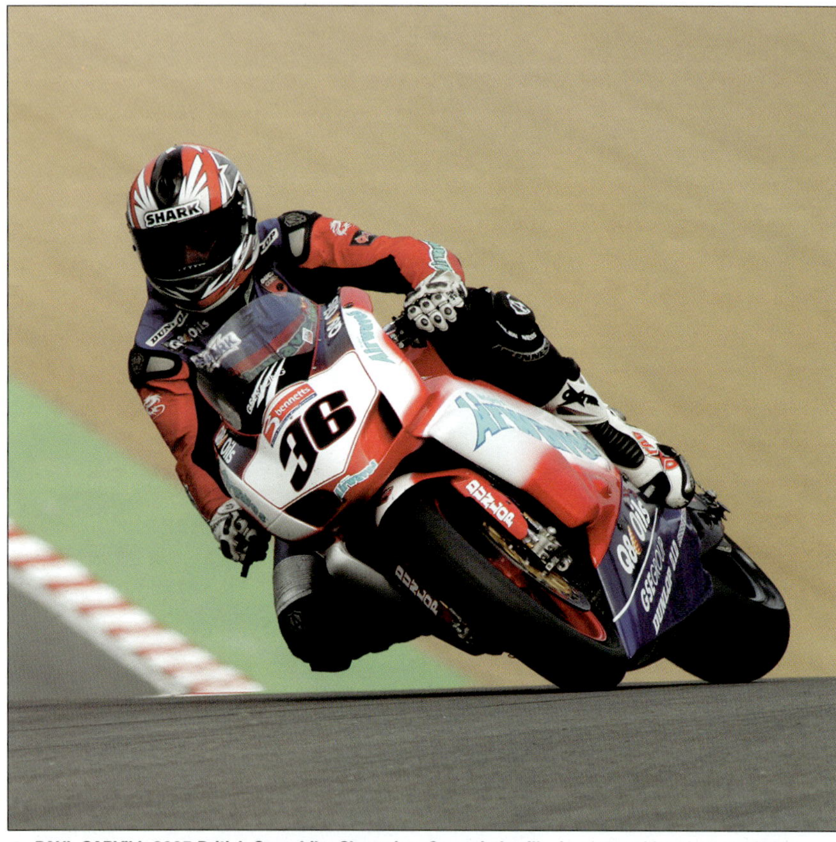

● PAUL CARVILL 2005 British Superbike Champion, Gregorio Lavilla, is captured head on at 1/640sec shutter speed against a pre-planned and uncluttered background.

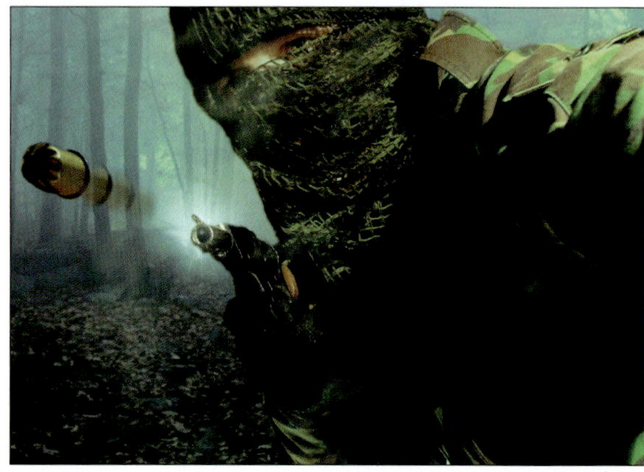

● STEVEN FRYER This digitally manipulated shot creates the illusion of a firing bullet. Our eagle-eyed members spotted it was a blank!

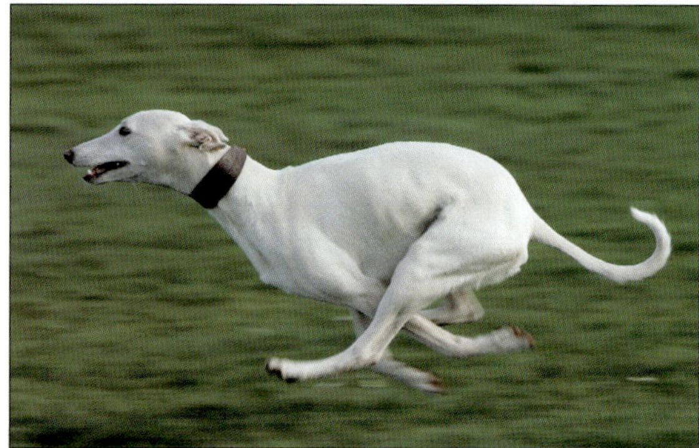

● PAT BASQUIL My nephew's whippet 'Blondie'. Canon 70-200 f/2.8L IS was pre-focused on an EOS-1Ds Mk II at f/10 and 1/320sec.

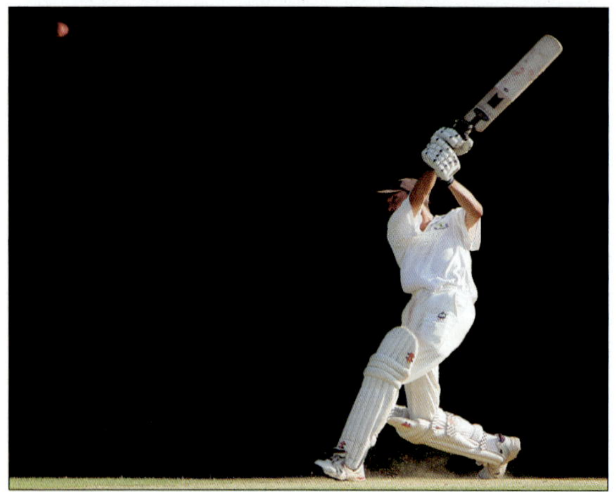

● MICHAEL ROGERS Chipperfield CC provides a perfect clean background for cricket shots with a wood surrounding the pitch.

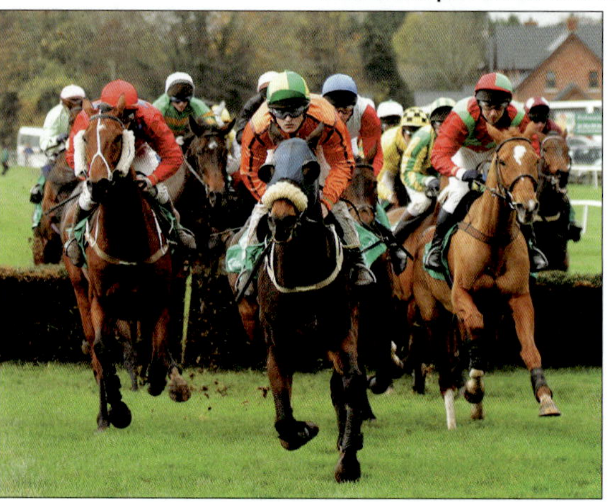

● NIGEL MOORE Standing up the racecourse and leaning over the rail gives the illusion of being in front of the horses on the course.

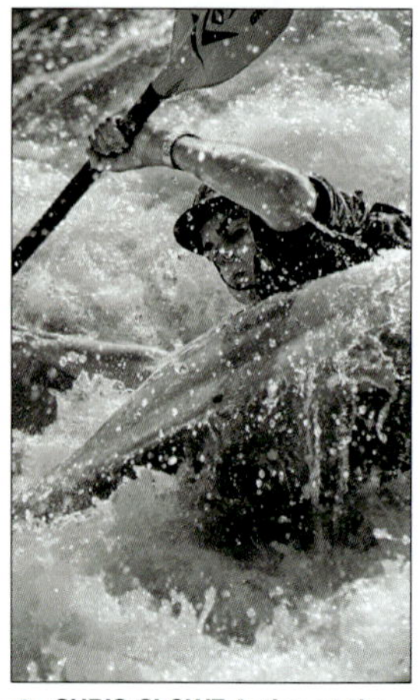

● CHRIS CLOWE Action at the White Water Centre, Stockton.

Sport & Action

From professional football stadiums to school playing fields, our members capture the action and we've around 9000 action photographs, covering everything from skateboarding to Formula 1 racing. This section highlights some of our favourites and combines these with useful advice to help you capture action with your camera.

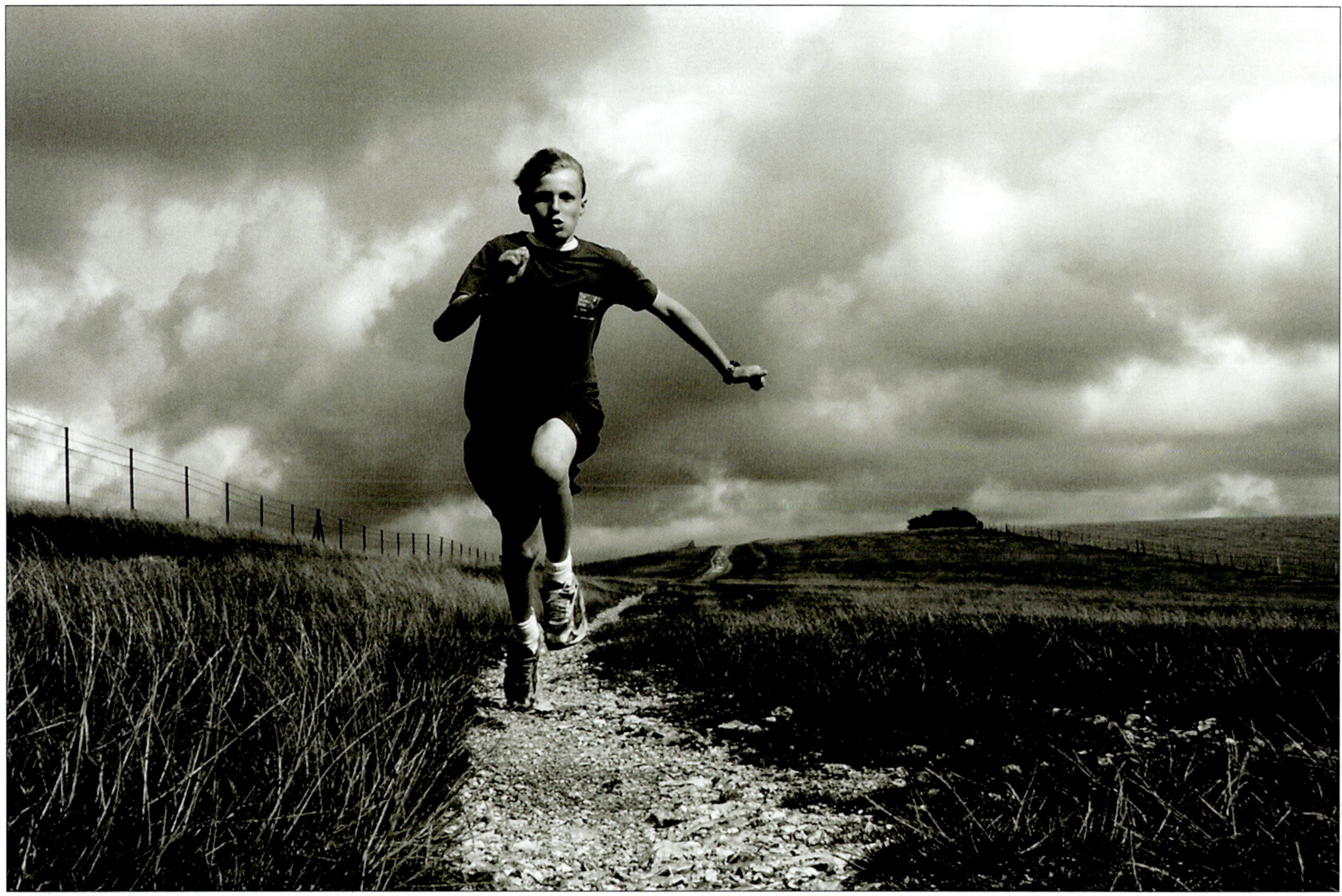

● **CHRIS MOLE** Boy running on the Downs near Ditchling Beacon, Sussex. The chosen low camera angle ensures a dramatic perspective and with the horizon placed on the lower third more emphasis is brought on the boy. The conversion to black & white also offers a strong impact that may not have been so effective in colour.

Sports photographs fill the back pages of just about every printed newspaper. Whether it's a ball sinking into the back of the net, the revealing bum shot of a female tennis player stretching to serve, or a spectacular crash at a race track, the moments are captured by the world's press photographers. These dedicated professionals sit at the sideline of events and record every worthwhile second, using huge lenses that poke out at the action.

Over the years the game has changed. Where photographers handed a film in to the paper for processing, images are now wired straight from the stadium/trackside to the desk. A photo can be in print in record time, but even so the principles of sports photography remain as they have always done and apply to any form of action photography. You could adopt techniques used by a premier division football photographer when photographing the school sports day, and the fill-in slow sync flash used by a pro cycle photographer would work equally well when shooting your child on a bike ride in the local wood.

There are a few things that apply in most action photography and knowing these simple rules will help you to improve and, hopefully, become as good as the pros.

One of the main things is knowing how to predict where the action will occur. Look at any pro at a football match and they'll pre-focus on the goal mouth. Nine times out of ten this is where the action will happen to create award winning photos. At a race track it also pays to find the best vantage points and pre-focus, firing the shutter when the action appears.

Timing is another very important aspect. It's no use showing a batsman swinging his willow without a ball either hurtling towards or away from the bat. And any goal scoring action either wants the ball sinking into the back of the net or showing the ball slipping through the goalie's grasp or just coming away from a leather boot. This is dependent on super responsive trigger action or a camera with continuous frame shooting that you can activate while panning the action. It's also a benefit if you know the sport you're photographing so you can understand when a particular peak moment is likely to occur and trigger a fraction of a second before, so when the shutter opens you're recording that perfect moment.

Next is a full understanding of shutter speeds and their influence on a moving subject.

Finally, there's dedication. Pro sports photographers generally didn't just get lucky, they had to work hard and often for little financial reward, gaining respect from the trade to take them from the local parks to the stadiums of the world. It's this dedication that gives them access to press-pass protected areas, ensuring the best viewpoints, free from crowded spectator areas and obstructive fencing.

Sports photography is one of the few areas where specific equipment is essential. You will need a long lens, whereas with most other subjects you can make do with shorter lenses and move closer. You will need fast lenses to ensure the action freezing shutter speed is possible and ideally you'll need a camera with a fast continuous shooting mode of around five frames per second.

Over the following nine pages you'll see ePHOTOzine's members applying their technical knowledge to a whole range of subjects. We've covered horse and greyhound racing, all kinds of motor sports, ball games, winter sports, climbing, underwater antics and even ringside action.

You'll learn how to pan to ensure a sharper moving subject and how to create digital motion blur, when your action photo isn't exactly shouting action at you. Plus, we'll explain about film speeds, shutter speeds and CCD sensitivity. ■

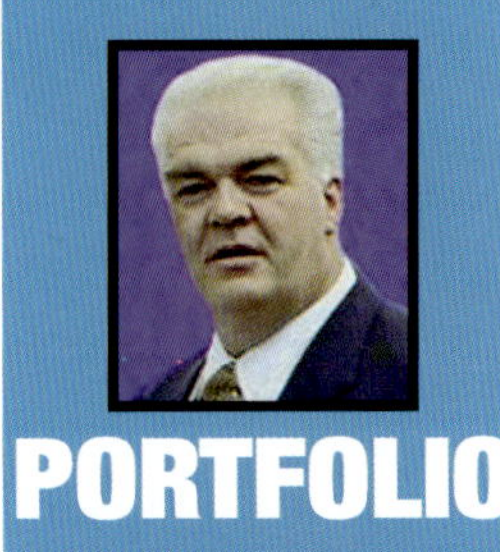

PORTFOLIO

Sean Byrne
Sean is a professional photographer working out of the small seaside town of Dungarvan, Ireland.

At 18 Sean painted landscapes in oils as a hobby and bought a Canon AE-1 SLR to photograph scenes that he wanted to paint. He soon became hooked on photography.

I used the camera's manual mode, which I would recommend to anyone starting out. I learned a lot through trial and error, joined a local camera club and studied at night school. I upgraded my camera to a Canon A-1 and then a T90.

In 1993, after about three years taking photographs of kids' weekend hurling and football matches, I made a serious decision to leave my secure employment at Waterford Crystal and become a full time photographer.

I bought an EOS-1, EOS-5 and Bronica ETRS to cover Gaelic matches, events, presentations and school events which I submitted to local papers. The shots were black and white, printed in my converted downstairs toilet.

The hardest part for any photographer starting out is getting established and gaining the respect of other professionals working in your area.

It took me eight years to get where I wanted to be, by building up a good client relationship with delivery of a quality service and product.

I now shoot digital and use the Canon EOS-1Ds MkII for everything from weddings, studio, events to presentations – the quality amazes me. I use a Canon EOS-1D MKII for sports with my 300mm f/2.8L, which I bought second-hand.

I take about 50 weddings a year and cover five matches a week for the local papers. My advice for anyone wanting to become a sports photographer is to start at kids' weekend matches where you can get close to the action. ■

www.seanbyrnephoto.com

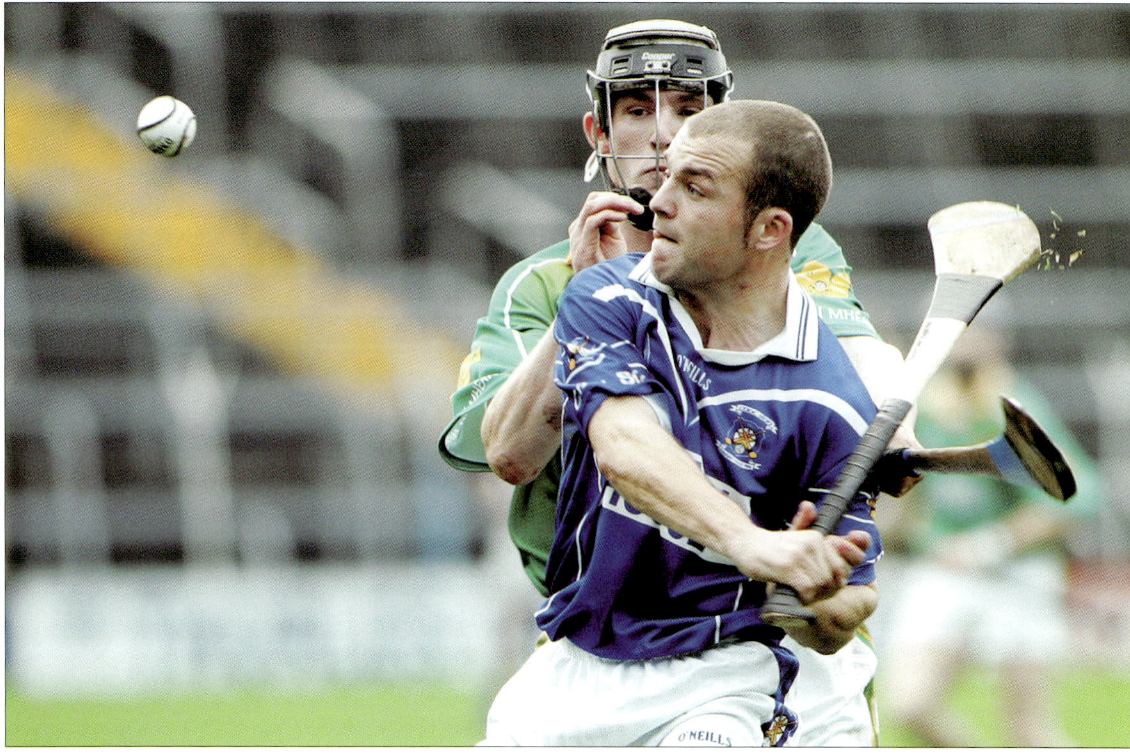

● The 2004 Munster Club senior hurling final between Waterford's Mount Sion and Tipperary's Toomevara. I love sport, especially Gaelic Football and Hurling, which I played a lot of myself. This gives me a great advantage when covering matches for the papers as I can anticipate the action.

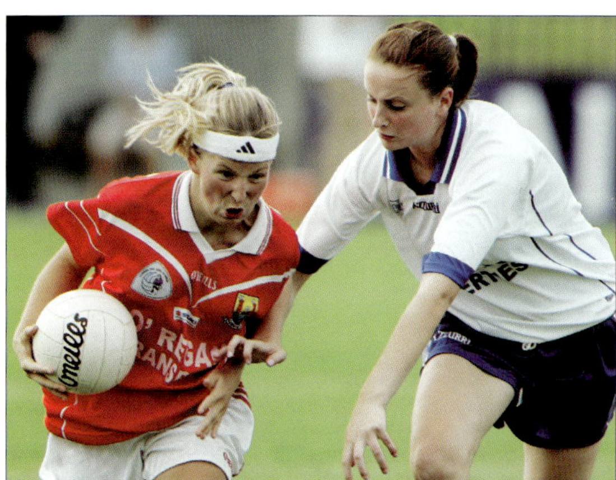

● Action from a Ladies inter-county gaelic football match between Cork and Waterford.

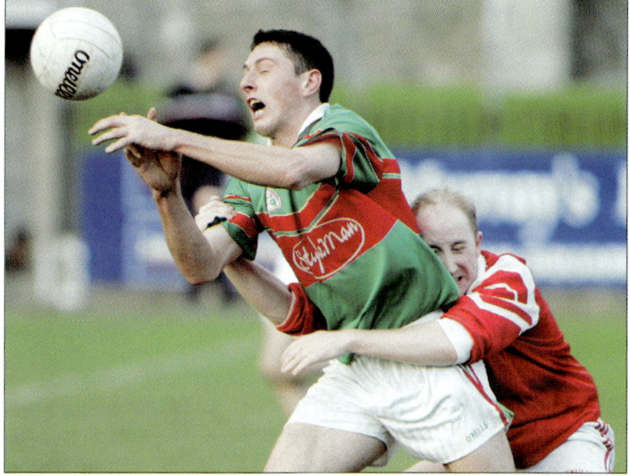

● Munster Club Football championship match between Stradbally, Waterford and Loughmoy, Tipperary.

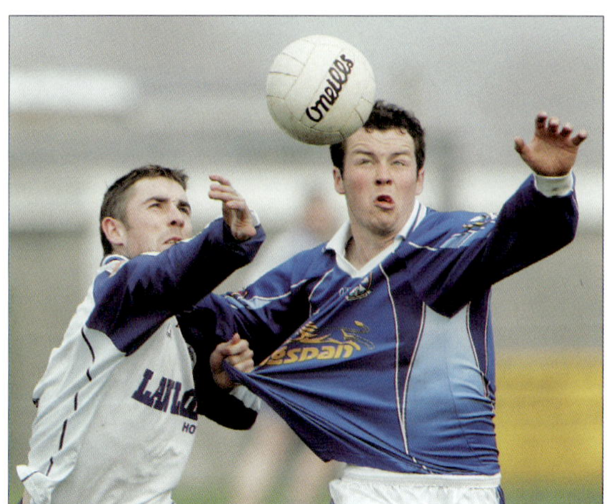

● A split-second moment captured at the 2004 National football league game between Waterford and Cavan.

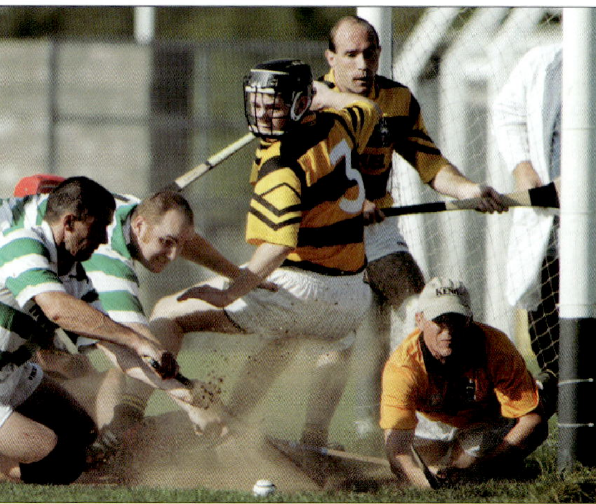

● Goal mouth action shot from the 2004 Waterford senior hurling championship between Lismore and Roanmore.

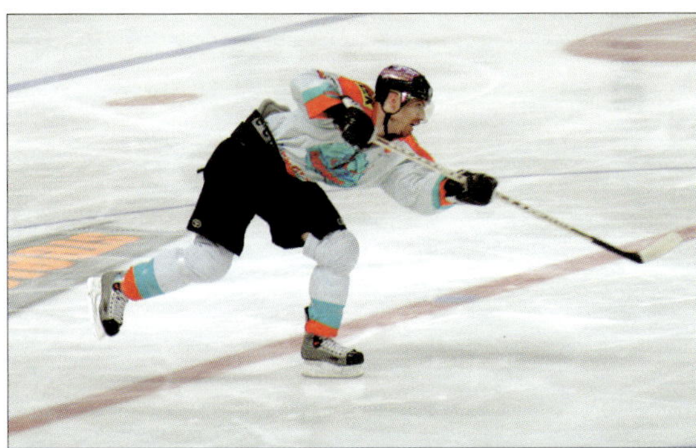

● ANTHONY HILL Mark Dutiaume at Sheffield Arena, taken on a Canon EOS 300D at ISO800 to give a 1/250sec speed at f/5.0.

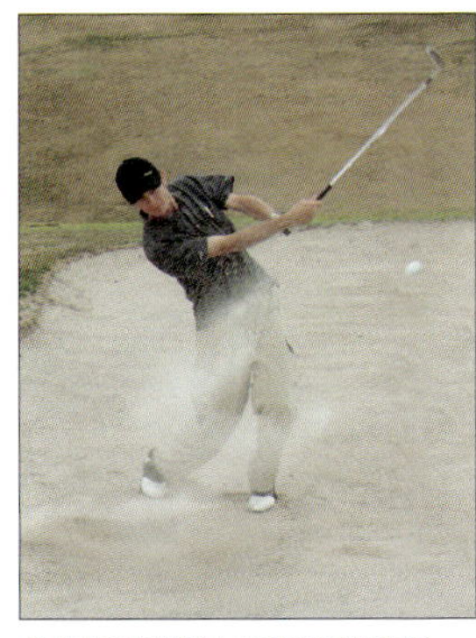

● ALEXANDRA LOWSON Golf swing at Howick Golf Club.

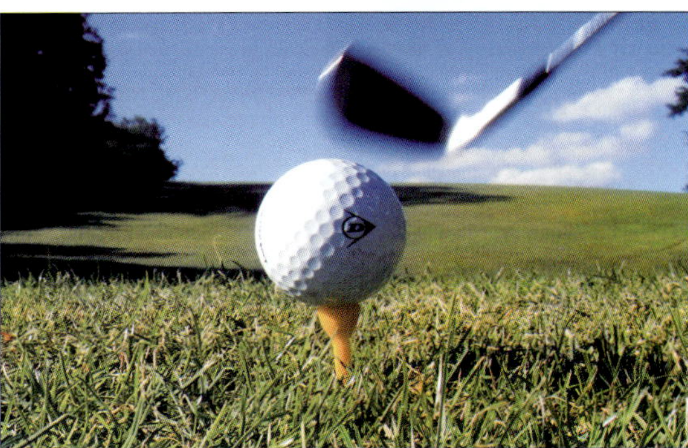

● KIM WALTON A set up shot with the club swinging backwards and a slow shutter speed to give the sense of movement.

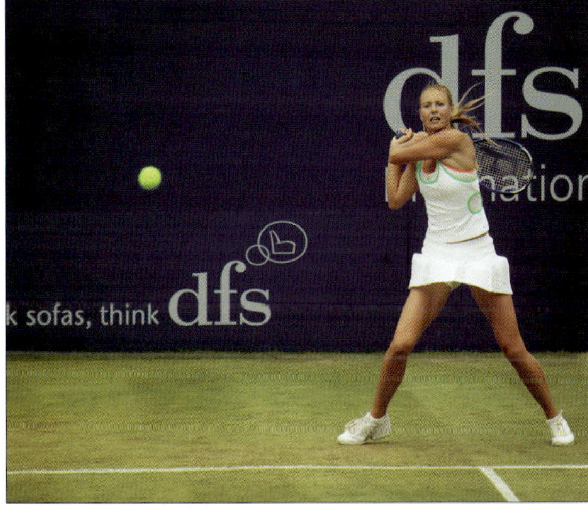

● KEITH HENSON Tennis – a fast moving, high speed subject where trigger reaction is critical. The ball is captured perfectly mid flight.

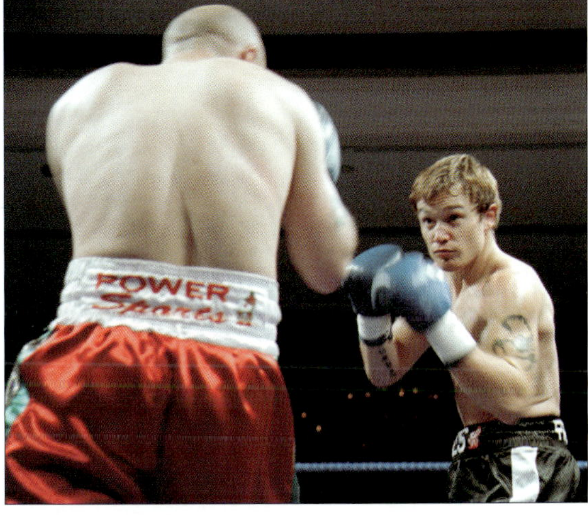
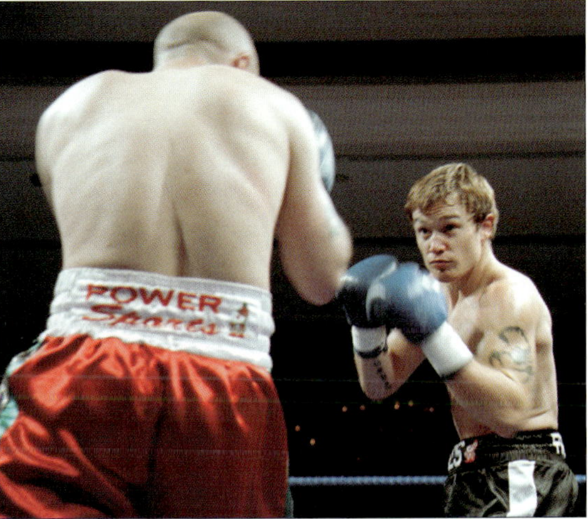

● MARTIN STEWART Although it's just a warm-up bout, the concentration on the young boxer's face shows his commitment.

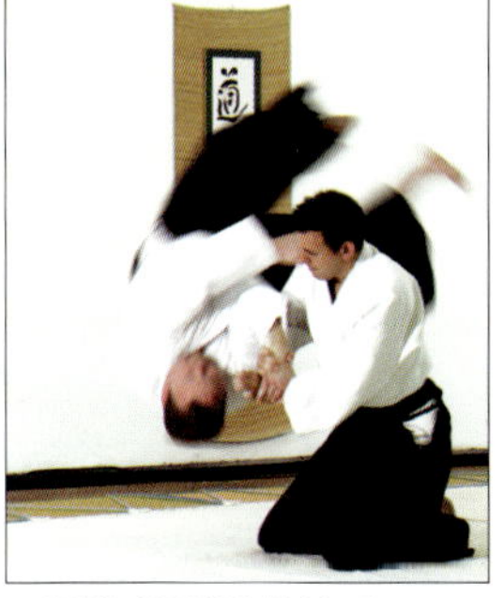

● PAUL GROOM Aikido from Bristol's Templegate Dojo.

2nd CURTAIN FLASH

■ When shooting fast moving subjects with long exposures using flash, motion trails appear in front rather than behind your target. This gives the impression that the subject is moving in the wrong direction.

■ To overcome this, consider using 2nd curtain flash (also known as rear-sync flash) if your camera supports it. The technique works by firing the flash at the end, rather than the beginning, of an exposure.

■ The result: a frozen subject at the end of motion and a trail showing the target's movement history.

■ Peter Graves' shot below shows the effect perfectly with the fire trail appearing behind the staff.

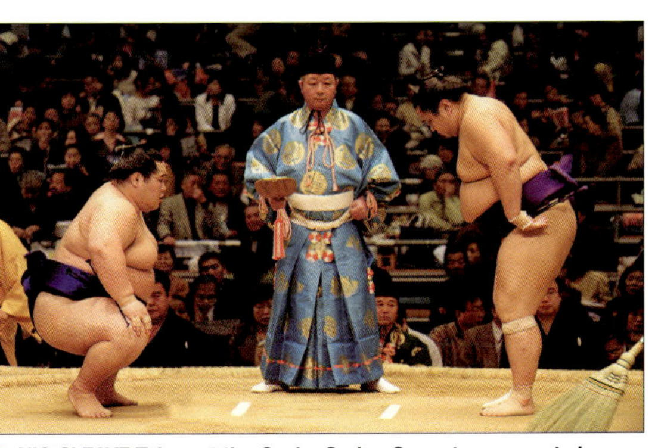

● NIC CLEAVE Taken at the Osaka Spring Sumo tournament, Japan, using Canon D30 and Sigma 170-500mm, ISO 400, 1/125 at f/4.5.

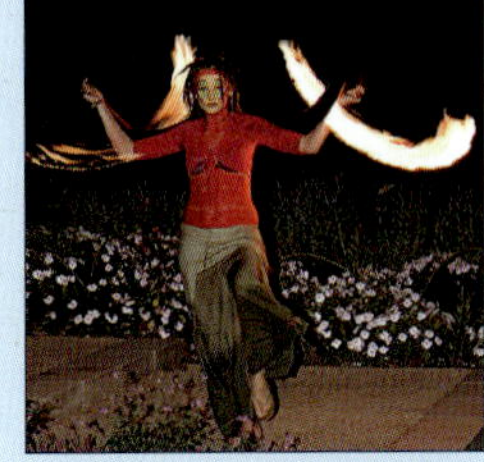

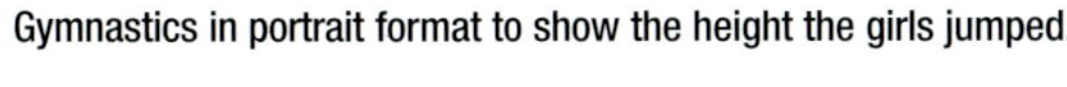

● DARREN BANKS Commonwealth Games 2002 Manchester. Gymnastics in portrait format to show the height the girls jumped.

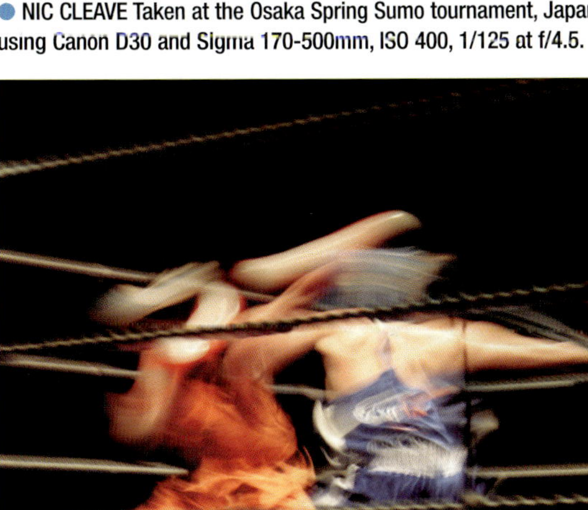

● ANDREW SHACKLEY Taken at an amateur boxing evening. Flash cannot be used, but a slow speed has introduced wonderful blur.

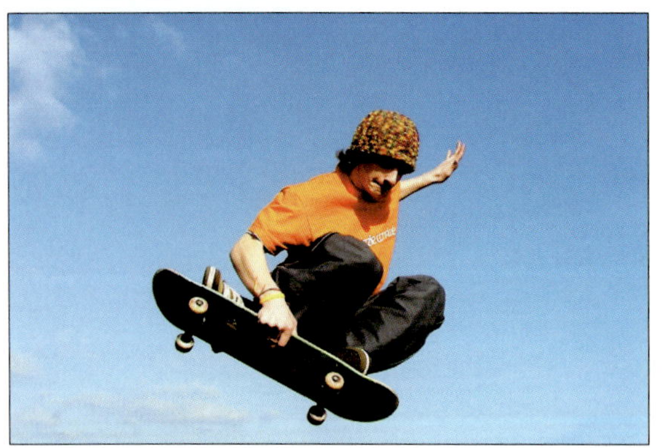
● CHRIS LOUDE Rob Ayton with this perfectly styled 'Tucknee' over the hip in Exeter, taken on a Fuji Finepix S5000.

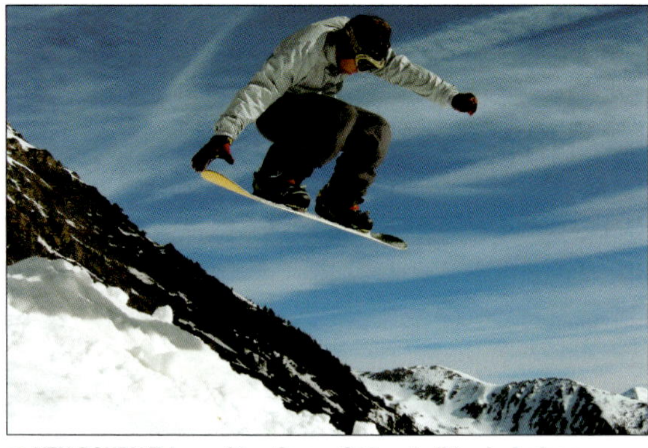
● KEN BOURN Taken with a Canon S45 on holiday in Andorra. Panning as snowboarders were taking off got a little dicey at times!

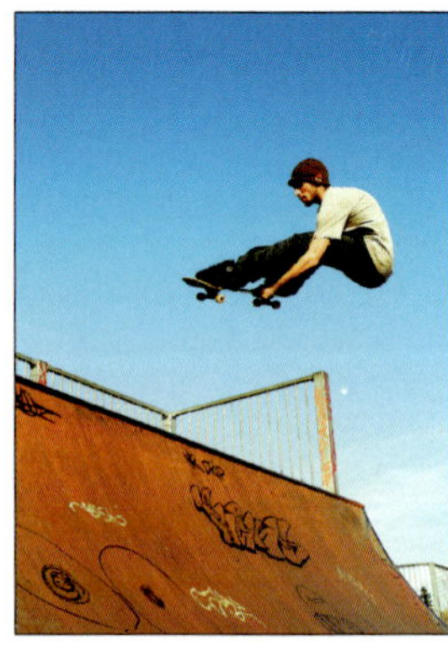
● CHRIS JOHNSON Skater, taken at the highest point.

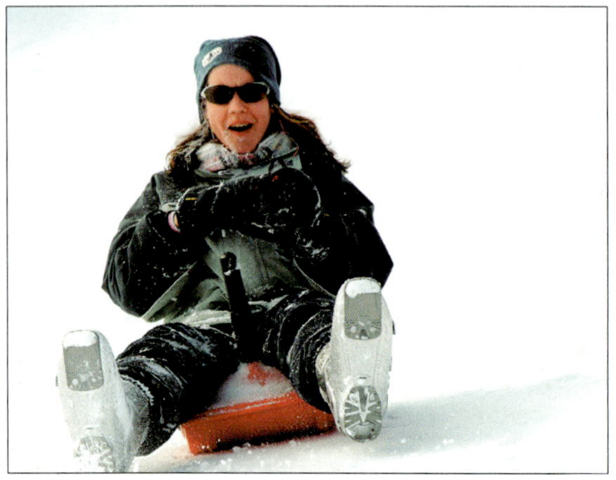
● RICHARD INGRAM PENROSE Alpine fun in the mountains of Austria, taken using a Fuji S2 Pro and Tamron 28-300mm zoom.

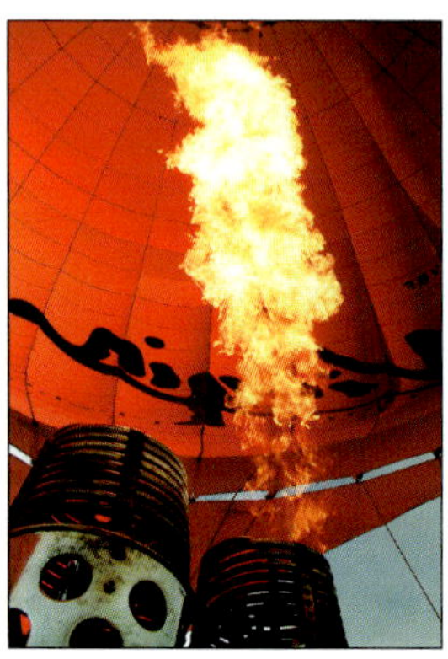
● PAUL SUTTON Close-up of a balloon burner in use.

● ANDREW CHANG Taken at a skateboard tricks competition in London. The camera was set to ISO100 and 135mm lens at f/2.8 to achieve the 1/4000sec shutter speed.

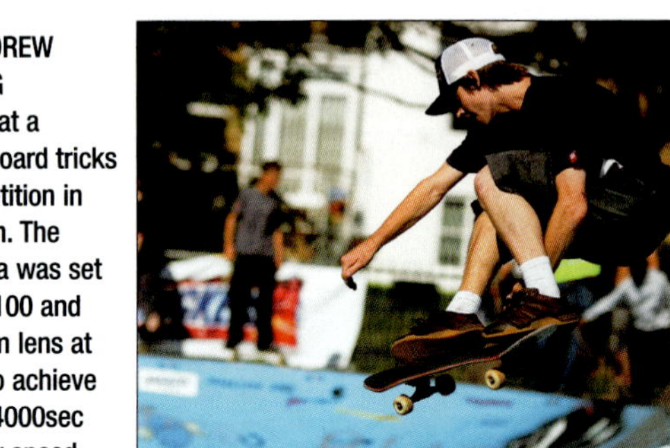

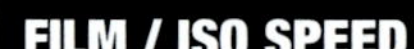

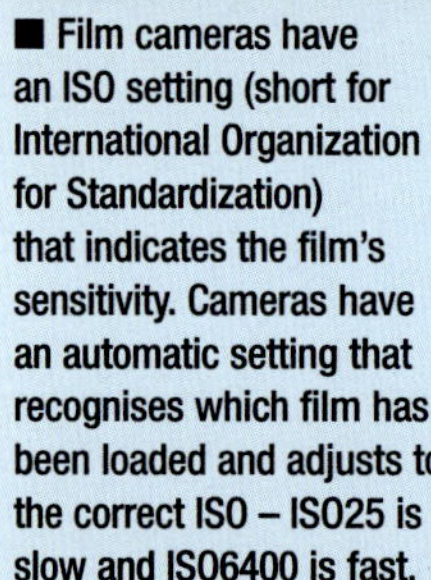

FILM / ISO SPEED

■ Film cameras have an ISO setting (short for International Organization for Standardization) that indicates the film's sensitivity. Cameras have an automatic setting that recognises which film has been loaded and adjusts to the correct ISO – ISO25 is slow and ISO6400 is fast.

You can load a film with a sensitivity that suits the shooting conditions – using slow speed film in bright conditions and fast film in low light. With some film it's also possible to change the ISO and compensate when processing the film.

The problem using faster film is photos become grainy and have less contrast.

■ Digital cameras have an ISO setting too. This adjusts the sensitivity of the recording sensor so similar advantages can be gained.

The disadvantage of setting a fast speed on a sensor is it creates noisy images. Noise reduction systems help here.

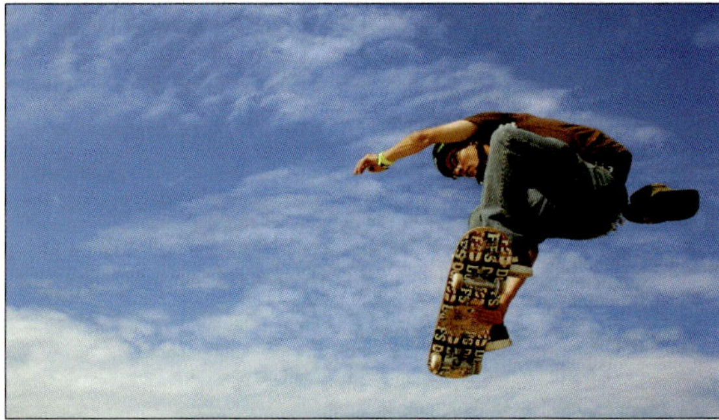
● GUY EPPEL Captured at the Sprite Urban Games 2004, the UK's version of the X-Games, an annual event held in London.

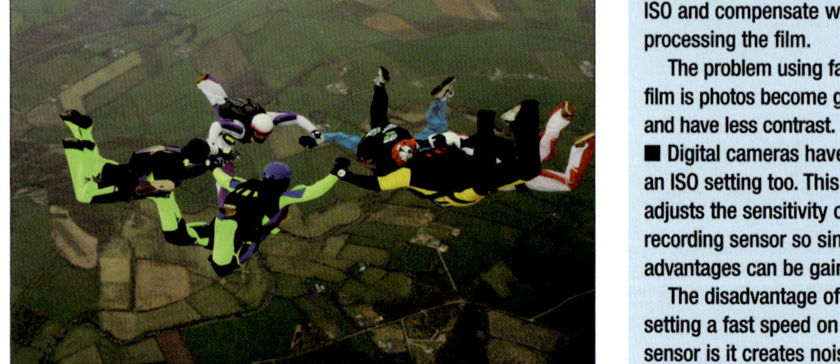
● ANDREW CRELLIN Dune Boarding on 90 Mile Beach, New Zealand. "The shifting sands under my feet made panning difficult."

● DAVID PRITCHARD Four-wheeler race on the frozen Pennessewasse Lake, Norway. With +0.7 exposure compensation in program mode.

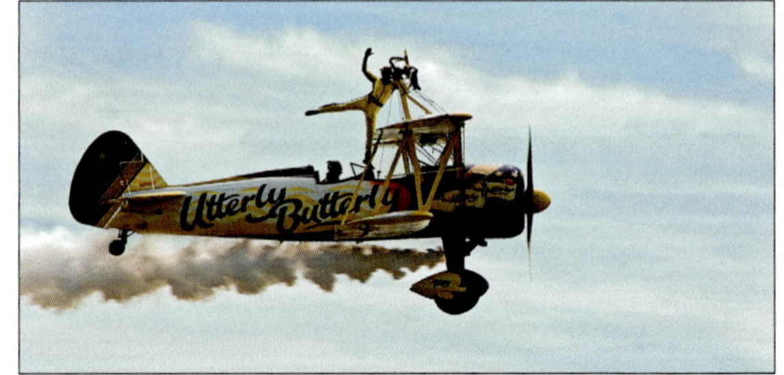

● MICHAEL MURPHY A six way speed star over the Wild Geese Skydiving Club, Co. Londonderry. 28mm lens and 1/750sec speed.

● STEVE CRAMPTON Wing walkers at an airshow. Shot at 1/400sec, f/9.0 with a Canon EOS digital SLR and a 28-300mm lens.

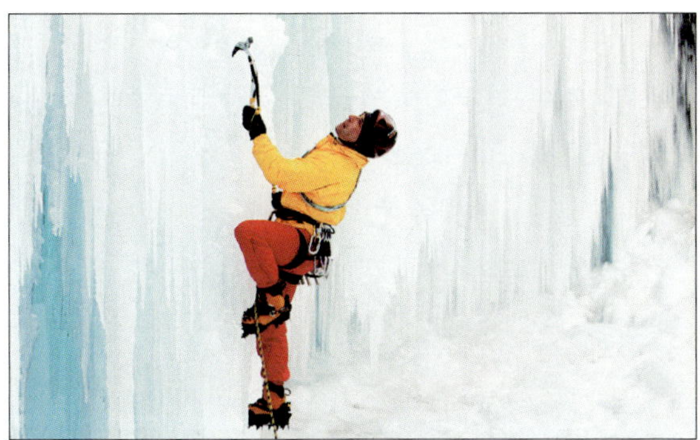

● JAKA ADAMIÈ The colourfully clothed ice climber, placed slightly off-centre, stands out from the white ice wall.

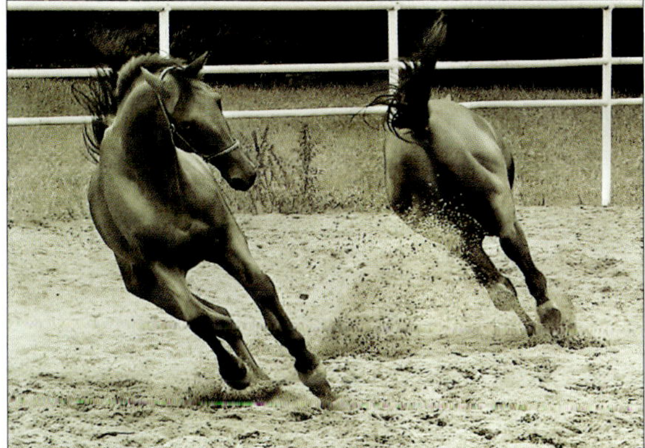

● JOANNA MARIA RYBCZYNSKA Horses at a riding club near Warsaw, Poland, taken on a Sony DSC-V1 at 1/500sec and f/4.0.

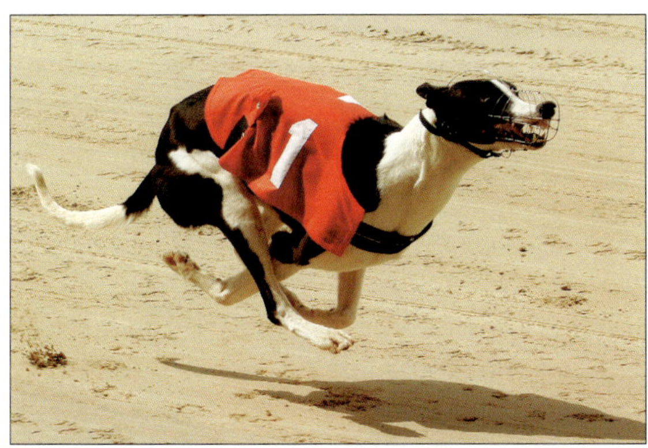

● STEVEN PRICE A fast shutter speed was used on the Canon EOS 20D to ensure the dog was caught in its tracks.

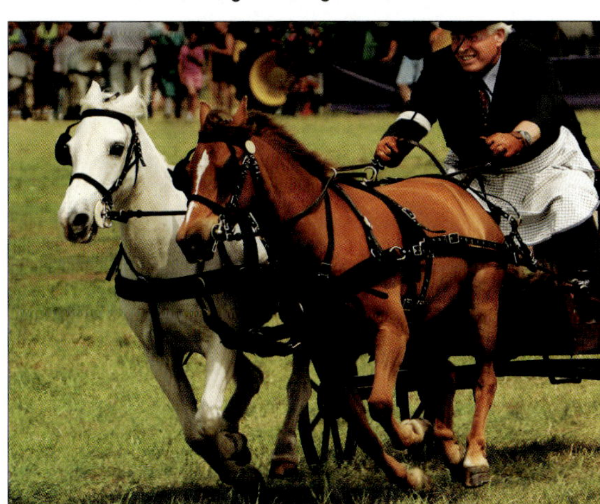

● MICHAEL STEVEN OSBORNE The background was burned in using Photoshop to help emphasize the subject.

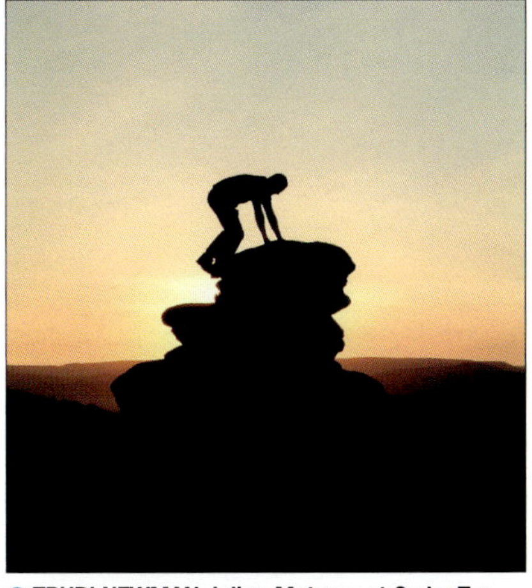

● TRUDI NEWMAN Julian Materna at Owler Tor, Peak District, against the setting sun backdrop.

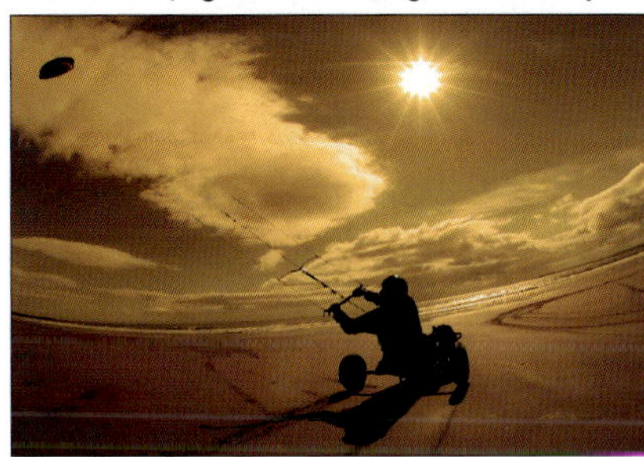

● JOHN WHITE A kite buggy taken with a 10.5mm fisheye lens at Aberavon Beach, South Wales.

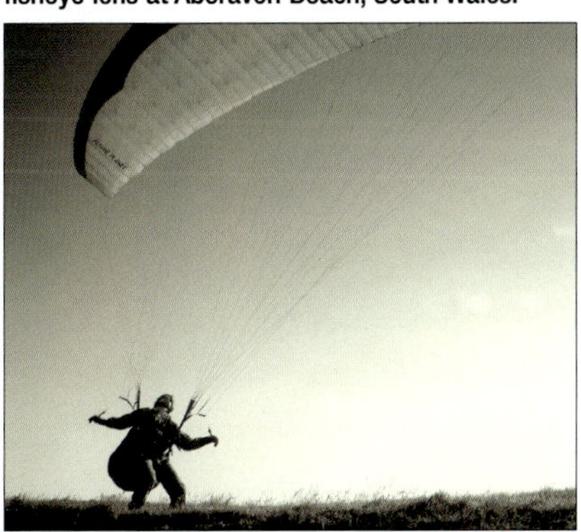

● KARL WOOD Converted B&W, taken at Mam Tor in the Peak District, using a Fuji602 digital camera.

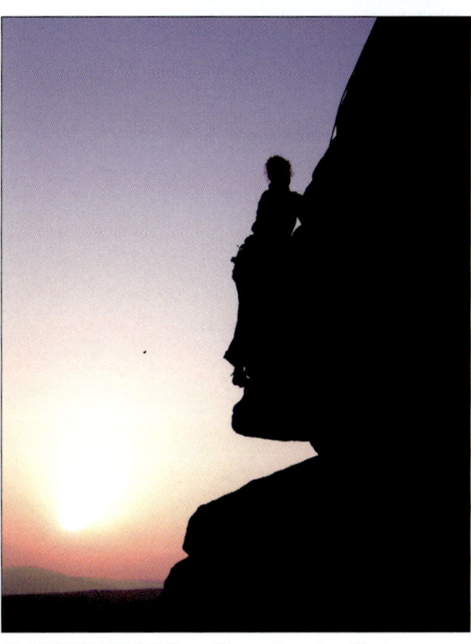

● ANDREW FYFE The silhouette of a climber on Wrinkled Rock with a colourful, twilight sky.

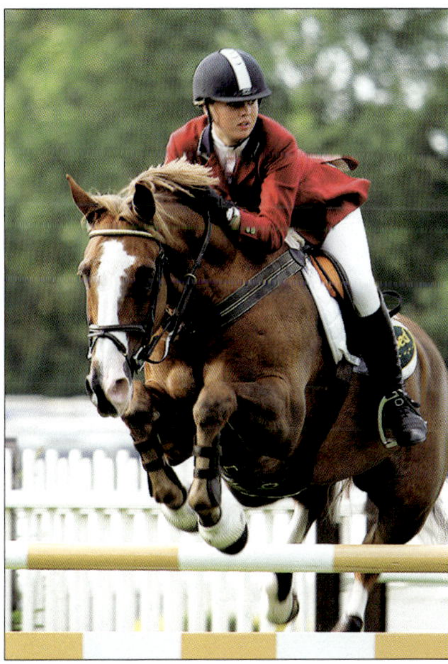

● SIMON THEO Ellen Whitaker at the Hickstead Derby 2005, taken for EQUIPhotos, using a Canon EOS 10D and 70-200mm plus 1.4x converter.

TECHNIQUE TIP – PANNING TO CREATE MOTION BLUR

■ If you follow the subject as it moves across your path and press the shutter, as you continue to follow, you are applying a technique referred to as panning. There's a necessary skill in making the most of this technique though and you have a few things to consider.

■ Firstly, the shutter speed. This needs to be at a speed that ensures the background is blurred, but not so blurred all detail is lost. A faster moving subject will need a proportionally faster shutter speed. You'll need to do a few test shots until you have some experience of what to set.

■ Next is the panning speed. You need a steady hand, an idea of where the subject is going to pass and a panning speed that matches the subject speed and direction. Get any of this wrong and you'll end

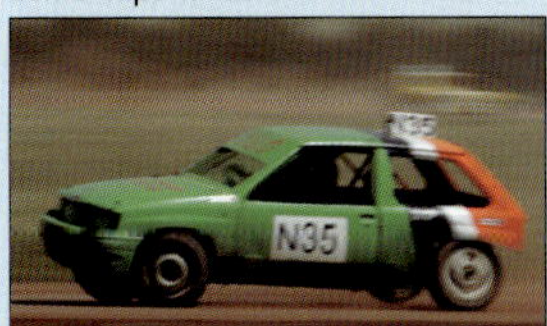

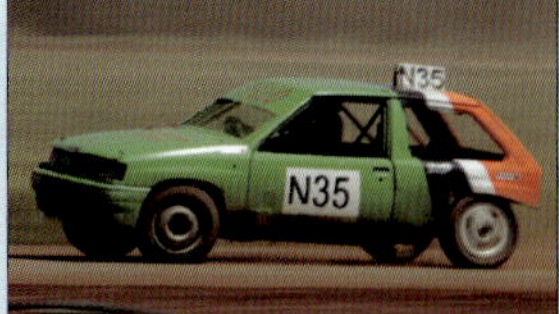

up with a shot like the one on the left where the subject is also blurred. The second shot is much better controlled, but, even so, there's some blur in the top number.

■ The focal length of the lens can have an effect too. A longer lens with a narrower angle means you have to be more accurate in your subject tracking, but once mastered will give the best results.

See the digital method of creating motion blur on page 177

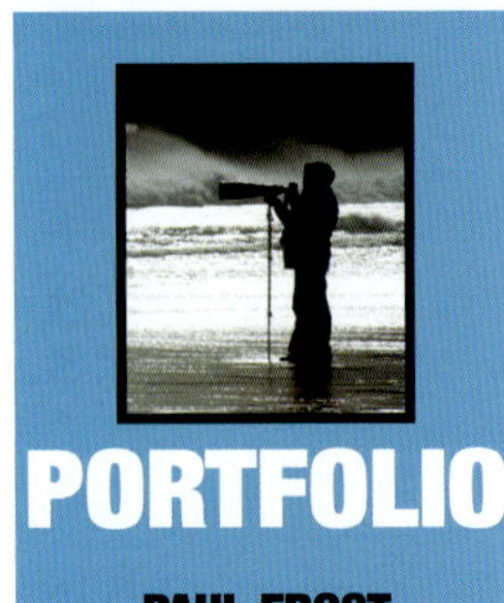

PORTFOLIO

PAUL FROST
Paul made the right move, switching from an archaeology course to a photography HND.

My first camera was a Zenith 35mm. I dabbled in photography, never doing anything special, until a work placement required me to photograph items at a local museum.

This sparked my interest in photography again and I bought a Canon EOS 1000F at auction. At this time I was also learning to kite surf and, watching other kite surfers around me, I thought what ideal material it would be to photograph.

Surfers liked what I was doing and bought my pictures, motivating me to get serious about photography. I switched from my archaeology course to an HND in photography and digital imaging.

I love photographing extreme sports – surfing in particular. For these I use the Canon EOS 1D Mark I body, with the Canon 600mm f/4 lens for sharp, fast focusing. I have a back-up body of an EOS D60, which these images were produced on.

Some believe the D60 isn't very good for sports photography, but it certainly works for me! I also use Ikelite underwater housing for water shots with an EOS 50E film body and sometimes use the Mamiya RB67 Pro medium-format camera for advertising work.

Anybody can have a go at sports photography, but getting that special shot does require much time and planning – knowing where to stand and where the action will be isn't easy. And you have to be prepared to suffer for your art – at a big competition I can be on the beach for eight hours or more, even ending up in the water at times!

For anyone wanting to take these kind of photos, good contrast and light helps to produce sharp images, which can be breathtaking

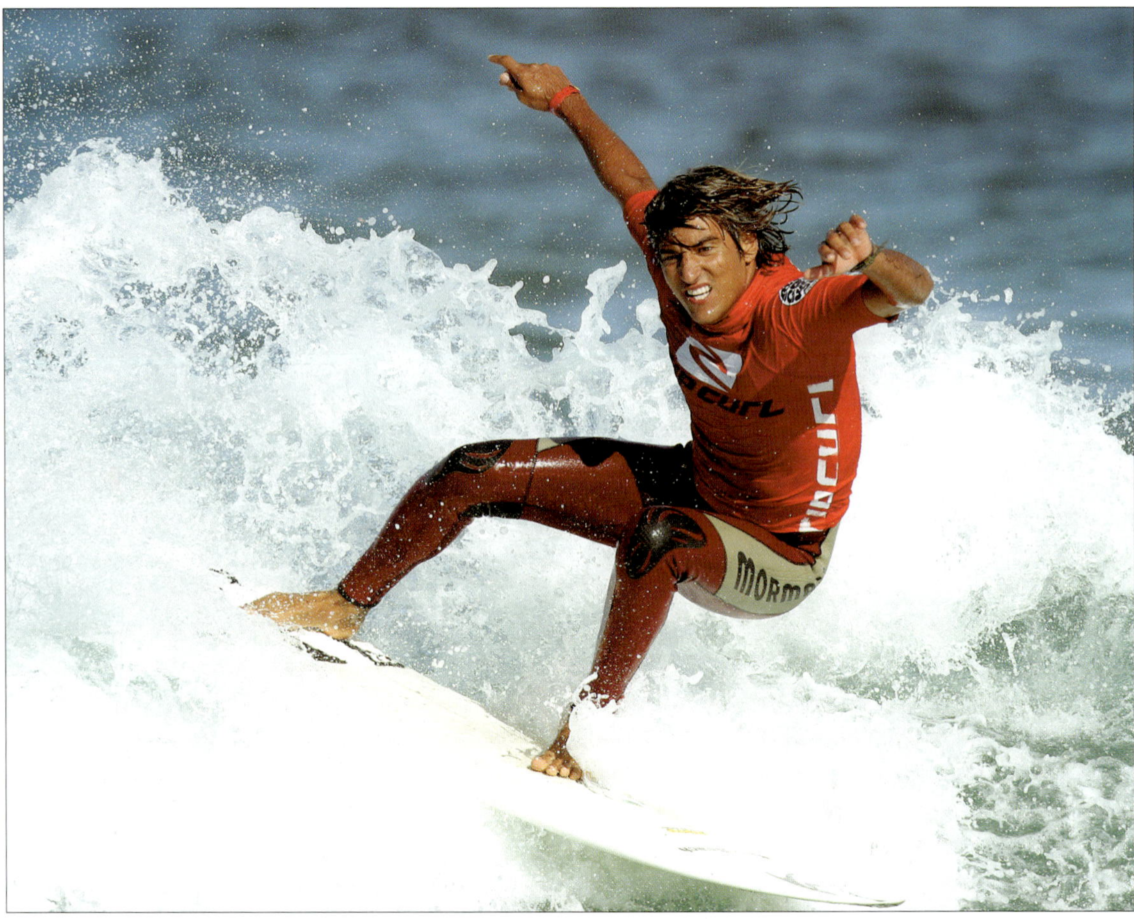

● Wait until you see the white of their teeth before you press the shutter button! I think this guy could be in an advert for toothpaste! A 600mm f/4 lens was attached to Paul's Canon EOS D60 to get this frame filling surfer.

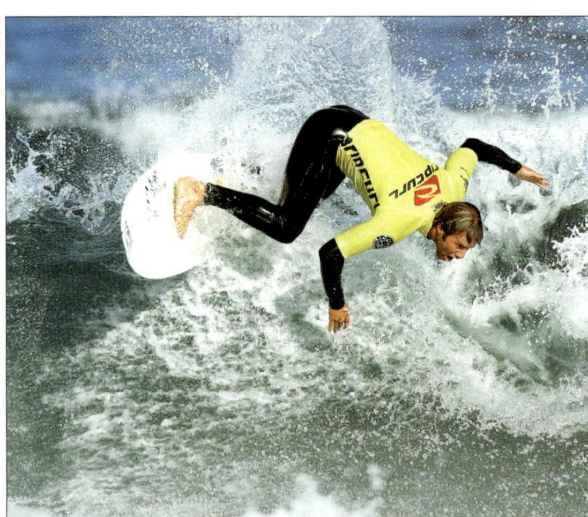

● This guy was really on a wing and a prayer to land this move from this angle, but he did and carried on to do more power moves.

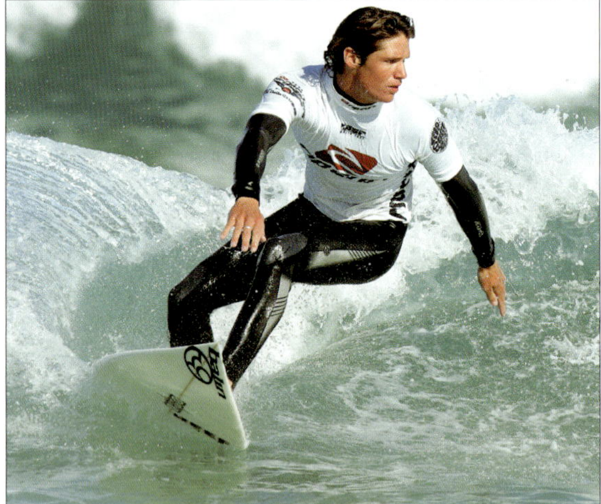

● A summer shot from the UK. The intensity of the guy's gaze, in the direction of his next move, helps make this shot.

on-screen. I love looking at the droplets of water thrown up by the movements of the surfer and his board.

I've had some great photography experiences but my most memorable was at the UK National Wakeboard Championships in Cornwall. I'd got a place on the tow boat but a couple of Wakeboard Magazine photographers and the editor got

me thrown off.

Undeterred, I changed into my wetsuit and swam out into the 70 foot deep lake with my water housing. As the tow boat came past me, the wakeboarder behind it jumped off a floating VW Beetle right in front of me. I snapped away, getting several shots including the guy taking off the Beetle, the cable trailing back to the boat and a perfect blue sky

with fluffy white clouds – and the photographers staring back at me!

Back on dry land, the editor of Wakeboard Magazine chased me for the pictures. Afterwards I was delighted to see my picture, the biggest printed in the issue, accompanying a two-page spread which opened the magazine.

I mainly use digital because it's much cheaper than using film and there's so much you can do with it

that I never leave an event without at least one picture. I still have film cameras, but I don't usually use them unless a client specifically requests film.

In future, I hope to expand my event photography and be able to travel to places like Hawaii and Fiji to film big waves and photograph sharks in their natural environment. ∎

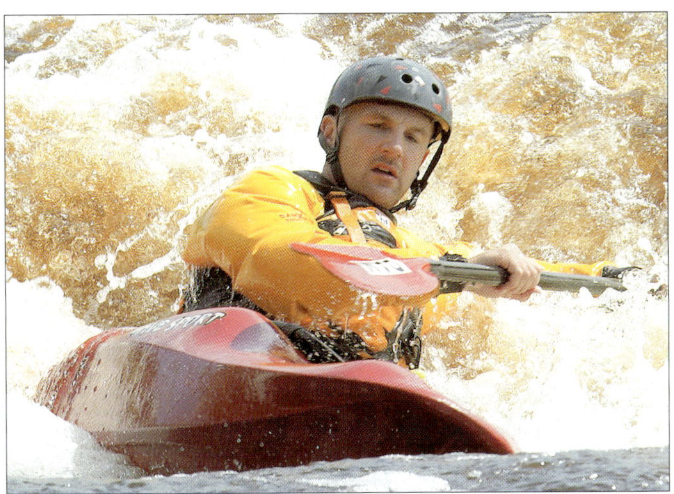

● JOHN SHORT The Canon 100-400mm zoom was attached to an EOS 10D to get this close-up of a white water slalom event.

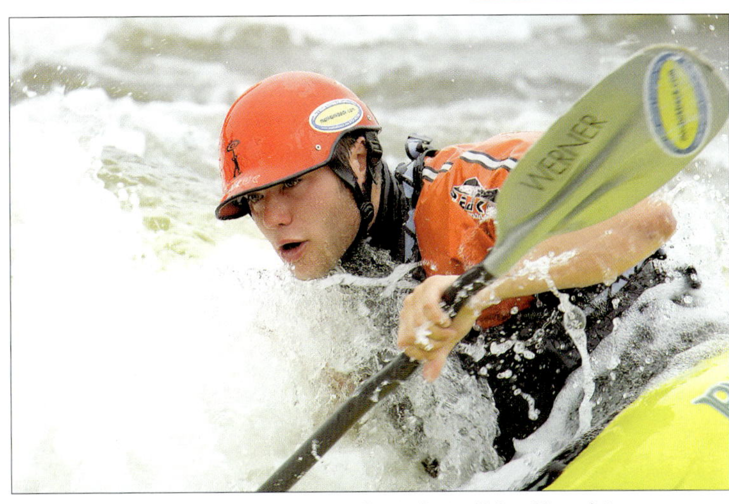

● MIKE NEALE Taken at the National Water Sports Centre, Holme Pierrpoint near Nottingham, using a Canon EOS 1d Mk2, and 100-400mm IS zoom lens.

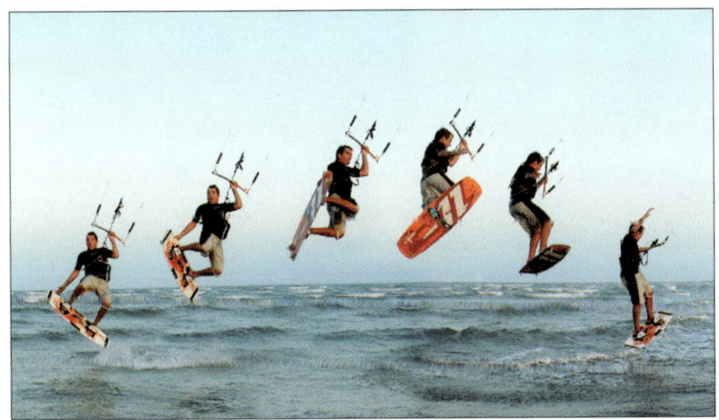

● MARK ABLE This kite surfing jump sequence was multi-layered and then blended and erased using Photoshop.

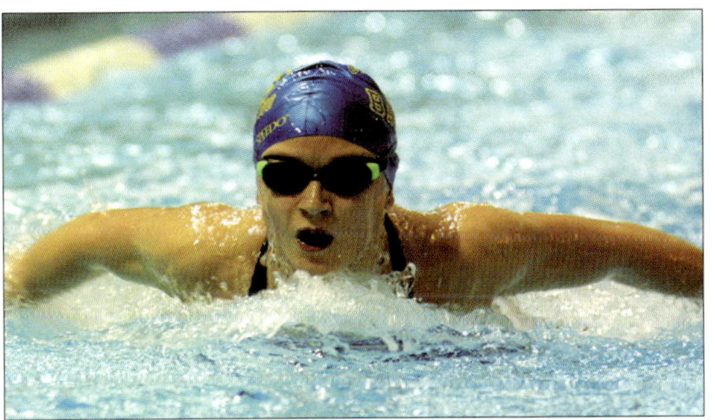

● PHIL SEARLE The low shooting angle has accentuated the swimmer, lifting her body out of the water, and f/2.8 blurred the background.

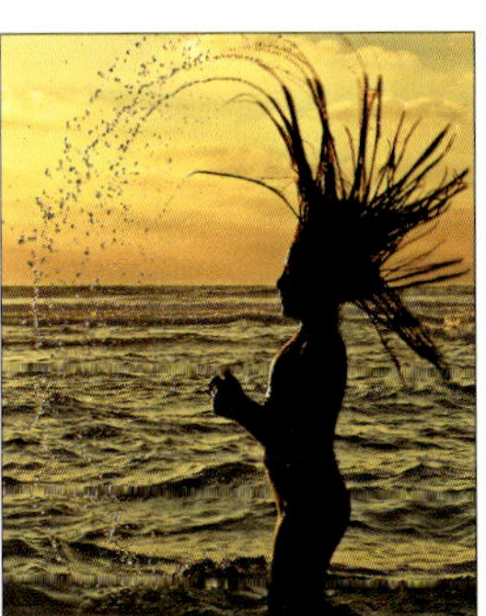

● HERMIN ABRAMOVITCH 1/1000sec freezes the back flip.

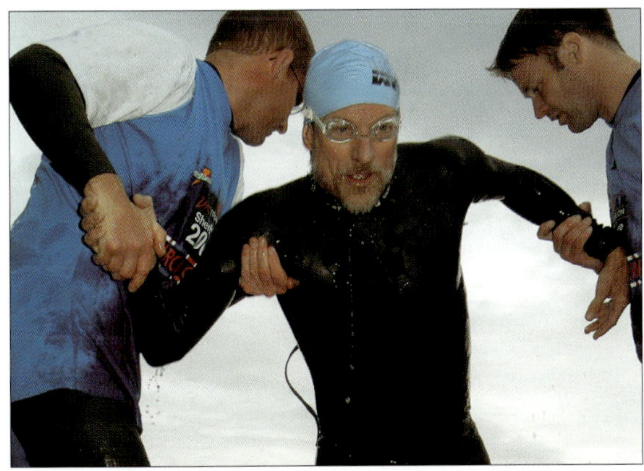

● JOHN COXON This plucky triathlete, competing at Half Ironman UK 2004, Sherbourne Castle lake, was captured by John lying down.

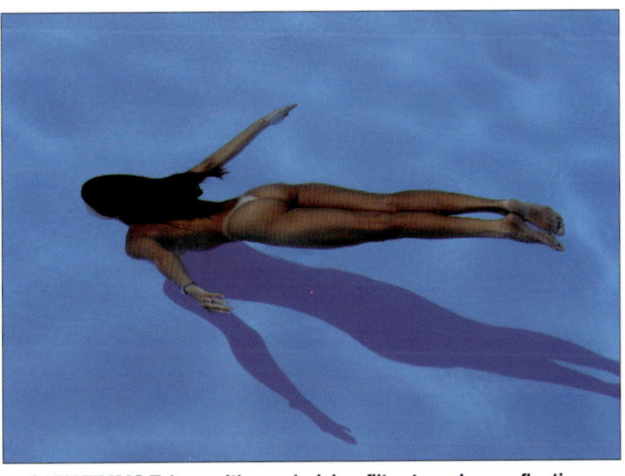

● GARY TIMMS Taken with a polarising filter to reduce reflections off the water's surface. Notice the way the shadow floats below her.

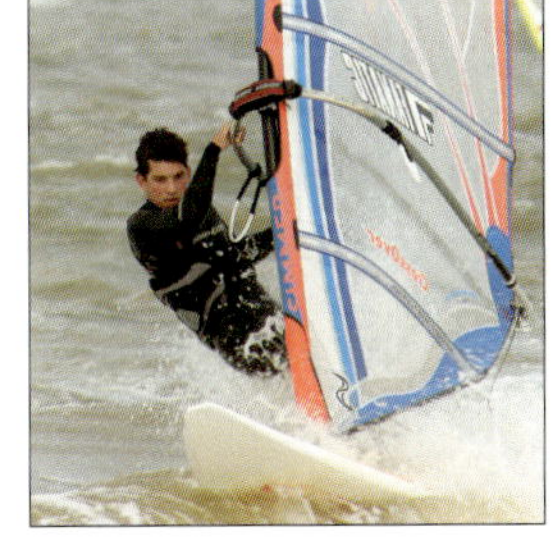

● MARCUS KEELER Tight crop on this dismal day for surfers.

SHUTTER SPEEDS

■ One of the most important considerations when taking action is the shutter speed. A fast shutter speed of 1/500sec or more will freeze most motion, while a slow shutter speed of 1/8sec or slower will emphasise motion by creating subject blur.

■ The shutter speed used needs to reflect the speed, direction and distance of the subject. If the subject is closer it will appear to be travelling faster than a distant subject, so a faster shutter speed is necessary. Some of the captions on these pages indicate the speed used.

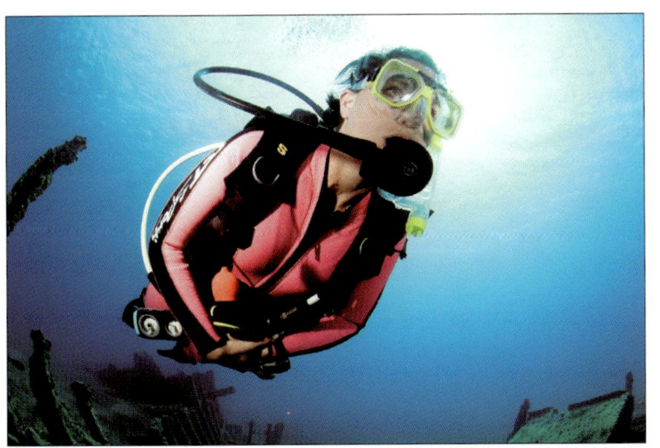

● ROBERT SMITH Diver, Iva Jedlikova, on wreck. Part of a series shot for the dive centre in the Elounda Bay Hotel complex in Crete.

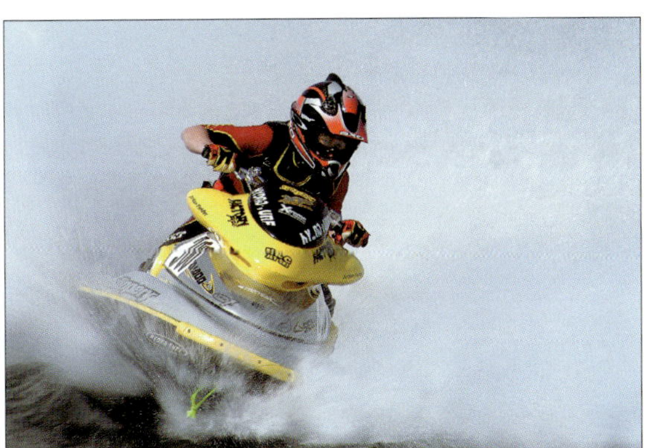

● JOHN TISBURY Jet skier takes a tight turn, captured using a Nikon D100 with a 300mm lens. The camera was mounted on a monopod.

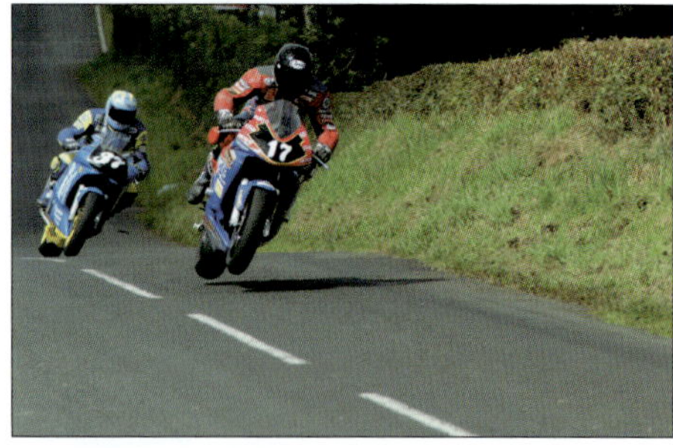

● DEREK CLEGG "I focused manually on the road, panning and firing the shutter at the focal point."

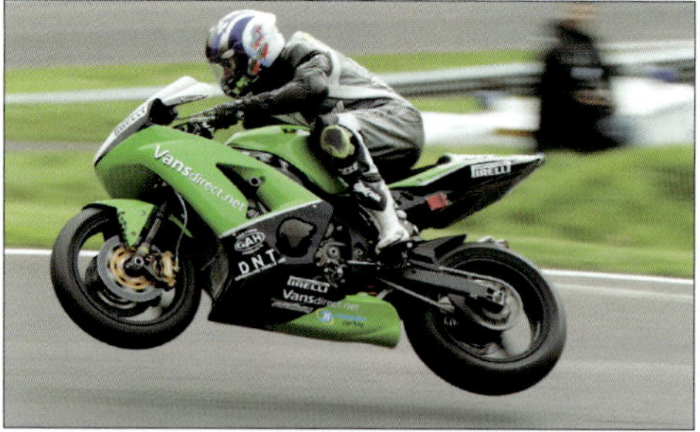

● MERV PAGE The notorious mountain section at Cadwell Park displays perfect panning technique.

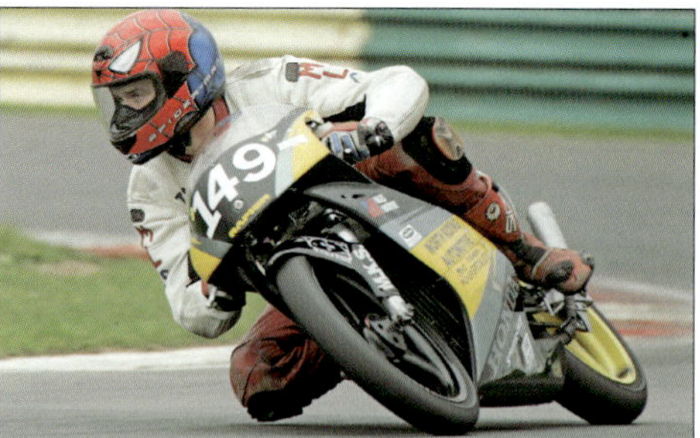

● IAN HARDY The Canon EOS 1D MKII was set at 1/250 sec and ISO400. The 100-400mm lens was at f/8.

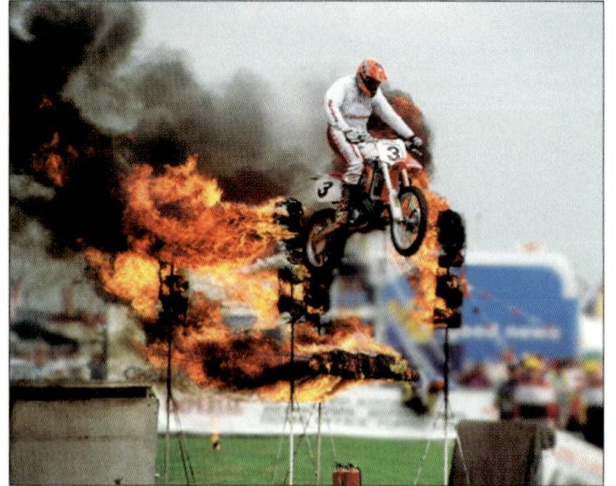

● PETE LOVATT Motorcycle jump at the Wirral Show, caught on a Canon EOS 50E with 75-300mm lens.

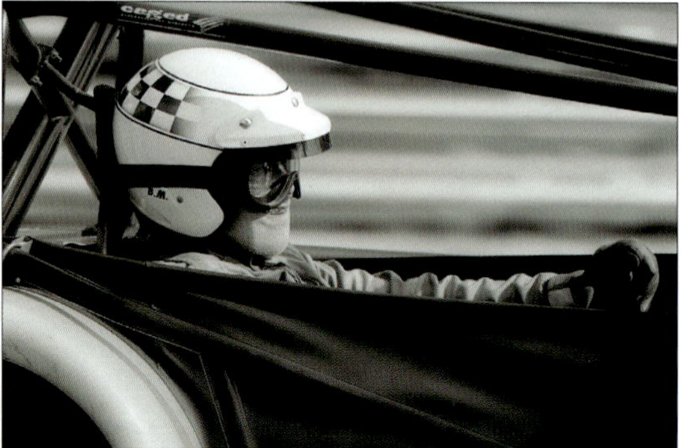

● GARY WILLIAMS On the approach to Druid's at Brand's Hatch. Shot on a Canon EOS 10D with a 100-400mm IS L at 400mm.

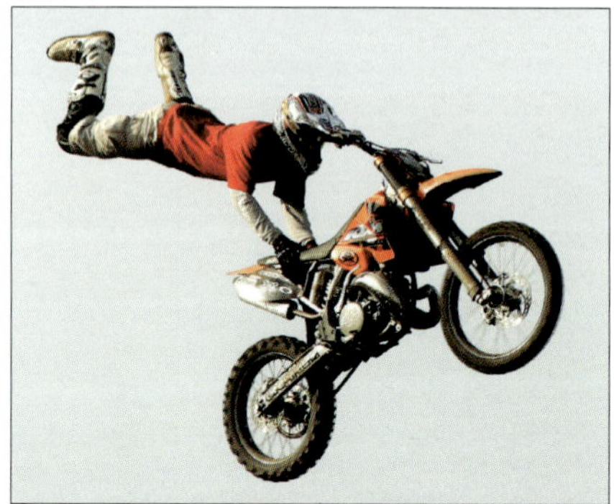

● STEVE HYDE The UK Freestyle Motocross team at the 2004 Moto1 event, Donnington Park.

MOTORSPORTS TIPS

■ If you know the track and have knowledge of styles of individual racers you will find it easier to anticipate where the action will occur.

■ Pre-focus on a point where action will occur and lock the focus at this point manually.

■ Invest in a long telephoto with a large aperture – you can't cut corners with sports photography.

■ You only have one chance so be very prepared and shoot using continuous frame mode so you have less chance of missing the moment.

■ If you need to use flash, take it off camera. Flash in daylight can be used as fill-in.

■ Learn to keep your eye that's not looking through the viewfinder open so you can look around and see what's coming into frame.

■ Experiment with panning speeds to see which works best for you.

■ Always attempt to stand in a safe place. The inside of a corner is safer than the outside, but find a spot where there aren't as many spectators.

■ Talk with event organisers to try and get a press pass and prime track positions.

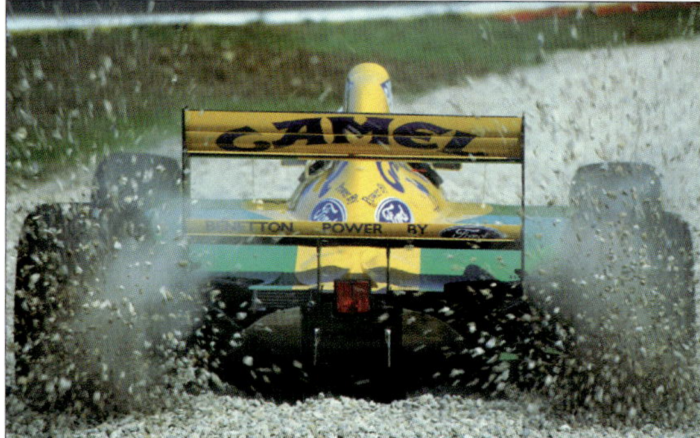

● STEVE TAYLOR A Benetton Formula One car spins off in the gravel trap during a practice session. A fast speed has frozen the gravel.

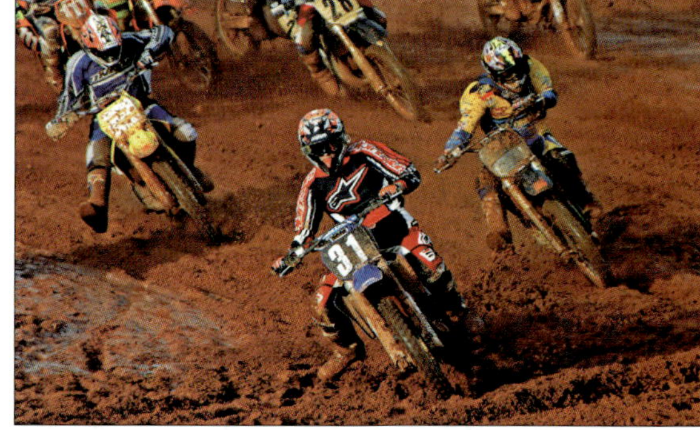

● STEVEN HANNA Riders heading into the first corner at a charity motocross, Desertmartin, on a Canon EOS 300D, 1/640sec at f/5.6.

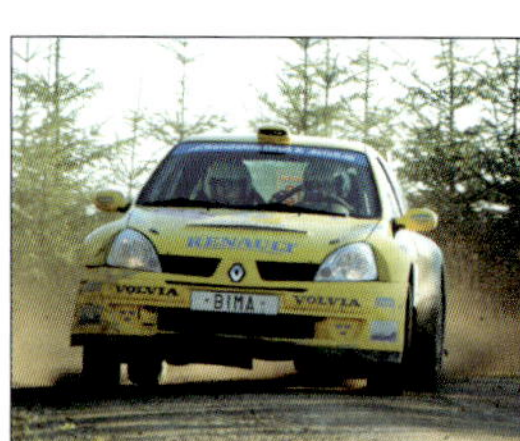

● DARREN COOMBS "A 170-500mm lens was used so I could remain at a safe distance from the rally car."

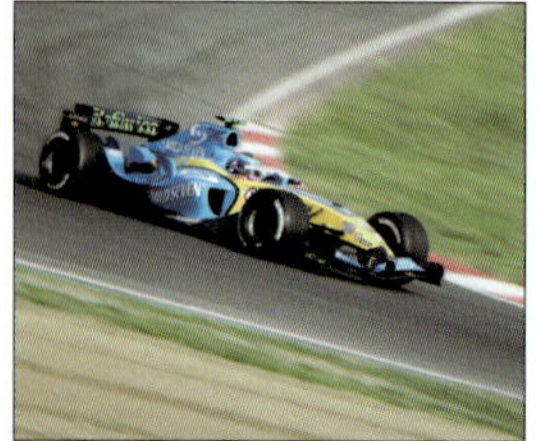

● ANTONIO ALOMAR Renault Formula 1 car captured at a training session in Barcelona.

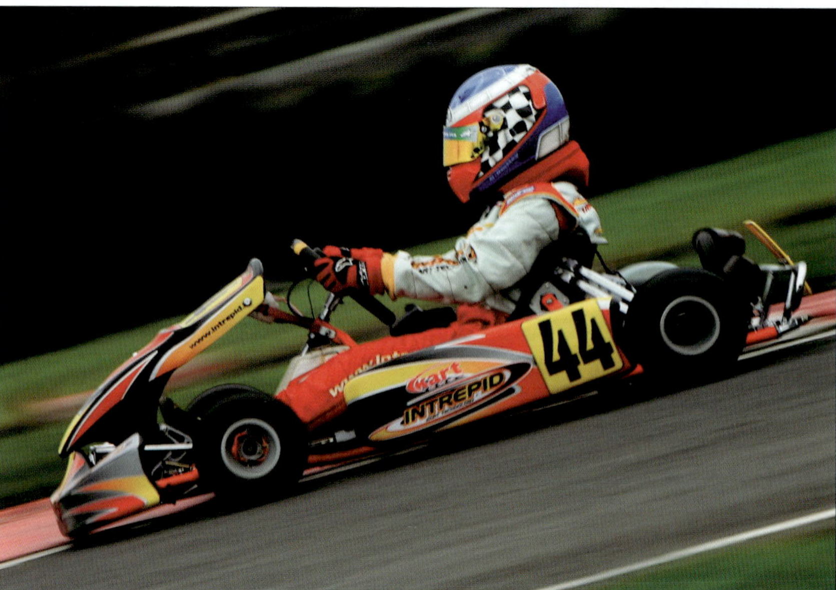

● STEVEN HANNA The photograph has been angled and subject panned at 1/125sec to emphasise the speed. Steven used a Canon EOS 10D at ISO200 with a 70-200mm f/4 'L' lens set at f/7.1.

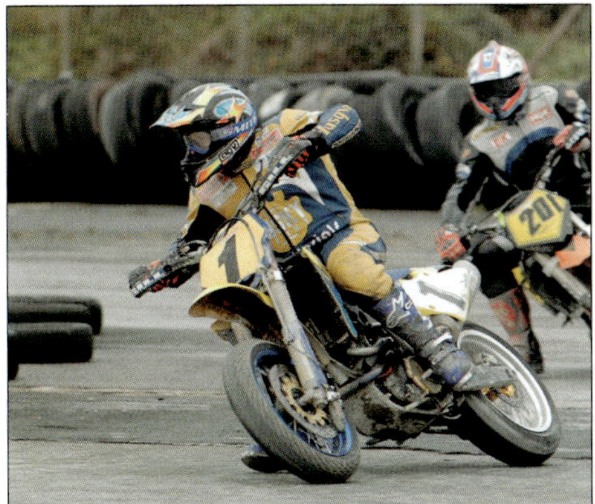

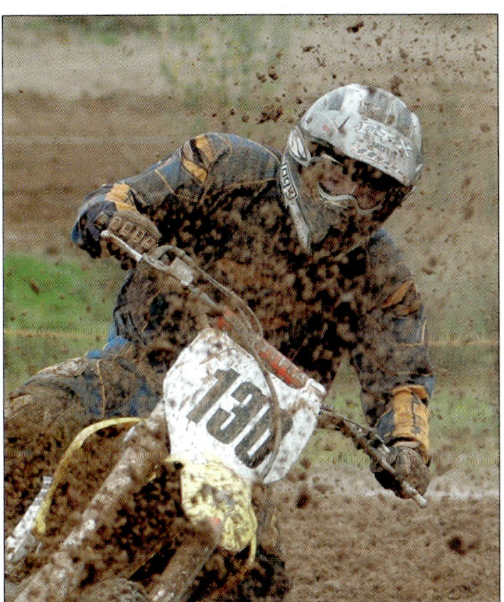

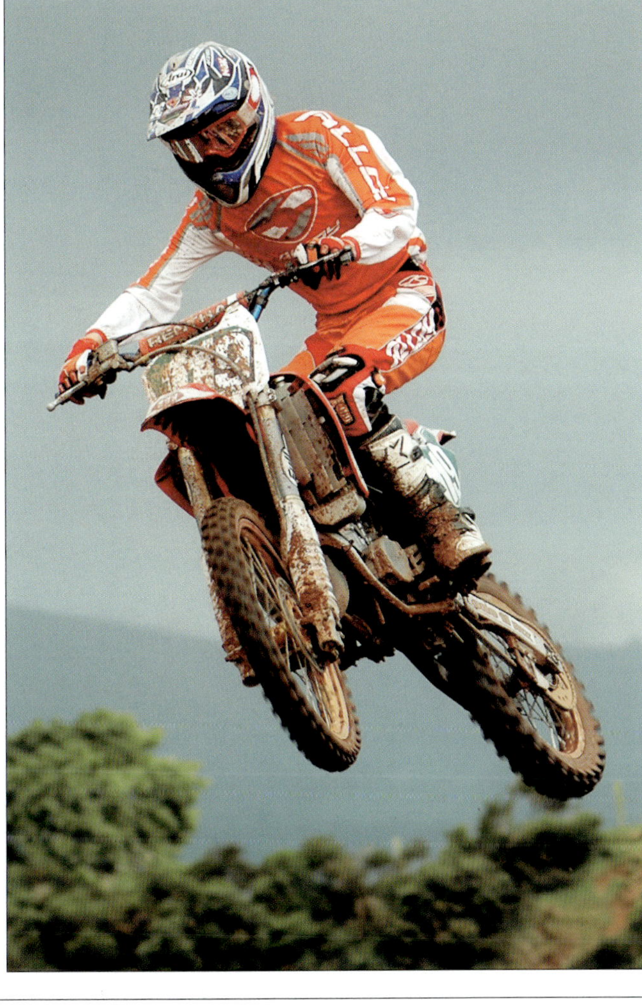

PORTFOLIO

JOE BEATTIE
Joe is a regular at Moto-X events and his work appears in national publications.

I got my first camera when I was 14 – a 110 format camera I got free after sending off tops from a few cereal packets!

I loved using this but after developing an interest in motorsport I realised I would need more suitable kit. I saved up and bought a Zenith E and a couple of lenses, which made a world of difference. I still didn't know much about things like settings, so went along to my local camera club and learned by listening to more experienced members.

After getting my first job I bought an Olympus OM10 and some zoom lenses. I used Olympus kit throughout the '70s, '80s and '90s, plus medium-format Bronica kit for studio work.

My photography improved and I became a regular at youth Moto-X events. My profile grew and local and national publications began using my photos for articles and rider profiles.

When photographing motorsports I walk around the course first in the opposite direction as the bikes will be going, which lets me scout for areas of maximum action potential. If I've been asked to cover a particular rider I keep in mind when they'll be coming into view, which requires a tremendous amount of focus and concentration.

I currently use Nikon D70 cameras, which have a great feel and solid build quality, with a range of lenses from 18mm to 400mm, both zoom and prime. For motorsport, my 18-70 zoom, 80-200 f/2.8 zoom & 300mm f/4 prime lenses are essential.

I prefer digital photography as it's cheaper and more convenient. In future I hope to become involved in sports photography on a semi-professional level. ∎
www.joebt.me.uk

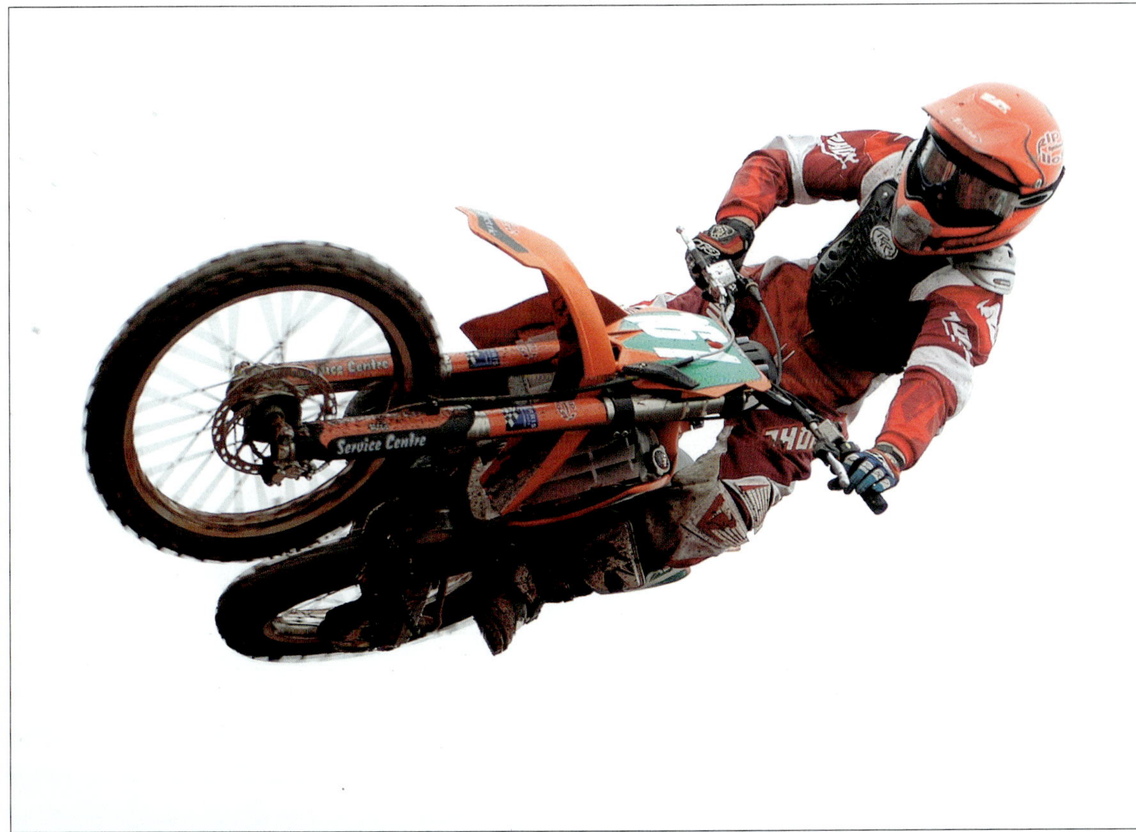

● The four photographs here represent the type of work Joe does at motorsports events around the country.

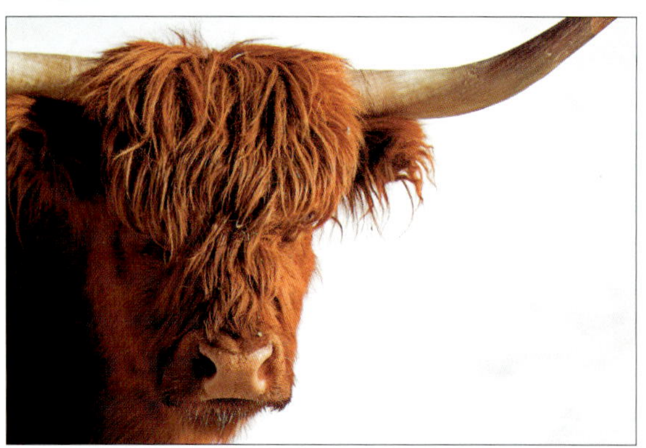

● ADAM BURTON A tightly cropped mug shot of a Scottish Highland cow, photographed on a farm in New England, USA.

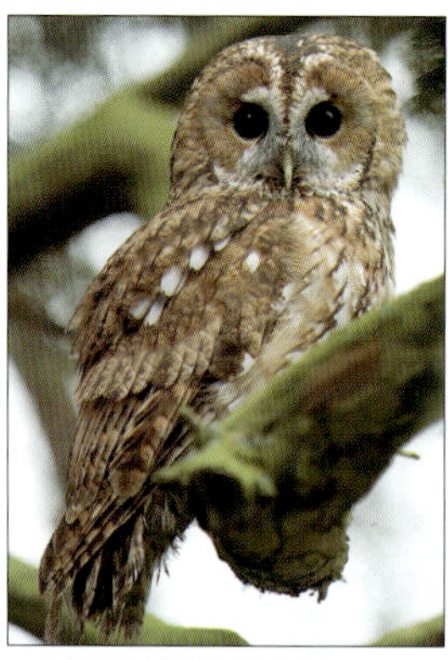

● SIMON SPARKES EOS20D with EF70-200mm IS lens at 148mm.

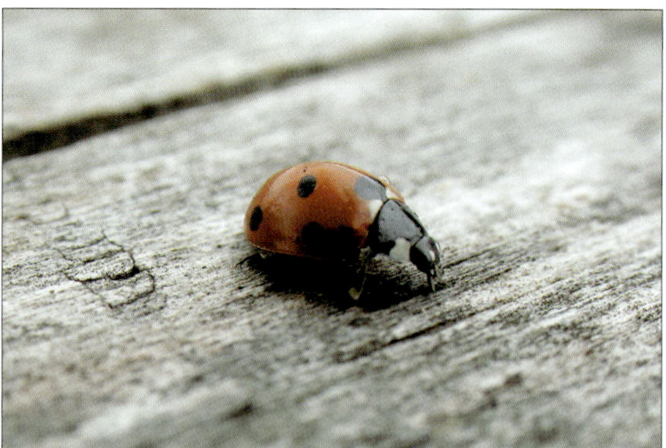

● TOM CHARLES The close distance and use of wide aperture has made the depth-of-field limited, drawing attention to the ladybird.

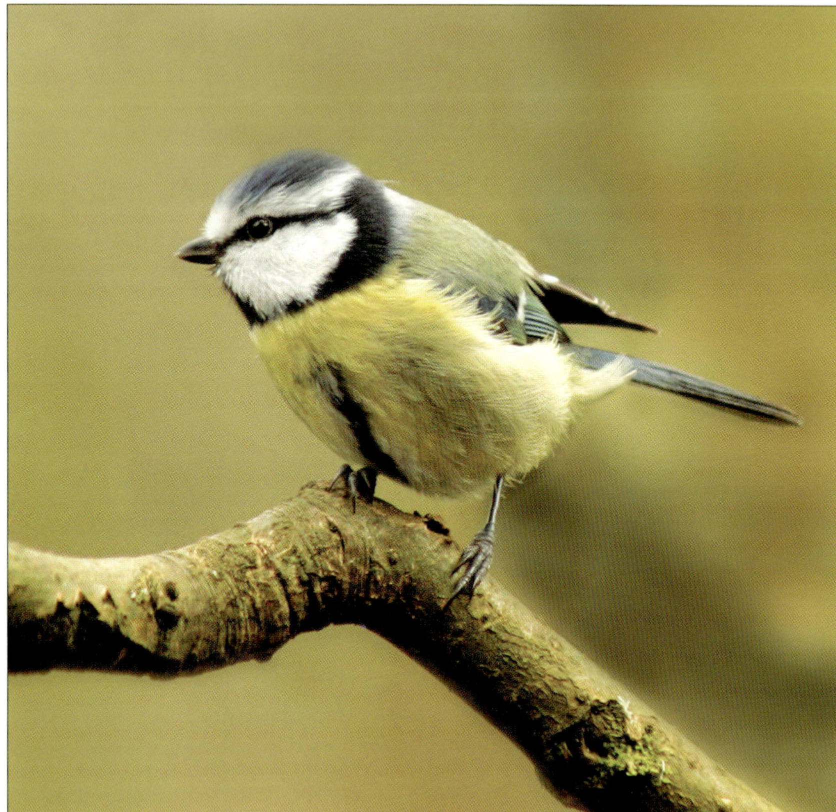

● MARTIN PETTINGER Peanuts were placed by a curved branch to tempt birds on a cold spring day. The focal length of the lens used to shoot this blue tit was 200mm.

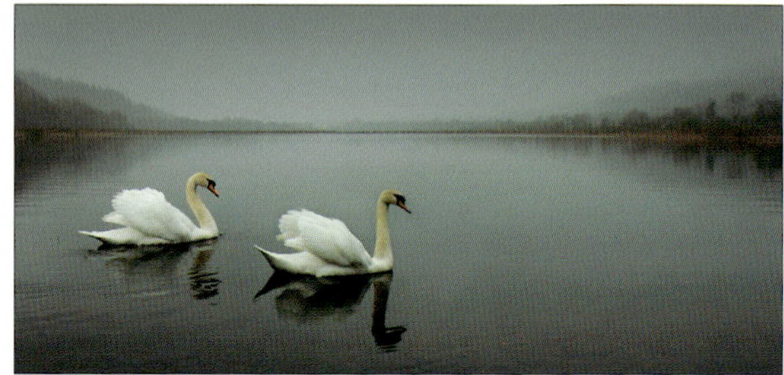

● ROBERT TAYLOR Swans taken at Rheola lakes, South Wales, using a Nikon D70 and 18-70DX lens.

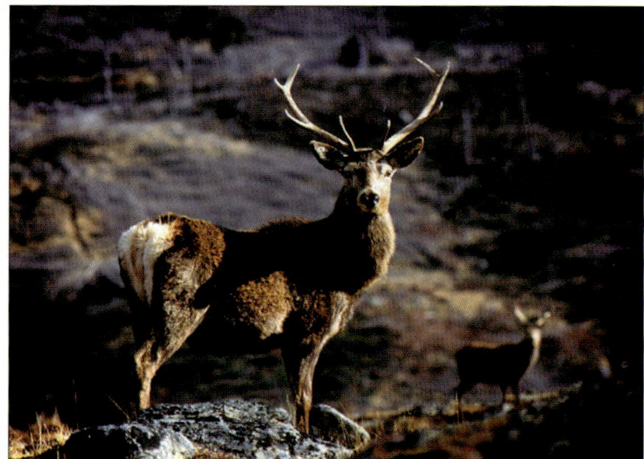

● BRIAN D CLARK Two red deer stags photographed on Velvia, using a Nikon F5 and 300mm Nikkor in Glen Cannich, Scottish Highlands.

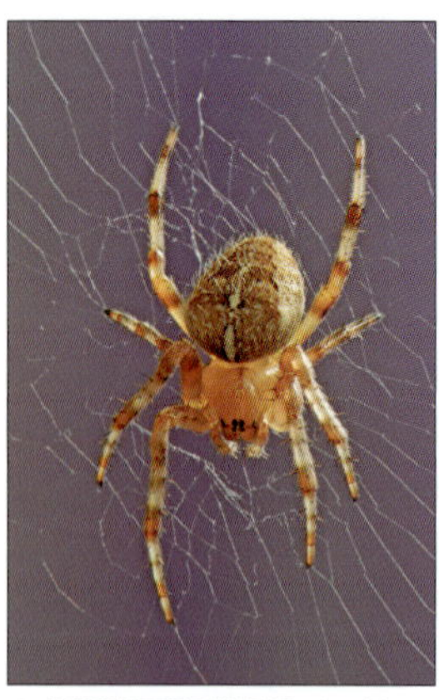

● GEMM FERRANE Shot with a Canon EOS 10D and 100mm f/2.8 macro in natural light with lilac curtains as a background. The exposure was 4sec at f/22.

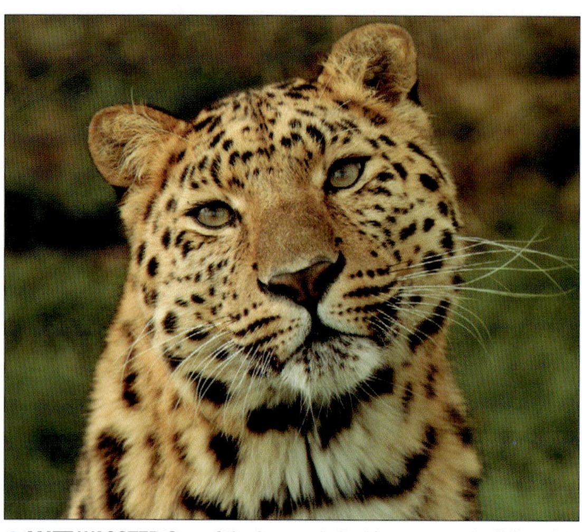

● MATT WAGSTER One of the Leopards lost in a moment of thought at the Wildlife Heritage Foundation in Kent.

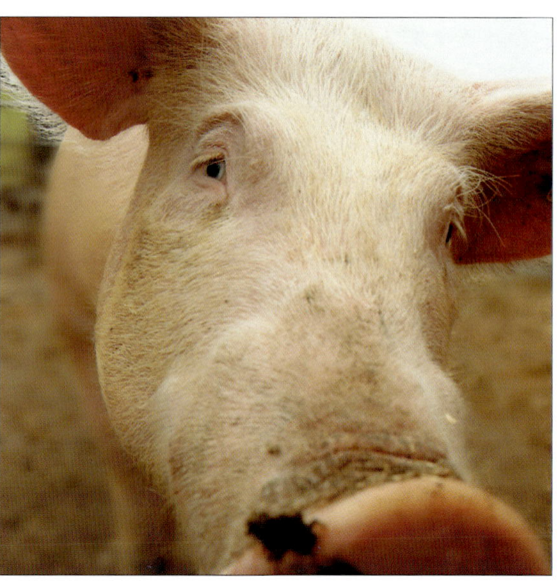

● MATT PAGE A farm pig, taken up close with a Pentax *ist-D and 16mm lens. Selectively blurred in Photoshop to increase depth.

Nature

Some would argue that nature is one of the hardest subjects to photograph. Okay, the category covers a broad range of subjects, from sleeping caged animals to cheetahs speeding along at 70mph in pursuit of their next supper. It does depend on the subject and here we've pulled together a huge variety of species – some easy, some incredibly hard to photograph.

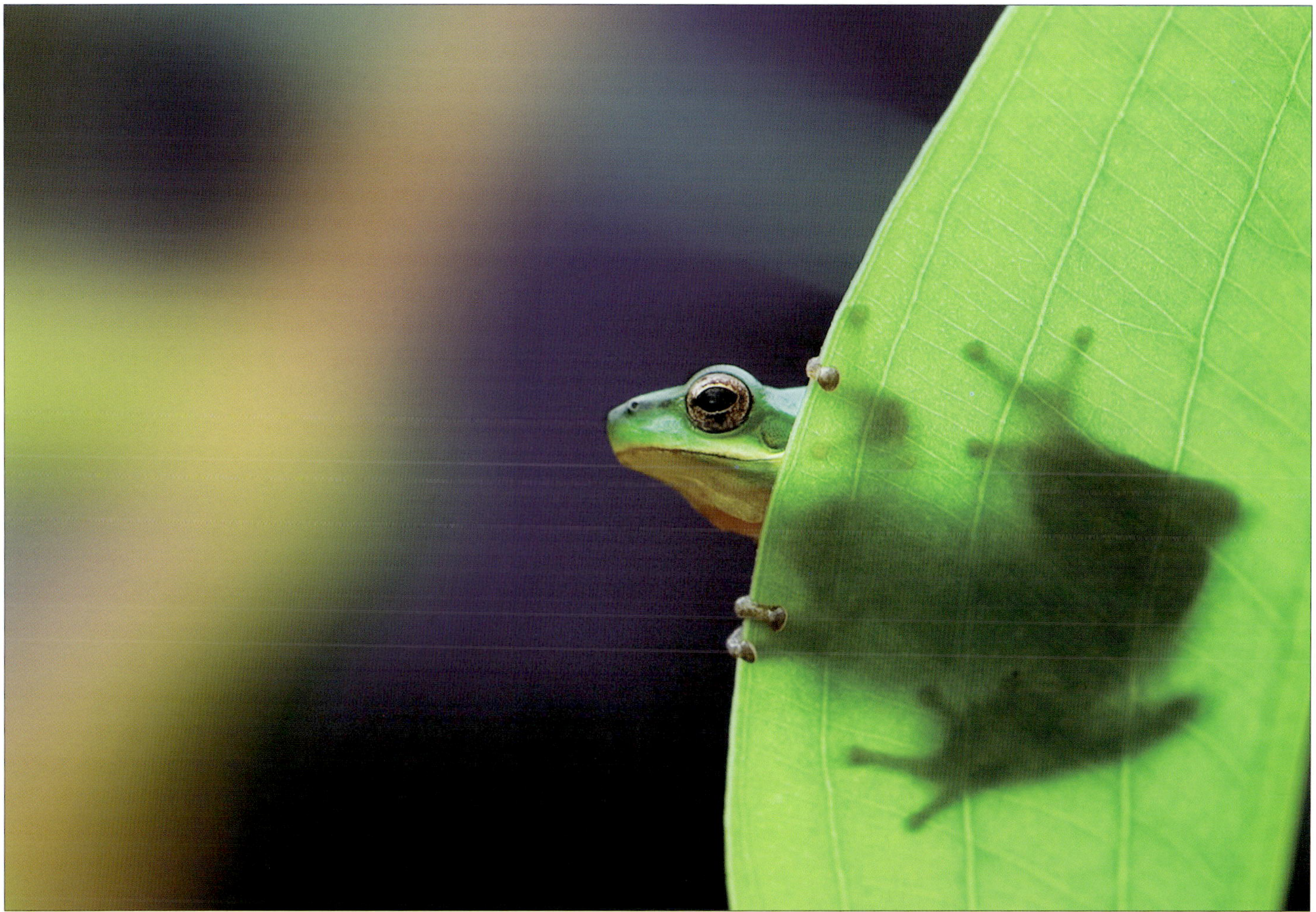

● STEVE NEIL Litoria Fallax (Eastern Sedge) backlit on a leaf, taken with a Canon EOS 10D with a 100mm Macro lens. This is one of the smallest tree frogs in Queensland. It can be difficult to see as it has the ability to change its colour very quickly to match what it's sitting on. This can vary from any shade of green to fawn.

There's a saying, "Never work with children and animals". Well, wild animals take that statement one step further into problematic territory for the photographer. Bird photographers, for example, may spend days in a hide waiting for the elusive kingfisher to land on the pre-focused perch. Safari photographers will be up before the crack of dawn and cover hundreds of miles in pursuit of a herd of elephants, while insect photographers may invest in complex bellows systems and remote triggering devices to allow them to hone in on minute creatures.

Our nature category covers everything from the tiny fairyfly to the gigantic African elephant. And while the caged owl may, in theory, be easier to photograph than a wild cheetah, even the bored owl can create problems when you're trying to take a natural looking shot.

So, what is it that makes a good nature photograph? Well, all the usual composition, focusing and exposure technicalities are still required, but, unlike a shot of a static landscape or building, the nature photographer also has to consider subject speed and its often-unpredictable movement.

Ideally, the wildlife subject should look natural so the cage bars, tethers and man made trappings need to be either carefully cropped when composing or edited out digitally later.

In zoos and safari parks it's often possible to place the camera close to the fence to throw it right out of focus so that it's undetected, but many creatures have bars behind too. There's also a problem with those housed behind glass where reflections and dirt are introduced or focusing problems occur.

Some reserve owners are aware of the photographer's needs and have special days where unique shooting spots are created to gain unfenced views of the creatures. Others hold special flying days so you can shoot birds of prey with natural looking backdrops.

Another aspect is light. Cages are often very dim and when you turn up on a dull day the slow shutter speed may result in either camera shake or subject movement.

The background can often be very distracting too so a good knowledge of technical aspects, such as adjusting the aperture to gain the necessary depth-of-field or focusing at a certain point will help throw the background subtly out of

focus, resulting in an almost three-dimensional subject.

In the wild, it pays to know the habitat and the type of creatures it attracts. Certain birds can be found in specific woodland and mammals will populate specific types of locations too. A good port of call for research is the Internet. Searching county wildlife trust sites often gives an indication of what you may find on your travels. Also, check out the gallery on ePHOTOzine to see where specific creatures have been photographed.

You don't, of course, have to go far from your doorstep to shoot nature. With the right plants in the garden you'll attract a host of insects. Add a few feeders and the birds will come flocking. Even closer to home are the family pets – check out the photographs our members have taken of their dogs, cats and small furry things. You could have a star attraction in the house as we speak!

Without a doubt, if you can get over the hurdles that surround nature photography, you have access to one of the most varied and colourful subjects going. Throughout this section we'll give you many ideas of what, how and where to shoot. ■

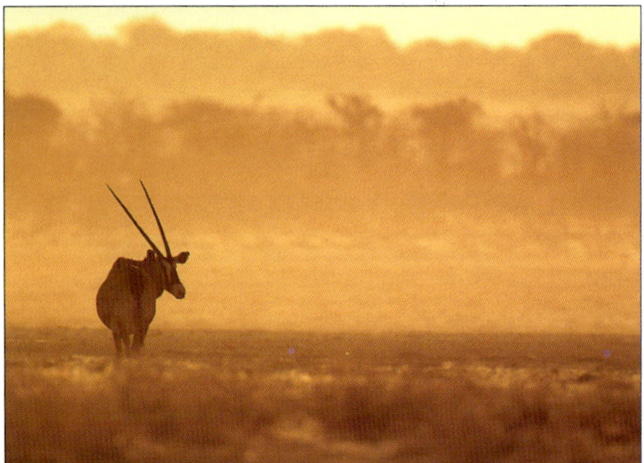

● BRIAN W MATTHEWS A silhouette of an oryx, also known as an African antelope, taken at sunset in Etosha National Park, Namibia.

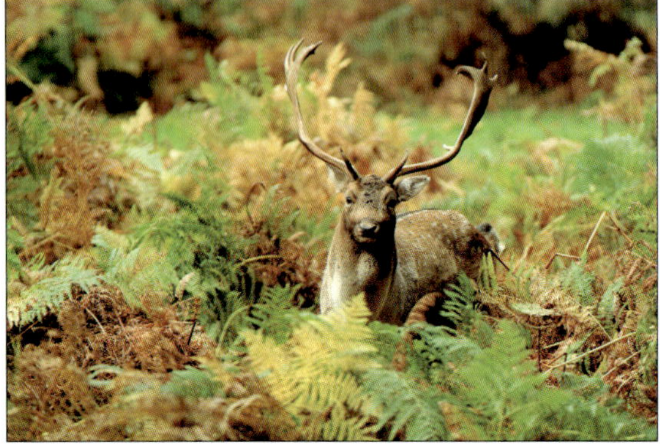

● MATT WAGSTER Dunham Massey Deer Park, during the rutting season. 200mm lens handheld at 1/90sec and f/3.3 with ISO400.

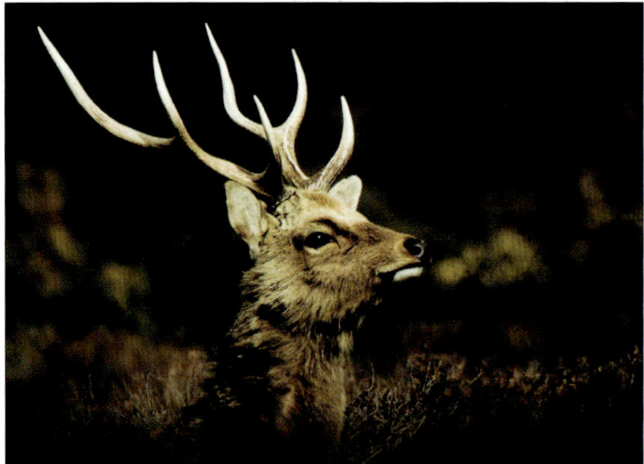

● PHILLIP DERHAM Taken at RSPB Arne in Dorset. "I felt the pose and alertness of this fine animal made it a stunning capture."

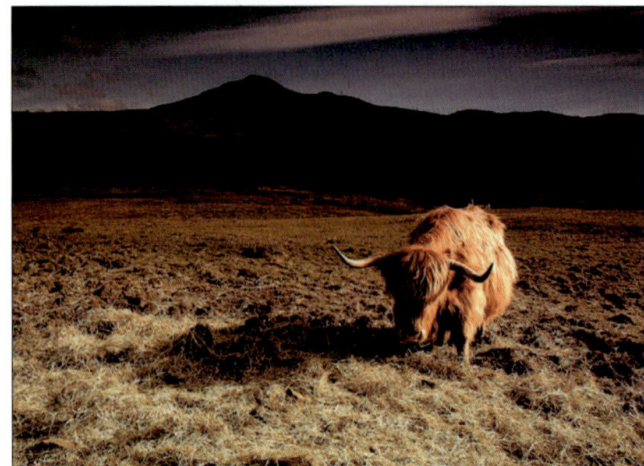

● DAVID WATSON A hairy Highland cow guards his patch with menace. Taken on the fields along the shores of Loch Lomond.

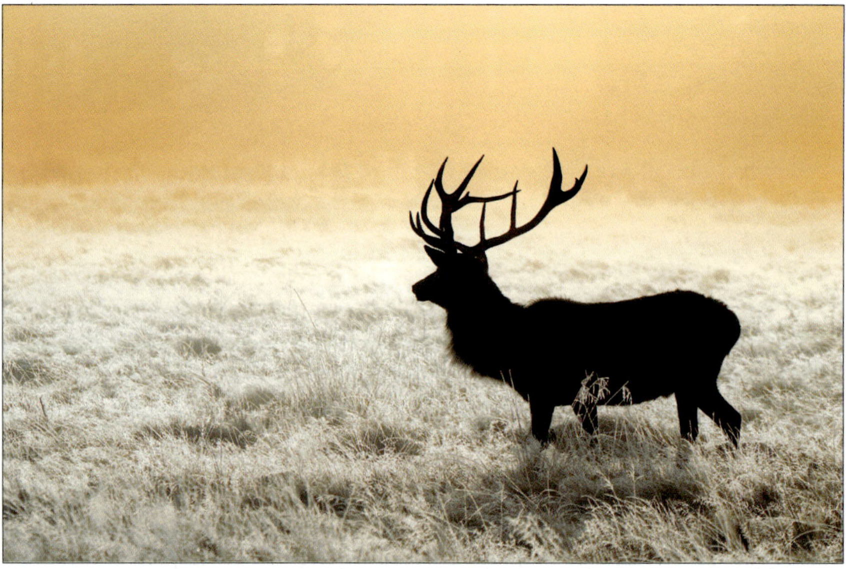

● HELEN DIXON A hoarfrost dawn in Richmond Park, recorded using a Canon EOS-10D and 70-300mm lens. The mist and light conditions were perfect for silhouettes.

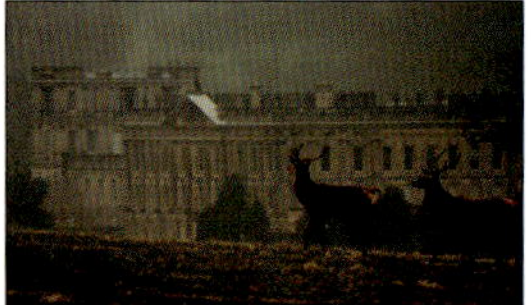

● DAMIAN LINLEY Deer at Chatsworth House, Derbyshire. "I knew the shot I wanted, It was just down to patience!"

WILDLIFE TIPS

■ For comical shots use an extreme wide-angle and move in really close to the nose to create a distorted view. Only do this on animals that won't headbutt you, and make sure you have a filter on the front, just in case the creature decides to lick the lens!

■ Use a long lens of at least 300mm when shooting wild animals. This will ensure the animal takes up a larger proportion of the frame.

■ When photographing deer and similar wild animals avoid wearing scent. Some photographers recommend you wash yourself and your clothes in baking soda.

■ Watch the wind direction. If it's going from you towards the animal you'll scare them off.

■ Shoot deer and similar animals early in the morning for more atmospheric images.

■ Take care not to disturb animals that are caring for their newborn.

■ Learning about the habits of wild animals will help you understand more about where to find them.

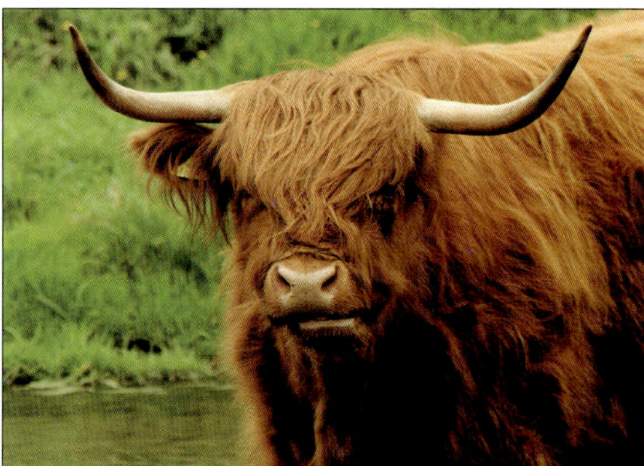

● SUE OSMANT Highland cattle, actually photographed in Kent, using a Sigma 70-300mm zoom lens.

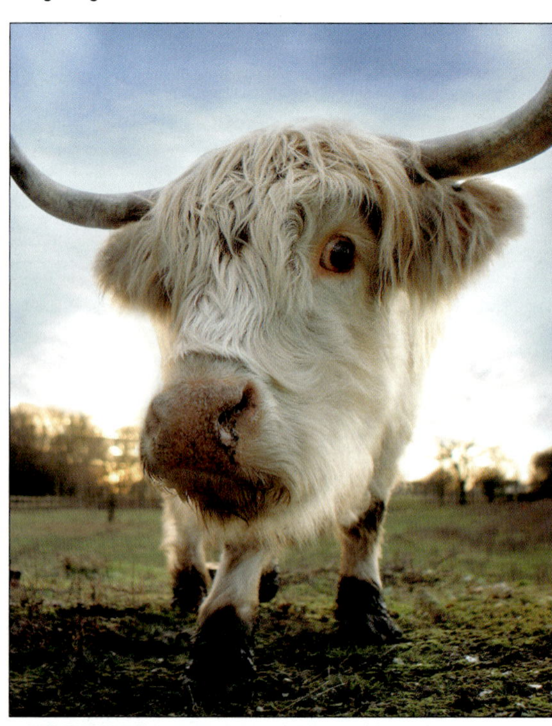

● TED TURNER Taken at a low and 24mm wide-angle to get a different perspective, using the Canon EOS 10D. 1/125sec at f/2.8.

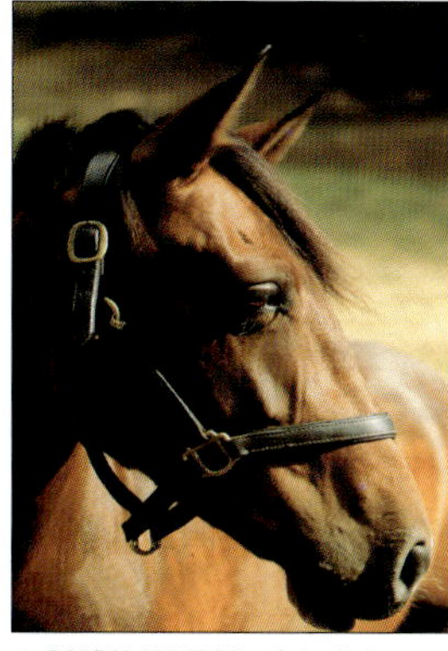

● MARK ABLE My sister's horse, Gloria, taken with a Nikon F90x.

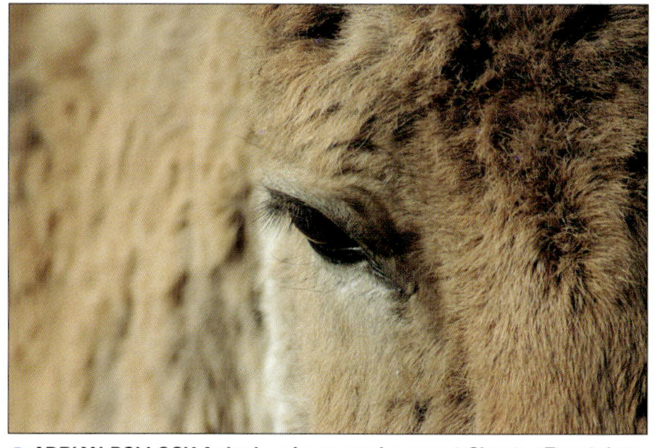

● ADRIAN POLLOCK A donkey in an enclosure at Chester Zoo, taken with a Canon EOS 300D and Sigma 75-300mm at 300mm and f/5.6.

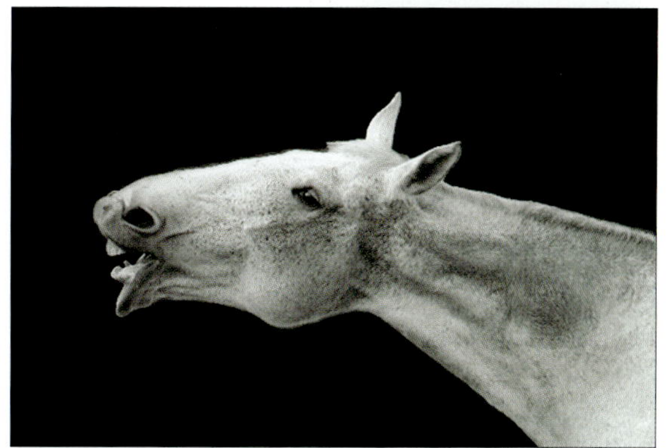

● ADRIAN CROOK Caught just at the right moment and converted to black & white to add emphasis to the strong, bold composition.

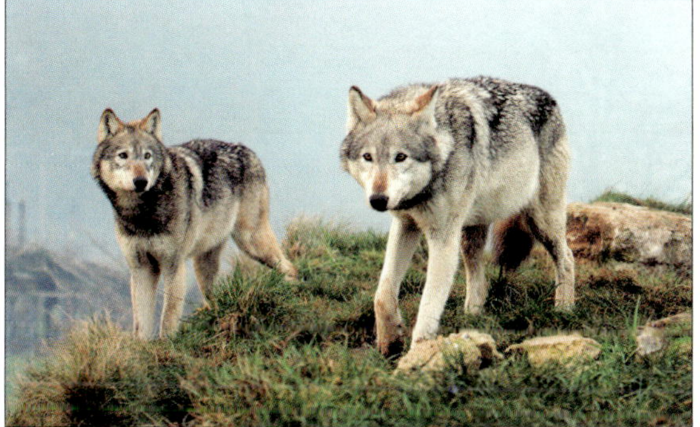

● PHILIP BEALE Shot through wire mesh at the UK Wolf Conservation Trust on a Canon 10D, with 100-400L lens at 1/180sec and f/6.7.

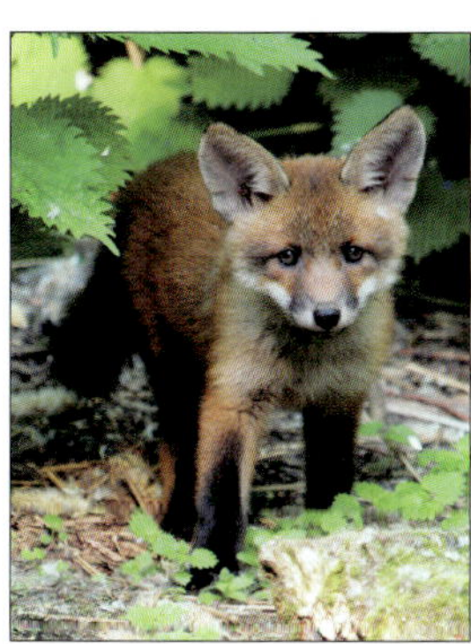

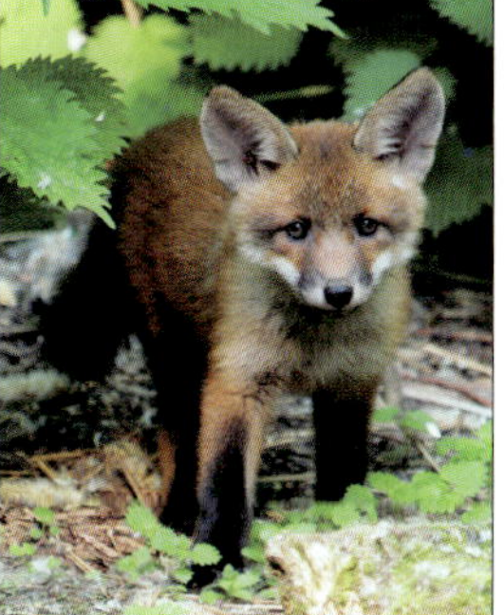

● BARRY POWELL This fox cub watched for 10 secs then ran off.

● HEATH CURNUCK This image was taken with a Fuji Finepix S7000. The exposure was 1/80sec at f/2.8 with the CCD light sensitivity set to ISO400.

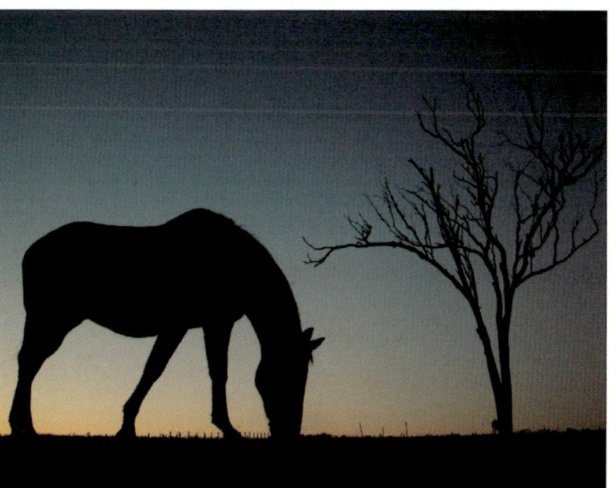

● NEIL SMYTH Happy as a pig in.....hay! Taken with a Canon EOS 300D and a Sigma 28-300mm lens at 300mm f/6.3.

SHOOTING TIPS – HORSE PHOTOGRAPHY

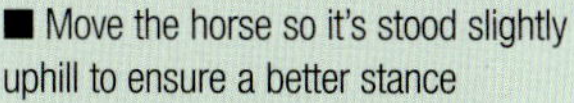
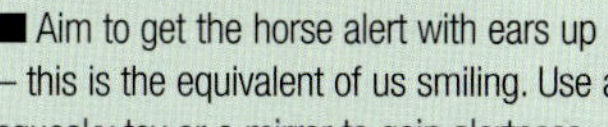
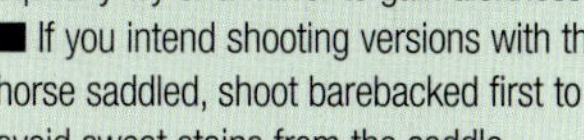
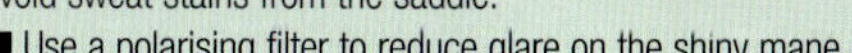
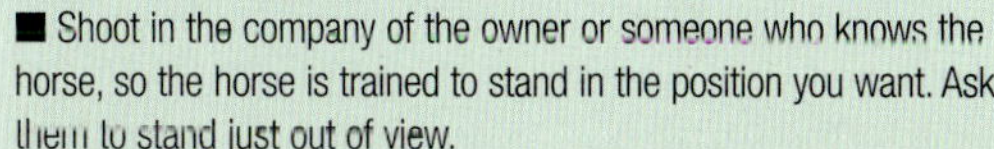
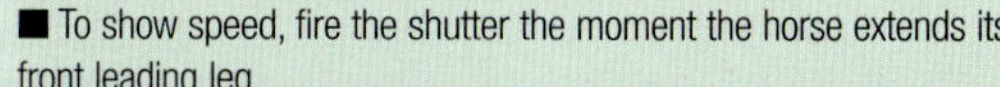

■ Move the horse so it's stood slightly uphill to ensure a better stance
■ Aim to get the horse alert with ears up – this is the equivalent of us smiling. Use a squeaky toy or a mirror to gain alertness.
■ If you intend shooting versions with the horse saddled, shoot barebacked first to avoid sweat stains from the saddle.
■ Use a polarising filter to reduce glare on the shiny mane.
■ Make sure grass does not obscure the feet.
■ Shoot in the company of the owner or someone who knows the horse, so the horse is trained to stand in the position you want. Ask them to stand just out of view.
■ To show speed, fire the shutter the moment the horse extends its front leading leg
■ To show power, capture the moment the horse brings up all of the legs under it.
■ When the horse is trotting take the photo when one of the front legs is totally extended.
■ Use a lower camera angle to make a horse look more muscular and a higher angle when you want a slender appearance.
■ Make sure you can see all four legs when taking a full shot. It's easy for one to by hidden and make the shot look less effective.
■ To avoid distortion stand further away and use a telephoto lens. This will prevent a big head, small rump.
■ Shoot with the sun at a low angle to emphasise detail and shape in muscles, especially on very dark horses.
■ Grooming before taking photos will result in more professional – looking images. Try washing the tail, plaiting the mane and oiling the hooves.
■ Ask the owner which is the best side and shoot that ideally against a clean background. Blurred trees are a good backdrop, but watch for stumps growing out of the head.

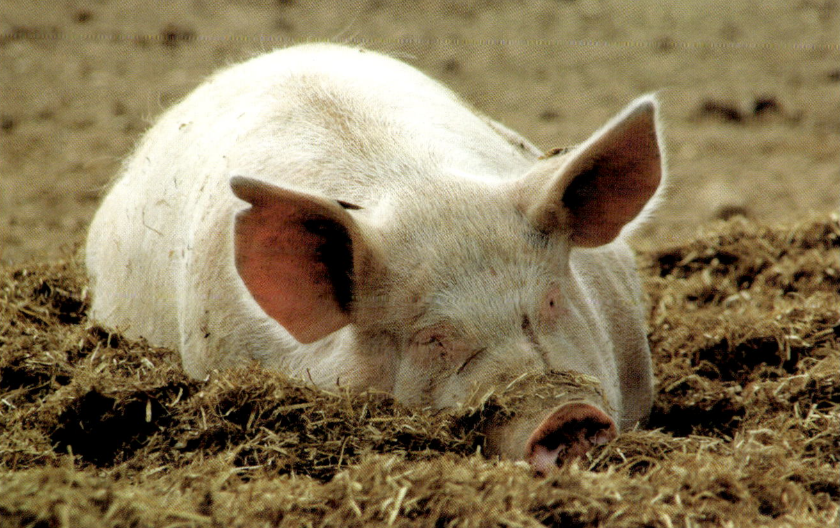

● STEVE SHARP A flash exposure on a grey day whilst on Skye, leaning over a fence. With camera held to the ground I clicked away.

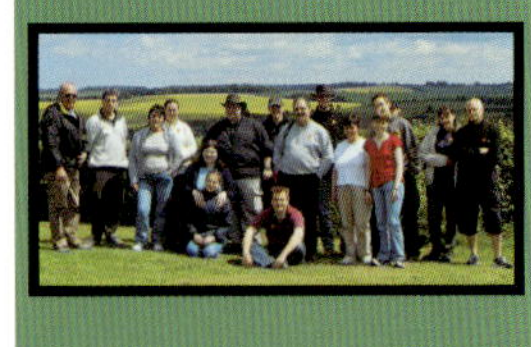

PORTFOLIO

SEEING
The South East England Independent Nature Group has made a positive impression on Wildlife Trusts.

When six photographers met up for the first time in March 2004 at Wildwood in Kent, organised through the ePHOTOzine members meeting forum, they discussed what they did with their pictures.

Most of them — four were already digital — just languished on their PCs. Knowing that there was a need for decent wildlife pictures by the Wildlife Trusts they decided to form a group, again through the pages of ePHOTOzine, to provide Trusts with good quality images.

A brainstorm session at their first meeting helped develop SENG into the South East England Independent Nature Group, so SEEING was born. Meetings were set up and attended so some early requirements could be established.

A list of aims and objectives were drawn up, along with a few rules to keep things on an even keel. One of the first Trusts on board was the one where the group had originally met and the Trust's Education officer introduced the Conservation officer.

Between them, they had an urgent requirement for pictures of small mammals, so a shoot was set up to photograph Water Shrews and Hazel Dormice. One of the reasons was the forthcoming BBC Britain goes Wild series, part of which was filmed with the Trust's staff and Dormice! Other images, such as body parts of these tiny creatures, were needed for the newly built Education centre.

The Kent Wildlife Trust then came on board with their full backing. Images have been supplied to them by SEEING for various publications and leaflets and used in their quarterly magazine *Wild Kent* as well as various appeal leaflets.

In return, they have allowed

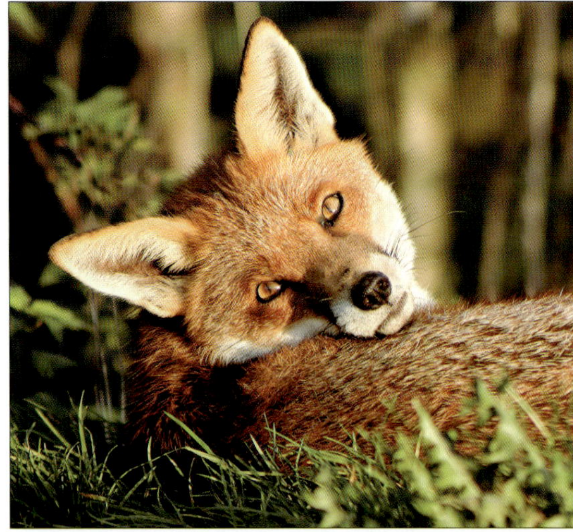

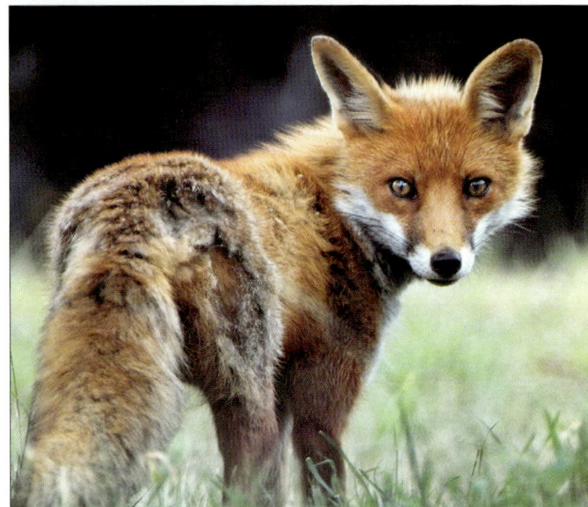

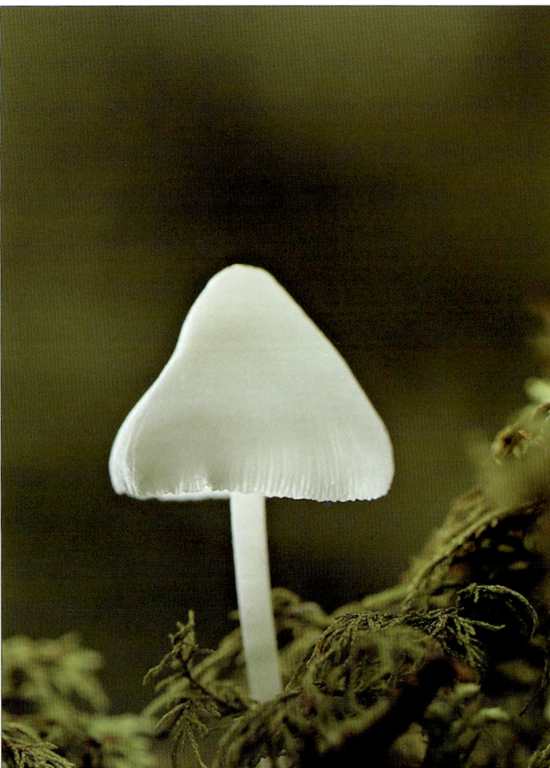

● TOP LEFT: SIOBHAN BOYD-LONGLEY Red fox (Vulpes vulpes), taken at the British Wildlife Centre. Canon EOS 300D, 75-300mm. Exposure: 1/200sec at f/6.7 ISO200. ● ABOVE: DAVID NEWTON This bonnet fungus was perfect for some flash lighting experimentation, using a Canon EOS 20D at a favoured reserve in autumn. ● LEFT IAN ANDREWS Red fox taken through wire mesh, using a Sigma SD9 and 170-500mm APO Zoom. Ian was pleased with the direct eye contact. ● BELOW: FRAN FRENCH Thistle head seeds and tall weeds are the main diet of this little goldfinch (Carduelis carduelis).

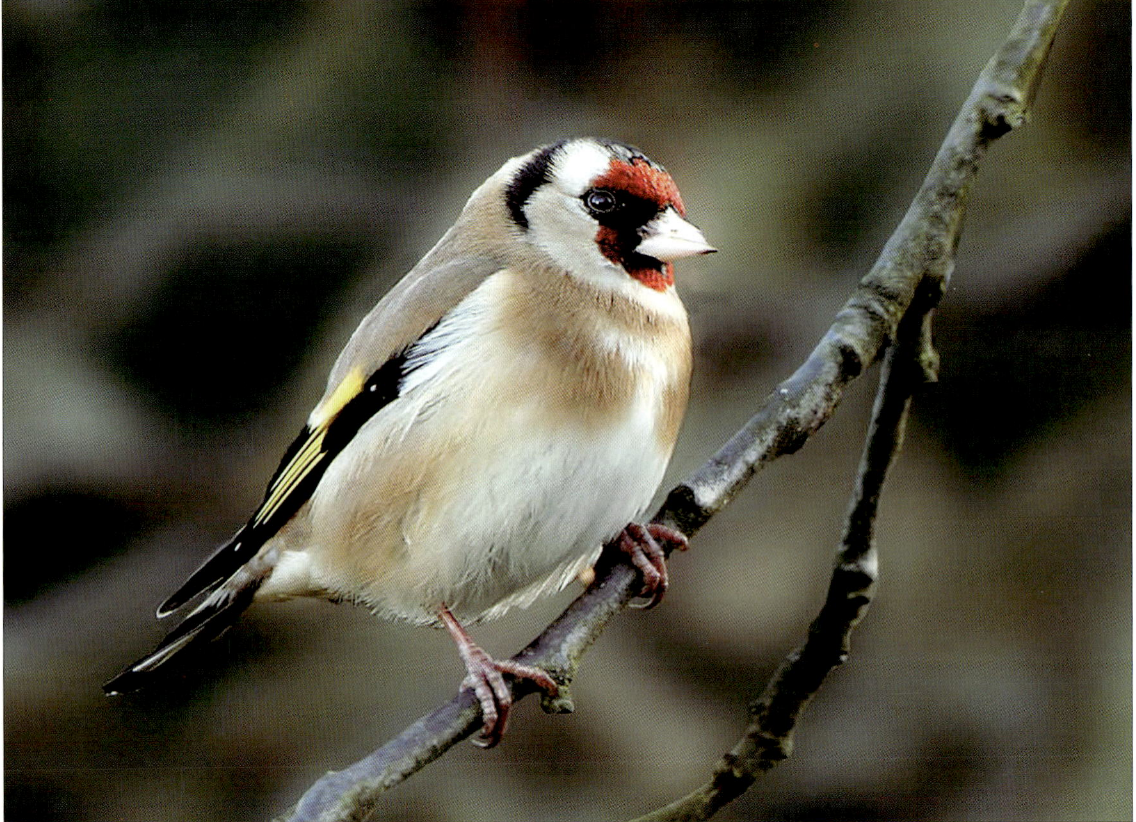

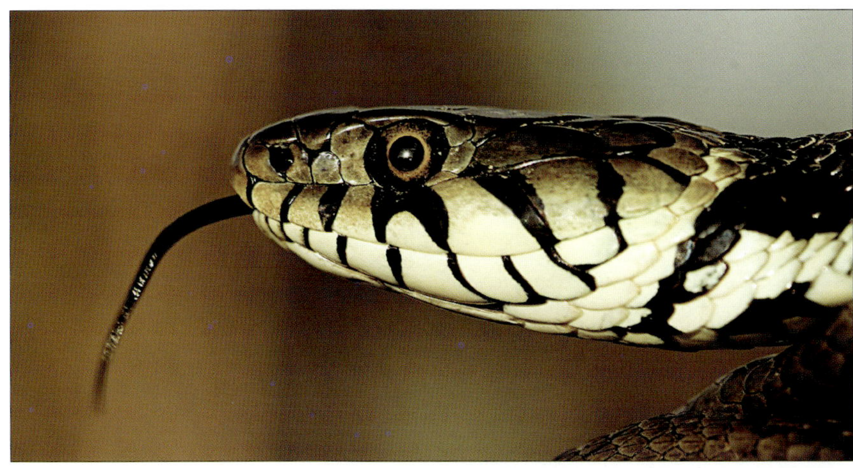

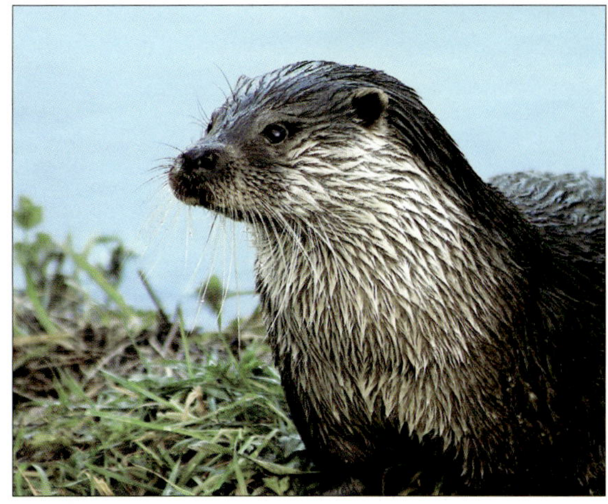

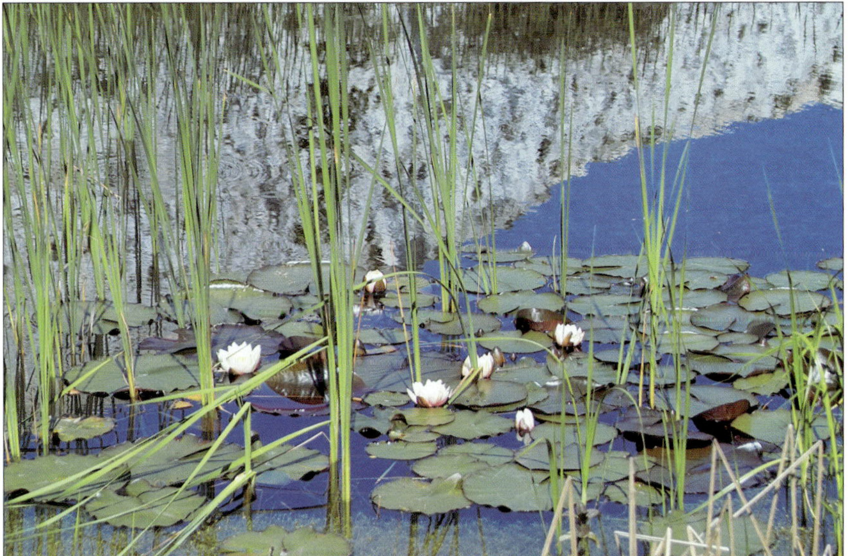

● CLOCKWISE: TERRY LONGLEY:
A grass snake (Natrix natrix), taken
at the British Wildlife Centre, using
a Canon EOS 10D with 100mm
Macro at 1/250sec at f/8-1/3, ISO
200. ● SHARON BOYD: Otter (Lutra
lutra), taken at the British Wildlife
Centre, using a Canon EOS 300D
with 75-300mm and an exposure of
1/250sec at f/8 ISO200. ● SHIRLEY
ANDREWS: tends to take shots the
boys miss when they're looking for
detail, such as this pond at Monkton
on a Minolta Z1 set to auto.
● MIKE TAYLOR: Broad-bodied
chaser, female (Libellula depressa),
taken on a Nikon CoolPix 4500 using
macro mode. Handheld exposure
1/167sec at f/4 and ISO100 with the
white balance set to cloudy.

SEEING access to some of their
more restricted reserves under
supervision.

Other small local trusts and
reserves have also welcomed
SEEING with open arms and
used images in newsletters and
information leaflets.

The group sorted out images
of rare breeds for a cross border
conservation project, including
Kent County Council and the Nord
Pas de Calais in France, where
information leaflets were produced
for distribution to farmers and
landowners to help in conservation
plans. Interest has also been
shown by a local coastal project
as well.

In May 2005, SEEING held an
exhibition of work at the Jeffery
Harrison Memorial Trust – a
wildfowl reserve in Sevenoaks, Kent.

By being professional in their
approach, while sticking to the
amateur ideals that they started
with, SEEING has made a positive
impression on the Trusts, a
reputation they intend to build on.

The group is not a closed shop
and is open to offers of help from
all directions, both to enhance the
existing relationships and to further
more of them.

They are adding to the fast
growing pool of images that are
made available to the Trusts
that they support. There is no
membership cost, you are just
required to put in a little time
and be active. The rewards are
manifold in the knowledge that you
are putting something back into
the natural environment that we all
tend to take a little for granted.

If anyone would like to offer
their help and/or join SEEING they
look forward to hearing from you
through the website. ■

www.wildaboutkent.co.uk

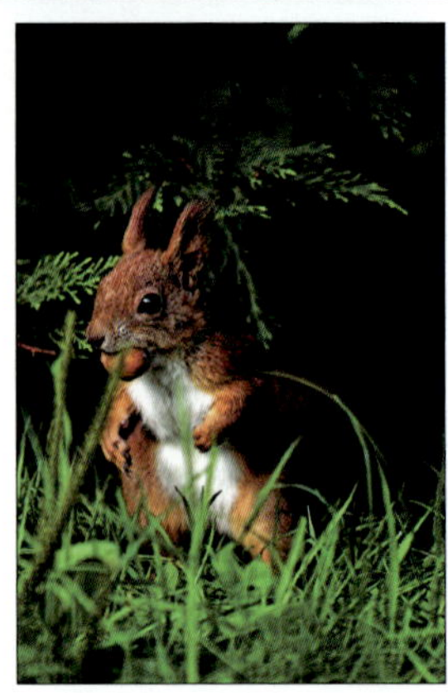

● COLIN MILL Taken with a 70-300mm zoom on an ePHOTOzine meet at the British Wildlife Centre.

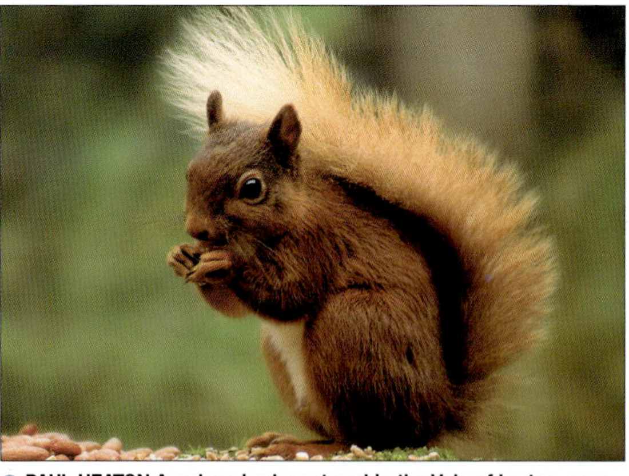

● PAUL HEATON A red squirrel, captured in the Vale of Lorton, near Buttermere in Cumbria, using a Canon EOS 5 with a 75-300mm lens set at 300mm to fill the frame and blur the background.

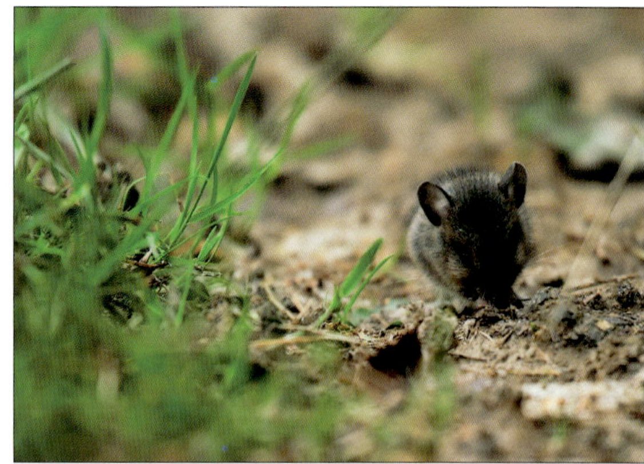

● EDWARD NORTON A chance encounter with a mouse on Ranmore Common, taken using a Canon EOS 10D with a 100-400mm L lens set at 400mm and f/6.3. ISO was at 400 and handheld at 1/125sec.

SHOOTING TIPS – SETTING UP A HIDE

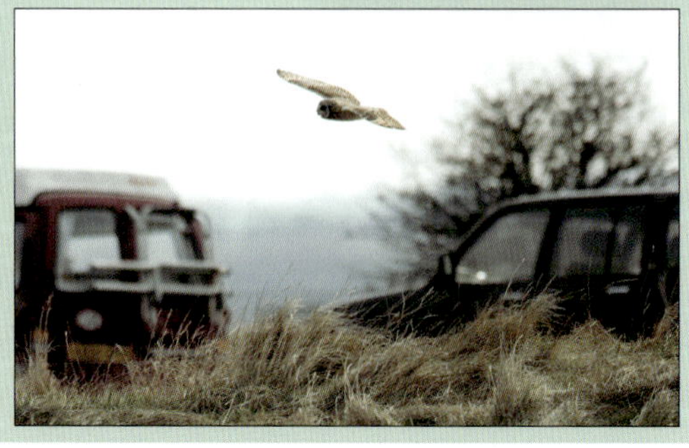

■ Hides come in all shapes and sizes, from a simple throw-over cover through to three storey buildings with lifts for wheelchair access and include every size in between.
They all serve the same purpose, to hide the occupant from the wildlife.

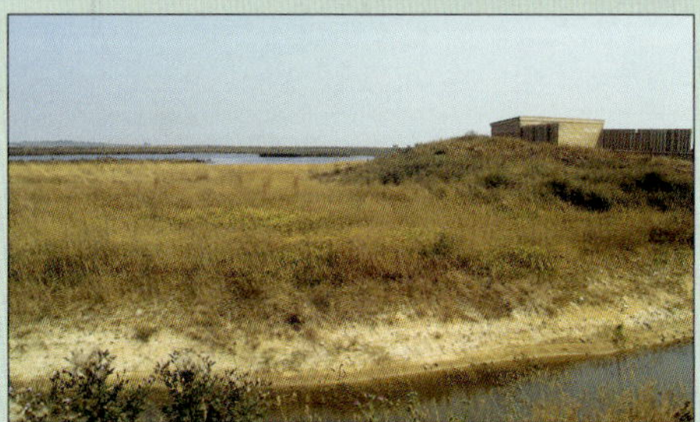

■ Permanent hides, most often found on nature reserves, can be elaborate buildings down to small sheds with a flap built in for viewing. Other kinds can include miniature tent type structures that pop up with FRP poles, bags made from camouflaged material, simple Hessian strung between two poles or, one of the most successful types, the motor vehicle.

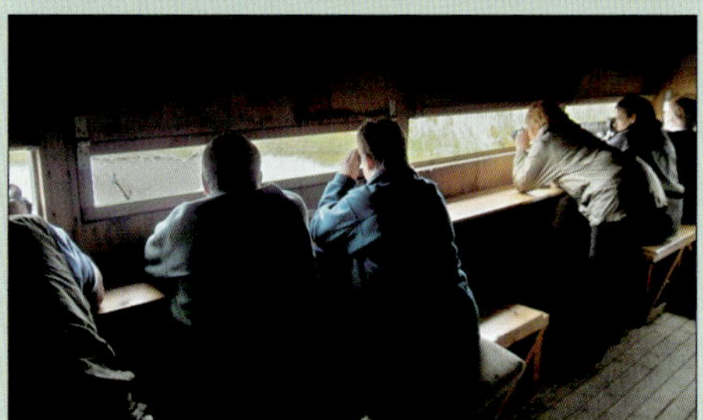

■ Birds and mammals take fright at the human form and the single, most important use of a hide is to disguise this. As long as the material from which the hide is made does not show a silhouette of the human form, it can be used for a hide.

■ Setting up a hide needs some thought. Firstly, you need the landowner's permission.
If the species you hope to photograph is protected in any way, you may well need a licence from the appropriate governing body, normally English Nature in England. Take the time to read and understand the Royal Photographic Society's Guidelines and Code of Conduct, agreed in conjunction with the statutory bodies. It will, at the very least, give you an understanding of what is required.

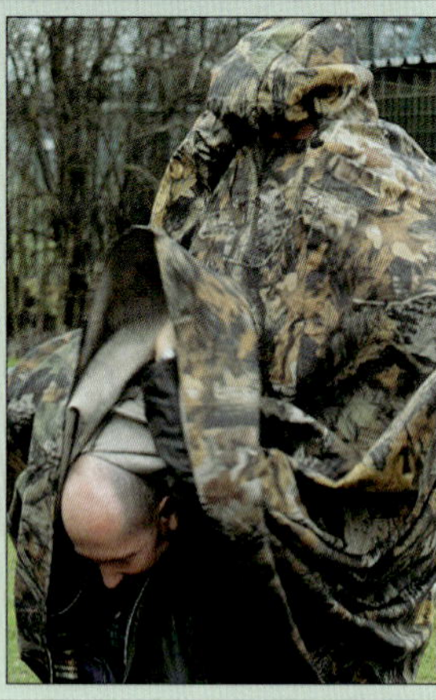

■ A public hide is normally easily approached, with paths shielded from the view of the hoped-for subjects. A private hide needs thought as to positioning, light angles, ease of approach, wind direction etc. It's possible to erect a hide and, slowly, over a week or so, move it closer to the subject. This is only possible nowadays, on private land, as it would not be advisable to leave a hide, possibly costing hundreds of pounds, where there is public access.

■ Birds and mammals are not renowned for their ability to count and a common practice is to have a 'putter-in', a second person that approaches the hide with you and then leaves you there. The subject has seen humans go in followed by humans leaving and thinks the coast is clear.

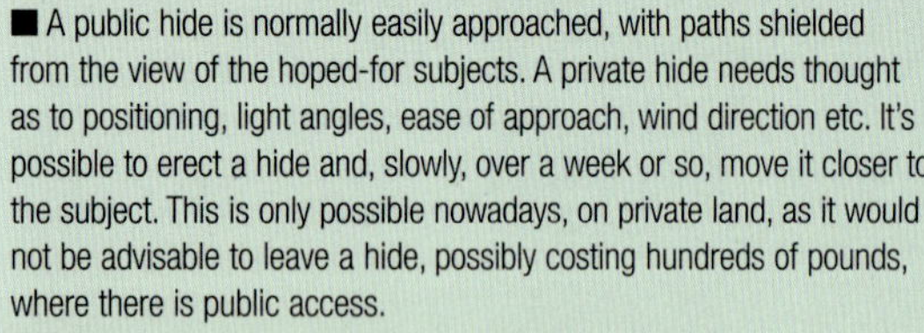

■ The motor vehicle, should not be ignored. Although responsible for many more animal deaths than anything else, mammals and birds do not fear them as much as they should and they are an excellent way of disguising the human form. **Words & Photos Ian Andrews**

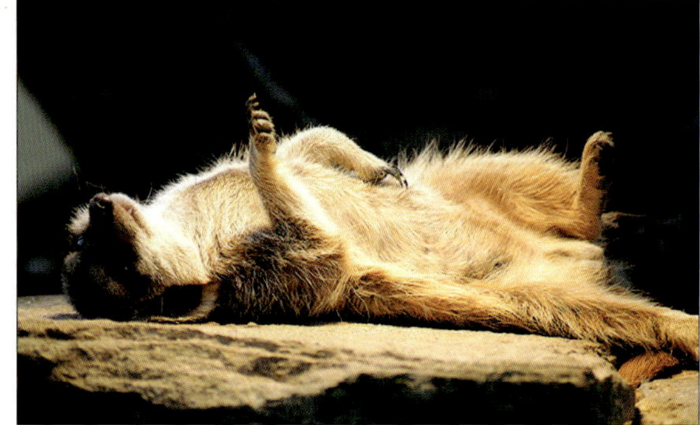

● PAUL HOFFMAN "I just loved the way the meercat was sunbathing under the lamp at Marwell Zoo."

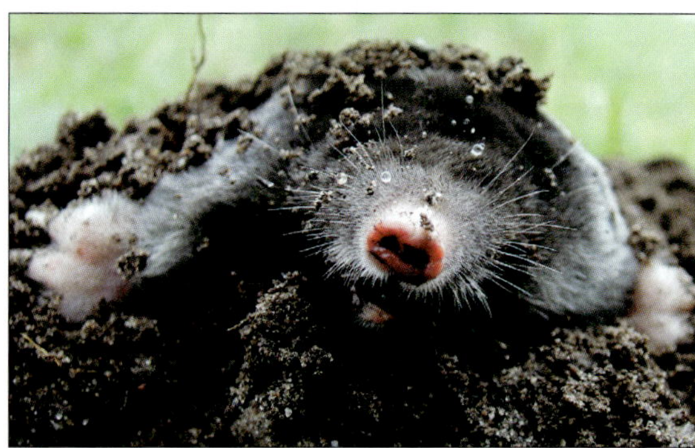

● ROSEY NORTON Taken in Lincolnshire for use to illustrate an article on moles. "I set ISO200 on the camera with an exposure of 1/105sec at f/2.8. It disappeared after two shots."

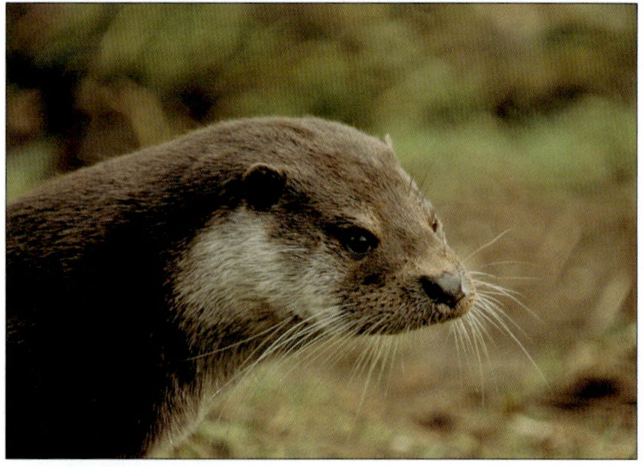

● VAL SAXBY This British otter was taken at the Owl and Otter Centre in the New Forest, using a Sigma 50-500mm on a tripod mounted Canon EOS 20D and fired by remote control.

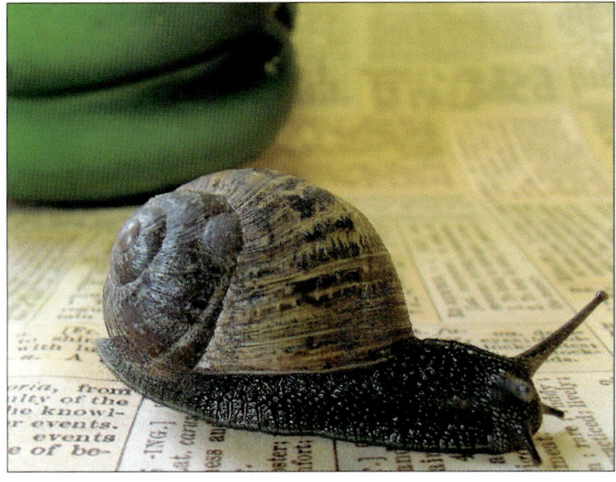

● LINDA PELLING You could bring bugs and snails indoors to photograph them in different surrounds. Linda even calls hers Brian!

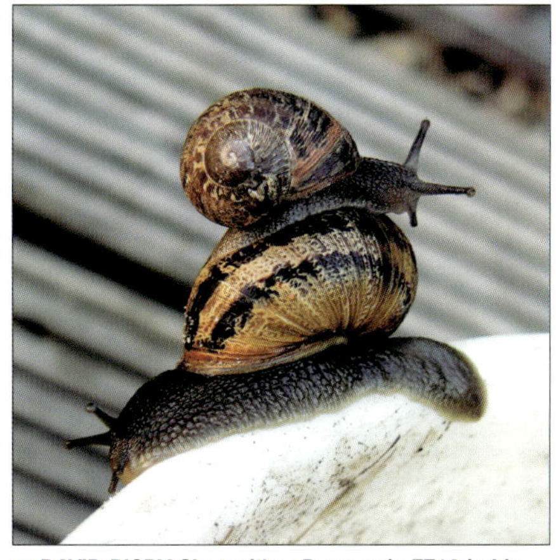

● DAVID RIGBY Shot with a Panasonic FZ10 in his garden, hand-held in Macro mode with manual focus.

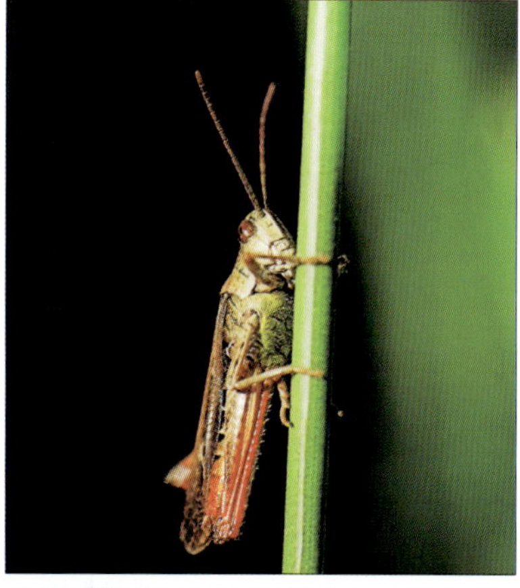

● K L KOH Handheld at 1/125sec at f/5.6 with ISO400 on a Canon 20D and Tamron 90mm.

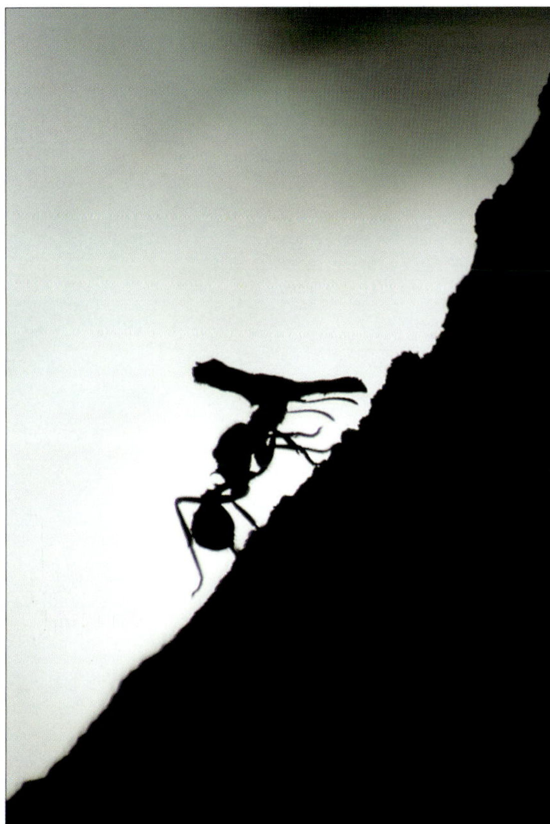

● RON THOMAS Taken indoors at Chester Zoo. The camera & lens were supported by a rolled-up sweater on top of a wooden barrier.

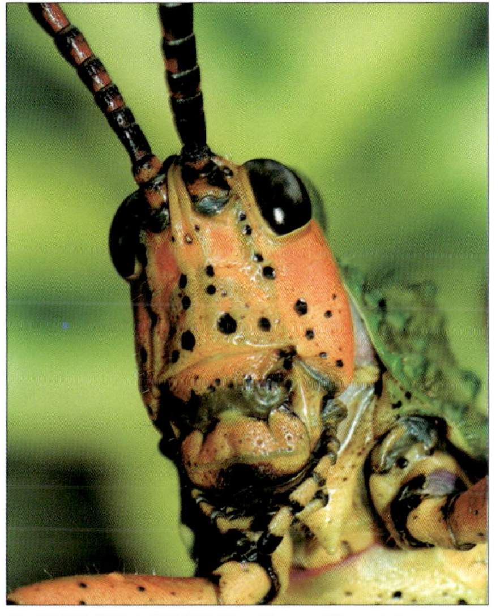

● JOGGIE VAN STADEN A milkweed locust in open shade, using a Nikon D70 and 105mm at f/32.

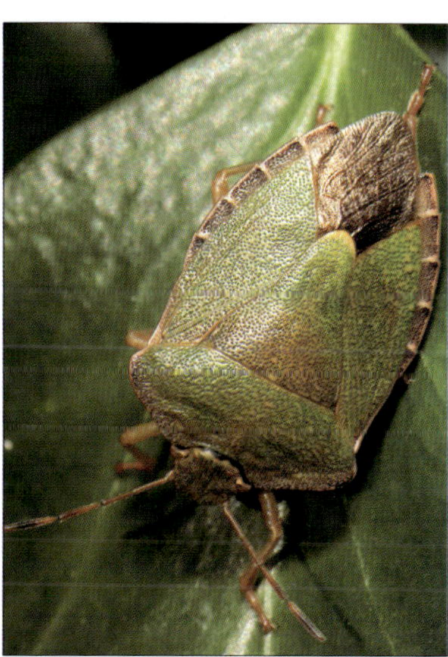

● CHRIS J SIMPSON Green shield bug, using flash with a Stofen diffuser on an EOS 300D.

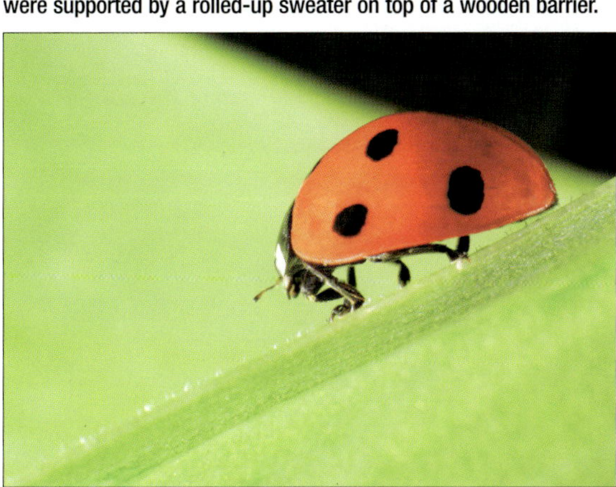

● ALISON PRINCE This ladybird shot was set up in a studio and taken using a Canon 20D and 50mm lens with extension tubes.

SHOOTING TIPS – USING RING FLASH

■ A ring flash has a circular flash tube that is positioned around the camera lens. It's usually mounted on a ring that attaches to the lens' filter thread.

■ It fires a circular shadowless light, making it perfect for close up photography where a single, directional light would cause harsh shadows.

■ This sort of flash is made by Sigma and Sunpak, while a model under the different names Vivitar, Centon and Starblitz can be picked up easily on eBay.

■ Some photographers feel the shadowless light is not natural and flash manufacturers have moved with these views to create more advanced units. These have more than one flash tube so you can adjust the ratio of flash and show some form of modelling on the subject, yet still gain the benefits of the ringflash position.

■ Konica Minolta introduced the Macro Twin Flash 2400 first, which was soon followed by Nikon's SB-R200 Remote Speedlight and Canon's Macro Twin Lite 24-EX. All three have small flash tubes that can be positioned directly on a ring, mounted on the lens. The output of each can be controlled independently so you really can balance the flash. All three manufacturers also have a standard ringflash option too.

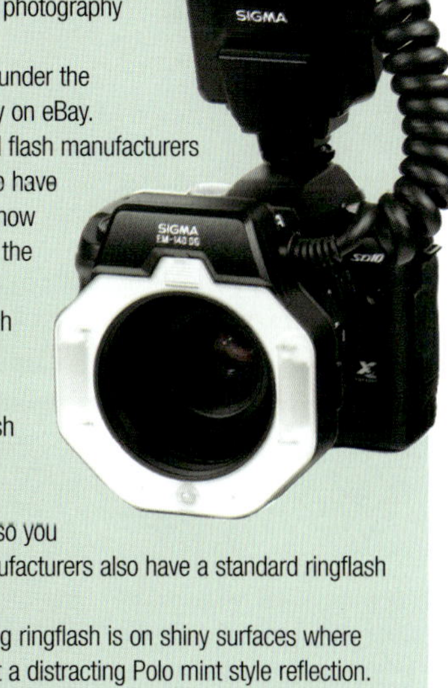

■ The main downside to using ringflash is on shiny surfaces where you get a distracting Polo mint style reflection. These can be cloned out in Photoshop. Some photographers use the ring flash off the camera at an angle to the subject to gain the shadowless light without the reflections.

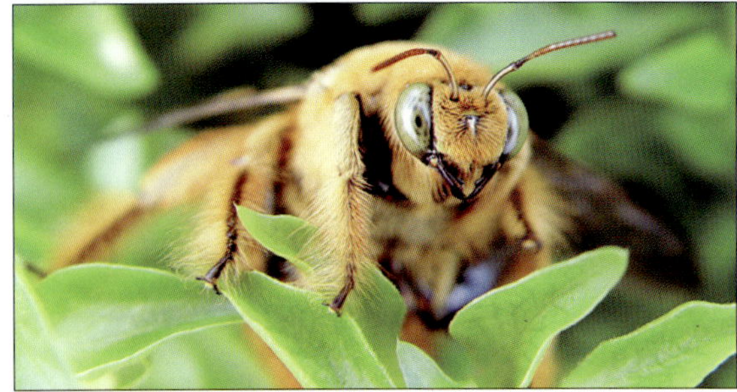

● STEPHANUS J BOTHA Head on shots, like this one taken using a Sony DSC-F717, can make the insects look more sinister.

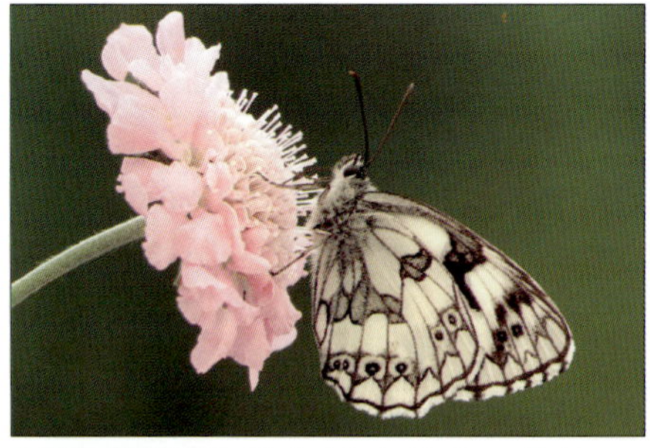

● MATT BERRY Marbled white butterfly on Field Scabious, taken with a Fuji S7000 in macro at f/4.

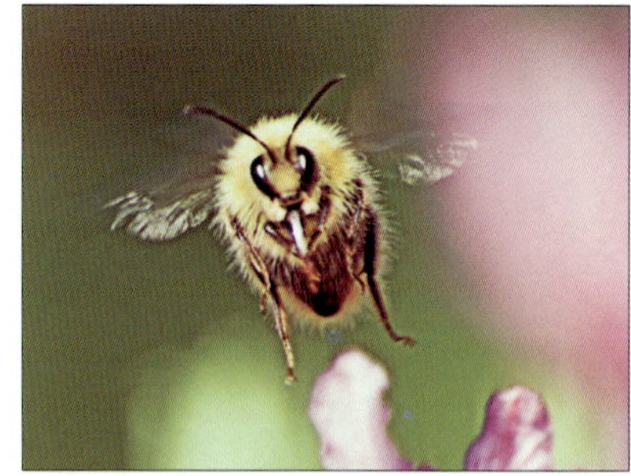

● BRIAN WADIE Handheld shot, using the Sigma 70-300mm macro at 300mm and f/8.

DIGITAL TECHNIQUE – USING THE REPAIR TOOLS

■ Image-editing programs, such as Photoshop, have a selection of useful repair tools. We'll show you how to use the Clone tool and the Patch tool on this photo of a dragonfly, caught resting on a dead iris.

1 You may or may not want to perform the first stage which involves using the Clone tool to remove the highlights on the insect's head. I find these distracting and remove them by sampling from a nearby area of similar colour. Do this on both sides to remove the hexagonal highlight. Incidentally, this is the shape of the aperture of the lens used to take the photo.

2 The Clone tool can also be used to patch up small areas of cobweb that are around the Iris head. Sample from nearby and follow the path of the web to remove it. The red arrow shows where the first sample point was taken and where it is currently.

3 Next step is to remove the chunky blob to the left in the background. This is an out of focus yellow flower, which distracts. Select a much larger brush size for the Clone tool and sample from below. Work upwards into the yellow blob to replace with the reeds below.

4 You may find this difficult to repair using the Clone tool, which is one reason Adobe created the Patch tool. With this selected you can draw around an area you want to "patch up" and drag the selection to the area you want to use to patch and let go. Photoshop then goes into action replacing and blending the area. It's a fantastic tool.

5 You may have a slightly messy area that now looks a little mottled and may not look real. Here's where the Motion blur filter comes in useful. Make a selection around the area you want to blur. Feather this selection – Select⇨Feather. I set 100pixels as the radius, and apply blur – Filter⇨Blur⇨Motion blur. Adjust the angle so it follows the reeds and increase the Distance slider making sure the Preview box is ticked. Adjust this so that the whole area streaks but still has texture.

6 Using the repair tools for jobs like this doesn't affect the ethical aspects of the photograph, it just enhances the subject.

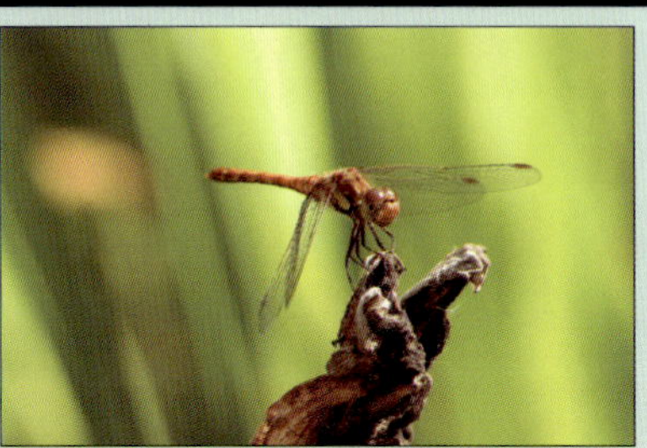

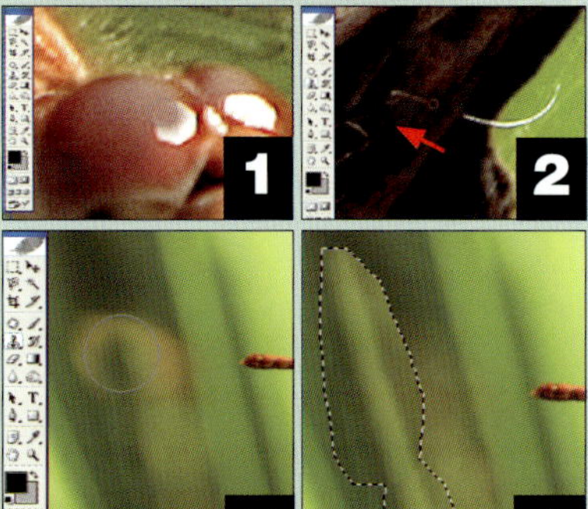

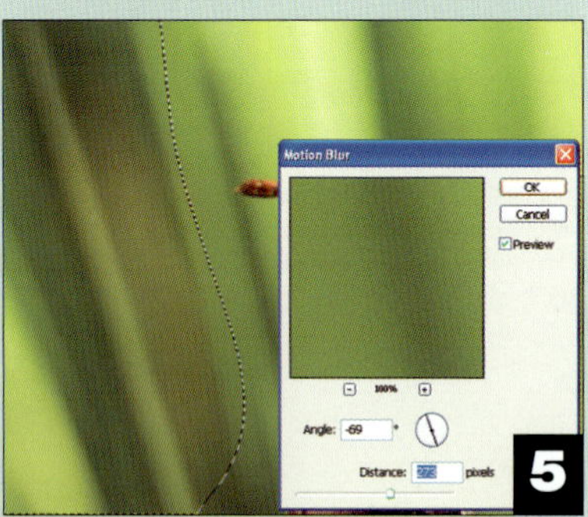

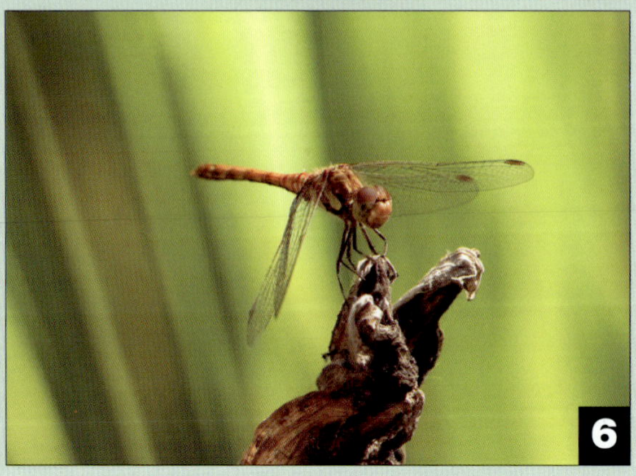

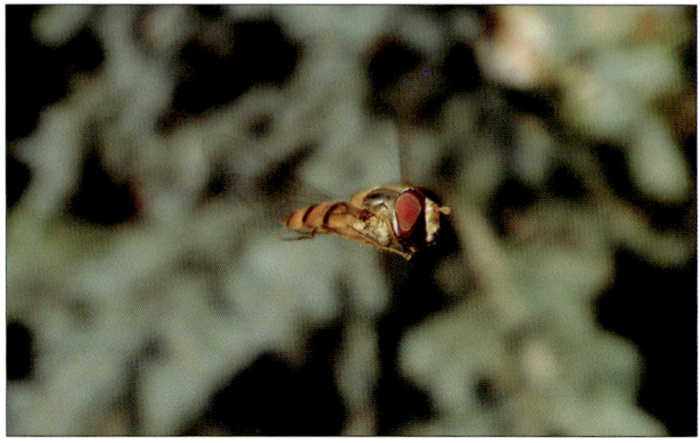

● MAREK RAPICKI "A hoverfly taken early morning in my garden. using a Fuji Finepix in macro mode at ISO100."

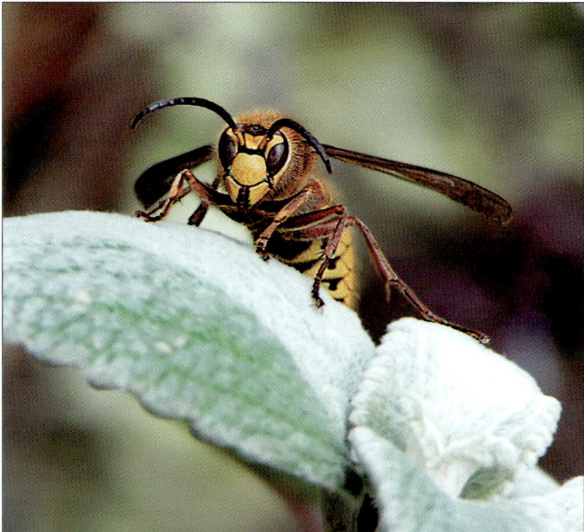

● GRAHAM MULROONEY "I felt very vulnerable with my face this close. Taken at f/4.0 and 1/100sec with a focal length of 50mm."

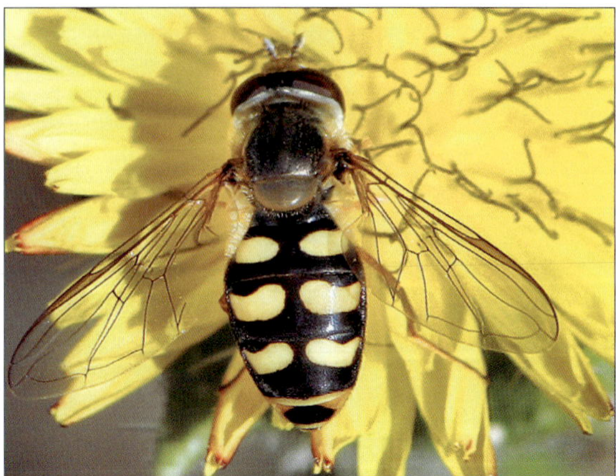

● ADE OSMANT A frame-filling close-up of a hoverfly, using flash to make the wings glisten.

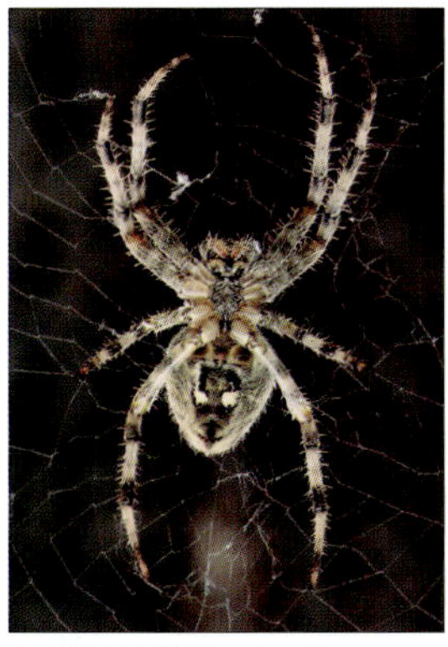

● PAUL RULE Used a Canon 100mm and MR14 EX Macrolite.

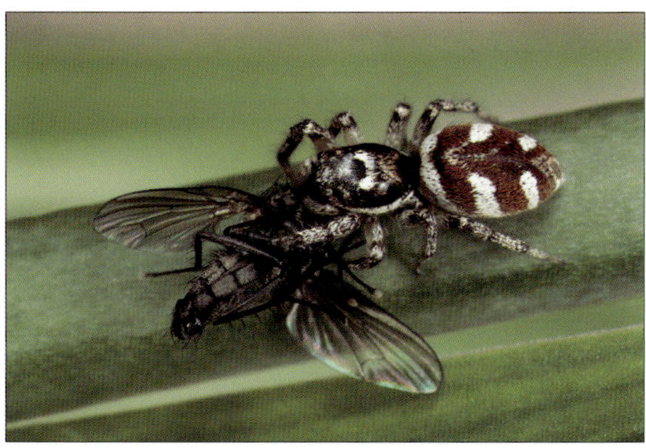

● KEITH ROWLEY The zebra spider jumps onto its prey rather than catching it in a web. Illuminated by off-camera flash.

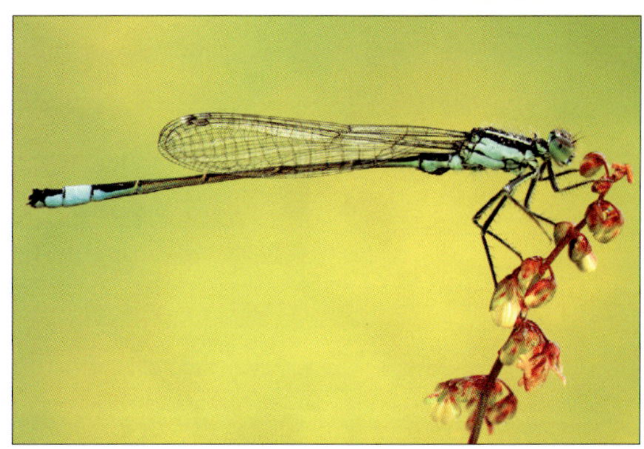

● PATRICK BENTLEY Blue tailed damselfly, photographed on the Avon River, Bath. The exposure was 1/125sec at f/7.1 using ISO400.

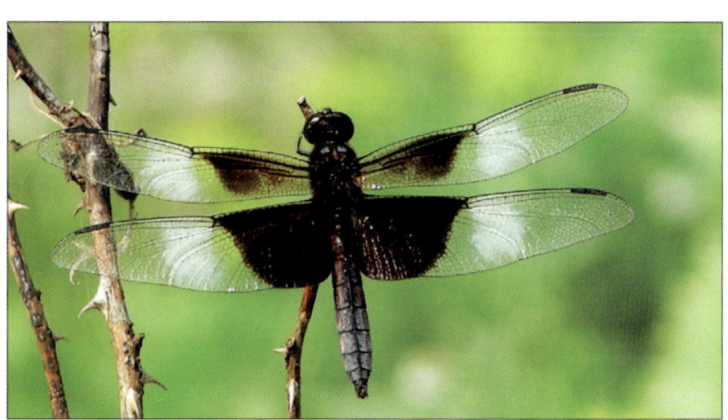

● SIMON TODD "The spider was actually underneath the leaf, but I found by simply turning the photo over gave the spider a menacing appearance."

● JENNIFER TAGGART Widow Skimmer against a fairly light and plain background to give it contrast and make it stand out.

SHOOTING TIPS – INSECTS   LOCATIONS – BUTTERFLY HOUSES

- Edinburgh Butterfly & Insect World, Midlothian, Scotland — www.edinburgh-butterfly-world.co.uk
- Buckfast Butterflies Buckfastleigh — www.ottersandbutterflies.co.uk
- Studley Grange Butterfly Farm, Swindon, Wilts — www.studleygrange.co.uk
- The London Butterfly House, Brentford Middlesex — www.butterflies.org.uk
- Mole Hall Wildlife Park and Butterfly Pavillion, Essex — www.molehall.co.uk
- Williamson Park and Butterfly House Lancaster — www.williamsonpark.com
- The Butterfly and Wildlife Park, Long Sutton, Spalding — www.butterflyandwildlifepark.co.uk
- Bedford Butterfly Park — www.bedford-butterflies.co.uk
- London Butterfly House — www.londonbutterflyhouse.com

SHOOTING TIPS

- Use a longer focal length lens so you are further away from the insect to prevent disturbance. A 100mm macro is a better choice than a 50mm, for example.
- Flash can be used to illuminate the subject but be careful, flash shots can look unnatural. An ideal method is to have two small units placed either side of the camera. Brackets can be used to support the guns. Canon and Nikon have special macro flash units that are positioned around the lens for such purposes.
- Insects are less active in the morning and evening, so during midday you need to be very mobile, making a monopod a better support than a tripod.
- Move slowly as most insects have compound eyes, so the saying "having eyes in the back of your head" is very true. They'll see you coming at any angle.
- If you are shooting in bright sunlight watch for your shadow being cast over the insect and scaring it off.
- A knowledge of the type of flower or plant that insects are attracted to is helpful if you're wanting to photograph them in your garden.
- Pre-focus on plants that are attracting insects and wait for one to land on the pre-focused spot. This requires more patience, but will deliver results.

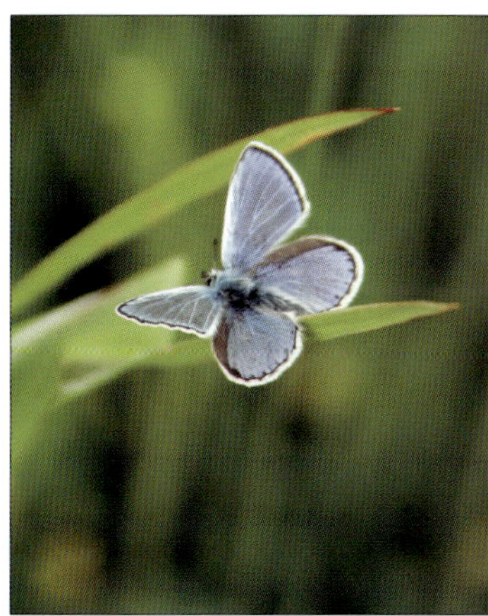

● PAUL EYRE Canon 300D with 28-200mm lens at 200mm and f/5.6.

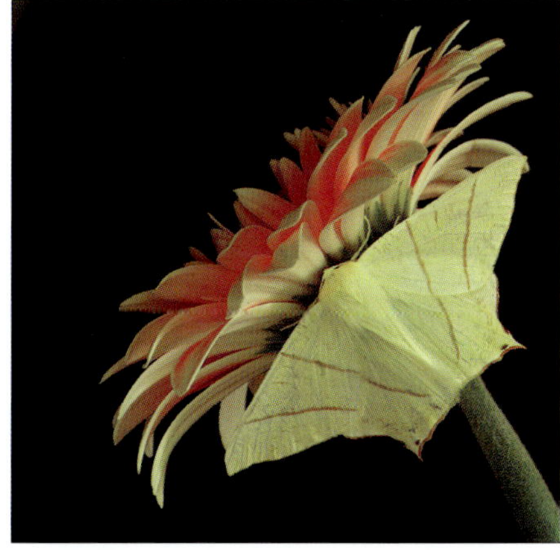

● MIKE TAYLOR Swallowtailed moth, taken with a tripod mounted Canon EOS 10D and 100mm macro.

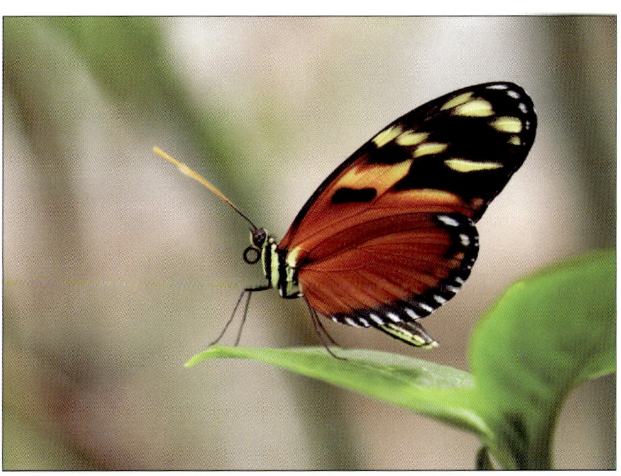

● JOE BOGLE Captured on a grey, rainy day at the Butterfly Centre, Statford-Upon-Avon, with a Canon EOS 10D and 100-400L IS at f/4.

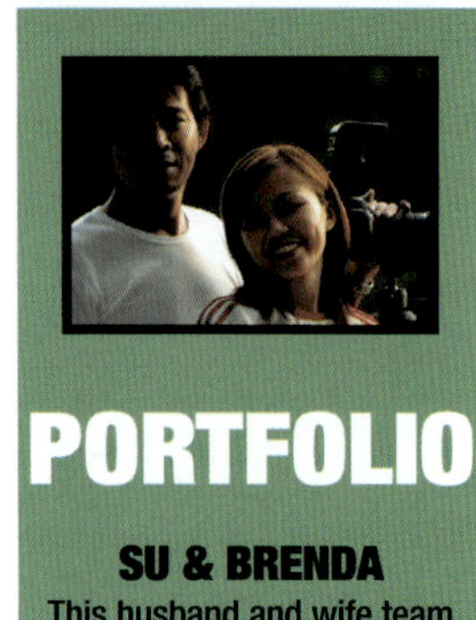

PORTFOLIO

SU & BRENDA
This husband and wife team are from Penang, Malaysia, and share a passion for digital photography.

The couple had been practising photography casually for two years, but they only got serious about it after joining ePHOTOzine in 2004.

"Our photography experiences have been a real rollercoaster ride so far and a steep learning curve. There's so much to learn, so much to do – but, unfortunately, so little time to do it in.

"We work solely in digital. Our first camera was a Nikon Coolpix 5000. We have since both upgraded, now having a Nikon D70 each. We prefer to work in digital as using film is too costly and time consuming, taking the film to be processed and then having to wait for the pictures.

"To us, post-processing with an image editor on our home computer is half the fun of digital photography.

"Our main interest is nature photography, allowing us to spend time together away from the stresses of work and everyday life."

Although this portfolio features incredible photographs of fish, you will also find a huge variety of damselflies, dragonflies, exotic butterflies and colourful birds on their ePHOTOzine portfolio too.

Su will think nothing of getting down on all fours in a shallow pond to get at the right level for the shot of a resting insect. The results pay off; at the time of writing the pair have eight Editor's Choices and 43 Highly Commended awards.

Many of the outdoor shots are shot in bright sunlight with reflectors and a polarising filter to enhance colours and increase saturation. The detail brought out of the subject is phenomenal and backdrops are always subtly thrown out of focus with careful control of depth-of-field. ■
Contact Su and Brenda by email at: **tradewin@streamyx.com**

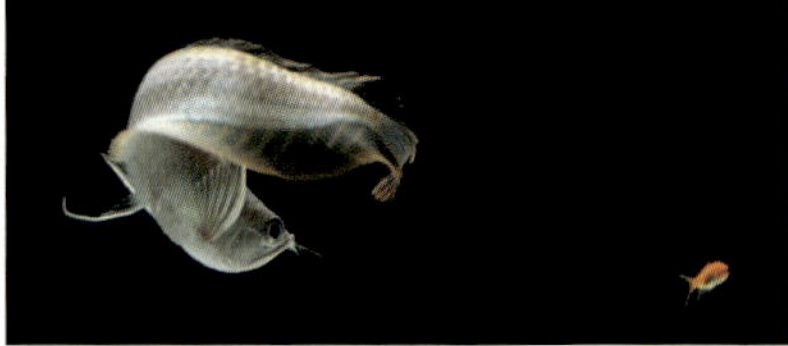

● Su particularly enjoys photographing his goldfish. To get the best results he photographs the fish in a small tank, which, unlike the main tank, is free of ornaments and other decorative features.

It's best to shoot the pictures in a dim or darkened room, as this helps to avoid any reflection on the glass of the tank.

"I use a variety of equipment when shooting these photographs, some photographic kit and other useful bits just from everyday life.

I use a black t-shirt for the background, hot-shoe flash connected to the camera via a sync cable, slave flash and aluminum foil for reflective light.

"The lens I use varies from the 60mm Micro Nikkor, 18-70mm zoom and the 105mm Micro Nikkor – this depends on the size of the goldfish being photographed and how much of that fish is required in the frame.

"I experiment with lighting quite a lot rather than using any specific method. I just like to try different things to find out what works."

For these three shots Su used rear curtain sync, with two low cost manual flash guns positioned left side & top side and a silver reflector on the right. The fish were in a studio 2x1x1ft glass tank. The wall of bubbles was created with an 8in flexible airstone.

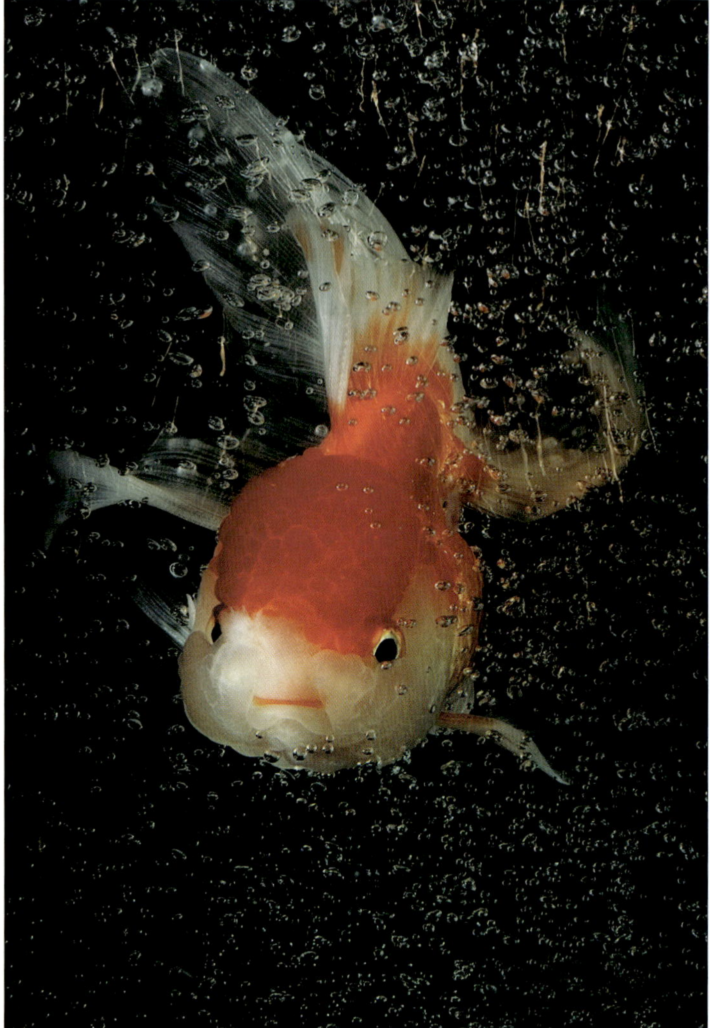

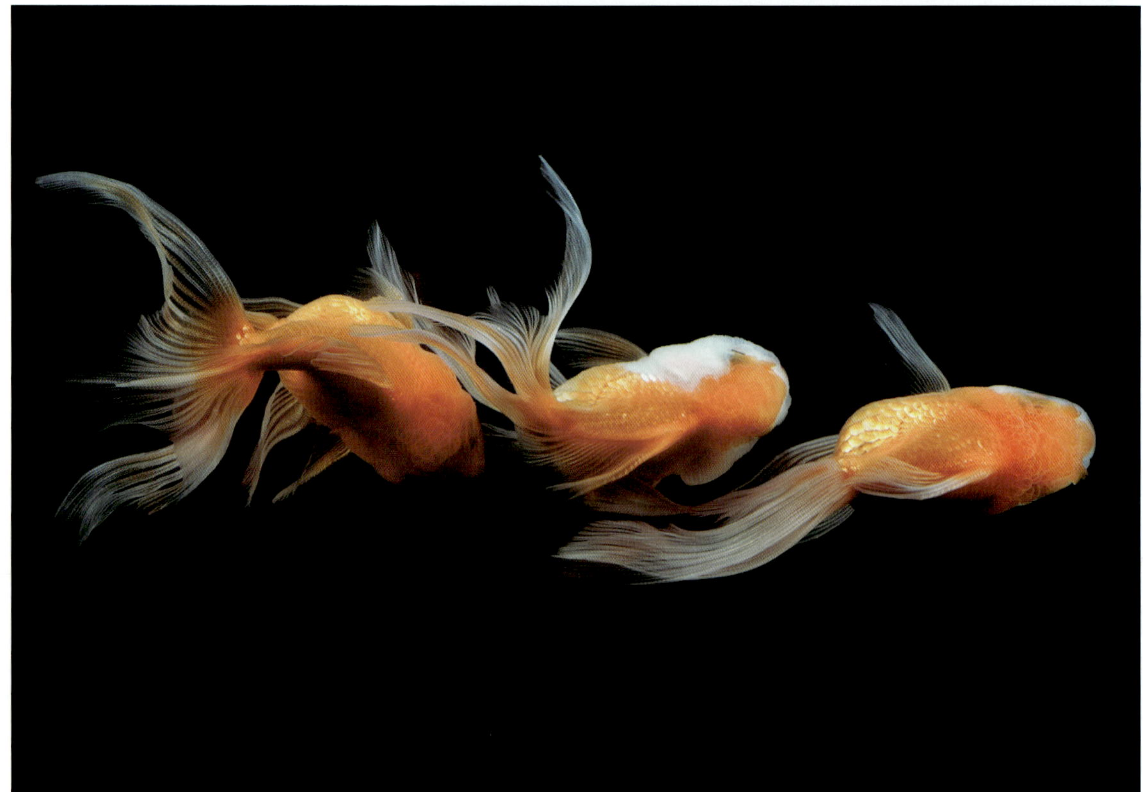

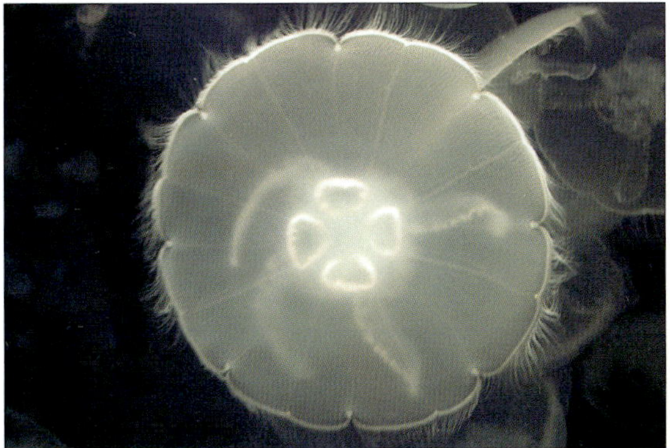

● JAMES STUBBS Taken in an aquarium of wall to wall jellyfish, handheld at a slow 1/4sec exposure, using a Nikon Coolpix 4500.

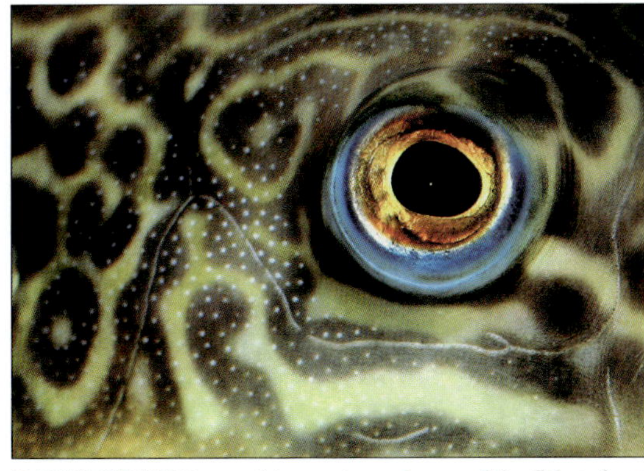

● PUAY-SZE LIM Cropped from a larger image of the fish swimming in an aquarium, taken with a flash on the Canon EOS 300D.

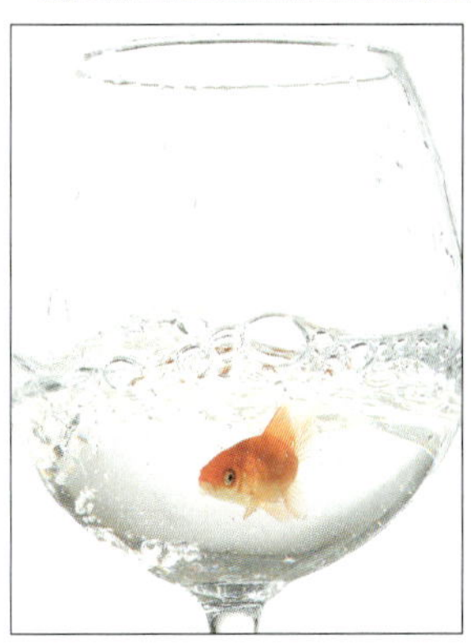

● TRISTAN POYSER Goldfish in a glass, lit with studio flash.

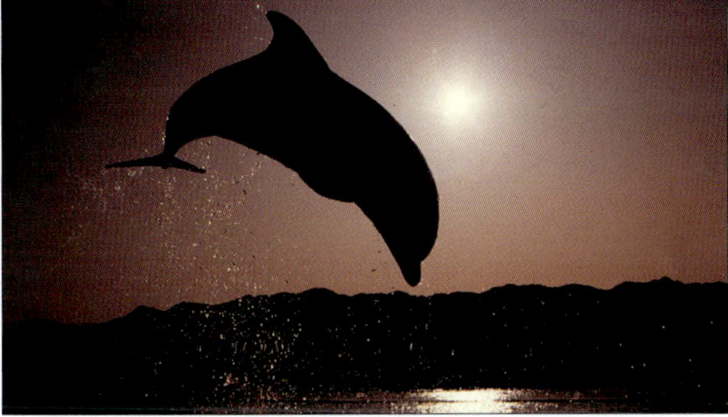

● PETER DALTON Taken at Dolphin Reef, in Eilat, with a Canon EOS 600 loaded with ISO100 slide film and aperture-priority at f/16.

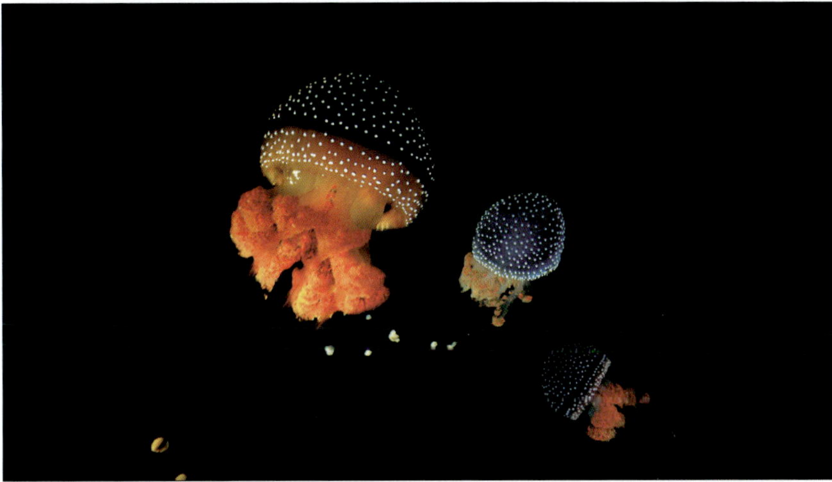

● ROY PRITCHARD Boston aquarium, taken with a Nikon D70 and 28-80mm lens set at 50mm. The exposure was 1/60sec at f/5. The resulting colours were saturated and the background darkened.

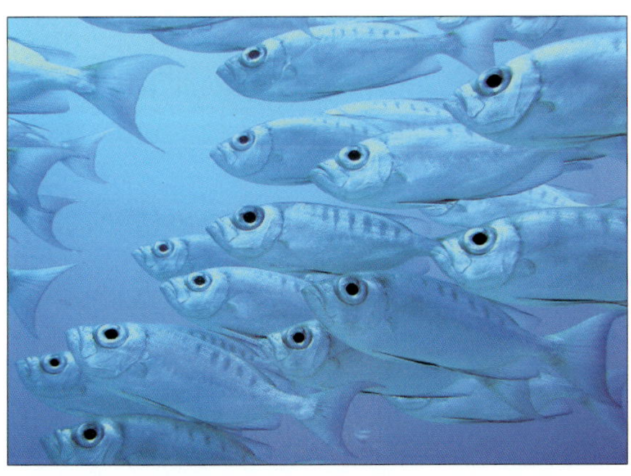

● EDDIE BLAGBROUGH A shoal of big eye, taken using an Olympus C-740 and underwater housing while scuba diving in the Seychelles.

THROUGH GLASS

■ At aquariums or zoos with glass walled enclosures you will be faced with a few problems that can be resolved with the right techniques.
■ When using flash place your camera at a 45° (or lower) angle to the glass to avoid flash reflections on the glass.
■ Place your camera lens up against the glass when it is not behind a barrier.
■ Use a lens hood to shield from stray light and prevent unwanted reflections.
■ Ask a friend to stand next to you and block stray light from behind reflecting on the glass.
■ Use a polarising filter to cut out reflections, but be aware that this can reduce the shutter speed by two stops. So you may need to increase the camera's ISO to compensate.
■ Wear dark clothing to avoid bright reflections.
■ Take a cloth to wipe smears off the part of glass you're shooting through.

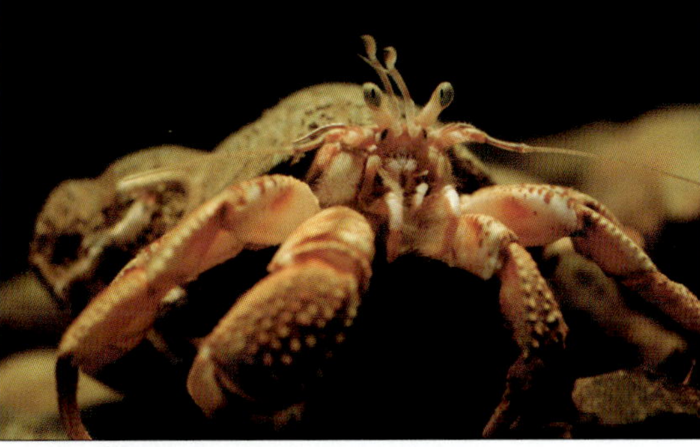

● PETER SMALLWOOD Hermit crab through glass using available light. A handheld Canon EOS 300D at ISO1600 with Sigma 50mm macro.

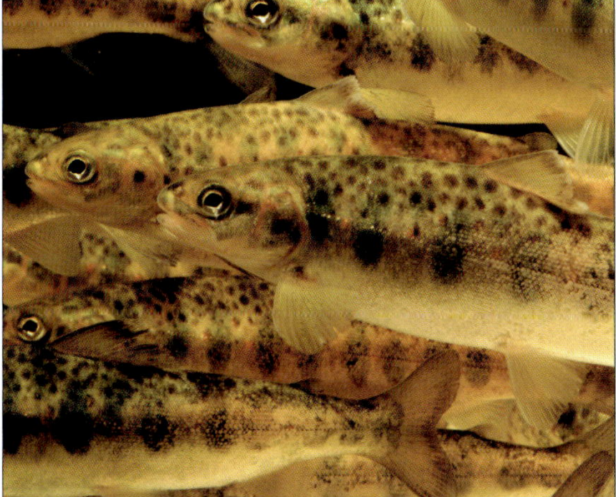

● ALAN DYKES Salmon parr, taken with a Fujifilm S2 Pro inside a specially constructed aquarium with flowing water.

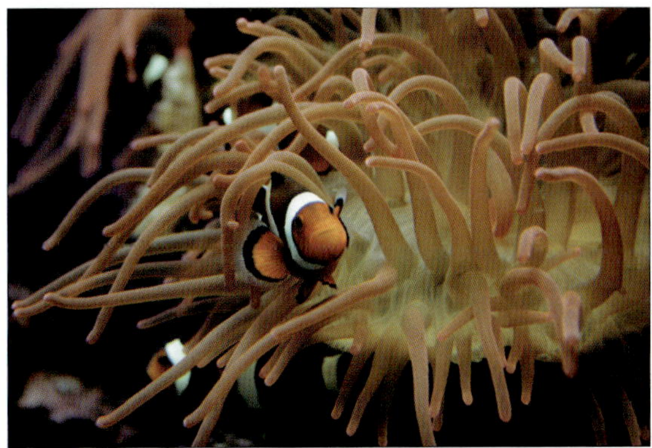

● CRAIG SEVIOUR Clown fish taken at Cape Town Aquarium with an exposure of 1/80sec at f/6.3 and the Canon EOS 300D set at ISO800.

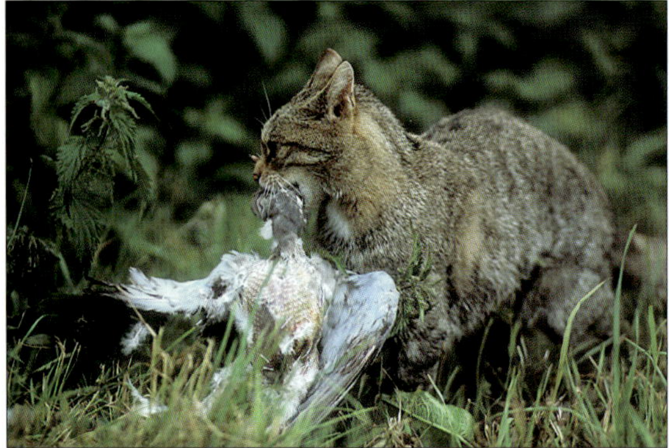

● RON THOMAS Taken in an enclosure at the British Wildlife Centre. "I tried for a shot that looked like it was taken in the wild."

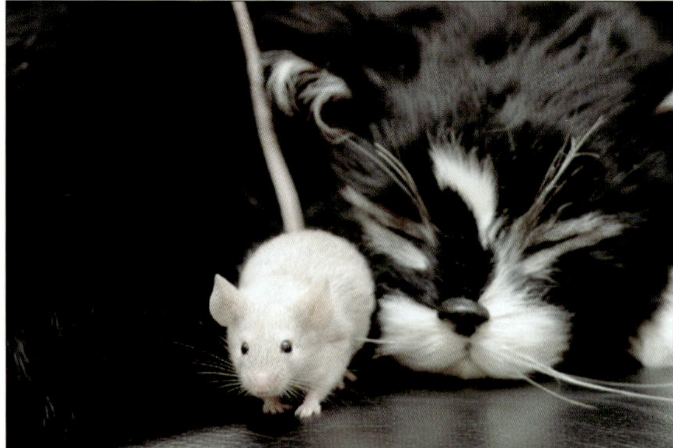

● JOHN MORLEY The cat wasn't going anywhere, but the mouse was all over the place. For a second, everything fell into place.

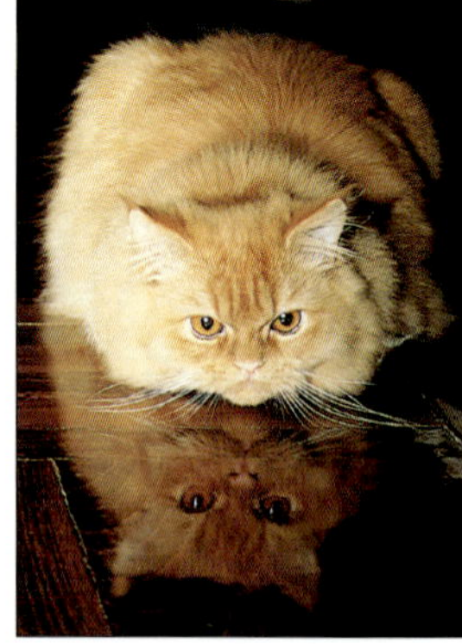

● STUART DAVIES Claude is in Travellers' Tails by Sue Poole.

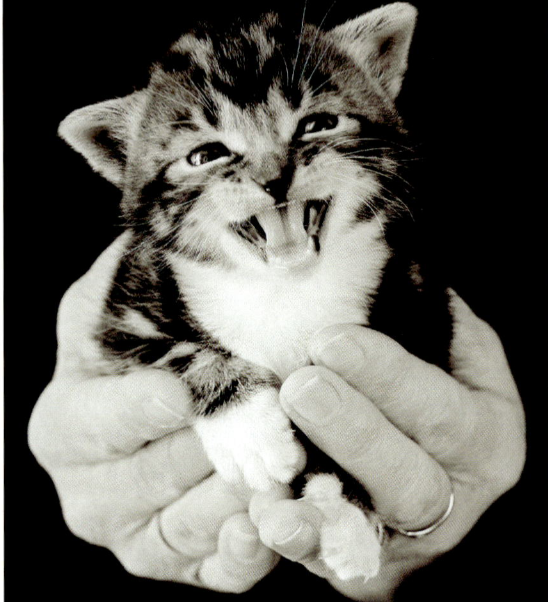

● LEE BEEL This kitten was being looked after by a lady for a cat protection group. "I photographed it for a people and pets theme."

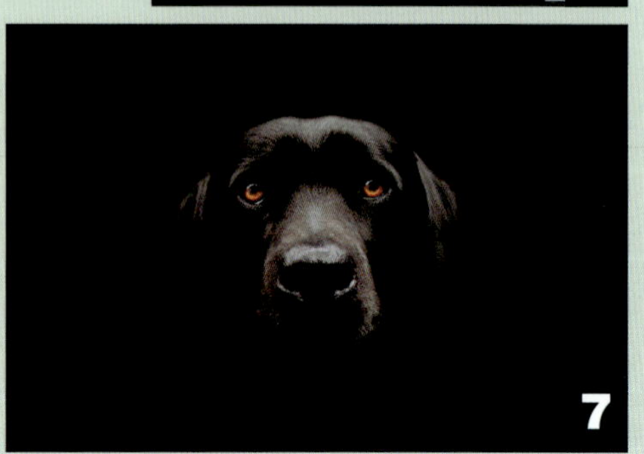

● STEVE SHARP "We had a visitor while enjoying a soup break. A grab shot that turned out well using a Coolpix 990 and infrared filter."

DIGITAL TECHNIQUE – SMARTEN UP YOUR PET PORTRAIT

■ Martin Wait has, with the aid of Photoshop, created the highest rated pet photo on ePHOTOzine. It's of Martin's wonderful dog, Max, who's now a celebrity on our site and we've used his photo on the cover of this book.
The original was little more than a point & shoot photo and here's how Martin transformed this simple snapshot into an image that immediately grabs attention. As you'll see, it's really simple to achieve.

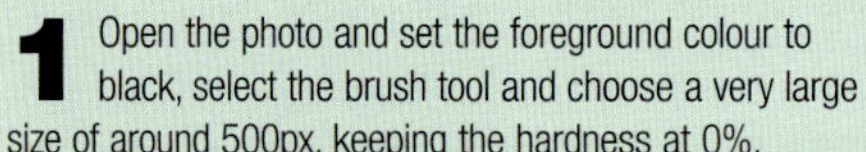

1 Open the photo and set the foreground colour to black, select the brush tool and choose a very large size of around 500px, keeping the hardness at 0%.

2 Paint black all around the subject, taking care not to go too close and catch the edges. Then bring the brush size down to around 100px and paint tightly around the head. Lower the brush size even further to paint into the narrow sections.

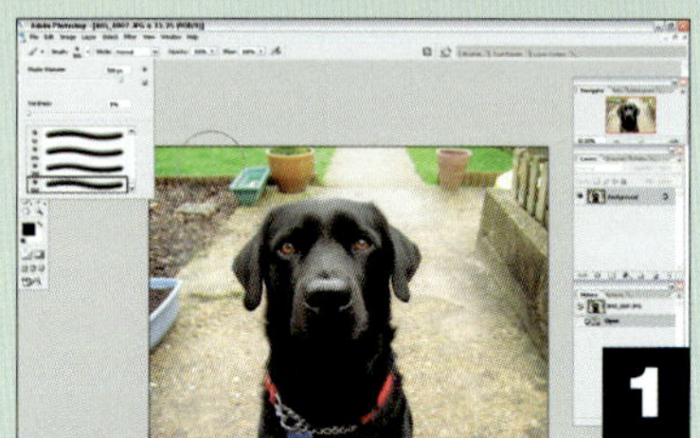

3 Now adjust the contrast using Levels – Image⇨Adjustments⇨Levels. This is the point that you really see the power of the image. I adjusted the sliders until it looked right on screen.

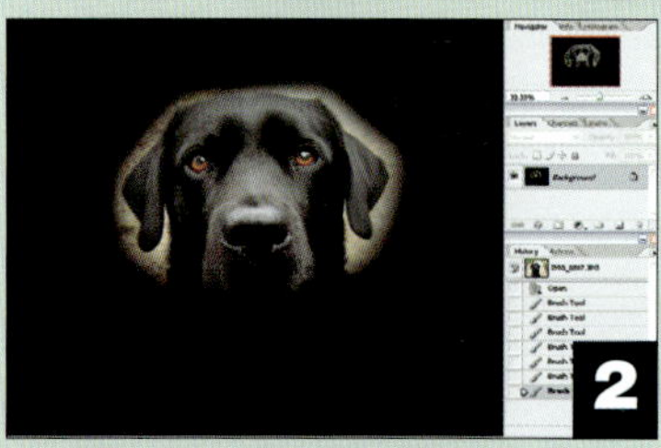

4 I then opened Curves – Image⇨Adjustments⇨Curves and adjusted the curve into an S-shape which has allowed for an extra boost of colour in the eyes and added contrast and a better blackness around Max.

5 Crop the image using the Crop tool to place Max central in the shot.

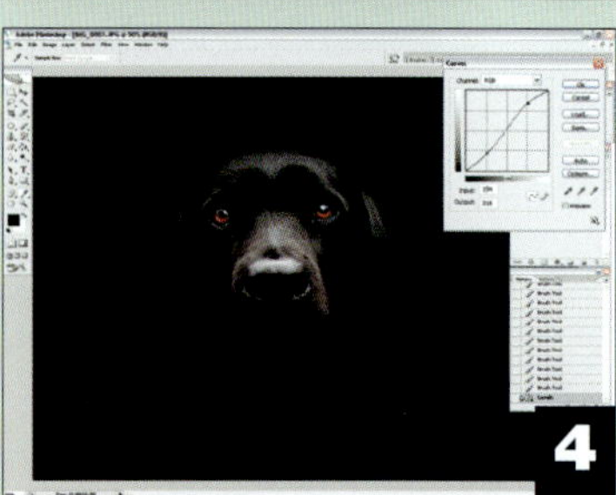

6 It was at this point I realised there was a reflection of my house in Max's eyes. Select the Clone tool and use it in nearby areas to remove traces of the house reflection and make the eyes appear more natural.

7 I also used the Clone tool and Healing Brush tool to take out unwanted patches of hair and other discrepancies, tidying up the image to arrive at the final photograph.

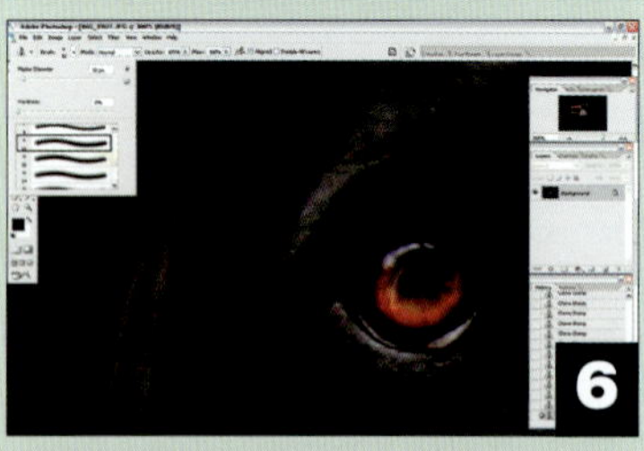

TIP: Getting the best capture of your dog will dramatically cut down your time spent in Photoshop. Taking the shot in a good light makes the process much easier. If your pet is clean and brushed and has a nice catch light in the eyes there will be less time spent cloning and healing.

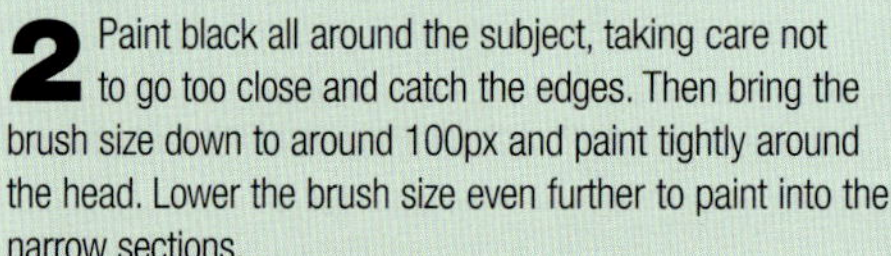

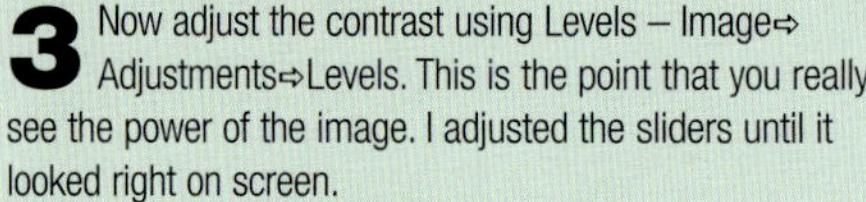

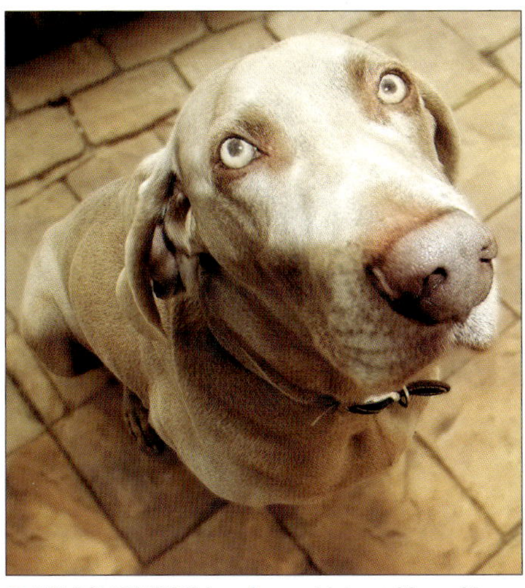

● MIZ POLATAJKO Taken from a high position with a wide-angle lens to obtain the different viewpoint.

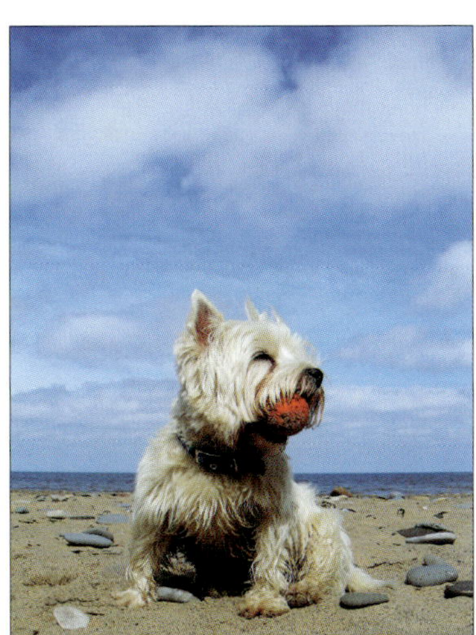

● MARK CURRY Low angle beach shot of Ally at Runswick Bay on a Canon Digital IXUS.

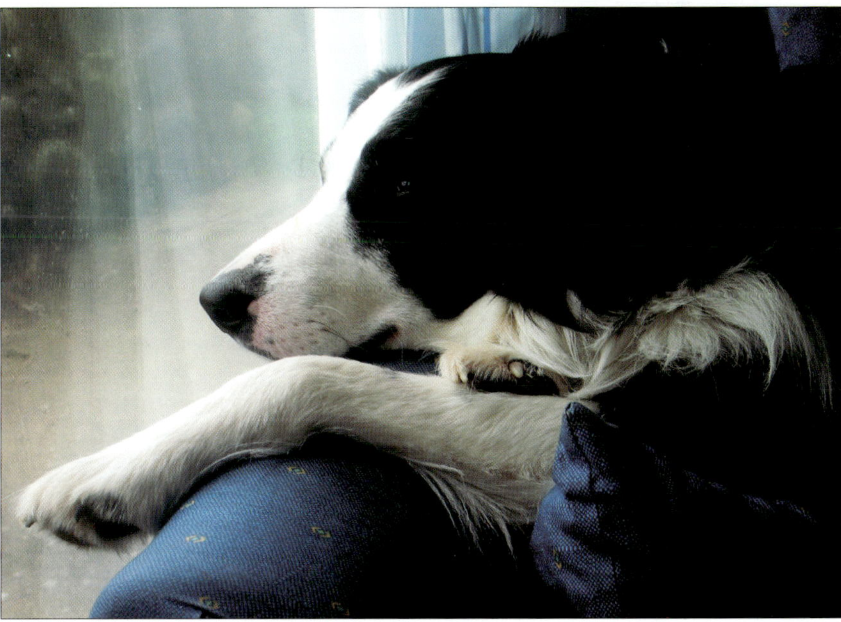

● MARI STERLING "My bored working sheepdog on holiday, waiting for the rain to stop so he could go for a walk. Taken using a Canon EOS 300D with an 18-55mm EFS lens."

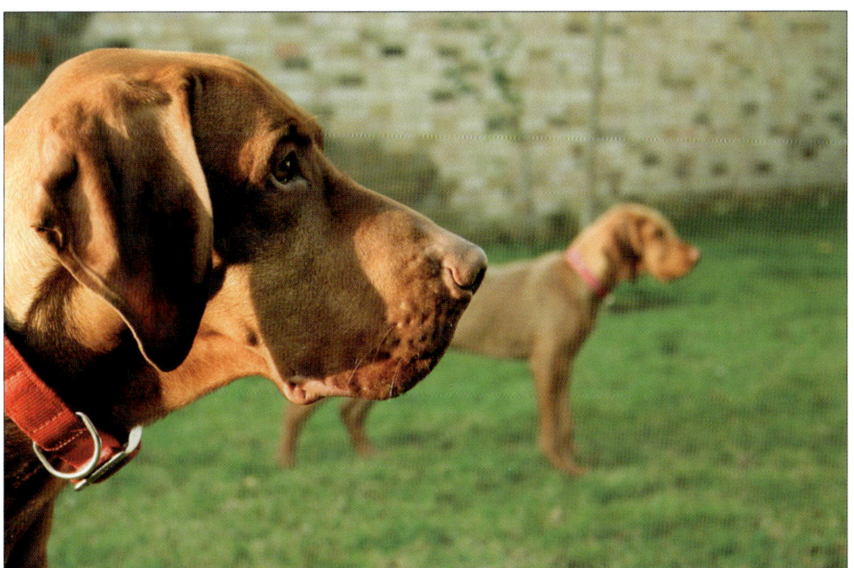

● NIALL COOK Titled 'Me and my Shadow', Boris is in the foreground and his sister Agi in the background. The lens was set at 55mm and an aperture of f/5.6 has thrown Agi out of focus on a Canon EOS 300D.

SHOOTING TIPS – PHOTOGRAPHING PETS

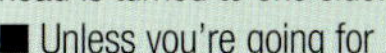

■ Use soft overcast light to avoid a shiny coat of fur having bright spots. A polarising filter will help reduce glare if it's sunny.

■ Focus on the eyes for the attention-grabbing shots, but don't forget a dog with a long snout will need more depth-of-field when shooting close up to prevent the tip of the nose being out of focus. Use a small aperture to avoid this or shoot when their head is turned to one side.

■ Unless you're going for unnatural distortion, place the camera at the same level as the animal.

■ Photograph them in familiar surrounds — maybe in a bed or on the window ledge where they usually like to sit. A cat basking in the sunlight will be an easy target.

■ Ask someone else to entertain the pet while you walk around taking photos. Try to keep the person out of the frame and the shots will be more natural. If part of the person is in shot, clone out later using your image editing program.

■ Make sure the animal is alert. A squeaky toy, nibbles or plaything will make their eyes open and ears stand up to give a better portrait. Place the distraction behind the camera so they look in the right direction.

■ Metering can be fooled by dark or light fur so it comes out greyer than it should be. If the pet is taking up most of the frame, over-expose by half to one stop for a light coat and underexpose by half to one stop for a dark coat.

■ Try using a slow shutter speed with flash, and panning with the animal as it moves, to create abstract slow-sync flash shots and a sense of action.

■ Humans are not the only ones who suffer from devilish looking eyes when flash is used. Pets eyes appear bright green when flash has reflected. Digital photographers can use the selection tools and colour saturation to banish the glaring colour. See the technique in the portraits section.

■ Use a piece of large white card or a purpose made reflector to bounce light into the shaded side of the pet when shooting outdoors.

■ Unless the pet is well trained you'll find it hard to shoot in a studio with a backdrop, but natural backdrops such as hedges or walls can be used to deliver an uncluttered portrait. Use a wider aperture to throw the background out of focus.

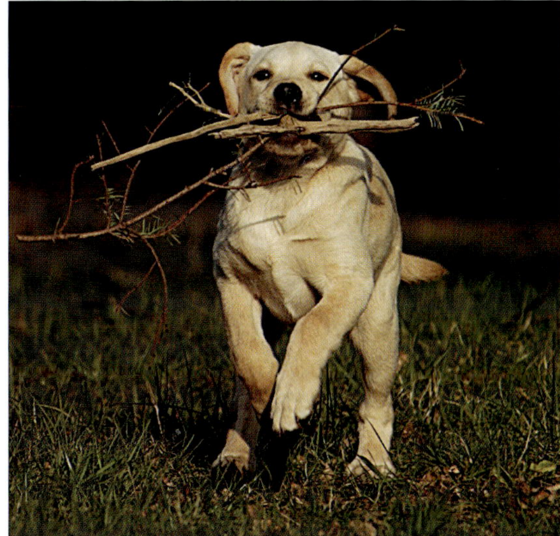

● PHILIP HIGGINS Fetch Dabley! Taken with a Nikon D1H, using spot metering to determine the 1/1000sec at f/5.6 exposure.

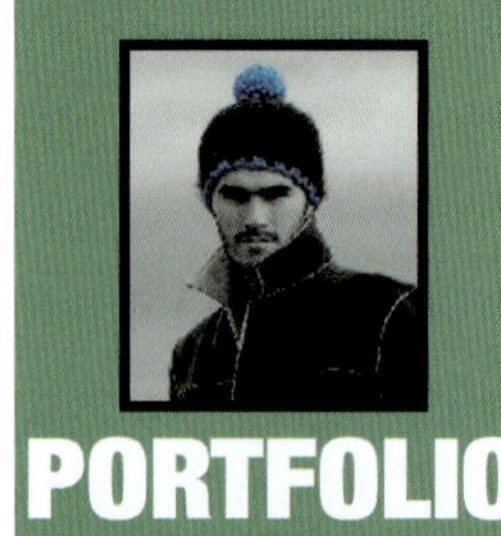

PORTFOLIO

GAVIN

Wildlife photography has taken Gavin to some beautiful places, including the Batu Caves in Kuala Lumpur.

Gavin is based in North Wales and has been into photography since 2001 when he bought his first digital camera – a cheap two Megapixel in November 2003. He's since purchased a digital SLR – the Canon EOS 300D – and that's when his real passion for photography kicked off.

The thing Gavin loves about digital photography is that you can take as many photos as you want without having the expense of getting them printed, and the results are immediate.

He also studied Computer Science at University so he enjoys the image manipulation side of digital photography too. Being able to create lots of different images from the one photo is a big plus for Gavin.

Since he bought his SLR he's added a selection of zoom lenses, including the Canon 16-35mm, 28-135mm and 100-400mm IS lens, and he's dabbled in most areas of photography, including wildlife, scenic, portraits, weddings, macro and infrared.

Digital Camera Magazine have published three of Gavin's shots in their Hotshots section – two of which won the title 'Shot of the Month'.

Gavin's main interest, however, lies with wildlife and scenery, which has taken him to some beautiful places – his favourite being a trip to the Batu Caves in Kuala Lumpur which produced three of the outstanding images in this portfolio.

Getting so close to the wild, free-roaming macaques was an experience he will never forget – especially when he and his wife were chased down a flight of steps by an angry male and female! ■

www.gndphotography.co.uk

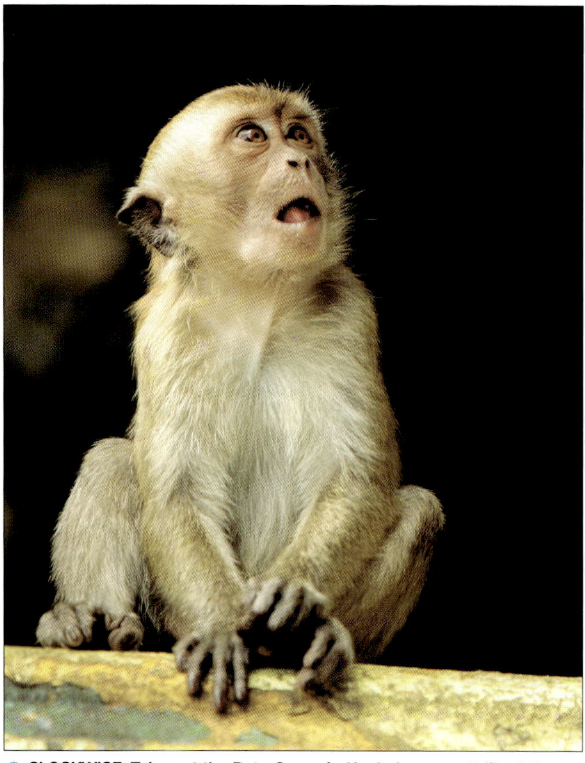

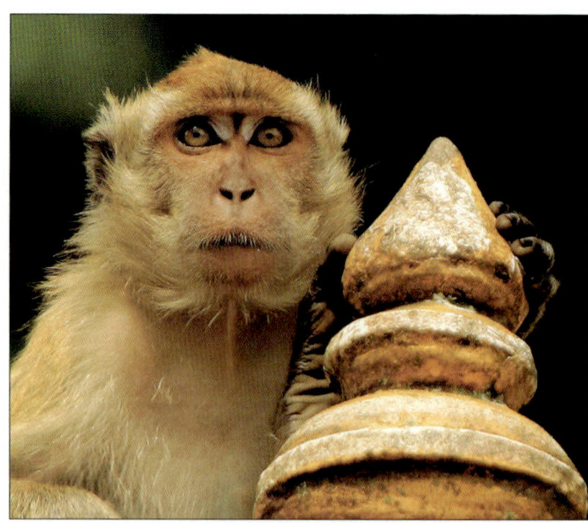

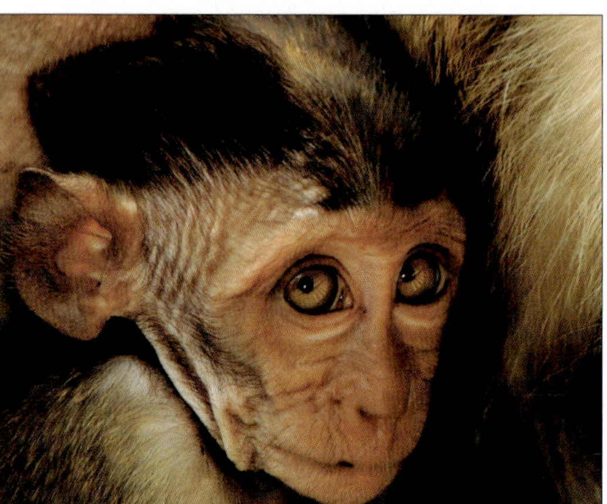

● CLOCKWISE: Taken at the Batu Caves in Kualu Lumpur. "I liked the bemused look that this macaque had on its face." ● Temple Guard!!! Taken at the entrance to the Batu Caves in Kuala Lumpur. ● Taken at the Batu Caves in Kuala Lumpur. The reflections in the eyes are of the steps that lead up to the temple. ● Penny for... I spent ages photographing these at Chester Zoo."

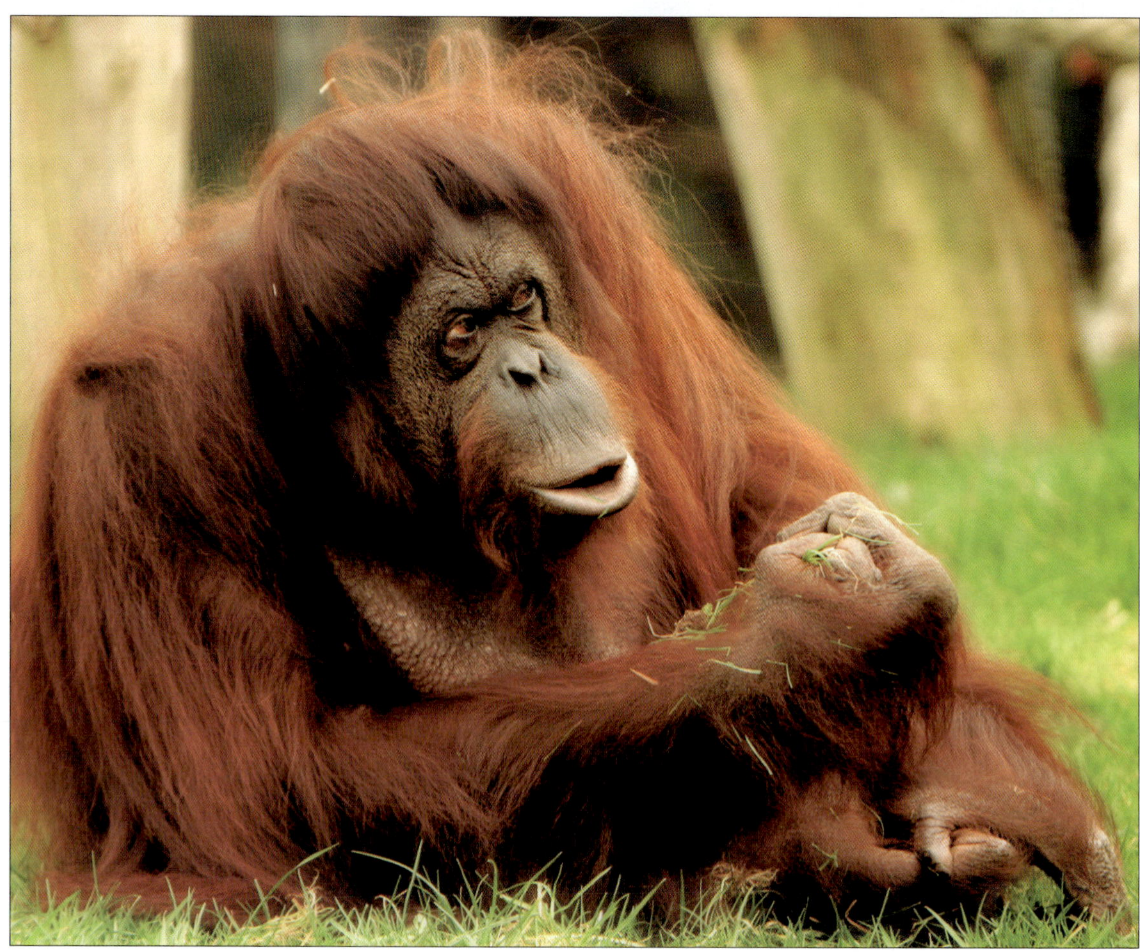

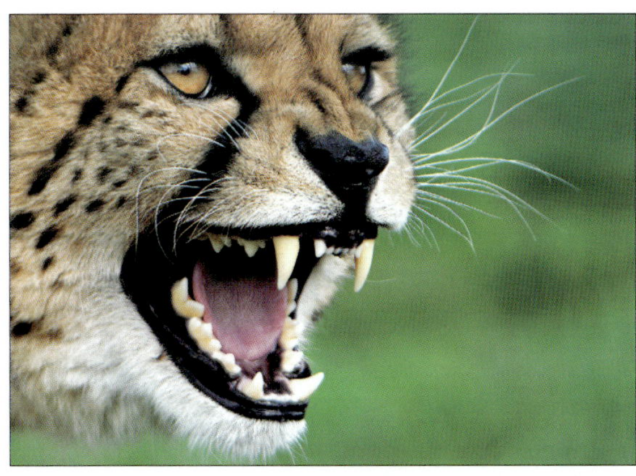

● ALISON PRINCE Male cheetah photographed at a conservation centre in Kent, with a Canon EOS 300D and Tamron 200-400 lens.

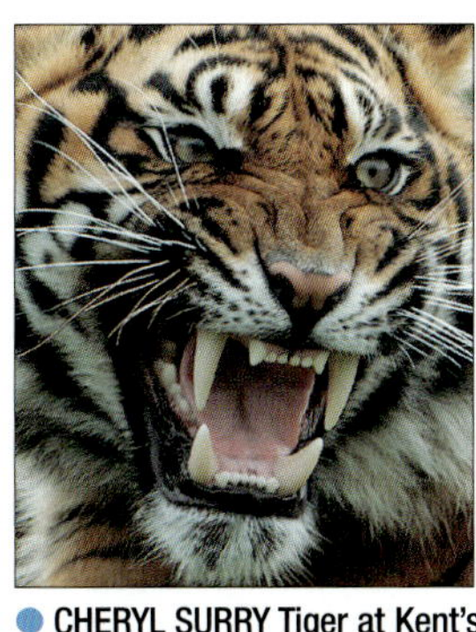

● CHERYL SURRY Tiger at Kent's Wildlife Heritage Foundation.

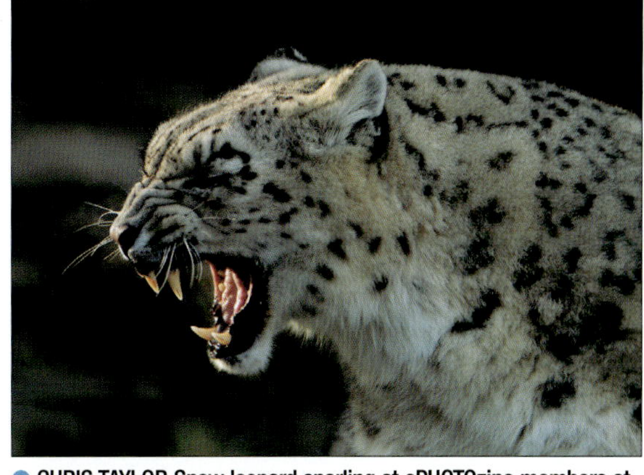

● CHRIS TAYLOR Snow leopard snarling at ePHOTOzine members at a Marwell Zoo meet. Taken with a Nikon D100 and Sigma 70-200mm.

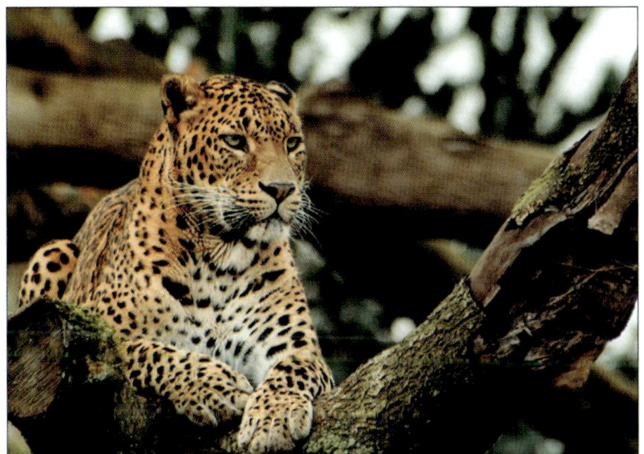

● NEAL LAVER Sri Lankan leopard shot through the glass viewing panel at Banham Zoo, Norfolk, using a Fuji S2 Pro and 70-300mm.

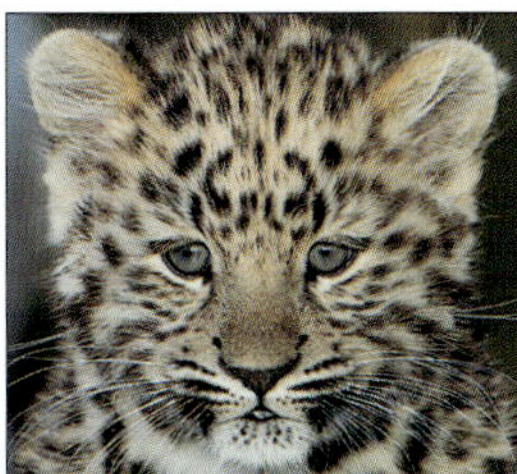

● PETER GRAVES Amur leopard cub at Marwell Zoo, Hampshire.

SHOOTING TIPS – BETTER PHOTOS AT ZOOS

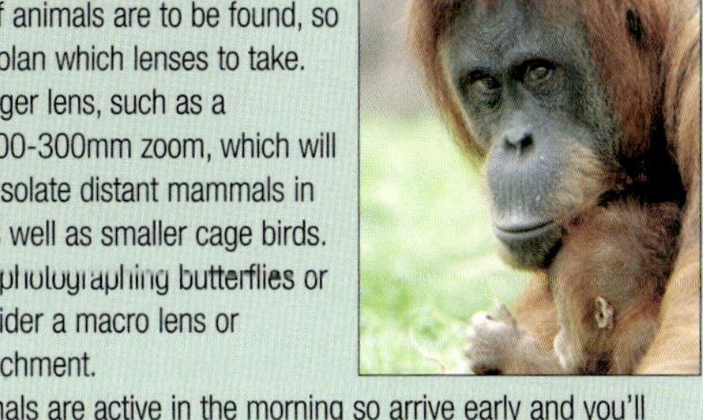

■ Check the website beforehand to see what types of animals are to be found, so you can pre-plan which lenses to take.

■ Take a longer lens, such as a 70-200 or 100-300mm zoom, which will allow you to isolate distant mammals in paddocks, as well as smaller cage birds. If you intend photographing butterflies or insects, consider a macro lens or close-up attachment.

■ Most animals are active in the morning so arrive early and you'll not only catch the action but you will miss the crowds too.

■ Check the plan for the zoo when you pay for your entrance ticket. It will often give you a guide of how to walk around to make the most of the trip.

■ Avoid holiday periods or weekends if you want to gain uncrowded views of the enclosures.

■ Look out for feeding times and head for the areas well in advance so you get a good vantage point.

■ Alternatively, find an enclosure near a feeding area and head for that at feeding time. The crowds will be drawn away from that area to the action, leaving you a few minutes of peace.

■ Put your lens right up to the cage and position it so a gap is in the centre of the lens. Use a wide aperture to throw the cage wire totally out of focus.

■ Move around to get the best background. There's often caging behind as well as in front so choose a position where the animal is in front of a bush or other cage-hiding background.

■ Try to get eye contact with the animal – making a noise not too harsh to disturb but enough to attract attention is all that's needed.

■ If you don't take a tripod use barriers/fences as supports.

■ See the panel on shooting through glass on page 87.

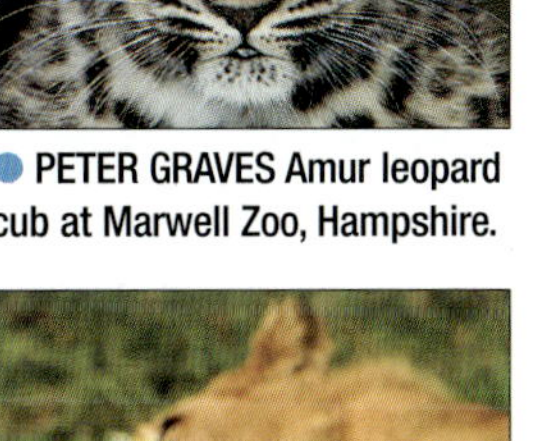

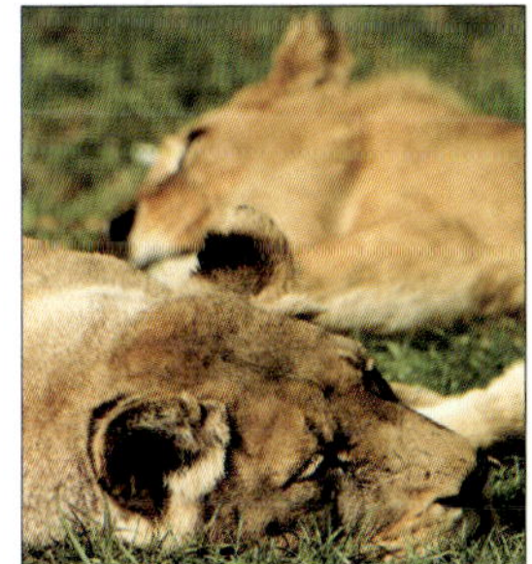

● MALCOLM JOHNS Two old lionesses relaxing in the sun.

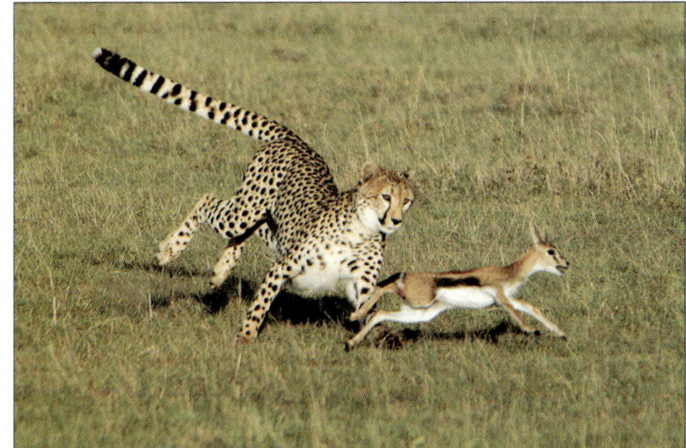

● PETER REAR Cheetah chase at Masai Mara, taken on a Nikon D100 with 80-200mm and 2x Teleconverter – 1/1000sec at f/5.6.

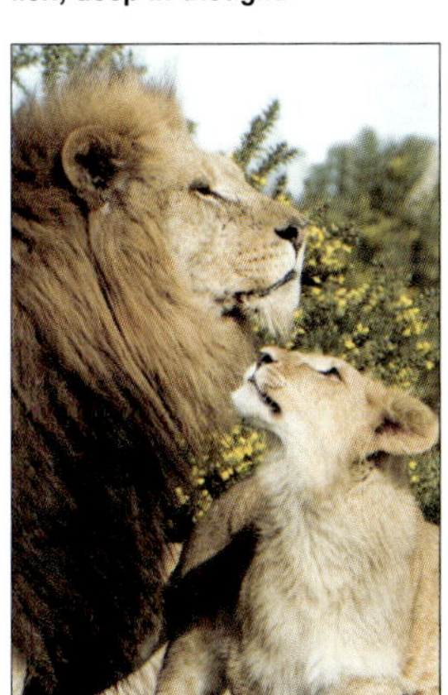

● CHRIS HARTLEY An Asiatic lion, deep in thought.

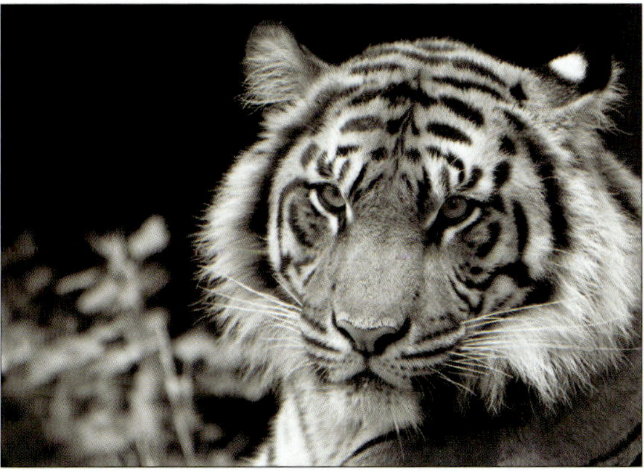

● WILLIE BANEHAM Tiger close-up, using a Canon 100-400mm at 400mm. Image converted to black & white and warm grey duotone.

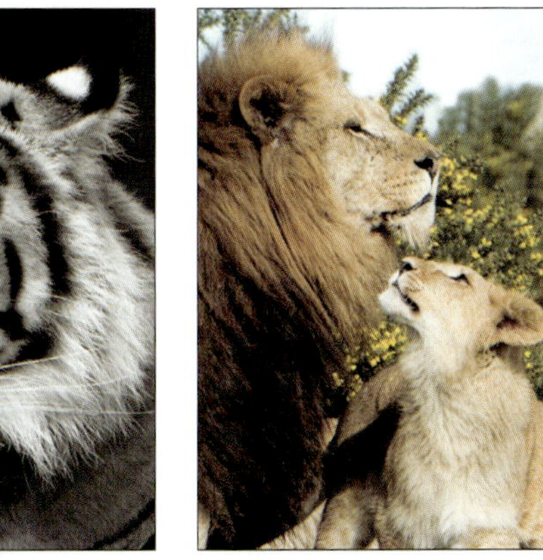

● ANDREW BRITTIN 170mm lens at f/6.3 and 1/400sec speed.

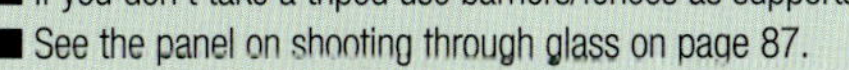

● MATT WAGSTER Pepo, a cheetah at the Wildlife Heritage Foundation in Kent, photographed against the natural background.

NATURE

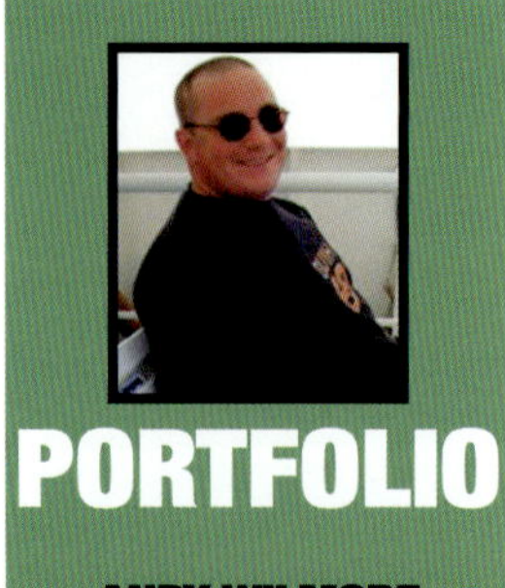

PORTFOLIO

ANDY WILMORE
has always had a fond love of wildlife and the natural world, so photographing animals was his natural choice.

Andy only started out in photography quite recently, in 2001, after being given an old Praktica BC1 by his grandfather. From there he moved on to the Canon EOS film system before deciding, in 2003, to take the plunge into digital photography and buy a Canon EOS 20D digital SLR.

Andy has always had a fond love of wildlife and the natural world, so photographing animals was his natural choice.

"Although my main goal, when photographing animals, is to do so in their natural environment, I also visit zoos, wildlife parks and private sanctuaries to take photographs. These allow me to get close to the animals and are a good base to use for practice.

"Time and money are also a big factor in my reasons for going to these types of places – it is not always possible to capture some of these animals in their natural environment, so zoos and wildlife parks are the next best thing.

I prefer to shoot in RAW format and use RAWShooter and Photoshop post-shooting to process my files as near to the captured image as possible, with little in the way of manipulation or any alterations.

"I enjoy photography, but I do not really have a main goal for it or any particular plans for the future. It's just a hobby at the moment and as long as I continue to enjoy it then I will be happy.

"Having said that, if my photography could be used to in any way promote or aid animal conservation then that would be a real bonus for me."

A few of Andy's favourite photographers include Heather Angel, Steve & Ann Toon, Rosemary Calvert and Moose Petersen. ∎

www.andywilmore.com

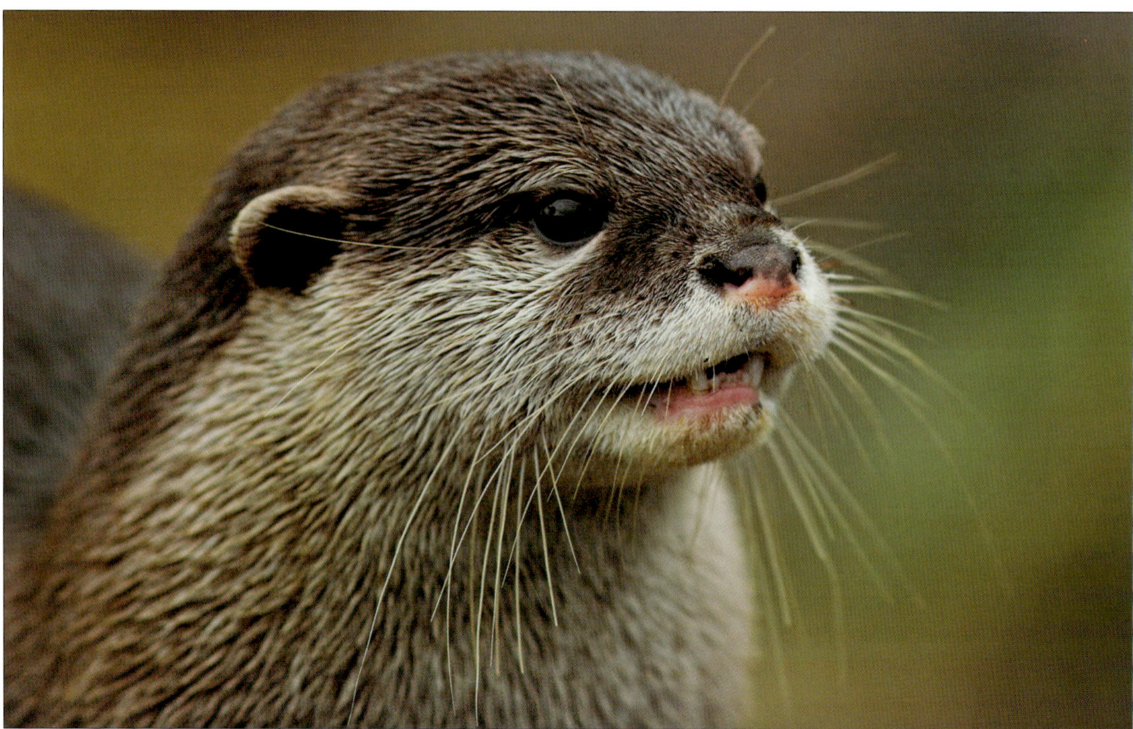

CLOCKWISE: All four photos were taken using a Canon EOS 20D Digital SLR ● ASIAN OTTER: Photographed at Chester Zoo using the Canon EF 300mm f/4L IS and the camera at ISO800 sensitivity. ● SNOW LEOPARD: This was one of the first shots Andy took while on a photo day at Santago Rare Leopard Project in Herts. The leopard had just woken up and was actually yawning. When pressing the shutter Andy had a feeling she was going to look fierce. The shot was captured using the 70-200 f/2.8L IS set at 200mm and an exposure of 1/500sec at f/4 with ISO 400 sensitivity. ● LEOPARD: Sheena is another cat at the Santago Rare Leopard Project, taken using the Canon EF 300mm f/4L IS and ISO 400. ● CANADIAN TIMBER WOLF: Madadh is one of the beautiful Canadian timber wolves from Wolf Watch UK, and quite a character. Tony, the owner of Wolf Watch UK, takes her out for walks with the photographers, which is a bit daunting. It was a pretty glum day, so Andy set ISO 800 and used a Canon EF 300mm f4L IS lens, but the exposure was difficult because the white on her cheeks would burn out if he wasn't careful!

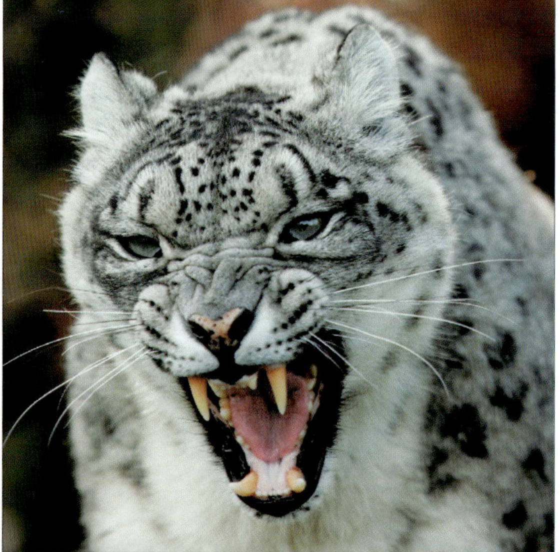

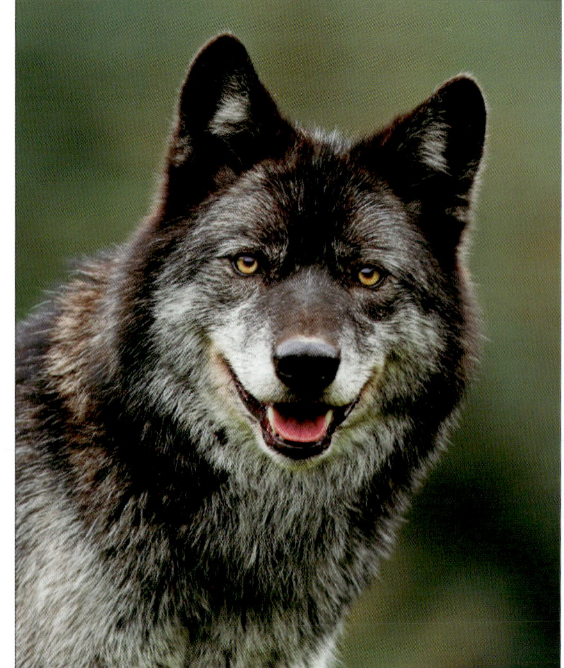

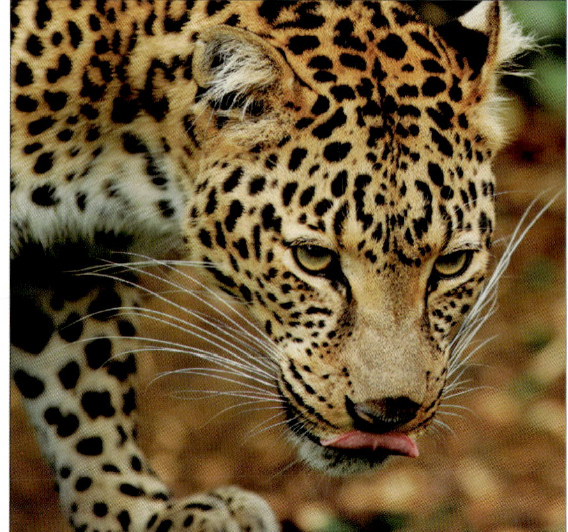

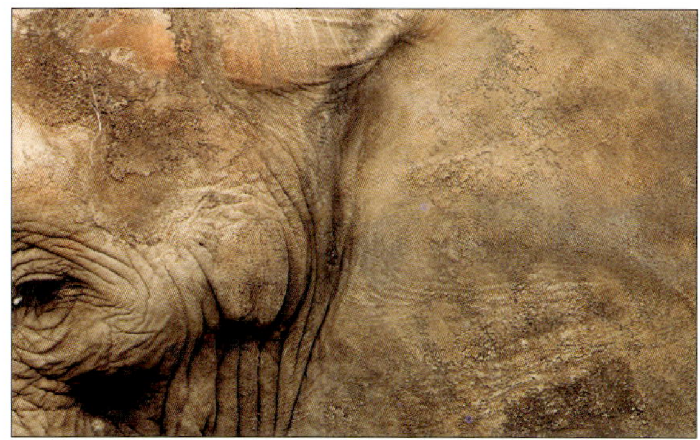

● COLIN CONSTABLE A Canon EOS 10D in aperture-priority was used for this tight-framed shot, with a Sigma 100-300mm at 300mm.

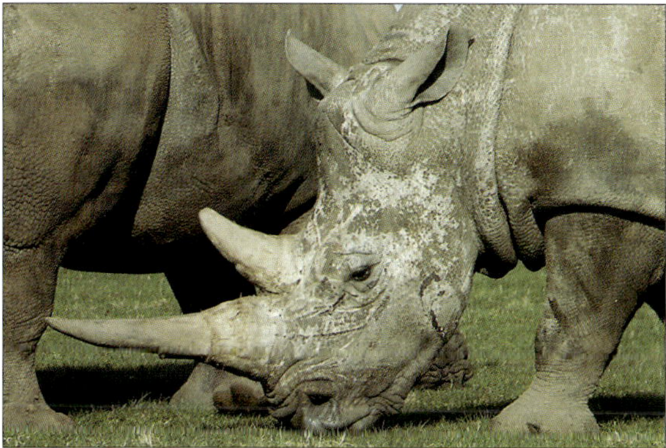

● ALAN DONAGHUE Getting in close and on the same level as these huge animals gives greater impact to the overall image.

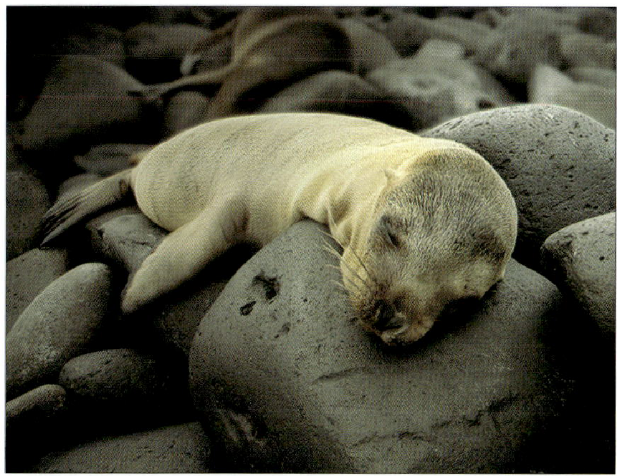

● ROBIN SLATER Age of innocence – a Galapagos sea lion fast asleep and completely ignorant of Robin's presence.

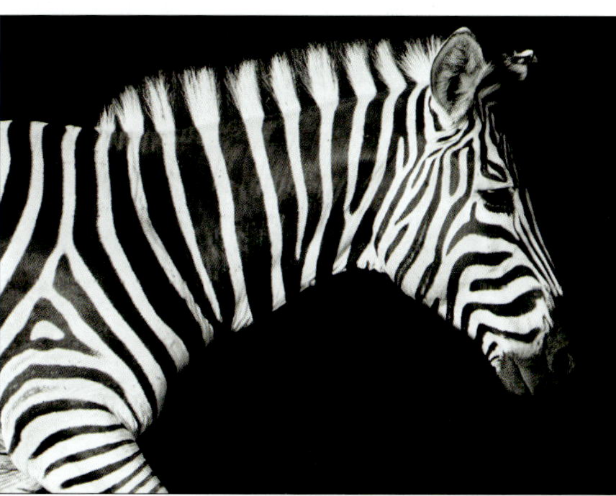

● ALEX KERR Taken in Botswana, using the Canon EOS 20D's black & white setting and high contrast to bring out the zebra's stripes.

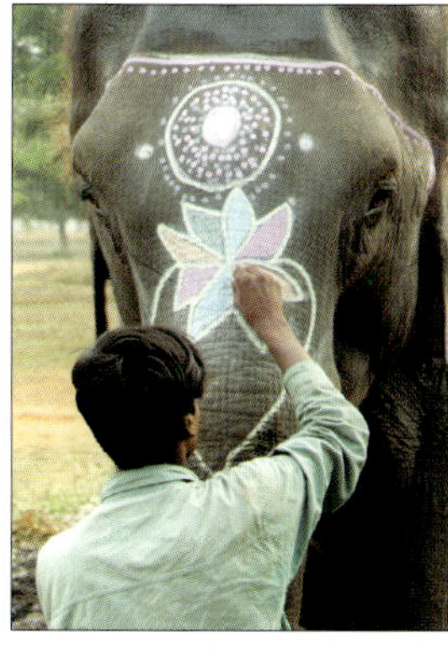

● DAVID KNOWLES Elephantine preparations before the photographic Tiger Hunt in Corbett National Park, India.

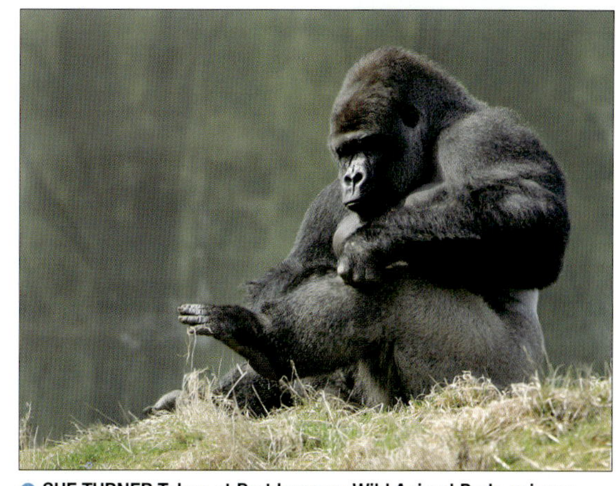

● SUE TURNER Taken at Port Lympne, Wild Animal Park, using a Canon EOS 300D and 100-400mm USM at 400mm and f/6.3.

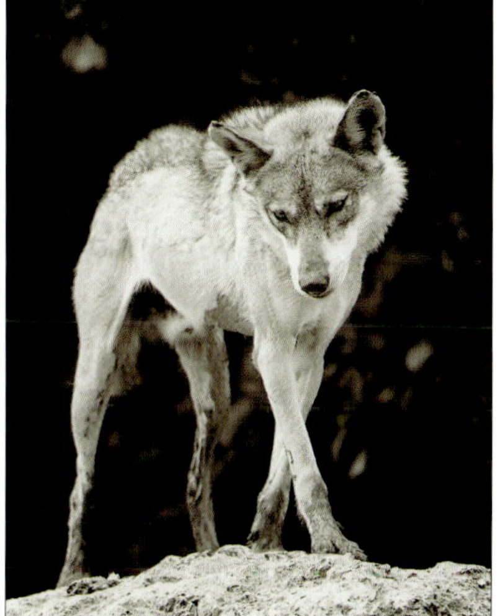

● YAIR LEIBOVICICH This wolf belongs to one of the smallest sub-species of the gray wolf (Canis lupus pallipes) that can be found in Israel.

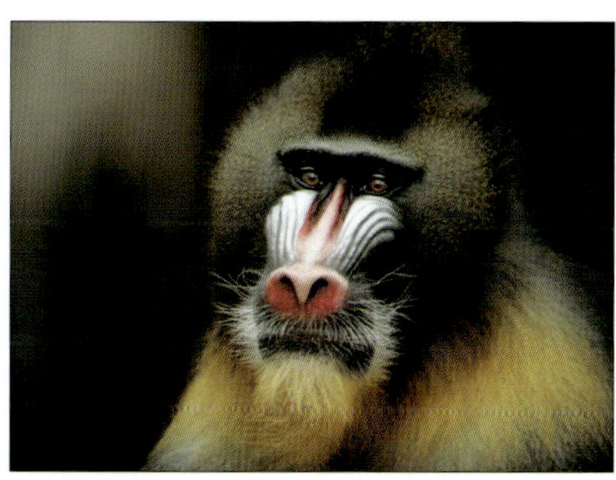

● PETER BARGH A mandrill taken through glass at Chester Zoo, using a hood and pressing up close to the glass to reduce reflections.

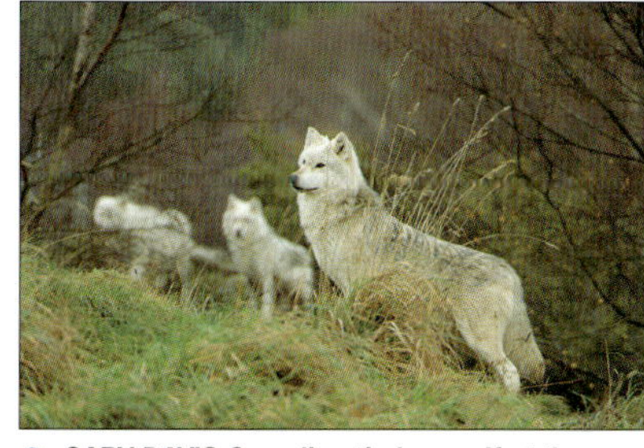

● GARY DAVIS Canadian timber wolf at the Highland Wildlife Park, taken on a Nikon D70 with a Sigma 170-500mm zoom lens.

LOCATION GUIDE – ZOOS & PARKS

■ Chester Zoo, Chester www.chesterzoo.org
■ Marwell Zoological Park, Winchester **www.marwell.org.uk**
■ Twycross Zoo, Atherstone Warwickshire **www.twycrosszoo.com**
■ London Zoo, London www.zsl.org
■ Blackpool Zoo, Blackpool Lancashire www.blackpoolzoo.org.uk
■ Galloway Wildlife Conservation Park **www.gallowaywildlife.co.uk**
■ British Wildlife Centre, Lingfield Surrey **www.british-wildlife.com**
■ Dunham Massey (Deer park), Altrincham, Manchester **www.nationaltrust.org.uk**
■ Lincolnshire Wildlife Trust, Horncastle Lincs **www.lincstrust.org.uk**
■ Whipsnade Wild Animal Park, Dunstable Bedfordshire **www.zsl.org**
■ Wildwood Trust, Herne Bay, Kent **www.wildwoodtrust.org**
■ Badger Watch Dorset, Dorchester Dorset **www.badgerwatchdorset.co.uk**
■ Highland Wildlife Park, Kingussie Scotland **www.highlandwildlifepark.org**
■ Blair Drummond Safari and Leisure Park, Blair Drummond Stirling **www.safari-park.co.uk**
■ Kirkcudbright Wildlife Park, Kirkcudbrightshire **www.safaripark.co.uk**
■ Island Farm Donkey Sanctuary, Wallingford Oxfordshire **www.donkeyrescue.co.uk**
■ Welsh Hawking Centre and Wildlife Park, Barry S Glamorgan **www.barrywales.co.uk/hawkingcentre**
■ Argyll Wildlife Park, Inveraray Argyll **www.safaripark.co.uk**
■ The Monkey Sanctuary, Looe Cornwall **www.monkeysanctuary.org**
■ The Wildlife Park at Cricket St Thomas Chard, Somerset **www.cstwp.co.uk**
■ Curraghs Wildlife Park, Douglas Isle Of Man **www.gov.im/wildlife**
■ South Lakes Wild Animal Park, Dalton-in-Furness Cumbria **www.wildanimalpark.co.uk**
■ Santago, Herts **www.santago.com**
■ Paradise Park Wildlife Sanctuary, Hayle Cornwall **www.paradisepark.org.uk**

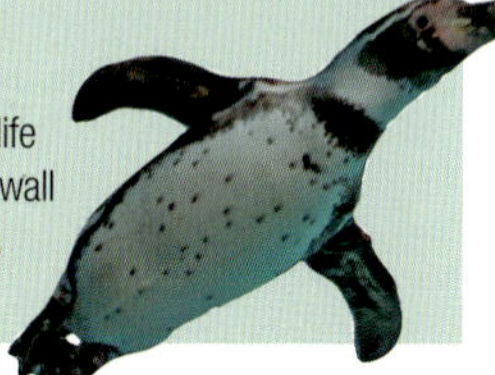

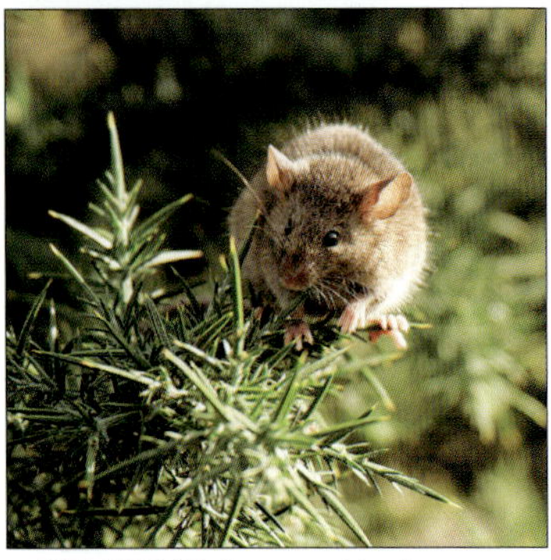

● MIKE TAYLOR A mouse tries to escape the adder enclosure.

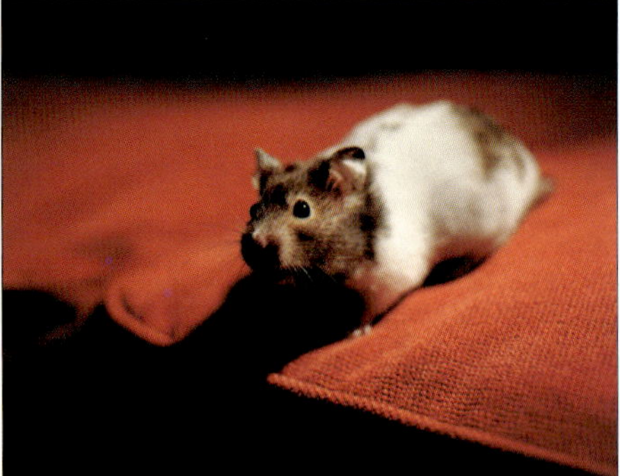

● SHAUN BALL Hovis running on the sofa, lit by a tungsten spot lamp and Canon EOS 10D at ISO800.

PLANNNG TIPS – BETTER RESULTS ON SAFARI

■ Planning a safari? Here's some advice to help you prepare and return with a better set of photos.

■ For a safari the most important thing is the lens. While it's possible to get fairly close to many animals there will be some that will be too far away for a short zoom lens of up to 70mm to fill the frame. Ideally, in these circumstances, you'd need a lens of 300mm or longer. A lens, such as Sigma's 50-500mm zoom, is a perfect choice for close-ups and distant subjects. As animals are more active at dawn and dusk faster lenses are more useful, otherwise you need to increase film speed or CCD sensitivity resulting in excessive grain or noise. Take a wide zoom for landscapes, river scenes and herds.

■ You can take a photograph with a 35mm camera and enlarge the centre portion, but this isn't advisable with a lower resolution digital camera (2mp or less), as you'll lower the quality too much. In such situations it's probably better to just enjoy the moment and try and take a shot on another day when you may be lucky enough to get closer to similar animals.

■ You may be going to one of the hottest countries in the world, but it's still cold at dawn, so take a jumper for the early morning safaris.

■ When travelling in a safari jeep there isn't much room to carry lots of gear so a tripod's out of the question. SLR owners shooting using 300mm or more could consider taking a monopod to support the camera, but in most cases it's better to use the roof bars of your vehicle as a sturdy support when it's stationary. Wait until no one is moving in the vehicle before you take a photo.

■ Take a pocket torch if you intend going on a night drive so you can see the controls on your camera.

■ If you've planned several safari treks don't go mad shooting all your film on the first day. You may have better sightings later.

■ Often, you only get a fleeting glance of certain animals, so be prepared to take the first shot quickly to avoid "the one that got away." Then spend time, if available, to get a better shot on your second attempt.

■ Become friendly with the guides, tell them what you're trying to do and they're often very flexible, but do bear in mind the needs of other passengers on your trip. Hiring a private guide may be a better option.

■ Scenes can confuse your camera's automatic metering. The camera may compensate if it is overall bright and light toned and make the picture too dark, resulting in the central animal becoming a silhouette.

■ Bright mid day sunlight will create harsh shadows that can be reduced using flash as a fill-in source. Set the flash to half power when the subject is backlit or has deep shadows. Set it to quarter power when the sun is out, but shadows aren't as harsh.

■ Make sure you avoid cutting off the horns, tail or other extremities unless there's a specific reason.

■ Include something in the foreground to add a sense of depth when shooting landscapes. A rock, tree stump or person will add scale and interest.

■ Use the focus lock when using an autofocus camera to shoot a subject that's off centre. Point the camera at the main subject, press the shutter release halfway down and hold, recompose and press fully down to take the picture.

■ Many cameras have an automatic flash. If you try to take a picture of a sunset or night scene the flash will probably fire. Most can be switched off for more natural results.

■ Don't be afraid to ask your guide to stop the vehicle if you spot something interesting.

■ Although cameras are light tight, and film can be loaded in daylight, it's best to load in the shade to avoid fogging the film. If you can't find a shaded area, use your body to shield the camera from the sun.

■ When it's dusty avoid changing lenses on your SLR as the dust can easily get inside the camera and cause damage. Dust on a CCD will appear on every photo and need editng out later. This applies to film too. If you need to change film take a small blower brush and clean the film chamber when you reload to avoid dust scratching the film.

■ Keep your exposed films in your hand luggage on the return trip home - airport x-ray machines are film safe, cargo ones generally aren't! Memory cards are not affected by airport security.

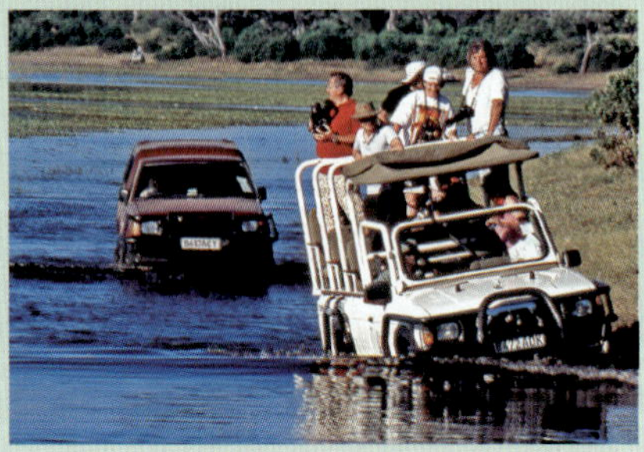

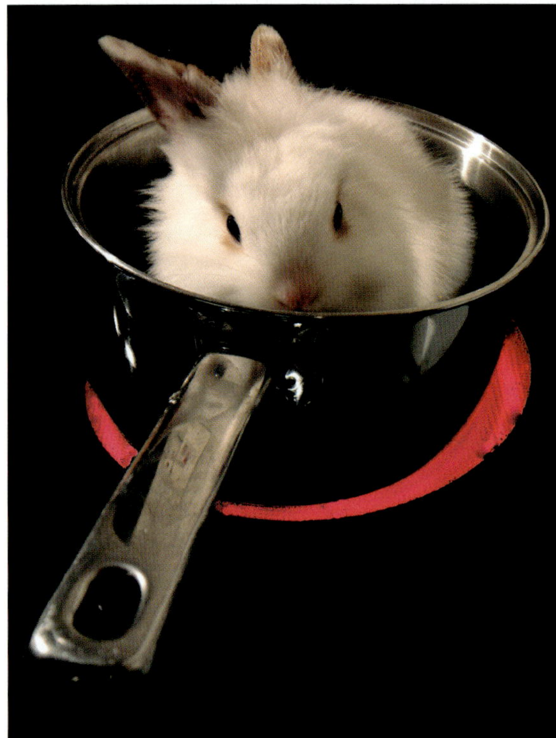

● MILES HERBERT Miles spent hours knelt in a gorse bush leaning on the tripod waiting for the rabbits to do something.

● KARL WOOD Taken using a Fuji 602 on a tripod and merging two shots. No animals were harmed in the making of this shot!

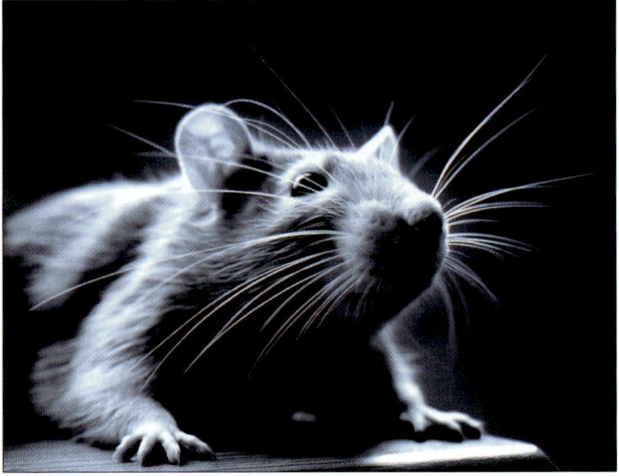

● LAUREN MALLEY Pet rat Beatrix, shot using a Canon EOS 300D and 18-55mm lens with natural window back lighting at f/5.6.

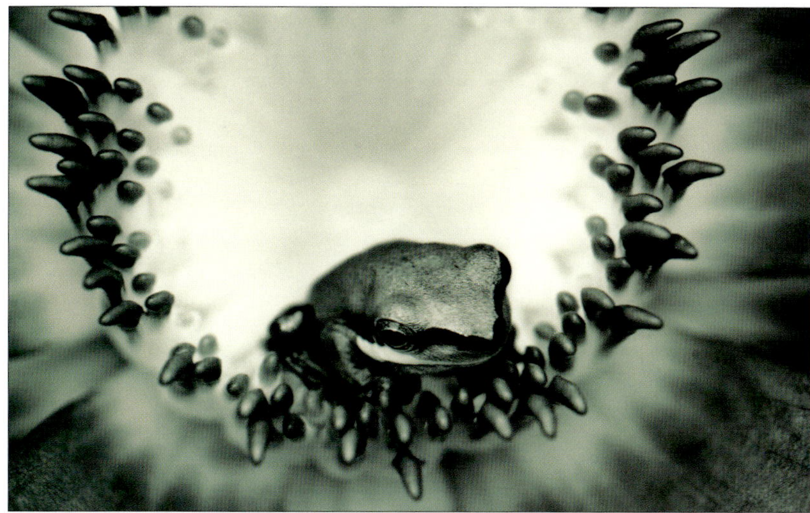

● STEVEN NEIL Steve's a designer in Australia and has produced some of the best frog photos we've seen. This Eastern sedge was sat inside a lily and has been cross-processed using Curves.

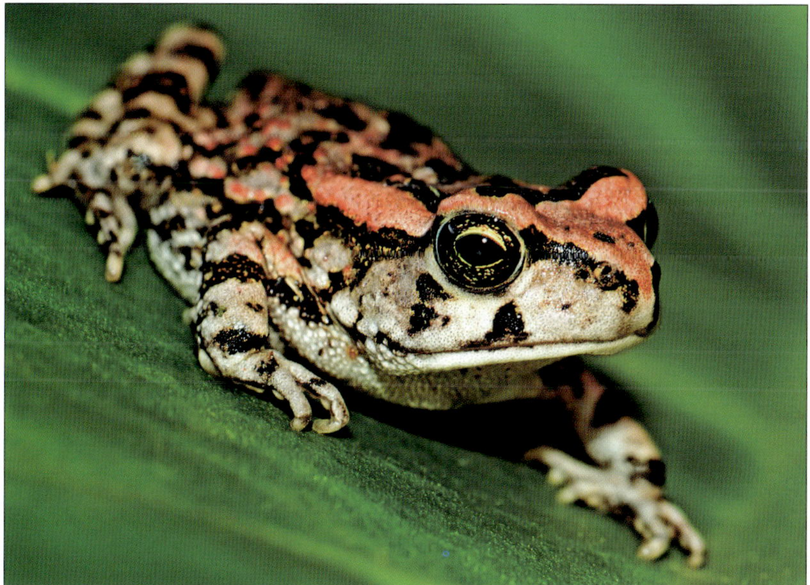

● JOGGIE VAN STADEN Juvenile rough-skinned toad is just 3cm long so the 105mm Micro Nikkor was needed on the Nikon D70. Built-in flash and an exposure of f/32 at 1/60sec.

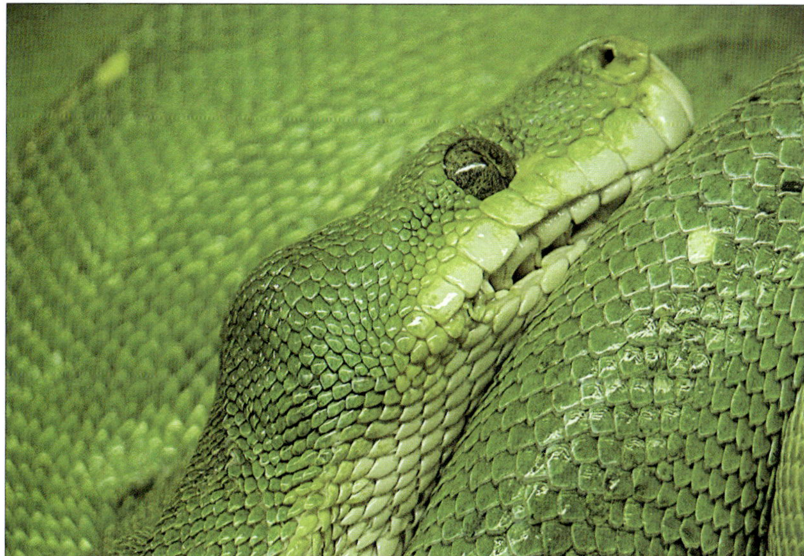

● JUDE GIDNEY A Nikon Coolpix 5700 was used with the zoom at the maximum length of 300mm for this shot at Chester zoo, taken through glass. Jude wanted the vivid green to fill the frame.

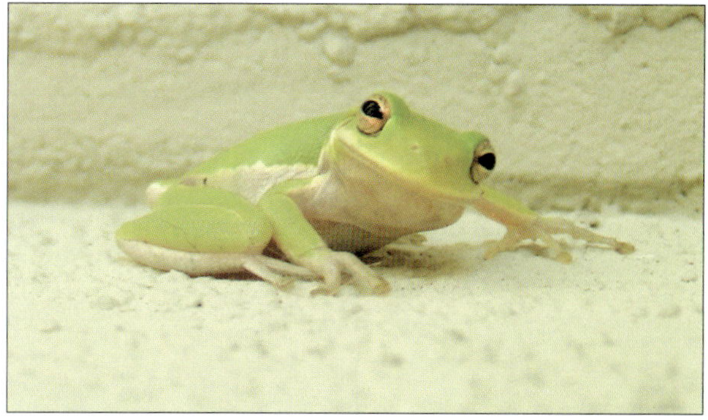

● DAVID CARTER Taken just after Hurricane Jean hit Florida in September 2004. I found this little chap sheltering in the doorway of the villa.

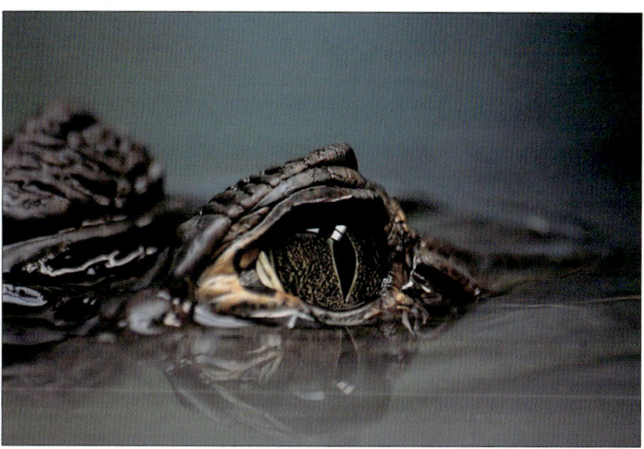

● JOHN BOGLE Low light and massively under-exposed at ISO800 to get 1/50sec on the Canon EOS 10D. Then enhanced in Photoshop.

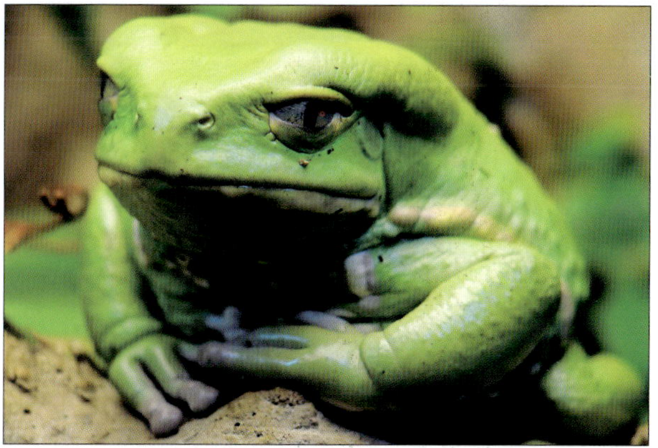

● PHIL DRINKWATER This is a waxy frog. I felt it was important to highlight its skin, so I waited until the lighting was correct.

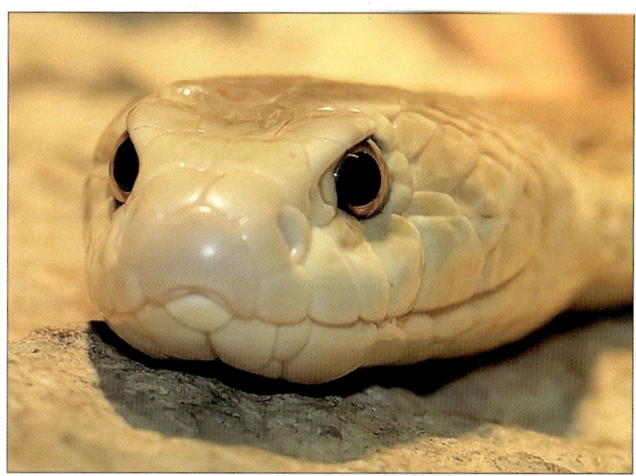

● RON REEVES The taipan up-close, using a Canon EOS 300D and Sigma 105mm Macro lens at f/6 and a shutter speed of 1/125sec at ISO400.

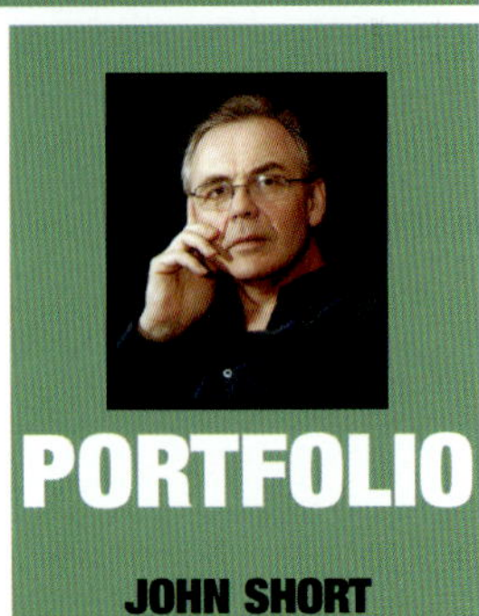

PORTFOLIO

JOHN SHORT
John's a wildlife photographer who started out with a Zenit B and home processing his photos.

John became interested in photography at 17. At that time, money was not available to fund his interest, so he learned his skills in a cupboard under the stairs developing Ilford FP4 film in a dish.

Eventually, John saved enough to buy a Zenith B with a 58mm f/2 Helios lens and exposure meter. He joined the local photographic society and borrowed books from the library, learning everything he could about photography.

Exposure readings were taken by hand, shutter speeds and apertures manually selected and focus was also manual. Taking pictures this way he learned the relationship of exposure, shutter speed and aperture in producing a successful print.

Today, as he looks through the viewfinder of his Canon EOS 20D digital camera, the exposure readings in the display are his bible, viewed and considered before he presses the shutter release each time.

John enjoys photographing wildlife and uses aperture-priority as he finds this the most flexible mode to cope with the variables associated with wildlife photography. He opens the aperture as far as necessary to provide the shutter speed he needs if the animal is on the move, while stopping down to gain depth-of-field when necessary.

John's advice to others would be to under-expose shots by ¼ to ½ a stop to retain detail in white areas of a subject. If the image is of a swan, or other primarily white animal, he recommends under-exposing by a full stop.

You can always increase the exposure with post-processing software without loss of quality, but an over-exposed image with blown highlights can never be recovered. ■

www.sigmaphoto.co.uk

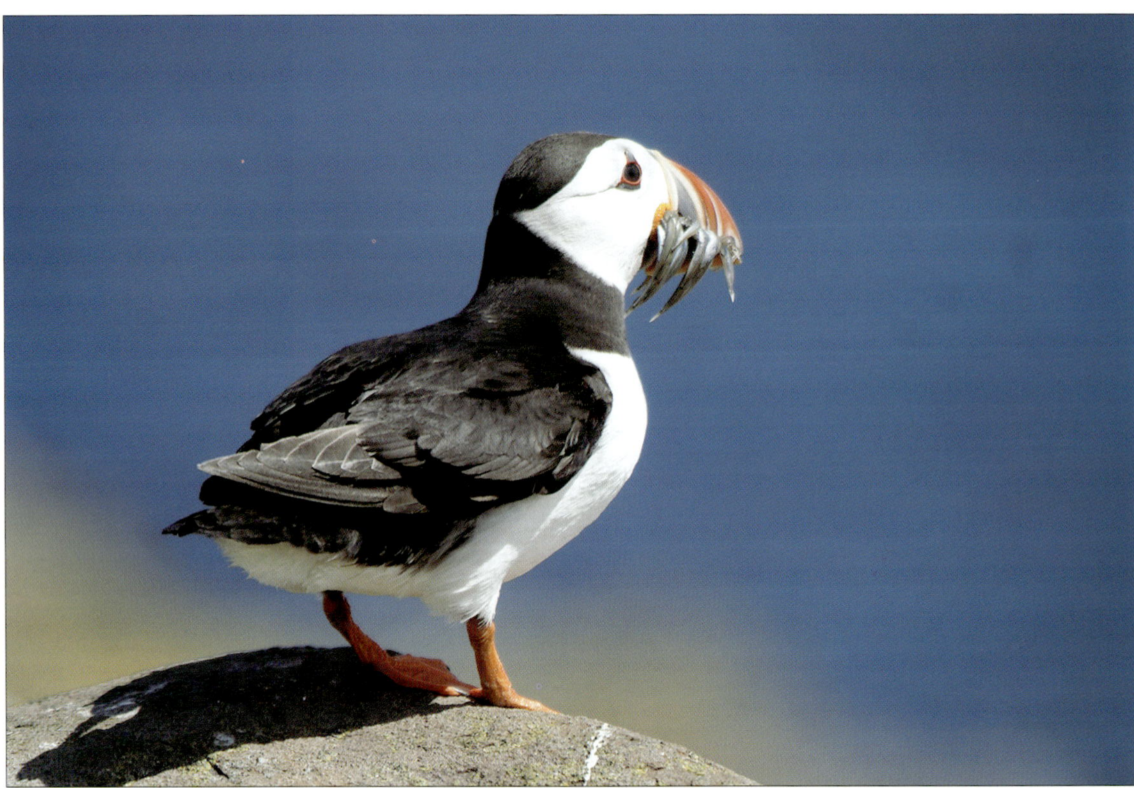

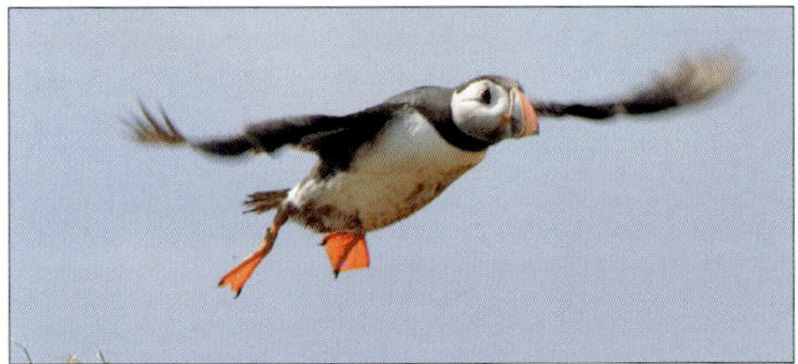

John's portfolio features three shots from his collection of Atlantic or common puffin (Fratercula arctica). The photographs were taken on the Farne Islands, two miles off the coast of Northumberland and the Shetland Islands. Puffins tend to spend time on the Islands between March and August, rearing chicks between June and early August. The best time to visit a colony is in the morning or early evening when the birds are not out fishing. ● ABOVE Admiring the view, with a mouth full of sandeels. ● LEFT: Puffin in flight ● BELOW: Shetland puffin.

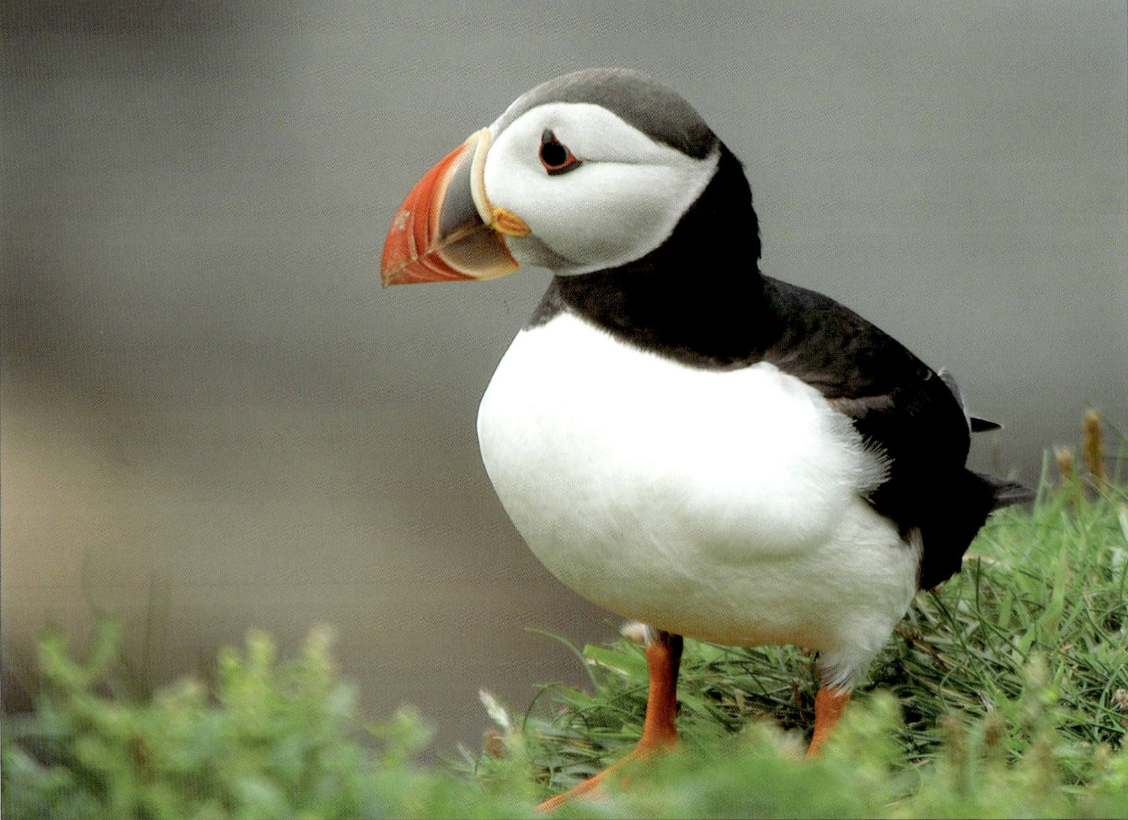

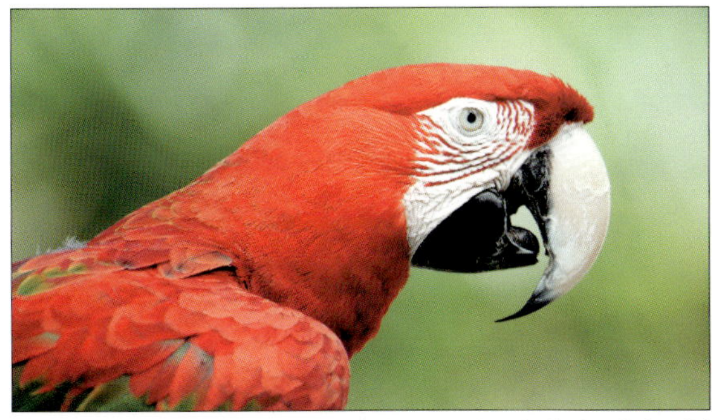

● JASON NEWELL A Green Winged Macaw, taken in Aruba. Colourful and entertaining to watch. Canon EOS 20D and 100-400L at ISO200.

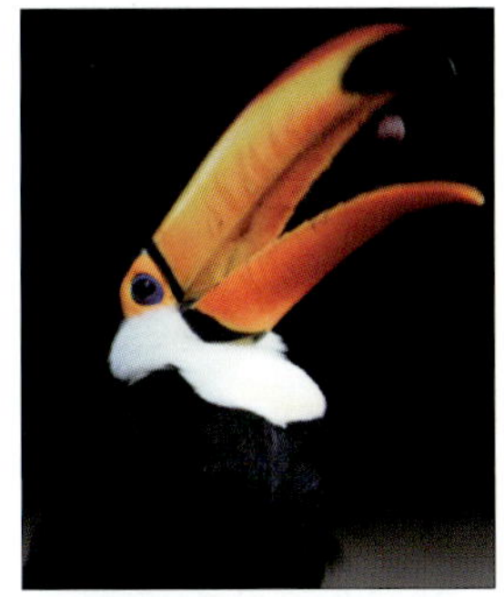

● PAUL GROOM "I waited ages for the Toucan to turn its head."

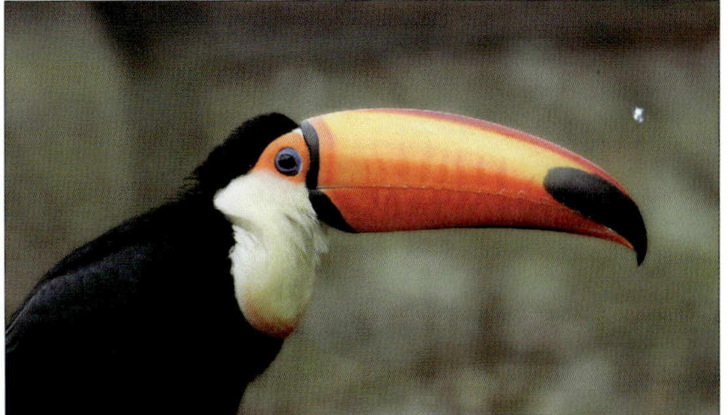

● NICK MOSS Toucan taken at Birdworld in Farnham, using a Canon EOS 20D and 70-200mm f/4 L at 120mm and f/4.

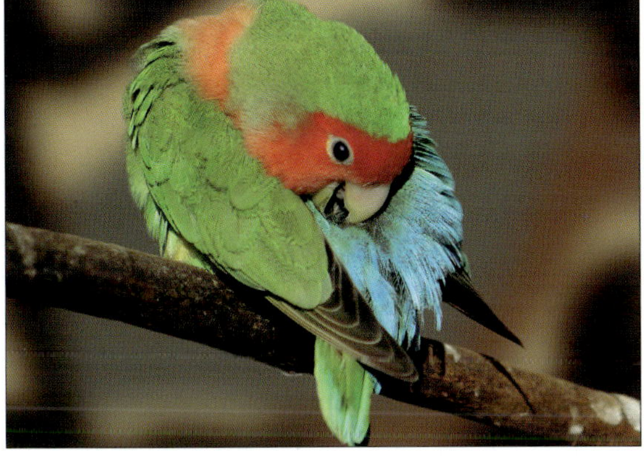

● SIOBHAN BOYD-LONGLEY Taken at Marwell Zoo, using a Canon EOS 300D and 75-300mm at f/8 and on-board flash.

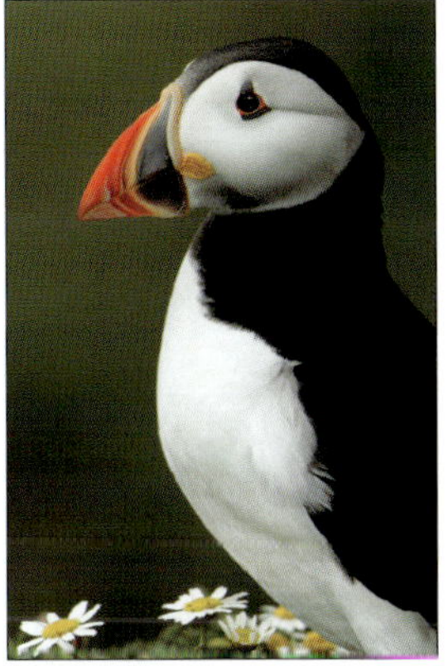

● GRAHAM ELLA Puffin on, Skomer Island, Pembrokeshire.

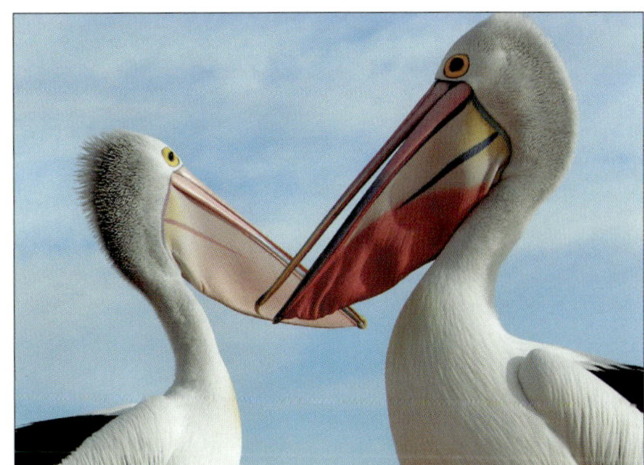

● KRISTINA SMITH Pelicans of Monkey Mia, Western Australia, using a Nikon Coolpix 8700 with an exposure of 1/4sec at f/6.5.

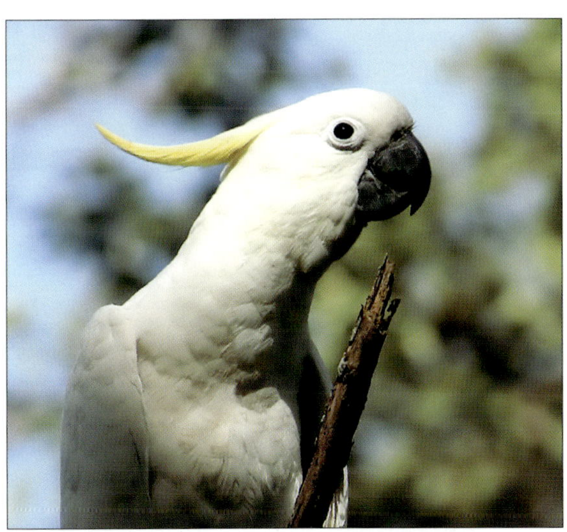

● NORMAN WRIGHT Wild sulphur crested cockatoo taken in Eungella National Park, Queensland, Australia.

EXPOSURE TIPS

■ Bird photography can, like many subjects, create problems for your camera's built in exposure meter. Here are a few tips to ensure better photographs:

■ Bird's often take up a smaller central portion of the frame. If your camera has a spot meter select it to ensure more accurate readings.

■ If the bird is taking up the whole frame you may need to compensate from the tones being averaged out by the meter. A white bird will need around one stop extra exposure to prevent it looking grey and a black bird will need around one stop less exposure.

■ Beaks tend to reflect more light and can easily be overexposed. Use exposure compensation, or switch to manual and reduce the exposure by half to one stop.

■ Similarly, if you shoot in bright sunlight you may find white birds have blown out highlights. Underexpose in these situations too.

■ When a bird is in flight against a light background you need to over-expose to prevent a dark subject.

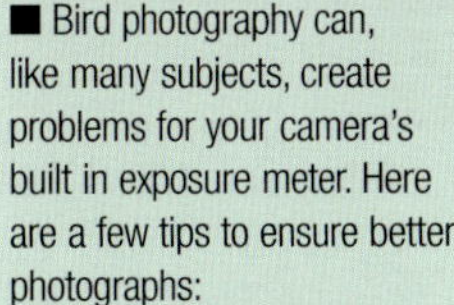

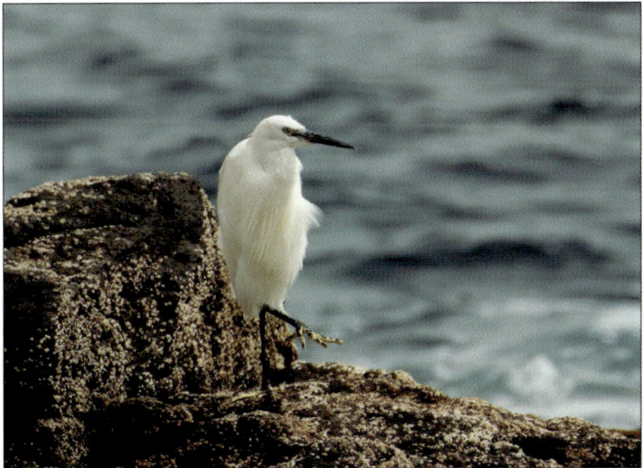

● IAN ROSS Little Egret on the rocky Fuerteventura coast at Caletta de Fuste, using a Canon EOS 300D and 170-500mm lens handheld.

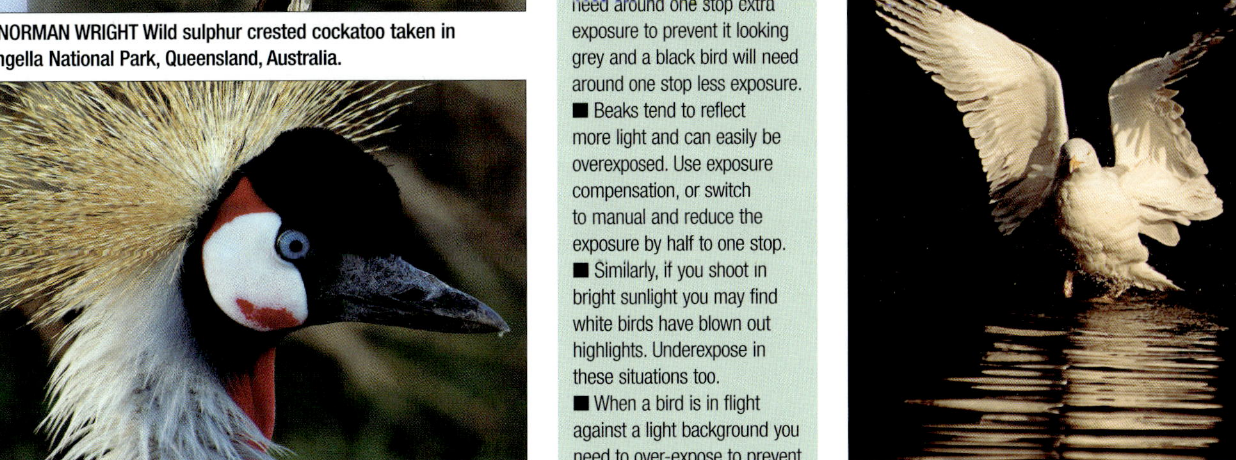

● ALBERT CONROY Taken at Martin Mere with an Olympus E300 and Sigma 55-200mm at f/8. A monopod prevented camera shake.

● MARK PHILLIPS Mark focused above the seagull and waited for it to fly up out of the water, using a Sigma 70-300mm APO lens at f/8.

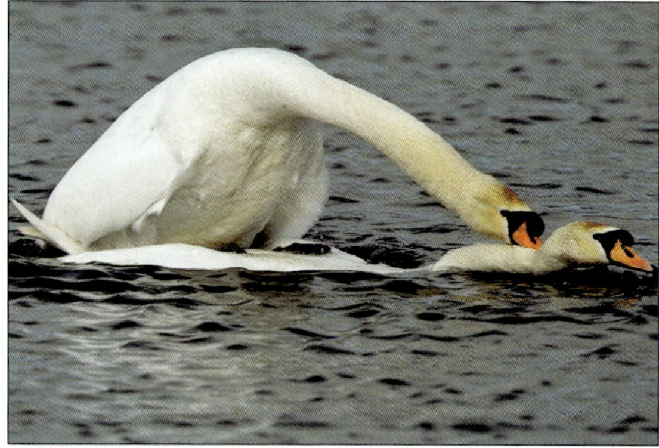

● IAN ANDREWS Ian watched these swans for days establishing the pair bond and seeing off suitors. Taken using a Sigma SD10 with a 120-300mm lens and exposure of 1/1250sec at f/7.1.

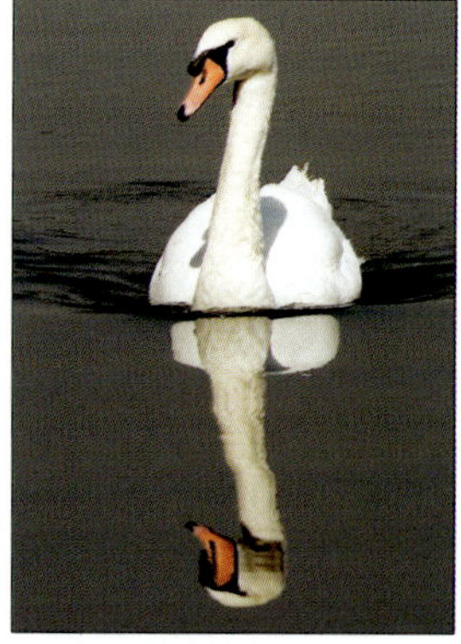

● ANDY MOORE Taken on a perfectly still day as a horizontal shot that was later cropped.

LOCATION GUIDE – GUIDE TO BIRD & WILDLIFE CENTRES AND RESERVES

- Liberty's Raptor and Reptile Centre, Ringwood — www.libertyscentre.co.uk
- The National Birds of Prey Centre, Newent, Gloucestershire — www.nbpc.co.uk/home.htm
- The Barn Owl Centre, Brockworth, Gloucester — www.barnowl.co.uk
- Gauntlet Bird of Prey, Eagle and Vulture Park, Knutsford, Cheshire — www.gauntlet.info
- Eagle Heights Bird of Prey Centre, Eynsford Kent — www.eagleheights.co.uk
- Birdworld, Farnham Surrey — www.birdworld.co.uk
- Bird of Prey Centre, Thirsk, North Yorkshire — www.falconrycentre.co.uk
- Kielder Water Bird of Prey Centre, Northumberland — www.discoverit.co.uk/falconry

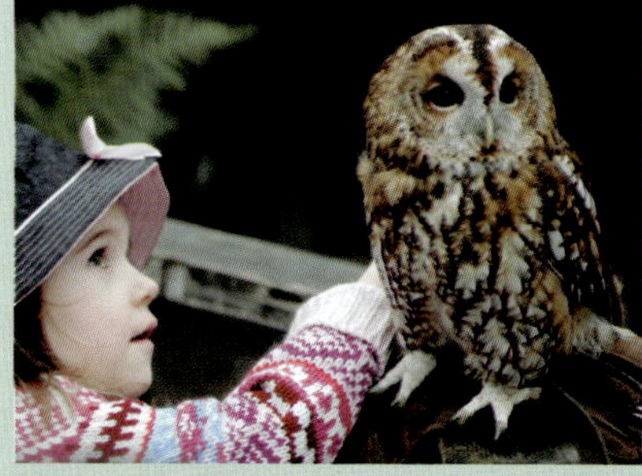

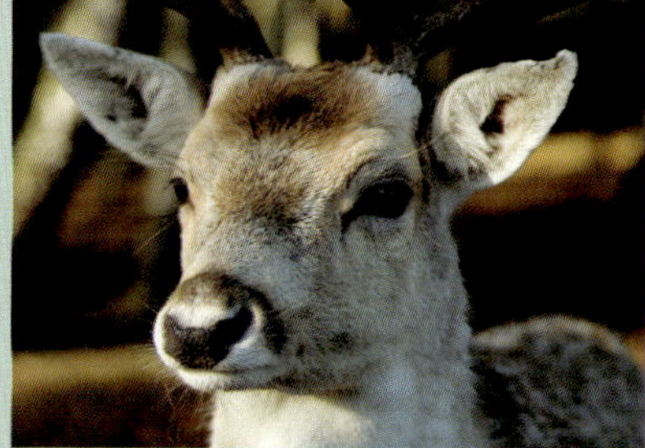

- The Wildfowl and Wetlands Trust in West Sussex, Dumfrieshshire, Co Down, London, Carmarthenshire, Cheshire, Lancashire, Gloucestershire, Tyne and Wear, Cambridgeshire — www.wwt.org.uk
- Donna Nook Nature Reserve North Somercotes — www.lincstrust.org.uk
- Pensthorpe Nature Reserve and Gardens, Fakenham Norfolk — www.pensthorpe.com
- Cheshire Waterlife and Falconry Centre, Northwich Cheshire — www.cheshire-waterlife.co.uk
- Wetlands, Nr. Retford Nottinghamshire — www.wetlandswildlife.co.uk
- Rutland Water, Rutland — www.rutlandwater.org.uk

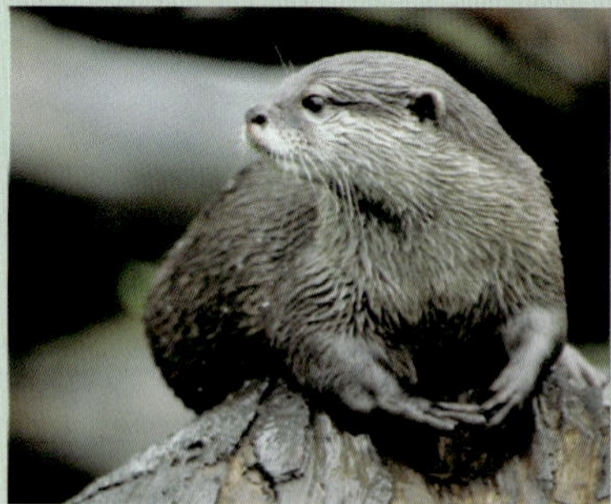

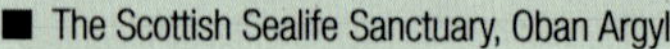

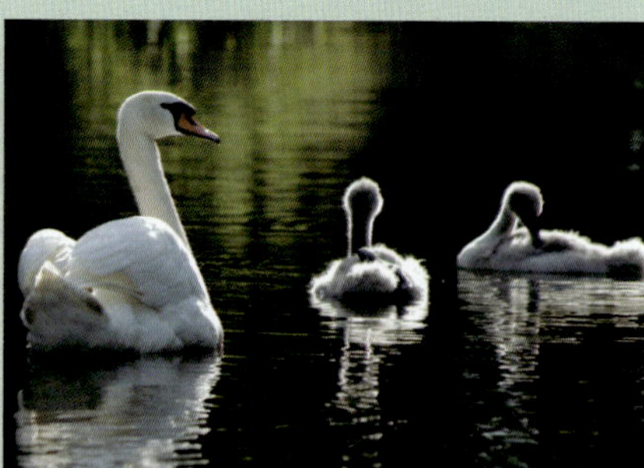

- The Scottish Sealife Sanctuary, Oban Argyll — www.sealsanctuary.co.uk
- The Otter Trust, Bungay Suffolk — www.ottertrust.org.uk
- Dartmoor Otter Sanctuary, Buckfastleigh — www.ottersandbutterflies.co.uk
- Chestnut Centre, Chapel-en-le-Frith Derbyshire — www.ottersandowls.co.uk
- Tamar Otter Sanctuary at North Petherwin, Launceston Cornwall — www.ottertrust.org.uk
- North Pennines Reserve Barnard Castle, County Durham — www.ottertrust.org.uk
- Wildlife Sailing Herne Bay — www.wildlifesailing.com

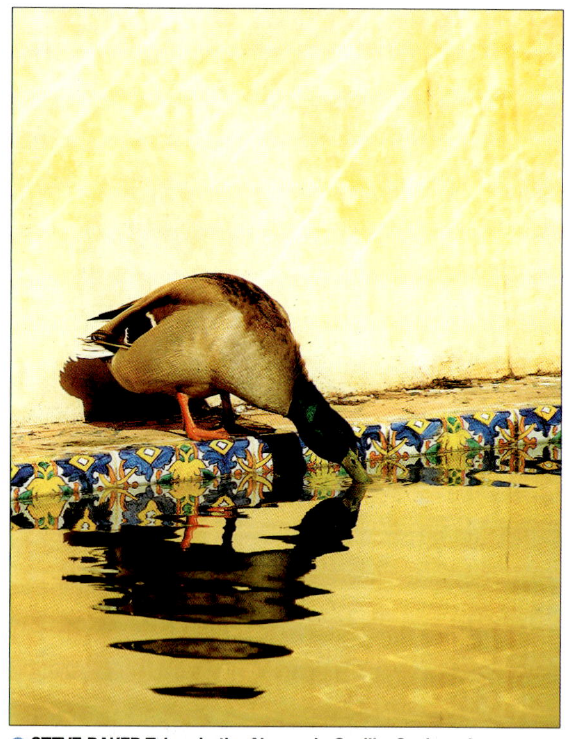

● GARETH BODRELL Two swans in the early morning light in Bushy Park, taken using a Canon EOS 300D and a 19-35mm lens.

● STEVE BAKER Taken in the Alcazar in Seville, Spain, using an Olympus 765UZ and a lot of luck with the timing.

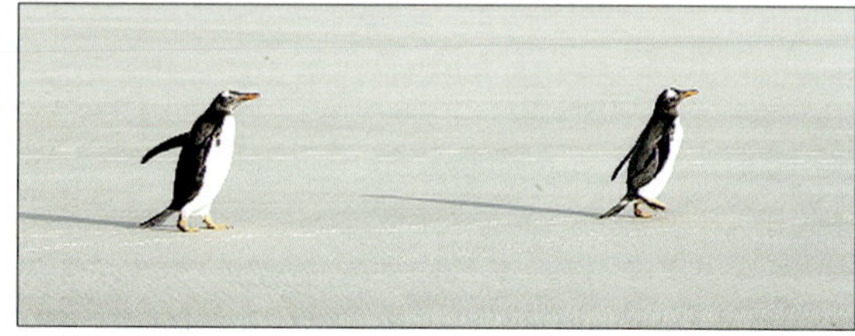

● BAZ PELLING Two penguins taken while Baz was in the Falkland Islands in the South Atlantic.

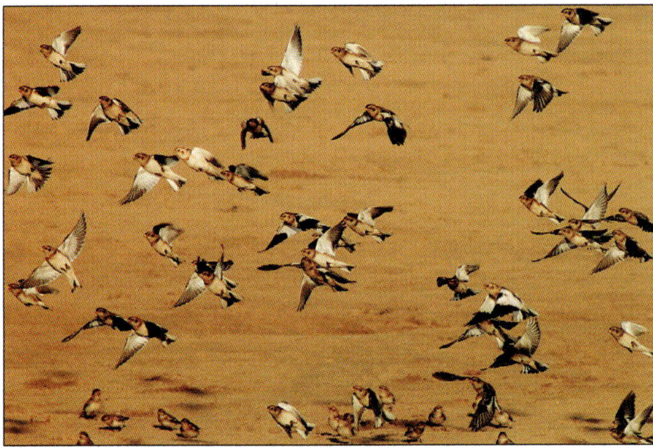

● STEVE CRIBBIN Snow buntings in winter plumage at Donna Nook. ISO800 gave 1/2500sec at f/8 for a flash-like motion freeze.

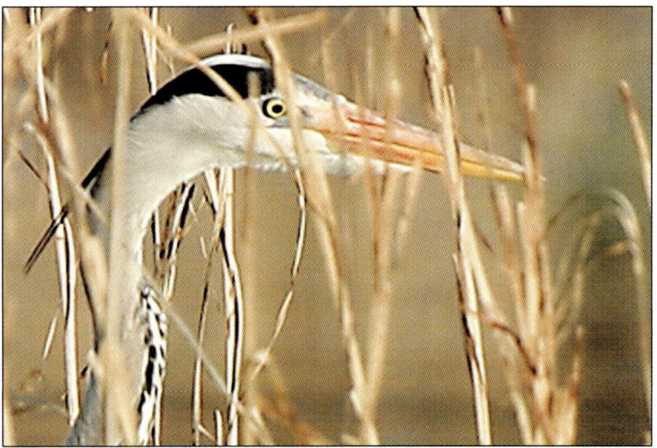

● PETER LOOSE A grey heron taken at Furzton Lake, Milton Keynes, with a Canon EOS 20D and 100-400mm IS lens.

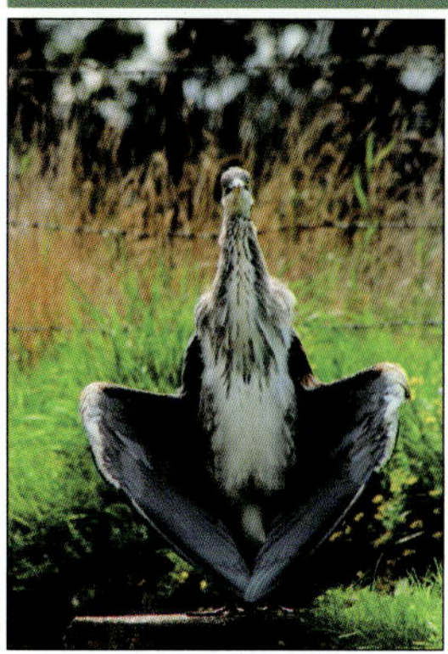

● STEVE BALL A heron posing on a tow path in Audlem.

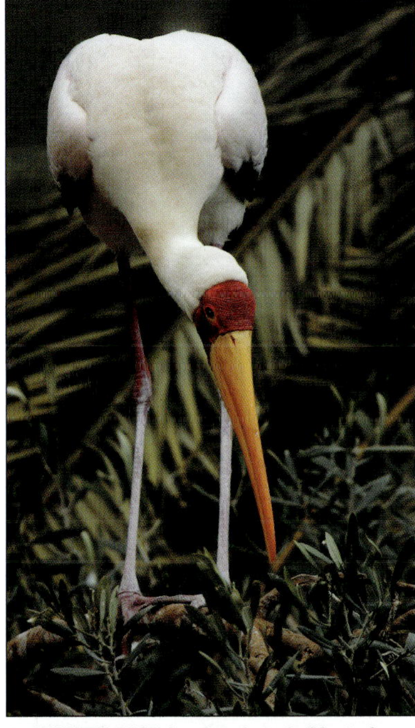

● ANNETTE EAST A painted stork (Mycteria Leucocephala), taken in the giant aviary at Vergel Safari Park in the Costa Blanca.

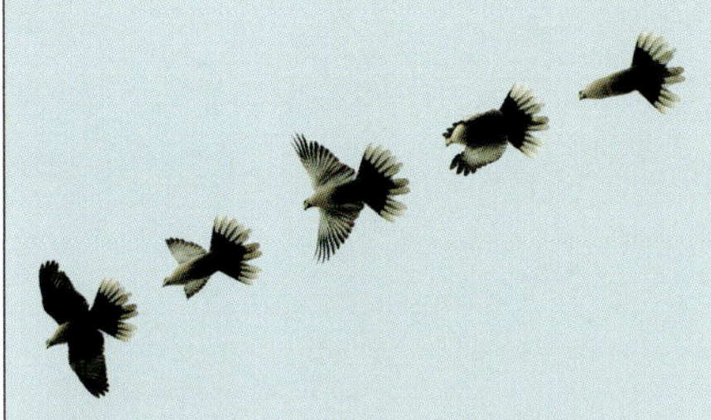

● GEMM FARRANE Composite of five shots of a collared dove in flight, using a Canon EOS 1D MkII and 70-200mm f/2.8L IS. Exposure 1/5000sec at f/4.

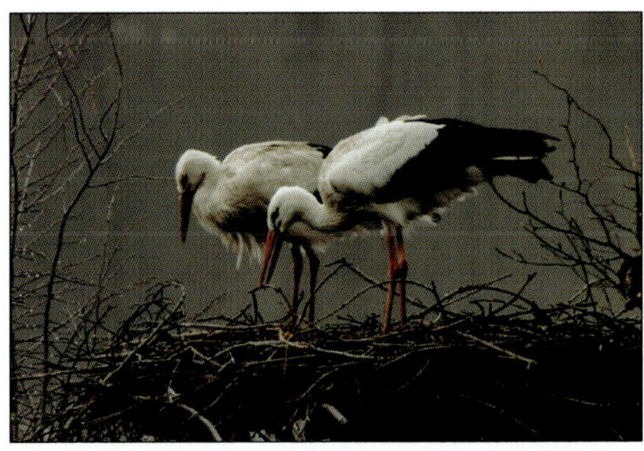

● PETER BARGH White storks, building a nest in the grounds of Harewood House, taken using a Pentax 80-320mm zoom at the 320mm setting on an *ist D.

SHOOTING TIPS – BIRD PHOTOGRAPHY

■ Use a long lens of at least 300mm. If you are limited it's better to stand further away and crop (right) than miss the shots because of a potentially timid bird.

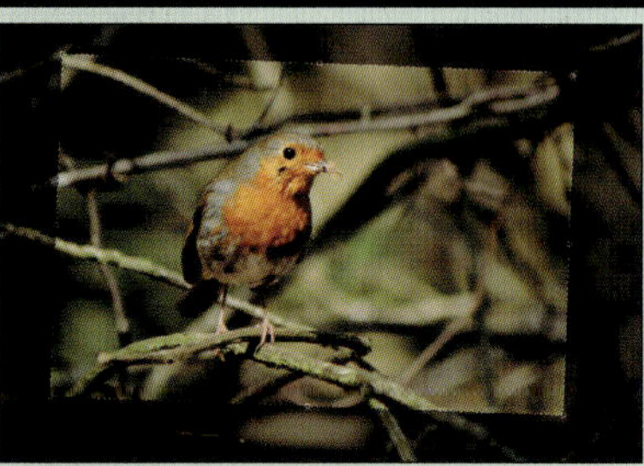

■ You can sit just a couple of feet away from many species, such as blue tits, wrens and robins, providing you're quiet and keep movement to a minimum.

■ Invest in remote release and a tripod so you can position your camera nearer the birds and not disturb them.

■ To isolate a close-up subject from a confusing background, throw the background out of focus. This may mean decreasing depth of field by opening up the aperture.

■ Artificial backgrounds can be used where the natural one is not suitable, but be aware that these don't always look authentic.

■ Leave some space around the bird as tightly framed subjects can look claustrophobic and unnatural.

■ When shooting a bird on a branch with the bright sky as a background you may end up with a silhouette. To avoid this, point the camera at something of similar tone to the main subject and either lock the exposure, manually change to the indicated reading or use exposure compensation.

■ Lard spread on a likely branch, or pushed into a crevice of a stump will be found by local birds and devoured. It has the advantage that, tucked away, it won't be seen by the camera. Replace it regularly and watch for your reward.

■ Pick a spot and be prepared to sit and wait for a while. As the birds get used to your presence they will come closer to you. Look out for reflections from water that can fool the metering, but also the reflections that can become part of the picture. Mirror images on flat water can be very effective.

■ Lighting from the side helps to create shadow, making a 3D subject appear more dramatic and effective.

■ Overcast conditions are excellent for showing off maximum detail and subtle colours.

■ Don't have loads of feeders in the garden. Having just one or two means the birds will queue to feed and will be encouraged to perch on nearby, equally photographic, points.

■ Make a resting perch using an old branch and place it near the feeding station, but in better light. This position will also be free from peanut cages and fat balls, giving your photos a more natural look.

■ Sandwich a bird feeder between a tree branch and a piece of wood that are just slightly thicker than the feeder. Position this so the branch is facing the camera. When a bird lands to eat from the feeder you'll just see the bird and the branch, making it look natural.

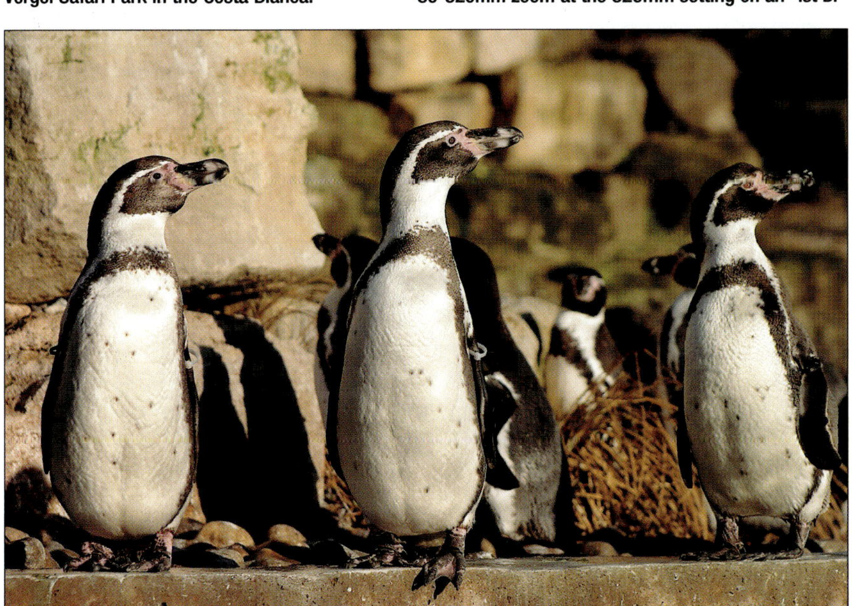

● BRIAN PRICE "This was a grab shot on the Canon EOS 10D and 28-135mm IS lens, taken when I noticed the three penguins all look to their left. The exposure was 1/1500sec at f/5.6 and ISO200."

BIRDS OF PREY

■ Bird of prey photography is similar to capturing any other bird on film/sensor. They are often bigger and much faster so these tips could help you obtain better shots.

■ **Practice** Bird of prey Centres are good places to practice techniques for occasions when you come across wild versions, where you won't have time to worry about your techniques. If you want the shot, it must be instinctive.

■ **Focus** Many cameras, including today's electronic marvels, aren't fast enough to keep up with a bird in flight, especially one coming towards you at speed. Learn to use manual focus; pre-set the focus and wait for the bird to fly into focus. It takes practice, but is one technique that can be learnt easily.

■ **Meter** Rather than get a black silhouette against a blank sky, use manual metering, especially if the light is fairly constant. Take a reading of a neutral zone, such as grass, and set the camera to the reading, ensuring as high a shutter speed as possible. This way the bird will be properly exposed even if 60% of the frame is sky – which confuses the auto-metering.

■ **Tracking** Learn to track the birds from the waist, keeping your shoulders and elbows as still as possible. Learn to move your feet too, if you are using a tripod/monopod.

■ **Observe** Watch flight patterns of birds that are too far away to take a decent photograph. Do they turn sharply or gently? Do they drop quickly or swoop down? If you know what they're likely to do when closer, you will have more chance of keeping them in the frame.

■ **Anticipate** Birds of Prey are mostly creatures of habit. They do the same thing repeatedly. Kestrels will fly a stretch of roadway, perhaps landing on alternate lamp-posts, three or four times a day, often at the same time of day. Buzzards and Harriers will quarter the same fields and marsh areas on a regular basis and Owls will often use the same fence post to perch on.
Words Ian Andrews

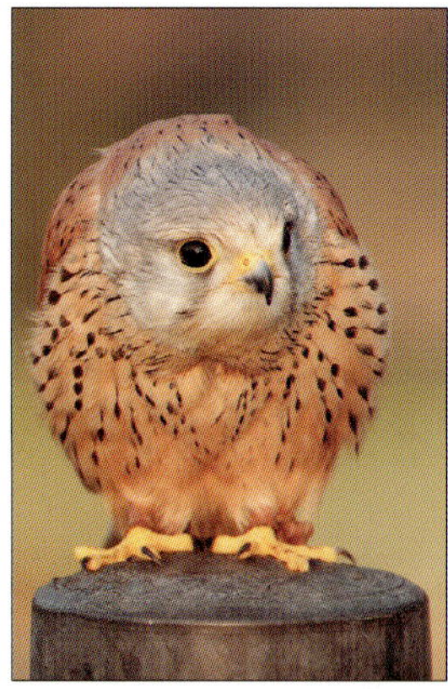

● JASON NEWALL Kestrel, enjoying early evening sunshine. Canon EOS 20D and 100-400L.

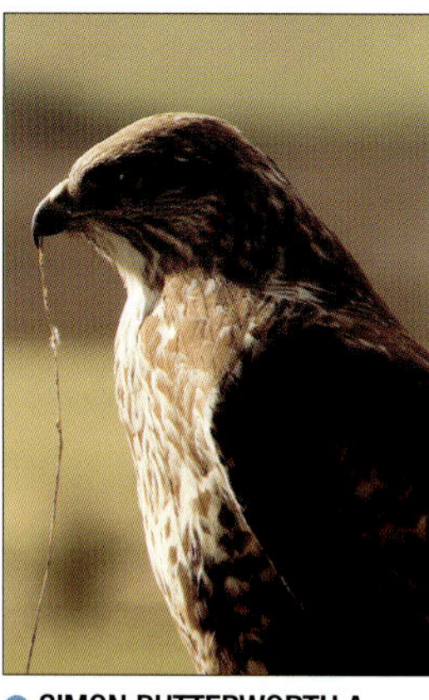

● SIMON BUTTERWORTH A wild buzzard, taken while in the Scottish borders.

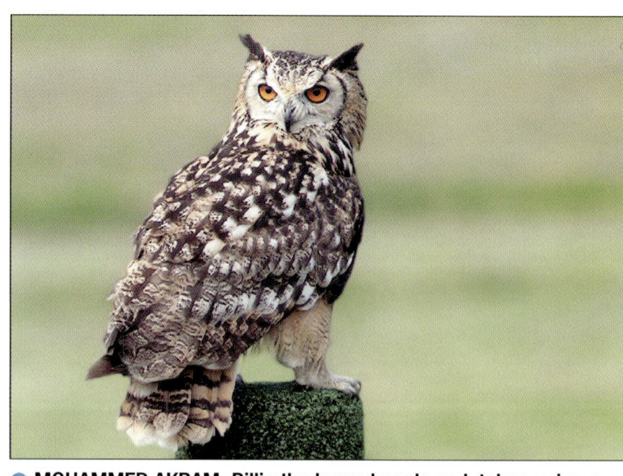

● MOHAMMED AKRAM Billie the bengal eagle owl, taken using a Minolta Dynax 7 with Sigma 28-135mm at 100mm on Fuji Superia ISO100 negative film. The exposure was 1/500sec at f/5.6.

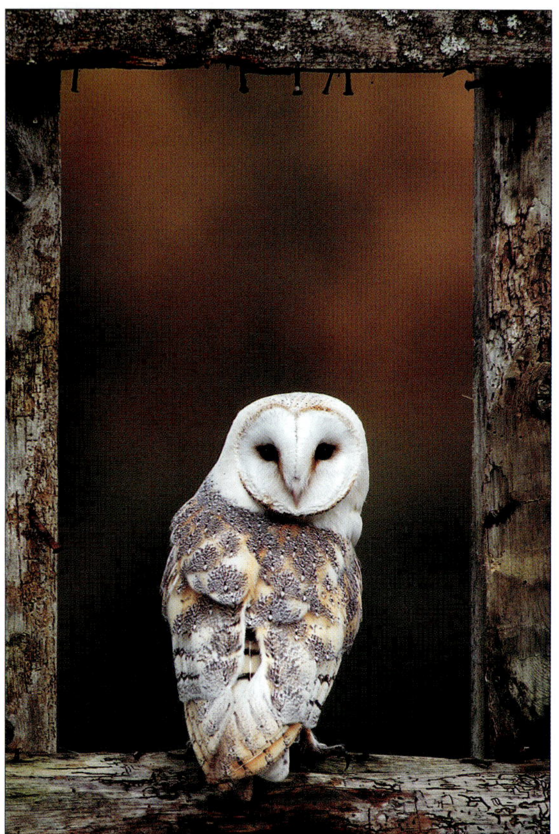

● CHERYL SURRY Captive barn owl in a window, taken while on a photography holiday near Kingussie in Scotland.

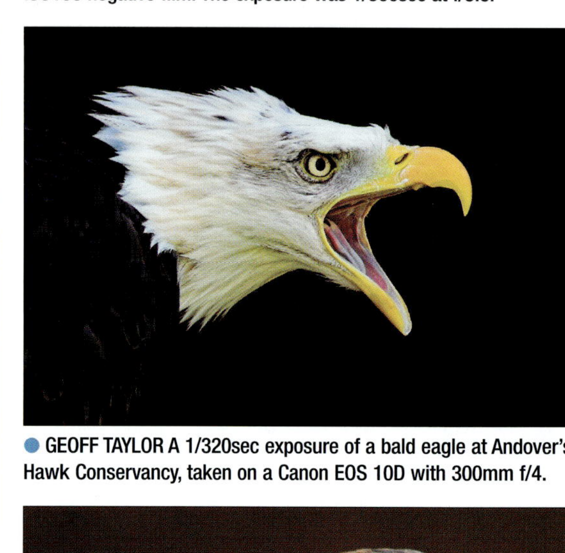

● GEOFF TAYLOR A 1/320sec exposure of a bald eagle at Andover's Hawk Conservancy, taken on a Canon EOS 10D with 300mm f/4.

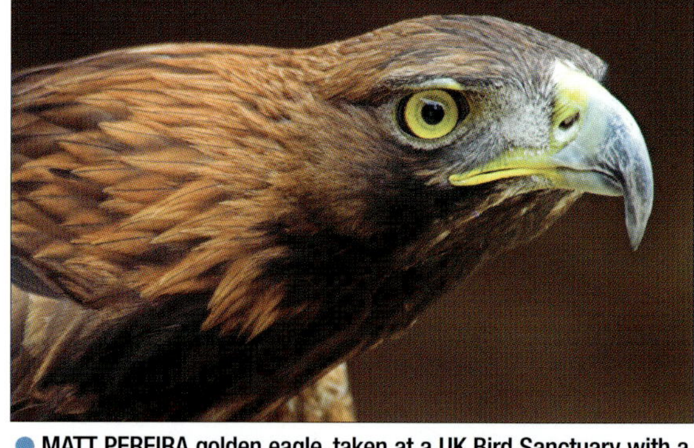

● MATT PEREIRA golden eagle, taken at a UK Bird Sanctuary with a Canon EOS 10D and EF100-400mm L IS USM lens at 400mm.

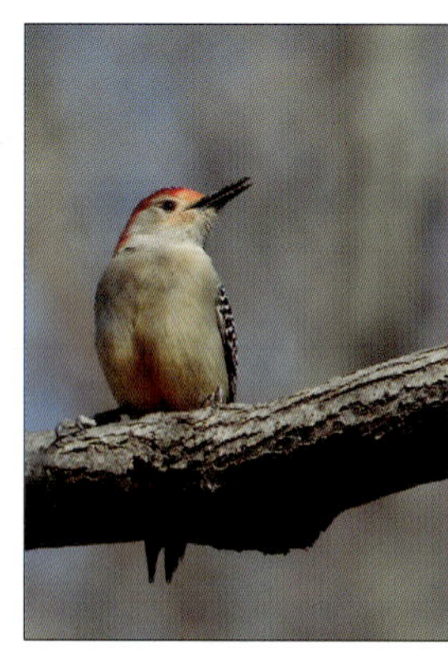

● CECILIA LAZZARO Woodpecker, taken with a Nikon 80-400mm.

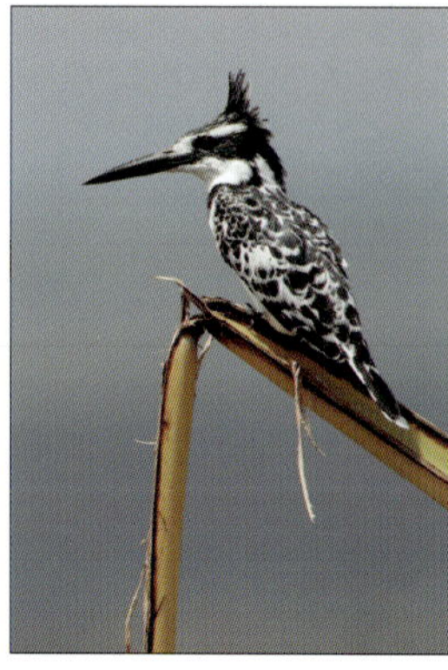

● IAN BUTLER A pied kingfisher scans Lake Naivasha in Kenya.

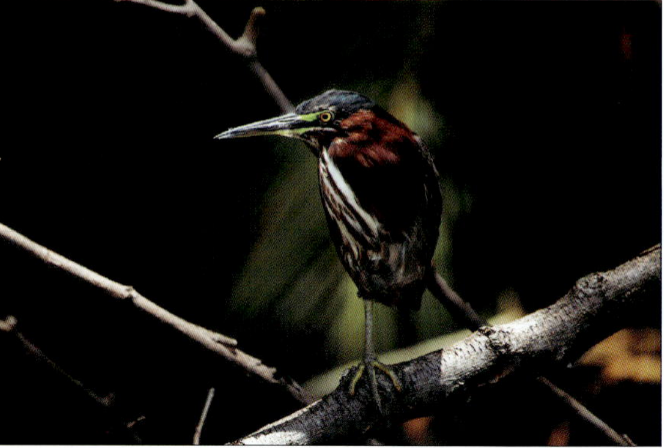

● DAVID BAILLIE Green heron at Indian River Com of Dominica on a Canon EOS 20D and 100-400L FL. The exposure was 1/500sec f/5.6.

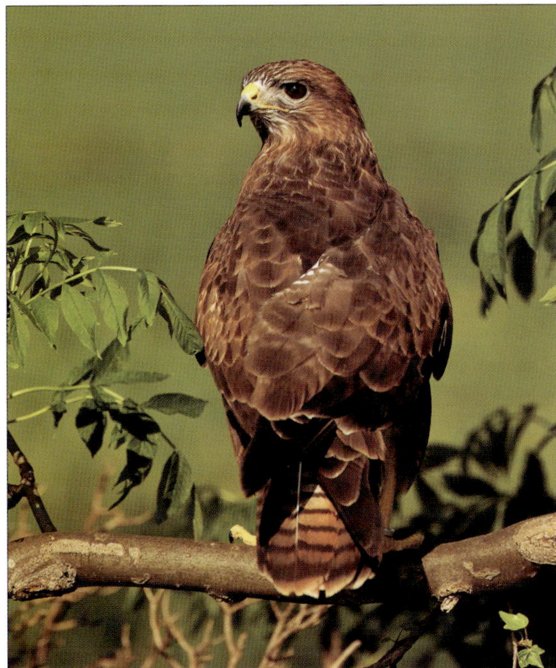

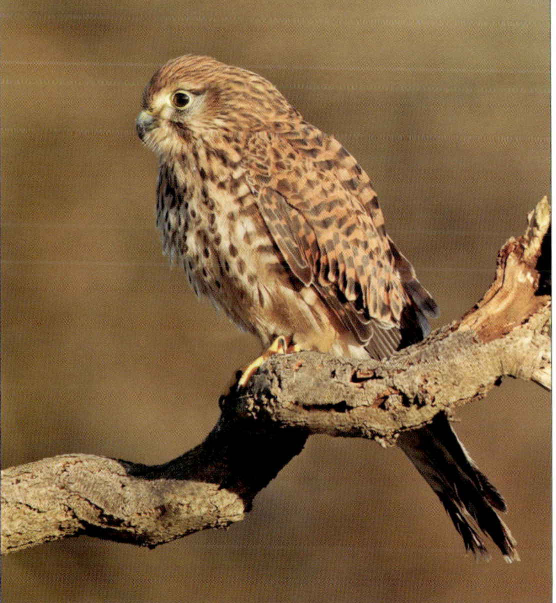

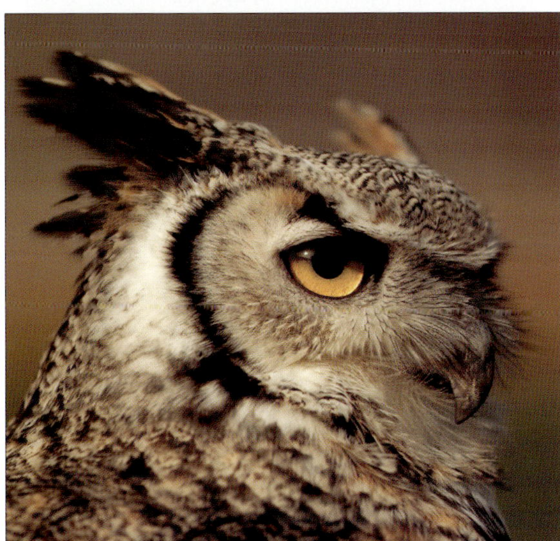

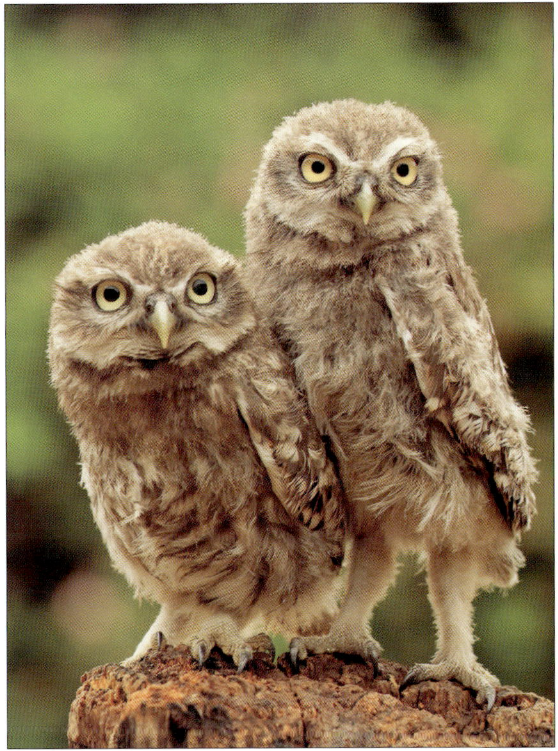

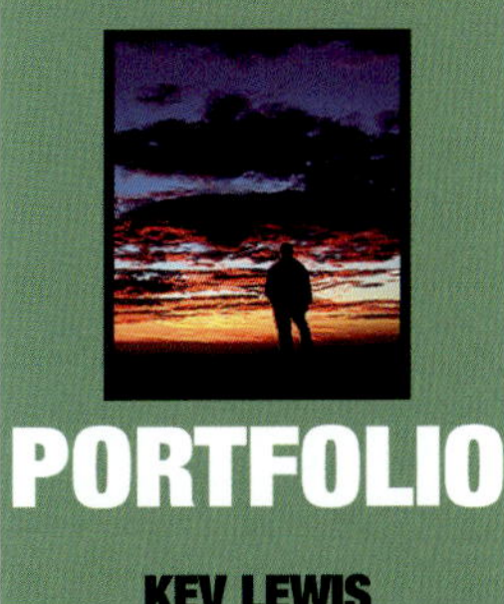

PORTFOLIO

KEV LEWIS

Kev has a wide range of lenses, including the 600mm f/4, and prefers nature not to be aware of his presence.

Kev picked up his first camera, a well used manual Praktica, when he was in his teens. It taught him all the basics – how to frame an image, how light and dark work together and the dying art of black & white developing & printing.

Since those first experiences he's spent hundreds of hours in a red lit darkroom surrounded by chemicals and photographic paper, enjoying the magical moments as a print appears on the paper.

Over the years Kev's experience and love of photography continued to grow. He upgraded to the Canon system, buying cameras like the A1 and F1, as well as all the lenses and accessories he could afford.

His hobby took a back seat during the '80s and '90s as work, marriage and family took precedence. Today though, his interest is stronger than ever. He still uses Canon equipment, which now includes the EOS 20D and a range of lenses from 10mm up to the beautiful, but very expensive, 600mm f/4 lens.

Kev's primary interest is wildlife photography and using this range of lenses allows him to photograph wildlife without disturbing the natural behaviour of the birds and mammals. If he can get an image and walk away, leaving the wildlife unaware of his presence, he feels he's achieved something.

Kev's a serious amateur so is not tied to any of the shackles of professional commissioned work. He can experiment, making mistakes and learning from them, taking his time and re-shooting as often as he likes until he's happy with an image.

Kev's one piece of advice would be don't be afraid to be different; it's only by being different that you can develop your own photographic style. ∎
www.photosbykev.com

● Five photographs taken on a Canon EOS 20D; CLOCKWISE: Buzzard (Buteo buteo), using a Sigma 120-300mm lens at 221mm The exposure was 1/1000sec at f/4. ● Orphaned little owls (Athene noctua) on a Canon 100-400L lens with a EFII x1.4 teleconverter at 560mm. The exposure was 1/160sec at f/11. ● European eagle owl (Bubo bubo) on the Canon 100-400L lens at 400mm and an exposure of 1/500sec at f/5.6. ● Great-horned eagle owl (Bubo virginianus), using a Sigma 150mm macro lens and exposure of 1/250sec at f/16. ● Kestrel (Falco tinnunculus), using the Canon 100-400mm L lens at 400mm. The exposure was 1/250sec at f/11.

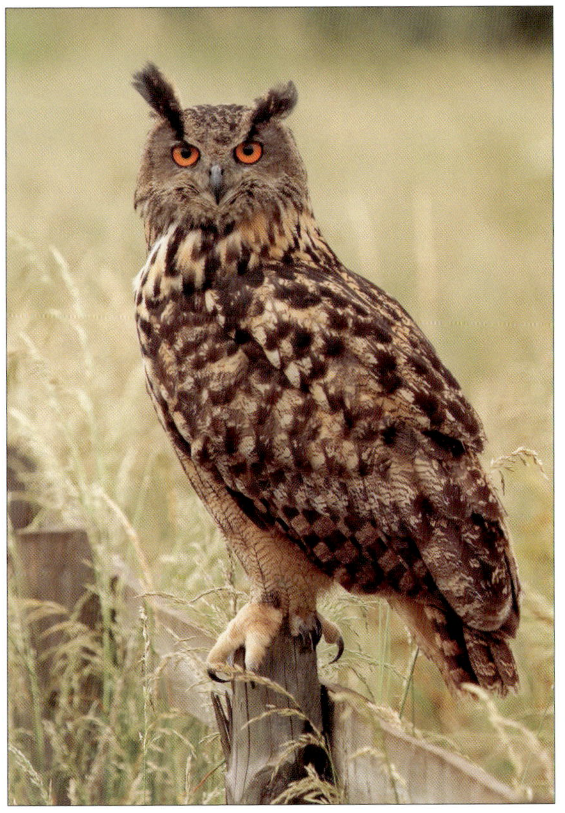

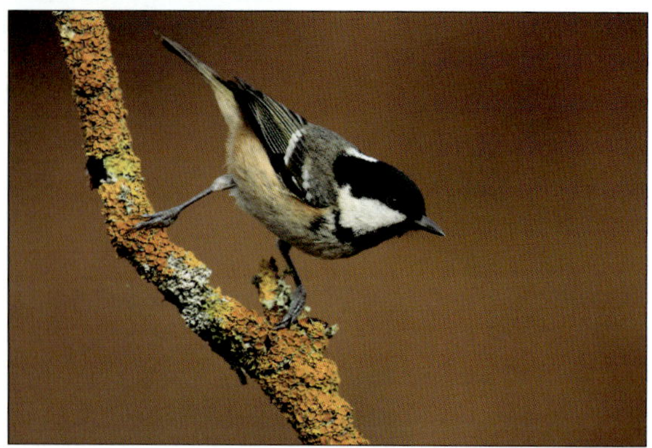

● JUSTIN COWTAN By putting out a regular supply of food during the Winter months, this coal tit became a frequent visitor.

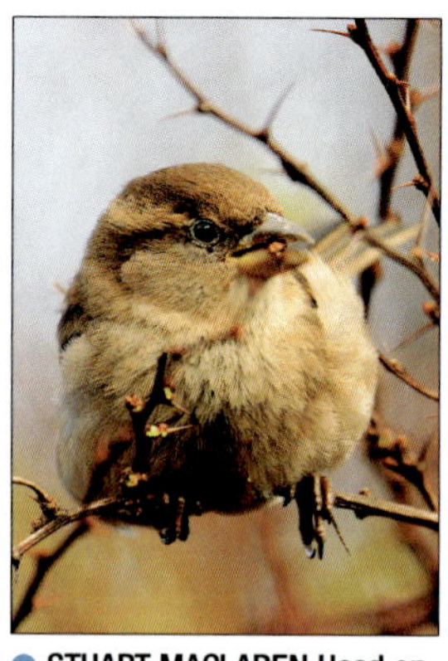

● STUART MACLAREN Head on shot with Canon 100-400mm.

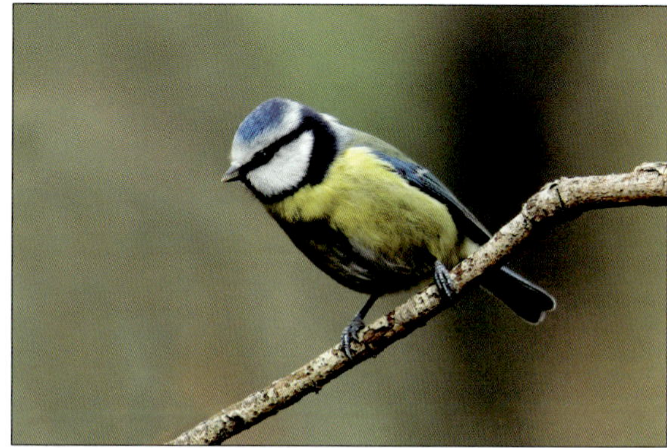

● MICHAEL BRACE Blue tit, taken at Stockgrove Country Park with a Canon EOS 300D and Sigma 100-300mm lens – 1/125sec at f/5.

DIGITAL TECHNIQUE – USING THE SHADOWS/HIGHLIGHT OPTION

■ Photoshop has a useful feature that makes it easier to adjust shadow and highlight areas of an image than using Levels or Curves. This method, found by going to Image⇨Adjustments⇨Shadow/Highlight, allows you to correct each pixel, based on the luminance values of neighbouring areas. Doing it this way allows image contrast to be increased in the shadows or highlights or both without sacrificing contrast in other areas. In this example of a snowy owl taken in a zoo. I exposed so the white feathers didn't burn out, but that's made the background black and the darker feathers are also too dark.

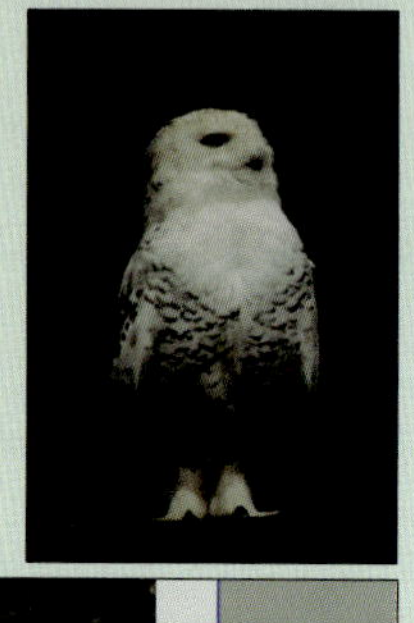

■ There are several sliders to make adjustments. The Shadows and Highlights sections each have Amount, Tonal Width and Radius sliders, found by clicking more options the first time you open the feature.

■ The **Amount** slider controls the steepness of a brightening or darkening curve. A zero value on both produces a straight line and no pixel modification, while a value of 100% produces a very steep curve with maximum change by lightening shadows and darkening highlights, making it best suited for severe backlighting with very dark subjects. The default is 50%, which is fine for most other backlit situations, but in this example has made the owl too light with bleached out detail.

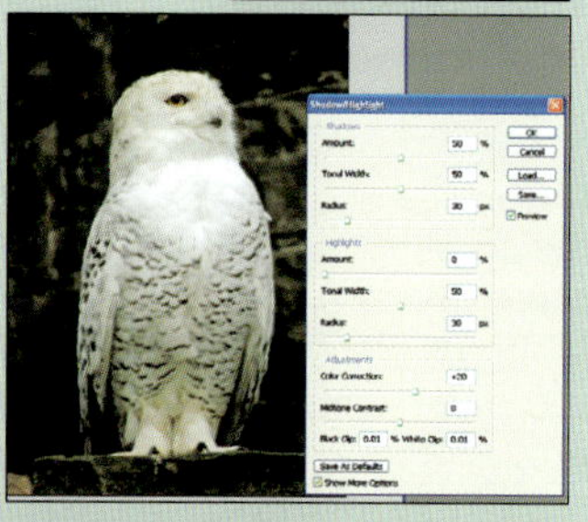

■ The **Tonal Width** slider adjusts how much modification you make to the shadows, midtones and highlights. Selecting a small value places emphasis on the darker regions while larger values place emphasis on midtones and highlights too.
The default is 50% and you'd move it to the left if you are trying to lighten a dark subject, but the midtones or lighter regions are changing too much. Doing so would only lighten the darkest regions. If you need to brighten up the midtones and shadows, move the slider to the right.

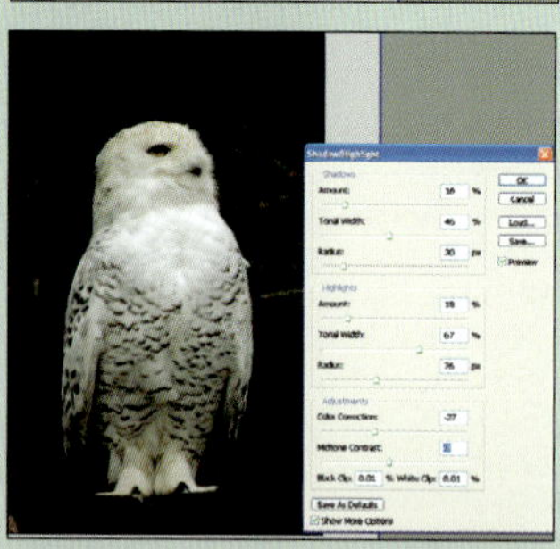

■ The **Radius** averages out the luminance of neighbouring pixels so that each pixel is modified according to its surrounding data. A larger radius increases the averaging range of neighbourhood luminance. Adjust the slider to obtain a good balance between subject contrast and its brightness value with the background.

■ The bottom sliders let you adjust **colour brightness** and **midtone contrast**. The **clip values** entered here determine how much of the extremes are clipped when you adjust the slider. A high value delivers dramatic adjustments, with highlight and shadow detail being clipped and lost.

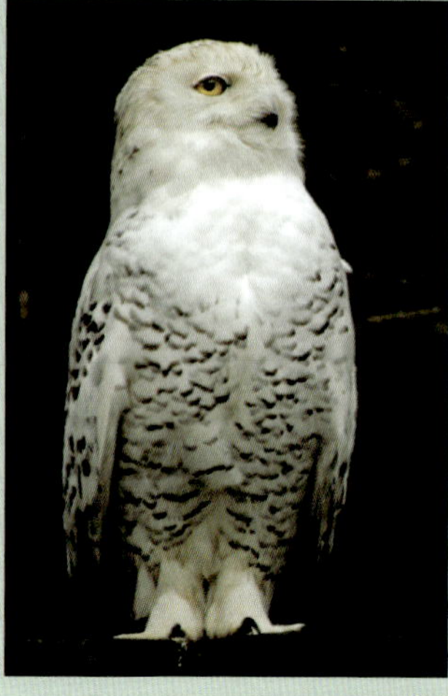

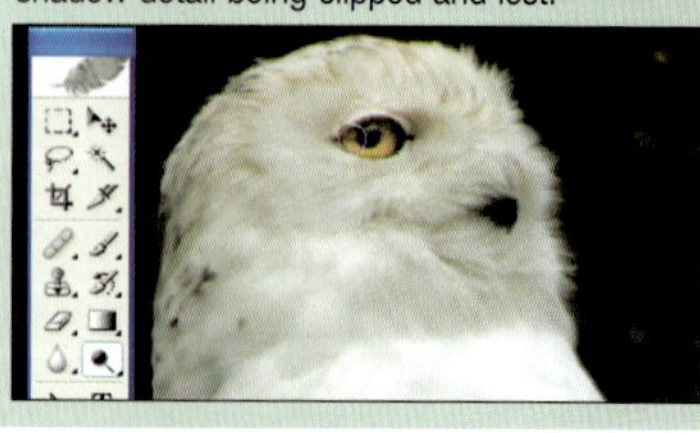

■ As a finishing touch I used the Dodge tool to brighten the owl's yellow eye and ran Auto Levels.

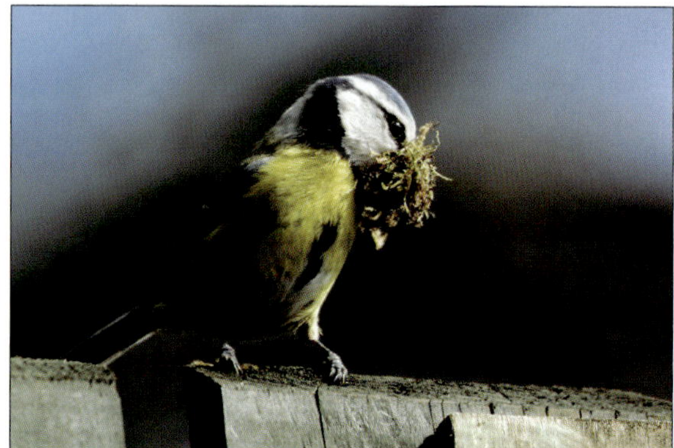

● STEVEN HANNA Canon EOS10D with 70-200mm f/4 L using ISO100 and an exposure of 1/800sec at f/4.

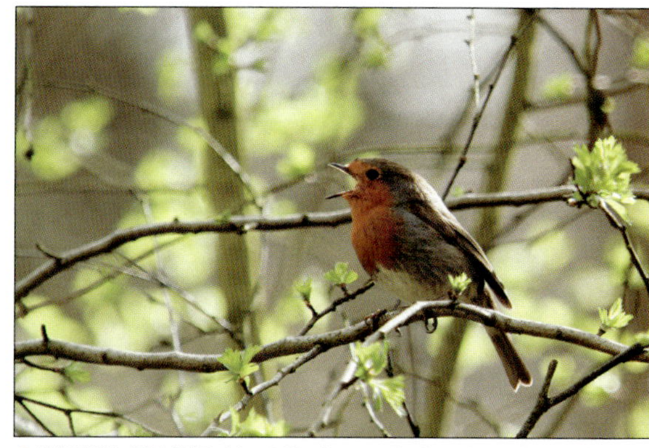

● MICHAEL BRACE Robin at Stockgrove Park, using a Canon EOS 20D and Sigma 100-300mm with 1.4x converter. 1/400sec at f/5.6.

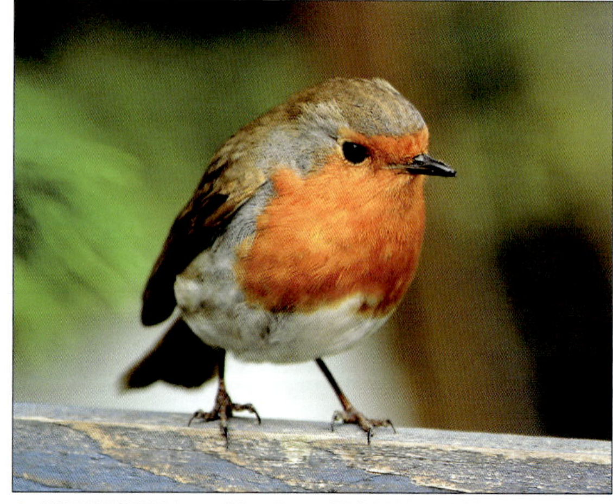

● JAN HANCOX Taken with a Canon EOS 300D and Sigma 70-300 Lens set at 150mm. The exposure was 1/125sec at f/4.5 and ISO400.

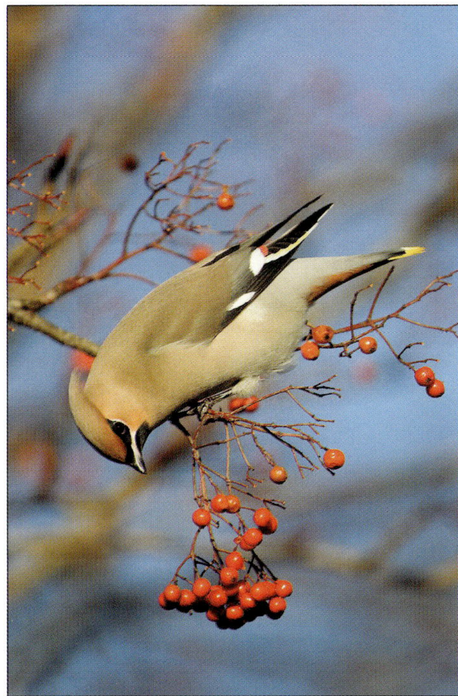

● SIMON BOOTH 2004 saw record numbers of waxwings in the UK. This individual was captured feeding on Rowan berries in Lancashire.

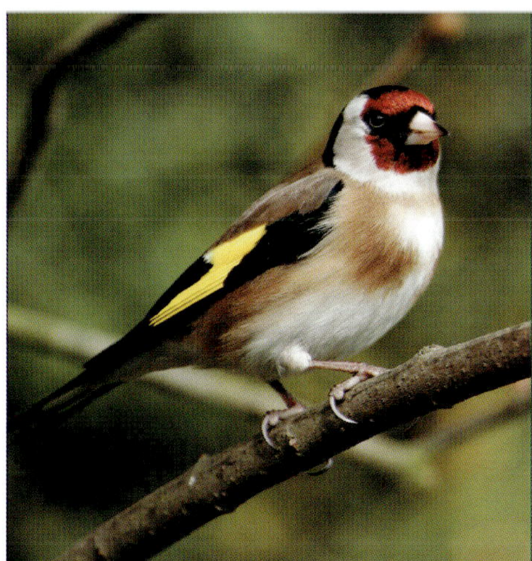

● STEVEN PRICE Taken with a Canon EOS 20D and 100-400mm L IS lens set at 400mm f/5.6 and a 1/200sec exposure at ISO400.

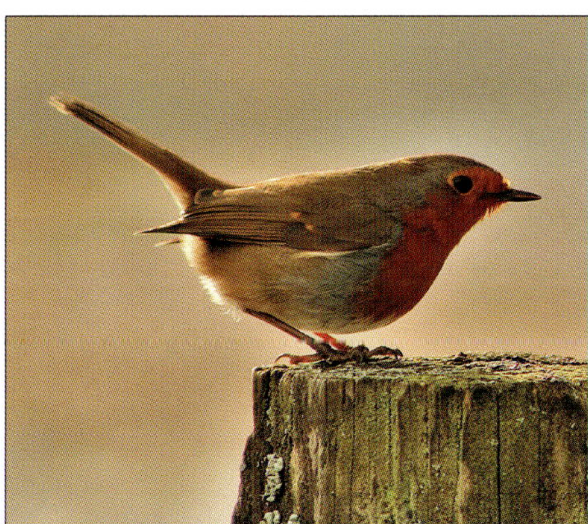

● ANDREW ROBERTS A little backlit robin taken in the Brecon Beacons, using a Canon EOS 300D and Canon 75-300 IS lens.

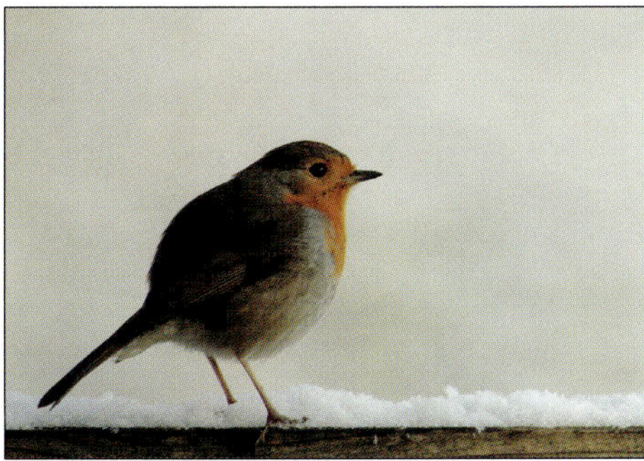

● STEVE LANGTON Robin in the winter snow. Canon EOS 10D and 300mm f/4 L with 1.4X converter.

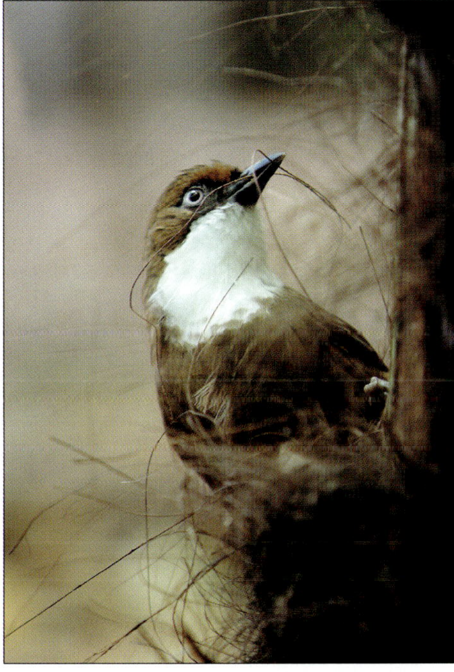

● SAM BASSAN This shot, on a Canon EOS 10D and 70-200mm IS needed lots of patience and stillness but it was worth it! 1/50sec at f/2.8 +2/3 and monopod.

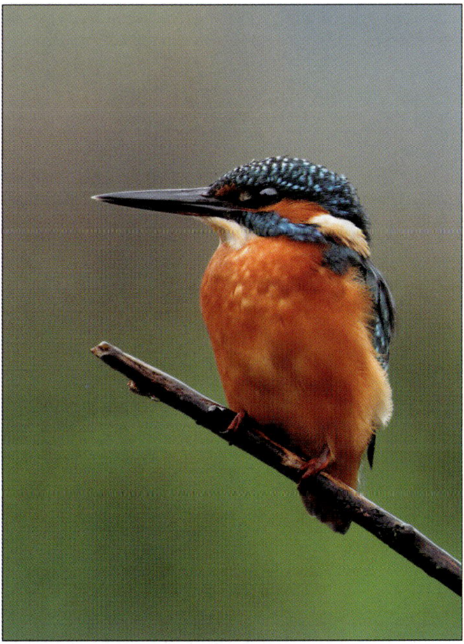

● JUSTIN COWTAN "Having set up a hide under the cover of darkness, it wasn't long before this kingfisher landed on the perch I'd provided."

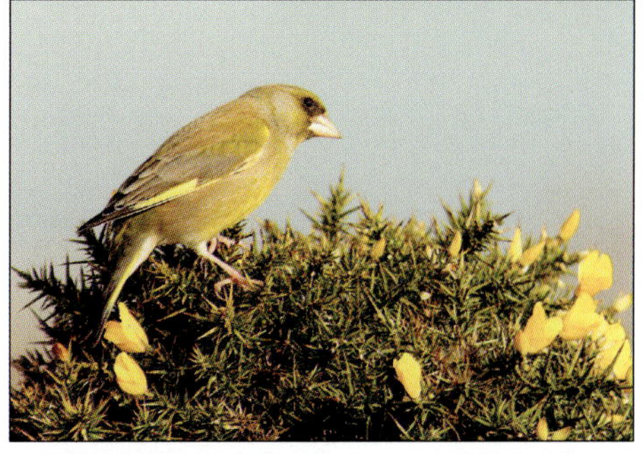

● BRIAN WADIE Greenfinch on gorse at Mudeford Harbour, using a Sigma 100-300mm EX f/4 on a Canon EOS 300D.

ATTRACTING GARDEN BIRDS

■ Blackbirds like areas with bushes, shrubs and trees and nearby open ground with short grass. They eat insects, worms and berries.

■ Bramblings are similar to chaffinches and can be found eating seeds in gardens in the winter months.

■ Blue Tits like gardens with oak and mature trees or nestboxes. They eat insects, caterpillars, seeds and nuts.

■ Bullfinches like thickets, hedgerows and mature gardens and eat seeds, buds and insects.

■ Chiffchaffs like mature gardens where there is thick undergrowth and eat Insects.

■ Coal Tits like gardens with conifers and eat insects, seeds and nuts.

■ Chaffinches go anywhere with trees and bushes including suburban gardens and eat insects and seeds.

■ Hedge Sparrows need areas with thick vegetation such as brambles and hedges. They eat insects, spiders, worms and seeds.

■ Greenfinch like tall hedges, conifer plantations, orchards, churchyards and anywhere with tall, fairly dense trees. Bird table food makes them common and they eat seeds and insects.

■ Goldcrests like large gardens where there are conifers nearby and eat insects.

■ Goldfinches like trees and bushes with areas of tall weeds nearby and eat seeds and insects in summer.

■ Great tits like hedgerow trees, parkland and gardens and mature trees with nest holes, although they will use nest boxes. They eat insects, seeds and nuts.

■ Grey Wagtails are found around garden ponds or searching for insects in damp gutters. It eats insects.

■ House Martins are common in villages and towns, and are more likely to be found in larger centres of population than swallows. They mainly nest on buildings, often forming colonies. They eat insects.

■ Jackdaws are found in gardens with areas of grassland nearby to feed on. In towns they will breed in roofs and chimneys and eat insects, seeds and scraps.

■ Jays appear in suburban areas where there are mature trees and eat acorns, nuts, seeds and insects.

■ Magpies like gardens with thick hedges or scattered trees and they are omnivores and scavengers.
Robins like gardens with plenty of undergrowth and eat worms, seeds, fruits and insects.

■ Starlings like suitable trees with nest holes and eat insects and fruit.

■ Thrushes like hedgerows and bushes and prefer gardens with cover. They eat worms, snails and fruit.

■ Tree Sparrows prefer large gardens, especially where nest boxes are provided. They eat seeds and insects.

■ Wrens are regular garden visitors, especially if there's thick undergrowth. They feed on insects and spiders.

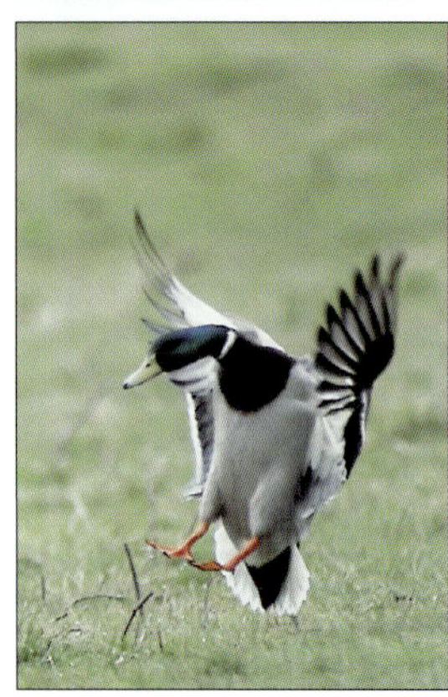

● JOHN DALY Mallard bouncing just after take-off from river.

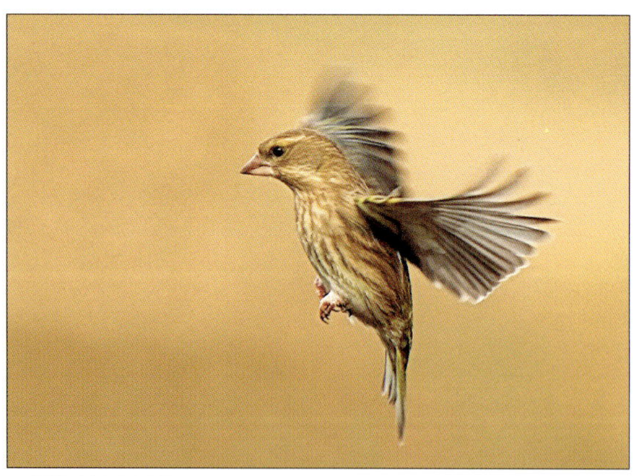

● ADE OSMANT Flaps up, brakes on! A 1/1250sec exposure at f/11, ISO800, tripod mounted with focus preset and remote trigger.

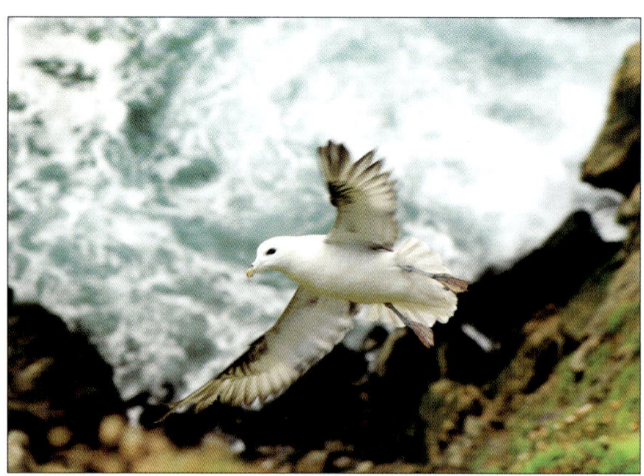

● BRAD CHAPPELL Taken from cliffs at Sumburgh Head, Shetland, using a Canon EOS 10D and 150mm lens. Exposure 1/100sec at f/8.

DIGITAL TECHNIQUE – BETTER BACKGROUNDS

■ As anyone who has taken bird photographs, or any discipline of wildlife photography, will know, there's seldom time to move left, right or even up or down, in order to achieve a better background. And, despite the right equipment and good technical knowledge, you will still get cracking shots of a subject that are ruined by a poor background.

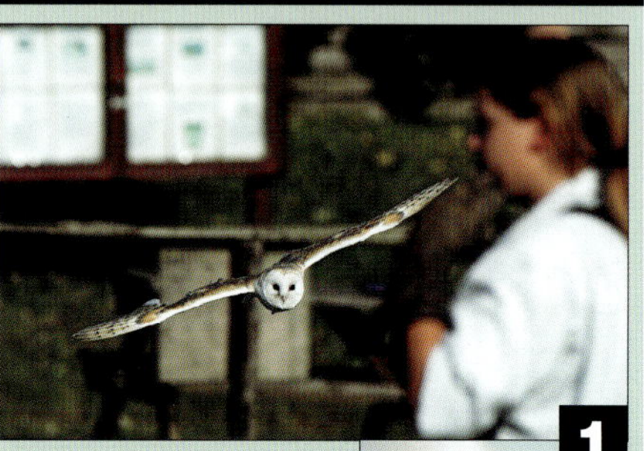

One of the most common occurrences is when shooting wildlife in a captive environment. Fences and stray people ruin the effect of an otherwise excellent shot. Software packages, such as Photoshop and Paint Shop Pro, have a number of tools that enable you to clone out, blur or erase distracting elements of the picture. My favoured method, especially if there's a fair amount of distraction in the picture, is to replace the background completely.

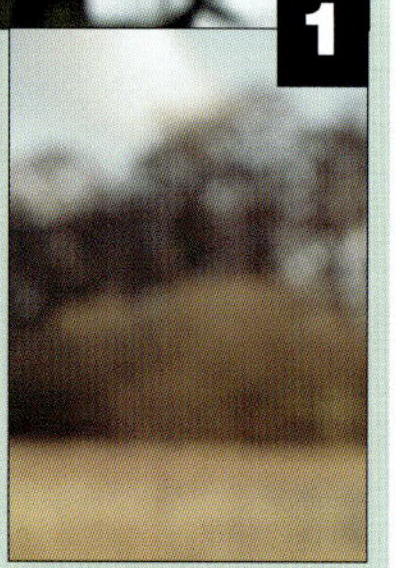

I have a folder entitled Backgrounds which contains a number of shots in landscape and portrait format, taken with the camera deliberately set wide open and well out of focus. These include photos of grass, trees and woodland, reed beds and the like, along with in-focus shots of blue skies/fluffy white clouds. When I get an image that has a distracting or bland background, I look through this folder for a possible replacement. There are a couple of ways to make this change using your image editing software. My favoured method is to use a layer mask.

1 Open the background and subject photos, making sure both are visible on the desktop. Go to the subject photo and roughly select around the subject with the Lasso tool. Then click on the Move tool and drag & drop the selected subject area across onto the background photo and position it roughly where you want it. Close the original image, selecting No when asked if you want to save changes to preserve the original file.

2 Create a Layer mask on the new layer by clicking the icon at the bottom of the layers palette. Select the brush tool and a suitable size brush with a feathered edge. Working at least at 100%, use the brush to mask out the areas of the subject that you don't want – change from black to white to paint the subject back.

3 When done, select Save as (so you can use the background file again) and rename the file choosing .psd file format.

4 Adjust each layer's levels and colours so it looks like a single picture and save. Once you've done this a couple of times, you will find it's the easiest way of achieving the desired effect in post production.

The secret is having a good selection of backgrounds and choosing the right one. Give it a try – your spoiled photographs could be turned into masterpieces. The only caveat is don't try to pass off your manipulated wildlife image as something it isn't. If it's of a captive animal, don't be afraid to say so. The subject may look as though it is in the wild, and that may well be the impression you intend, but it is still a captive creature and that fact should be stated.
Words and photos Ian Andrews

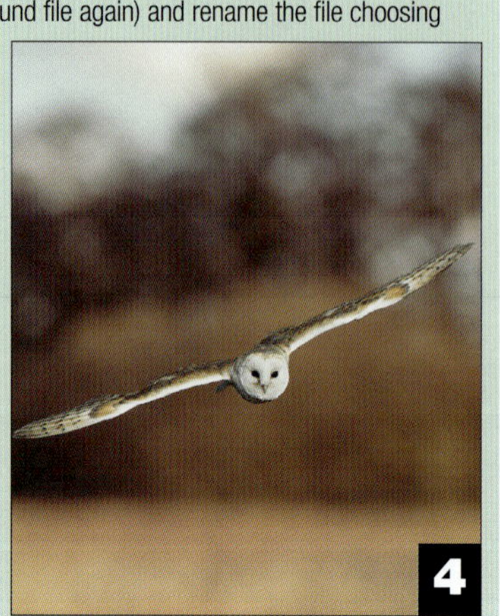

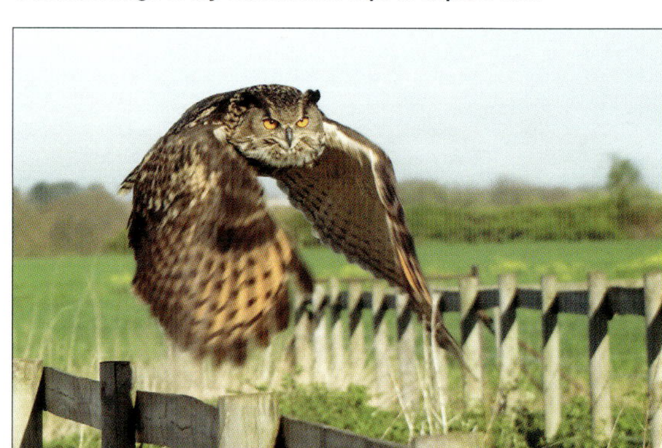

● MARTIN JORDAN "From the beach bar I had seen this pelican do a couple of 'fly pasts'. I went and grabbed my camera and waited. I took advantage of my Canon 20D's 5fps to capture this."

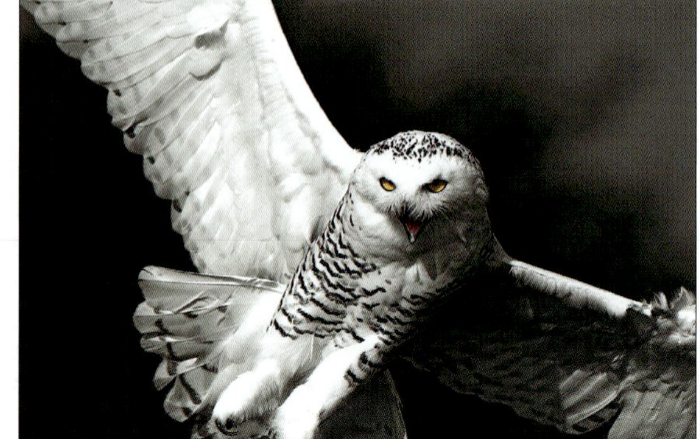

● VINCENT JONES A powerful European eagle owl in flight, showing determination and flight power. Taken with a Nikon D1X and Sigma 50-500mm at 1/500sec and f/7.1 with ISO200.

● IAN ANDREWS A tightly framed shot of a snow owl, taken with a Nikon 300mm VR lens on the Nikon D2H.

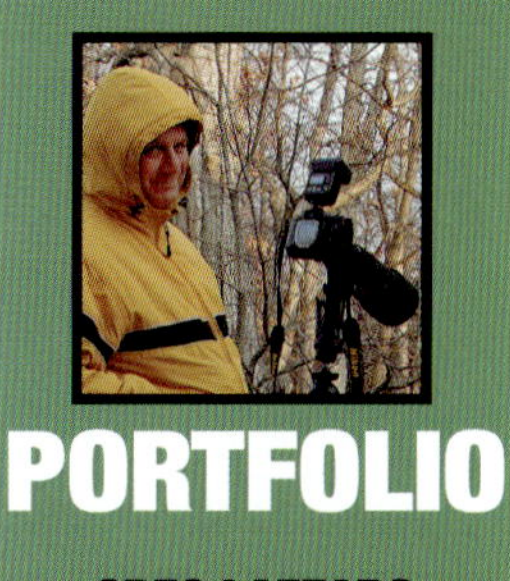

PORTFOLIO

GREG LAZZARO
Greg is from Delaware and spends much of his time in a hide gathering an amazing collection of bird photos.

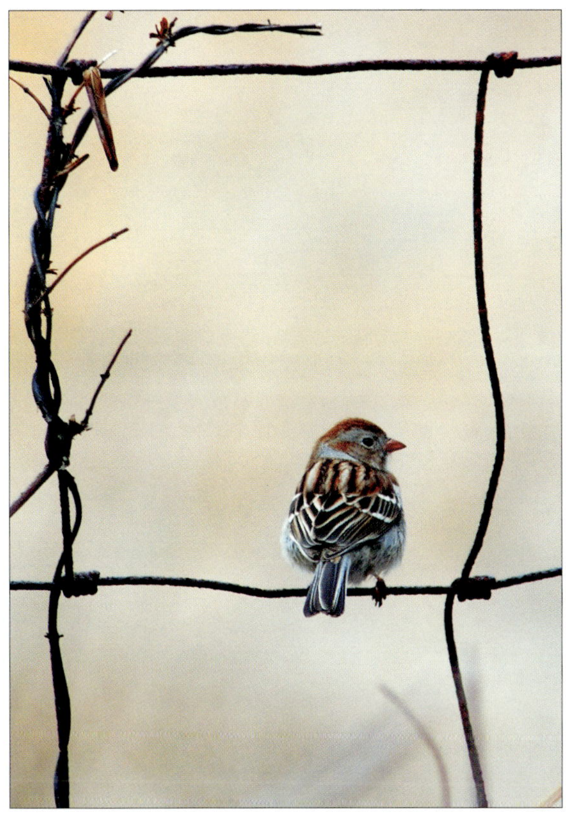

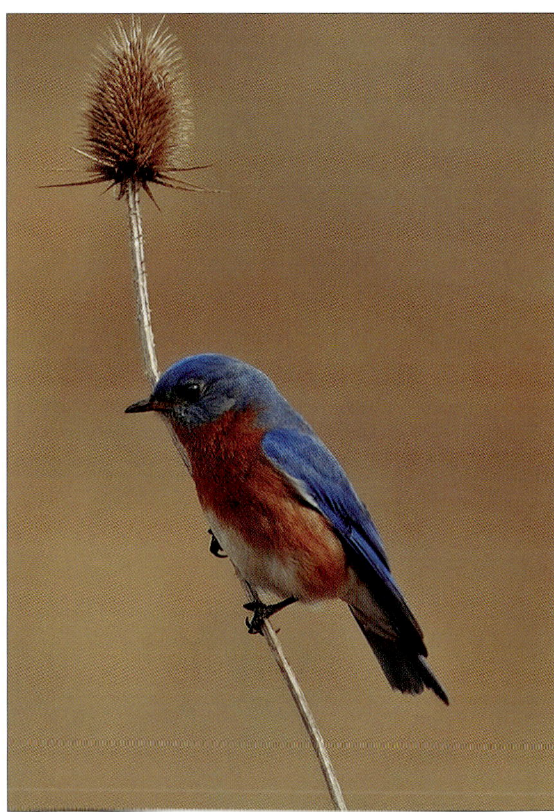

● CLOCKWISE Chipping sparrow taken at a local abandoned farm, fenced off field on a sunny day, 1/500sec, f/5.6 and ISO200, focal length 300mm ● Eastern bluebird taken in an open field of tall grass on a sunny day, 1/400sec, f/6.3, ISO200, focal length 500mm ● Female redwing blackbird, taken at a fresh water marsh on a sunny day, 1/1350sec at f/9, ISO200, EV -0.07, focal length 600mm.

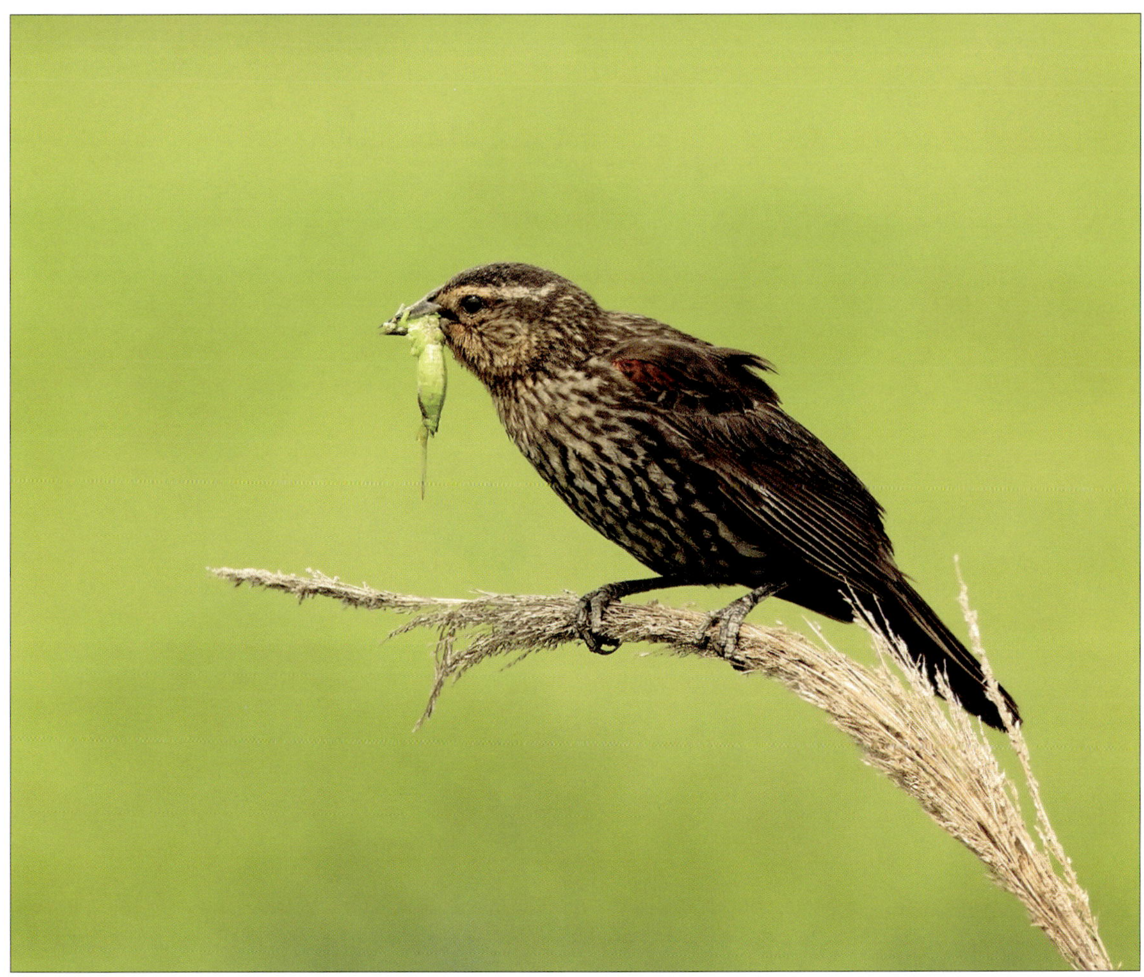

Greg's greatest passions in life are his family and nature photography. His family nurtures his soul and inspires him to excel in life. Being behind the camera provides him an outlet to explore, learn and experience new things. That is because photography broadens ones view of their environment, forcing you to really look, plan and execute.

Through photography he seeks to capture nature's natural beauty, its creatures and events within nature as he sees them and to share with others the beauty and diversity of that environment.

As the images of other photographers have inspired him to explore his world, he hopes his own contributions will inspire others to do the same. But, most of all, to inspire others to pick up a camera, learn, and have fun doing it. After all we only get one shot at life; lets go out with a smile.

Greg's shooting tip: When shooting birds, in particular the little seed eating variety, find a good location for a shoot, one that would be advantageous to the camera and sprinkle the area with bird seeds at least a day before the planned shoot. Then, on the day of the shoot, sprinkle the area again, find a nice seat and be prepared to get a variety of bird shots.

Greg's editing tip: Most folks do not realize how much more detail there is in the eyes of birds when editing, that is because at a glance there appears to be nothing. Reflections, detail and colour can be brought forth with little effort. Select the eyes, then in whatever editing program you use, reduce shadows between 10 – 50%, a whole new window of detail will be made available. ■

You can view Greg's amazing portfolio on ePHOTOzine.

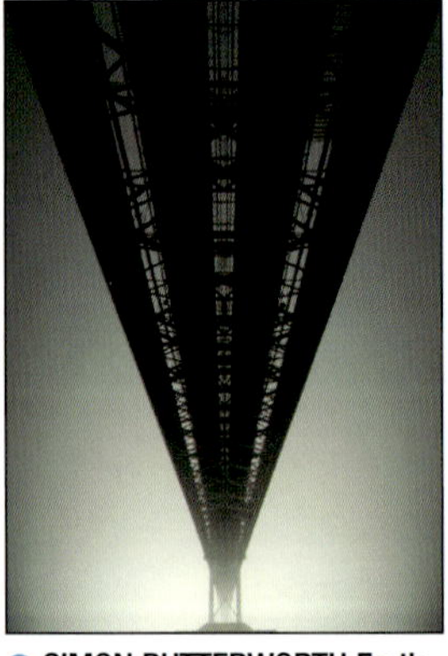

● SIMON BUTTERWORTH Forth Road Bridge on a foggy morning.

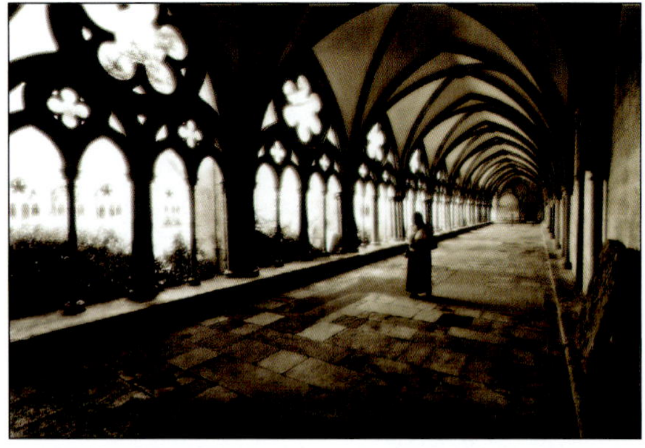

● NIGEL SHARMAN Cloisters at Salisbury Cathedral with Canon EOS 20D and 10-22mm, 1/25sec at f/10. Toned and diffused digitally.

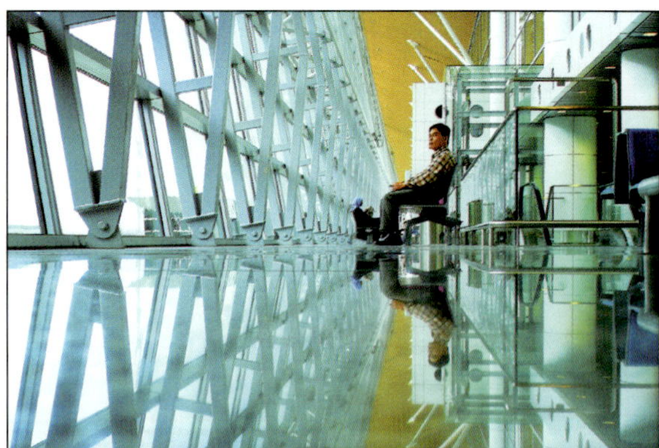

● ADRIAN LUNSONG A Sony Cybershot DSC-W1 was positioned at floor level to shoot Kuala Lumpur Airport in Malaysia.

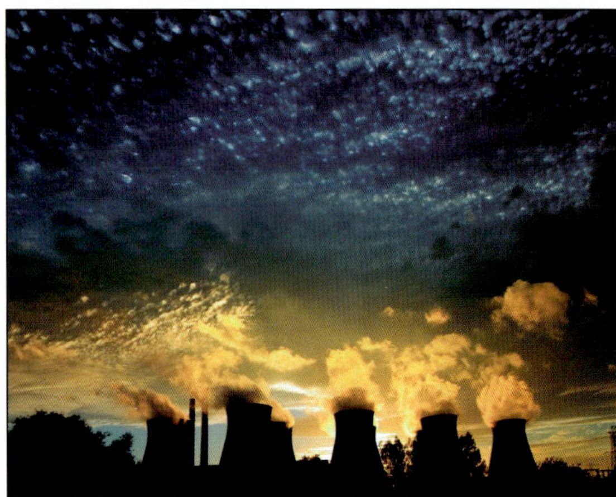

● ADRIAN WILSON Ferrybridge Powerstation taken from the A1 road during a superb September sunset.

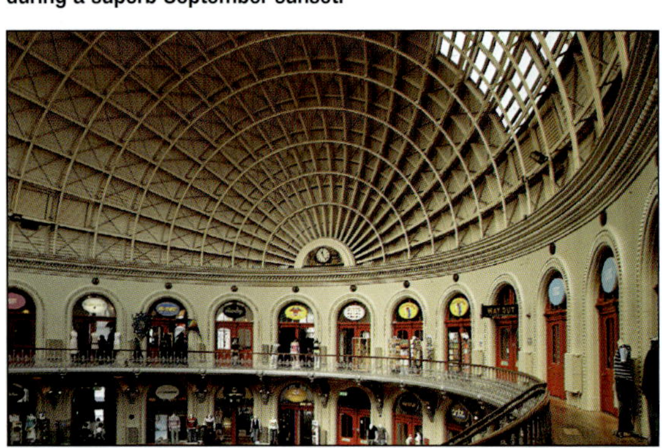

● STEVE MAIDEN Leeds Corn Exchange using the Canon D60 and 16-35mm f/2.8 L and a handheld exposure of 1/90sec at f/5.6.

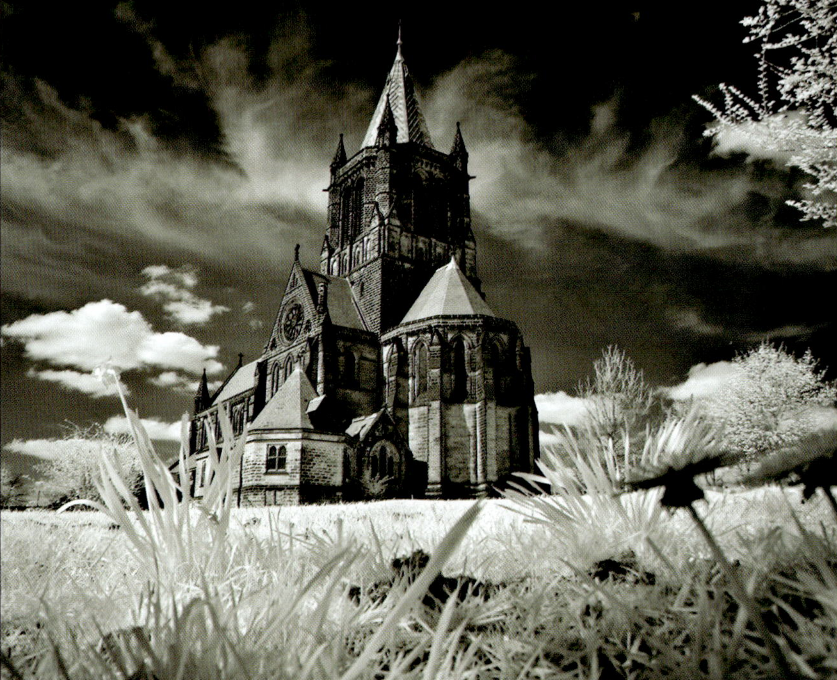

● STEVE SHARP Nikon's Coolpix 990 was one of the best digital cameras for infrared as demonstrated in this shot, taken at St. Barts, Armley, Leeds, with a Hoya RM90 IR filter attached.

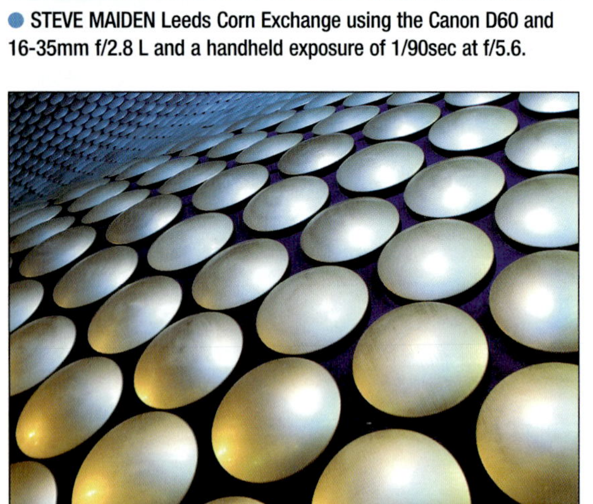

● NEIL PASKIN Selfridges building in Birmingham taken with a Konica Minolta 7D and 17-35mm lens. Exposure was 1/6sec at f/3.5.

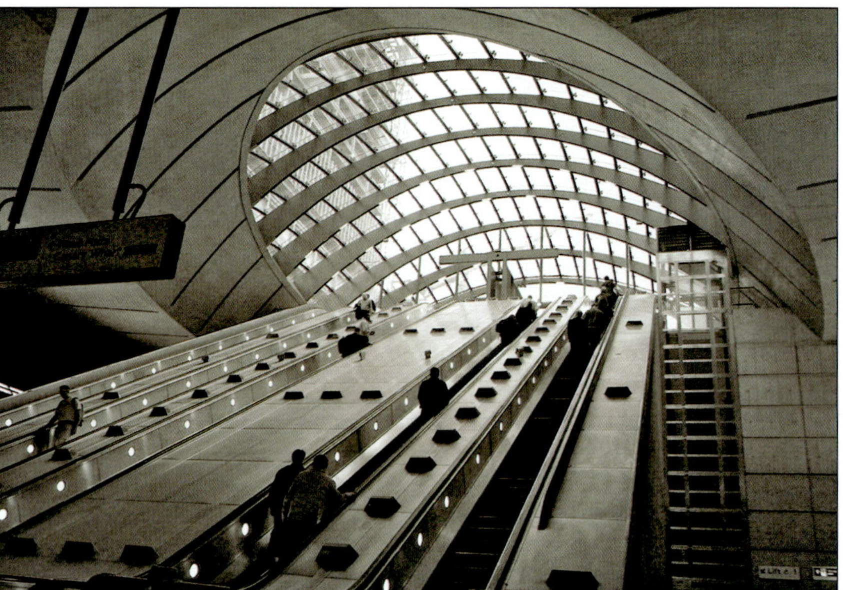

● TONY CREFFIELD Canary Wharf Station taken using a Canon EOS D30. The exposure was f/11 at 1/250sec and the Sigma 28-300mm zoom was set at 30mm.

Architecture

Whether you shoot to record the detail created by an architect or to add your own creative slant, buildings provide tremendous photographic scope. From the crude monolithic structures through to the intricate detail of Victorian designs to the abstract shapes of the latest modern constructions, architecture is waiting for us to capture in colour or black & white.

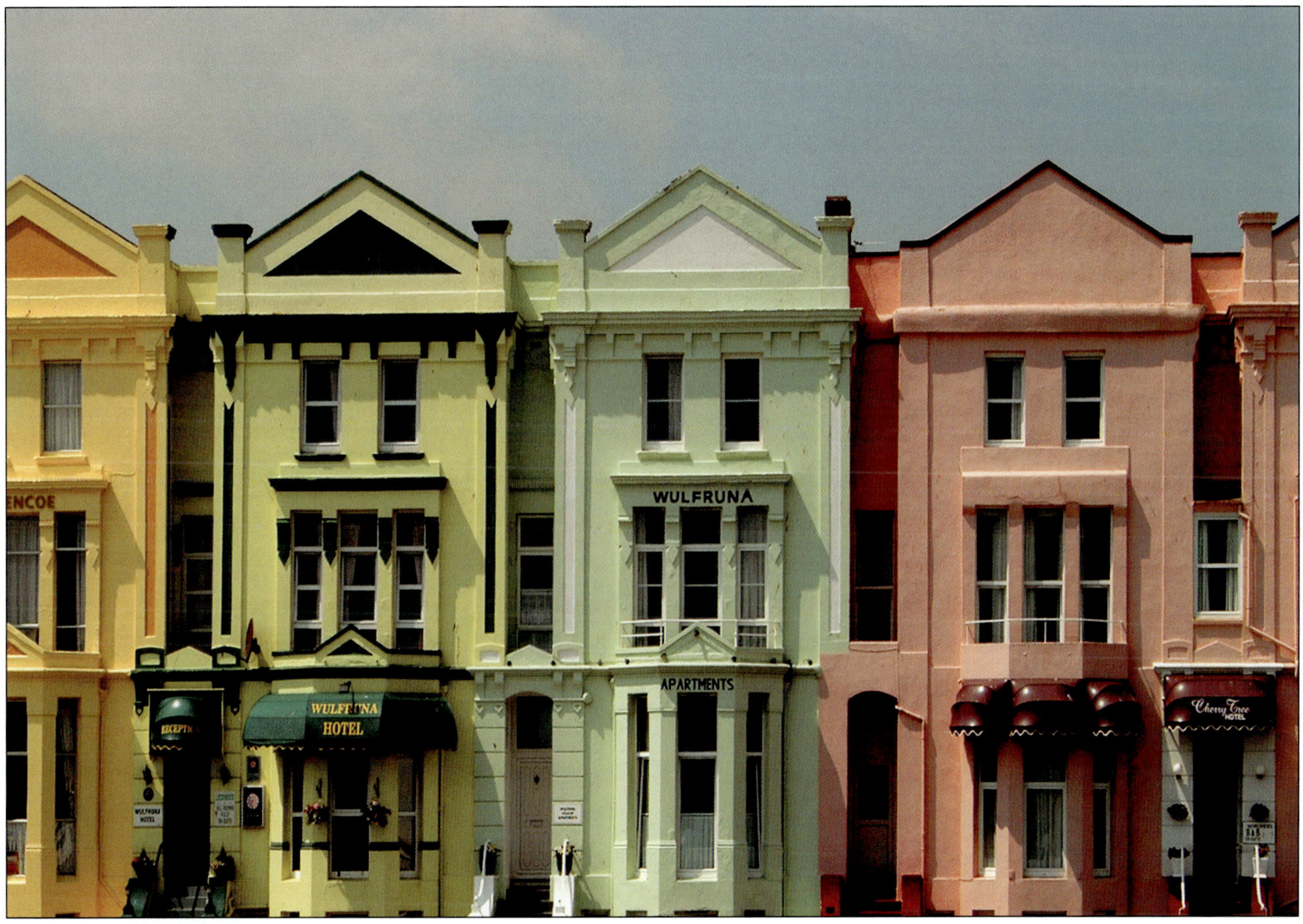

● TIM COOPER Taken with a Nikon D70 and a 24-120 VR lens, these are part of a parade of colourful hotels on Paignton seafront.

Although we are often surrounded by the most spectacular buildings, much of the population take them for granted. These structures provide a home, a work place, a reference centre, a store and they even keep some of us out of trouble! But unless you have a photographic eye, or a real interest, most of the detail goes unnoticed as people go about their daily duties. Those subtle angles, built to reflect light and surrounds at certain viewpoints, the amazingly detailed carvings, the beautiful windows, arches and steps, are all waiting to be recorded.

You may have noticed when you first became interested in photography that certain details you had previously taken for granted started to appear, as if by magic, before your eyes. Door knockers, panelling, light fittings, ceilings, staircases, start to take on a whole new photographic meaning. The beauty with buildings, and their furnishings, is they don't blink, get bored or jump about and, in most cases, they will still be in the same place, day after day, year after year. So, if you do make a mistake and don't get the photograph you'd hoped for there's always another day.

It's not all a bed of roses though! You do have a few technicalities in the way to prevent you getting a good photograph. Just like landscape photography, light can make or break a good architectural shot. Strong sunlight will create harsh shadows in alcoves, doorways and arches. The extreme contrast will mean the photograph will be either too light or too dark in certain areas.

This harsh contrast can be perfect, though, when shooting a modern glass building where you may want the sun illuminating the chromework and creating sparkling highlights. But it's also essential to lift the stonework of churches and historic buildings and to create 3D depth in carvings. The trick is to use daylight conditions to suit the subject you're shooting.

Another concern is leaning walls, caused because the building towers above you and the sloping verticals curve inwards toward the top. This is exaggerated the further the walls are from you and the nearer you are to the base of the building. You can reduce the effect by standing further away, gaining a higher viewpoint or using a longer lens.

Special perspective control lenses are available to correct this too, but digital imaging software has also helped because you can adjust the frame and correct the verticals using devices such as Photoshop's transform tool.

Another problem you may encounter is getting the whole building in the frame. It's easy when you can stand further away and use a wider angle lens, but what if you have restricted movement and are already at the widest setting of your zoom lens? Again digital comes to the rescue. You can take several shots of different parts of the building and assemble them in a grid, using your image editing program. You have to be careful of perspective and you may need to use the transform tool to make the individual photos align.

Throughout this section of the book we've selected a wide range of buildings that have been photographed by ePHOTOzine members. We have everything, from abstract close ups to those showing the building in its surrounds. We've also added a range of tips to help you take better architectural shots and introduce you to a few digital techniques to help you rescue shots that went wrong. ■

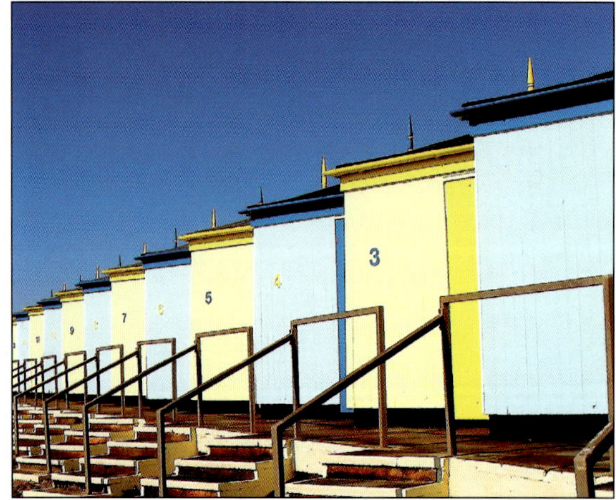

● IAIN JOHNSTONE A simple shot, but the bold, contrasting colours and the strong lines of these beach huts was too much to resist.

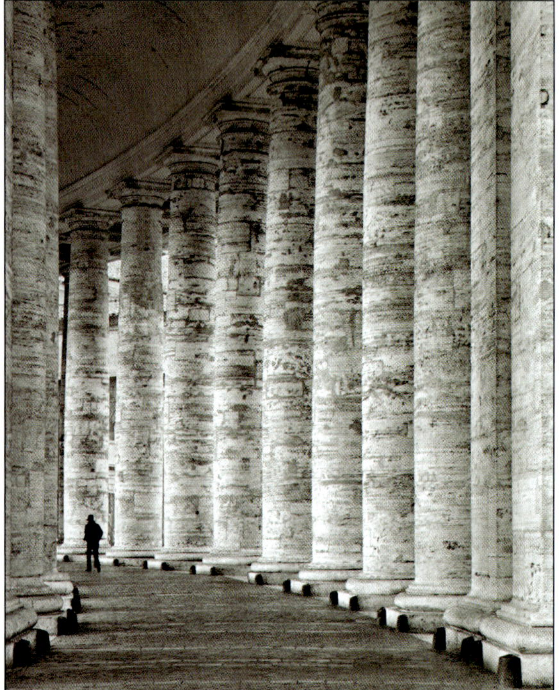

● LEVENTE TOTH Bold lines created by the columns in St. Peter's Square, Rome. The lone figure gives a sense of dramatic scale.

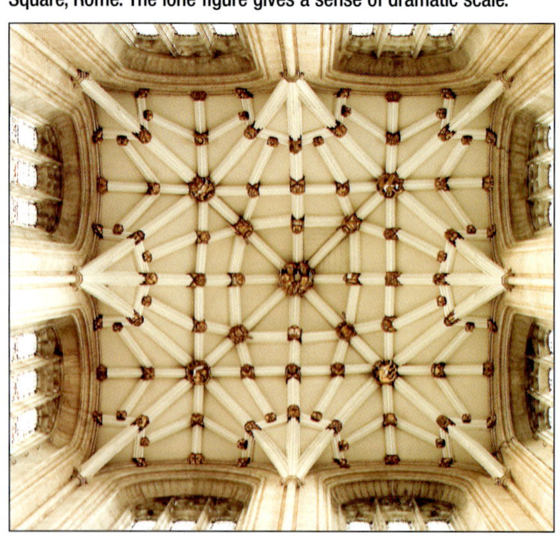

● ANDREW FINDLAY Canon EOS 10D was placed on the floor of York Minster and triggered using the self timer. Exposure; 1/15sec f/2.8.

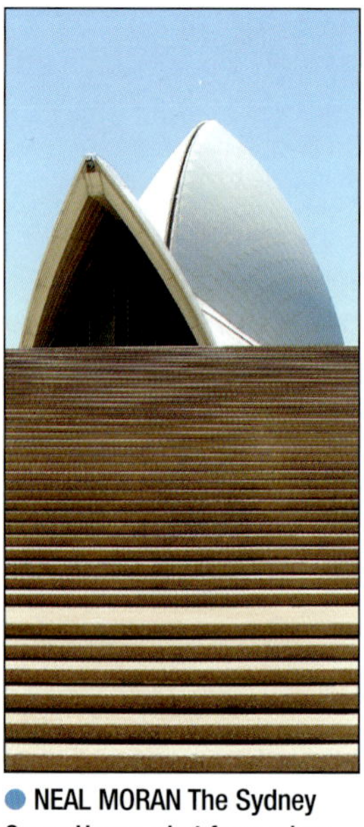

● NEAL MORAN The Sydney Opera House, shot from a low viewpoint to give an unusal view of this popular tourist spot.

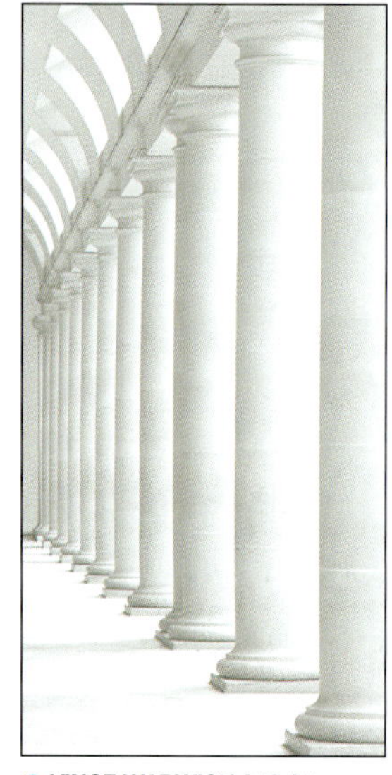

● VINCE WARWICK A tight crop on columns at Covent Garden.

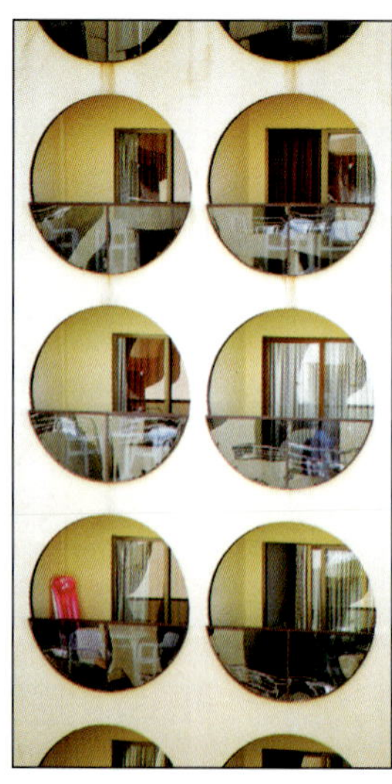

● MARTIN JANES Unusually shaped hotel balconies.

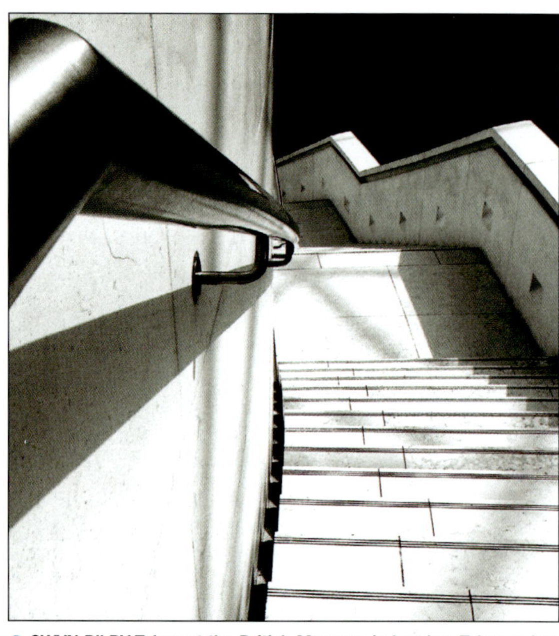

● GWYN BILBY Taken at the British Museum in London. Taken using a Fuji S5000, converted to B&W in Photoshop Elements.

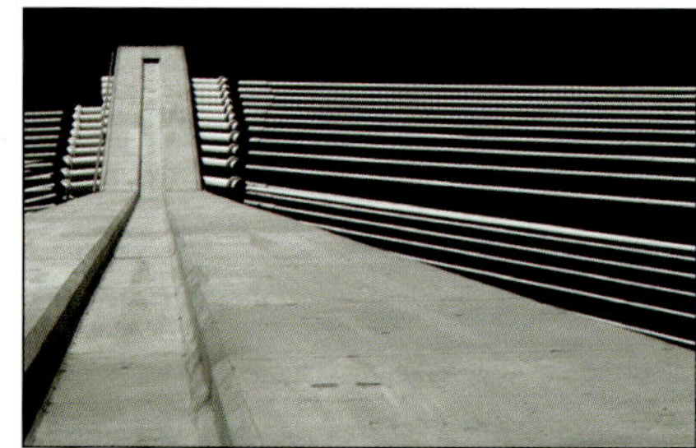

● ELA WLODARCZYK Swietokrzyski Bridge, Warsaw, Poland, taken with Sensia 100 film in a Canon EOS 300V and converted to B&W.

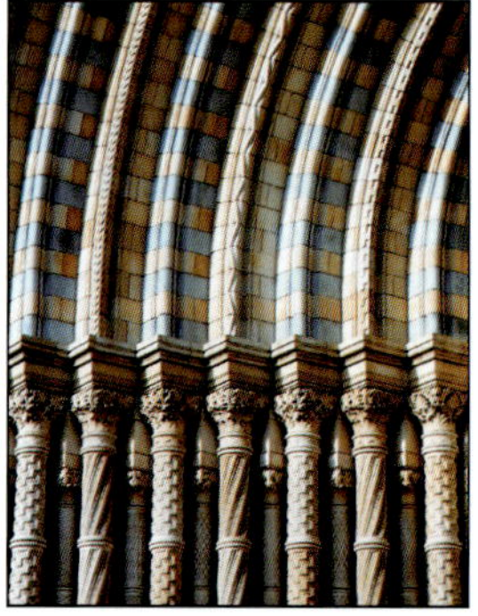

● STEVE BRIDDON The Natural History Museum's entrance.

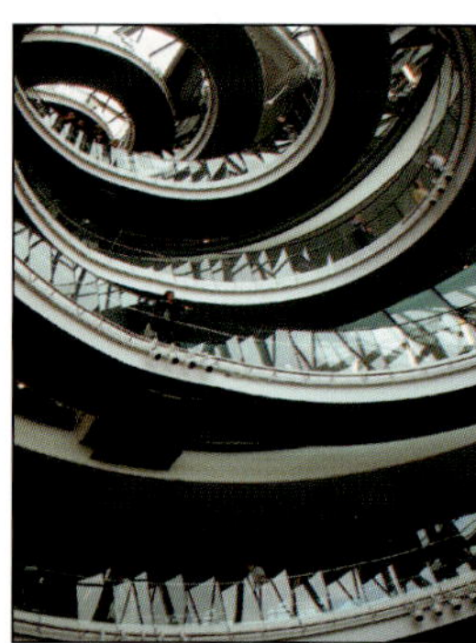

● IAIN GILFILLAN London City Hall, Sir Norman Foster's design.

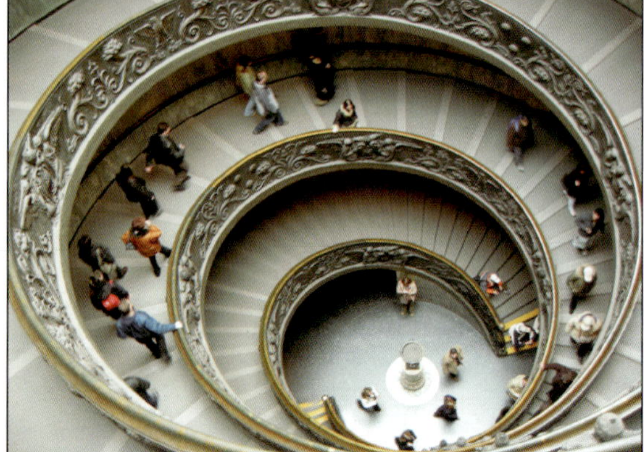

● ELIZABETH BARNETT A spiral staircase, like this one in the Vatican City, is a perfect subject for almost hypnotic patterns.

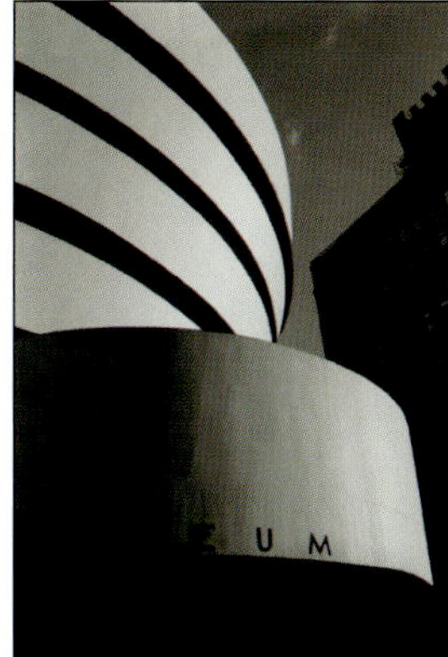

● HELEN POLSON Spiral gallery at the Guggenheim Museum in New York, shot on grainy B&W film and a wide-angle lens.

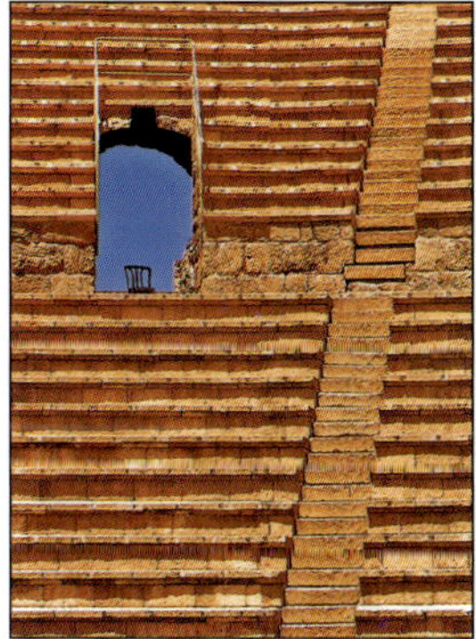

● HERMIN ABRAMOVITCH Light play on Roman amphitheatre stairs.

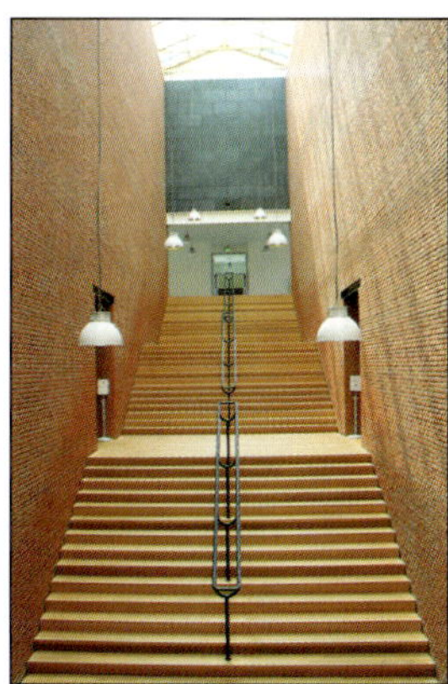

● ERNST VAN LOON Central stairs of Bonnefanten Museum in Maastricht.

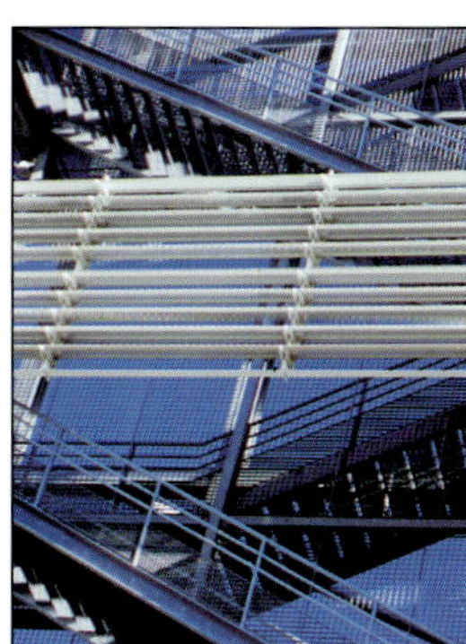

● MIKE QUINN Abstract in steel and glass in Montpellier.

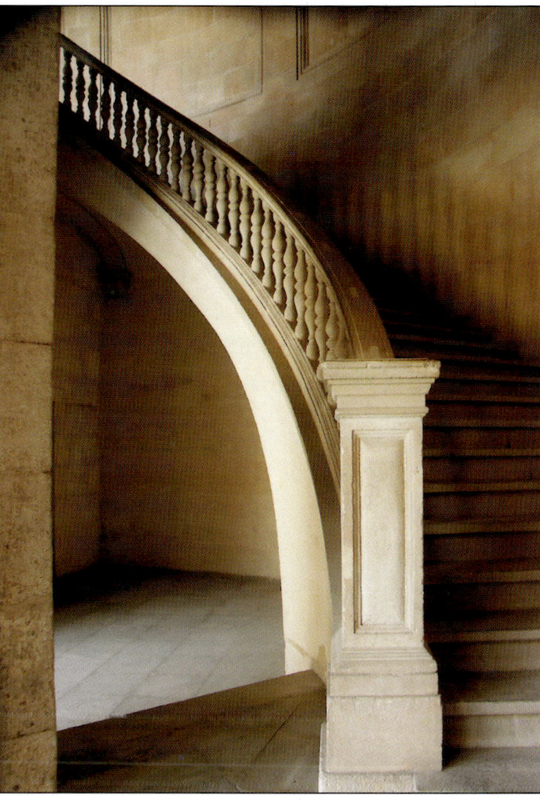

● JAN VAN DER KLUGT The Alhambra, Spain has over 7000 visitors daily. Fortunately, there was nobody in the way for this shot!

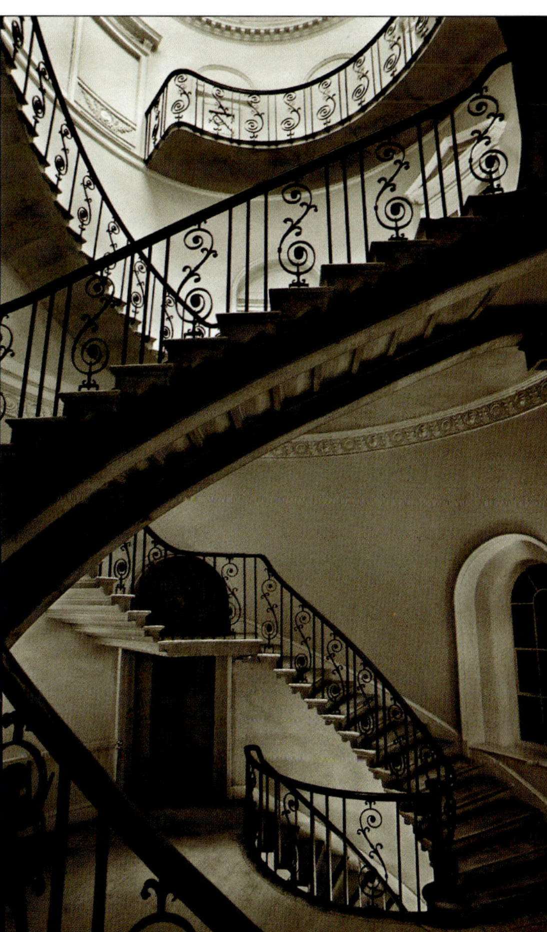

● LEVENTE TOTH Nelson staircase in Somerset House, London. The staircases crossing the shot create a feel of a work by MC Escher.

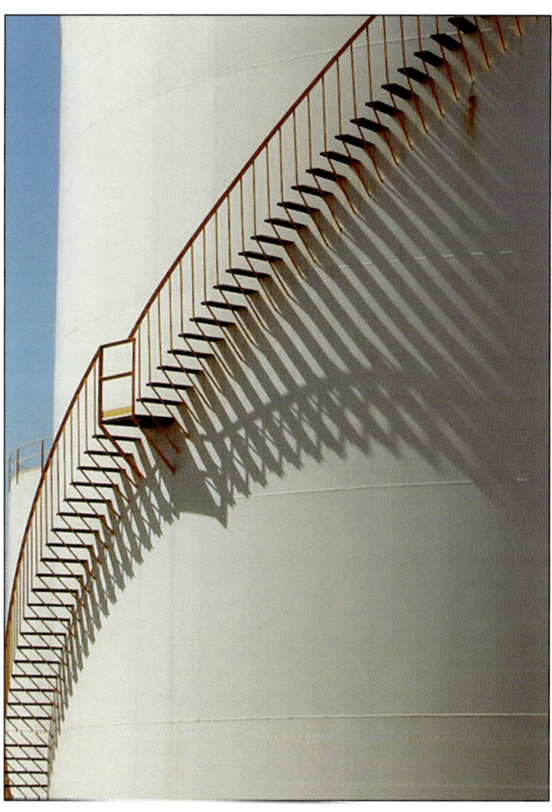

● TIMOTHY LUBCKE "I like how the shadows of the stairs on this oil storage tank became longer due to the curvature of the tank."

SHOOTING TIPS – INTERIORS

■ Where possible use a tripod. The light in most indoor locations will require the use of a longer shutter speed to cope. If you are hand-holding, the shot may suffer from camera shake. If you don't have, or are not permitted to use, a tripod look for a sturdy rest – railings, walls or pillars all come in handy.

■ Use a slave flashgun to light dark crevices or alcoves.

■ Watch the colour temperature! Interiors illuminated by artificial light will have a colour cast when you shoot with normal daylight film or digital set to the wrong white balance setting. Tungsten lighting, such as household lightbulbs, creates a very strong orange cast. An 80 series blue filter can be used to correct this. Fluorescent lighting usually delivers a green cast and this is corrected with a magenta filter. Digital cameras have an automatic white balance setting, but to be on the safe side switch to the suitable option.

■ Watch out for bright window light overexposing or causing the camera's meter to make the interior too dark. If the detail you require is inside, make sure you meter without the window in the frame. Ideally take two shots – one for the highlights and one for the shadows – and blend the two digitally.

■ When taking photos of busy staircases, in places such as stately homes, ask a friend to go up the stairs out of view and stop people walking back down while you take the shot. You can be waiting a long time otherwise.

■ Look for a high vantage point to reduce sloping verticals on taller buildings. Nearby multi storey carparks, hills or steps up to other building's doorways are ideal. Some photographers carry step ladders to gain height.

■ Set the camera on B and fire a flash several times to build up light.

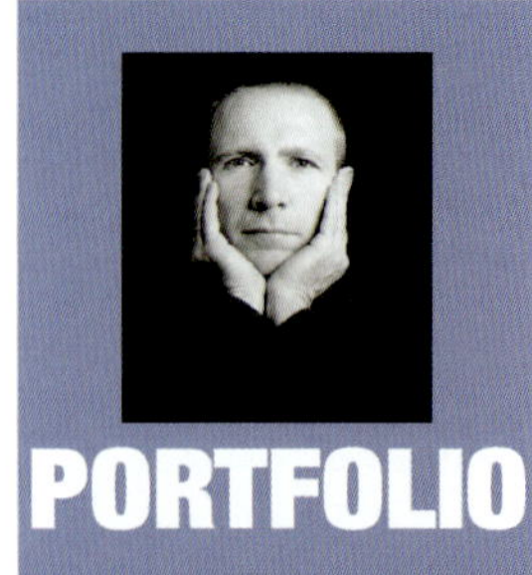

PORTFOLIO

PAUL STEFAN
Studying building design
has given Paul an insight
into what makes a good
architectural photo.

**From an early age I've been
one of those people who
likes to frame a scene in
my head. Whenever looking
at people, places, objects, I
tend to observe what's there
and consider how I could
reproduce it photographically.**

I used to take my first camera,
a Canon EOS 500 with a couple of
average lenses, everywhere and
take hundreds of shots, but was
continually frustrated with wasting
film with trial and error images.

I decided to enrol on a City &
Guilds photography course and my
enthusiasm and knowledge sky
rocketed. The course enabled me
to learn about what made a good
photograph, to understand the
fundamentals of how a film image
is created and to discover and
perfect new techniques.

I love all kinds of subjects,
from landscapes to still life, to
portraiture. However, I studied
building design at college and
have always had an interest
in architecture. I therefore love
photographing any form of
construction, from traditional to
contemporary.

Since joining ePHOTOzine and
gaining a wealth of knowledge
and enthusiasm from other very
talented photographers, I have
moved to digital and now use a
Canon EOS 20D. Like many others,
shooting digital provides much
faster feedback on the results and
therefore enables me to get the
shots I really want.

But, my camera aside, I
wouldn't ever go on a shoot
without my tripod and set of filters
– absolute tools of the trade!

The result of all this is I'm
now able to provide photography
to paying customers, which is
something I always aspired to. ■

www.paulstefan.co.uk

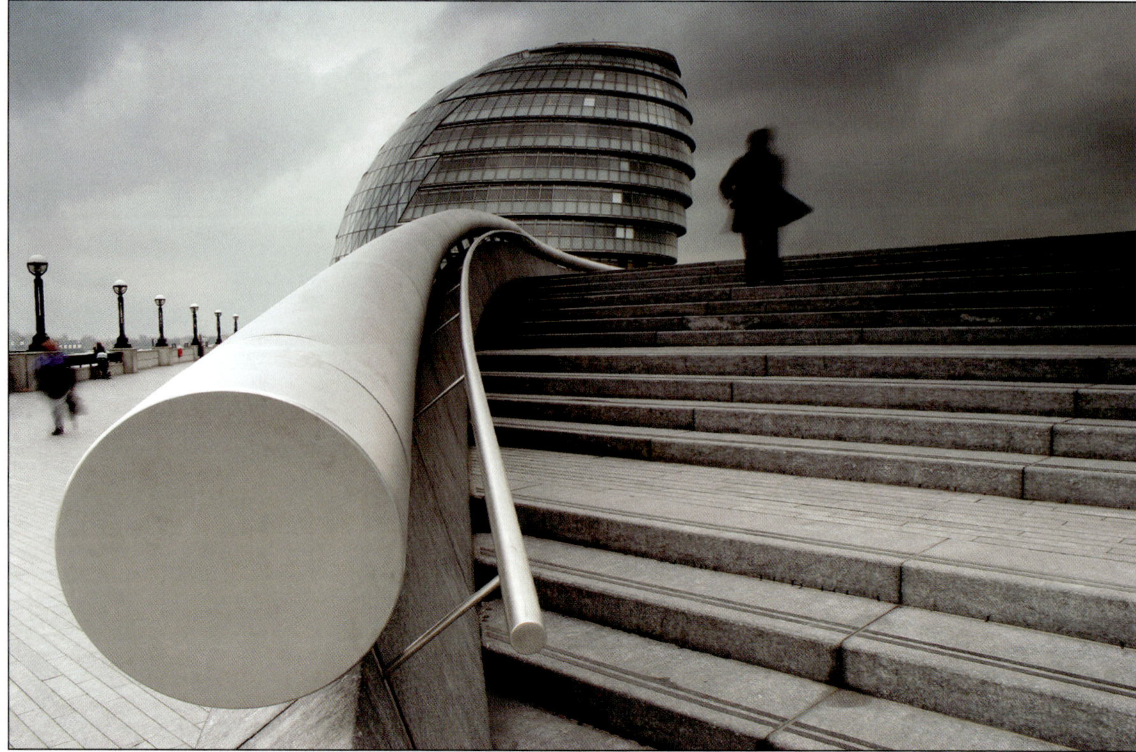

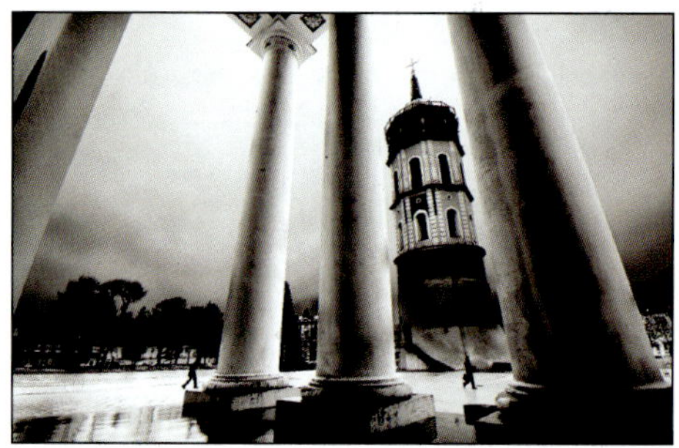

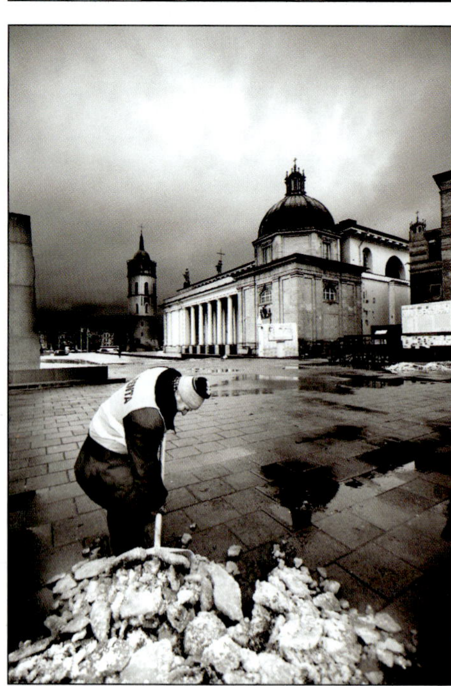

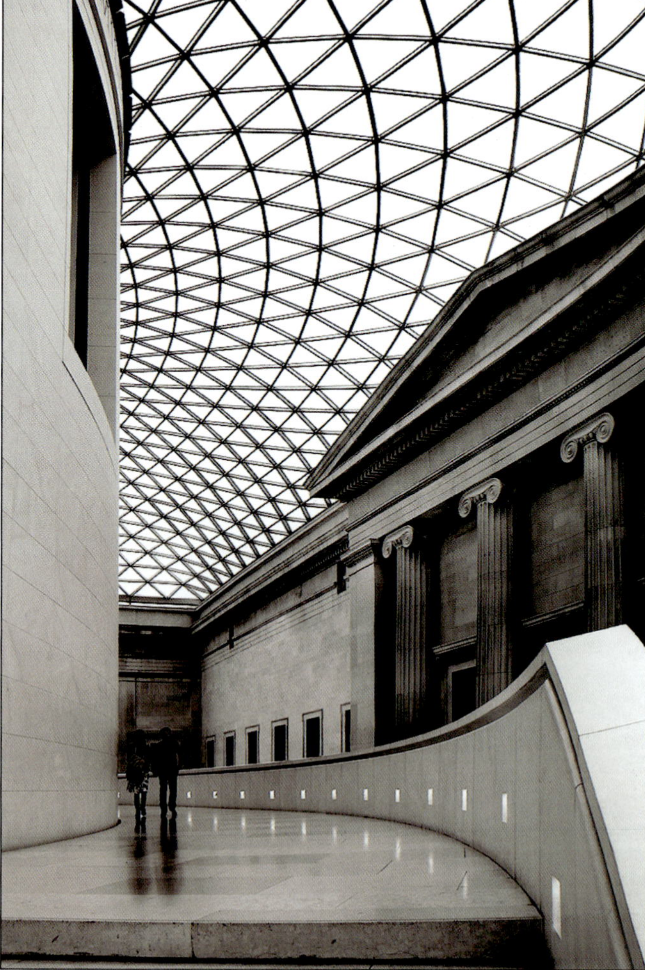

● Paul also has a passion for landscape photography and often tries to apply similar techniques in the architectural composition that he
would when composing a landscape. So his shots provide good lead in foregrounds, plenty of depth-of-field and, if lucky, a couple of solitary
people in the scene. Top: The much photographed mayor's office in London. Middle: Vilnius cathedral Lithuania. Above left: Ice clearer in
front of the cathedral in Vilnius. Above: The British Museum in London during a quieter moment.

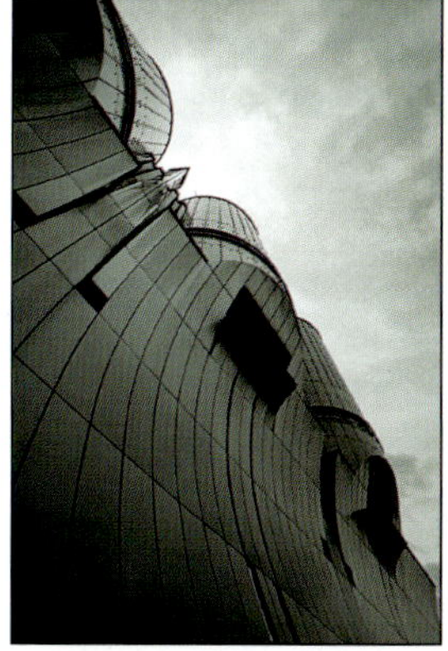

● LEE ANTHONY DOBSON Ferry Terminal at Sakai Minato, Japan.

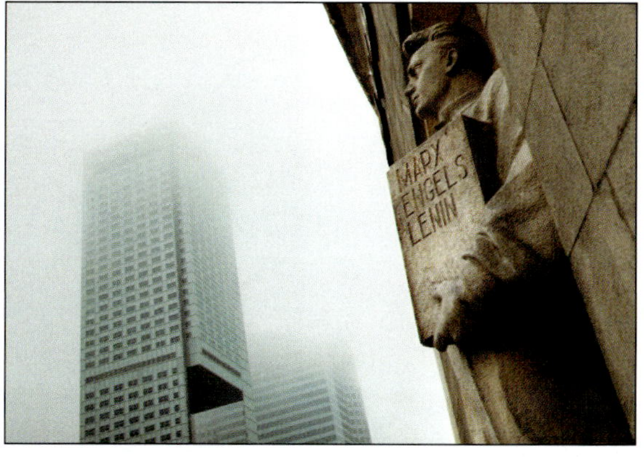

● ELA WLODARCZYK Warsaw, Poland, using Canon EOS 300V. The image was then converted to B&W and toned for past vs present feel.

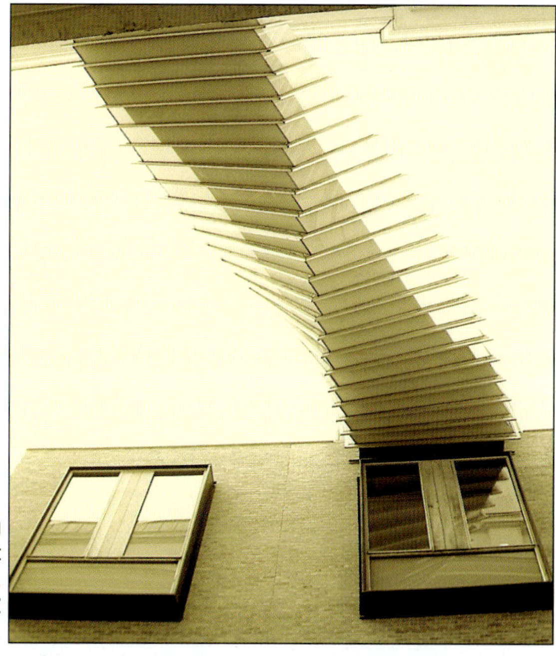

● PUAY-SZE LIM The Dancing Bridge linking the Royal Ballet School & Royal Opera House. Shot with Fuji FinePix F601Z and toned with Photoshop.

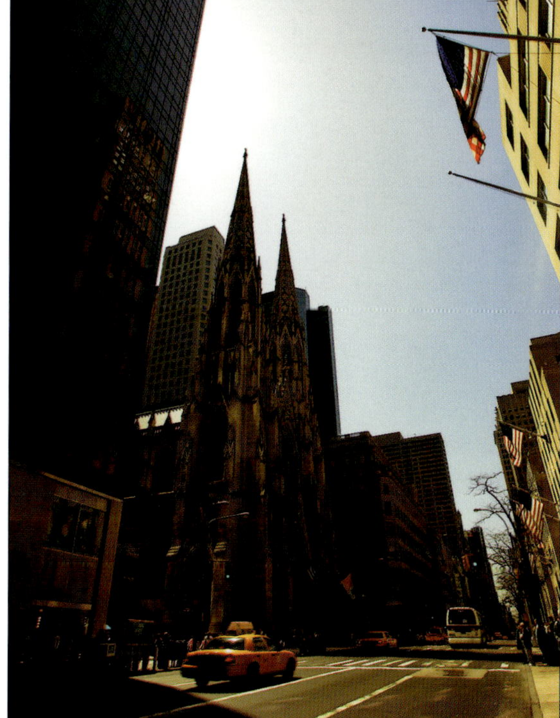

● PHIL SMITH Arches & curved wall, Laggan Dam, Glen Spean.

● JAN GEE Glass tower building reflecting the cloudy sky.

● EDWARD NORTON New York icons – Skyscrapers, St Patrick's, yellow cab, stars and stripes – taken at 5th Avenue.

DIGITAL TECHNIQUE – CORRECTING VERTICALS

■ Buildings look as though they are thinner at the top when you shoot from a low viewpoint. This perspective distortion is affected by the angle of view and focusing point. Digital image-editing programs, such as Photoshop and its budget version, Elements, have a transform tool that lets you pull the picture in different directions. Doing this allows you to make areas thicker or narrower to correct or enhance distortion. In this example, stepping back any futher would have taken the photographer onto a dangerous main road so the walls lean inwards slightly.

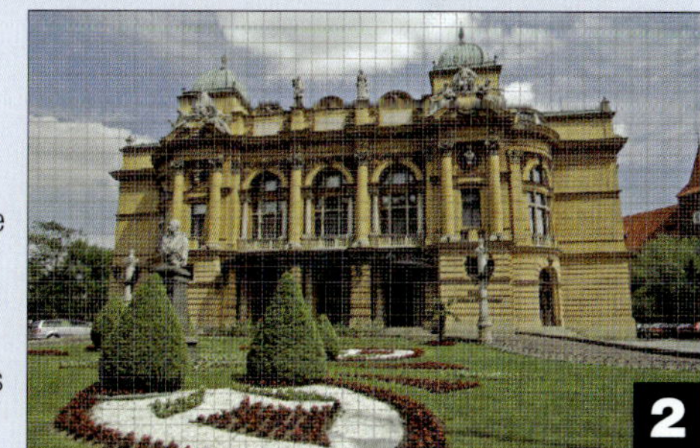

1 Go to Select⇨All to put a marching ants selection around the whole picture.

2 Now go to View⇨Show Grid to display a grid of horizontal and vertical lines over your photo. These are only present when the picture is being displayed and not when the picture is saved for web, printing or viewing in different software. You can change the colour of the grid or the number of lines and spacing of the grid via Edit⇨Preferences.

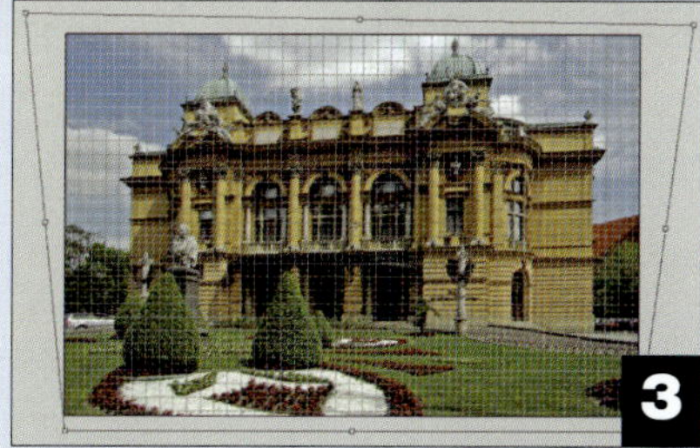

3 Select Image⇨Transform⇨Distort and, with your cursor over one of the square corner markers, click and drag to extend the box. Pull it so that the wall on the side that you are pulling becomes straight. Repeat with the opposite side.

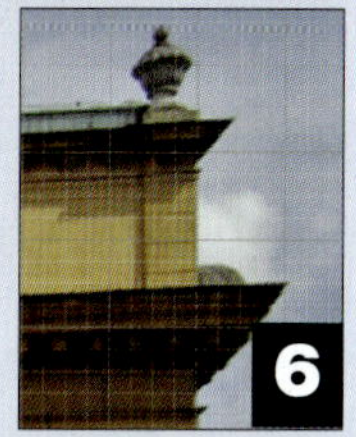

4 The image may now look too squat, so we need to stretch it by clicking on any of the top three markers or bottom and drag up or down to make the picture elongated and more natural.

5 Pull one side higher than the other if the image is still not square on and play around pushing and pulling on any of the markers until the image looks natural.

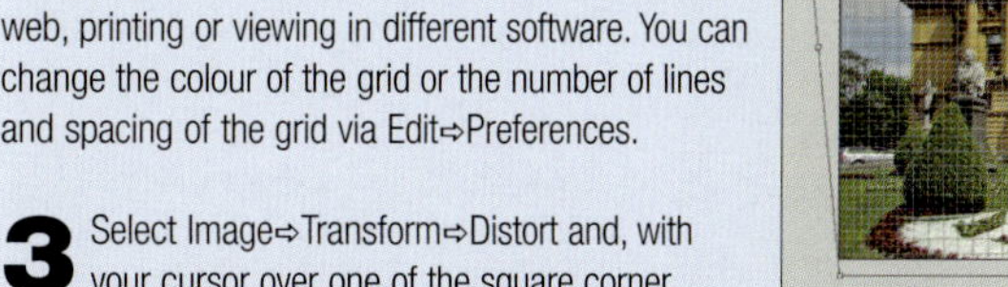

6 Magnify the image to check for perfect alignment using the grid. When you are satisfied, click inside the image area or press the Return key to process the transformation.

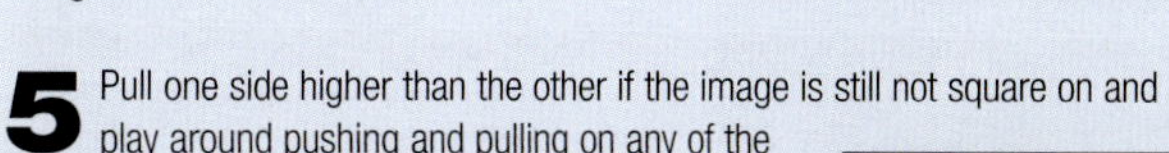

If you drag the picture inwards on the canvas, use the Crop tool to remove blank canvas and square up the photo.

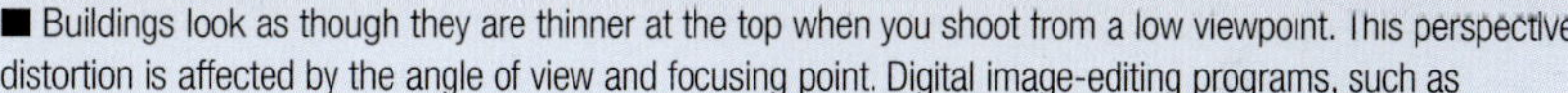

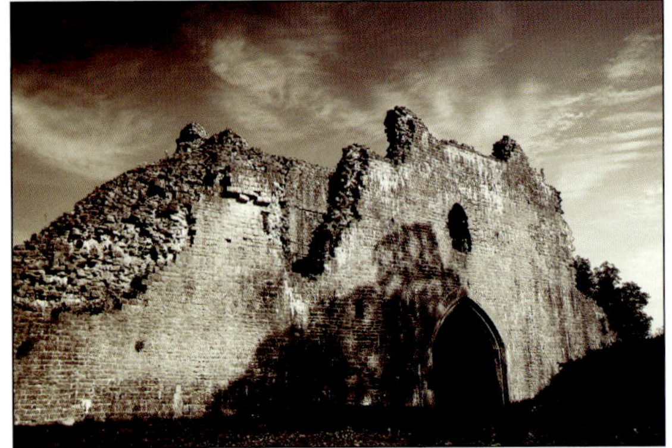

● MARI STERLING St Quentins Castle, Llanbleddian, Cowbridge, Vale of Glamorgan. Recently restored remains of an old castle.

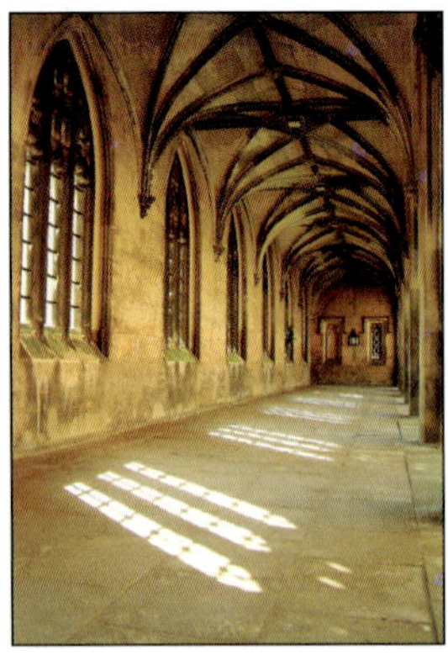

● CHRIS GIRLING The cloudy WB setting was used as a warm up.

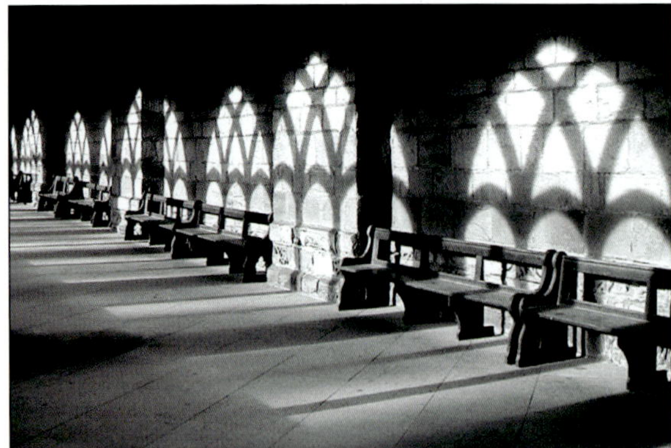

● GARY BRIGGS This was taken at Durham Cathedral as the sun broke through to show the building detail outside the frame.

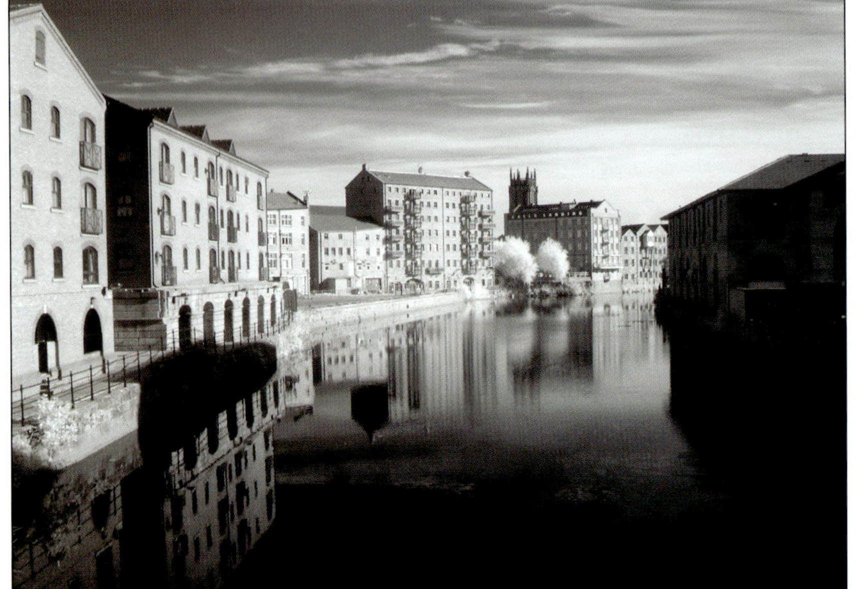

● STEVE SHARP Call Landings, Leeds. Taken with Nikon Coolpix 990 with Wratten 87 IR filter attached.

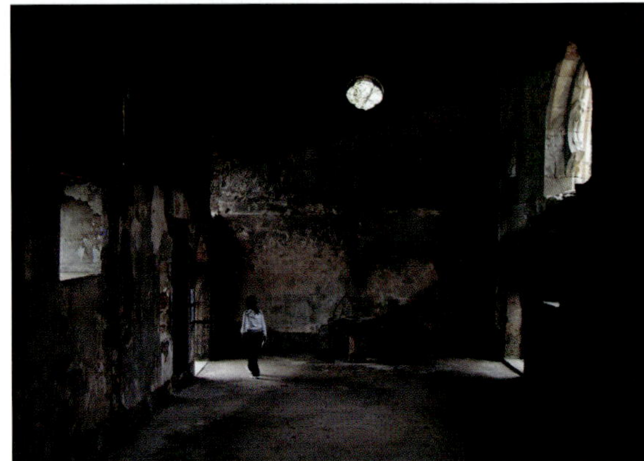

● IAN WILSON This old church is within the grounds of Skipton Castle. It was taken handheld with an Olympus C50 digital compact.

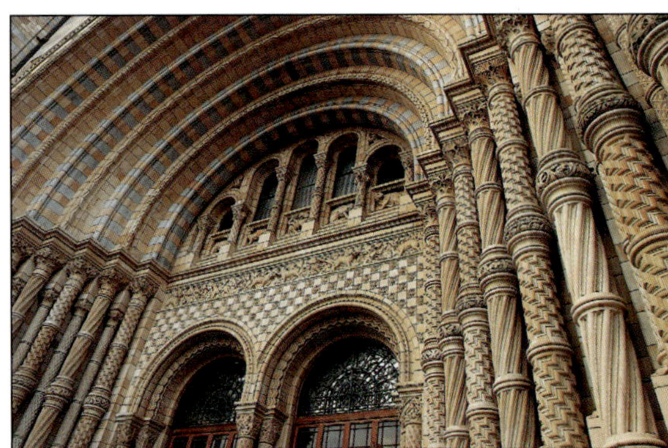

● BRIAN PRICE The 17mm lens meant depth-of-field was OK even at f/4.5. Angled upwards to make converging verticals less obvious.

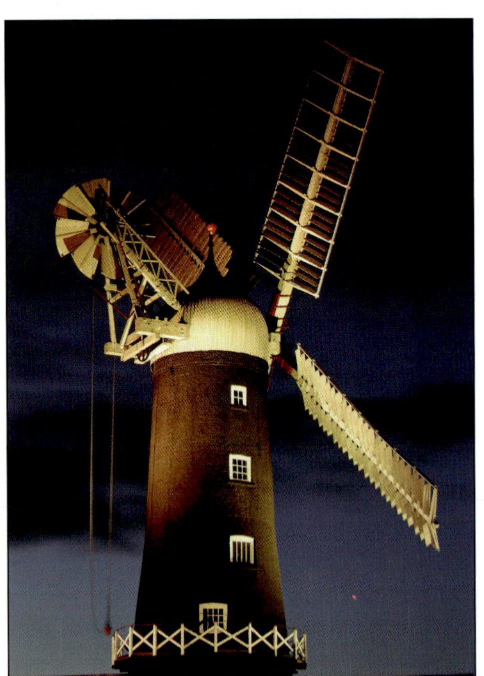

● PAUL GIBBINS Skidy Mill, East Yorkshire using a Canon EOS 300D, 18-55 lens at 55mm and a 6sec, f/8 exposure.

HISTORICAL HOUSES

■ Two of the best sources of information about historical houses are The National Trust and English Heritage. Both have reduced entrance fees for members, but photography is not always permitted.

■ English Heritage cares for about 400 sites which includes properties such as Battle Abbey in East Sussex, Leeds Castle near Maidstone in Kent, Tintagel Castle in Cornwall, Castle Rising Castle in Norfolk, Bolsover Castle in Derbyshire, Fountains Abbey in North Yorkshire and Castle Howard in York. **www.english-heritage.org.uk**

■ The National Trust has around 300 historic houses and gardens and includes properties such as St Michael's Mount in Cornwall, Charlecote Park in Warwick, Calke Abbey in Ticknall, Derby, Dunham Massey in Altrincham, Lindisfarne Castle on Holy Island, Berwick-upon-Tweed and Tattershall Castle in Lincoln.
www.nationaltrust.org.uk

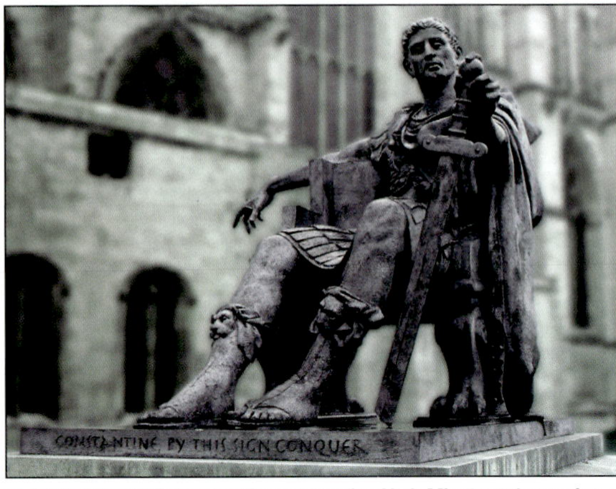

● PAUL WILLOWS Constantine overseeing York Minster taken using a Fuji S602 with adjustments to colour and background in Photoshop.

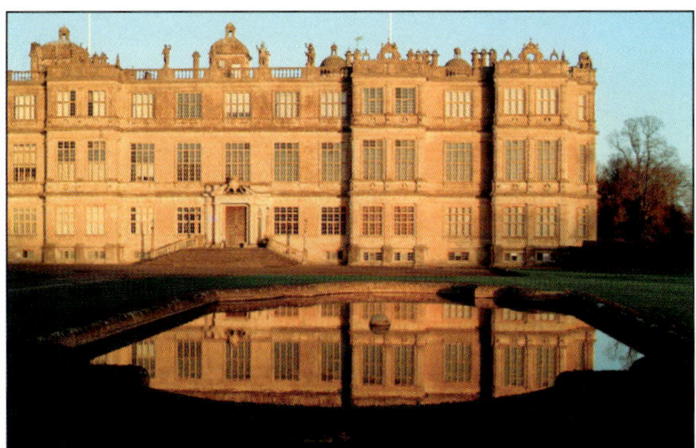

● ALAN BENSON Longleat House, Wiltshire, taken as the sun was rising, lighting up the house and casting a reflection across the water.

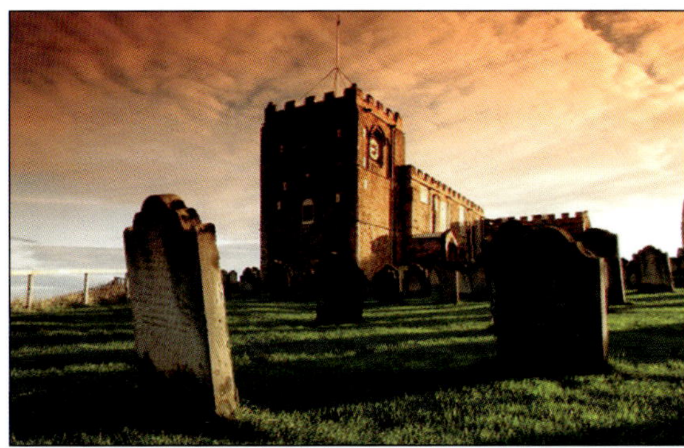

● MARTIN WESTON The church stands on the cliffs above Whitby harbour. I used a wide-angle lens set at f/16 and a grad filter.

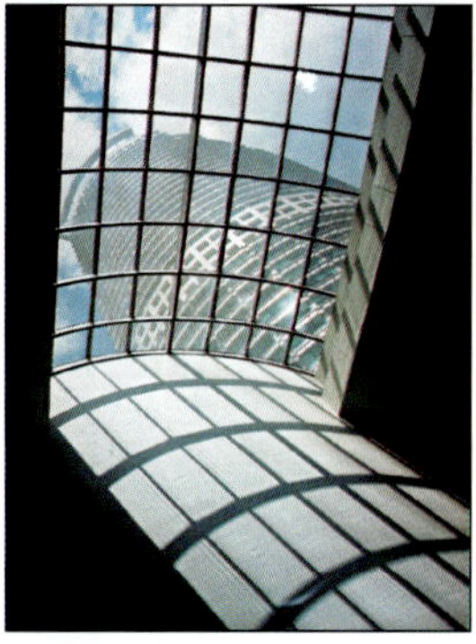

● MATT ZAIN ABDULLAH Pattern formed by shadows.

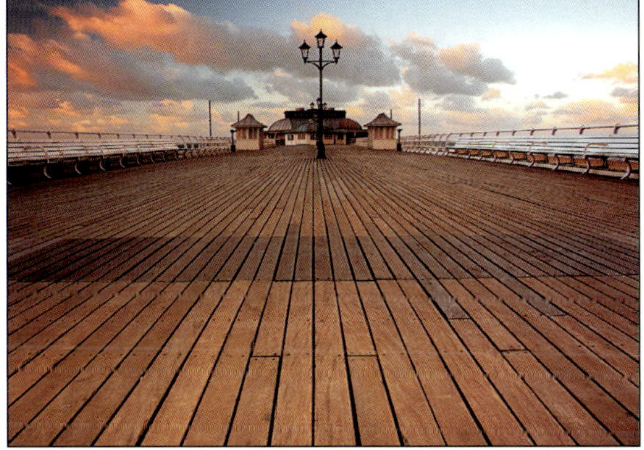

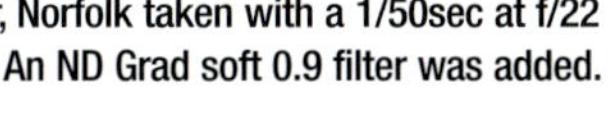

● KATE BARCLAY Cromer Pier, Norfolk taken with a 1/50sec at f/22 exposure in RAW and ISO200. An ND Grad soft 0.9 filter was added.

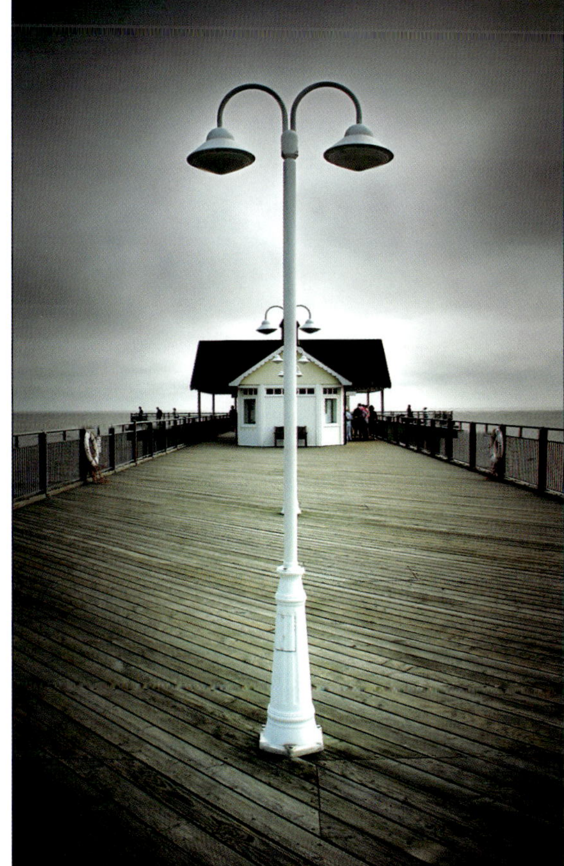

● KATHY WRIGHT Bat willows in the Waveney Valley, on the Norfolk/ Suffolk border. Taken using a Canon 300D, Canon 35-135mm.

SHOOTING TIPS – INFRARED WITH FILM & DIGITAL CAMERAS

■ Infrared photography offers some unusual, but very interesting, characteristics for creative photographers. Infrared is outside the visible spectrum, but it can be captured on special film and on some digital cameras.

■ **Film options** include Kodak High Speed Infrared, Konica R750, Ilford SFX 200 and Rollei IR820.

■ **Which filter?** Infrared films also see visible light so you need to block it out using a filter. Some photographers use a normal 8x red, but for the best results you need a special, almost opaque, R72 infrared filter. They are available in glass from Hoya and B+W or in Gels from Kodak and Lee.

■ **Which film camera?** Most film cameras will work unless the pressure plate, that's on the hinged film back, is dimpled or has an aperture cut out to allow data to be recorded. Both these will cause patterns or shapes to appear on film. Shoot a test roll to see. Another problem is the auto film advance that uses an infrared sensor to count sprockets when advancing each frame on many Canon EOS SLRs and a few Minolta Dynax models. This fogs the edge of the frame.

■ **Which digital camera?** Infrared style photos can be created using some digital cameras. One of the best was the 2 megapixel Nikon Coolpix 950, but other newer models may be as successful. Most models have a special infrared-blocking filter in front of the CCD and, because of this, deliver limited brightness in the foliage and a huge colour cast when an infrared filter is attached. Check the Internet for camera recommendations.

■ **Which subject?** Foliage reflects much more infrared light so you start to see interesting glowing effects and blue skies become almost black so landscapes are among the favourite subjects. You can also produce great effects when photographing people, especially their eyes, which go black while veins can appear to be on the surface of the skin, which goes pure white. Nudes are popular. Overgrown grave stones look spooky, as do stone circles and derelict buildings.

■ **What's the best time of day?** Infrared light appears at its best in bright sunlight, especially the hours just after sunrise and before sunset, because of the angle of the sunlight through the atmosphere. You won't find much infrared light when the sky is overcast. Take photographs with the sun either behind or at most 90 degrees to the camera – the area of deepest blue is the area that is more likely to go black.

■ **How do I focus?** Infrared light does not focus on the same plane as daylight so this throws out the camera's automatic focusing and the subject will be blurred. If you have an autofocus camera switch to manual and, as a guide, set the focus so it's about 50cm closer than the indicated distance and use a small aperture to ensure maximum depth-of-field. Shoot a trial first using your various lenses and make notes so you can refer back and see what does and doesn't work.

■ **What about exposure?** Cameras with automatic metering adjust the exposure to compensate for the dark filter being placed in front of the lens. For cameras without meters, or ones that don't read through the lens, allow the following: Orange 4x 2 stops, Red 8x 3 stops, Infrared R72 3.5 stops. On digital cameras it depends on the infrared blocking filter. Do a trial first.

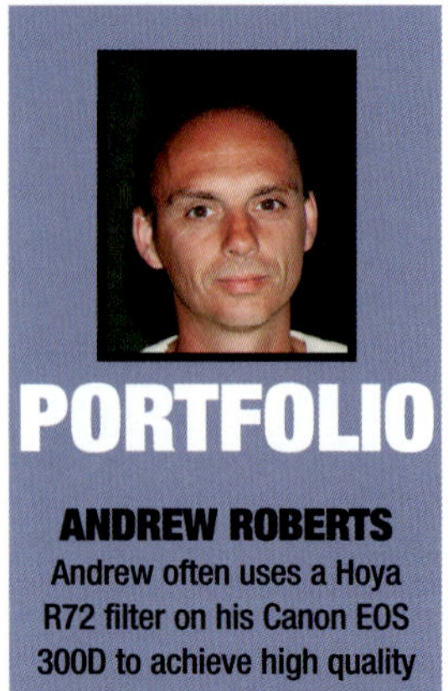

PORTFOLIO

ANDREW ROBERTS
Andrew often uses a Hoya R72 filter on his Canon EOS 300D to achieve high quality infrared photographs

I got my first camera, a Praktica MTL5, at 14 but I didn't become serious about photography until a friend introduced me to ePHOTOzine.

My main interest is architectue and I enjoy photographing castles, standing stones and burial chambers. I look for castles with a moat around them and fluffy white clouds to add interest to the image. I prefer infrared photography, which seems to have punchier tones than black & white. It also produces a surreal effect when used with long shutter speeds on my EOS 300D!

To get the best from my photographs I start off by walking around the subject, which allows me to get a feel for the place, finding the best angle or viewpoint.

I've been fully digital since Canon introduced the EOS 300D and I was able to switch from a 35mm EOS. Apart from the camera, the equipment I consider essential for my photography is a tripod or bean bag.

I also enjoy landscape and wildlife photography and occasionally some macro work.

My interest in wildlife was awakened on safari in Namibia. I won an all-expenses paid trip as first prize in the Panasonic Photo Awards 2004. It was a real dream come true and my proudest photographic achievement.

Photography has always been just a hobby for me but in the future I would love to be able to make a living from it. ■
email: dalamans@aol.com

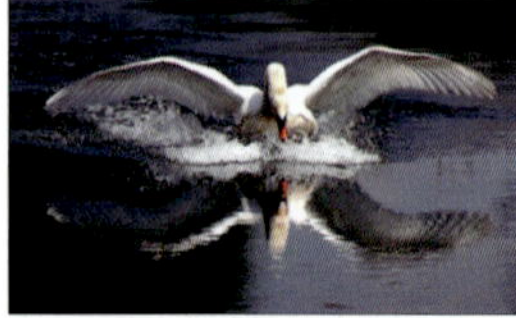

● Andrew's winning photo was selected from over 5000 entries.

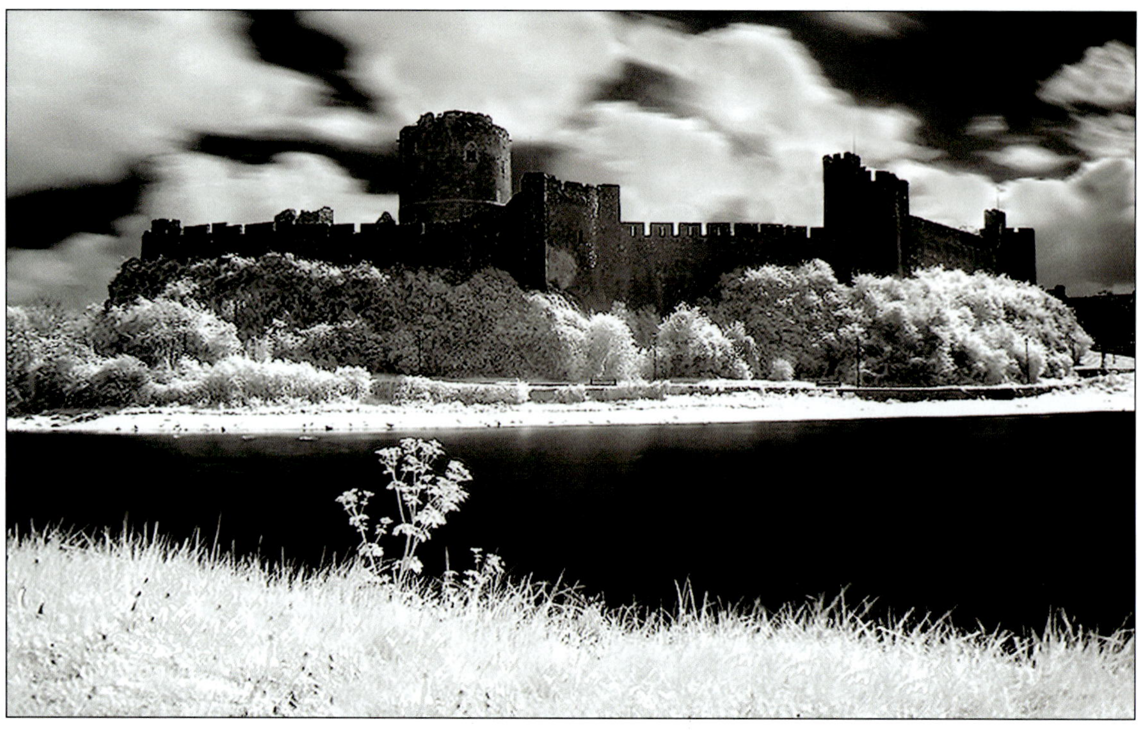

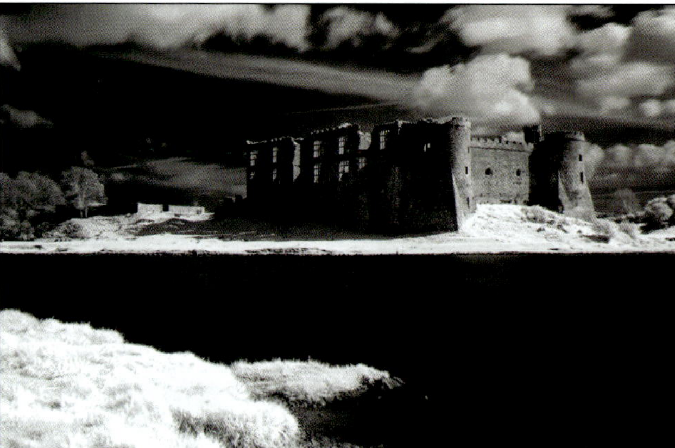

● Three photos, all Welsh castles, taken using a Hoya R72 filter and a long exposure of around 25 seconds to achieve the surreal infrared effect. Andrew used a Canon EOS 300D and a Sigma 18-50mm zoom lens set at f/4.5.

Top: Pembroke Castle in West Wales. In this shot the wind was strong and the moving clouds help to give the photograph a timeless feel.

Middle: Carew Castle West Wales. The infrared effect lightens all vegetation, so the grass around the castle and in the foreground becomes much brighter and almost glows.

Bottom: Carew in West Wales. Infrared darkens blue so the areas of clear sky become almost black and a total contrast to the clouds, making the scene much more dramatic.

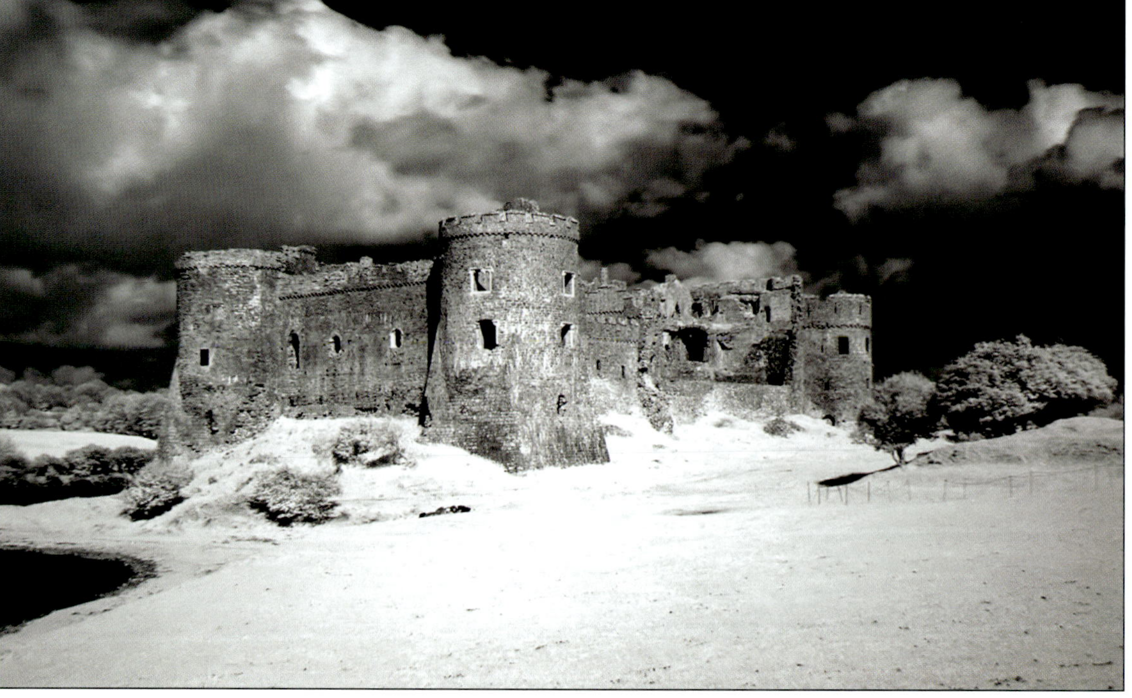

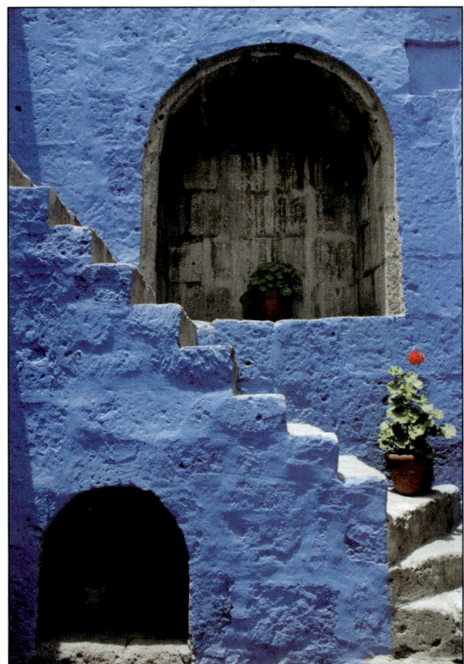

● MELISSA WEIR Santa Catalina monastery, Arequipa, Peru. Taken using Nikon D70 and 18mm lens at f/6.3.

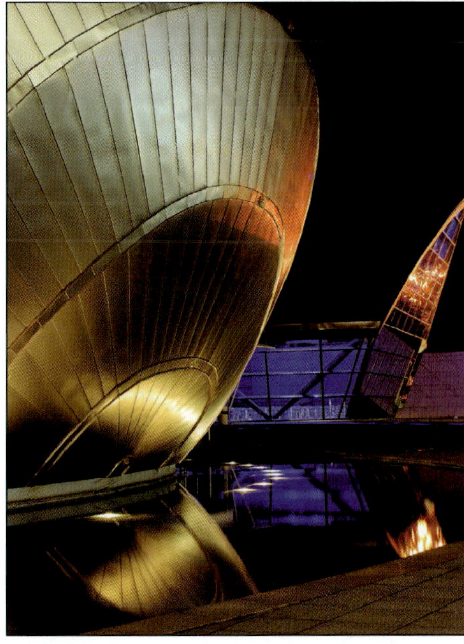

● STUART MACLAREN Glasgow Science Museum with an exposure of f/8 at 20secs and tungsten white balance.

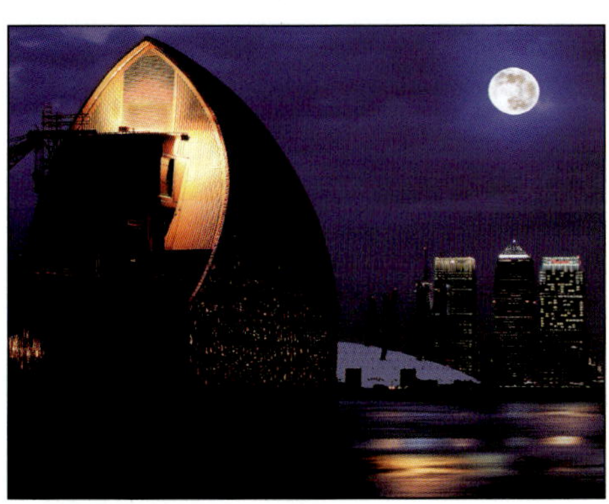

● TONY HEPWORTH Canary Wharf from the Thames Barrier, shot with a Canon EOS 10D and Sigma 15-30mm.

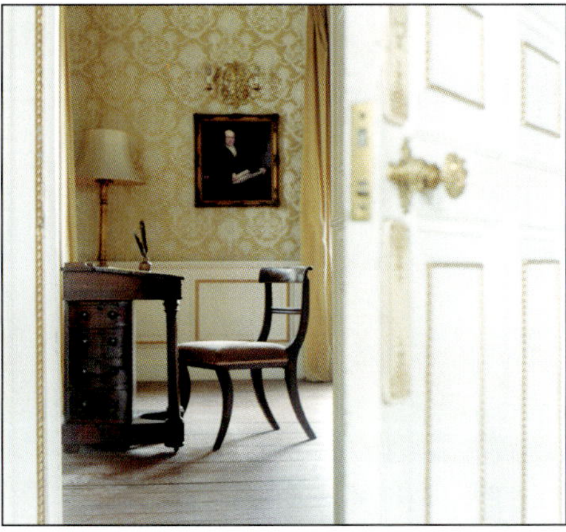

● MARTIN STEWART Boston Manor House, a 17th Century stately home in west London. Shot with a medium-format camera and window light.

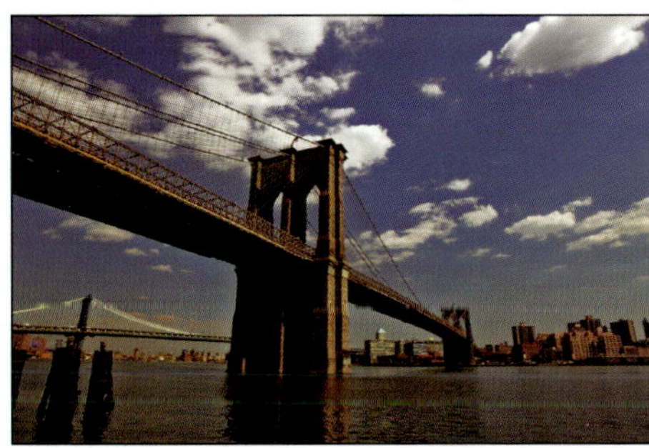

● EDWARD NORTON Roebling's legacy, taken using a Canon EOS1DII with 17-35mm L at 17mm.

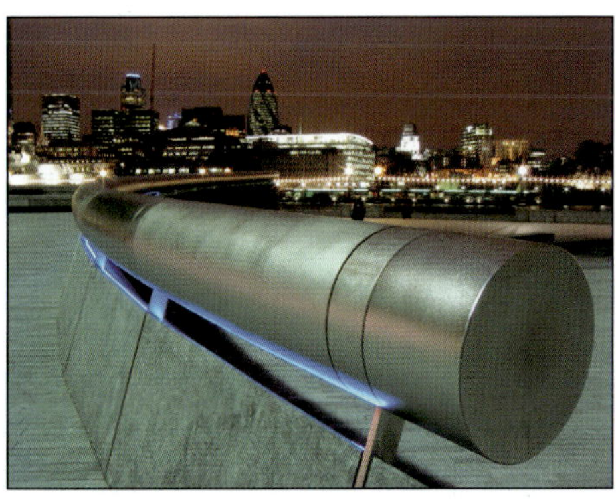

● KEN BOURN City of London from the south bank of the Thames – along exposure was set to avoid flash.

LOW LIGHT EXPOSURE GUIDE

■ There are certain illuminated scenes that are similar in brightness value wherever they are photographed, so exposure values listed in the table below can be used as a guide. If your camera doesn't have an f/2.8 lens adjust the shutter speed as necessary.

Floodlit building	1/2sec	f/2.8
Shop window	1/8sec	f/2.8
Typical street scene	1/2sec	f/2/8
Christmas light street scene	1/15sec	f/2.8
Brightly lit theatre districts	1/30sec	f/2.8

The settings are based on cameras loaded with film or digital CCDs at ISO100. You can compensate for different film speeds. Don't forget to set the white balance or use the correct filter to avoid a colour cast.

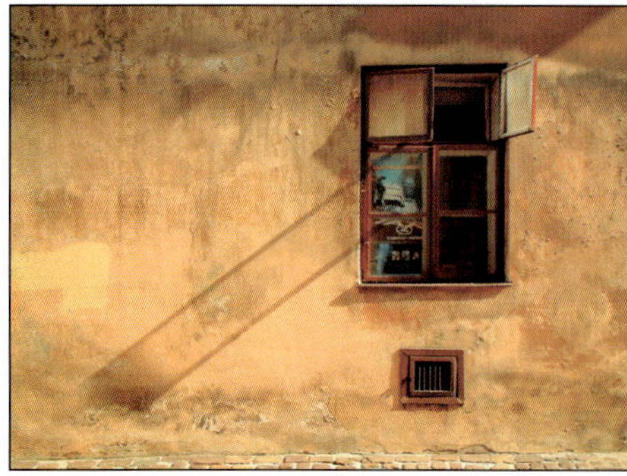

● PAWEL ZASUN Jagiellonska Street in Krakow, Poland. "I waited 20 minutes for the sun to create this shadow."

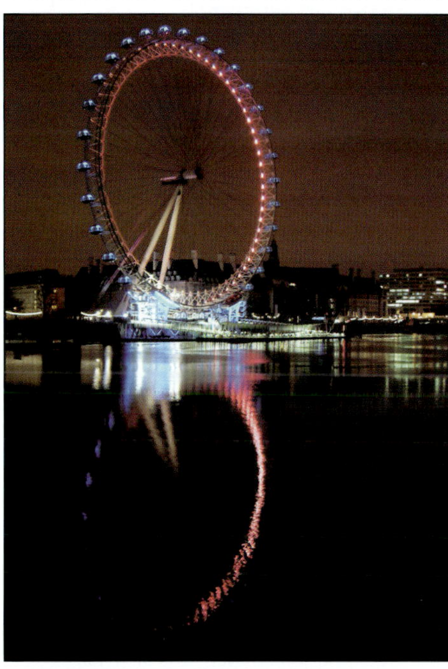

● TONY MARSH London Eye lit in pink for Valentine's Day. A 1sec exposure helped retain detail in the reflection.

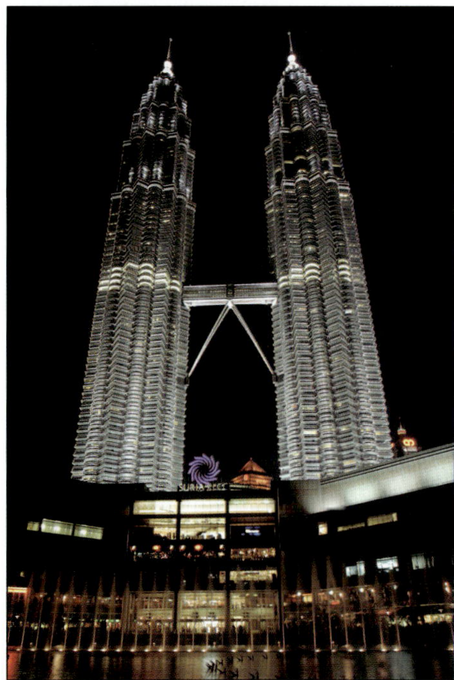

● NIC CLEAVE Petronas Towers, Kuala Lumpur, using Canon EOS 10D and 17-40mm L. 3sec exposure at f/5.6.

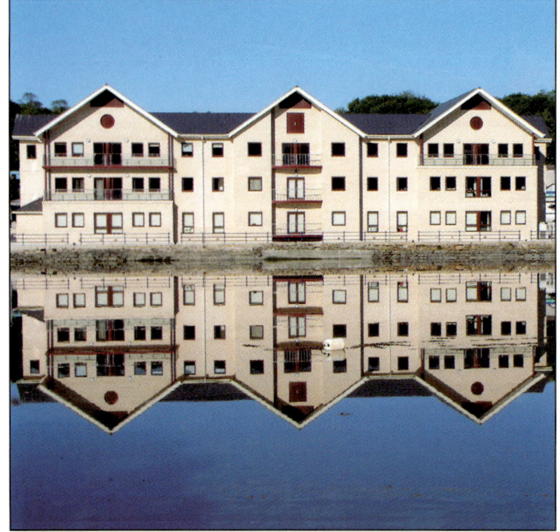

● RICHARD INGRAM PENROSE An early morning shot of Truro River. Soft light and hardly a breath of wind gives the smooth reflection.

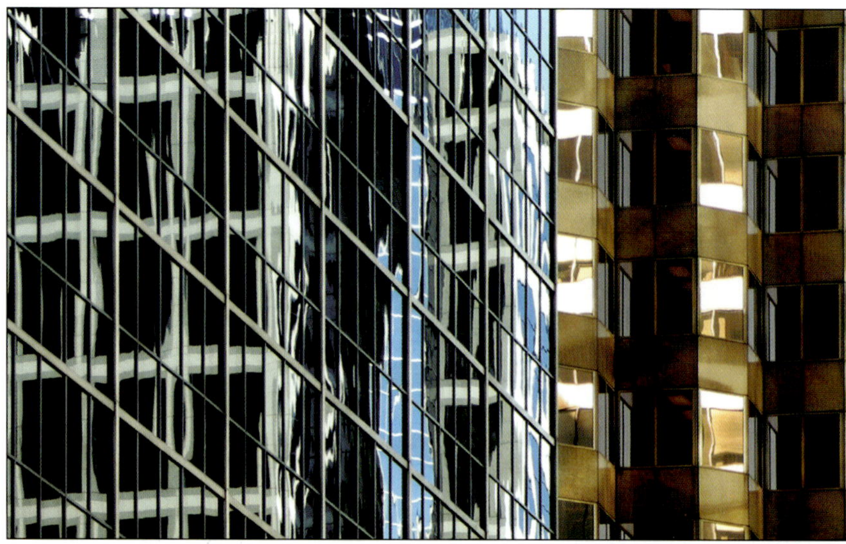

● ARTHUR CHAN Several downtown buildings in Vancouver and their reflections, taken on a Canon EOS D60 with the lens set at 74mm. The exposure was 1/125sec at f/5.6 on ISO200.

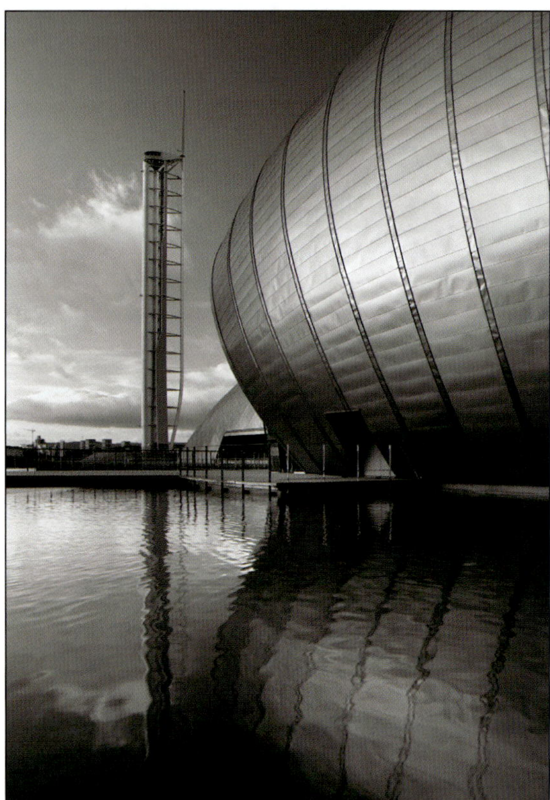

● PAUL GAUGHAN Glasgow Science Centre & Glasgow Tower. Inspired by B&W photographs I saw of these amazing structures.

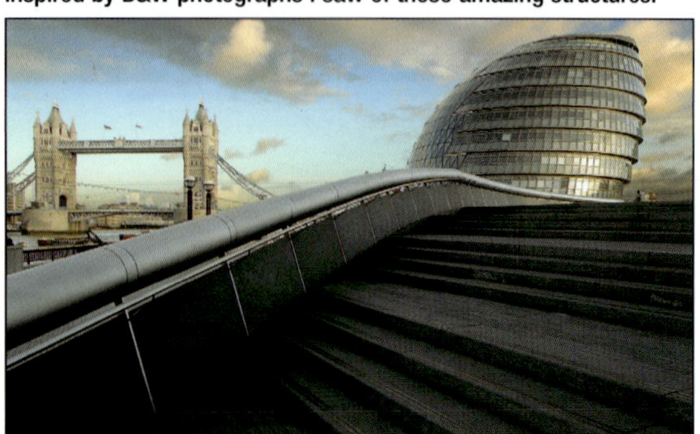

● PAUL BROWN London's City Hall, the Mayor's Office, at dusk. Taken during a walk after work. Exposure f/6.3 and 1/90sec, ISO400.

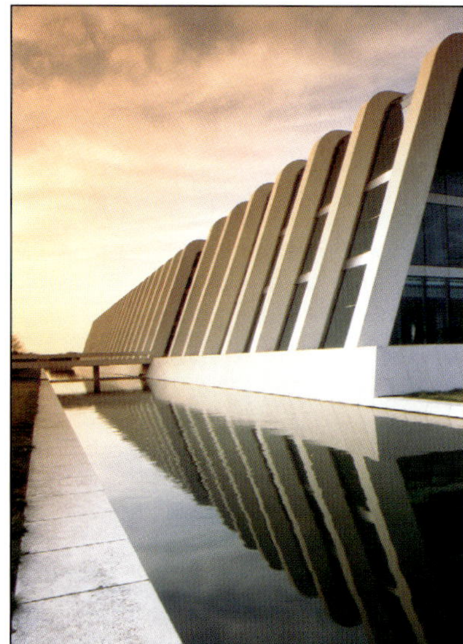

● RICHARD ALLEN Taken at the Cambridge science park using a graduated tobacco filter on a Nikon FA and a 24mm Nikkor lens.

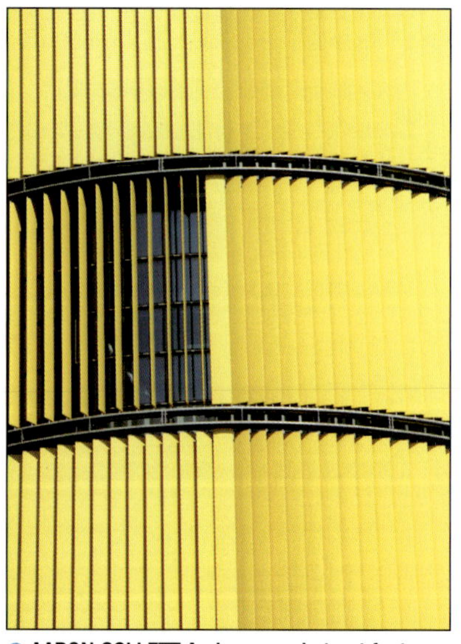

● AARON COLLETT A close-up abstract feature on a building in Berlin.

ARCHITECTURE SHOOTING TIPS

■ Take photographs in the early morning or late afternoon when the light is at its best.

■ Avoid photographing in the bright sun at midday, unless the subject is glass or a modern sculpture. In those cases, the sun can help to highlight features.

■ Many buildings are too tall to capture in one frame, so don't ruin your shot trying to squeeze it all in. Instead, pick out an interesting feature on one segment of the building and home in on that.

■ Alter viewpoint. Get on your knees and shoot upward or go across the street and photograph the building from a high window or roof-top.

■ Try photographing historical buildings like libraries, museums or older hospitals, which often have interesting pillars and decorative stonework.

■ Cathedrals and churches offer many interesting opportunities, such as gargoyles and other decorative stonework, stained glass windows and tall spires.

■ The building doesn't have to be the main focal point – focusing on something interesting in the foreground, such as a stairway or path, can add interest and lead the eye naturally into the image.

■ Make use of the surroundings to help tell a story by placing the building in context within its environment.

■ If the building you photograph is on private land gain permission before attempting to take photos.

■ If your photography is for commercial use you must make this clear before taking pictures as you may require permission for this.

■ Many well-known buildings are copyright-protected, especially if you're a commercial photographer.

■ Do your research on the building – knowing a bit about its history could help you to pick out interesting features that you may have previously overlooked.

■ Walk around the building first to pick out the best angle and find which parts get the best light.

■ Avoid getting people in your photo by taking it early in the morning, when fewer will be around.

■ However, lots of people milling around can make an image seem more real, creating a bustling scene with the building at its centre.

■ If photographing modern architecture, try shooting in black & white for an interesting contrast image.

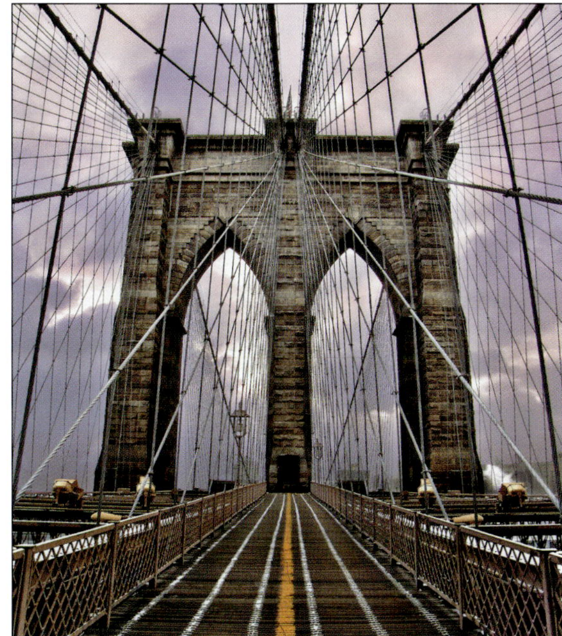

● DAVID PRITCHARD Brooklyn Bridge, 8am and snowing. The exposure was 1/60sec, f/6.3 and perspective corrected in Photoshop.

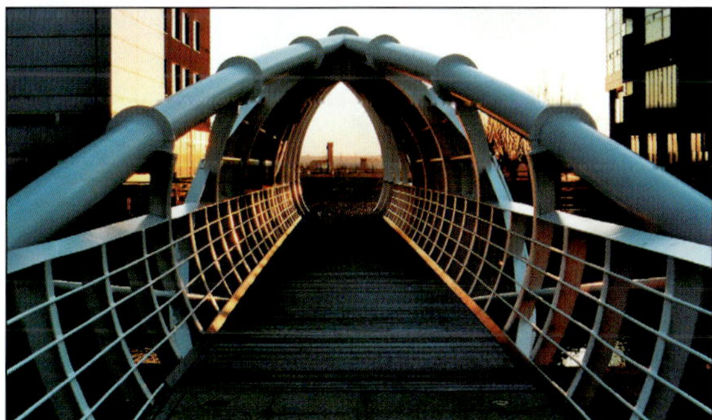

● ERIC FARAGHER Sunlit bridge at Liverpool waterfront on Olympus OM10/50mm. Appears with permission of Chapter Thirteen Photography.

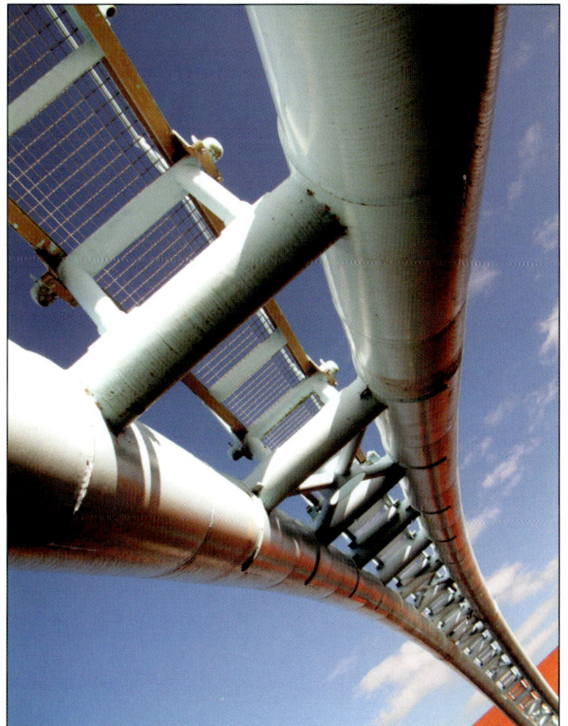

● MARK CAVENDISH Water Pipes, Ely River, Cardiff. Acting on ideas from ePHOTOzine members, I revisited this location and reshot.

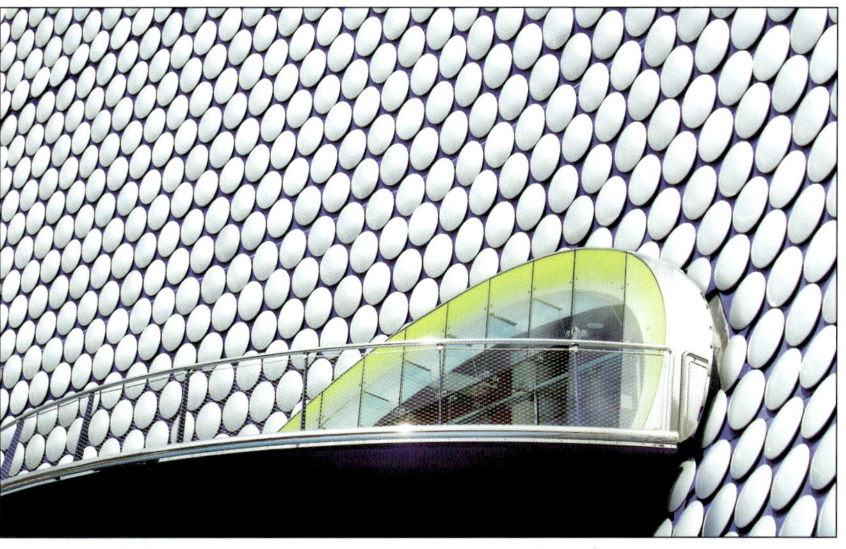

● LUCREZIA HERMAN Exterior detail of Selfridges in Birmingham, taken with an Olympus 5050 at f/8.

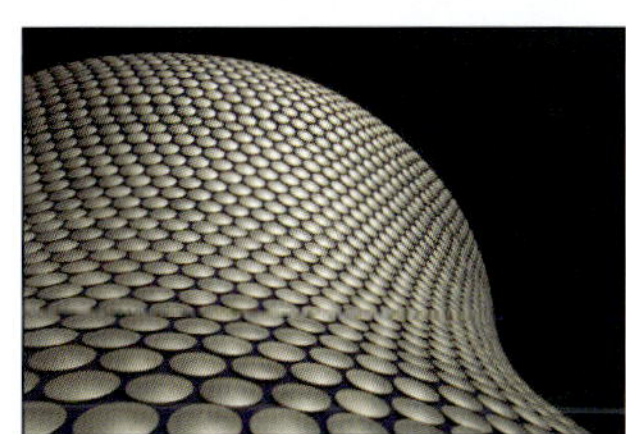

● PETER BARGH Selfridges building is also superb for creating abstract patterns against a blue sky, but beware, you may be questioned by the security team!

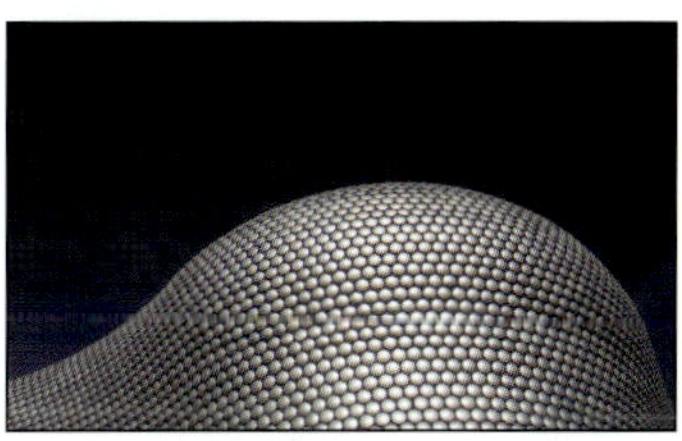

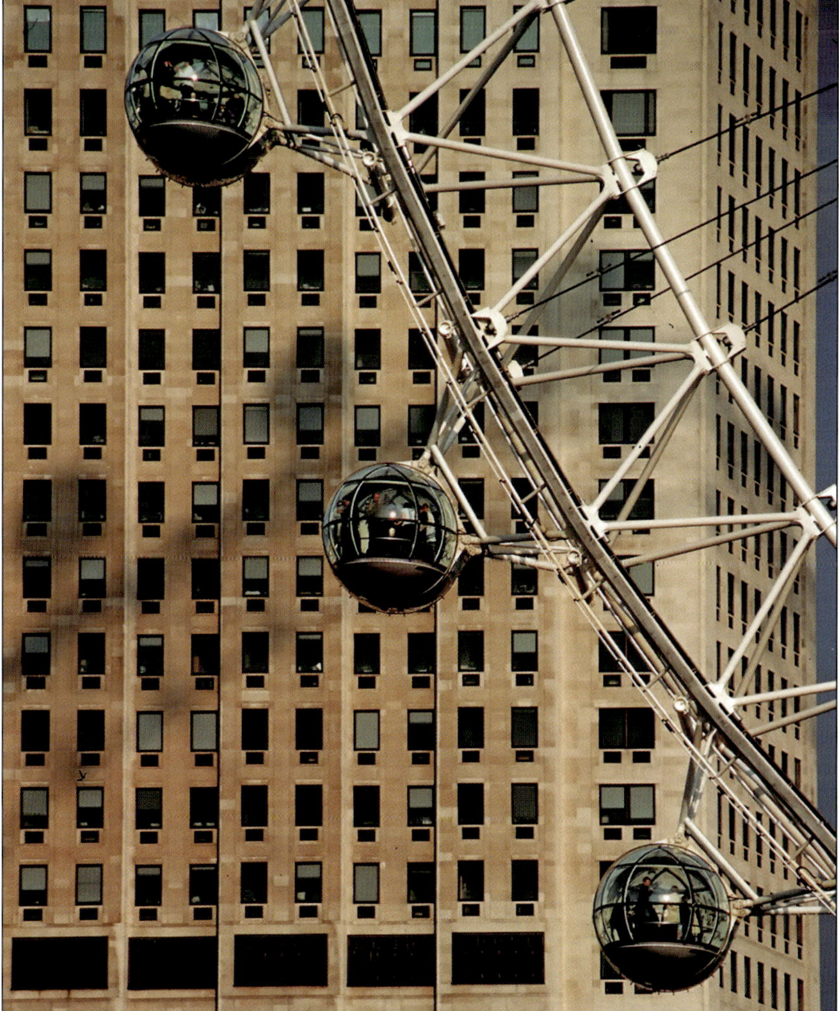

● BARRY REID "The effect of the shadow behind the wheel inspired me to take this shot on a Canon T90 with 70-210mm lens. The perspective was corrected in Photoshop."

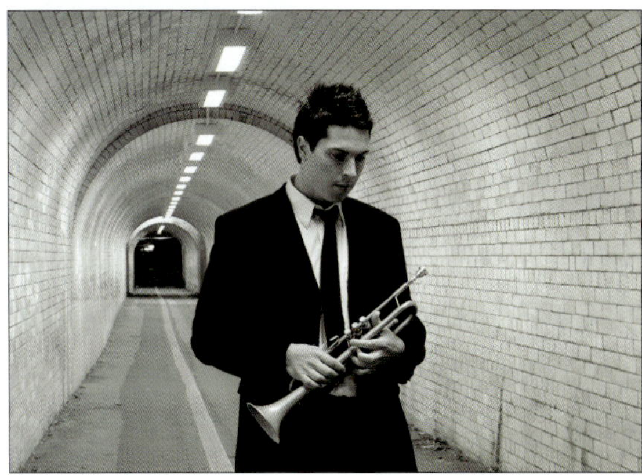

● FUNKELDINK Taken as part of a shoot for an album for singer/songwriter Danny Gough.

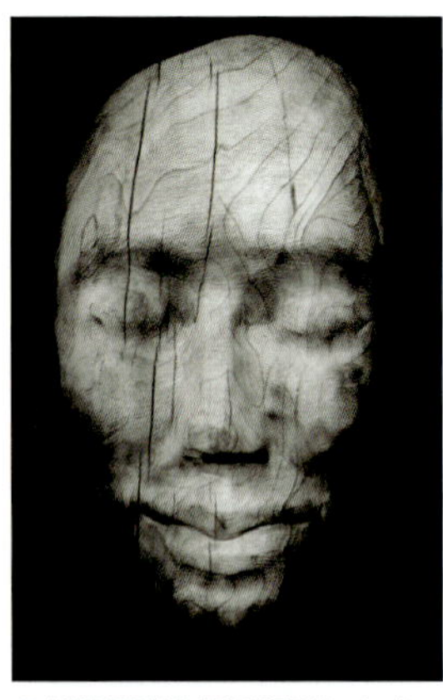

● ANDREW GARDNER Part of The Big Tree in Paignton.

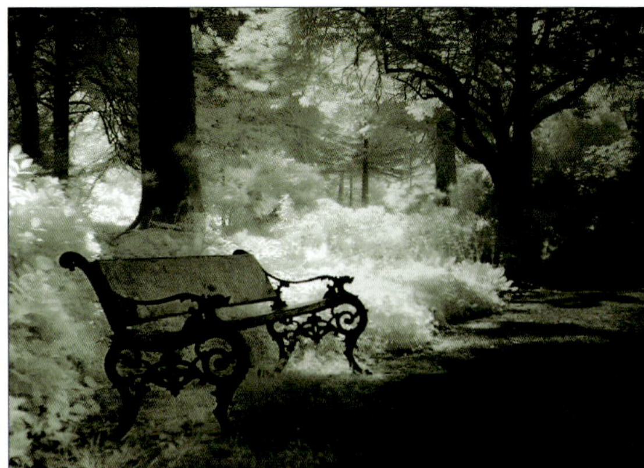

● ANGIE BARNETT Infrared shot of Torosay Castle Gardens, Isle of Mull, Scotland, using 89B Cokin IR filter and toning with Photoshop 6.

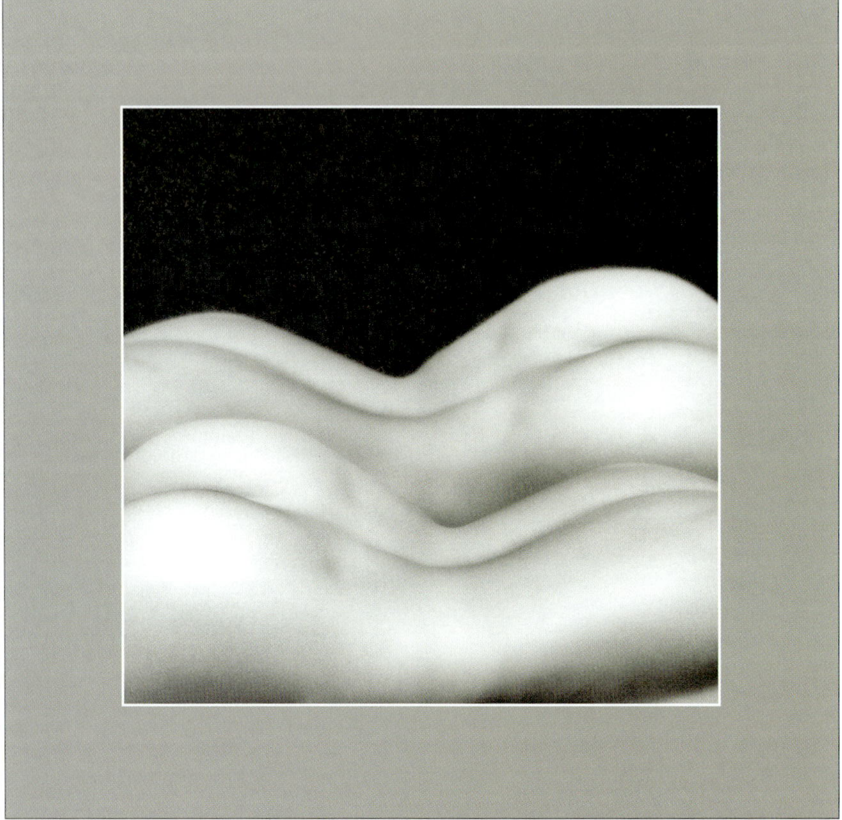

● VICTOR HABBICK A three feet square window light was suspended over models and a Nikon D100 with 35mm lens was used. Retouched in Photoshop CS to create the reticulation effect.

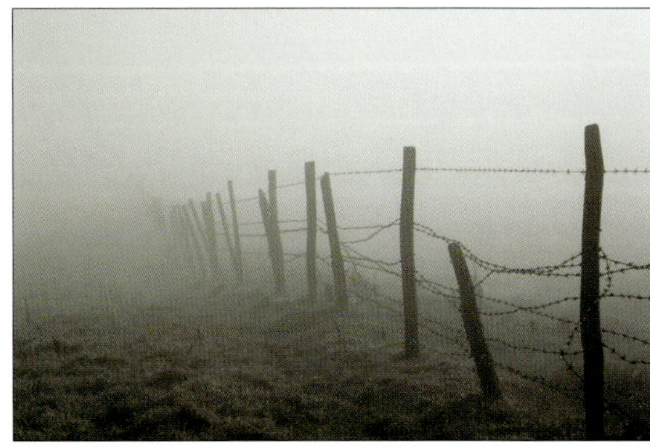

● DENNIS REDDICK Taken on Ditchling Beacon, South Downs. "It was very wet and windy, so I covered the camera with a dustbin bag."

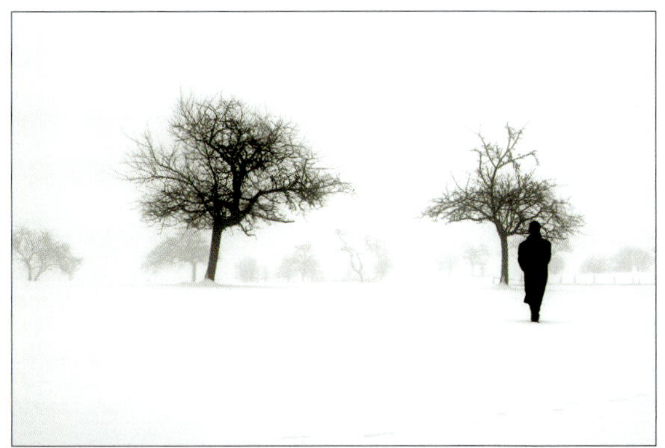

● IIONA WELLMANN Digital capture taken using the camera's B&W setting and 1/250sec at f/6.4. Contrast adjusted in Photoshop.

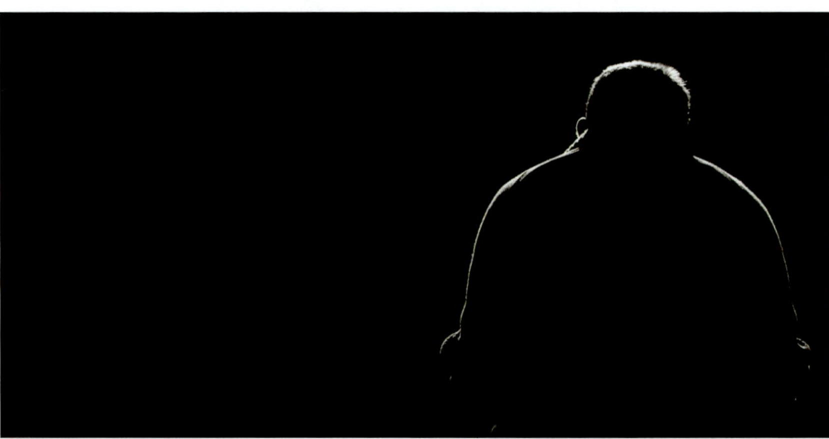

● LUCREZIA HERMAN This rim-lit person was taken with an Olympus 5050 outside London's City Hall. The image was converted to black & white using Channels in Photoshop CS.

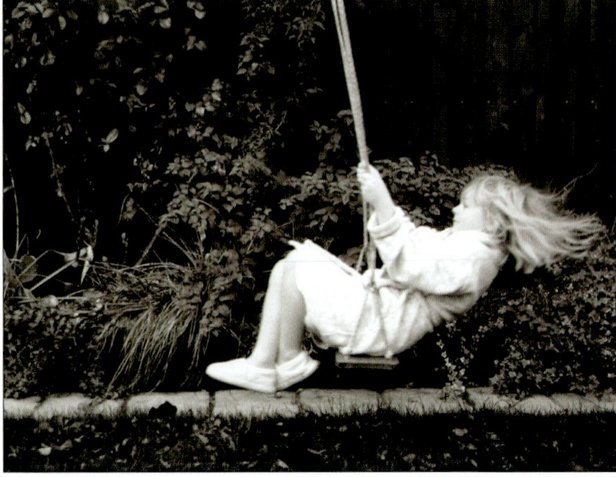

● JEANETTE LAZENBY "It felt good to see such simple pleasures are still enjoyed today – Beth loves her swing!" Exposure 1/250 at f/4.5.

Black & white

Since the invention of photography, images of our colour world have been recorded in a series of greyscale tones. Names such as Ansel Adams, Bill Brandt, Irving Penn, Bob Carlos Clarke, David Bailey and Elliot Erwitt have continued to tantalise our visual tastebuds with outstanding black & white photography. Our ePHOTOzine members have been doing so too!

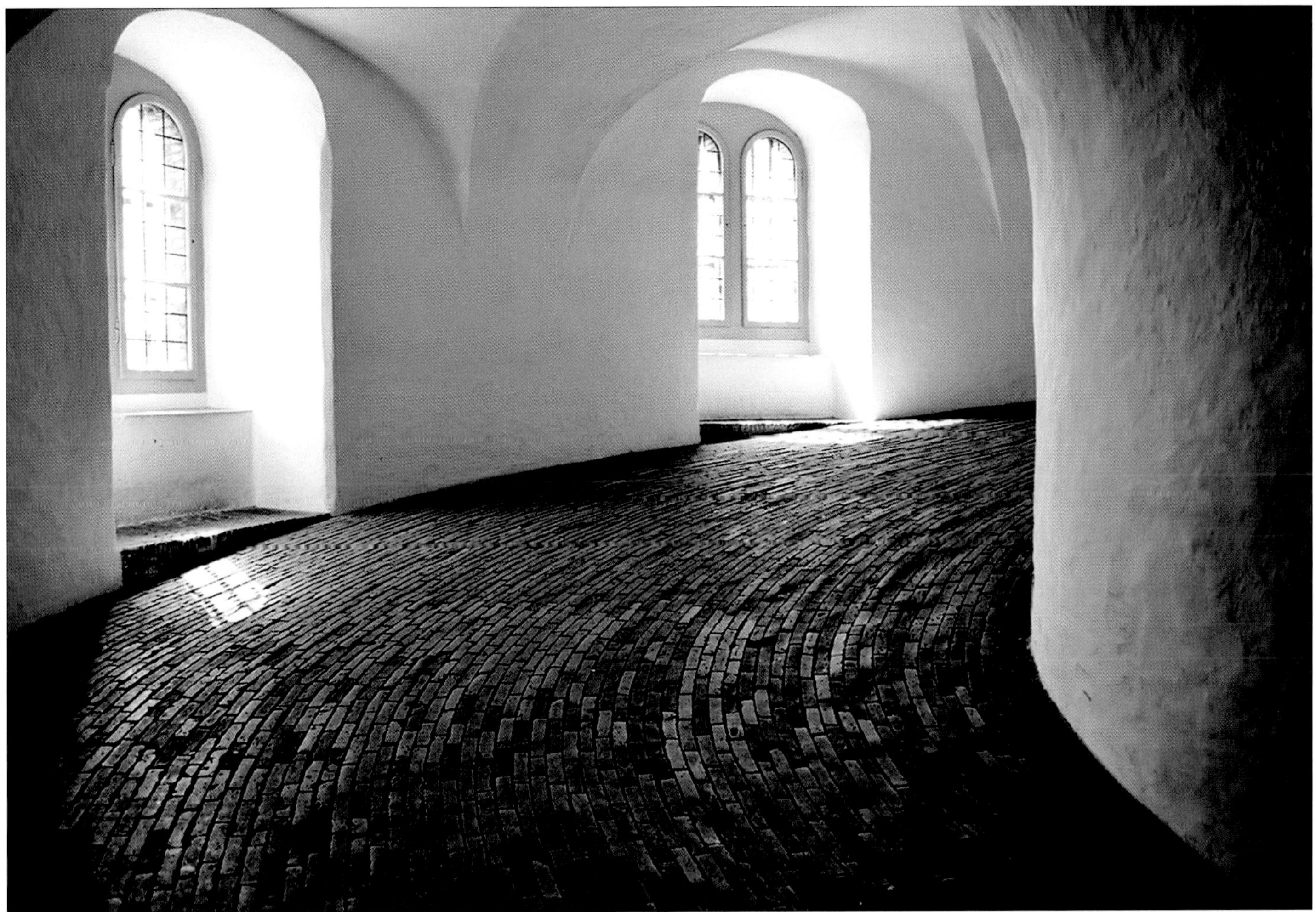

● STEVE BRIDDON The Rundtarn, Copenhagen, taken with available light, using a Canon 50mm f/1.8 lens on an EOS 33 loaded with Kodak Supra ISO400 film. The photograph was converted to black & white to place more emphasis on the texture of the walls.

The pioneers of photography, such as Henry Fox Talbot and Louis Daguerre had no choice but to record our world in black & white, but by helping create the photographic process they also helped many photographers see things differently.

Although our world is in glorious colour, the conversion to black & white gives us opportunities to see the world in a new way. With our senses not being influenced by the colour we start to appreciate the shapes, patterns and textures.

This dramatic transformation was what made Ansel Adams' views of the Yosemite Valley so magical. The colourful greens of the vegetation being replaced by subtle tonal differences and textures that leap off the print.

Ansel Adams took his exposure so seriously that he developed a whole new way of exposure and processing to ensure that each photograph captured a complete tonal range. This system, known as the Zone System, was the reason why many photographers invested in a darkroom.

Today digital photography has more or less killed the darkroom, with historic companies such as Agfa falling by the wayside. Fortunately, despite a rocky few years, film manufacturer Ilford survived and continues to provide a superb range of film and chemicals for lovers of black & white processing.

And for the masses now embracing digital technology, you have the option to shoot digital in colour and convert to black & white, or scan in old colour or black & white material and convert. From there the computer replaces the darkroom, allowing you to achieve a whole load of things that only the alchemist could have done in the darkroom. There are no smelly chemicals, no complicated chemical mixing and no dark rooms. More or less anything that was possible in the darkroom is possible with an image editing program.

You can create antique printing effects, dodge and burn, create lith effects, special effects and masking techniques. You can adjust contrast as you could using variable-contrast papers and you can tone in any shade of colour you like.

You can even recreate the tonal ranges that Ansel Adams would have achieved using his Zone System and can replicate contrast control filters, such as red and orange.

Once you've edited the image so it looks bright and punchy, you can either send the file to a processing lab to output or use an inkjet printer to create an enlargement for your album or wall. It's here where many darkroom users have become despondent. While the photograph on screen may look more stunning than anything created in the darkroom, with subtle tonal differences, great detail in the shadows and brilliant highlights, the inkjet output may have inherited a colour cast with a flattened tonal range.

To overcome this, inkjet manufacturers work hard to develop substitute inksets for printers made by companies such as Epson, Lyson and Permajet. For example, a set of black inks of varying intensity is made to replace standard CMYK inks and help recreate the tonal gradation delivered by silver halide products. Darkroom users are happy again!

If you've never tried black & white, at least have a go at one of our suggested conversion techniques on one of your colour photos. Once converted you'll start to shoot and see the world like the pioneers, and maybe you'll discover a whole new world of photography to experiment with. ■

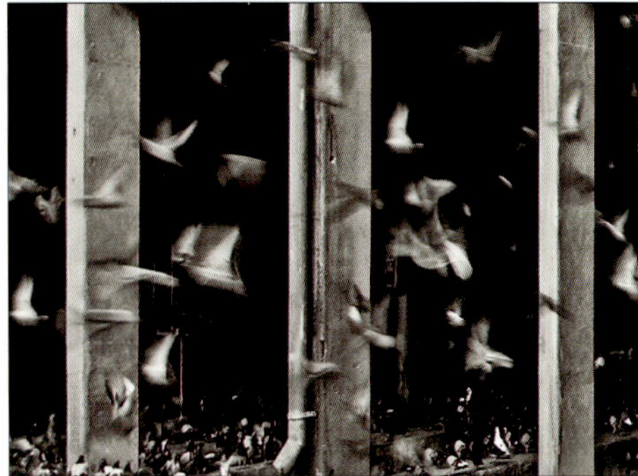

● HERMIN ABRAMOVITCH Pigeons in a grain warehouse at ISO100 and an exposure of f/8 and 1/20sec.

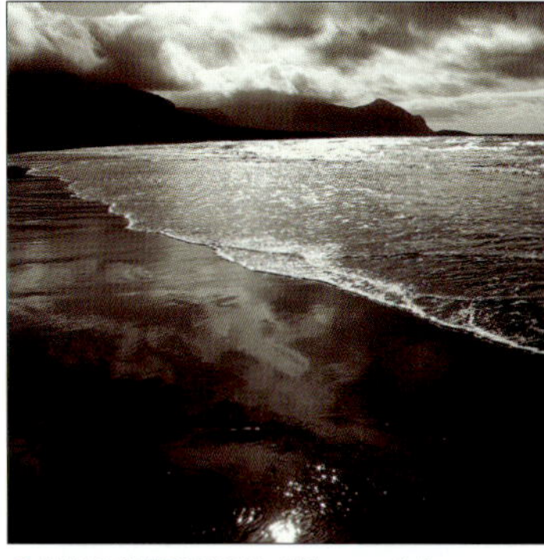

● MARI STERLING Yr Eifl mountains, shrouded in cloud from Lleyn Peninsula.

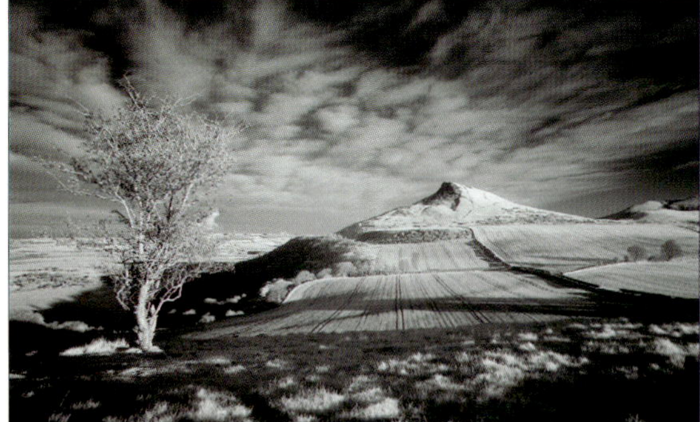

● STEVE SHARP Roseberry Topping, bathed in morning sunlight, and captured using a Nikon Coolpix 990 and Hoya RM90 Infrared filter.

DIGITAL TECHNIQUE – CONVERTING COLOUR TO BLACK & WHITE

■ One of the great things about digital photography is that you don't need two camera bodies – one loaded with colour film, the other with black & white. You can now shoot everything in colour and convert the ones you think will work well as black & white later using an image editing program.

There are several ways to convert colour photos to black & white – the most common are detailed below:

1 The quickest method is to convert to greyscale – Image⇨Mode⇨Grayscale. This removes all colour by converting the photograph to 256 tones of grey. Those with a good eye for tone will find this option too limited.

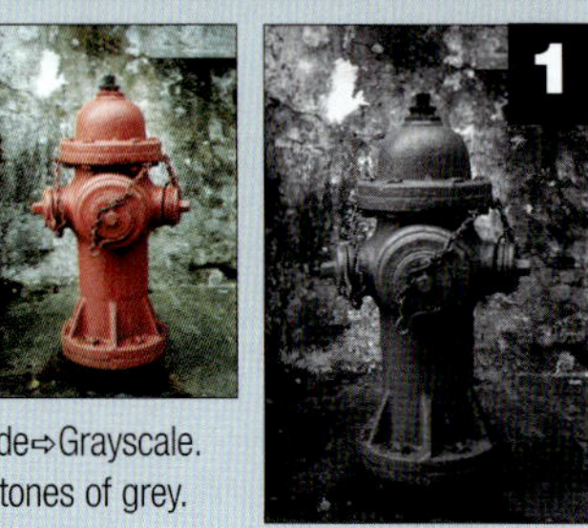

2 A better, but still basic option is to desaturate the image, removing colour, but still keeping three channels – Image⇨Adjustments⇨Destaurate. In this mode you can easily apply a colour tone to the RGB channels using Hue/Saturation.

3 The next option is to split the channels. Open the channel palette and right click on the arrow to the top right to see the Split channel option. Once applied, your image opens as three individual channels of Red, Green and Blue, all appearing as greyscale. You'll see a vast difference in tonal range between each channel. Close the two you don't like and save the third. In this example Blue was the best.

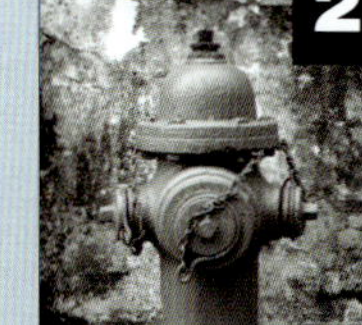

4 On a similar vein to splitting channels, but with far more control, is Photoshop's Channel Mixer – Image⇨Adjustments⇨Channel Mixer. This is like having a set of contrast control filters and by adjusting each of the red, green and blue channel sliders, in conjunction with the Constant slider, you can simulate just about any filter you would have attached to the lens when using film.

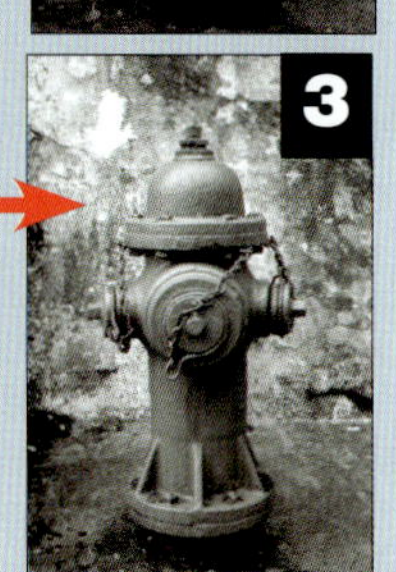

5 Another favourite of many photographers is to convert to Lab colour and delete the A and B channels. Go to Image⇨Mode⇨Lab Color and then select the channel palette and delete the A and B channels to leave an Alpha 1 channel. Then go to Image⇨Adjustments⇨Curves and adjust the curve to gain contrast.

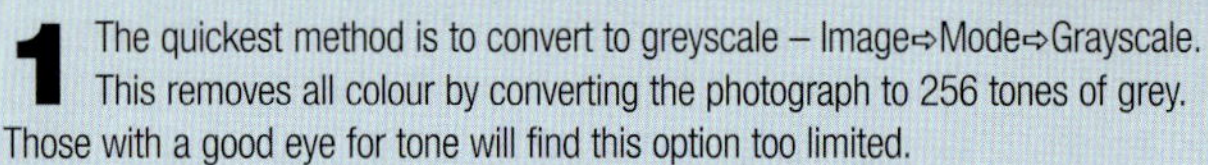

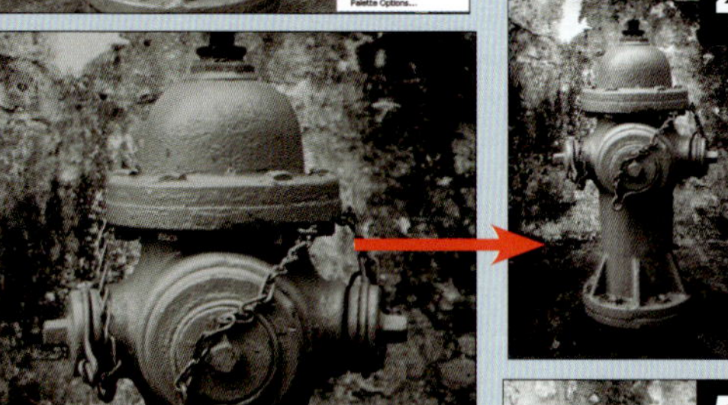

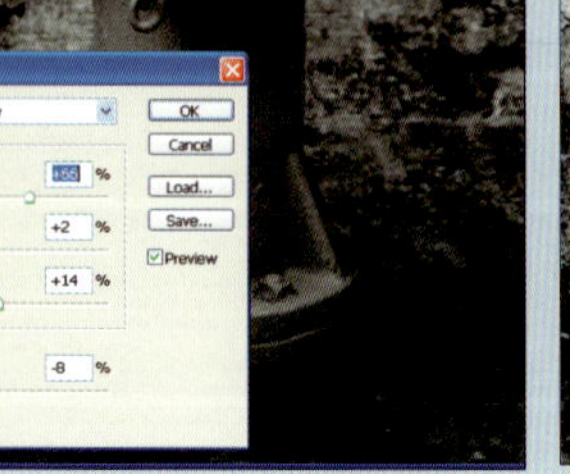

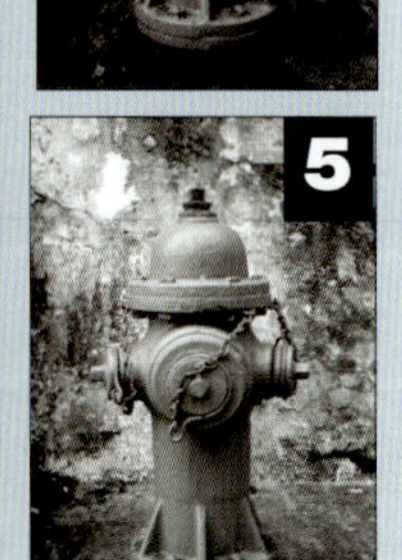

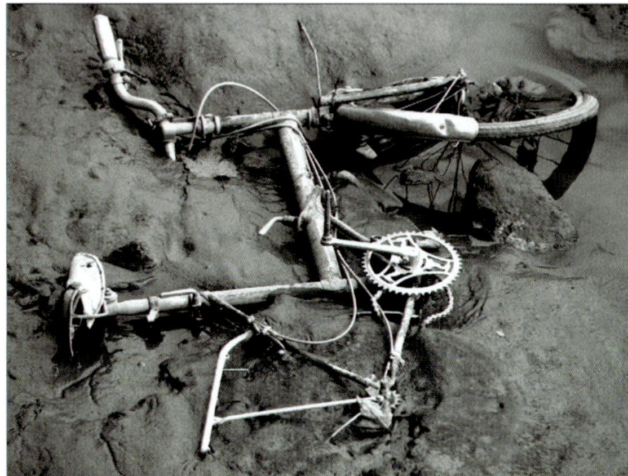

● KATIE RYDE A bicycle in the Thames mud at low tide, taken on a Canon EOS 3 with a EF 100-300mm zoom lens.

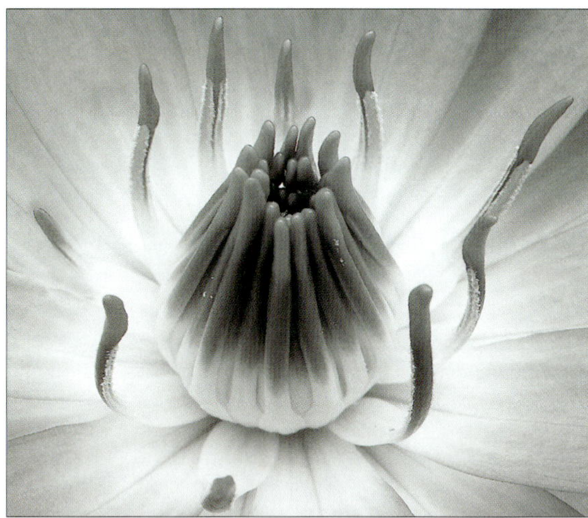

● TREVOR SLATTER Taken at Kew and converted to black & white.

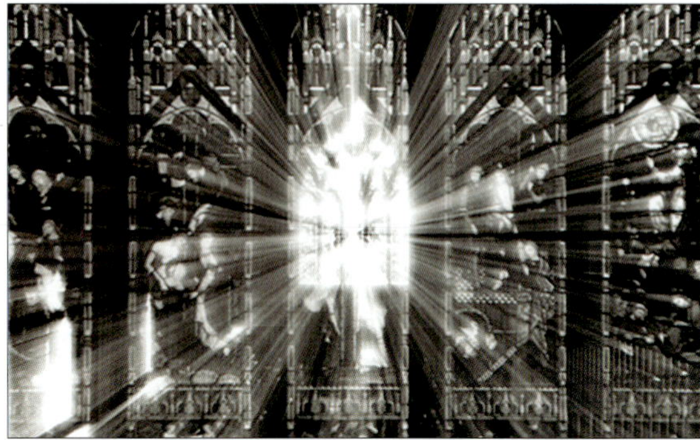

● PAUL GARDHAM I achieved this while trying out long exposures and quick zoom outs. Diffuse Glow has been added after.

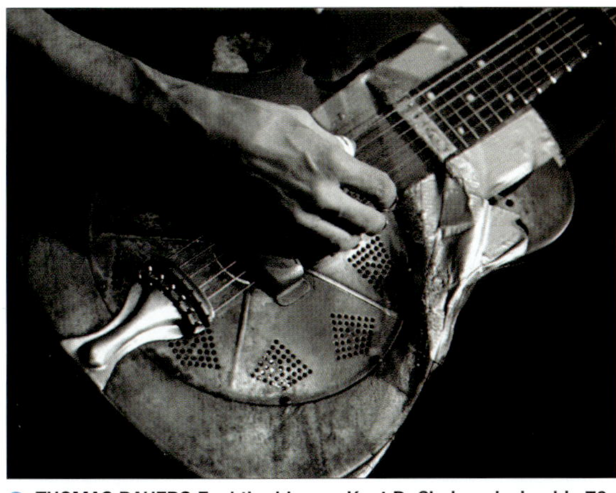

● THOMAS RAUERS Feel the blues – Kent DuChaine playing his 70-year-old steel guitar live. Taken on ultrafast Kodak T-Max 3200 film.

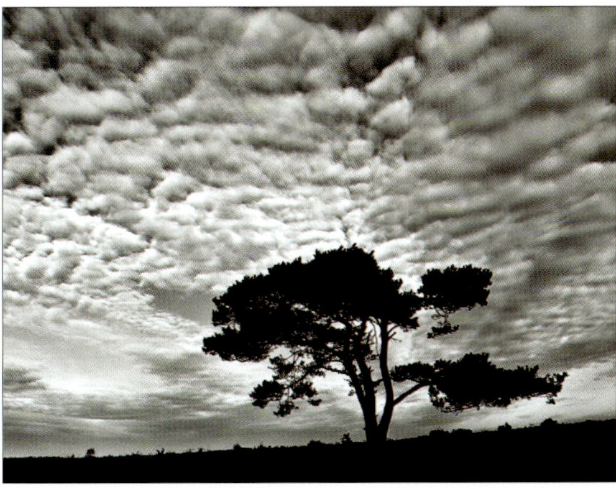

● PETER HORNER A cloud formation creating a perfect backdrop for a long standing tree in the New Forest.

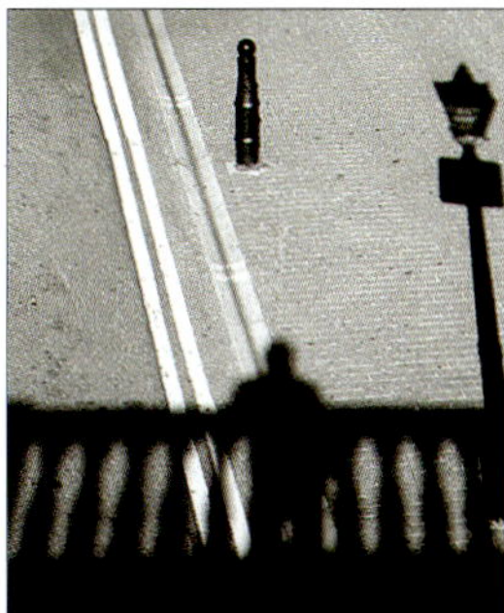

● IVAN HARRIS "My shadow and not me", taken on a Sony DSC P71. The colour file was changed to greyscale and contrast and gamma adjustment.

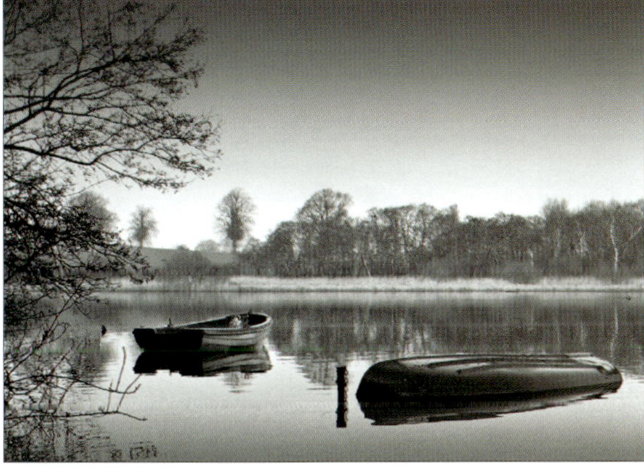

● FRANK MARSH Budworth Mere in Cheshire, taken using a Nikon D70 and 18-70mm lens. Changed to black & white in Photoshop.

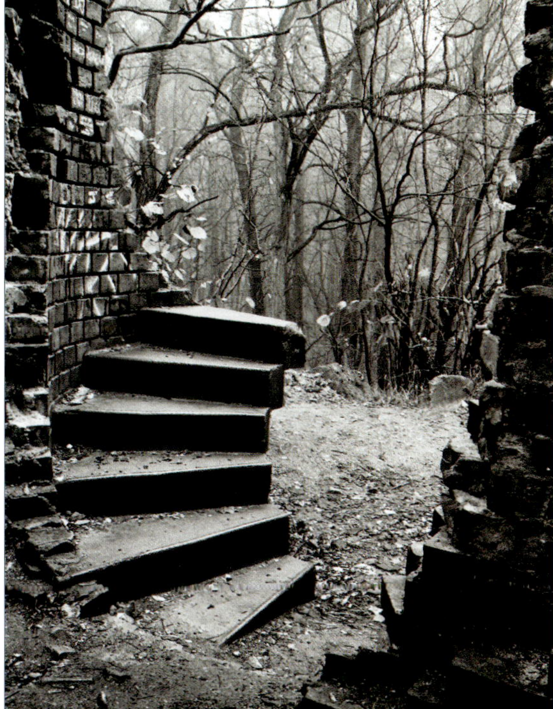

● MAREK JEZIERSKI Remains of Quistorp's Tower, Szczecin, Poland destroyed during WWII, using a Minolta Dynax 5 with Agfa APX100.

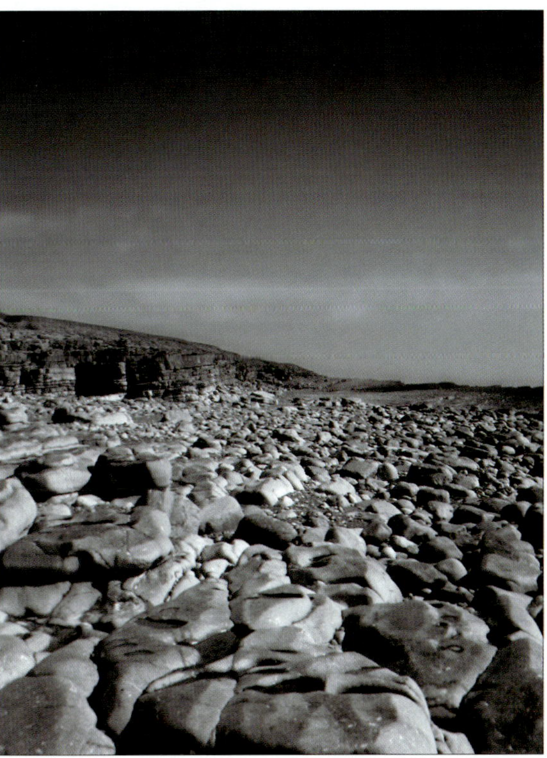

● PETER CHARLES TURNER Ogmore Beach in South Wales. A Photoshop Photo filter was added, along with levels and contrast adjustment layers and a black to transparent gradient from the top.

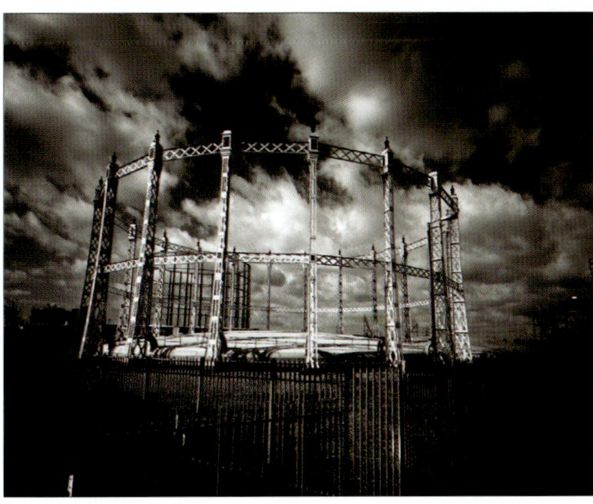

● GERRY SEXTON Gas holder at Bekton, London, using Fuji Acros film in a Mamiya 7II. A red filter was used on 43mm lens at f/11.

B&W FILTER GUIDE

■ **Yellow** introduces a subtle change to yellows, oranges and red, which become slightly lighter. This filter ensures any light sky areas have a slight tonal value to differentiate them from the white border. It hardly affects exposure so is a good all-round protection filter.

■ **Orange** lightens oranges and reds and darkens blue. This increases contrast to give prints more punch. As it lightens reds it is often used by portrait photographers to reduce freckles and skin blemishes.

■ **Red** is a popular choice for creative photographers who like contrasty results, as tones are dramatically affected. It's also used by infrared photographers as an alternative to the true infrared filter and very popular with landscape photographers who are after really moody shots, as it makes blue skies go almost black and darkens foliage.

■ **Green** is used by landscape photographers looking to ensure foliage comes out accurately, with each tone being distinguishable.

■ **Blue** is not widely used, but can work as a contrast reducer.

■ **Infrared R-72** An almost opaque filter that blocks out most of the visible light and only allows infrared light to penetrate. Used with special infrared film or digital cameras that have suitable CCDs.

■ Many other filters, such as **neutral densities, polarisers, graduates, close ups, starbursts** and **diffusers,** can also be used for black & white photography.

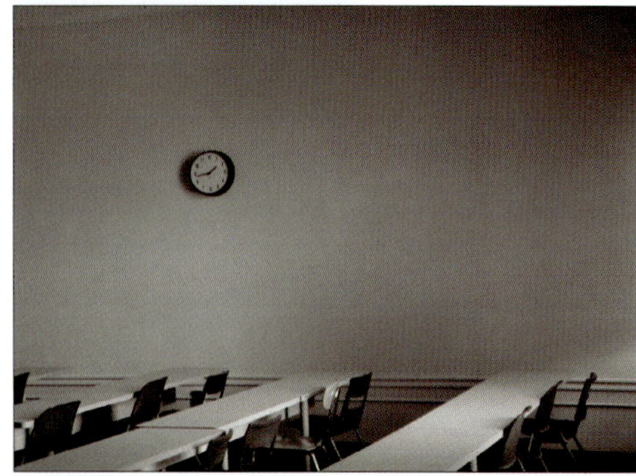

● BENJAMIN GAJEWSKI "I captured the feeling of school by being as stark as possible."

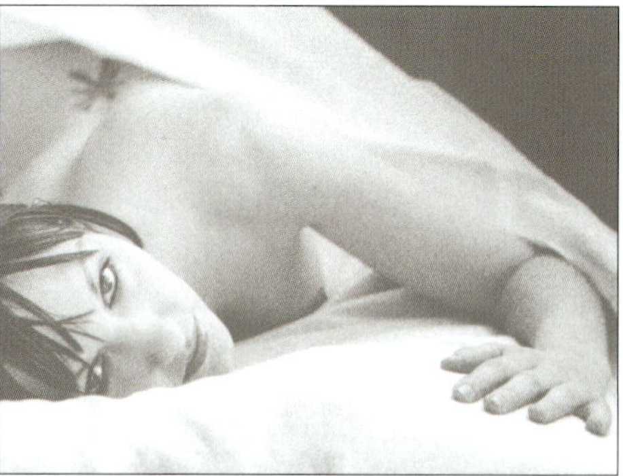

● JOHN DUDER Vikkx, taken in a cold studio! She'd only been modelling for a few months.

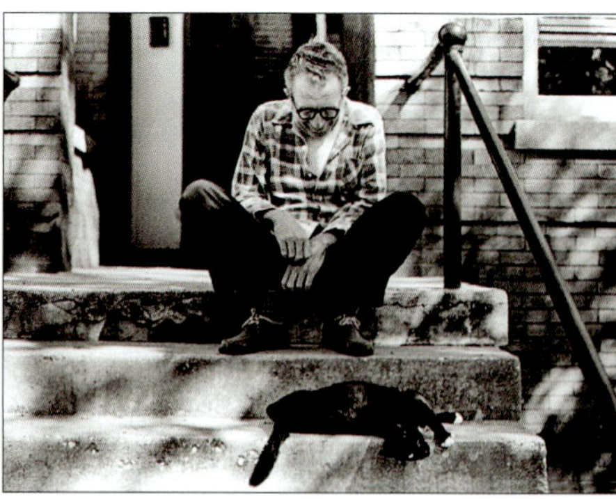

● TUNA ONDER A cat and his owner caught in an unguarded and happy moment.

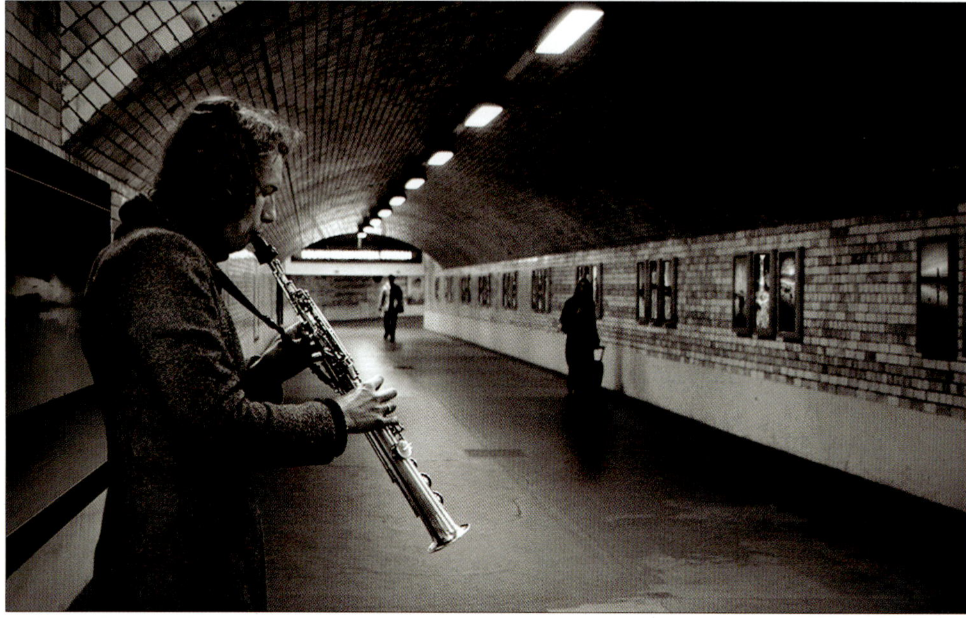

● PAUL STEFAN A busker performing at South Kensington tube station in London. It was shot on a Canon EOS 20D, set at ISO3200 and an EF-S 18-55 lens at 37mm. The grain and contrast were then increased in Photoshop.

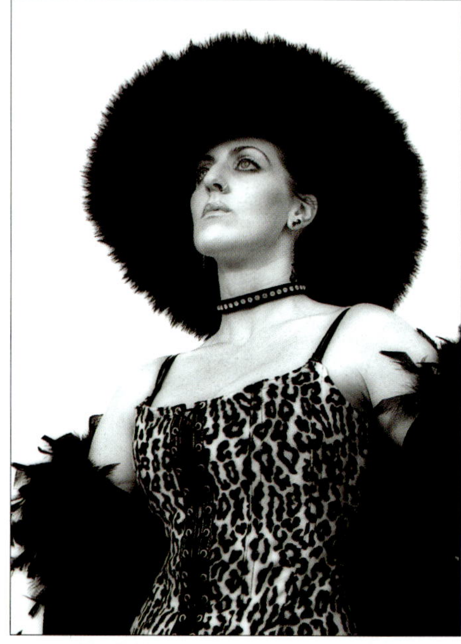

● BILL STEVENSON Taken at Elgol, Isle of Skye, using a tripod mounted Canon 10D and 28-135mm zoom.

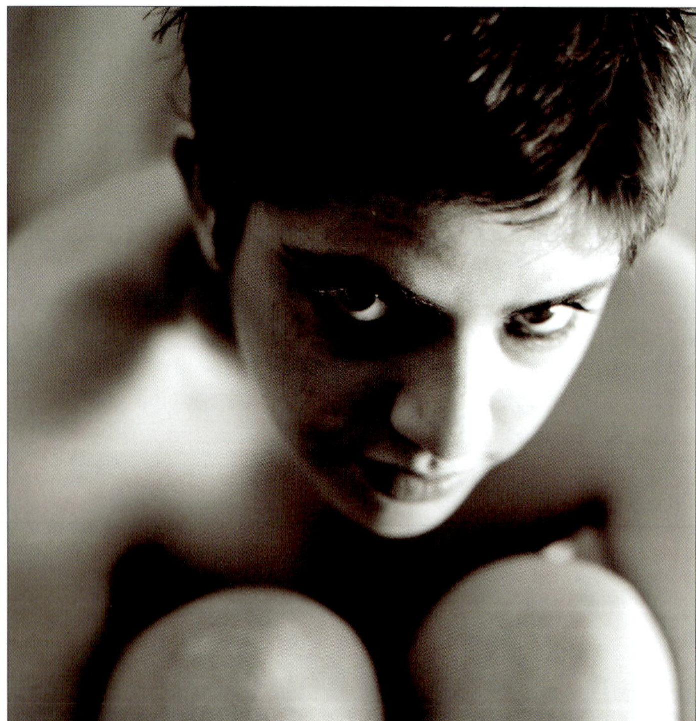

● FABIO BORQUEZ The girl is Juliana, taken at a photo-shoot in Buenos Aires. "I was using Kodak ISO400 film in my Mamiya RB67."

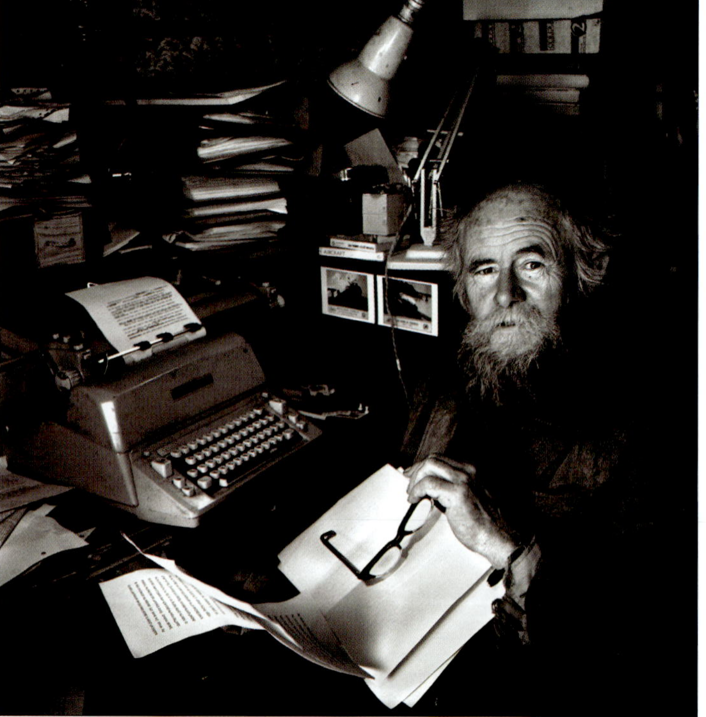

● LUKE SMITH A fascinating portrait of a writer by his typewriter, taken using an old Mamiya C33 twin-lens camera and 80mm lens on Ilford FP4 film.

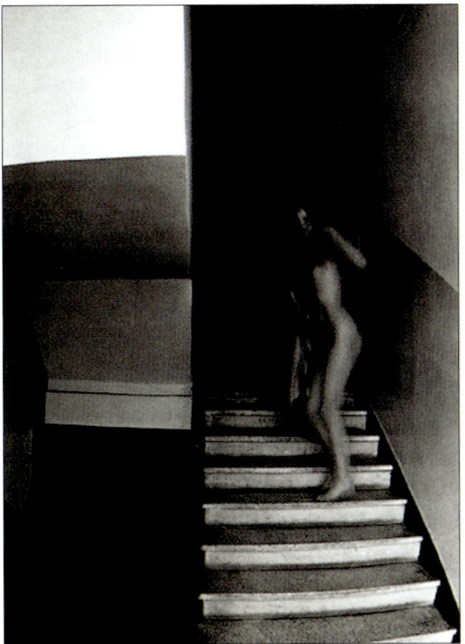

● STANISLAW TRZASKA Shot at 1/2sec, available light, 20mm lens at f/5.6 – by accident!

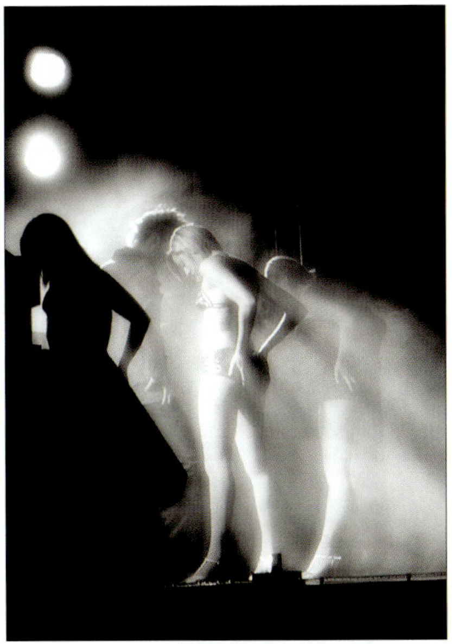

● DAWN KAY Entertainment staff doing their routine, taken at a South Wales holiday resort.

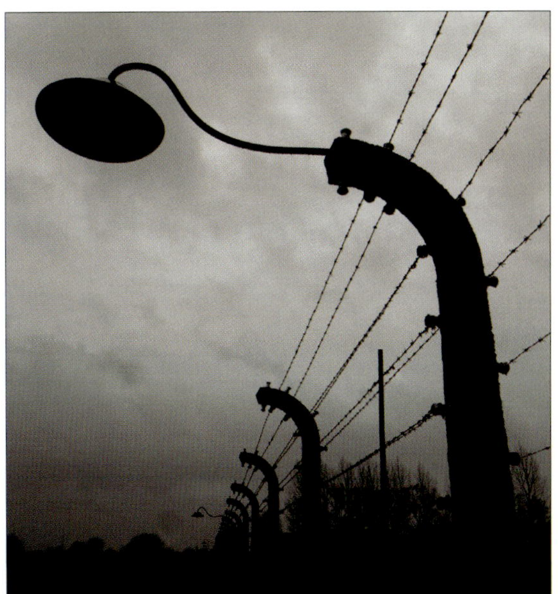

● BILL HUNT Taken in January 2005 at the 60th commemorations of the liberation of Auschwitz-Birkenau.

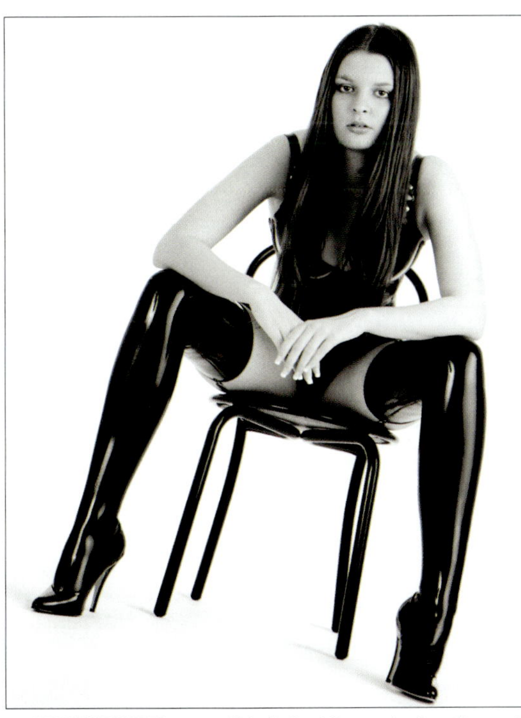

● JOHN TISBURY The use of black & white emphasises line and form in this studio shot.

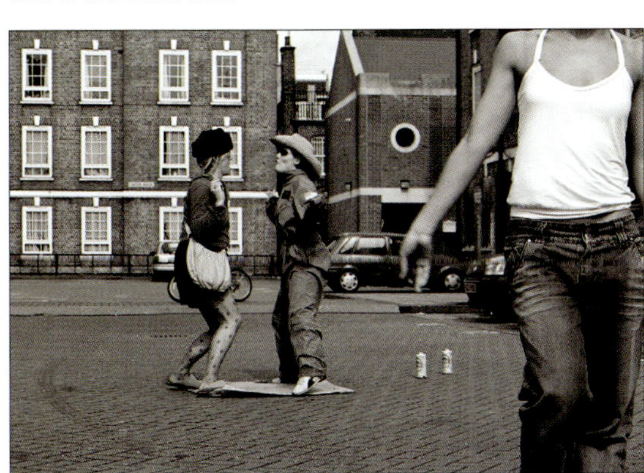

● IZZY ELTREKI Shot spontaneously during a two day party in an estate of east-central London.

DIGITAL TECHNIQUE – SHOOTING AND ENHANCING INFRARED LIGHT

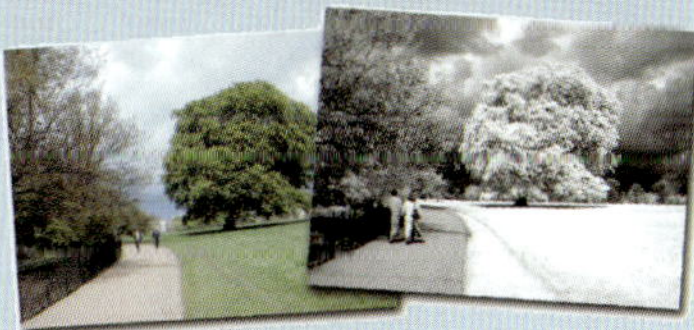

■ Digital photography has made it easier to shoot infrared pictures. A digital camera's CCD can capture infrared light, unlike conventional film (unless the camera has an infrared blocking filter over the CCD). To make infrared prominent you block out the visible lightwaves using a special infrared filter placed over your camera's lens.

1 Your camera's built-in exposure meter will be fooled by the infrared light so you need to make some exposure tests, previewing the results on the LCD until you get it right.
Most cameras have an auto ISO adjustment that will increase the ISO to compensate for the lack of visible light passing through the filter. Switch to manual and set the lowest ISO for best quality or turn on Noise reduction if available.

Autofocusing may be tricked too. Magnify the preview on the LCD to check whether it's sharp. If not, switch to manual and adjust until you have the correct sharpness. Set a small aperture to ensure maximum depth-of-field. Mount the camera on a tripod to prevent camera shake during the long exposure.

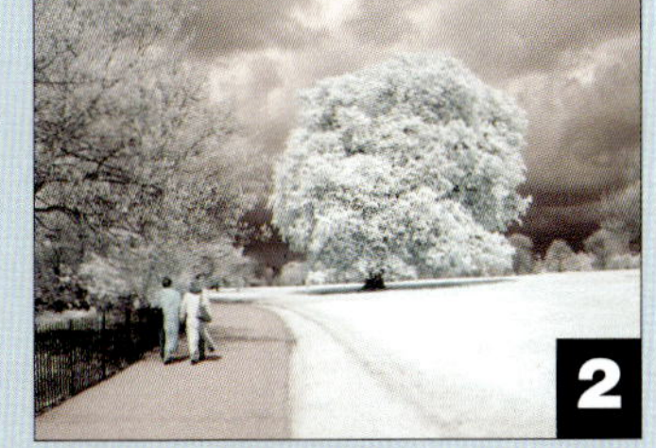

2 The pictures you get will have a colour cast. This can be removed in your image editing program. Go to Image⇨ Adjustments⇨Desaturate to knock out all the colour.

3 Now to give the shot characteristics of a film-based infrared image. For starters, we need some typical coarse grain to make it look more atmospheric. You could go to Filter⇨Noise⇨Add Noise, select Monochrome with Gaussian distribution and adjust the slider to add grain, but I prefer to use a different option that also accentuates another infrared characteristic.

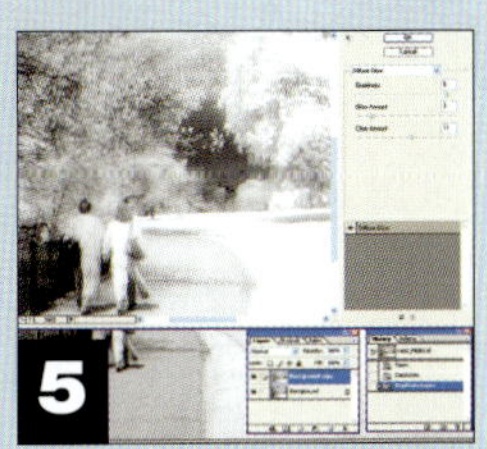

4 Duplicate the layer by clicking on the existing layer in the layers palette and dragging it over the Layer icon at the bottom of the palette.

5 With the new layer active, go to Filter⇨Distort⇨Diffuse Glow. Here you can make areas of the image glow while adding really cool grain at the same time. You can adjust the three sliders while watching the preview to deliver the ideal result.

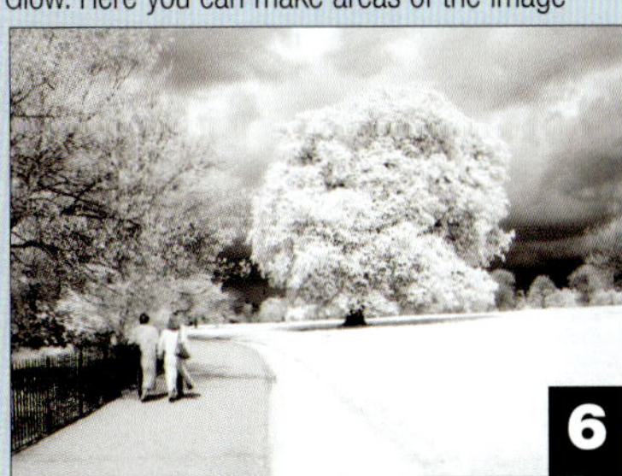

6 Photoshop allows Layers to interact using the blend modes and there are several options to change how the top layer affects the one below. Try Normal blend mode and reduce the diffuse glow intensity by dragging the top layer opacity down slightly to 85% or Soft light at full opacity, which was used here.

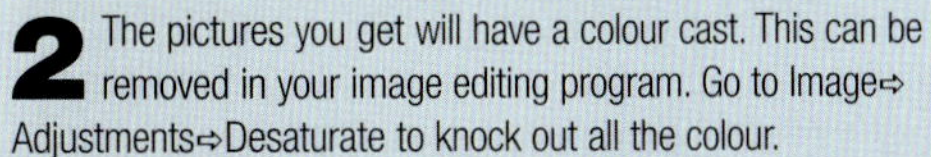
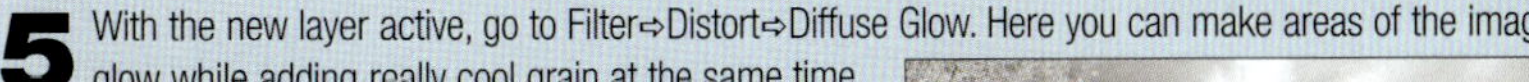

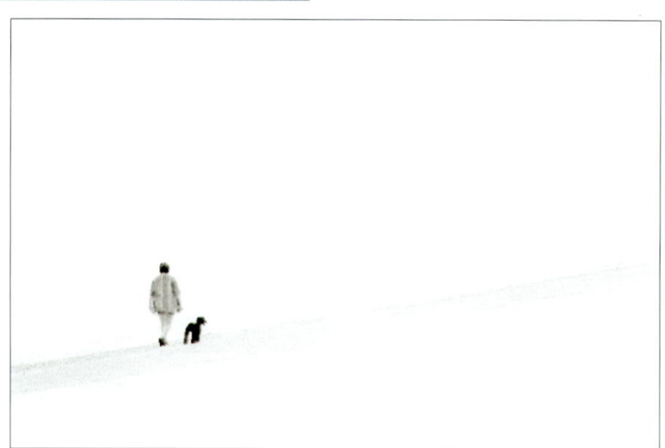

● ALEXANDRA LOWSON Solitude – an evening walk on a beach in Auckland, taken with a Fuji S5000 and manipulated in Photoshop.

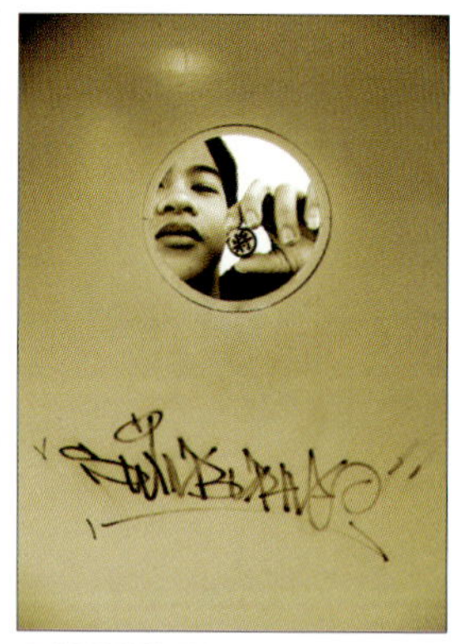

● ZARNIKO Friend with Chinese chess piece through a toilet door.

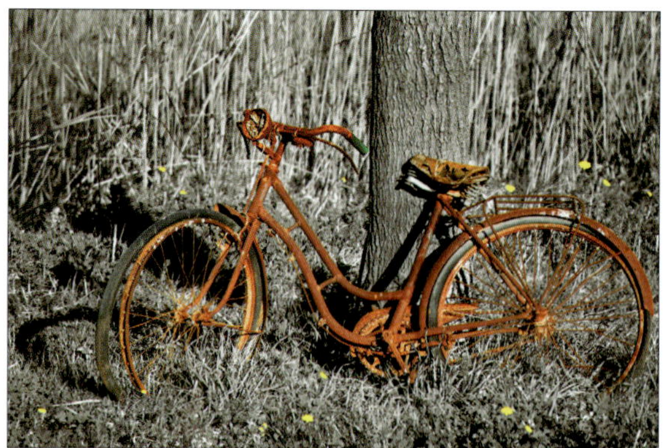

● ANTONIO ALOMAR A black & white shot that's been selectively coloured to highlight the rusty bicycle.

DIGITAL TECHNIQUE – CREATING A CYANOTYPE EFFECT

■ The cyanotype process, discovered by English inventor Sir John Herschel, uses ammonium ferric citrate and potassium ferricyanide as a light-sensitive coating. The resulting rich, deep blue prints are still made today by advanced darkroom users, along with other early processes. Here's how to recreate the cyanotype effect digitally:

The main thing to strive for is a full tonal range with deep shadows, detailed highlights, overall deep blue tone, a creamy appearance in the highlights and a texture that makes it have a painterly feel.

1 This interior of Bolsover Castle was a tricky exposure – bright sunlight bursting through the window was the only illumination the corridor received. It was taken on a Nikon D100 with a 24mm lens set to f/3.5. I exposed for the back wall, making the window slightly over exposed, but there was still plenty of detail in the shadows. After a bit of work in Photoshop, cloning, dodging and burning, I had a shot ready to be given the cyanotype treatment.

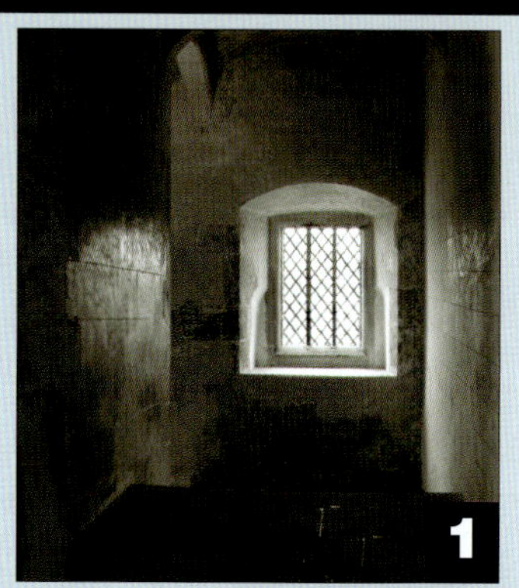

2 Use Curves to make colour changes. Go to Image⇨Adjustments⇨Curves (Ctrl+M) and select the individual channels. Pull the curve up or down to create the desired Cyanotype style – vivid Prussian Blue. With the Red channel selected, click on the Curve at around the 100 input value and either drag the curve or key in the following: input should be around 100 and set output to around 40. The photo will now have a cyan/blue hue, but it's not deep enough yet.

3 Click ok and select the Blue channel. Click around 192 and drag downwards so the output is around 175. Click lower down on the curve at around 65 and drag this point up to around 80.

4 Click ok and select the Green channel and input points of around 97 while adjusting the output to around 73. Now you should have a photo with a very realistic looking Cyanotype blue tone with creamy highlights.

5 Now we need to give the photograph a realistic grain appearance using the Photoshop Noise filter. Create a duplicate layer by dragging the existing layer to the Create a new Layer icon or Layer⇨Duplicate layer from the menu.

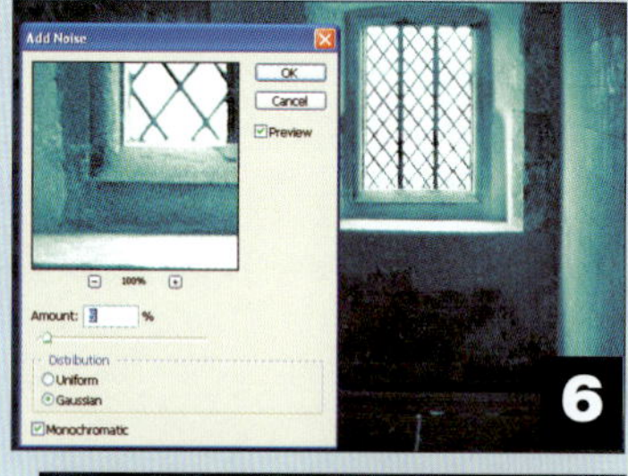

6 With the new layer selected go to Filter⇨Noise⇨Add Noise, Set Gaussian, Monochromatic and drag the Amount slider to around 5% to introduce a noise/grain effect. Click OK and save the photograph.

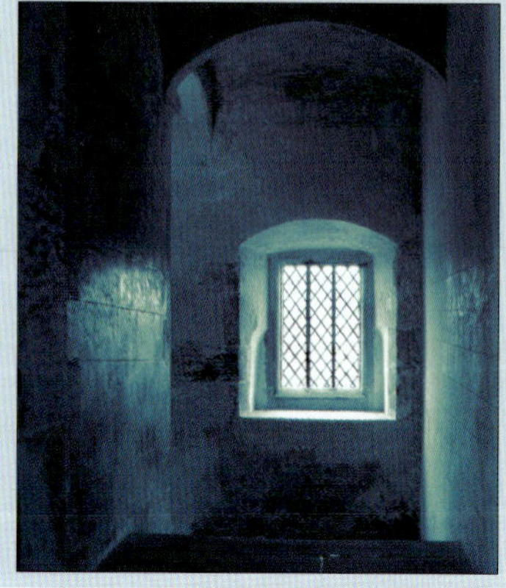

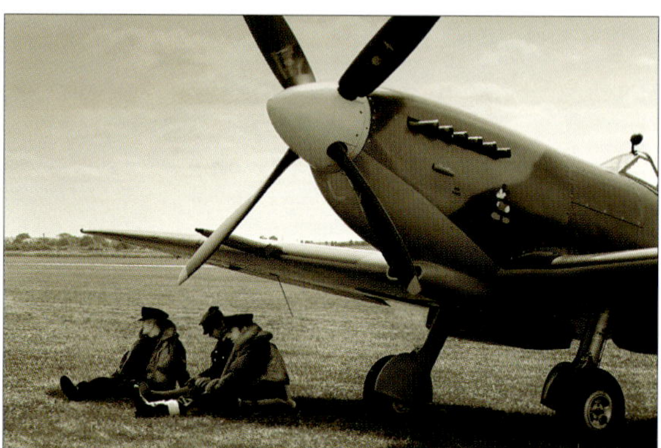

● MILES HERBERT Spitfire with volunteers in period flight dress, toned to give a suitably aged look.

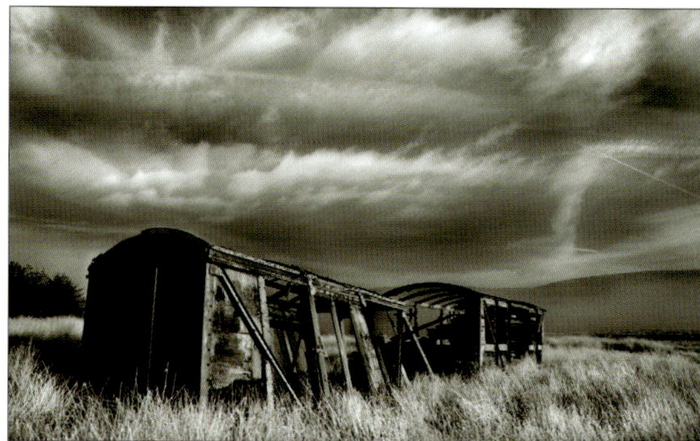

● ALEX HYDE A circular polarizing filter was used to bring out the dramatic sky in this scene in the Yorkshire Dales.

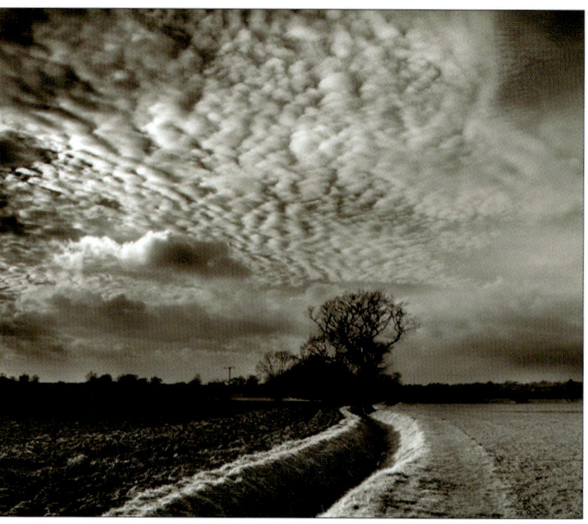

● KATHY WRIGHT Captured on a Canon 300D with EF-S 18-55mm lens while out walking on a winter afternoon in Norfolk.

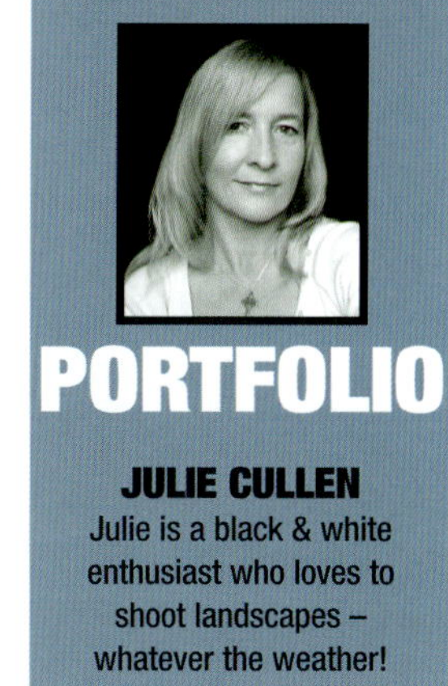

PORTFOLIO

JULIE CULLEN
Julie is a black & white enthusiast who loves to shoot landscapes – whatever the weather!

I love all aspects of photography, but my biggest passion lies in black & white photography, with a particular emphasis on landscapes.

When composing a landscape image, the first thing I look for is an eye-catching sky. I try to include as much of the sky as possible in the shot, while still keeping foreground interest.

I usually use manual mode and, to me, a red 25A filter is also a must as this helps to bring out the tones and darken the sky. I often under-expose a shot by at least half to one stop, if not more. I then do some work post-shooting in Photoshop, for example darkening the neutral tones. I then sharpen up the image using the unsharp mask option.

My advice to people having a go at landscape photography would don't be put off by dull, misty and wet days – you can still achieve great results.

My shot, 'Creeping Mist' (above left), was taken under these conditions, using a red filter. Also, when you see the shot you want, it is worth persevering and pushing the camera to its limits.

There's nothing like taking in a beautiful scene and feeling the excitement rise within you as you set about composing that image in your mind and camera.

I enjoy experimenting with other subjects, but landscape remains my first love. I take most of my photographs in black & white, as I feel it creates powerful and emotive images. Most of my work was shot using the Fuji S7000, but I have now upgraded to the Canon 350D, giving me more scope with use of lens.

Recently I have experimented with Infrared photography as well as photographing wildlife – both can be very challenging. ∎

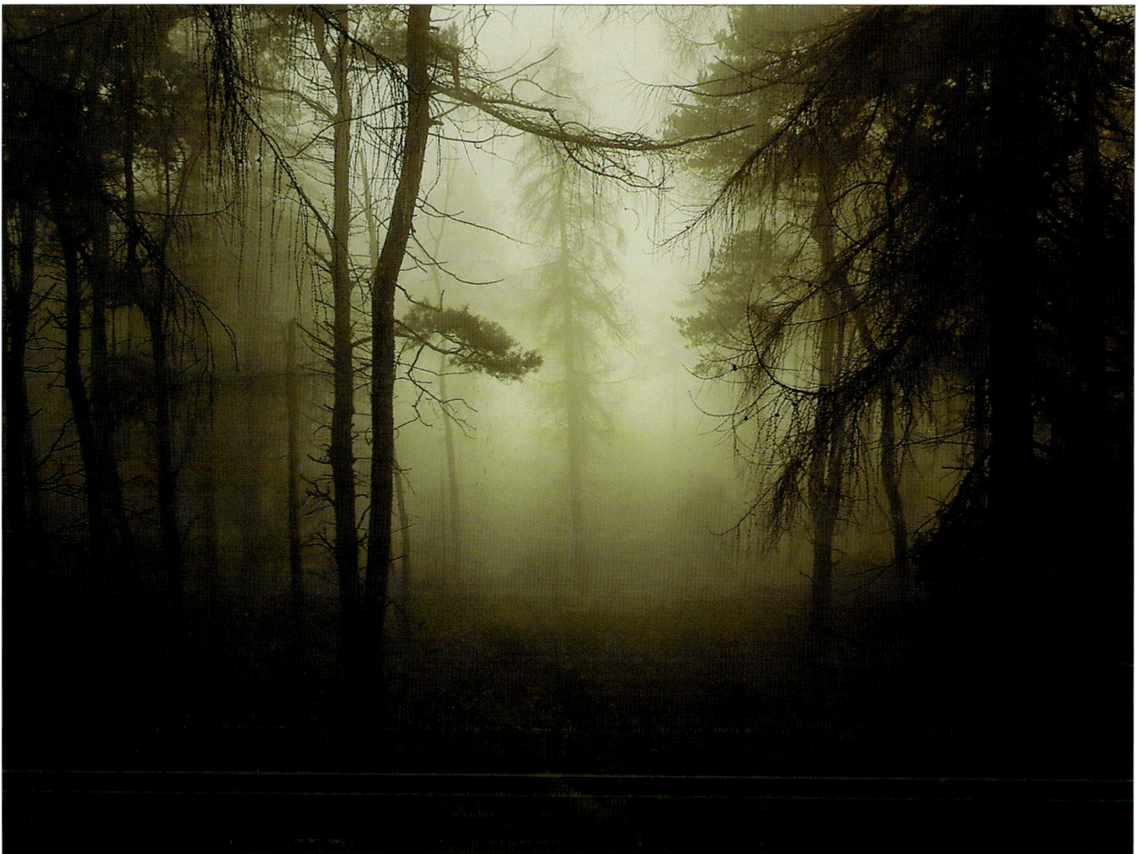

● This misty forest scene was taken on a wet, foggy day in the Forest behind Julie's house. A Red 25A filter was attached to the Fujifilm S7000 camera and the exposure was 1/20sec at f/8 with the CCD sensitivity at ISO200.

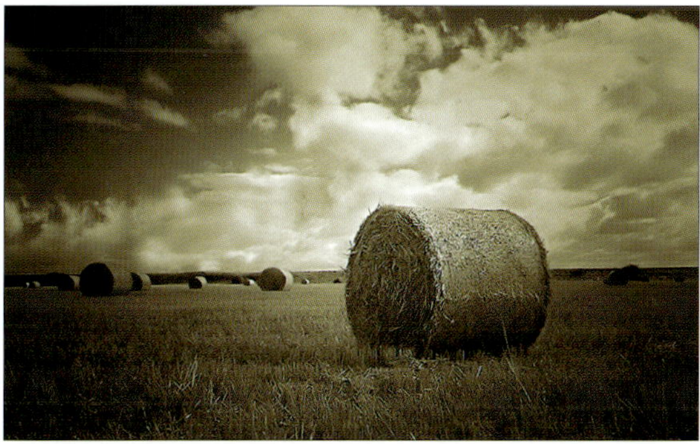

● Freshly cut bales of hay taken using a Fuji S7000 with a red filter and a 1/1250 sec at f/2.8 exposure. The CCD was at ISO200 and the result was toned in Photoshop to add the sepia colour.

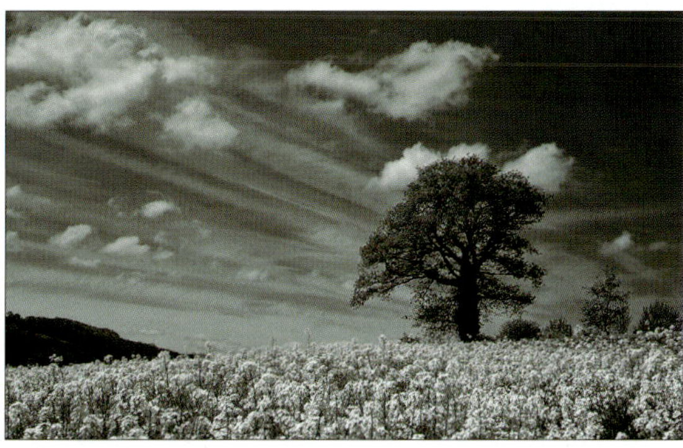

● The cloud formation and tree is a focal point of the shot, taken using a Fuji S7000. The blue colour tone was added later in Photoshop using the colorize adjustment in Hue/Saturation.

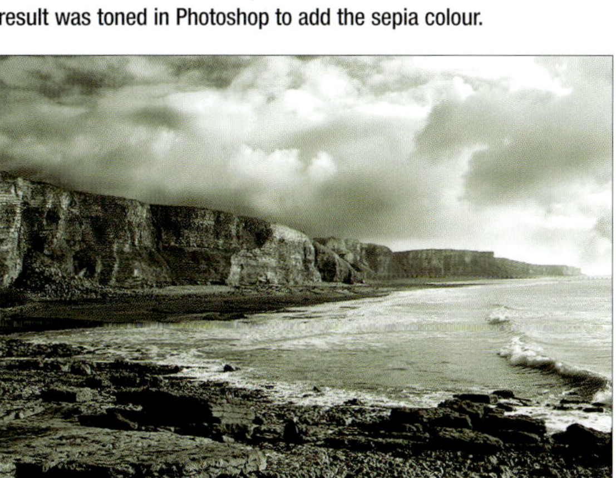

● The Fuji S7000 was used with a red filter and the shot was underexposed by one stop to add mood. A slight blur was then added to the sky, using the Magic Wand selection tool in Photoshop.

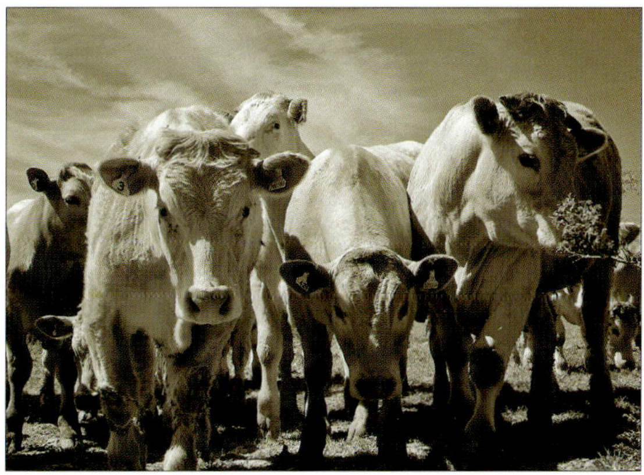

● Taken on the ground looking upwards with the Fuji S7000 and a Red 25A filter. The sepia colour tone was created using Hue/Saturation in Photoshop.

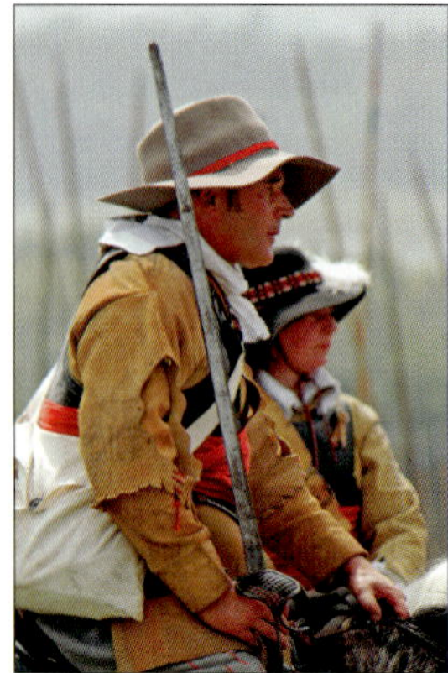

● PETER BARGH You'll find ample candids at reenactments.

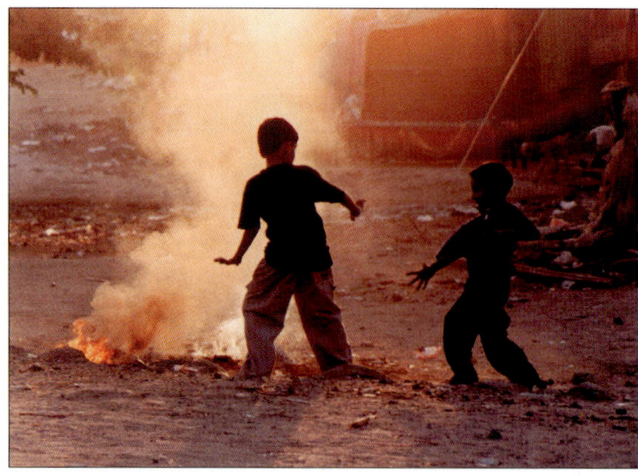

● SURESH KHAIRE A Nikon F90X was used in Silhouette mode with a 70-300mm AF ED lens and exposed on Kodak Gold 100 film.

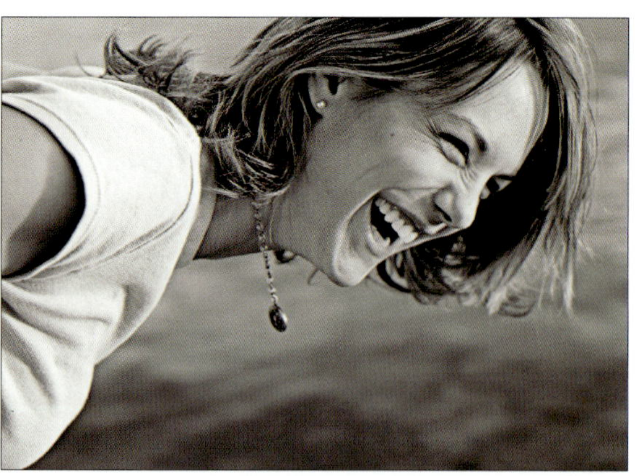

● ERIN VEY Erin's younger sister Shannon is full of life and laughter, with expressions just waiting to be caught on camera.

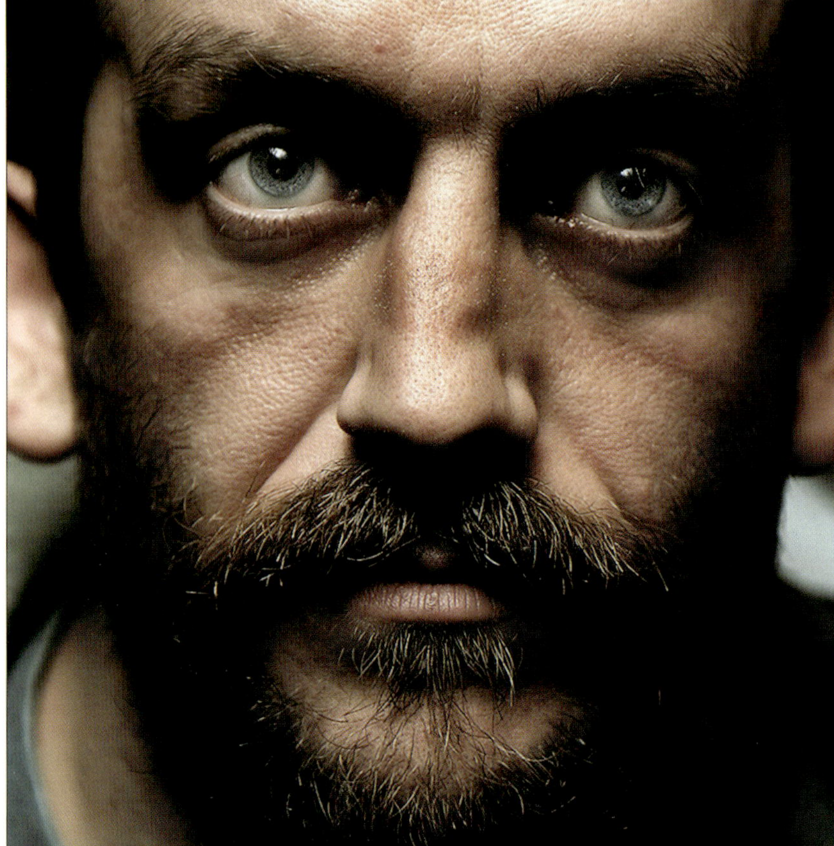

● CHRIS ROBERTS A self portrait using a Canon EOS 10D on a tripod with remote capture software on the PC, to help with focus. The 24-70mm f/2.8 lens was set at f/4 and flash was bounced off the ceiling.

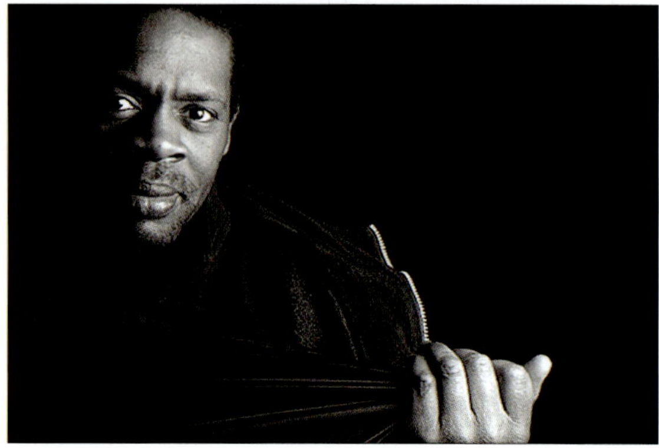

● ROD EVANS Professional photographer Rod sadly passed away in September 2005. This portrait of his friend Michael Campbell was taken in a studio in a converted barn using one softbox at f/8.

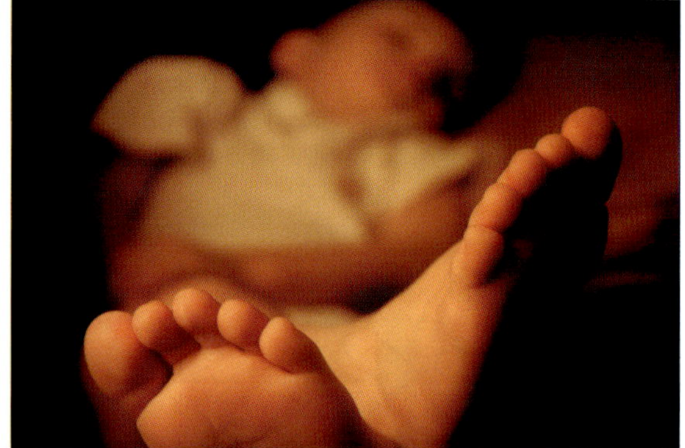

● SHAUN BRADFIELD After a hard day at school, taken using a Nikon D70 with 18-70mm zoom at 70mm f/4.5 and 1/5sec speed.

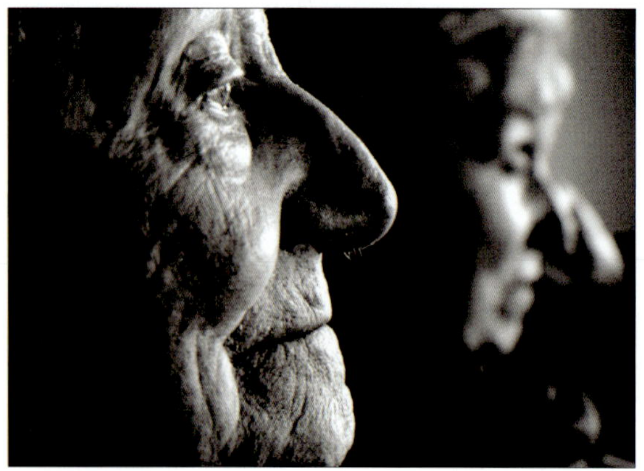

● MICHAEL BURNELL Taken using only available light, thereby producing a grainy image, showing off the age of the subject.

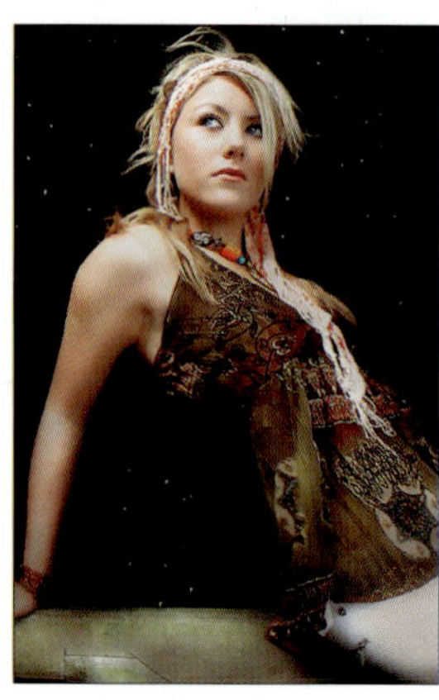

● LYNE EDESON Maria-Louise with Photoshop background.

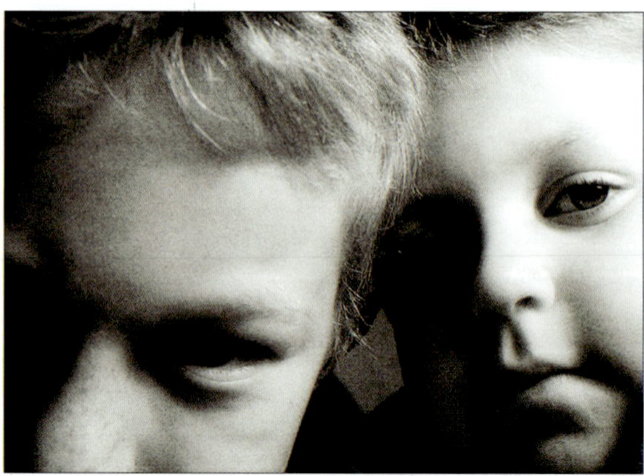

● PETER BARGH I got the kids to stare into the lens by asking them to look for the little man inside who operates the camera.

Portraiture

Whether it's the close up of your child's expression taken in a fleeting moment, a candid of a street performer snatched while you're out and about or a staged model shoot, portraiture delivers one of the widest range of options and meanings in the photographic world. Here we take you through some of the best from ePHOTOzine's gallery pages.

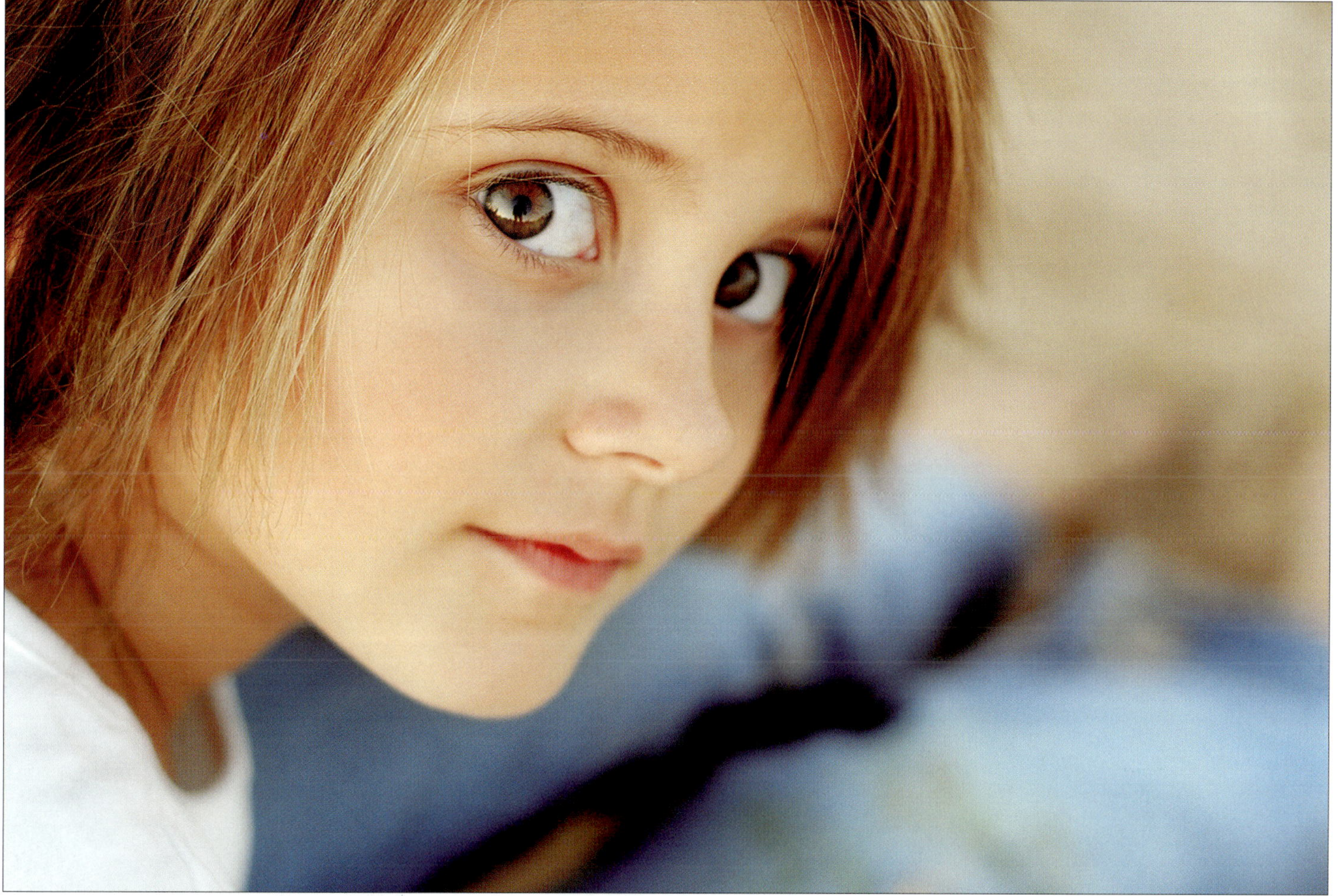

● GABRIEL BIENCZYCKI "Avery is a girl I photographed in Houston, Texas, in the fall of 2004; she is a very cool model. The scene was illuminated with light from a sunset and I used a prime 50mm lens set at f/2.2 on a Nikon D70." The tight crop and left position of Avery's head ensures our attention goes to her big, bright eyes.

From family snapshots to holiday pictures, whatever the special occasion, we all like to capture it in a photograph. And what is the one thing that most of these images have in common? People.

We all like to take pictures of our loved ones, hoping to capture a person, a time, even a feeling, which will last for eternity. But there is no reason why your photographs of people should be restricted to just snapshots. There is more to the genre than snapping a hurried photo of Dad as he dozes off in front of the television!

The art of photographing people is known as portraiture and this area offers photographers a number of creative and artistic ways to include people in their pictures.

For many of us, the idea of a portrait tends to conjure up bad memories of our days posing for school photographs, frozen into a stiff, characterless pose. Or of the type of factory-line portraiture often churned out for family portraits, where an entire branch of a family tree is organised together, posed in a formal and unnatural way.

But it does not have to be like this – portraiture has so much more to offer the photographer than these stereotypical impressions. While a portrait is intended to show a person's physical likeness, a good portrait should go that extra mile and also give an impression of the subject's personality and character.

Great photographs are evocative and we should be able to look at photographs of our loved ones (and even people we do not know) and really see their individuality and celebrate the life coming from within the photograph.

Whether posed or candid, portraits are an extremely powerful expression, literally allowing us to freeze time and capture a sense of that person forever. We can use it to make a permanent record of our lives, and of those around us who touched our lives, creating powerful and emotional memories that will last a lifetime.

Over the following section you will see a superb range of styles, lighting techniques, and subjects. We will look at candids, people at work, children at play, studio sets, artistic creations and much more.

We hope that the photos will inspire you to look at your work colleagues, partners or relations in a whole new light. Your photographs of people don't have to be staid uncomfortable poses or grabbed party pics taken across the table at your local pub/restaurant. Consider going out especially to take portraits. Look for interesting venues – gardens or historical buildings never fail to deliver suitable surrounds, while ruins, subways, colourful walls or modern architecture make great backdrops.

Read our tips panels throughout this section to help you find all the necessary knowledge and study the photos to inspire you. Could you do similar shots? Post your results on ePHOTOzine and ask for our members' opinions. There's a wealth of help and advice on offer.

The most important thing is to be creative. Successful portraits capture emotion or character, and with the help of good composition, careful use of exposure and focusing it's possible to capture those important moments forever.

Don't be afraid to break rules, though. You'll learn that once you understand them, they are there to be broken. If you're new to portraiture we'd suggest you start by trying some of the ideas on these pages and then move in your own direction to develop a distinct style that will set you apart from the crowd. ■

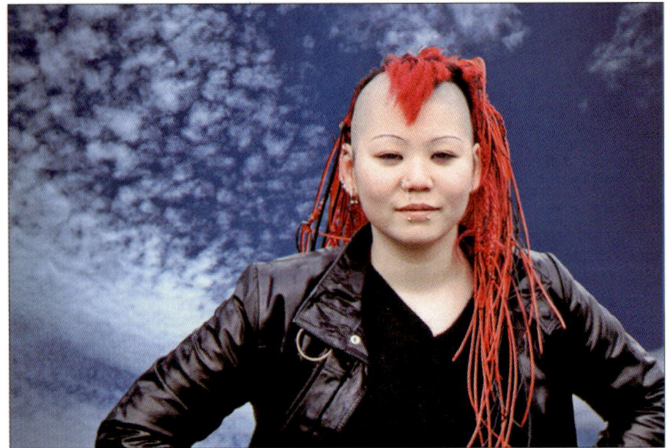

● BILL STEVENSON Taken at a Whitby Goth Weekend using a Canon T90 and 70-210mm zoom. The original background was replaced.

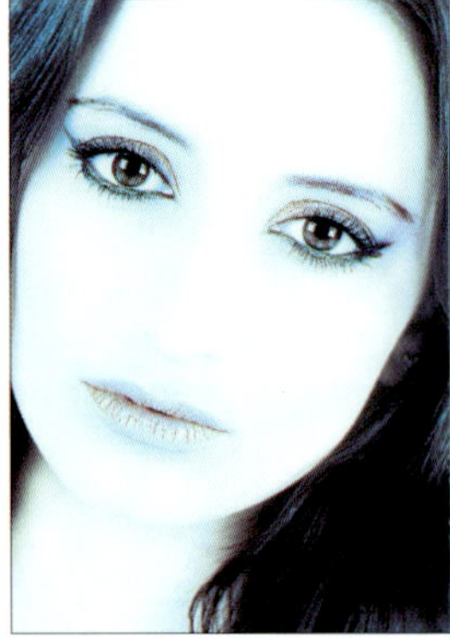

● KAREN BACON Model lit with two softboxes. Digitally toned.

DIGITAL TECHNIQUE – GOLD TONING

■ Many portrait photographers shoot in colour and, with maybe a digital crop or a slight tweak to the contrast, they often leave the photo as shot. Occasionally a quick conversion to black & white may be applied or a subtle tone so here's something to stir things up a bit. In the style of James Bond, we're going to apply a Goldfinger tone to our portrait.

1 The original of model Jasmine was taken using a Pentax *ist D and Tamron 90mm lens. It's shot in RAW mode and illuminated using Bowens studio lights with softbox. It's a great version to use as the sharpness of the lens has picked up the texture of the make up, which will look like paint when we finish.

2 First we'll go to Image⇨Adjustments⇨Hue/ Saturation (Ctrl+U) and click Colorize. On the sliders, reduce the Saturation and Lightness to make the photo darker and flatter in tonal range and then adjust the Hue to make the photo go blue. I find this treatment gives a better gold hue later, but you could experiment with different hues to get your desired colour.

3 Now we go to the Image⇨Adjustments⇨Colour Balance (Ctrl+B) and play around with the sliders in each of the individual tonal areas, including Shadows, Midtones and Highlights. These are activated by clicking each one in turn at the bottom of the Colour Balance palette. Dragging the Cyan/Red slider to the right increases red, and the Yellow/Blue to the left increases yellow and the combination creates our desired shift to orange. Only make minor adjustments to the Magenta/ Green channel.

4 The next stage is to go to Image⇨Adjustments⇨ Curves (Ctrl+M) and Drag the RGB curve downwards to darken the tones. Then make adjustments in each of the Red and Blue channels. Take the Red curve up slightly and the Blue down, which will emphasise the gold colour we are now creating. At this stage you may want to go back to the Hue/Saturation sliders and tweak the tones, pulling the saturation up a touch and increasing the lightness to make the photo brighter.

5 The final adjustment was to crop the photo, drawing our attention to Jasmine's eyes. And, while we're on the eyes, I used the Saturation tool, set to desaturate, and painted over them to remove the colour and ensure the whites of the eyes are bright and fresh.

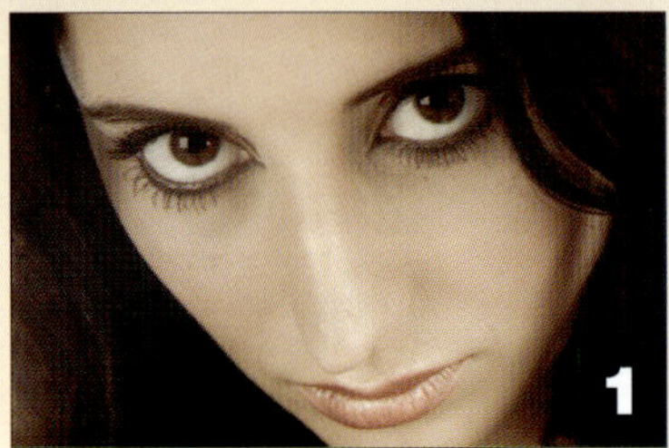

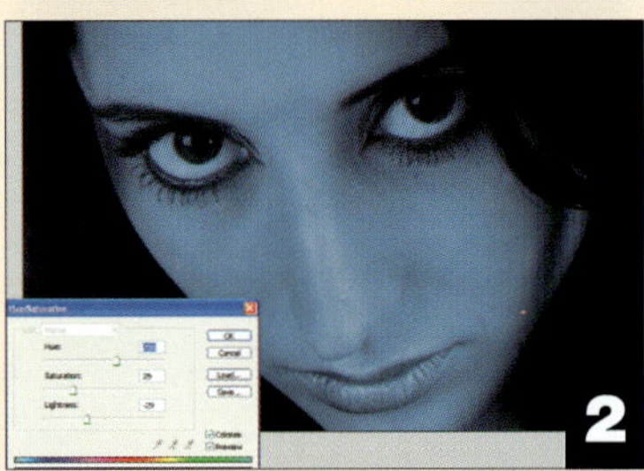

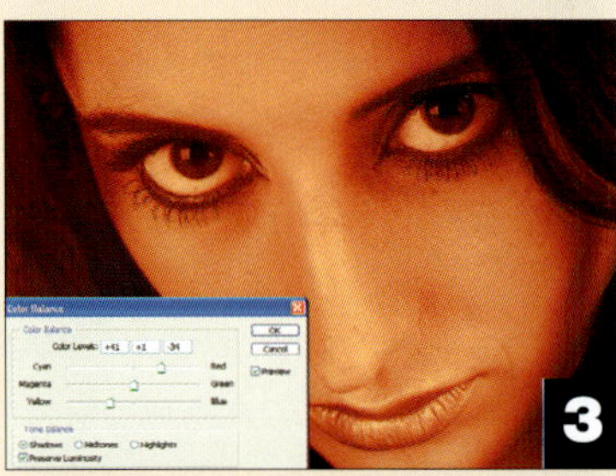

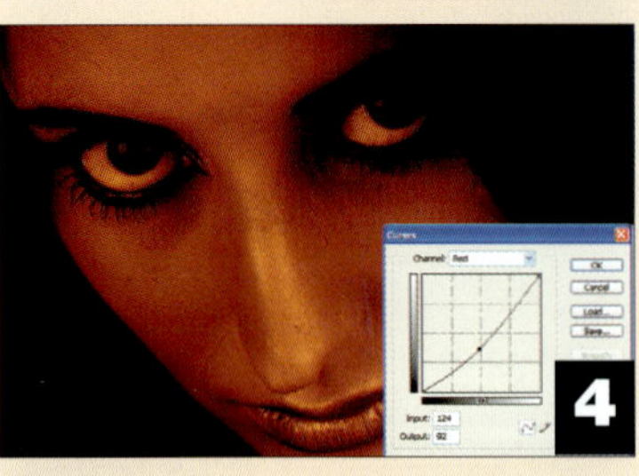

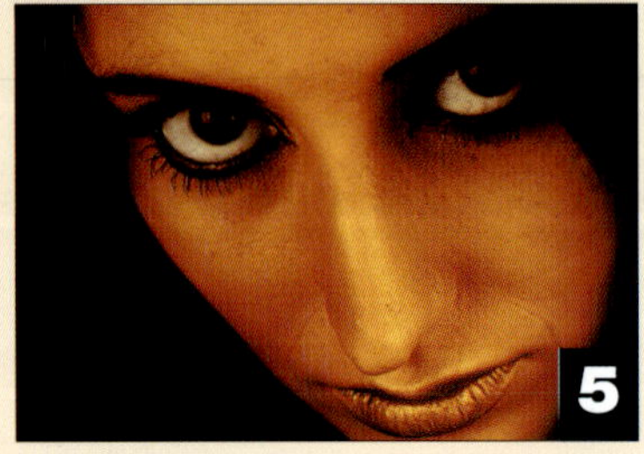

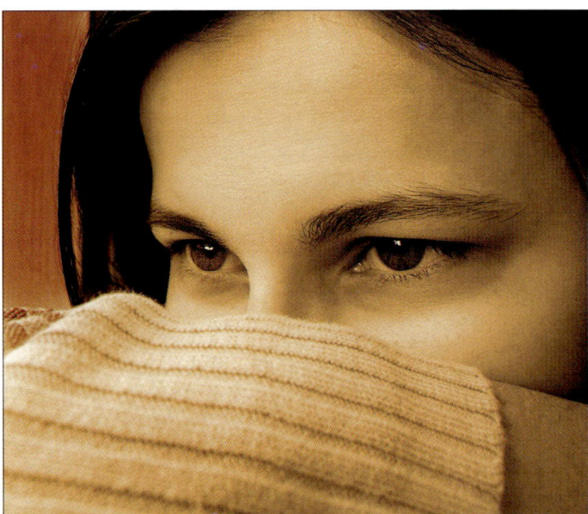

● ANGIE BARNETT Angie's fascination with mermaids shows with this self-portrait, using a flat bed scanner, fishing rope and seaweed.

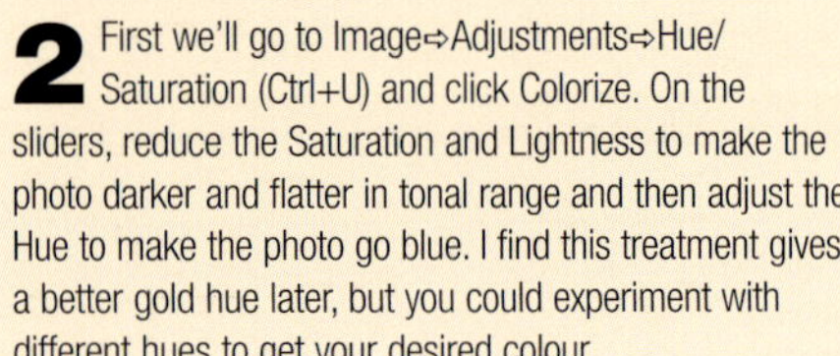

● INKA PATTERSON This shot was taken with available light in front of a window to give a lively picture with a natural feel.

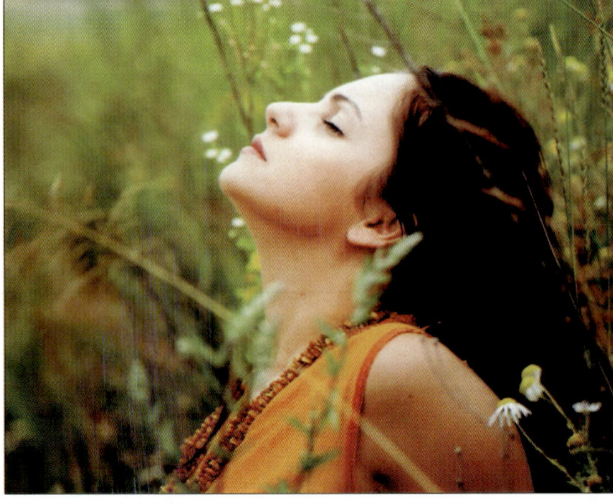

● ANETA LACORSA The expression shows this girl clearly enjoying relaxation in the sun, taken in a field in Poland using a Nikon F801.

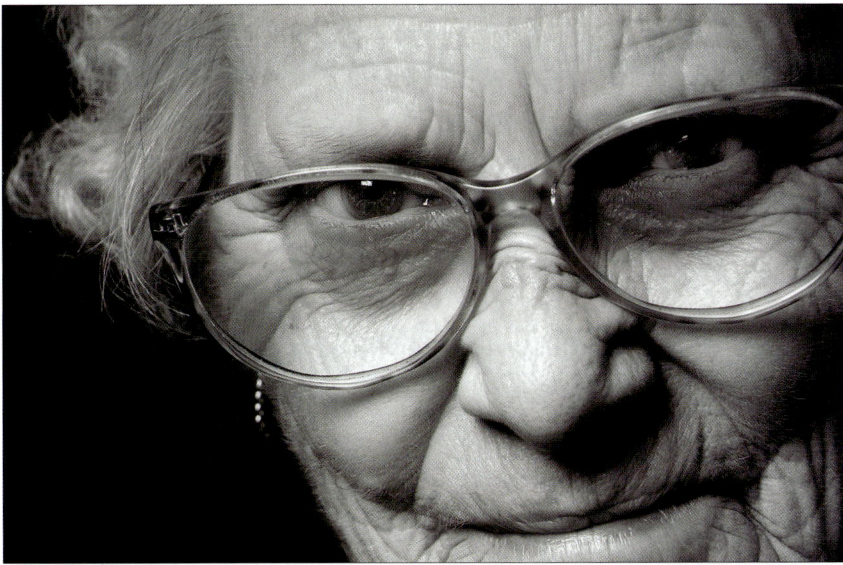

● RAB LETHAM "My lovely Mum Nancy, shot in the studio in colour and converted to black & white."

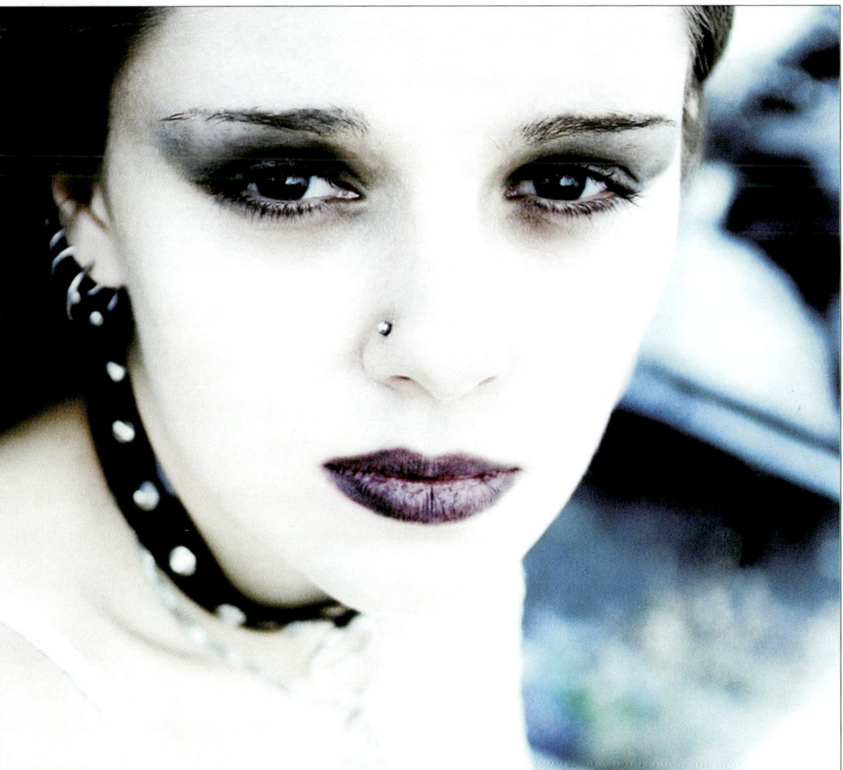

● ARNE HOFFMANN Arne titled this one White Goth. The tight crop and Photoshop editing have created a stark image with plenty of impact that suits the subject.

DIGITAL TIPS – DUOTONES

■ Photoshop has a very good, but underused colouring tool that's perfect for creating monocolour images. To get to this from a colour image you first go to Image⇨Mode⇨Greyscale to remove the colour. Then Image⇨Mode⇨Duotone which brings up a dialogue box where you pick colours for your Duotone, Tritone or Quadtone. Try experimenting with the various options using the Tritones mode. Click in the right-hand Ink 1 box to pick a colour instead of black and you will see that all the black areas of the

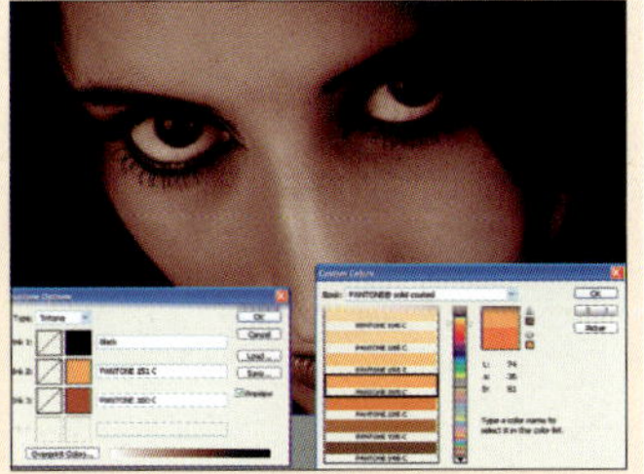

photo become the colour you select. For this reason it makes sense to choose a dark colour. Clicking on the colour box of Ink 2 (currently set at white) adds an overall colour to mid-tones too and this can be blended with the colour in Ink 3 to produce an amazing variety of tones. The box on the left of each ink lets you adjust the curves for each colour so you can create split tone effects over the highlights and shadows.

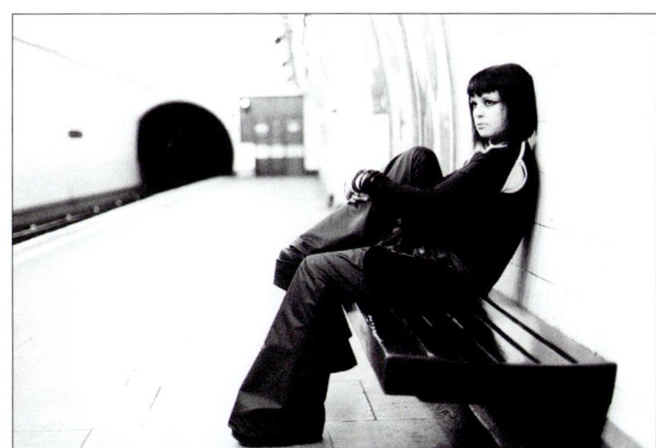

● CHARLES SCHMIDT "My friend Ruth, taken at Highgate underground station, using a Nikon F80 and 50mm lens."

EQUIPMENT TIPS – USE A REFLECTOR

■ Many photographers making their first steps into studio work often believe that they need to invest in a complex multi studio light set up. The fact is you can take really good portrait photos with just one flash head, especially if you add a reflector.

■ A reflector is a flat-surfaced gadget that is positioned so it reflects light from a point source towards the subject. There are many kinds available, in all shapes and sizes. The surface will be either white, silver or gold. White produces a natural bounced light while silver increases contrast and gold introduces a warm tone.

■ Most are made of material with holes in each corner that are stretched and attached over a frame to make it into a large flat panel. The frame often has a tripod mount so a stand can be used to hold and position the flat surface in the right position near your subject.

■ Lastolite came up with a novel approach with a patented fold away method that has since been used on pop up tents, bird hides and projector screens. The idea is that the material is framed with a collapsing metal hoop that folds in on itself to reduce the overall size by around two thirds. When it springs open to full diameter it creates a taught reflective surface.

■ Another ingenious product from Lastolite is the Triflecta. This comprises three reflective panels on an adjustable frame.

This was made popular by fashion photographer Stu Williamson who used it in the '80s to produce fantastic portraits with great catchlights.

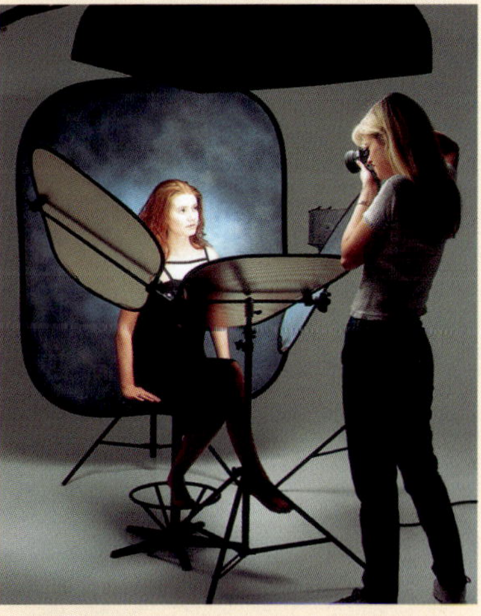

■ Do it yourself. There's nothing complex about a reflector. If you don't mind taking a Heath Robinson approach you can use a large sheet of white card to act as a simple reflector.

Take this concept a stage further and spray mount cooking foil onto the surface and you have a handy silver reflector. Some photographers crunch up the foil first so it creates a more diffused reflective surface.

For smaller subjects, even a sheet of glossy inkjet paper is fine to throw some light into the shadow areas.

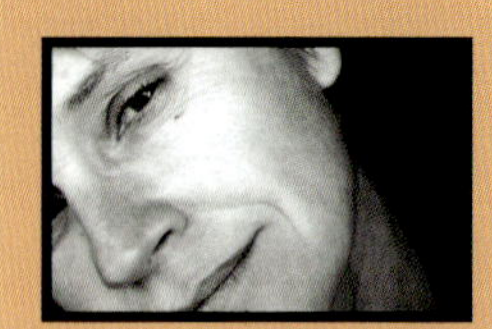

PORTFOLIO

JILL COLEMAN
This self-taught photographer uses her artistic background to compose vivid portraits.

I am a Zimbabwean-born South African, living in the Klein Karoo in the Western Cape region of South Africa. It is only two years since I took up photography seriously and I am basically self-taught.

I am also a painter and my artistic background has helped me immensely, particularly with colour, composition and expressions.

I studied photography for a brief time 20 years ago at Durban Technikon and during that time film was the only method available. Now, however, I work solely in digital, which I find to be just as rewarding as well as being much cheaper and quicker than using film.

My predominant interest in photography is portraiture, most often taking pictures of people within their natural surroundings. My images are simple, with sometimes unusual compositions. My main love is black & white photography, though I also shoot some portraits in colour. I shoot all my images in colour, converting selected images to black & white in Photoshop. I don't usually know what pictures will be black & white until after editing, it really depends on the mood. I use the gradient map rather than the greyscale option when converting, which seems to give much better tones.

The thing I enjoy most about portraiture is capturing emotion. I like my pictures to show reality and normal, everyday life. This means that sometimes my images can be very raw, but I would rather have that than glossy, perfect photographs.

In portraiture it's essential that the subject trusts you and feels at ease. I often take up to a year on my projects, gradually getting to know the person and gaining their trust. During the actual shoot

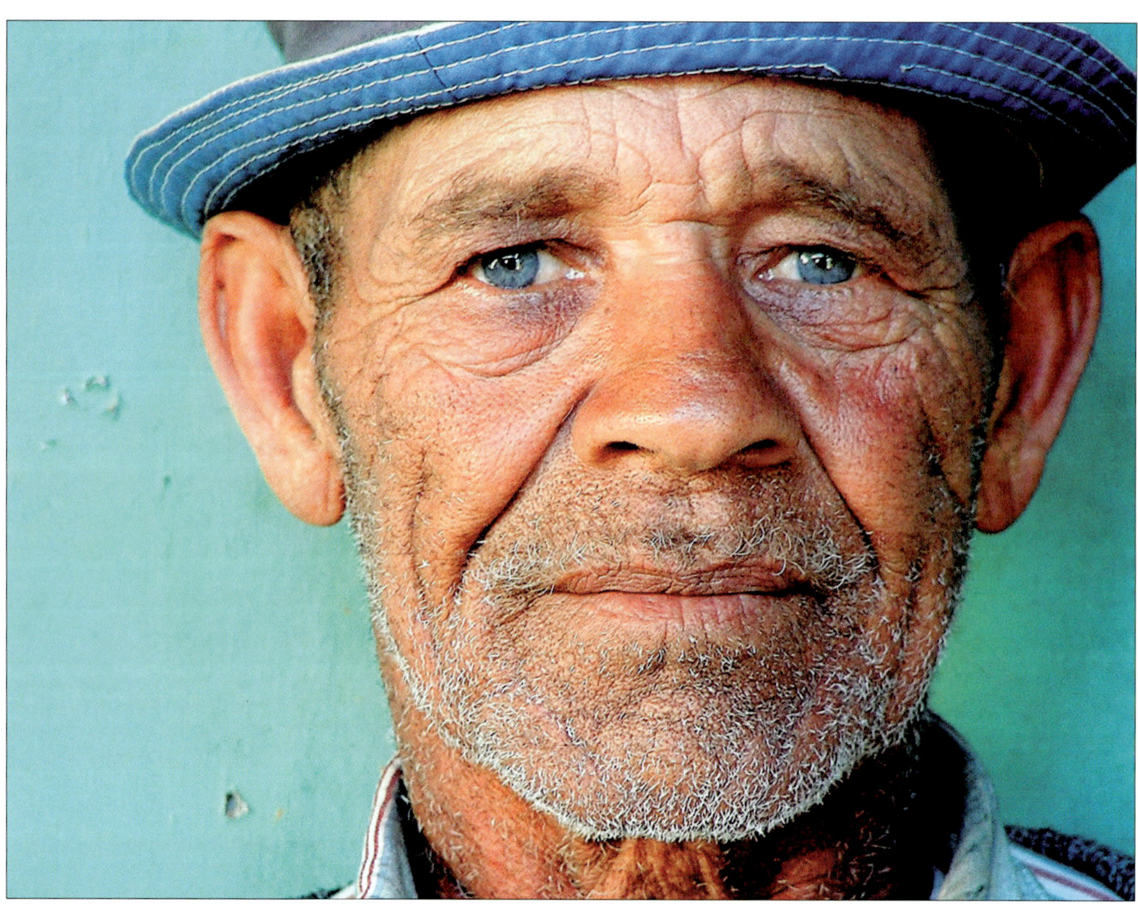

● Ol' Blue Eyes – Jan, a face of The Klein Karoo, taken near Uniondale, Western Cape.

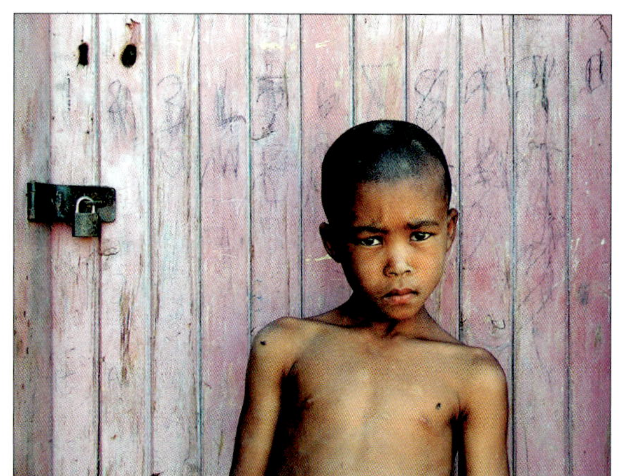

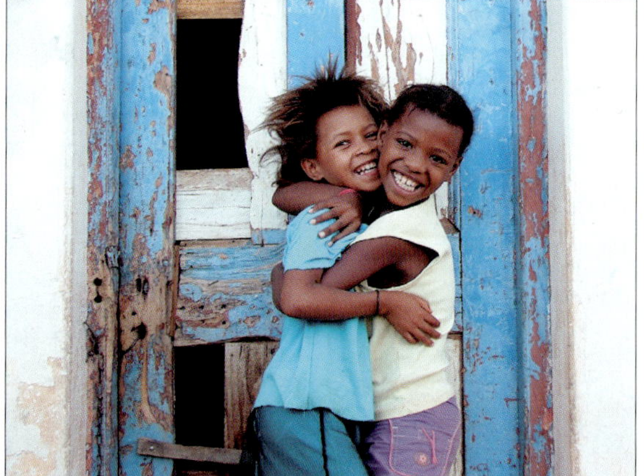

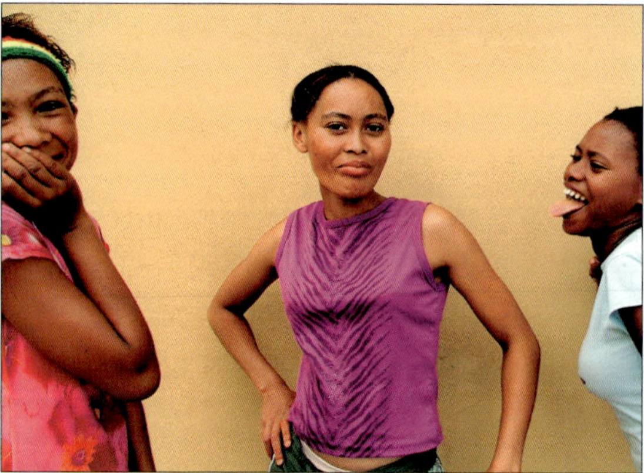

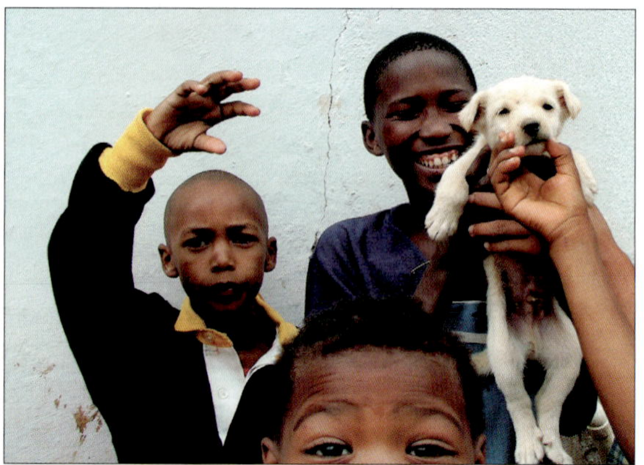

● Top left, clockwise 1: The Counting Door - A young farm boy from The Klein Karoo. 2: For Life – As in "Friends For Life". 3: Dog – Children on the Ostrich Farm, part of the People of the Klein Karoo Series. 4: Girls On Film – Angelina and the girls, taken in De Rust, Klein Karoo. These three tease each other when I shoot, so there is a lot of laughter and fun. I often tease them too and it seems to relax them.

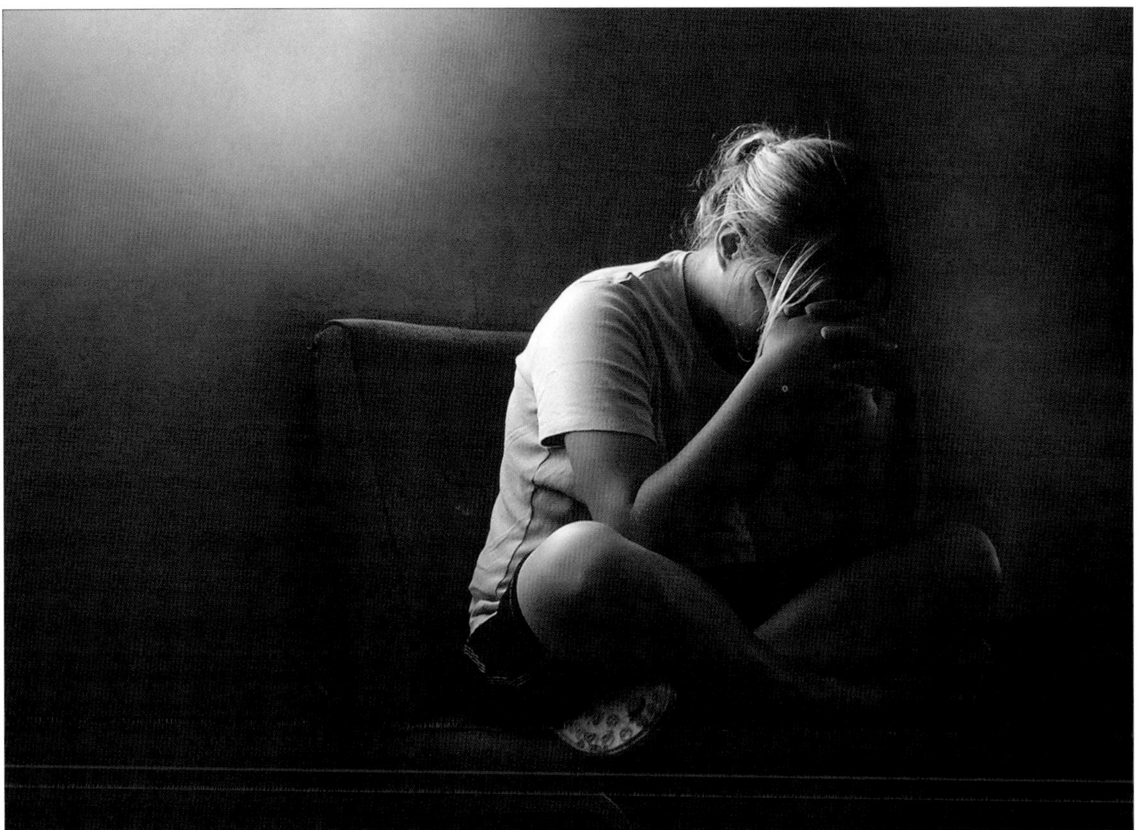

A recovering heroin addict, taken at an informal Church Service at Serenity Care Centre, South Africa. It's part of my recovery series. To me the photograph portrays everything that is wrong with addiction – it is very sad and very lonely.

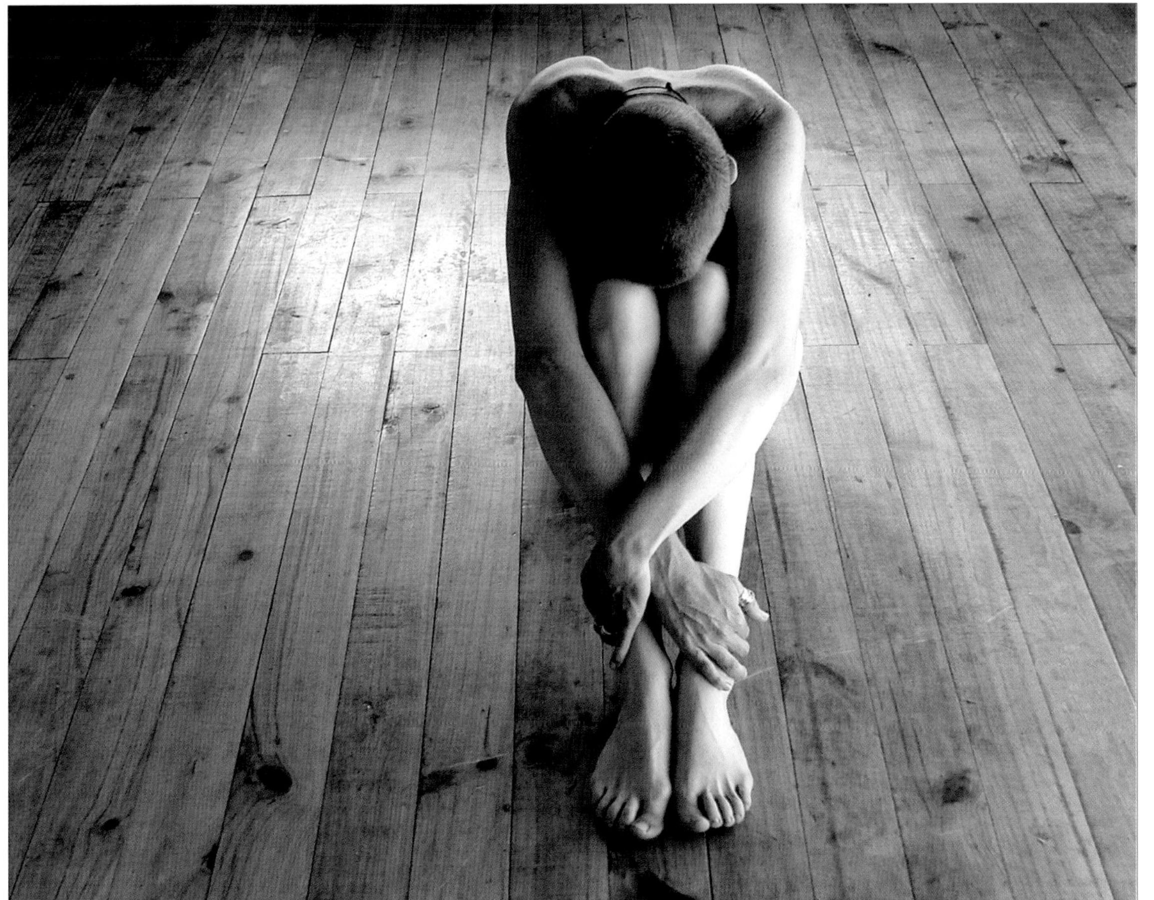

Another from my recovery series. One rape is committed approximately every 83 seconds in South Africa. Most are not even reported.

I work quickly, usually setting my camera on Automatic so I don't have to spend time setting up pictures. Shooting quickly means the subject doesn't have time to get uptight or start feeling shy. I find talking to the subject throughout the shoot also helps the mood and having a sense of humour always breaks the ice.

As well as portraits I also enjoy shooting flowers and nudes and I'm a great fan of good still-life, though I'm still learning that. Overall, I have the greatest respect for photo journalism and real life photography.

Because of my artistic background, my eyes tend to see things in a certain way and, as a result, some of my crops tend to be very unconventional.

My main influences in photography are National Geographic photographers like Steve McCurry and the well-known South African photographer, Obie Oberholzer. These photographers do inspire me but I am very much a person who likes to develop their own style and retain individuality. For that reason I don't read any how-to books, preferring instead to experiment in order to develop my own style.

The only essential equipment to me is the camera and lens, I don't really use anything else. In fact I still like some of the photos I took on a tiny little Olympus – I truly believe good photography is in the eye.

I do however find Photoshop extremely useful and think it's very important to have a good computer set up, especially the monitor. I am a recovering alcoholic and have found photography to be very therapeutic.

I put some of my pictures up in the rehab centre for the patients, which were then seen by a local magazine. The magazine then approached me and it resulted in my producing an article for them on the subject of drug addiction, alcoholism and the recovery process, accompanied by about eight of my photographs. This was great exposure for me but mainly I just hoped it would be of help to other recovering addicts. ∎

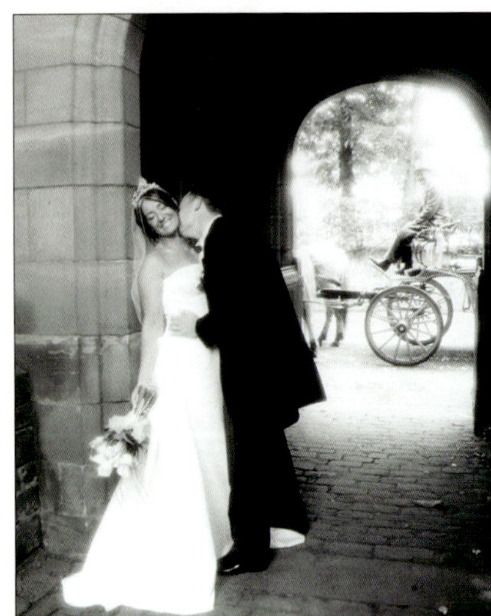

● JAMIE CARTER A moment of passion, captured in a reportage style at a wedding.

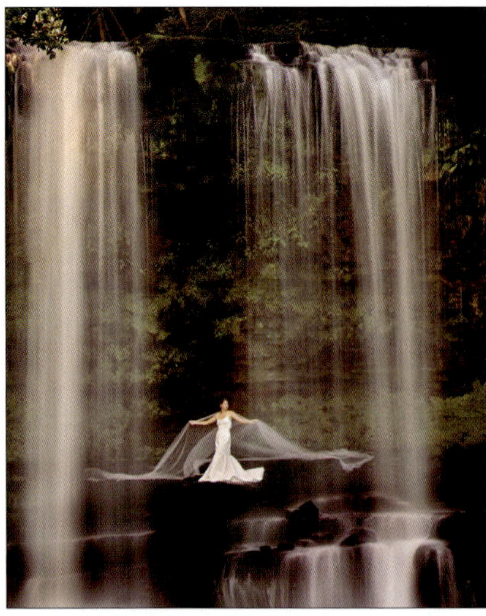

● KIM WALTON Bride behind the Famous Sgwd y Eira waterfall, Brecon Mountain National Park.

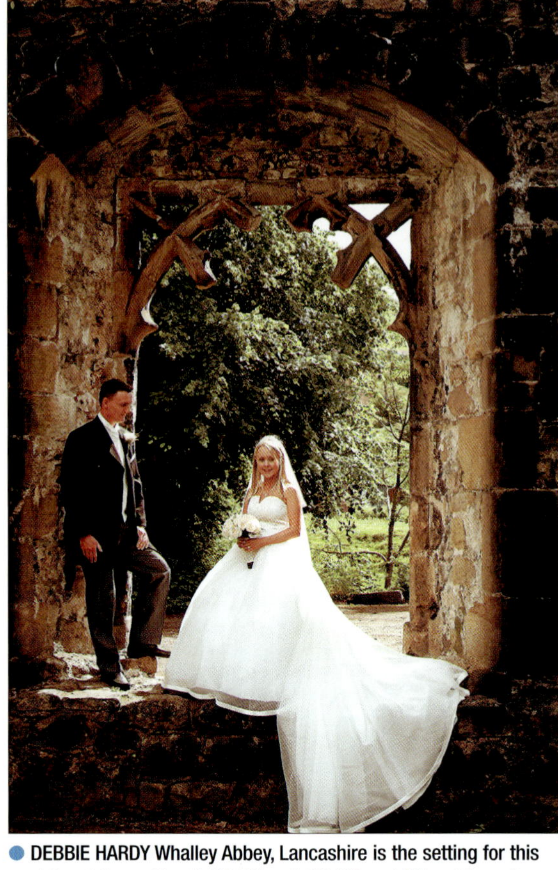

● DEBBIE HARDY Whalley Abbey, Lancashire is the setting for this wedding, taken with a Fuji S2 Pro at ISO100 and Nikon 85mm lens.

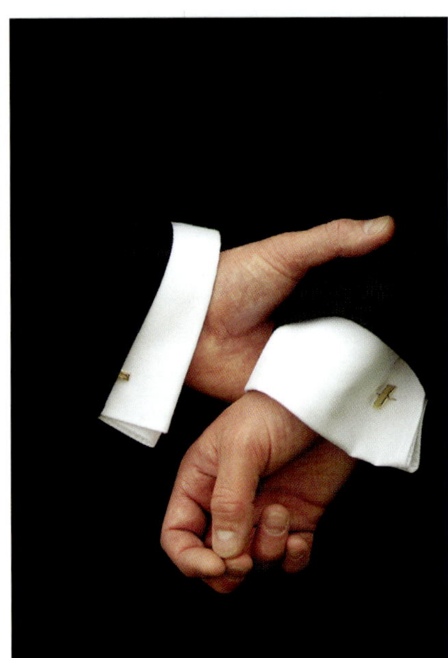

● MIKE FRENCH Reportage image showing the groom's anticipation as he waits for his bride.

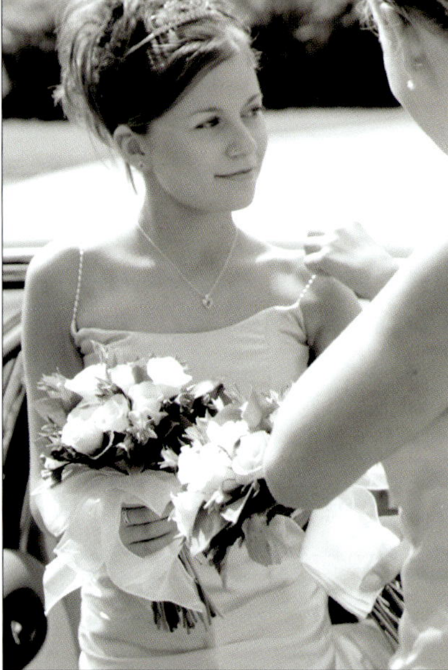

● ALAN ROXBURGH Shot in high summer with strong sun from the left to add to the challange.

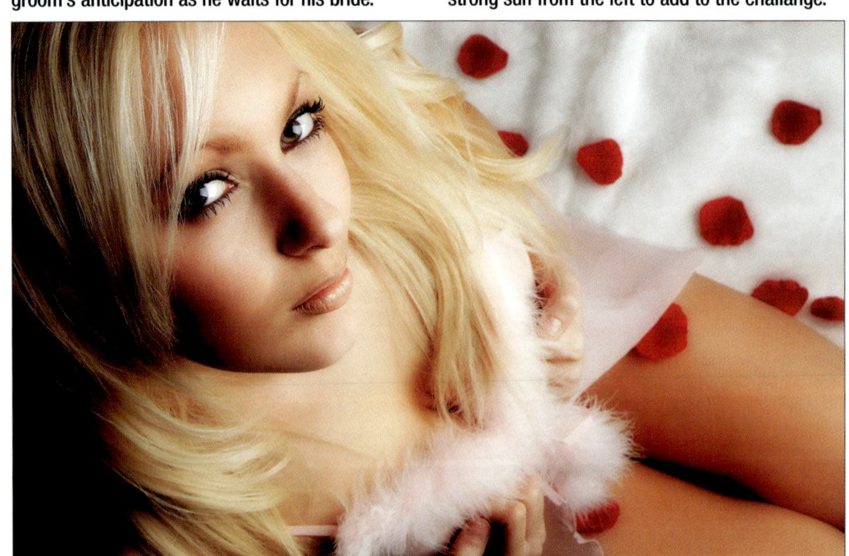

● PHIL DRINKWATER I chose to take this picture of HayleyAnn from a high angle to concentrate on her eyes and create more depth. A single softbox was positioned on the right.

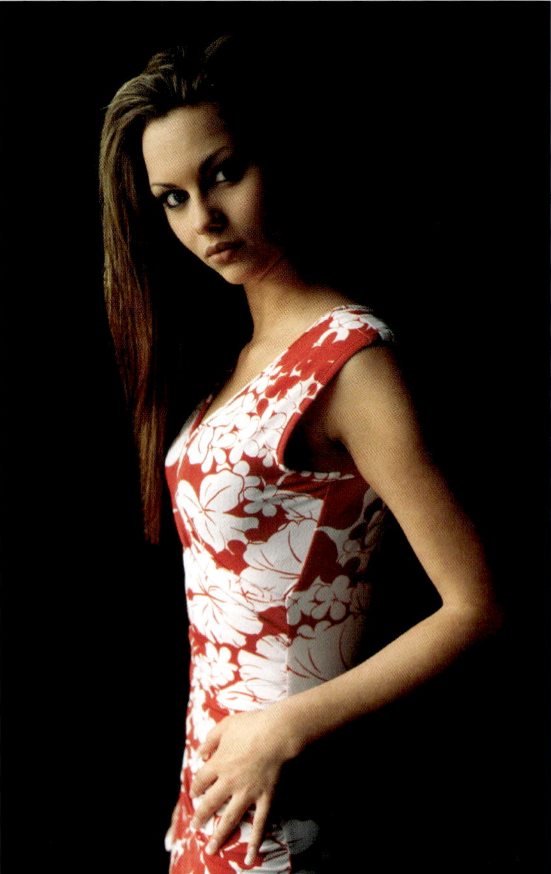

● ALAN BOOTH This shot of glamour model, Jessica, was taken using an old Pentax MG manual camera and just window light.

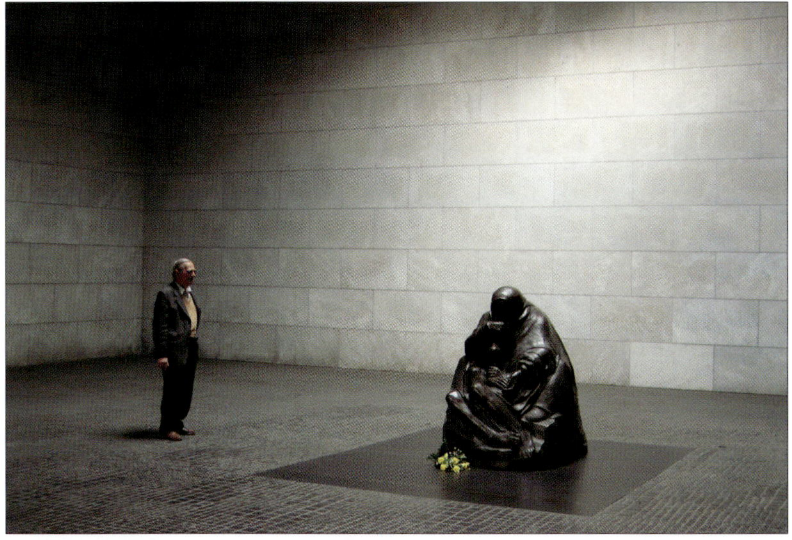

● PENFOLD MERTON One of Berlin's less crowded war memorials. It's almost empty most of the day, but those who do visit tend to stay quite a while. It's illuminated by a single skylight.

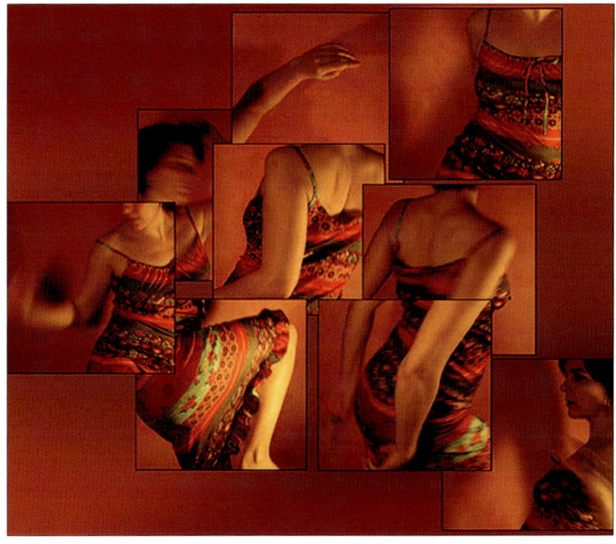

● LUCIE NADEJOVA A selection of self portrait photographs of Lucie dancing, then arranged in Photoshop to produce this interesting collage.

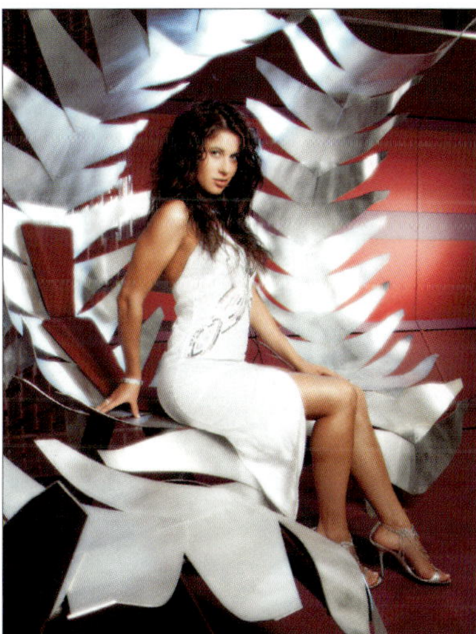

● AL MULROONEY This shot was taken on the set of a sci-fi film. It was lit by two flash heads at 1/160sec, and f/10 using the CCD set at ISO200 and an 18mm lens.

● PAUL WARD Taken for a local rap artist using a Canon EOS 1Ds and 17-40mm L lens for extreme perspective, single softbox plus backlights.

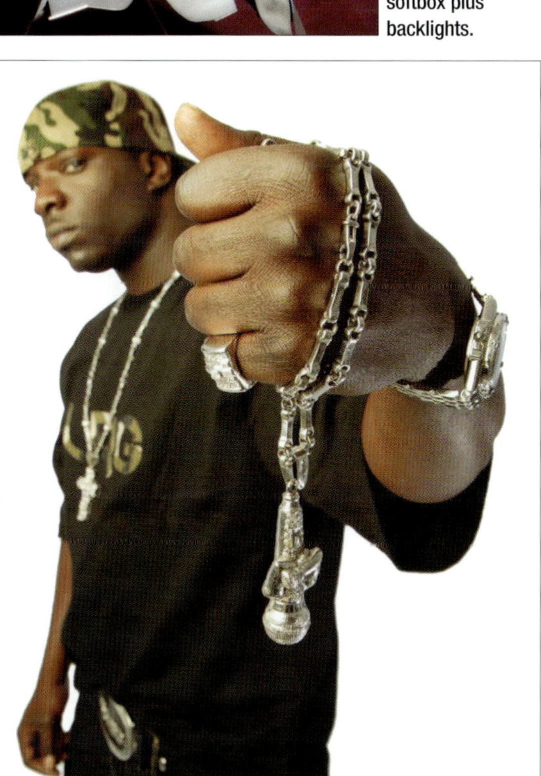

DIGITAL TECHNIQUE – CREATING A VIGNETTE

■ Portrait photographers have used filters or darkroom masking techniques for years to create light or dark vignettes around their subjects. Once a standard stock item in the wedding album, this technique can be applied with ease and much variety using a digital editing program.

1 This photograph of rock singer Beverly, taken using studio lighting against a grey fabric backdrop, will be used to create a dark vignette.

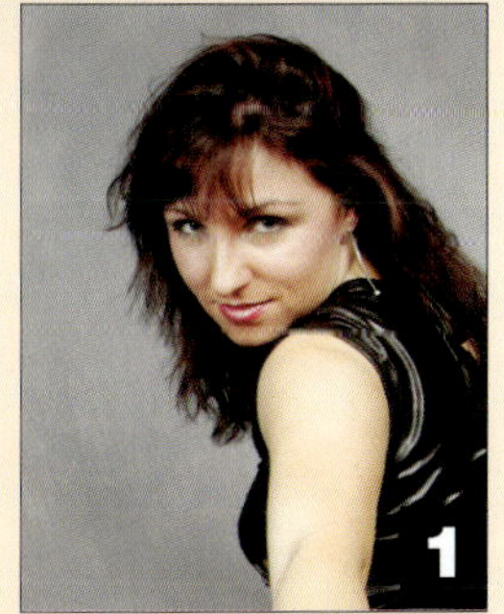

2 Choose the Elliptical Marquee from the tool bar (Shortcut key M), click top left and drag down to bottom right to create an oval dotted line around the subject. Click on the inside of the oval (with the Marquee tool still selected) and move the oval so it's positioned perfectly over the subject.

3 Go to Select⇔Inverse (Select+Ctr+I) to turn the selection from the oval area in the middle to the surround.

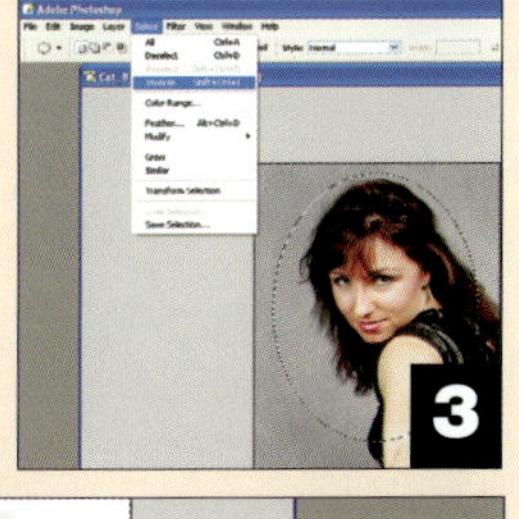

4 Feather this selection to ensure the vignette has a soft edge when applied later, Select⇔Feather (Alt+Ctr+D). The size you set the feather radius to depends on the number of pixels in the image. I usually choose a feather of around 3 to 5% of the longest side. So in this example, where the height was 1600 pixels, I selected 60 pixels as the radius – just under 4%. If you are too far out you can always undo using the History palette and reapply.

5 Now to change the Lightness using the Hue/Saturation option (Ctrl+U). Leave the Hue and Saturation sliders and adjust the lightness to the right for a high-key, white, vignette or to the left for a low-key, black vignette.

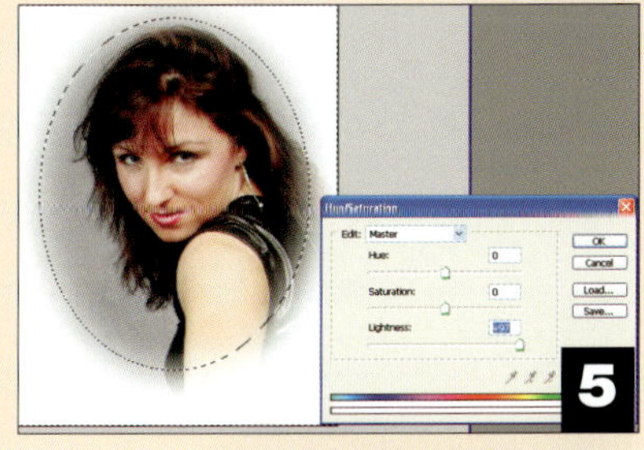

6 Whether you choose a high-key or low-key vignette will depend on the subject. In this example a harder more 'rocky' low-key was preferred, while a wedding portrait of a bride will often look better with a high-key vignette.

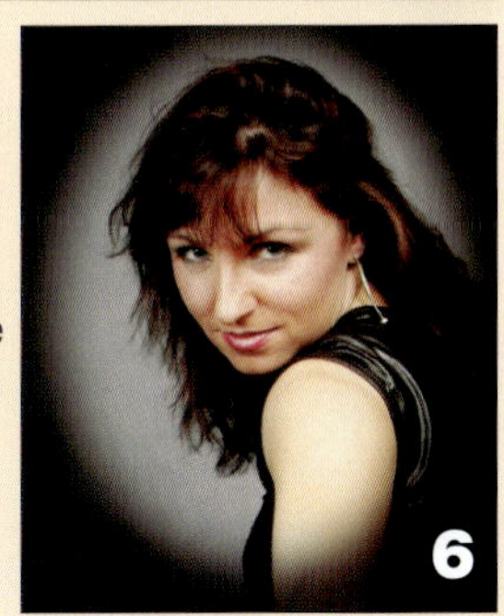

7 You can also use this technique to create many other filter effects. Using Gaussian Blur – Filter⇔Blur⇔Gaussian Blur at the final stage will make the photo look as though it's been shot with a soft spot filter. Using a new layer and a colour fill will make it look more like one of the Cokin Centre Spot filters and, with the image editing colour wheel, will give you infinite variation of colours to compliment the subject, if that's your kind of thing!

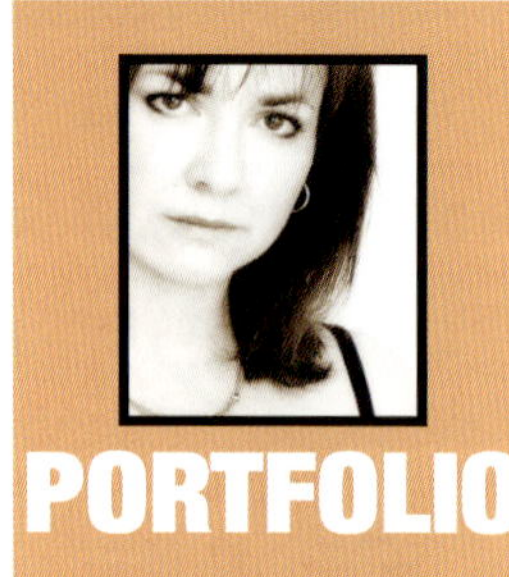

PORTFOLIO

KAREN BACON

Karen's not afraid to try her hand at any photographic subject, but portraiture will always be her passion.

I've always had a camera and enjoyed capturing snapshots, but they were just that, until I discovered ePHOTOzine and its wonderful members.

I was stuck in the house in the evenings. Being a full-time working single parent doesn't provide much of a social life or spare cash to spend on luxuries. But I bought a small compact digital camera and Photoshop Elements and I've never looked back.

Soon I was paying attention to more than just the subject in a photograph – once where my son would have had furniture sticking out of his head, he now had a perfect background. A background which was just a black dress – I had to improvise.

My passion for photography, especially portraits, grew. Eager to learn and to progress I borrowed a digital SLR and a whole new technical world opened up, from F-stops and shutter speeds to white balance and shooting in RAW. It's all a big learning curve and an ongoing process.

But my biggest learning curve was stopping myself concentrating on one subject, albeit a subject I loved. In order to learn I had to photograph everything, from dripping taps to standing track side at a Motocross event – I can still taste that dirt – but this step was essential for me in understanding the various genres of photography. By doing that I have a better understanding and appreciation of those who excel in different areas.

ePHOTOzine is a continual inspiration to me, it has opened my eyes again to a whole new world. I would now be lost without my camera; I've come to realise that the world is definitely worth photographing. ∎

www.dandelionphotographic.co.uk

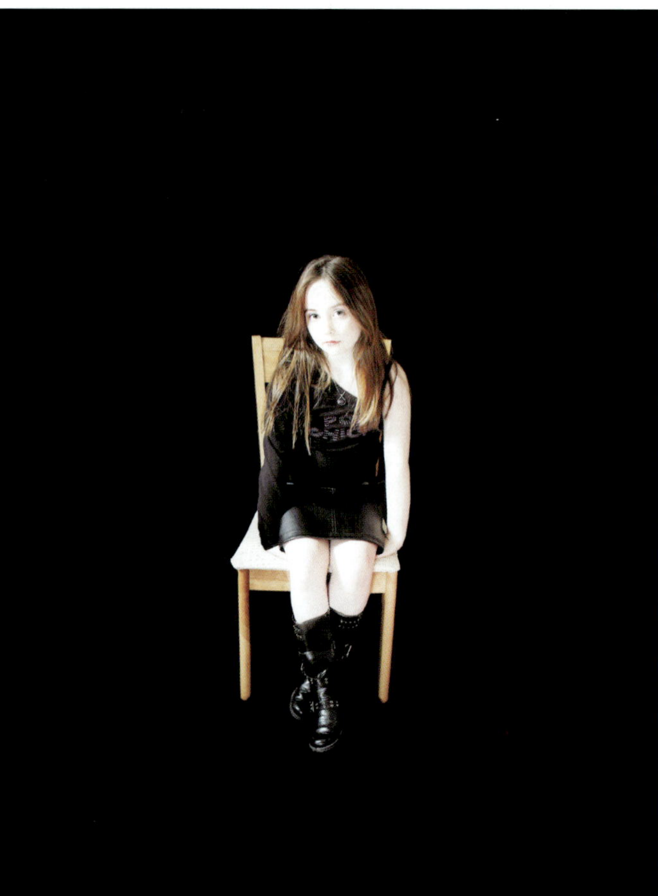

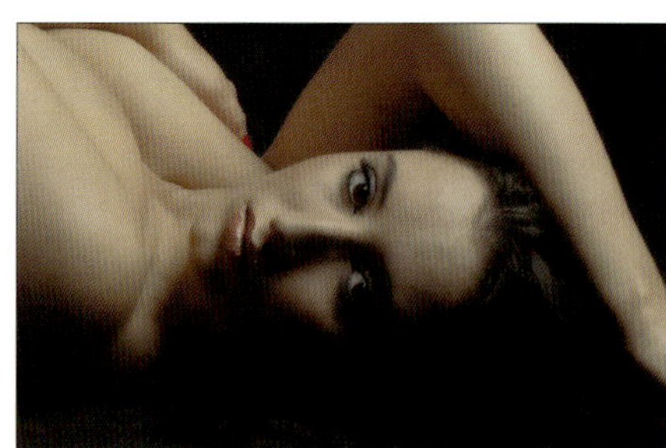

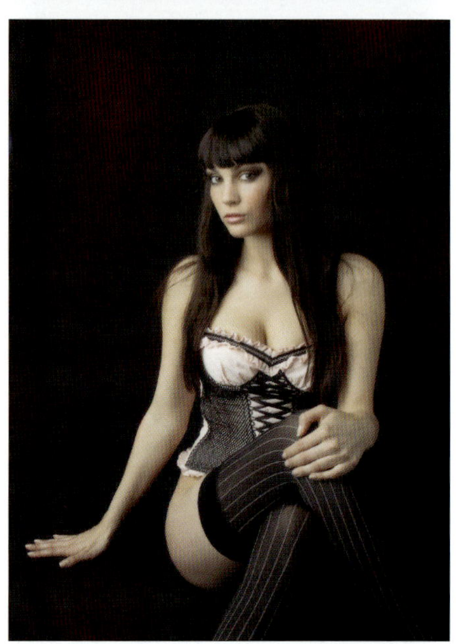

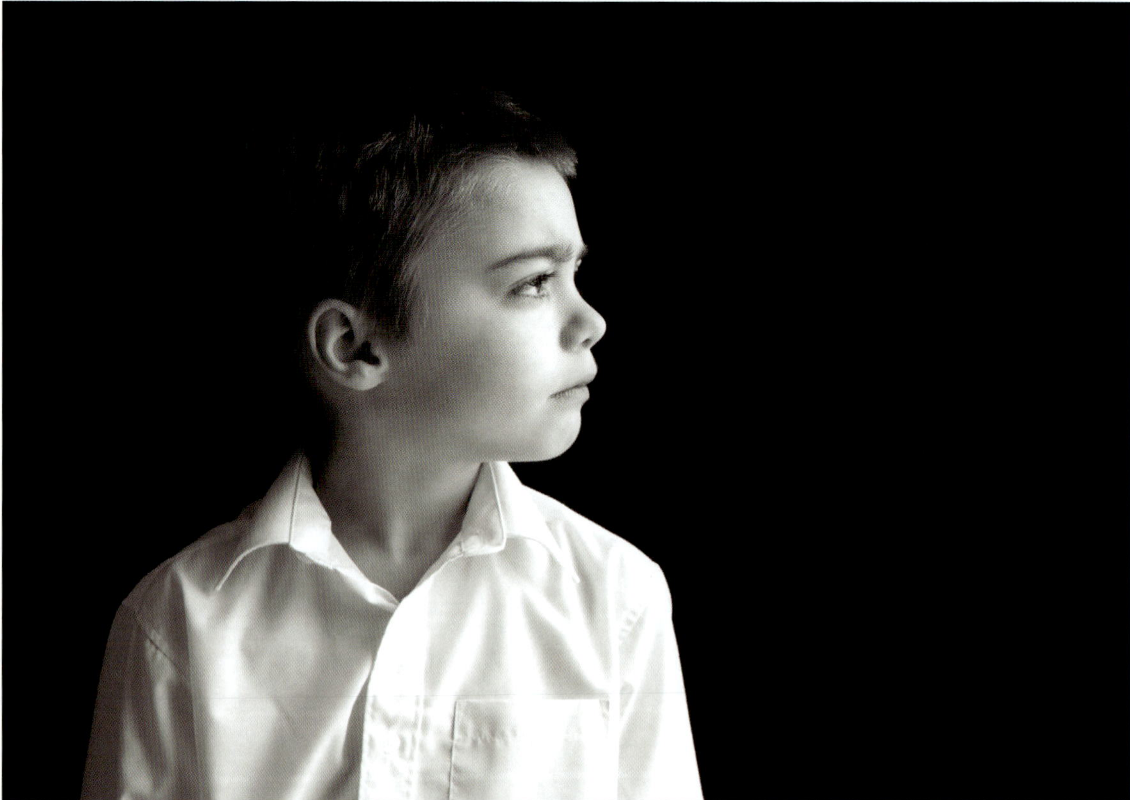

● Karen proves that you don't need to have access to lots of expensive equipment to take good quality studio style portraits. The photos top left and below were taken using either window light or basic Jessops Portaflash studio kit. The backgrounds are bits of material. These shots also show you can be more creative with your family photos – the willing models are her children. Top right was Karen's first venture into a studio using Worksop studios and model Jasmine. Middle right is Angelina, taken using a Bowens flash fitted with an Octo 150 softbox. The photos have been edited using Photoshop.

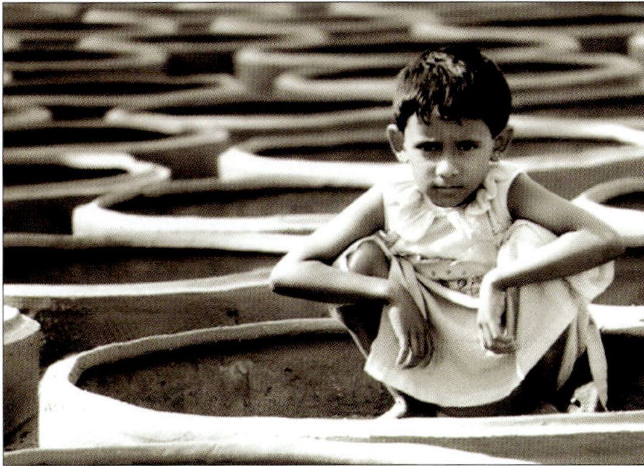

● RUDRA MANDAL Boy in Calcutta, taken with a Vivitar SLR with 70-210mm and an exposure of 1/60sec at f/8.

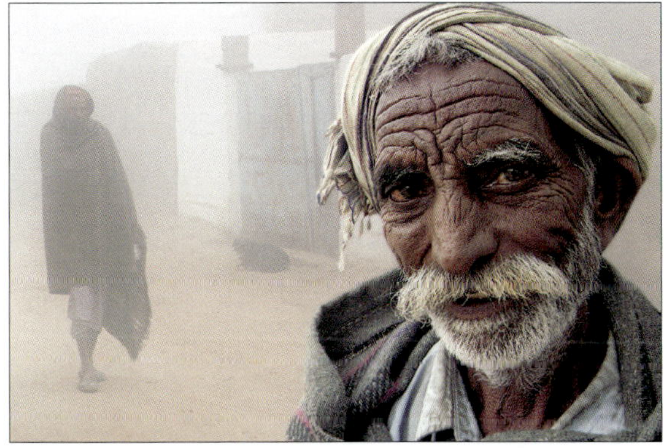

● ALAN BROWN Taken one morning in a Rajasthan village. Most of the village came out to see the stranger and be photographed.

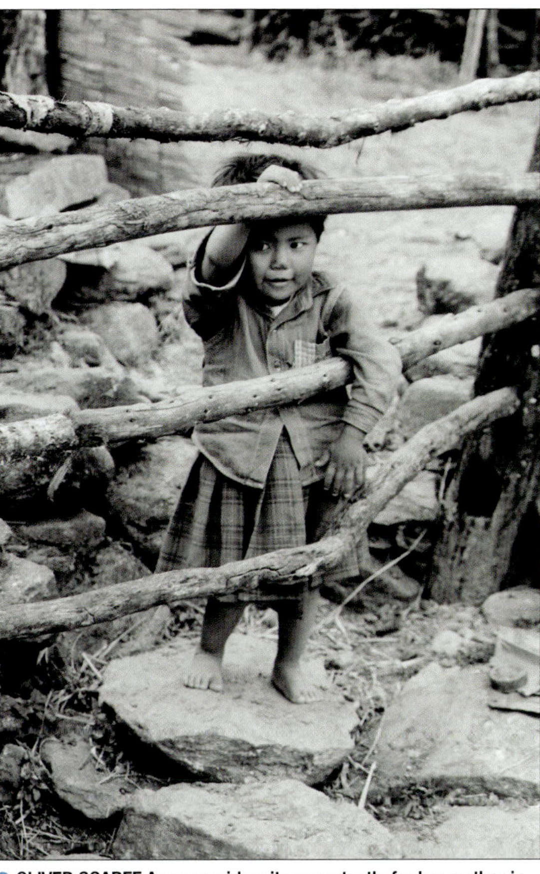

● OLIVER SCARFF A young girl waits expectantly for her mother in the Khumbu region of Nepal, Himalayas.

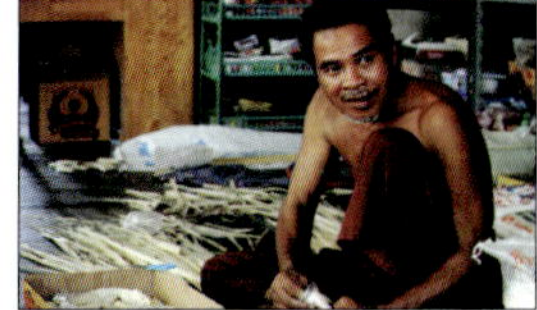

● NIC DUNCAN Man making cigarette papers from palm leaves. Koh Phangan, Thailand.

TRAVEL TIPS

While travelling you'll come across a wide variety of characters, from the wealthy to the famine-stricken. Each offers photographic potential, but you must be sensitive to people's situations and cultures.

■ Taking photos of people without permission can be a problem in some countries. If you're unsure, ask before taking. If you don't speak their language, holding the camera up while pointing at it and smiling may work.

■ Learn a few phrases, so you can say hello, goodbye, please, thank you, yes and no. If photography's an important part of the trip, knowing how to ask "May I take your photo?" will help no end.

■ Always thank the person when you have taken their photo and do so with a smile!

■ In some countries be prepared to pay for a photo; a small gift such as a pen or can of pop may please kids, while small amounts of money are very welcome to adults.

■ Look out for signs that request you not to take pictures – usually in museums and tourist houses.

■ Go on an organised trip to a village if you are concerned about safety. These are slightly more touristy, but you still get some interesting shots of locals in traditional dress.

■ Don't photograph military or police personnel, unless you have done research. In some countries you will be arrested for pointing your camera in their direction.

■ Take care for your safety when walking away from the main tourist areas. Expensive equipment attracts thieves.

■ Some downtown areas and back streets should be avoided, especially after dark. Your hotel will offer advice on which areas are safe.

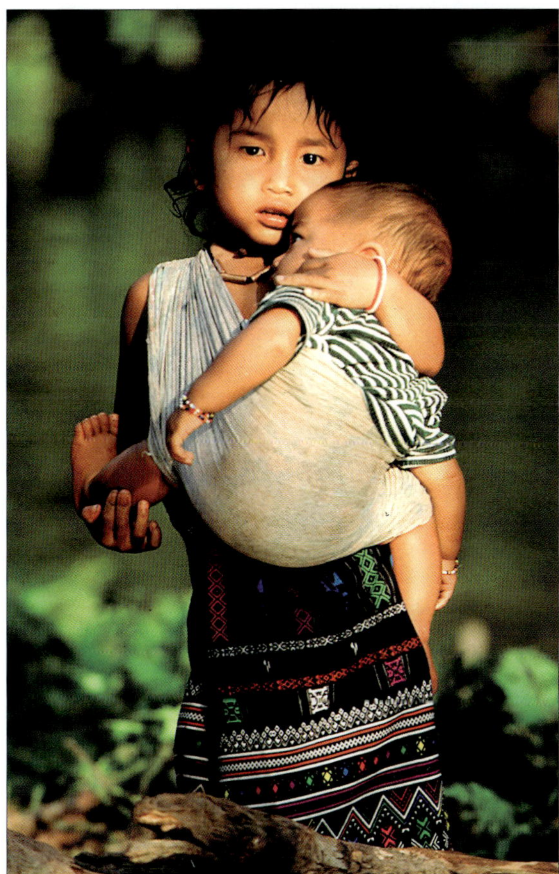

● DARRIN JAMES This shot of a young girl taking care of her younger brother was awarded Photo of The Year in a US Competition.

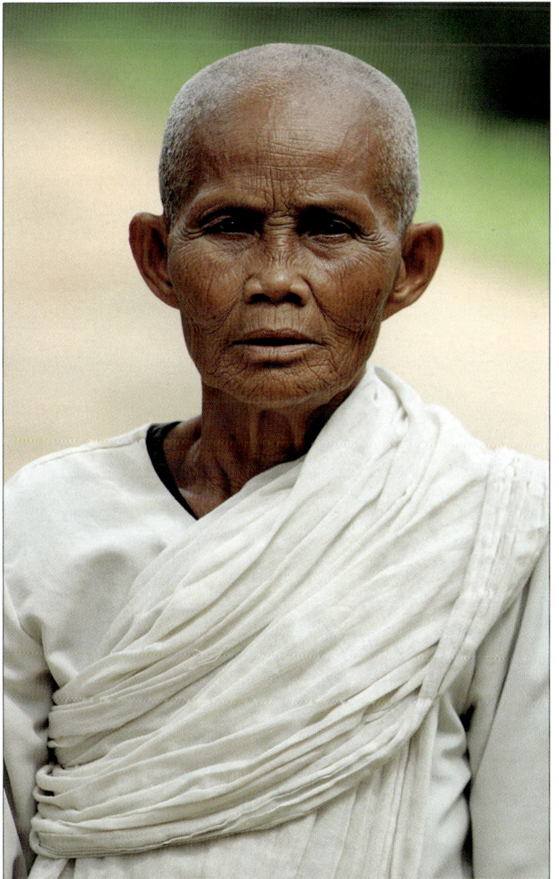

● NIC CLEAVE Cambodian village woman, Angkor village, Siem Reap, taken using a Canon EOS 10D, 70-200mmL at 184mm and f/4, 1/180sec.

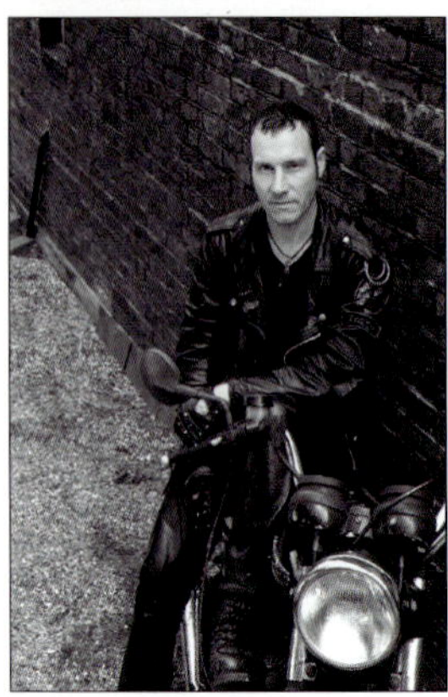

● DAVID BAILIE Biker taken at f/18 for maximum depth-of-field. A reflector was used too.

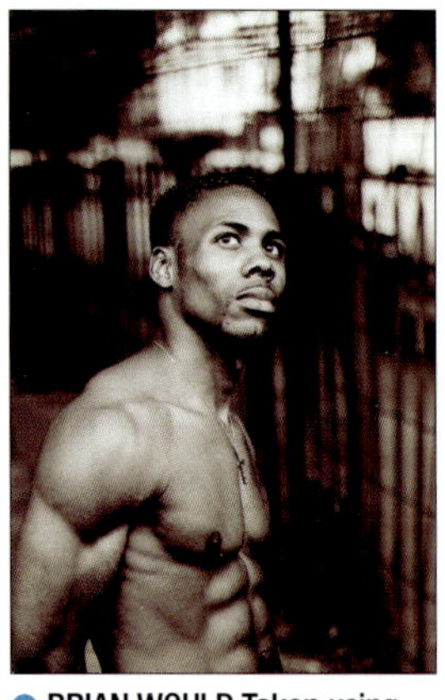

● BRIAN WOULD Taken using available light on XP2 film, loaded in a Canon AE1.

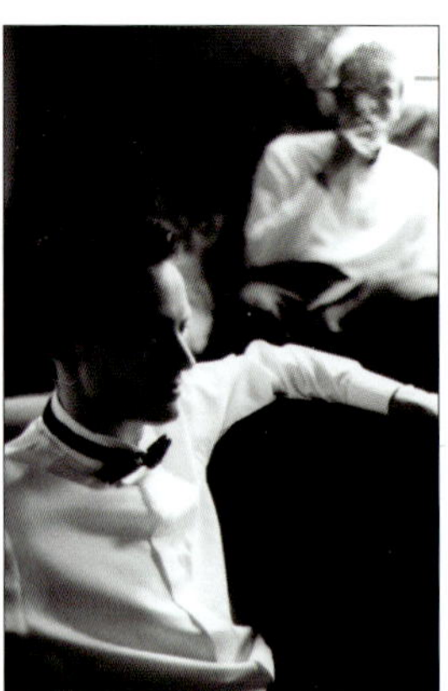

● JOHN PEAURT Pentax Asahi SLR using Ilford 200 B&W film. Natural light and steady hand.

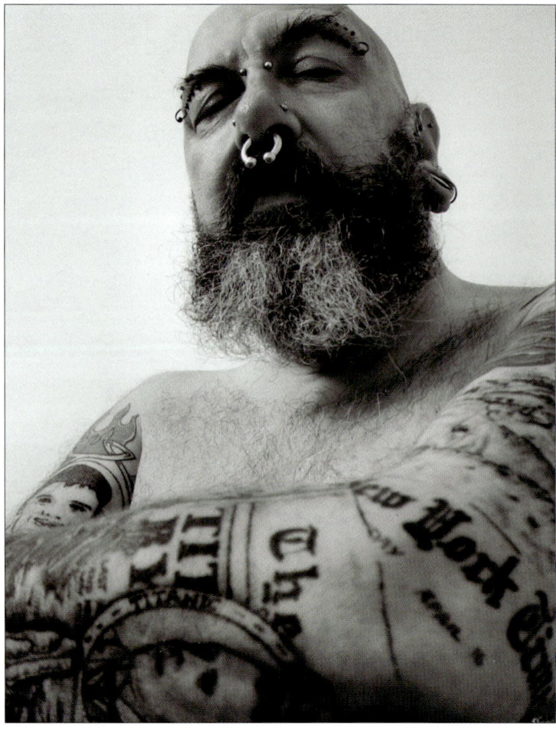

● STUART WEBSTER A 1/4sec exposure at f/2.8 using a Fuji S2 Pro. The image was then converted into B&W using Paint Shop Pro.

SHOOTING AND DIGITAL TIPS – DEALING WITH FLASH RED-EYE EFFECT

■ When you take a photograph of a person or animal using your camera's built in flash or one very close to the camera, you may end up with photos where the eyes are red or, in a an animal's case, green or yellow. This is because the flash reflects off the blood-filled capillaries in the back of the human eye or the tapetum layer behind the animal's retina that's used to enhance an animal's night vision.

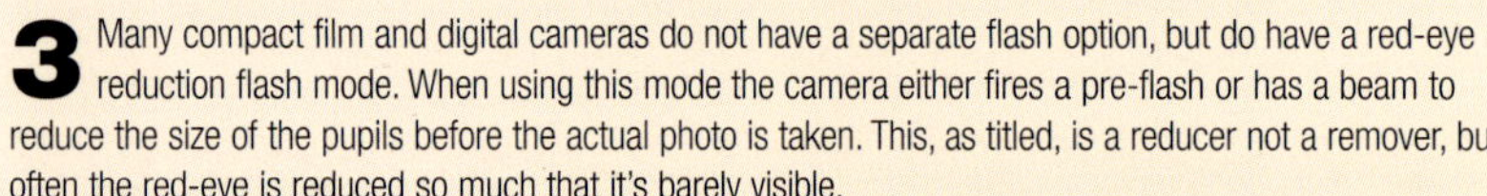

1 Red-eye effect can be removed digitally with relative ease, as explained later, but it's better to reduce it when you take the photo to save you time and effort. There are several options.

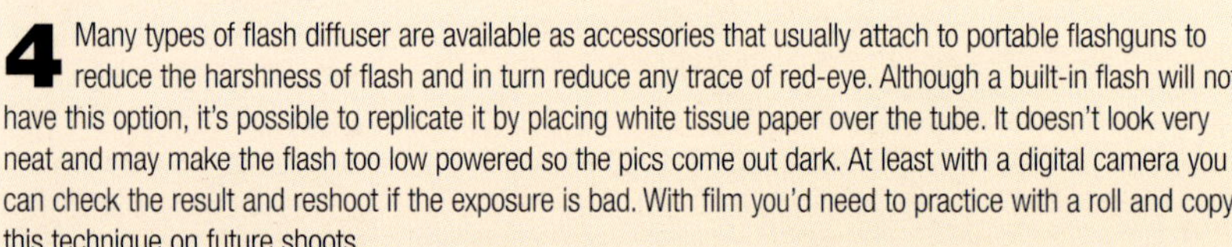

2 The built-in flash is almost on the same axis as the lens and that's when the effect is strongest, as the light is bouncing directly back. Some cameras have a flash socket or hotshoe to allow an optional off-camera flash to be used. This usually removes the problem totally.

3 Many compact film and digital cameras do not have a separate flash option, but do have a red-eye reduction flash mode. When using this mode the camera either fires a pre-flash or has a beam to reduce the size of the pupils before the actual photo is taken. This, as titled, is a reducer not a remover, but often the red-eye is reduced so much that it's barely visible.

4 Many types of flash diffuser are available as accessories that usually attach to portable flashguns to reduce the harshness of flash and in turn reduce any trace of red-eye. Although a built-in flash will not have this option, it's possible to replicate it by placing white tissue paper over the tube. It doesn't look very neat and may make the flash too low powered so the pics come out dark. At least with a digital camera you can check the result and reshoot if the exposure is bad. With film you'd need to practice with a roll and copy this technique on future shoots.

5 One of the most simple methods is to ask your subject to look at a bright light just before you take the photo. This has the same effect as the camera's beam version of red-eye reduction and reduces the pupils to reduce red-eye. To make this even easier, stand with a brighter light near you so that the pupils are automatically reduced.

6 You often read advice suggesting that you take the shot when the subject is looking away from the camera. This sometimes helps and can make the photo look more natural and less staged, although some cameras still produce red-eye even when the subject is at a 90° angle to the camera.

7 If all else fails use your image editing software! Select a small area around the red pupil using the Eliptical marquee or Lasso tool and Feather the selection by a small pixel radius. Then go to Image⇨Adjustments⇨ Replace Colour. Click on the eye and adjust the fuzziness slider so all the red part is selected. Adjust the sliders below to a suitable colour.

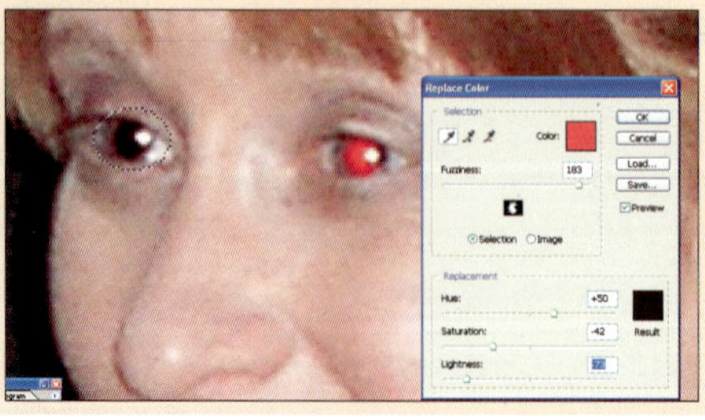

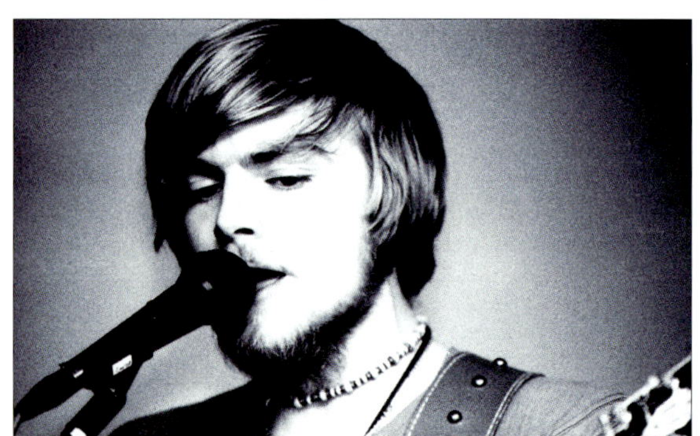

● ROBERT ANTHONY Hand-held Pentax P30 at 1/60sec on Ilford HP5+ film with 80-200mm lens at 200mm. Blue toned in Photoshop.

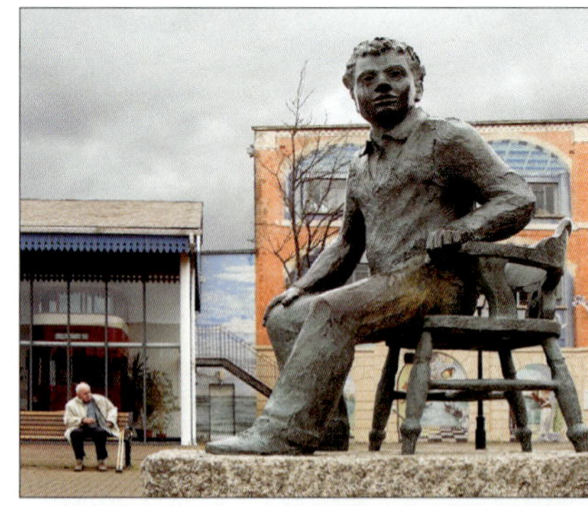

● ADRIAN R TURNER Abstract relationship between Dylan's statue and the elderly gent.

● CHRIS JOHNSON I like the dim lighting, the dark straight lines and the No Right Turn sign.

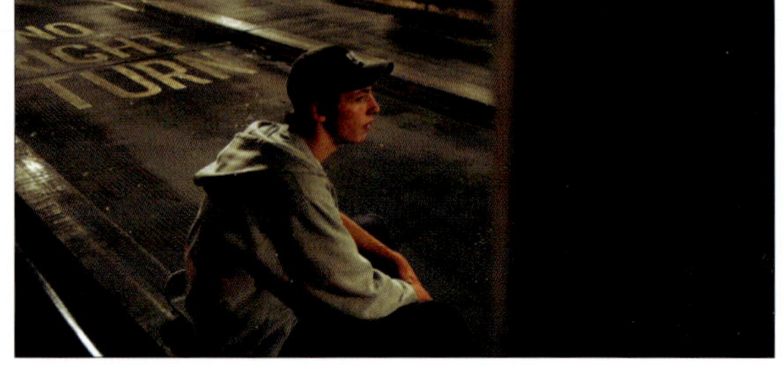

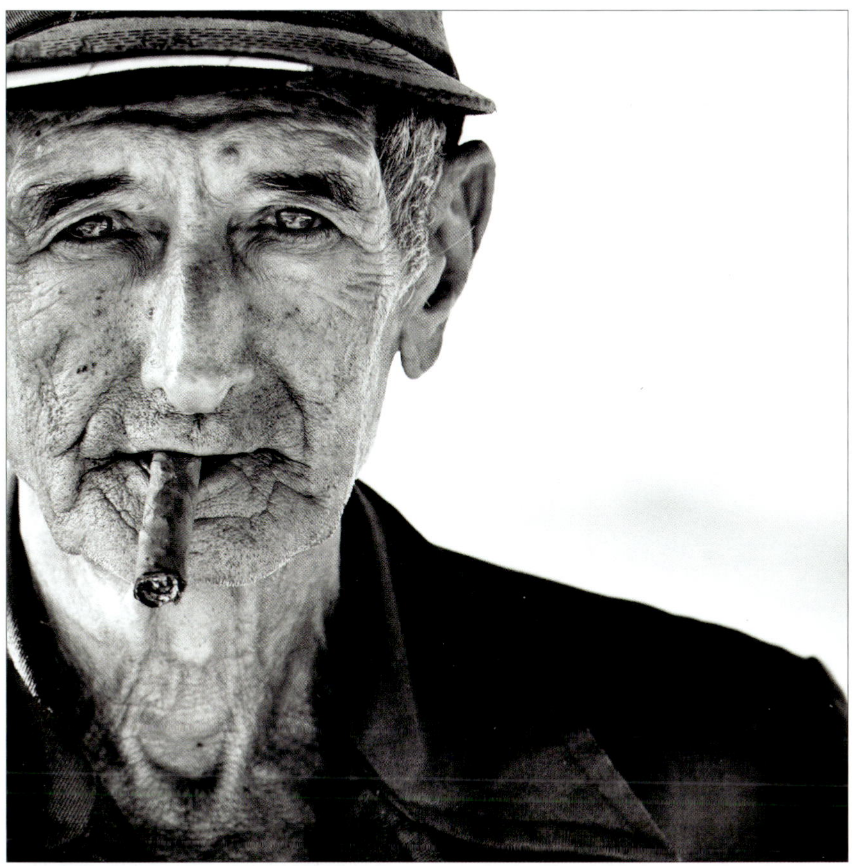

● OISTIEN THOMASSEN A very friendly fisherman at Playa Giron on the south coast of Cuba. He was on duty this afternoon, guarding the boats. Tight crops like this can have much more impact.

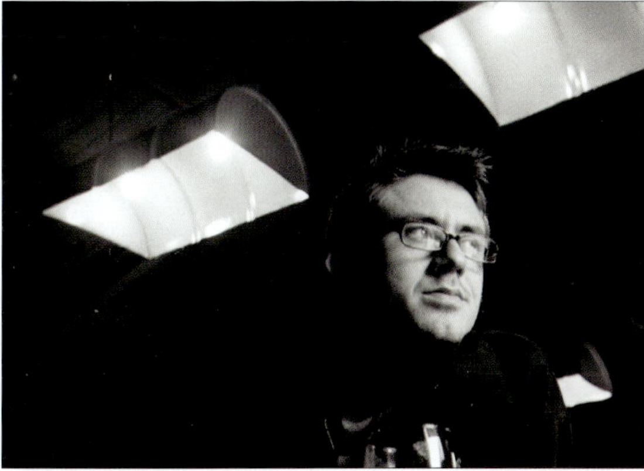

● ANTHONY S HAMILTON This was my first shot using a Lubitel 166B medium format with a Kodak TX400 film, taken at a local pub.

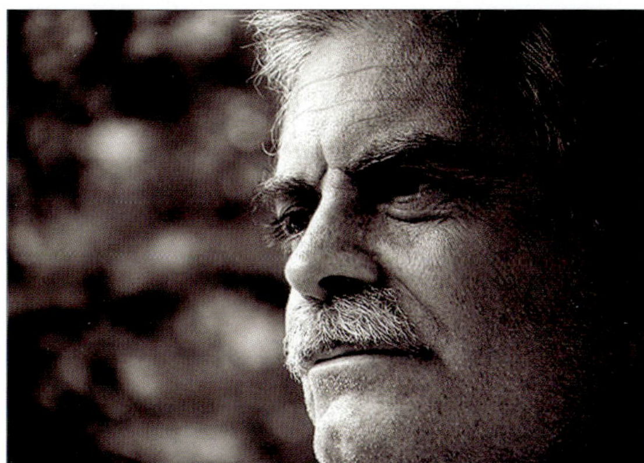

● BRAD D'AMICO This is a picture taken of my dad and one of the first taken after purchasing my new Fuji S5000.

UNUSUAL CROPS

■ Several of the portrait photos in this section go against the normal portrait where the head is bang in the centre of the frame. Although it's often an automatic approach to shoot with the head in the middle, a tightly cropped and off-centre portrait can, as you'll see, be much more dramatic.

■ You don't have to crop in camera. Use your image editing program's crop tool to remove detail later. Or, on film cameras, ask for a hand print, indicating what you want in the cover letter to the processing lab.

■ When tight cropping, it's better to have the subject looking in to the frame rather than out.

■ Don't be frightened of cropping into the head or chin, but leave enough to make the portrait complete. The photos bottom left and top left of this panel are good examples.

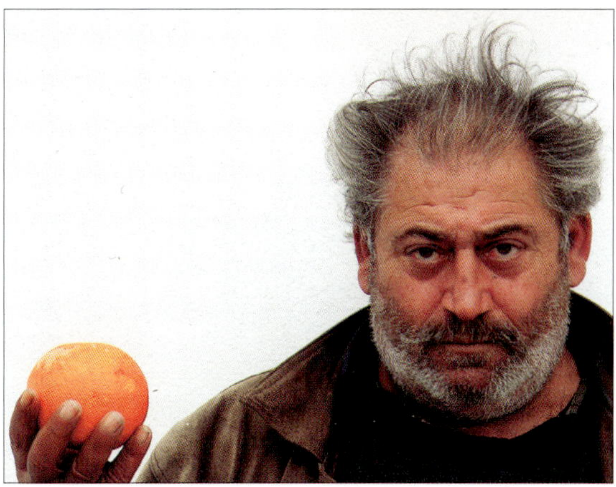

● LYDIA MOORE Georgie is a rather eccentric character and very happy to pose holding an orange, without even asking why!

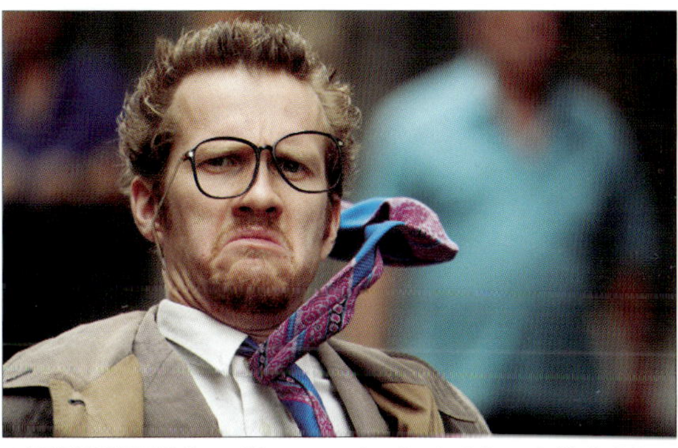

● KEITH HENSON One of the many street entertainers in York, taken using a Canon EOS-1Ds and EF100-400mm L lens set at 400mm.

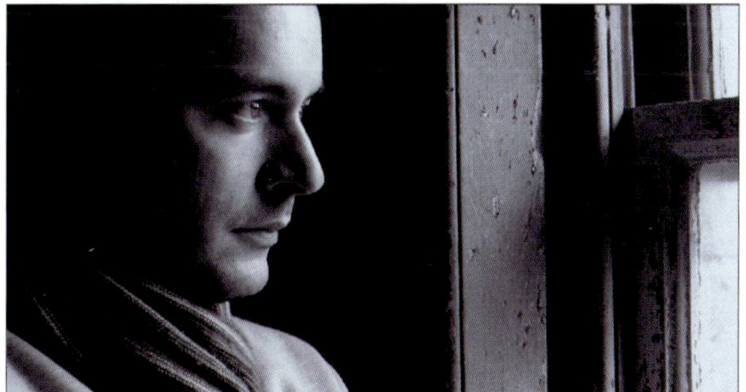

● TOM MARRIOTT Taken using a Sony DSC-P73 with 1/50sec speed and f/2.8. A cooling filter was added in PS to enhance the winter feel.

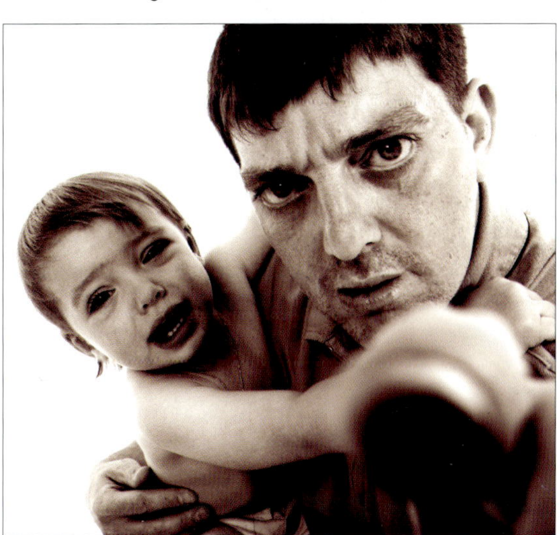

● JOHN PARRIS "Shot in our studio. The Dad wasn't really angry. I just clicked at the perfect time when he picked up his crying child."

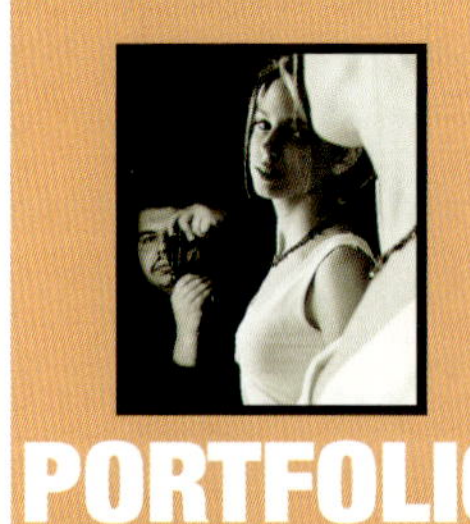

PORTFOLIO

BARTOSZ KLIMASINKI
Bartosz uses unusual angles and unconventional crops to make his photos more interesting and different.

My first photography experience was four years ago. I shot just two rolls of film of landscapes, using a Kiev 4, and realised it wasn't what I wanted to do, so I left photography.

Some time later I had problems forming a band, but I thought I would stay in music in another way and started to take pictures at concerts using a Zenit 12XP. This lead me to take portraits and I soon found it was what I liked best. I started looking for people who could pose and two or three years ago I met my first model. I shot some fashion photographs and started education in art school.

Now I'm writing a diploma in fashion photography and I want to continue studying photography.

In the beginning, I looked for models on the internet and in my school and many are just my friends. I now know some professional models in my city that work with fashion designers.

To make the session with a particular model easier, it's a good idea to talk before and during the shoot, not to hurry, and to have some music if it is possible.

Many times I use unusual angles and unconventional crops to make my photos more interesting and different. I was told first in music school and then in art school that if you know the rules you can break them. I want to be recognisable, to show how I see things and people, to have something to say. The world is full of look-a-like photos.

I now use a Nikon digital camera, but I still love to use 35mm film, especially if the developed photos are going to be used big. The grain looks fine and I prefer it to big pixels from digital photos. In my opinion medium-format cameras are still useful – I

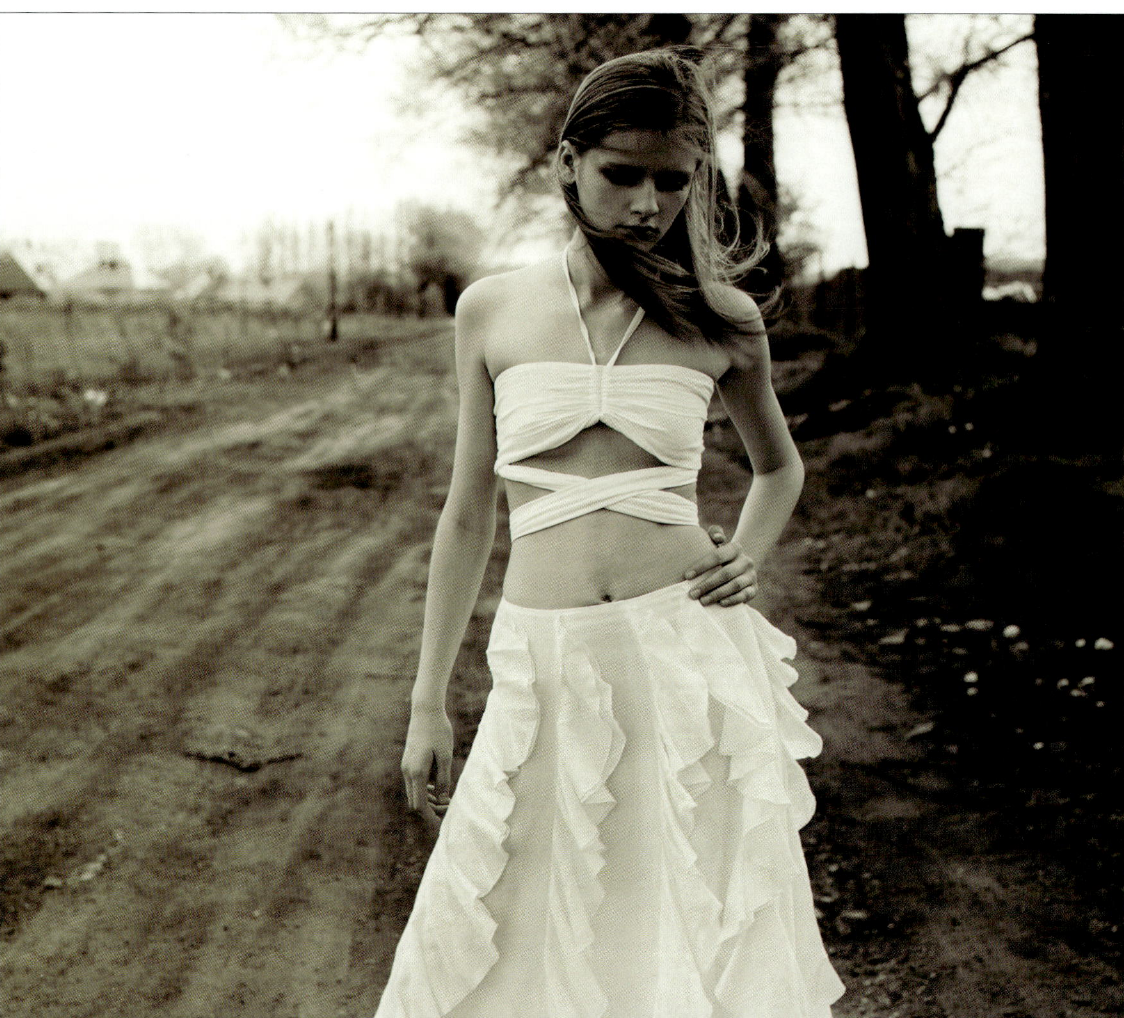

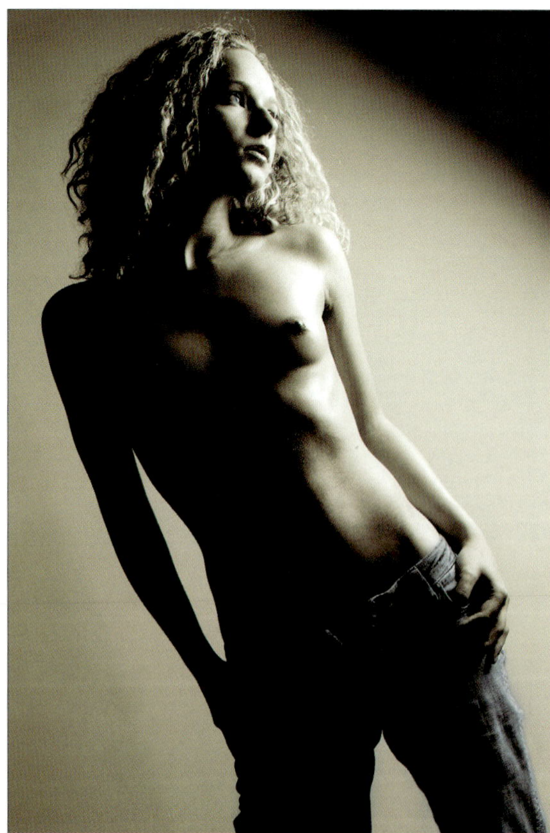

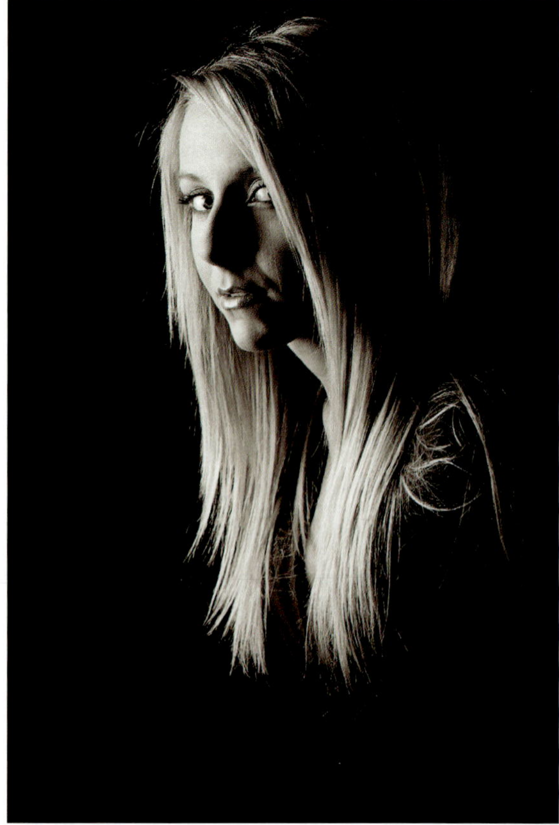

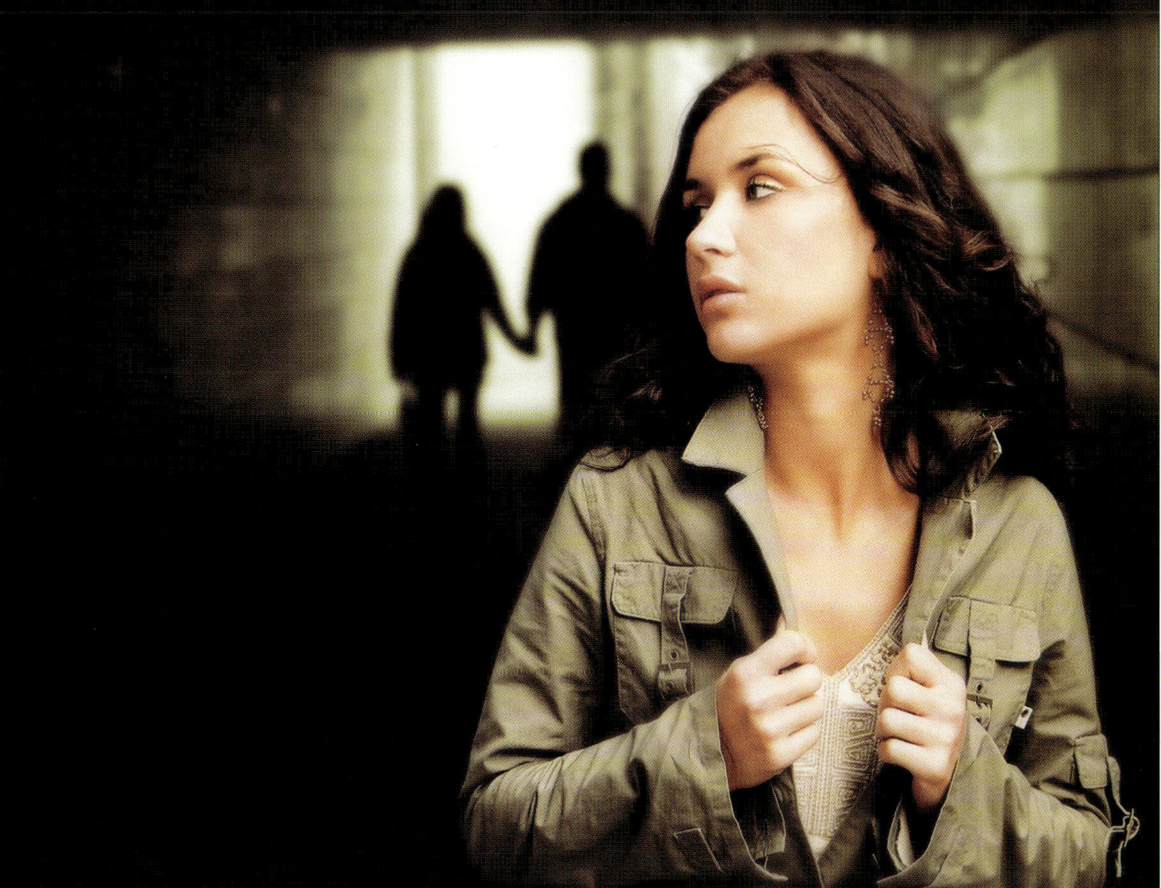

used a Kiev 80 and now have a Bronica. I love the quality and the nobility of the film, especially black & white.

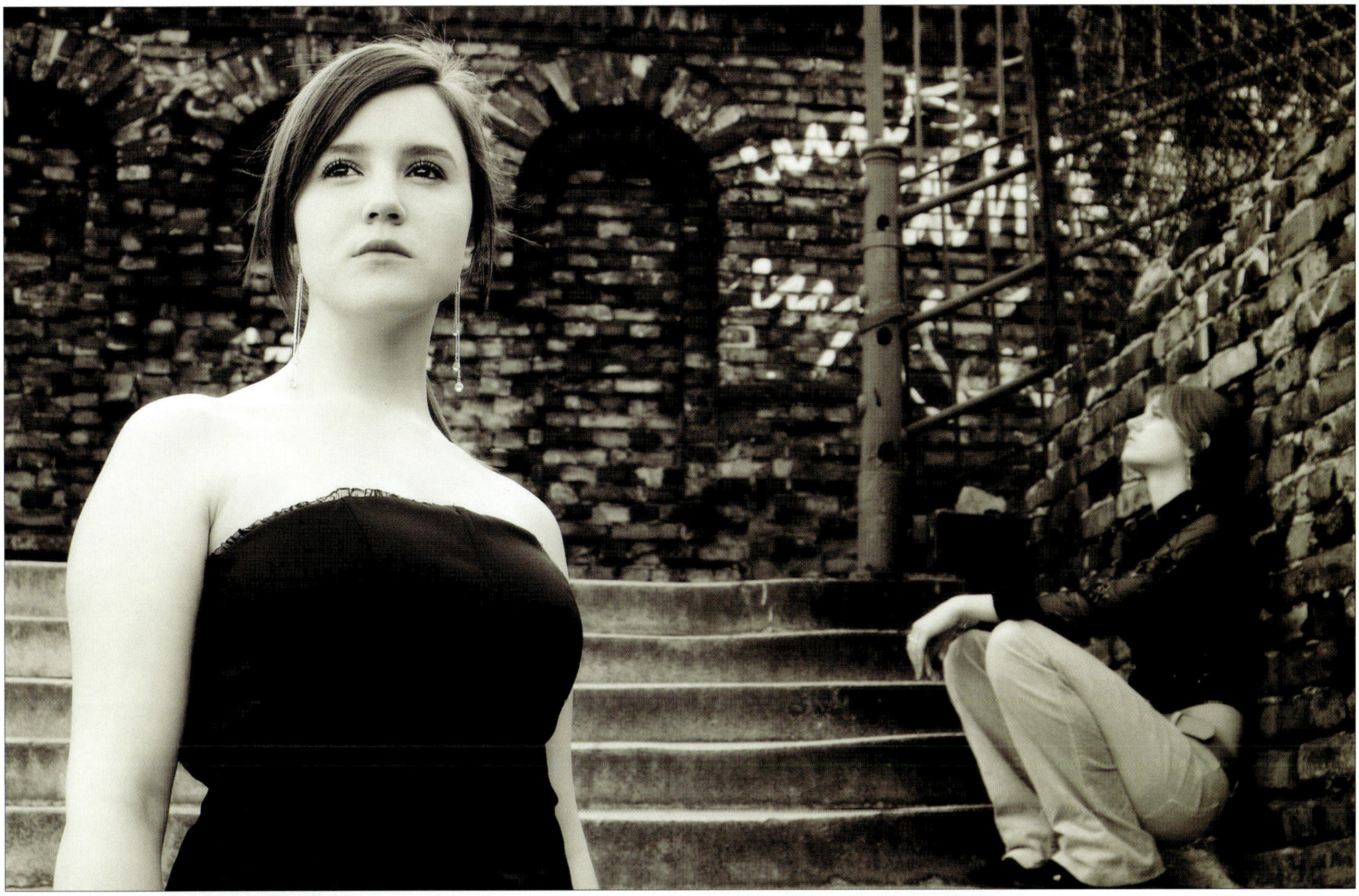

My favourite lighting set up is using just one light with a softbox. This gives great shadows and lighting that an umbrella can't give me. Some people say that it's not natural because of the dark shadows, but I like it and it's similar to outdoor in full sun or indoor with only window light. I sometimes use a white or silver surface to light the shadows on the face.

For the next few years I plan to write diplomas in photography and computer science at my technical university. I would like to study to improve my knowledge of making and directing films in a cinematography course. I also intend to do some magazine and advertising photography.

The five photographs here were taken using either the Nikon F80 film camera or the Nikon D70 digital SLR. ■

www://feliz.pl
email: f@feliz.pl
tel: +48 600948441

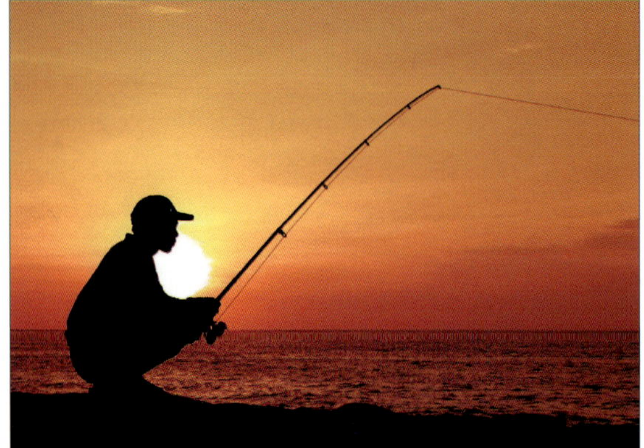

● MAX ADIYUNIARKO I took this photo of a fisherman in Kuta, Bali, using my Nikon Coolpix 2500 set at ISO100.

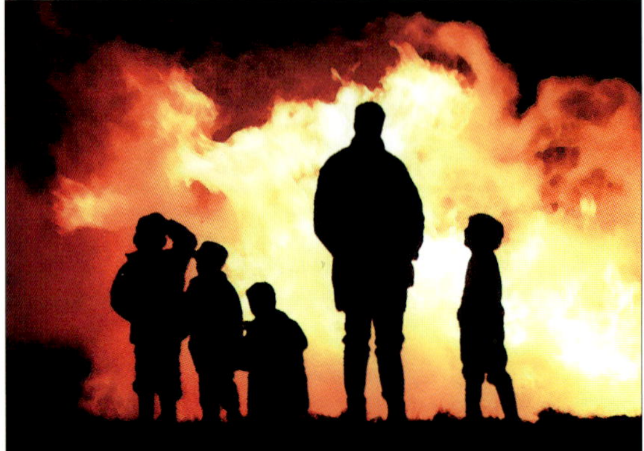

● CHRIS MOLE Silhouettes at a Guy Fawkes Night bonfire. A watercolour filter was used to accentuate the pattern of the flames.

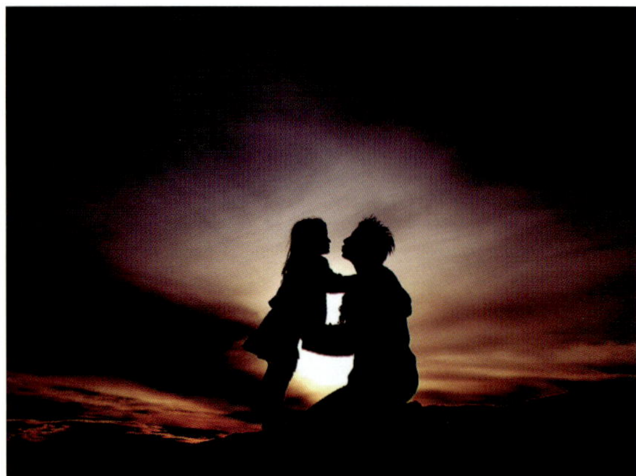

● FUNKLEDINK "A mother's love", taken in the evening at Lights Beach, Western Australia. Levels and colour adjusted in Photoshop.

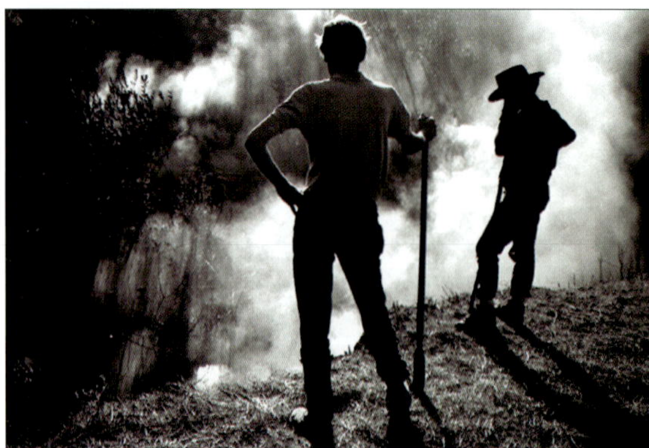

● VICTOR BURNSIDE Backlit workers burning Scrub, with wonderful rim lighting taken in the Spanish mountains near Alicante.

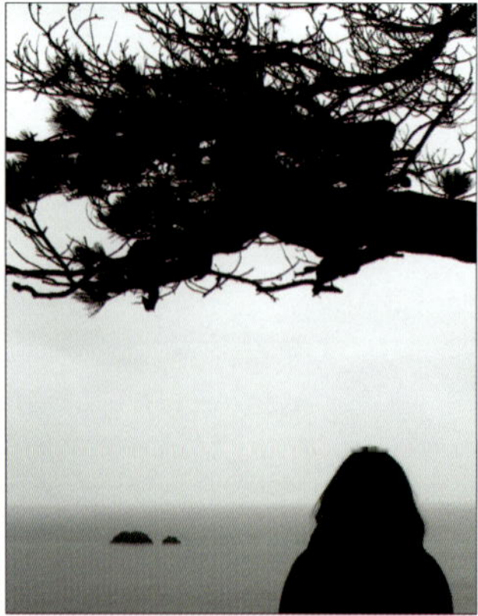

● JOHN COE "Taken from the grounds of Coleton Fishacre, Devon, using a Canon IXUS V2. I increased contrast in Photoshop CS."

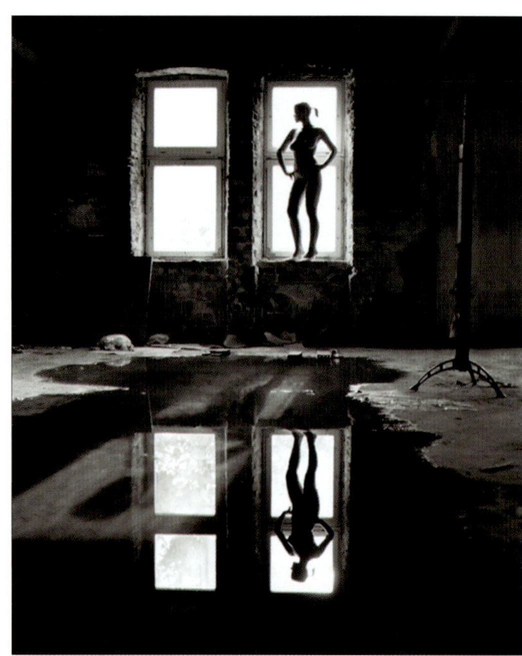

● STANISLAW TRZASKA Architecture plus model study at a painter's workplace after rain, taken using an 18-35mm lens and fill-in flash.

SHOOTING TIPS – MODEL PHOTOGRAPHY

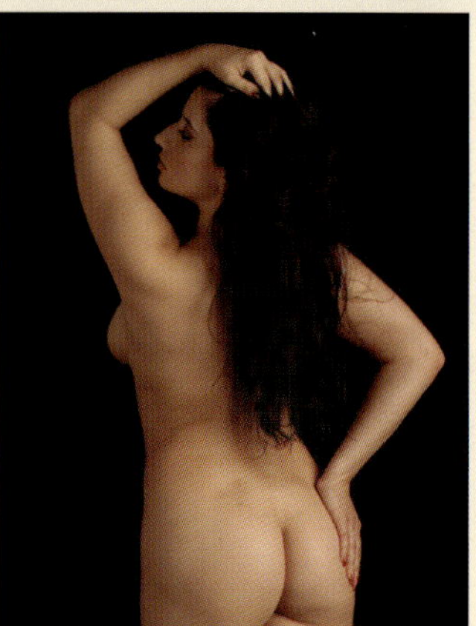

■ Taking nude or semi-nude model pictures is an aspect of photography many would like to try, but haven't a clue how to go about it. What follows are a few ideas and tips to help you make the move to find a model, hire a studio and be creative.

1 Let's look at getting a model first. There are many model hire businesses where you can find a range of models, offering everything from fashion to glamour to nude to mens mag and fetish. You decide what you want to shoot and choose a model to suit. Basically, the more clothes they take off the more they charge – from £15 to £50 per hour is about the going rate.

2 The web is a good place to look. Useful links: **www.uk-new-media.co.uk**, **www.themodelsclub.co.uk**. **www.net-model.com** and **www.photographyheaven.net**

3 Many models have access to a studio, but if not you need to consider that cost too. Hiring a studio and a model on your first attempt at glamour could be a bad idea. It would be good to ask an obliging friend to see if they'd do some test shots and practice before you spend lots of money.

4 When you eventually go ahead and hire a studio and model, have some pre-planned ideas of what you want to get out of the session. Sketching a few ideas up, or taking in cuttings from magazines can help you explain to the model what you want to do.

5 Select a studio whose owner will assist you with lighting and metering. Most will help beginners out in the hope that you will return and use their facilities again. Or consider clubbing together with a friend or two to make the day less embarrassing and less costly.

6 Choose a suitable model for your idea. A plump person may not suit that acrobatic shot you have in mind. Equally a skinny model won't be much use if you're trying to recreate Renaissance art!

7 Professional models are used to dealing with beginners so don't feel you have to relax them. If anything they'll be relaxing you, although it does help if you're friendly and talk through the session. Some photographers play music to make the mood more relaxing. Ambient, not death metal!

8 Make sure you take along a model release form and ask the model to sign it before you leave. You are then free to use the photos as you wish, according to the stipulations on the release form. You can download one of these from the ePHOTOzine website.

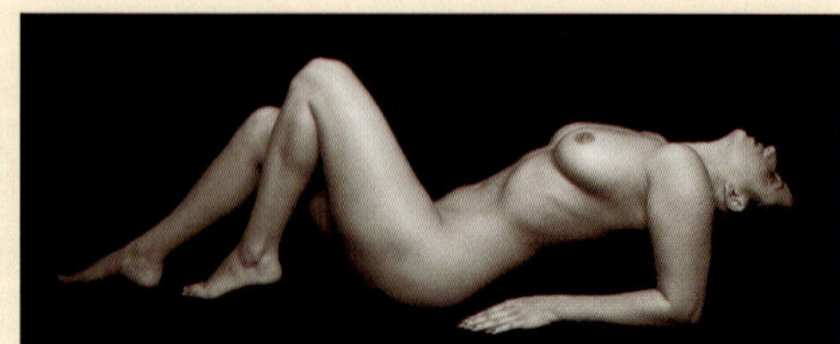

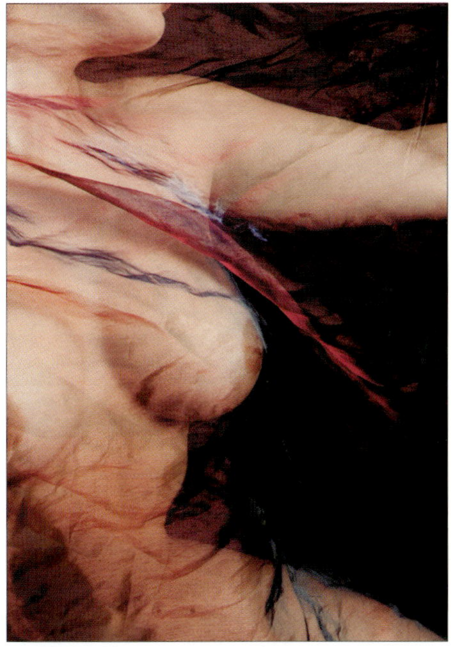

● KAREN BACON Illumination by single softbox of model draped with translucent material.

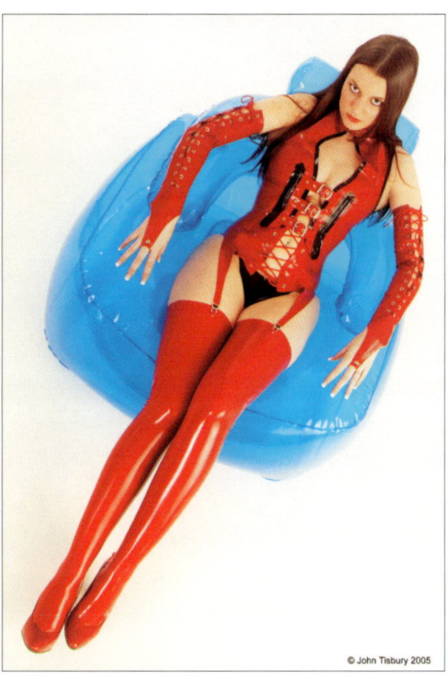

● JOHN TISBURY Colourful studio shot of Claire, dressed in red latex, and illuminated with four lights.

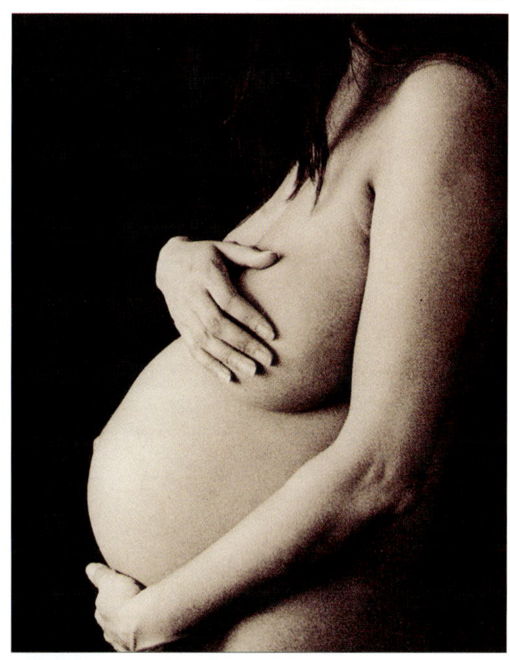

● TINA BOLTON Lith print capturing the stillness and peace of pregnancy. Ilford Delta 400 film pushed one stop.

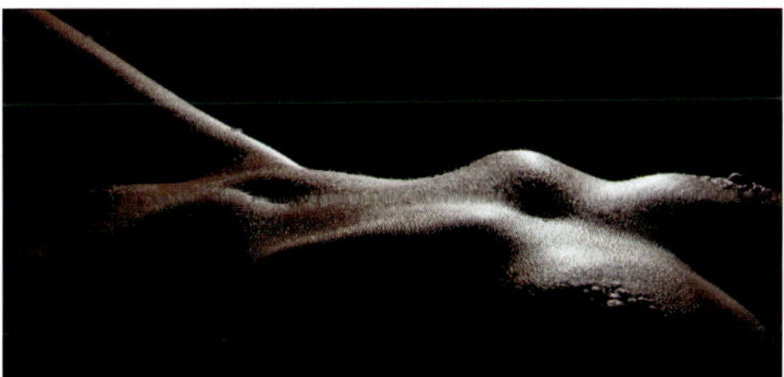

● DEAN WHITE Taken with a Canon 20D in RAW mode with a single key light. The droplets were created with oil and water spray.

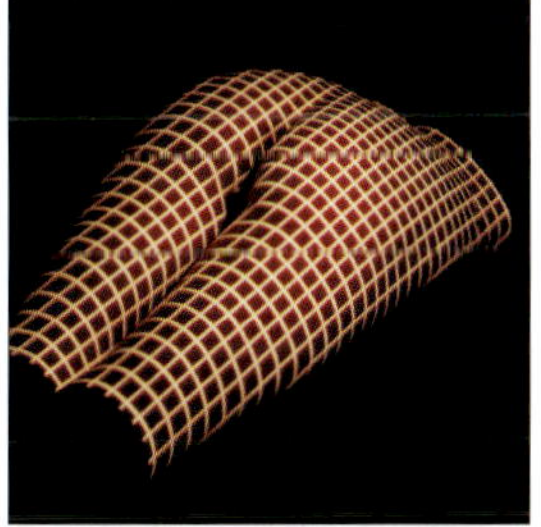

● DAVID GREEN Slide projector used to impose the grid pattern.

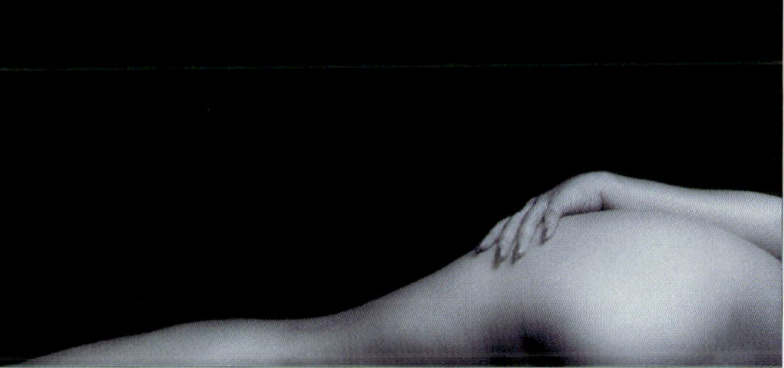

● PETER BARGH Studio shot of a model, lying on black material backdrop, cropped into panoramic format and toned in Photoshop.

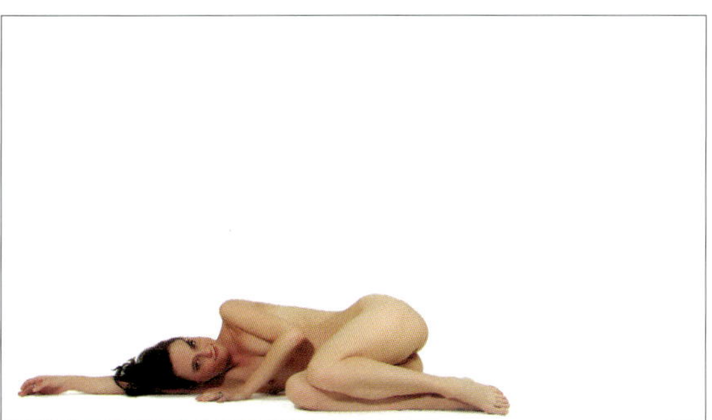

● ROBERT HIRSCHI Annwvyn was photographed on a white paper, seamless background. A telephoto lens was used for a tight DOF.

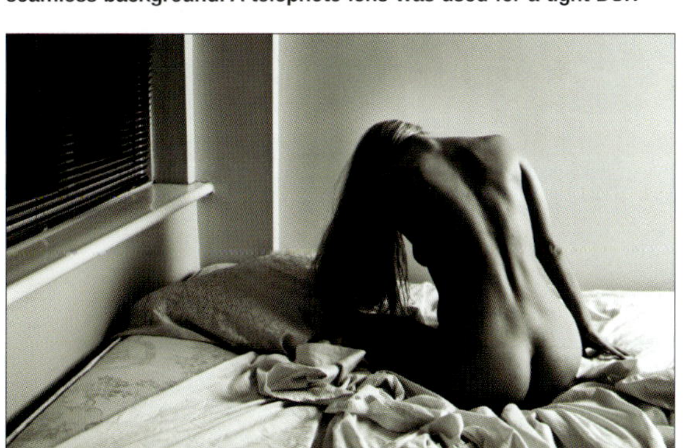

● PAUL STONE A softbox angled towards the wall gave slight spill on the background and soft light to accentuate the models back.

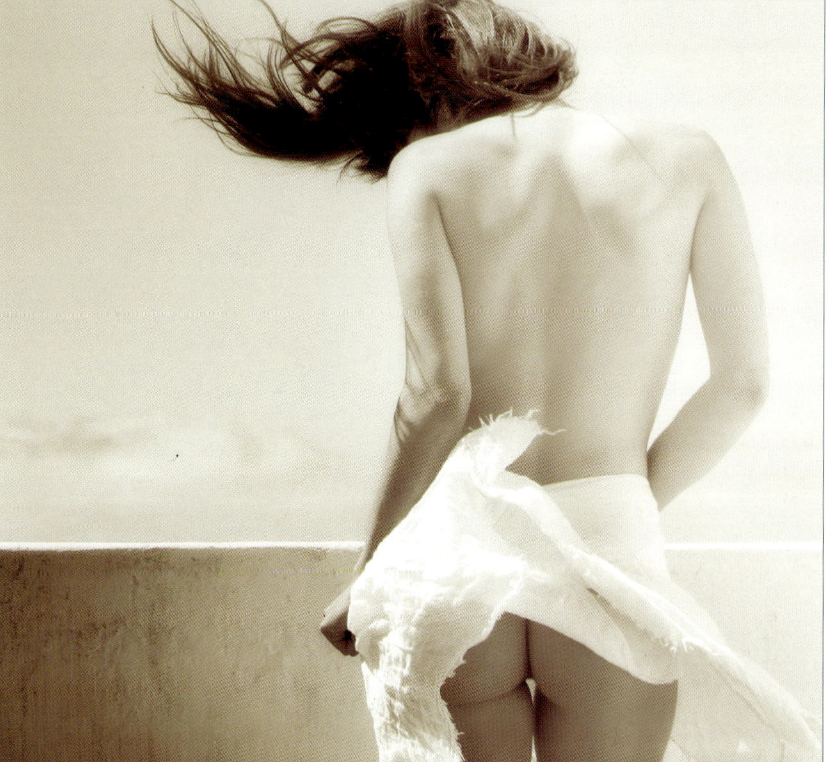

● GASPAR CABRERA We spent time on the terrace, enjoying the sun and the summer breeze.

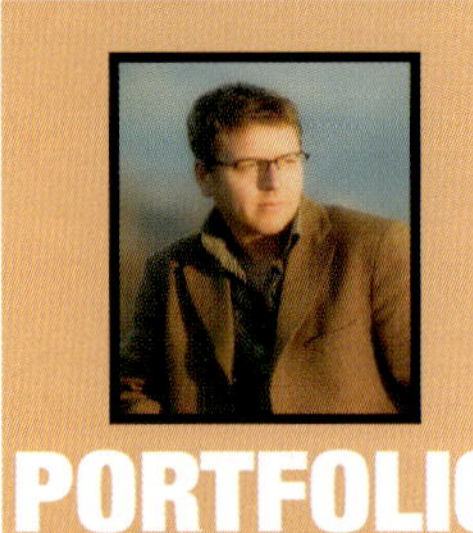

PORTFOLIO

JOHN PARRIS
John and his wife put every penny they had to their name and started Parris Photography.

Since primary school I always had an eye for drawing wildlife and landscapes in the classroom. In my late teens I fancied having a crack at photography, instead of drawing what I saw I tried to capture it on film. That is when my passion began.

I joined camera clubs and won several local competitions before studying photography for a couple of years at college. Soon after I started shooting weddings and portrait shots at weekends to build up experience.

After five years shooting local weddings I decided it was time to go for the big one! I tried my hand at full time wedding and portrait photography. I worked with my girlfriend (who is now my wife) and together we put every penny we had into a business venture called Parris Photography.

We have found our own style by experimenting over the years. Many of our images have strong saturated colours which have visual impact, but you have to be careful with this technique as it doesn't work on every shot.

When our clients see the shots for the first time, they are always amazed. They love our approach because it looks different, and we always give our clients variety. This helps move the visual flow as they won't get bored looking at the same style throughout their photo album.

Our kit consists of: Canon EOS 1DS, Nikon D1X, Fuji S2, and various lenses. The reason we use Digital SLRs is because they are fast and easy to carry. My Canon EOS 1DS is great – having over 11MB inside it can handle all the image detail that we need for shooting various jobs.

We are now achieving many of the goals we have aimed for from

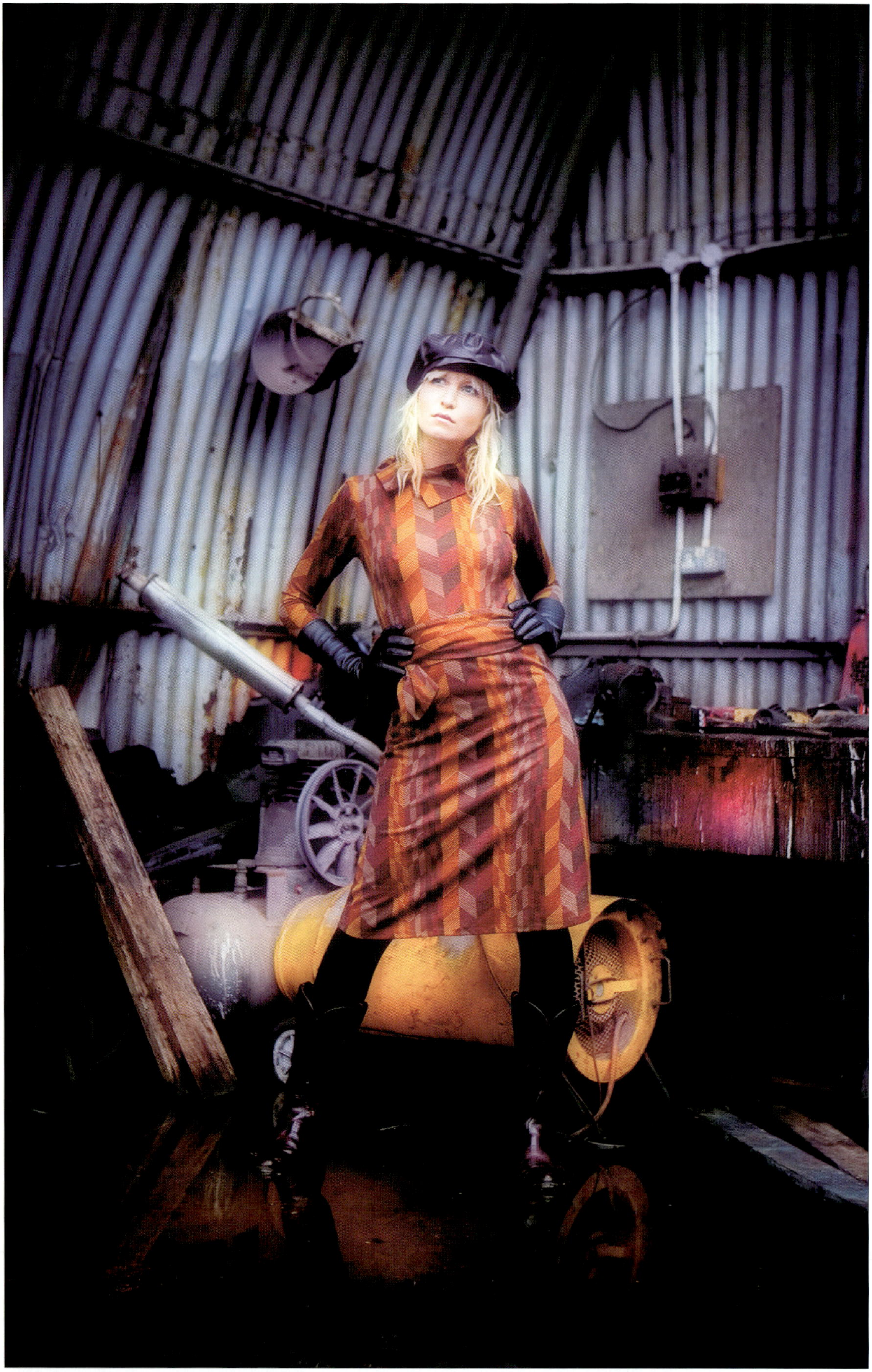

● John won gold awards at the British Institute of Professional Photographers Scottish Annual Awards 2005, for four photographs, and a silver for another which helped gain him the overall title of BIPP Scottish Photographer of the Year. The photo above, shot in a scrap yard, using natural light, was one of the gold winners. John really liked the colours of Shell's dress working with all the background colours.

the beginning. One of the best moments was when I won 1st, 2nd and 3rd in the Kodak Wedding and Portrait Awards. I was told that I am the only photographer in the UK to ever win all these within one portrait category. Since then I have also been awarded Scottish Photographer Of The Year 2005 through the British Institute Of Professional Photographers, Scotland.

I look back to when we started our business, and just trying to make enough money to provide our family with a decent living (we have two kids and a mortgage) was the hardest thing we have had to deal with. We really struggled for many months and money was near non-existent by the time we had paid our bills, but we just tightened our belt as tight as it could go and battled on.

From starting with only eight weddings and various other jobs in the first year, we now shoot around 50 weddings a year, and have gained a very high reputation in the social photography business.

The best advice I can give is learn to operate your camera manually, even if it is a digital automatic SLR. Once you master how to control the light meter in the body this makes life much easier, as sometimes you will run into tricky lighting situations and the automatic setting won't be able to help you.

Becoming a professional photographer is not just about taking pictures – it's about being a business person. This means organising bookings, orders, making albums, providing accounts, paying bills, keeping the inland revenue happy and dealing with clients. Once you master all this you should be on the right track.

Also, photography at the highest level needs passion. Passion adds a spark to the images, and you can always see it in the photographer's eyes when you meet them. Mine are on fire; but the amount of whisky I drink probably helps!

Sandra and I will continue to go for the goals we want to achieve and so far they have all been achievable through our passion for photography. It's taken a number of years to get where we are now and, if it continues this way, we should have many good years in the business to look forward to. ■

Parris Photographic Studio
tel: 01450 370523
www.parrisphotography.co.uk

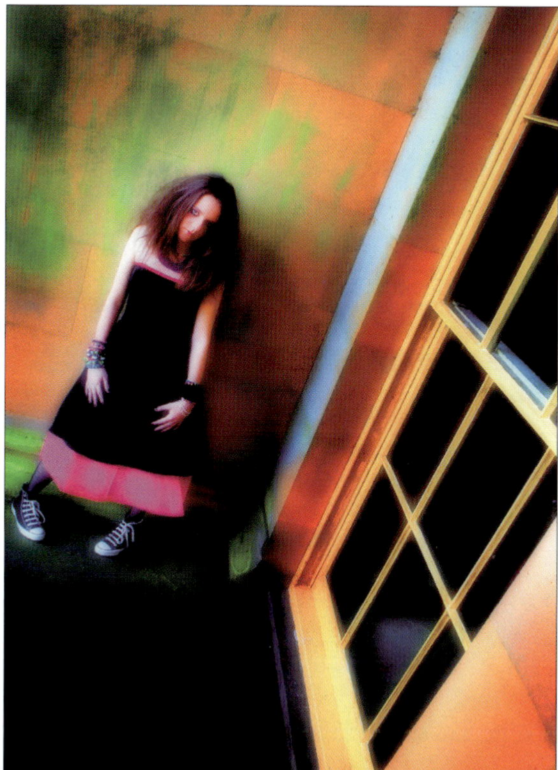

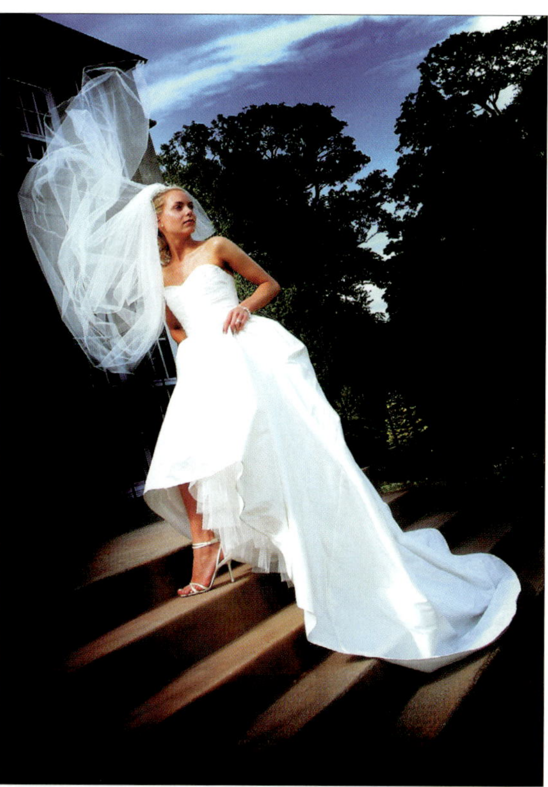

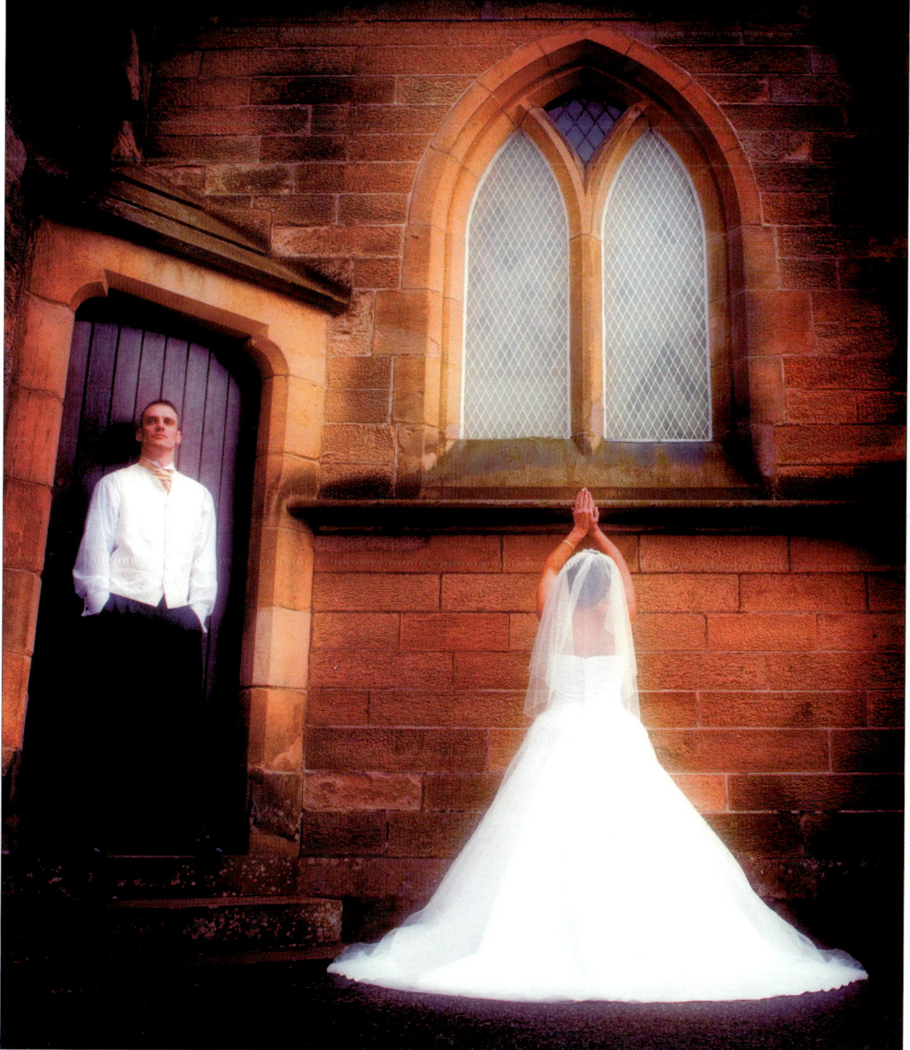

● **Above: Another Gold Winning photo from the Scottish Annual Awards 2005. John was trying to create a disturbing looking image. This was part of a shoot he had been working on.**

Above right: John had the bride running up the stairs as the wind caught her veil. This has produced a much more creative look and also added lots of saturation to give a more 'fashionable' feel.

Right: John always tries to make wedding images interesting and creative, but still does traditional to keep the couple's parents happy.

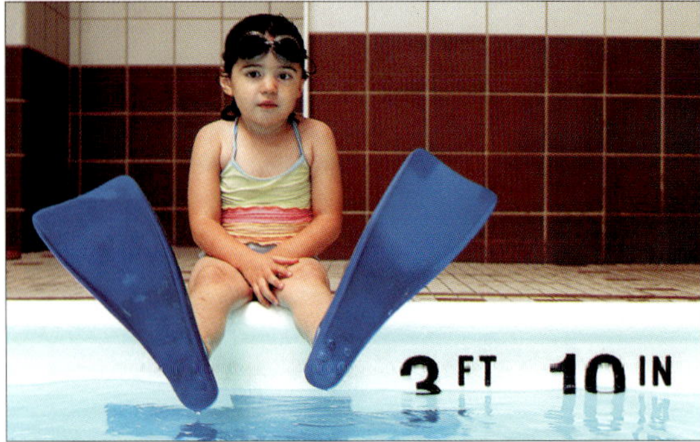

● A J TORRES The diver student, taken with a 1/40sec at f/4 exposure on a Nikon D70 with Nikon 28-80mm lens and ISO320.

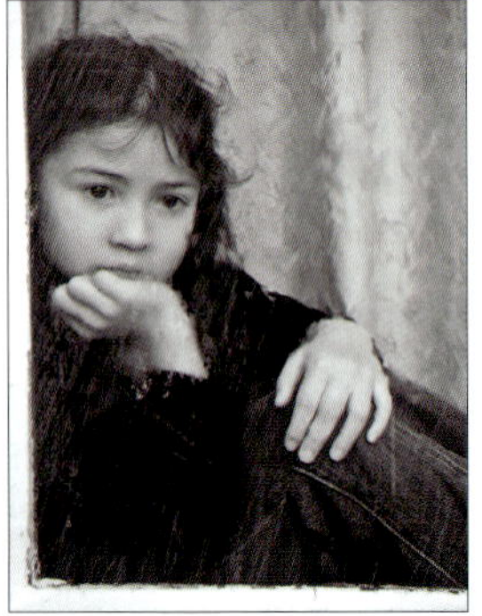

● CLIFF HUBY Shannon waiting for the rain to go away.

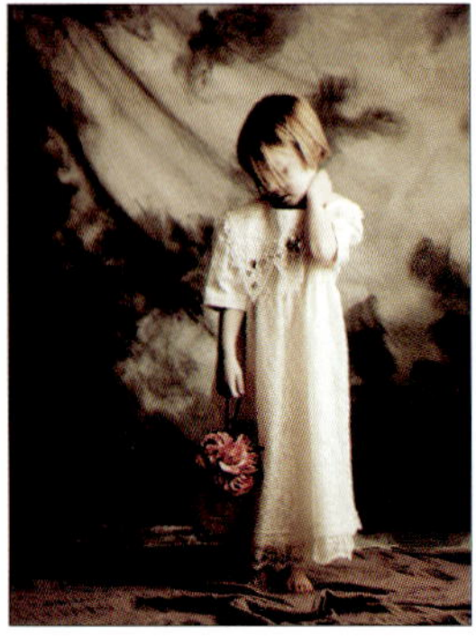

● SHERRY MARSHALL Two mins earlier she was spinning around.

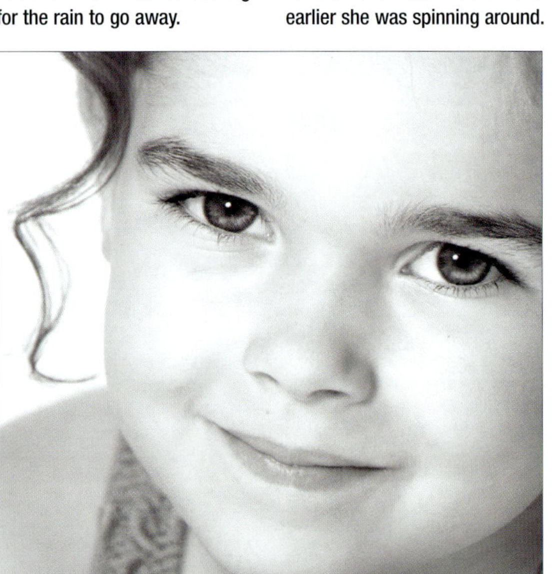

● PAUL GROOM Using a combination of tungsten lamps and a reflector underneath her chin. Canon 10D with 70-200mm f/2.8 L.

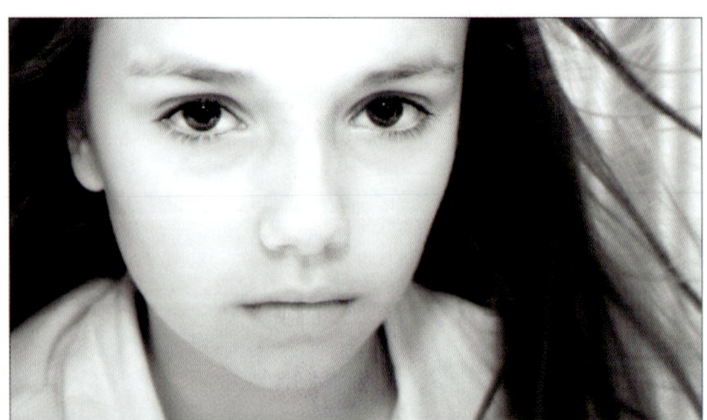

● GAVIN DAVIES "This is a photo of my cousin, Kate. Lighting consisted of a lamp behind and a bounce flash off the ceiling."

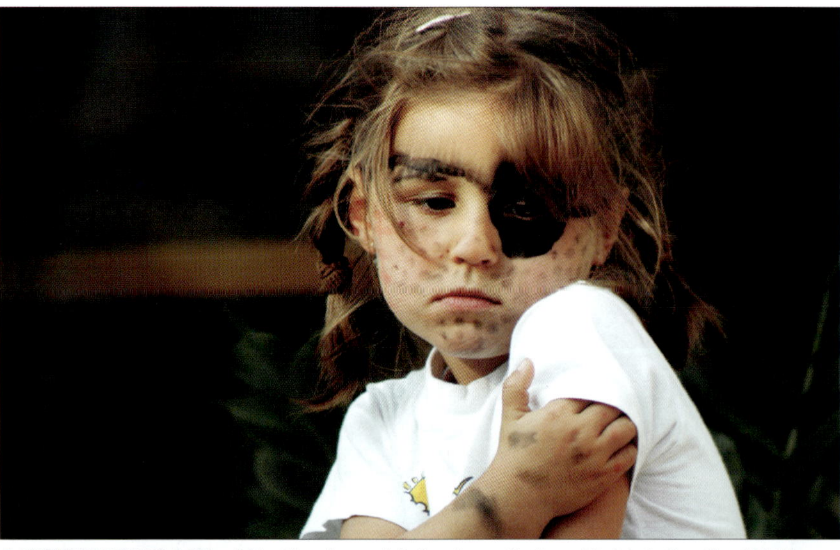

● THOMMIE LEHANE A little girl had her face painted and wasn't allowed to join in the other kids' fun.

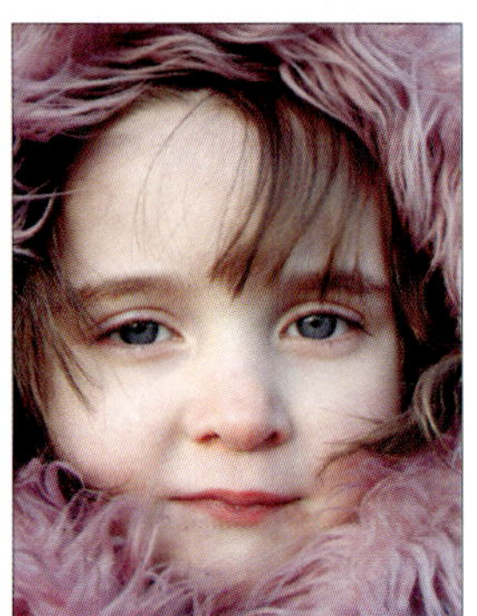

● SUSAN COLLINS Cold day in March, using a Fujifilm S602Z.

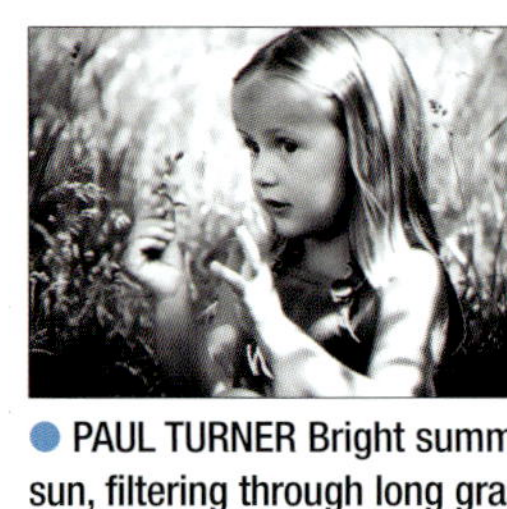

● PAUL TURNER Bright summer sun, filtering through long grass.

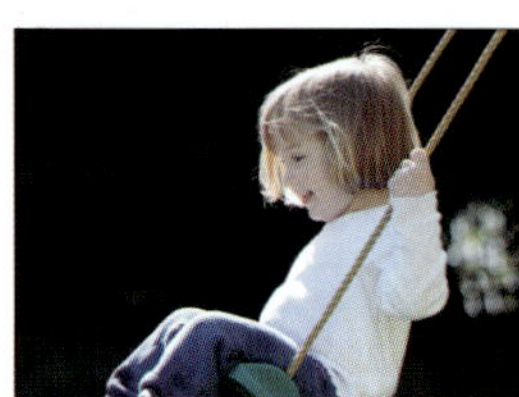

● NICK MOSS Amelia, enjoying her favourite past time. 1/500sec.

HOW TO SEPIA TONE

■ The photograph, bottom right, has a sepia tone. This technique has been used for decades; first in the darkroom, then with optical filters and recently by adjusting colour digitally.

1 Darkroom Sepia toning involves placing a processed black & white print into a toning solution that used to smell of bad eggs because of the sulphur content. Modern sepia toners are odour-free. Try Paterson Acutone Sepia.

2 Adding a filter over the lens makes colour photos come out with a sepia hue. It's less variable than darkroom toning but easier to do. Try the Cokin 005 filter.

3 Use Colour balance or Hue adjustments to make digital sepia toning very simple. Also, try the more advanced Duotone option.

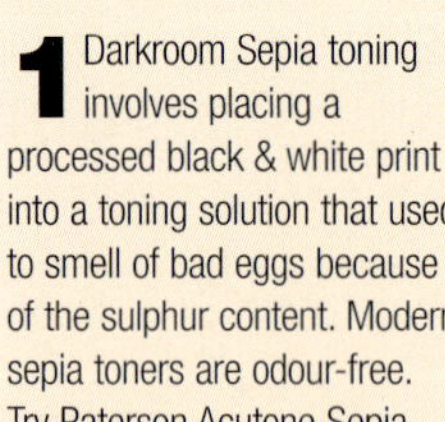

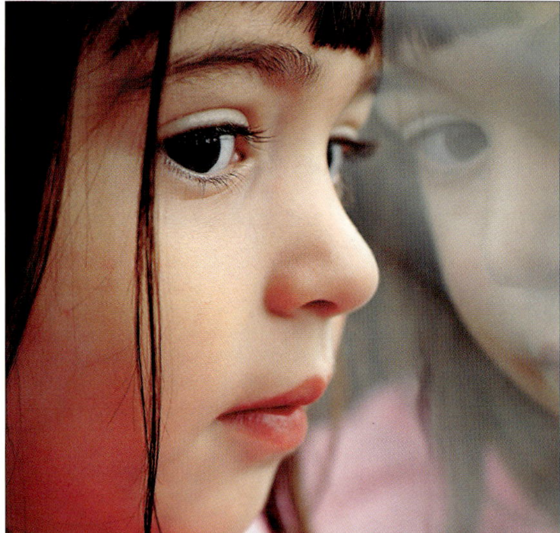

● A J TORRES Reflection in a train window, using a 50mm f/1.8 lens.

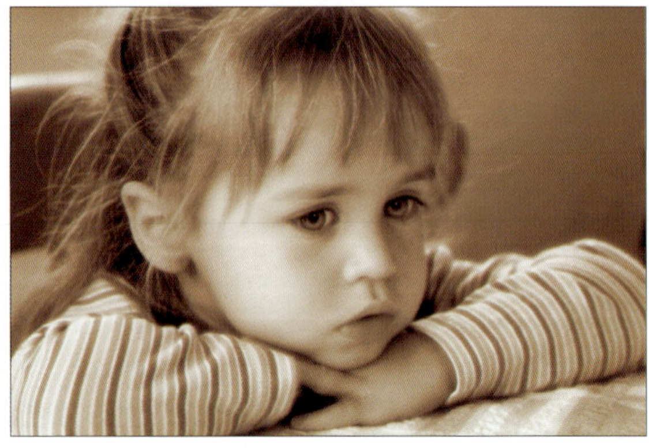

● CLIVE BURROW "My daughter Jessica, sitting at a table unaware that I was taking her picture. I just loved her bored expression."

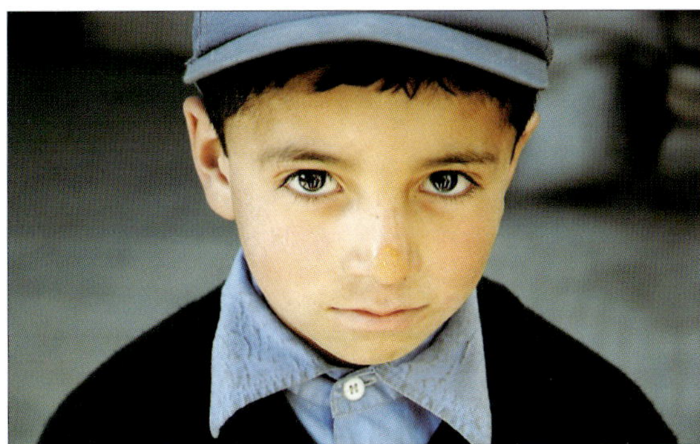

● TORWONG SALWALA Boy at Ladahk, Himalaya, India, taken on a Nikon D70 with 18-70mm AF-S DX lens.

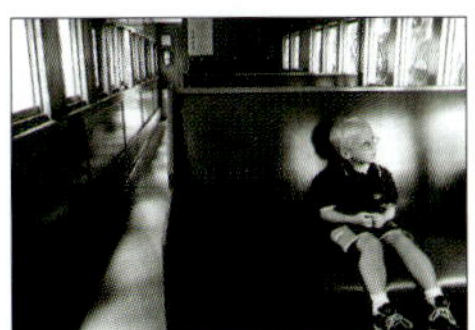

● LYDIA GARTNER Taken on the historical Kuranda Train.

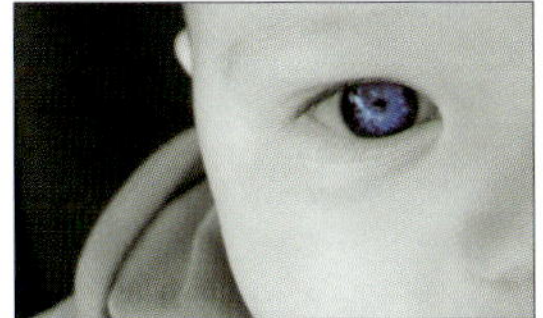

● CHRIS CLOWE Eye copied on new layer and base layer B&W.

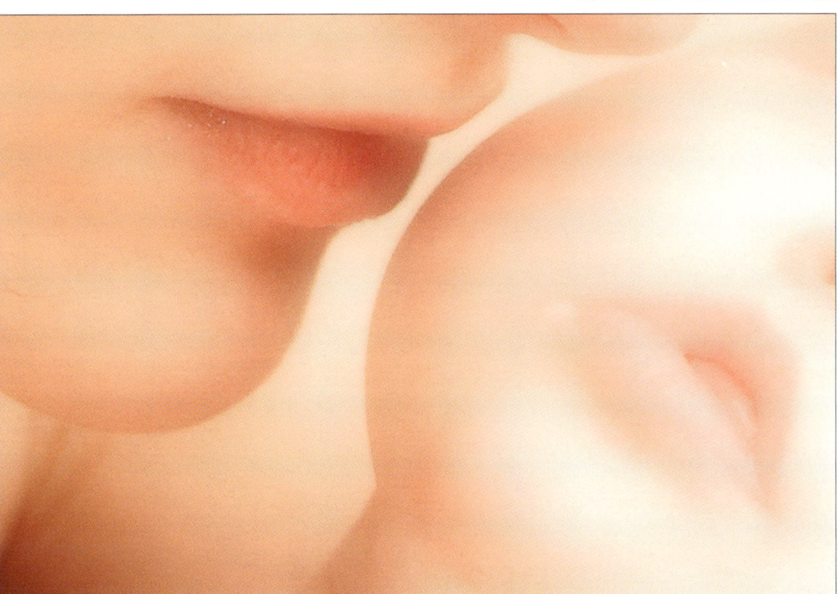

● JOHN SHORT 'The touch of your lips' is a tight crop from one of Karen and baby Emily's pictures, taken on a Canon EOS 10D with 28-200mm zoom lens. The softness has been added using Photoshop.

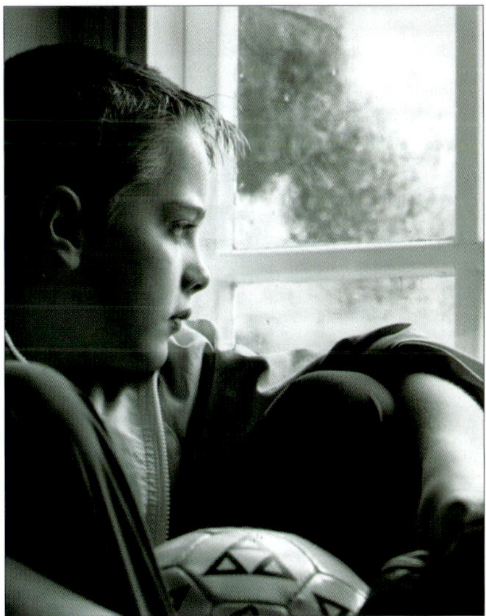

● LEWIS BUCKLE A window of our house, using a hose to create the rain. Shot using a Mamiya RB67.

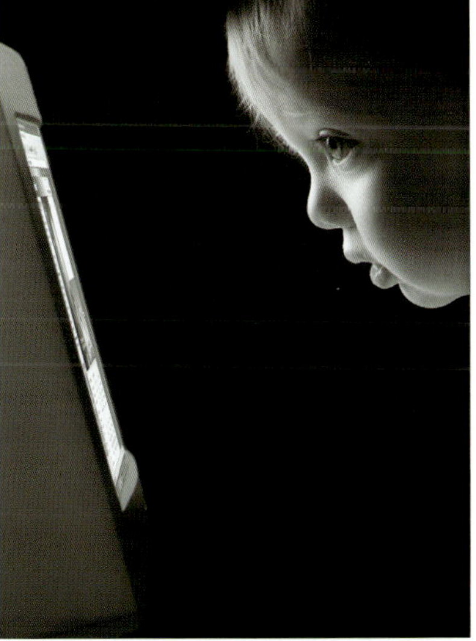

● CHRIS CLOWE The Canon 20D was set at ISO1600 to record the low light of the PC screen.

SHOOTING TIPS – PHOTOGRAPHING CHILDREN

■ It's often said that child photography is one of the more difficult aspects of portraiture, but there are things you can do to make life easier when attempting to frame the young.

■ The main thing to do is keep them entertained. Children tend to get bored really quickly, so if you're lucky you may get a 5-10 minute sitting before their attention drifts.

■ One way of holding the attention of younger children is to introduce toys and let them play while you shoot away. You'll get some great relaxed candid shots.

■ When taking the portraits add a friend. They will then compete to get the best photo and, hopefully, the boredom won't kick in.

■ Take them out to climb trees or play in the park. Once again, the activity will keep them entertained while you snap away. You'll need a longer lens to ensure frame-filling shots.

■ Place a mirror behind the camera to encourage fun expressions.

■ Adults tend to be at a much higher level, so you're always pointing down to take photos. Kneel down so you're on the same level and the shots will look less distorted.

■ If you want the children to look into the camera, ask them to look for the miniature man inside the camera who makes it work. If you say he's behind the lens they'll be looking to see him. Shoot away: the expressions will be great.

■ Take photos regularly – your children soon grow up and you'll miss some great moments.

■ Get your kids involved and let them take photos of you too.

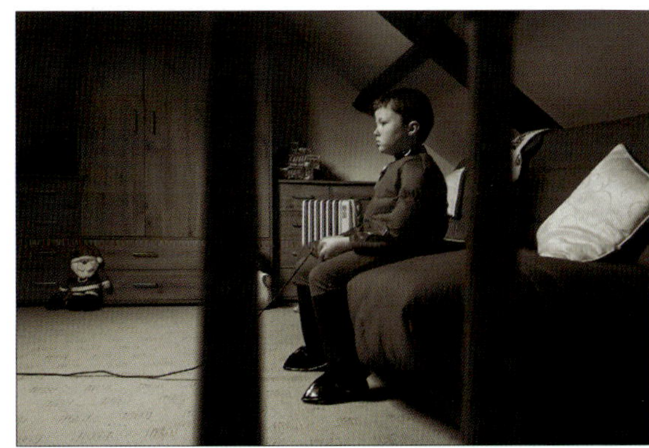

● ROBERT TAYLOR Christmas Day 2004. "With a house full of people, my son Matthew escaped to the loft for a bit of solitude."

● ALAN HUGHES An impromptu, unposed and almost grab shot, using only window light. It was handheld at 1/20sec at f/8 and then levels and tones were adjusted in Photoshop.

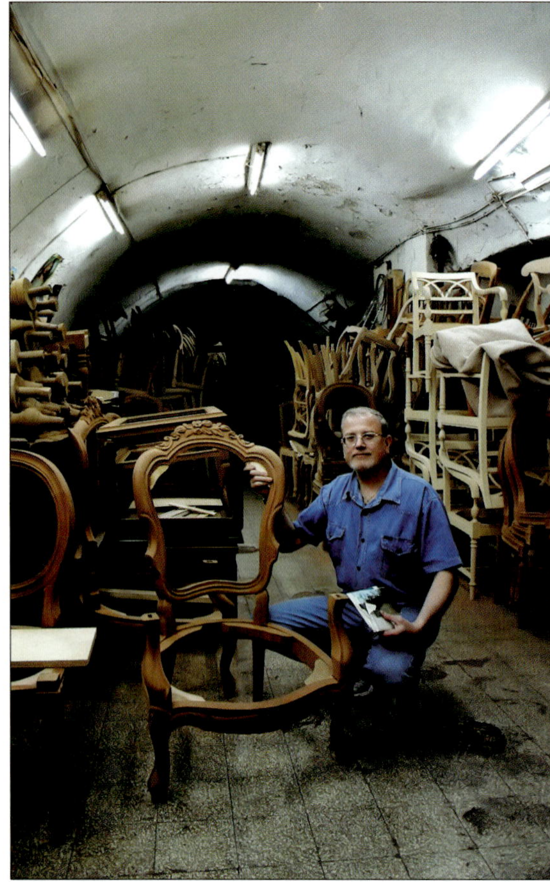

● THOMMIE LEHANE This chairmaker, seen at work in the back streets of Naples, was taken without flash at ISO 1600.

PLACES TO GO – REENACTMENT

■ Reenactment is a fast growing hobby for those who enjoy history. With groups around the world re-living various wars, the participants, and often their families, can escape reality for a moment while learning something about their history. As well as being a very entertaining day, a visit to a reenactment provides a fantastic opportunity to photograph people dressed in period clothing. Events usually take place between March and October.

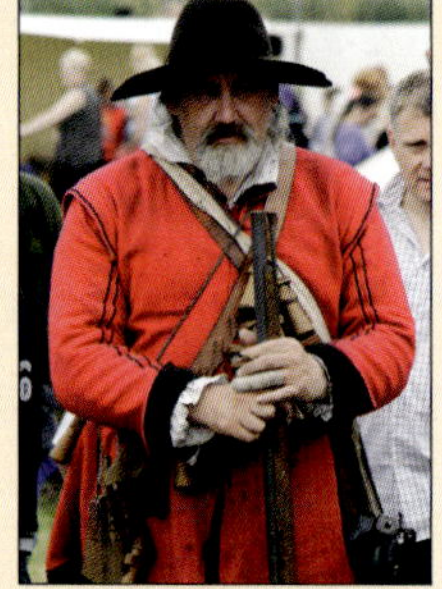

■ To find out more visit **www. tudortimes.org** and click on event guide. This covers events throughout Great Britain and Europe.

■ The Sealed Knot is a registered society that re-enacts the Civil War. The example photo above was taken at an event at Rother Valley near Sheffield, with the aim of encouraging interest in our heritage. Visit their website to find out all about them and events they are running this year. **www.sealedknot.org**.

■ Events usually provide an opportunity to get up close to interestingly-dressed participants, so a standard zoom lens is fine – a wide-angle is helpful to shoot full length in the often crowded spectator areas. When the battles commence you're often much further away from the action and a tele zoom lens is the only way to get decent shots. A 75-300mm is ideal for these occasions.

■ When arriving, get a program of the day's events/battles and walk around the site looking for the best vantage points. The crowds start to build when a battle is about to commence, so make sure you set up in advance to get a decent view at the front.

■ Asking the organisers and speaking to reenactment members can help you find the best vantage points.

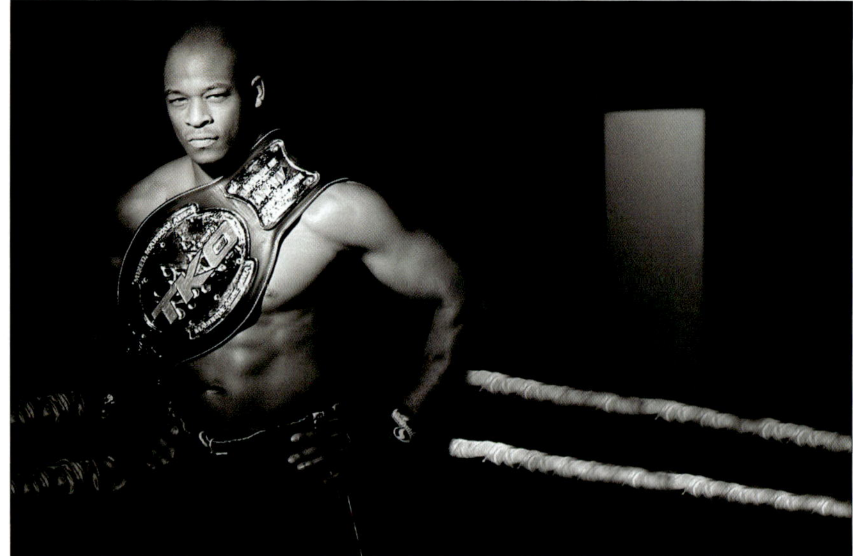

● PATRICK DI FRUSCIA Portrait of David Loiseau a Canadian World Champion Ultimate Fighter. Pat used Kodak T-Max 400 rated at ISO 320 in his Minolta Dynax 7, with the 24-105mm f/3.5-4.5 lens attached.

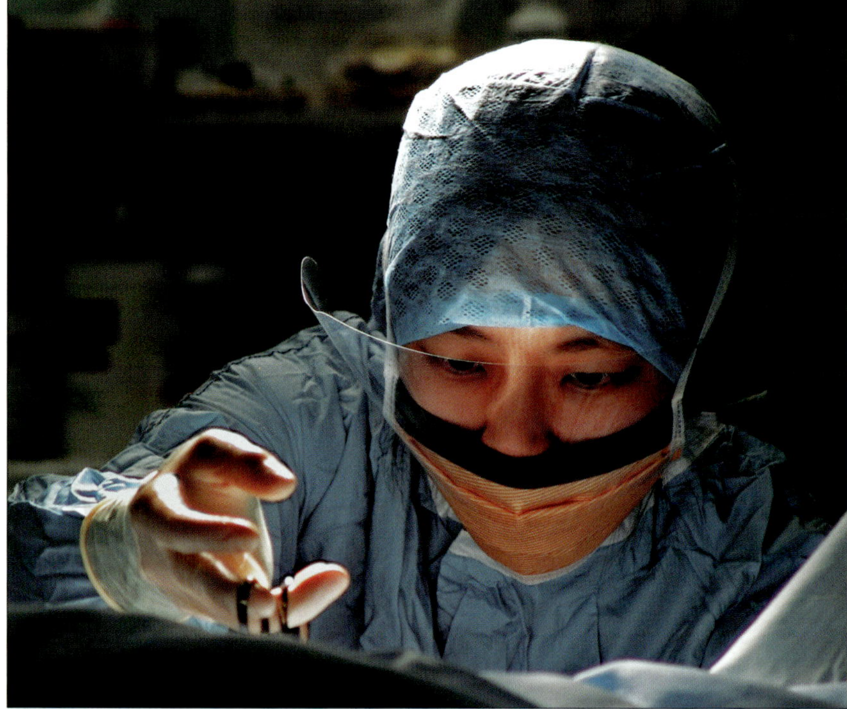

● DANNY TUCKER A surgeon photographed using a Sony DSC-F828 with an aperture of f/2.8 and speed of 1/800sec. This moment captures the deep concentration of Danny's work colleague.

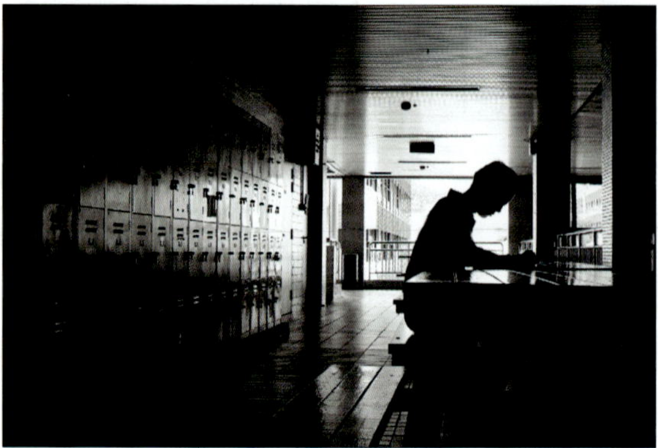

● COLIN YEO Self portrait taken at the National University Singapore, using a Minolta Dynax 7, Tamron 28-200mm lens and Ilford XP1 film.

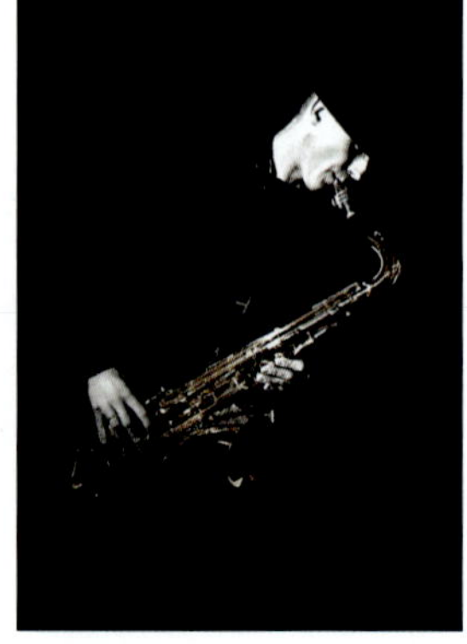

● RICHARD HOWELL Ilford FP4 film was used in a Mamiya 645S.

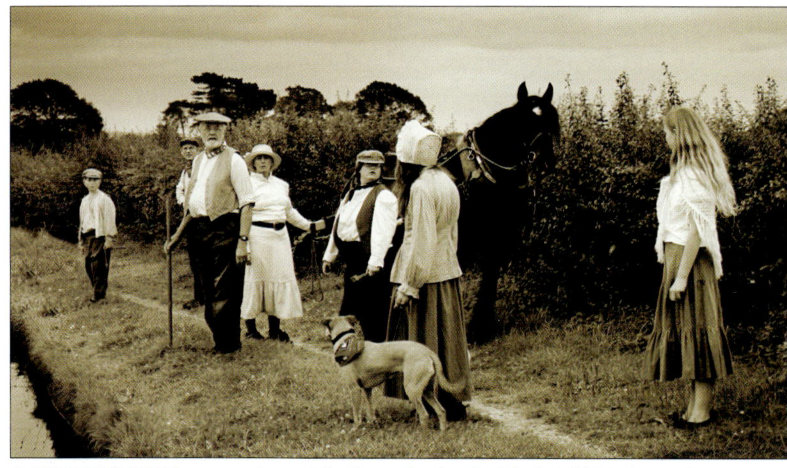

● ADRIAN WILSON These members of the Horse Boating Society, in full Victorian costume, were en route to Preston Brook Festival. Sepia toned to make the scene even more realistic.

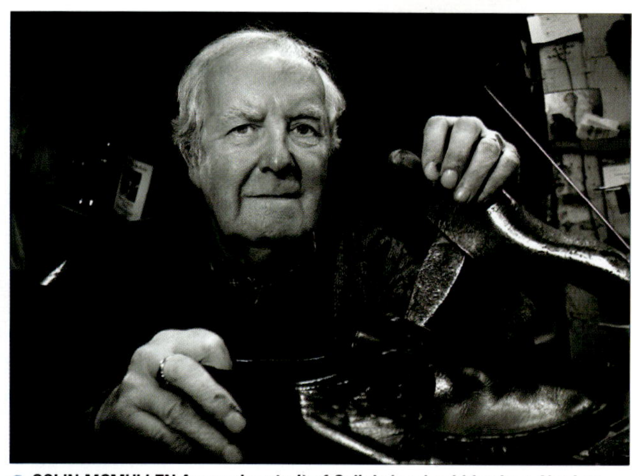

● COLIN MCMULLEN A posed portrait of Colin's local cobbler, Ivan Abraham, using a Sigma 17-35mm EX wide angle zoom on the Canon EOS 30D.

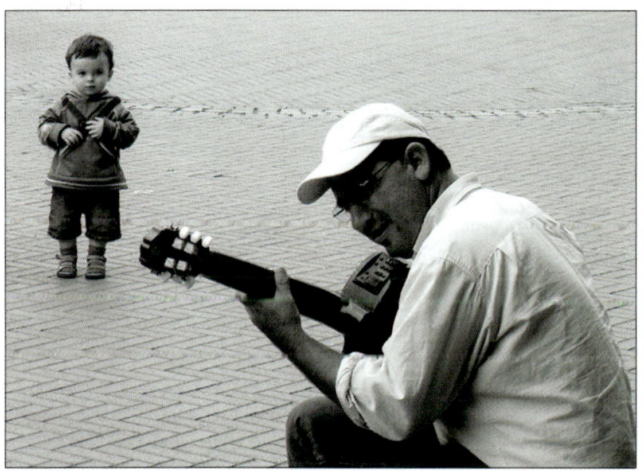

● MILES HERBERT A candid Bournemouth street scene. One of those hard to find moments in time.

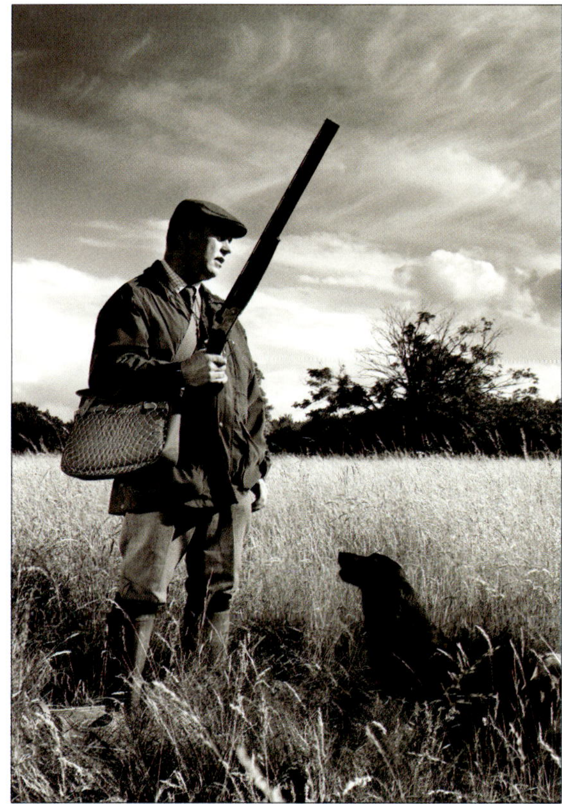

● NICK HILL Shot in North Lincolnshire on a Hasselblad 501CM, with 80mm lens and a Phase One H20 digital back. Converted to B&W.

DIGITAL TECHNIQUE – SELECTING AROUND HAIR

■ When you want to replace a subject's background where there's a complicated outline, such as a girl with whispy hair or an animal with spiky fur, it can be difficult to make a quick and detailed selection. The result will be a subject that looks cut out on the new background. Here's a quick fix: use the Background Eraser tool.

1 Firstly, make things easier by removing most of the unrequired background. Notice I've created a new layer filled with black and made the background layer active by clicking on it to allow transparency and then switched layers in the palette so the new background layer is the newer black fill layer.

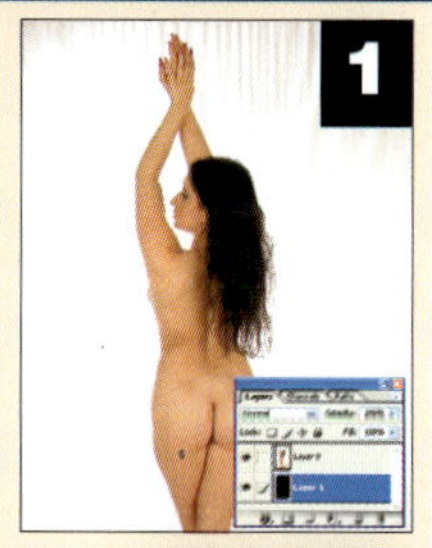

2 To speed things up, make a selection around the model using the freehand lasso tool. Then invert this selection and press the delete button. You should have a large black mass surrounding the freehand cut out shape.

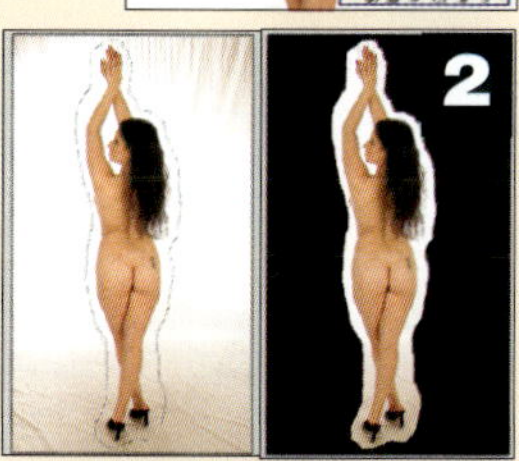

3 Now use the Background Eraser tool, with the toolbar that appears across the top, set with Limits to Discontiguous, Tolerance at about 20%, Protect foreground colour ticked and Sampling to Once. Paint around the model to fill in the remaining surrounding white areas. You may have to go over some areas two or three times clicking in different start points to pick up the whole range of tones.

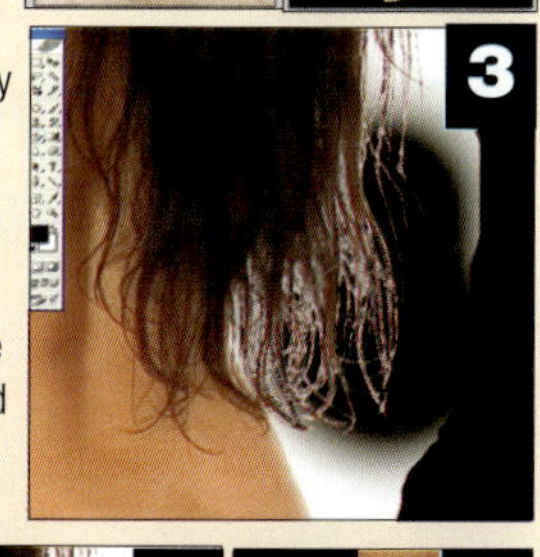

4 If we turned off the background you'd see the transparent background displayed as a chequered area. It's harder to determine how the erasing job is going like this and that's why background was filled with black earlier.

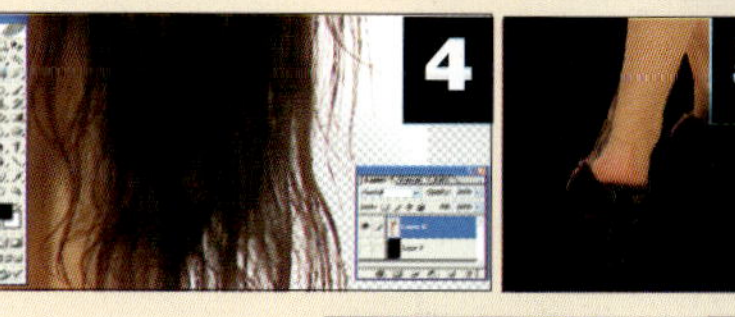

5 While painting around with the Background Erasor take care on areas of the background that have a similar tonal value to the subject. This shot shows what happened when I went a bit fast around the leg areas. The erasor has removed some of the leg. If this happens hit Ctrl-Z to undo or revert to a previous stage on the History palette.

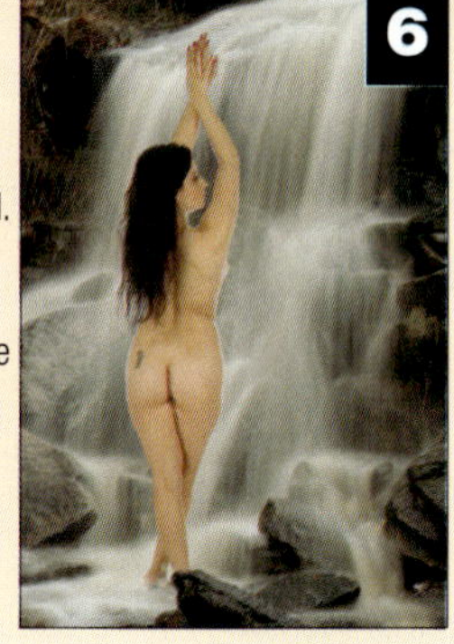

6 When you've gone around the whole photo you should have a good cut out, especially around the hair. This layer can then be copied and pasted onto a new suitable background. In this case I've selected a waterfall. I added a layer mask and painted out the feet so they look submerged. I also used Photoshop's Match colour adjustment to ensure the skin tones matched the background scene and flipped the girl to make her look into the waterfall rather than away from it.

The whole thing took less than five minutes to create and use as this illustration. Further improvements could be made by editing the outline on the body that's come from lights at each side to make the girl look even more naturally placed.

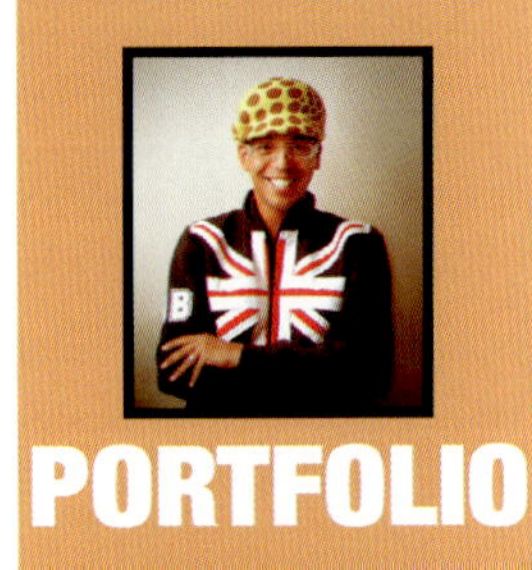

PORTFOLIO

JOHANN PINTO

Johann brings interpretations of his dreams, fantasies and inspirations to life in carefully staged pictures.

Johann is an amateur photographer who imprints his images with a touch of surrealism and theatrical feeling.

He likes bringing to life the interpretation of his dreams, fantasies and inspirations in carefully staged pictures covered in light and details.

He has participated in several theatre workshops in his native Venezuela, which allows him the ease to stage his photography. The use of light, colour and, for that matter, all technical details are self-taught.

Photography quickly evolved from a hobby to an almost full-time passion once he emmigrated to Canada. The fascinating changes in light and colour through the seasons made him study and perfect ways of capturing the natural scenarios he marvelled at from coast to coast.

"My approach to taking pictures is to have respect for the subject. I have a desire to explore it to its limits. I prefer natural light, but if the situation requires it I am willing to compromise. No matter how simple or complicated the image, it must draw the viewer to a new world, a new feeling or an old feeling they haven't fully explored. My interest in self portraits came to fruition with a project I set myself called 'Boys will be Boys'.

Inspired by the desire to send a Valentine's Day image to my friends I produced several self-portraits.

I quickly became fascinated with the idea of exploring 'myself'; my capabilities and limitations, my joys and my fears. Self portraits give me so much opportunity. I am able to confront myself, take a journey of self discovery, recreate my past and erase its faults, stage

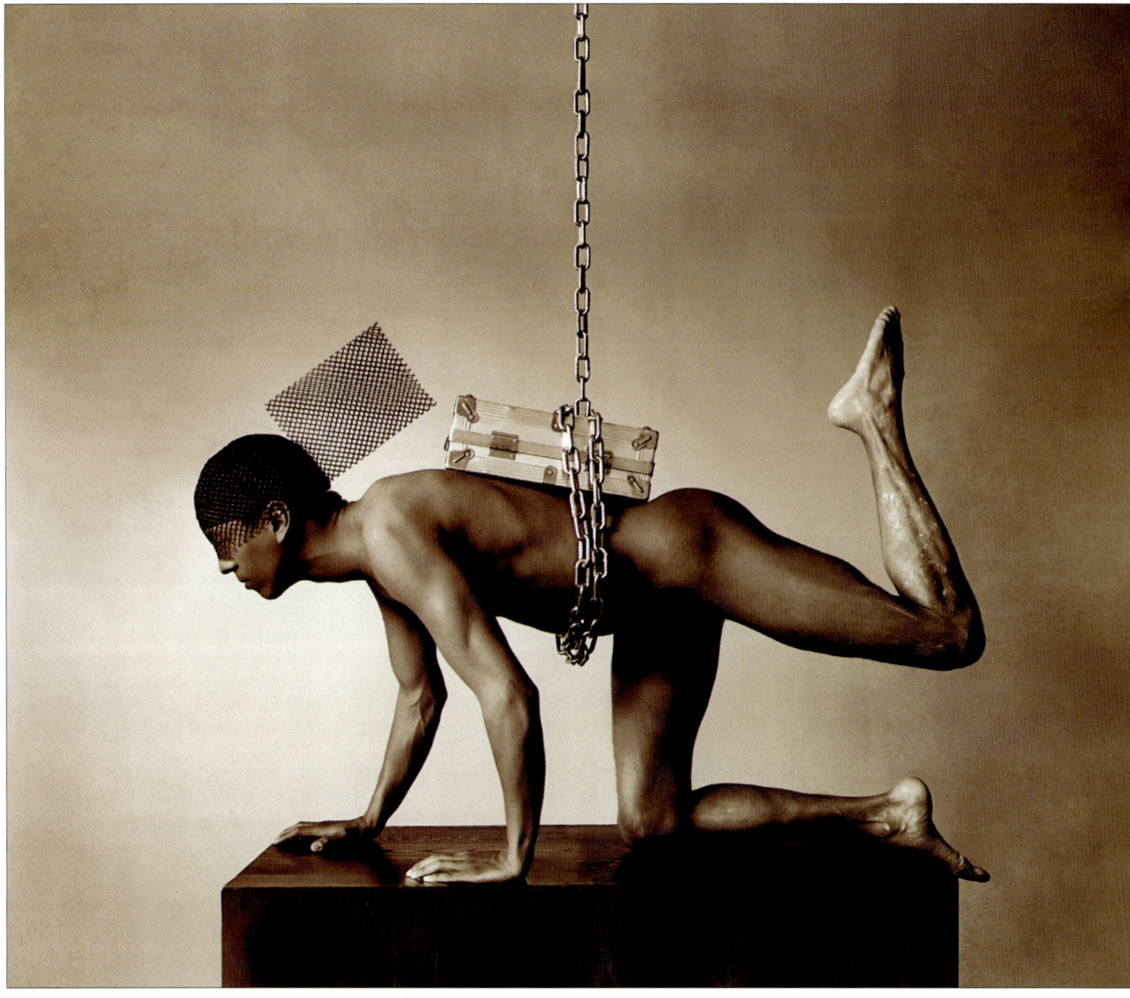

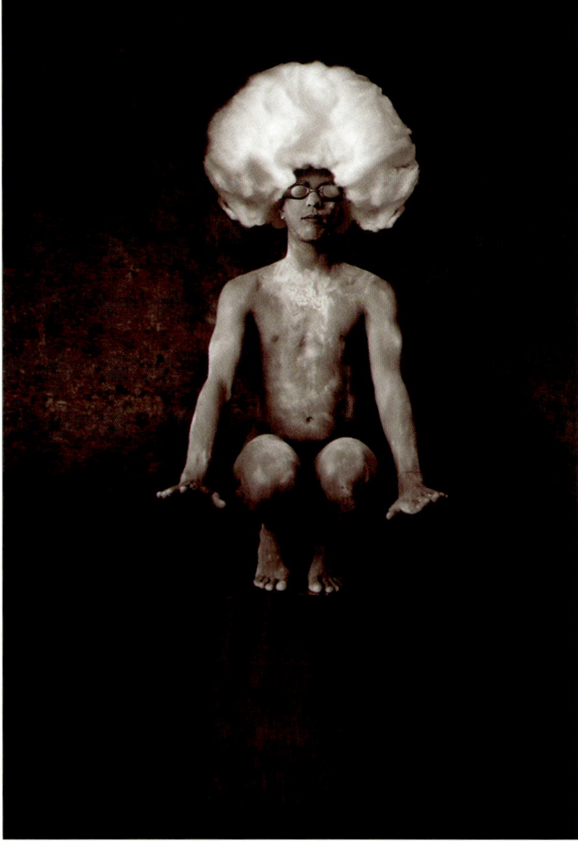

● Here is a selection of five of the images from Johann's self portrait project 'Boys will be Boys'. They were all captured on a Sony Cyber-Shot 8.0 megapixel camera and edited using Photoshop.

Top: "Dumping Depression", Left: "Unplugged", Below: "Vertigo"
Opposite page, top: "The Last Breath Burglar", Johann dedicates this image to all the people in Tim Burton's Underworld. Opposite page, bottom: "The Alchemist".

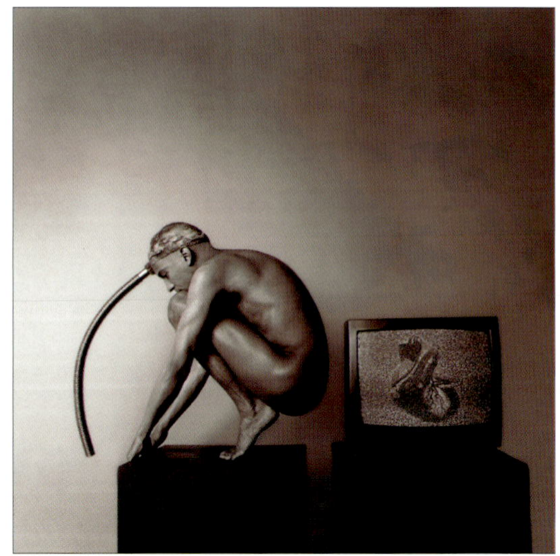

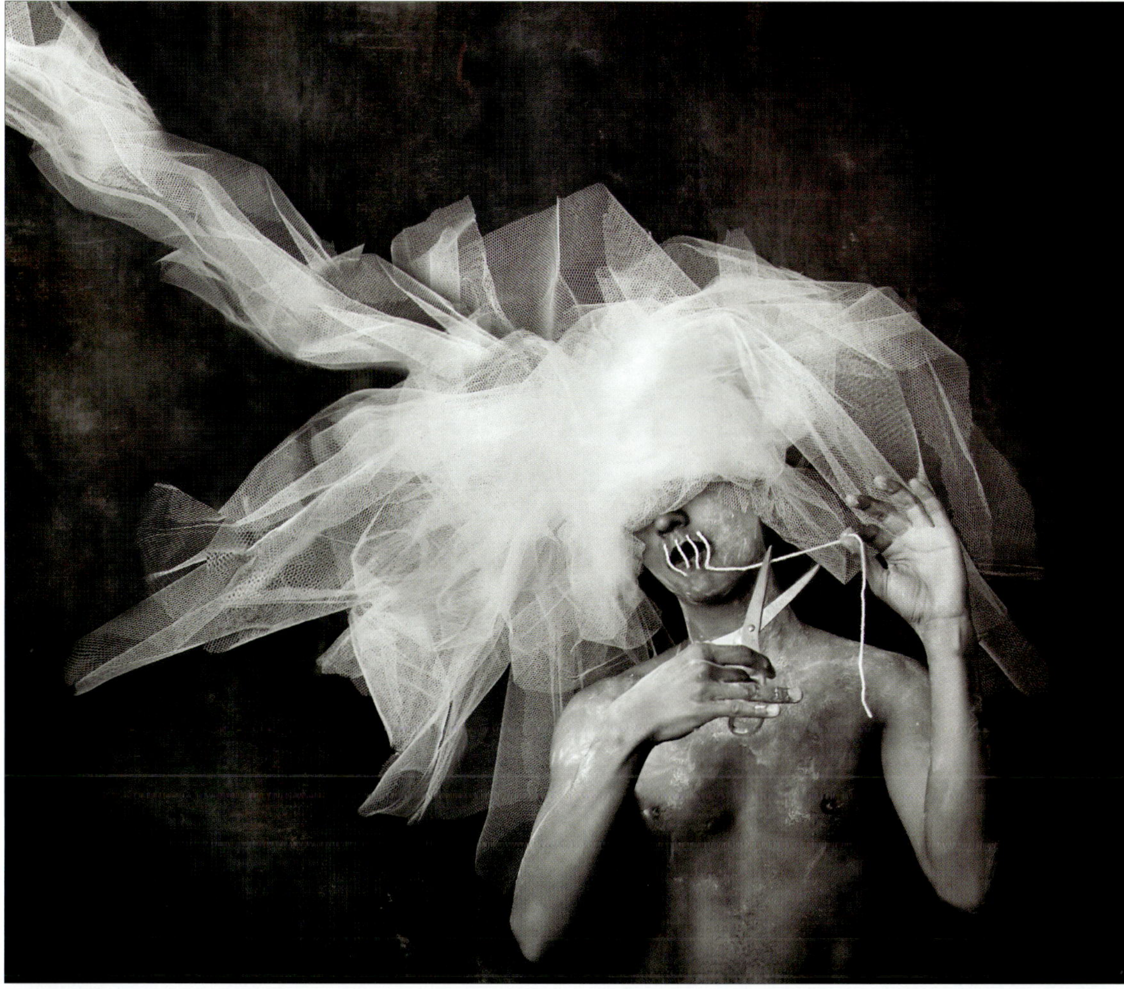

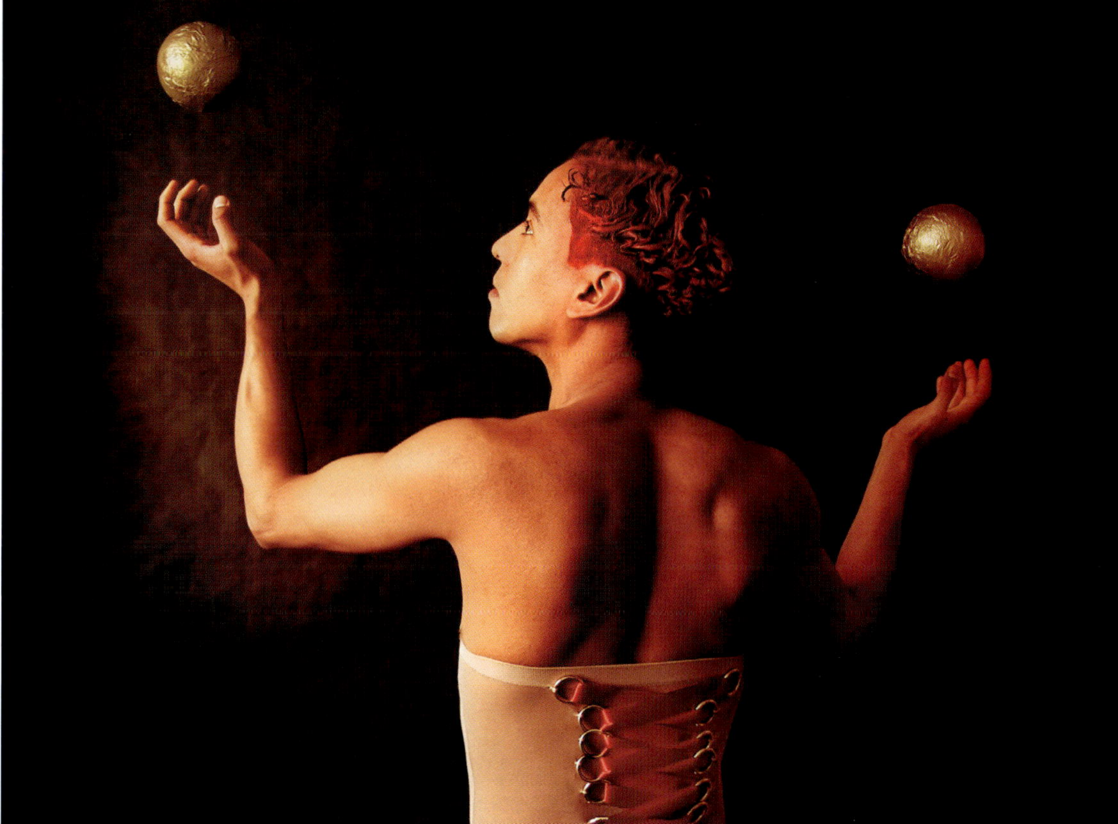

my dreams and make them reality and to stage my future and make it come true.

It became a spiritual journey, and although I plan to explore other styles it's an experience that will remain with me forever and I'm aiming to do a couple of self portrait shoots each year throughout my lifetime. They are a way of letting me step back from myself and leave me feeling empowered.

First of all, I compose the image in my mind and consider a way to convert my vision into a photograph. My intention is to produce an exciting image that draws the viewer into my world.

On the day of the shoot I decide on the best lighting to use and fine-tune other details. I like to be spontaneous and go with the feeling rather than rely on preconceived ideas. Natural light is always my preference but, depending on the subject and idea behind the image I'm trying to create, I utilise other approaches.

Do I use Photoshop? I ike any modern digital photographer, of course. It helps enhance the image and can transform the most abstract ideas into reality. The amount of work I have to do on the computer depends on the complexity of the idea.

I am very disciplined with my editing. I like to begin the process as soon as possible after the shoot so that the material is still fresh in my mind, and the idea doesn't slip away.

Although the nature of my work necessitates constant evolution, there is always an underlying satisfaction that I get from my images. I hope to explore different ways of reproducing beauty, but the intimacy of portraiture is something that will always bring me back to the medium.

The world around me is a big inspiration. My South American heritage gives me an innate ability to explore and develop beyond face value. My background means that I rely primarily on my own creativity, and supplement it with technology only when necessary.

I admire the work of artists like Richard Avedon, David LaChapelle and Cecil Beaton, they are a constant source of inspiration to me. One day I hope to emulate their mastery of the art form, but for now I just view their work with envy and produce the best compositions I can." ∎

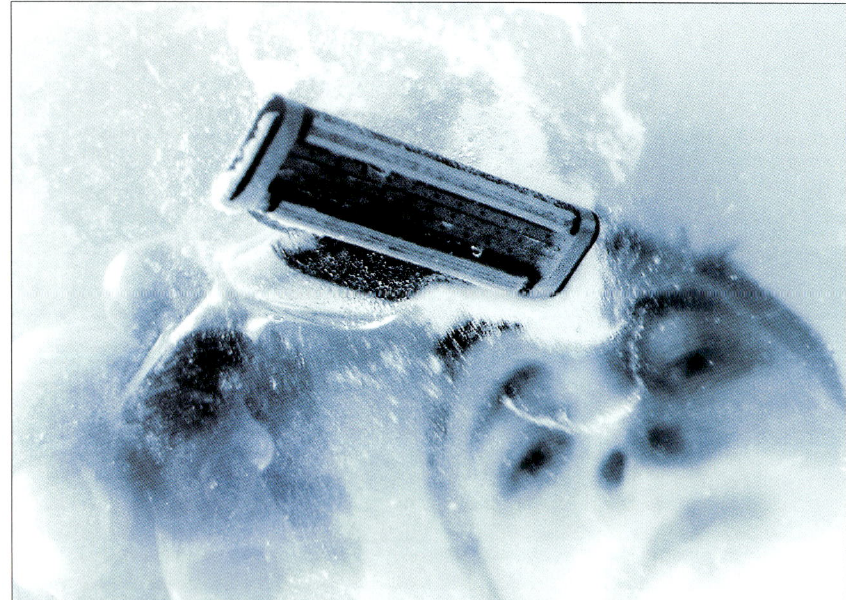

● DANIEL WARBURTON Self portrait, having a very rare shave. "The things you put yourself through for art! Taken using a basic digital camera, placed below a glass bowl full of water."

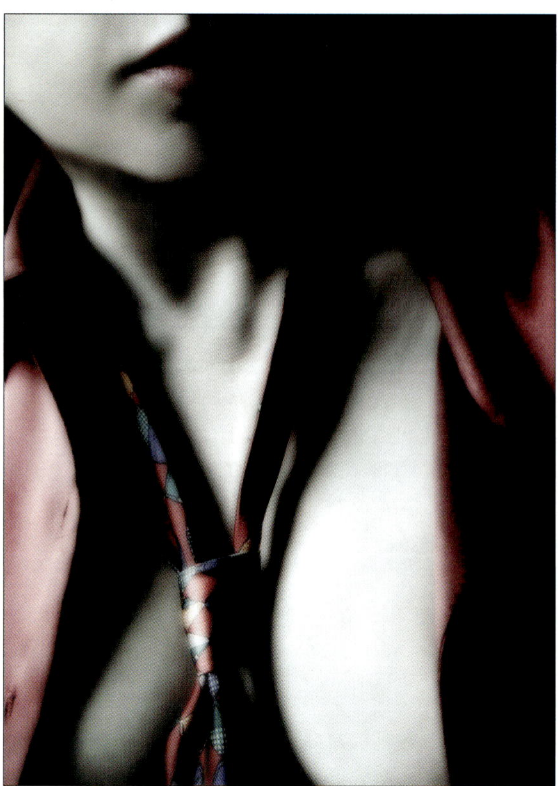

● ILONA WELLMANN Self portrait, taken with a tripod mounted Canon EOS 300D at 1/50sec. The pastel colours and dreamy look were created in Photoshop.

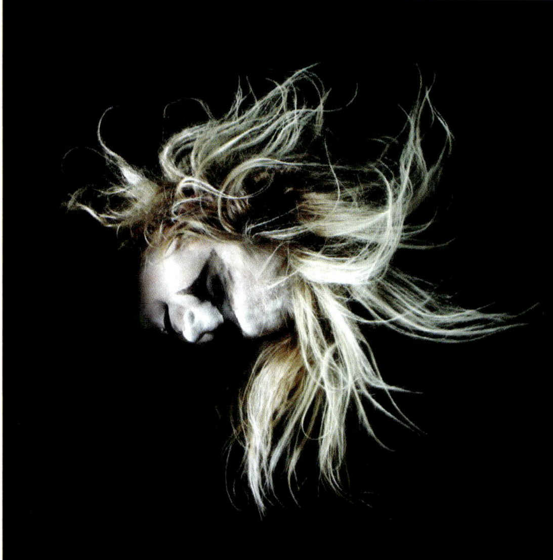

● LEE SEARLE The ingredients for this shot were loud music and lots of movement. My subject danced around in front of the camera.

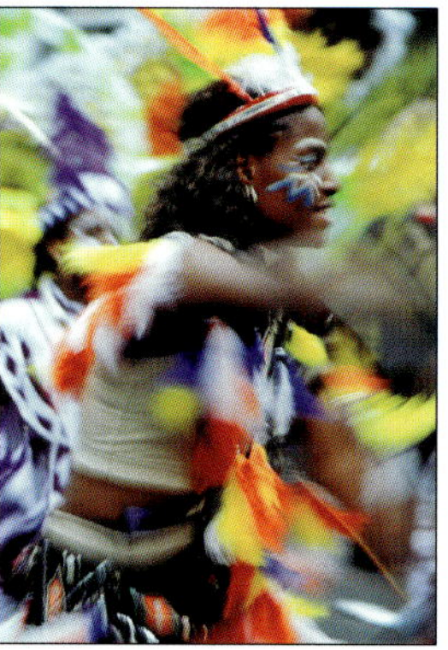

● MARK GOLDSTEIN Notting Hill Carnival in London, handheld using a slow shutter speed to blur the dancer's movement.

USING A GREY CARD

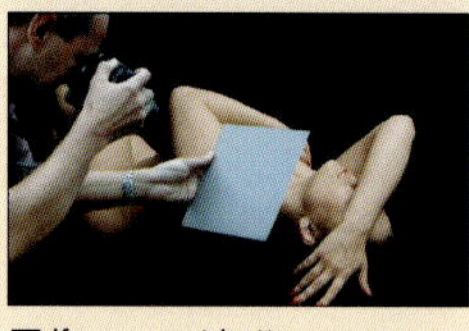

■ If you want better exposures from your camera's meter, buy a grey card. This 18% grey card is the same tone that a camera meter scrambles to.

■ Taking a meter reading from a grey card, placed in front of the subject, gives a similar exposure to an incident meter reading as it isn't fooled by the subject's reflectivity.

■ Position the card in the same light that's falling on the subject and take a reading. Set this and the exposures will, 99 times out of 100, be spot on.

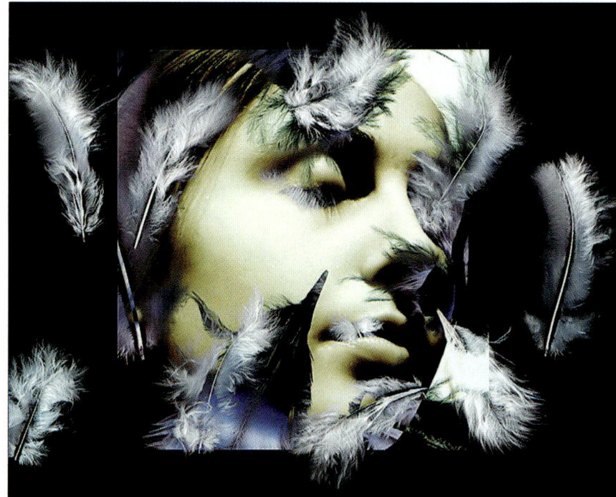

● CLAIRE MORGAN A self portrait lit from above by spotlights. Feathers scanned directly into Photoshop then added as a layer.

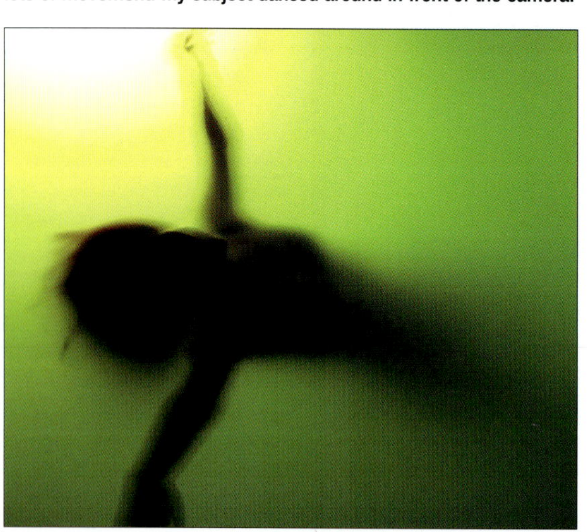

● TOM PEACEY Girlfriend in pool in Rio de Janiero, with Canon Ixus Digital V2 and slow-sync flash. The pool had lights and green algae.

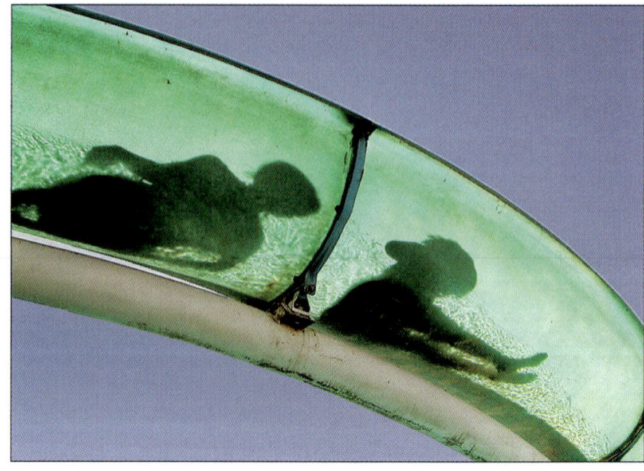

● HERMIN ABRAMOVITCH A silhouette of children in a watershoot, taken using a Nikon E990 at, 1/1000sec at ISO100.

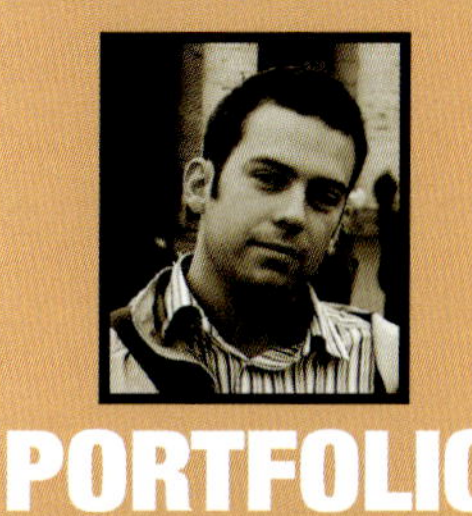

PORTFOLIO

MICHAL MURAWSKI
Often uses the sky, as one of
the most accessible, perfect
and natural backgrounds,
for his model photography.

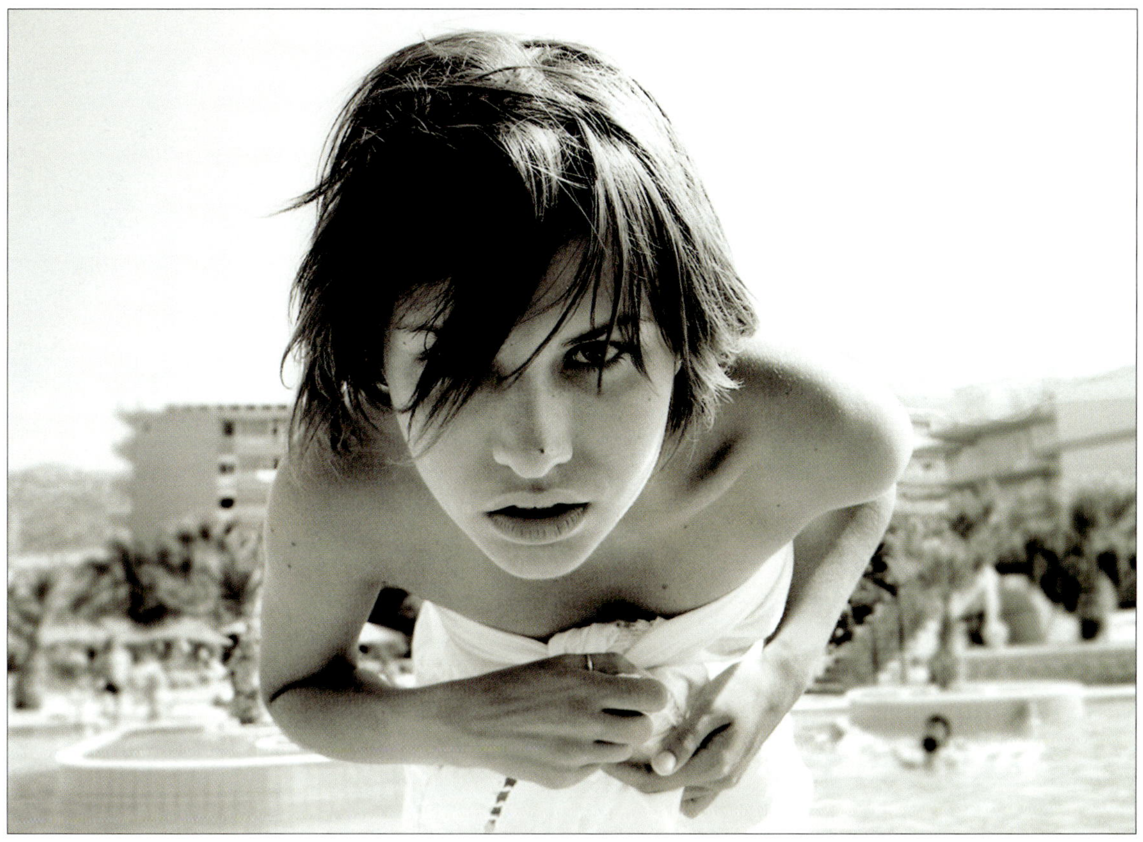

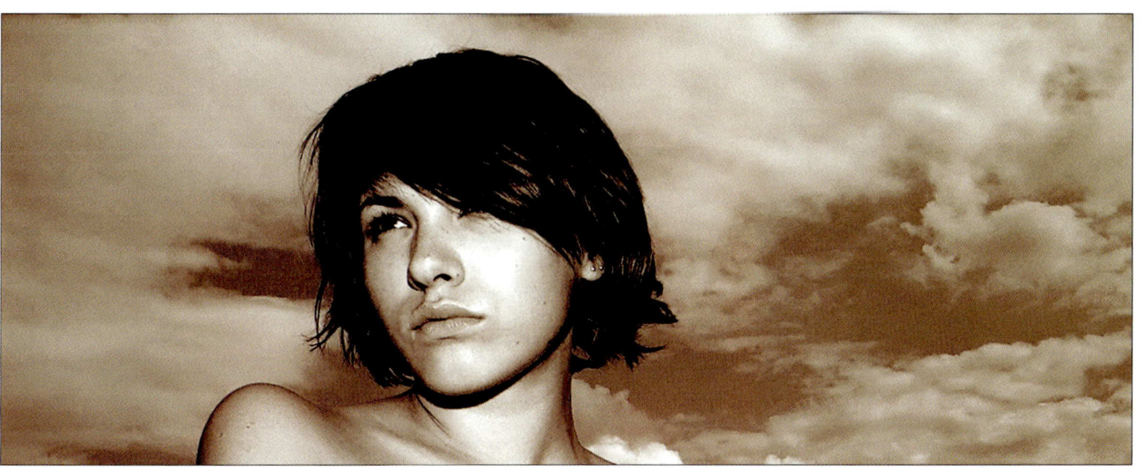

**I started out in photography
when I was aged 13 or 14,
using two lenses with my
Lubitel 166B camera and then
my Zenith 122.**

Between three and five years
ago I began to get serious about
my photography and decided
to buy my first digital camera, a
Nikon Coolpix 4500. These days
I'm using a Nikon 8700 and SB-
800 flashlight and I plan to buy a
Nikon D70.

My main interest in photography
is portraiture and I especially enjoy
shooting portraits of my fiancee. I
love how each portrait is a record,
showing her in a different state of
mind, a different mood and at a
different part of her life.

I like to shoot portraits in both
black & white and colour, but I
think it is much harder to shoot a
good colour portrait – it is easier
to retouch and present a black &
white photograph and gain a lot of
good comments.

Most of my portraits featured
here place the subject against the
sky. Though not all my photographs
feature this background, I think
the sky can sometimes be one of
the most accessible, perfect and
natural backgrounds which lets
both you and the viewer of the
photographs focus on the person
or their face. I also like to connect
the person in my portraiture with
the landscape or location details,
which I think helps to show a
little more about the mood of the
subject and the photograph.

Though portraiture is my main
interest I also enjoy shooting more
contemporary subjects like club
scenes, music concerts, city life
scenes and fashion.

In future I hope to develop
my fashion photography and I've
started a course with one of the
best Polish photographers. ■
www.clubbing.waw.pl

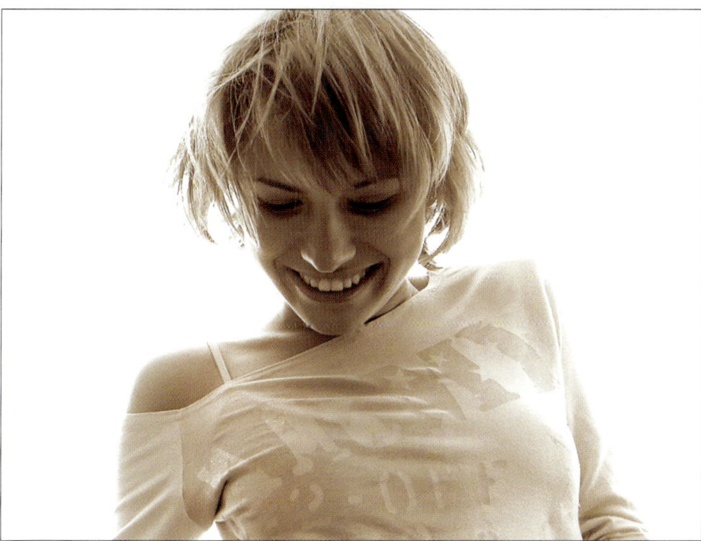

● Just a few of the photos in Michal's fantastic
portfolio which can be seen on ePHOTOzine.
Unusual angles, unusual crops, unusual
compositions and interesting toning treatments
feature highly throughout his photos.

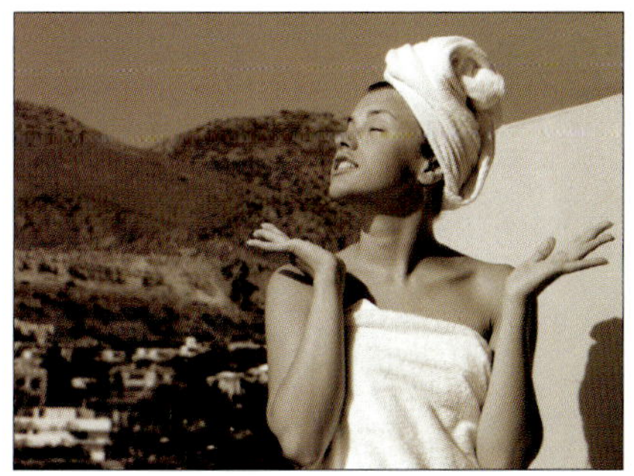

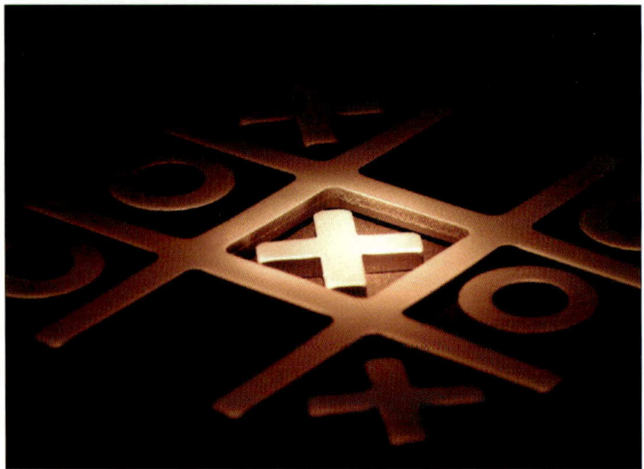

● MATT WAGSTER Tic-Tac-Toe travel set placed on black card, lit by a small torch that had the front coloured in with a red marker.

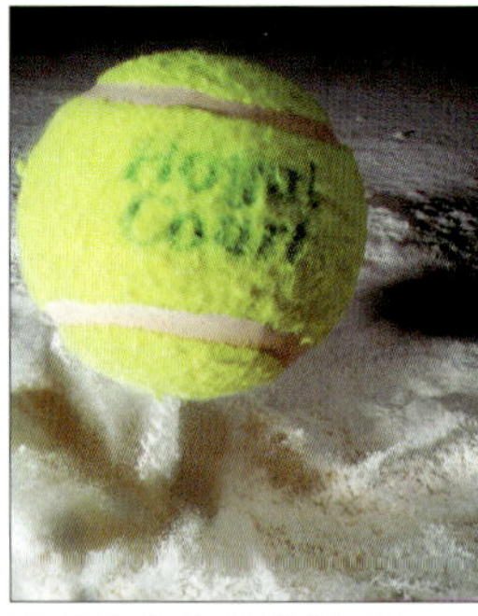

● GARY WOLSTENHOLME An experiment to capture the motion of a ball bouncing. The dust is there to help show the motion of the ball.

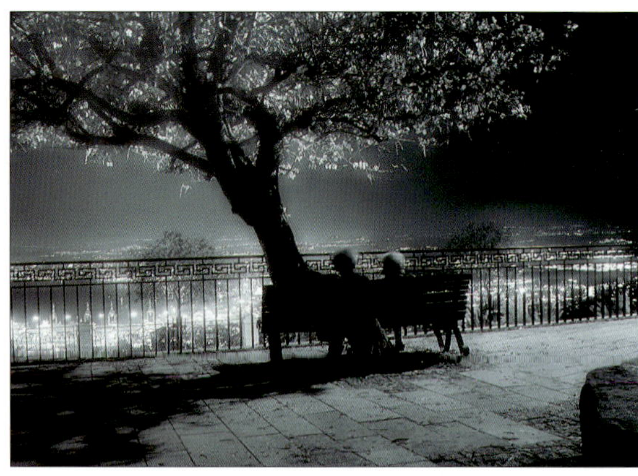

● HERMAN ABRAMOVITCH City lights in the distance give a magical glow to both the scene and the backlit tree leaves.

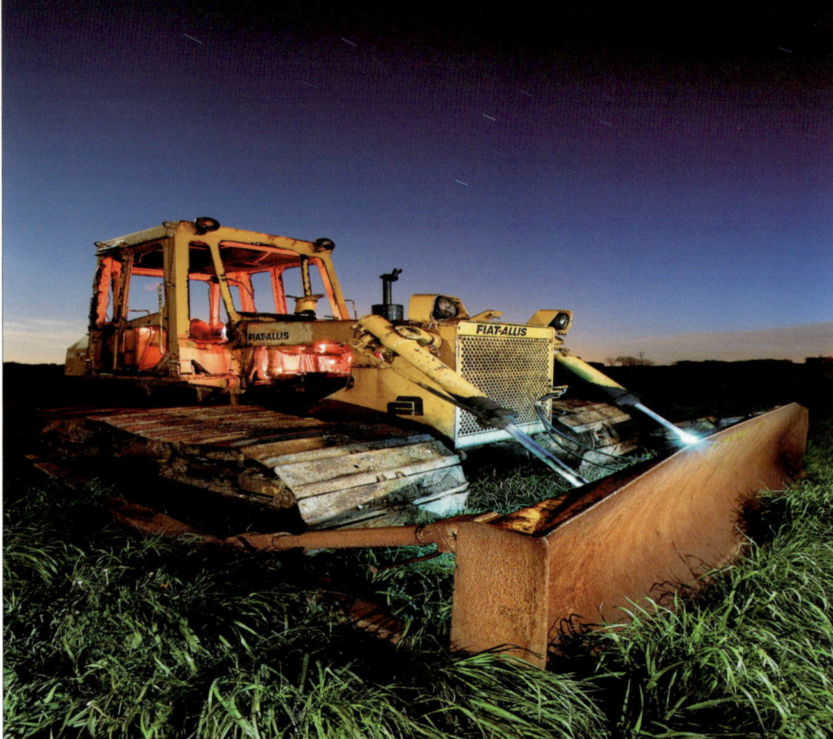

● STEVE SHARP "A lengthy 305 second exposure at f/10.0 allowed me to walk around the machine, flashing it with and without coloured gels."

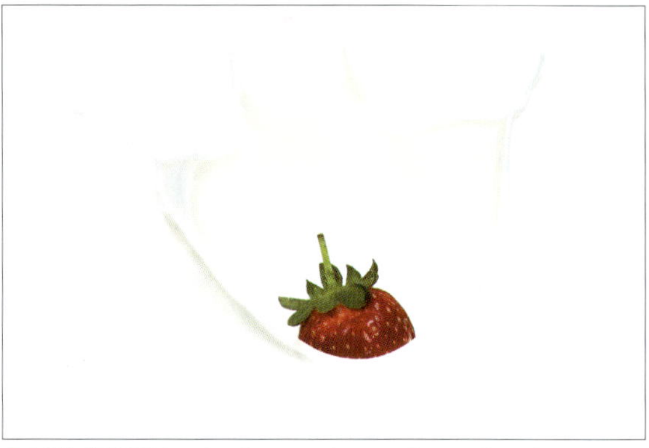

● PAUL GROOM Caught after countless re-plops and making a mess of his living room! Canon 10D with 28-135mm and Multiblitz flash.

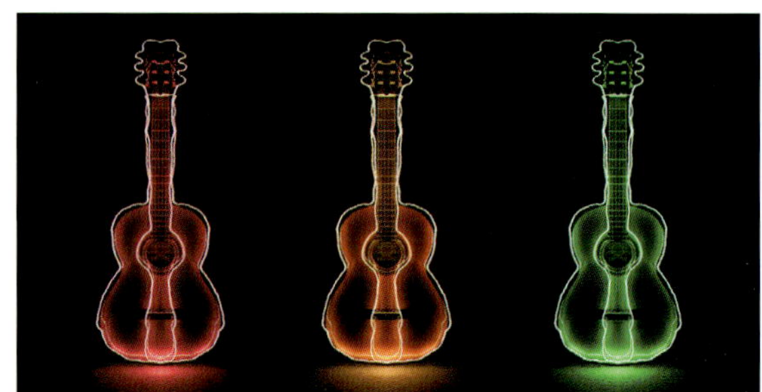

● VICKY HAMMERSTEIN I traced around the guitar with a torch while the camera was on B. Duplicated and adjusted hue/Saturation.

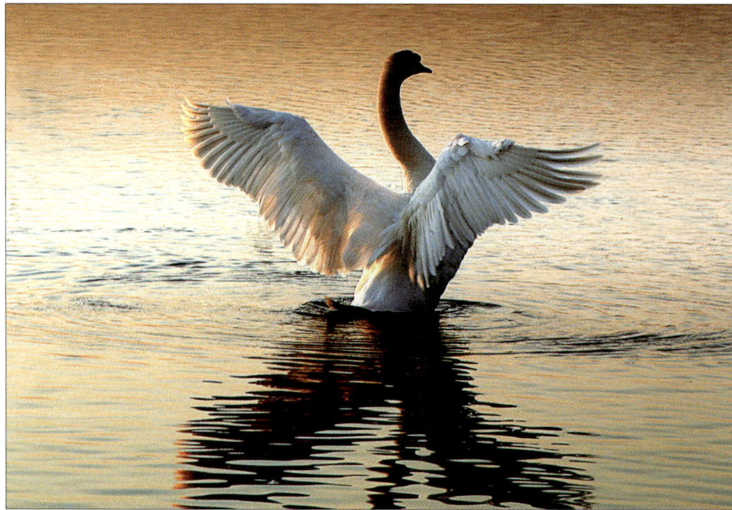

● ARFON JOHN Contre-joure shot using warm evening light and a helpful swan, taken using a Canon EOS D30 at 1/350sec and f/8, ISO200. Saturation was boosted in Photoshop.

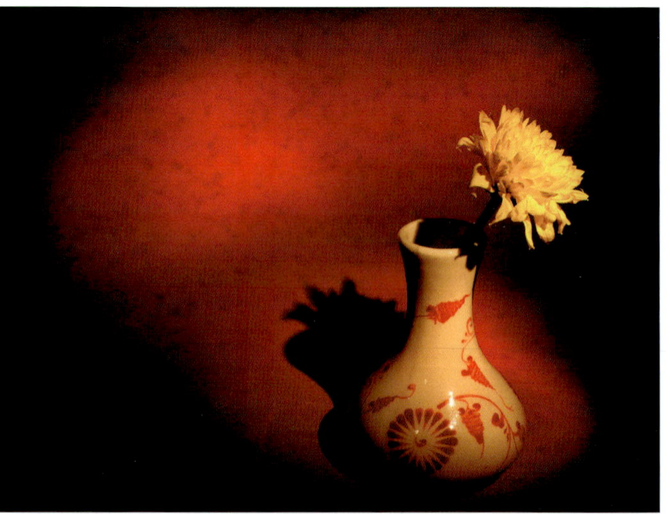

● MICHAEL MERCER This image was painted with light using a small, hand-held torch. The aperture was f/16 and the shutter set to bulb and opened for 25secs.

Flash/lighting

One of the key elements in any good photograph is lighting. Whether it's taken indoors using artificial light, outdoors in natural daylight or with flash, a subject has to be lit well to make it leap off the page. In this section, we look at photographs taken using a wide variety of lighting, each in very different creative ways.

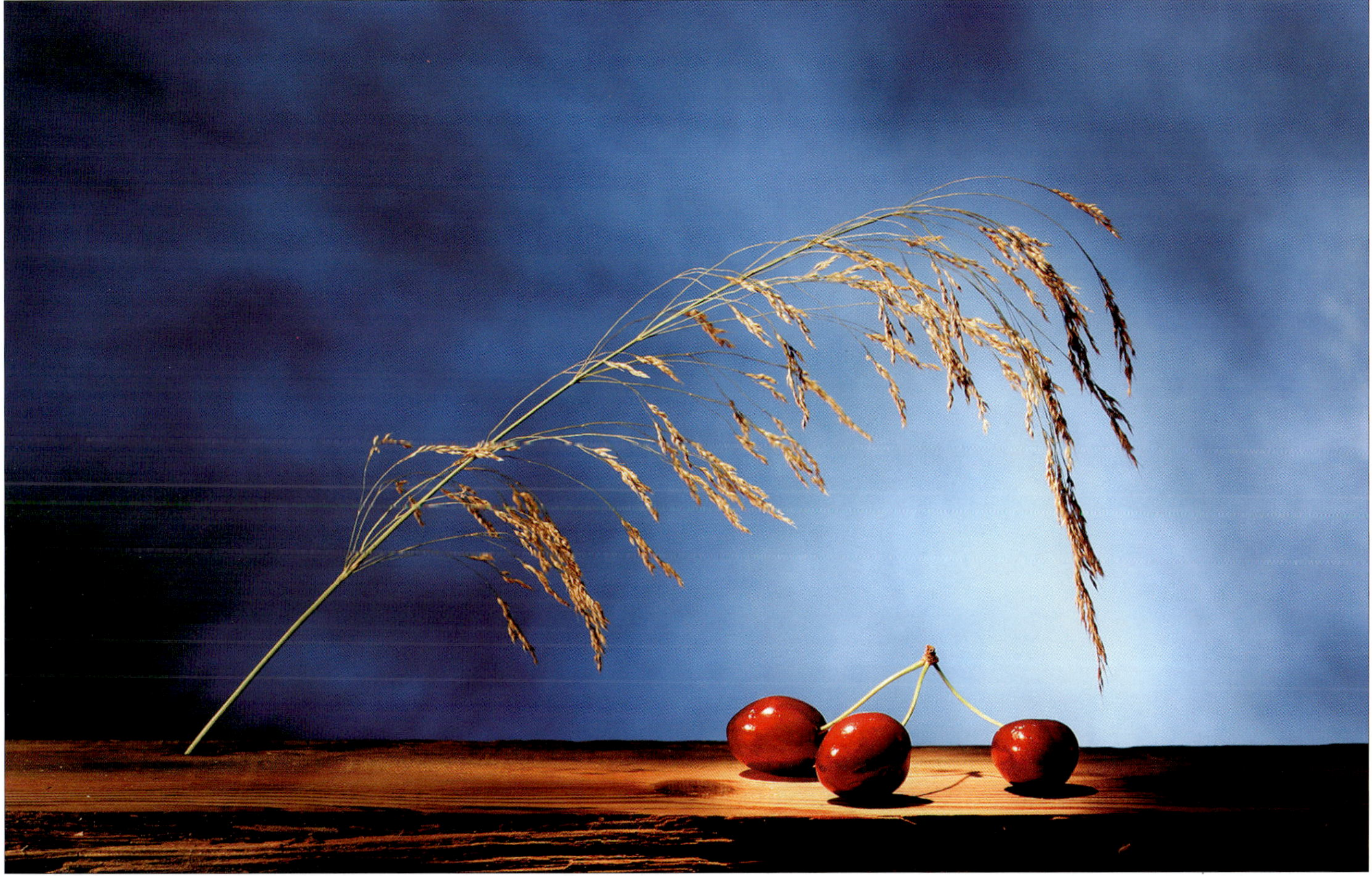

● STEPHEN GALEA Lighting is essential for good studio photography. This is the result of a three light setup. One was positioned direct at the background as a backlight, which gives the circular gradient effect. A second one was set to one side to help reveal texture and the third was a spotlight, positioned above to illuminate the cherries.

We normally think of lighting as the stuff that illuminates our homes, streets or work places. It's also vital in photography and is often undervalued. While beginners concentrate on getting the subject sharp and well exposed they often miss out on how to control the lighting.

The most natural form is the sun and it's probably also the most misused. Any good landscape photographer will be up at the crack of dawn to capture the light at its best, and midday is often missed to avoid harsh contrast.

They'll use filters to adjust tonal range between the ground and sky and wait around for hours for the right moment. While they are in the hands of the gods, so to speak, they do use time and location to control the light as far as humanly possible.

Reflectors and black masks are also used to shape the light outdoors as well as in the studio, adding light into shadows or taking away glare from subjects.

In the studio photographers will use similar techniques when working with flash or tungsten light. They will also use devices to soften the artificial light or make it harsher. The person who grasps the way light works will generally produce more pleasing images.

We cover most of the techniques using light in the relevant sections, but using light is not just about producing natural looking images. It can also be used creatively for special effects. A mirror introduced outdoors on a bright sunny day can create a second sun, bouncing brilliant light at the subject. Try this with flowers and they'll sparkle.

A torch or flash gun can be used to paint with light. Attach an inverted cone on the front of a torch and you can create a narrow beam for pencil-like drawings around the subject.

You could use several flash guns to create pockets of light in larger interiors, such as churches. These will fill in shadow areas in alcoves etc, while adding a coloured gel over the light source will introduce a hue to the photo or a background.

Flash can be used in daylight at half or quarter power to fill-in shadows and create less harsh results. Under-exposing the shot and using flash at full power will create a dark background with a perfectly exposed foreground. This can result in very moody shots.

Flash can also be used with the camera set at a slow shutter speed to create slow-sync flash shots, where the flash freezes the subject momentarily while the rest of the exposure appears blurred. Panning with the subject gives a great sense of speed.

Then consider the effect the subject has on the light. Surely everyone remembers the legendary Pink Floyd Dark Side of the Moon album that shows the spectrum created when white light travels through a prism. Well you could do similar experiments photographing the light projected through a wine glass, or crystal ball. Or how about creating a series of shadows?

Another option is to place the light source behind the subject and create a rim light. This works really well with glass bottles as it creates a fine highlight around the bottle – also on hair, especially blonde, as it illuminates the surroundings of the face, lifting the portrait into another dimension.

And then there's high speed flash. A little more specialised, but with digital it's easier to get the desired shots. Use flash to freeze the movement of a dart bursting a balloon, a champagne cork popping or the splashes as an object hits water or paint.

Don't take light for granted. Your subjects will look a lot better with just a bit more thought. Have a look at the following pages for some ideas created by our members. You'll find many more examples throughout the book in the subject based sections. Light – shape it, craft it, make it. ■

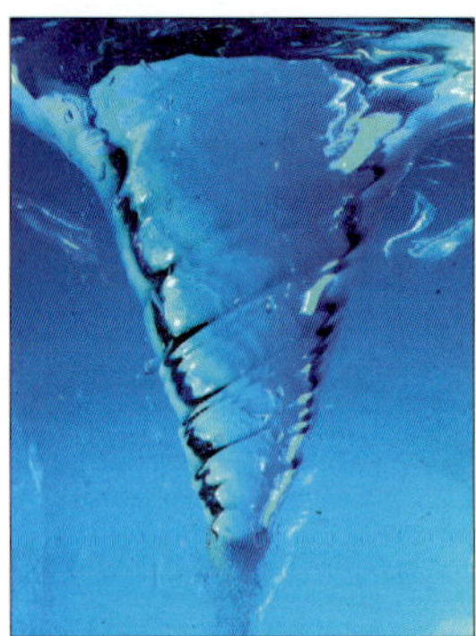

● DAVID BAILIE This whirlpool was created with an electric drill and paddle, back lit by the sun and gelled flash. Taken using a Canon EOS 10D 1/180sec at f/22.

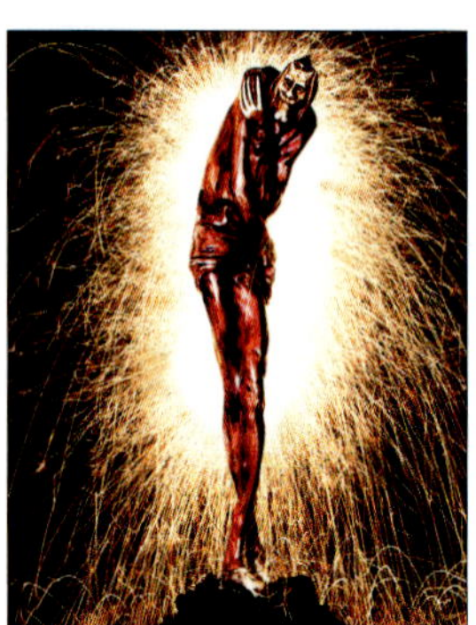

● ROB FREEMAN Sparkler lit, shutter opened, flash fired and sparkler was then left to burn before closing the shutter.

RIM LIGHTING

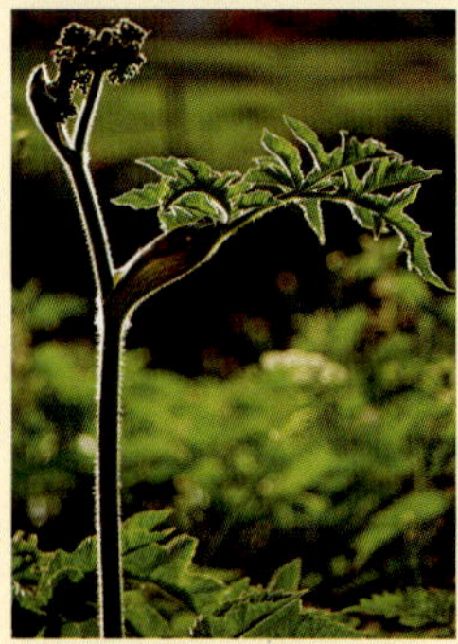

■ When the light source is positioned behind the subject it's referred to as backlighting. If it's in such a position to highlight the edges of the subject, it's called rim lighting.
■ Rim lighting works best when the subject's edges are thin so you get light bursting through, creating wonderful outlines.
■ To ensure a sparkling rim over-expose it slightly.
■ Move around to position the subject against a darker background to enhance the effect of the rim light.

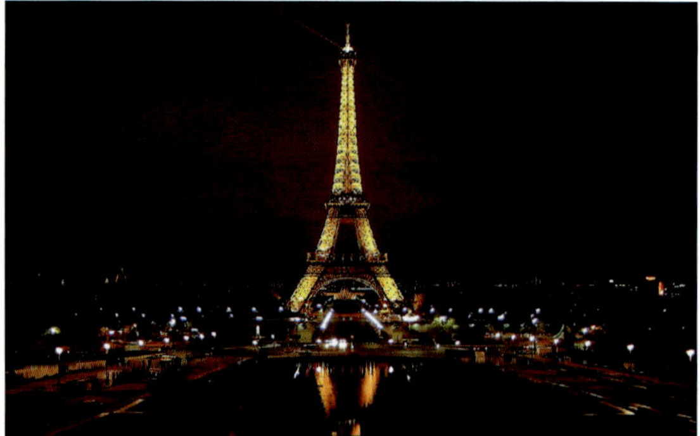

● JOHN DUCKETT ISO1600 was set to allow a hand-held shot. It was then run through the Neat Image programme to remove noise.

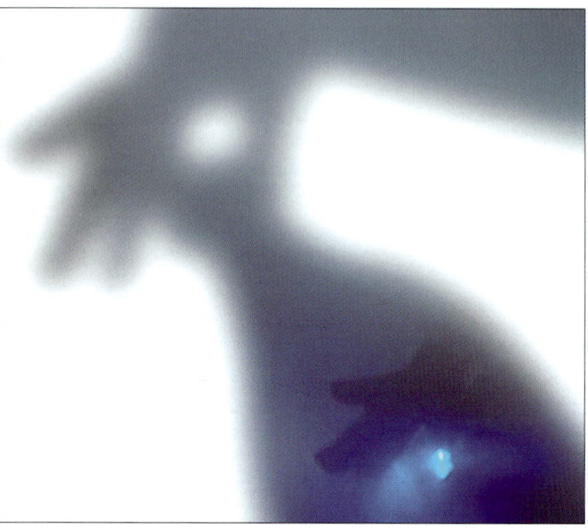

● SUZANNE BOSWORTH A shadow in full sun on a white card. Gaussian blur at 40%, using a soft brush to reveal the highlights.

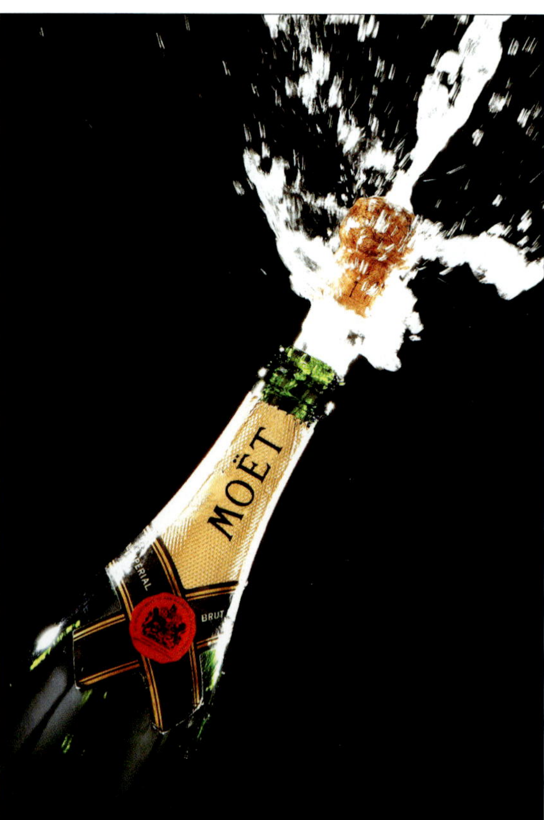

● KEVIN GOODCHILD Captured at a still life studio. The bottle, with the bottom cut off, is fixed upside down against a black background.

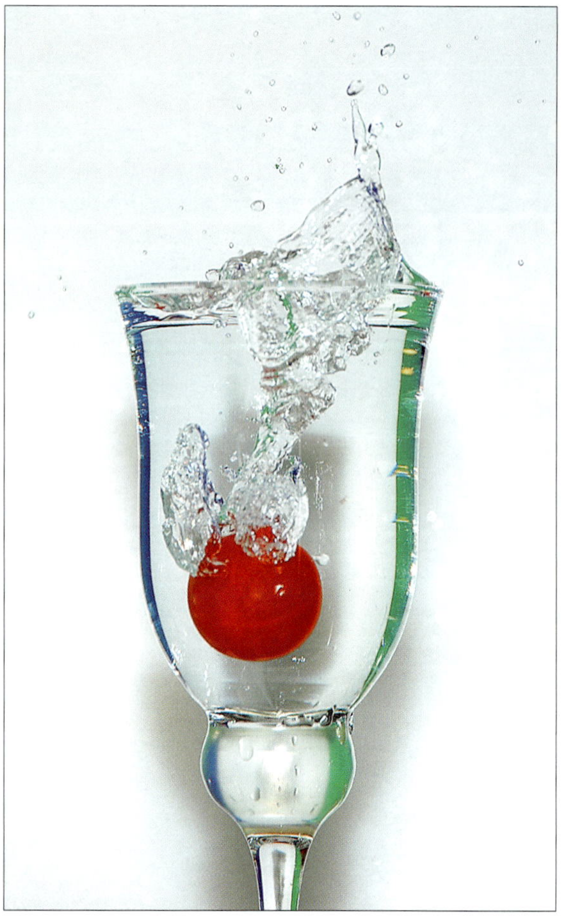

● TIM COOPER A cherry tomato dropped into a glass of water, two bright chopping boards providing the colour. Nikon D70 and SB800.

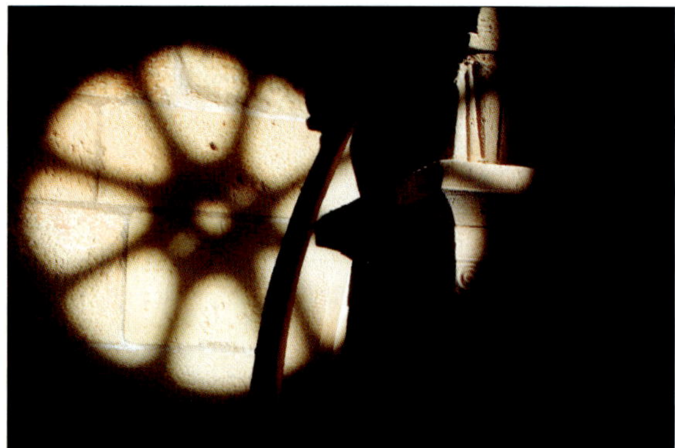

● ANTONIO ALOMAR A window in the cloister of the Monastery of Santa Maria de les Monjes, reflected on the stone wall.

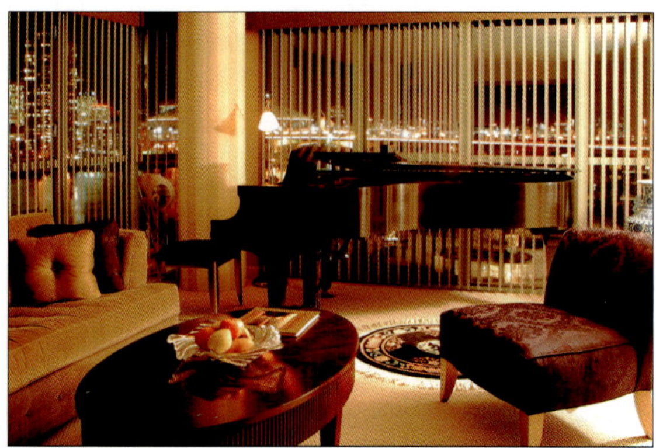

● ARTHUR CHAN Attempted to balance the light from outside and inside the room. Taken using a Canon EOS D60 and 20sec at f/11.

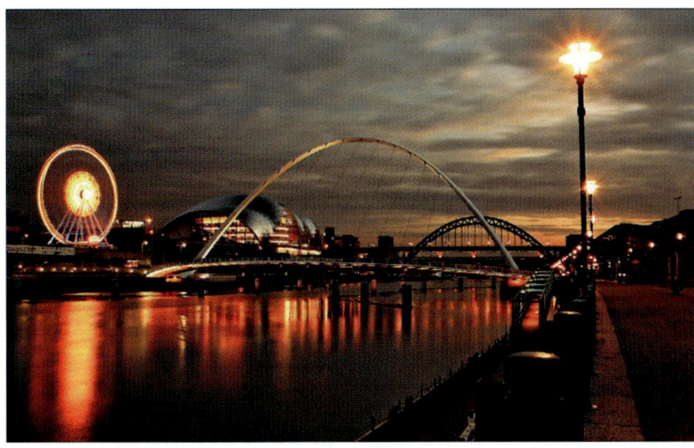

● JAMES BURNS Newcastle Quayside captured on a Nikon D70 with a Sigma 18-50mm, ND Grad and Circular Polariser. The exposure was 20sec at f/25.

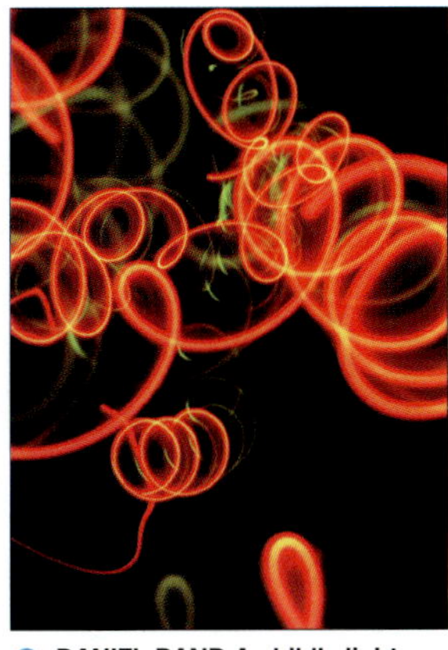

● DANIEL BAND A child's light-up toy, taken with a Canon A70.

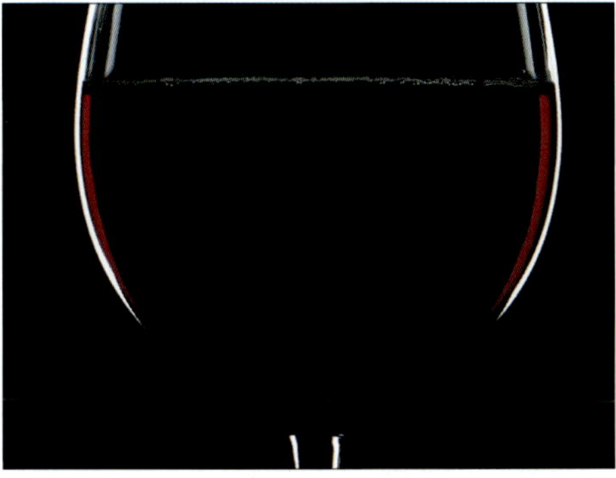

● ANNETTE EAST A backlit wine glass, using a Sigma 105mm macro set at f/11.

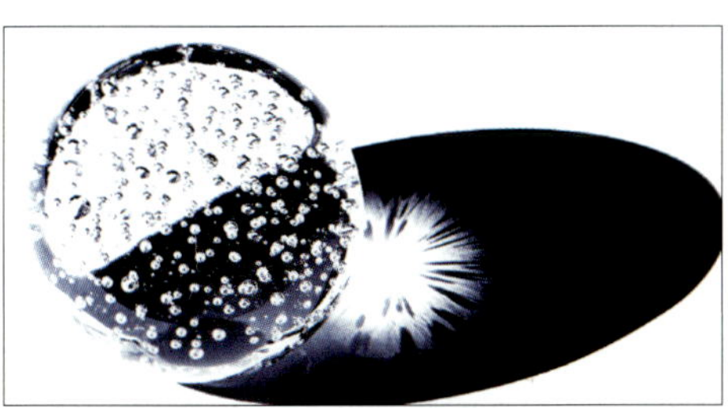

● TOM SANDERSON A glass paperweight. Strong side lighting and spot metering were used to capture this.

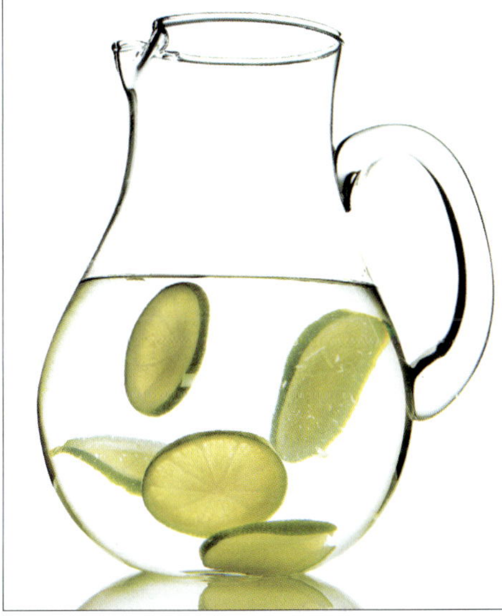

● MIKE CHAJECKI Three lights positioned left, right and back with black boards at each side. Flash freezes the limes in motion. Fuji FinePix S2 at 1/125sec and f/8.0.

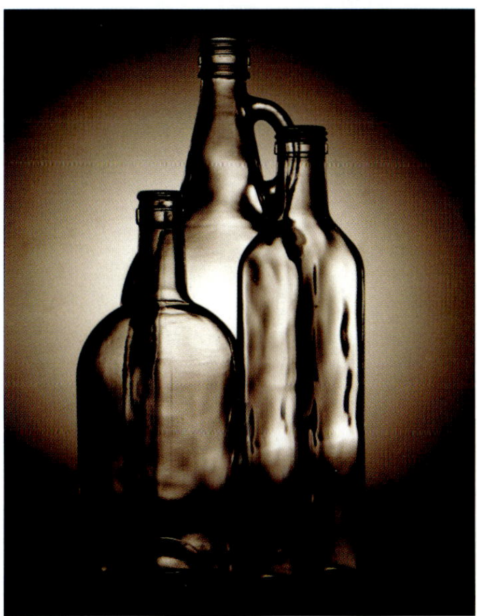

● ANTON HEIBERG The modelling lamp and honeycomb on a studio flash, directed through paper background.

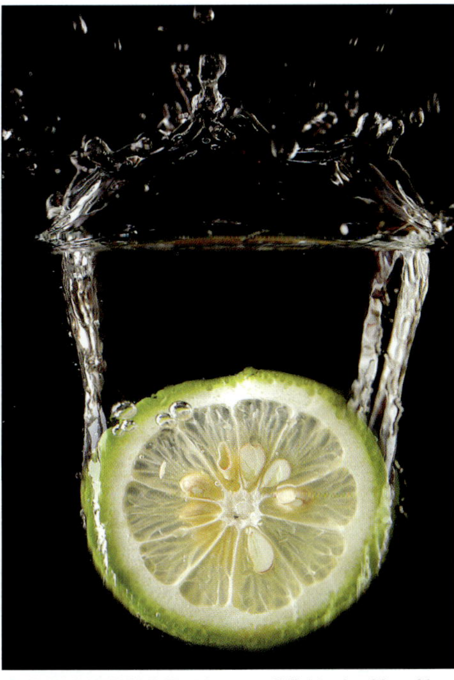

● ANTON HEIBERG Shot in a small fishtank with softbox from the left and white reflector from the right.

SHOOTING TIPS – USING A TORCH

■ Using a small pocket torch as a light source can be the recipe for some very creative lighting effects.

The technique, known as painting with light, allows you to illuminate precise areas of the subject by pointing a torch at it during the exposure. The trick is to build up the amount of light on the subject so that it is correctly exposed. Or draw around the subject to create a glowing outline, like Vicky did with the guitar on the opening page of this section.

■ Any standard torch will do but the powerful compact models, from the likes of Maglite, are perfect. You can also often adjust the beam from a wide spread to quite intense, making it useful for different types of subject. You could use a cone made from black card to make an even more precise point light source.

■ This technique can be achieved with any camera, although digital is much easier as the exposure is quite tricky to calculate with a film camera and you need to bracket to stand a chance of getting good shots.

■ Mount the camera on a tripod so you can control the torch with one hand while tripping the shutter with the other. Use a cable release or remote control to make it even easier to fire the camera.

■ Set the camera on auto exposure and bracket two stops over and under, making notes so you can refer to them when your photos are printed. With a digital camera you can preview the photo after you've taken it and shoot again if the result isn't quite right.

■ Focus and set the camera on focus lock so that it isn't fooled by the uneven light.

■ A torch has a colour temperature that's warmer than daylight so subjects illuminated with it will appear orange. You can use a blue 80 series filter to correct this with film, whereas a digital camera has an automatic white balance control that adjusts to make the picture look like daylight. When necessary, you can override the white balance and set the colour correction manually.

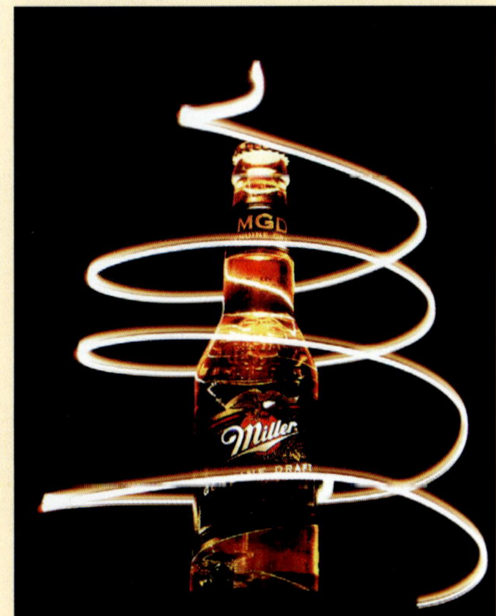

● PAUL MITCHELL A bottle of Miller beer on a torch with a yellow Y2 filter. A Maglite was used to create the light trail, with an 8sec shutter speed.

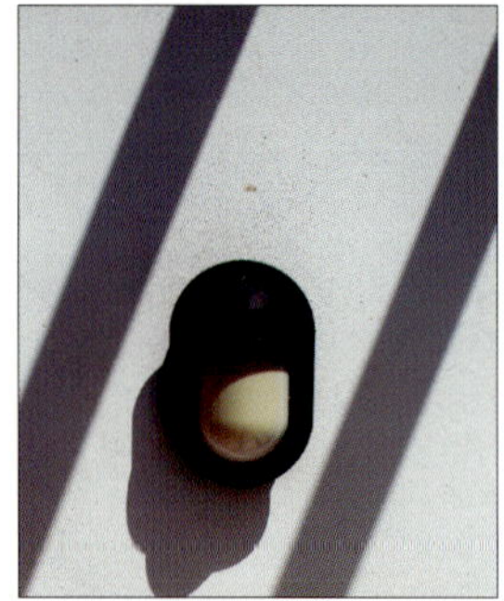

● JIM MACBRAYNE An interesting shadow cast by the midday sun on the balcony of a Canarian hotel. Taken with a Canon EOS 20D and 18-55mm.

FLASH TIPS

■ Flash is most commonly used on cameras with a built-in unit and at night it will activate automatically, firing to give harsh results with no detail in the dark background. To overcome this you would turn it off and make use of the ambient light from either the moon or outdoor street lighting or tungsten/fluorescent indoors.

■ Another option would be to invest in a slave flash which is triggered by the on-board flash and can be used to illuminate the dark background. Some photographers have several to ensure all the shadow areas receive some exposure.

■ The power of your built-in flash is often too low to illuminate larger subjects that are further from the camera – a church, for example. With your camera set on B it's possible to fire the flash several times with the camera's shutter open to build up to the correct exposure. After each flash cover the lens with card while the flash recycles to prevent the ambient light causing over-exposure.

■ Red-eye is more likely when you shoot at night. Ask the person to stare at a bright light for a few moments before you take the shot to reduce the effect.

■ Avoid covering the flash with your fingers when using a compact camera. It's easy for fingers to rest over the tube.

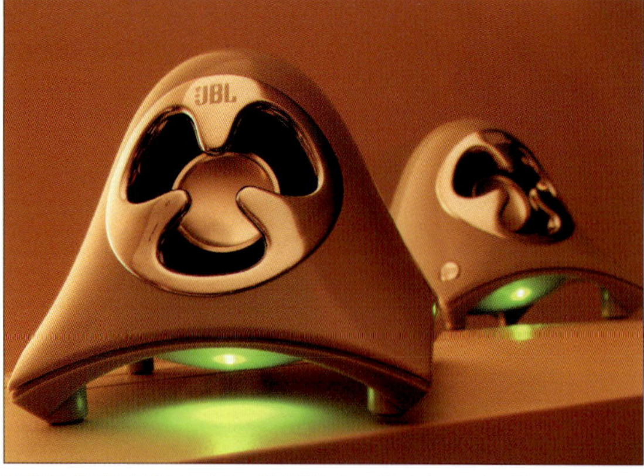

● IAIN GILFILLAN used low light from a desk lamp to allow green lights from his speakers to show up. DiMage Z3 at 15secs and f/8.0.

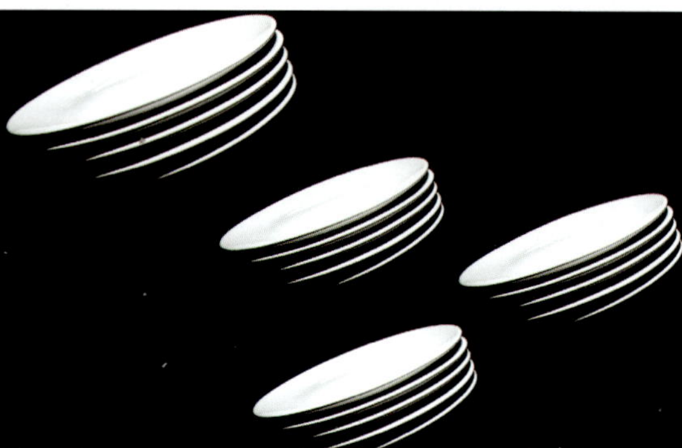

● BRAD BUCHANAN Plates stacked in a dark room with a halogen lamp, taken on a Canon EOS 300D at ISO100, 1/125sec and f/5.6.

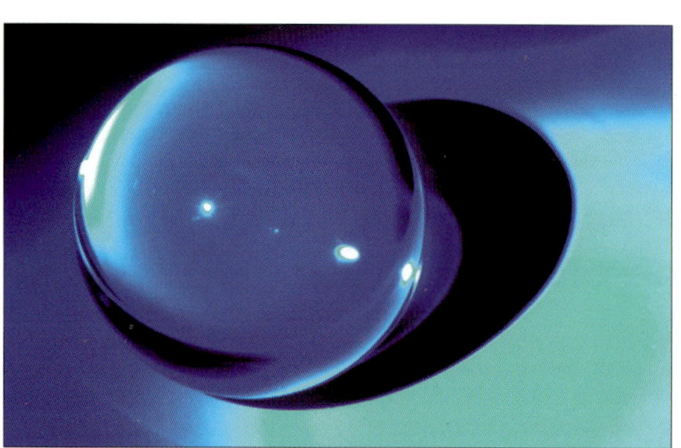

● GLENN JOHNSON Taken in darkness using a crystal ball with a blue LED flashlight shining through it and a one second exposure.

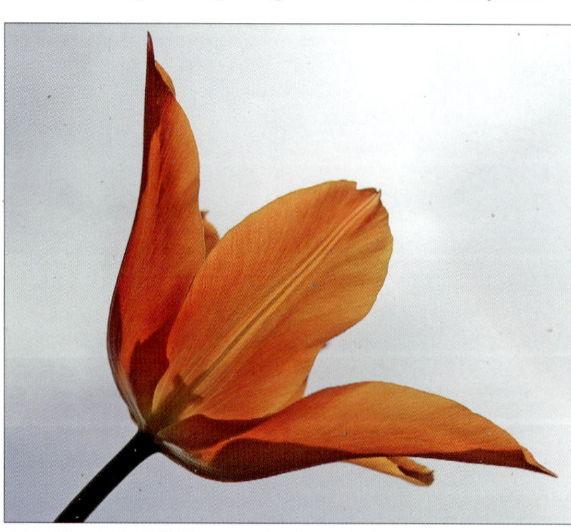

● TREVOR SLATTER Taken on his friend's balcony on a very sunny day, using an Olympus C8080WZ at 1/2000sec and f/3.2, ISO50.

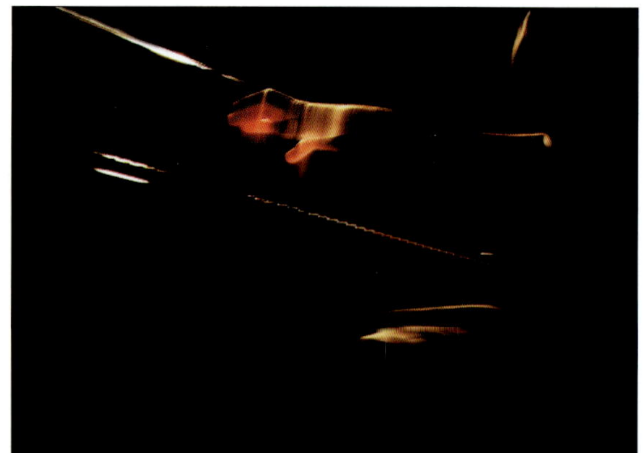

● CLAIRE MORGAN Pianist performing in an Orchestra. The shot was taken from floor level and was lit from above by a single light.

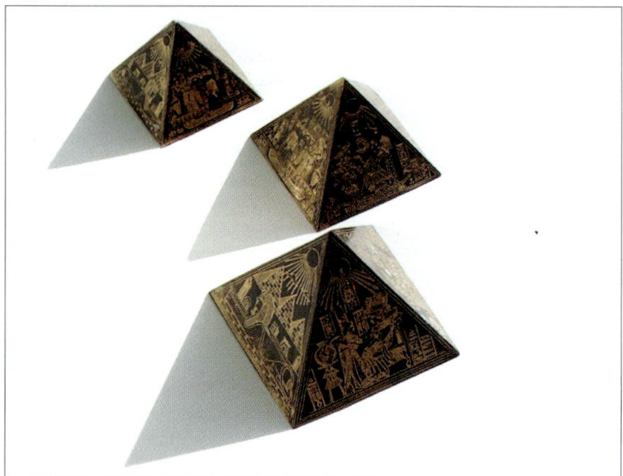

● DANIEL VIDAL Taken on a white table and lit with sunlight from the right. A white card was placed on the left as a reflector.

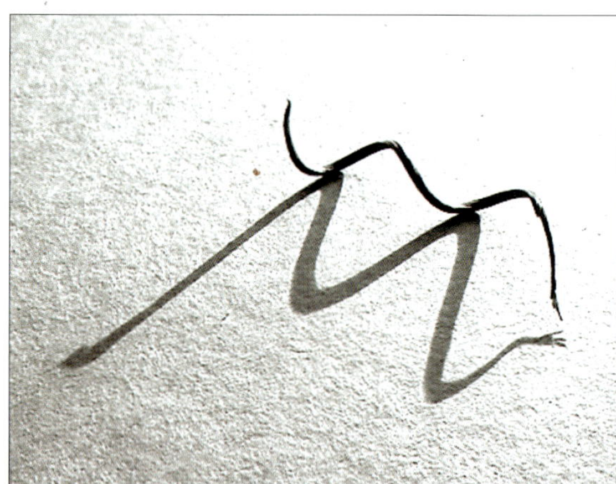

● ANNE RICHARDSON Experimenting with light and shadows. A piece of curly grass on white paper, taken using window light.

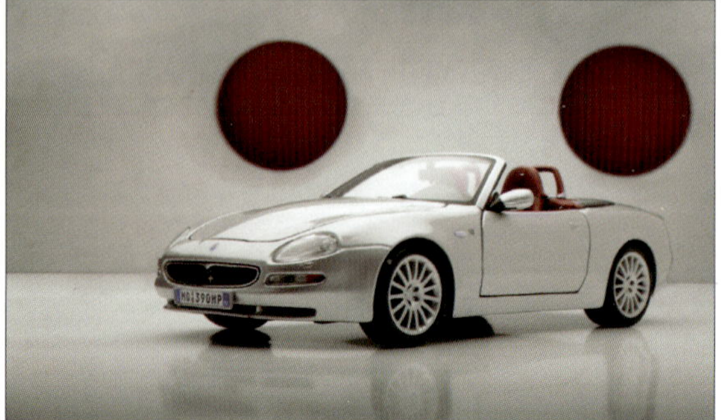

● PETE IRELAND I bought this 8in model from Tesco on a rainy day, itching to test out my lighting and softbox. Canon EOS 20D at f/16.

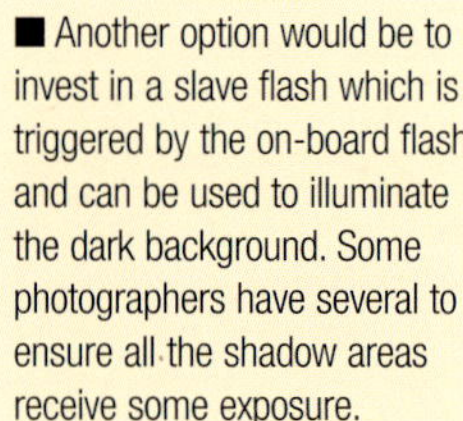

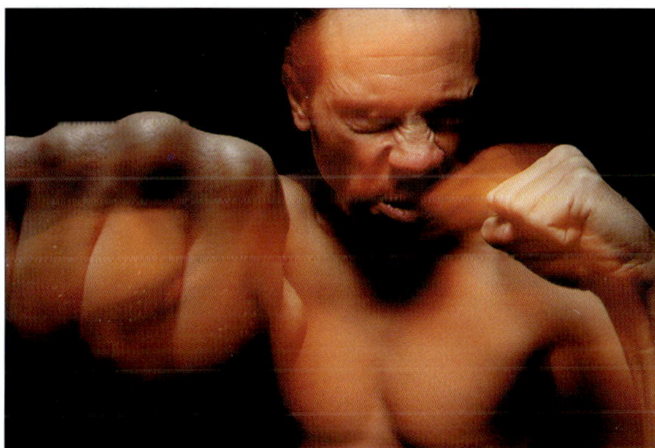

● SUZANNE GALLOWAY Studio light fitted with a soft box at 45 degrees onto the face and a spot on the background.

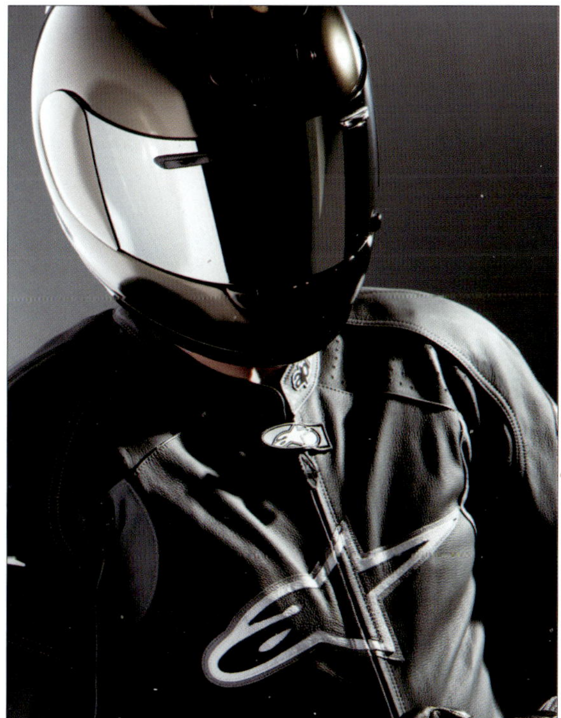

● RAB LETHAM Shot using rear sync flash at 4secs. The model moves causing blur and flash freezes the action as the lens closes.

● NICK HILL Shot in studio using three lights, taken using a Canon EOS 1Ds MkII and a 200mm lens at f/14 and 1/250sec.

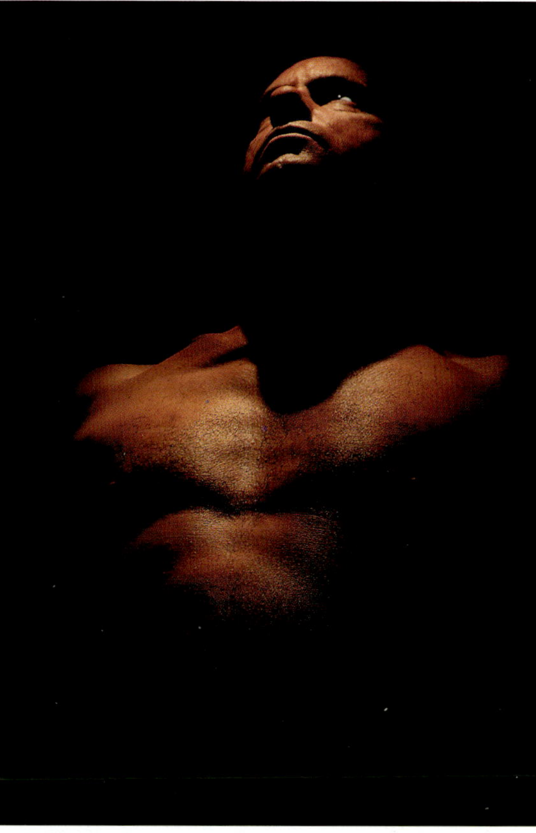

● MIKE DEGASPERIS Lighting does play an important role in the final outcome of any image. Here it's a single light from above.

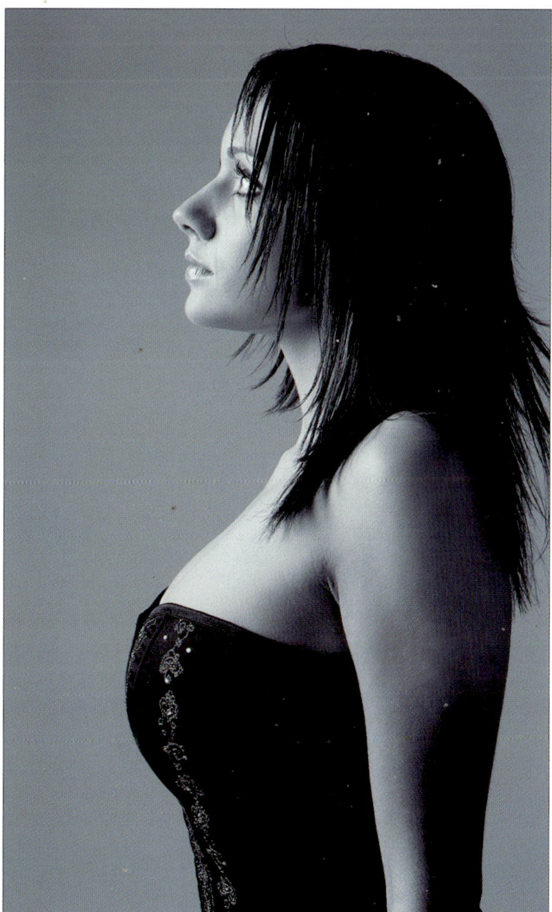

● GARY TIMMS This was shot with a simple setup – a 1m softbox overlooking the subject. The image was toned slightly in Photoshop.

FILL-IN FLASH TIPS

■ You don't only have to use flash at night. Your camera's flash can be a great friend in bright daylight when used as a fill-in option.

■ The idea is to expose as normal, but fire the flash to fill in shadow areas. Compact cameras usually have a fill-in flash mode, called forced flash. The results are usually too harsh because you really need to use the flash at a lower ratio to daylight.

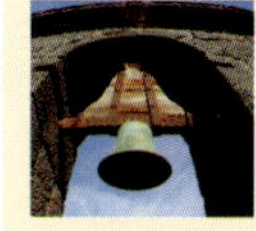 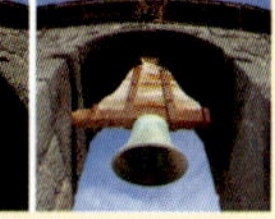

■ SLR users have much more control, especially when using a portable flash with automatic settings. Models such as the Vivitar 283 have been around for about 30 years and still provide many photographers with the best option. This one, like many auto guns, has auto aperture settings. Most have one or two, the Vivitar has four and some Metz guns have six!

■ The idea is that you meter as normal for the ambient light, which may be f/8 and set the flash to f/5.6. The flash then gives enough exposure for f/5.6, but the lens at f/8 means the flash under-exposes by one stop. This is fine for shots taken in bright sunlight where shadows are harsh.

■ On more overcast days it would be better to have quarter power with an aperture of f/4 – this is when it helps to have a flash with more auto settings. Some of the latest cameras look after all the ratios automatically.

■ You will see many photographers on TV at news events with a bounce flash pointing upwards. You'll also see the head has a small translucent cube over it. This is a flash diffuser, made by Sto-fen, called the Omni Bounce. It spreads the light to reduce the harshness of flash so the result looks like it's been illuminated by daylight.

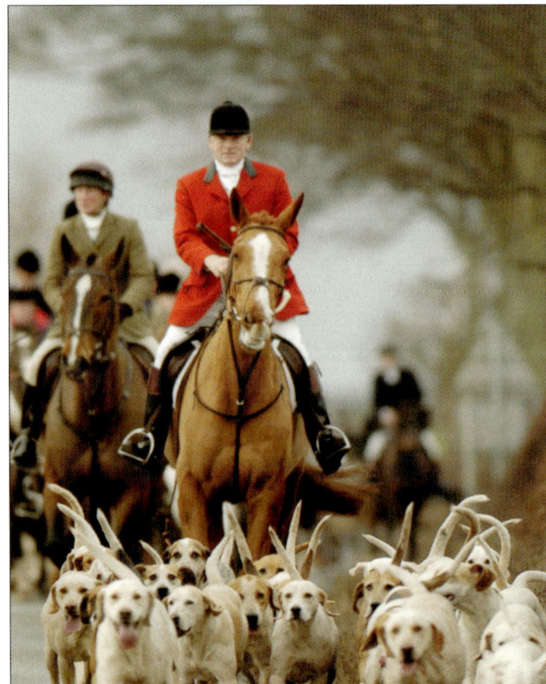

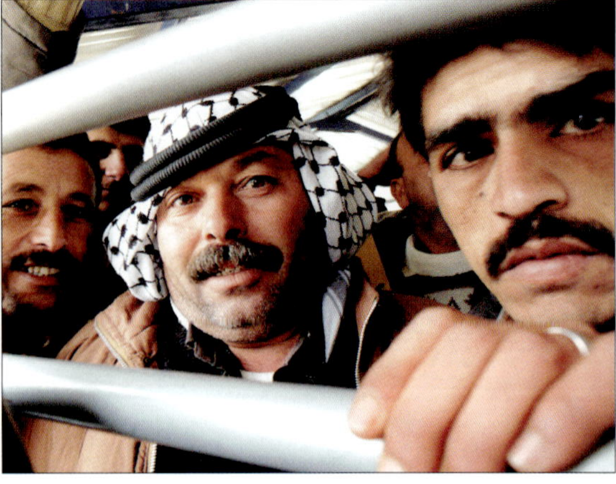

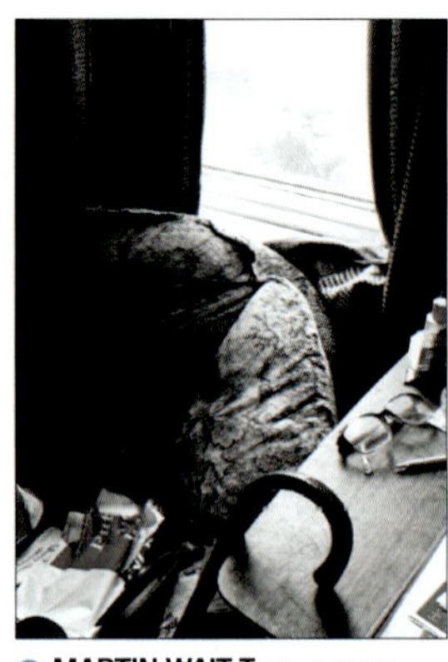

● FRANCOIS LEPINAY Travel restrictions. Palestinians with Israeli ID cards are caged while waiting to be processed back through the Israeli border. Those without ID cards are not allowed in.

● MARTIN WAIT Tom, a man of great character, sat in this chair for many years. Sadly he passed away shortly after this photograph was taken.

● ROB GRAY Hunstmen at Berwickshire Hunt on New Years Day 2005, taken on a Nikon D2H with 300mm f/2.8 and ISO400.

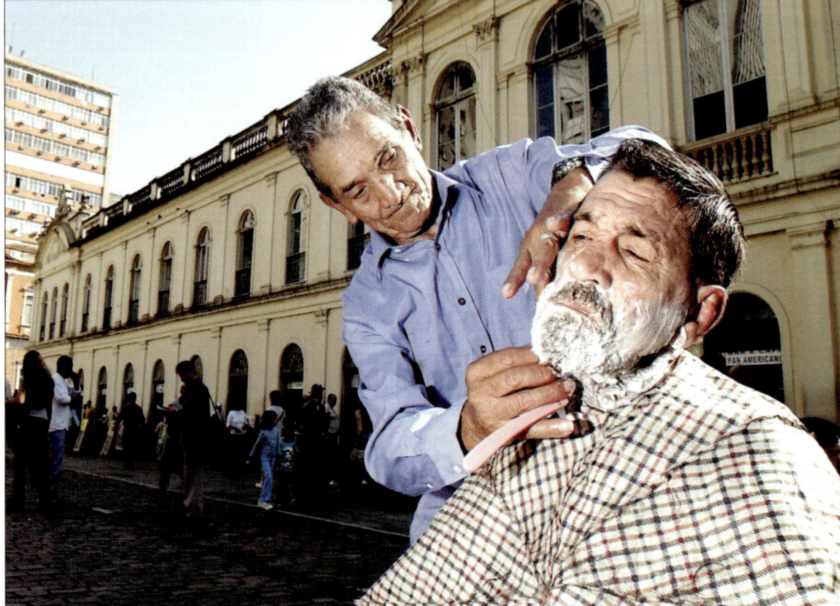

● ANDREA GRAIZ Barber shop in the street in the city of Porto Alegre, south of Brazil. A Nikon D1 digital camera was used with a 17-35mm lens and fill-in flash to bathe the barber with light.

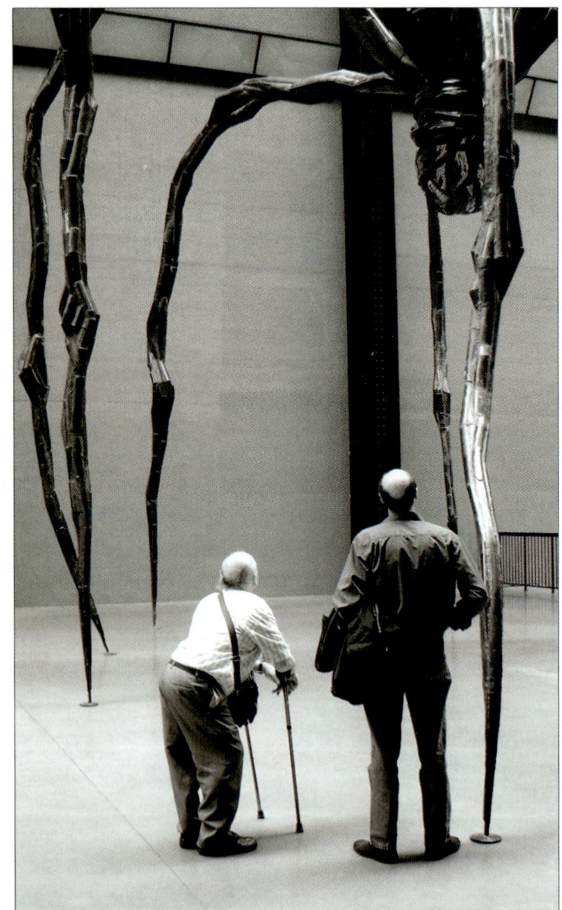

● CHRIS MOLE Tate Modern, London." I was drawn by the parallel between the legs of the spider and the man's walking sticks."

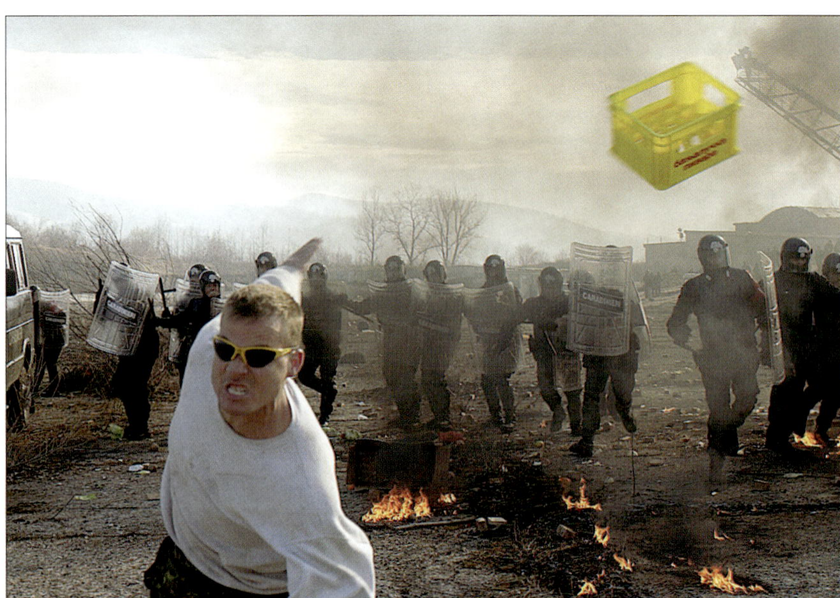

● BRAD CHAPPELL Whilst running from the Carabinieri, the rioter still managed to throw the crate at them. Taken in Bosnia on a Nikon D1.

Photojournalism

Photojournalists turn their cameras to the pursuit of news, an essential function in any democratic society. With the advent of affordable digital technology comes the opportunity for anybody with the determination, and a modicum of skill, to get involved and photograph real-life as it happens. In this section, ePHOTOzine members do just that.

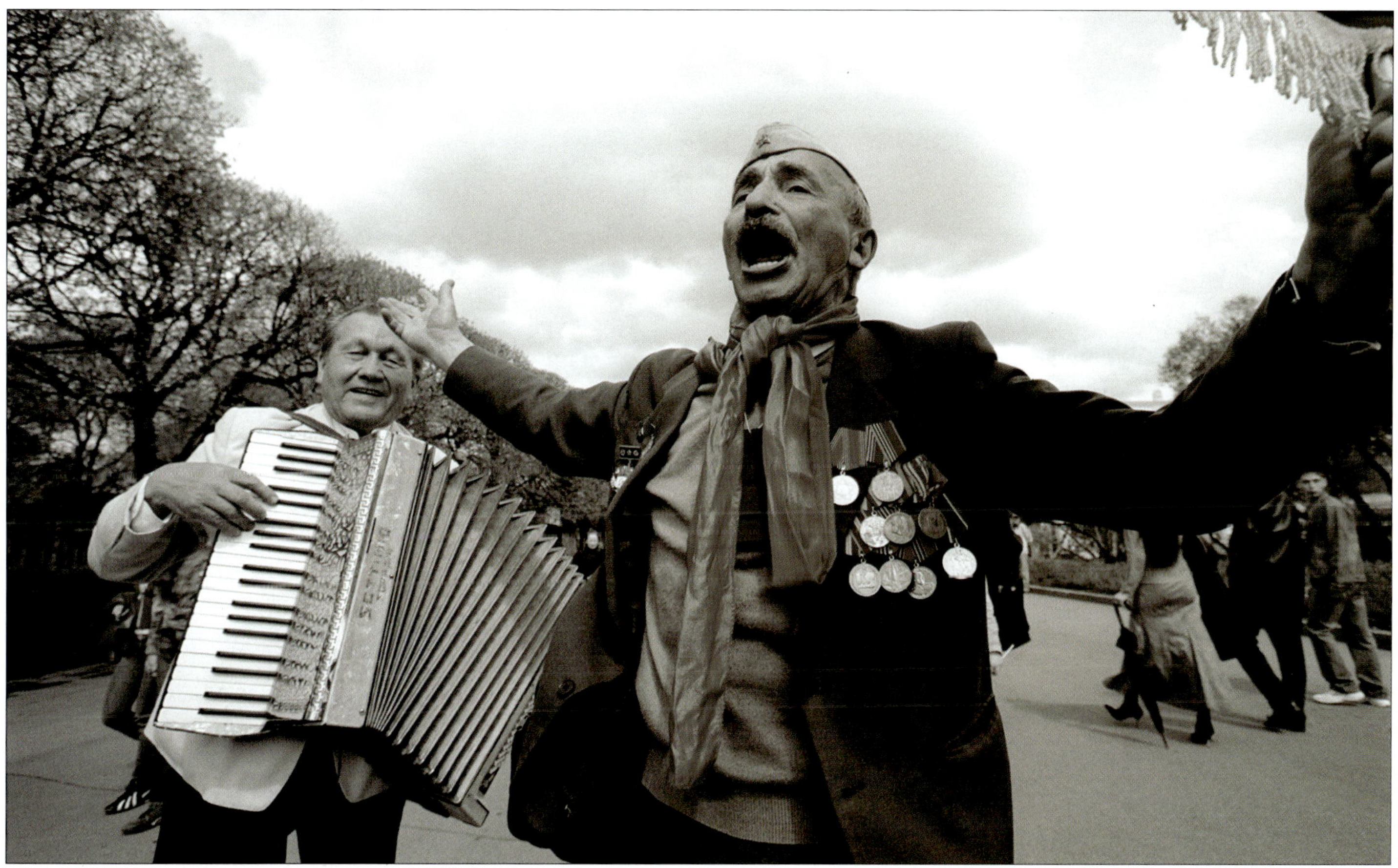

● ALEXEY AISTOV Titled Song of Victory, this shot portrays a veteran of two World Wars singing a song with his friend, a front-line soldier. Taken using a Canon EOS 1n with a 17-35mm zoom on Kodak black & white film.

Photojournalists use their cameras to document the world, capturing reality in a way that may shock or surprise, but will always ultimately inform. Their pictures take the viewer to places they might not ordinarily go, to see things they might not (or weren't supposed to) see.

Pictures can have a dramatic impact on everyone's lives. Who could forget the student who stood in front of a tank in Tiananmen Square 1989 or the many pictures of the September 11 attacks on the World Trade Centre in 2001? Photojournalists often endanger their own lives to bring us the pictures that could change a generation.

A precise definition of photojournalism is somewhat troublesome, but in broad terms a photojournalist is somebody who tells a story through pictures. He is a visual reporter of the facts.

At the most serious level, for democratic society to function correctly, photojournalists must be allowed to get their pictures across to audiences so that corruption, scandal and abuses of power can be exposed.

On a lighter and less vital note, there's the tabloid photographer with his telephoto lens snapping away at D-list celebrities as they emerge from the latest premiere; offering as he does a form of entertainment to the red-top reader.

Of course, it's not just a job for the professionals: anybody with a camera in the right place at the right time can make a contribution. News is now a 24-hour concern, and the demand for pictures has never been greater. Indeed, major organisations, including the BBC, are making increasing use of opportunist shots when covering breaking stories.

That isn't to say that photojournalism is an easy profession to break in to – far from it. As the demand for pictures grows, so too does the number of people competing for a shot. Although almost anyone can do it, to do it well is another matter entirely.

Along with the power to make a difference inevitably comes much responsibility. Although it's a cliché, a picture really can say a thousand words and leave a lasting impression on the viewer. Images transcend cultural and linguistic boundaries; they are immediately understandable.

There are legal matters to consider too. Although UK law has nothing defined in statute concerning privacy, the more determined photojournalist might fall foul of harassment laws or contravene the European Convention of Human Rights if he causes distress in the course of his endeavours.

Globetrotters also need to make sure they're aware of the law in whichever country they're documenting, because even the most complete understanding of UK legal issues offers no protection on foreign shores. An awareness of ethical issues and local custom also serves the travelling photojournalist well to ensure he doesn't cause unintentional offence.

As a photojournalist you'll need specific kit to capture your images. The hardened pros prefer pro-spec cameras with weatherproof bodies and ones with faster film advance/buffer refresh rates to capture five or more shots per second. A quiet camera is preferred by those shooting in difficult conditions – one reason why the rangefinder was a preferred choice of the '70s/'80s documentary photographers. Now, digital cameras deliver similar noise-free operation.

You'll see Metz and Quantum flash competing with Speedlites as methods of illumination, and often a Stofen diffuser on top to soften the light and give natural looking flash shots. Don't forget mini step ladders – cumbersome but essential if you want to get a view above the crowds.

Paparazzi photographers use long lenses and shoot from a distance, while those in the crowd will have 17-35mms attached to cope with the limited space. You'll rarely find a tripod in sight; if any support is used it will be a monopod.

Although the tools of the trade are important, the most crucial thing is having the eye! A good photojournalist will be able to compose through instinct alone; if it looks right then it usually is. The opportunity for photojournalism is all around us, you just have to open your eyes. ■

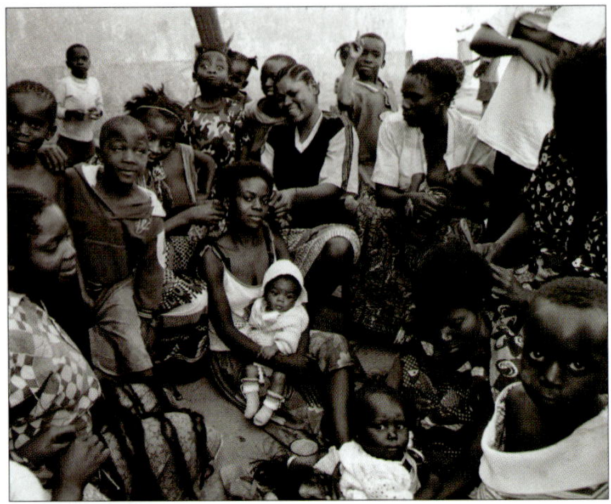

● PETE ELGAR Taken at the Calgary Stampede, Canada, on a Pentax Club trip with a Pentax LX, 300mm Hanimex lens and XP1 film.

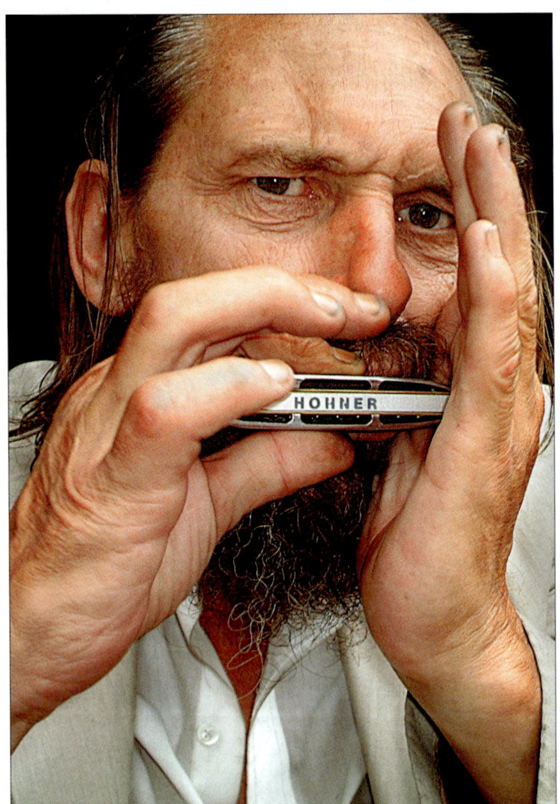

● JOHN WEARING Women and children in a disused abattoir refugee camp in Congo. Ilford XP2 film was used in a Nikon F4s.

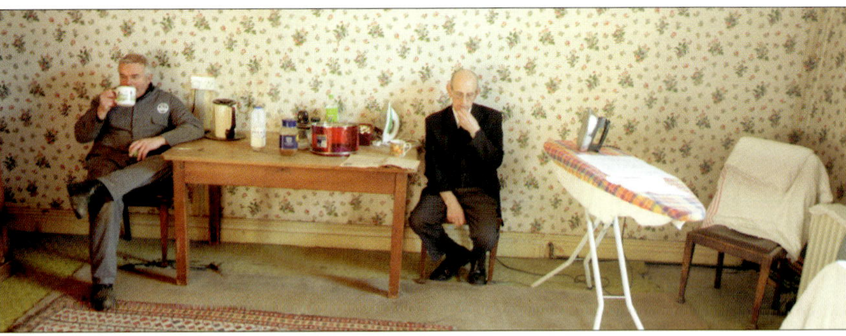

● MATTHEW NOBLE Coffee break at the Abbey, the chauffeur and the butler take a morning break. Photographed on a Hasselblad XPAN loaded with Fujicolour NPS.

HOW TO MAKE IT

In these technological times virtually anybody with a camera can become a 'photo journalist'. To help you stand out from the crowd, consider the following:

■ There are now fewer jobs available for photojournalists, particularly those who take only still pictures. Try to add other strings to your bow, such as video capture and editing.

■ When sending your work to editors, don't just submit images on their own. Consider writing an article to accompany them, making sure it's informative and relevant to the publication in question.

■ Make sure you have a website with examples of your work and contact details. A professional looking site needn't cost the earth — build it yourself using open source software and refer to online web design tutorials.

■ Don't be disheartened too easily! You will receive rejections before (and, indeed, if) you get your break. Remember, even the pros didn't start out at the top.

■ The British Press Photographers Association website is a useful online photojournalism resource: **www.britishpressphoto.org**

■ The National Union of Journalists web site **www.nuj. org.uk**. has useful information, including rates to charge for picture usage.

■ Obtain tips and leads from Freelance Photography Made Easy: **www.fpme.co.uk**

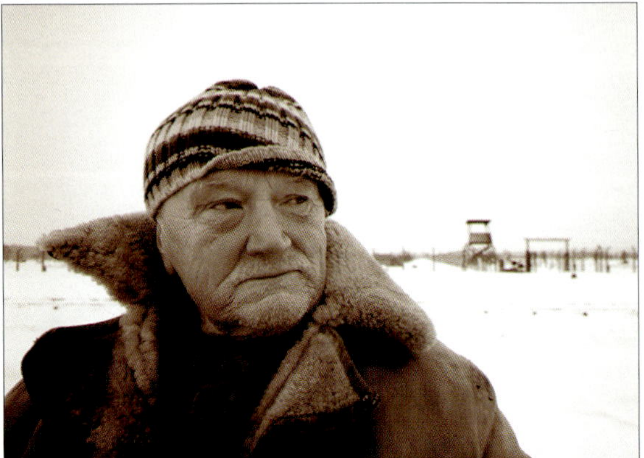

● OVIDIU MOLDOVAN A former prisoner of Auschwitz II – Birkenau, Poland. 27 January 2005 was the 60th anniversary from liberation.

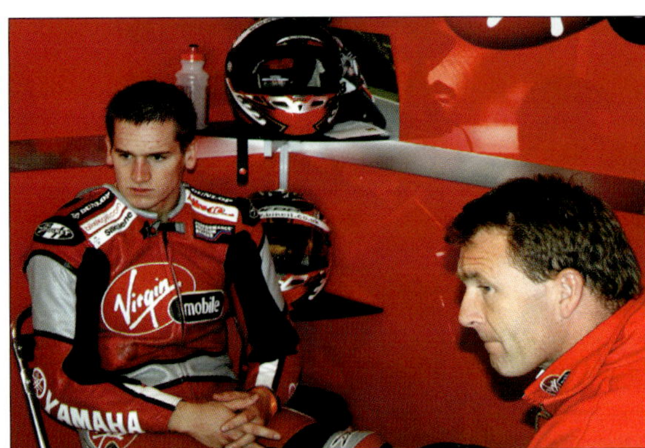

● PAUL CARVILL A moment of tension captured between Tommy Hill and his boss at the Donington British Superbikes 2005.

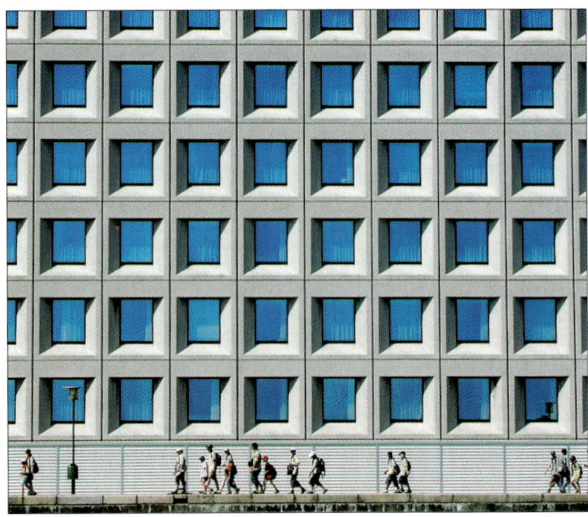

● STEVE BROOKWELL Windows and workers, taken in Copenhagen as passengers disembark a ferry and stroll past the dockside office.

● PATRICIA FENN "Drawn by a melancholy tune I dropped a dollar into his tin. His eyes crinkled a thank you. I captured the moment."

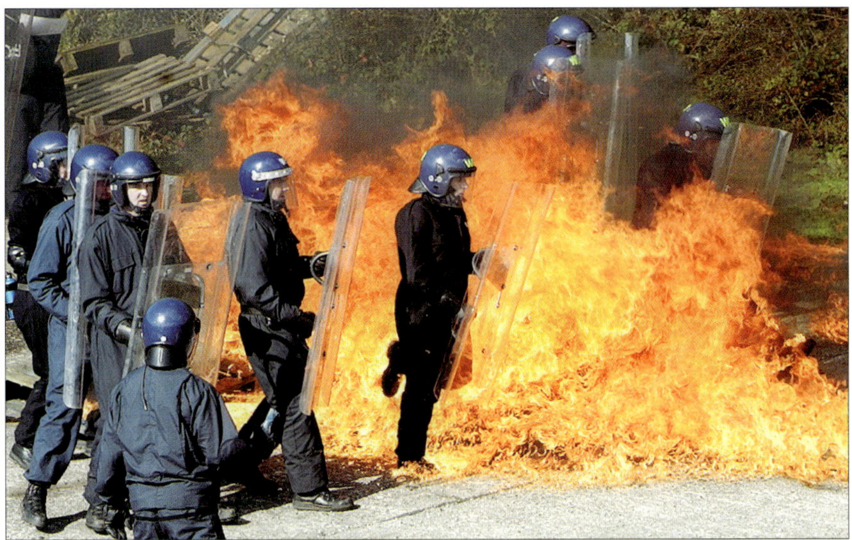

● CARL RYAN A major riot training scenario to test police personnel and their effectiveness in coping with the stress of disorder/riot events. Fire bombs, missiles and bricks are being thrown at the officers.

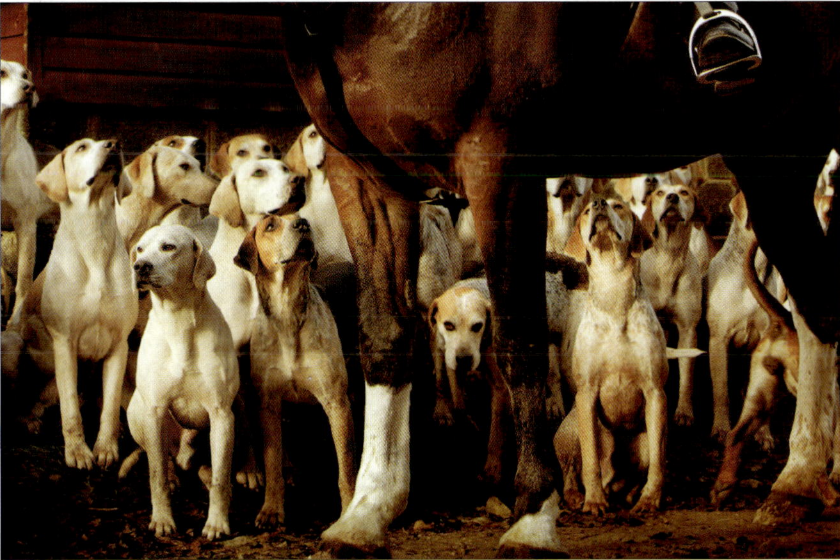

● JONATHAN EVANS Foxhounds awaiting the start of the Surrey Union Hunt on 19 November 2004.

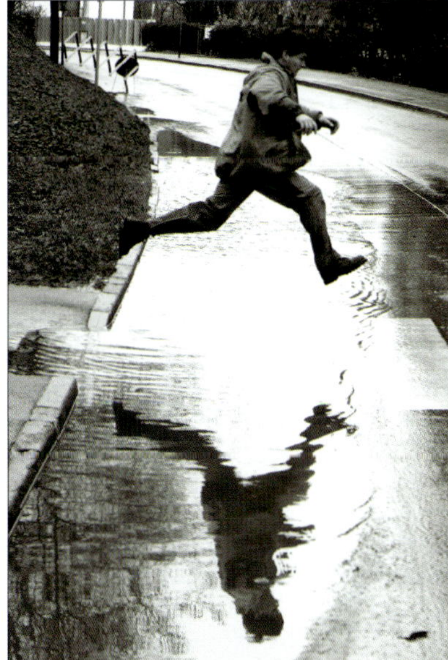

● JAKA ADAMIÈ Man jumping over a puddle is influenced by Henri Cartier-Bresson.

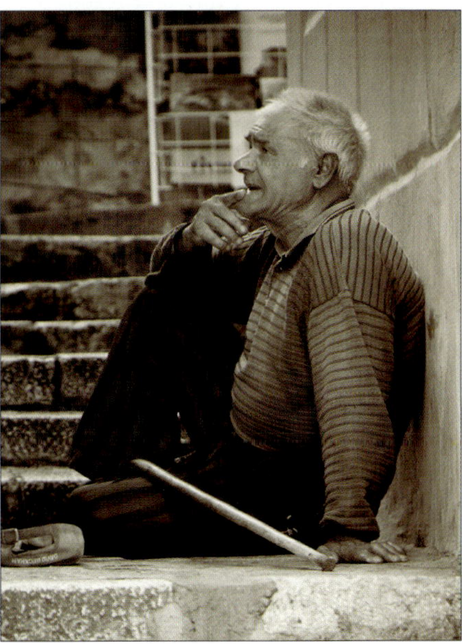

● ZORAN DJEKIC A candid shot of gypsy life on the streets of Bosnia.

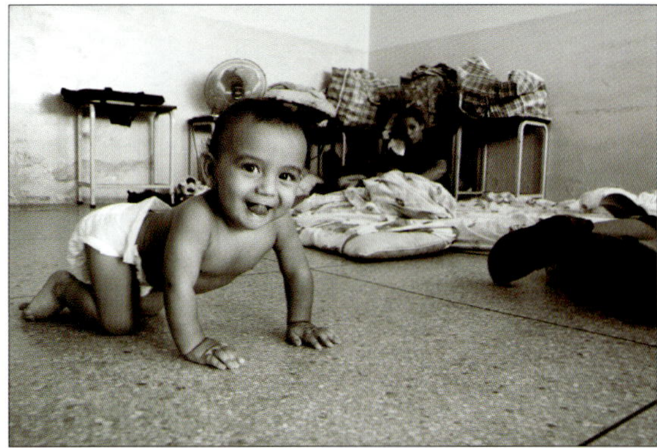

● RAQUEL CHAVEZ Children in refuge, having lost their homes following a flood, taken on a Canon EOS 20D and 17-35mm.

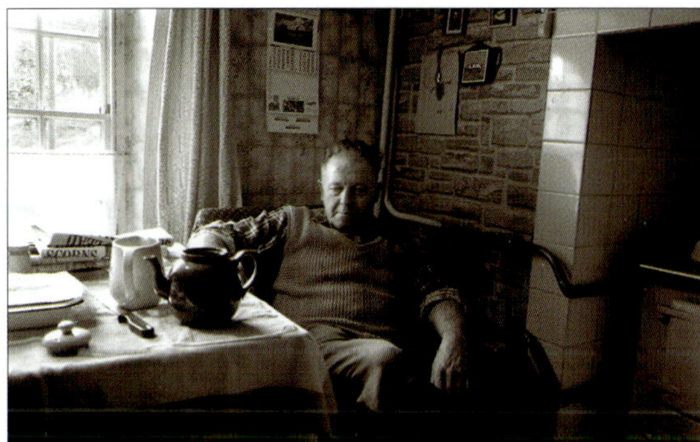

● LUKE SMITH This Cornish farmer having his tea is part of a series Luke has recorded on farm life.

LEGAL ADVICE

A judge once ruled that there is "no law against taking a photograph" but in practice photographers need to be aware of UK law - and make sure they stay on the right side of it!

■ Be aware of the law concerning private property: photography is prohibited in many museums and stately homes, for example, and most concert venues.

■ Using a telephoto lens to take a photo of someone in their home, or other private property, without their consent is probably an invasion of privacy, even though the photo is taken from a public place.

■ There is no statutory UK law concerning privacy, so photographers are theoretically free to take pictures of people in public places as long as their photos are not used for commercial purposes.

■ Having said that, taking a photograph could be classed as harassment if the subject didn't consent to the picture and the photographer's actions caused distress. This only applies to a "course of conduct", i.e. photographing them on two or more occasions.

■ To complicate things further, the European Convention of Human Rights states that everyone is entitled to "respect for his private and family life, his home and his correspondence". It is still unclear what this actually means in practice, so if in doubt tread carefully!

■ Obtaining a model release is not a requirement under UK law but most photo libraries and stock agencies sell to an international market and will not accept images of people without a release. In many countries, including the US, a model release is a legal requirement.

■ It is illegal to take a photograph of a UK bank note unless permission has been given in writing by the "relevant authority", e.g. the Bank of England.

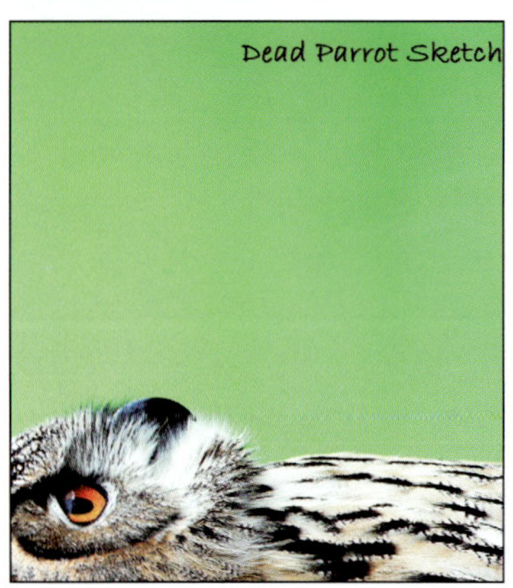

● STEVE BALL Background colour changed, rotated 90 degrees and text added.

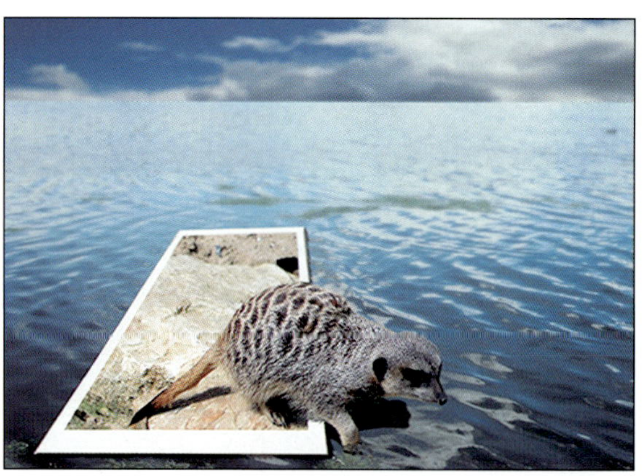

● BOYD A composite of three photographs. "This mongoose really didn't want to have his picture taken, so I imagined him escaping."

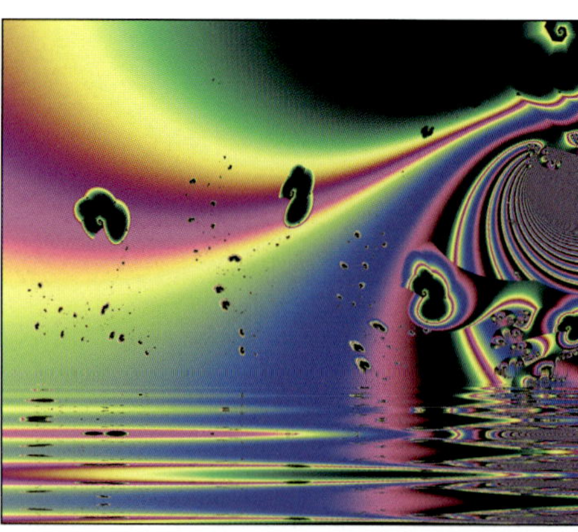

● MIKE ARSENAULT Fractal image generated from a mathematical formulae and a computer program.

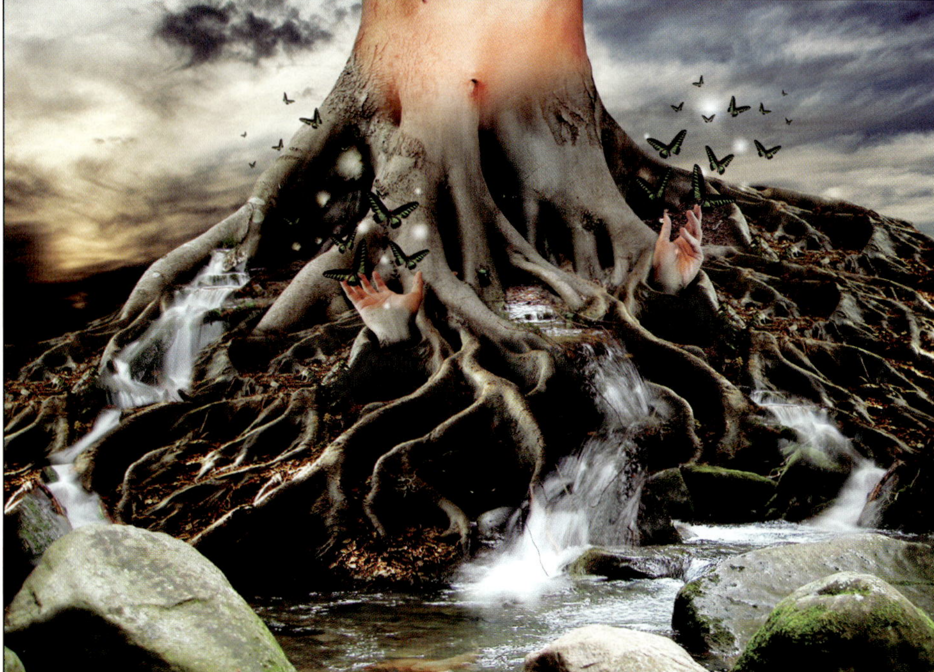

● RYAN FORESHAW "I wanted to create a fantasy tree that was able to create life."

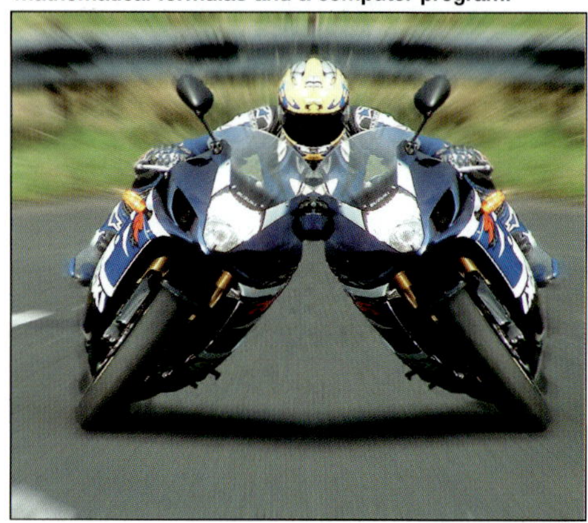

● JOE BEATTIE Image copied and flipped to give mirror effect, blended, detail cloned out and radial blur added.

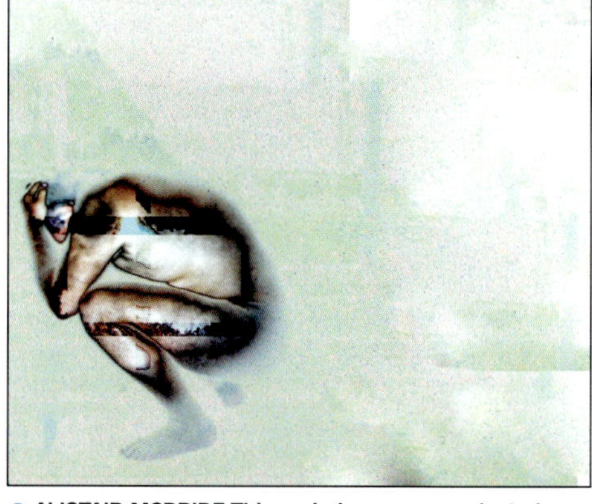

● ALISTAIR MCBRIDE This main image was selected from its background and a hand-painted layer was made and overlaid on top of the original.

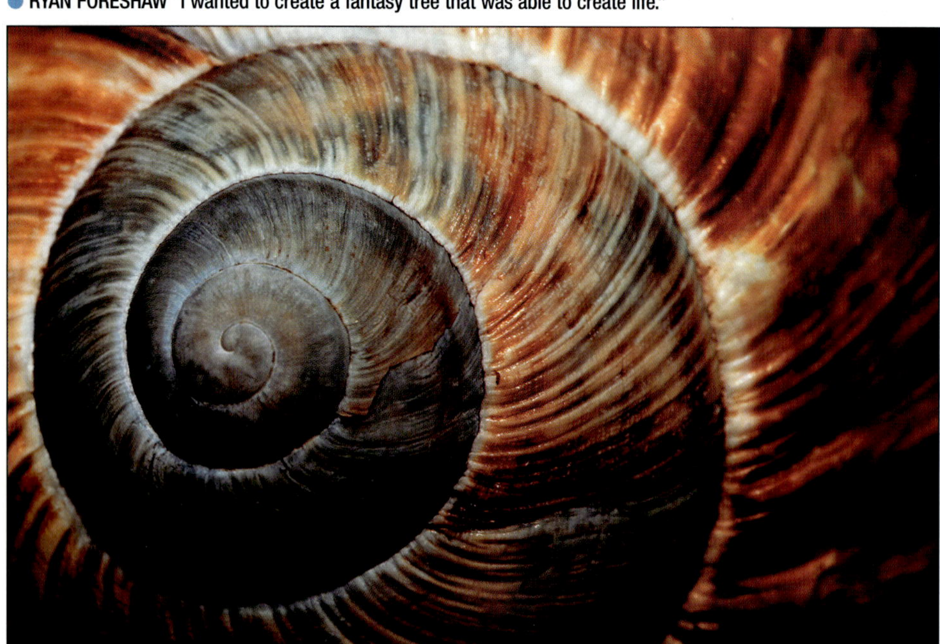

● EDWARD NORTON Roman Snail. An experiment with white balance. Canon EOS 10D with Sigma 180 Macro f/22 1s ISO 100 tripod and kitchen lights.

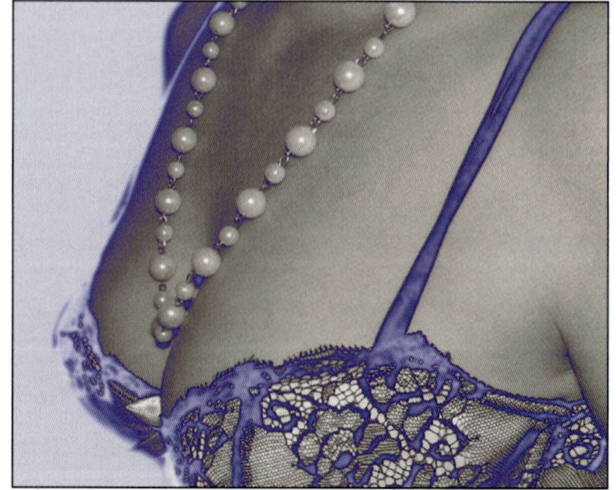

● TEENA RANDALLS A colour self portrait that has been desaturated and selective colour reintroduced.

Digital

Digital photography has changed the way we take, view, process and share images. We no longer have to worry about the cost of film and processing. And, with an image editing program, we can correct most exposure errors, change the composition, adjust focus, colour or content of a photograph. Arguably it's the most powerful media to hit the art scene.

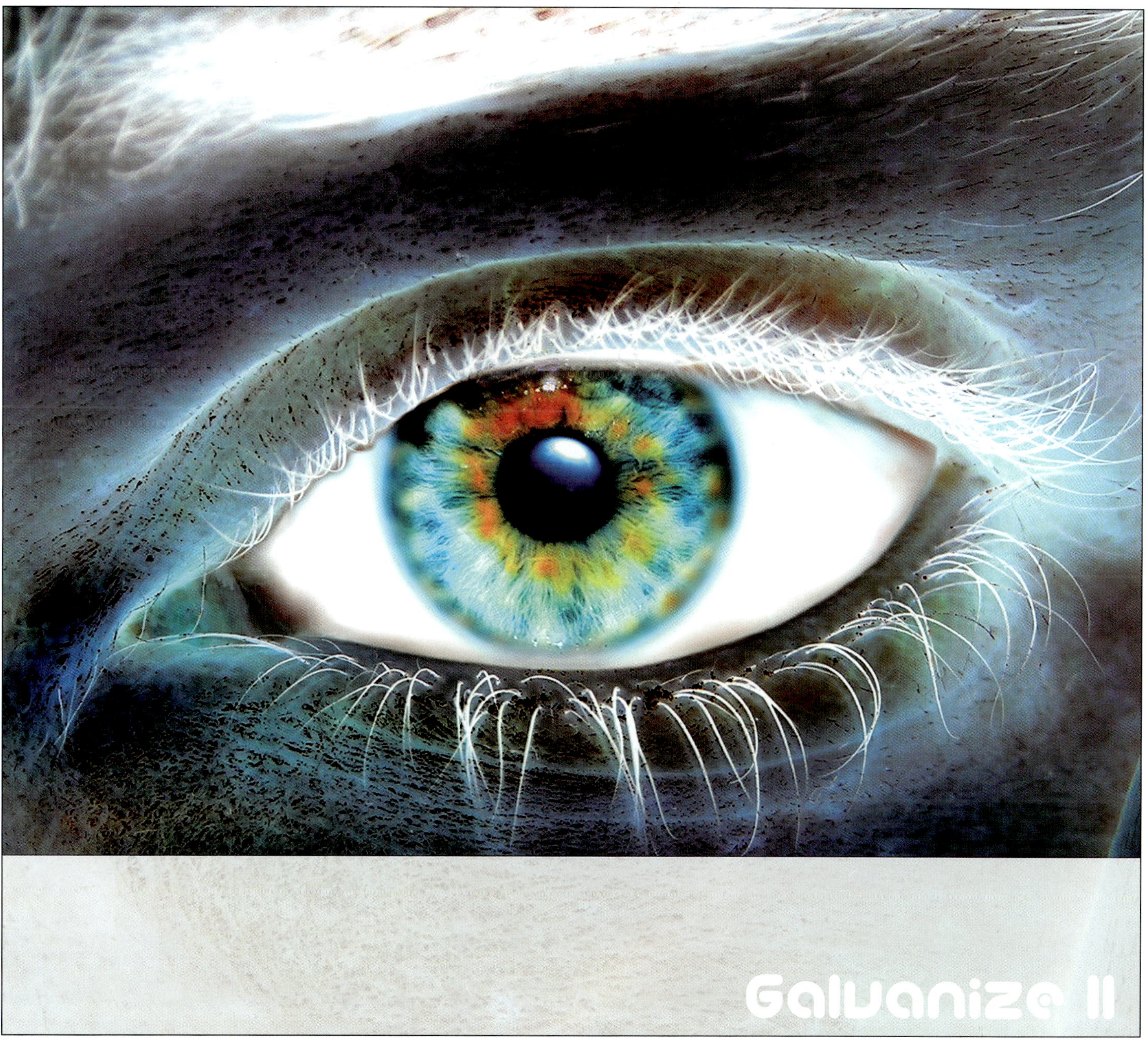

● ANJA MUELLER A digital shot taken on a Nikon Coolpix 8700 and manipulated with Corel PhotoPaint.

Just over a decade ago the only people who could really afford a decent setup to cope with digital editing were professional photographers and design studios. Computers were clunky and software was expensive.

Thanks to the speed of technological development there are hundreds of image-editing applications to choose from, including the free programs such as Gimp and FxFoto to highly sophisticated graphics packages, such as Photoshop and Paint Shop Pro. With programs like this you can do everything from simple sharpening and colour tweaks to advanced multiple layer collages using complex blending.

We used to paint with oils, now we can paint with pixels and create images in our minds rather than what the camera sees. Of course, with this relatively new media we create a whole load of new issues about integrity, originality, worth and appeal.

It's easy to get carried away with digital, just like photographers did with special effects filters in the 80s. When applied, some effects really turn a photograph into a mess. However, used with skill, a whole range of styles and treatments can be developed to do no end of things with your photos. You may just want to subtly edit a picture to remove

a blemish or you can go the whole hog and create pictures that are highly surreal.

On ePHOTOzine we have some highly imaginative artists using programs like Photoshop to create unique images that could never have been created with traditional film and the darkroom. Some verge on being paintings, but most come from a photographic origin and remain that way. Enjoy the selection over the following pages and the various step-by-step guides that you can follow using your computer and image editing software. Check out ePHOTOzine's technique pages for many more useful tutorials like these. ■

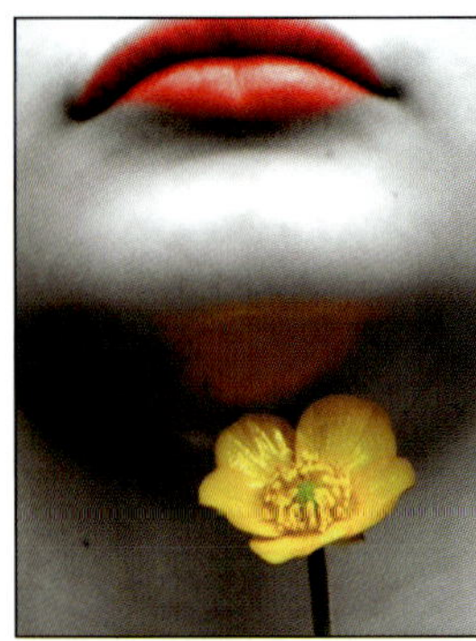

● JUDE GIDNEY Taken with a Nikon D70 camera. Manipulated in Photoshop using masks and layers.

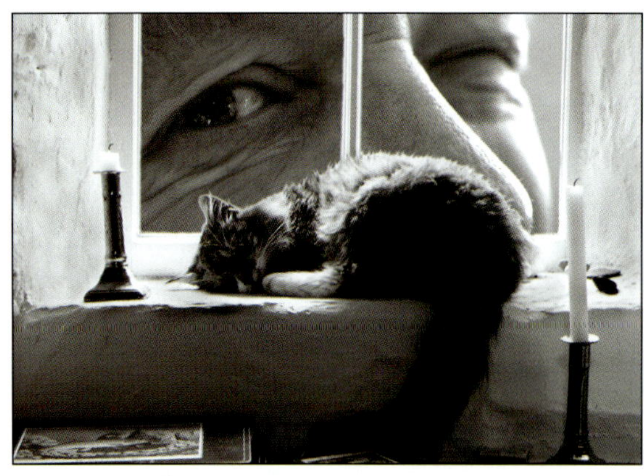

● TANYA HAMES Image created from two slides which were imported into and then digitally manipulated in Photoshop 7.

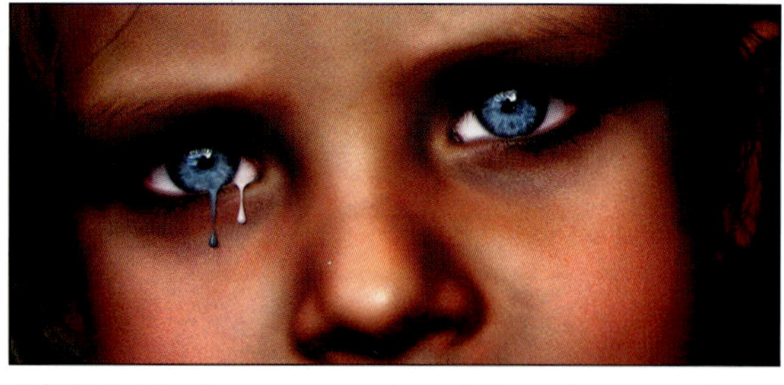

● STEVEN NEIL The eyes were enhanced, then noise was applied and a dark shadow. A drip filter was used to create the tears.

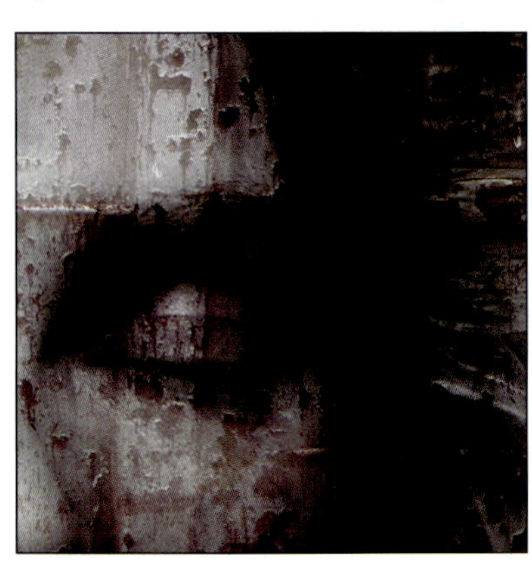

● LUCIE NADEJOVA A self portrait combined with an old rusty garbage container using Photoshop's Displacement map feature.

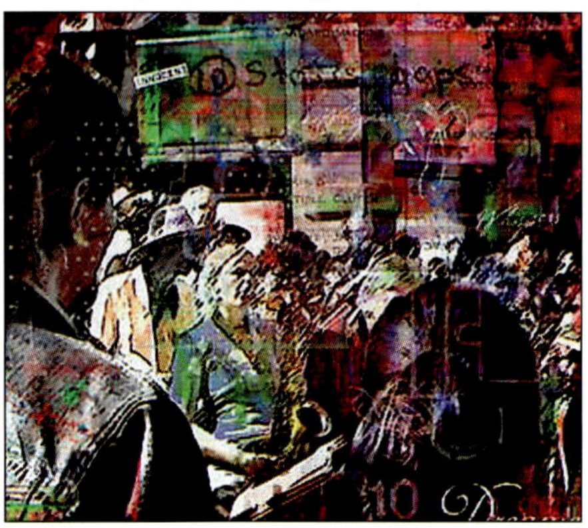

● ANDREW CHAMBERS One of a series of images using the grunge technique explained over the page. This one takes a more colourful approach.

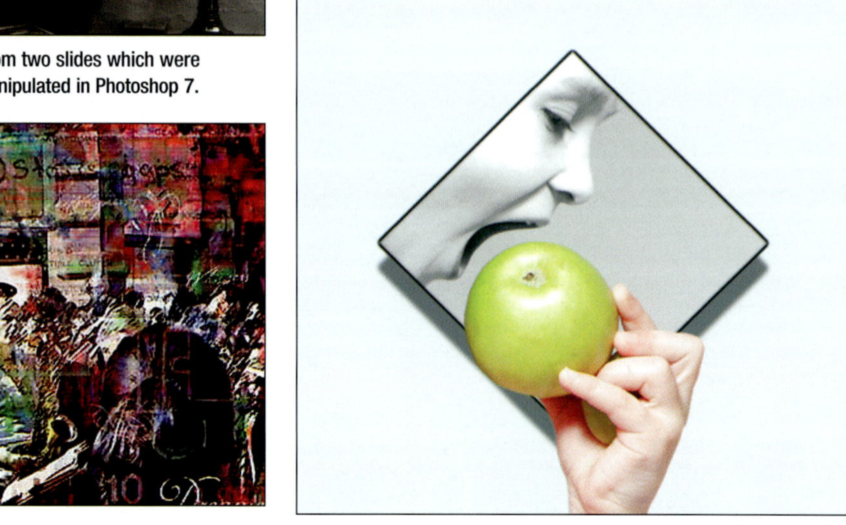

● TONY Taking a photograph and being original with the framing is just one of the many creative things you can achieve digitally.

DIGITAL TECHNIQUE – USING THE CROP TOOL

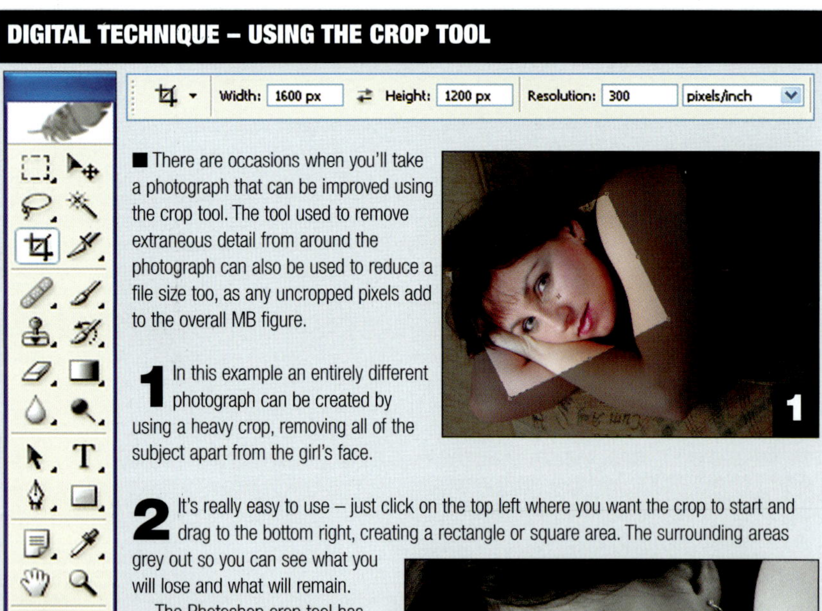

■ There are occasions when you'll take a photograph that can be improved using the crop tool. The tool used to remove extraneous detail from around the photograph can also be used to reduce a file size too, as any uncropped pixels add to the overall MB figure.

1 In this example an entirely different photograph can be created by using a heavy crop, removing all of the subject apart from the girl's face.

2 It's really easy to use – just click on the top left where you want the crop to start and drag to the bottom right, creating a rectangle or square area. The surrounding areas grey out so you can see what you will lose and what will remain.

The Photoshop crop tool has an option to rotate the crop box, as illustrated above in Pic 1, and alter the size by dragging on the corners. You can also fix the size so the inner cropped area creates an image of specified dimensions and resolution.

In this example I converted to black & white as a final stage. ■

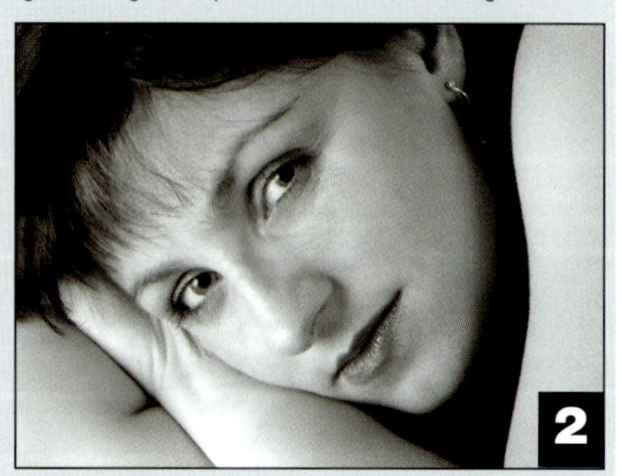

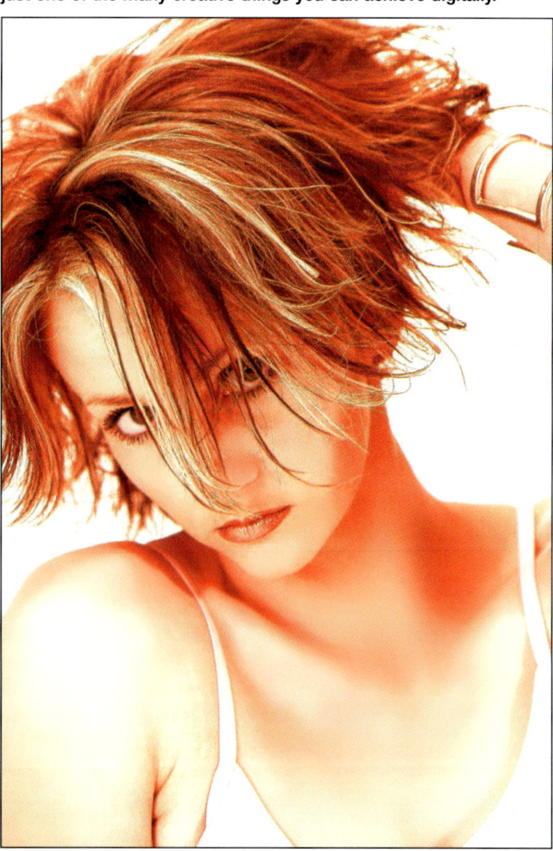

● ROBERT HIRSCHI Photograph of Mandy, taken with hot lights behind a translucent background. Replace colour was used, along with tweaks using Noise>Median and texture addition.

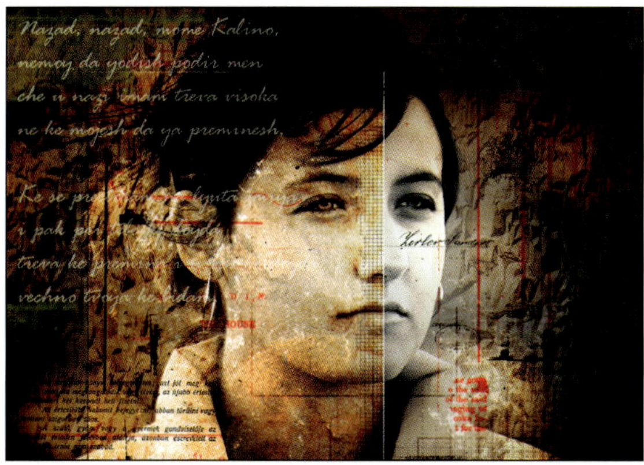

● **GASPAR CABRERA** This was one of the first in the series of Digital Grunge Style, a mix of a romantic postcard and urban gothic.

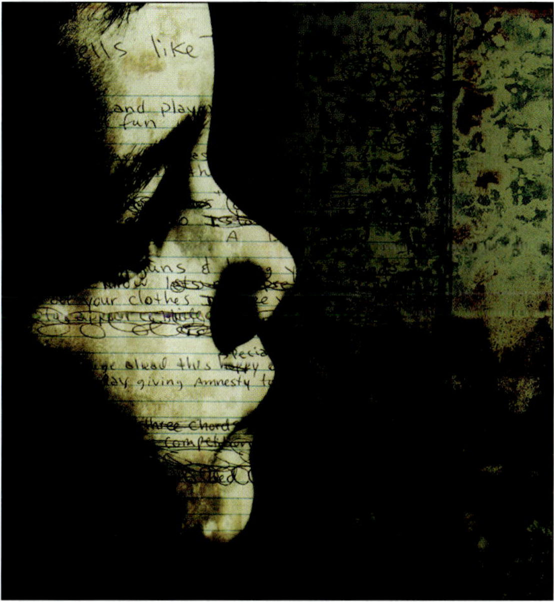

● **SIMON LOACH** The face in the image is that of my beautiful son Nico. The feel of the image flowed naturally from his look of pathos.

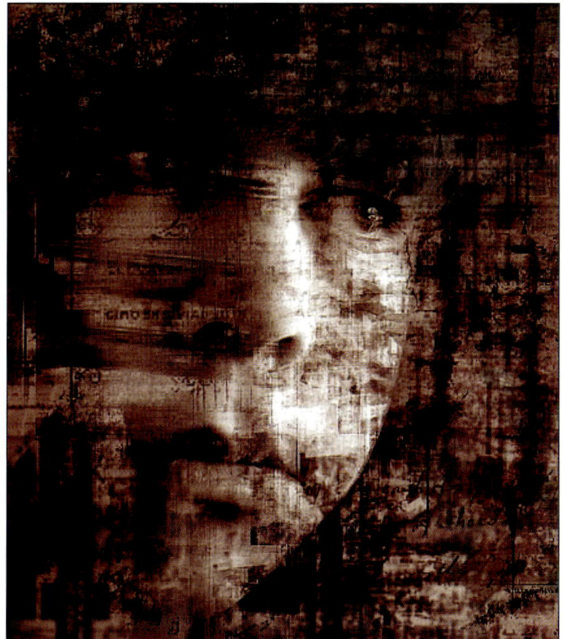

● **BRAD D'AMICO** A picture of myself, with an added layer of grunge produced in Photoshop 7.

DIGITAL TECHNIQUE – CREATING A GRUNGE STYLE EFFECT USING LAYERS

■ The grunge style technique was first introduced to ePHOTOzine members by Gaspar Cabrera. Here he shows us how to create the effect using Photoshop's Layers feature and two photographs.

1 Open up a suitable photo as the main subject - flowers, animals or portraits work well. Place the picture in a new Photoshop layer.

2 Open up a suitable texture photo. Any texture will work, but normally I prefer rocks, old walls or recycled paper, as they give interesting effects when blended. If you need textures look at **www.mayang.com/textures** or make your own by taking specific shots of walls, material etc. Copy the texture. Make a new layer on the original and paste the texture on to it. Resize and adjust the texture position as necessary.

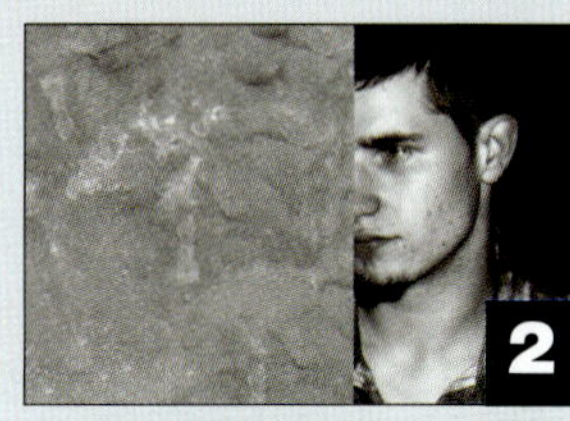

3 Then I set the Blending Mode to Overlay. Notice the line in the face made by the Texture layer. Fix this by making a layer mask and use the gradient tool to soften the edge.

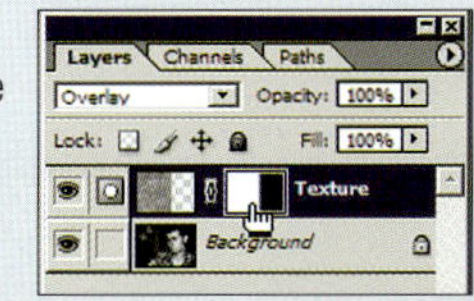

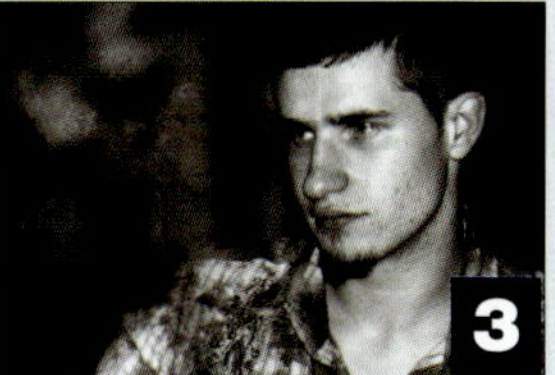

4 Add a third fill layer to provide the colour. Choose a suitable colour from the picker and set the layer to Soft Light blend mode. I've used an orange colour fill which has given the image a sepia hue. Merge all the layers.

5 Add a new texture and set the blend mode as Hard Light. Use the Layer Mask/Gradient Tool technique to erase spots that do not look right over the face. A radial gradient may be better for this. Merge the layers.

You could continue this process with different textures and blending modes forever — as many as your creativity tells you, but in this case we will keep it simple and start adding some details.

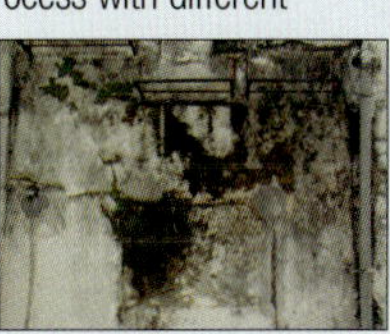

6 Here is when you will need to get hold of some PS Brushes, or make them yourself which is always better. To make them you will need either a texture, a picture of some old document or anything that can give details to the image.

To make the brushes open an image with some interesting detail, make a selection on the detail and then go to Edit⇔Define Brush Preset and you are set!

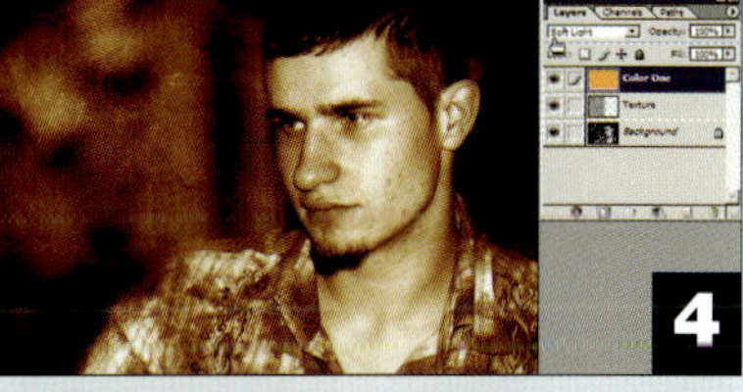

7 For the next steps I used an old document in JPEG format copied and pasted into a new layer. Move, contract or expand the document as you see fit and then set the Blending Mode to Linear Burn.

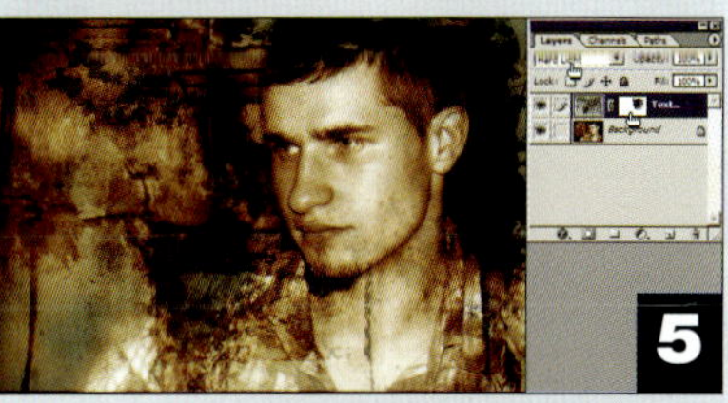

8 Next, more brush work with the brushes in greyscale. Even if you made the brush from a coloured selection, its colour can be changed like any other brush. In this case I will sample colours from the image to retain colour consistency. Notice that each brush stamp is made in a new layer, just in case you want to change colours or step back to earlier in the editing process.

9 That's it, unless you want to add some more patterns or textures and play with the Burn / Dodge Tools to darken or brighten some areas of your image. If you enjoyed this tutorial and would like to contact Gaspar his email address can be found on his website: **www.takuineko.com**

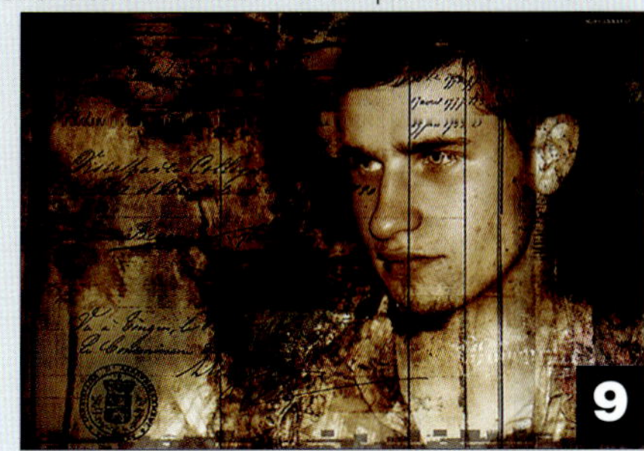

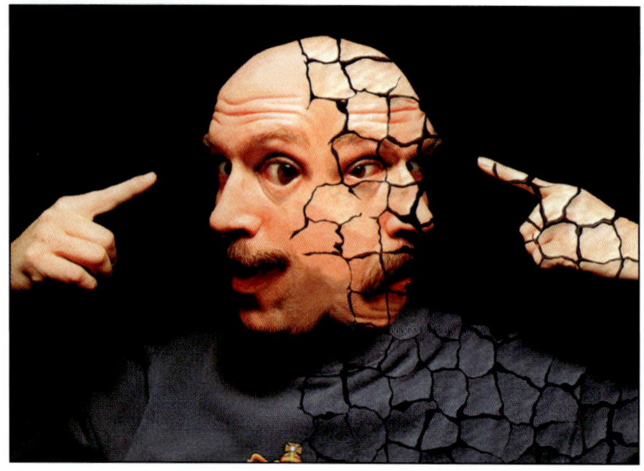

● BRIAN WATERS I find the best way to get creative is to randomly select one of my images, and experiment with the tools at hand.

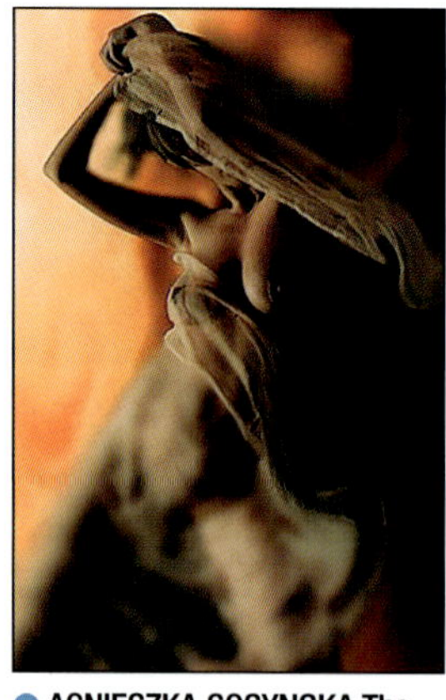

● AGNIESZKA SOSYNSKA The smudge tool put to good use.

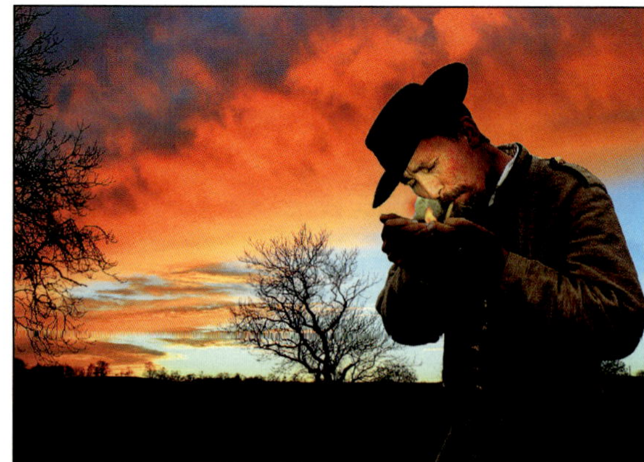

● BILL STEVENSON Two combined shots taken on a Canon EOS 10D with 28-135mm. The back of his hands were darkened and face lightened.

DIGITAL TECHNIQUE – CREATING A CROSS PROCESSING EFFECT

■ Look at any old photography special effects book written before digital came along and the chances are it will include a technique known as cross processing. This creative technique is achieved by developing a film in the wrong chemicals. E6 film, that should be processed in reversal chemicals, is processed in those for a C41 negative/print film and vice versa. This is how the technique gets its name and the results can be quite unusual, as we'll demonstrate with this shot of Jessica.

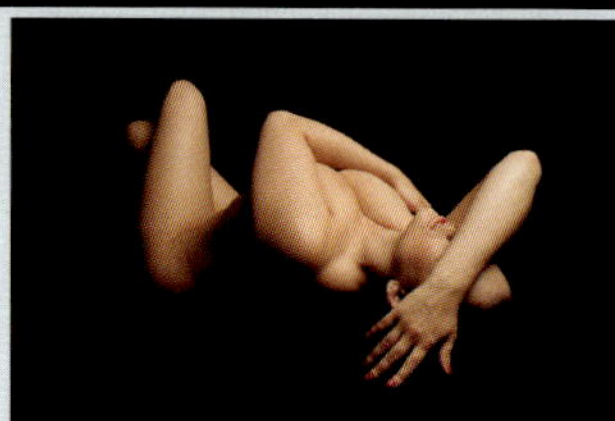

1 To recreate the effect of a slide film being processed in a print developer we need to end up with a photograph with creamy highlights and blue milky shadows. It's easy using Photoshop's curves adjustment. First, create a new adjustment layer. Layer⇨New Adjustment Layer⇨Curves. Doing this allows you to make as many changes as you like without affecting the original. Changes will only affect the original when you flatten the layers.

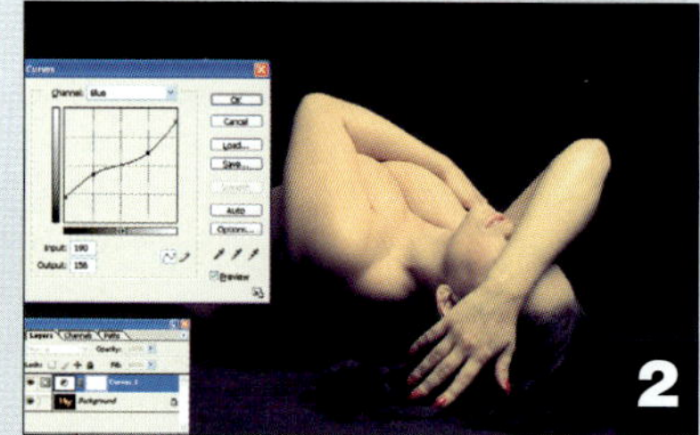

2 From the channel drop down list in the Curves palette select the blue channel. Drag the bottom left corner of the curve graph upwards and the top right down to reduce the contrast in the highlights and shadows. Then click on the graph at the second and fourth grid line and drag up and down respectively to create a reverse S curve. Notice how the black/shadow areas become blue and almost foggy and the highlights become creamier.

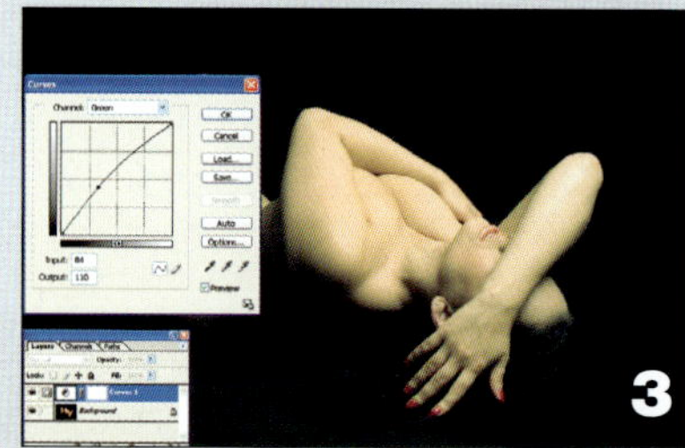

3 Now go back to the channel drop down and select Green. Grab a point near the centre of the graph and drag up and left to increase the green content which makes the skin tones go even creamier.

4 It's still not looking like a cross processed shot yet. It's the red channel where things start to take shape. By creating another reverse S shaped curve on the red channel you'll now see shadow areas take on the blue/green hue and highlights become creamy yellow – both characteristics of cross processing.

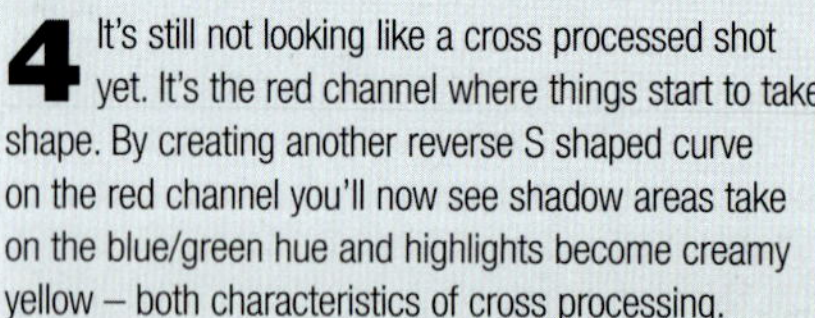
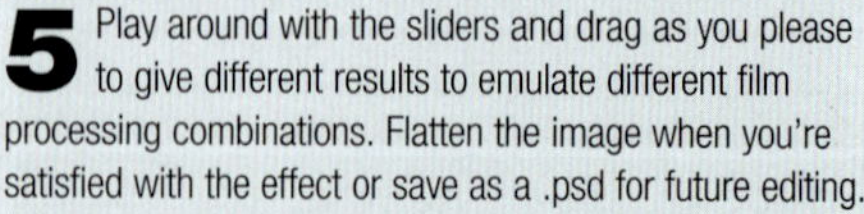

5 Play around with the sliders and drag as you please to give different results to emulate different film processing combinations. Flatten the image when you're satisfied with the effect or save as a .psd for future editing.

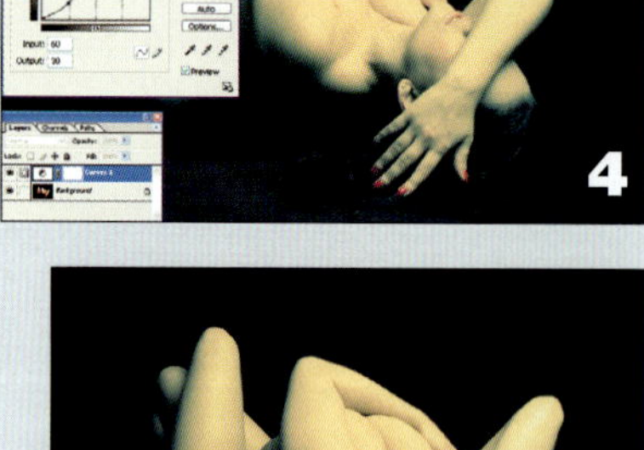

■ If your program doesn't have a Curves feature, similar results can be achieved using a Colour balance editor. Increase yellow/green in the highlight areas and a combination of blue/green/cyan in the shadows.

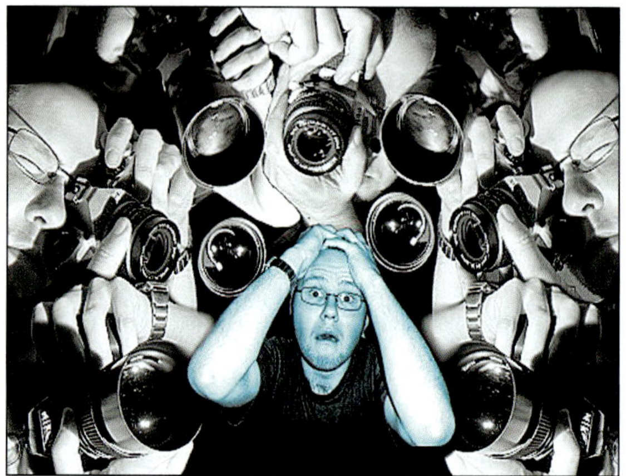

● GARY WOLSTENHOLME I tried to recreate a favourite piece of art by Winston Smith, using myself, a Nikon digital camera and Photoshop!

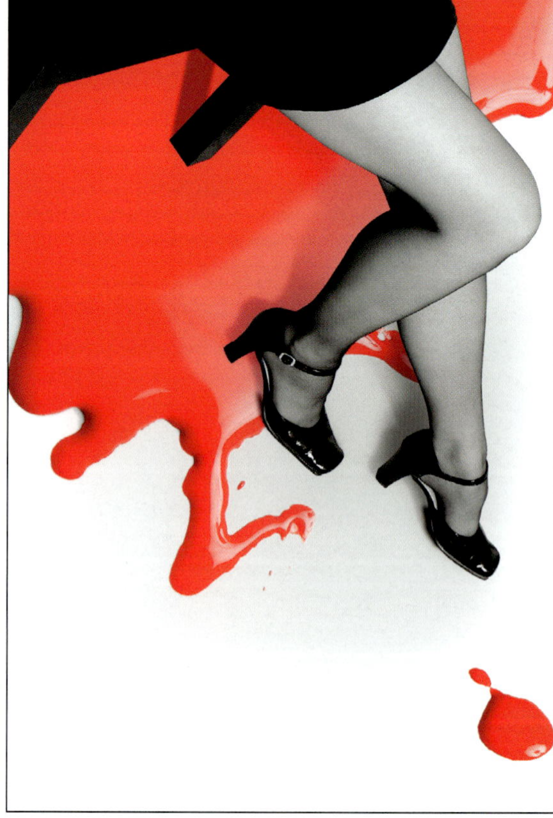

● MAREK KOMISARUK I used a Fuji S1 digital camera with 28-80 mm lens and studio flash light. Then I edited it in Photoshop.

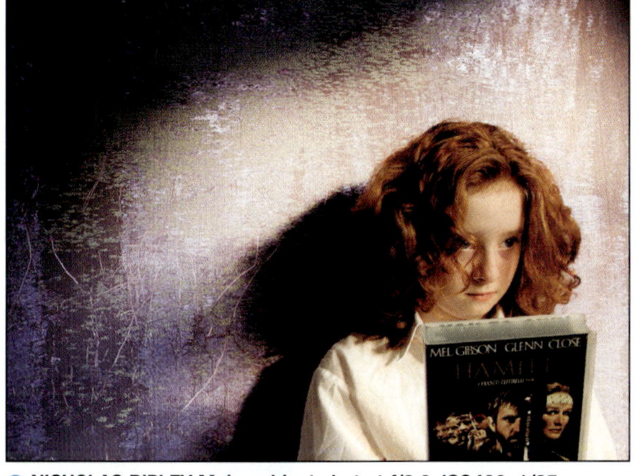

● IAN ANSTEY A washed out sky in Venice. "I cropped it, then desaturated and brought the colour back on one gondola."

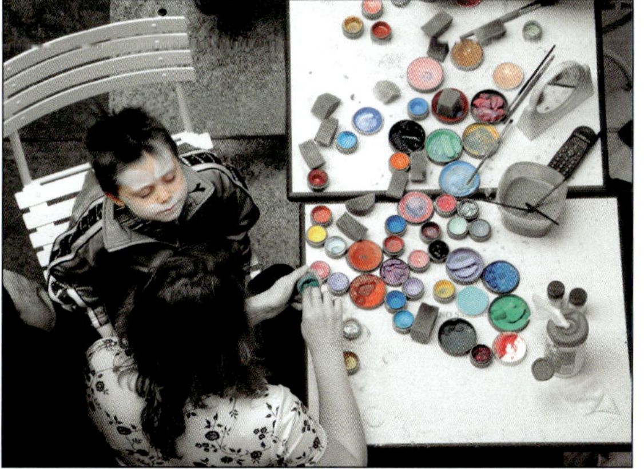

● NICHOLAS RIPLEY Main subject shot at f/2.8, ISO400, 1/25sec, on a Fuji S7000. "I was inspired by Dante Gabriel's Rosseti's Ophelia."

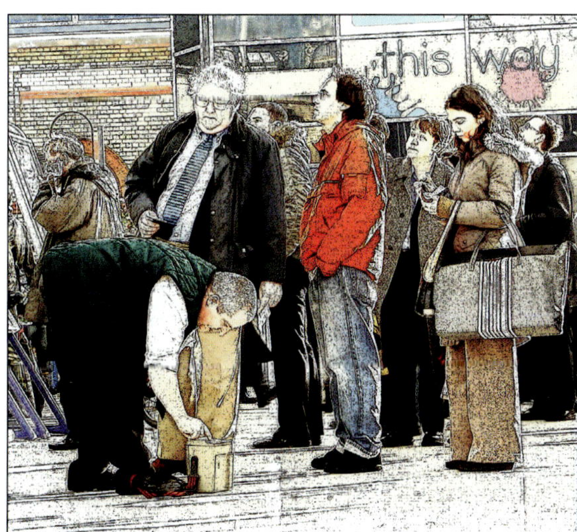

● STEVE DOREY "The film Pleasantville gave me the idea for this colour popping treatment, using Photoshop layers and desaturate."

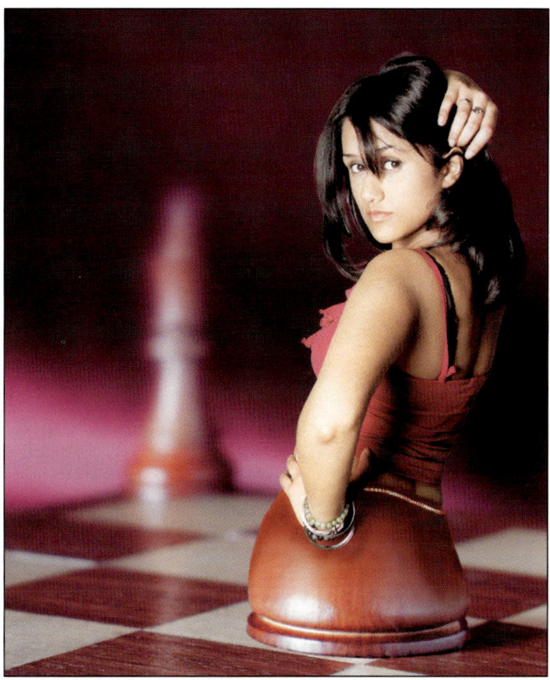

● MIKE BOWES Model photographed on Fuji Reala with EOS 50E. The chess piece was shot and assembled digitally.

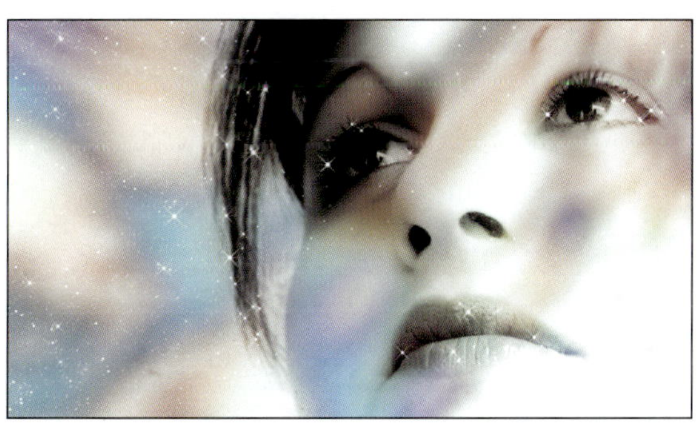

● SCOTT HARRISON Portrait taken then a cosmos effect overlaid to create an even tone. Stars added to emphasize the features.

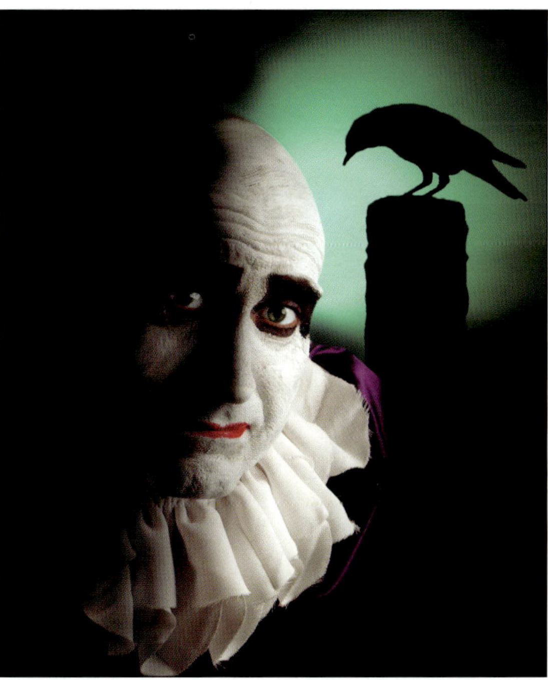

● ANTON HEIBERG Combined shots taken using a Pentax *ist D, with 28-70mm lens and lit using Prolinca lights and softboxes.

● JOHN BALLANCE A watercolour sketch effect of Brighton Station Concourse, created using filters in Corel PhotoPaint 8.

SELECTIVE COLOUR

■ Several digital photographs throughout this book use a technique often referred to as colour popping. It's where the colour of the original is removed and then part of the image is recoloured. This selective colour technique is useful when you want to draw attention to a particular part of the image. In our example below we will desaturate the traction engine and sky.

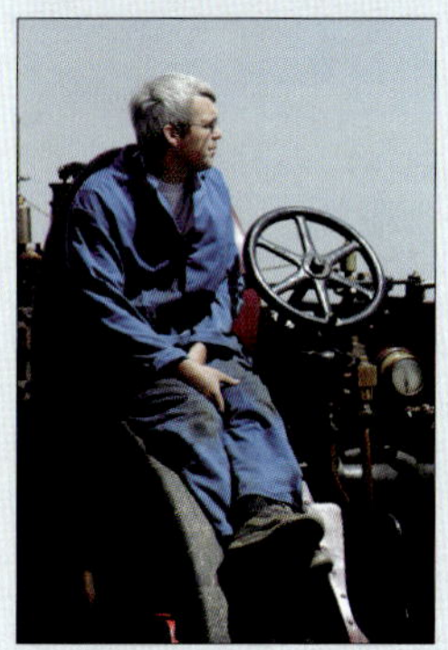

1 Open the colour image and desaturate. Image⇨Adjustments⇨Hue/ Desaturate (Shift+Ctl+U). This makes the image greyscale but it still has the three colour channels in use.

2 Now click on the left square to the side of the Open state in the History palette to add a History Brush Icon, and select the History Brush from the toolbar.

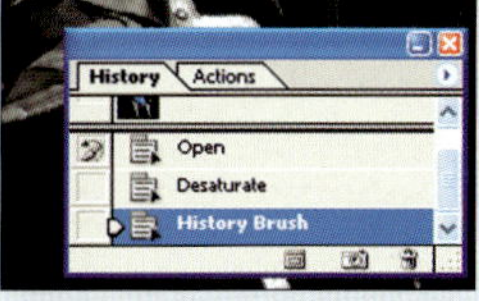

3 Paint over the area you want to bring back the colour to, using a small brush for detailed outlines and a large brush for the inner areas. If you make a mistake either click undo or click to the left of the Desaturate stage to add the History brush and paint back to this desaturated state.

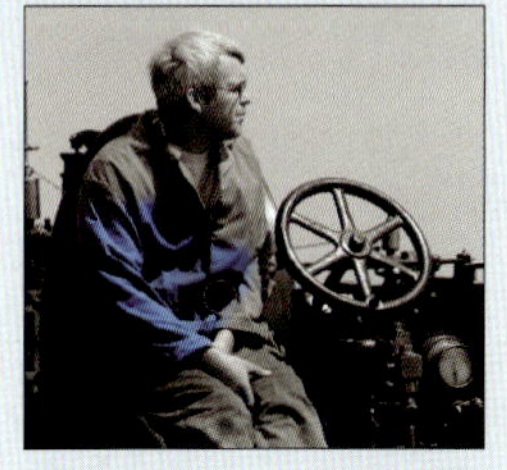

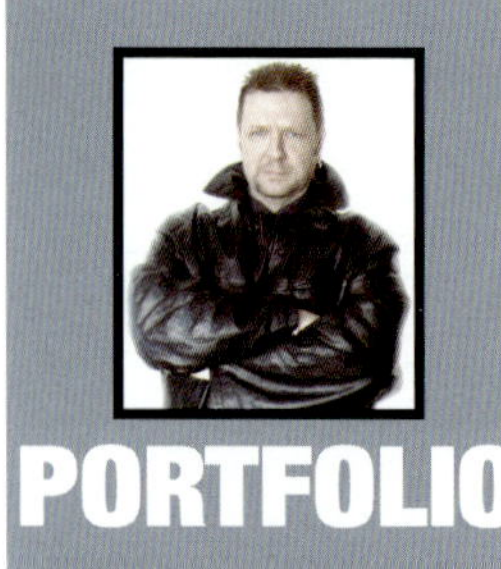

PORTFOLIO

VICTOR HABBICK

Victor has a worldwide client base and stock library to keep him busy with his conceptual photography.

After 28 years in the design and photography business, self employment came as a natural progression rather than a preconceived career move.

For 10 years my commercial business has grown steadily with a worldwide client base and a stock library keeping me busy with conceptual photography. This freedom has enabled me to venture down a different route, exploring ideas and emotions of a more personal nature. The irony is I have attracted a much wider audience than I could ever have hoped for, so perhaps my own take on life through photography and art has resonated beyond my own personal inner world.

I've little time for the arguments for and against digital photography. Without this leap in technology I doubt I could have achieved as much as I have, while still retaining control of the creative process from start to finish. I suppose this thinking originates from my school days when one of my art teachers was always telling me to never get hung up on the tools of the trade, to use and, at times, abuse anything that produced the result I was after. I have never forgotten these words of wisdom.

Inspiration is derived from many areas, from movies to Manga, painters to writers. The biggest influence on my style is from artists Dali and Magritte and photographer Bob Carlos Clarke. All have carved out individual creative paths that go beyond the norm to force and assault our senses.

The advice I would give to any aspiring photographer is never stop looking at and studying light, shade and composition. Without mastering these disciplines you will never achieve anything more than average and all of us, with time, are capable of so much more. ■

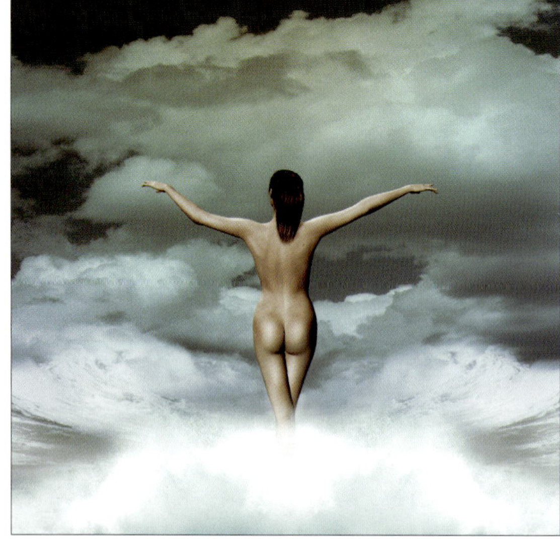

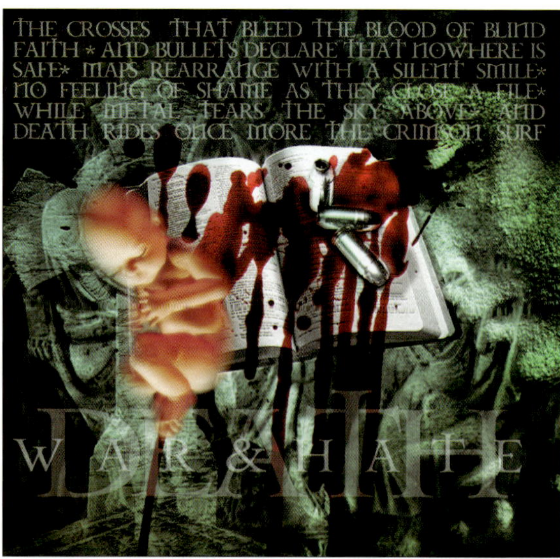

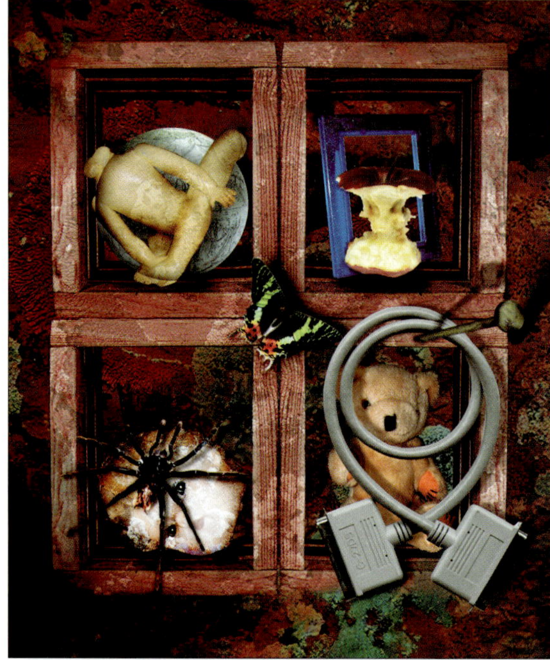

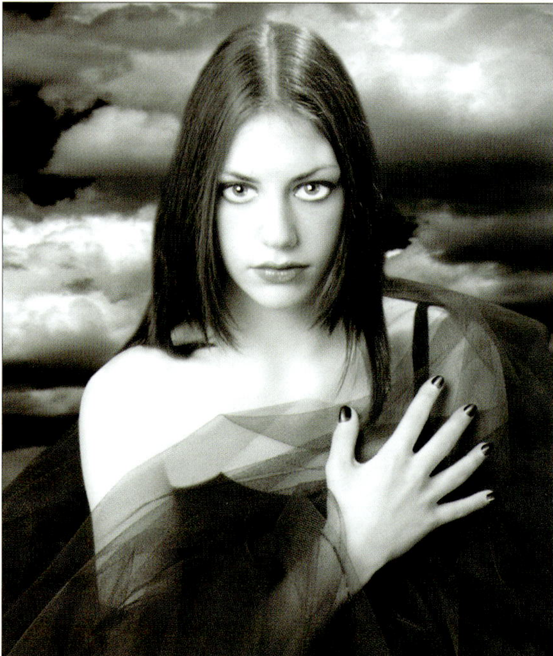

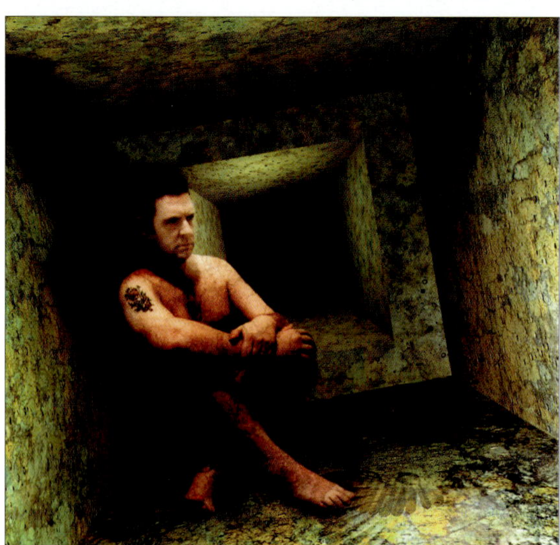

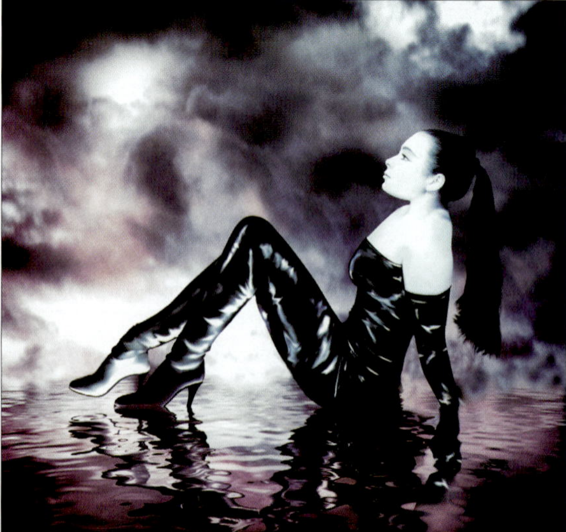

● A small selection of the many amazing images created by Victor that can be found on ePHOTOzine. Many are taken to meet briefs created by clients and often feature strong messages through powerful composites. Victor's personal work is equally thought-provoking and his use of software, such as Photoshop and Painter, takes his images into a world of visuals usually only found in dreams. www.victorhabbick.co.uk

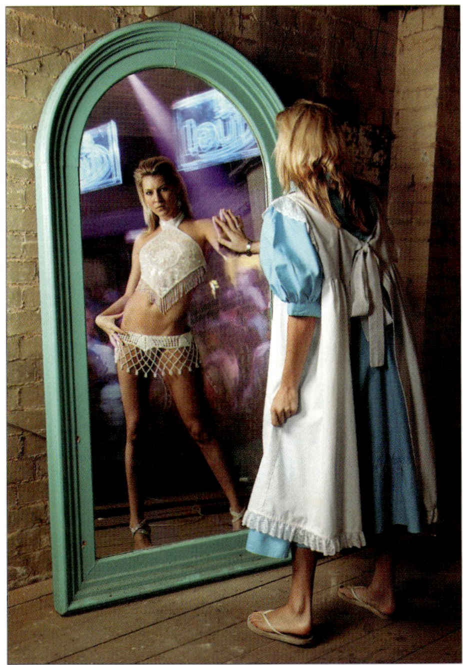

● PAUL WARD This Alice in Wonderland shot was done in Photoshop using three images. Two of the girl in the two outfits in front of the mirror and one of a night club.

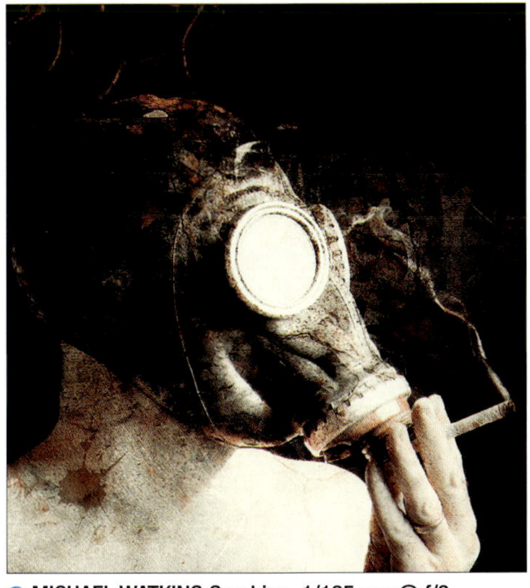

● MICHAEL WATKINS Smoking. 1/125 sec @ f/9, manual, softbox and reflector. Texture layers blended in Adobe Photoshop CS.

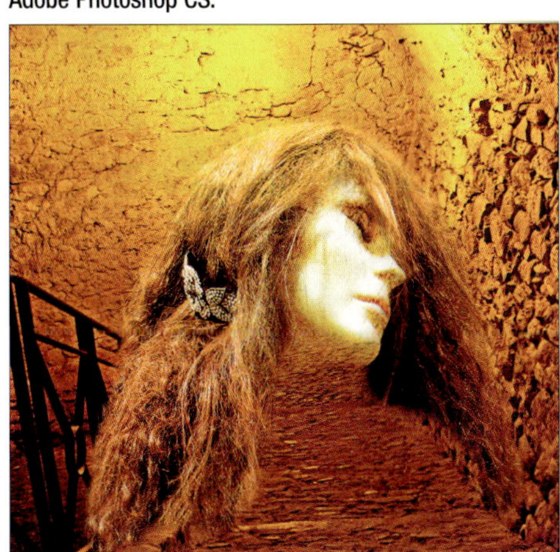

● ARIEL ALEXANDRE Tries to recreate the atmosphere of childhood and dreams in his photographs.

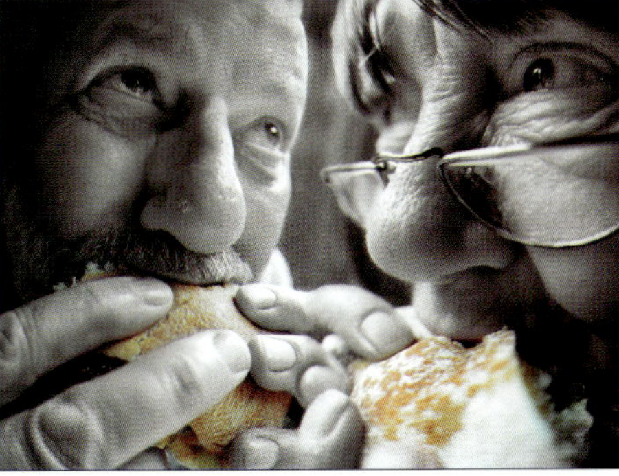

● STEVE SHARP Two semi fish-eye shots merged, then desaturated and the colour was painted back in via the History brush in Photoshop.

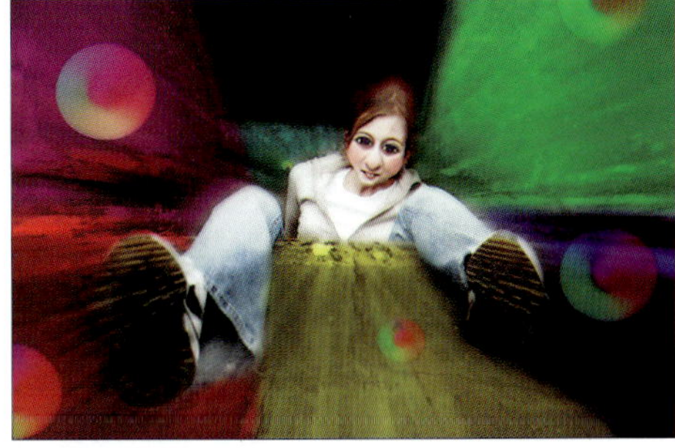

● ANNALIESA BENDING Wacky shot using layers, colour adjustments, zoom motion blur and liquified eyes.

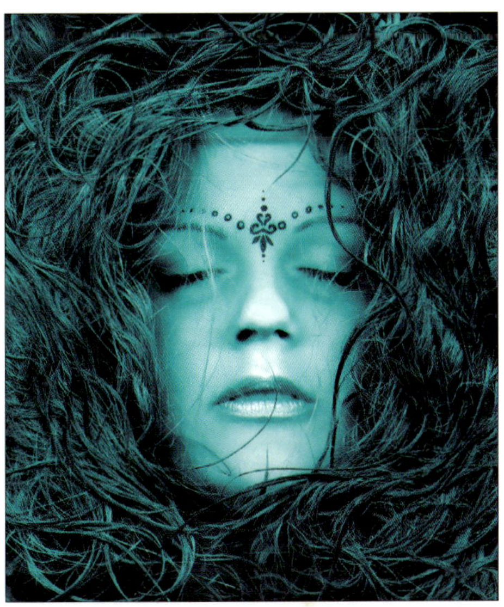

● ANGIE BARNETT A self portrait with fishing rope done on a flatbed scanner as part of Angie's mermaid series.

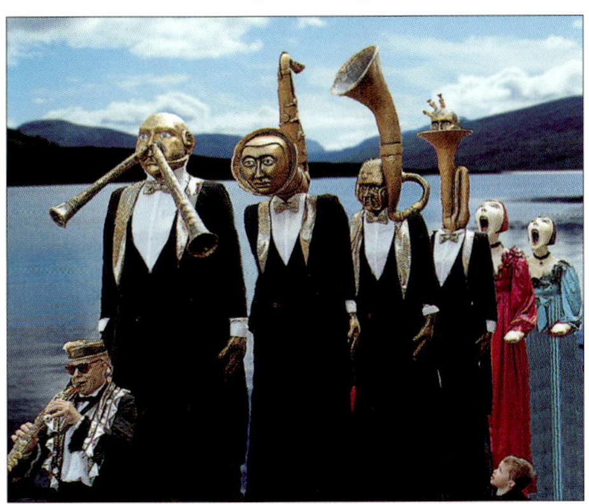

● RAYMOND KING Street performers, captured using a Fuji 6900, were cut and pasted on a new background.

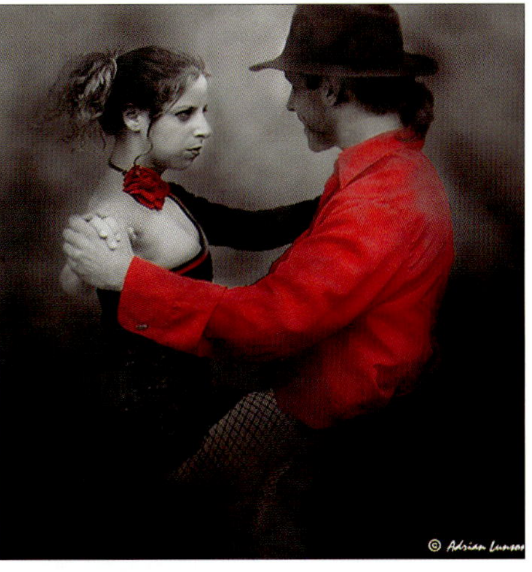

● ADRIAN LUNSONG Taken with a Sony Cybershot DSC-W1 at the Edinburgh Fringe Festival 2004. Used Photoshop CS2 for digital manipulation.

PHOTOSHOP FILTERS

■ While programs such as Photoshop and Paint Shop Pro have some amazing built-in effects there are many more made by third party companies to expand the software's versatility. What follows is a selection of these popular "plug-ins". Add them to your program's plug-ins folder and access them from the filter menu.

■ **www.neatimage.com** A filter designed to reduce visible noise and grain in photographic images produced by digital cameras and scanners.

■ **www.xaostools.com** Paint Alchemy transforms your images with paint effects like Coloured Pencil, Impressionist, or Pastel. Choose from 75 built-in brush stroke effects, 36 editable brush styles and complete versatile controls.

■ **www.autofx.com** Photo/Graphic Edges, Mystical Lighting and Dream Suite. Photo/Graphic Edges has thousands of ready made edges to enhance your photos, including all those specials you could originally create using Polaroid.

■ **www.alienskin.com** EyeCandy and Xenofex special effects plug ins are joined recently by Exposure, a great film characteristic emulator.

■ **www.ononesoftware.com** Genuine Fractals is an image scaling plug-in that helps you increase the image up to 800% without loss in quality.

■ **www.flamingpear.com** A range of filters including the Flood filter that creates realistic ripples.

■ **www.theimagingfactory.com** Convert to B&W Pro offers highly controllable colour to black & white conversion so you don't lose valuable tonal detail.

■ **www.extensis.com** Mask Pro 3 helps you make precise selections around difficult edges, such as hair.

■ **www.corel.com** KPT Collection – an amazing collection of plug-ins to be creative with. Highlights include the lightning filter and a good lens flare editor.

■ **powerretouche.com** Pro Pack of plug-ins includes various editors to provide advanced control of Noise, Tone, Softness, Sharpness, Brightness, Saturation, White balance and colour as well as an anti-aliasing mode , histogram repair and lens correction.

■ **www.andromeda.com** A collection of great tools that are geared more towards photographers than most, with filters, among many, to solve problems with red eye, depth-of-field and lens distortion.

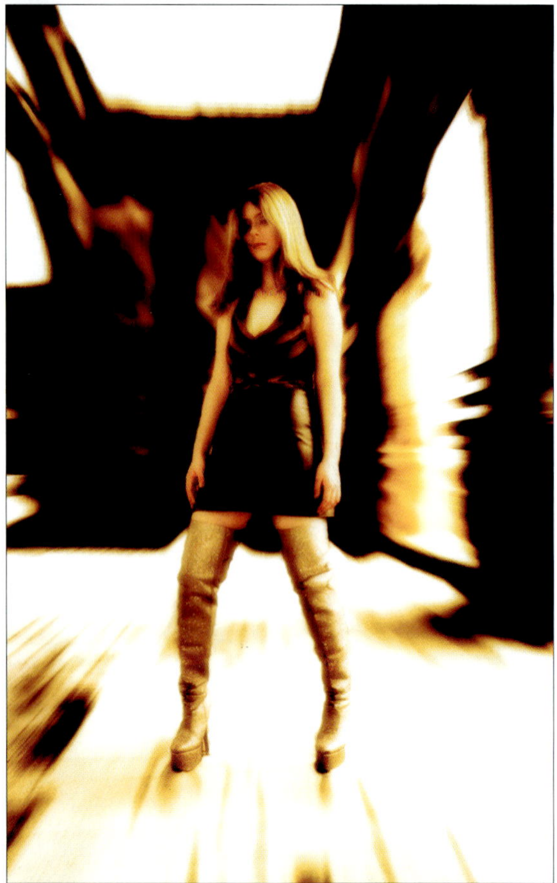

● ANTHONY STEWART HAMILTON Shot for 'My Fashion' on location and manipulated in Photoshop CS.

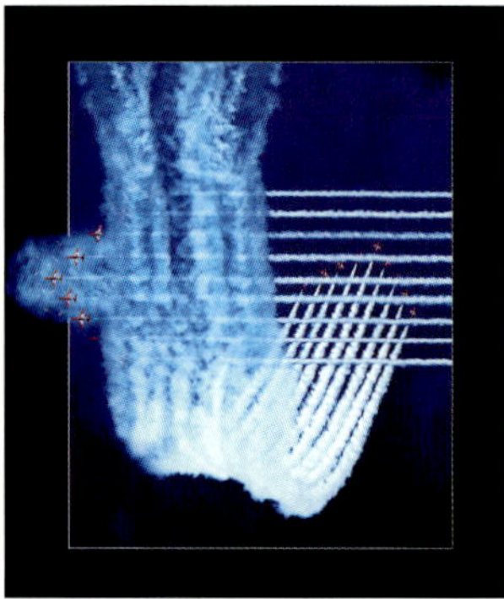

● BRIAN CLARKE A clever use of breaking out of the frame.

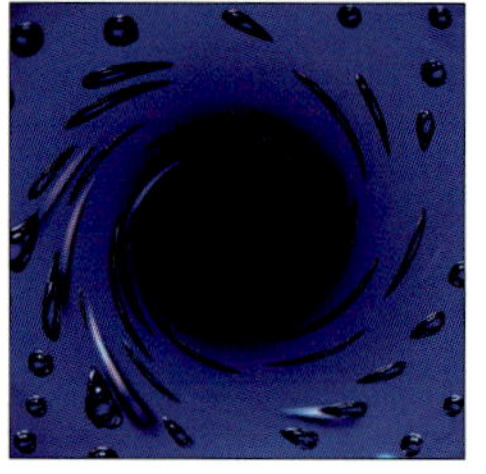

● JIM MACBRAYNE A paperweight, taken on a Canon EOS 20D fitted with a 18-55mm lens in tungsten light. The exposure was 1/15sec at f/8.

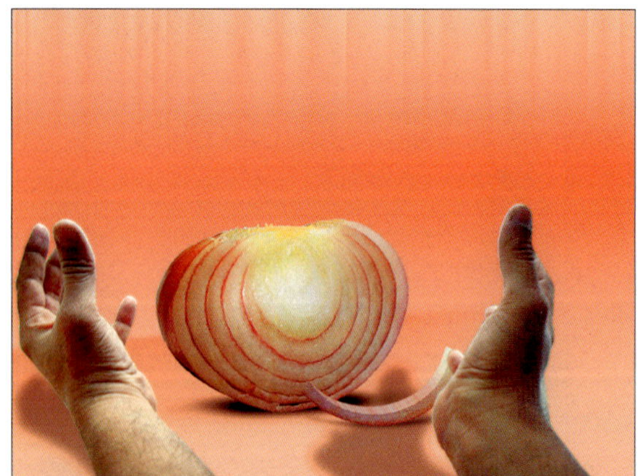

● MUNIR RAHOOL Conceptual composition done in Photoshop of snaps taken using a Canon PowerShot A300.

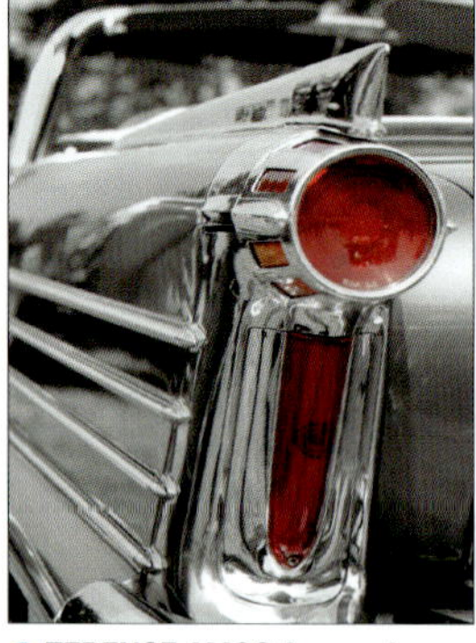

● TERENCE AMOS A copy layer was desaturated and eraser used to bring back red lights. Shot on a Canon EOS 10D.

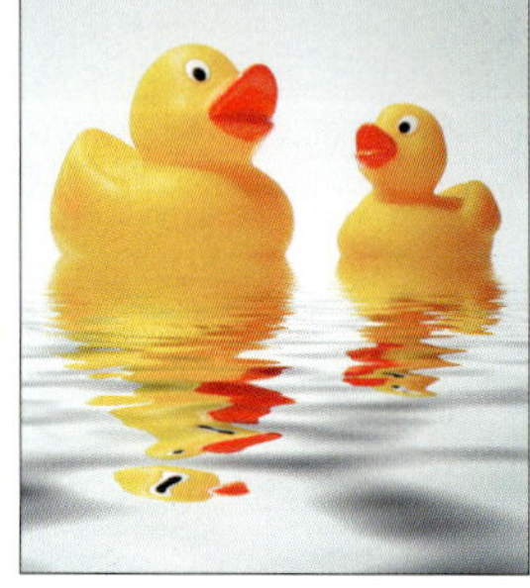

● EMMA TUMMAN Two rubber ducks, lit with a halogen lamp. Flood filter added in Photoshop.

FREE RESOURCES

■ The Internet is a great place to find freebies and low cost products to help photographers do things better. Here are some useful options to check out:

■ **Image editors**
www.irfanview.com
www.gimp.org

■ **Photoshop plug-ins**
www.thepluginsite.com
www.freephotoshop.com
photoshop.pluginsworld.com
www.grafnet.com.pl

■ **Web design**
www.nvu.com

■ **Images**
www.freefoto.com
www.bigfoto.com

■ **Clip Art**
www.free-graphics.com

■ **Fonts**
www.free-fonts.com
www.1001freefonts.com

■ **Image organiser**
picasa.google.com

■ **Internet spell check**
www.iespell.com

Various other resources
www.download.com
www.tucows.com
www.freewarehome.com
www.passtheshareware.com
www.freeware-guide.com

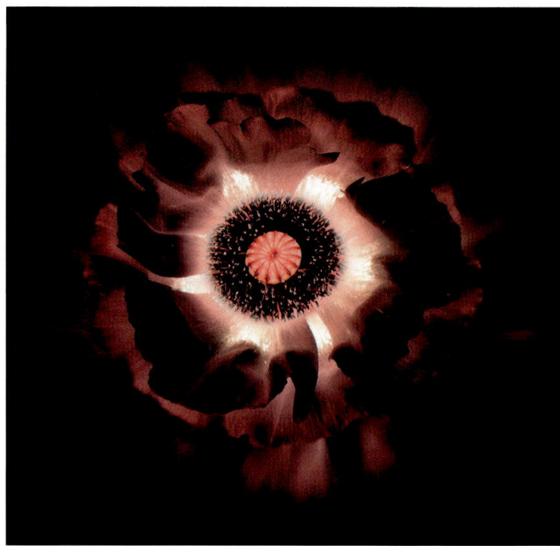

● JOHN EDWARDS One of a series of ethereal images created in Photoshop, using an original photo of a white oriental poppy.

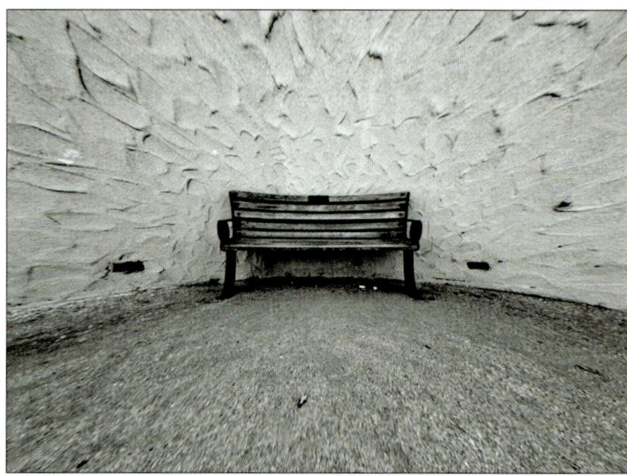

● HEIDI LEE This was manipulated in Photoshop Elements using Pinch & Spherise. The camera exposure was 1/20sec at f/2.8.

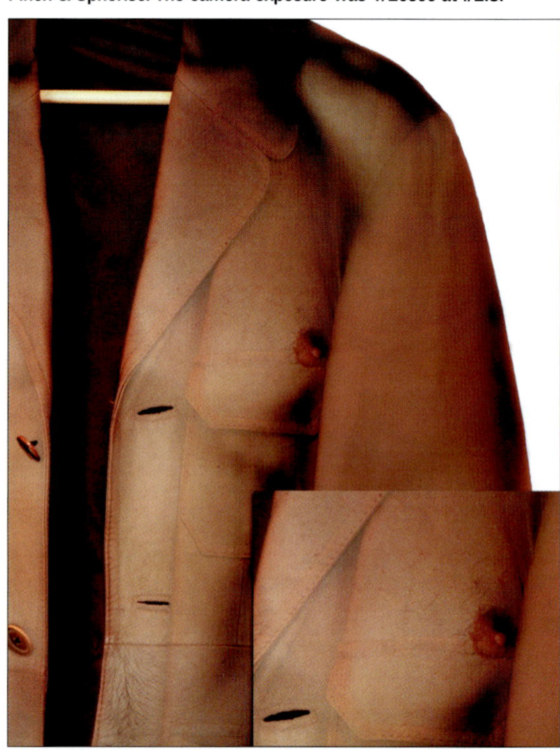

● DANIEL BUXTON Addressing concepts of fashion and the figure, this layered digital shot is part of a zipped series.

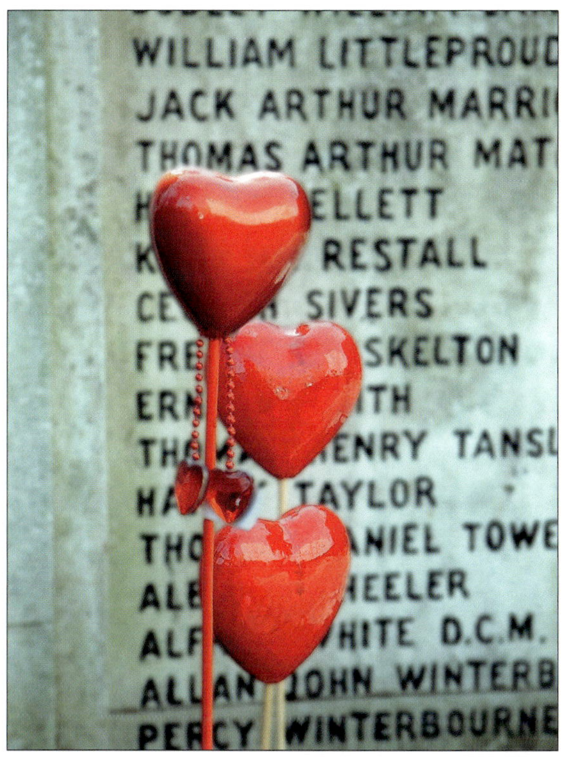

● JOHN FLYNN A slightly tweaked digital image of plastic hearts at a war memorial.

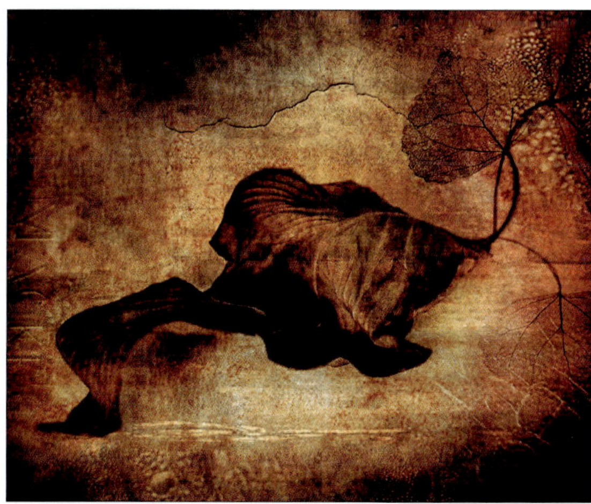

● JOHANN PINTO Textures were added on Photoshop to give a more dramatic effect, especially to the background.

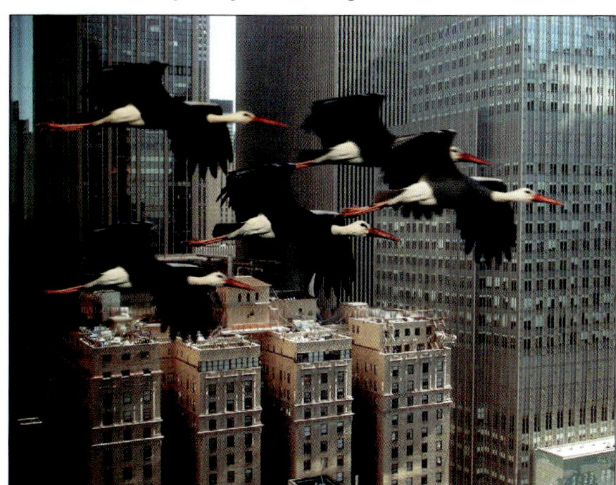

● GEORGE CRAMER Shot from a hotel-room window in New York, using an Olympus E1 with 4-54mm lens. The photomontage was done in Photoshop with several layers.

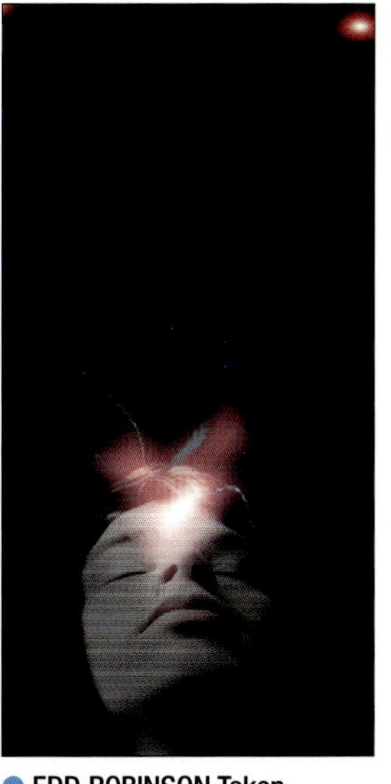

● EDD ROBINSON Taken indoors with natural light and a hood over head. The lights were manipulations of standard Photoshop lighting effects.

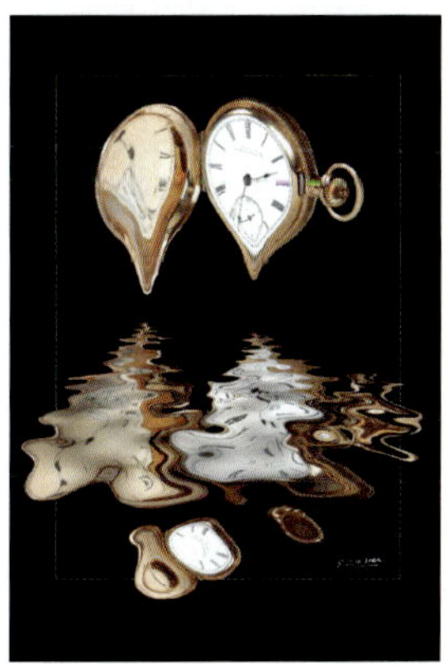

● SIMON MITCHELL "I created this image using liquify and reflection filters. Distorting the reflection and adding a border increased depth."

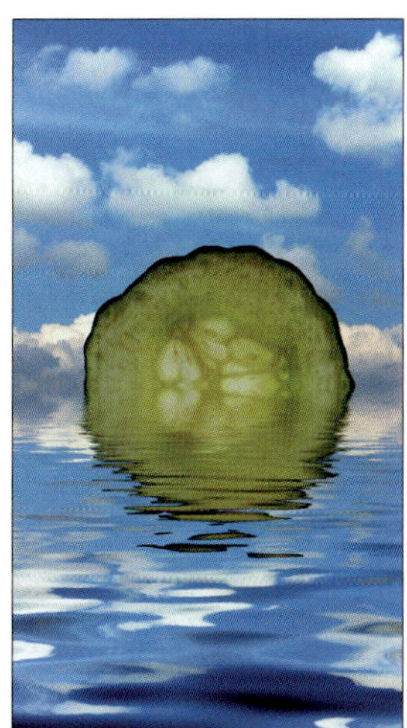

● LEWIS BUCKLE "One thin cucumber slice, one sky stock-shot and the Flaming Pear flood filter. It was simple to do, taking just 20 mins from start to finish."

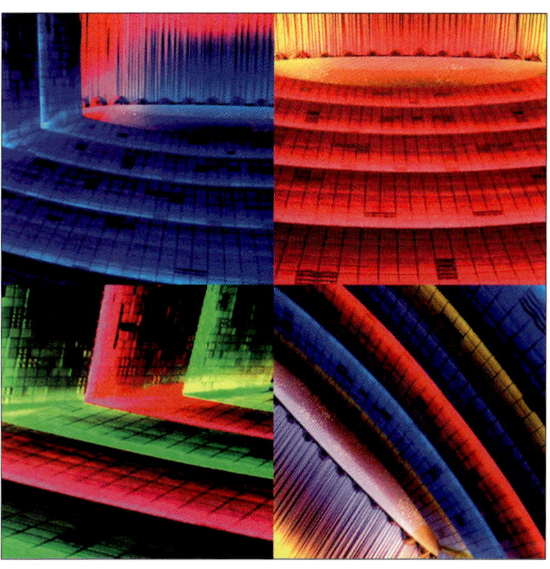

● TARA MCNAMEE This abstract comprises four architectural patterns, individually coloured and combined in a grid.

DIGITAL TECHNIQUE – RIPPLE EFFECT

■ The ripple effect has become very popular on ePHOTOzine since Flaming Pear gave a demo version of their plug-in on a magazine cover CD. Here we show you how to create the effect using a Photoshop Distort Filter.

1 Choose a photograph that will be suitable for a ripple effect. This otter, taken on an ePHOTOzine members' meeting at Chester Zoo is perfect. He's resting on a log and we'll create a reflection in some water below and then add a ripple.

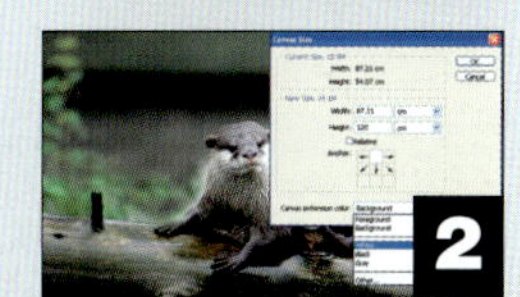

2 Extend the canvas – Image⇨ Canvas size. Select white as the canvas colour and make it at least twice as big. Click in the top square of the nine square grid so the canvas is extended below the existing area.

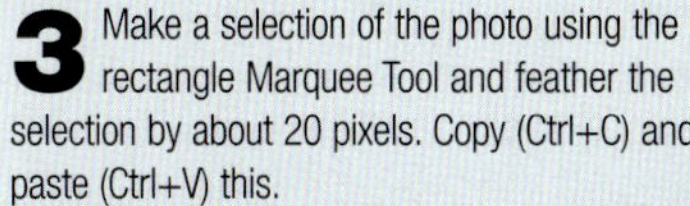

3 Make a selection of the photo using the rectangle Marquee Tool and feather the selection by about 20 pixels. Copy (Ctrl+C) and paste (Ctrl+V) this.

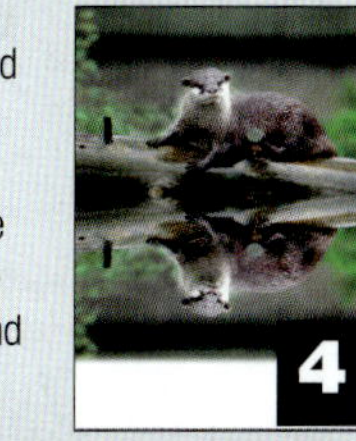

4 Flip the pasted Image Edit⇨Transform⇨Flip Vertical and use the move tool to reposition it in the extended canvas area. Align precisely with the original using the up and down keyboard arrows so that you don't see a join.

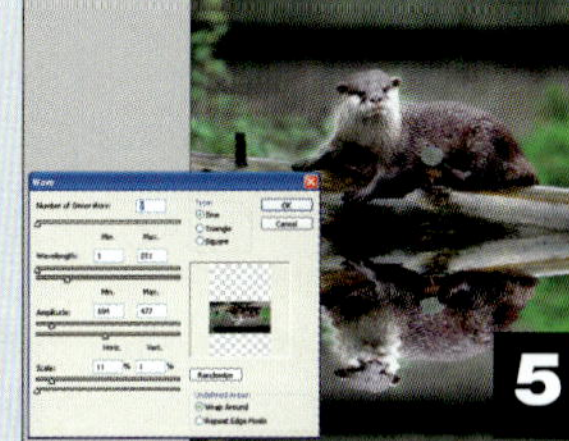

5 Now to create the ripple: Go to Filter⇨Distort⇨Wave and adjust the sliders until you have a natural looking effect.

6 To make it more realistic, add a touch of Gaussian blur or Motion blur from the Filter⇨Blue menu and adjust the brightness and colour so it looks more like a water reflection than a mirror.

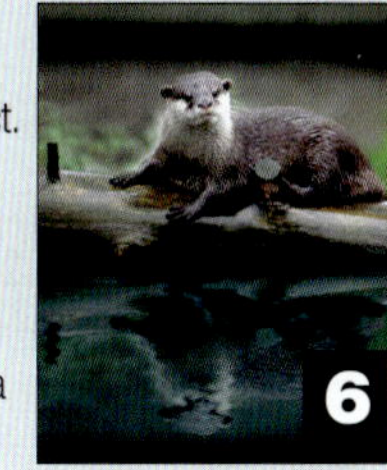

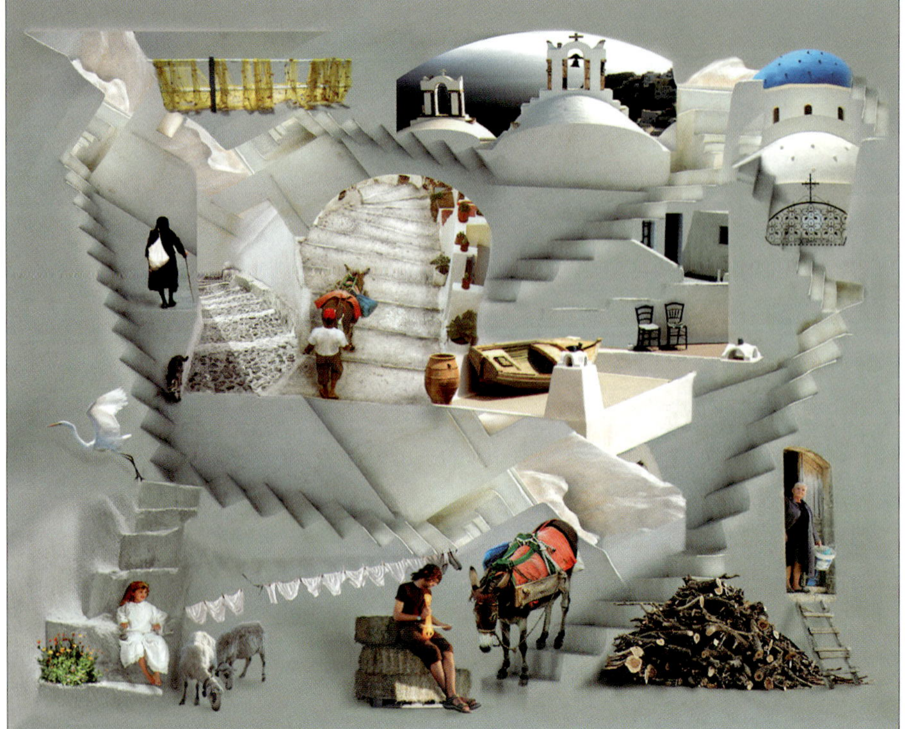

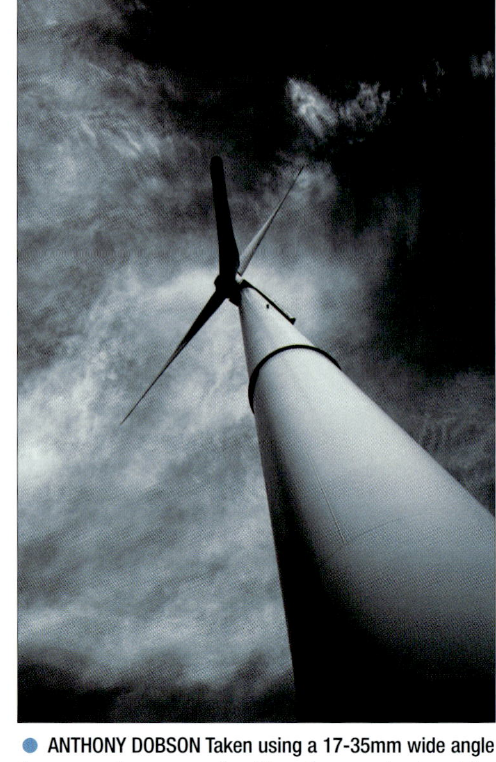

● PATRICIA FENN "Having always admired the works of M.C.Escher (so precise and orderly) I was inspired to try a Greek version (where nothing is precise or orderly). It was a huge amount of work in Photoshop combining all the different photographs using layers, the clone tool and lots of patience."

● ANTHONY DOBSON Taken using a 17-35mm wide angle from a very low perspective. Given the mono treatment in Photoshop using the hue/saturation channels.

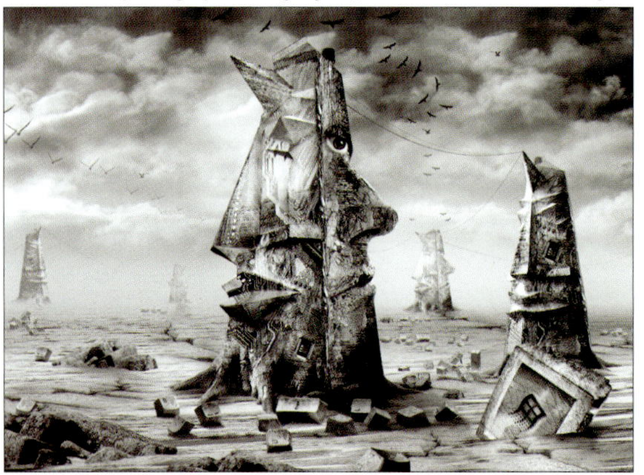

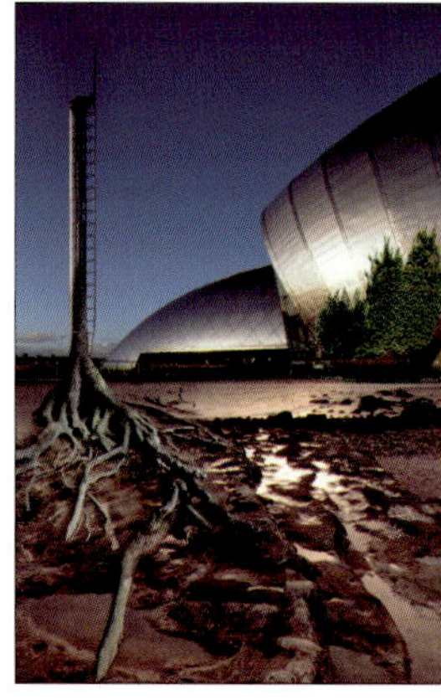

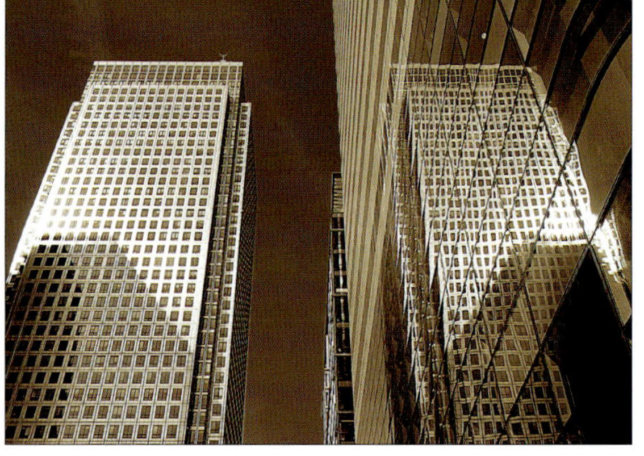

● MAREK KOMISARUK "I have used parts and whole frames of 20 photographs merged into about 310 layers in Photoshop."

● CHRIS STOBBS The Glasgow Science Centre returned back to nature with a little help from Photoshop and a handful of other images.

● BRIAN USHER Reflection of 1 Canada Square on the HSBC building, taken using a Canon EOS 10D with 16-35mm and 1/180sec at f/11 exposure. Desaturated to increase contrast and impact.

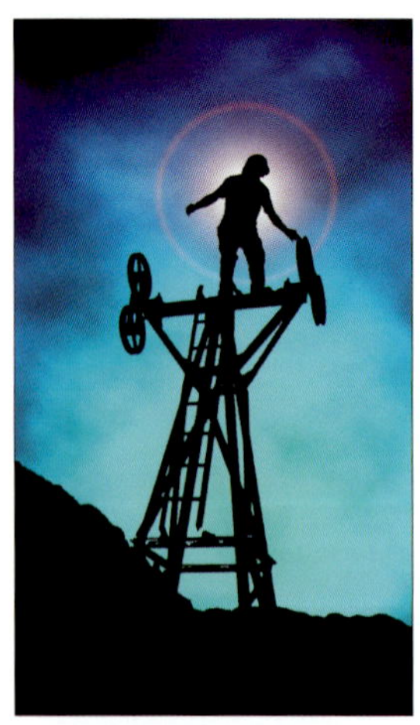

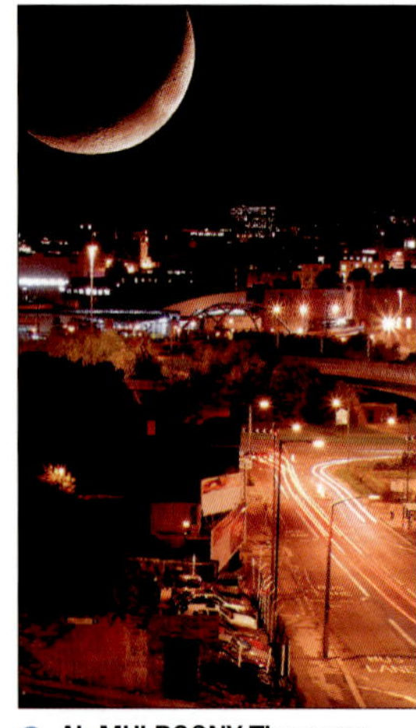

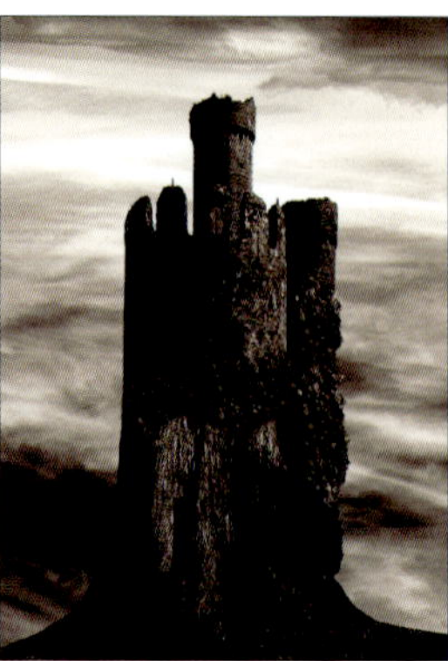

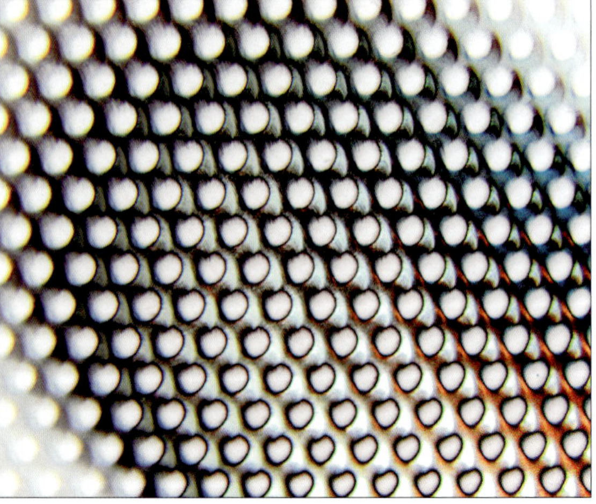

● DAVE ELLISON A silhouette placed on a new layer on a computer generated background.

● AL MULROONY The moon was added to this night scene of Sheffield city centre.

● RICHARD INGRAM PENROSE "I was inspired by the work of Jerry Uelsmann."

● STEVE NEIL A close up of metal mesh with the colours inverted in Photoshop to create the interesting abstract pattern.

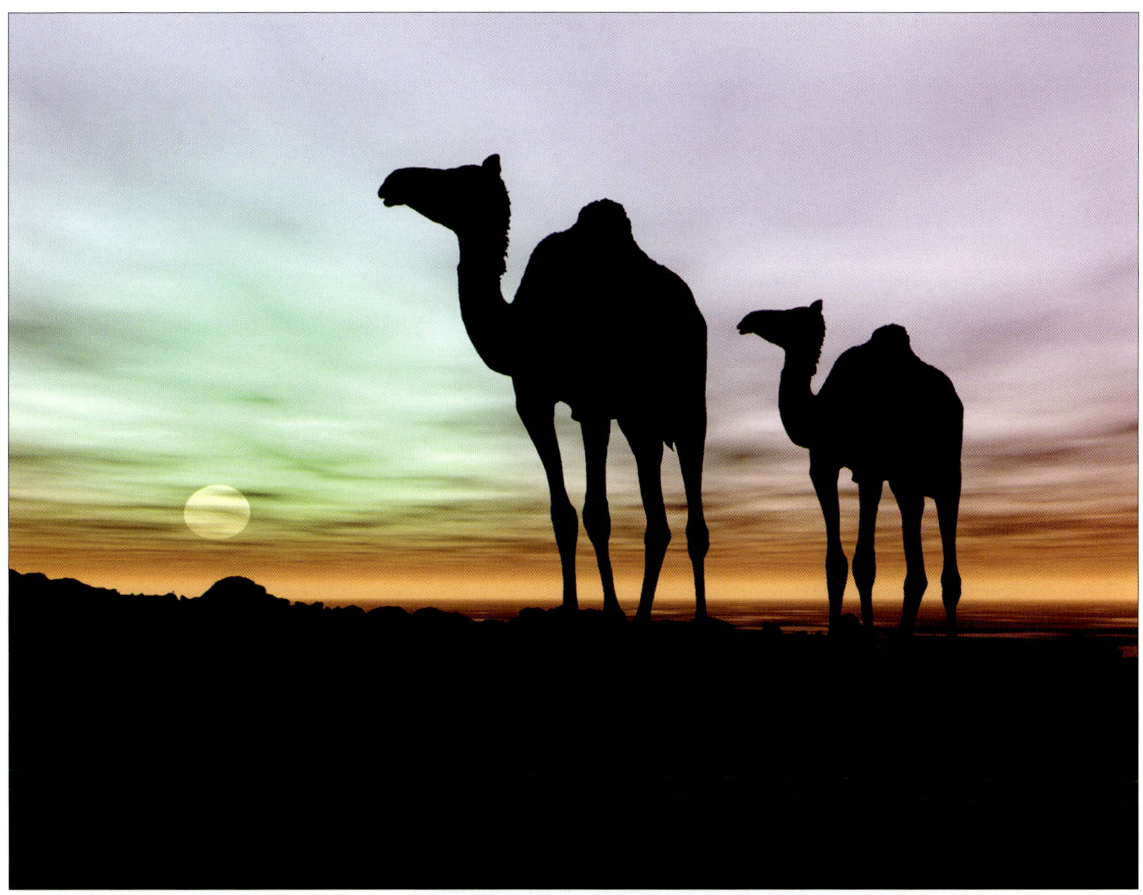

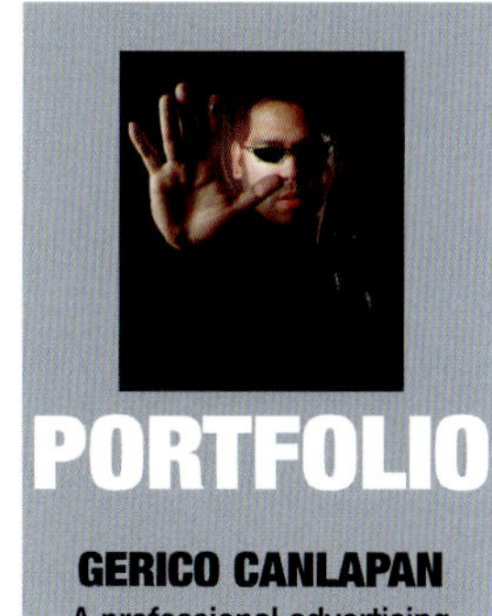

PORTFOLIO

GERICO CANLAPAN
A professional advertising photographer from the Philippines shooting on all formats from 35mm to 5x4.

Filipino advertising photographer Gerico Canlapan works with the likes of Saatchi & Saatchi and McCann Erikson on projects for a wealth of companies such as Sony, Shell and various Saudi banks and breweries, creating photographs with a difference.

As well as the usual range of studio pack shots that advertising photographers tend to shoot, Gerico ventures into the world of conceptual portraits, fashion and glamour and has, for the last few years, turned his hand to digital photography.

"I conceive, I capture, I create. From the stark realities heralded by monochromatic prints to the animated revelry of coloured images, the transcending nature of photographs has transfixed man for many generations.

My fortune has been that of being one among those who have built a vocation in photography – a destiny I treasure dearly, a journey from an old hand-me-down rangefinder to a state-of-the-art digital SLR camera.

Digital technology has spawned a new genre that stirs our mindset. Digital art challenges the boundaries of convention.

The images displayed here are snapshots of my forays into the realm of digital art."

Gerico is one of just 12 Filipinos to be bestowed the Bagong Bayani Award 2005, for the category on Culture and Arts. The award seeks to recognise and pay tribute to overseas Filipino workers for their significant efforts in fostering goodwill among peoples of the world and enhancing and promoting the image of the Filipino as a competent, responsible and dignified worker. ∎

www.jerishoots.com

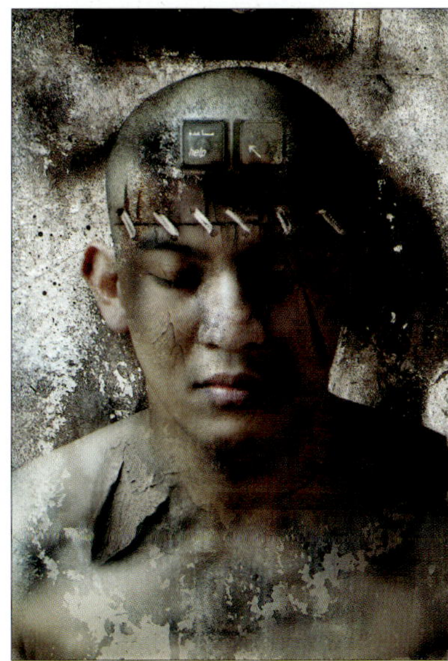

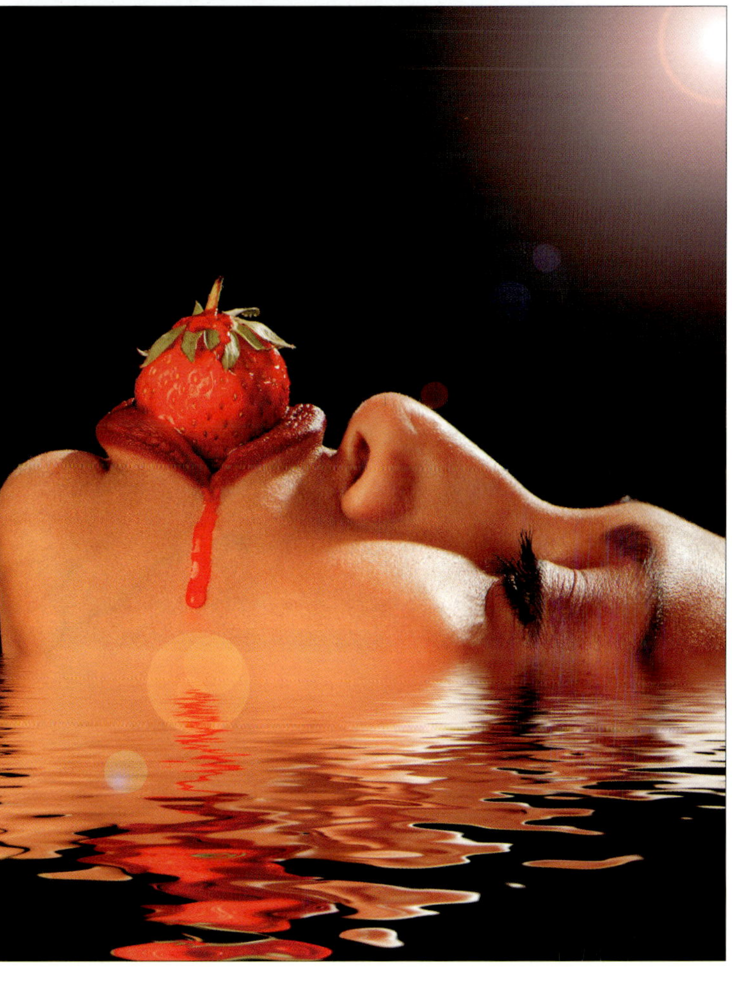

● Top: Two images combined in layers. The camel layer has been turned into a silhouette and the background layer's saturation increased to ensure the dramatic colours.

● Above left: Titled "Help", this surreal art is a combination of five images, using blending modes, to create the stitching and cracked forehead.

● Right: The water reflection was done using Flaming Pear's plug-in flood filter for Photoshop. There are plenty more fascinating images just like these on ePHOTOzine.

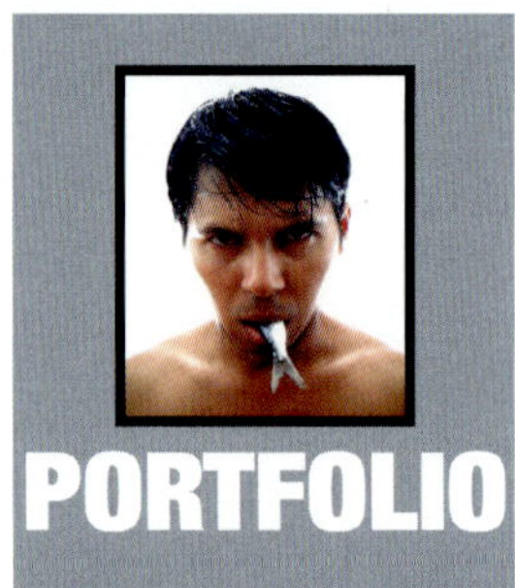

PORTFOLIO

ABDUL KADIR AUDAH

Abdul is a successful freelance photographer, based in Germany, working for US and UK stock agencies.

My father, who was a keen amateur, introduced me to photography, but it wasn't until I was working as a business analyst in Indonesia that I really developed a passion for it. I travelled a lot with this job and the number of different places and people I saw sparked my interest.

Since moving to Cologne, my passion has become stronger and since 2001 I have participated in many photographic competitions, receiving a number of awards and commendations.

I've never had any formal education in photography, learning instead from books, the internet and, most importantly, by experimenting with various styles to achieve different results. I don't have a specialist area – I will shoot any subject as long as it's artistic.

I work mostly in digital format, though I still use an analog camera occasionally for black & white. Digital art has now become part of my work, because I find it to be very challenging and it demands a high standard of creativity to achieve unique results.

Once I was confident that my work was up to professional standards, I started to look for publishers. Of course I had work rejected at times, rejection is part of this business, but I try to learn from the experience and would never stop submitting my images to various publishers.

I'm now a freelancer for US and UK stock agencies and do assignments and designs based on my original photos. My images are published and sold in many formats, including magazines, book covers, brochures, advertising banners, greetings cards, postcards, fine art posters and canvasses around the world. ■
www.audah.com

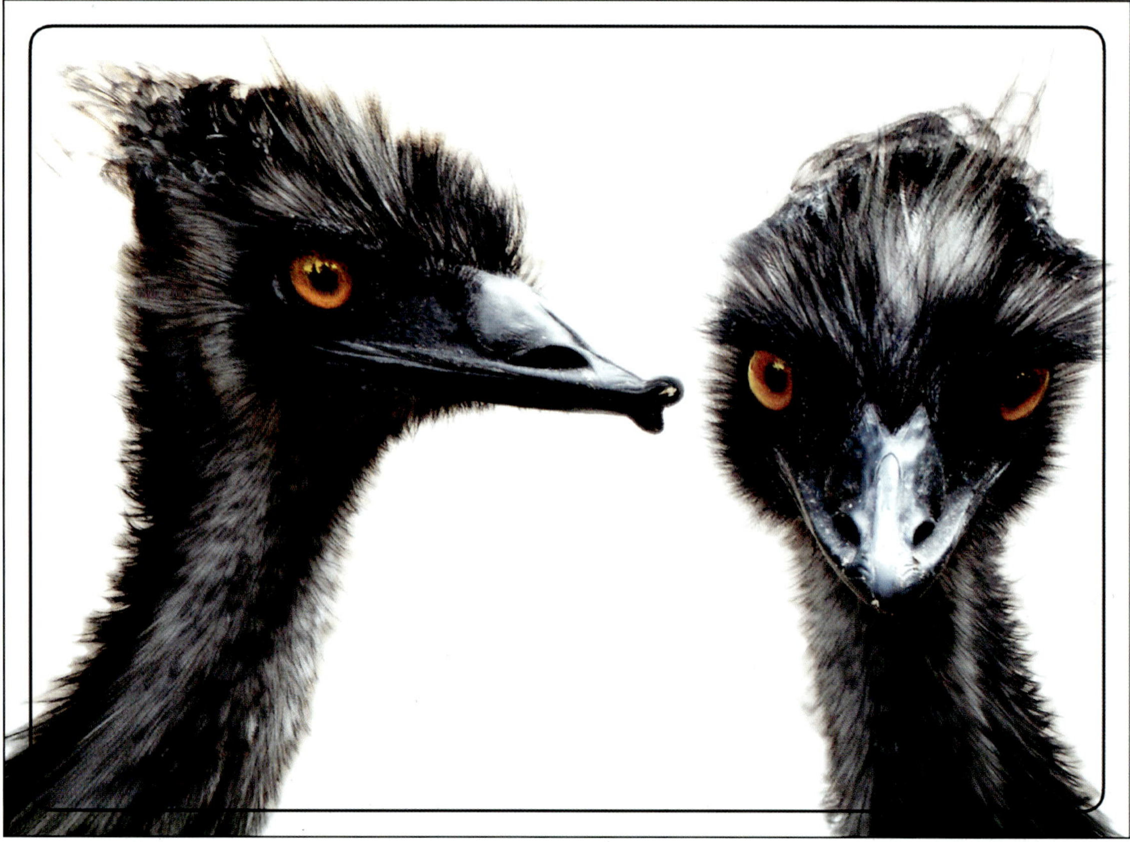

● These emus were taken at Artis Zoo in Amsterdam. The backgrounds were removed and replaced with white. Several designs like this one can be seen in Abdul's portfolio on ePHOTOzine and they were produced for a series of greetings cards.

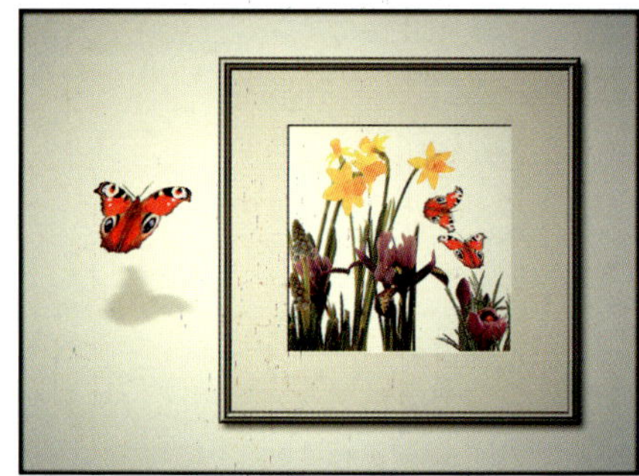

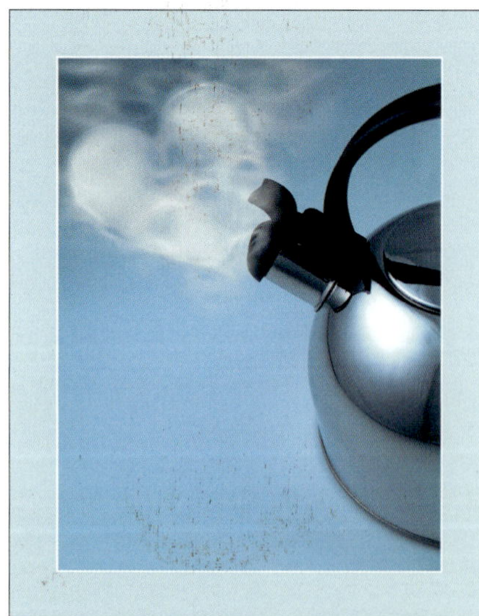

● Top: One from the series "Butterflies in the Gallery". Bottom: Heart shaped steam was created in Photoshop for this greetings card image.

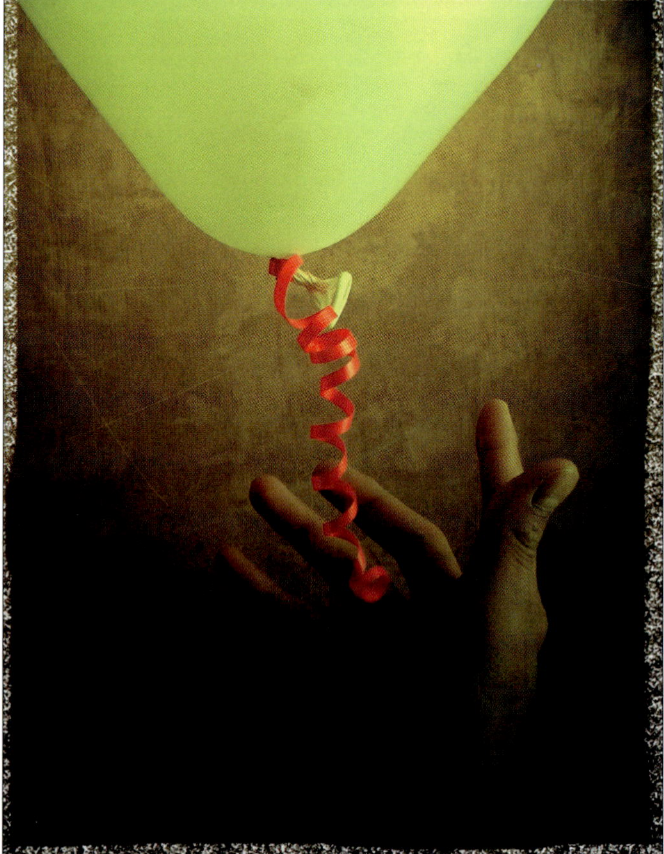

● The green colour on this was created naturally by shooting using a green filter that you would normally use to change contrast on black & white film. The surrounding frame texture was made using Photoshop brushes.

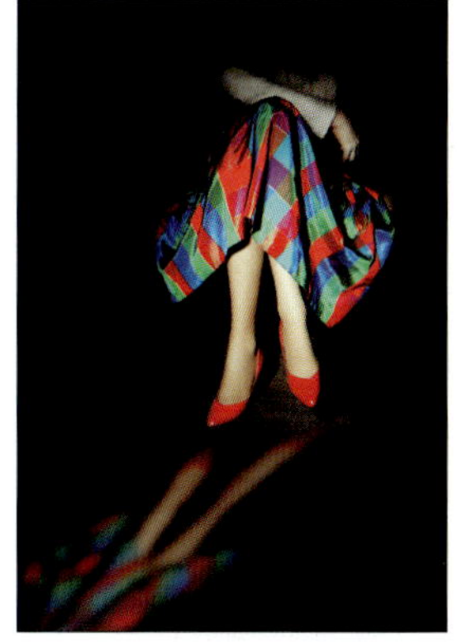

● PETER KENT Flipped and blurred to create a reflection.

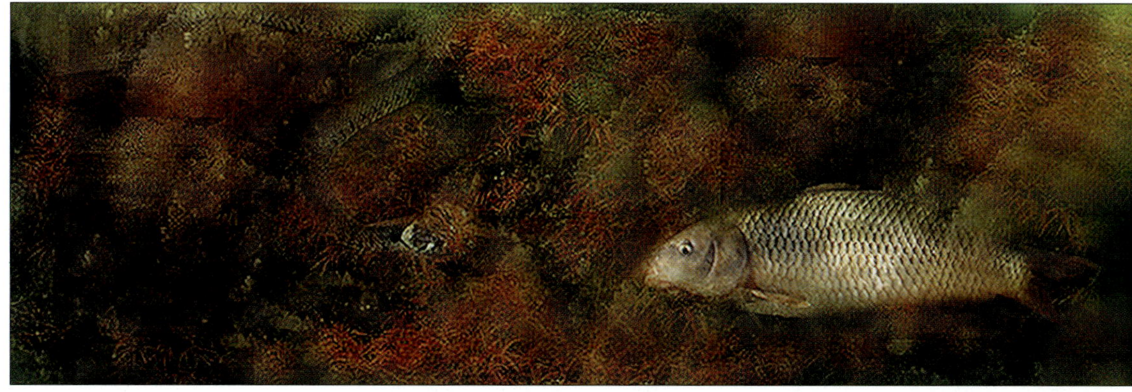

● PAULINE WHITE This comprises five individual images, each cloned at a different density to retain the quality of light in the final image.

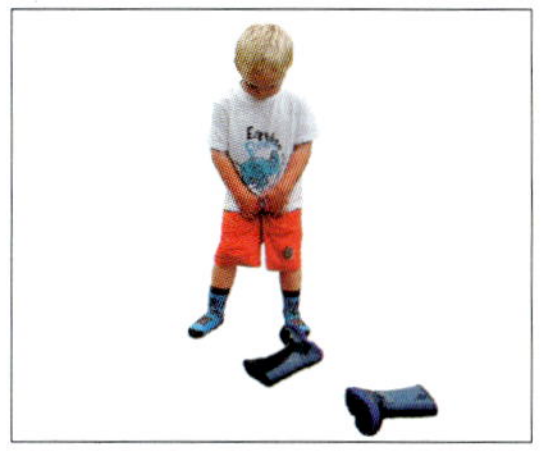

● IAIN JOHNSTON The original has been improved by removing the background in Photoshop.

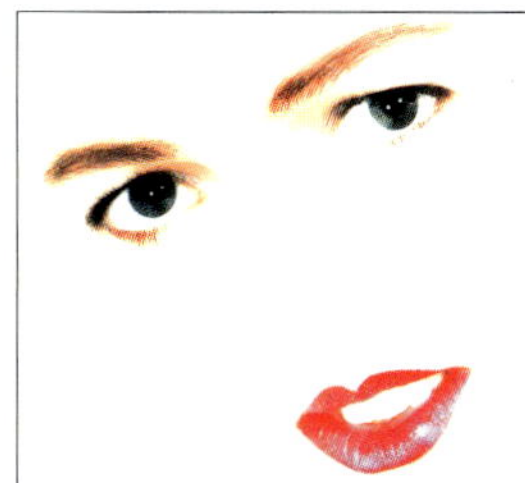
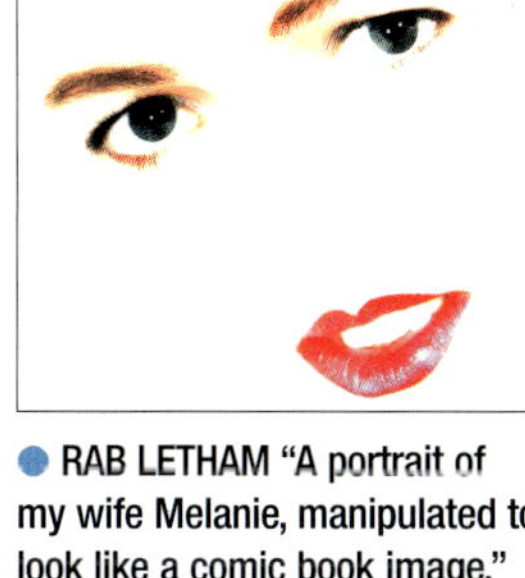

● RAB LETHAM "A portrait of my wife Melanie, manipulated to look like a comic book image."

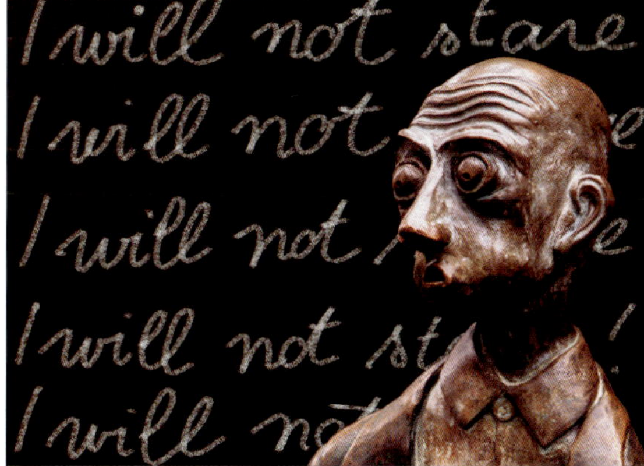

● STEPHANIE BELTON I found this unusual statue in the streets of Melbourne and added background using a chalk effect brush.

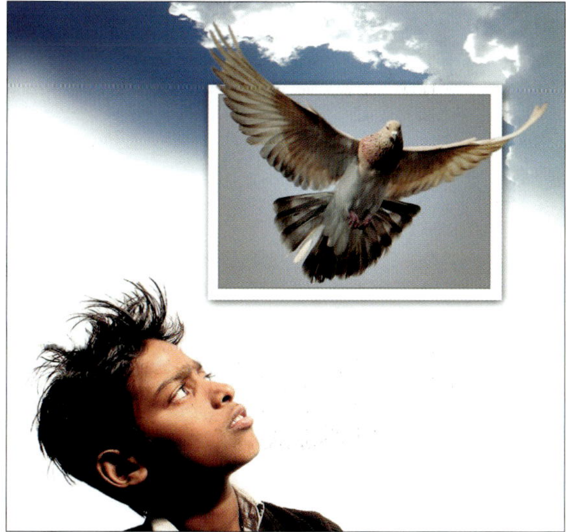

● RUDRA MANDAL Individual shots of the portrait, bird and sky were taken on a Nikon Coolpix 3100 and combined in Photoshop.

DIGITAL TECHNIQUE – CREATING A SILHOUETTE EFFECT

■ Here's a simple technique using your image editing program to turn a colour or black & white photograph into a silhouette. We will use the Threshold control to take out all of the colour from an image and turn it into a complete silhouette.

1 First, choose a picture. It should be one that's already lacking in tone so it's easy for the software to remove the grey tones and replace them with black or white. This typical misty winter landscape, taken in the grounds of Chatsworth House, Derbyshire, will suit this technique perfectly.

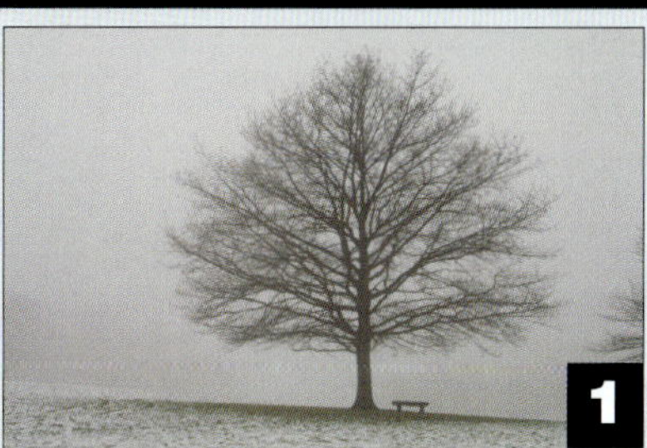

2 Go to Image⇨Adjustments⇨Threshold and the picture will immediately change to black & white with no mid tones. You will also see the Threshold graph showing the range of tones in the picture. If we drag the white marker to the left the tones that are visible will be predominantly white. This may be good for some subjects but I need more detail in the tree, and some ground would be nice!

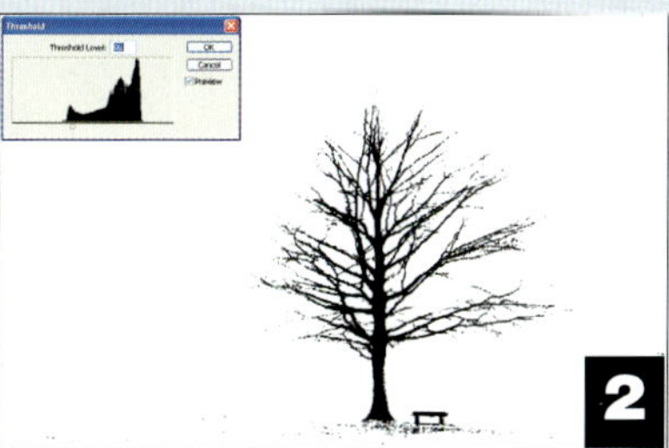

3 If we drag the white slider to the right the picture will become predominantly black, as illustrated. In this example you can now hardly make out the tree in the black mass that's been created. This is far too heavy for our silhouette so we need to drag the slider back to a more appropriate mid-point.

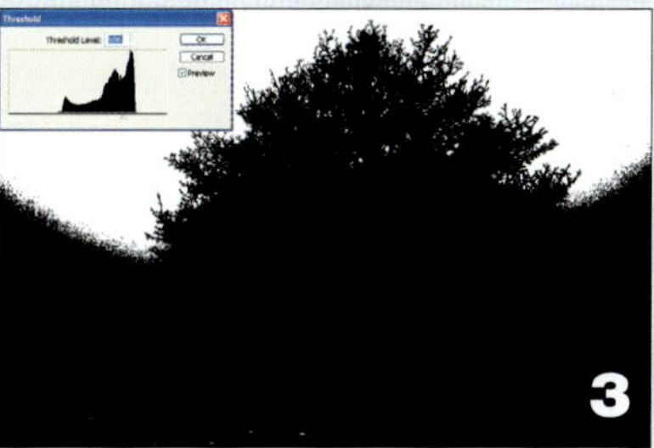

4 Setting a threshold somewhere between the two extremes of the graph will create the best result and this point depends on the photo you're using. 148 is about right for our example. With a mid-way threshold value you gain enough detail in the tree and ground to create a strong silhouette, without affecting the background.

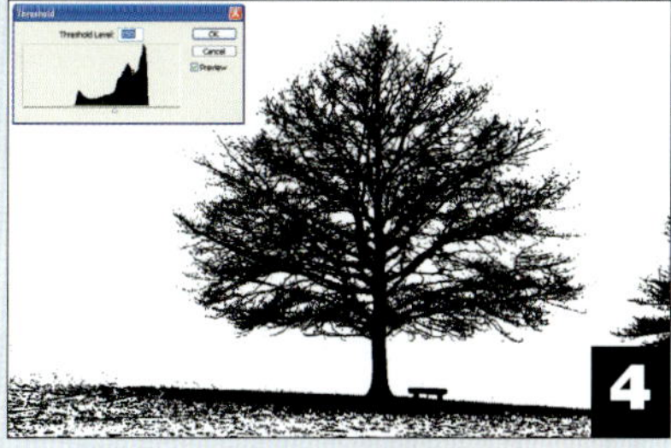

5 You could save the photo or go one stage further. We'll take it to a new level using layers. I thought the photo would look good with a sunset style graduation and applied the gradient tool with the foreground set to orange and the background white. Drawing down the photo with the tool creates the orange sunset effect with ease. You can choose any colour — blue and grey being good alternatives.

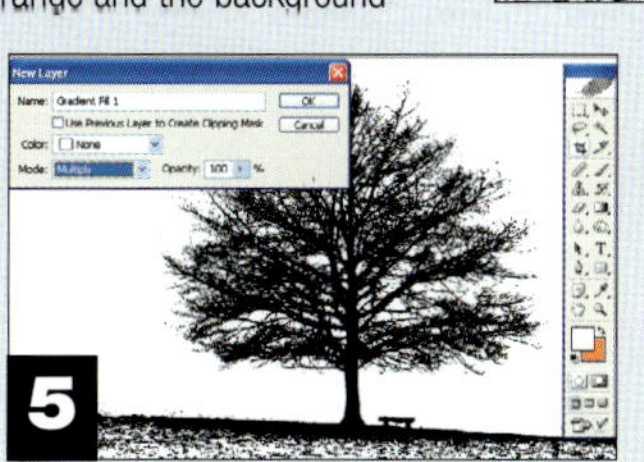
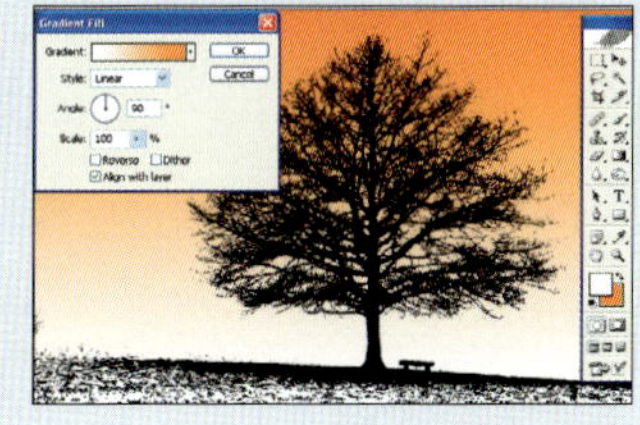

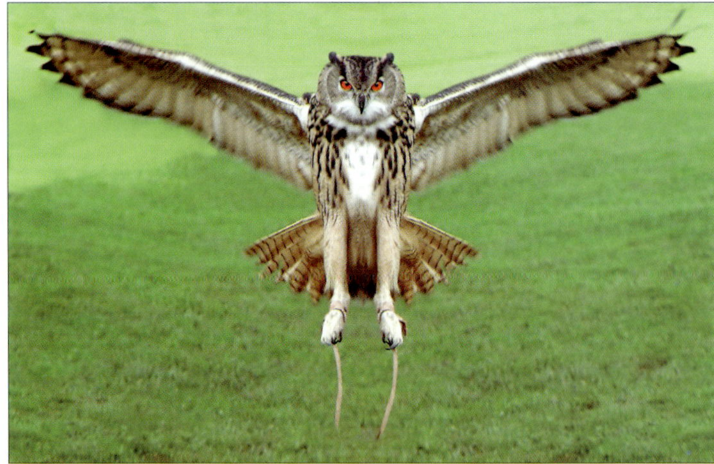

● KEV LEWIS An eagle owl taken at the National Bird of Prey Centre in Newent. The owl was mirrored about the vertical centre line to create a symmetrical image.

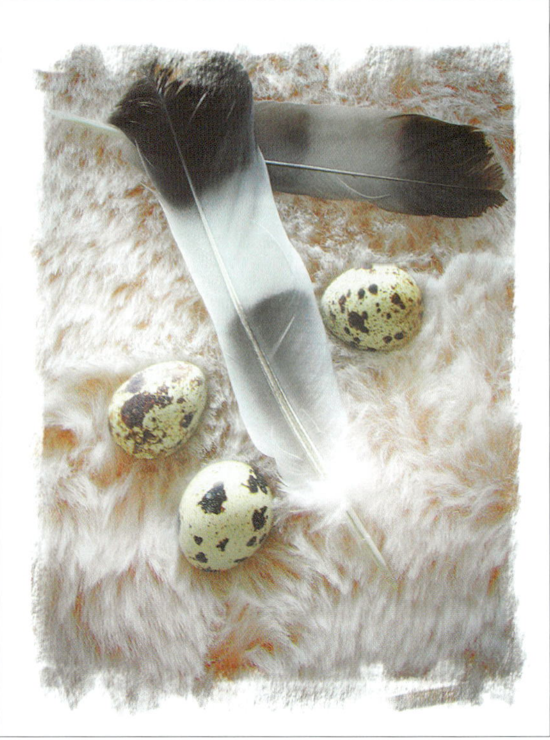

● ANNETTE EAST A texture brush was used to paint around the edges and give the ragged effect that compliments the photo.

DIGITAL TECHNIQUE – CREATE A RAGGED EDGED BORDER

■ You don't have to buy expensive border making plug-ins if you own an image editing program. Here we show you how you can create the effects using one of Photoshop's preset brushes. Other editing programs should have similar tools.

This photograph of a poppy field is a 3 million pixel digital image with a 2048 x 1536 pixel resolution. Follow the technique with one of your photographs and use the same settings that we use. If your file is bigger or smaller adjust the settings by a similar percentage.

1 Create a new layer: Layer⇨New⇨Layer or Shft+Ctrl+N. This is where we will add the frame border.

2 Make a selection using the Rectangular Marquee tool. Click in the top left corner where you want the selection to start, hold the mouse down and drag to the bottom right corner where you want the selection to end. The dotted rectangle is where we will create the ragged border, so make sure this is where you want the effect to occur and take care not to cut into the main image. Change the selection from the inner area to the border Select⇨Inverse.

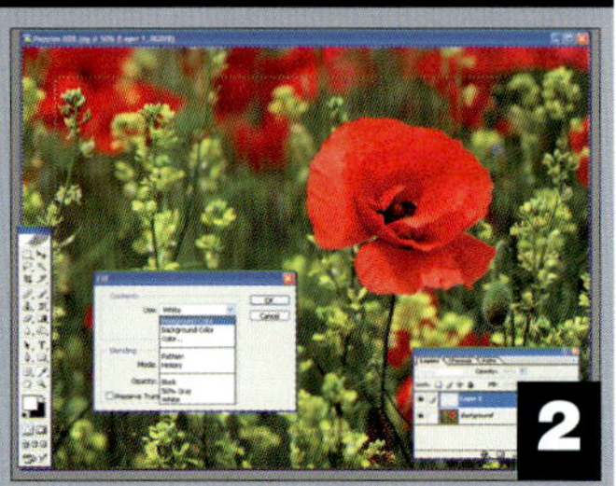

3 Go to Edit⇨Fill and, depending on whether you may want the outer part (frame) of the photo black, white or a colour, select the desired fill colour from the pop up box. Click OK. The photo will then have a layer with just a border in it and will appear as a surround on the photo. For best results use black when the inner area has light tones and white when, as in this example, the inner area has darker tones.

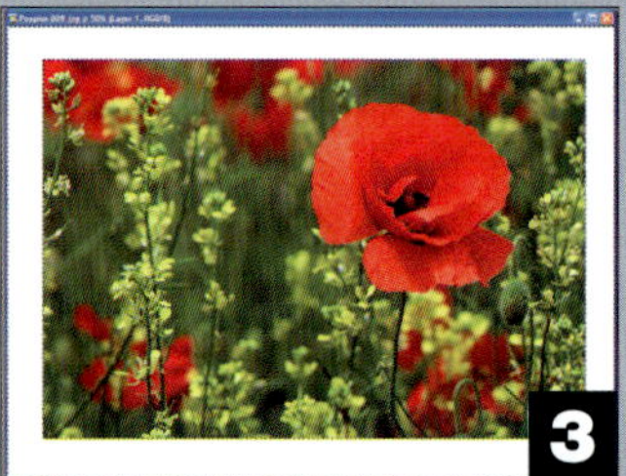

4 Now the creative bit. Select the frame layer and the Eraser tool from the toolbar. At the top of the page you'll now see various brush options under the normal menu. Click on Brush to bring up the brush preset picker. From here, click the little arrow, top right, to take you to a list of brush styles and from the list select Dry Media Brushes. You will be asked if you want to replace the current set. Click OK. Don't worry, you can go back to this point and reset the default set or choose different ones at a later stage. Select the Pastel Medium Tip brush indicated by the red arrow to the right and adjust the diameter of the brush to 75 pixels to give you a decent ragged effect.

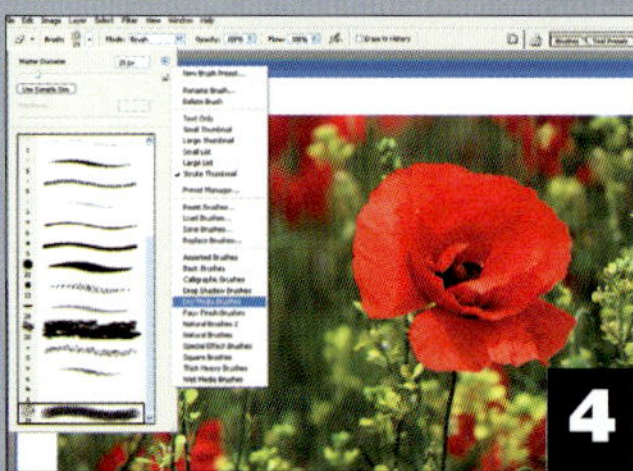

5 Magnify the photo on screen, so just a small area of the border is showing, and begin to paint using the Eraser brush on the border layer. Work from inside the picture so the edge of the brush creeps into the border area. You will see that the white is erased so the background shows through and it will have a ragged effect. You can do this really quickly by erasing around the edge following an uneven line, but to get best results take your time and change the brush size to vary the evenness of the ragged edge.

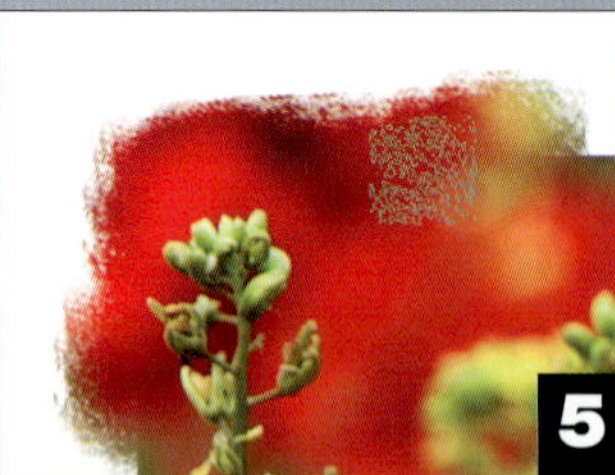

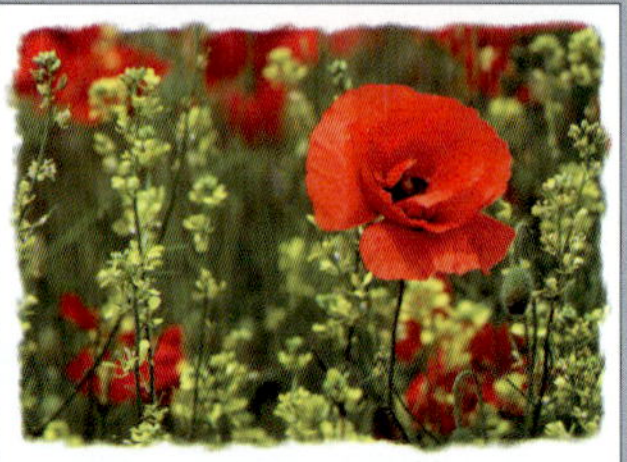

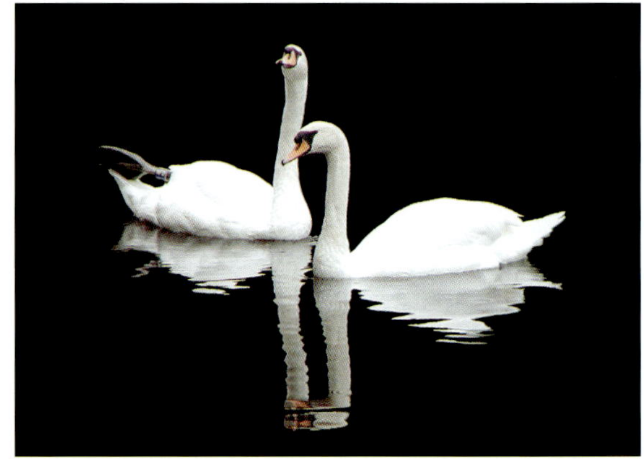

● IAN HOMEWOOD Swans at Elterwater were removed from a dark background and placed on a totally black one for striking contrast.

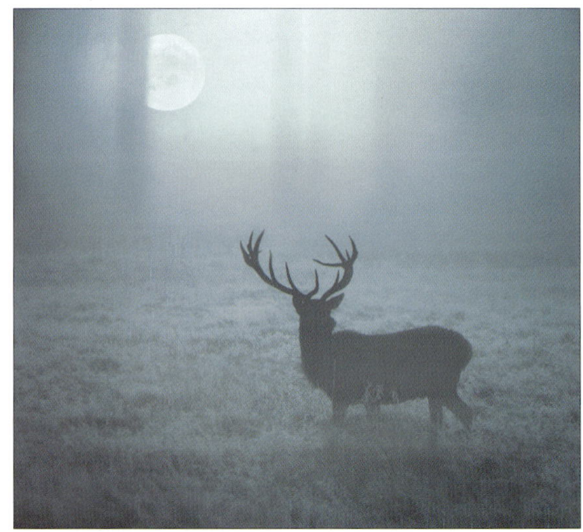

● HELEN DIXON A hoarfrost dawn in Richmond Park. The mist and light were perfect for this silhouette on a Canon EOS 10D. 70-300mm.

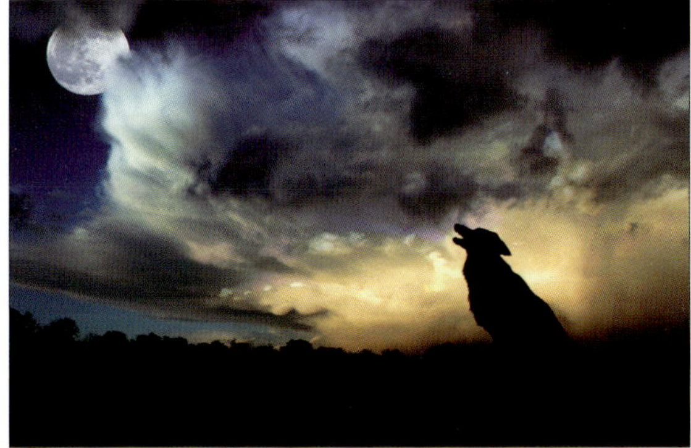

● KATHY WRIGHT "Separate photos of the moon, sunset, a cloudscape and a silhouette of my dog were placed on individual layers which were then blended and merged in Photoshop."

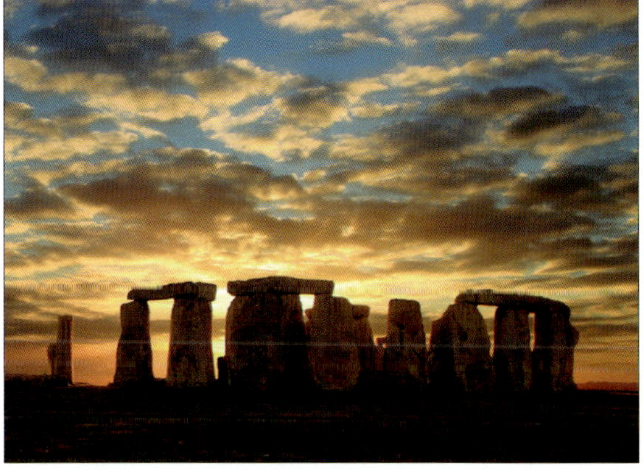

● BRIAN PRICE "The foreground was first lightened. Then the sky was duplicated and merged in Multiply blend mode to add density. I finally tidied it up by cloning out six people and a fence."

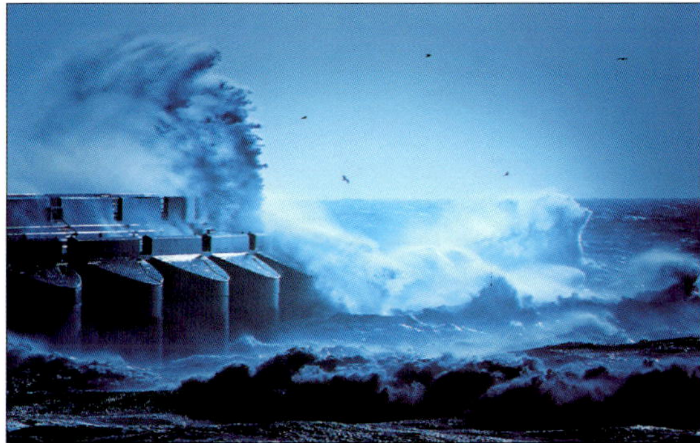

● DENNIS REDDICK "I wanted to give an overall cold tone to the image, so I manipulated in Photoshop using the colourise option in the Hue/Saturation adjustment mode."

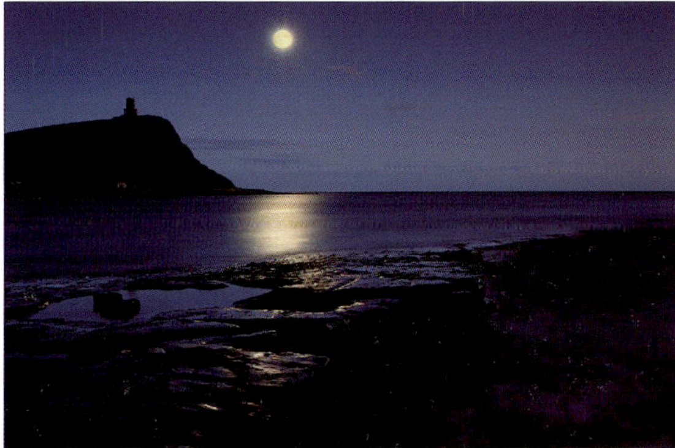

● MILES HERBERT A full moon at Kimmeridge Bay created by merging two different exposures of the bright moon and dark scene.

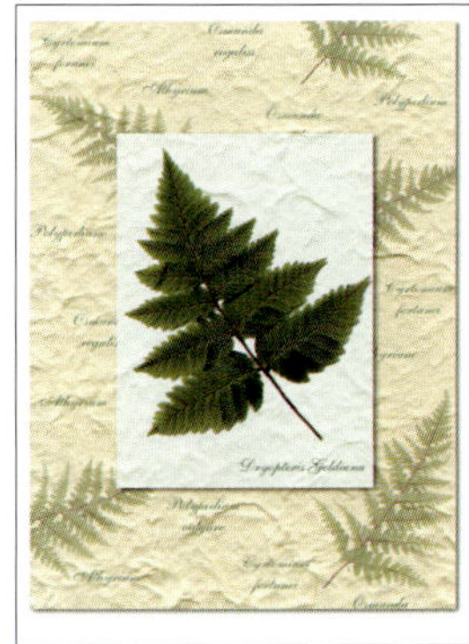

● CHERYL SURRY Above: This original fern leaf was scanned with a flatbed scanner and then used at lower opacity as the background.

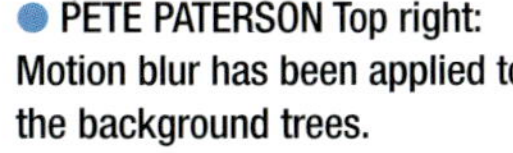

● PETE PATERSON Top right: Motion blur has been applied to the background trees.

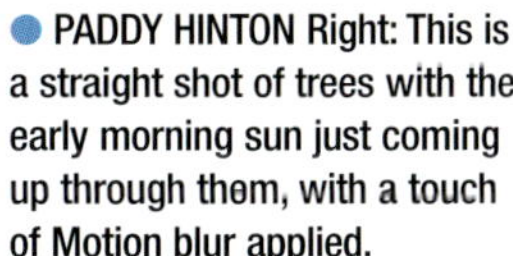

● PADDY HINTON Right: This is a straight shot of trees with the early morning sun just coming up through them, with a touch of Motion blur applied.

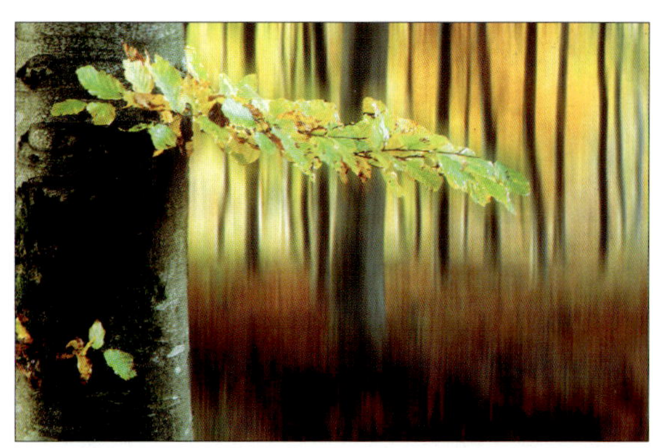

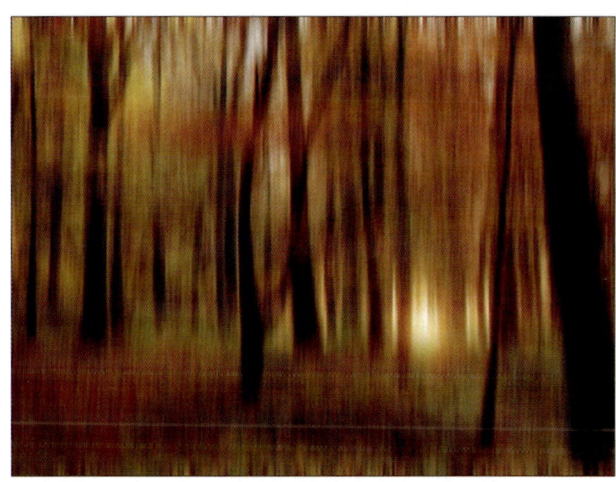

DIGITAL TECHNIQUE – ADDING MOTION BLUR

■ The two photos above have both been changed using one of Photoshop's blur filters. While these shots apply the treatment to similar subjects, the filter can be used for all kinds of images. In the landscape section we showed you a similar technique using the sea and clouds as a subject instead. Here we make a motocross bike appear to move faster. In this shot a fast shutter speed was used and the photographer panned with the subject, resulting in a bike frozen mid-air. While the exposure is good it could do with a stronger feeling of motion.

1 Open the photograph and go to Layer⇨ Duplicate Layer. The layer palette will now show the same image on two different layers. Select the new top layer.

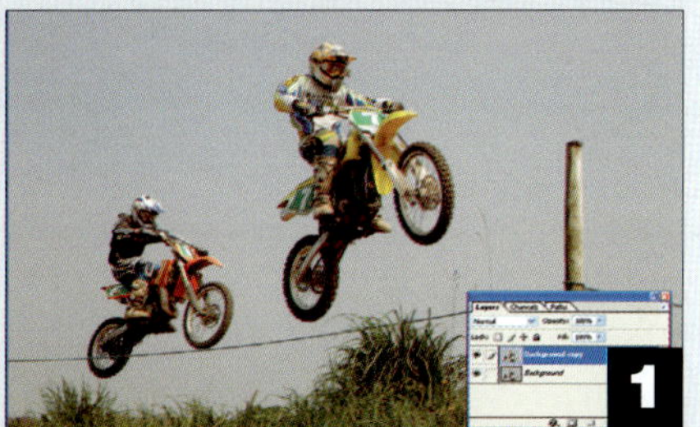
1

2 We will add motion blur to this layer Filter⇨Blur⇨Motion blur. When the Motion Blur palette opens make sure the preview option is selected. Now adjust the angle of blur so it matches the direction the subject is travelling. In this example the bike's heading upwards at about 40 degrees toward the top right corner. Adjust the distance while watching the preview until the bike looks blurred, but just enough that you still see detail and recognise the subject. Click OK.

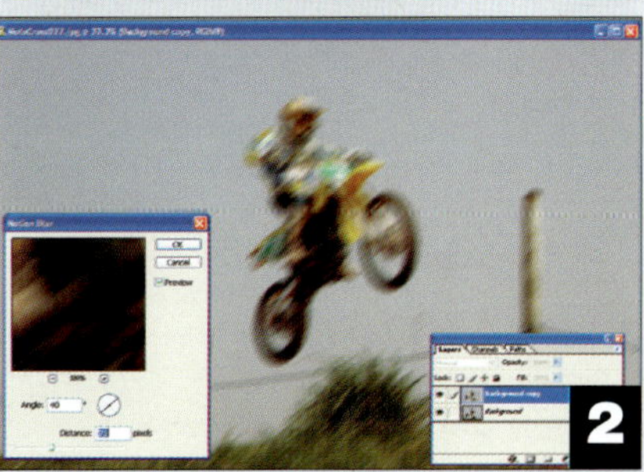
2

3 Now select the Eraser tool and a brush size that's about the size of the rider's helmet. And with the blurred layer still active start to paint with the Eraser over the front of the bike. This removes blurred detail in the top layer so the detail in the sharp layer below shows through. You could erase over the whole bike so the whole thing appears sharp but I've just done the front section to give a touch more motion.

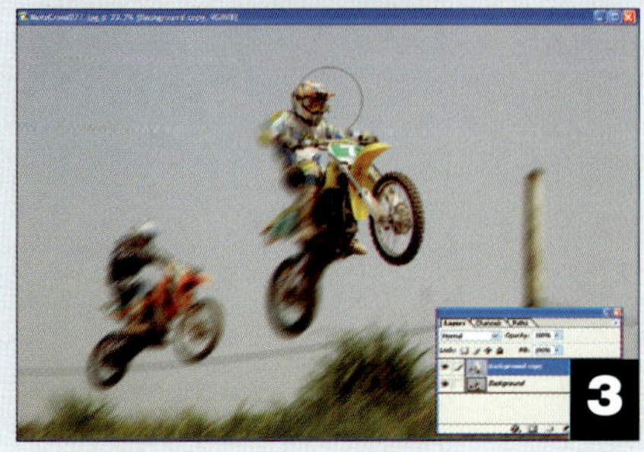
3

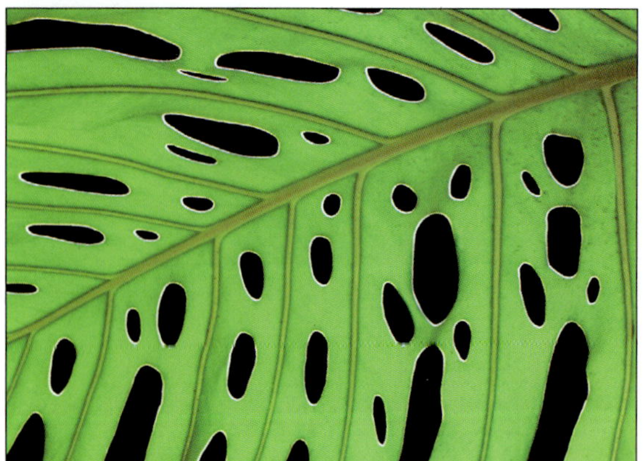

● EVAN ROBERTS "This leaf took on an illuminating glow as the backlight of the sun provided me with an image I had to capture."

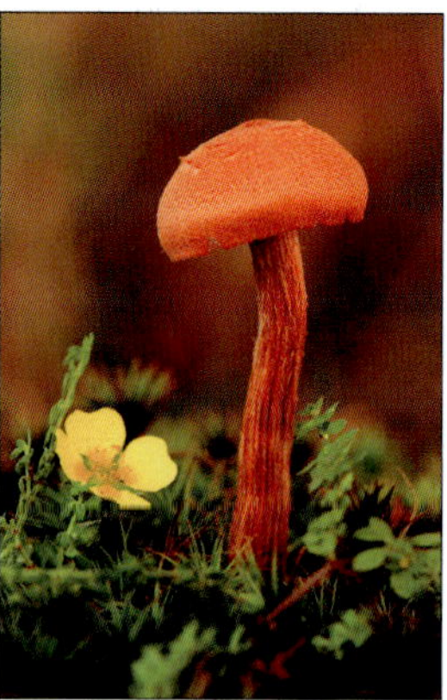

● MIKE TAYLOR Daylight shot, with fill-in from a reflector.

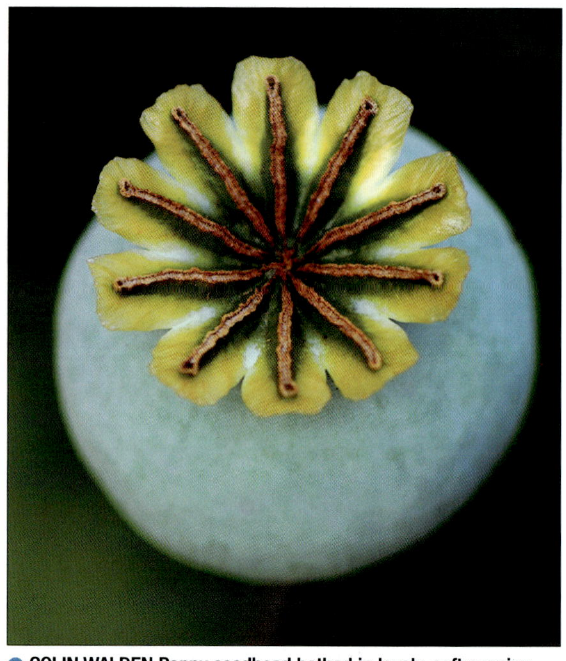

● COLIN WALDEN Poppy seedhead bathed in lovely, soft evening light, using a Konica Minolta Dynax 7D and 100mm f/2.8 macro.

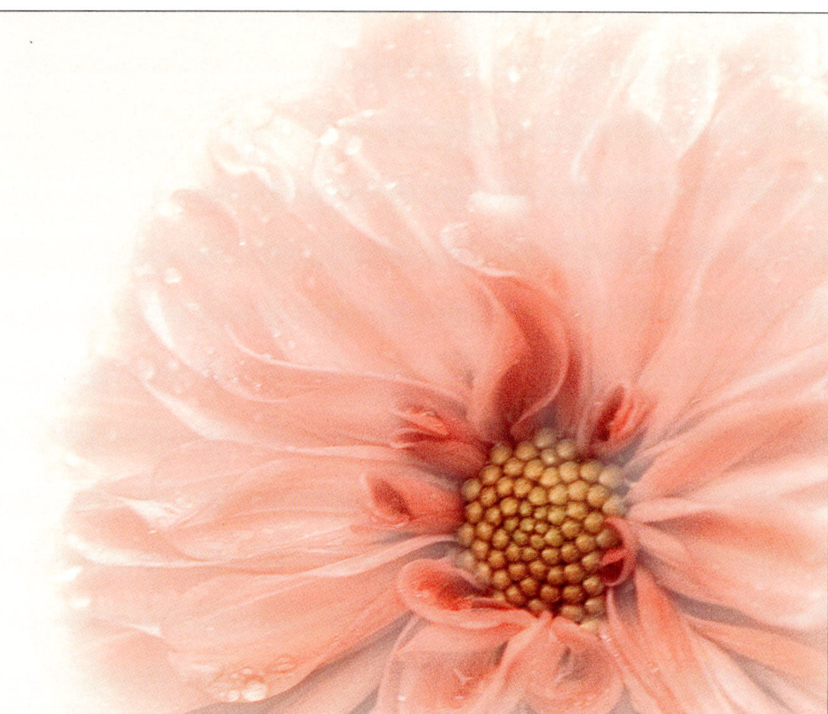

● MATTHEW PAGE Close up taken using the Pentax *ist D with 100mm f/2.8 macro lens set at f/4. The high key effect and lighter background have been added in Photoshop.

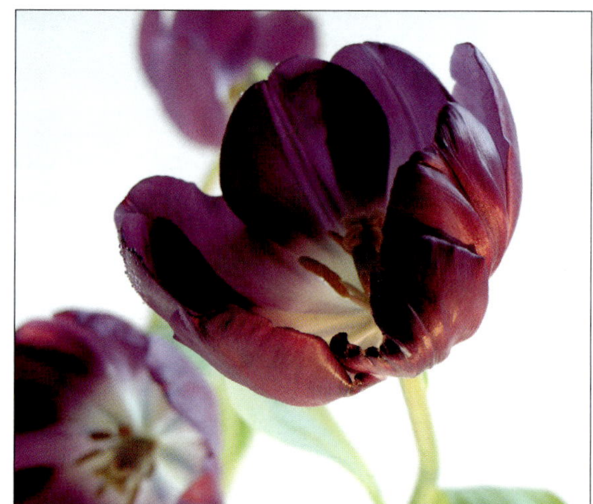

● JANE SMITH Simple tulips – an exercise in lighting and in using depth-of-focus to get an abstract feel, taken with an Olympus 8080.

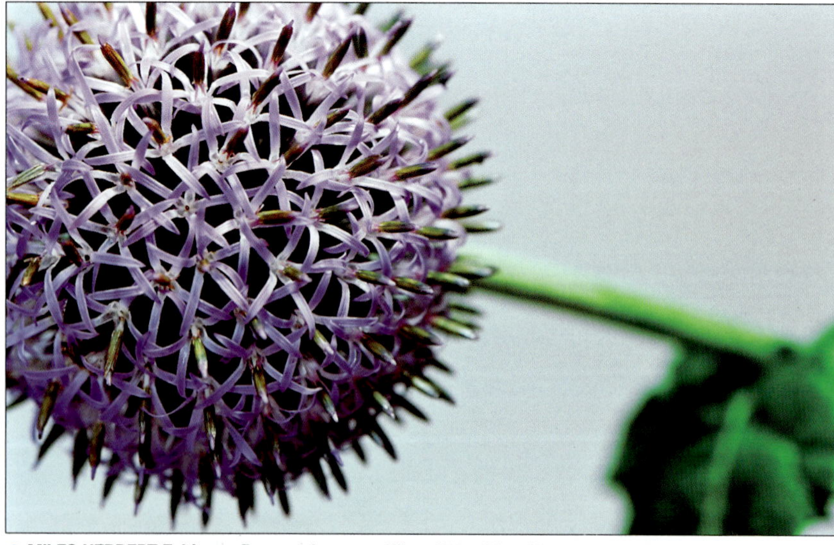

● MILES HERBERT Echinops flower, taken on a Nikon F80 with a Sigma 105mm Macro lens as an experiment to show depth-of-field. The image was shot on Kodak HD 200 film.

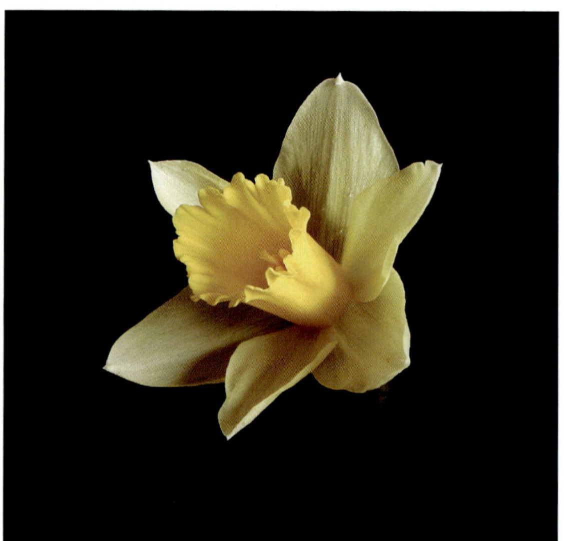

● SARAH BROOKE "First daffodil of the year in my garden, taken with a Canon EOS 300D, 18-55mm at f/22 and a 3.2secs exposure."

FLOWERS

Without doubt flower photography is one of the easiest subjects to attempt. You can shoot them indoors when the weather's bad or outdoors in gardens and parks. You don't need special equipment to fill the frame and the colours can make your photos super bright. But, like any form of photography, put your heart in it and your results will stand out from the crowd.

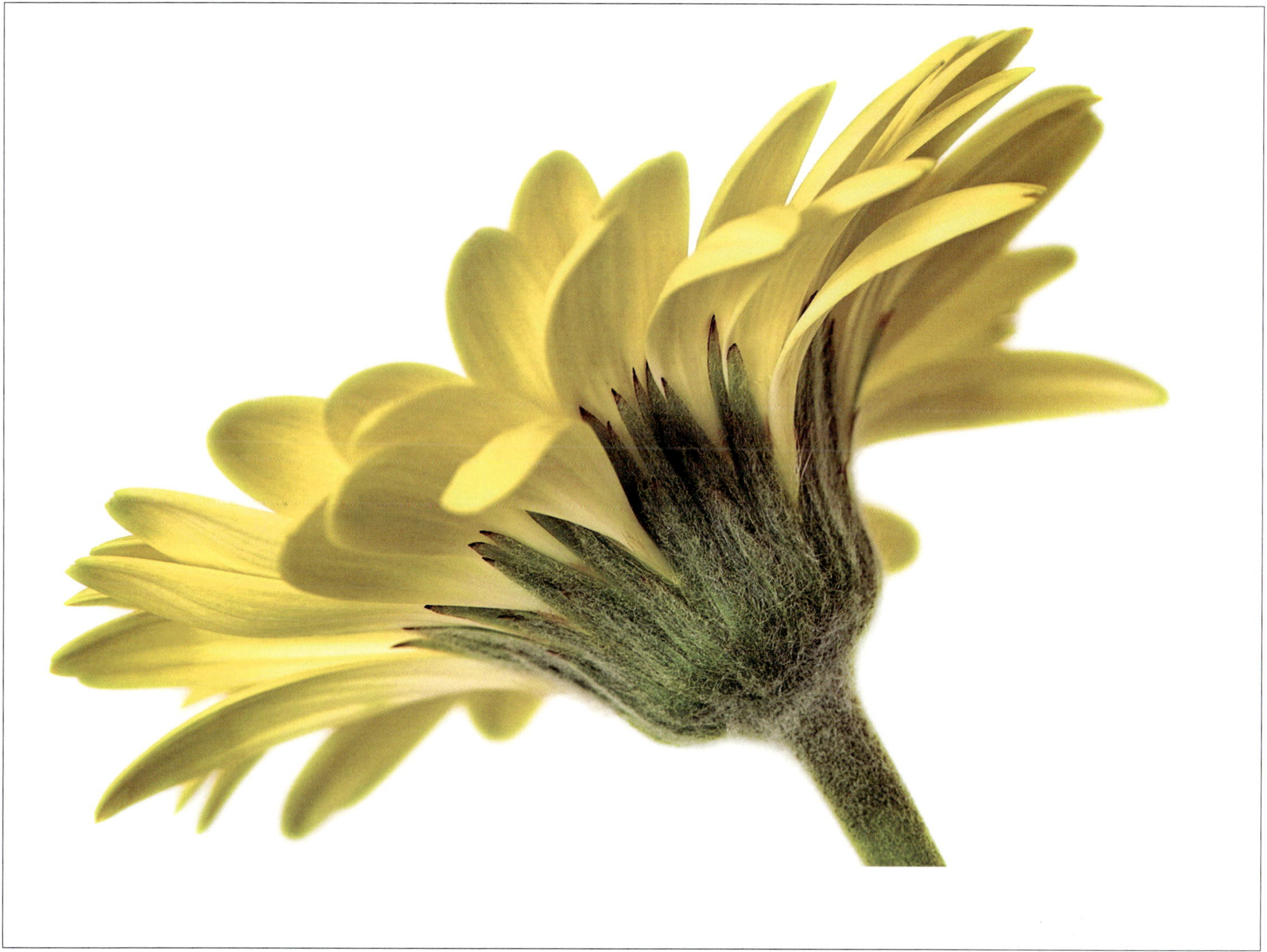

● **VINCE WARWICK A** softbox was used to obtain the subtle lighting on this flower, taken using a Sigma SD10 camera and 105mm f/2.8 Macro and ISO100.

Flower photography can be tried by anyone, with even the most basic camera kit. Nearly all compacts have a close focus feature that will allow you to fill the frame with the larger blooms, while the latest digital compacts with their 2-4cm focusing will let you tackle more minute specimens.

Most of us have a garden or window box to record the flowers we grow, while those who don't can visit the nearest supermarket buy a bunch and arrange them in a vase to get interesting shots. We also have access to thousands of parks and gardens, tended by horticulturists who have a knack of arranging the beds in colourful arrays, making prime subjects for our flower photography.

Venture into the wild and our landscape is a mass of pretty wild flowers, from the common dandelion to more rare species, like orchids. Seek and you shall find.

So, it's a common subject, but how you approach it will decide if your pictures are common or a little more unique. In this section of the book you'll find a wide variety of styles, techniques and ideas to help you take your flower photography to a new level.

We will explain how you can vary the background to add emphasis to the colours of flowers, show you a few digital techniques and suggest where you can go to find examples of specific flowers.

Don't expect to get the best without a little effort though. Like all aspects of photography nature has its way to hinder quality and technical issues can create problems too.

One of the main problems with outdoor flower photography is the wind. Even a gentle breeze can cause a flower to sway uncontrollably – anything stronger and you may as well pack up and go home. Well not quite: you can build a shield around the flower to block the wind, but you may not always have such devices to hand. Another issue is the sun. While the great ball of fire increases contrast and makes the colourful blooms vibrant, it plays havoc with the film or digital sensor causing areas in direct sunlight to have bright spots and shadow areas to go black. So you need to expose very carefully. It's much easier if you shoot on an overcast day. The colours may be more muted but the shot will often look far better.

Then there's nature taking its toll on the blooms. Look at a colourful bed of roses from a distance and you'll have a fine set of specimens, move closer and you may find those pretty flowers are actually ragged around the edges. Digital photographers have the benefit of being able to patch things up using the clone tool or healing brush to spot out the blemishes. Film photographers should walk around the bed and look for the tidiest bloom.

As well as the ideas in this book, have a look at books on growing plants to give you thoughts on the types of flowers you'd like to photograph. Plants are rarely imaginatively photographed in practical gardening books, but at least you'll know what varieties to look for and can start to think how you could do things more creatively. ■

SHOOTING RAW

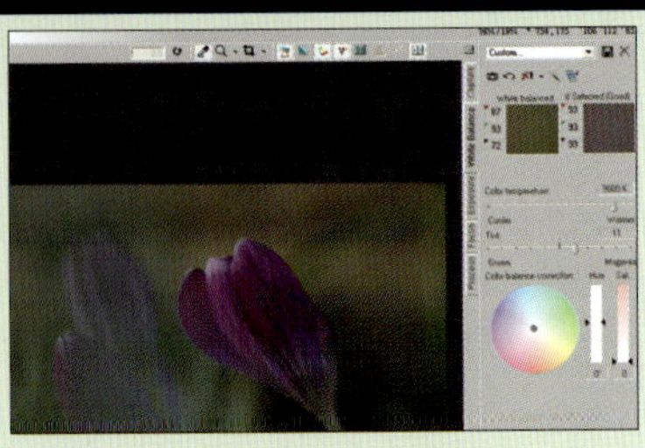

■ RAW is an option that appears on most digital SLRs and some advanced compacts. It's selected instead of Jpeg as a shooting option and when used it records the photograph as it was taken, without any in-camera processing that would take place when a Jpeg or tif file is shot.

■ RAW has the advantage of the user being able to convert the file in a RAW program, such as Adobe Camera RAW, Capture One or RAW Shooter. All these

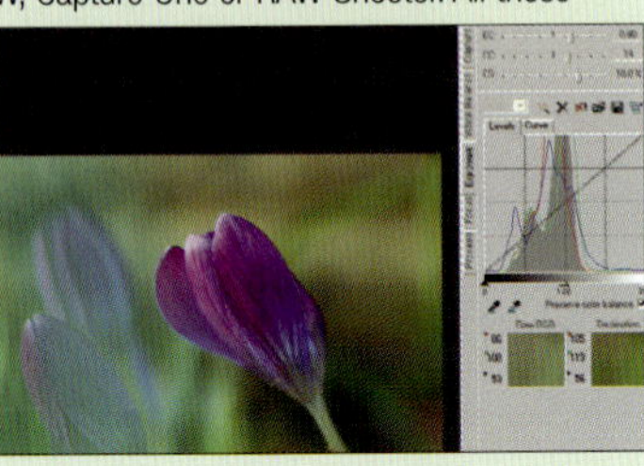

programs give you access to a range of controls to adjust criteria, such as contrast, sharpness, white balance, exposure and noise after the photograph has been taken and stored.

■ Doing it this way not only allows you to get the maximum quality out of a file but also allows you to create a photograph that has the right elements to

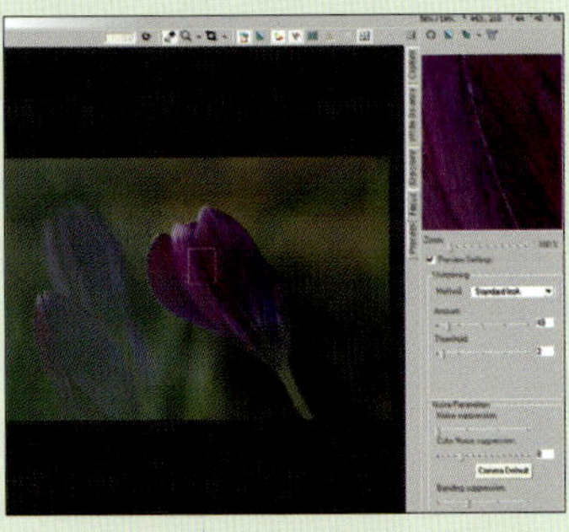

appeal to you, and not the camera's automated processing. It gives you much more flexibility and results are usually far better.

■ Some cameras' auto processing cannot cope with certain colours, bright red being one example, and as a result you get overly saturated tones. Shooting in RAW prevents this.

■ You can also find situations where you weren't sure of the exposure – using a RAW program lets you adjust this later, almost as well as you would have done using exposure compensation in camera.

■ For those who've processed films before, treat the RAW file as the exposed but undeveloped image. Where you would choose a developer and time combination to get a particular grain/contrast/sharpness for your processed negative, here you'd use RAW to do the same. The benefit with RAW over a negative is that your latent RAW image can be redeveloped as many times as you like, in as many ways as you like.

■ The main disadvantage with shooting in RAW is the file size is much bigger so you fill memory cards much quicker and you have to do the processing when you get back to the computer.

Capture One: www.phaseone.com
Raw Shooter: www.pixmantec.com
Camera Raw: www.adobe.com

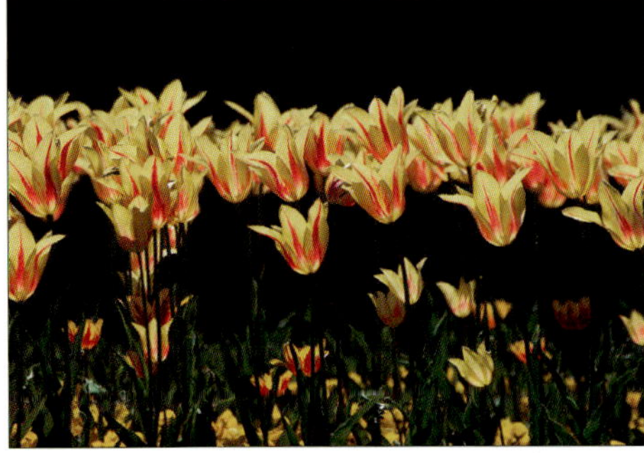

● ANDY FLOWERDAY A flower bed of backlit tulips with a backdrop of dark-green foliage in shadow. Taken with a Pentax Z-1P and Sigma 70-300mm on Fuji Astia 100.

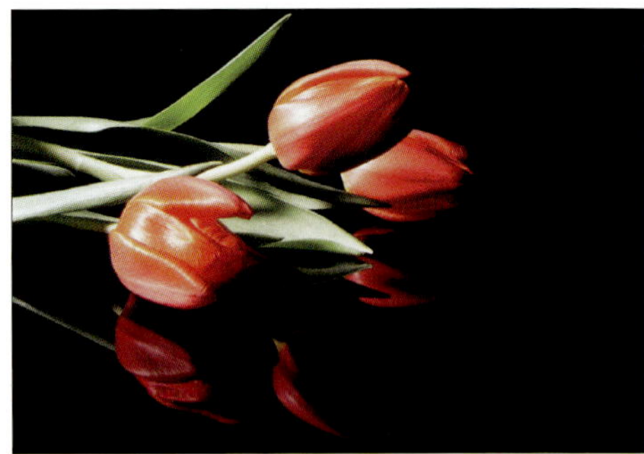

● FRANK THOMAS This photo was taken by placing the tulips on a black acrylic sheet which was lit from the left by a 320WS studio flash.

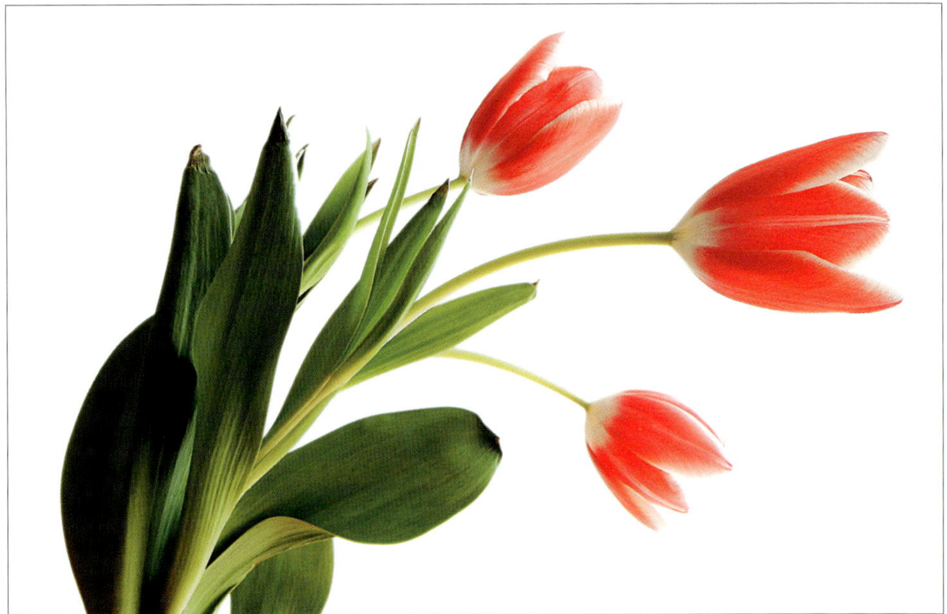

● IAN WALKER The flowers were back lit using a lamp and shot against a white card, using a Canon EOS 20D and a 17-40mm f/4L lens. The exposure was 1/6sec at f/8 with +1 exposure compensation to help create the glow effect.

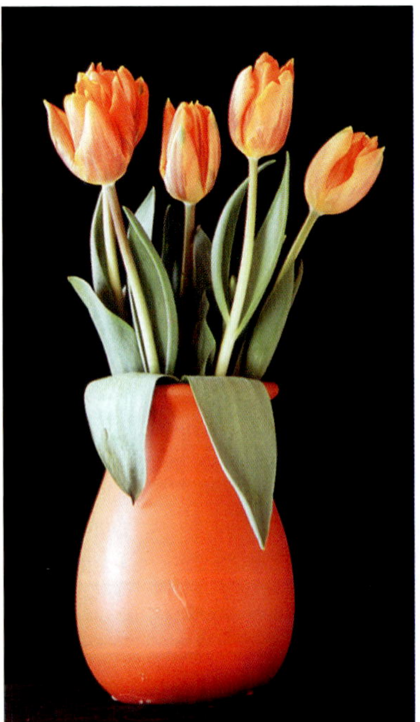

● CERI EVANS Velvet backdrop and Windowlight with home made reflector to bounce light back. Prakticamat with 50mm lens and 1sec at f/11.

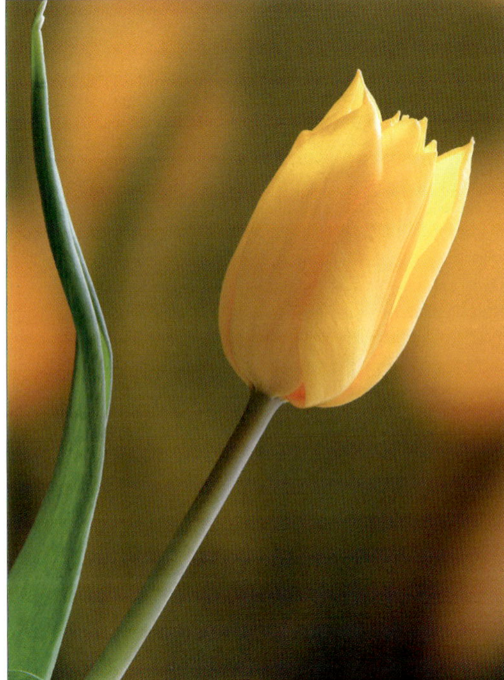

● JASON NEWELL Two shots of cut flowers were combined digitally in Photoshop to emulate a field of Tulips in spring.

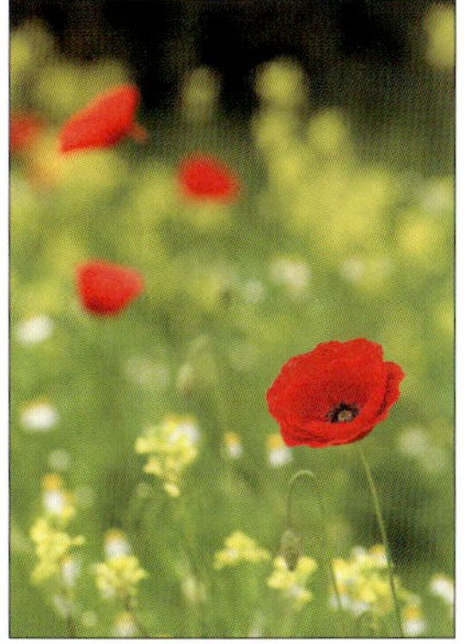

● HELEN DIXON Wild poppies taken along the roadside, using a Canon EOS 10D at 1/30sec.

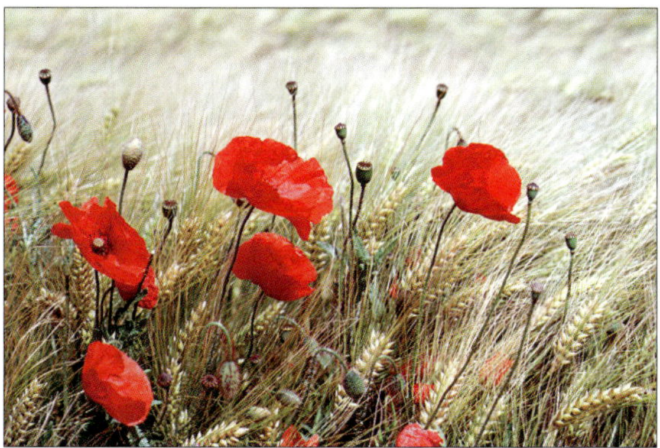

● IAN OLIVER One of those unplanned shots that was taken hand-held on a Canon AE-1. It was a windy day so there's some movement in background crops.

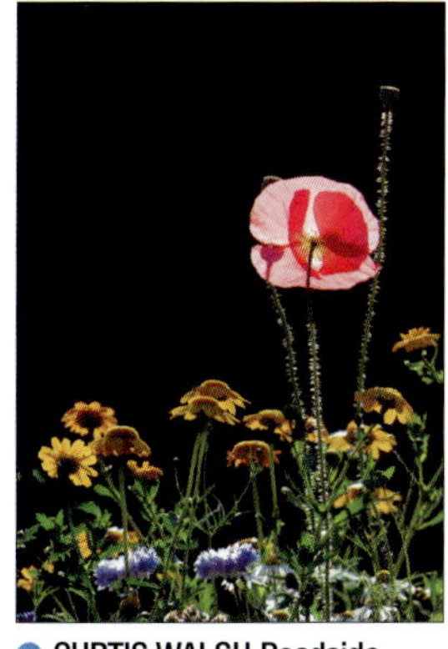

● CURTIS WALSH Roadside colour in a wild flower bed at Earlston in the Scottish Borders.

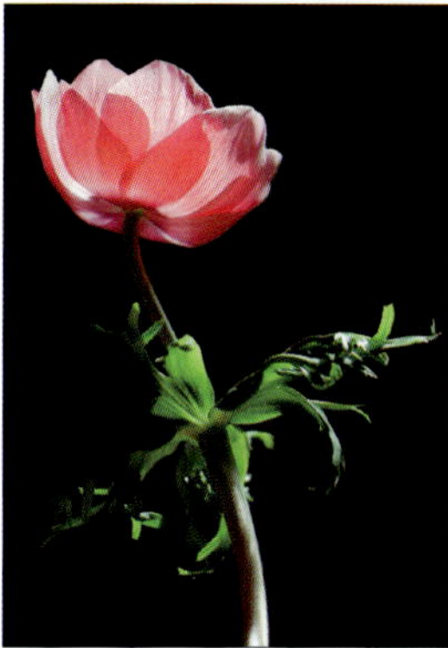

● SAM BASSAN The anemone was placed by a window and lit by natural evening light.

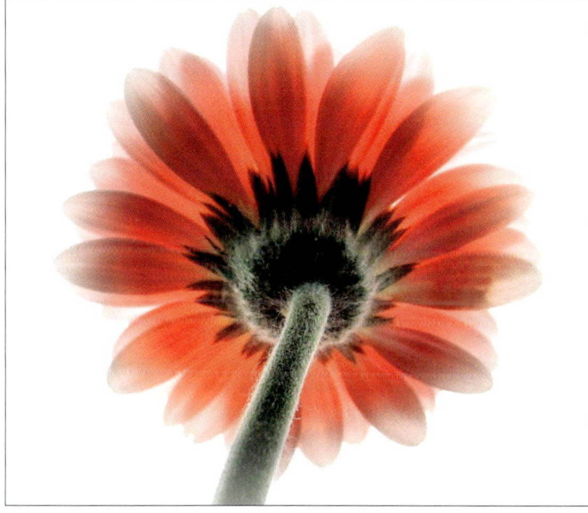

● LINDA PELLING "This gerbera was illuminated from below using a lightbox. I wanted something a little different with the back view."

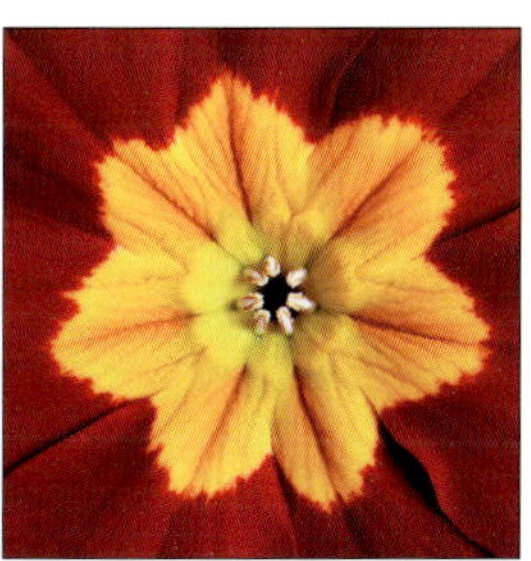

● JUSTIN COWTAN "I liked the near symmetrical composition." Canon 10D and Tamron 90mm.

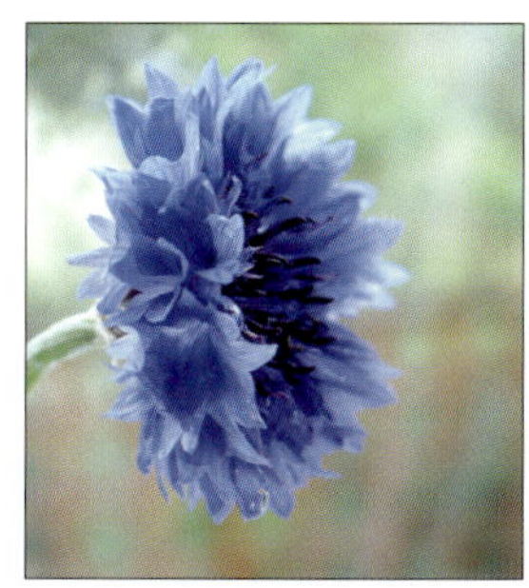

● MARGARET BARTON Cornflower shot in profile.

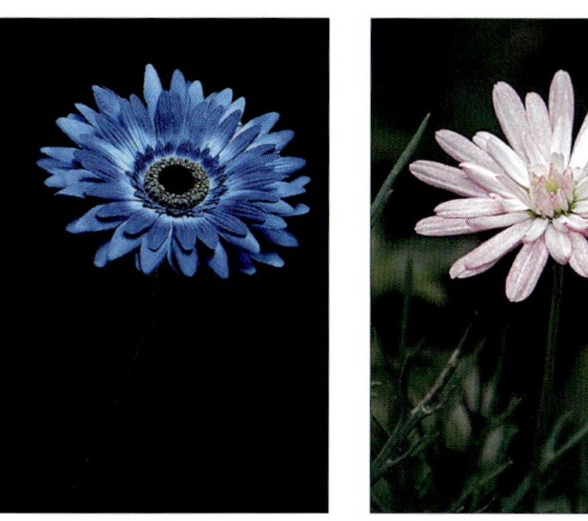

● DEREK STEIN "My entry for a competition at Musselburgh Camera Club, using a Fuji S602."

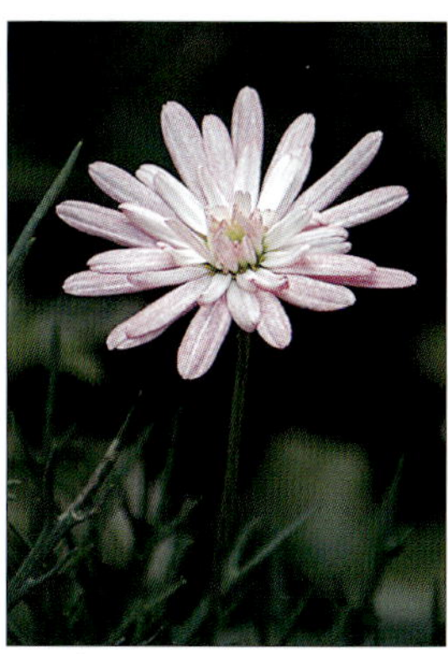

● KEN FOWLER The aperture was set to f/5.6 so it rendered the background out of focus.

DIGITAL TECHNIQUE – PHOTOSHOP LIGHTING FILTER

■ One of Photoshop's hidden secrets can be found in the filter menu Filters>Render>Lighting Effects. This handy filter lets you simulate various forms of light, from spotlight to tungsten. There's plenty of choice so it's a case of picking a suitable image and dragging the various slider while watching the preview to see the effect being applied. If you don't like the result, select undo (Ctrl+U) or click on the previous History state. Almost any lighting effect is possible using this filter on any kind of subject. Landscapes, portraits and interiors provide plenty of scope but really fun stuff can also be done with flowers.

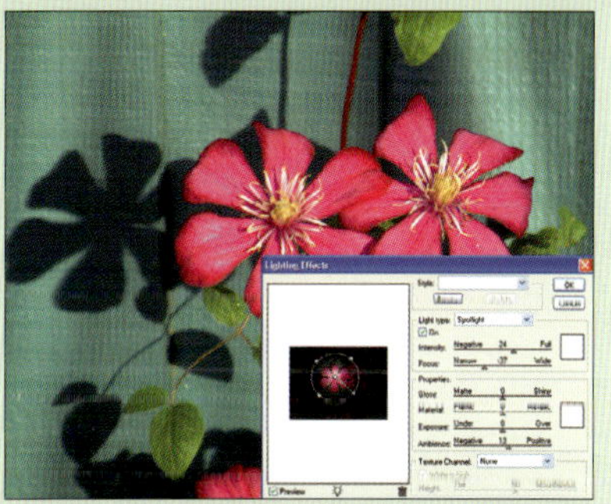

■ There are several Adobe presets already in the Style menu, but using the default and creating your own is where the fun starts.

■ To do this, select Omni, Spotlight or Directional from the Light type drop down menu. Then pick a colour by clicking on the square to the right and choosing from the colour picker.

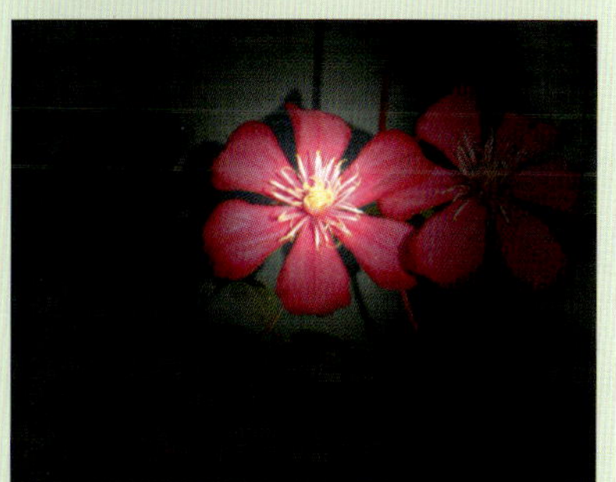

■ The Intensity slider controls the brightness of the light. Moving towards Full simulates bright sunlight style effects, while dragging towards Negative makes the appearance darker and more like moonlight.

■ The Properties controls adjust the lighting so it emulates real life objects and how they appear with light. Gloss makes the object's surface reflectivity low when you slide left towards Matte or high towards Glossy.

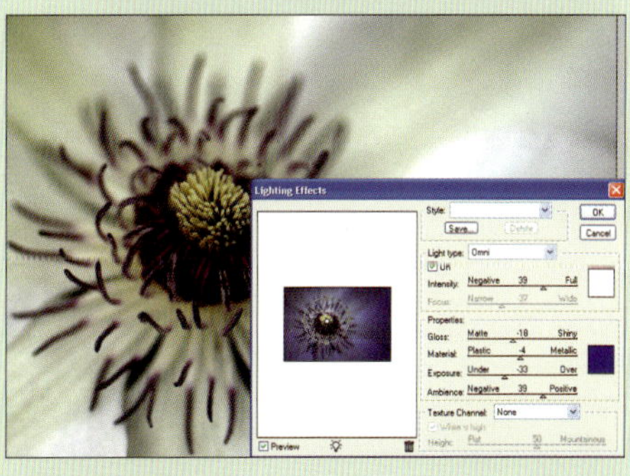

■ Material controls whether the light or object reflect more light. Plastic reflects the light's colour and Metallic reflects the object's colour.

■ Exposure works like a camera – over exposure increases the intensity of light and under exposure decreases the light. There's no effect at 0.

■ Ambience adjusts the balance of the light with a background lighting colour that you select by clicking on the colour square. A 100 value puts full emphasis on the light source while a −100 value removes the light source. Values between these create an interesting balance of the property and light colours.

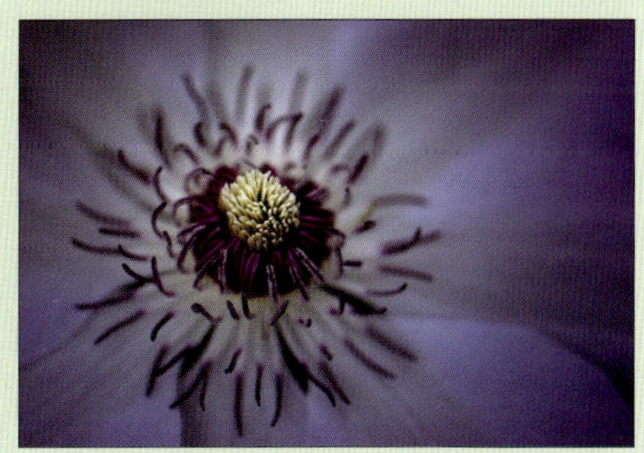

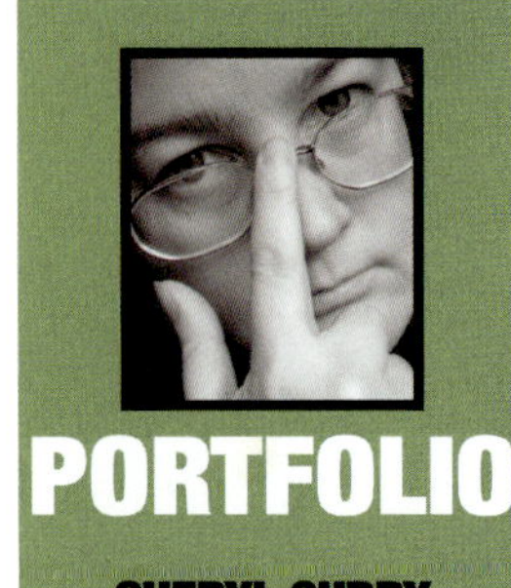

PORTFOLIO

CHERYL SURRY
A photographer happy to turn her attention to any subject, Cheryl likes nothing more than to experiment.

I have been interested in photography for the last 20 years on and off, but only began to get serious about it during the last three. In this time many other hobbies have come and gone, but I have always found myself returning to photography.

My favourite subject is anything in the world of nature, though I will generally try my hand at most subjects (landscape being my weakest area). A key feature of my work is experimentation and I am always on the look out for a different angle to photograph from, or a new perspective from which to approach an old subject.

For anyone who is interested in this, or any other type of photography, my tip is do not be afraid to experiment. There are no 'wrong' results and only you will know if the photograph does not turn out as you intended.

Experimenting is easier when shooting with a digital camera as for film users the cost issue can be prohibitive to extensive experimentation. However, it is not impossible – get the shot that you are happy with first and then try a little experimenting. Try a new angle, a wider aperture - it is surprising what you can achieve by utilising this simple principle.

Another useful piece of advice I would offer is to get to know your equipment, which will allow you to use it to its full potential. If you are using digital also get to know your post-shooting workflow. Try and keep changes to your workflow to a minimum – this will reduce the time you need to spend sat at the computer and allow you to maximise the time you can spend behind the camera. ∎

www.cherylsurry.com

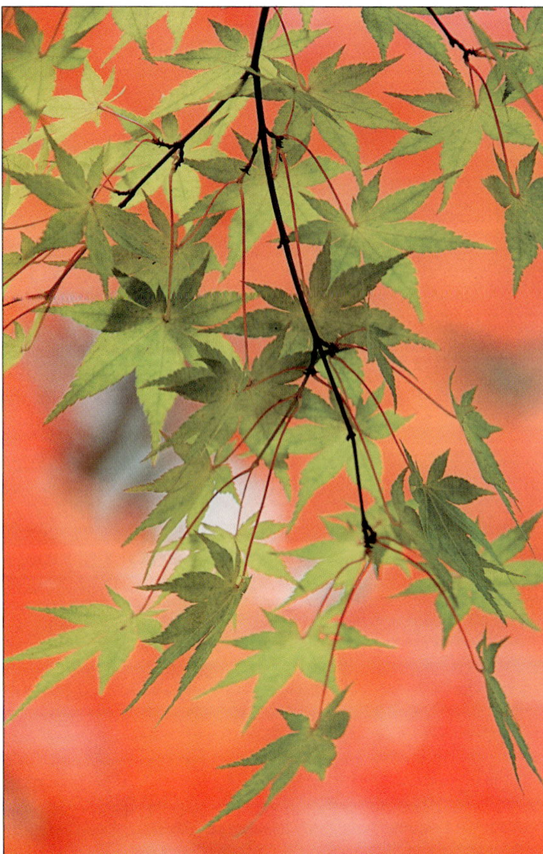

● A study of colour contrasts in Autumn foliage, taken at Westonbirt, using a Nikon D100 and 24-120mm lens. Orange and green work well together to create a fusion of vivid colour.

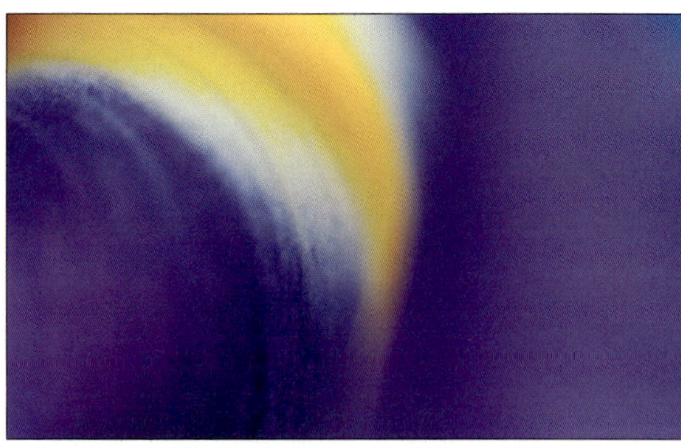

● The Nikon D100 was used with a 60mm Micro Nikkor lens to take this Iris. The idea was to isolate the colours from the petal to create an abstract where no point is actually in focus.

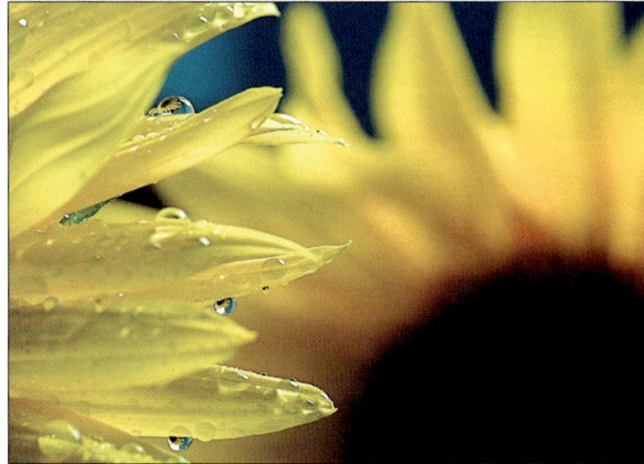

● A reflection of the rear sunflower is caught in water droplets taken on a Nikon D100 with a 60mm Micro Nikkor lens set at a wide aperture to throw the background sunflower out of focus.

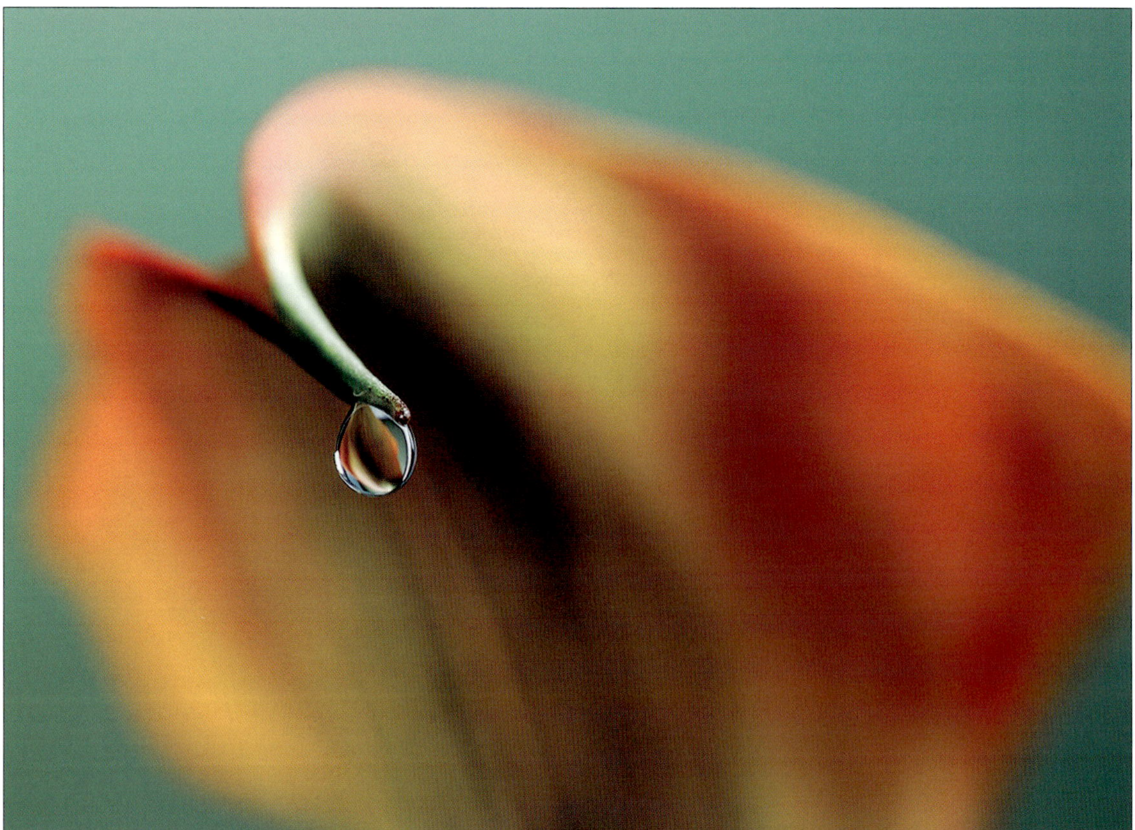

● I was experimenting with extremely limited depth-of-field when taking the dew drop on the tip of this Calla Lily (Zantedeschia). By setting a wide aperture and making a precise selection of the focusing point it's possible to create stunning abstracts with diffused colours. Notice the lily is reflected in the droplet, which is acting like a lens.

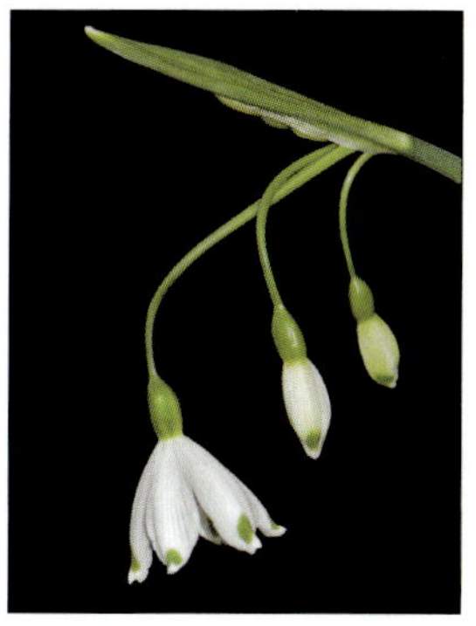

● KAREN BACON Snowdrops against dark background.

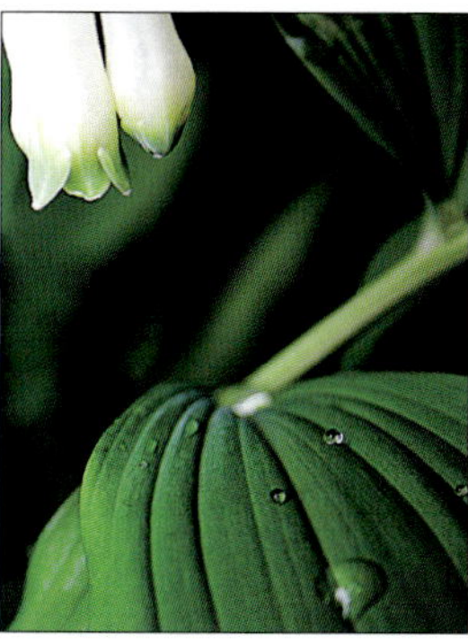

● MARI STERLING "I laid flat to get this parallel perspective."

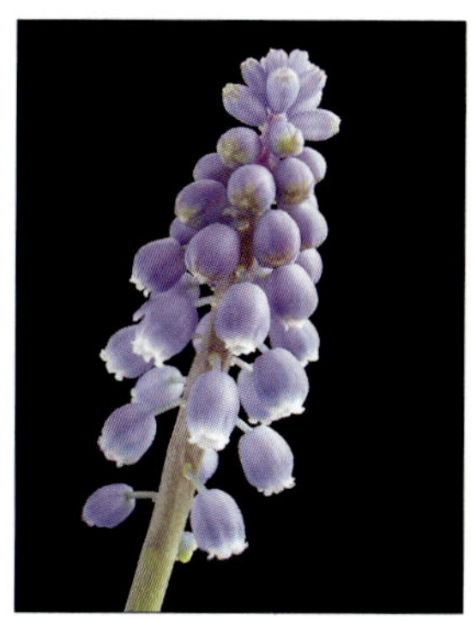

● CHRIS GEORG Grape Hyacinth lit by large diffused window.

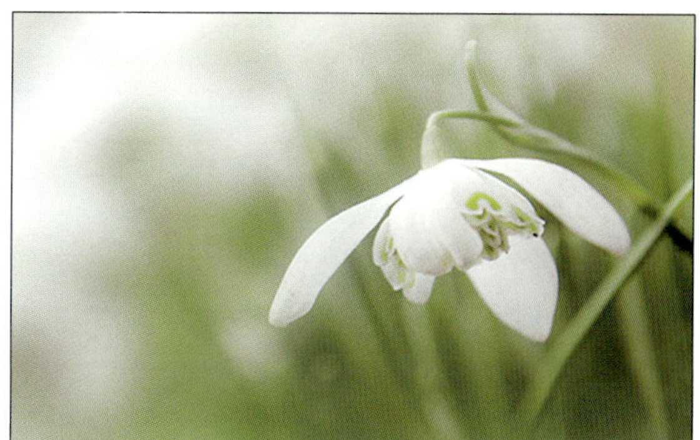

● PETER BARGH This snowdrop had many more in the background, so I used heavy Gaussian blur to simulate shallow depth-of-field.

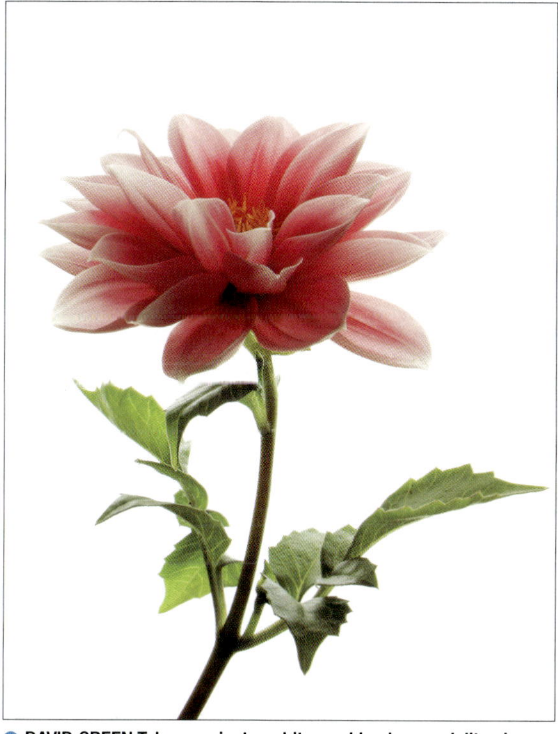

● DAVID GREEN Taken against a white card background, lit using a studio flash with a softbox for soft illumination.

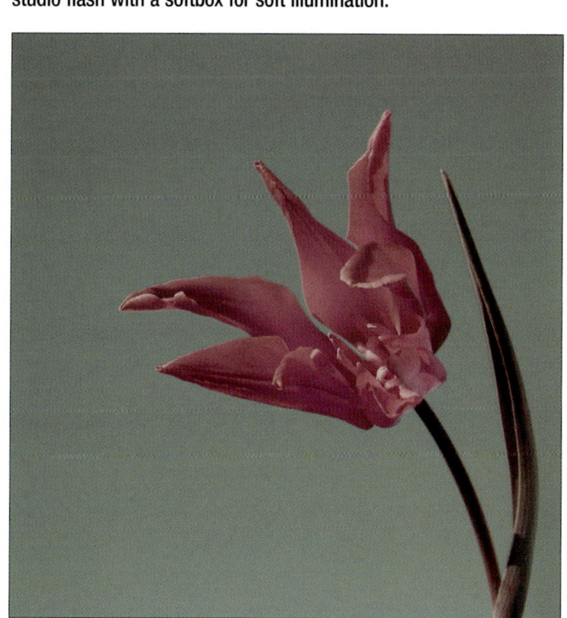

● COENRAAD HEIJDEMANN Orange tulip, hand-held against a clear sky. Captured with a Canon EOS 300D and 18-55mm lens.

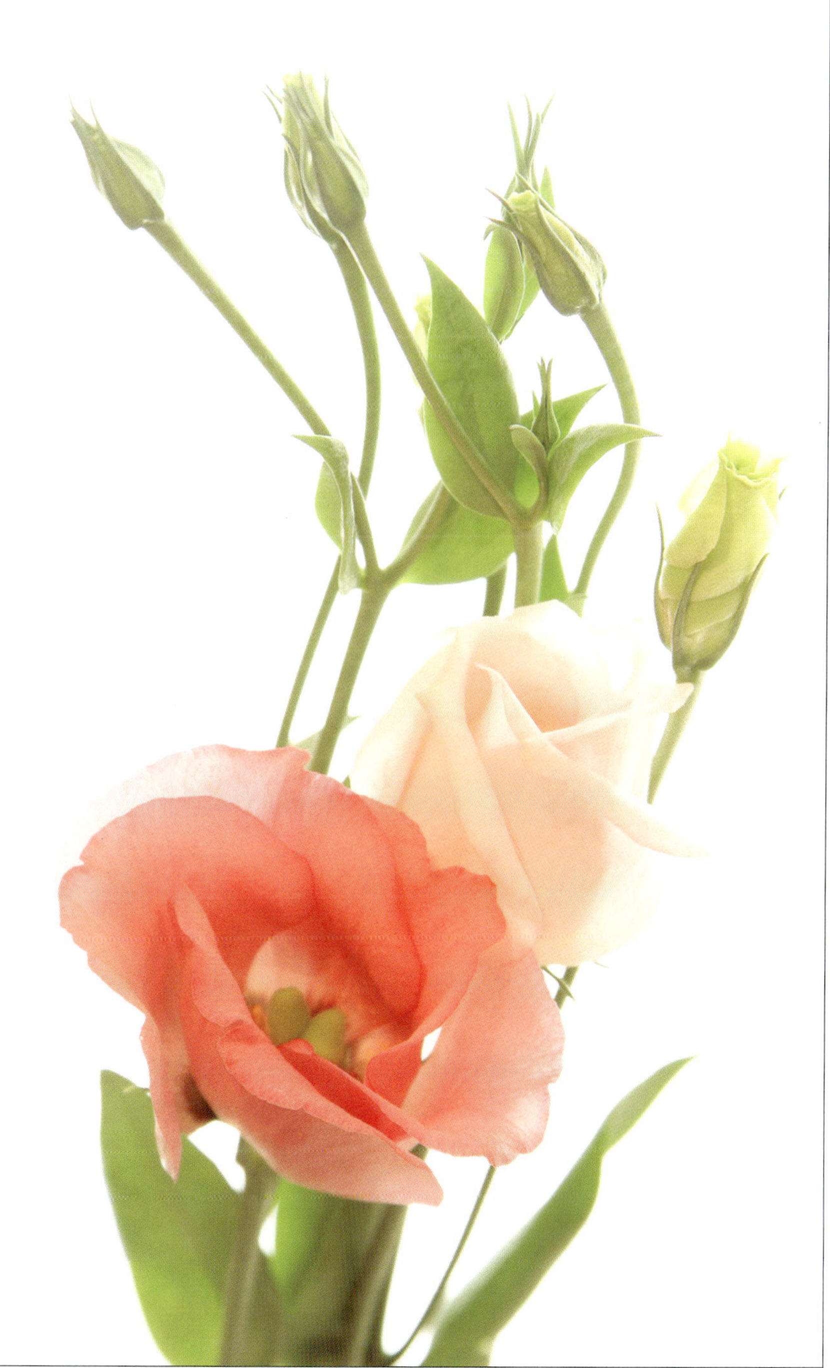

● EWAN STEVENSON Lisianthus using a lamp held quite close to the lens caused flare which reduced the contrast, giving the soft effect against a white background.

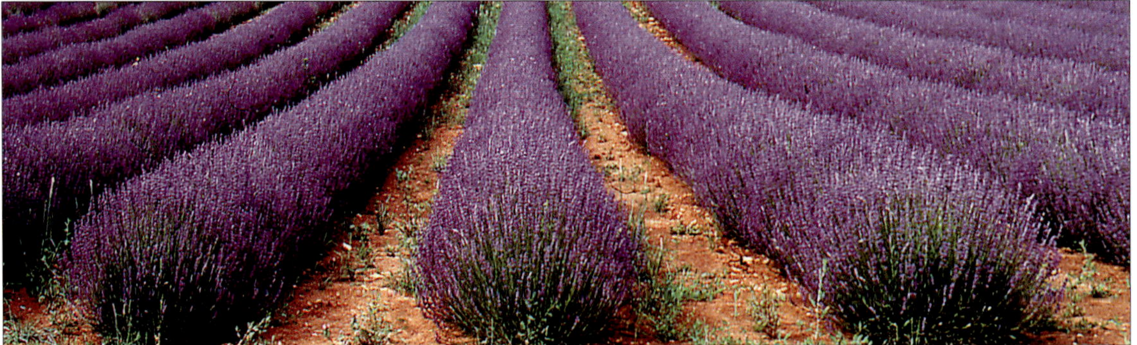

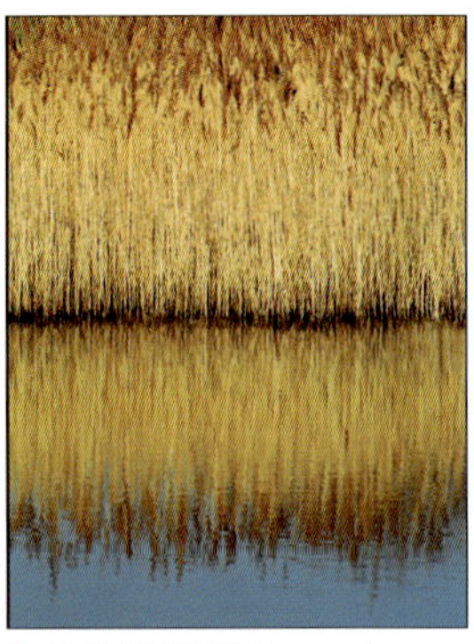

● PAUL HOFFMAN Hidcote Lavender taken at Snowshill Lavender fields in the Cotswolds. The image was cropped to gain the panoramic shape, which suits the colourful rows. Try cropping your landscapes too – it's amazing what the letter box format can do.

● GEOFF BAKER Taken at Cardiff Bay on a Dynax 7D.

SHOOTING TIPS – GARDEN AND FLOWER SHOWS

Flower shows
■ The Chelsea Flower Show May. Tel: 020 76491885 (Recorded information line) www.rhs.org.uk
■ Harrogate Flower Shows, 4a South Park Road, Harrogate, North Yorkshire HG1 5QU. Tel: 01423 561049
www.flowershow.org.uk
Spring Flower Show, end of April Autumn Flower Show, mid September

Gardens
Royal Horticultural Society Gardens www.rhs.org.uk
■ Wisley, Woking, Surrey GU23 6QB. Tel: 01483 224234
■ Harlow Carr, Crag Lane, Harrogate North Yorkshire HG3 1QB. Tel: 01423 565418
■ Hyde Hall, Rettendon, Chelmsford, Essex CM3 8ET. Tel: 01245 400256
■ Rosemoor, Great Torrington, North Devon EX38 8PH. Tel: 01805 624067.

Royal Botanic Gardens www.rbgkew.org.uk
■ Kew, Richmond, Surrey TW9 3AB.
■ Wakehurst Place, Ardingly, Nr. Haywards Heath, West Sussex RH17 6TN.

Birmingham Botanical Gardens & Glasshouses, Westbourne Road, Edgbaston, Birmingham B15 3TR. Tel: 0121 4541860. **www.birminghambotanicalgardens.org.uk**

The National Botanic Garden of Wales, Llanarthne, Carmarthenshire SA32 8HG. Tel: 01558 668768. **www.gardenofwales.org.uk**

Westonbirt, The National Arboretum, Tetbury, Gloucestershire GL8 8QS. Tel: 01666 880220 **www.forestry.gov.uk/forestry/infd-5y4f5k**

Bedgebury, The National Pinetum, Park Lane, Goudhurst, Kent TN17 2SL. Tel: 01580 211781 **www.forestry.gov.uk/website/oldsite.nsf/byunique/infd-5y7hy6**

English Heritage Gardens www.english-heritage.org.uk. Tel 0870 3331181
■ Audley End House & Gardens, Essex
■ Kenwood House, London
■ Mount Grace Priory, North Yorkshire
■ Brodsworth Hall & Gardens, South Yorkshire
■ Kirby Hall, Northamptonshire
■ Walmer Castle & Gardens, Kent

Places to find snowdrops
Rococo gardens, Painswick, near Stroud, Gloucestershire.
Hodsock Priory, Blyth, near Nottingham
Hopton Hall, Derbyshire
Anglesea Abbey, Cambridgeshire

Places to find bluebells
Emmetts Gardens, near Westerham in Kent
Hodsock Priory, Blyth, near Nottingham
Bedelands Nature Reserve, Mid Sussex
Hambleden Estate, near Marlow, Oxon
Cwm Pennant in Snowdonia
Skomer Island
Bowdown Woods, Greenham Common
Moors Copse, near Theale
Rococo gardens, Painswick, near Stroude
Goblin Coombe at Cleeve
Blaise Castle, Forest of Avon

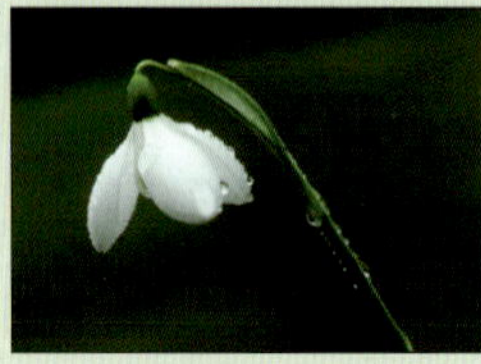

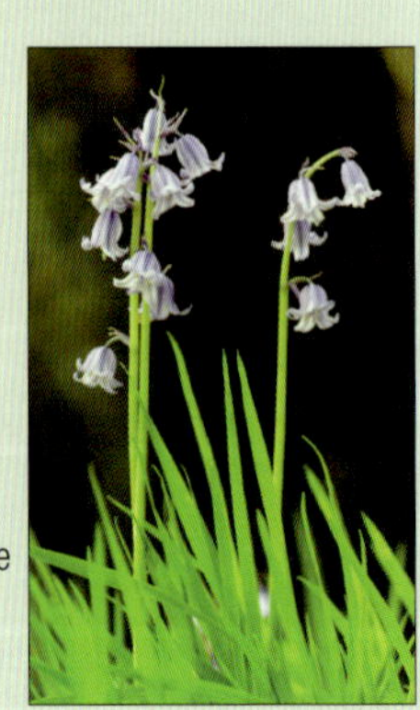

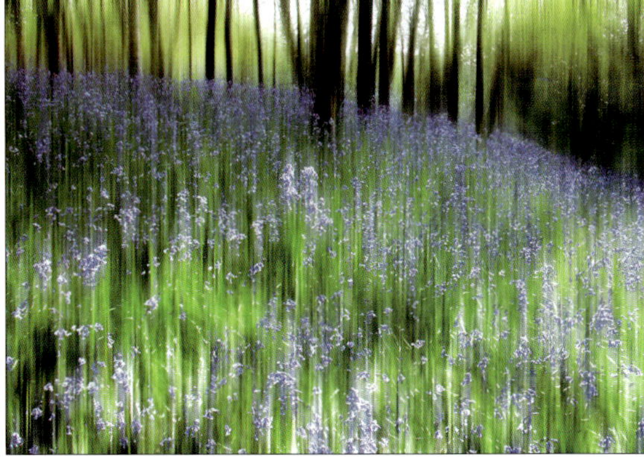

● CHRIS MOLE Bluebells taken at Heaven Farm in Danehill, Sussex. A touch of motion blur has created the vertical streaks.

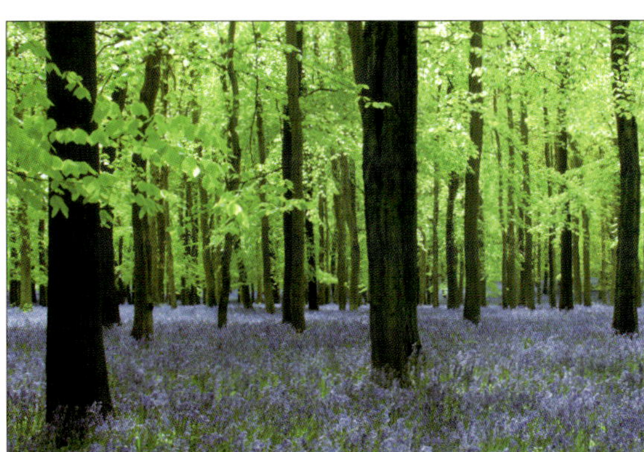

● MICHAEL BRACE This was taken in Spring Wood on Ashridge Common, Hertfordshire, using an Olympus E20 mounted on a tripod with an exposure of 1/5sec at f/10 and ISO80.

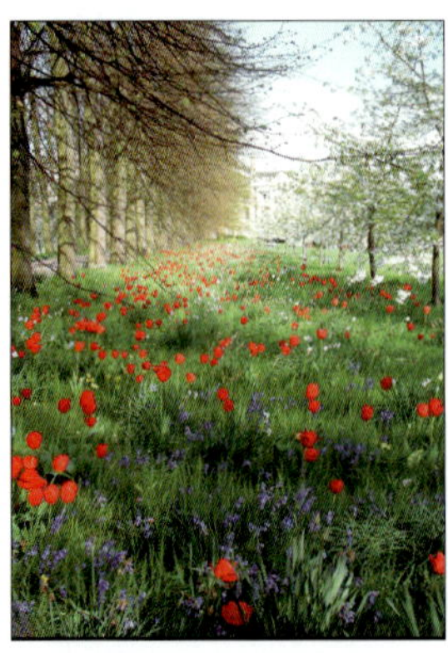

● CHRIS GIRLING Taken at the 'Backs' of the Cambridge Colleges on a Fuji S602Z. Levels were tweaked in Photoshop.

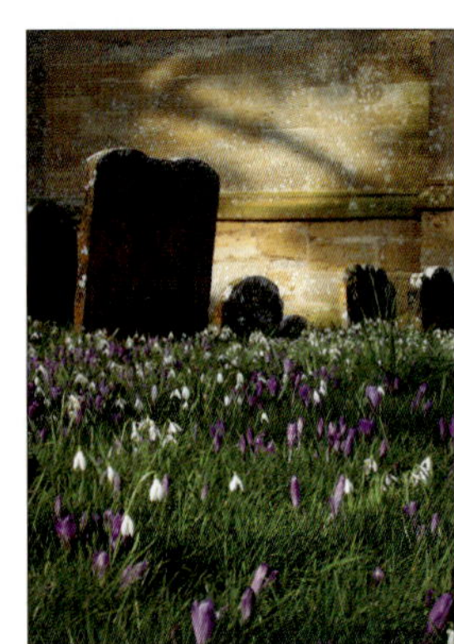

● WILL BREALEY Spring at Birlingham."To ensure the crocuses and sunlit wall were sharp I set a small aperture."

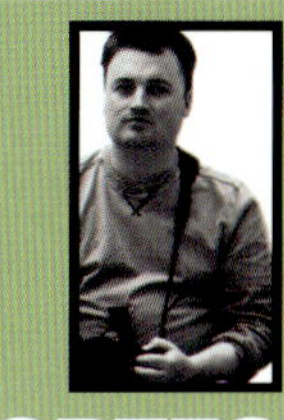

PORTFOLIO

EDWARD NORTON

Edward dreams of becoming the next Colin Prior, and can still be found snapping away in the Surrey wilderness.

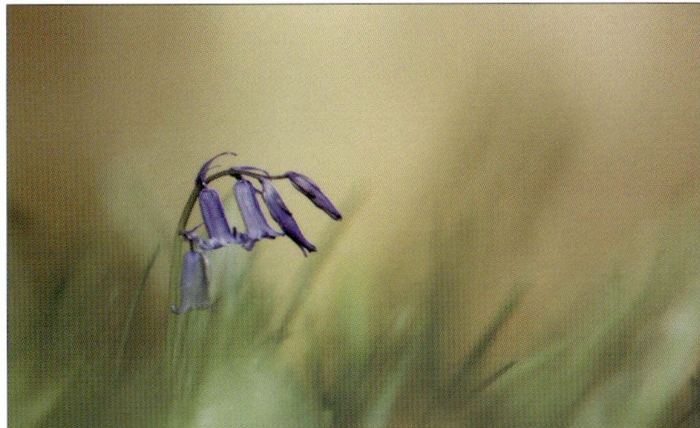

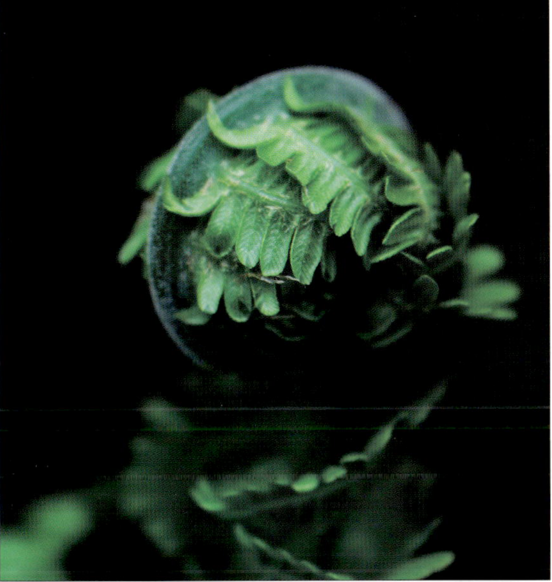

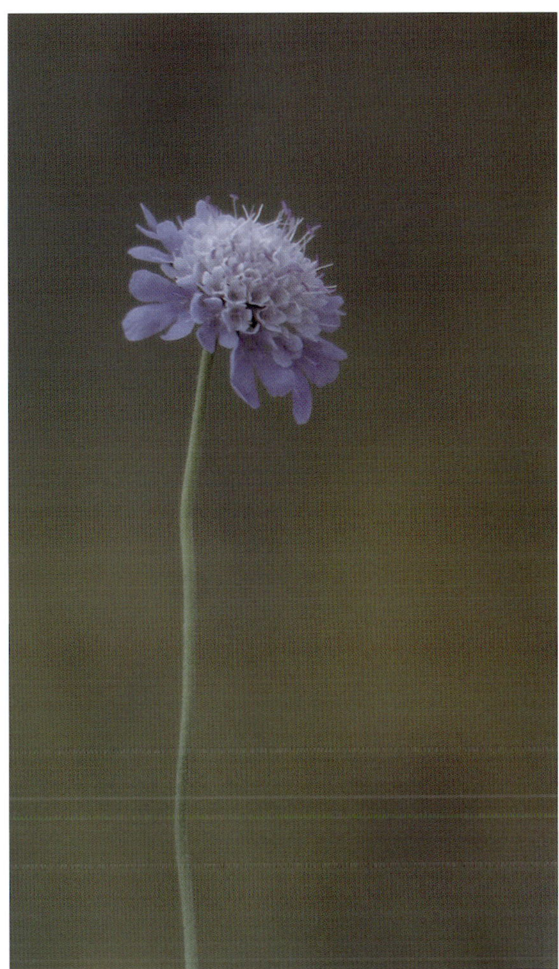

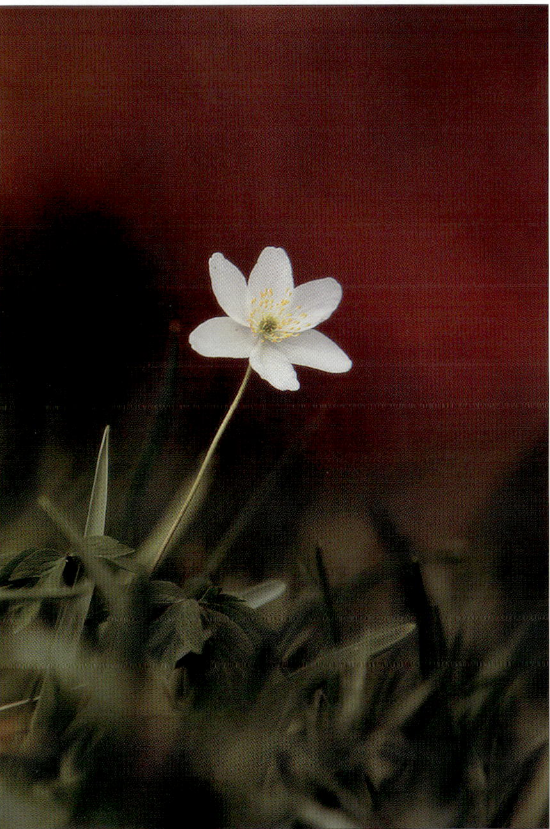

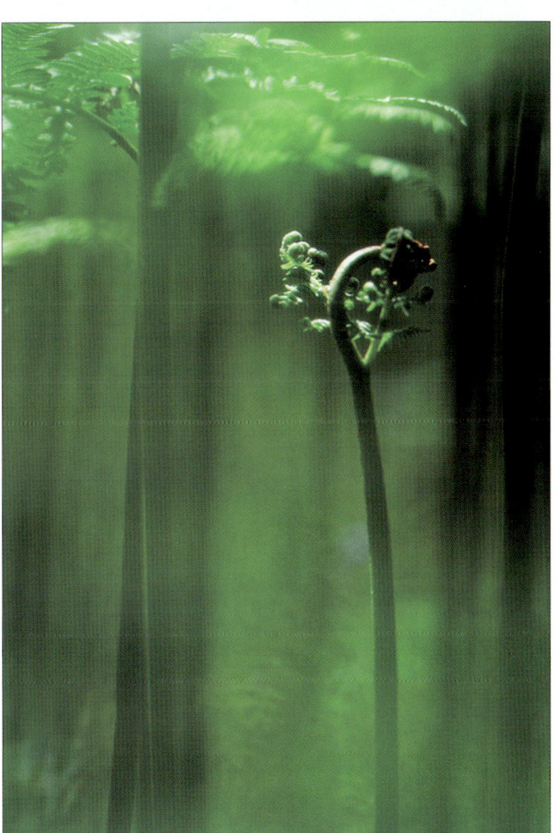

My childhood is full of photographic memories: standing in the Verona traffic aged 11, trying to fill the frame with the Colosseum, marvelling at the split prism of an OM10 and my uncle's heavy black Nikons.

In my twenties I dreamed of being the next Colin Prior and eventually bought an SLR as I approached 30. I went digital after my son was born, buying a compact to keep family and friends updated. I loved the freedom of using digital but missed the functionality of the SLR.

After Canon released an affordable DSLR my dream returned to landscapes and a possible career. Then I discovered ePHOTOzine and my view of photography changed forever. I had no idea how little I knew!

For the past two years I've immersed myself in photography, devoting most of my free time and money to it. My passion is macro photography and photography that isolates the subject. I'm lucky in that where I live in Surrey, geology has created many wonderful micro-habitats from sandy heath to chalk hills and clay bogs.

These images all use very narrow depth-of-field to isolate the subject. I use either a macro lens close to my subject or a longer lens to isolate the subject from its background.

A beanbag, groundsheet and angled eyepiece help me get low to the ground with a degree of comfort and I occasionally use filters, tripod or flash. I like to work quickly as I find if I have time to think I often don't get the shot. This works well for me and very often the first shot I take is the keeper. ■

● This selection of photos demonstrate Edward's love of using longer lenses with a wide aperture to throw his backgrounds totally out of focus, allowing our eye to rest on the main subject of the photographs. The bluebells, top left, were his first attempt at this technique.

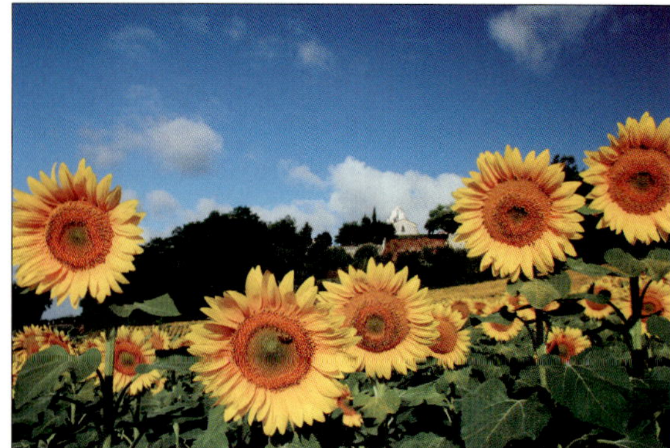

● JEANETTE LAZENBY Taken at 9am near Monsegur, Bordeaux, with a polariser on a Canon EOS 300D and a 1/250sec at f/10 exposure.

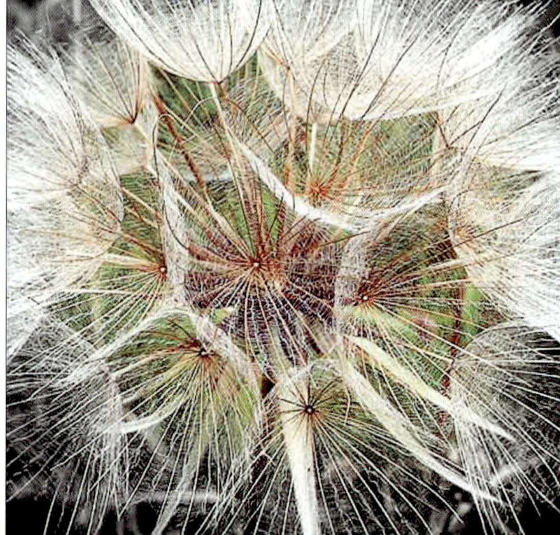

● TONY HUMPHREYS Background duplicated and made black & white. Then a layer mask was used to bring back areas of colour.

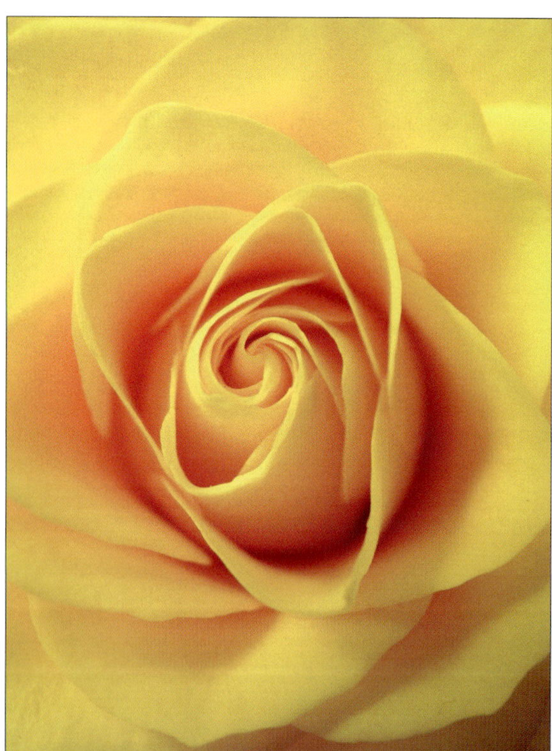

● LUCY BIRNIE Petals provide great abstracts when tightly cropped. Taken in daylight with a Canon EOS 20D and 100mm Macro lens.

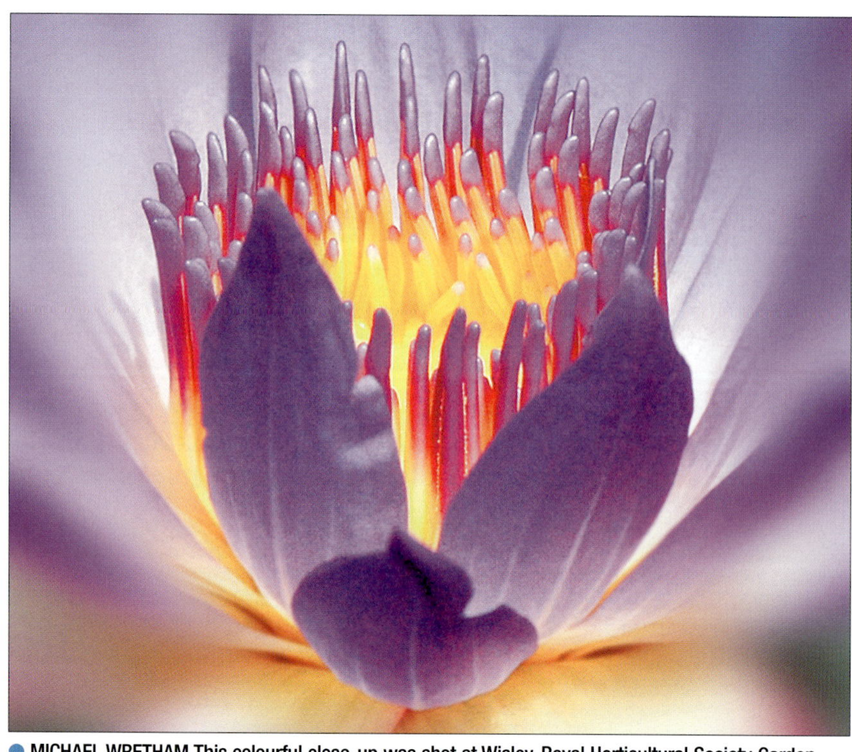

● MICHAEL WRETHAM This colourful close-up was shot at Wisley, Royal Horticultural Society Garden, using a Nikon D70 with a Nikon 18-70 zoom lens.

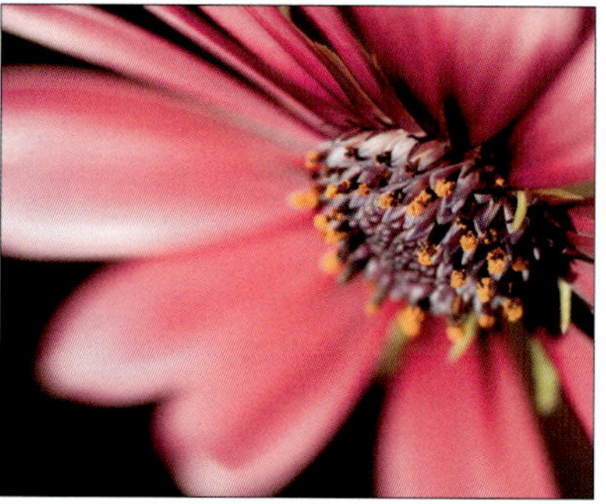

● MICHAEL WILSON An interesting angle and crop, using a Nikon D70 with 70-300mm zoom.

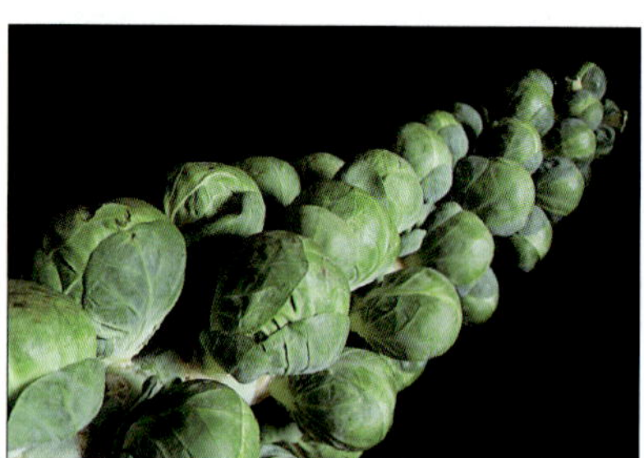

● ANGELA SANDERSON Taken using a Canon Powershot A70. Burn tool darkened background.

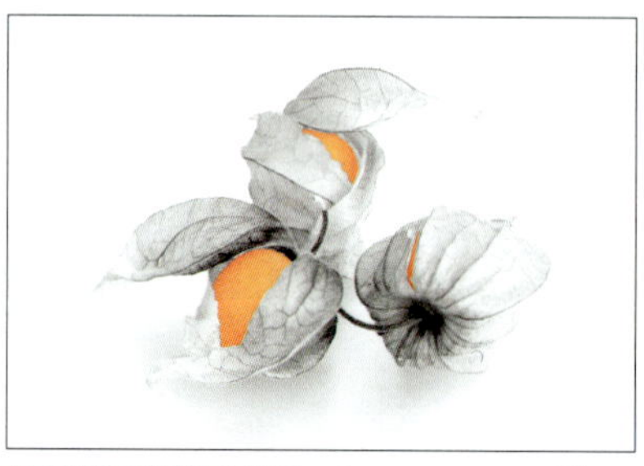

● ANDREW FINDLAY Two layers were used in Photoshop; one colour, the other black & white.

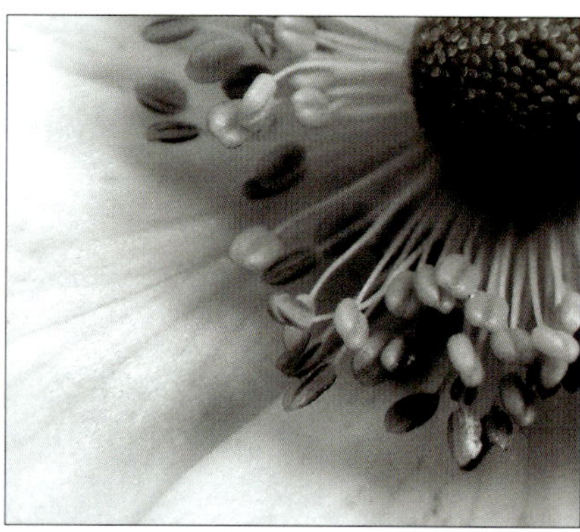

● FUNKELDINK Tight crop and converted to black & white for a different take on flower photography.

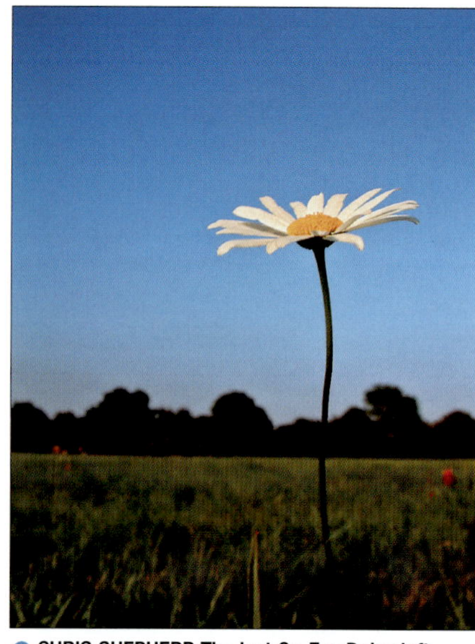

● CHRIS SHEPHERD The last Ox-Eye Daisy left standing in Roding Valley at the end of summer.

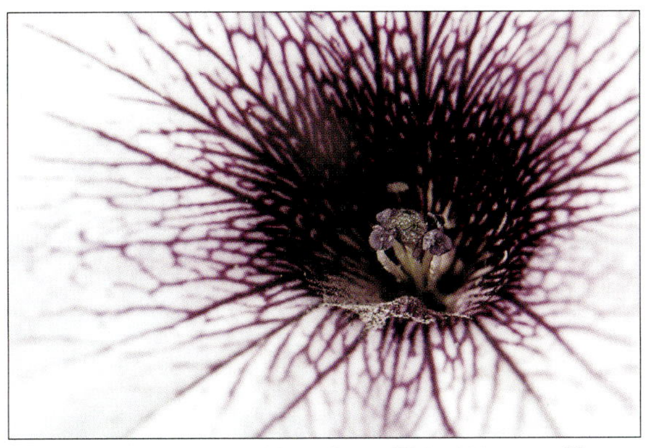

● RICHARD NIXON Canon EOS 10, Canon EF 35-105 zoom with extension tubes, Kodak Elitechrome 100. Taken under natural light.

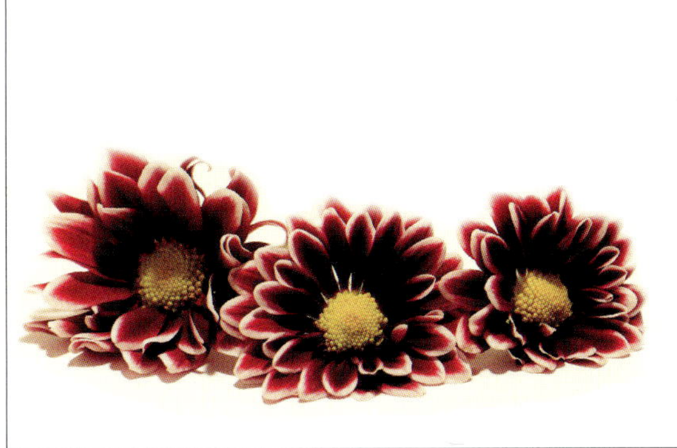

● NIAMH BALDOCK Taken using simple desk lamps projected through white muslin.

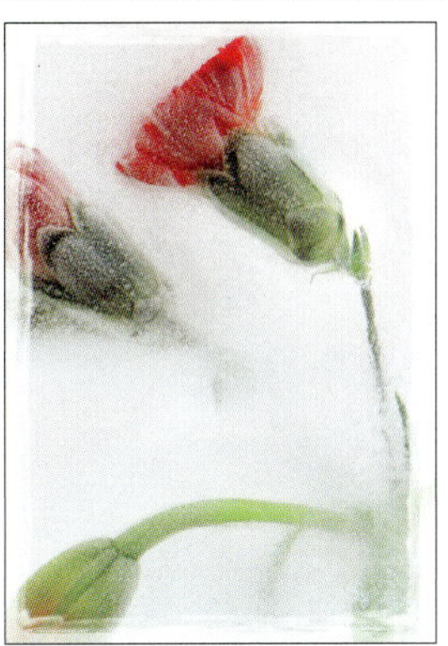

● STEVE LE PREVOST Frozen in a glass dish overnight.

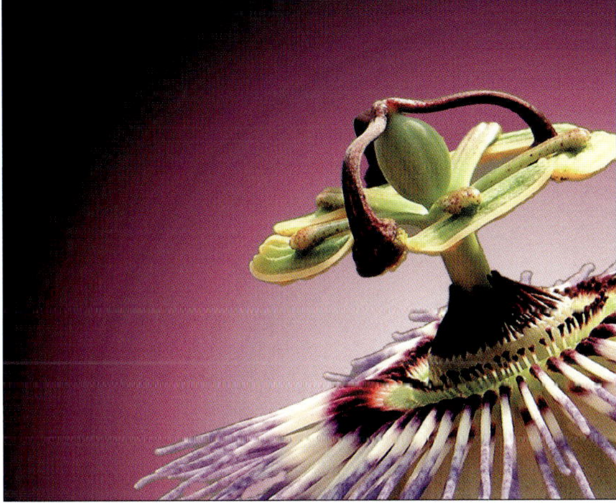

● ALAN MITCHELL Taken using a Fuji S7000 in macro mode with a white background so a colourful one could be added in Photoshop.

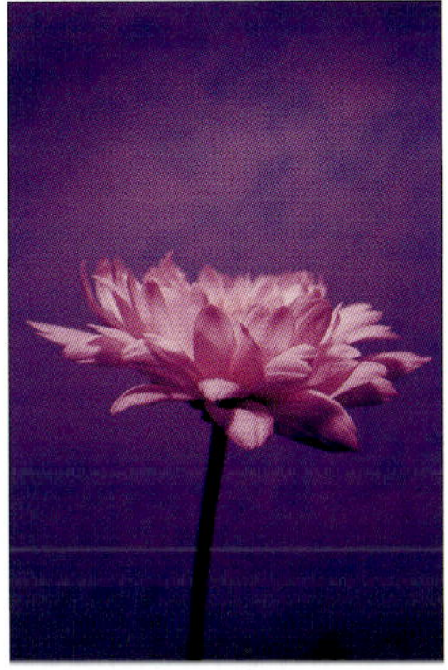

● BARBARA WILCOX Taken using a Nikon D70 and a Sigma 50mm f/2.8 Macro lens, spotlight and backing card.

SHOOTING TIPS – ARTIFICIAL BACKGROUNDS

■ Sometimes, no matter what lens/aperture/position combination you use, you end up with a distracting background. With flower photography here's a little tip to get you a clean background: Simply place a piece of matt card positioned behind the flower – choose a colour that compliments the bloom (see colour wheel on page 211) In this example the background was a square pot and appears as an ugly right-angled line in the background. The same flower head shot with no digital manipulation shows a much cleaner example.

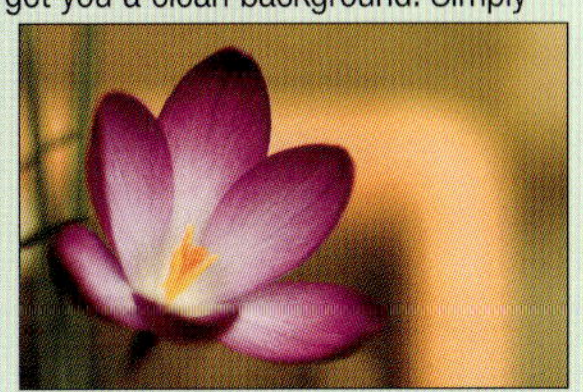

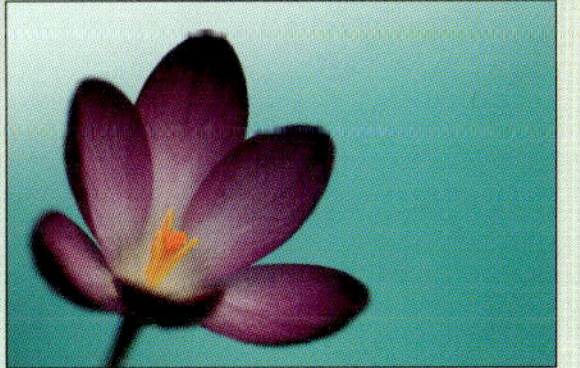

■ If you choose a colour that doesn't appear in the flower or stamen you can, at a later stage, go into Photoshop and select Image⇨Adjustments⇨ Replace color and, using the +eyedropper, click on areas of the background to totally select it. Then change the hue/ saturation or lightness to create a background of any colour you like. In this example I went for white by turning lightness up to 100%.

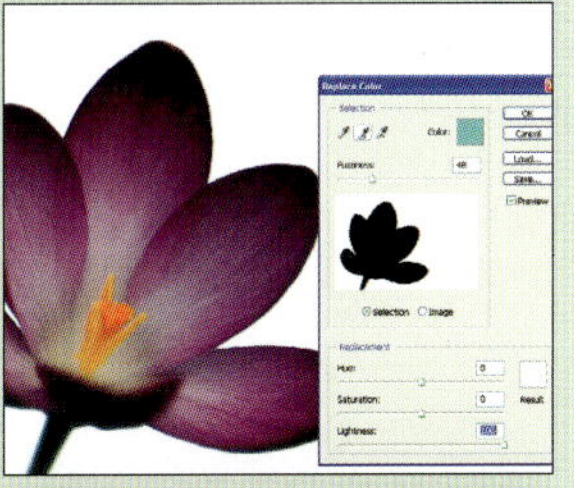

■ Want a natural background? Place a small mirror behind the flower and reflect nearby stalks or blooms. At the right distance they will appear suitably blurred.

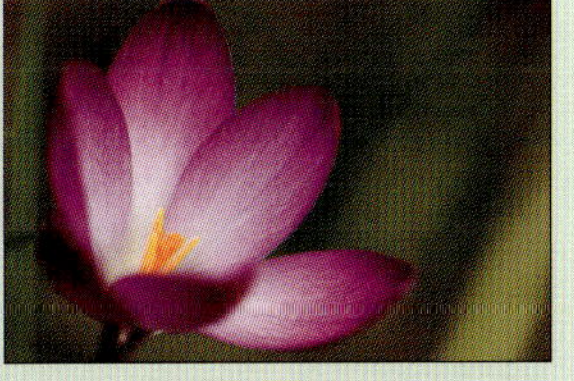

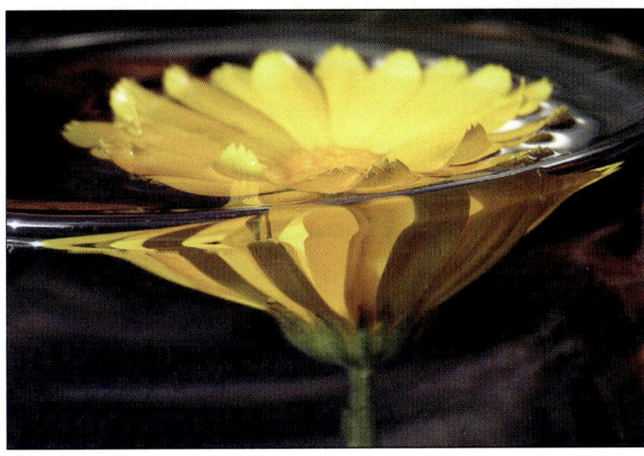

● SYLVIA ADAMS Flower floating in a vase and using refraction to create a different view of the subject.

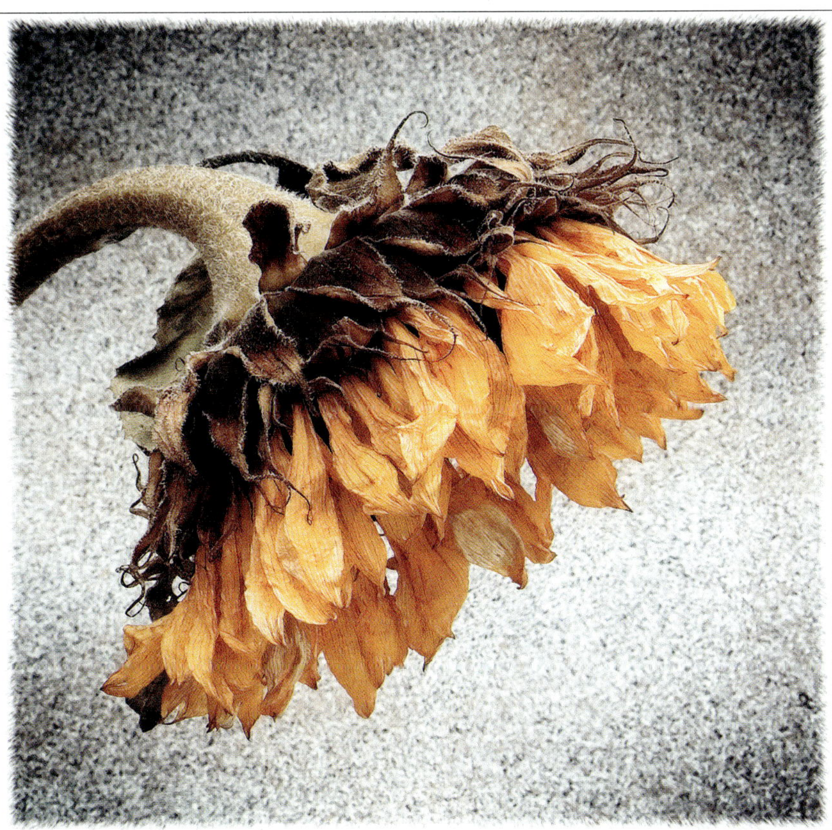

● PETER PATERSON This sunflower was past its best which gave a paper texture to the petals. A suitable textured background was chosen to compliment the texture in the petals.

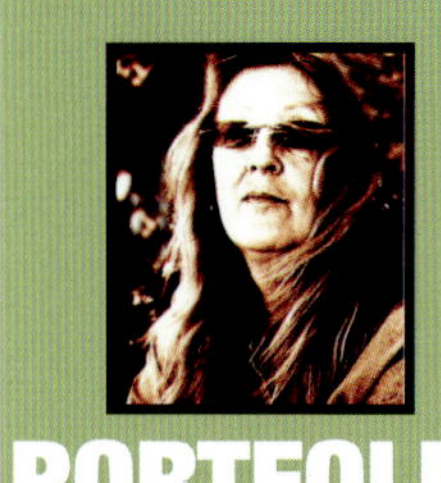

PORTFOLIO

LYDIA MOORE

The picturesque setting of Crete provides Lydia with plenty of scenery to point her camera at.

After escaping the London rat race five years ago, I now live a simple life in an old Cretan village. This suits me perfectly as I love travelling and discovering different cultures.

I'd always travelled with a point and shoot film camera, but after discovering ePHOTOzine two years ago I bought an Olympus C-5000 digital camera. Using this helped me to learn more about composition of images, the importance of light and the use of Photoshop.

A year ago I acquired the Konica Minolta A2 camera, which is sufficient for my current needs. Hopefully, the next step will be to buy a digital SLR.

I like my pictures to be a bit out of the ordinary, preferring to take shots of things that are quirky or unexpected, and will often wander around with flowers and place them where they don't belong in order to photograph them.

I find the contrast of placing fresh, vibrant, living flowers against textured old wood or rusting metal particularly appealing. I will certainly never run out of things to photograph here – Crete has an abundance of wild flowers and ancient villages as well as strong, unpolluted light. The strong summer sun with the reflective light of limestone and whitewashed houses is also particularly challenging.

As well as flowers I also enjoy photographing the local architecture, close-ups of dilapidated doors and windows, chairs, cats and people. I'm not interested in only photographing beautiful people – I like a face with character, a face that has lived and shows it.

My only regret is that I didn't discover photography, and what I could do with it, a lot earlier. ■

www.colour-me-crete-photography.com

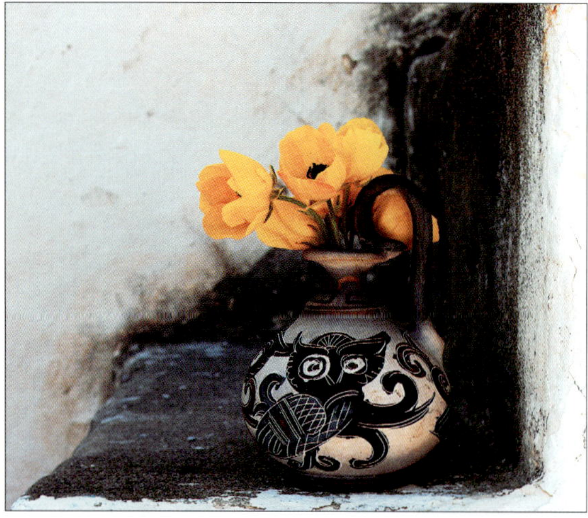

● A typical Greek pot filled with wild rununculus spotted on an old step. Positioned on a third intersection for dramatic composition.

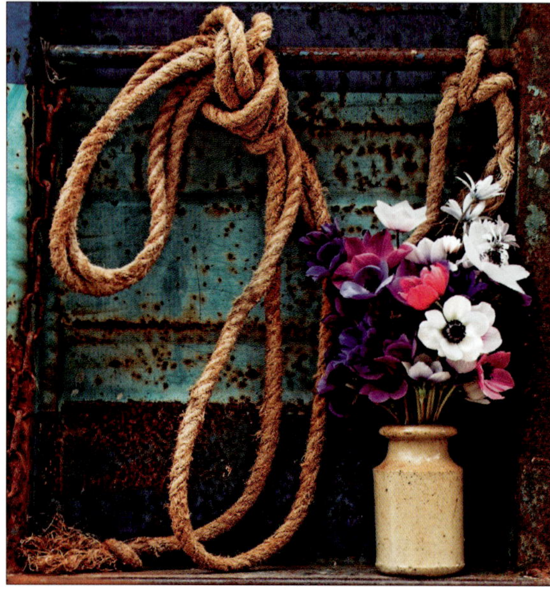

● Cretan wild anenomes on a side panel of an old lorry. The old rope was a big bonus to the texture mix and colour.

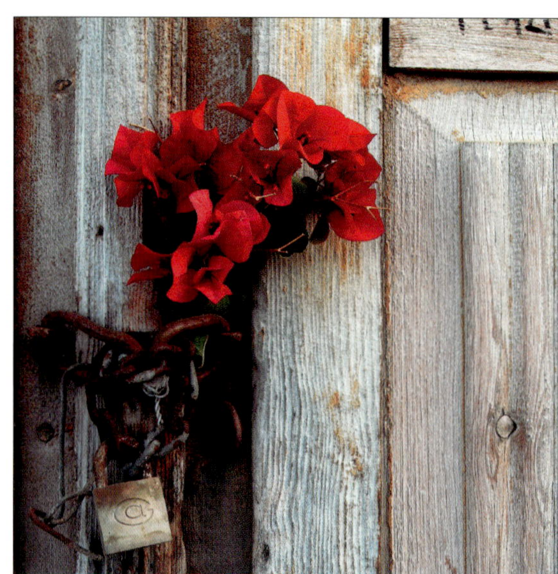

● A bright and vibrant sprig of bouganvillea, placed to contrast with the old and worn door with its rusty padlock and chain.

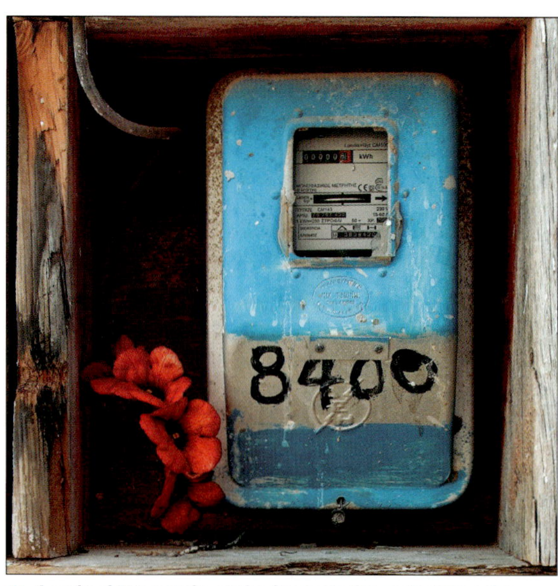

● A sprig of trumpet vine and a Greek electric meter. This offers great textures and colours – it just seemed to belong there.

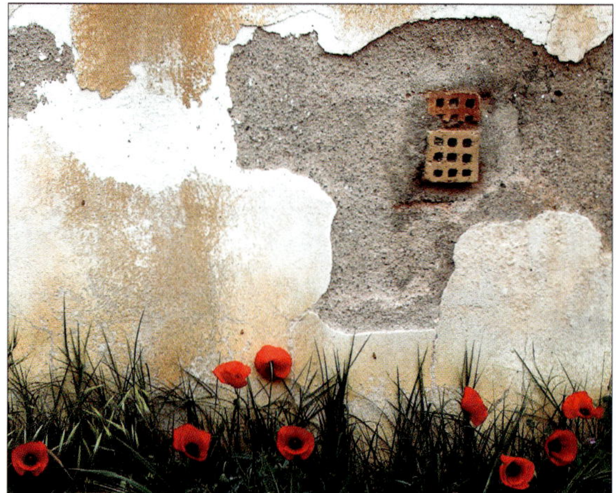

● There are no poppy fields as such in Crete. This lot were growing on scrub land in the local co-op car park.

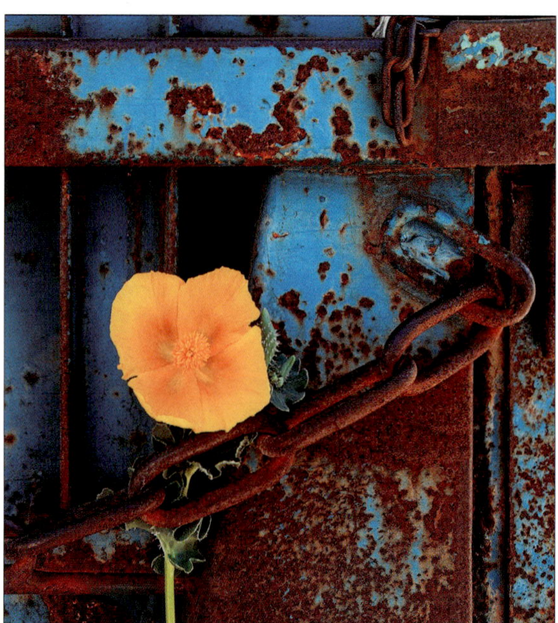

● I couldn't resist adding a yellow horned poppy to the side panel of an old lorry. The blue paint contrasts really well against the yellow.

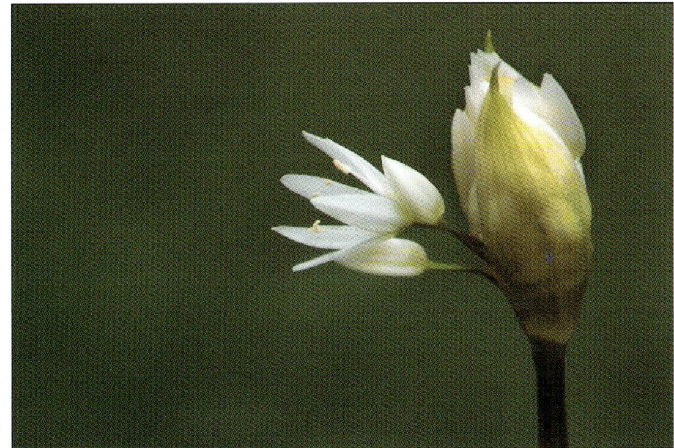

● CHRIS MILES Allium Ursinum (Ramson). Cromford Canal, Derbyshire, taken using Nikon D70, Nikon 50mm f/1.8 at f/8 and 1/30sec.

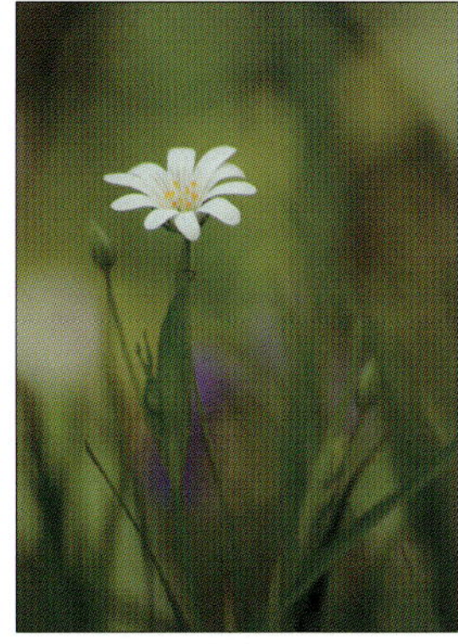

● PAUL EYRE Stitchwort taken with a tripod mounted Canon EOS 300D and Sigma 70-300mm APO at 300mm and f/5.6.

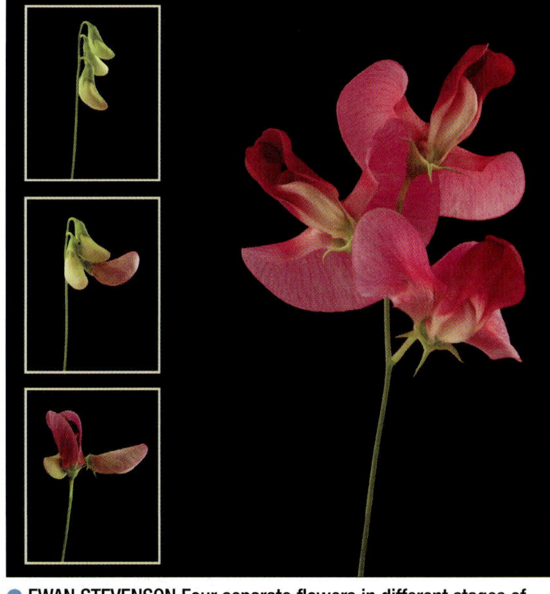

● EWAN STEVENSON Four separate flowers in different stages of opening were photographed against a black background.

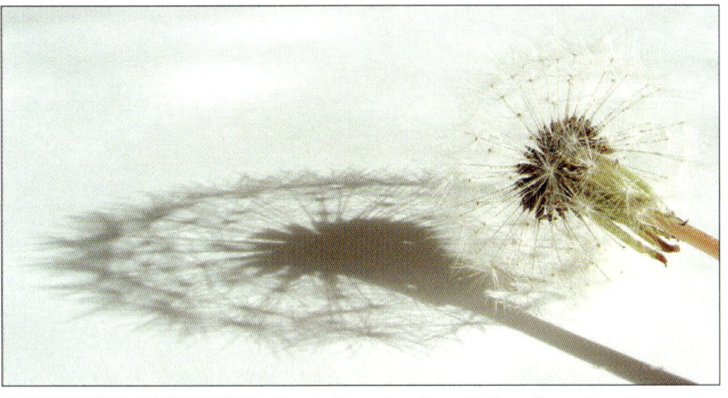

● DEMELZA ANDREOLI A dandelion shadow, taken in natural sunlight on a Fuji Finepix S3000 digital camera.

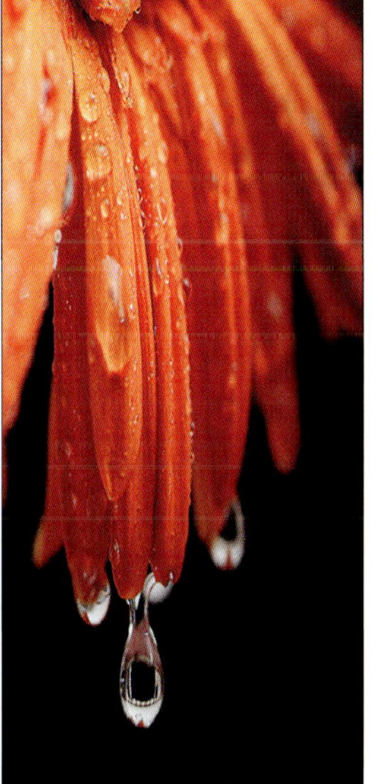

● JOHN MORLEY Gerbera are very popular flowers to photograph and always give good results. 1/250 at f/4 using a Sigma 105mm EX macro.

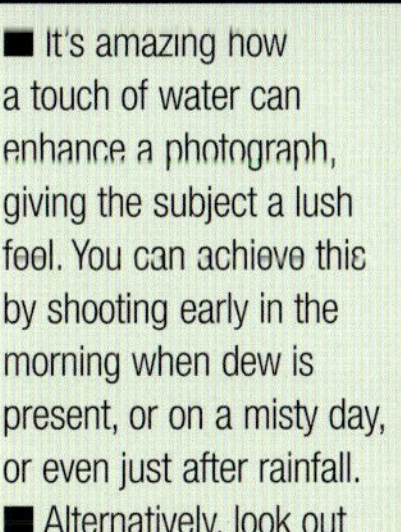

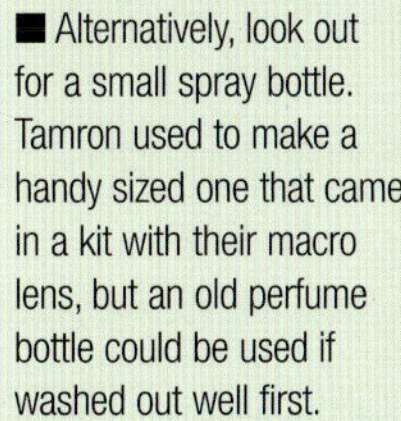

● MIKE DEGASPERIS Bleeding Hearts, shot from the front of the stem, using a wide aperture to introduce the progressive sharpness fall off.

TECHNIQUE TIPS – WATER DROPLETS

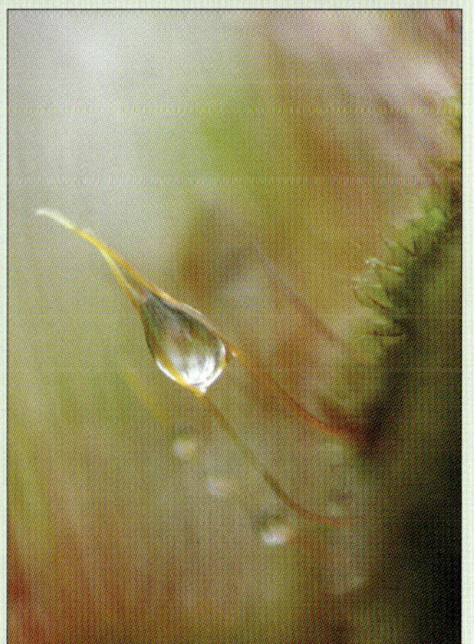

■ It's amazing how a touch of water can enhance a photograph, giving the subject a lush feel. You can achieve this by shooting early in the morning when dew is present, or on a misty day, or even just after rainfall.

■ Alternatively, look out for a small spray bottle. Tamron used to make a handy sized one that came in a kit with their macro lens, but an old perfume bottle could be used if washed out well first.

■ A pipette is another useful accessory to place single droplets of water. Add a touch of glycerine to the water and it will ensure the drop stays as a drop and doesn't flow away.

■ Don't just use drops on flowers. Some of the best shots on ePHOTOzine have been taken with drops on feathers, fruit or metal.

■ When focusing on a droplet you can either focus on the droplet itself, making sure the edge is sharp, or use the droplet as a lens and focus on the reflected image through it. This will mean the droplet may be out of focus, but the upside view through the water can be fascinating. Some photographers have make good use of this technique by creating purpose-made backgrounds to be reflected.

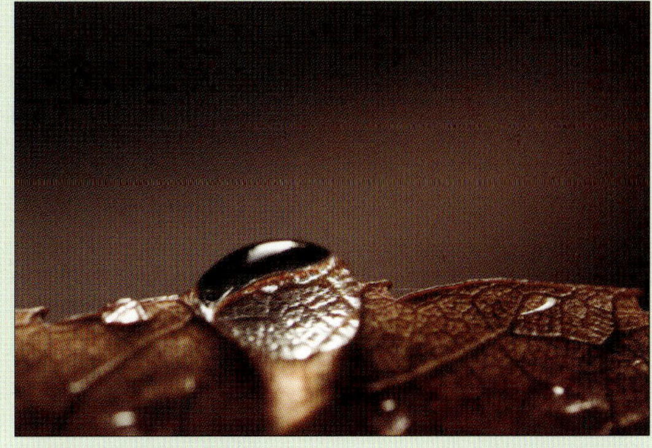

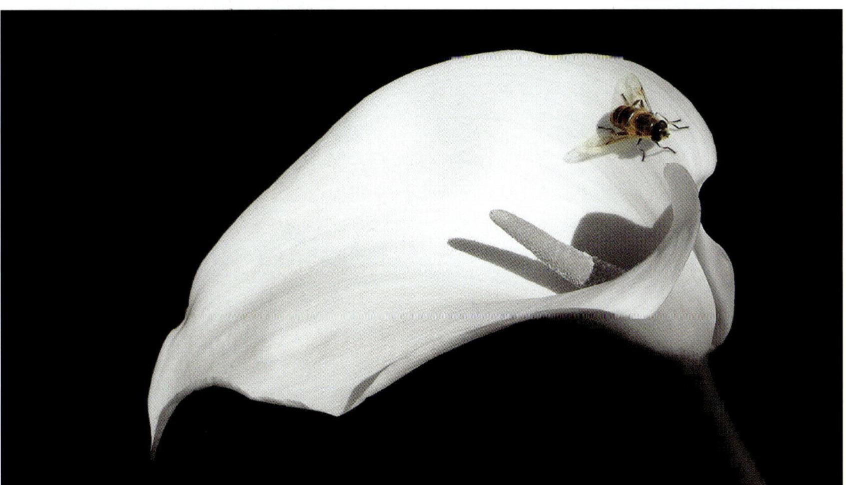

● GWYN BILBY This was taken at Wisley Gardens, Surrey, in colour mode on a Fuji Finepix S5000. It was then converted to black & white and selectively coloured in Photoshop.

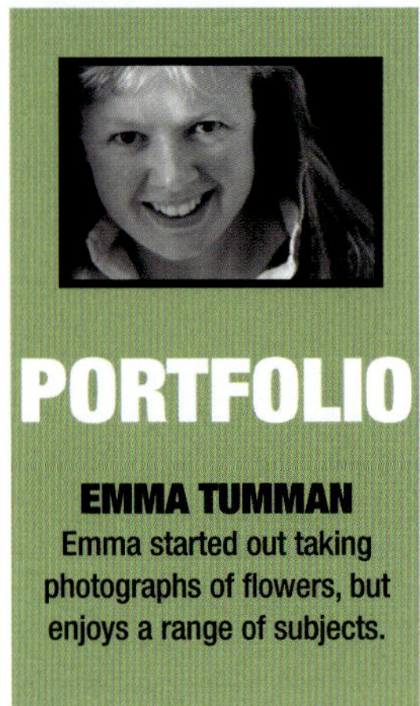

PORTFOLIO

EMMA TUMMAN

Emma started out taking photographs of flowers, but enjoys a range of subjects.

My interest in photography began after I was given an SLR camera for my 18th birthday. After many years of snapping away, learning by trial & error and getting through hundreds of rolls of film, the camera was put away in a cupboard and almost forgotten about.

However, after discovering digital cameras I began to get serious about photography again. My first digital camera was a Canon Ixus I, but I found it could be quite limiting in its functions, with no proper zoom and no control over aperture or shutter speed. It did, however, have a good macro function and this is how I began taking photographs of flowers.

Photographing flowers was a good way to start as they were easily accessible and easy to photograph, mainly because they couldn't run away like some other subjects! I have since upgraded my camera and am now using a Canon EOS 300D.

Lighting is a very important part of photography, but I do not use anything fancy or expensive. Most often I will use a single halogen spot lamp, a light-box (the slide viewing type) or even just daylight. I do have a soft light studio, which diffuses the light nicely, and also find that a piece of white cardboard comes in handy as a reflector. The backgrounds I use are also cheap and cheerful; using black or coloured card, black velvet or the light box, as well as a few backgrounds that I created and printed off myself.

I still photograph flowers, but there are lots of other subjects that I also enjoy. As for the future, I'm not sure where my photography is heading – I am just happy to wait and see where it will take me. ■
www.emmatumman.co.uk

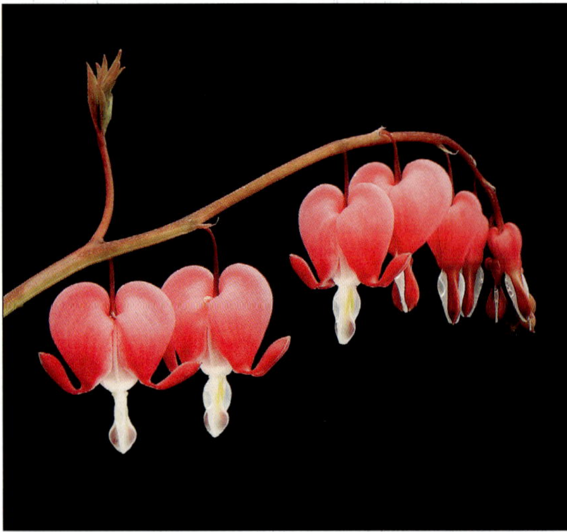

● This was lit with daylight and diffused by the Maplin Soft Light Studio. Taken using a Canon EOS 350D with 18-55mm at ISO400 and an exposure of 1/20sec at f/25.

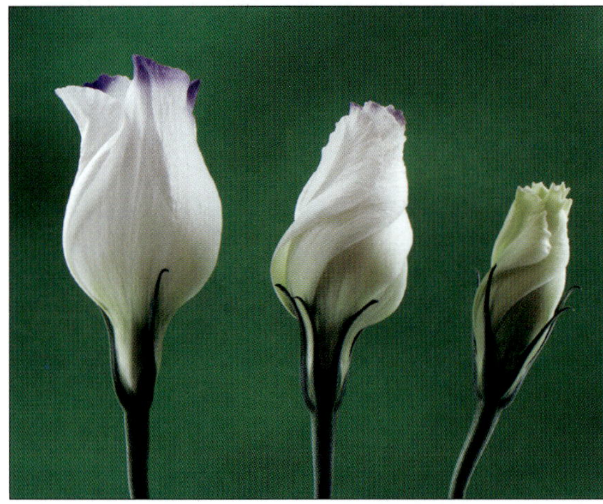

● I printed the background and stuck it onto the window behind the flower heads. I then bounced some light back with white paper and took the shot with a Canon 350D and 18-55mm lens.

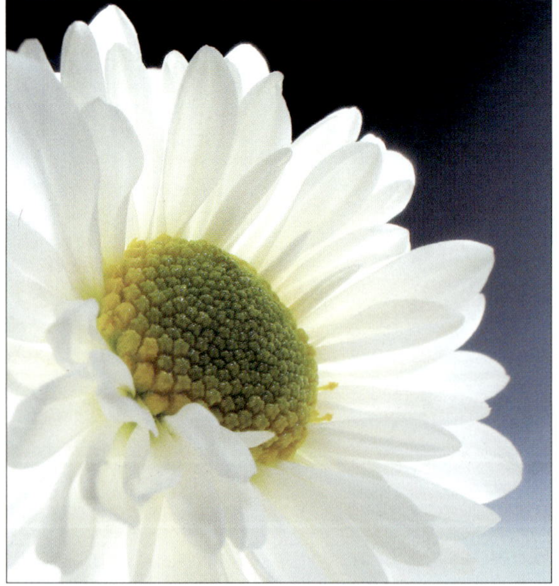

● Lit with a single halogen lamp and taken using a Canon Digital Ixus I from a low viewpoint. The gradient effect can either be created by printing out a graduated sheet or digitally in Photoshop.

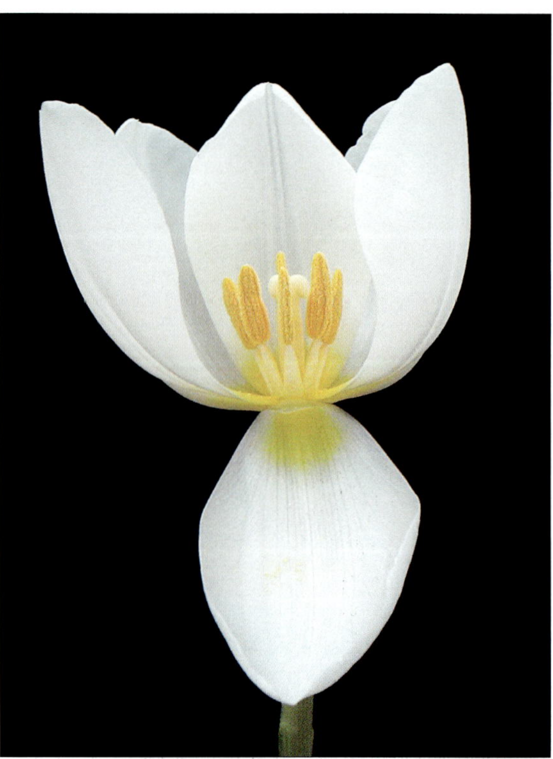

● Lit with a halogen lamp and diffused with the Soft Light Studio. One of the petals was dropped to reveal the stamen and the shot was taken using a Canon Digital Ixus I.

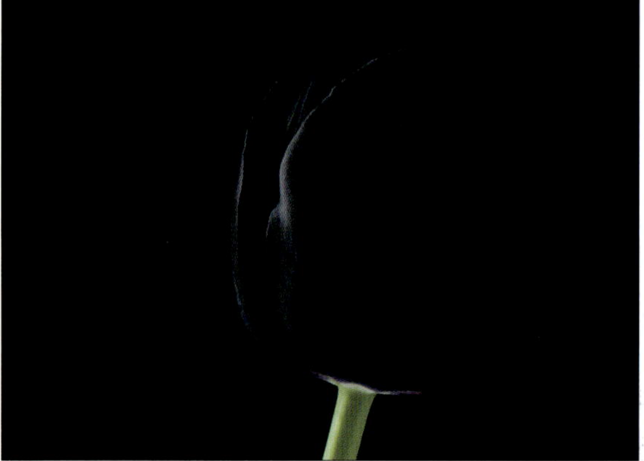

● Black card was taped to a window behind the tulip which was lit with natural light. The Canon EOS 350D was set to ISO200 for a 1sec at f/22 exposure.

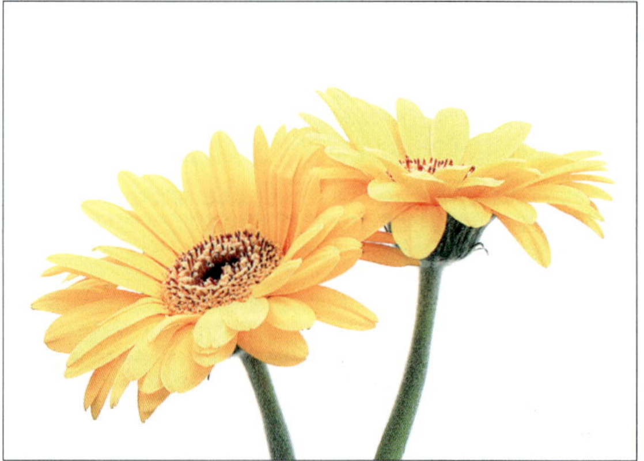

● The background is a daylight-balanced light box and the flower heads were lit with bounced natural light. Taken using a Canon EOS 350D and 18-55mm lens.

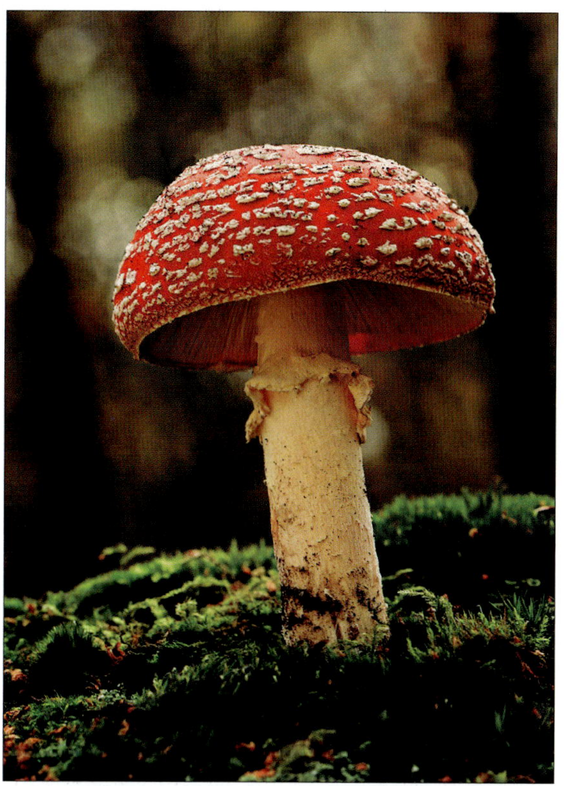

● TERRY LONGLEY Fly Agaric, taken on a Canon EOS 10D and 100mm Macro with 1sec at f/16 exposure. Gold reflectors have lit the underside.

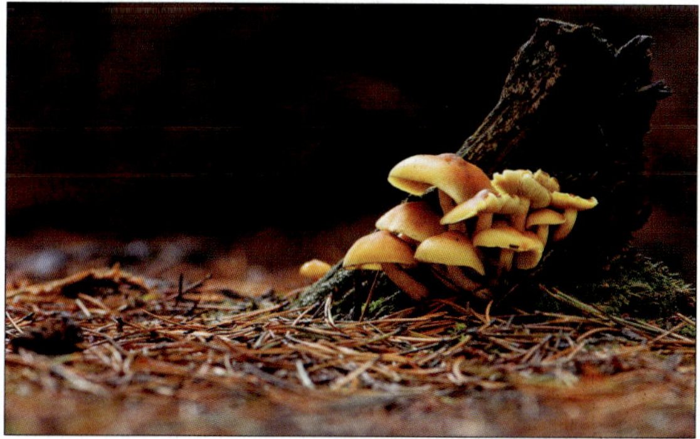

● IAN DAISLEY Velvet Shank mushrooms surrounded by fallen pine needles in Farley Woods, Matlock. Sigma 105mm Macro at f/5.6

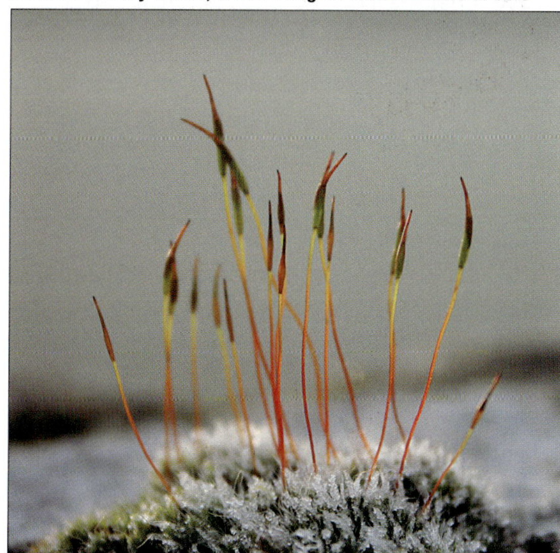

● ANNE RICHARDSON "My first shot using a Canon EOS 300D, of moss starting to thaw. Taken early in the morning on an ePHOTOzine meet."

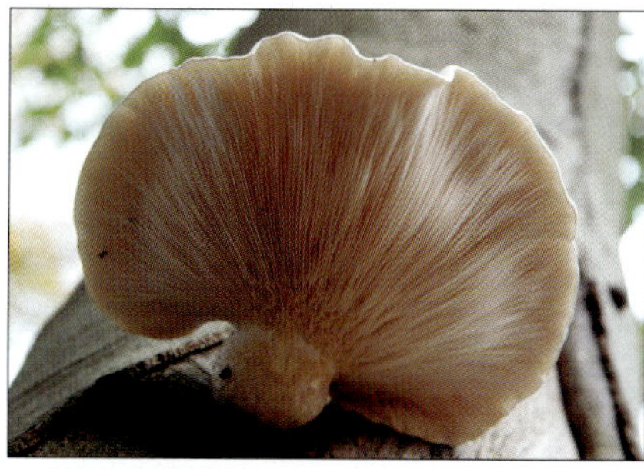

● CARABOSSE Bracket fungus should be shot from below to appreciate the wonderful patterns.

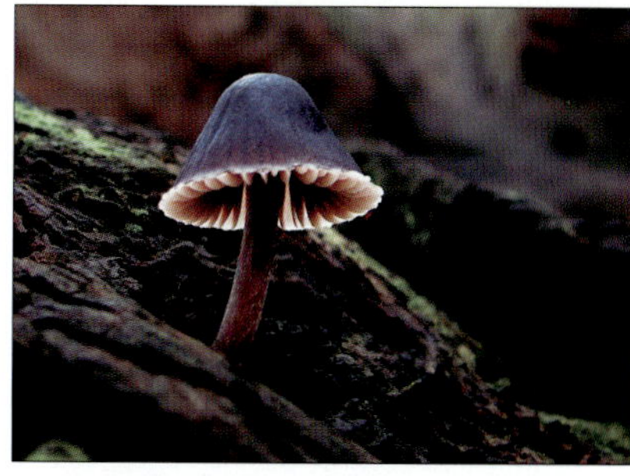

● MATT BERRY Small mushroom fruiting from a large log. Taken with a Fuji S7000 in macro mode.

DIGITAL TECHNIQUE – CLEANING UP MUSHROOMS

■ Getting down at a low angle is what usually makes fungi photographs special. The interesting angle is a winner, but they usually need cleaning up too. First thing to notice when taking shots of a toadstool is the head will pick up reflections from the sky, causing parts of the cap to be burnt out while the stem will often be in shade and dark.

A useful shooting tip is to cover the mushroom with a cloth. I use a coat and nearby sticks to make a tent above the specimen to reduce the glare. This also reduces the exposure, so a tripod is essential.

1 You'll also find that there will usually be a collection of soil on the cap. I prefer to leave this on to ensure it looks natural, but you could go around cloning out the bits. I prefer to use the Clone tool to remove grass stems cutting over the stalk. The heal tool is even better. Select a brush size a touch larger than the grass that you're going to remove and sample from a nearby point.

2 Although I used a wide aperture, the background isn't blurred enough. Create a duplicate layer – Layer⇨Duplicate layer and add a layer mask – Layer⇨Layer Mask⇨Reveal all. Blur the new layer – Filter⇨Blur⇨Gaussian blur and adjust the slider to give a preferred degree of blur to the whole image.

3 Click on the layer mask and paint over the cap of the mushroom using the Eraser tool set to a large feathered brush size. This will reveal the sharp layer below. If you make a mistake you can remove the mask using the paint brush.

4 Now to lighten the shadow area on the cap. Draw around the darker area using the Freehand lasso tool. Once the selection is made go to Select⇨Feather and set a 30 pixel feather. Make sure the background layer is selected and open Curves – Image⇨Adjustments⇨Curves. Pull the curve just enough to lighten the shaded area so it's close in tone to the non-shaded areas. Avoid taking the curve too far or you'll clip the highlights and lose detail.

5 With the background layer still selected, use the Dodge tools set to Highlight and a low exposure value and paint over the stalk to brighten it up. You can go over it several times to build up the brightness. Do the same over the cap to pick up the flecks of white.

6 Flatten the layers – Layer⇨Flatten image and make any further tone adjustments using Levels or Curves. At this stage, I also added a warm filter using the Image⇨Adjustments⇨Photo filter option set to Warming 81, and adjusted the saturation – Image⇨ Adjustments⇨Hue/ Saturation (Ctrl+U) to give the cap the vivid red tone.

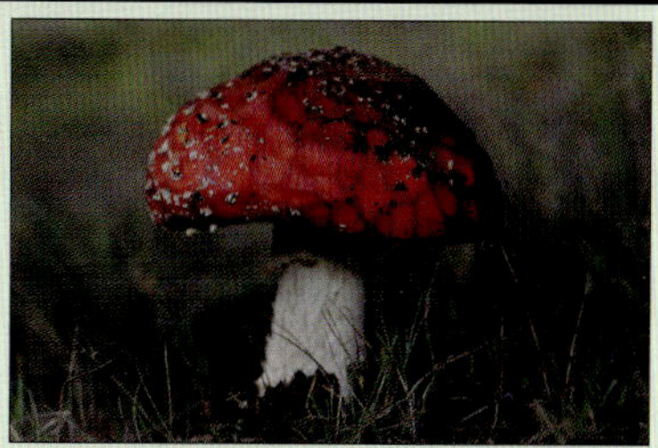

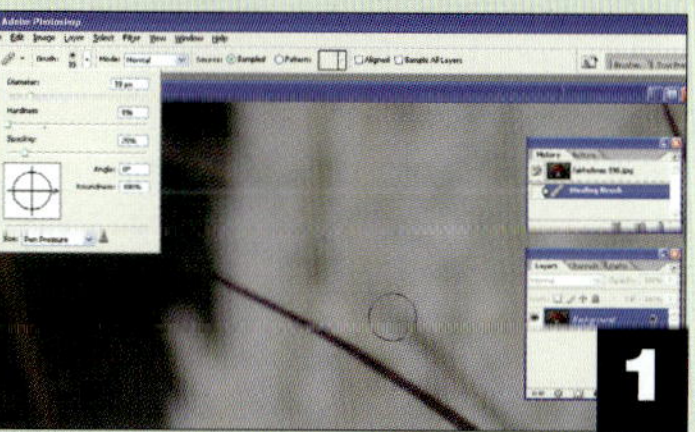

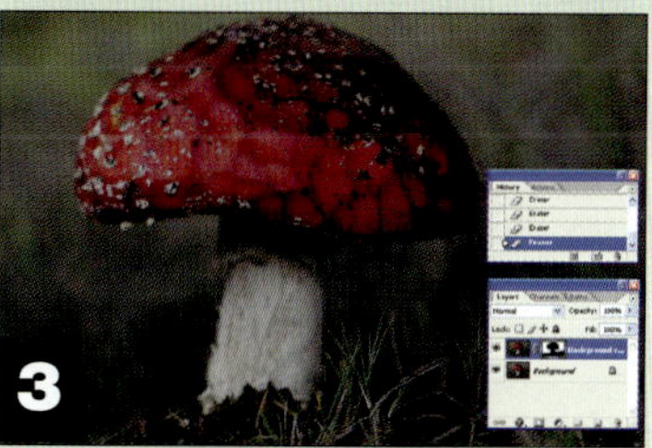

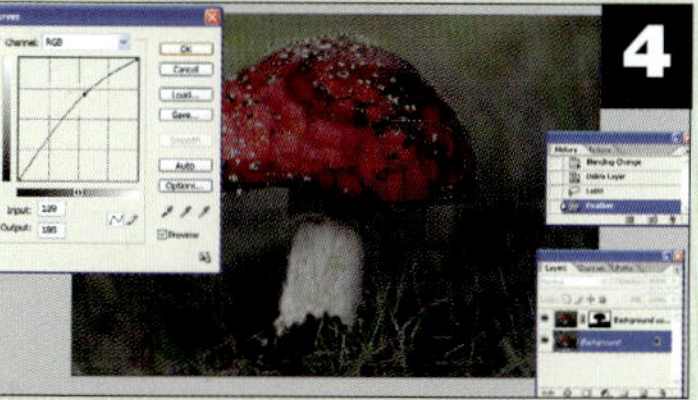

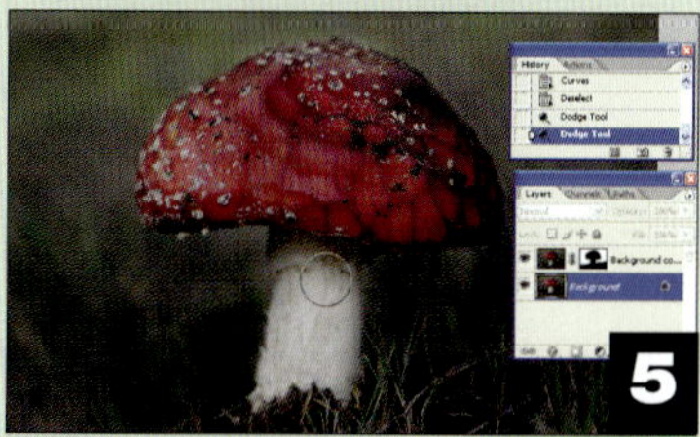

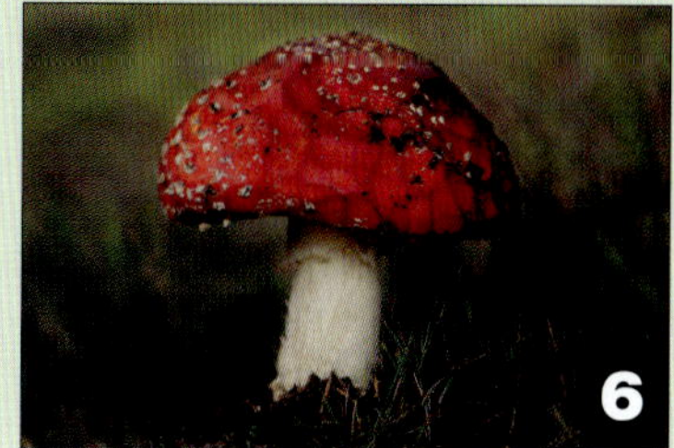

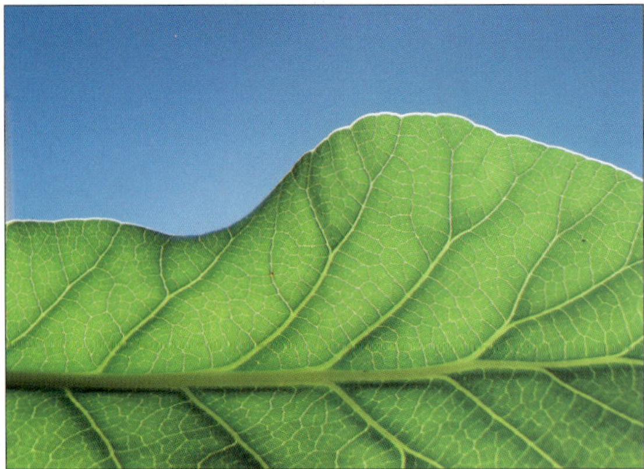

● ALAN DRUMMOND Puka leaf taken in New Zealand, using a Canon Powershot G3 with an exposure of 1/1250sec at f/4.

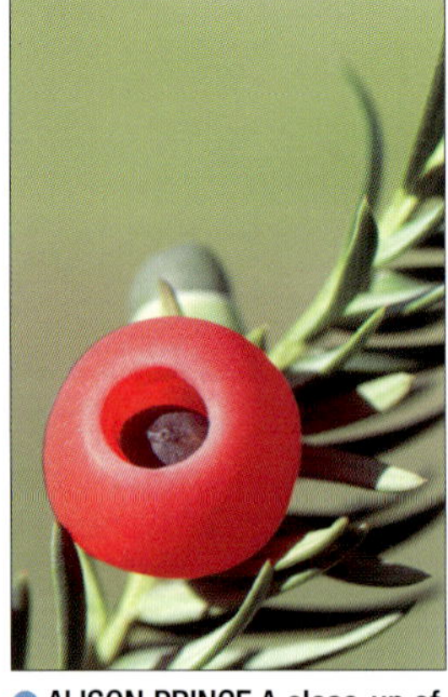

● ALISON PRINCE A close-up of a berry, shot in overcast light.

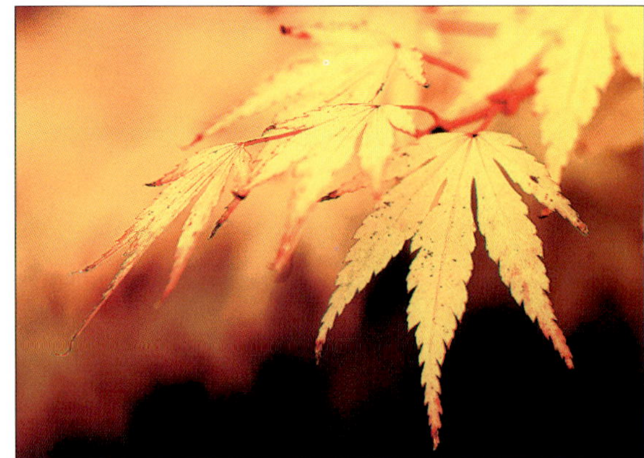

● BILL CAMM Acer leaves in Autumn, shot using a Fuji S2 Pro with Sigma 105mm. Hand-held, manual focus and 1/180 sec at f/3.3.

DIGITAL TECHNIQUE – SCANNING LEAVES

■ You can buy a good flatbed scanner for around £70 which, as well as being useful for scanning documents and photos, can also be used creatively to make digital photos of objects.

■ The scanner uses a CCD to record data. The CCD is driven across the scanner bed and uses a fluorescent tube to illuminate the path it travels over.

■ By placing objects on the glass above you can create interesting photos of any surfaces that touch the glass. The CCD's lens offers enough depth-of-field to ensure close parts of any three-dimensional object appear in focus. The further away the part is from the glass, the softer it appears and also darker the exposure.

■ You can scan various things, including leaves, jewellery, flowers and rocks to come up with interesting results. Leaves are a perfect subject, because you can pick up all the individual patterns and textures and use these as backdrops to pages, or digital collages.

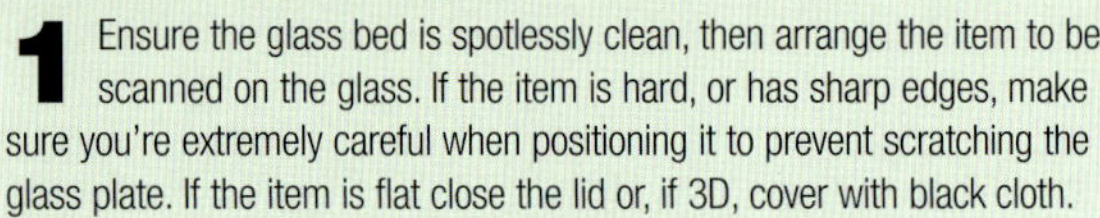

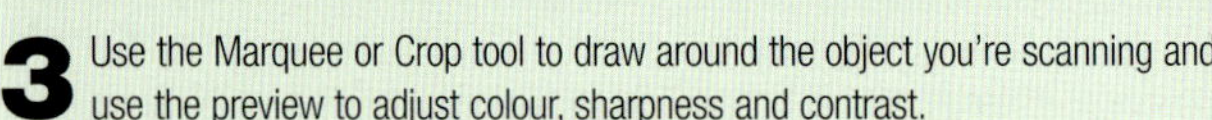

1 Ensure the glass bed is spotlessly clean, then arrange the item to be scanned on the glass. If the item is hard, or has sharp edges, make sure you're extremely careful when positioning it to prevent scratching the glass plate. If the item is flat close the lid or, if 3D, cover with black cloth.

2 Open the scanning software to bring up the dialogue box with its preview button. Click this button to make the scanner scan the area quickly and show a low-resolution version of the entire glass plate.

3 Use the Marquee or Crop tool to draw around the object you're scanning and use the preview to adjust colour, sharpness and contrast.

4 Select the size you want the image to appear, click on scan and wait a minute or so for the full scan to finish.

5 Now view the image in your image-editing program and make any final adjustments to contrast, colour or sharpness. At this stage you can also clone in bits that are missing or damaged using other parts of the leaf.

TIPS

■ Use the leaf scans to make interesting photographs. Try enlarging a section to magnify the pattern, then use that as a background by blurring it and lightening the colour. Like the example to the right.

■ When scanning leaves try using reflective (lit from front) and transparent (lit from behind) modes if you have a transparency adaptor. Each delivers very different results.

■ Try scanning both sides of the leaf as each side gives a slightly different texture and pattern.

■ Leaves can be scanned when new or old. New ones are moist and need extra care when arranging on the glass to avoid creases – old ones are quite brittle so care should be taken that they don't break. Also, look out for ones that don't have bug bites because you'll have more work retouching these later.

■ When you've scanned a leaf try making interesting crops which could be used as a reduced opacity border, header or footer on letter headed paper, or as part of a collage.

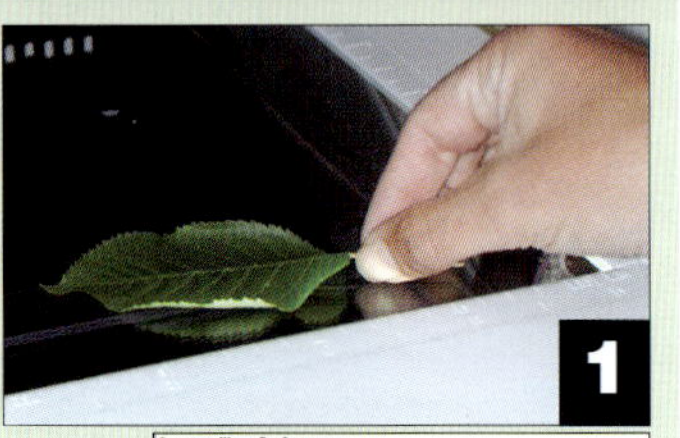

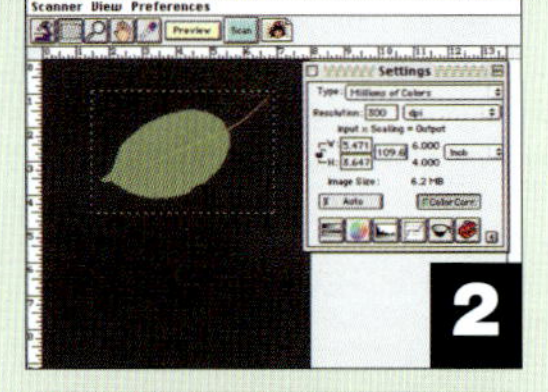

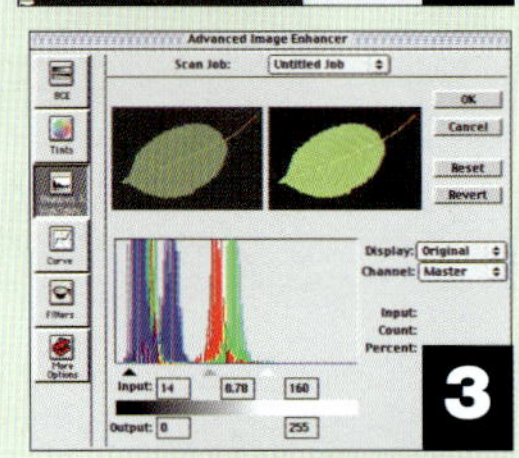

● SURESH KHAIRE Palm shot on Kodak Gold 200 film in a Nikon F90X with 70-300mm.

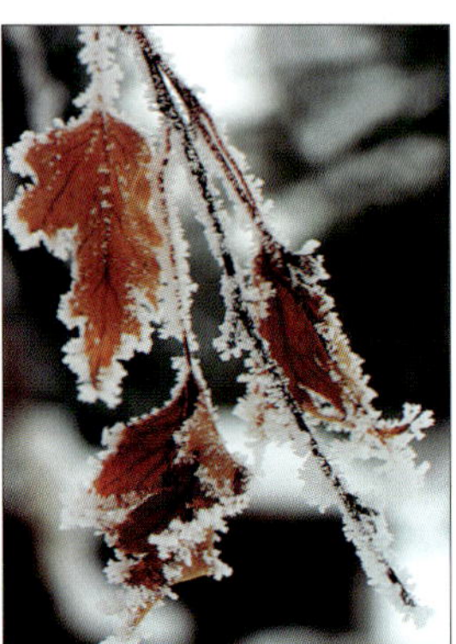

● BILL MATSON Frosted leaves, taken in a cemetery on a cold winter day. f/6.3 at 1/1600sec.

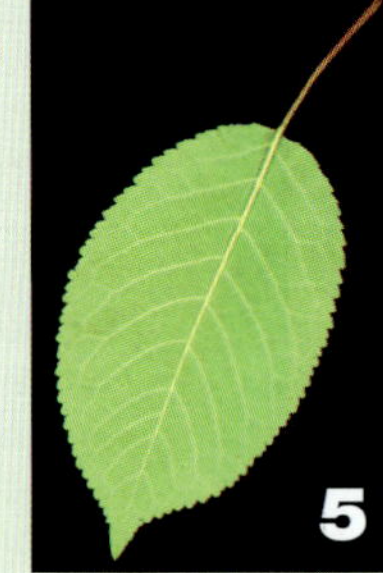

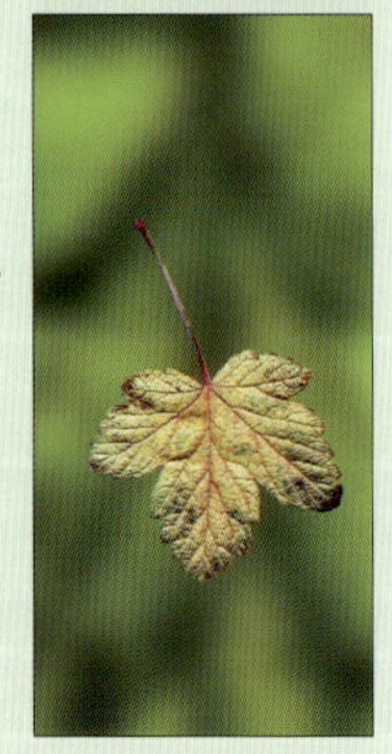

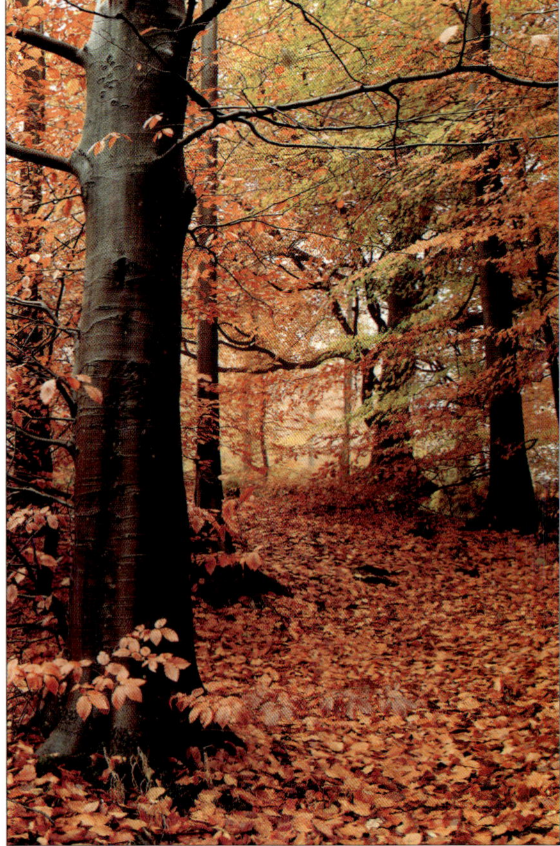

● GERWYN GIBBS St Gwynno's Forest in South Wales, taken using a tripod mounted Fuji S2 Pro with Tamron 28-75mm at 28mm.

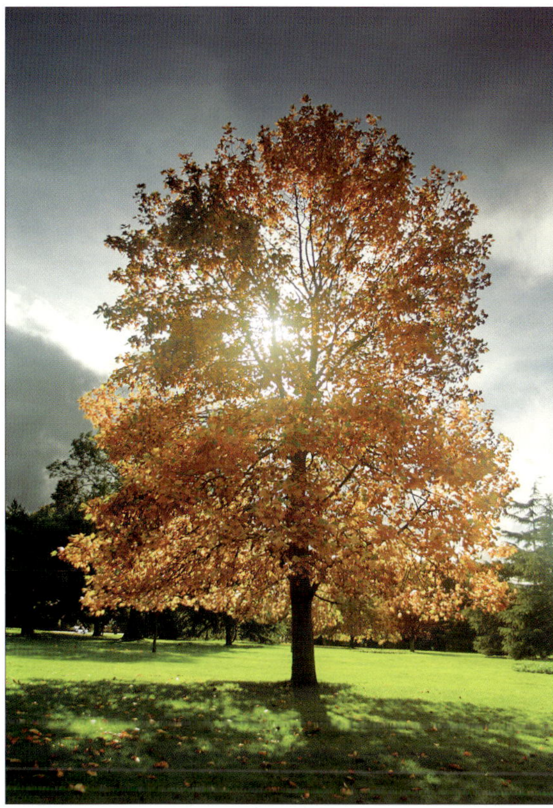

● GARETH BODRELL Composite of two shots – "I exposed once for the sky and once for the tree, then blended them both in Photoshop."

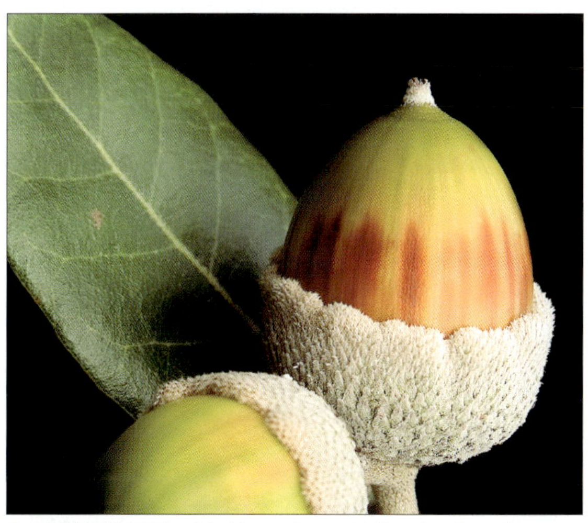

● GEOFF TAYLOR Hand-held on a Canon 300D, using Canon's 28-135mm image stabilized lens at 135mm and 1/60sec exposure.

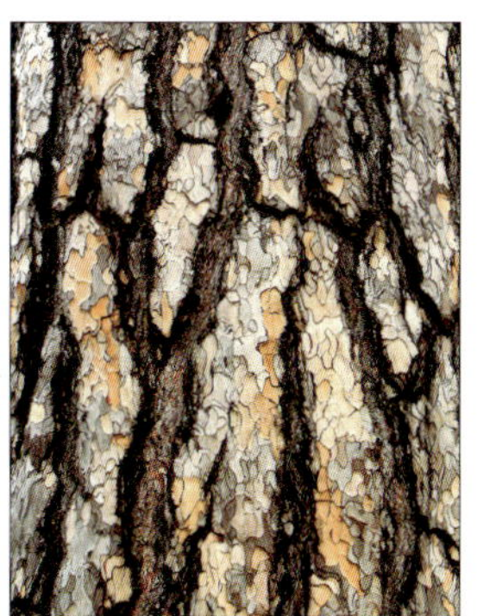

● PUAY-SZE LIM Canon 300D and 18-55mm lens at full zoom, to isolate the jigsaw-like details.

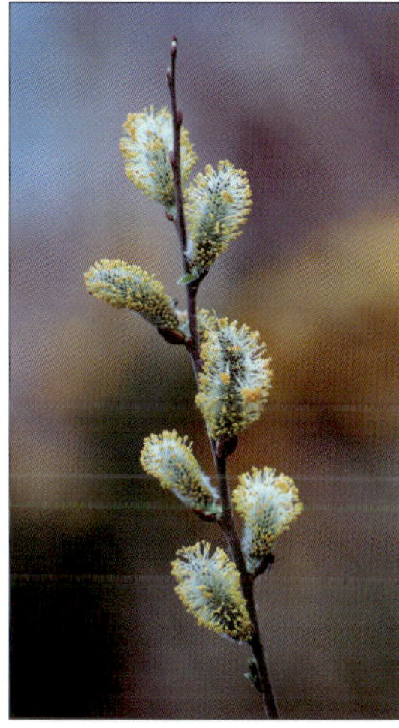

● ROBERT TAYLOR "The background colour cast was accidental, but I liked the effect."

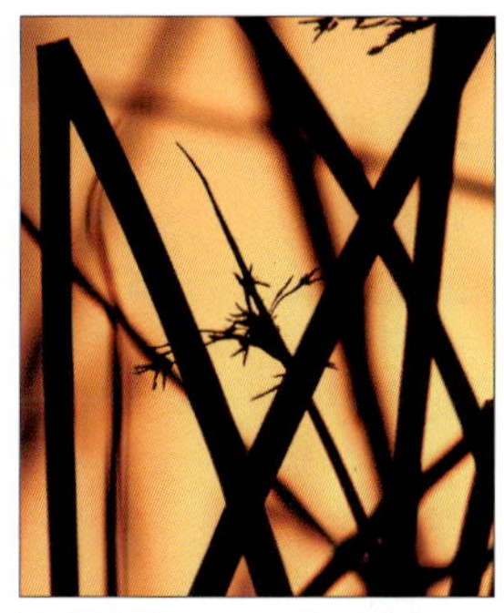

● JAN GEE Reeds, backlit by desert sunset in Utah.

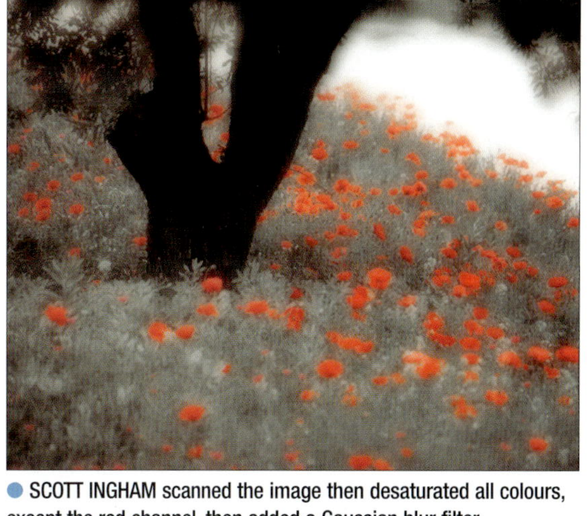

● SCOTT INGHAM scanned the image then desaturated all colours, except the red channel, then added a Gaussian blur filter.

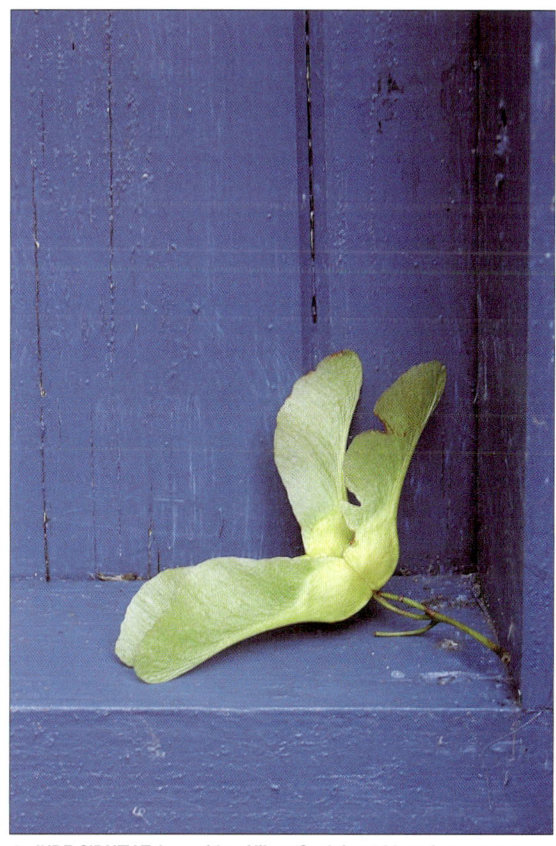

● JUDE GIDNEY Taken with a Nikon Coolpix 5700 and an exposure of 1/30sec at f/4.1. Levels and saturation enhanced in Photoshop.

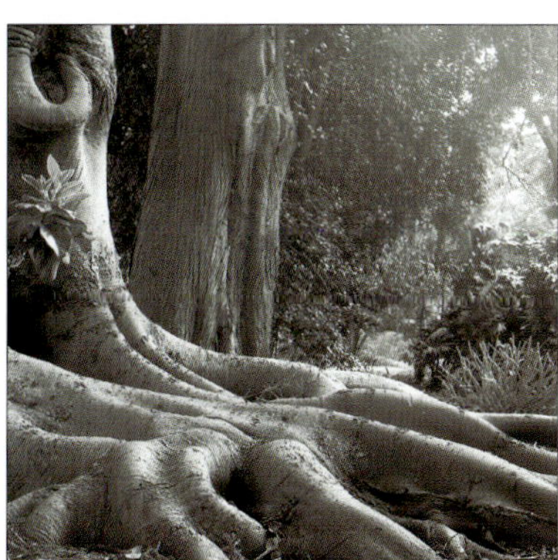

● MARC MOREL Tree in the Geelong Botanical gardens, using a Rolleiflex and Ilford Delta 400.

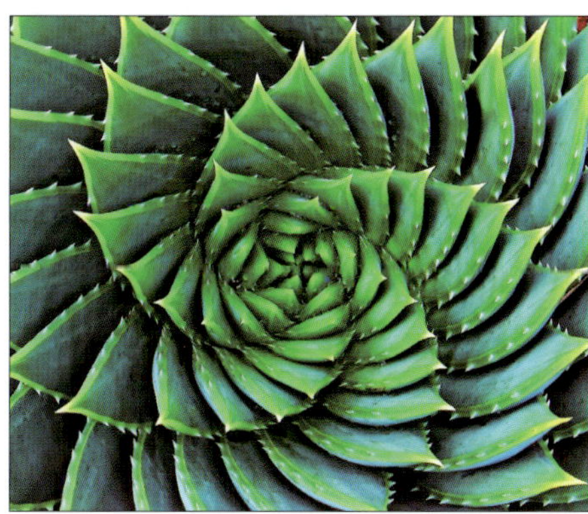

● PATRICK SMITH Aloe polyphylla at Berkeley Botanic Gardens on a cloudy day. It's almost 1m wide!

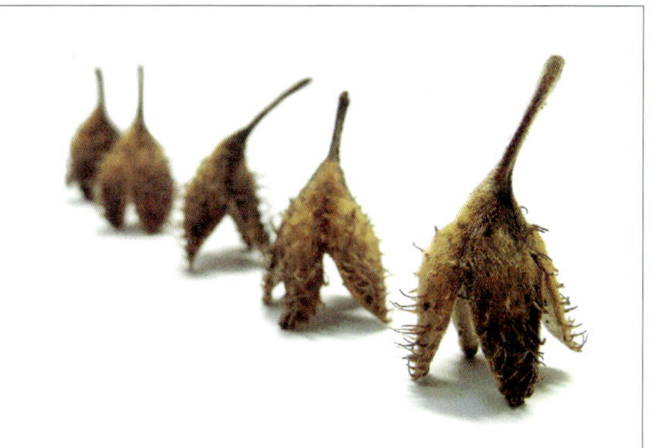

● NEAL MORAN Taken with a Fuji S5000 and standard lens in macro. "I liked the way these guys look like headless chickens."

SHOOTING TIPS – FLOWERS

■ Shoot from a low angle to ensure a better profile of the bloom. Use a right-angle findor 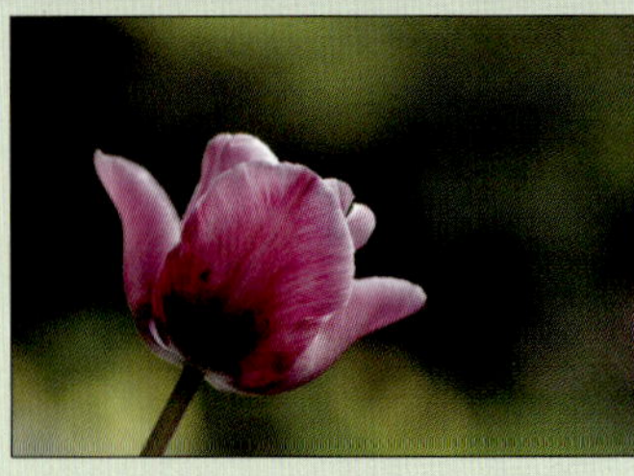 to improve comfort while looking through the viewfinder at such a low angle.

■ Shoot with low angle lighting to increase depth of the subject and make it more three-dimensional.

■ Take shots with the sun behind the subject for a rim lighting effect. Backlighting works well on leaves, which take on a translucent look.

■ Move in close to concentrate on patterns and textures rather than the flower as a whole.

■ Set the camera up on a tripod and take a shot at intervals to record a flower opening. The length of time you leave between shots depends on the speed the flower opens.

■ Use a reflector to bounce light back into shadow areas of the flower. The aluminium foil used for cooking can be taped to a piece of cardboard to make an effective reflector. Crumple before you attach it to get a more diffused reflective light.

■ Use a mini clamp to stop a stalk swaying or shield it from the wind.

■ Make a flower stand out from its background by using a wide aperture to ensure shallow depth-of-field. 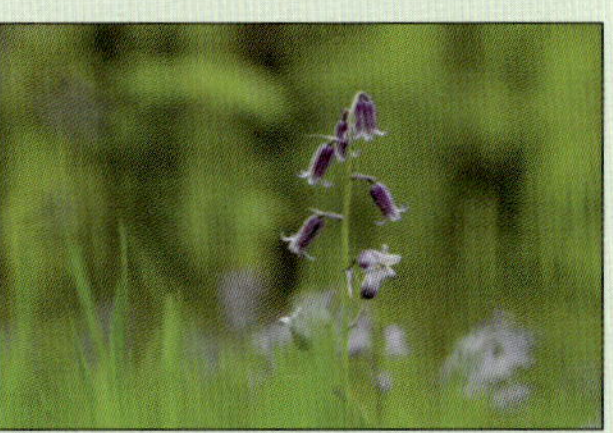

■ Use a light tent or cube to create a wonderful soft diffused light around the flower. Maplins sell a low cost one. See Emma's portfolio on page 190 for such shots.

■ Try a zoom burst. Set the zoom at one end of the range, focus on the flower and then, using a long exposure, adjust the zoom as you fire the shutter.

■ To ensure a sharp flower from front to back shoot two photos - one focused on the front, the other on the back and combine both in Photoshop using layers and masks.

■ Use filters – an 81A warm up filter can be used on cloudy days to make the photo look more pleasing. Use a polarising filter to cut glare and increase saturation.

■ Carry a large plastic bag around with you. This can be used to kneel on when shooting from ground level. Take things a stage further into the comfort zone and use a gardeners' kneeling pad.

■ Move any obstructing branches and leaves and hold them out of the way while you take the shot. Use string to tie branches and stalks temporarily out of view.

■ Use foreground leaves or stalks to provide an out-of-focus frame around the main bloom. These can be positioned for great effect. 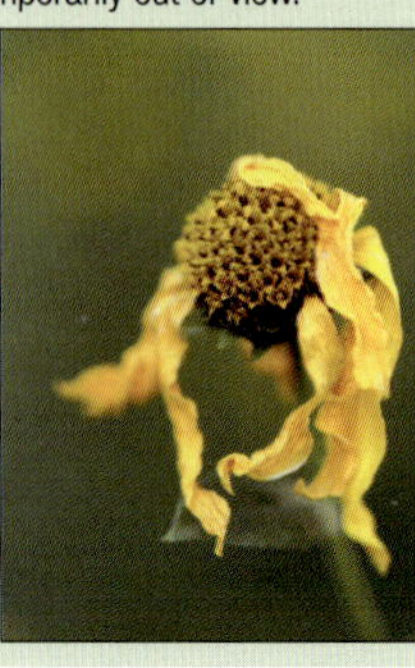

■ Try allowing more space around the flower head to let it breathe in the photo.

■ Don't just shoot fresh blooms – withered and dried plants can also look artistically attractive.

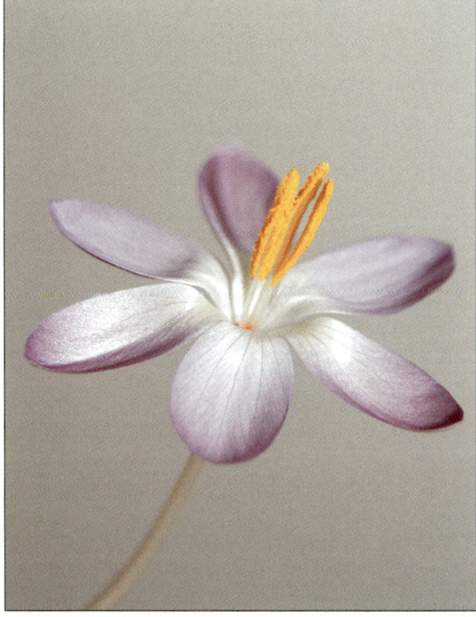

● MELANIE LETHAM Crocus against white background, under-exposed to produce a mid grey. Lit by window.

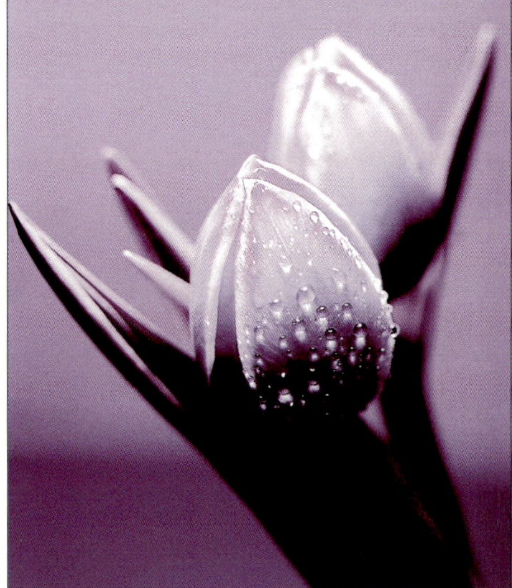

● CLAIRE MORGAN Shot on Fuji Provia 100 at ISO25 in a Bronica ETRS and then cross processed.

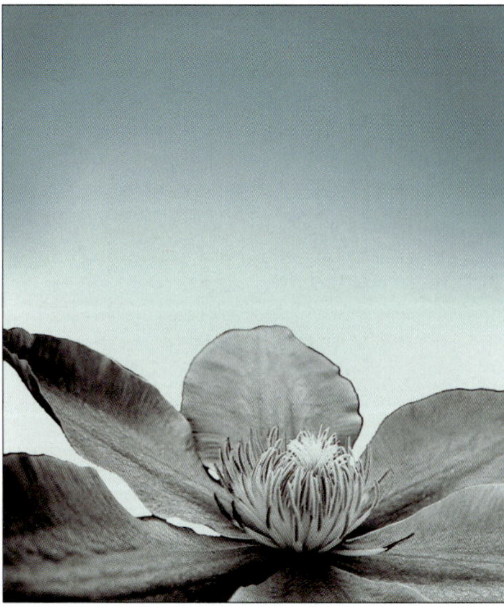

● TONY HUMPHREYS Clematis taken with a Fuji 602 Pro. Blue-toned and graduated background in Photoshop.

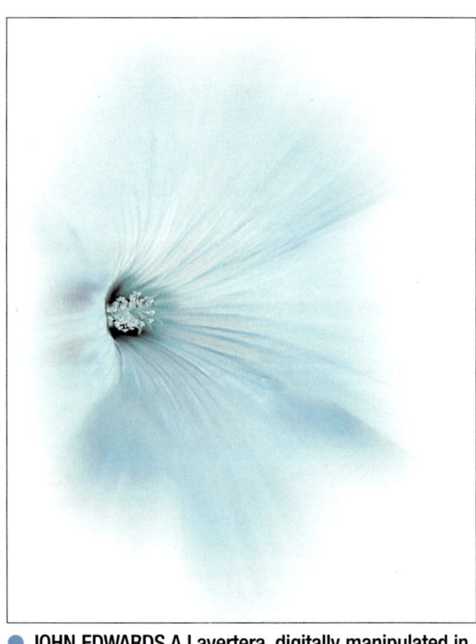

● JOHN EDWARDS A Lavertera, digitally manipulated in Photoshop using zoom blur and a change of hue.

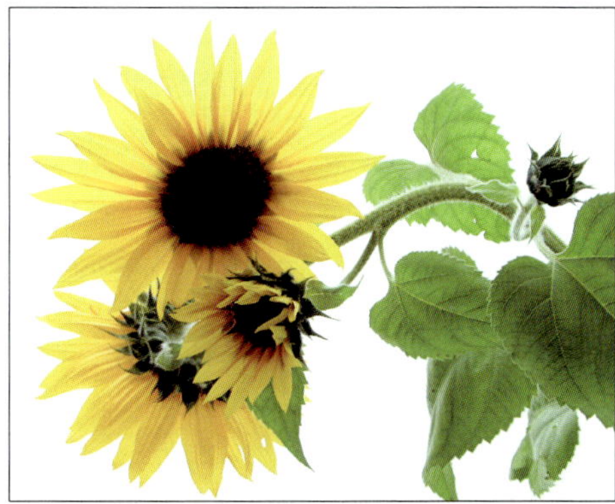

● ALISON GUPPY Sunflower taken against glass patio doors with a muslin curtain pulled across.

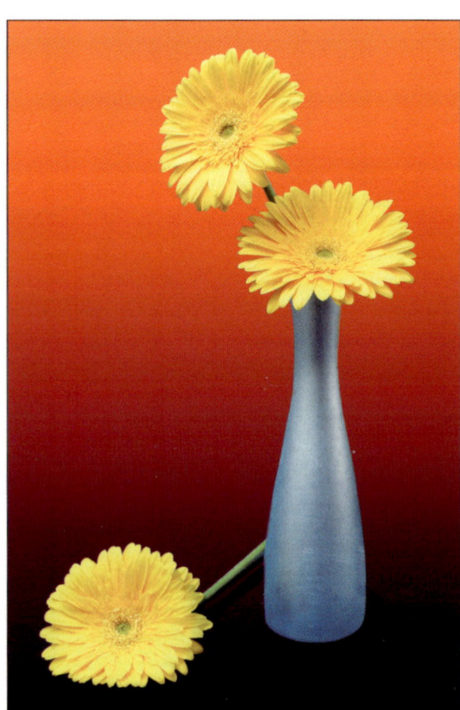

● TONY HEPWORTH Taken with a black background for easy exchange to graduated background in Photoshop.

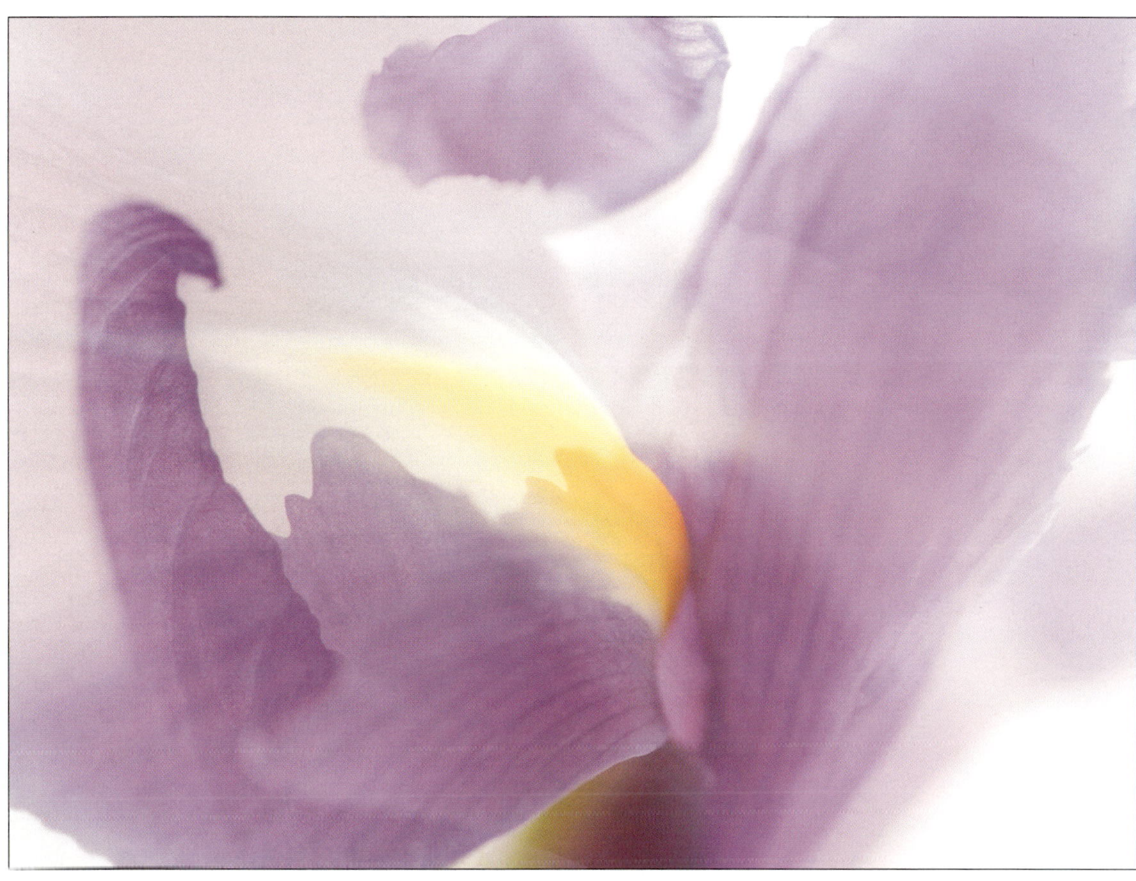

● These two beautiful examples are from a series of macro photos of flowers, taken using a Canon EOS 300D and Sigma 105mm Macro lens. The results were then layered and manipulated using Photoshop to create the soft and textural abstract images.

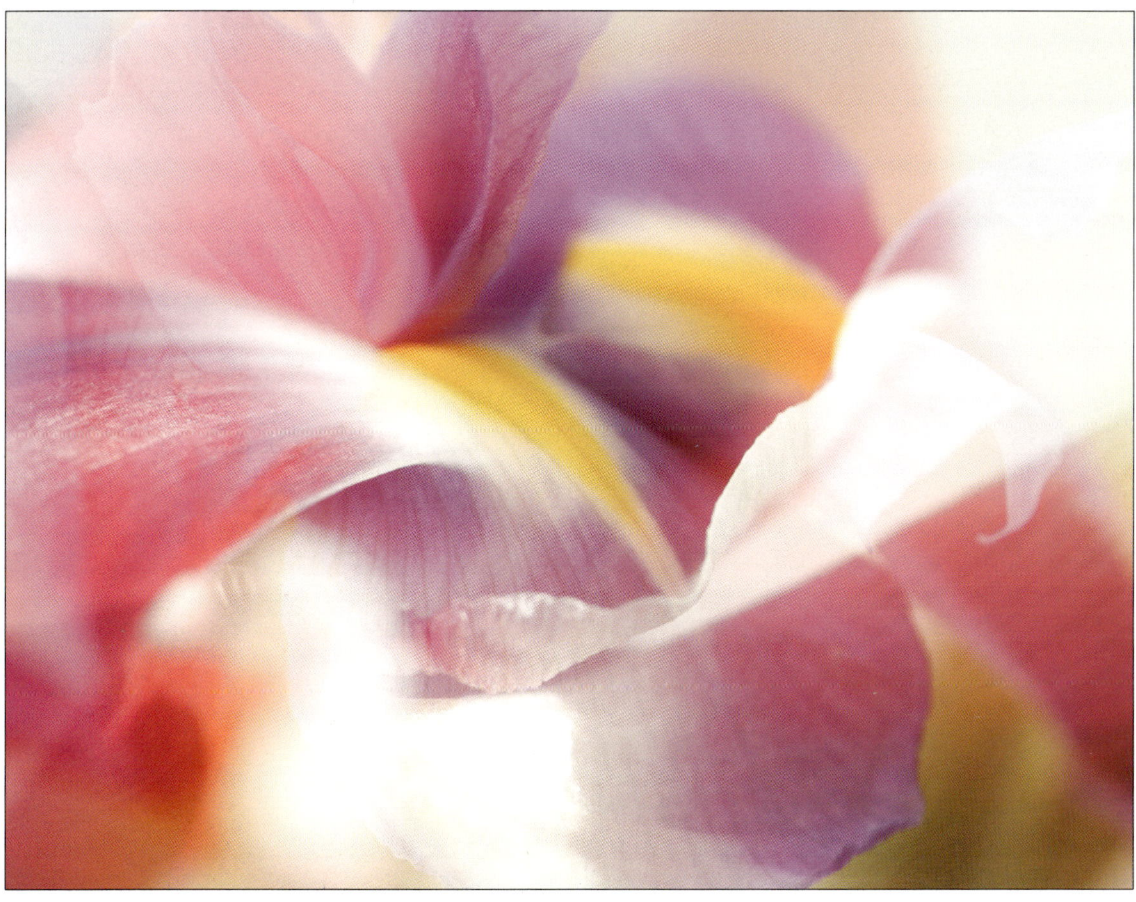

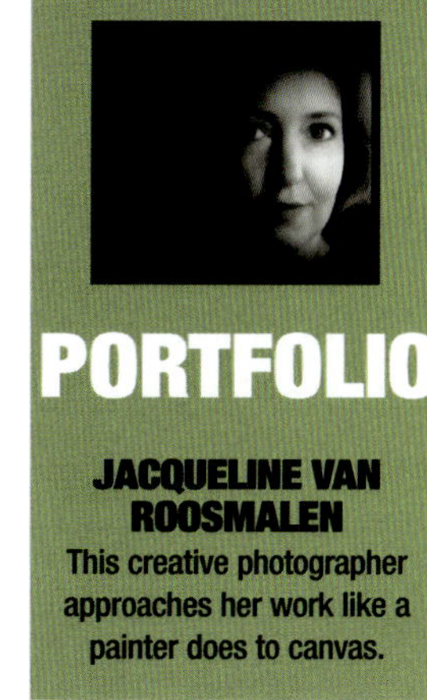

PORTFOLIO

JACQUELINE VAN ROOSMALEN
This creative photographer approaches her work like a painter does to canvas.

My brother introduced me to photography in my teenage years. Since then it has always been a part of my life.

I am very much aware of the world around me, the fragility of our environment and the way we live.

Seeing so much can be overwhelming and sometimes I just need some time to narrow my focus, isolate thoughts and concentrate on small details. These are the times that I grab my camera. I literally zoom in on small parts of safe and known surroundings, only to discover the beauty that lies there, so near yet almost overlooked in our busy lives.

Looking through the lens, the beauty of nature, and especially flowers, so close-up can literally take my breath away!

The texture of flower petals, the curves, colour and shapes form the most beautiful pictures that lift my spirit and leave me in awe.

Photography enables me to capture that beauty, but it is very real; it records every fault as well. That is the reason I like to go a step further. I tend to filter out the imperfections of the reality and emphasise parts of the photograph that correspond with the image that forms in my mind. I like to manipulate the image to make it match my vision.

Digital photography has given me the tools to manipulate the images from their real world appearance to my own interpretation. Colours are changed, some details erased, new parts added, images combined. Reality is sculpted to my vision. The photograph does not dictate the outcome, I become the creator of the image, just like a painter creates his painting. ■

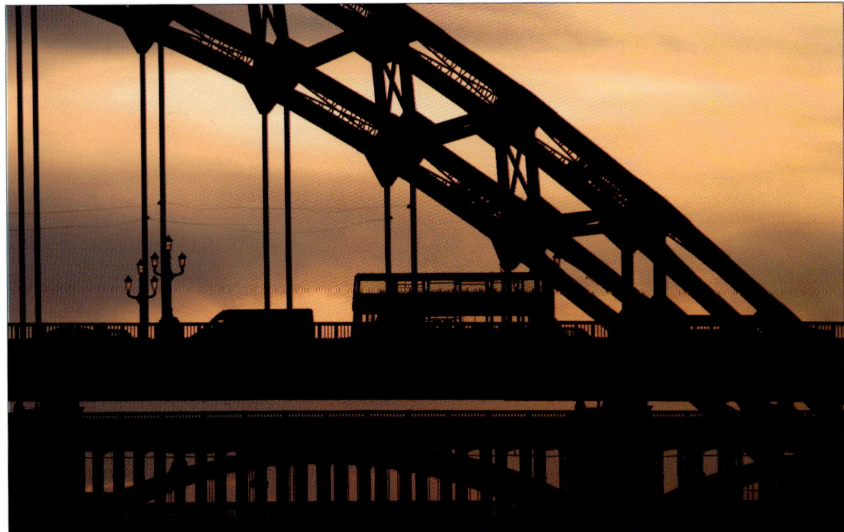

● DAVE FLETCHER Taken one evening in Newcastle. The colour has been tweaked slightly, but is more or less how the setting sun appeared.

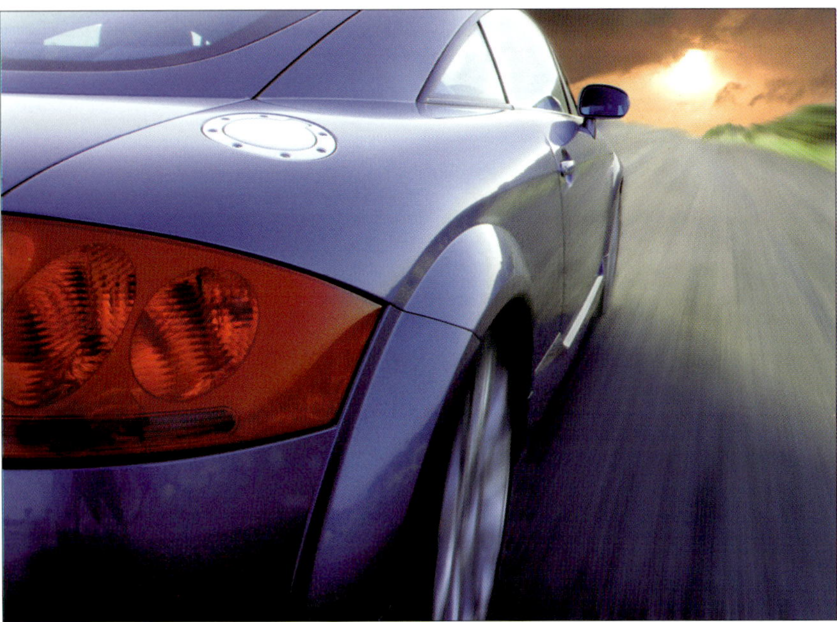

● MARTIN WESTON An Audi TT, taken at sunrise, using a Leica Digilux camera at the wide-angle setting.

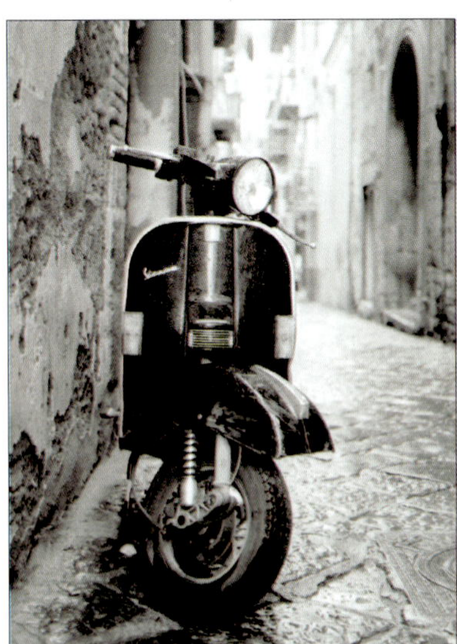

● MATT WITTINGHAM Battered Vespa, taken in Naples and converted to black & white.

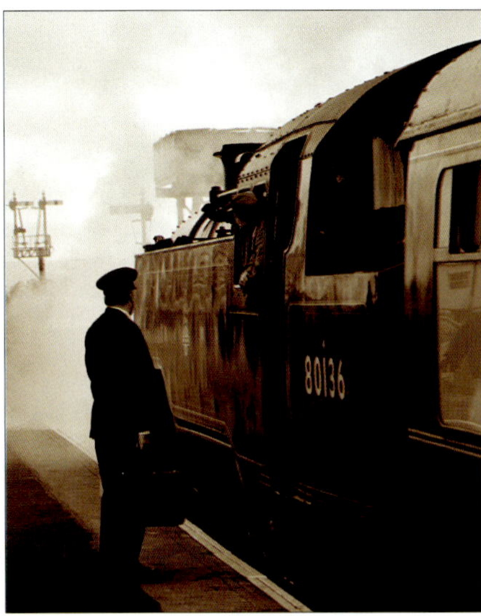

● DARRYL HOUSTON A steam engine driver chats to the station guard while waiting for the signal to leave.

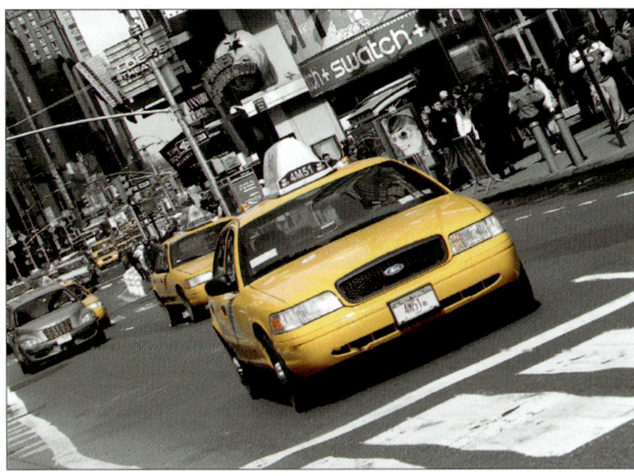

● DAVID JELLY Times Square, New York City. All the colour was removed and the yellow tones of the taxis were brushed back.

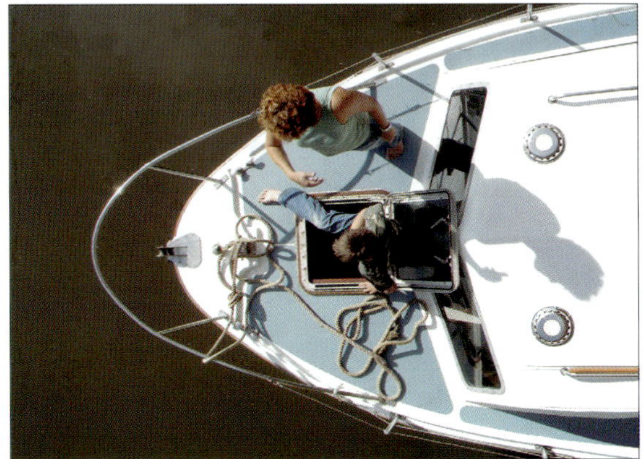

● KEVIN LOWE A shot taken leaning over a bridge as this boat came out from underneath.

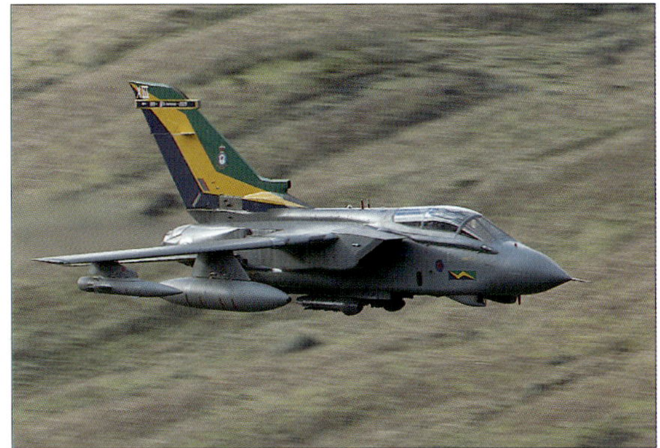

● ALAN WORSLEY A Tornado taken on the LFA17 (Low Flying Area) from a hilltop in the Lake District, about 250ft above ground.

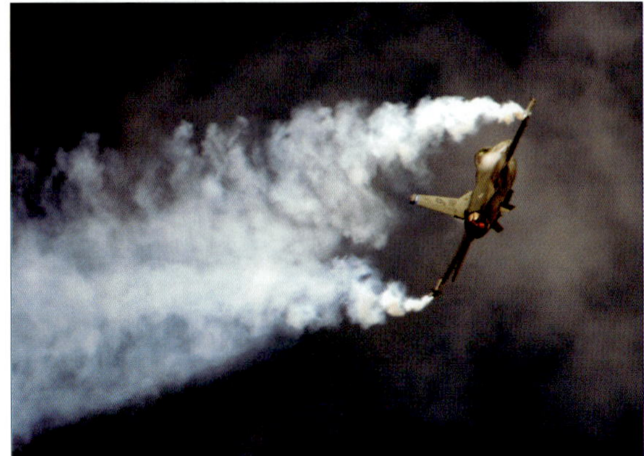

● MATT ADAMS A Lockheed Martin F-16 in tight turn at Farnborough. The vapour is coming from the leading edge of the wings.

Transport

Despite offering some great photographic opportunities, transport remains one of the least active galleries on ePHOTOzine. As you'll see from the selected photos your work could encompass bygone vehicles with intricate details, air displays, rusty relics, modern sleek sports machines or even good old horse and cart or cycle.

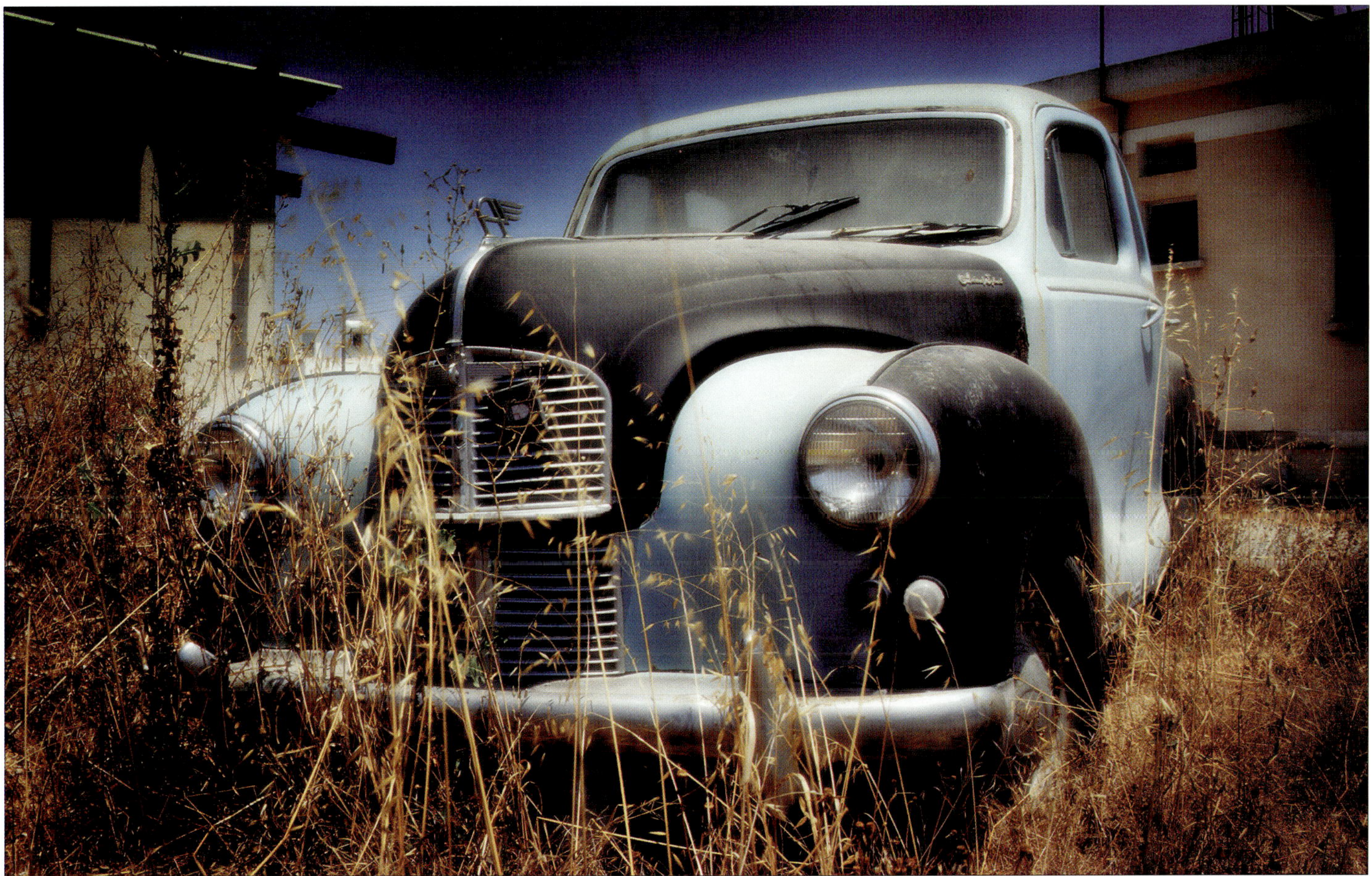

● **TREVOR SPEID** This photograph of Trevor's dad's old car was taken in Cyprus almost three years ago. In such a warm climate there was no rust whatsoever. The negative was scanned on a Nikon 4000ED film scanner and the vignetting was created using Photoshop's Burn tool. A small amount of Diffuse glow has delivered a softening of the tones.

From the early days of photography we've seen the rise of the steam engines through to the latest high speed trains. As Victorians we rode about on Penny Farthings and now we have the latest aerodynamic cycles. We've been enthralled by the flying antics of the Wright Brothers in their Flyer to the unusual GlobalFlyer, taken around the world without refuelling by Steve Fossett.

Throughout history the latest travel inventions have been recorded for news purposes, but one other thing that drives many photographers to transport is an unrivalled passion for the subject they are photographing. This passion is so high that trainspotters became known as anoraks. This slang has since spread to anyone with a 'nerdy' interest in any subject, but still appears to be extreme in transport.

The fact is transport provides a perfect subject to take an interest in. What other subject could create such a buzz – from a historical point of view through the adrenalin rush of the latest super speed device to the sexy curves of an Italian-designed dream car.

Apart from the day to day opportunities to shoot planes, trains and automobiles, enthusiasts around the country hold rallies, events and displays to bring together a wide mix of transport, presenting us with great photo material – all in one place.

Although transport is often one of the easier subjects to photograph, like all subjects, it has its complications. If you shoot it static it will look just that, yet a moving vehicle can be more difficult to photograph well.

Then there are shows and rallies. Check out any classic car show and the field or hall will usually only allow enough space to line cars up side by side. As the photographer you rarely have the space to isolate individual cars in your shot. And then there are the visitors, who tend to want to look at the details of the exhibits, which means you rarely get a moment without a body in the way, either in front or behind the vehicle. Fortunately, digital allows us to clone out people or unwanted backgrounds so you can end up with shots you wouldn't have got.

A wide-angle zoom lens is the ideal choice for most types of static vehicle. With this lens you can exclude the surroundings by moving close and choosing a wider focal length. If it's an air-display or a motor race event you'll need a lens in the telephoto range, 300mm often being the minimum useful length.

Practice your skills at panning with moving subjects using cars on the road before moving to a special day out where you're only going to get one chance. There are tips on panning in the sports and action section.

While you're doing so, select interesting cars to shoot and you'll get some good stock shots in the process. I have a collection of shots of taxis taken while on a visit to Japan. The colours were amazing and against streaky neon backgrounds create a fusion of colour. I've done similar with Red London Buses in Piccadilly Circus and cyclists in Cambridge.

A hot air balloon festival is a must if you're after colourful graphic images. Once again, a wide-angle's needed for the ground shots and a telephoto for the in-air antics. These days one lens that will look after all your needs is the super-zoom. You can buy a 28-300mm that will cover all eventualities. The downside is that they don't have wide apertures so they tend to be slower to use and there's more chance of camera shake or subject blur. A tripod or monopod will bail you out of camera shake or you can increase the ISO setting to reduce subject blur.

Anorak or not, there's a huge amount of variety in transport to keep your photographic tastebuds tantalised. Enjoy our selection of photos and keep an eye on the local paper and the web for forthcoming events near you. ■

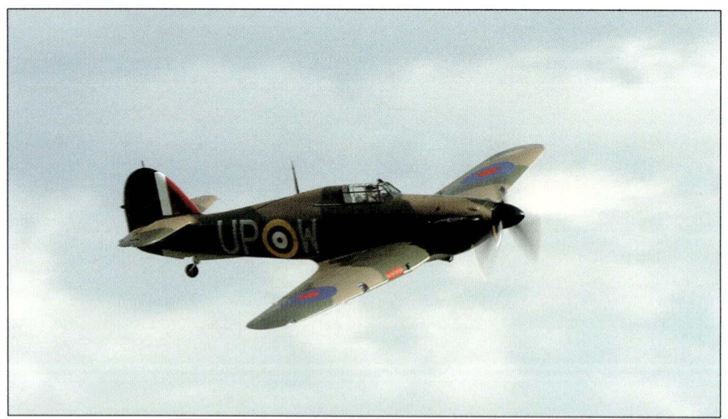

● DOUG VICKERS Hawker Hurricane MK1 at Duxford. A Canon EOS 20D and Sigma 70-300mm lens were used to pan at 1/200sec shutter speed and capture prop blur.

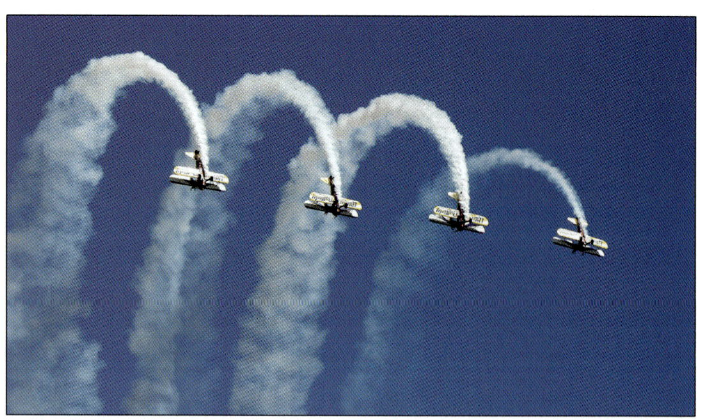

● ANDY DAVIS The Utterly Butterly display team at Duxford Airshow. Take care with exposure: here the sky is a similar tone but when it's light it can fool the camera.

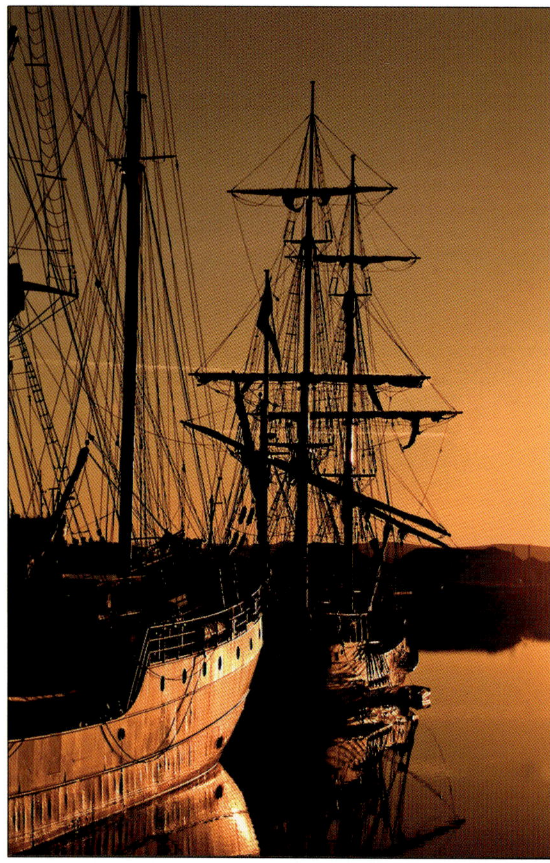

● ANDY KIM DIPPIE Tall ships taken using a Moose filter, which is a polariser and a warm-up filter combined, along with ND Grads.

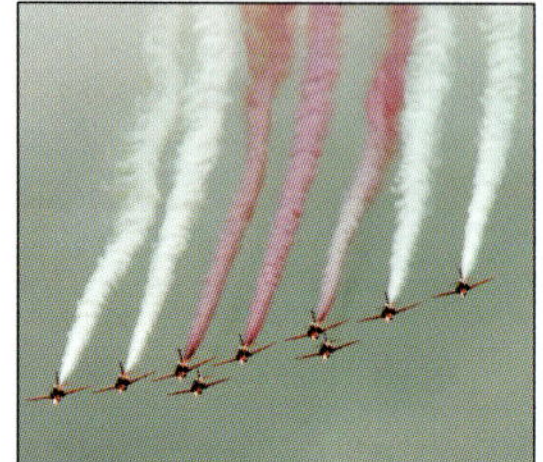

● SAM STANDERWICK Taken in foul weather at Yeovilton air day earlier this year.

AIR EVENTS

■ Some web addresses that you'll find useful when looking for events around the country:
■ Pendle Balloon Flights Clayton-le-Dale Blackburn **www.pendle-balloon-flights.co.uk** ■ Red Arrows Air Displays, Lincolnshire **www.raf.mod.uk/reds/dates.html** ■ Northants Balloon Festival **www.northamptonballoonfestival.com** ■ Devon and Somerset Balloons, Pewsey, Wiltshire **www.balloon-flights.ne**t ■ Cameron Flights Southern Pewsey, Wiltshire **www.cameron-flights.co.uk** ■ Hot Air Balloon festivals **www.eballoon.org/festival/balloon-festivals-uk.html** ■ Royal International Air Tattoo, Fairford Gloucestershire **www.airtattoo.com/airtattoo** ■ Shuttleworth Collection, Nr. Biggleswade **www.shuttleworth.org** ■ Imperial War Museum, Duxford **duxford.iwm.org.uk** ■ Biggin Hill Air Displays, Kent **www.airdisplaysint.co.uk** ■ Newark Air Museum, Winthorpe, Notts **www.newarkairmuseum.co.uk** ■ Redhill Airshow, Surrey **www.redhillairshow.co.uk**

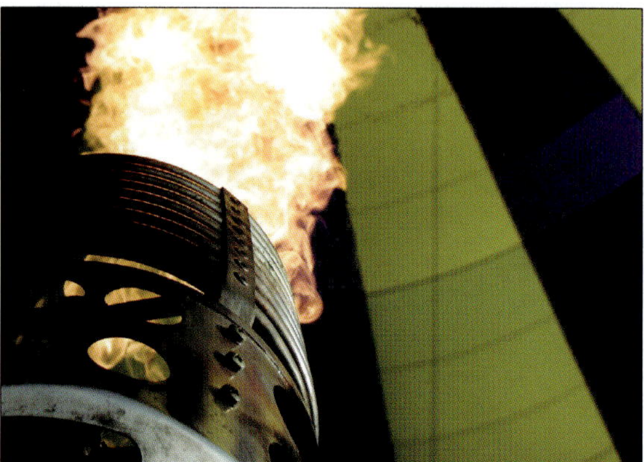

● GARY WILLIAMS An alternative view on a balloon flight. Wait until the burners ignite and shoot away against the colourful balloon.

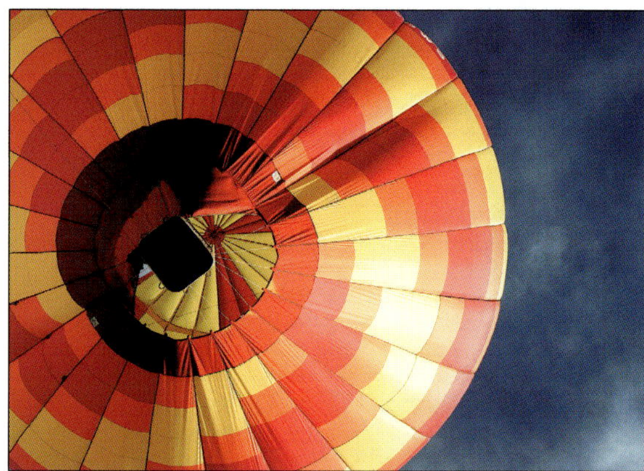

● PAUL STEFAN Paul had a press pass for the main arena at Bristol Balloon Fiesta, enabling him to get under balloons as they launched.

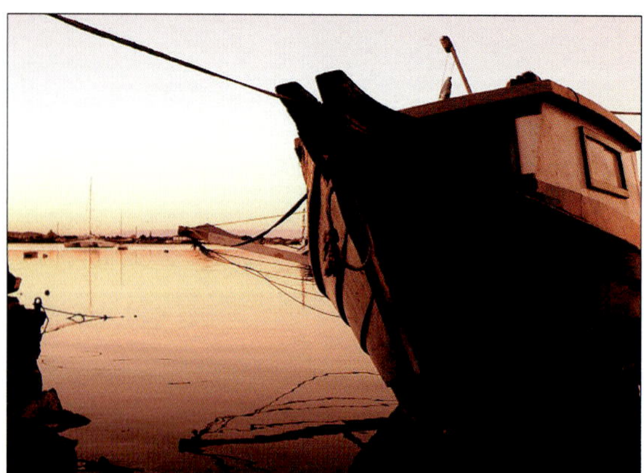

● EDUARDO MARQUETTI A boat in maintenance at the Saco da Fazenda, Itajaí, Santa Catarina in Brazil.

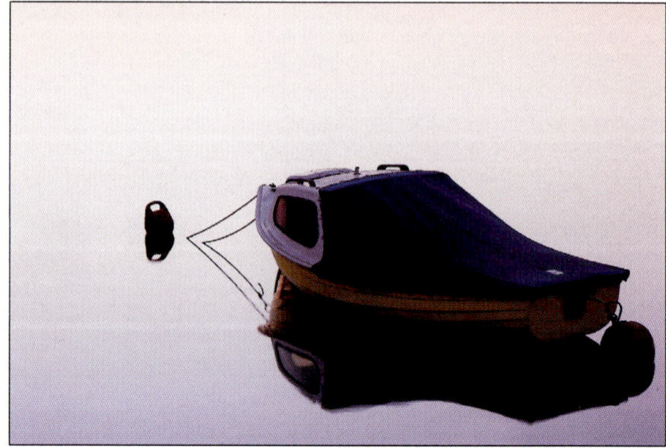

● CHRIS FROUD The calm water allowed Chris to capture a near perfect reflection, which he feels is the key to this image's success.

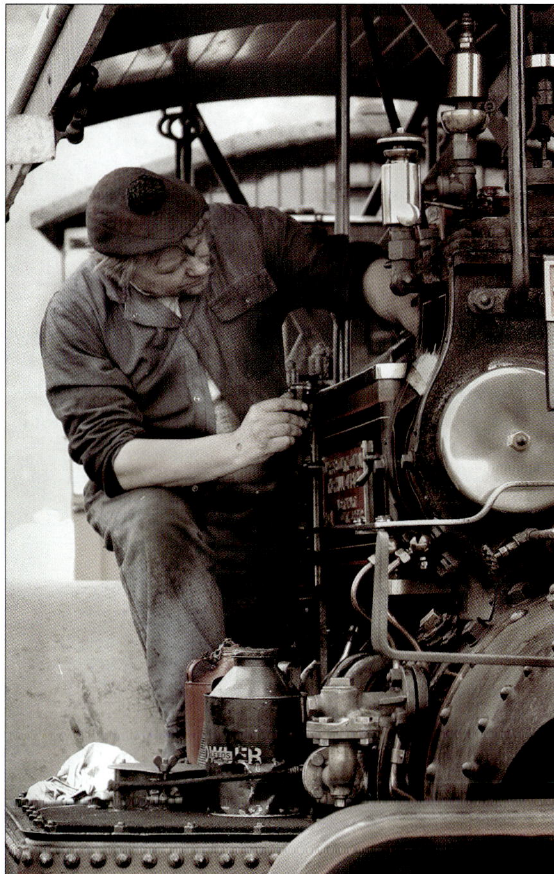

● KEV BOOTH This man was fixing his steam engine with such loving care while Kev caught him on candid camera.

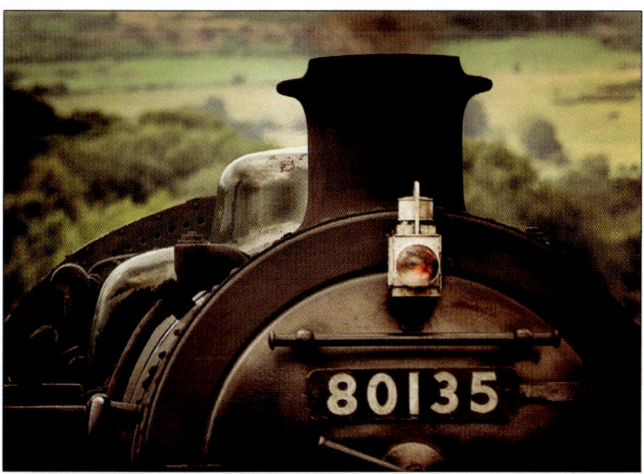

● MATT PAGE This train on the North Yorkshire Moors Railway is used in the TV programme Heartbeat. Dodged and burned.

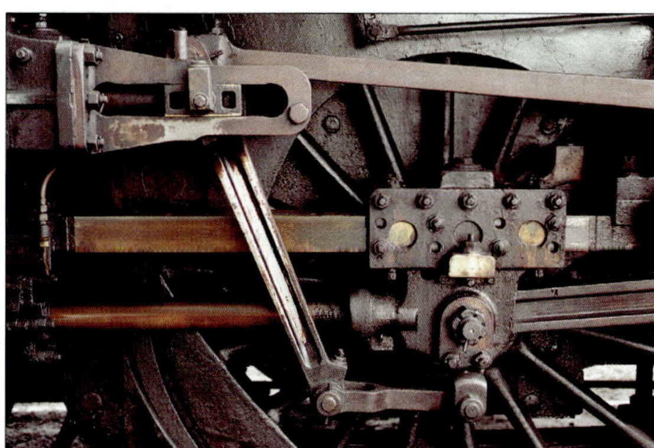

● CHRIS WALKER Steam engines provide plenty of close-up details. Here the wheel and its mechanisms are the focal points.

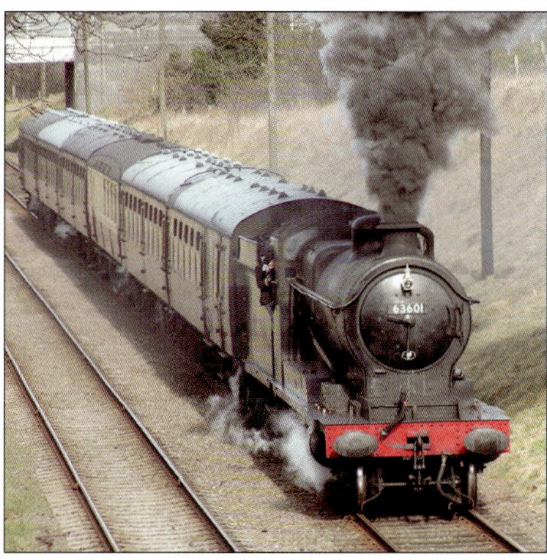

● ALLEN COOK The 63601 locomotive taken as it pulls away at the Great Central Railway.

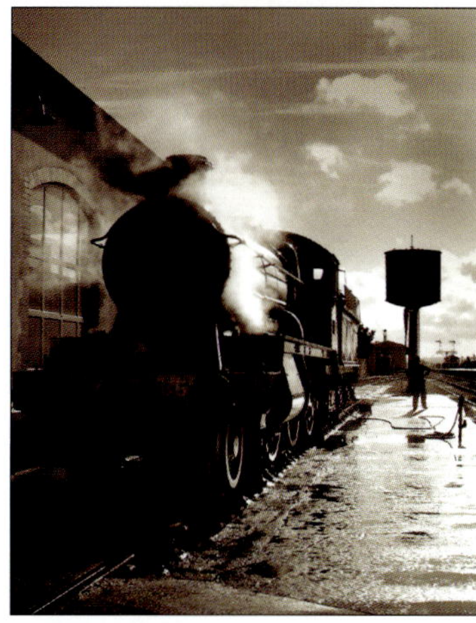

● PETE MURRELL A steam loco of the West Somerset Railway takes on water.

DIGITAL TECHNIQUE – ENHANCE A CLASSIC CAR SHOW SNAP

■ Vehicles are often cramped into tight spots at car shows and a touch of digital cloning is usually required so why not go a stage further and lift it into a new, more atmospheric setting?

1 Open the car photo and create a duplicate layer – Layer⇨ Duplicate Layer. Go back to the background layer and fill with white – Edit⇨Fill. I also added an ePHOTOzine number plate using the Type tool and Edit⇨Transform⇨Distort so it follows the plate's angle.

2 Add a layer mask to the duplicated layer – Layer⇨Add Layer Mask⇨Reveal All and click inside the white mask box that appears alongside the normal layer thumbnail.

3 Click on the Lasso tool and draw a rough selection around the car. Don't worry about being right up to the edge. We will erase any unwanted edge detail next.

4 Once you've gone all the way around the car go to Select⇨Inverse (Shift+Ctl+I) to invert the selection.

5 Go to Edit⇨Fill and select black to add a mask on the top layer and allow the white from the layer before to show. You should now have your car surrounded by a rough white vignette.

6 Now, with the mask still selected, use the eraser and brush set to small size to paint or erase the mask around the car. On straight edges use the Polygonal lasso and fill with black (mask) or white (unmask) Once complete (don't forget the windows too) you should have a perfect cut-out.

7 Select the background, make it a transparent layer by double clicking on and then deleting the white. Select⇨All and hit the delete button.

8 Go to Layer⇨Merge Visible and Copy (Ctrl+C) and Paste (Ctrl+V) onto a suitable background. I chose a coastal scene that had already been enhanced by merging a sunset with a drab grey coast.

9 The colours may differ, making it look unnaturally placed, so go to Image⇨Adjustments⇨Match Color and select the original coastal shot as the match. This adds colours from the sunset onto the car. I then tweaked curves to make it more dramatic.

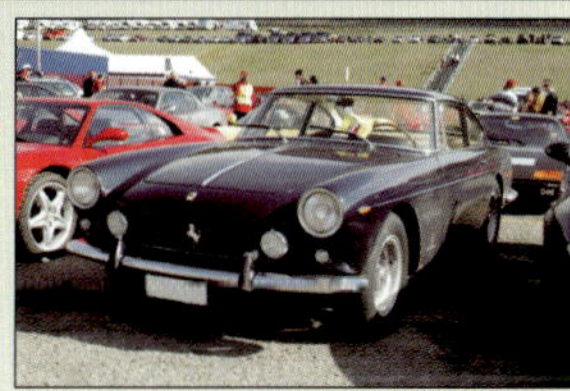

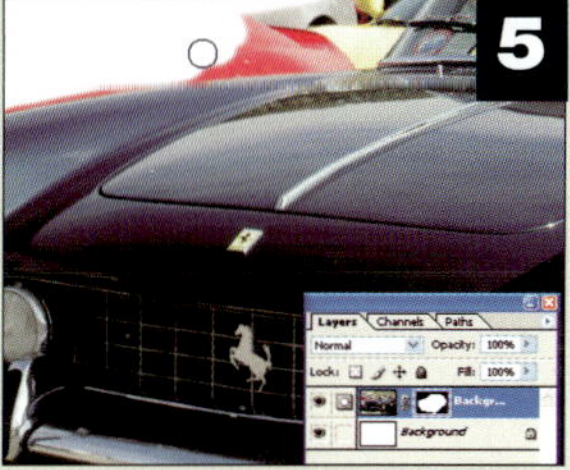

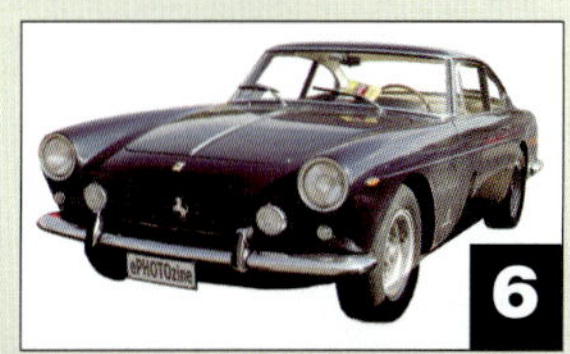

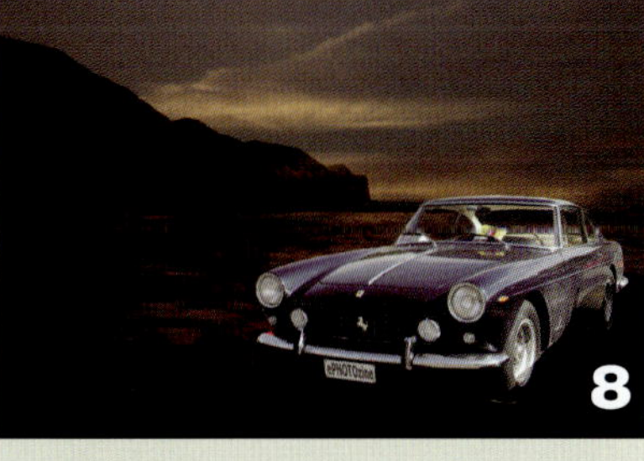

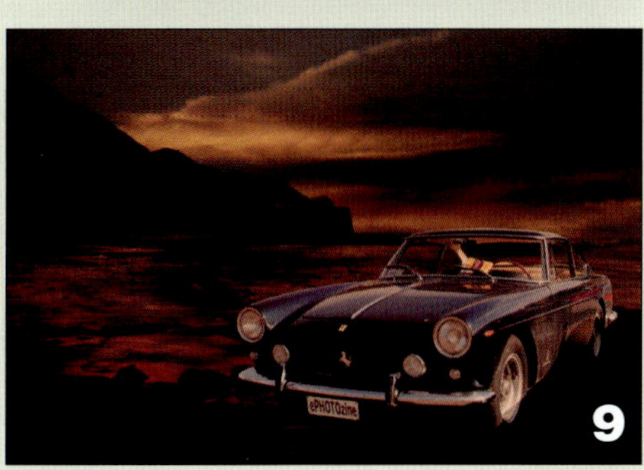

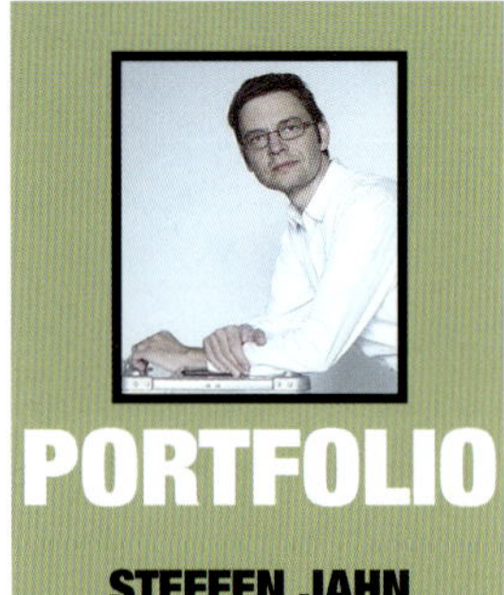

PORTFOLIO

STEFFEN JAHN
A Germany-based car photographer who works for international clients in studio and on location

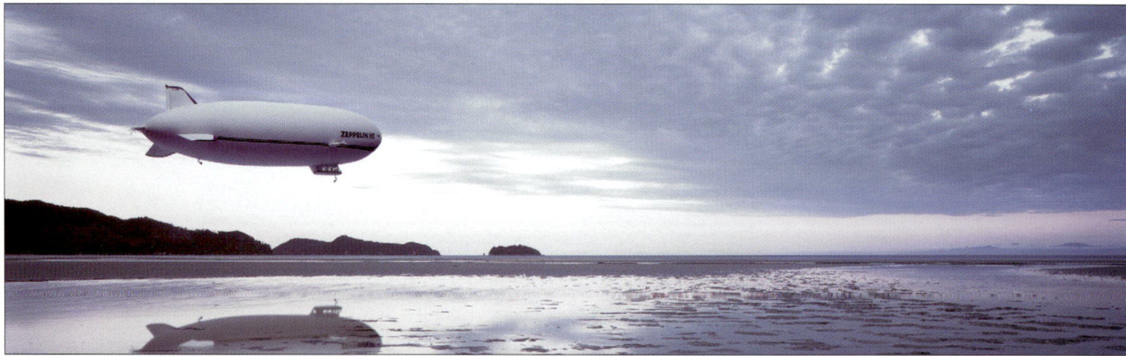

Steffen's career began as a teenager through an apprenticeship in one of Europe's largest car photo studios, where he assisted many great photographers. He specialises in shooting technical images – you get the best results when you know the subject well.

Ten years ago he opened a studio in Stuttgart, strategically based between the HQs of Mercedes and Porsche.

Out of all the projects he's worked on one stands out above the rest: The client wanted a brand new Mercedes standing in front of a MD9 jet. His company rented an airport in the Mojave desert, along with a huge passenger jet. Being the owner of a private jet for 24 hours was quite an experience.

Whether Steffen shoots on his X-Pan or 8x10in camera his most valued item is a tripod. A tripod forces you to think about the picture before you even look through the finder. You need to decide about angle, perspective and lens with great care. It leads you to the one perfectly balanced image, rather than dozens of average pictures.

In professional photography, one of the most common sayings now is; "Don't worry! We fix it in post-production!" Although pushing, pasting and pampering pixels will make some images look passable, you can seldom create a perfect photo out of bad design.

Advertising photography is mainly a fight against schedule, budget, client, agency and weather, but sometimes you get an unexpected gift – your flash-system fails, a rain shower is coming in or the driver puts the car in the wrong position. Always be open to see an image beyond your imagination. ■
www.steffenjahn.com

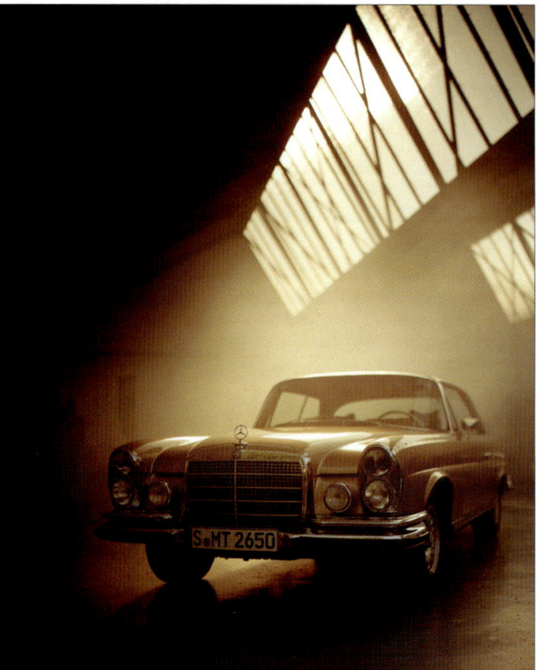

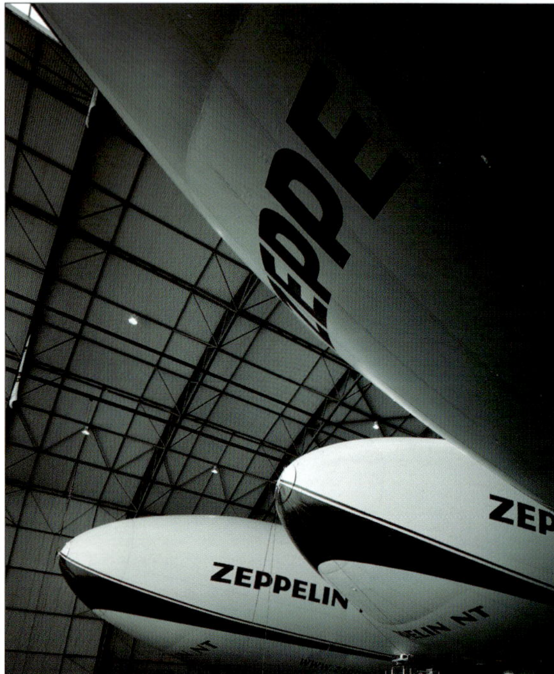

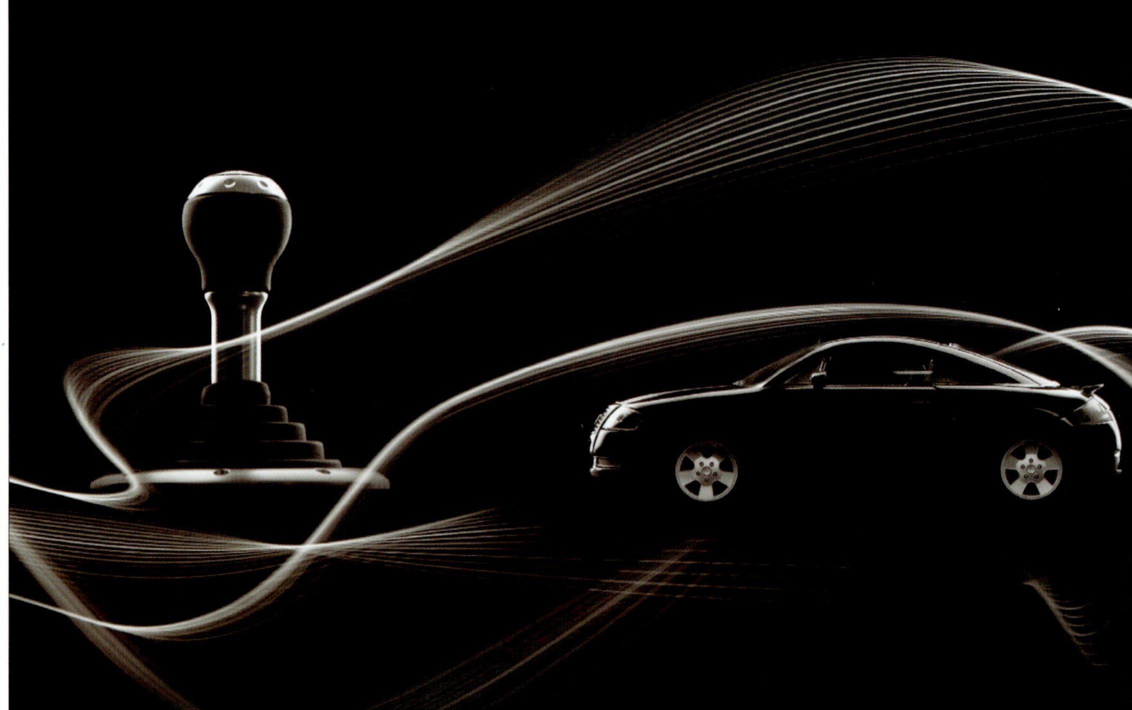

● Top: The Zeppelin NT (New Technology) captured soaring over a New Zealand beach very early in the morning. Middle left: Steffen waited six hours until the sun was in the right position, added a little studio fog and came up with this shot. Middle right: Zeppelin's lined up in a hanger, blue toned for effect. Bottom: Composite shot, featuring the sexy Audi TT. Black & white ensures it has a very graphical feel.

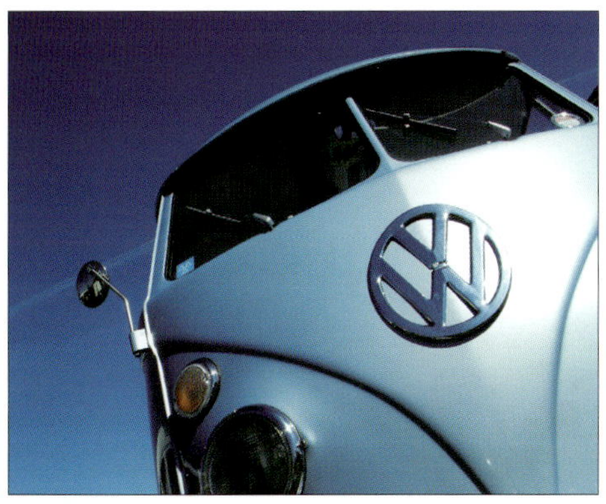

● MICHAEL BOSANKO A VW Caravanette, shot with a wide angle lens from a low viewpoint.

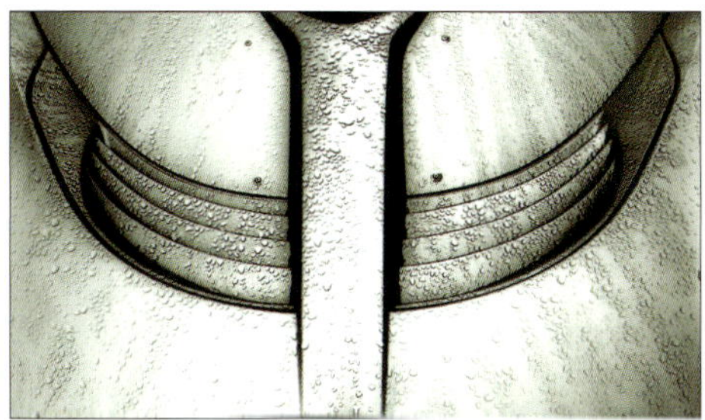

● MIKE OTLEY. The radiator exhaust vents on the front bonnet of a Lotus Elise Sport 135R in pouring rain.

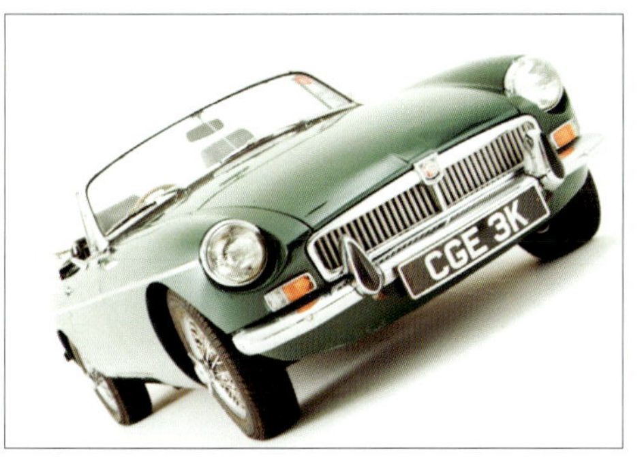

● TRACEY SIMPSON The camera was tilted to gain the dynamic angle – a technique often used by car magazines.

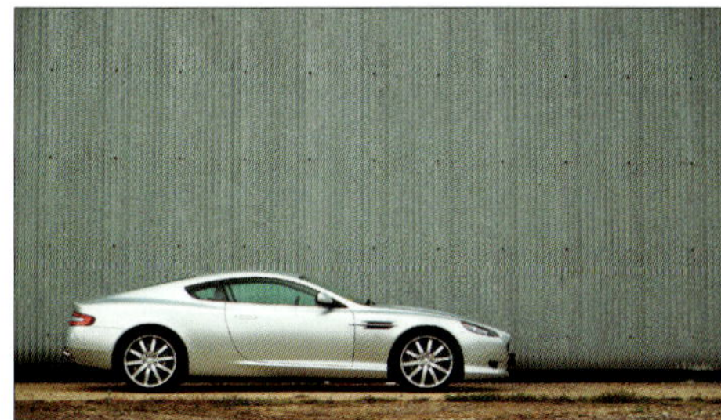

● STEPHEN HALL Stunning lines of the gorgeous Aston Martin DB9 against a suitable, non-distracting backdrop.

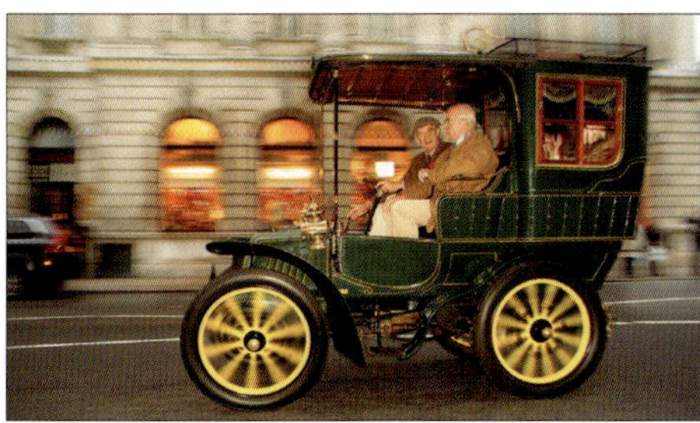

● PETER SIMMONDS A 1903 *Panhard et Levassor* in Pall Mall, using a Nikon D100 and balanced fill flash.

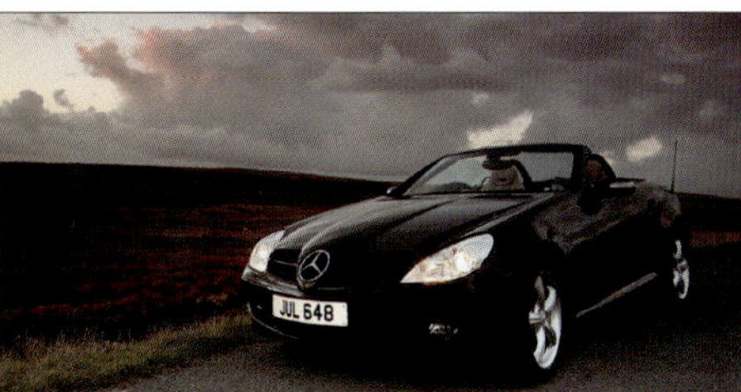

● STEVE LANGTON Fill-in flash and 1/6sec exposure balance the SLK against its West Lancs Moors backdrop.

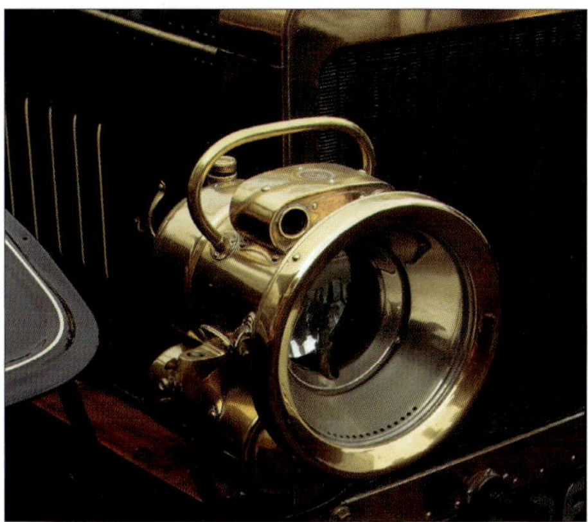

● MIKE OTLEY A detailed shot of an acetylene headlamp on an Edwardian 1910 Standard.

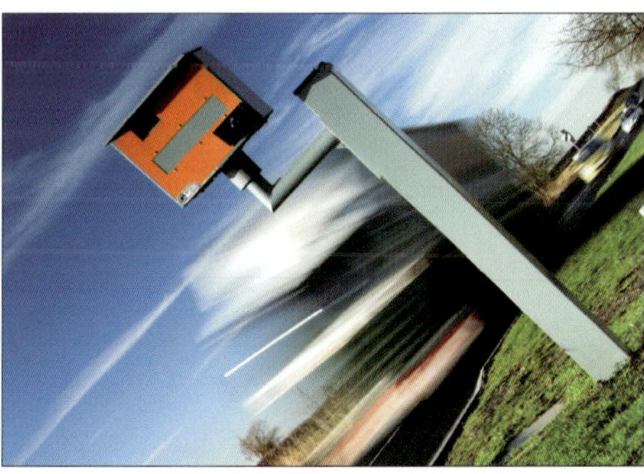

● STEVE SANT A speed camera taken at a low shutter speed to show movement in the passing vehicles.

SHOOTING TIPS – CAR TRAILS

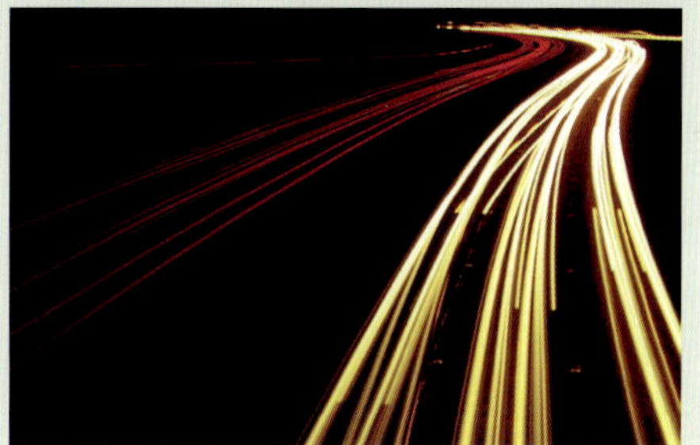

■ A long shutter speed can be set at night to record car headlights and rear lights as colourful trails.

1 Choose a safe position on a suitable bridge over a busy road and mount the camera on a tripod.

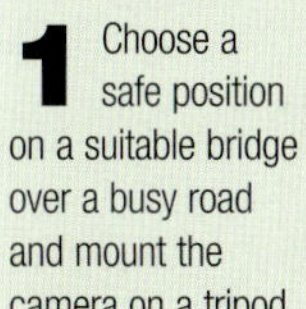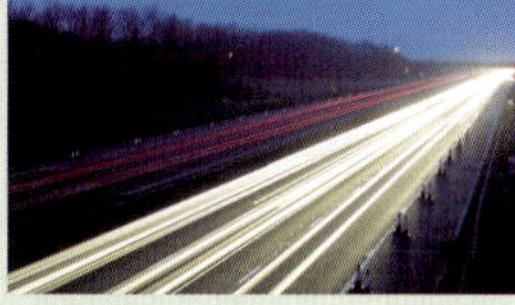

2 Set the camera to manual and select a long shutter speed of between 1 and 15 seconds, depending on the length of streak you require.

3 If you want multiple streaks and the road is quiet select the camera's B-setting, trip the shutter using a cable release with a shutter lock and record the first approaching car. Then cover the lens and wait for the next car to appear before uncovering the lens again. Repeat this until you have a suitable number of streaks.

4 Roads with a bend ahead provide more interesting S-shaped streaks.

■ An alternative option is to ask a willing driver to take you out on the road and record trails from inside the car. You'll also pick up trails of street lights and neon signs. Sit in the passenger seat and point the camera out through the window or sit in the back and use slow-sync flash to illuminate the driver and balance with the outside streaks.

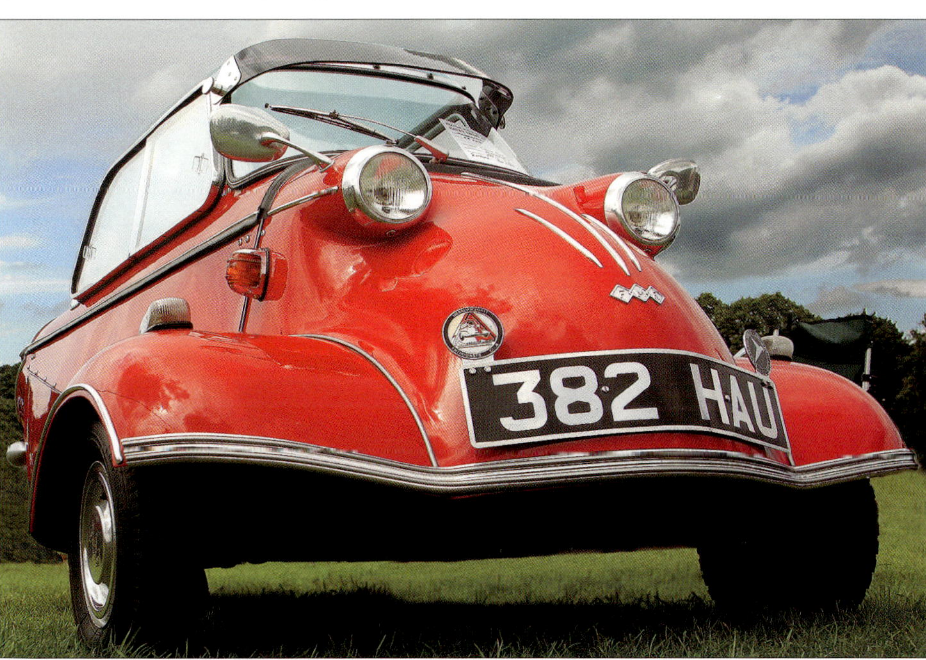

● ROGER PRESCOTE A low, wide-angle shot of a Messerschmitt three wheeler at Autokarna, Wollaton Park.

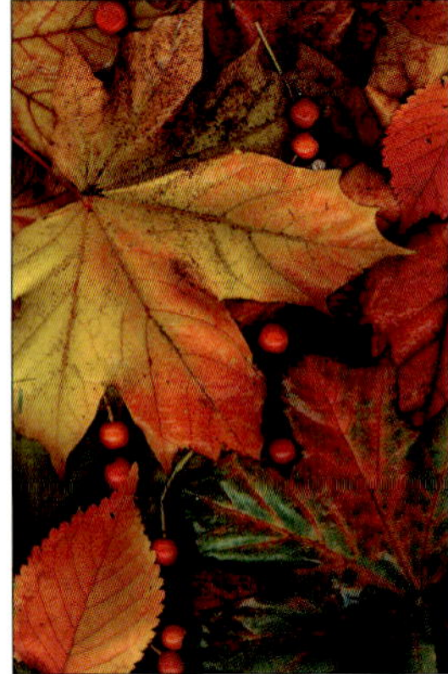

● CALEB DANIELS Leaves scanned on a Canon 8000f.

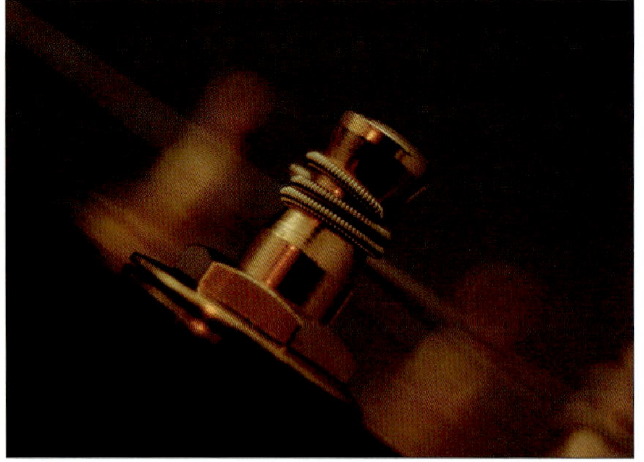

● ERICA CAMERON An experimental picture of a guitar using a 1/60sec shutter speed and a 90mm macro at f/5.6 and ISO400.

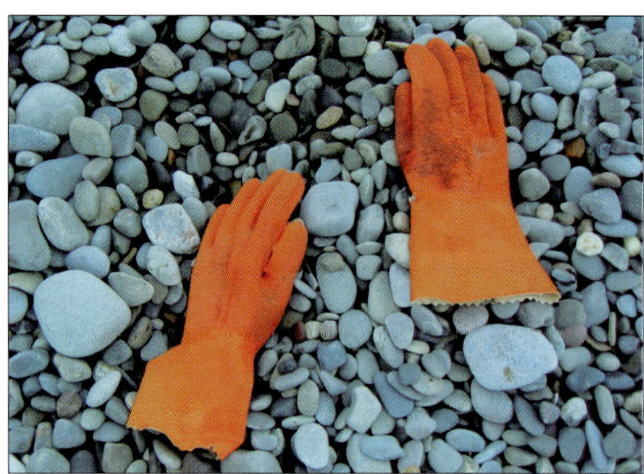

● PHILIP HENDY Items washed up on a beach can be perfect subjects for close-ups, using the pebbles or sand as a backdrop.

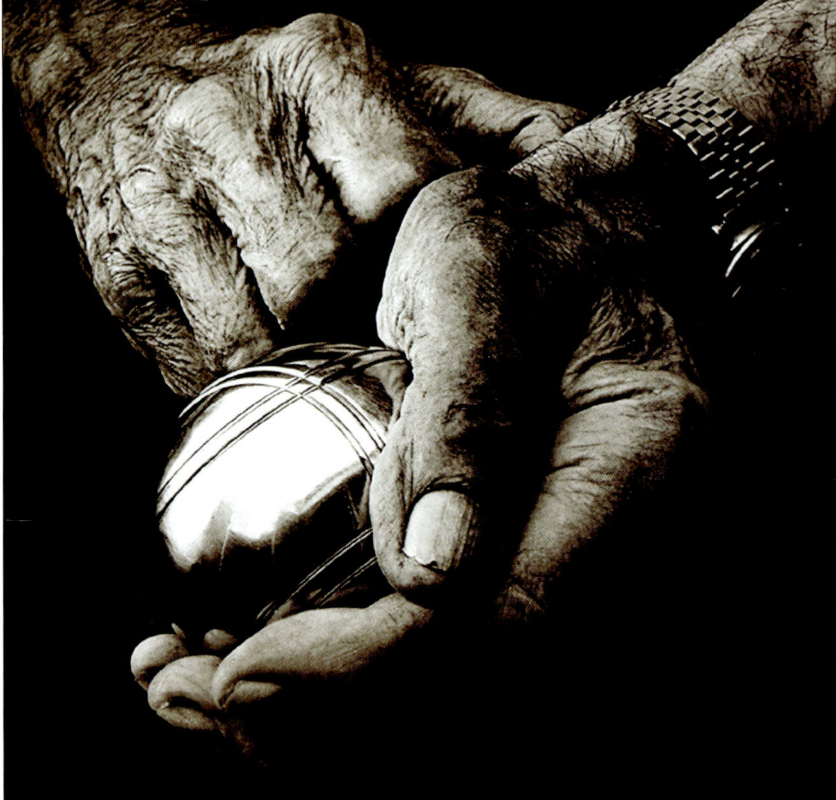

● TONY PERRYMAN "Waiting to Play" is a natural light shot taken using an Olympus E20 in aperture-priority mode and 100mm lens at f/8. The result was converted to sepia using Photoshop.

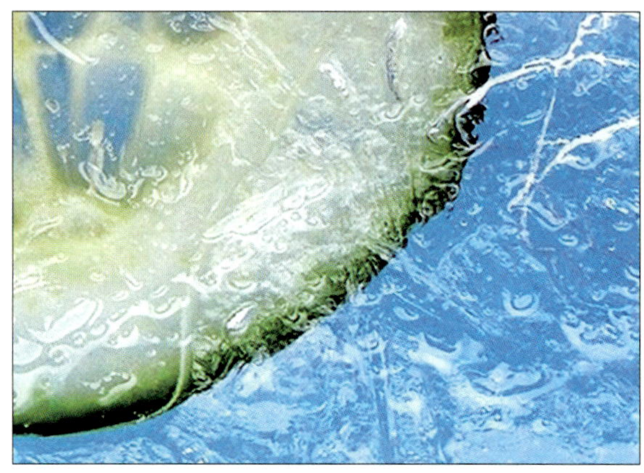

● CLARE LAMBERT Sliced fruit and vegetables, such as this cucumber frozen in ice, make colourful subjects for indoor shots.

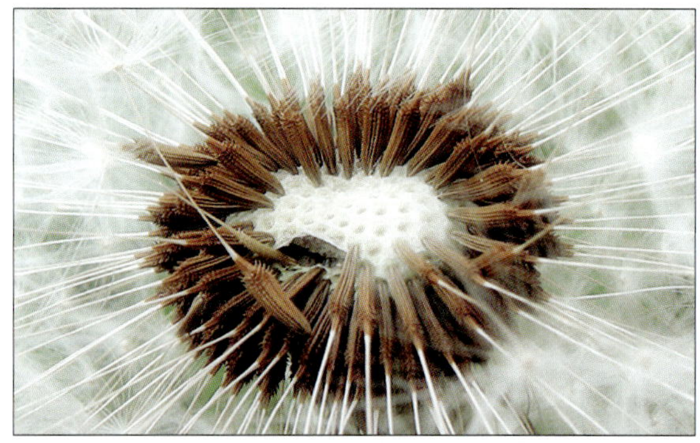

● MARTIN WAIT Taken hand-held with a digital compact. Diffuse glow was added to bring out the white in the seeds as they flew off.

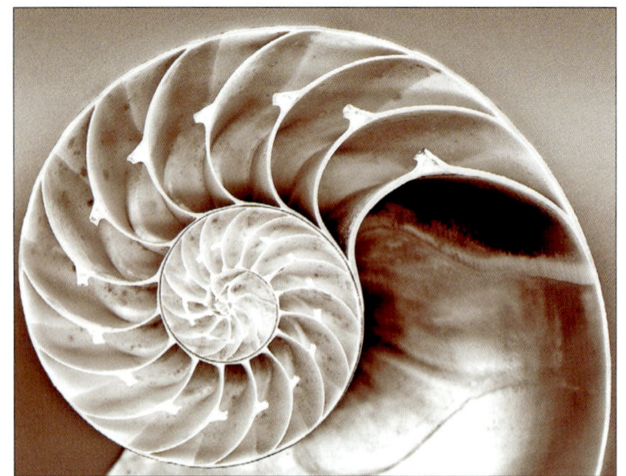

● TONY HUMPHREYS Image showing the internal structure of a Nautilus shell. Turned to black & white and then toned.

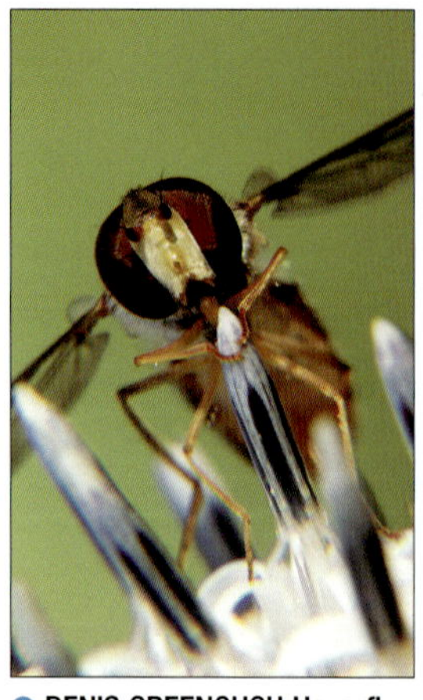

● DENIS GREENOUGH Hoverfly on a globe thistle.

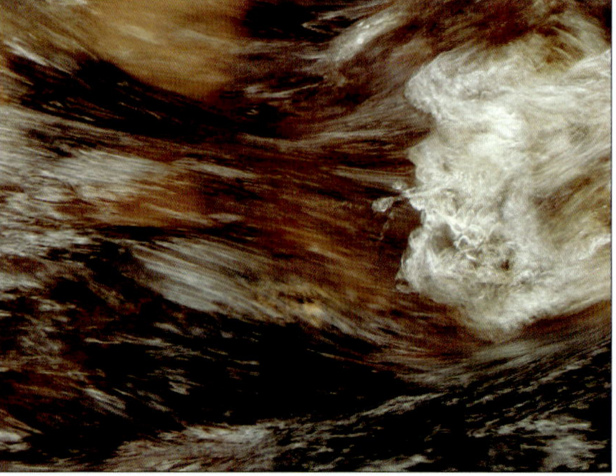

● KATH HILTON One of a sequence taken lying at the side of Wycoller Beck using my trusty Fuji S5000, hand-held on the macro setting.

Close-ups

Our world presents a very different view when seen close-up. With the aid of a close-up lens or macro mode our cameras can be used to record patterns and textures, graphic detail, incredible colours and fascinating features that our eyes may normally skim by in our day to day activity. This section gives us a glimpse into an amazing miniature world.

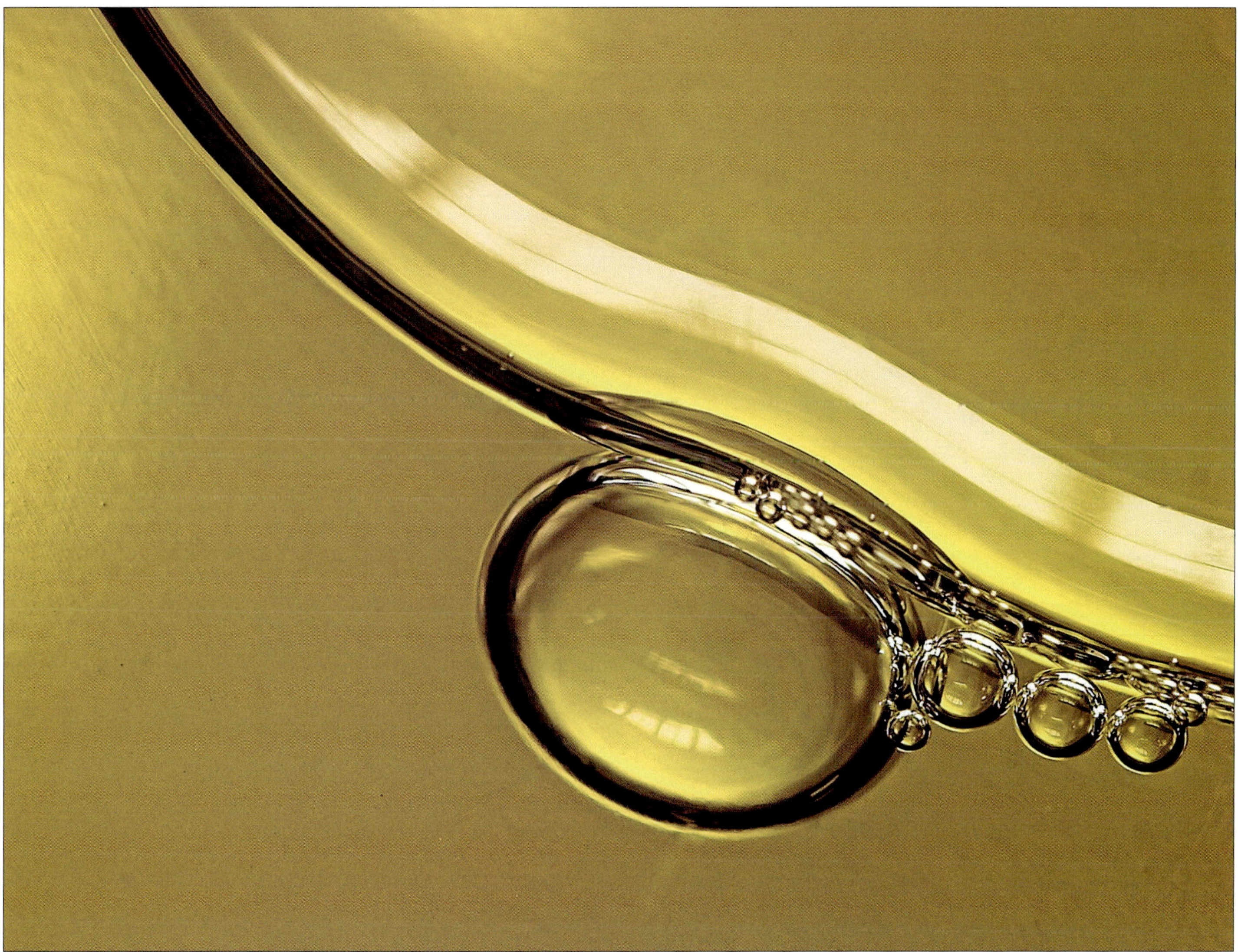

● COLIN MILL A bubble in a wine bottle, lit by a north facing window, taken on a Canon EOS 10 and a Sigma 105mm macro lens. When taking shots like this, consider the direction of the light. Varying the camera to subject and subject to illumination position can result in some very different results.

Close-up photography allows you to shoot things that you may not have previously thought possible – a close-up of your diamond engagement ring, bees in the garden or flower stamens. You could also record your stamp collections for insurance purposes or hone-in on patterns and create textured backgrounds for your new web site, newsletter or project. Any subject that's seen from near can be classed as close-up while macro takes things a stage further offering magnifications greater than lifesize. The list of practical and creative applications is endless.

The subject reproduced on the film or CCD is measured as a ratio of life-size. For example, a camera that can record pictures at half life-size means that the subject will appear recorded on the film or CCD half the size that it is in real life. This, of course, changes when an enlargement or print is made, as the subject then appears larger than life.

To achieve close-up or macro photography your camera must have a focusing system that lets you produce sharp pictures from distances closer than 20cm, ideally closer.

Very few compact digital cameras now come without a macro or close-up lens that's usually indicated with an icon of a flower. Some allow you to go as close as one or two centimetres from the subject, allowing you to fill the frame with a subject that's just 15mm wide. As a result, macro photography is far less of a complication than previously experienced in the film user's world.

Compact film cameras have a macro setting. This normally gets you to around 60cm from the subject, so true macro photography isn't an option, but they are usually adequate for taking photos of larger flowers and similar-sized subjects.

The SLR is the most versatile option and manufacturers produce a range of lenses for their SLR cameras that also allow macro photography. The standard zoom lens supplied with an SLR will focus close enough to give quarter life size (1:4) results, but the true macro lens gives you either half life size (1:2) or life size (1:1) sometimes with an extension tube.

When you shoot a close-up it may be just to crop out background details, for example when taking photos of flowers. A single tightly framed head is often better than a shot of a bed of flowers. While taking things into the macro realm means you may be photographing abstract shots of petals or detailed shots of the stamen.

For many of us, flower photography or insects is the first step we take into the world of macro. However, once you've looked through this section of the book you should be inspired to shoot a whole host of close-ups.

If you're unsure what equipment to use we have explained this in the panel on page 205. ■

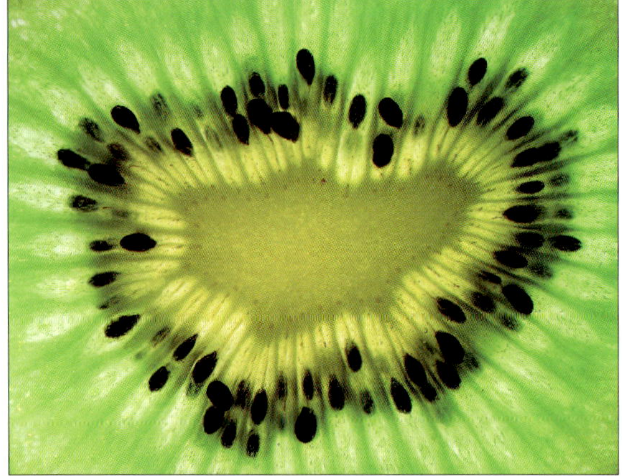

● EMMA TUMMAN A slice of Kiwi Fruit on a lightbox, taken with a Canon Digital Ixus I camera. Try using a variety of fruit like this.

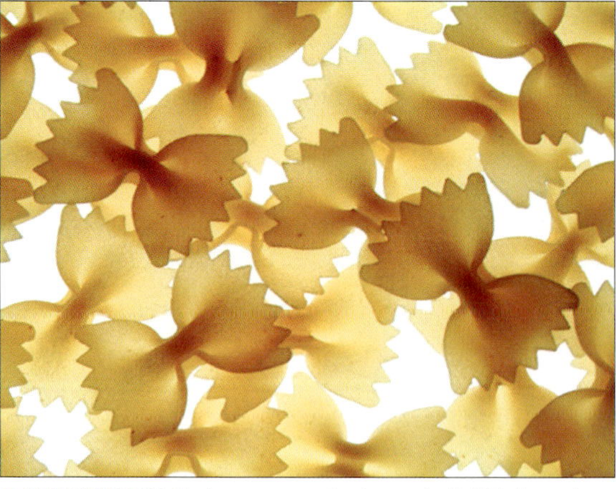

● FRANK THOMAS Pasta was spread out on a daylight-balanced lightbox. The FinePix S602's histogram was used to check exposure.

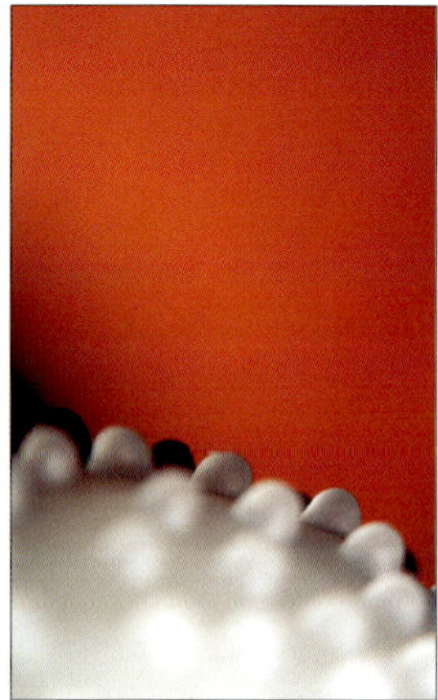

● AARON COLLETT Shallow depth-of-field for abstract shot.

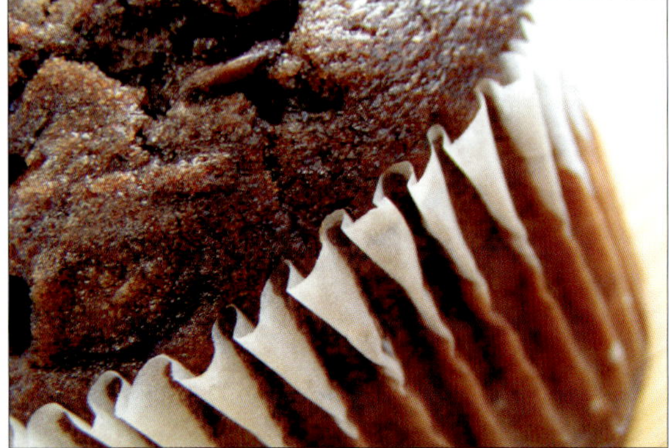

● AL MULROONEY Tried to capture the moistness of this Muffin using natural light from the window and the camera's macro mode.

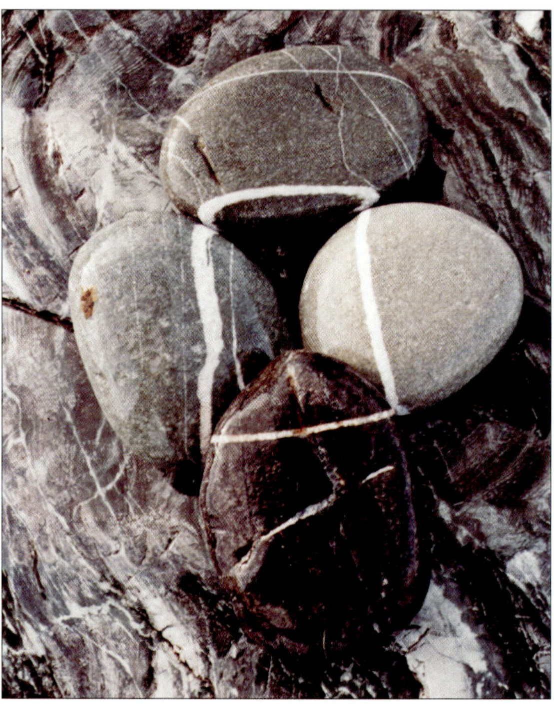

● SUSAN COLLINS Taken with a 20 year old Olympus OM10. Stones arranged, photographed and then left behind in Goldsworthy style.

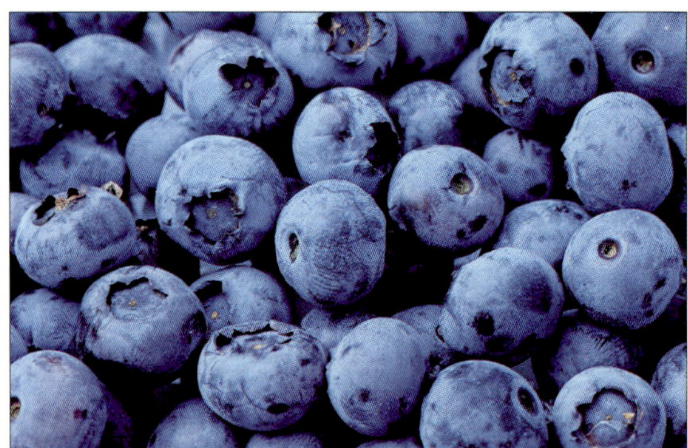

● KEITH ROWLEY Blueberries taken under soft overcast lighting at f/16 with a Canon 100mm macro lens. Fujichrome Velvia film.

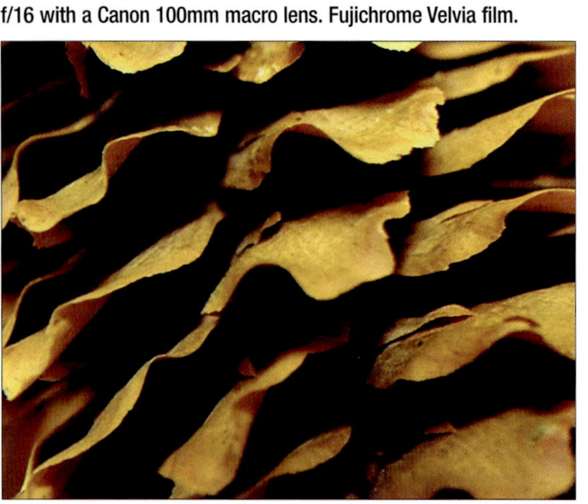

● LINDA AINSLIE Detail in a pine cone, taken with Fuji Finepix S7000 using its macro setting. Patterns are found in many subjects.

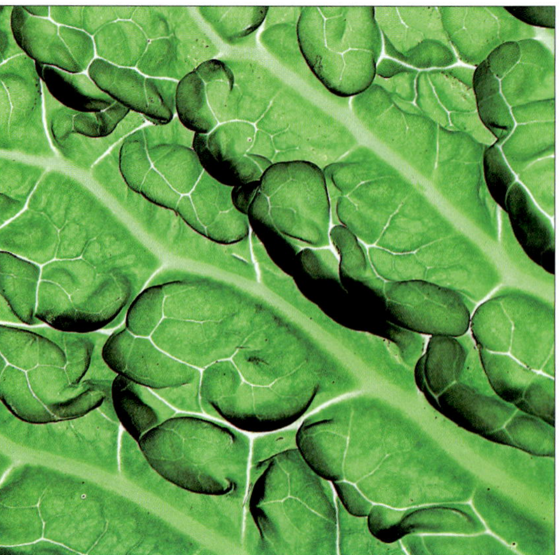

● ALAN PARKINSON Close-up of a savoy cabbage, taken with a Canon EOS 300D and 18-55mm lens. Cropped in Photoshop.

KILL REFLECTIONS

■ While reflections may sometimes be desired, in close-up photography they're often so big they distract from the subject and should be removed. Reflections can be reduced or removed in a number of ways.

■ **Polarising filter** is the easiest and most convenient option. This screws onto the lens or slots into a filter holder and rotates in the mount to offer a variable reflection remover. Like polarising sunglasses, it's perfect for reducing reflections in water so you can see under the surface, but also ideal to remove glare from foliage so the natural rich green shows through. It doesn't work on bare metal, but is good for killing reflections on painted objects, glass and natural reflective surfaces.

■ **Matt sprays** can be used to spray over the object to add a matt coating that reduces reflectivity. Although this works, it's a messy and clumsy way.

■ **Black paper/card** placed between the light source and the object reduces directional light falling onto it. This is an effective way, but blocking light reduces the exposure, so a tripod is more often needed. The subject can also become flat and lack 3D form, where the unblocked light source would have given it depth and shape. One way around this is to use tracing paper to diffuse the light source and reduce hard reflections.

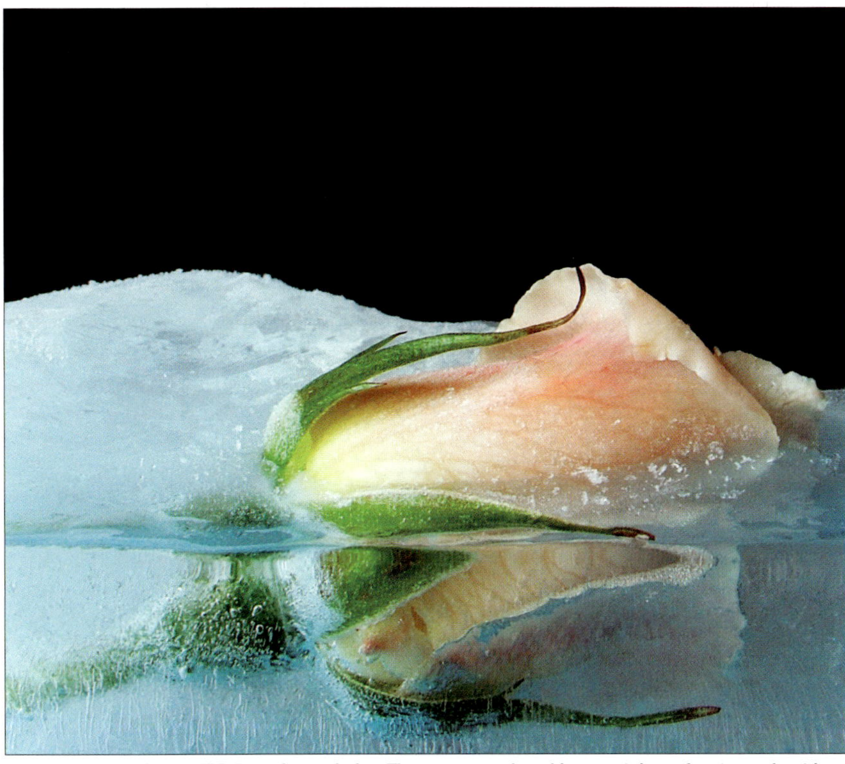

● MATT DILLON-SHEPHERD Rose frozen in ice. The rose was placed in a container of water and put in the freezer and then shot using natural light. This technique can be used for all kinds of subjects.

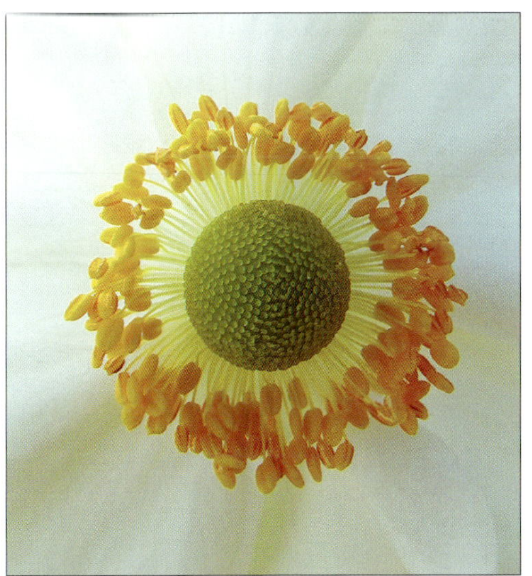

● TREVOR SLATTER An Anemone, taken at Great Dixter, using a Fuji S7000 at ISO200 and a f/6.3, 1/400sec exposure.

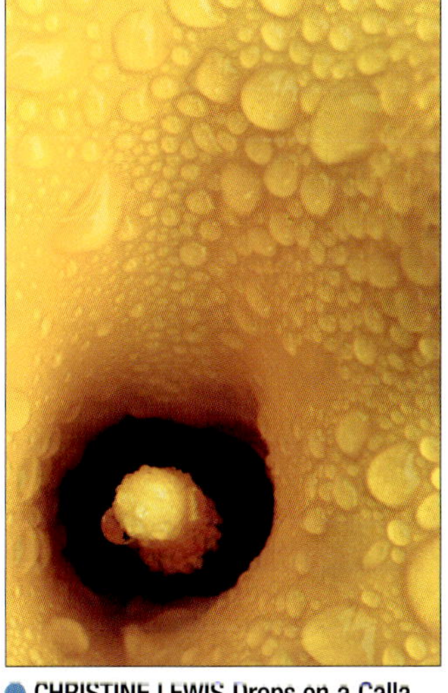

● CHRISTINE LEWIS Drops on a Calla, using Nikon FM3a and 105mm macro.

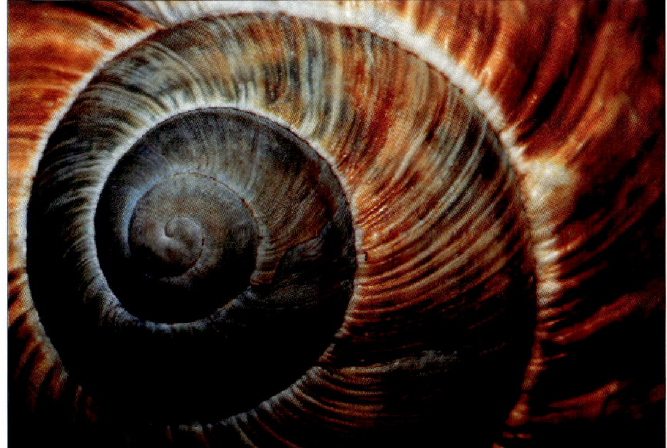

● EDWARD NORTON An experiment with the Canon EOS 10D's white balance. Sigma 180 Macro at f/22, 1sec, illuminated by kitchen lights.

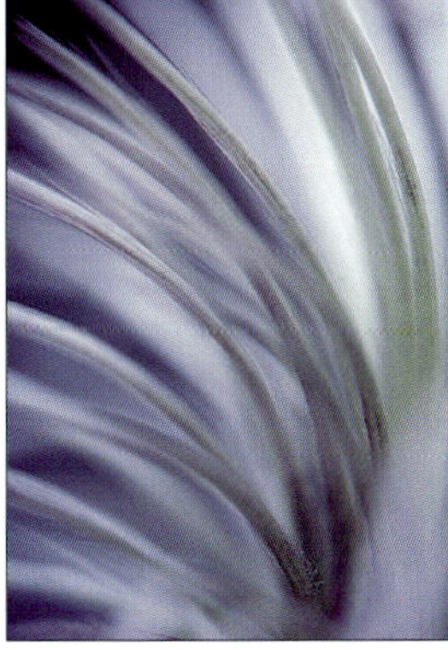

● BRIAN WADIE Clematis seed head, using a reversed 50mm.

ESSENTIAL CLOSE-UP ACCESSORIES

■ If you have an SLR you can add a whole host of accessories to get you close to the subject. Below are some options you can consider

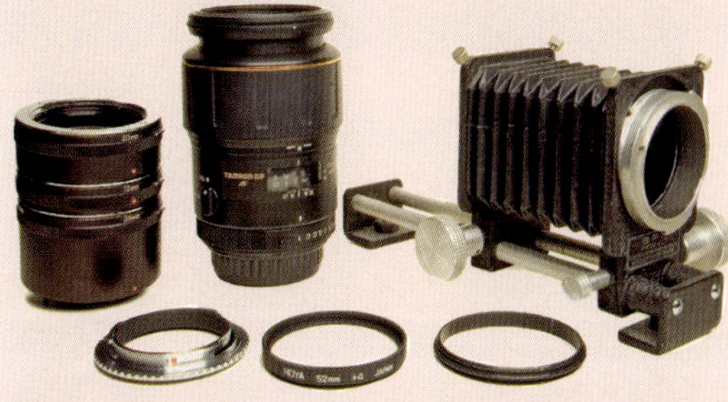

■ **Macro lens £100+** All dedicated close-up photographers either own or lust after a real macro lens. They offer a near-perfect performance and gain the close-up ability just by rotating the lens barrel. With most of the other options you have to attach the accessory to do close-ups and remove it to go back to distant photography. All fiddly stuff! You'll achieve at least 1:2 half life-size ratio and, on many, 1:1 lifesize.

■ **Reversing ring £10 to £15** This reverses the lens on the camera body. Buy one that matches your body mount and the lens' filter thread. All auto coupling is lost so program exposure and shutter-priority modes are not possible, but most cameras will work okay in aperture-priority or manual mode using stop down metering. Canon manual focus cameras need a small adaptor placed on the rear of the lens to lock the aperture down, while screw thread lenses need the aperture's coupling pin holding down if there isn't a manual switch. A reversing ring offers a life-size image that's razor sharp in the centre, but a little softer at the edges compared with a macro lens, but the price is excellent. Distance from subject: 10cm.

■ **Extension tubes £65+** A set of three tubes in different lengths that go between the camera and lens to offer a choice of macro ranges. They can be used in any combination to give six different lengths and ratios from around 1/3rd to lifesize. Their only real drawback is that there is a loss of light in the tubes which is adjusted automatically by through-the-lens metering and, as there are no elements inside the tubes, quality is as good as the original lens. Distance from subject: 5.5cm.

■ **Close-up lens £8+** A small dioptre lens that's available in several magnifications: +1, +2, +3, +4 and +10 to screw onto the lens' filter thread. They can be used in combinations to increase magnification. They're ideal for larger subjects, such as flowers, or for anyone wanting to copy old photographs and they don't affect the exposure. The quality is on a par with a reversing ring. Distance from subject: 20cm.

■ **Macro converter £100** A seven-element 2x converter with the added benefit of a macro mode which extends out to offer a 1:1 life-size ratio. You lose two stops of light, but the metering coupling is maintained so your camera will take care of the exposure. The results produced are the closest you'll obtain to having a true macro lens. Use it with a telephoto lens and you have a powerful magnifier from close-up and afar. Distance from subject: variable.

■ **Bellows £70+** The most versatile, but also the most bulky, cumbersome and fiddly to use. They consist of a rack with a set of rubber or cloth bellows mounted on front and back frames with a lens mount on one end and a camera mount on the other. To increase magnification you extend the bellows. When the bellows are extended you really need a TTL meter or you will have to manually compensate for the loss of light reaching the film. The further you extend the lens, the more light lost. Distance from subject: variable.

■ **Coupling ring £5+** A double sided thread that lets you reverse a lens and attach it to the lens on your camera. This method offers the closest focus of all, but care is needed when choosing lens and aperture combinations. The best results are obtained when a smaller focal length lens, such as a 50mm, is reversed on the front of a longer one, say 105mm. Results are sharp at the centre, but there's considerable fall off in quality towards the edges of the photo. Distance from subject: 4cm.

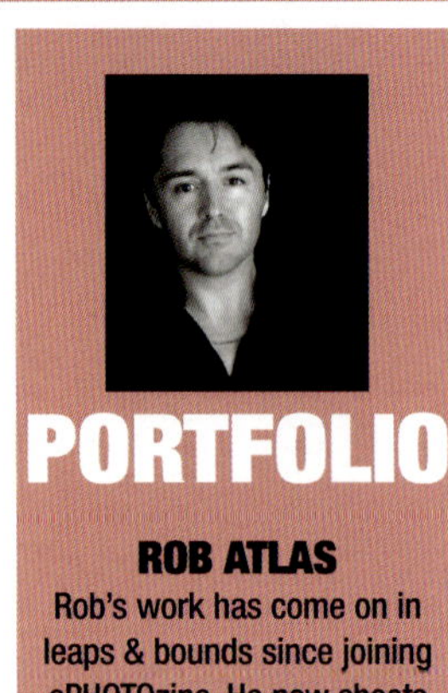

PORTFOLIO

ROB ATLAS

Rob's work has come on in leaps & bounds since joining ePHOTOzine. He now shoots some amazing still-lifes.

I started taking pictures aged eight or nine, taking close-up pictures of my toy cars so they looked real. As I got older though I became more of a casual snapper, taking holiday photos and the occasional portrait.

I got serious about photography a couple of years ago after buying a digital camera. Digital was ideal for me as I could experiment without wasting film, taking close-up shots of any household item I could think of. I decided to upgrade my camera to a Fuji 602, as this gave me all the manual control I needed. I'm now using a Nikon 8700, which I won in an ePHOTOzine competition.

Lighting is crucial. At first all I had was a halogen desk lamp and pieces of paper and card to diffuse and reflect light. I decided to take the plunge and splash out on studio lighting and now have a large 2ft x 2ft lightbox, large soft box, two studio flash heads with brollies, slave flash, reflectors, flash meter and various other bits.

The soft box is my most used item. It's ideal for both commercial and creative close-up work and is also ideal if you fancy doing a bit of portraiture. Lighting can be expensive but it's definitely worth it in the long run.

A subject doesn't have to be complicated in order to be effective – most of my images feature simple objects, like balloons and snooker balls. Make sure the light and reflections are right, clone out any specks of dust in Photoshop and make sure the colour is how it should be.

My photography has now improved enough to sell my images, win prizes and awards and I've even had a photo exhibited at the Royal Albert Hall in London. ■
www.robgatlas.co.uk

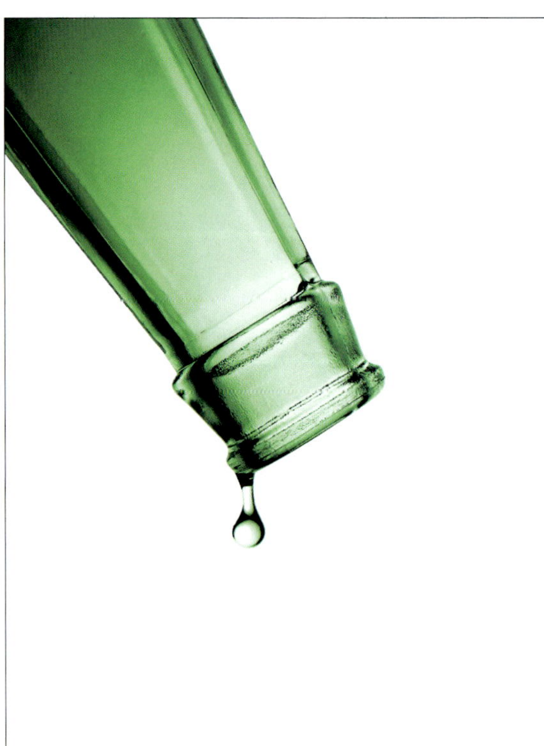

● Drips and splashes feature heavily in Rob's pictures, adding interest to a shot. These are quite simple to do but require a lot of patience to get right – shooting frame after frame to get the exact shot you want. Digital is best for this, as there's no need to worry about the cost of constant shooting. The bottle had a hole drilled in the bottom with an airline inserted, feeding a slow, but constant, supply of water for drips.

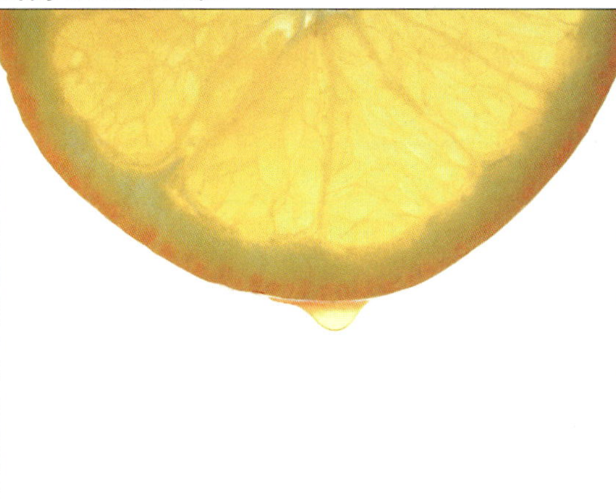

● A slice of orange with a drip captured. This was set directly in front of a large lightbox with two small reflectors close in front.

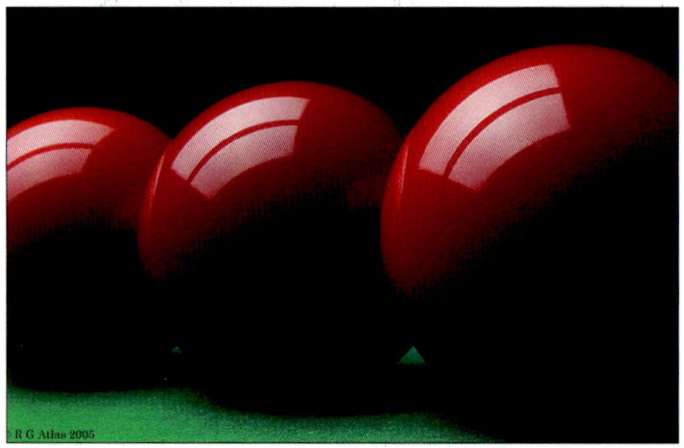

● Three snooker balls taken at an angle to alter scale and allowing the window reflection to add an interesting and repeated pattern.

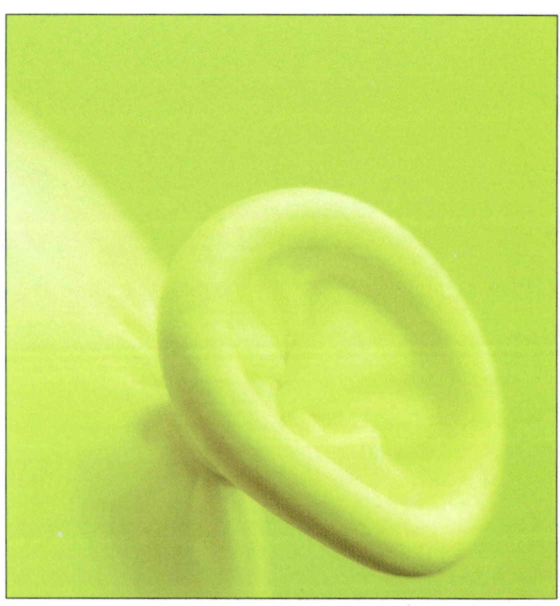

● The tied valve of a yellow balloon was placed in front of a yellow background so the whole thing becomes very graphical. Look around you and many things you've never considered can make good subjects when a close-up lens is attached.

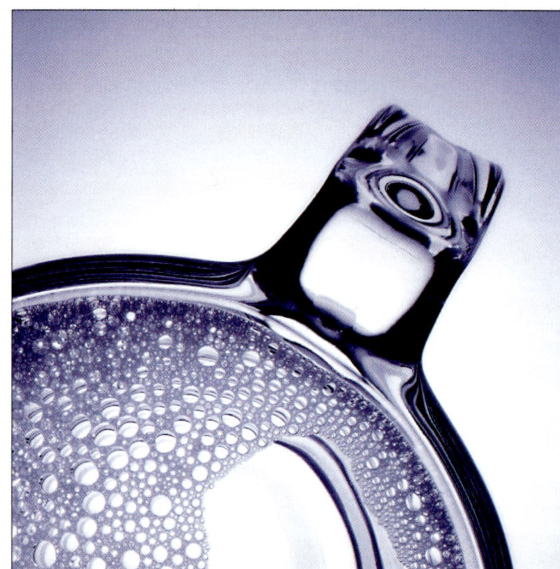

● This is simply a Pyrex measuring jug on a lightbox from above, with water and soap bubbles. Some thought it was a bottle.

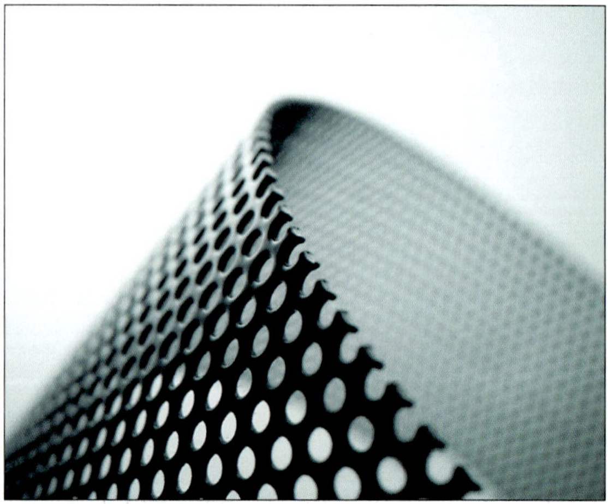

● Cylindrical mesh from a halogen ceiling light fitting, mono toned in Photoshop, giving quite a nice effect from an old piece of scrap.

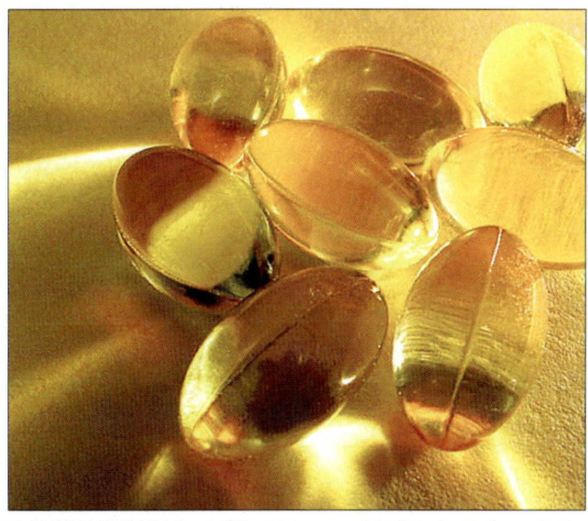

● BRIAN HALHEAD A small torch was used to illuminate these Cod Liver Oil capsules and the light refraction was the desired result.

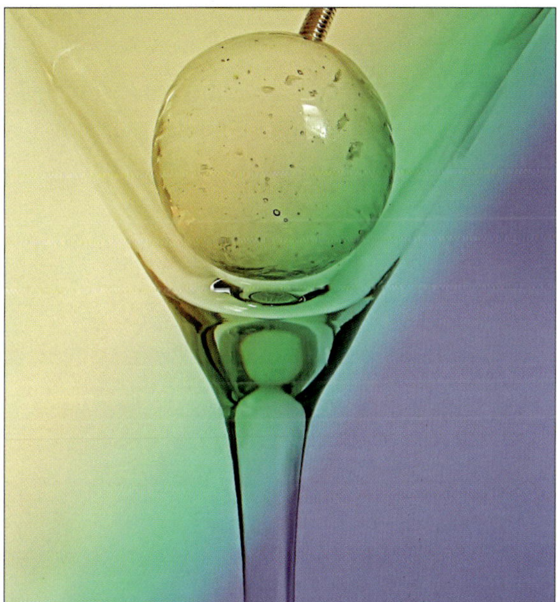

● ANGELA SANDERSON A Canon A70 was to used to shoot the glass against a white background. A Photoshop gradient was added after.

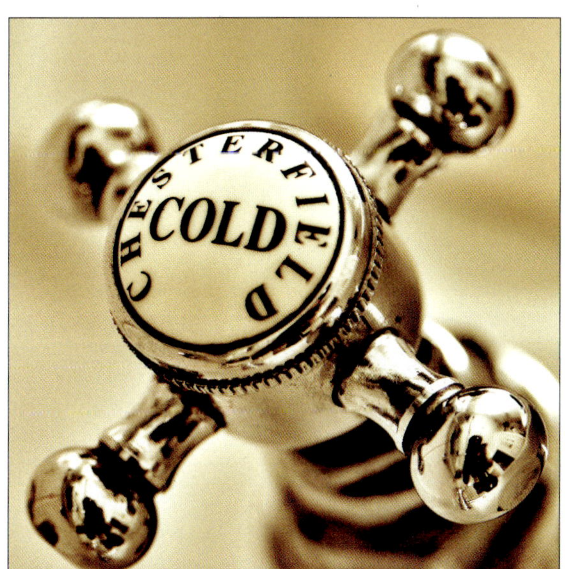

● BEN MERCER Lit using an anglepoise lamp and shot with a Nikon D1 and 28-105mm lens. Tone & contrast tweaked in Photoshop.

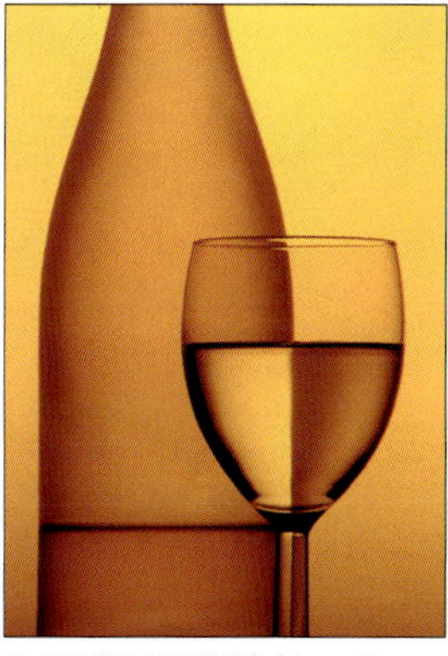

● ANTON HEIBERG Glass lit from behind with tungsten fired through draftsman paper.

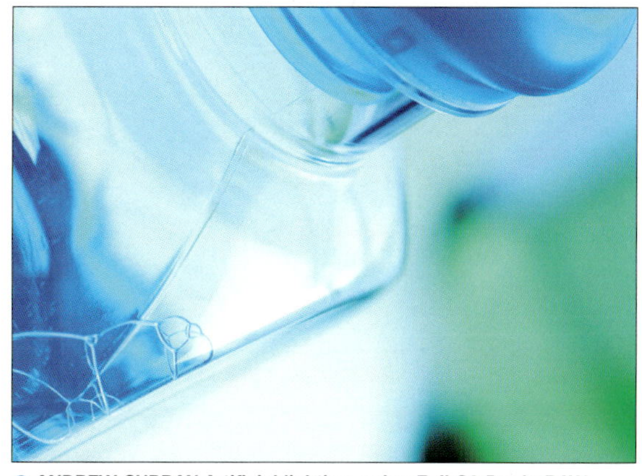

● ANDREW CURRAN Artificial lighting, using Fuji S2 Pro in RAW mode and a 90mm Macro lens set at f/2.8.

CREATIVE SHOOTING – CROSS POLARISING TECHNIQUE

■ When the weather or short daylight hours restrict your outdoor photography, here's something you can try at home to create vividly colourful photos with loads of impact.

■ By using two polarising filters – one at the light source and one on the camera – spectacular images can be created from clear plastics. The effect is achieved when rotating the camera polariser, which causes

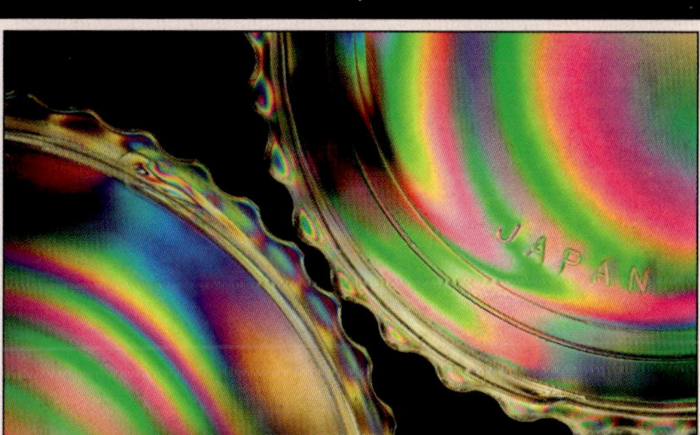

'cross polarisation', and the darkening of the light source polarising filter. To the right is a simple but effective arrangement of round filter cases that are supplied from the likes of Hoya and Jessops. The colours seen in the plastic are the result of diffraction of white light into various parts of the spectrum. The closer the cross polarisation the stronger and more saturated the colours.

■ To attempt this type of photography you need a light source which could be an electronic flash, either portable or studio, or tungsten light. The advantage of using studio flash over a normal flashgun is that you have a modelling light to see the effect you will create. Tungsten light or a slide projector will produce the same visual effect, but if daylight film is used a colour correction filter is required to prevent a yellow cast. With digital, just set the white balance to the lightbulb (tungsten) setting.

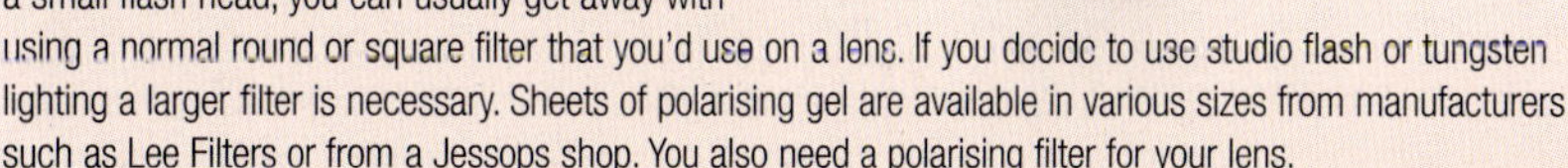

■ You also need polarising material. This must cover the light source. So, if a projector is being used, or a small flash head, you can usually get away with using a normal round or square filter that you'd use on a lens. If you decide to use studio flash or tungsten lighting a larger filter is necessary. Sheets of polarising gel are available in various sizes from manufacturers such as Lee Filters or from a Jessops shop. You also need a polarising filter for your lens.

■ The subject matter should be placed between the camera and light source. Plastic that cracks when flexed seems to produce the most vibrant colours. Items such as rulers, cassette and CD cases, plastic catering cups, measures, camera filter cases and even some transparency mailing boxes produce marvellous effects. Attach a lens to the camera that will fill the frame with the subject – a macro lens is the best solution, but a close-up lens added to a non-macro lens will reduce the cost. When selecting film pick a slow speed for sharp, fine grain results or fast film for grainy effects and preferably slide film to give the best saturation of colours. Print film may confuse the automatic processor, resulting in disappointing images.

■ If you use the camera's built-in meter make sure you use the correct polarising filter. There are two types, circular and linear, and because of the latest technology some cameras give incorrect readings when a linear filter is used – check the instruction book or ask your dealer. As a guide, autofocus or multi spot reading cameras need circular polarising filters and older manual cameras need linear. You can use the wrong one providing you compensate for the metering error. Take a test film and bracket exposures making a note of the settings so they can be repeated.

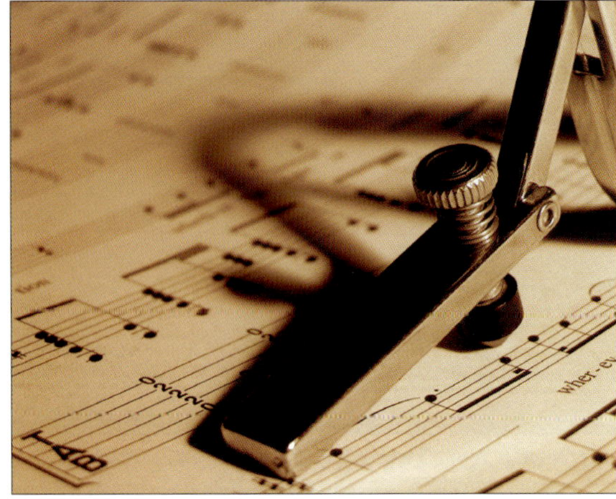

● ANDREW CLARK A Capo on some printed music with carefully placed anglepoise, shot using the sepia option on a Minolta Z1.

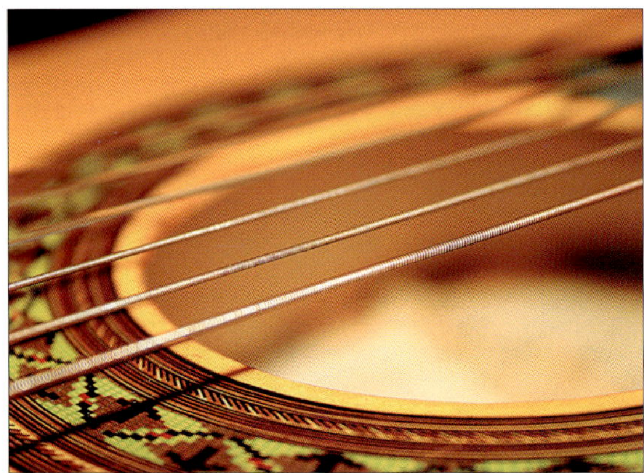

● CRISTIAN PHILPOTT Colourful digital close-up of his son's guitar. Canon EOS 300D with EF-S 18-55mm lens. ISO400 and 1/60sec.

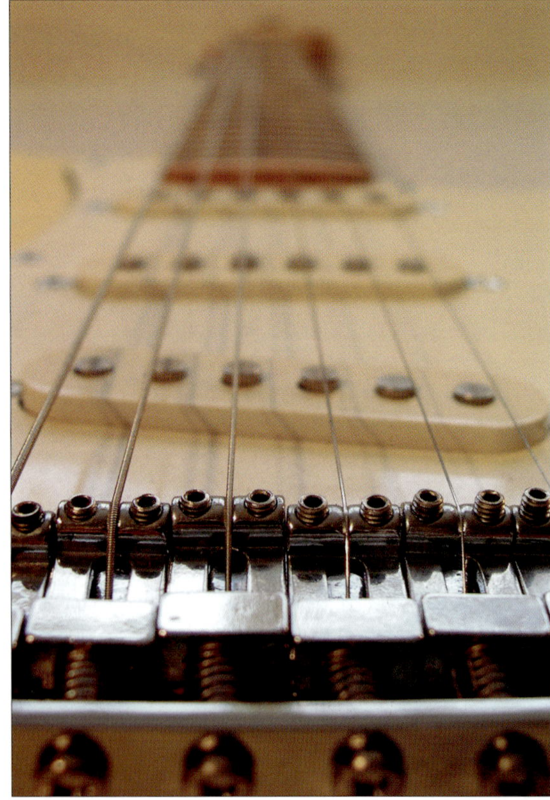

● ELLA VAN RADERS "Fender Stratocaster – while my guitar gently sleeps", taken using the close-up setting of a Nikon Coolpix 4300.

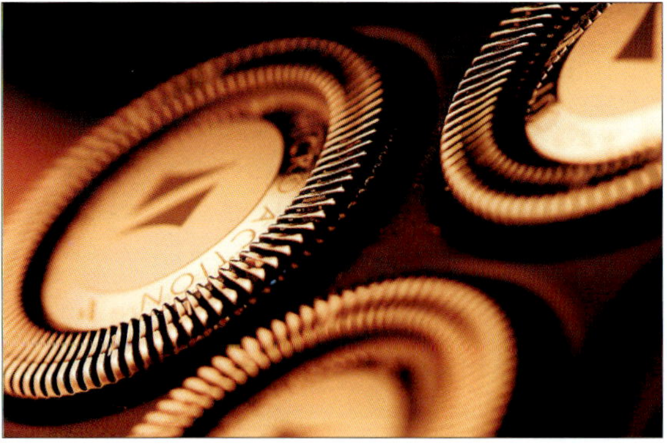

● CHRIS ROBERTS Razor lit with a 500W security light and diffused by a sheet of A4 paper pegged over it. A 105mm macro lens was used.

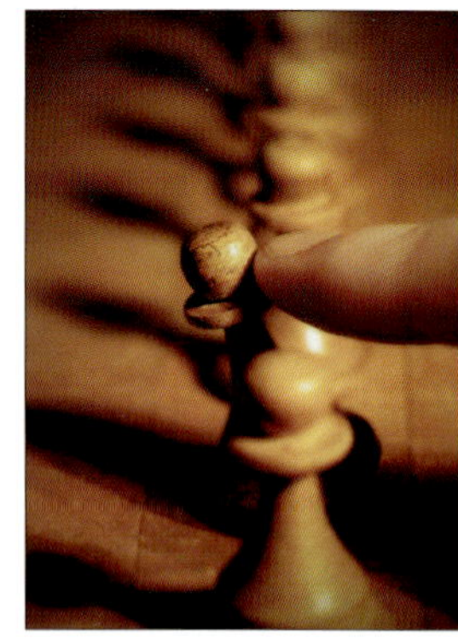

● ARAM AVETISYAN Lined up and side lit chess pawns.

FLAMES & SMOKE

■ Candlelight and smoke from matches and incense sticks provide rewarding subjects for simple home studio photography.

■ Make sure the item is lit in a safe environment – any inflammable material should be at a safe distance, including a backdrop of paper or material.

■ By the nature of exposure of a candle the background will probably be dark and the candle flame could easily be over-exposed. Setting the camera exposure compensation to - 2 will help bring out detail in the flame.

■ The shutter speed could be around half a second so shoot in a draft free location and make sure the camera is supported to prevent camera shake.

■ A shorter duration is needed to capture smoke, so many photographers use flash.

■ Several ePHOTOzine members have used incense sticks to create a natural smoke trail, like the example below. All you need is a dark background and a flash firing from the side to illuminate.

■ To make the smoke create interesting patterns gently waft your hand seconds before taking a photo.

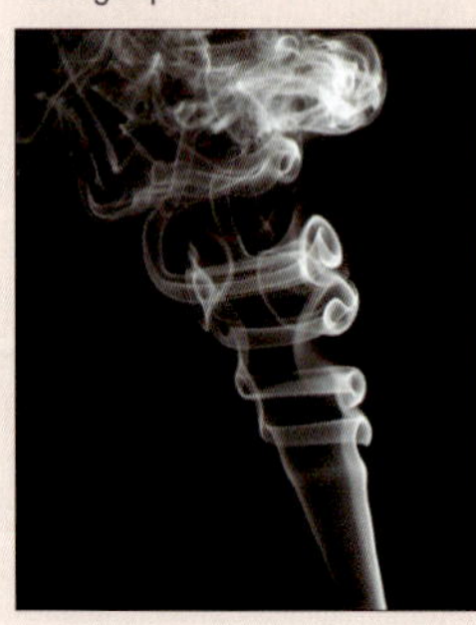

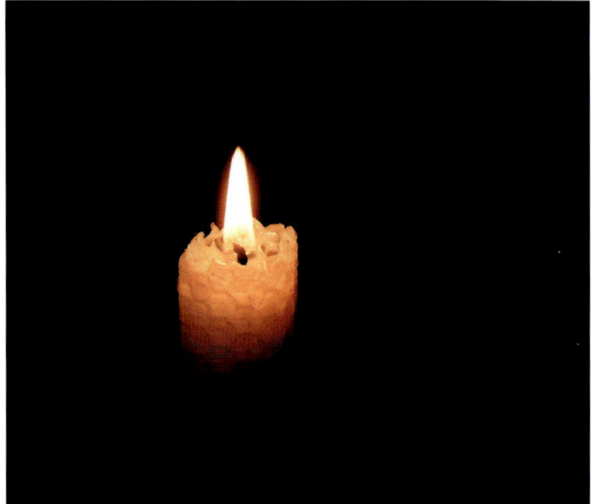

● CLIVE BURGESS Beeswax candle, taken with an Olympus C5050Z. 1/100sec at f/2.3 with -2 stops exposure compensation.

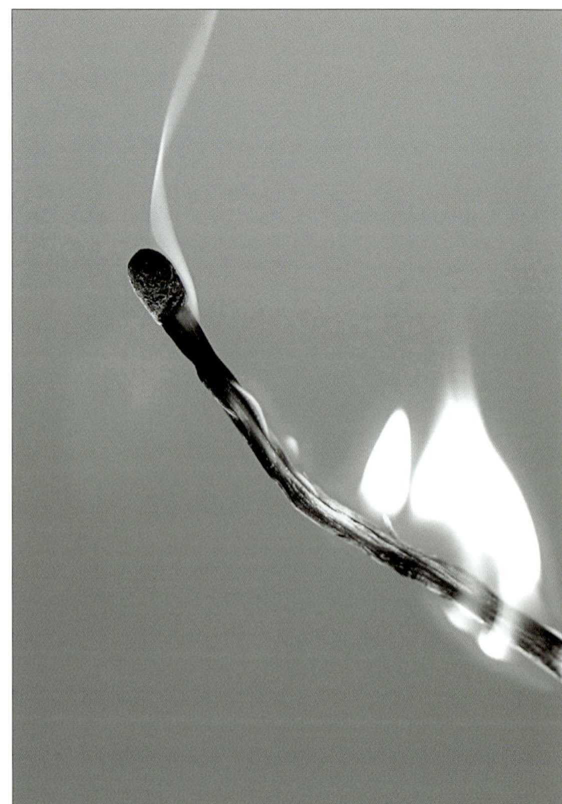

● CHERYL SURRY This flame and smoke trail, from a match, was converted to black & white to focus attention on the smoke.

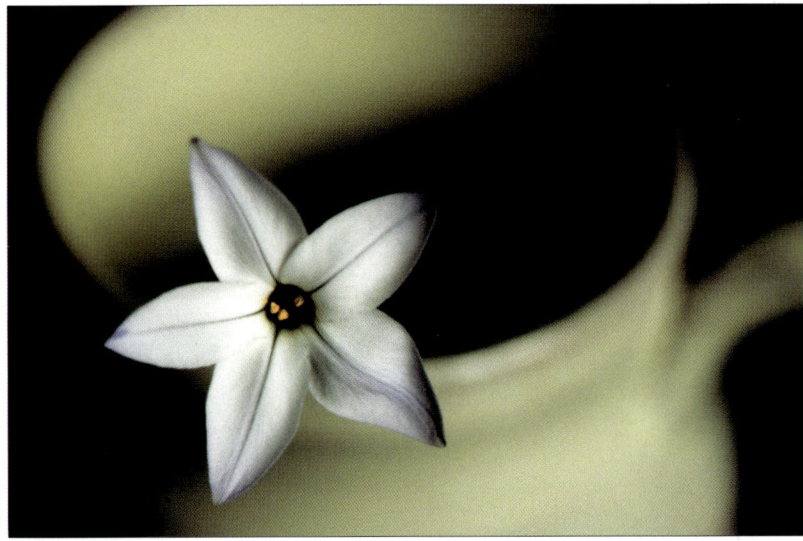

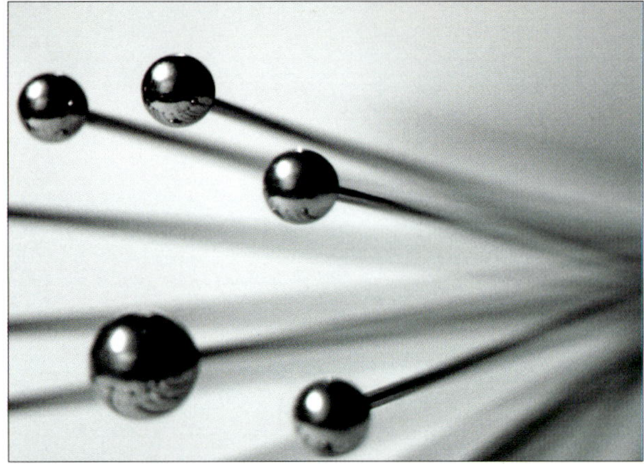

● BRANDON B JENKINS A macro shot of a wire whisk, taken with a Canon EOS 300D at f/5.6 and 1/100sec shutter speed. It was then desaturated using Adobe Photoshop.

● GEOFF BANKS This flower in a coffee mug was taken using a Pentax MX with bellows and a 35mm lens on Fuji Sensia slide film. The shallow depth-of-field ensures the mug is out of focus.

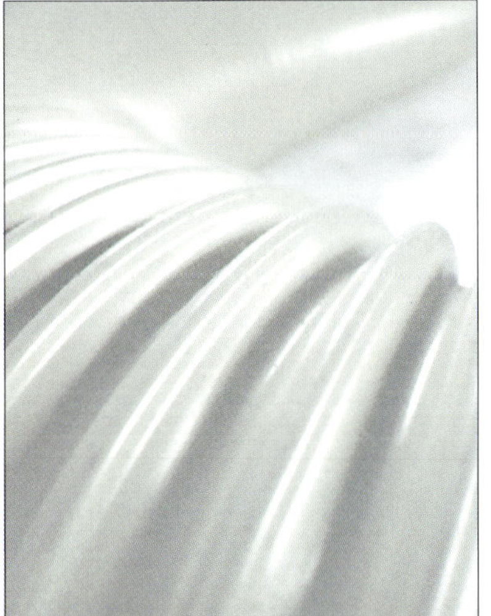

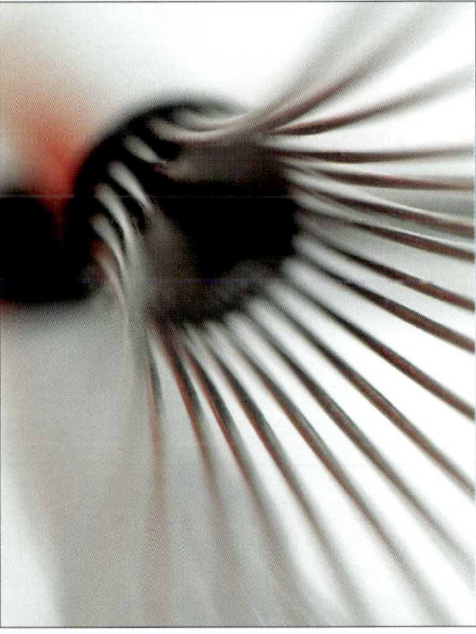

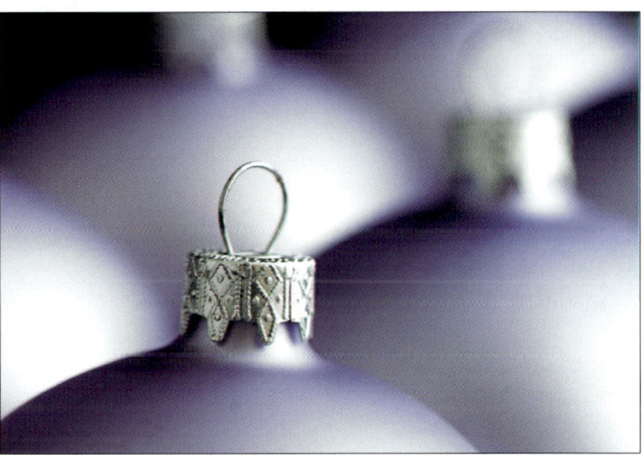

● COLIN MILL Christmas baubles grouped together on a black background in a light tent. Lit by diffused light from a north facing window.

● ANNE RICHARDSON From a series Anne took in an old factory before it closed.

● ANDREW CURRAN Egg whisk, using a Fuji S2 Pro on RAW and a 90mm macro lens at f/2.8.

SHOOTING TIPS – SELECTIVE FOCUS

■ A focusing technique that's often used by close-up photographers is to selectively focus on one point of the subject and, using shallow depth-of-field, throw other areas out of focus, like the examples on this page.

■ The trick is to do this so the overall photograph doesn't look out of focus and the eye is drawn to the main area of the photograph.

■ There are three main ways to control the depth-of-field. You can either move closer, use a longer focal length lens or select a wider aperture. Which option you use depends on how selective you want to be and where you want the elements in the subject to appear.

■ You then need to choose the point that you want sharp. If the subject is off-centre you can either switch to manual focus or use the camera's focus lock. Some cameras have multi-point focus and will automatically detect the point the camera thinks you want to focus on, although this is often hit and miss when using the selective focus technique.

■ If your camera has a depth-of-field preview button activate this and adjust the aperture while looking through the viewfinder. Look at the various elements you want sharp or unsharp and adjust position, focus point or aperture until everything is as desired.

■ Sometimes it's not possible to focus selectively and get all the elements you want unsharp how you would like. In such cases you can use techniques in an image editing program to do the camera's job for you. These are covered in other areas of the book.

■ An option not covered above is to adjust the plane of focus using lens movements. These are normally found on large-format cameras with front and back tilt & swing panels, but Canon, for example, create Tilt/Shift lenses offering similar facilities for their EOS cameras. With these you can force an area to become the only area in focus, even when using smaller apertures.

■ A similar gadget, produced by Lensbabies to fit several SLR mounts, is a lens on a flexible bending tube that you adjust to create graduated blur around the point of focus.

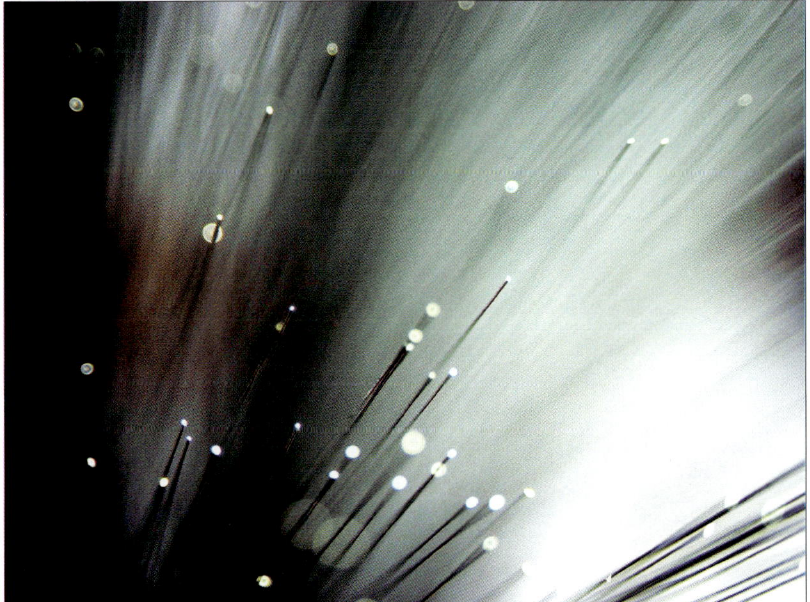

● BEN MERCER A close-up of a fibre optic lamp, with an exposure of 1/60sec at f/4.5 on a Nikon D1 SLR and 28-105mm lens. Using a higher ISO gives noise similar to grain, which can enhance a shot.

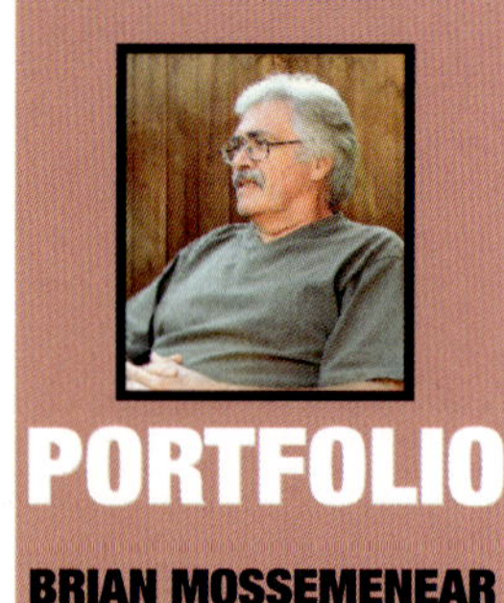

PORTFOLIO

BRIAN MOSSEMENEAR

Brian has been taking photographs for the best part of 50 years, starting with his father's old Box Brownie.

Once I was bitten by the photography bug, I saved my pocket money so I could buy a camera of my own and, before long, I was developing my own films and contact printing 2.5 x 2.5 images.

As my creativity grew it called for something more, so my parents bought me a second-hand Voigtlander Brilliant TLR and basic enlarger. With a makeshift darkroom in the attic I was really on my way, making up my own chemicals, developing films and toning prints.

By this time 35mm photography was starting to come into its own and I could see the advantages it offered. A year or so later, I got a part time job during the school holidays, which enabled me to acquire my first 35mm camera – an Ilford Sportsman. This new format gave me scope to experiment with the production of transparencies, both in colour and black & white.

However, over the next 40 years, my equipment became more sophisticated and my photography often had to take a back seat, apart from during the annual holidays. It was not until I bought my first digital camera three years ago that the magic really came back into photography for me.

I was surprised at the kind of results that could be achieved with a fairly basic piece of equipment, provided that I worked within its limitations.

I enjoy digital photography as there's so much scope to be adventurous, both when taking the shot and afterwards, without consideration of cost. And whilst I do not manipulate my images to any great extent I do take advantage of the available technology to tidy up the images a bit. ■

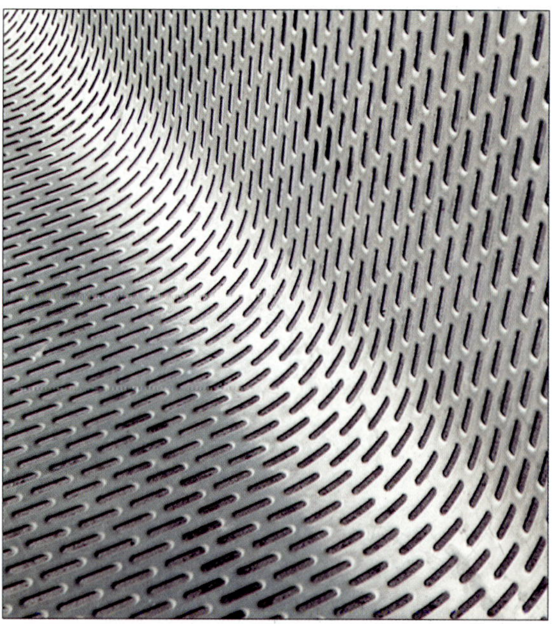

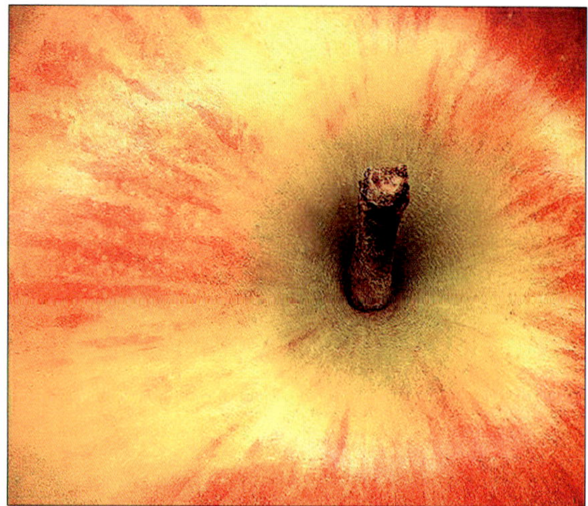

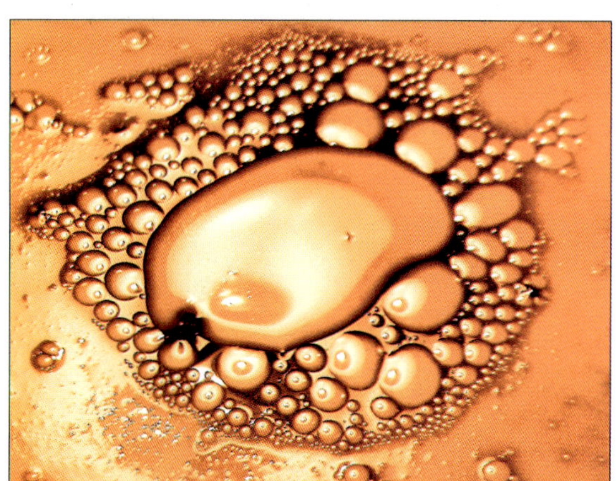

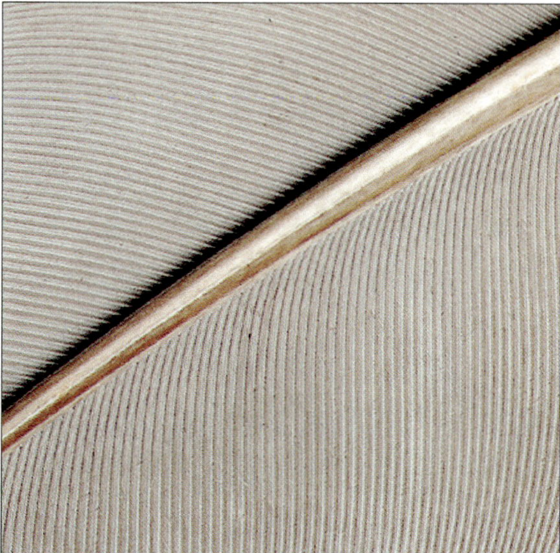

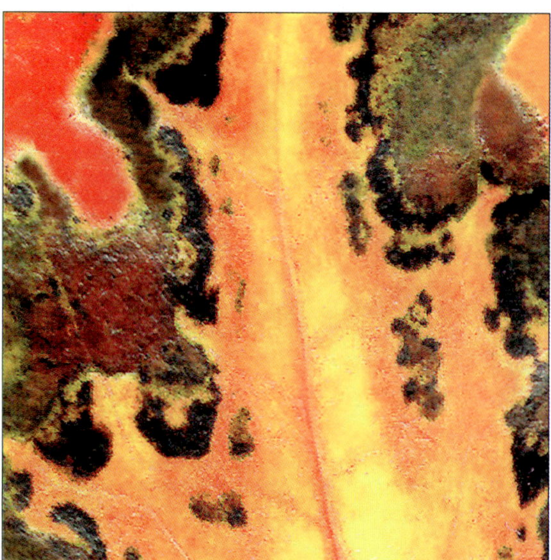

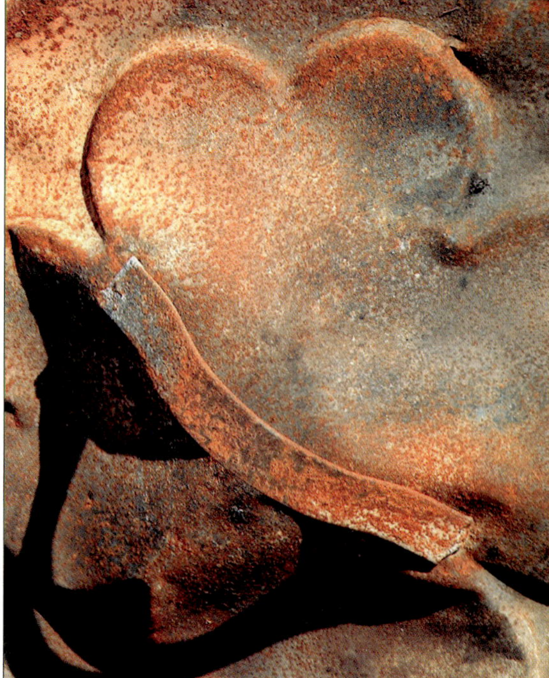

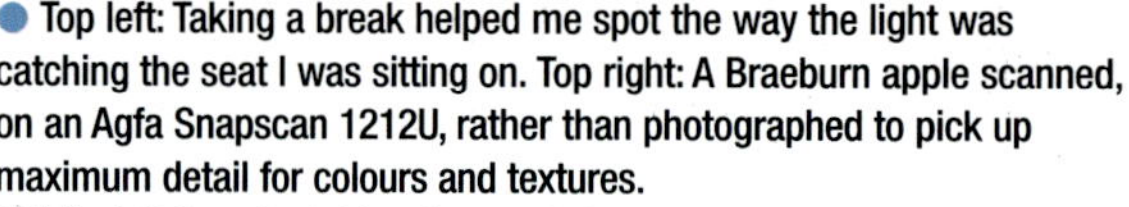

● Top left: Taking a break helped me spot the way the light was catching the seat I was sitting on. Top right: A Braeburn apple scanned, on an Agfa Snapscan 1212U, rather than photographed to pick up maximum detail for colours and textures.
Middle left: I spotted this mixture of oil and balsamic vinegar left on a plate after a dinner party. Camera - Fujifilm FinePix 2600Z. Middle right: The lines and patterns in the feather caught my eye. Bottom left: I was intrigued by the flame-like patterns and colours in this fallen evergreen leaf. Bottom right: Out walking I spotted this rusting dustbin lid lying in the grass. Captured with a Fujifilm FinePix 2600Z.

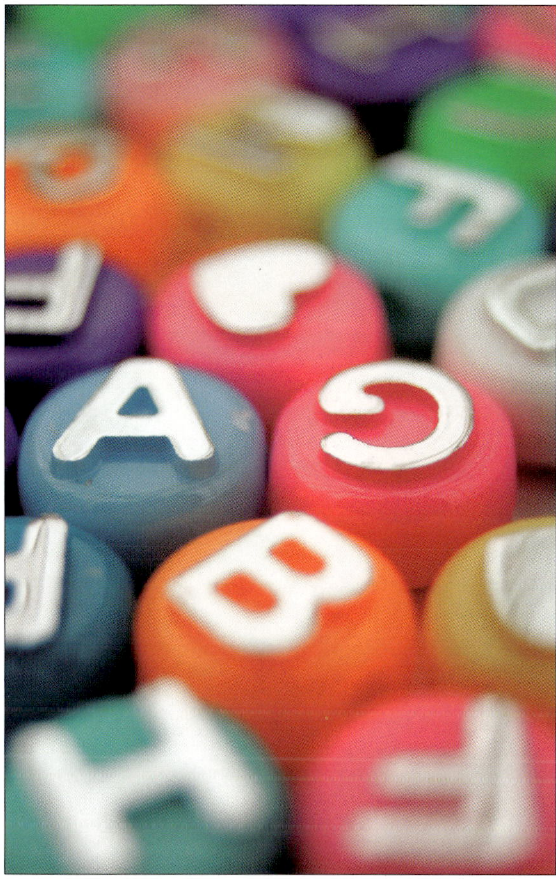

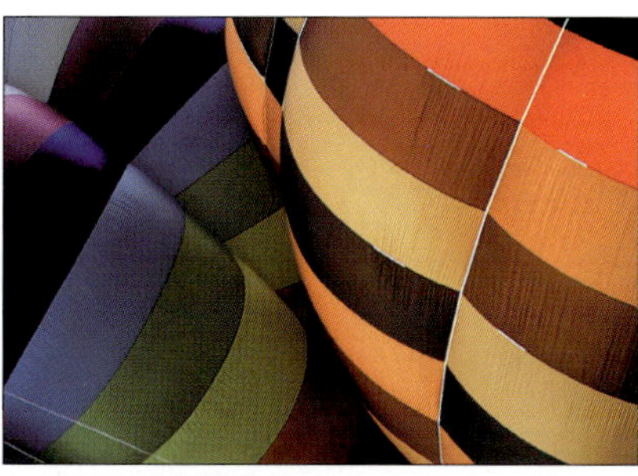

● ELA WLODARCZYK Tight abstract crop of Bristol Balloon Fiesta, using a Canon 300V and 28-90mm.

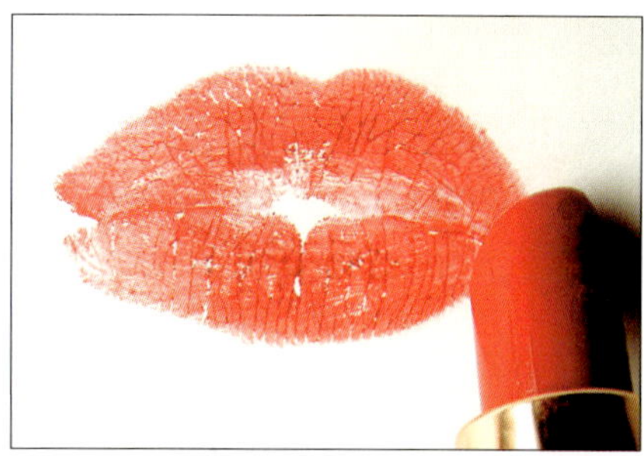

● DEMELZA ANDREOLI 'Lips kiss paper'. The stick was added and side-lit using a lightbox.

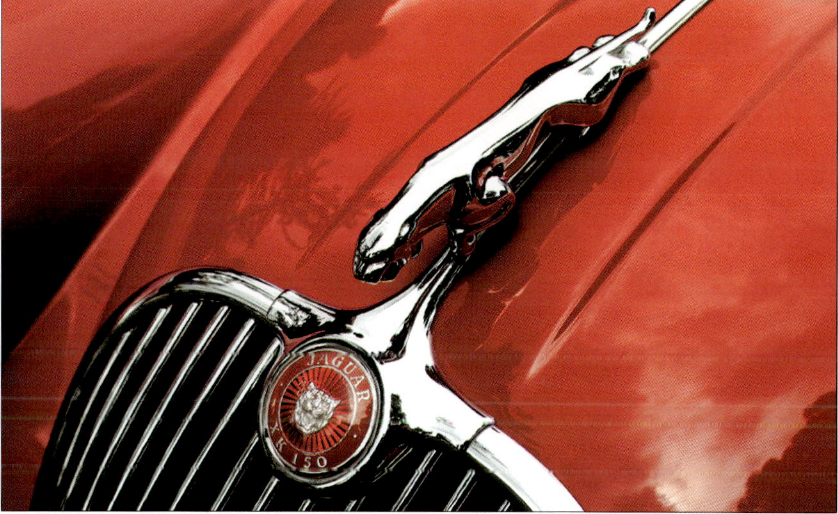

● DAVID KEY Playing around with a few coloured beads purchased at a craft shop. The wide aperture ensures attention on A and G.

● ARTHUR CHAN A close-up of a classic Jaguar XK-150, taken with a Canon EOS D60 and an exposure of 1/500sec at f/6.3. Classic car shows provide lots of opportunities like this. Use a polariser to kill reflections.

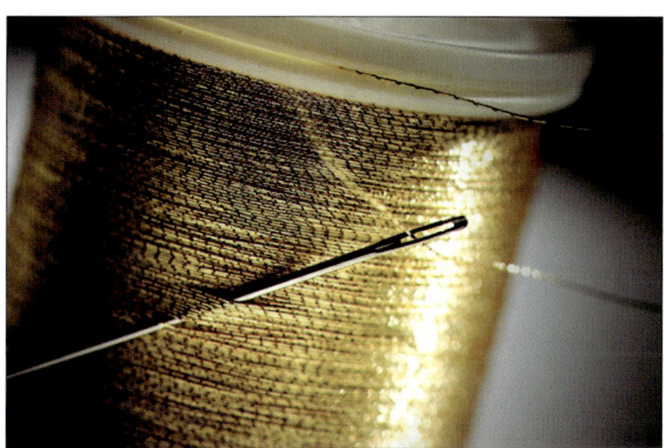

● ANNETTE EAST Even the simple household items can make interesting subjects. A cotton reel, taken with a Sigma 105mm macro.

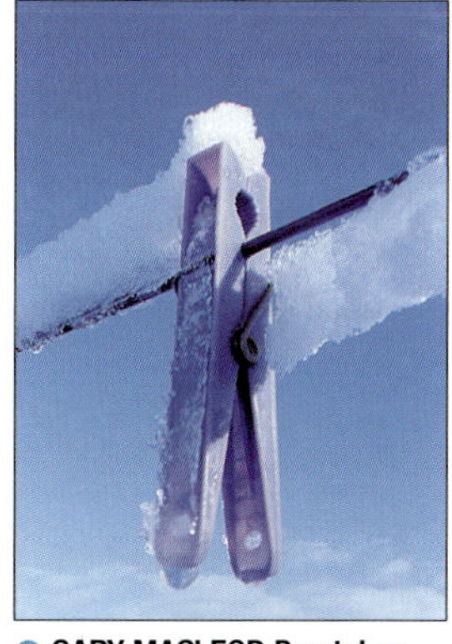

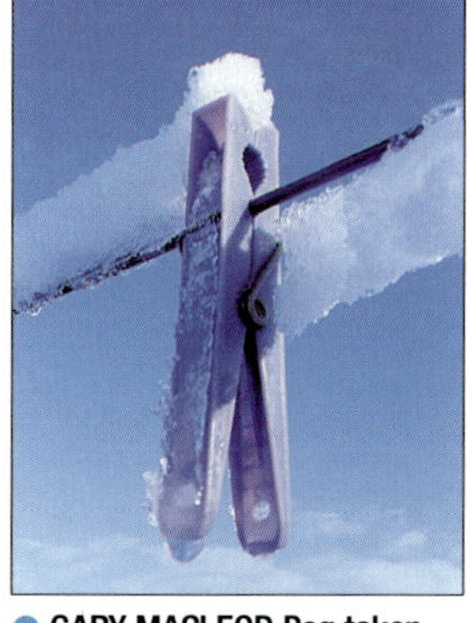

● GARY MACLEOD Peg taken just after a heavy fall of snow.

SHOOTING TIPS – COLOUR AND CONTRAST

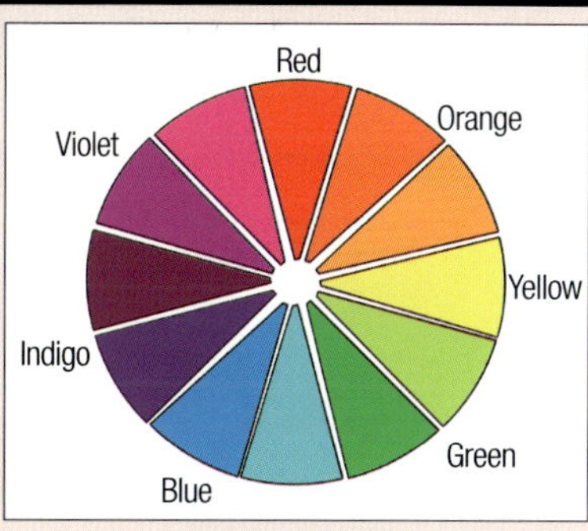

■ When setting up colourful close-ups it pays to take note of which colours work well together and which don't. Interior decorators and fashion designers have a good sense of the colours that harmonise and those that clash.

To help understand the relationship of colour it's worth having a colour wheel to hand. This wheel, devised by Sir Isaac Newton, has the colours of the spectrum arranged in a circle. From this you can work out which colours will and which won't work well together.

■ Complementary colours are directly across from each other on the wheel and produce a strong contrast, especially when placed side by side. Generally, our eyes have difficulty focusing on contrasting colours at the same time so they should be used with care.

■ Analogous colours are next to each other on the colour wheel. They provide harmony but may not provide enough contrast, so the subject won't stand out as well.

■ Photos with warm colours, from the red, orange and yellow segments, express positive and extrovert thoughts and are associated with sunshine and warmth to create a strong, dynamic mood. Cool colours, including violets, blues and greens, can express coolness, stability and calmness making the viewer feel relaxed or spiritual.

■ Monochromatic colours are those with shades or tones of the same colour. Converting a colour photo to black & white and using the Hue/saturation set to Colorize is a quick way to achieve this.

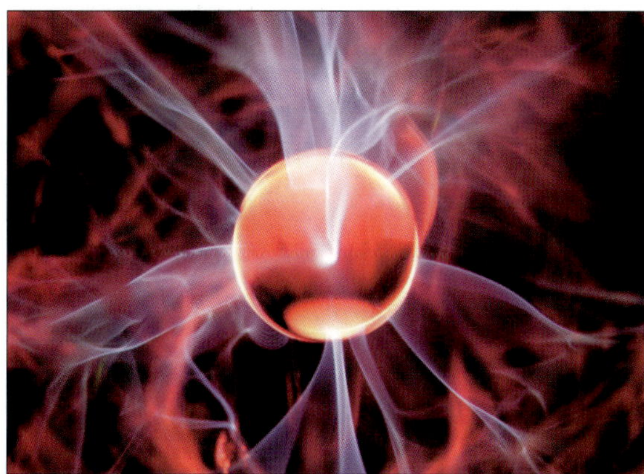

● MATT TILGHMAN Plasma balls create amazing colours. Using a long exposure ensures you capture even more rays and colour.

● EDWARD ROBINSON Simple objects can make striking images.

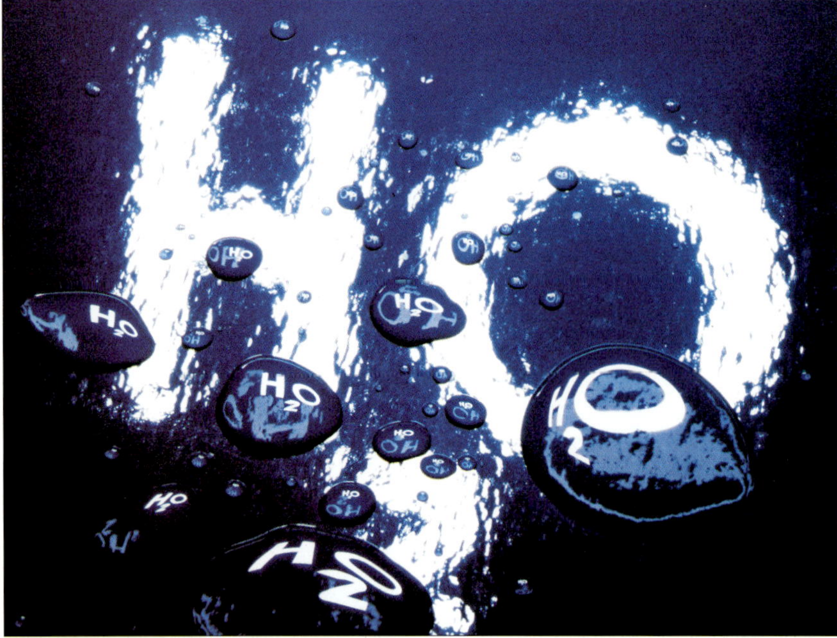

● DAVE FLETCHER Water on a blue plastic background with letters H2O cut from card and placed back-to-front, upside-down on a light box at 45°. Taken on Kodak EBX 100 in a Minolta Dynax 500si Super.

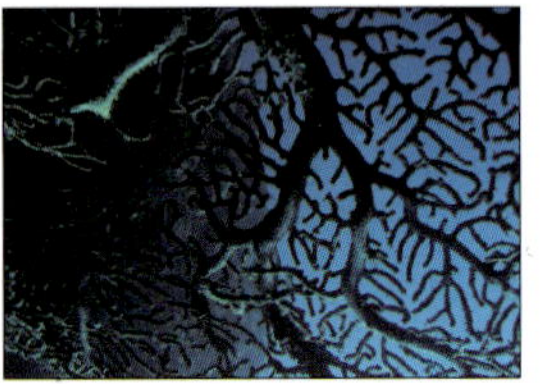

● EDDIE BLAGBROUGH A back-lit Gorgonian fan in the Great Barrier Reef, Australia, taken looking up from the sea-bed.

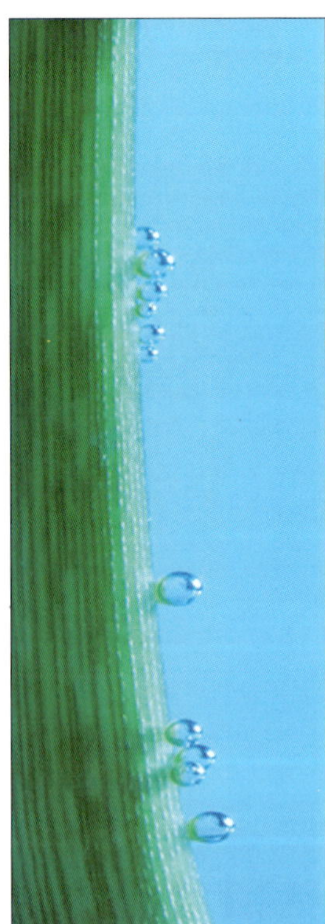

● ISABELLE ANDERSON A stem with bubbles, taken with an EOS 300D and 100mm macro at f/2.

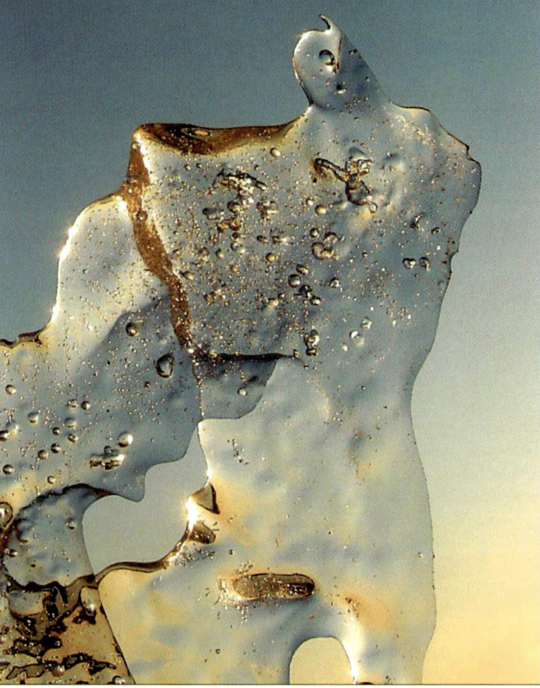

● BENEDICT LANDTMAN A tiny floe of ice that I found rather interesting. Captured in southern Finland, using a Sony P10.

EXPOSURE TIP – ICE AND WATER

■ The highly reflective tones of ice and water can fool the camera's metering system. This is because your camera's built in meter is designed to deliver a perfect picture assuming the contrast range is normal. It does this by scrambling the tones and adjusting so the scrambled colour brightness is a mid grey or average value. This is fine when the subject has a wide tonal range with everything from black to white being present, but when the subject is predominantly white the camera underexposes so that the white becomes grey.

All you need to do is override the camera's automatic setting using the exposure compensation setting, or manual, and plus 1 or 2 stops depending on the amount of ice/water in the picture.

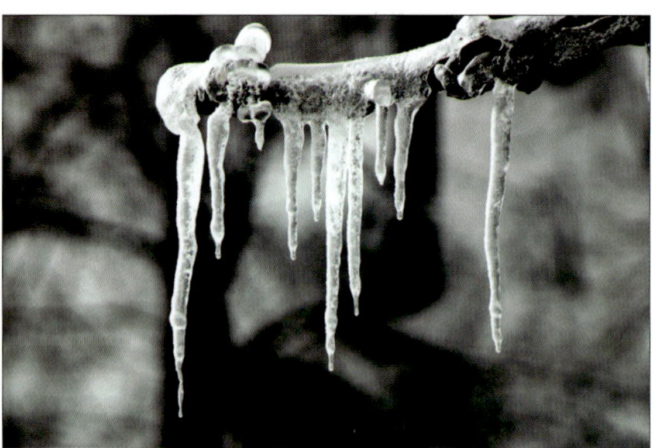

● ANDY GRANT Icicles taken on the Canadian side of Niagara Falls, using a Canon 300D and Sigma 28-300mm and converted to b&w.

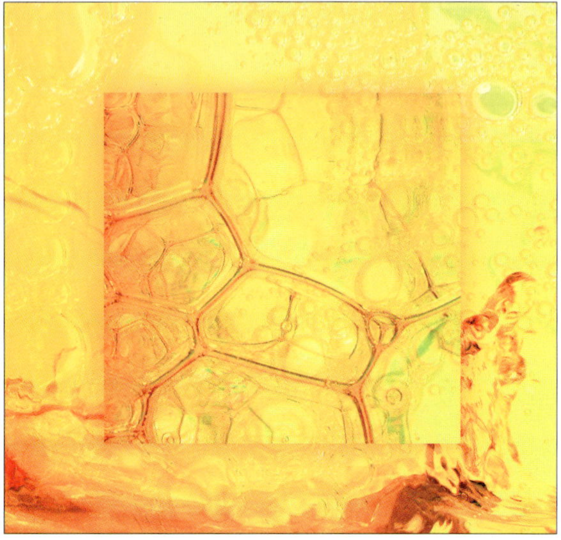

● MAREK KOMISARUK I used a Fuji S1 Pro with a 28-80mm lens, a close-up +2 filter and Multiblitz studio flash light.

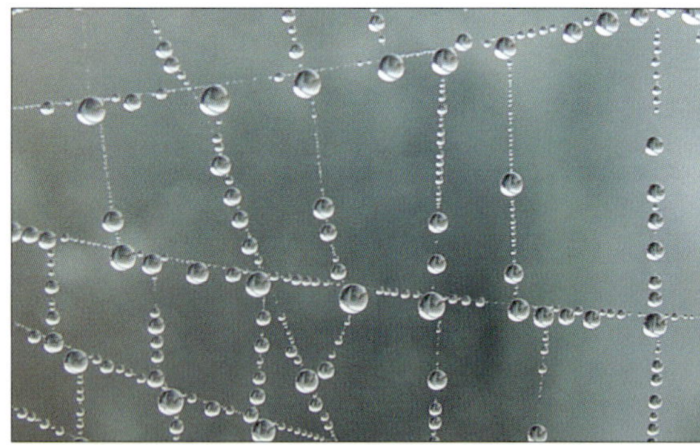

● DAVID BATEMAN A web taken early one misty morning on a Sony DSC-F717, 1/160sec, f/4, ISO200. Cropped and sharpened slightly.

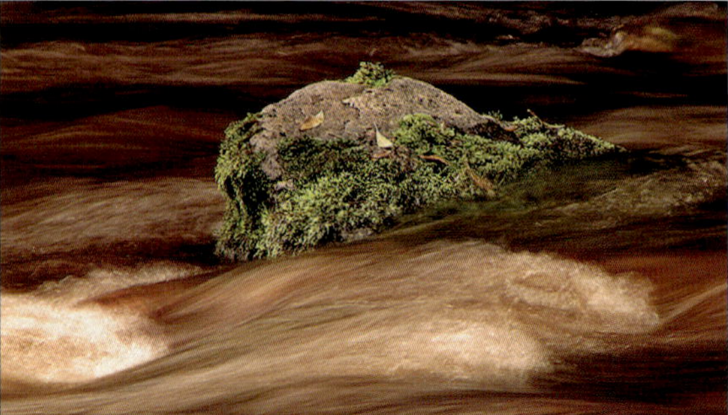

● ANDREW ROBERTS Moss covered rock at Ystradfellte waterfalls, taken with an ND4 filter to ensure a slow 1.5sec shutter speed.

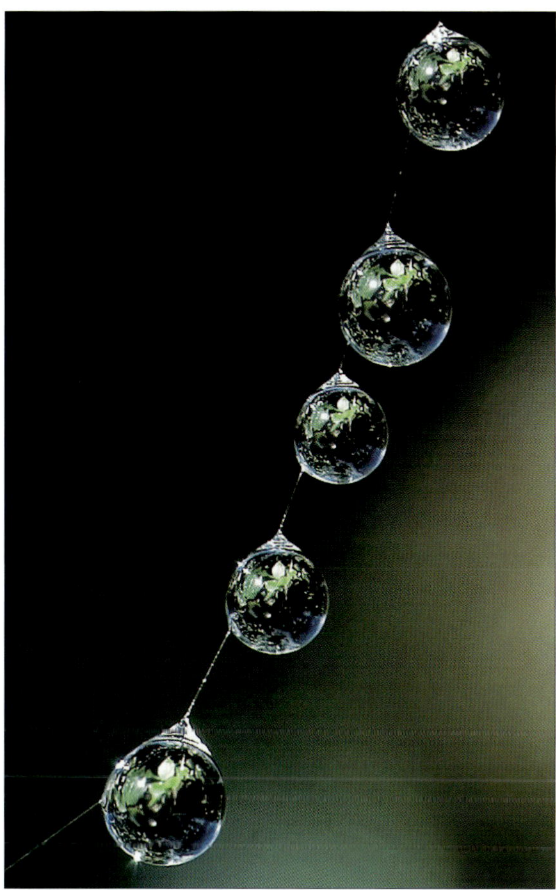

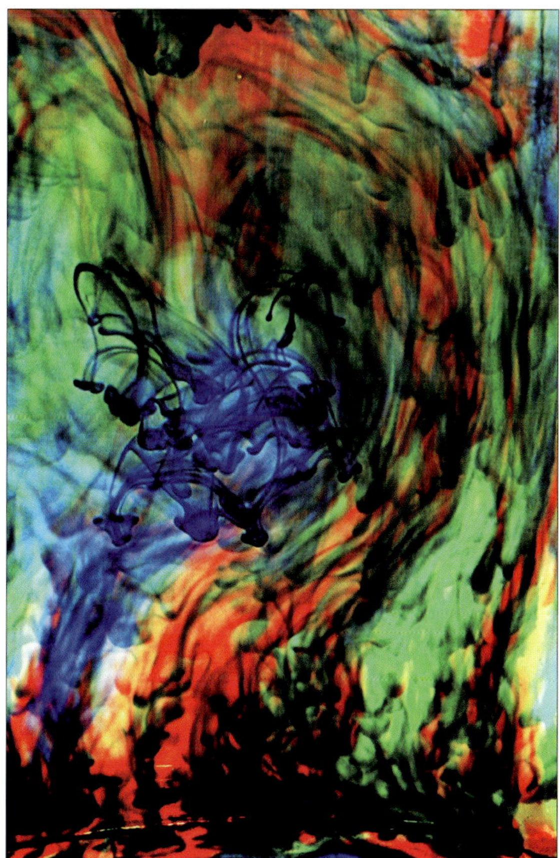

● HARJONO DJOYOBISONO Water droplets on a spider web, using a Canon EOS 300D and Tamron 90mm. Exposure was 1/100sec at f/10.

● KEITH LEWIS A photo of printer ink dropped into a vase of water, taken on a Canon EOS 300D with a 50mm f/1.8 – 1/60sec at f/5.6.

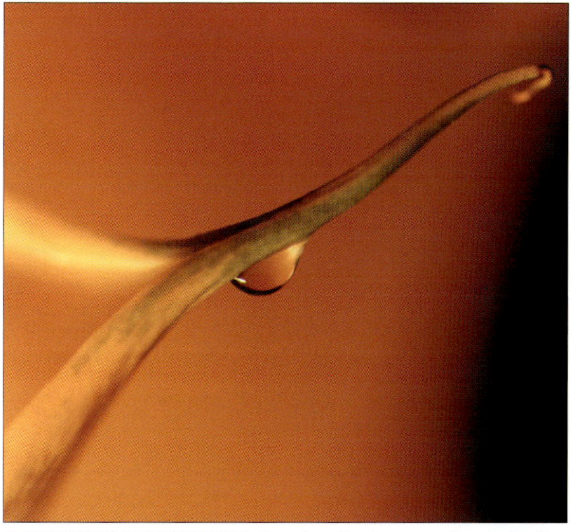

● COENRAAD HEIJDEMANN A drop dangling from a yellow calla lily, with a calla as backdrop. Taken with Canon EOS 300D and Sigma 105mm EX DG macro lens.

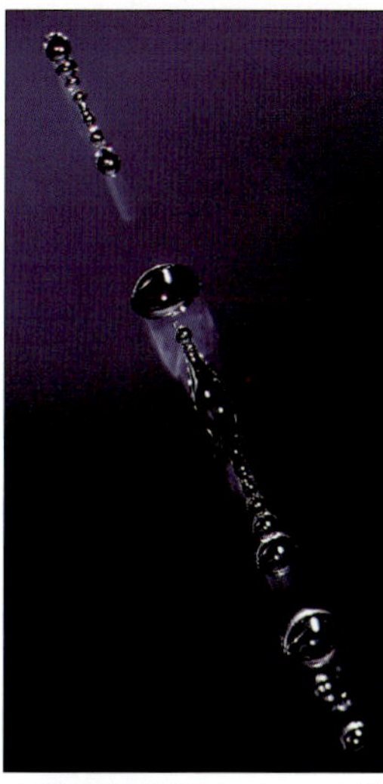

● HELEN DIXON The Canon G5's built-in flash was used to freeze dripping tap water. Then toned.

TECHNIQUE TIPS – DRIPS & SPLASHES

■ Freezing water as it drops or splashes can create fascinating photos. It's a fairly easy thing to shoot indoors, providing your camera has a responsive shutter and you have a good sense of timing. All you need is a camera, possibly a flash, (preferably off camera) and a macro/close-up feature, along with a bowl or glass full of water and a supply of water to provide the droplets.

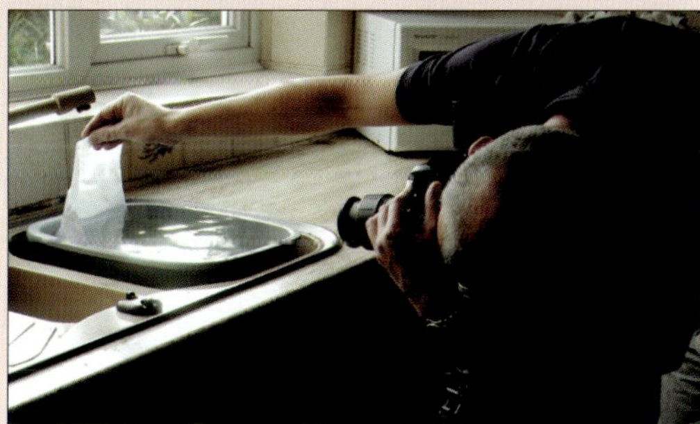

■ Set up the bowl in a suitable place – ideally under a tap. If you don't have a tap nearby you could always get a bottle of water, tape a straw to the neck and pour the water very slowly through the straw. The flow needs to be at drip speed with an interval of a second or two between drips.

■ Make sure the background is plain. In this example I used a piece of white tracing paper and held it at the back of the bowl so part of it was submerged in the water.

■ Mount the camera on a tripod and position it at a slight angle to the water. This way, you get the drip almost head on but with slight angle to give a full 3D effect.

■ You need to catch the droplet a fraction of a second after it's hit the water, which is why flash may be needed. It would be very hard to freeze the water using the shutter speed you'd achieve with daylight, unless you are by a window or using a fast ISO. Flash provides a brief duration which is enough to freeze the droplet. In this example a shutter speed of 1/125sec was enough to provide some movement to create the rising water column, yet fast enough to get the single droplet mid air.

■ Position the flash to one side to get more shape/outline to the splash.

■ If you're using a film camera shoot a roll at all different exposures and focusing points and make notes of what you've done. Process the roll and see what worked best by referring back to your notes.

■ Digital users can take a shot and check the LCD before continuing with necessary adjustments. Be prepared to take dozens of photos to get just one with the droplet in the right position.

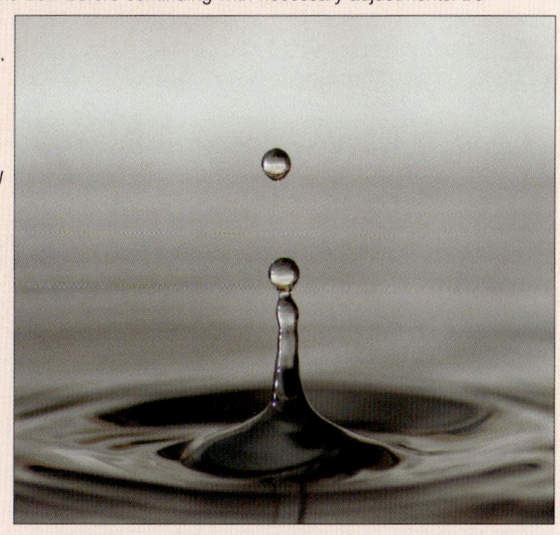

■ Once you've perfected splashes with water try milk, juice or paint. Try moving on to dropping fruit or objects into fluid or paint. Also have a go at shooting from below the surface as the subject penetrates the surface. A glass vessel, such as a goldfish tank or vase, will make life easier here.

■ If you find the subject enjoyable, and you want to get better and more accurate-timed shots, consider buying a photogate trigger. This is a light emitter and detector that creates a beam between the two. When the droplet splits the beam it fires the shutter. The device has a delay to allow for the drip to reach the water and bounce back.

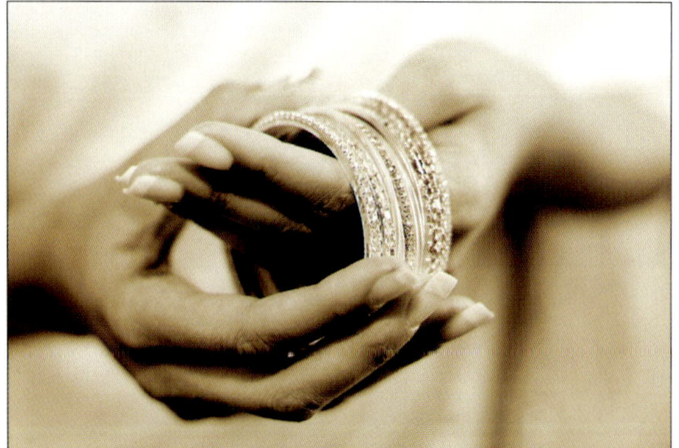

● DARRIN JAMES A Mauritian bride puts on her Grandmother's bracelets as she prepares for her traditional wedding.

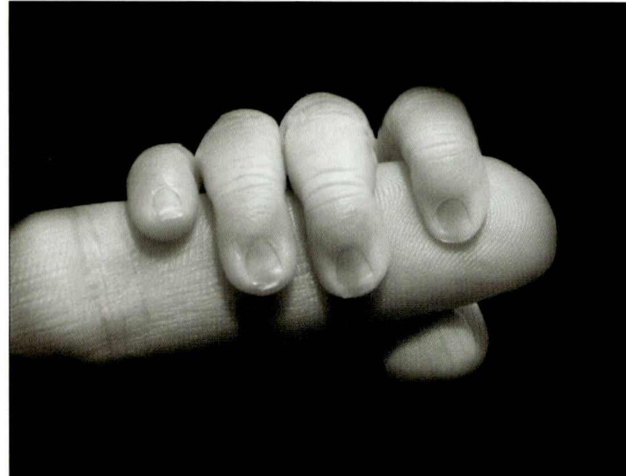

● SHAUN FOSTER-HENSON Taken of Shaun's newly born little boy. It was originally in colour, but he preferred the black & white tones.

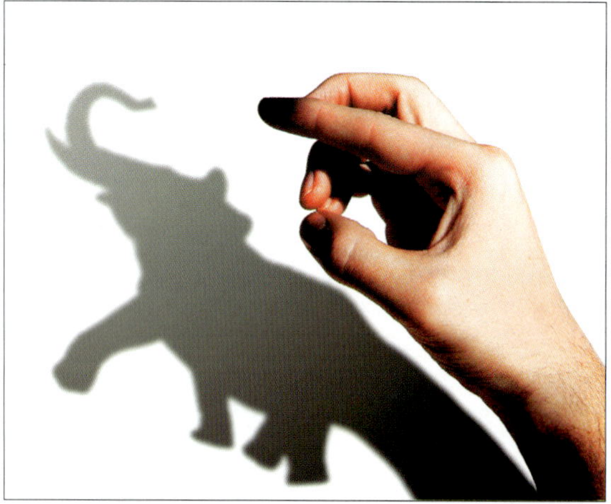

● DANIEL WARBURTON Trying his hand at a bit of hand puppetry, no pun intended, with a little help from Photoshop.

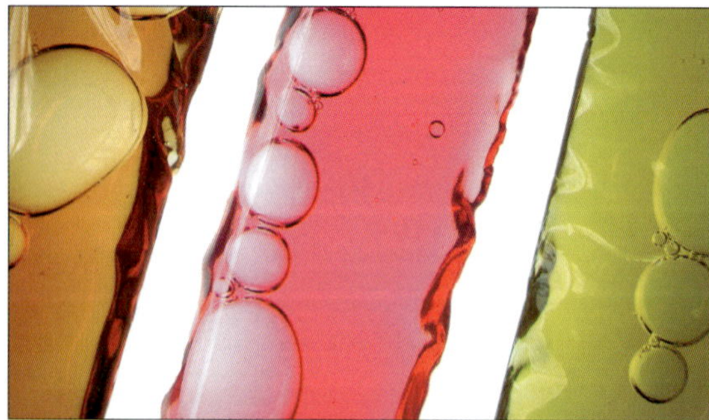

● TIM SMITH Ice pops placed on a lightbox to allow a backlight effect. Shake them up to increase the bubbles before taking a shot.

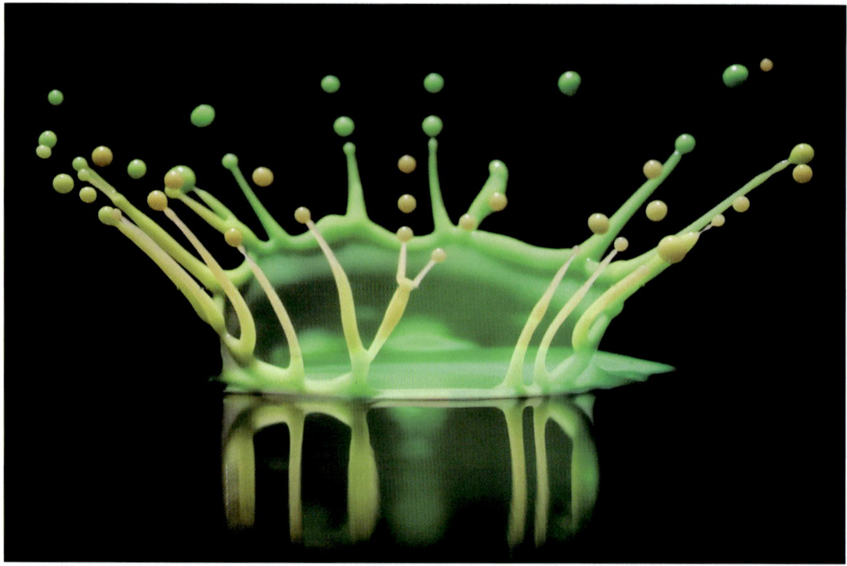

● MARC WHITBURN Neon paint caught as it splashes off black formica. Marc has built a set-up to create colourful shots like this, using a Vivitar 283 flash and Schmitt trigger photogate with delay.

DIGITAL TECHNIQUE – CREATING A RING FLASH EFFECT

■ Studio photographers sometimes use a ringflash to create a subtle shadow around the subject, which appears like a dark halo. The normal ringflash you get for macro photography, mentioned in the flash/lighting section, is not suitable because the diameter of the ring is too small and it may not have high enough power. The flash the pros tend to use costs an arm and a leg! Fortunately, digital photographers can create a similar effect by manipulating their originals. Here's how...

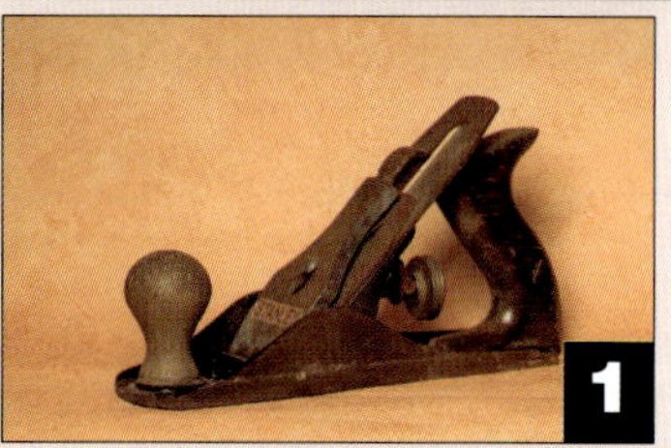

1 Take a photo of a suitable subject against a background illuminated with diffused window light, or a soft diffused flash/tungsten source. This vintage woodwork plane was photographed on a roll of wallpaper, so I had a continuous backdrop with texture. Notice that there's a slight shadow.

2 Make a selection around the plane using the Magic Wand or one of the Lasso tools. Select⇨Modify⇨ Contract and set 1 or 2 pixels, which will take the 'marching ants' inwards and ensure when you cut you don't carry any of the background with the plane. Copy (Ctrl+C) & paste (Ctrl+V) onto a new layer. Repeat this so you now have the original background layer and two new layers, both with an image of the plane. If the plane drops slightly out of register use the move tool and adjust the position so it fits in the exact spot that it came from. It's almost like matching up a two piece jigsaw. You can also use the arrow keys to move the item, which is often easier than trying to control it with the mouse.

3 Now remove the original shadow. Make the background layer active, select the Clone tool and choose a large brush size. Sample an area of background without any shadow and paint over the shadow area. You'll see that the plane doesn't appear to be affected, because that's now also sitting safely on the pasted layers.

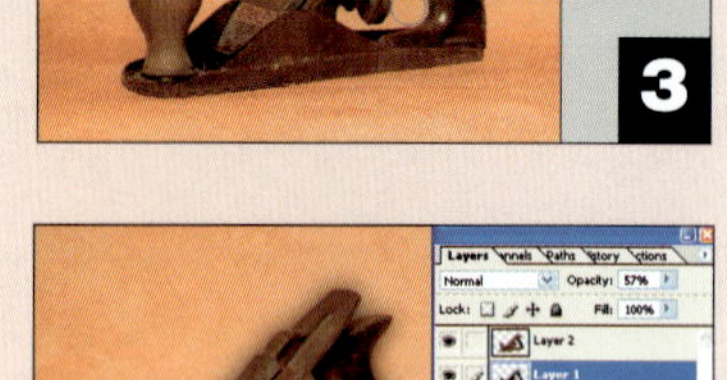

4 Click back on Layer 1, select Image⇨Adjustments⇨ Curves and drag the curve so the image becomes black. Then select Gaussian Blur from the menu – Filter⇨Blur⇨Gaussian Blur. Adjust the slider so that the layer is very blurred - a radius of around 30 pixels will do. What we are doing is blurring the middle layer so it spreads out beyond the top sharp layer and becomes visible as a dark halo.

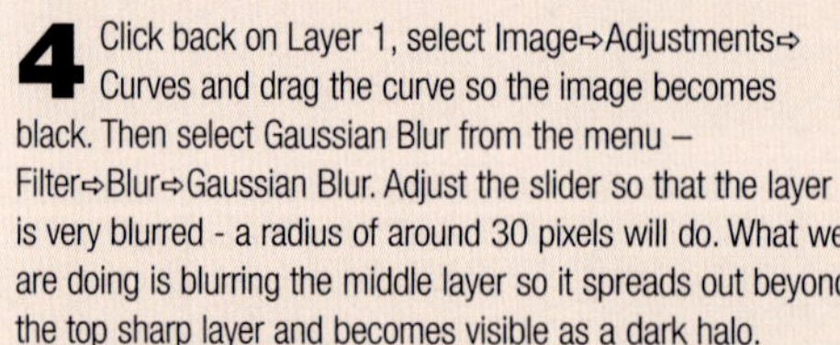

5 As the background, plane and shadow are on individual layers you have plenty of control. You can strengthen or weaken the shadow and alter the colour of the background or plane. In this case I added a background vignette using a feathered and inverted oval selection, made using the Elliptical Marquee tool, followed by a Curves adjustment and colour tweak using Hue/Saturation. I also erased the shadow at the base of the plane to stop it looking as though it's floating.

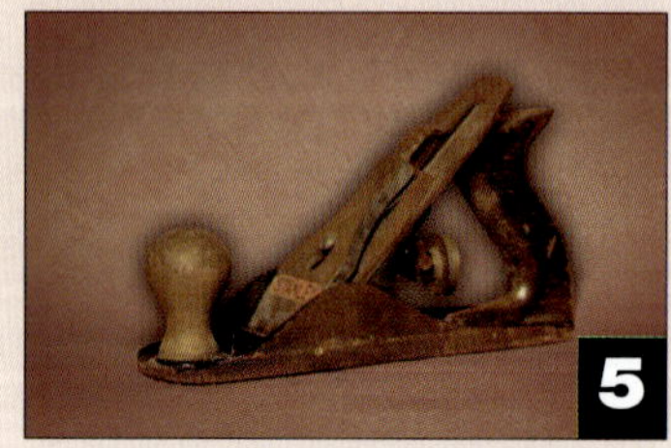

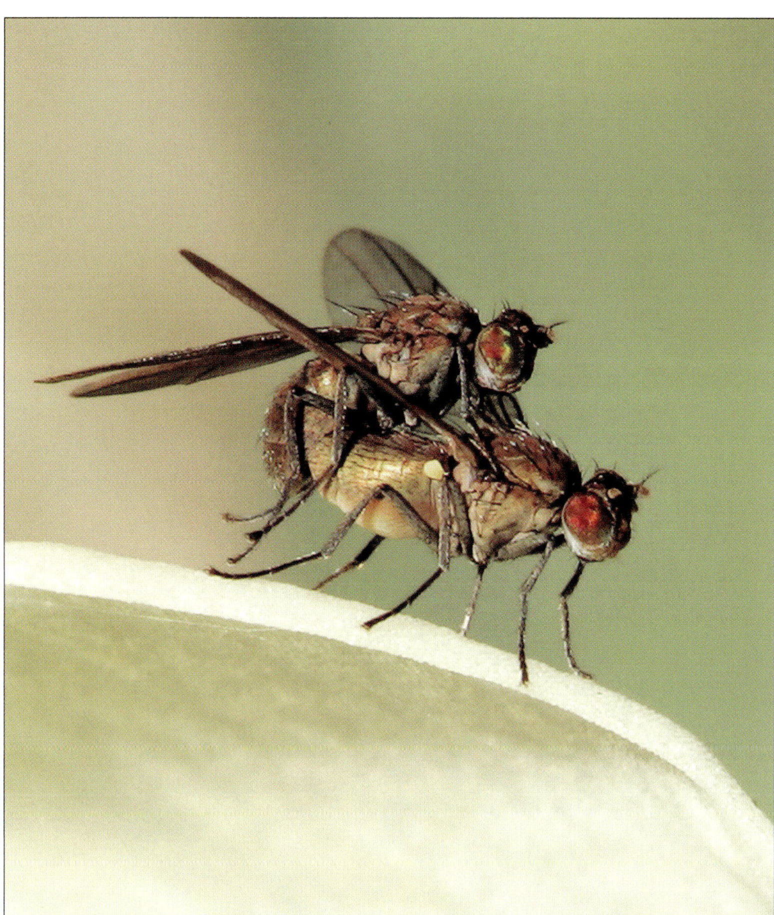

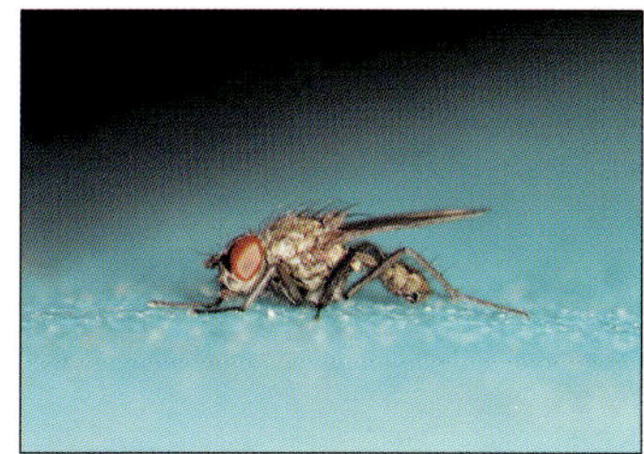

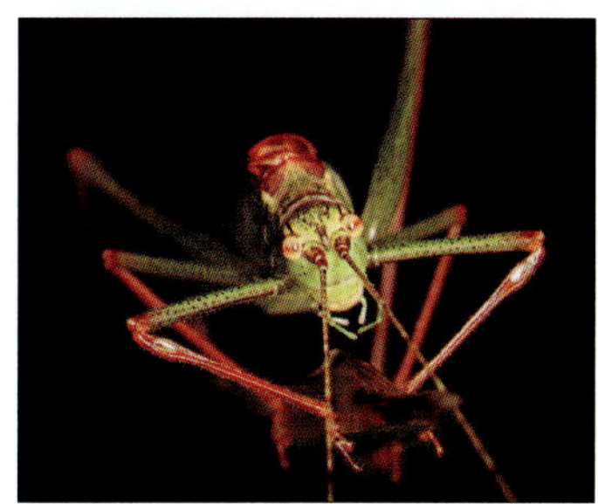

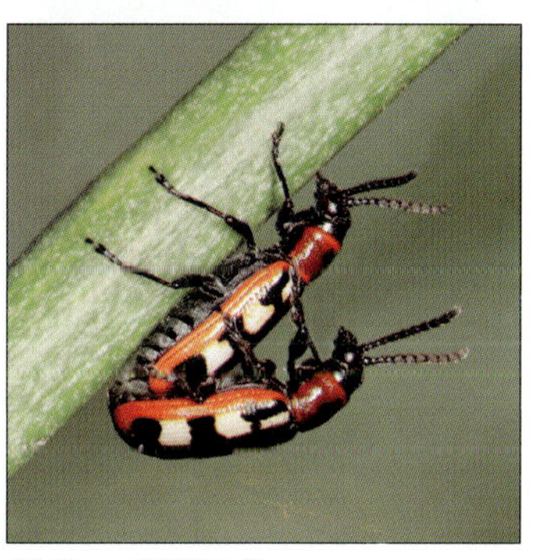

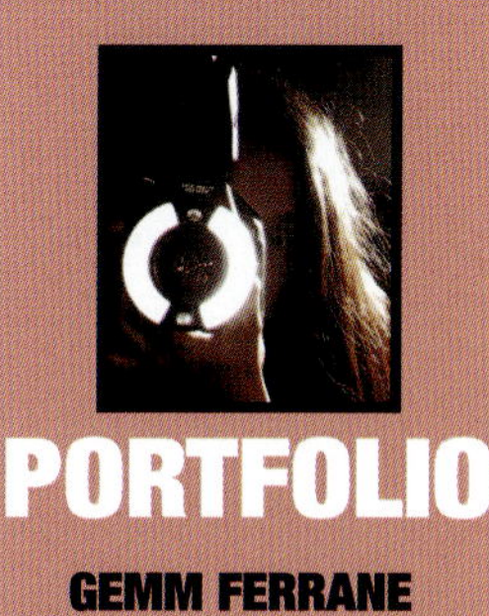

PORTFOLIO

GEMM FERRANE

Gemm is fascinated by the close-up world of insects and uses a combination of flash guns to achieve these images.

I was seven when I first held a camera, an old Canon Canonet passed on to me by my journalist father. I remember snapping away happily, taking snapshots of us on holidays or other special occasions, although I have no recollection of the kind of results these first formative attempts yielded!

Around 10 years ago I rediscovered my passion for photography and my snapshots developed into something more serious. Switching to digital also changed my perspective of photography and has helped make it even more enjoyable.

One of my favourite subjects is nature photography, with a particular emphasis on insects, flowers and birds. I use macro to capture images of flowers and insects, primarily in their natural environment. I find close-up detail fascinating and easily overlooked.

My inspiration comes from wandering around the garden, often with my nose pressed to the ground! I don't know what my neighbours think when they see me crawling around the garden, but I'm just glad they can't see the big grin on my face when I capture insects mating!

My technique usually involves hand-held shooting using a ring Canon MR-14EX flash, often together with a Canon 550EX fired off-camera with Canon ST-E2 wireless transmitter. Wireless off-camera flash is a godsend, especially when working with flowers. Generally, I don't use a tripod as they can be too restrictive to the speed I need to work at. Also, I regularly photograph moving subjects so my movement has to be flexible and therefore hand-held shooting is preferable – a tripod wouldn't allow me the freedom to move around. ∎

● **Top-left:** Canon EOS 1D MKII with 100mm f/2.8 Macro lens. Exposure 1/200sec, f/16, ISO100, lit with Canon 550EX off-camera.
● **Top-right:** Canon EOS 1D MKII with Canon 100mm f/2.8 Macro lens. Exposure 1/200sec, f/8, ISO100, lit with Canon Macro Ring Lite MR-14EX. ● **Middle right:** Canon EOS 10D with Canon 100mm f/2.8 Macro lens. Exposure 1/160sec, f/16, ISO100, lit with Canon Macro Ring Lite MR-14EX. ● **Bottom right:** Canon EOS 1D MKII with Canon 100mm f/2.8 Macro + extension tube. Exposure 1/160sec, f/16, ISO100, lit with Canon MR-14EX. ● **Below:** Canon EOS 10D with Canon 100mm f/2.8 Macro lens. Exposure 1/200sec, f/22, ISO200, lit with Canon 550EX.

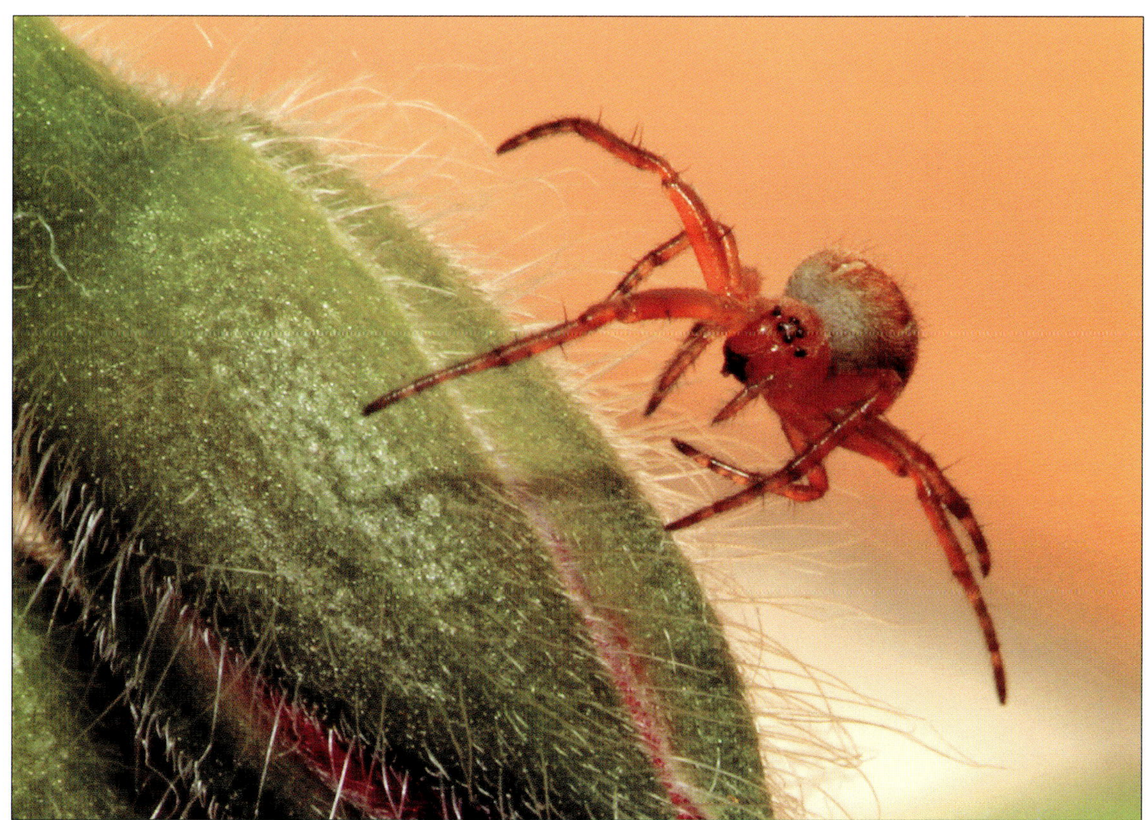

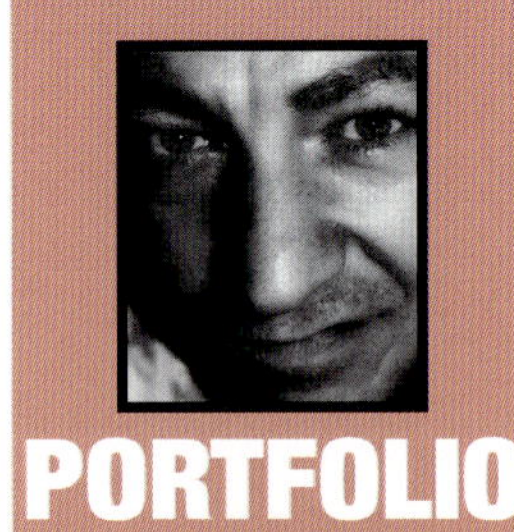

PORTFOLIO

STEVEN NEIL
Steve runs a design business in Brisbane, Australia, and enjoys macro, panoramic joiners and abstract photography.

My journey into photography has been a long one. I left school at 16 and studied engineering for four years, then worked in Seismic Exploration for almost 10 years.

I left Exploration after the birth of my first child and, by chance, began working for a London repro house doing high resolution drum scanning, retouching and colour correction for clients such as the BBC, Arri Cameras, Marks & Spencer and British Airways. Later, I progressed into freelance design and photography – the skills I first learned during my time in reprographics proved invaluable.

I left England for Australia five years ago, set up a design business and bought my first real camera – an Olympus 5050 to assist me with my design work.

I soon progressed to a Canon EOS 10D digital SLR and photography is now an important part of my business. There are many different flavours I enjoy – macro, panoramic stitching and abstract are probably the most enjoyable, but I've always had a creative mind and so am always open to other perspectives.

Whether it's design or photography, the one thing I always keep consistent in my work is balance. It's essential that a photograph, no matter what style, must balance. So, colour and composition are absolutely critical but I tend not to worry about the technical aspects – these can be learnt by trial and error. The key element is your eye – the camera is just a tool. If you are creative and willing to experiment the rest will fall into place eventually.

The biggest mistake I see is people trying to break into photography before they're ready. Don't rush – if you take your time and allow yourself to evolve you will eventually reap the benefits. ■
www.oxign.com.au

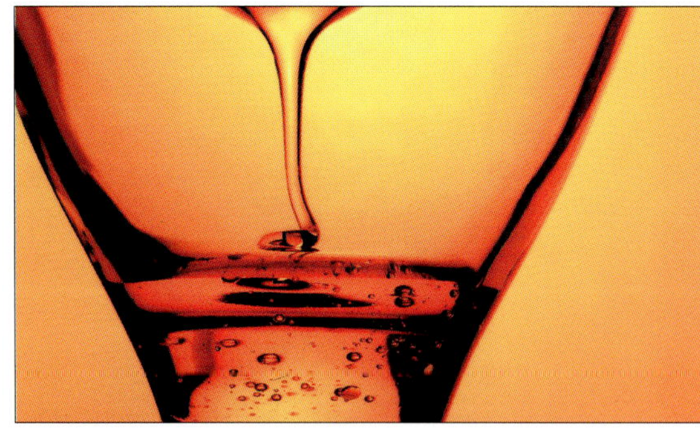

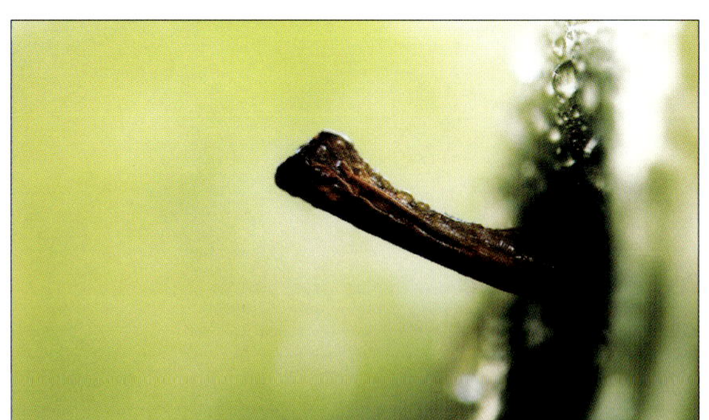

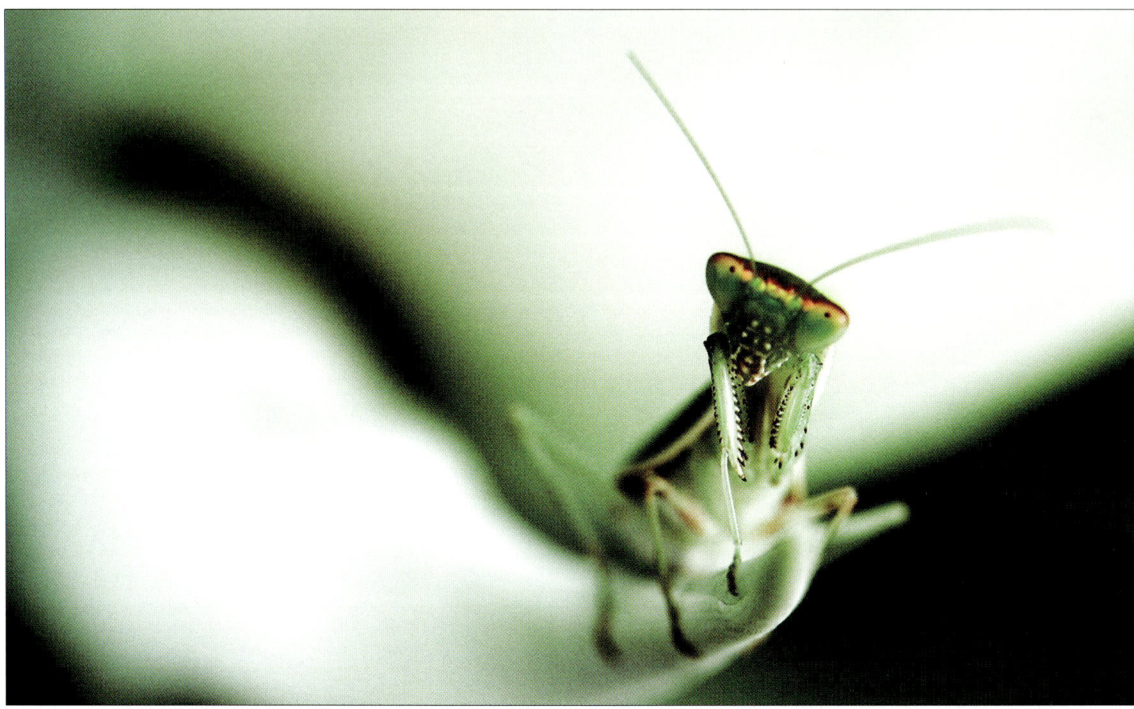

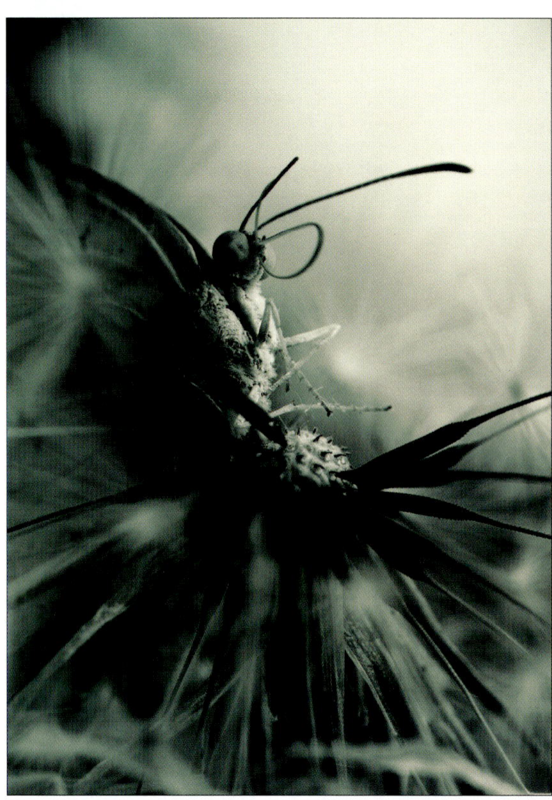

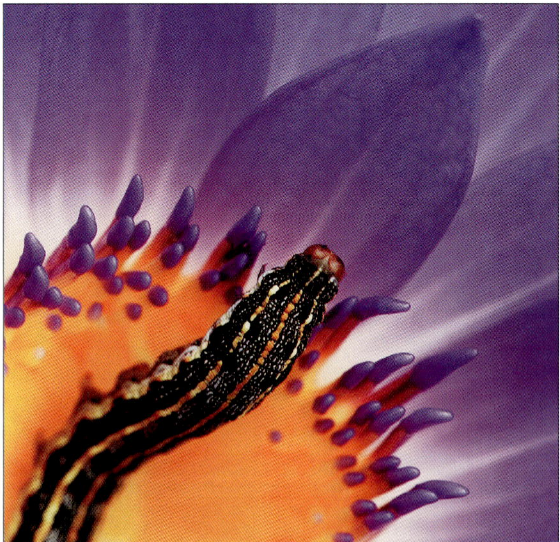

● Top left: Golden Syrup pouring into a glass with an orange lamp shade behind, using an Olympus 5050. Top right: A simple Apple Core, taken on a Canon EOS 10D and 100mm macro lens. Middle: These amazing insects have the most captivating expressions. Colour removed from the leaf to enhance the subject. Bottom left: A butterfly entangled in a dandelion seed, using a Canon EOS 10D and 100mm macro lens. Cross process technique used for colour. Bottom right: A caterpillar eating a lily, taken on a Canon EOS 10D and 100mm macro lens.

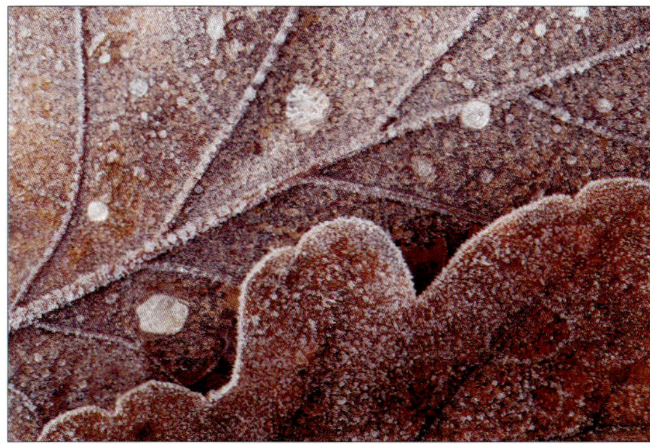

● JOHN TISBURY Frosted Oak leaves, taken using a Nikon D100 with 105mm lens on a tripod and an exposure of 6secs at f/40.

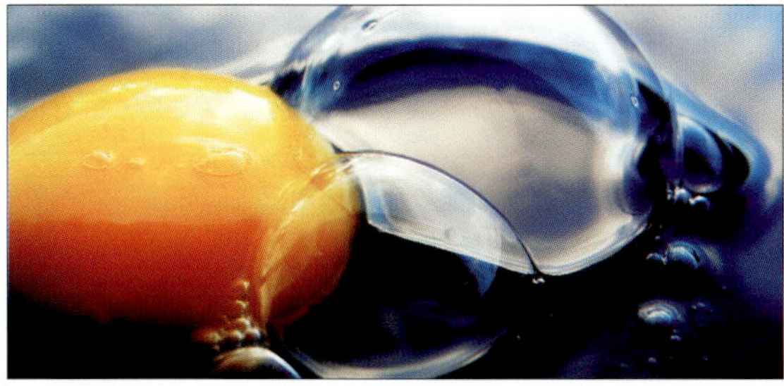

● STEVEN NEIL A cracked egg, taken with an Olympus 5050. The Overlay layer in Photoshop was used to soften and saturate colours.

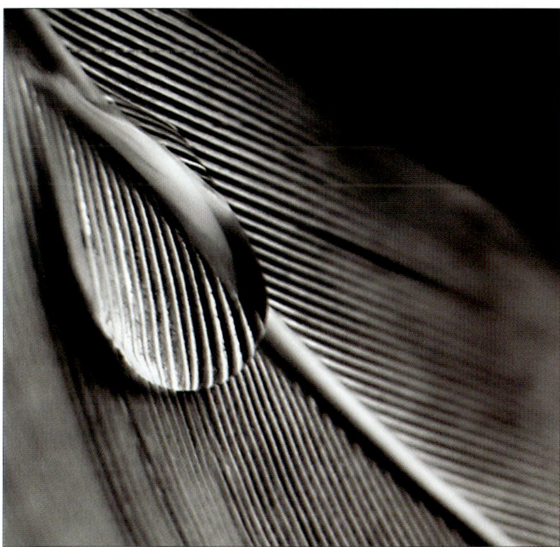

● IIONA WELLMANN Water on a feather, taken with a Nikon Coolpix 5700 in manual and 1/30sec at f/3.1 Desaturated in Photoshop.

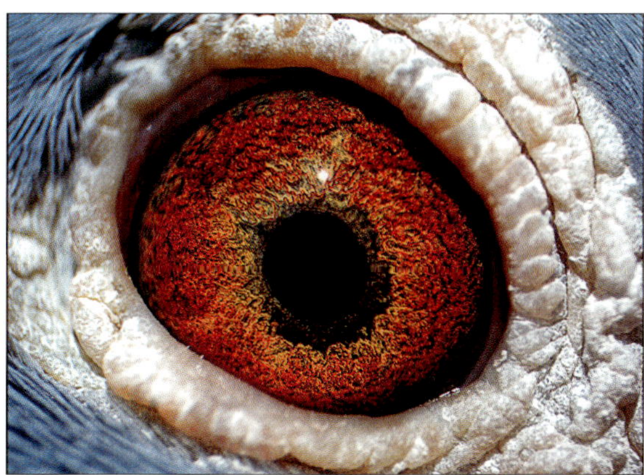

● JOGGIE VAN STADEN The eye of a racing pigeon, taken with a Pentax K1000 & 10X Leitz microscope lens mounted on a PVC pipe.

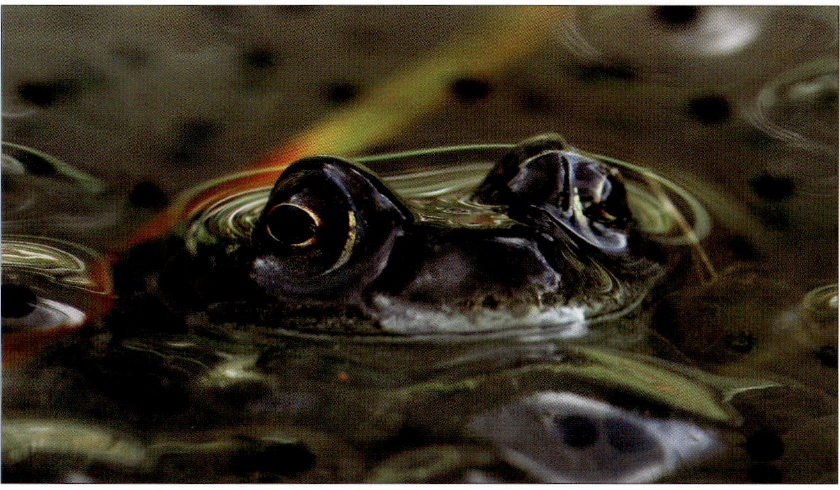

● CELI AZULEK A male frog looking for females and surrounded by frogspawn. This was taken with a 180mm lens at f/9 on a Canon EOS 10D at ISO200 and a shutter speed of 1/80sec.

SHOOTING TIPS – HOW TO USE A LIGHT TENT

■ Using a light tent helps when shooting reflective subjects, such as silverware and glass, where any light point will be reflected causing either distracting patterns or exposure problems. You place your subject inside the cube and the camera points in through a hole at the front. The idea is it allows you to illuminate and shoot reflective subjects without reflections and provides shadowless lighting.

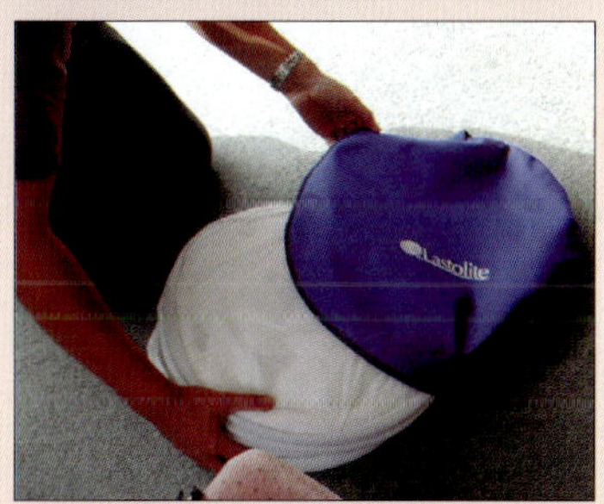

■ For those photographers who are tight on space there are now collapsable versions available — the Cubelite from Lastolite is one such gadget. It's an extremely lightweight cube, made from translucent material that you can fire light through, and is flat packed in a 38cm diameter storage pouch.

■ Opening the Cubelite, like many of the Lastolite folding products, is easy. Just unzip the case, pull out the item and run like heck! Well not quite, but the springy metal frames that are used tend to spring into shape as soon as they get the space, so one minute you have a small circular item in your hand and the next, in this case, you have two sides of the cube in your face! Then lift the third side out and the whole thing pops into shape.

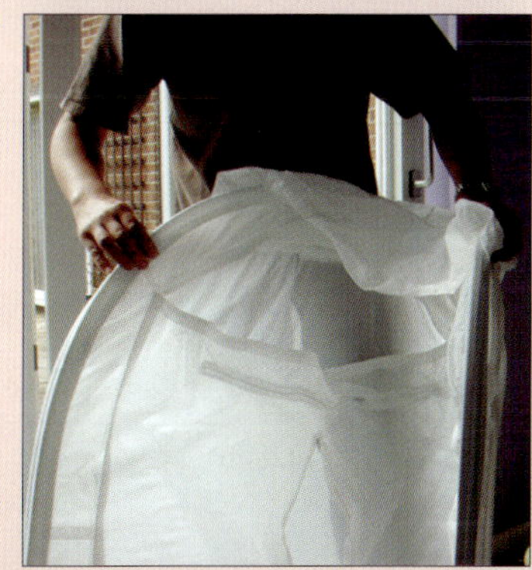

■ When erect you'll find the front – it's the side that has a removable Velcro panel. The panel also has horizontal and vertical slits that have zip fastenings. The idea is to remove the panel, place your subject inside and then attach the panel.

■ Once the panel is in place you unzip the slit where you poke your camera lens and, once in the best position, zip up so that the lens is snug in the aperture.

■ Now you're ready to light the subject. I used a room with good window light. You could also point studio lights from any direction, including underneath if you have the cube on a suitable glass table or product bench.

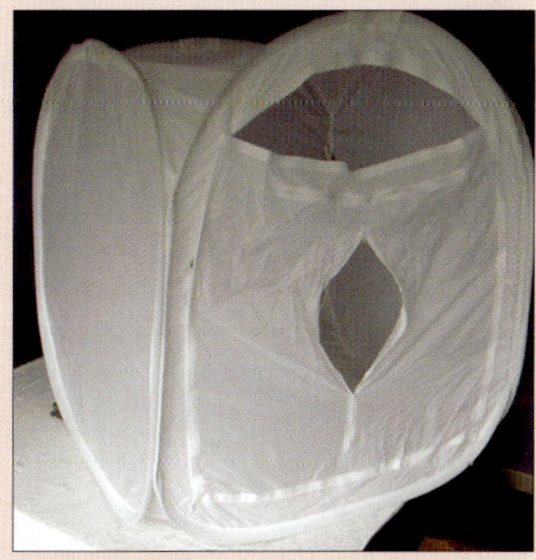

■ Another feature that's useful is a pair of crocodile clips that are positioned at the top, on each side of the back panel, on elasticized straps. These can be used to grip a background which would then be extended from the top to the base front to provide a continuous tone for the subject's background. I used a cut down vinyl sheet for this shot of a Guinness bottle, but paper or cloth can also be used.

■ Although the diffused light does kill all reflections it also dulls down the brilliance of glass, making shots look clean but sometimes lacking a little in sparkle. What it does well is provide shadowless lighting that would be difficult to control in normal studio conditions. It's also great for photographing less reflective items, such as fruit and vegetables, which would normally pick up a distracting highlight or two.

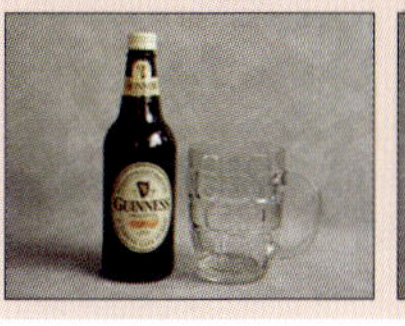

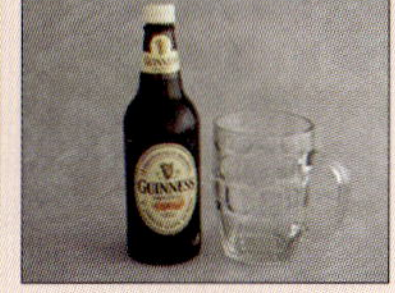

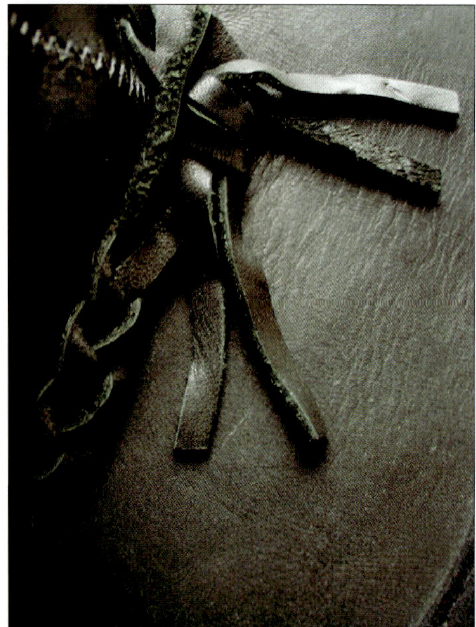

● PETER CHARLES TURNER Shot of a hat on an Olympus Camedia C2500L, converted to B&W and curves adjusted.

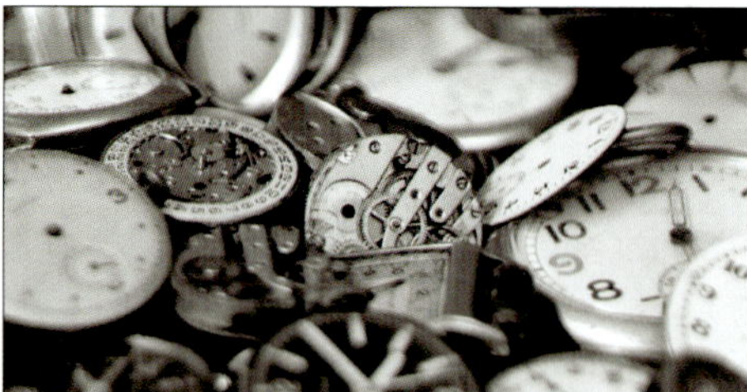

● NEAL LAVER Frozen in Time – broken watch parts, taken on a Fuji S2Pro and Sigma 24-135mm zoom.

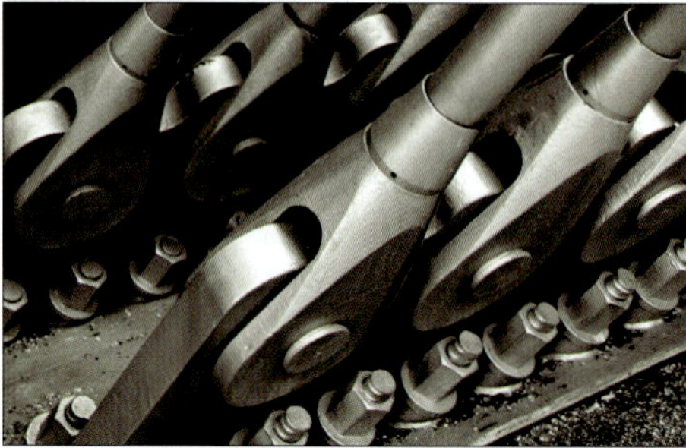

● LEVENTE TOTH Detail of the Millennium Bridge, London, shot on Agfa Scala B&W film in a Canon EOS33.

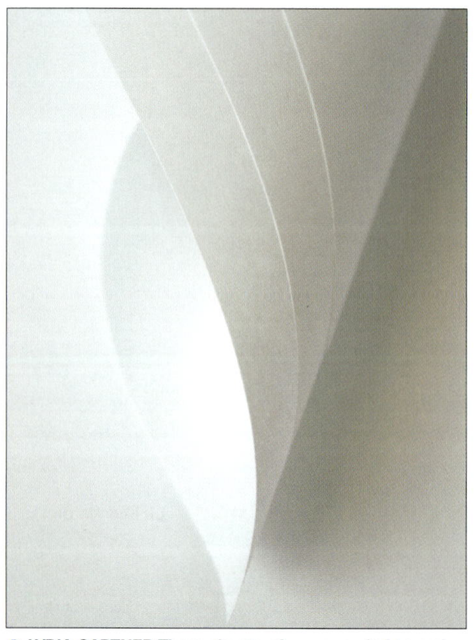

● LYDIA GARTNER Three sheets of paper curled to make the intended look and shot using natural outside lighting.

TECHNIQUE TIPS

■ Close-up photography is the perfect medium in which to emphasise colours, patterns and textures, making it ideal for experimenting with more unusual and interesting images.

■ Keep the background simple and crop out distractions.

■ Isolate close-up subjects from confusing backgrounds by opening up the aperture to throw the background out of focus.

■ Take care when choosing a background – a pale object against a bright background will draw attention to the background rather than the main subject.

■ Artificial backgrounds may be used where the natural one is not suitable and the subject is immovable, but be aware that these do not always look authentic.

■ Look for patterns and unusual shapes.

■ Keep it simple – don't include anything that breaks up a pattern as this will ruin the effect of the picture.

■ Photograph brightly coloured objects in bright sunlight to create bold and vivid images.

■ The closer you go the more limited the depth-of-field becomes. Set an aperture of f/16 or less to combat this.

■ Don't let a rainy day put you off. Capture droplets of rain hitting a puddle or running down a glass window.

■ Polarizing filters can be used to create a dramatic effect without ruining images.

■ If photographing in natural light, avoid the low-angled sunlight of dawn and dusk as it casts extreme shadows.

■ Artificial light can be moved to create the best image. Whereas, with sunlight you must judge when the best light will be provided to get the most from the photograph.

■ Lighting from the side helps to create shadow, making a 3D subject appear more dramatic and effective.

■ Lighting from behind can help to give some subjects a glowing appearance.

■ Avoid taking pictures of metallic and shiny objects in bright sunlight – the reflections will prove too distracting in a close-up image.

■ Winter provides many opportunities for the close-up photographer – frosted leaves, footprints in pristine white snow and a glistening, dripping icicle all make for interesting and effective images.

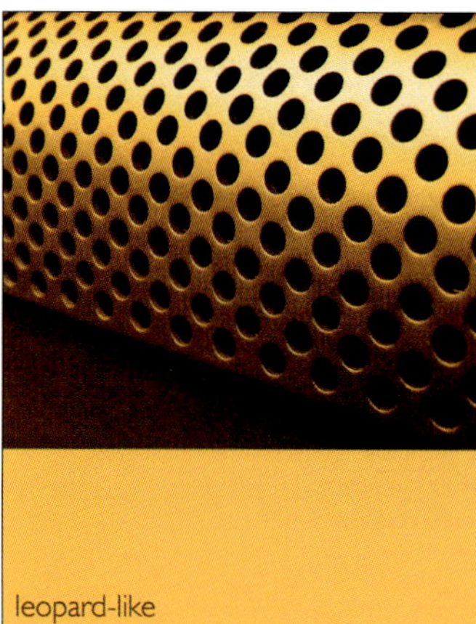

● NEAL MORAN 'Leopard-like' – a graphic approach to this shot of an Apple Mac G5.

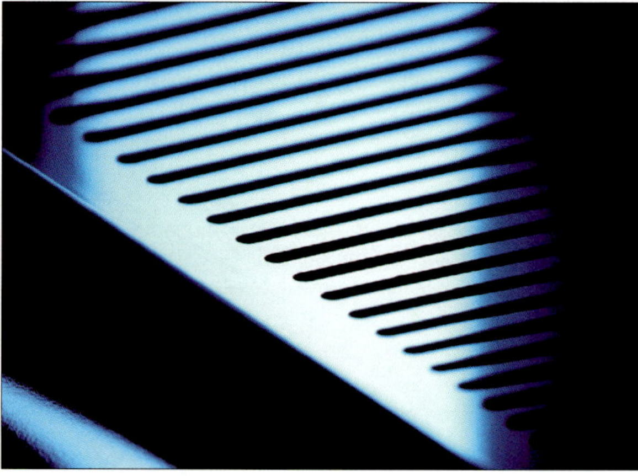

● EMMA JONES An abstract image of a radiator, shot on Kodak E100SW and cross-processed to give the vivid surreal colour.

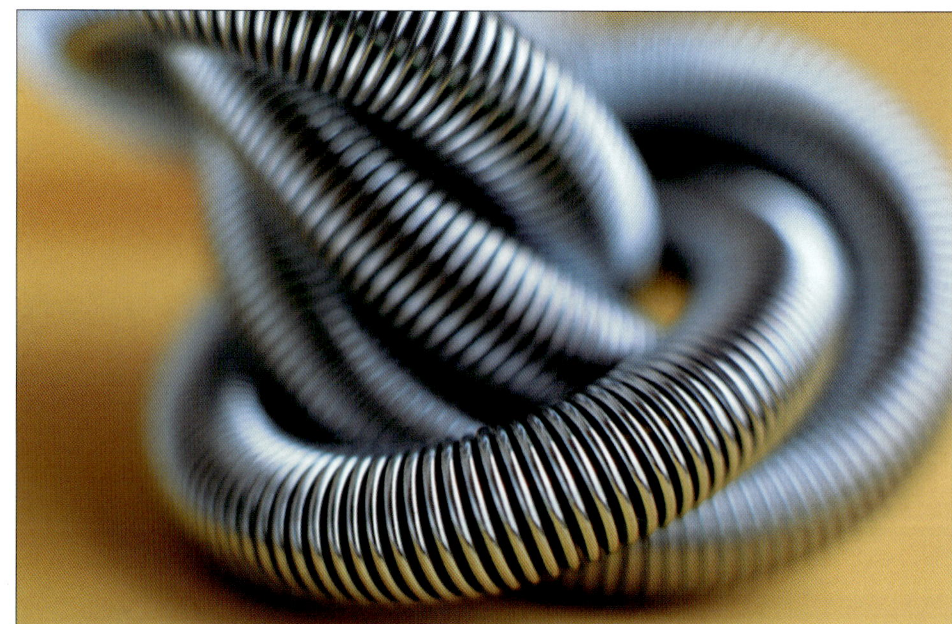

● HUGO DENBY-MANN A long metal, coiled spring lit by window light. Shot on Fuji Velvia with a Canon A1, using a 50mm lens plus an extension tube.

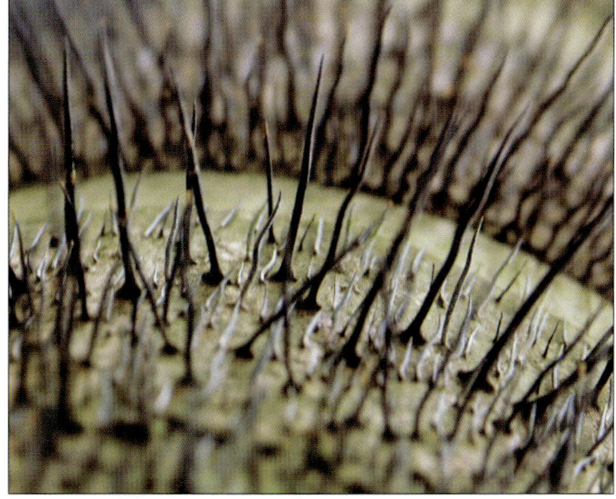

● DAVE DEWHURST A macro shot of a tree bark, taken at Kew Gardens Palm House at 200mm, f/3.5 on Minolta Dimage A1.

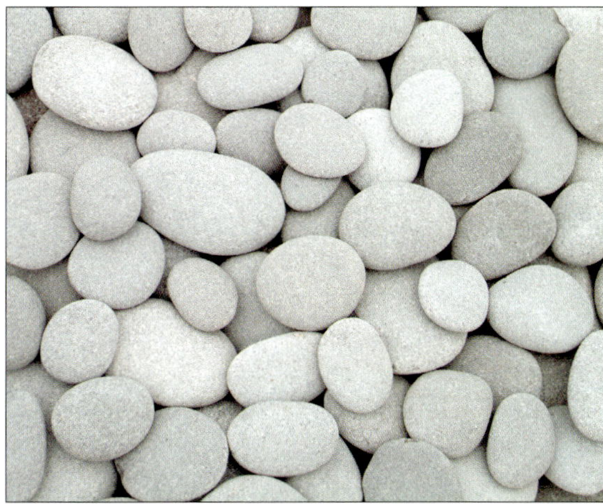

● ALETHEA HOLLIS Grey beach pebbles collected and arranged to show the smooth shapes and nature's many different shades of grey.

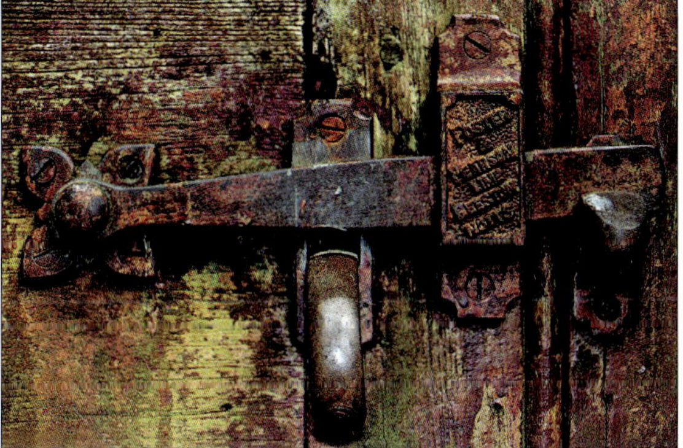

● ERIC FARAGHER Greenhouse latch at the Botanic Gardens, Southport. Appears with permission of Chapter Thirteen Photography.

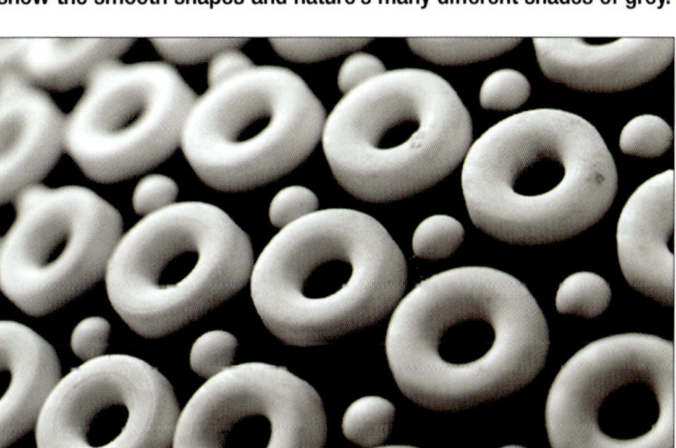

● DAN LARC A macro shot of his sister's 'Powerpop!' running shoe. Many kinds of clothing provide patterns and textures when up close.

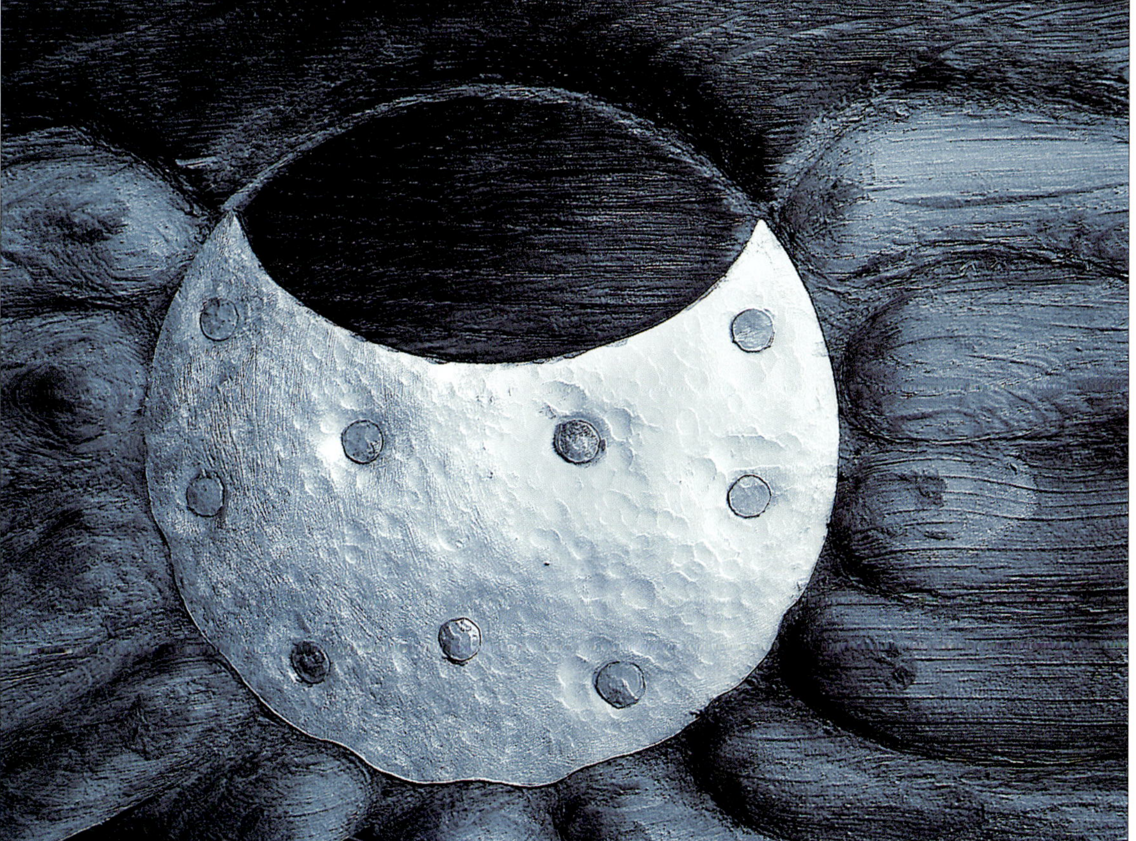

● CHRIS SHEPHERD Detail from a carving hidden in the depths of Hainault Forest, Essex. Fuji-S602 image converted to greyscale and toned.

USING QPCARD

■ Your digital camera may have a white balance control or you may shoot in Raw and adjust settings yourself, but you're either relying on the camera getting it right or the accuracy of your eye. In most cases neither do a perfect job. That's where colour calibration targets, like QPcard, come in.

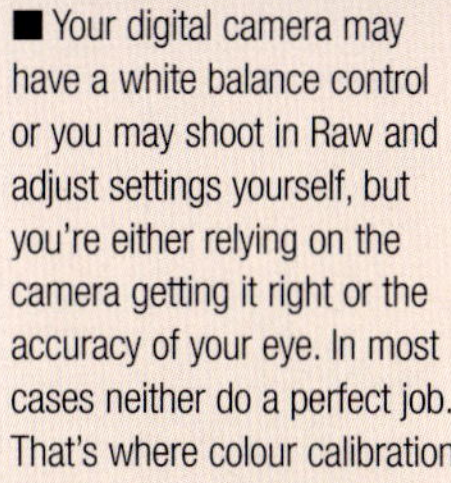

■ It's a small card with a set of 30 colour, grey, white and black patches that you place in the photo on your first shot.
■ Take a photo with the card parallel to your camera's sensor/film plane and evenly lit.
■ Shoot the rest of the photos under the same lighting without the card.
■ Open the photo that includes the QPcard in QPcolorsoft 501
■ Make a selection around the card with the marking tool.
■ Click Create Profile to create a colour correction profile. This compares the captured colours with the real colours and creates a correction profile.

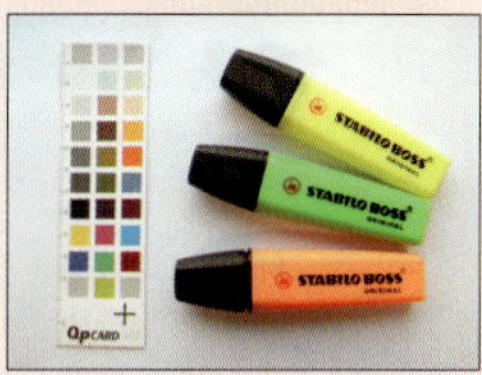

■ Correct colours by clicking the Convert Image icon.
■ Save the profile.
■ Batch convert the rest of the photos automatically.

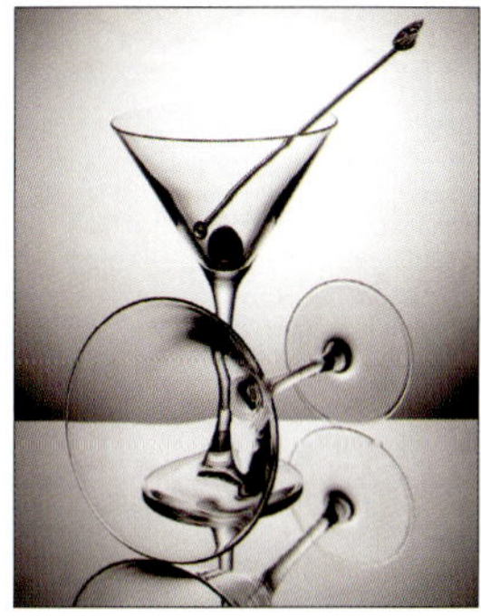

● LAURA MCLEARY Mirror card was placed underneath the glass to give reflections. The background is tracing paper with a harsh lamp behind.

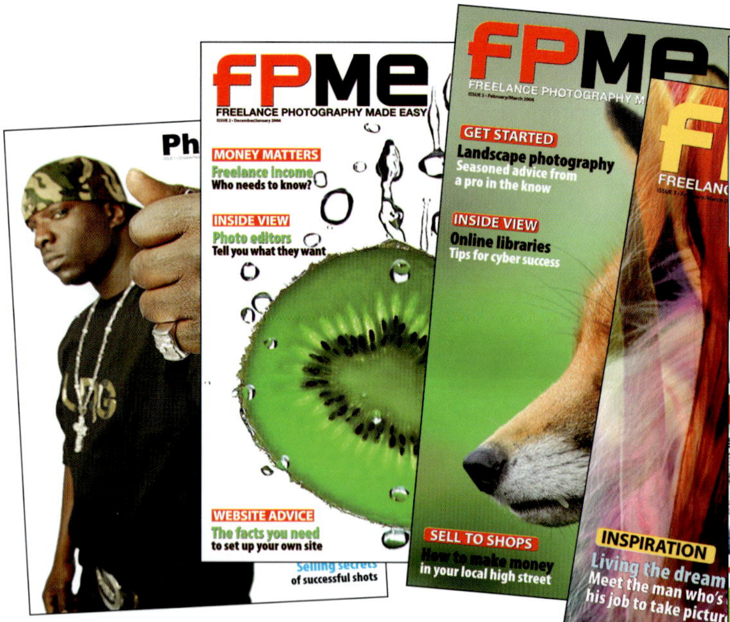

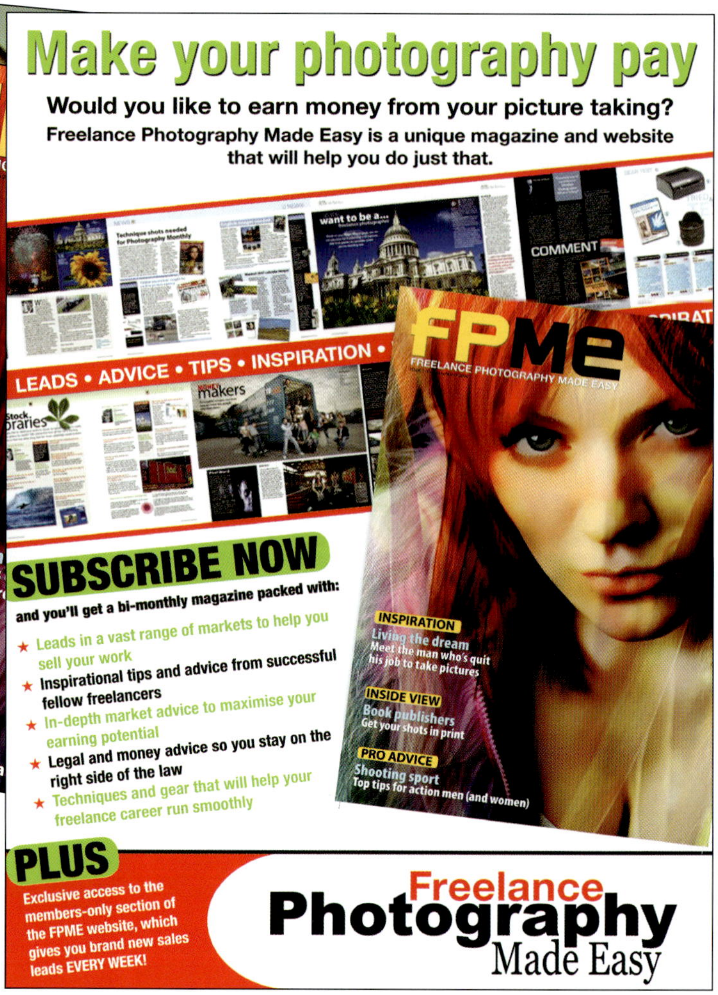

● *Freelance Photography Made Easy* is a subscription-based club with a bi-monthly magazine. The magazine has loads of facts, articles and leads to help you sell your photographs and become a successful freelance photographer.

The magazine is edited by Roger Payne, a respected journalist who's edited several newsstand magazines including *Photo Answers* and *Max Power*. Roger now runs his own company, Jump Media, with his partner Jules.

The concept of *FPME* was created to satisfy a growing number of ePHOTOzine members who had a thirst to see their pictures in print and be rewarded for the experience. It also aims to help those considering setting up a freelance business to cope with the legal aspects and help them understand the business side of the venture, rather than just what makes a successful and marketable photograph.
You can find out all about it at the web site: **www.fpme.co.uk.**

● IAN ANDREWS is proof that being proactive is the best way to be if you want to be successful. Ian has been a member of ePHOTOzine for over three years. He soon realised our website could be a useful self-promotion vehicle and started to write pieces for the articles section.

His monthly series "What to shoot in..." showed he had writing skills and could deliver copy on time to meet monthly deadlines. This lead to him being commissioned by us to write some equipment tests and then, when we set up our lens test service, we commissioned Ian to front it and provide us with a whole series of reviews.

Piggybacking off this success, Ian has been able to secure work with several newsstand titles including *Amateur Photographer*, *Digital Photography* and, most recently, a series in *Photography Monthly*.

● Many ePHOTOzine members have created their own websites using template systems from the likes of Amazing Internet **www.amazinginternet.com**, ClikPic **www.clikpic.com** and Photium **www.photium.com**. With links from their ePHOTOzine portfolios they are able to deliver a high class preview of their abilities. These type of websites allow the members to show and, hopefully, sell their images to a huge audience. We've listed many of our members' websites on the thank you page (p224).

Here are just a few examples of members' websites that we've visited recently:
1 Kathy Wright **www.overlookedimages.com**
2 Annaliese Bending **www.annaliese.co.uk**
3 Victor Habbick **www.victorhabbick.co.uk**
4 Paul Ward **www.paulwardphotography.com**
5 Anthony Stewart Hamilton
www.theblobphotography.com
6 Keith Henson and Andy Dippie
www.northscape.co.uk
7 Karen Bacon
www.dandelionphotographic.co.uk
8 Terry Longley **www.boyd-longley.co.uk**
9 Takui Neko **www.takuineko.com**
10 Paul Stefan **www.paulstefan.co.uk**

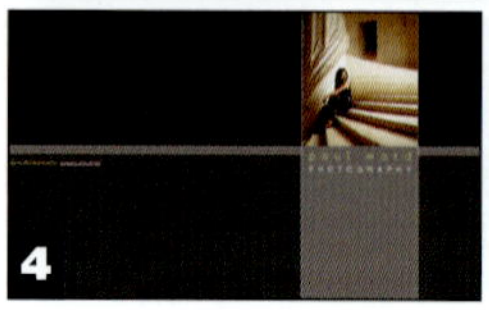

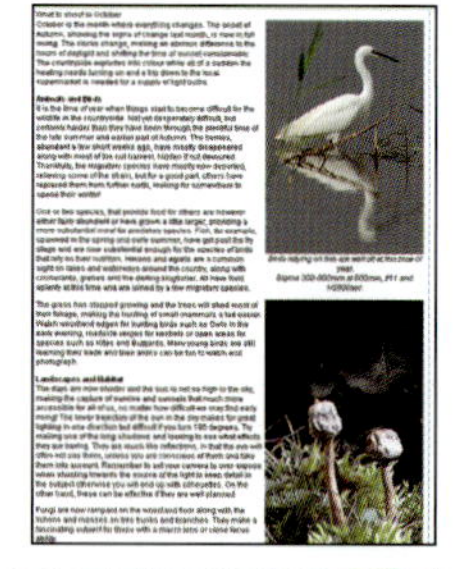
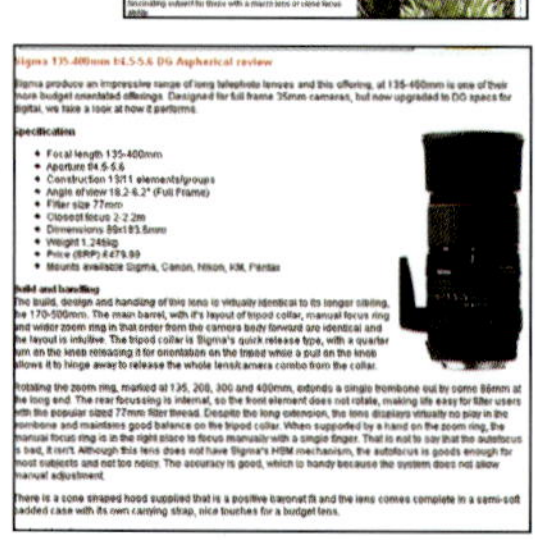
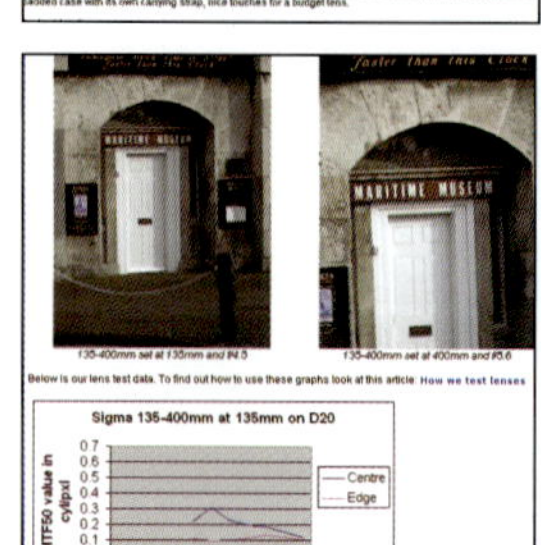
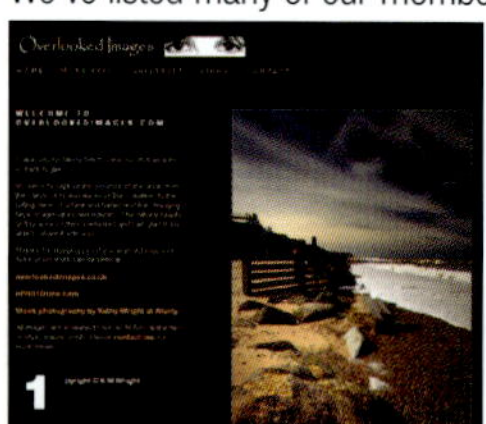
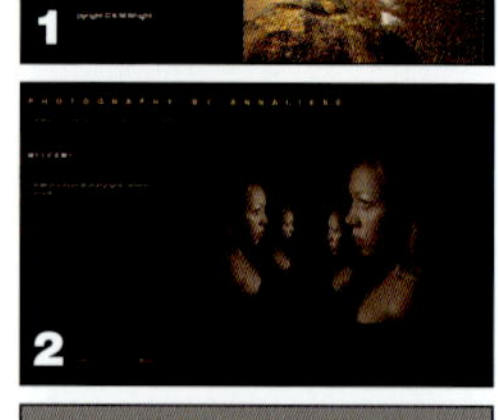
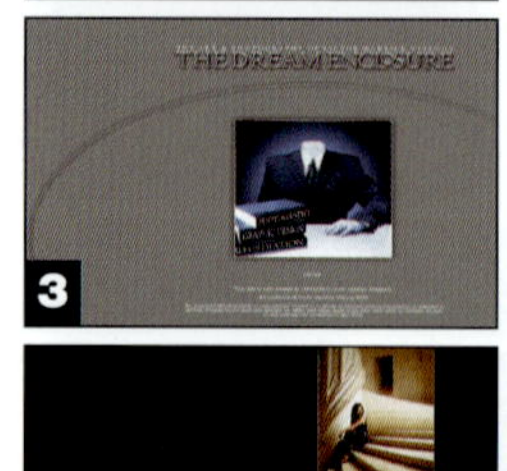
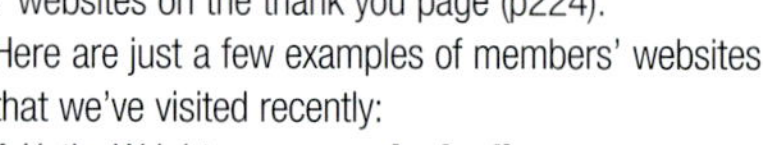
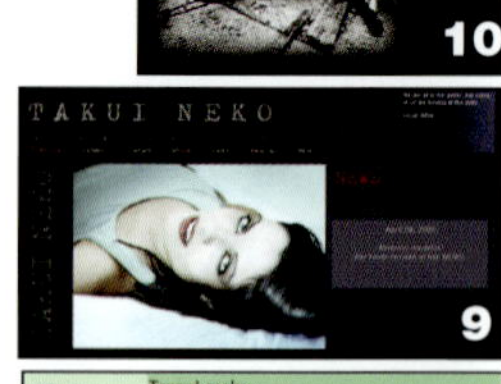
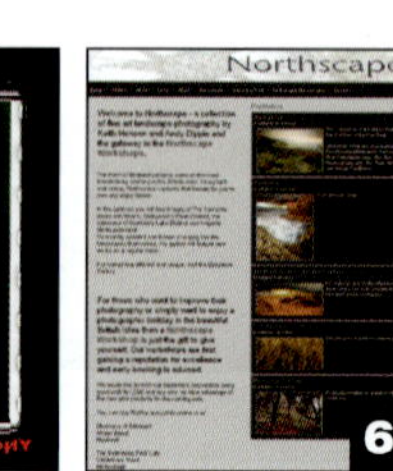
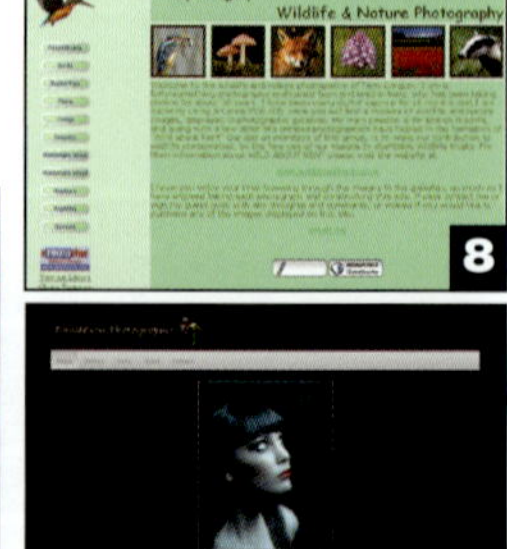
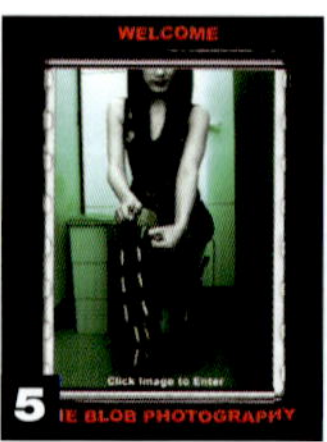

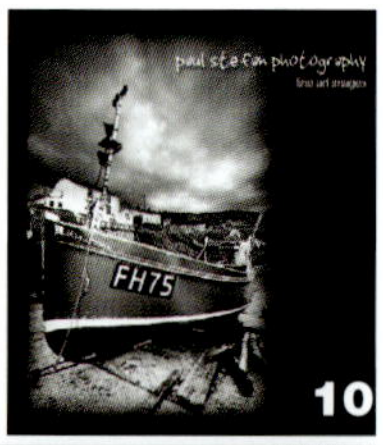

And that's about it

Well this is the end of the book, and we hope you thoroughly enjoyed it. But, for our members, it's possibly just the beginning. Many are starting to see their work improve dramatically, and some, from very point & shoot beginnings, are now starting to see their work in print in magazines, books and publications around the world.

ePHOTOzine tends to be used by many publishers as a resource to find new talent. Our members' profiles are often perused by editors to find photos for their publications. In the last few years we've heard many tales of members being contacted via their portfolios to request the use of their photographs in a number of publications.

Almost every week one of the ePHOTOzine members posts up a message to say their work or another members work is appearing in one of the magazines on the newsstand.

Below are just a few success stories of members' photographs being used after they'd been spotted on ePHOTOzine. ■

● NICHOLAS RIPLEY Heartbreak Productions is a professional theatre company, based in Leamington Spa, that has been operating successfully for 15 years. They specialise in producing classical pieces for outdoor production.

Heartbreak are undertaking four productions this year; The Railway Children, Twelfth Night, The Importance of Being Earnest and Romeo & Juliet.

The company regularly use photographers for their publicity production shots, but were looking to try some different approaches this year for two of their productions – The Railway Children and Twelfth Night.

In November 2005 they approached Nicholas to discuss a commission, having seen his work on ePHOTOzine. With a background in professional theatre he could quickly understand the approach they required, and discussed a brief to produce pre-tour publicity shots for use on their website: www.heartbreakproductions.co.uk, and for advance booking information.

The company were pleased with the results which has led to subsequent work producing rehearsal shots of The Railway Children.

Nicholas posted the shots he was unsure of on ePHOTOzine's gallery to gauge general members' reactions before choosing his preferred images for the client.

● DARREN SMITH was contacted through ePHOTOzine by another member, Paul Turner (p-tee), who was working on a project for a book cover for "Sports Journalism, A Practical Guide" by Phil Andrews, published by Sage Publications.

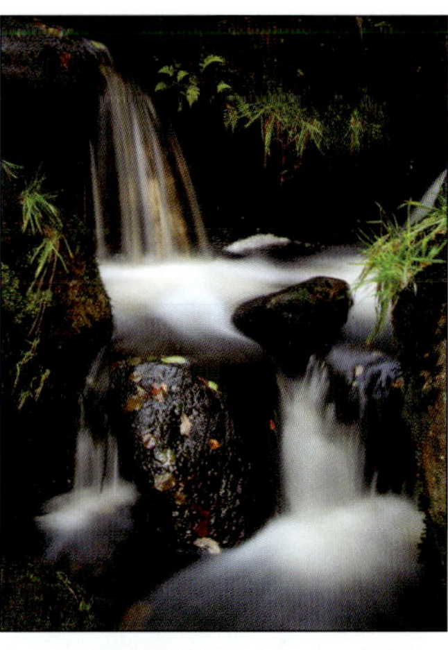

"Paul was looking for an image of a cyclist for the top of the cover to go with pictures of a swimmer and a footballer. He took an image that I'd shot of the men's cycling at the Olympic Games, in Athens 2004, and a few others as samples to his client who approved the image. The image was manipulated by the designer, but it's still obvious that it's mine." says Darren

● MARTIN WEST had four photos chosen from his ePHOTOzine portfolio last November by *What Digital Camera* for use in their Jan 06 issue. They appeared in a double page spread, along with a photo of Martin and a brief biography which included a mention of ePHOTOzine. "It was a good feeling to have my work in a national magazine. On from that, and with my photographs doing well on ePHOTOzine, I'm hoping to set up a website, when I get time," says Martin.

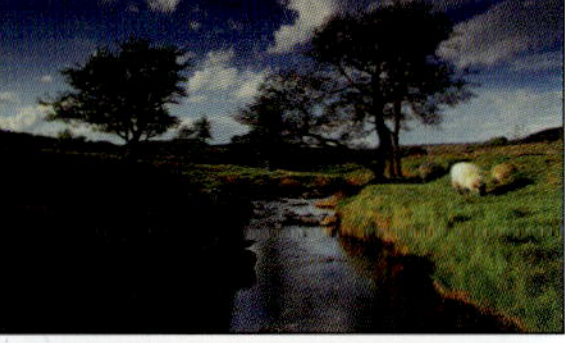

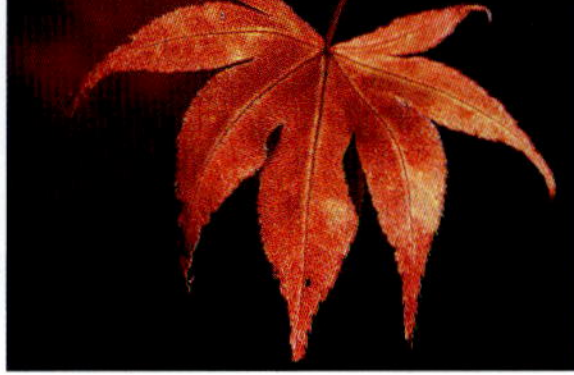

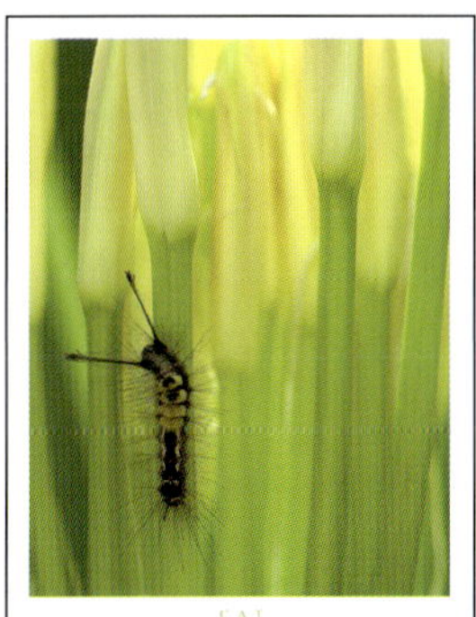

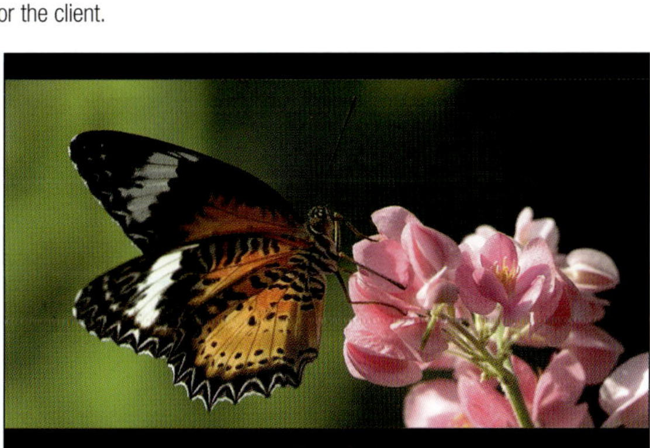

● KEN SU was approached by *What Digital Camera* magazine and they requested three photos that were selected from his ePHOTOzine portfolio. "I didn't ask what they would pay, but they sent me a cheque for £50 after receiving the high resolution pictures and all three were published in the July 2005 issue. This was my first ever publication – I never cashed the cheque!"

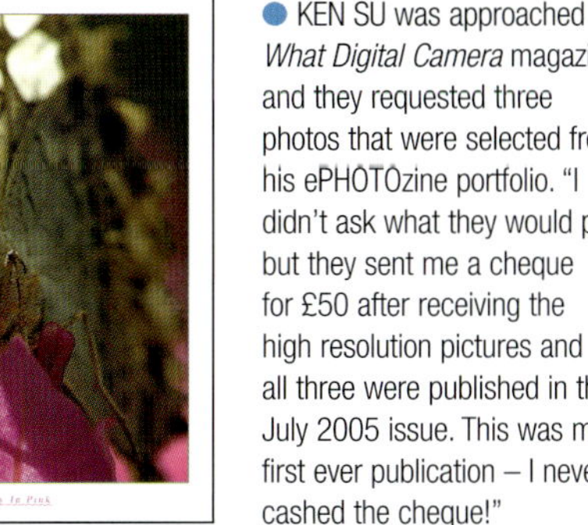

● We asked Nigel Atherton, Editor of *What Digital Camera* magazine, why he uses ePHOTOzine: "ePHOTOzine is one of the first places I visit when I'm looking for great photography taken by amateur and semi-pro photographers. The design of the site makes it easy to navigate, the standard of some of the work is quite outstanding and most images also include that all-important (for us) technical information (camera, lens etc). I often go to the Editor's Choice section first, where most of the best pictures usually are, but often link through from there to the photographers' portfolios (by clicking on their names). The ability to send private messages to photographers whose work I'm interested in clinches the deal for me."

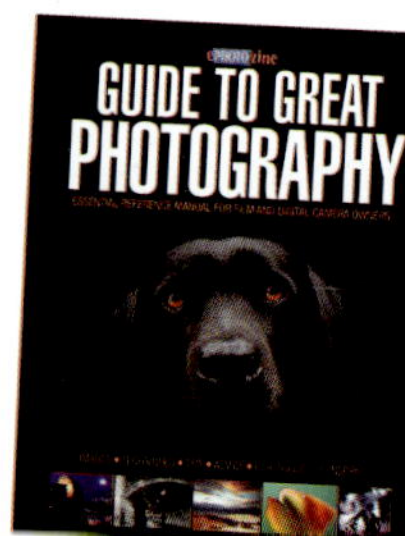

When we announced the planned production of the *ePHOTOzine Guide to Great Photography* the following members kindly paid in advance. We would like to thank these, and all the other members who didn't supply contact details but also paid, for helping us to get the project off the ground. Without your support, amazing patience and commitment this book would never have happened.

We have provided the members' names, followed by their ePHOTOzine user names in brackets, followed by either an email and/or web address. Please have a look at the portfolios of these members on ePHOTOzine by visiting the Reader Portfolio index page and using the alphabetical lists.

Adrian Lunsong (messhai) adrianlunsong@gmail.com
Adrian R Turner (digiart) adrian@artvision.co.uk www.artvision.co.uk
Ady Gell (towerbends) ady@towerbends.com www.towerbends.com
Alan Benson (alben) alben57@hotmail.com www.alanbensonphotography.co.uk
Alan Booth (A Booth) alan@booth6774.fsnet.co.uk
Alan Humphris (alife) al@ambientlife.net www.earthrise.co.uk
Alan Mitchell (amps) photoservices@btconnect.com www.alanmitchelldp.co.uk
Alan Skyrme (alansskyrme) alansskyrme@yahoo.co.uk www.alanskyrme.com
Alan West (wcluk2002) wcluk2002@yahoo.co.uk
Alastair Frieda (ala_fred) ala_fred@ndirect.co.uk
Alastair Holloway (aholloway) al@flamstead.freeserve.co.uk
Alejandro Torres (ajtorres) ajtorres67@lycos.com
Alex Allen (alex.allen) alex.allen1@btinternet.com
Alex Kerr (alexkerr) cooper_s_works@hotmail.co.uk
Alison M (cattyal) alisonguppy@btinternet.com www.alison-m.co.uk
Andrew Findlay (trahern) afind2000@hotmail.com
Andrew Fyfe (andrewfyfe) andrew.fyfe@btinternet.com
Andrew Jenkins (andrewjen) andrewjen40@yahoo.co.uk
Andrew Vizard (andrew vizard) athegreat@talktalk.net
Andy Crellin (andycrellin) andycrellin@gmail.com
Andy Marland (AndyM) andy.marland@btinternet.com
Angela Barnett (arwensgrace) www.celtic-photography.com
Angela Joel (angej) angela.joel@centaur.co.uk www.landscapeimagery.co.uk
Angela Sanderson (funkymarmalade) funkymarmalade@lycos.com
Angela Wareing (beaniebabe) angel@beanie.fslife.co.uk
Anthony Holloway (aj_h) ajh@jb.man.ac.uk
Anthony Smith (Anthony) mail@tony-smith.co.uk www.tony-smith.co.uk
Barry Powell (bppowell) bppowell@computate.co.uk www.computate.co.uk
Ben Rawson (BenHur) brawson021078@hotmail.com www.pbase.com/benhur26
Bill Camm (bill c) william@camm8798.fsnet.co.uk
Bill M (billip) w_mccudden@btconnect.com
Boyd (Boyd) seasider@gmail.com
Brad D'Amico (insanebmx312) brddmco@gmail.com
Brian D. Clark (bravo charlie) briandavidclark@hotmail.com www.briandclark.com
Brian Mossemenear (BrianM) brian@mossemenear.freeserve.co.uk
Brian Wadie (brian1208) bj.wadie@ntlworld.com www.imagesfromnature.co.uk
Bruce Dorricott (dodo_returns) bruce10_oaks@btinternet.com
Brynmor Jones (bj007a3664) brynmor@blueyonder.co.uk
C Heijdemann (conrad) mail.me@easy.com http://cameramad.columnar.com/
C Daniels (C_Daniels) Calport@AOL.com Calport@aol.com
Carrie Bugg (carriebugg) carriebugg@hotmail.com
Cathy Illsley (Cathyl) cathyillsley@gmail.com cathyillsley@gmail.com
CB (Carabosse) pm@londonmail.com
Charlie Yates (twistor) moonbiscuit@gmail.com
Cheryl Surry (csurry) csurry@ukgateway.net www.cherylsurry.com
Chris Clowe (kidda) info@chrisclowe.co.uk www.chrisclowe.com
Chris Girling (vfr400) c.girling@talk21.com
Chris Simpson (seejayess) seejay.ess@virgin.net www.seejayessphotography.co.uk
Chris Mole (ccmole) christopher.mole@uk.ibm.com
Chris Roberts (croberts) chris@crobertsphoto.com
Chris Shepherd (lobsterboy) chris@shepherdpics.com www.shepherdpics.com
Christine Balshaw (christabella) cbalshaw@btinternet.com
Christine Lewis (chrissieL) c.m.lewis@virgin.net
Claire Morgan (clairabella) claire.morgan@laposte.net www.claire-morgan.com
Clare McHale (rosegold) brokenpalette@claremc.co.uk brokenpalette.claremc.co.uk
Colin Mill (BigCol) grapher@colinemill.co.uk www.colinemill.co.uk
Colin Walden (ColWal) col@cwalden.karoo.co.uk
Cristian Philpott (Cristian) cristian@cristianphilpott.wanadoo.co.uk
Dave Clarke (dclarke5) dclarke5@lycos.co.uk www.oseagallery.co.uk
Dave Newton (davefolky) daveanewton@ntlworld.com
David Brighten (daveb) david_brighten@hotmail.com
David Carter (david carter) david.carter28@ntlworld.com
David Dunn (ddunn) day_dunn@ntlworld.com www.djld.co.uk
David Green (david j. green) djgreen@dsl.pipex.com
David Jelly (david_jelly) david_jelly@hotmail.com
David Knowles (dave knowles) dalyn@blueyonder.co.uk
David Watson (davewat) davewat@gmail.com www.scot-pics.co.uk
Debbie Hardy (debbiehardy) debbie@dvdreams.co.uk www.studio-25.co.uk
Debbie Legg (debster) debbie.legg1@ntlworld.com
Declan Higgins (declan) epz2004@hisdancingleg.com www.hisdancingleg.com
Dennis Reddick (den2il) den2il@ntlworld.com
Dewey J. Barker (starman1) dbarker12@cox.net
Donald Firth (Portknockie) dsfirth5356-photos@yahoo.co.uk
Doug Vickers (dougv) doug.vickers@btinternet.com
Dozi Design (afyfe) afyfe@dozi.co.uk www.dozi.co.uk

Duncan Robins (duncs) duncanrobins@hotmail.com duncanrobins@hotmail.com
Edward McKillop (Nicholl) emn@enicholl.com www.enicholl.com
Edward Robinson (edd robinson) www.edward-robinson.co.uk
Elizabeth Murphy (starliz) astroliz13@tiscali.co.uk
Emma Jones (missphotography) www.missphotography.com
Emma Tumman (ejtumman) ejtumman@gmail.com www.emmatumman.co.uk
Ernst van Loon (ernst) ernst.van.loon@xs4all.nl www.xs4all.nl/~loone
Ewan Rayment (ewanrayment) ewan@webleaf.co.uk
Ewan Stevenson (Ewan) ewan@oaktreephoto.co.uk www.oaktreephoto.co.uk
Francesco Cristofaro (ckristoff) ckristoff@aol.com
Frank Thomas (FrankThomas) frank@fttphoto.com
Gary Davis (gary900r) garyadavis@msn.com www.garydavisphotography.co.uk
Gavin Conlan (gav conlan) gavinconlan@aol.com
Gavin Davies (davies) gav_davies@hotmail.com www.gndphotography.co.uk
Gemm Ferrane (gemm) gemmferrane@dsl.pipex.com www.pbase.com/gemmf
Geoff Taylor (geoffash26) gpt@ntlworld.com
George Aitken (gma) ga.foto@ntlworld.com
George Alan Forster (galanfor) galanfor@aol.com
George White (geegee) geegee31@fsmail.net
Georgina Jackman (Dinda) gr@jackman53.freeserve.co.uk
Gill Brett (GillyB) gill.brett@btinternet.com
Glenn Harris (sabretalon) glenn@foto-graph-e.co.uk
Graham Anstey (ganstey) ganstey@mpc-data.co.uk
Gwyn Howells (gwyn h) gwyn.howells@gmail.com
Helen Dixon (digipal) hjd360bb@hotmail.com www.helendixonphotography.co.uk
Hugh McCluskey (shuggy67) hughmccluskey@blueyonder.co.uk
Hugo Denby-Mann (Hugo) hellohugo@hotmail.co.uk
Iain (IainH) Iain.Hutchinson@ntlworld.com www.IainHutchinson.co.uk
Iain Johnstone (claret) iain.johnstone1858@btinternet.com
Ian Anstey (iansamuel) ian@anstey.com www.pbase.com/iananstey
Ian Homewood (digicammad) digicammad@gmail.com
Ian Hunter (Ian Hunter) ian.cpa@btinternet.com
Ian Oliver (IanO) ian.oliver@freenet.co.uk www.ianoliverphoto.co.uk
Ian Walker (ian walker) walkerian@tiscali.co.uk
Ian Wilson (Ian G W) iangwilson@gmail.com
J.E. Morris (threave) jemorris@blueyonder.co.uk
Jane Smith (jane smith) illionsldg@aol.com www.janesmithphotography.co.uk
Janet Shippen (jana) janet_shippen@hotmail.com
Jason Newell (jasonewell) j_newell@btinternet.com
Jeanette Lazenby (jeanie) skyebeardie@blueyonder.co.uk
Jeanette Wise (jeanette) wise1@btinternet.com
Jeff Silvers (silvers106) jeffrey.silvers@ntlworld.com
Jenni Alexander (jennialexander) jennialexander@yahoo.com
Jim MacBrayne (old timer) jim@intermac.co.uk www.intermac.co.uk
JoAnne Dunn (baby jo) joanne@joannedunn.it www.joannedunn.it
Joe BT (snapbandit) jb@joebt.plus.com www.joebt.me.uk
John Carroll (johnc1711) www.johncarrollphotography.com
John Duckett (scallop) www.jduckettimages.com
John Edwards (johnjohn01) serendel@btopenworld.com www.johnfedwards.co.uk
John Monaghan (county) donnyhatter@blueyonder.co.uk
John Riley (johnriley1uk) johnriley@riley17.freeserve.co.uk
John Salmon (Just Jas) justjas2@btinternet.com
John Simmons (strawman) www.clutching-at-straws.co.uk
John Tisbury (johntisbury) info@johntisbury.co.uk www.johntisbury.co.uk
John Wearing (john wearing) johnwearing@ntlworld.com
Jon Gibbs (jon gibbs) info@jon-gibbs.co.uk www.jon-gibbs.co.uk
Jude Gidney (femin2003) jude.gidney@virgin.net www.judegidney.co.uk
Julian Mitchell (julesm) julesm@ip242yh.plus.com www.focal-perfection.com
Kai Roger Jensen (Kaikern) kaikernmail-ephotozine@yahoo.co.uk
Karen Bacon (answersonapostcard) www.dandelionphotographic.co.uk
Karen Morgan (frogsrcool) kfrogmorgan@aol.com ephotozine user=24377
Kate Barclay (katieb) kate@kbarclay.fsnet.co.uk www.katebarclay.co.uk
Kathy Wright (flybabe) flybabe@madasafish.com www.overlookedimages.com
Ken Fowler (deeken) ken@deeken.co.uk www.deeken.co.uk
Ken Jenkins (ken j) ken.jenkins@btinternet.com
Kevin Lewis (klewis) gallery@thelewiss.co.uk www.photosbykev.com
Kevin Lowe (nanpantannan) kevin.lowe@ntlworld.com
Kris Dutson (Ex) ex@dsl.pipex.com www.southernscenicphotography.com
Laura (laura16) sisterb@breathe.com
Laura Bryant (laurab) bbryantfamily@ntlworld.com www.feathered-friends.co.uk
Lee Hair (ScotSkin) mail@leehair.co.uk www.leehair.co.uk
Lucrezia Herman (lucrezia) www.dont-blink.net/lining_up.htm
Lydia (Lydia) lydia123@otenet.gr
M. D. Pontin (mdpontin) mdpontin@blueyonder.co.uk
Malcolm Johns (maljohns) malcolmdjohns@lineone.net www.pbase.com/maljohns
Marc Bowker (marcbowker) marcbowker@ntlworld.com www.onebigpicture.com
Marcus Keeler (marcuskeeler) marcus@mkeeler.com www.mkeeler.com
Margaret Barton (meggsy) tony.barton@aol.com
Mark Cavendish (markulous) markulousuk@yahoo.co.uk
Mark Curry (mcc28_x) mcc28_x@yahoo.co.uk
Mark Harrop (markharrop) markinessex@gmail.com
Martin Duke (martinduke) martinduke@yahoo.com
Martin Wait (frodo) martinwait@uwclub.net
Martin West (martin.w) martin@west78.fsnet.co.ukMartin Weston
Martin Weston (MartinWeston) martin.weston2@ntlworld.com
Mary Westlake (marineview) marywestlake@f2s.com
Matt Page (mattmatic) epz@photon.me.uk www.photon.me.uk
Matt Dillon-Shepherd (mdillon-shepherd) www.dillon-shepherd.co.uk
Matt Wagster (mattwaggie) mattwaggie@gmail.com www.mattwagster.com
Meg Langton (Meg) meg@meg76.co.uk
Melanie Letham (mellyleth) mel@rab-photo.com
Michael Amison (MikeA) MikeA@mja.eclipse.co.uk
Michael Brace (cameraman) michael@mk64lb.fsnet.co.uk
Michael D Callaghan (mrcal) mrcal@zoom.co.uk
Michael Murphy (skydivemike) michael@murphy7280.freeserve.co.uk
Michael Wilson (mttmwilson) mttmwilson@btinternet.com
Michiel Meyboom (m_meyboom) m_meyboom@yahoo.co.uk

Mike Hart (MikeH) michael@harts50.freeserve.co.uk www.mikehartimages.co.uk
Mike Otley (Mike Otley) mdotley@hotmail.com www.mophotos.co.uk
Mike Taylor (greyheron53) www.wildaboutlondon.co.uk
Mike Woodland (mwoodland) woodlandcm@fsmail.net
Miles Herbert (Miles Herbert) pesky_polecat@hotmail.com www.captive-light.com
Mo Akram (MoWiz) mo.akram@btinternet.com tel: 07800 800 831
Nadia Isakova (Nadia) nadia@raznoimport.u-net.com www.photosbest.com
Natalie Harrison (tigs) natalie@tigscreations.com www.tigscreations.com
Neal Moran (Nelly_77) lemonshed@gmail.com www.lemonshed.com
Neil Paskin (pask) n_p@talk21.com www.neilpaskin.com
Nic Cleave (nicanddi) nic@niccleave.com www.niccleave.com
Nicholas Hilton (Nick_Hilton) nicholas.hilton@btinternet.com
Nick Moss (malum) nick.moss@virgin.net
Nigel Moore (tully) tullyroe@nireland.com www.nireland.com/tullyroe
Nik Holgate (chuff) nickholgate@online24.co.uk Tel: +44 (0)7870 677140
Norman Wright (normanw) nswright_uk@yahoo.co.uk
Ovidiu Moldovan (ovi) ovidiu_moldovan@yahoo.com
Pat Collingwood (pcollingwood) p_collingwood@hotmail.com
Patrick Smith (PatrickSmith) patrick_d_smith@yahoo.com
Paul Bailey (bill777) p7a7u7l7@hotmail.com www.pbpgalleries2.co.uk
Paul Brown (paul162brown) www.paulbrownsphotography.co.uk
Paul Groom (paulgroom) paul@paulgroom.com www.paulgroom.com
Paul Heskes (wing) paulheskes@ntlworld.com paulheskes.com
Paul Hoffman (Hoffy) phof929403@aol.com
Paul Smith (Beardy) paul@rockandwateradventures.com
Paul Stefan (paulstefan) paulstefanphotos@hotmail.com www.paulstefan.co.uk
Paul Tilley (ptilley) paul@paultilleyphotography.com www.paultilleyphotography.co.uk
Pauline White (exposure) forbes@cytanet.com.cy www.whimages.com
Pete Poland (foggytwo) polandlillian@hotmail.com
Peter Dalton (diver pete) www.peterdaltonphotography.com
Peter Garwood (pgarwood) peter.garwood@bbrclub.org
Peter Graves (Pete_g) www.petergraves-photography.co.uk
Peter Paterson (peterpaterson) www.peterpaterson.com
Peter Shilton (peter shilton) peter@petershilton.co.uk www.petershilton.com
Phil Matthews (panda) philip.matthews@virgin.net
Phil Nightingale (phil_1975) philnightingale@ntlworld.com
Phil Smith (amaryllis) phil@aboyne.demon.co.uk
Philip Beale (phil beale) philipbeale1@aol.com www.wildlifelandscape.co.uk
Philip Hendy (iscramble) philip.hendy@ntlworld.com www.phil-hendy.co.uk
Rebecca Wilson (bexter) bexter84@yahoo.co.uk www.bexphoto.com
Rob Smith (scotdiver) scotdiver@hotmail.com www.scotdiver.co.uk
Robert Hirschi (hirschi) ranxx@comcast.net www.hirschiphoto.com
Robert Taylor (bobsy) roberttaylor008@aol.com
Roger Prestcote (ziggy) roger.prestcote@ntlworld.com
Roger Staten (rogerstaten) www.rogerstatenphotography.com
Ron Thomas (ron thomas) ronald.j.thomas@btinternet.com
Rosey Norton (roseyn) rosey@lincolnshirecam.co.uk www.lincolnshirecam.co.uk
Roy Pritchard (kaybee) roy_pritchard@hotmail.com
S Standerwick (samstan) www.standerwick-images.com
Sam Bassan (bassan) sam@ssbmarketing.co.uk
Sandy F (cameragirl) sandyfung@hotmail.com
Sarah (Sezzy) sarah@dawson04.plus.com
Sarah Brooke (whipspeed) whipspeed@tesco.net
Scott Secker (Scotty) sasecker@aol.com
Shane Kelly (Hazard) shane_kelly@ntlworprld.com
Shaun Ball (shaun) shaun.ball@dsl.pipex.com ephotozine user=11690
Shawn Haslgrove (coolpics) sphwt@aol.com
Simon (dusted) simonsays@dsl.pipex.com
Simon Falconer (SimJam) simjamfalc@supanet.com
Simon John Harvey (xanda) xanda@talk21.com www.studioxanda.co.uk
Simon King (siderath) siderath@hotmail.com
Simon Mitchell (mitchellhatpeg) mitchellhatpeg@netscape.net
Stephen Brightman (Tooth) stephenbrightman@eircom.net
Stephen R Butler (srbutler) contact@stevebutler.me.uk www.two42.com
Stephen Smith (corin45) bacchus04031958@aol.com
Stephen Websdale (seven21) srwebsdale@btinternet.com
Steve Ball (stevieb) borlyworly@gmail.com
Steve Briddon (ardbeg'77) stephen.briddon@nottingham.ac.uk
Steve Crampton (CanonMan) steve@electric-image.co.uk www.electric-image.co.uk
Steve Cribbin (Steve Cribbin) steve.cribbin@ntlworld.com
Steve Langton (stevie) langts@midthird.demon.co.uk
Steve Maiden (stevem) smaiden@wakefield.gov.uk
Steve Newport (Stevo) steve.newport@blueyonder.co.uk
Steven Fryer (fastshot1) www.smfcreativeimagingstudio2004@k9fry.fsnet.co.uk
Stewart Caie (stewartcaie) www.scotlandscenicphotos.com
Sue Turner (SueTurner) suemacdonald@indoors1594.fsnet.co.uk
Susan Collins (a11sus) a11sus@gmail.com
Tanya Chadderton-Evans (tce5) tanyaevans.photium.com
Tanya S Wrey (Tanya_Wrey) tanyaphotographyservices@yahoo.co.uk
Teresa Hill (TeresaH) ladymacbeth6868@aol.com
Terry Amos (TTT) info@terenceamos.com www.terenceamos.com
Terry Longley (Terry L) terry@boyd-longley.co.uk www.wildaboutlondon.co.uk
Tim Gambrill (bigbed) ephotozine@timandangela.com
Tina Bolton (tinabolton) info@tinabolton.co.uk www.tinabolton.co.uk
Tony Humphreys (akh) akh43@tiscali.co.uk
Trudi Newman (tn) trudi.newman@virgin.net
Val Prowse (Val Prowse) valprowse@yahoo.co.uk
Vicky Hammerstein (vickyh) vrh@misnet.co.uk www.vicspix.com
Vinny Parmar (vparmar) vines.parmar4@mail.com www.bvphotography.co.uk

Our thanks also go to everyone who submitted photographs for use in this book. It truly is one of the best collections of images to appear in one book.